www.wadsworth.com

www.wadsworth.com is the World Wide Web site for Wadsworth and is your direct source to dozens of online resources.

At *www.wadsworth.com* you can find out about supplements, demonstration software, and student resources. You can also send email to many of our authors and preview new publications and exciting new technologies.

www.wadsworth.com
Changing the way the world learns®

TWENTY QUESTIONS

AN INTRODUCTION TO PHILOSOPHY

Sixth Edition

G. LEE BOWIE
Mount Holyoke College

MEREDITH W. MICHAELS
Smith College

ROBERT C. SOLOMON
University of Texas, Austin

THOMSON

WADSWORTH

Australia • Brazil • Canada • Mexico • Singapore • Spain
United Kingdom • United States

Twenty Questions: An Introduction to Philosophy

G. Lee Bowie, Meredith W. Michaels, and Robert C. Solomon

Publisher: Holly J. Allen
Philosophy Editor: Steve Wainwright
Assistant Editors: Lee McCracken: Barbara Hillaker
Editorial Assistant: Gina Kessler
Technology Project Manager: Julie Aguilar
Marketing Manager: Worth Hawes
Marketing Assistant: Alexandra Tran
Marketing Communications Manager: Stacey Purviance
Creative Director: Rob Hugel
Executive Art Director: Maria Epes

Print Buyer: Karen Hunt
Permissions Editor: Bob Kauser
Production Service: Interactive Composition Corporation
Copy Editor: Michelle Gaudreau
Cover Designer: Yvo Riezebos
Cover Image: Antar Dayal, *Vice Versa*
Compositor: Interactive Composition Corporation
Text and Cover Printer: Malloy Incorporated

ExamView® and ExamView Pro® are registered trademarks of FSCreations, Inc. Windows is a registered trademark of the Microsoft Corporation used herein under license. Macintosh and Power Macintosh are registered trademarks of Apple Computer, Inc. Used herein under license.

Thomson Higher Education
10 Davis Drive
Belmont, CA 94002-3098
USA

For more information about our products, contact us at:
Thomson Learning Academic Resource Center
1-800-423-0563
For permission to use material from this text or product, submit a request online at
http://www.thomsonrights.com
Any additional questions about permissions can be submitted by e-mail to
thomsonrights@thomson.com

Library of Congress Control Number:
2005937319

ISBN: 0-495-00711-0

PREFACE

The favorable response to *Twenty Questions: An Introduction to Philosophy* has provided us with the impetus to bring philosophy into conversation with other intellectual traditions and activities. The format of this sixth edition is the same as that of earlier editions. We have added new material in order to keep up with developments in the field and with developments in the world. There is a chapter on philosophical issues around violence and terrorism (Chapter 12), and we have added material on stem-cell research and cloning to the chapters on abortion (Chapter 10) and personal identity (Chapter 8). And, because of a heightened interest in philosophy and elsewhere in issues of gender, race, class, and culture, we have been able to choose among a large body of interesting work that incorporates these perspectives into traditional philosophical concerns. We have deleted some selections in response to suggestions from students and teachers throughout the country. Finally, the book is accompanied by an instructor's manual for teachers, and an interactive website for students.

This book is the product of many years of teaching successful introductory philosophy courses. By "successful courses" we mean courses that engage and sustain the students' attention in genuine philosophical activity. We have tried to recreate here some of the elements that have made for success in the classroom.

First, we have included a large number of "classics" philosophical texts, both old and new. Philosophy builds heavily on its own tradition, and the introductory student profits from joining in that tradition. However, philosophers are not the only people who address philosophical questions. The student will also find here pieces on philosophical themes written by scientists, novelists, journalists, political activists, poets, religious figures, economists, and others. We are, along with Socrates, convinced that philosophical questions permeate so-called ordinary life. Students benefit from and appreciate the philosophical reflections of those outside the philosophical profession.

Second, in assembling the selections we have kept in mind that, although most traditional philosophers are white males, many students are not. All students need to know that people like themselves sometimes do philosophy. We have tried to represent a full range of human perspectives and voices.

We have arranged the selections in each chapter to create a natural philosophical conversation from the beginning of the chapter to the end. In many cases this order is antichronological. Instructors will certainly want to take liberties with our arrangements and create "conversations" that are different from the ones we envisaged. Other instructors might wish to gather material from several chapters into groupings that are quite different from what we thought natural. We believe that the design of the book allows a full range for the expression of idiosyncrasy.

We have developed an extensive companion website for this edition of Twenty Questions at *http://philosophy.wadsworth.com*. The site includes tutorial quizzes, weblinks, and internet activities for each chapter, in addition to many other resources for students who want to clear up confusions, or explore further.

Because we have been so concerned to include historical and contemporary material from both philosophical and nontraditional sources, this is a large book. Consequently, there is enormous flexibility in the design of a course that uses this book. One could diverge from the intention of the authors and teach a course entirely from historical materials. A course could focus on women writers. A course might be constructed very traditionally, or it might achieve eccentricity of truly epic proportions. There is no substitute in the classroom for the instructor's enthusiasm for the material; to make that enthusiasm possible, we have offered a broad range of options.

Because this book draws from such a range of sources, it has been in the process of revision since it began. This process will continue. For the book to be improved by use, we hope that instructors will pass on to us their complaints, their praise, and especially their suggestions.

In our experience using this text and talking with others (both instructors and students) who have used it, we have discovered that good students browse through it, reading selections that have not been assigned. We regard this as a significant measure of our success. Accordingly, we urge students to read freely through the readings gathered here. Philosophy is a field that typically (although not always) responds well to different views about what is philosophically engaging.

A number of people have helped us enormously with the creation of this book, both at Harcourt and at Wadsworth, especially Steve Wainwright and Barbara Hillaker. Also we would especially like to thank the reviewers of the sixth edition: Eric Cave, Arkansas State University; Lynn Holt, Mississippi State University; Mark Lance, Georgetown University; Linette Lowe, Bellarmine University; D. A. Masolo, University of Louisville; Jennifer McErlean, Siena College; Ronald Sandler, Northeastern University; Mary Schatz, Palomar College; Edward Schoen, Western Kentucky University; Michael Strawser, University of Central Florida; and Lynne Tirrell, University of Maryland, Baltimore. We would also like to express our gratitude to the reviewers of the previous edition of this book: Sherrill J. Begres, Indiana University of Pennsylvania; James M. Humber, Georgia State University; Peter Hutcheson, Southwest Texas State University; Stephen Leach, Minnesota State University, Mankato; Richard Shoaf, Tidewater Community College; and John S. Vassar, Louisiana State University–Shreveport. Finally, we thank our thousands of former students: Their enthusiastic responses as well as their blank looks have made this book far better than it otherwise might have been.

INTRODUCTION

At certain times in your life, you have undoubtedly stumbled across a peculiar sort of question, a question to which you haven't got a straightforward answer, a question that provokes head-scratching or that leaves you feeling slightly out of sorts. Suppose that you are sitting outdoors with a friend on a beautiful spring day. Both of you are looking up at the sky. "Isn't the sky amazingly blue today?" remarks your friend. "Yes," you respond, but just as you answer, a problem occurs to you. *How do you know that you and your friend are seeing the same color?* Well, your friend is seeing blue, and you are seeing blue, so doesn't that settle it? Not really, because now you can push the question further. Even if you both use the word "blue" to *describe* what you see, it's still possible that what you see is not what your friend sees. At this point you may begin to get a headache (and not from looking at the sky) and turn your attention to a more manageable question, such as "Is it time for lunch?" Indeed, one of the characteristics of the peculiar question about the color of the sky (the "Color Question") is precisely that it seems so unmanageable. How would one go about trying to answer a question such as that?

All of us have well-developed strategies for answering most questions. If you want to know whether it is time for lunch, you check your watch. If you haven't got a watch, you ask someone who does. If nobody around has a watch, you call the operator, find a sundial, or decide that, no matter what the actual time is, you'll follow the dictates of your stomach. (This last point shows that we also have a sense of when to give up.) But in the case of the Color Question, it is simply not clear what strategy you ought to adopt in attempting to answer it. It's tempting to give up before you even begin.

If the Color Question isn't one that has crossed your mind, perhaps you'll find this one more familiar. Imagine that you have spent the day chasing down various pieces of paper that are required for you to register for your classes. After standing in one line for twenty minutes, you are told that you belong in another line. After filling out four green cards, it turns out that you were supposed to fill out yellow cards. After gathering all your course books at the bookstore, you discover that the store doesn't accept checks. After waiting for your chance to order a sandwich, you are informed that there is no more bread. After carefully choosing your courses, your advisor tells you that three of them are closed. Returning home, you think to yourself, "What a useless day. What was the purpose of standing in all those lines? Nothing works out. I'm like a rat in a maze, running crazily around chasing its tail. In fact, *what is the point, the purpose of life? What does it all mean?*" Most of the time, we just do what we do, content to believe that the purpose in buttering the bread is simply to make it taste better. We don't then ask: *But what is the point in making it taste better?* But sometimes, when we are particularly frustrated or defeated in our attempts to perform ordinary activities, those activities appear in a different light. They appear futile, disconnected from the particular purposes they are designed to serve. Because they fail to achieve their immediate purposes, it is not surprising that the purposes themselves begin to look futile, utterly lacking in meaning. That is when the "Life Question" is likely to strike.

If the Color Question appears unmanageable, then the Life Question, being the biggest question of all, seems even less likely to yield to our ordinary strategies. Where would you begin to answer it? How would you know whether you had arrived at an answer? Perhaps the strangest thing about these peculiar questions is that they are clearly important and fundamental questions, even *profound* questions, and yet it is equally clear that people normally lead most of their lives without answering them, indeed, without giving them more than a passing glance.

There are some people, however, who take these and other questions like them very seriously. Socrates, one of the earliest Western philosophers, said, "The unexamined life is not worth living." As we all know, to examine something is to look at it very carefully. Of course, we can't look at life in the same way we look at a virus under a microscope. In the case of life itself, there is more to it than meets the eye. The process of examination, then, involves thinking about different aspects of life, focusing now on the color of the sky and later, for example, on the existence of God or the importance of truthtelling. Socrates is suggesting that there is something wrong with a life that does not subject itself to scrutiny, at least from time to time. Although his claim doesn't provide an answer to the questions we've been considering, it does suggest that we forge on in our attempt to answer them. That is precisely what he did, and what philosophers since then have done.

There are as many ways of thinking about these questions as there are philosophers. What unifies philosophers as a group, and philosophy as a field of study, is the belief that these questions deserve systematic attention. As a result, philosophy is a discipline that seeks to provide strategies for answering these questions, for seeing how they are related to one another and to our more ordinary beliefs and values. For example, if you believe that there is a God, then your answer to the Life Question might be quite different from that of a person who doesn't.

There is no one strategy that appeals to every philosopher. Different strategies yield different answers, and different answers inevitably lead to new questions. Some philosophers think that some questions, the Life Question being a good example, are so general and vague as to be meaningless. In fact, a favorite strategy of some philosophers is to show that something that looks like a question really isn't. It is like going to the doctor, only to discover that your symptoms are psychosomatic. You think that you are sick, but you really aren't. Or, if you are sick, your illness is not at all what you thought it was. Other philosophers believe that most philosophical questions are really about language. They might try to answer the Color Question by urging us to consider the way in which we use such words as "blue." If you and your friend always use the word in the same way, then there is no further interesting fact about whether what the two of you see is the same or not.

As you read through this book and discuss the issues it raises in class, you will begin to discover that you have certain philosophical inclinations. You will find the strategies of some philosophers congenial or persuasive. You will undoubtedly find, too, that some of them seem to you to miss the point, or to avoid it by distracting you with another issue. Sometimes, you will simply find that the question being considered isn't terribly pressing to you at this moment. People have philosophical preferences just as they have preferences for other things. Some people, for example, are particularly interested in ethical questions (see Chapters 13, 15, 19, and 20) because such questions are closely connected to choices that all of us have to make every day. Although these ethical choices may not be very serious, even the decision of whether or not to skip class has ethical consequences!

Other people are drawn to questions that never explicitly arise in the course of ordinary experience (except when they're doing philosophy), but that nevertheless underlie and inform our ways of thinking about that experience. You can get through the day without having to question whether your mind is something over and above your brain (Chapter 5). You can't however, get through the day without there being some relationship between your mind and your brain. Philosophy permits you to think seriously and systematically about the nature of that relationship.

As you may have noticed, Socrates' claim about the importance of looking "at the inside of life" is itself a philosophical claim. After you have had a chance to do some philosophical thinking, you will be able to decide whether you think that he was right. You might even develop some good reasons for thinking that he was wrong. If so, Socrates would have been proud of you. Showing that a great philosopher is mistaken can be an enormously productive and gratifying experience.

SOME ADVICE ABOUT STUDYING PHILOSOPHY AND USING THIS BOOK

Philosophy is notoriously difficult. Philosophers use an array of unfamiliar concepts and don't always do a good job of letting us know what they mean by those concepts. Also, in their attempt to be logical and rigorous, they sometimes leave out such things as examples, cases, and stories that might help us to judge whether we are following their reasoning. Nevertheless, when you read philosophy, always begin by trying to understand a philosopher on his or her own terms. Remember that no matter how strange what you are reading appears to be, it was written by an ordinary human being with a mind roughly like your own. You simply need to accustom yourself to seeing the world from the perspective of another person whose central concerns, at least initially, appear to be very different from your own. Once you've climbed inside the head of a philosopher, it is much easier to see the world in his or her particular way. Doing so doesn't mean that you will like what you see, nor does it involve adopting that way of seeing as your own, but it does give you a better chance of being able to understand and evaluate what you read.

To help you make that first step into a philosopher's world, this book presents a bit of biographical information at the beginning of each essay or story. Be sure to read it before you plunge into the text. Remember that if somebody lived from 1596 to 1650, that person is not going to be worried about nuclear war, nor will she or he have heard of robots or of the Equal Rights Amendment. It may well be, however, that what such a person has to say will help you understand the philosophical issues raised by these and other phenomena of the world in which you live.

In addition to the biographical information provided for each author, each chapter of this book has an introduction designed to give you an idea of the questions that chapter explores as well as some sense of what each author in that chapter is trying to accomplish. Because these introductions attempt to situate philosophical questions in a setting that is familiar to you, it is a good idea to read them carefully before you read the selections themselves. Remember, too, that rereading the introductions may help you to reorient yourself if you begin to get lost midway through a difficult essay.

Finally, you will notice that not every selection in this book is written by a philosopher. The book also contains fiction, scientific writing, newspaper articles, and essays from popular magazines. By setting strictly philosophical writing in a more familiar context, this book allows you to see the ways in which philosophy creeps into ordinary life. It also allows you to see that people other than philosophers are capable of great philosophical insight (and sometimes are more fun to read!).

Long after you've finished this course, you may find yourself reading an article in the newspaper and saying "Hmmm . . . I wonder what Plato would say about this." Philosophy is everywhere, once you learn how to recognize it. An introductory philosophy course is designed to show you how to do just that.

CONTENTS

PART 5   Living a Good Life   455

PART ONE

RELIGION AND THE MEANING OF LIFE

CHAPTER ONE

DOES RELIGION GIVE MY LIFE MEANING?

What do you believe in? What gives your life meaning? It is true that most of your days are filled with things to do, people to see, assignments to be completed, promises to be kept, and special events to be anticipated and then enjoyed. But what does all this add up to? What makes it significant? Why does it make a difference whether you are alive? These are the questions that are often summarized under the heading "the meaning of life," and they are among the oldest and most important questions in philosophy.

Religion is as old as these questions, and the various religions of the world are, in part, answers to these questions. The primary function of religion is to give our lives meaning, to show us how we fit into the world and God's plan. But there are many religions and conceptions of religion, and they explain life's meaning in very different ways. Judaism and Christianity insist that life has meaning because there is an Almighty God who created us and looks over us. There are, however, other ways of making sense of our existence, and some of them do not involve a being such as the Judeo-Christian God at all.

How does religion give meaning to life? Steven Cahn suggests that it is a combination of theory and practice, rituals, prayers, metaphysical beliefs, and moral commitments. But, he argues, it is not necessary that such theories and practices be part of an established traditional religion, nor is it necessary for a person who is religious to believe in a single supreme being or an afterlife—two fundamental tenets of Christianity but relative rarities among the various religions of the world. There are great religions in the East, as old as Judaism and Christianity, that explain the meaning of life without appealing to any conception of God like our own. And any number of "spiritual attitudes" to life exist that are not part of any particular religion. Religion may make life meaningful, but no particular religion does so exclusively, and many if not all of the ingredients of a meaningful life—rituals, moral commitments, metaphysical beliefs, and even prayers (to whom or what?)—might also be part of someone's strictly secular life. What is essential is that a person's life involves some sensibility that goes beyond the ordinary and everyday concerns of life, and it is the sense of "beyond" that gives life meaning.

Some of the great thinkers have suggested that what is central to religion is not belief in a particular deity, but rather a transformation of one's self, a rising "above" ordinary, everyday concerns to an appreciation of the nature of the cosmos as a whole. Believing in God is one way to do this, but there are other ways of viewing the world that make such "awakening" or "transcendence" possible. Tibetan Buddhism is a complex set of philosophical reflections on the nature of knowledge and reality. It is committed to the significance of ordinary human experience and yet insists that we can move beyond it. John Powers' essay on Buddhism provides a comprehensive account of the central doctrines of Buddhism in order to make them compelling both to those who love a philosophical challenge (what is the nature of causation?) and to those whose tendencies are more toward the spiritual (is this life my only life?). There are "many paths to the same summit," writes Ramakrishna. It would be a mistake to think that there is only one religion or one way to make life meaningful. But then, neither can one simply embrace all religions at once, because it is the particularity of the "path" that makes meaningfulness possible. A Christian should be a Christian, a Hindu a Hindu, but this does not mean that there is or should be any conflict between them. In this spirit, we take a brief look at two religions in which the God of the Judeo-Christian-Muslim tradition is not the issue. The first is discussed by Japanese Buddhist philosopher Keiji Nishitani. The second is summarized by a few verses from Lao-tzu, the author of the *Tao Te Ching,* the classic text of Chinese Taoism.

But then, it has also been argued that religion does not provide meaning to life at all; it rather gives us a distraction *from* life and a set of excuses for not taking life's problems seriously. So conceived, religion may *take away* rather than contribute to life's meaning. Bertrand Russell, for instance, once described the history of Christianity as a horrifying story of protracted violence and intolerance. Even more damning are the two excerpts from Friedrich Nietzsche, who first announces "God is dead" and then attacks Christianity for its continuing "war against the higher man," by which he means creative individuals who are constricted by Christian morality and religion. Mary Daly considers the *gender* of the Judeo-Christian God. bell hooks discusses the "ethic of love" and contrasts it with the efforts of both blacks and whites to overcome the ravages of racism and white supremacy. She is particularly concerned to establish love, and to oppose hate, as a motivating force in freedom struggles of all kinds.

Finally, it may be that life has no meaning and that the attempts of all religions to provide that meaning are just denial and refusal to accept the facts. H. L. Mencken makes his point about the illusory character of religion by listing the names of gods and goddesses who were once feared and revered. Albert Camus argues that the sensibility of the current age is that life is really "absurd" and religion cannot undo that single, overwhelming truth.

STEVEN M. CAHN
Religion Reconsidered

STEVEN M. CAHN *is a professor of philosophy and dean of the City University of New York. He teaches and publishes in the philosophy of religion and education.*

MOST of us suppose that all religions are akin to the one we happen to know best. But this assumption can be misleading. For example, many Christians believe that all religions place heavy emphasis on an afterlife, although, in fact, the central concern of Judaism is life in this world, not the next. Similarly, many Christians and Jews are convinced that a person who is religious must affirm the existence of a supernatural God. They are surprised to learn that religions such as Jainism or Theravada Buddhism deny the existence of a Supreme Creator of the World.

But how can there be a non-supernatural religion? To numerous theists as well as atheists the concept appears contradictory. I propose to show, however, that nothing in the theory or practice of religion—not ritual, not prayer, not metaphysical belief, not moral commitment—necessitates a commitment to traditional theism. In other words, one may be religious while rejecting supernaturalism.

Let us begin with the concept of ritual. A ritual is a prescribed symbolic action. In the case of religion, the ritual is prescribed by the religious organization, and the act symbolizes some aspect of religious belief. Those who find the beliefs of supernaturalistic religion unreasonable or the activities of the organization unacceptable may come to consider any ritual irrational. But, although particular rituals may be based on irrational beliefs, nothing is inherently irrational about ritual.

Consider the simple act of two people shaking hands when they meet. This act is a ritual, prescribed by our society and symbolic of the individuals' mutual respect. There is nothing irrational about this act. Of course, if people shook hands in order to ward off evil demons, then shaking hands would be irrational. But this is not the reason people shake hands. The ritual has no connection with God or demons but indicates the attitude one person has toward another.

It might be assumed that the ritual of handshaking escaped irrationality only because the ritual is not prescribed by any specific organization and is not part of an elaborate ceremony. But to see that this assumption is false, consider the graduation ceremony at a college. The graduates and faculty all wear peculiar hats and robes, and the participants stand and sit at appropriate times throughout the ceremony. However, there is nothing irrational about this ceremony. Indeed, the ceremonies of graduation day, far from being irrational, are symbolic of commitment to the process of education and the life of reason.

At first glance it may appear that rituals are comparatively insignificant features of our lives, but the more one considers the matter, the more it becomes apparent that rituals are a pervasive and treasured aspect of human experience. Who would want to eliminate the festivities associated with holidays such as Independence Day or Thanksgiving? What would college football be without songs, cheers, flags, and the innumerable other symbolic features surrounding the game? And those who disdain popular rituals typically proceed to establish their own distinctive ones, ranging from characteristic habits of dress to the use of drugs, all symbolic of a rejection of traditional mores.

Religious persons, like all others, search for an appropriate means of emphasizing their commitment to a group or its values. Rituals provide such a means. It is true that supernaturalistic religion has often infused its rituals with superstition, but nonreligious rituals can be equally as superstitious as religious ones. For example, most Americans view the Fourth of July as an occasion on which they can express pride in their country's heritage. With this purpose in mind, the holiday is one of great significance. However, if it were thought that the singing of the fourth verse of "The Star-Spangled Banner" four times on the Fourth of July would protect our country against future disasters, then the original meaning of the holiday would soon be lost in a maze of superstition.

A naturalistic (i.e., non-supernaturalistic) religion need not utilize ritual in such a superstitious manner, for it does not employ rituals in order to please a benevolent deity or appease an angry one. Rather, naturalistic religion views ritual, as Jack Cohen has put it, as "the enhancement of life through the dramatization of great ideals." If a group places great stress on justice or freedom, why should it not utilize ritual in order to emphasize these goals? Such a use of ritual serves to solidify the group and to strengthen its devotion to its expressed purposes. And these purposes are strengthened all the more if the ritual in question has the force of tradition, having been performed by many generations who have belonged to the same group and have struggled to achieve the same goals. Ritual so conceived is not a form of superstition; rather, it is a reasonable means of strengthening religious commitment and is as useful to naturalistic religion as it is to supernaturalistic religion.

Having considered the role of ritual in a naturalistic religion, let us next turn to the concept of prayer. It might be thought that naturalistic religion could have no use for prayer, since prayer is supposedly addressed to a supernatural being, and proponents of naturalistic religion do not believe in the existence of such a being. But this objection over-simplifies the concept of prayer, focusing attention on one type of prayer while neglecting an equally important but different sort of prayer.

Supernaturalistic religion makes extensive use of petitionary prayer, prayer that petitions a supernatural being for various favors. These may range all the way from the personal happiness of the petitioner to the general welfare of all society. But since petitionary prayer rests upon the assumption that a supernatural being exists, it is clear that such prayer has no place in a naturalistic religion.

However, not all prayers are prayers of petition. There are also prayers of meditation. These prayers are not directed to any supernatural being and are not requests for the granting of favors. Rather, these prayers provide the opportunity for persons to rethink their ultimate commitments and rededicate themselves to live up to their ideals. Such prayers may take the form of silent devotion or may involve oral repetition of certain central texts. Just as Americans repeat the Pledge of Allegiance and reread the Gettysburg Address, so adherents of naturalistic religion repeat the statements of their ideals and reread the documents that embody their traditional beliefs.

It is true that supernaturalistic religions, to the extent that they utilize prayers of mediation, tend to treat these prayers irrationally, by supposing that if the prayers are not uttered a precise number of times under certain specified conditions, then the prayers lose all value. But there is no need to view prayer in this way. Rather, as Julian Huxley wrote, prayer "permits the bringing before the mind of a world of thought which in most people must inevitably be absent during the occupations of ordinary Life: . . . it is the means by which the mind may fix itself upon this or that noble or beautiful or awe-inspiring idea, and so grow to it and come to realize it more fully."

Such a use of prayer may be enhanced by song, instrumental music, and various types of symbolism. These elements, fused together, provide the means for adherents of naturalistic religion to engage in religious services akin to those engaged in by adherents of supernaturalistic religion. The difference between the two services is that those who attend the latter come to relate themselves to God, while those who attend the former come to relate themselves to their fellow human beings and to the world in which we live.

We have so far discussed how ritual and prayer can be utilized in naturalistic religion, but to adopt a religious perspective also involves metaphysical beliefs and moral commitments. Can these be maintained without recourse to supernaturalism?

If we use the term *metaphysics* in its usual sense, to refer to the systematic study of the most basic features of existence, then it is clear that a metaphysical system may be either supernaturalistic or naturalistic. The views of Plato, Descartes, and Leibniz are representative of a supernaturalistic theory; the views of Aristotle, Spinoza, and Dewey are representative of a naturalistic theory.

Spinoza's *Ethics,* for example, one of the greatest metaphysical works ever written, explicitly rejects the view that there exists any being apart from Nature itself. Spinoza identifies God with Nature as a whole, and urges that the good life consists in coming to understand Nature. In his words, "our salvation, or blessedness, or freedom consists in a constant and eternal love toward God. . . ." Spinoza's concept of God, however, is explicitly not the supernaturalistic concept of God, and Spinoza's metaphysical system thus exemplifies not only a naturalistic metaphysics but also the possibility of reinterpreting the concept of God within a naturalistic framework.

But can those who do not believe in a supernaturalistic God commit themselves to moral principles, or is the acceptance of moral principles dependent upon acceptance of supernaturalism? It is sometimes assumed that those who reject a supernaturalistic God are necessarily immoral, for their denial of the existence of such a God leaves them free to act without fear of Divine punishment. This assumption, however, is seriously in error.

The refutation of the view that morality must rest upon belief in a supernatural God was provided more than two thousand years ago by Socrates in Plato's *Euthyphro* dialogue. Socrates asked the following question: Are actions right because God says they are right, or does God say actions are right because they are right? This question is not a verbal trick; on the contrary, it poses a serious dilemma for those who believe in a supernatural deity. Socrates was inquiring whether actions are right due to God's fiat or whether God is Himself subject to moral standards. If actions are right due to God's command, then anything God commands is right, even if He should command torture or murder. But if one accepts this view, then it makes no sense to say that God Himself is good, for since the good is whatever God commands, to say that God commands rightly is simply to say that He commands as He commands, which is a tautology. This approach makes a mockery of morality, for might does not make right, even if the might is the infinite might of God. To act morally is not to act out of fear of punishment; it is not to act as one is commanded to act. Rather, it is to act as one ought to act. And how one ought to act. And how one ought to act is not dependent upon anyone's power, even if the power be Divine.

Thus, actions are not right because God commands them; on the contrary, God commands them because they are right. But in that case, what is right is independent of what God commands, for what He commands must conform with an independent standard in order to be right. Since one could act in accordance with this independent standard without believing in the existence of a supernatural God, it follows that morality does not rest upon supernaturalism. Consequently, naturalists can be highly moral (as well as immoral) persons, and supernaturalists can be highly immoral (as well as moral) persons. This conclusion should come as no surprise to anyone who has contrasted the life of Buddha, an atheist, with the life of the monk Torquemada.

We have now seen that naturalistic religion is a genuine possibility, since it is reasonable for individuals to perform rituals, utter prayers, accept metaphysical beliefs, and commit themselves to moral principles without believing in supernaturalism. Indeed, one can even do so while maintaining allegiance to Christianity or Judaism. Consider, for example, those Christians who accept the "Death of God" or those Jews who adhere to Reconstructionist Judaism.

Such options are philosophically respectable. Whether to choose any of them is for each reader to decide.

JOHN POWERS
Some Important Buddhist Doctrines

JOHN POWERS *teaches in the Religion Department at Wright State University. A specialist in Indo–Tibetan philosophy and meditation theory, he has published widely on various topics in Buddhist thought and practice.*

KARMA AND REBIRTH

AMONG the most basic and pervasive of these are teachings attributed to Buddha concerning karma and rebirth. These ideas were already present in the culture in which Buddha was born, and he accepted them in much the same way that his contemporaries did. According to Tibetan Buddhists, Buddha taught that one's present life is only one in a beginningless series of rebirths, and each of these is determined by one's actions in previous lives. These actions are collectively referred to as "karma." This idea specifically refers to one's volitional actions, which may be good, bad, or neutral. The Buddhist concept of karma is similar to Newton's Third Law of Motion, which holds that for every action there is a reaction. Similarly, in Buddhism, actions give rise to concordant effects: good, bad, and neutral experiences are the direct results of good, bad, and neutral karma. This is presented as a universal law that has nothing to do with abstract ideas of justice, reward, or punishment. Every action produces a concordant reaction, and this occurs automatically. It does not require the control, intervention, or modification of any outside power, and as long as one remains within cyclic existence one performs actions (karma), and these inevitably produce concordant results.

Karmas, therefore, are being made all the time. When one speaks with a good motivation, a friendly atmosphere is created as an immediate result; also, the action makes an imprint on the mind, inducing pleasure in the future. With a bad motivation, a hostile atmosphere is created immediately, and pain is induced for the speaker in the future. Buddha's teaching is that you are your own master; everything depends on yourself.

Powers, John, "Some Important Buddhist Doctrines" from *Introduction to Tibetan Buddhism,* Snow Lion Publications, Ithaca, NY, 1995.

This means that pleasure and pain arise from virtuous and non-virtuous actions which come not from outside but from within yourself.

As long as one fails to recognize the cyclical nature of karma and rebirth, one will continue to transmigrate helplessly in cyclic existence. As we have seen in the life of the Buddha, however, it is possible to break the vicious cycle and escape from the sufferings that repeated births bring. The cycle is driven by ignorance, and the key to liberation lies in overcoming ignorance. The Buddha is the paradigm of a person who has accomplished this, and so devout Buddhists strive to emulate his example. The first requirement is the development of dissatisfaction with cyclic existence. As long as one is basically comfortable within cyclic existence, there is no possibility of release. One must develop a profound revulsion, looking back on one's beginningless births with disgust and vowing to break the cycle by any means necessary. According to Lama Thubten Yeshe, this attitude

indicates a deep, heartfelt decision definitely to emerge from the repeated frustrations and disappointments of ordinary life. Simply stated, renunciation is the feeling of being so completely fed up with our recurring problems that we are finally ready to turn away from our attachments to this and that and begin searching for another way to make our life satisfying and meaningful.

Next, one must emulate Buddha's example and develop the positive moral qualities that he cultivated. This leads to mental peace and equanimity, which are necessary to successful meditation. Without developing mental calm, one's thoughts will be so agitated that meditation will be impossible. Meditation is the key to overcoming ignorance, for through meditation one can develop insight into the true nature of reality, which acts as a counteragent to ignorance. Successful development of insight allows one to transcend the influence of karma, to end the ignorant engagement in actions that bind one to continued transmigration, and eventually to end the cycle altogether.

THE FOUR NOBLE TRUTHS

Since Buddhism holds that the problem is a cognitive one, the solution lies in cognitive restructuring. Buddhism teaches that one has transmigrated helplessly since beginningless time under the influence of ignorance and that ignorance has led to performance of actions that have created connections with cyclic existence. In order to break this pattern, one must reorient one's thinking to accord with reality.

One of the greatest obstacles to this lies in the fact that worldly existence is full of traps that beguile the unwary and blind them to the harsh realities of the world. The world is full of suffering, aging, and death, but most of us overlook these and focus on momentary pleasures. Those who view cyclic existence in accordance with reality, however, understand that all who are caught up in it must inevitably suffer over and over again. This truth was recognized with full existential clarity by the Buddha on the night of his enlightenment, and he expressed it in a set of propositions that are referred to by Buddhists as the "four noble truths." These are: (1) the truth of suffering, (2) the truth of the origin of suffering, (3) the truth of the cessation of suffering, and (4) the truth of the eightfold path which overcomes suffering.

The truth of suffering holds that all of cyclic existence is inevitably connected with suffering. It is important to note that the term translated here as "suffering" has a wide range of connotations. *Duhkha*, or suffering, refers not only to physical pain, but also to emotional turmoil, discomfort, dissatisfaction, and sorrow. The truth of suffering is a recognition that these things are found in the lives of ordinary beings and that they generally view them as being unpleasant.

It should be noted that Buddhism does not deny the presence of happiness in human life. What it does deny is that happiness can be permanent for those enmeshed in cyclic existence, which is characterized by constant change. Even when one finds happiness, it must inevitably end, only to be replaced by loss, longing, and unhappiness. This state of affairs is considered to be unacceptable, and Buddhism teaches a path by which this unsatisfactory situation may be transcended.

Suffering is generally divided into three types: (1) the suffering of misery, which includes physical and mental sufferings; (2) the suffering of change, which includes all contaminated feelings of happiness (called sufferings because they are subject to change at any time, which leads to suffering); and (3) compositional suffering—the suffering endemic to cyclic existence, in which sentient beings are prone to suffering due to being under the influence of contaminated actions and afflictions.

The first type is easily identifiable and includes ordinary pains, such as headaches, physical injuries, and emotional pain. All beings naturally wish to be free from this type of suffering and to experience its opposite, which is physical and emotional pleasure.

The second type is more difficult to identify, since it includes things that ordinary beings mistakenly think of as being pleasurable, such as buying a new car. Looking at a desirable car for the first time, most people view it as something that will bring pleasure and happiness, not even considering the fact that all cars break down, often in inconvenient places. Moreover, they cost money for the initial purchase, for taxes, insurance, maintenance, gas, etc., and from the moment they are driven out of the dealer's lot they begin their inevitable progress toward the junkyard. What begins as a gleaming high-performance machine begins to rust, leak oil, and require repairs, until finally it becomes unusable and has to be discarded. As the Dalai Lama points out,

> When you first get it, you are very happy, pleased, and satisfied but then as you use it, problems arise. If it were intrinsically pleasurable, no matter how much more you used this cause of satisfaction, your pleasure should increase correspondingly, but such does not happen. As you use it more and more, it begins to cause trouble. Therefore, such things are called sufferings of change; it is through change that their nature of suffering is displayed.

Anything impermanent inevitably leads to suffering, since eventually it breaks down, leaving one with a sense of disappointment and loss.

The third type of suffering is the basis for the first two, since it refers to the fundamentally unsatisfactory nature of cyclic existence, which is so constituted that it entails suffering for all who are caught up in it. The Dalai Lama says that

> it is called pervasive compositional suffering since it pervades or applies to all types of transmigrating beings and is compositional in that it is the basis of present suffering and induces future suffering. There is no way of getting away from this type of suffering except by ending the continuum of rebirth.

Transmigrating beings experience sufferings as a result of their previous negative actions, actions motivated by afflictive emotions *(nyon mongs, klesa)*. The primary afflictive emotions are ignorance, desire, and aversion. These motivate people to engage in negative actions that inevitably rebound on them, and they also tend to produce concordant mental states, leading to a vicious cycle.

The cycle can only be broken through eliminating the motivating negative emotions. Although we have been caught in transmigration since beginningless time, it is possible for an individual to bring her own transmigration to an end. This is the focus of the second noble truth. Buddha recognized that suffering has a basis, and he identified this basis as desire motivated by ignorance. Beings suffer due to their afflicted desires, and the way to overcome suffering lies in eliminating them. In a discussion of the first two noble truths, Kalu Rinpoche indicates that Buddha

> taught these subjects extensively and in great detail, and it is important for us to understand them in order to recognize the limitations of our present situation. We have to understand our circumstances and know that, given the nature of cause and effect . . . we can look forward to nothing but suffering. We have to realize that we are enmeshed in the various factors of cause and effect, which lead first to one state of suffering and on that basis to another, and so on.

When we have seen the inherent limitations of this situation, we can begin to consider getting out of it. We can begin to look for the possibility of transcending samsaric existence and all its attendant sufferings, limitations, and frustrations.

Desire is divided into three types: (1) desire for pleasure, (2) desire for continued existence, and (3) desire for non-existence. The first type is the result of contact with sense objects that one finds pleasurable, and it creates the seeds of future attachments. The second type is the common wish that one's existence will continue forever and the tendency to live as if this is the case, despite the overwhelming evidence that one will inevitably die. The third desire arises from the belief that everything comes to an end in death, and so it is wrong to find happiness in material things, or in the present life, since death is inevitable. Buddhist philosophy holds that all three kinds of desire are mistaken and that all must be overcome in order to find lasting happiness.

The third noble truth indicates that it is possible to bring suffering to an end through overcoming afflicted desire. Suffering depends on causes, and if one removes the causes, suffering will disappear. The problem is cognitive, and so the solution is also cognitive: we suffer due to false ideas about what is pleasurable, worthwhile, or desirable, and the truth of the path indicates a way to restructure one's cognitions in accordance with reality in order to bring suffering to an end.

The path is commonly referred to as the "noble eightfold path" because it is divided into: (1) correct view, (2) correct intention, (3) correct speech, (4) correct action, (5) correct livelihood, (6) correct effort, (7) correct mindfulness, and (8) correct meditative absorption.

The eightfold path outlines a course of practice aimed at overcoming suffering. The root of suffering is said to be desire based on ignorance, and the primary concern of the path is overcoming this basic cause of all cyclic existence. The parts of the path are commonly divided into three groups (called the three trainings because each represents a particular aspect of the training program of the path). The first two members of the eightfold path are grouped under the heading of "wisdom," since they entail a basic cognitive reorientation that is necessary as an initial prerequisite for the path. The next three are classed as "ethics," because taken together they are concerned with training in moral actions and attitudes. Morality is seen as a necessary prerequisite for progress on the Buddhist path, since a person with good morality is calm and self-assured. The last three are grouped under the heading of "meditative absorption" because they are concerned with developing concentration.

Correct view consists of both positive and negative aspects: on the positive side, correct view involves knowing certain key Buddhist concepts, such as the four truths and the operation of dependent arising, or understanding what actions lead to good and bad effects. It also involves getting rid of wrong views, the most important and dangerous of which is the "view of true personhood," the view that the elements of the psycho-physical personality constitute a truly existent person. Wrong views are to be avoided not merely because they are philosophically or logically untenable, but because they are conceptual manifestations of ignorance, desire, and aversion. Holding them leads to further desire, hatred, ignorance, and ultimately to further suffering.

Correct intention involves developing a proper orientation, that is, a mental attitude that aims at following the Buddhist path to enlightenment. In cultivating correct intention, a person decides what is ultimately important, what he or she will work at. In a Buddhist context, the ultimate goal is enlightenment, and a person who has correct intention will take this as the goal of religious activity. This decision is of fundamental importance, because in order to achieve something difficult (such as enlightenment) it is necessary to devote oneself to it single-mindedly. A person with correct intention cultivates an attitude of renunciation of worldly things, avoids harming others, and engages in activities that are concordant with the goal.

A person with correct speech avoids abusive, coarse, and untruthful speech, speaks what is correct and true, speaks gently and nonbelligerently. Since one's speech is an outward manifestation of internal mental states, cultivating truthful and pleasant speech also leads to gradual development of concordant mental attitudes.

For monks and nuns, correct action involves keeping the rules of monastic discipline outlined in the system of "individual liberation," and for laypersons it involves keeping the lay precepts of individual liberation, which forbid killing, stealing, lying, sexual misconduct, and ingesting intoxicants. These rules are not simply arbitrary strictures, and they are said to have a practical basis: cultivating morality results in mental calm, and this calm is a prerequisite for later concentrations and advanced meditative states. In order to attain the higher meditative states, one must overcome the mental troubles and disturbances that agitate the minds of ordinary beings and that impede their ability to concentrate. Correct action is mainly concerned with avoiding the physical expressions of negative mental attitudes.

Correct livelihood is also connected with moral training: it consists in avoiding occupations that result in breaking the precepts, occupations that lead people to kill, lie, cheat, steal, or engage in sexual misconduct. Prohibited occupations include hunting, fishing, meat-selling, making weapons, prostitution, and other activities that involve people in evil deeds. These are to be avoided because they create negative mental states as well as bad karma, and this combination prevents a person from successfully practicing meditation.

The next three aspects of the path are concerned with meditation. A person who has cultivated the previous aspects of the path has created a foundation consisting of proper attitudes and actions. Based on morality and the calm mental states that it produces, a person has the prerequisites for pursuing the higher levels of meditative practice. Correct effort involves properly orienting the mind toward the desired goal of liberation. In this practice, a yogin overcomes negative feelings that inhibit equanimity and meditation, such as impatience, slothfulness, excessive pride, vengefulness, concern with unimportant things such as wealth, power, etc. The yogin then focuses on the goal of liberation through concentrated meditative practice. This involves steady effort rather than spurts of enthusiastic activity.

Correct mindfulness is emphasized in Buddhist meditation manuals as being of fundamental importance in meditation. In order to attain liberation, one must initially develop awareness of what one is doing and why one is doing it. In addition, one must learn to control and regulate the mind. A person seeking liberation must move from his or her present state of confusion and random thoughts to a state of clarity and mindfulness in which he or she is aware of mental processes and attitudes and, more importantly, is in control of them.

Correct concentration requires the previous steps. Without a concentrated mind that can fix itself calmly and one-pointedly on a single object without being distracted by laxity or excitement, one cannot properly enter into the concentrations, which are advanced meditative states in which one's attention is fully concentrated on one's object of observation.

Taken together, the four noble truths constitute a summary of the Buddhist path. The truth of suffering indicates the basic problem that Buddhism proposes to overcome, and the truth of the origin of suffering shows the cause of the problem. The third truth holds that the negative elements of the human condition are not immutable, and the fourth truth indicates how a person may bring about a cognitive reorientation and transcend suffering.

APPEARANCE AND REALITY

According to Buddhist meditation theory, the basic causes of suffering are cognitive in origin. We mentally create a vision of reality, but because of ignorance this vision is skewed and does not reflect things as they are. Some of our wrong ideas are harmless, but others lead to the creation of negative mental states, such as ignorance, desire, or hatred. One of the most dangerous of these wrong ideas is the false notion of a self, which Buddhist meditation theory contends is innately present in all human beings. On a very basic level, every person believes in a self or soul that is un-created, immortal, unchanging, and permanent. Contrary to some other religious systems, Buddhism denies the existence of such an entity and contends that in order to attain liberation one must eliminate the false idea of a self or soul.

There has been some disagreement among western scholars of Buddhism concerning whether or not Śākyamuni Buddha ever really advocated this idea, but there is no debate among Tibetan scholars, who view the concept of selflessness as a cornerstone of Buddhist thought and practice. In Tibetan meditation texts, the concept of a self or soul is said to be based on a false imputation, and techniques to examine this concept in order to eradicate it are an important focus of meditation literature.

But if the concept is common to all human beings, where do we get it? And if it is a false concept, why is it so universally accepted? The answer, Buddhist texts suggest, is that although there is a basis for this idea of a self the imputation is still a false one. The basis for the imputation of self is the collection of elements that together constitute the psycho-physical personality, which Buddhism divides into five "aggregates": (1) form, (2) feelings, (3) discriminations, (4) composi-tional factors, and (5) consciousness.

These are the constituents of all imperma-nent phenomena and are the basis on which we impute the notions of "I" and "mine." Taken together, they are the constituents of the indi-vidual, but we mistakenly impute something more, an essence, a self or soul. When one ana-lyzes this concept to locate its basis, however, all that one finds are these five aggregates, none of which can constitute a self because they are con-stantly changing, whereas the self that sentient beings imagine is self-sufficient and enduring.

Form refers to things that constitute the physical world, which includes the sense organs (eye, ear, nose, tongue, body, and mind) and their objects. These are material things composed of

the four great elements: earth, water, fire, and air. *Feelings* are our sensations of things, and these are divided into three types: pleasant, unpleas-ant, and neutral. They result when the senses come into contact with objects. *Discriminations* are the differentiations we make regarding objects of perception as a result of contact. They cause us to discriminate between colors, sounds, smells, tastes, tangible objects, and mental images. *Consciousness* includes the six types of consciousnesses: eye, ear, nose, tongue, body, and mind. *Compositional factors* are volitional activi-ties, both good and bad. Karma is included within compositional factors, since it directs the mind in particular directions, thus influencing the content of future mental states.

Taken together, these five aggregates consti-tute the sum total of the psycho-physical per-sonality, and Buddhist teachers claim that the totality of an individual is included within this group. Ordinary beings, however, impute some-thing more, an enduring, uncreated "self" that exists apart from and independently of the aggregates, but this is nothing more than a label imputed to these constantly changing factors. This mistaken notion leads to grasping and attachment, which in turn result in harmful actions, and so the mistaken belief in a self is said to be one of the most powerful factors that keep ordinary beings enmeshed in cyclic existence. According to Lama Zopa,

> The door that leads us out of samsāra is the wisdom that realizes the emptiness of self-existence. This wisdom is the direct remedy for the ignorance which is both a cause and effect of clinging to the self, and which believes the self or "I" to be inherently and in-dependently existent. . . . We then become addicted to this phantom I and treasure it as if it were a most precious possession. Wisdom recognizes that such an autonomously existing I is totally nonexistent and thus, by wisdom, ignorance is destroyed. It is said in the Buddhist scriptures that to realize the correct view of emptiness, even for a moment, shakes the foundations of samsāra.

This is not as easy as it might at first appear. The false notion of self is deeply ingrained, and every sentient being has cultivated it not only in the present lifetime, but for countless past lives. Since it has been reified and strengthened over such a long period of time, it is deeply embedded in our basic assumptions and consequently very difficult to dislodge. Because of its strength, it is not possible to eradicate the idea of self all at once through simply recognizing that the concept is untenable (although this is an important first step). One initially understands selflessness conceptually, through a process of reasoning. The reasoning begins with a consideration of how the self appears to us, that is, as something that is autonomous, enduring, and independent of the psycho-physical continuum.

The reasoning process begins with an analysis of whether or not the self can exist in the way that it appears. The meditator first determines that if there is a self, it must be either separate from or identical with the psycho-physical aggregates. If it is different from them, then there is no connection between the self and the meditator, since they are different factualities. The self appears to consciousness as something enduring and self-sufficient, but all of us are impermanent and only exist due to causes and conditions that are external to ourselves. The only constant in human life is change, and all the constituents of the psycho-physical personality are changing from moment to moment; thus the meditator should conclude that even if there were a self different from the aggregates, it would be unrelated to him, since an autonomous, enduring self could have no conceivable relation with an impermanent being. The Dalai Lama concludes that

> if the self or the person exists independently, separate from the aggregates, then after mentally disintegrating the aggregates one should be able to point out a self or person existing independent of these aggregates—but one cannot. If the self or the person is a totally different and separate entity from the aggregates, then there should be no relation between the self and the aggregates at all.

Having eliminated the possibility of a self that exists independently of the aggregates, one then considers the possibility that there might be a self that is the same as the aggregates. If there is such a self, it must be the same as at least one of them; but when one examines each in turn one realizes that they are all impermanent, changing from moment to moment, and there is no underlying unity or essence that remains throughout the ongoing process of change. The Dalai Lama points out that the idea of a self that is identical with the aggregates is untenable because

> if the self exists as single or totally one with the aggregates, then the contradiction arises that just as the aggregates are many, the self should also be multiple. Also, when this present life ceases at the time of death, the continuity of the self should also cease right then. And, if the self or the person is totally one with the aggregates, how can one have the natural feeling of the self being the master of these aggregates and the aggregates being the subjects and possessions of that self?

The only conclusion that can legitimately be reached is that the self is a fiction, a mere label superimposed onto the constantly changing aggregates, a self created and reified by the mind, but lacking any substantial reality. This reasoning process alone does not eliminate the idea, however; it merely weakens it. Because it is so deeply ingrained, the idea of self is only eliminated through repeated meditation on the reasonings of selflessness, which enable the yogin to become progressively more familiar with the understanding that there is no self or essence. The Dalai Lama concludes that "when such a realization is maintained and reinforced through constant meditation and familiarization, you will be able to develop it into an intuitive or direct experience."

Many Westerners reject this notion, contending that it would be a sort of cognitive suicide. The idea that the self (which is assumed even by people who reject religions that propound the idea) does not exist is profoundly disturbing to many non-Buddhists, but in Buddhist thought the denial of self is not seen as constituting a loss, but rather is viewed as a profoundly liberating insight. Since the innate idea of self implies an autonomous, unchanging essence, if such a thing were in fact the core of one's being, it would mean that change would be impossible, and one would be stuck being just what one is right now. Because there is no such self, however, we are constantly changing, and thus are open toward the future. One's nature is never fixed and determined, and so through engaging in Buddhist practice one can exert control over the process of change and progress in wisdom, compassion, patience, and other good qualities. One can even become a buddha, a fully enlightened being who is completely liberated from all the frailties, sufferings, and limitations of ordinary beings. But this is only possible because there is no fixed and static self, no soul that exists self-sufficiently, separated from the ongoing process of change.

Such intellectual understanding is not enough by itself, however. Even when beginning meditators gain a conceptual grasp of the doctrine of emptiness, it does not weaken the strength of the appearances of inherent existence. People and things still appear to exist from their own side, independently of external causes and conditions. On a personal level, even when one intellectually recognizes that there is no basis for the mistaken concept of "I," this false idea still appears. As an analogy, a physicist might recognize that the table in front of her is mostly composed of space and that the matter of the table consists of infinitesimally tiny particles in a constant state of vibration, but the table still appears as a solid, hard object.

Because intellectual comprehension of a concept is not the same as fully grasping it, Buddhist texts make a distinction between three levels of understanding, which are called respectively "wisdom arisen from hearing," "wisdom arisen from thinking," and "wisdom arisen from meditating." The first type is the superficial understanding one gains from simply hearing someone else teaching something. It does not involve a great deal of analysis, but is primarily based on listening to someone and understanding the meaning of the words. Wisdom arisen from thinking comes from pondering the significance of what one has heard and gaining a deeper understanding, although this is still only conceptual. Wisdom arisen from meditating occurs when one fully internalizes what one has learned and pondered, through comprehending with direct perception on a level that transcends merely conceptual understanding. At this level of understanding, one moves beyond dependence on the mere words of the teaching and perceives the truth directly.

DEPENDENT ARISING

Closely connected with the idea of selflessness is the doctrine of "dependent arising," which holds that all compounded phenomena arise due to causes and conditions external to themselves, remain in existence due to causes and conditions, and eventually pass away due to other causes and conditions. The classical formulation of this doctrine expresses it as follows: "Because this exists, that arises; because this is produced, that is produced." The first line indicates that effects arise from conditions unalterably, and the second states that objects are produced from conditions that are themselves impermanent. This process is broken down into twelve steps, which are referred to as the "twelve links of dependent arising":

1. ignorance
2. action
3. consciousness
4. name and form
5. the six sources
6. contact
7. feeling
8. attachment
9. grasping
10. existence
11. birth
12. aging and death

In this process, the primary factor is *ignorance*. This is not just an absence of knowledge, but is also a consciousness that perceives reality incorrectly. It motivates beings to engage in actions, but since the basis of the actions is mistaken, the actions lead to negative reactions. The most basic type of ignorance is the belief in an inherently existent self, which leads to thoughts of acquiring things for this self to possess.

In the context of the schema of the twelve links of dependent arising, *action* generally refers to a defining action that determines one's future rebirth. If this action is meritorious, one will be reborn in one of the three good transmigrations—human, demi-god, or god. If it is a negative action, one will be reborn in one of the three lower transmigrations—animal, hungry ghost, or hell-being.

The defining action conditions one's *consciousness*, since each type of transmigration has a distinctive type of consciousness. (All are characterized by basic ignorance, however, and ignorant thoughts tend to perpetuate themselves.) At the beginning of a new life, one acquires a particular sort of consciousness, and this is determined by one's past deeds. If one is born as a human, one will have a human consciousness, which will be conditioned by one's past actions. Moreover, a human who engaged in acts of violence in a past life, for instance, will be predisposed toward violence in the present life, and unless he does something to reverse this trend, he will likely engage in violence in the present life, leading to negative karma and a lower rebirth.

Consciousness conditions the next link, *name and form*. *Name* refers to the aggregates of feelings, discriminations, compositional factors, and consciousness. *Form* refers to the aggregate of form. Together these constitute the psychophysical personality, and this is conditioned by the predispositions that have been inherited from past lives. According to Kalu Rinpoche, these are influenced by the false sense of self, which all of us have cultivated since beginningless time.

From this basic dualistic or discursive consciousness there arises the sense of self, of "I." At the same time, whatever forms are seen, whatever sounds are heard—in short, whatever phenomena are experienced—are perceived as some version of "other." In this way there occurs a definite split into self and other. At this point, although there is no physical basis for consciousness, there is nevertheless a sense of embodiment, of identity coalescing. There is also the sense of naming things in the phenomenal world.

The *six sources* are the sense powers of eye, ear, nose, tongue, body, and mind. As the form aggregate develops, these also mature, and the process is influenced by the previous four members. As the sense powers develop, one begins to have contact with external things, and this contact is also conditioned by the previous stages. *Contact* is the coming together of object, sense faculty, and consciousness. It conditions the next link, *feeling*, which has the function of discriminating some things as pleasant, some as unpleasant, and others as neutral in accordance with how they are distinguished in contact.

All of these are conditioned by ignorance, and so they are all mistaken with respect to their appearing objects. As one develops ideas of pleasure, pain, and neutrality, one begins to grasp at things that are pleasant and avoid things that are unpleasant. Thus one experiences *grasping* and *attachment*, the eighth and ninth links of the process.

These in turn create the basis for continued *existence*. Existence results from grasping and attachment: when one becomes attached to the things of cyclic existence, one assures that in the future one will again be reborn in cyclic existence. This is a predisposition that began with ignorance, which in turn led to actions, and these led to contact and grasping.

All of these taken together constitute the link to future *birth*. Due to the force of previously generated desires, a being who is about to be reborn feels desire toward its future parents. If the being is to be reborn as a male, it will feel desire toward its future mother, and if it will be a female, it will feel desire toward its future father. Moreover, the type of being for which it will feel desire is determined by the nature of its past karma. If its karma destines it for rebirth as a human, then it will feel desire for human parents, and if it will be reborn as an animal, then it will feel desire for animal parents, and so forth. It will be drawn toward a male and female who are about to copulate and who are appropriate for its future life situation.

The completion of the process of rebirth occurs when the future father impregnates the future mother, and the being takes rebirth in the appropriate life situation. The moment of physical birth is the culmination of this process.

The final factor, *aging and death*, begins at the moment of birth. Everything that is born is moving toward death, and in each moment cells are dying and being replaced by new ones. Eventually the process begins to break down and one's physical condition degenerates. The inevitable result is death, and so Sogyal Rinpoche asks,

What is our life but this dance of transient forms? Isn't everything always changing: the leaves on the trees in the park . . . the seasons, the weather, the time of day, the people passing you in the street? And what about us? Doesn't everything we have done in the past seem like a dream now? . . . The cells of our body are dying, the neurons in our brain are decaying, even the expression on our face is always changing, depending on our mood. What we call our basic character is only a "mindstream," nothing more.

Most beings are beguiled by the transitory things of cyclic existence and seek to acquire those that are perceived as pleasant. They are blind to the inevitable results of such actions, which only bind them to continued existence.

RAMAKRISHNA
Many Paths to the Same Summit

RAMAKRISHNA *(1836–1886) is perhaps the best-known Hindu saint of modern times. He had his first experience of spiritual ecstasy at the age of seven. He worshipped Rama, Krishna, Shiva, Kali, Allah, and Jesus.*

GOD has made different religions to suit different aspirants, times, and countries. All doctrines are only so many paths; but a path is by no means God Himself. Indeed, one can reach God if one follows any of the paths with wholehearted devotion. One may eat a cake with icing either straight or sidewise. It will taste sweet either way.

As one and the same material, water is called by different names by different peoples, one calling it water, another eau, a third aqua, and another pani, so the one Everlasting-Intelligent-Bliss is invoked by some as God, by some as Allah, by some as Jehovah, and by others as Brahman.

As one can ascend to the top of a house by means of a ladder or a bamboo or a staircase or a rope, so diverse are the ways and means to approach God, and every religion in the world shows one of these ways.

As the young wife in a family shows her love and respect to her father-in-law, mother-in-law, and every other member of the family, and at the same time loves her husband more than these; similarly, being firm in thy devotion to the deity

Ramakrishna, "Many Paths to the Same Summit" from *The Religions of Man* by Huston Smith, New York: Harper Brothers, 1958.

of thy own choice, do not despise other deities, but honour them all.

Bow down and worship where others kneel, for where so many have been paying the tribute of adoration the kind Lord must manifest himself, for he is all mercy.

The devotee who has seen God in one aspect only knows him in that aspect alone. But he who has seen him in manifold aspects is alone in a position to say, "All these forms are of one God and God is multiform." He is formless and with form, and many are his forms which no one knows.

The Saviour is the messenger of God. He is like the viceroy of a mighty monarch. As when there is some disturbance in a far-off province, the king sends his viceroy to quell it, so wherever there is a decline of religion in any part of the world, God sends his Saviour there. It is one and the same Saviour that, having plunged into the ocean of life, rises up in one place and is known as Krishna (the leading Hindu incarnation of God), and diving down again rises in another place and is known as Christ.

Every man should follow his own religion. A Christian should follow Christianity, a Mohammedan should follow Mohammedanism, and so on. For the Hindus, the ancient path, the path of the Aryan sages, is the best.

People partition off their lands by means of boundaries, but no one can partition off the all-embracing sky overhead. The indivisible sky surrounds all and includes all. So common man in ignorance says, "My religion is the only one, my religion is the best." But when his heart is illumined by true knowledge, he knows that above all these wars of sects and sectarians presides the one indivisible, eternal, all-knowing bliss.

As a mother, in nursing her sick children, gives rice and curry to one, and sago arrowroot to another, and bread and butter to a third, so the Lord has laid out different paths for different men suitable to their natures.

Dispute not. As you rest firmly on your own faith and opinion, allow others also the equal liberty to stand by their own faiths and opinions. By mere disputation you will never succeed in convincing another of his error. When the grace of God descends on him, each one will understand his own mistakes.

There was a man who worshipped Shiva but hated all other deities. One day Shiva appeared to him and said, "I shall never be pleased with thee so long as thou hatest the other gods." But the man was inexorable. After a few days Shiva again appeared to him and said, "I shall never be pleased with thee so long as thou hatest." The man kept silent. After a few days Shiva again appeared to him. This time one side of his body was that of Shiva, and the other side that of Vishnu. The man was half pleased and half displeased. He laid his offerings on the side representing Shiva, and did not offer anything to the side representing Vishnu. Then Shiva said, "Thy bigotry is unconquerable. I, by assuming this dual aspect, tried to convince thee that all gods and goddesses are but various aspects of the one Absolute Brahman."

KEIJI NISHITANI
What Is Religion?

KEIJI NISHITANI *(1900–1990) was a famous Japanese philosopher and representative of "the Kyoto School," who was conversant in Christianity, Buddhism, and Existentialism.*

"WHAT is religion?" we ask ourselves, or, looking at it the other way around, "What is the purpose of religion for us? Why do we need it?" Though the question about the need for religion may be a familiar one, it already contains a problem. In one sense, for the person who poses the question, religion does not seem to be something he needs. The fact that he asks the question at all amounts to an admission that religion has not yet become a necessity for him. In another sense, however, it is surely in the nature of religion to be necessary for just such a person. Wherever questioning individuals like this are to be found, the need for religion is there as well. In short, the relationship we have to religion is a contradictory one: those for whom religion is *not* a necessity are, for that reason, the very ones for whom religion *is* a necessity. There is no other thing of which the same can be said.

When asked, "Why do we need learning and the arts?" we might try to explain in reply that such things are necessary for the advancement of mankind, for human happiness, for the cultivation of the individual, and so forth. Yet even if we can say why we need such things, this does not imply that we cannot get along without them. Somehow life would still go on. Learning and the arts may be indispensable to living well, but they are not indispensable to living. In that sense, they can be considered a kind of luxury.

Food, on the other hand, is essential to life. Nobody would turn to somebody else and ask him why he eats. Well, maybe an angel or some other celestial being who has no need to eat might ask such questions, but men do not. Religion, to judge from current conditions in which many people are in fact getting along without it, is clearly not the kind of necessity that food is. Yet this does not mean that it is merely something we need to live *well*. Religion has to do with life itself. Whether the life we are living will end up in extinction or in the attainment of eternal life is a matter of the utmost importance for life itself. In no sense is religion to be called a luxury. Indeed, this is why religion is an indispensable necessity for those very people who fail to see the need for it. Herein lies the distinctive feature of religion that sets it apart from the mere life of "nature" and from culture. Therefore, to say that we need religion for example, for the sake of social order, or human welfare, or public morals is a mistake, or at least a confusion of priorities. Religion must not be considered from the viewpoint of its *utility*, any more than life should. A religion concerned primarily with its own utility bears witness to its own degeneration. One can ask about the utility of things like eating for the natural life, or of things like learning and the arts for culture. In fact, in such matters the question of utility should be of constant concern. Our ordinary mode of being is restricted to these levels of natural or cultural life. But it is in breaking through that ordinary mode of being and overturning it from the ground up, in pressing us back to the elemental source of life where life itself is seen as useless, that religion becomes something we need—a *must* for human life.

Two points should be noted from what has just been said. First, religion is at all times the individual affair of each individual. This sets it apart from things like culture, which, while related to the individual, do not need to concern each individual. Accordingly, we cannot understand what religion is from the outside. The religious quest alone is the key to understanding it; there is no other way. This is the most important point to be made regarding the essence of religion.

Second, from the standpoint of the essence of religion, it is a mistake to ask "What is the purpose of religion for us?" and one that clearly betrays an attitude of trying to understand religion apart from the religious quest. It is a question that must be broken through by another question coming from within the person who asks it. There is no other road that can lead to an understanding of what religion is and what purpose it serves. The counterquestion that achieves this breakthrough is one that asks, "For what purpose do I myself exist?" Of everything else we can ask its purpose for us, but not of religion. With regard to everything else we can make a *telos* of ourselves as individuals, as man, or as mankind, and evaluate those things in relation to our life and existence. We put ourselves as individuals/man/mankind at the center and weigh the significance of everything as the *contents* of our lives as individuals/man/mankind. But religion upsets the posture from which we think of ourselves as *telos* and center for all things. Instead, religion poses as a starting point the question: "For what purpose do I exist?"

We become aware of religion as a need, as a must for life, only at the level of life at which everything else loses its necessity and its utility. Why do we exist at all? Is not our very existence and human life ultimately meaningless? Or, if there is a meaning or significance to it all, where do we find it? When we come to doubt the meaning of our existence in this way, when we have become a question to ourselves, the religious quest awakens within us. These questions and the quest they give rise to show up when the mode of looking at and thinking about everything in terms of how it relates to *us* is broken through, where the mode of living that puts us at the center of everything is overturned. This is why the question of religion in the form, "Why do we need religion?" obscures the way to its own answer from the very start. It blocks our becoming a question to ourselves.

The point at which the ordinarily necessary things of life, including learning and the arts, all lose their necessity and utility is found at those times when death, nihility, or sin—or any of those situations that entail a fundamental negation of our life, existence, and ideals, that undermine the roothold of our existence and bring the meaning of life into question—become pressing personal problems for us. This can occur through an illness that brings one face-to-face with death, or through some turn of events that robs one of what had made life worth living. . . .

Nihility refers to that which renders meaningless the meaning of life. When we become a question to ourselves and when the problem of why we exist arises, this means that nihility has emerged from the ground of our existence and that our very existence has turned into a question mark. The appearance of this nihility signals nothing less than that one's awareness of self-existence has penetrated to an extraordinary depth.

Normally we proceed through life, on and on, with our eye fixed on something or other, always caught up with something within or without ourselves. It is these engagements that prevent the deepening of awareness. They block off the way to an opening up of that horizon on which nihility appears and self-being becomes a question. This is even the case with learning and the arts and the whole range of other cultural engagements. But when this horizon does open up at the bottom of those engagements that keep life moving continually on and on, something seems to halt and linger before us. This something is the meaninglessness that lies in wait at the bottom of those very engagements that bring meaning to life. This is the point at which that sense of nihility, that sense that "everything is the same" we find in Nietzsche and Dostoevski, brings the restless, forward-advancing pace of life to a halt and makes it take a step back. In the Zen phrase, it "turns the light to what is directly underfoot."

In the forward progress of everyday life, the ground beneath our feet always falls behind as we move steadily ahead; we overlook it. Taking a step back to shed light on what is underfoot of the self—"stepping back to come to the self," as another ancient Zen phrase has it—marks a conversion in life itself. This fundamental conversion in life is occasioned by the opening up of the horizon of nihility at the ground of life. It is nothing less than a conversion from the self-centered (or man-centered) mode of being, which always asks what *use* things have for us (or for man), to an attitude that asks for what *purpose* we ourselves (or man) exist. Only when we stand at this turning point does the question "What is religion?" really become our own.

LAO-TZU
A Taoist View of the World

LAO-TZU *(6th century BC) was a Chinese philosopher, a Taoist who thought that the most important thing in life is to get in touch with our true natures and our place in nature as a whole. His concept of religion, therefore, was not focused so much on God or gods but on "the way" (Tao) of nature. To know the world and to know God (although these are not so distinct in Chinese philosophy) are not to have true and provable beliefs but rather "to know the way," being able to course through the cosmos—like a driver or a charioteer—without encountering any unnecessary obstacles. What follows is a brief selection from Lao-tzu.*

THE LAO-TZU*

You carry the spiritual and sentient souls and
    unite them as one,
But can you keep them together?
You concentrate your vital forces and attain
    pliancy,
But can you assume the bearing of a child?
You cleanse the dark mirror of your mind,
But can you be free of imperfection?
You love the people and order the country properly,
But can you be anarchic?
Your senses are open to the world,
But can you act the female?
You are clear and penetrating in all things,

But can you be ignorant?
The most excellent ruler—the people do not
    know he's around;
The second most excellent—they love and
    praise him;
The next—they fear him;
And the worst—they look on him with contempt.
When his integrity is inadequate,
There will be those who do not trust him.
Relaxed, he is economical with his words.
When his accomplishments are full and the
    affairs of state are in proper order,
The common people all say, "We are naturally
    like this."

Lao-Tzu "A Taoist View of the World" trans. by Roger Ames. Reprinted by permission of the University of Hawaii Press and the author.

*Translated by Roger T. Ames.

You have to be bent to be made whole;
You have to be warped to be straightened;
You have to be hollow to be filled up;
You have to be broken to be renewed;
You have to have little to get a lot;
You have to have much to become confused;
Thus the Sage embraces One to be the model
  of the world.
It is because he does not show himself that he
  is brilliant;
It is because he does not assert himself that he
  is distinguished;
It is because he does not boast that he is
  accomplished;
It is because he is not conceited that he is
  enduring.
It is only because he does not compete that no
  one in the world is able to compete with him.
As the ancients said, "You have to be bent to be
  made whole."
How can this be empty talk?
This is really returning to it whole.

One who understands masculinity and
  preserves femininity
Is the river gorge of the world.
As the river gorge of the world,
One's constant potency does not quit one,

And one returns to a state of infancy.
One who understands white and preserves
  black
Is the model of the world.
As the model of the world,
One's constant potency does not err,
And one returns to a state of boundless-ness.

One who understands glory and preserves
  disgrace
Becomes the valley of the world.
As the valley of the world,
One's constant potency is thus sufficient,
And one returns to a state of unworked wood.
When unworked wood is splintered,
It becomes vessels.
The Sage uses it,
Only to become the chief of the officials.
Therefore, the best organization does not
  divide things up.
Tao engenders one,
One engenders two,
Two engenders three,
And three engenders the myriad things.
The myriad things shoulder the *yin* and
  embrace the *yang,*
And in blending their psychophysical vapors,
  they achieve harmony.

FRIEDRICH NIETZSCHE
God Is Dead

FRIEDRICH NIETZSCHE *(1844–1900) was one of the most controversial philosophers of the late nineteenth century. He famously attacked Christianity and proclaimed "the death of God." In the passages that follow, he portrays a madman making that announcement and then in a book polemically entitled* The Anti-Christ *expresses some of his own doubts about the capacity of religion to enhance our lives. To the contrary, he says, religion can impoverish life as well.*

Nietzsche, Friedrich, "God Is Dead" from *The Gay Science,* trans. W. Kaufman, Random House (p. 181).

HAVE you not heard of the madman who lit a lantern in the bright morning hours, ran to the market place, and cried incessantly: "I seek God! I seek God!"—As many of those who did not believe in God were standing around just then, he provoked much laughter. Has he got lost? Asked one. Did he lose his way like a child? Asked another. Or is he hiding? Is he afraid of us? Has he gone on a voyage? emigrated?—Thus they yelled and laughed.

The madman jumped into their midst and pierced them with his eyes. "Whither is God?" he cried; "I will tell you. *We have killed him*—you and I. All of us are his murderers."

"I have come too early," he said then; "my time is not yet. This tremendous event is still on its way, still wandering; it has not yet reached the ears of men."

FRIEDRICH NIETZSCHE
The Anti-Christ

ONE should not embellish or dress up Christianity: it has waged a *war to the death* against this *higher* type of man, it has excommunicated all the fundamental instincts of this type, it has distilled evil, the *Evil One,* out of these instincts—the strong human being as the type of reprehensibility, as the "outcast." Christianity has taken the side of everything weak, base, ill-constituted, it has made an ideal out of *opposition* to the preservative instincts of strong life; it has depraved the reason even of the intellectually strongest natures by teaching men to feel the supreme values of intellectuality as sinful, as misleading, as *temptations.* The most deplorable example: the depraving of Pascal, who believed his reason had been depraved by original sin while it had only been depraved by his Christianity!—...

Christianity is called the religion of *pity.*—Pity stands in antithesis to the tonic emotions which enhance the energy of the feeling of life: it has a depressive effect. One loses force when one pities. The loss of force which life has already sustained through suffering is increased and multiplied even further by pity. Suffering itself becomes contagious through pity; sometimes it can bring about a collective loss of life and life-energy which stands in an absurd relation to the quantum of its cause (—the case of the death of the Nazarene). This is the first aspect; but there is an even more important one. If one judges pity by the value of the reactions which it usually brings about, its mortally dangerous character appears in a much clearer light. Pity on the whole thwarts the law of evolution, which is the law of *selection.* It preserves what is ripe for destruction; it defends life's disinherited and condemned; through the abundance of the ill-constituted of all kinds which it *retains* in life it gives life itself a gloomy and questionable

Nietzsche, Friedrich "The Anti-Christ" from *Twilight of the Idols* by Friedrich Nietzsche, translated by R. J. Hollingdale with an introduction by Michael Tanner, pp. 47–53 (Penguin Classics 1968, this edition with a new introduction 1990). Translation and Translator's Note copyright © R. J. Hollingdale 1968. Introduction copyright © Michael Tanner 1990. Reproduced by permission of Penguin Books Ltd.

aspect. One has ventured to call pity a virtue (—in every *noble* morality it counts as weakness—); one has gone further, one has made of it *the* virtue, the ground and origin of all virtue—only, to be sure, from the viewpoint of a nihilistic philosophy which inscribed *Denial of Life* on its escutcheon—a fact always to be kept in view. Schopenhauer was within his rights in this: life is denied, made *more worthy of denial* by pity—pity is *practical* nihilism. To say it again, this depressive and contagious instinct thwarts those instincts bent on preserving and enhancing the value of life: both as a *multiplier* of misery and as a *conservator* of everything miserable it is one of the chief instruments for the advancement of *décadence*—pity persuades to *nothingness!* . . . One does not say "nothingness": one says "the Beyond"; or "God"; or "*true* life"; or Nirvana, redemption, blessedness. . . . This innocent rhetoric from the domain of religio-moral idiosyncrasy at once appears *much less innocent* when one grasps *which* tendency is here draping the mantle of sublime words about itself: the tendency *hostile to life.* Schopenhauer was hostile to life: *therefore* pity became for him a virtue. . . . Aristotle, as is well known, saw in pity a morbid and dangerous condition which one did well to get at from time to time with a purgative: he understood tragedy as a purgative. From the instinct for life one would indeed have to seek some means of puncturing so morbid and dangerous an accumulation of pity as that represented by the case of Schopenhauer (and unfortunately also by our entire literary and artistic *décadence* from St. Petersburg to Paris, from Tolstoy to Wagner), so that it might

burst. . . . Nothing in our unhealthy modernity is more unhealthy than Christian pity. . . .

I make war on this theologian instinct: I have found traces of it everywhere. Whoever has theologian blood in his veins has a wrong and dishonest attitude towards all things from the very first. The pathos that develops out of this is called *faith:* closing one's eyes with respect to oneself for good and all so as not to suffer from the sight of incurable falsity. Out of this erroneous perspective on all things one makes a morality, a virtue, a holiness for oneself, one unites the good conscience with seeing *falsely*—one demands that no *other* kind of perspective shall be accorded any value after one has rendered one's own sacrosanct with the names "God," "redemption," "eternity." I have dug out the theologian instinct everywhere: it is the most widespread, peculiarly *subterranean* form of falsity that exists on earth. What a theologian feels to be true *must* be false: this provides almost a criterion of truth. It is his deepest instinct of self-preservation which forbids any part of reality whatever to be held in esteem or even spoken of. Wherever the influence of the theologian extends *value judgement* is stood on its head, the concepts "true" and "false" are necessarily reversed: that which is most harmful to life is here called "true," that which enhances, intensifies, affirms, justifies it and causes it to triumph is called "false. . . ." If it happens that, by way of the "conscience" of princes (*or* of nations—), theologians stretch out their hands after *power,* let us be in no doubt *what* at bottom is taking place every time: the will to the end, the *nihilistic* will wants power. . . .

bell hooks

Love as the Practice of Freedom

bell hooks *is a professor of English at City College of New York. Her work focuses on cultural politics, feminism, critical race theory, and media criticism. Among her most recent books are* Real to Reel: Race, Sex, and Class at the Movies *(1996) and* Communion: The Female Search for Love *(2002).*

I
N this society, there is no powerful discourse on love emerging either from politically progressive radicals or from the Left. The absence of a sustained focus on love in progressive circles arises from a collective failure to acknowledge the needs of the spirit and an overdetermined emphasis on material concerns. Without love, our efforts to liberate ourselves and our world community from oppression and exploitation are doomed. As long as we refuse to address fully the place of love in struggles for liberation we will not be able to create a culture of conversion where there is a mass turning away from an ethic of domination.

Without an ethic of love shaping the direction of our political vision and our radical aspirations, we are often seduced, in one way or the other, into continued allegiance to systems of domination—imperialism, sexism, racism, classism. It has always puzzled me that women and men who spend a lifetime working to resist and oppose one form of domination can be systematically supporting another. I have been puzzled by powerful visionary black male leaders who can speak and act passionately in resistance to racial domination and accept and embrace sexist domination of women, by feminist white women who work daily to eradicate sexism but who have major blind spots when it comes to acknowledging and resisting racism and white supremacist domination of the planet. Critically examining these blind spots, I conclude that many of us are motivated to move against

domination solely when we feel our self-interest directly threatened. Often, then, the longing is not for a collective transformation of society, an end to politics of dominations, but rather simply for an end to what we feel is hurting us. This is why we desperately need an ethic of love to intervene in our self-centered longing for change. Fundamentally, if we are only committed to an improvement in that politic of domination that we feel leads directly to our individual exploitation or oppression, we not only remain attached to the status quo but act in complicity with it, nurturing and maintaining those very systems of domination. Until we are all able to accept the interlocking, interdependent nature of systems of domination and recognize specific ways each system is maintained, we will continue to act in ways that undermine our individual quest for freedom and collective liberation struggle.

The ability to acknowledge blind spots can emerge only as we expand our concern about politics of domination and our capacity to care about the oppression and exploitation of others. A love ethic makes this expansion possible. Civil rights movement transformed society in the United States because it was fundamentally rooted in a love ethic. No leader has emphasized this ethic more than Martin Luther King, Jr. He had the prophetic insight to recognize that a revolution built on any other foundation would fail. Again and again, King testified that he had "decided to love" because he believed deeply that if we are "seeking the highest good" we "find it through love" because this is "the key that unlocks the door to the meaning of ultimate reality." And the point of being in touch with a transcendent reality is that we struggle for justice, all the while realizing that we are always more than our race, class, or sex. When I look back at the civil rights movement which was in many ways limited because it was a reformist effort, I see that it had the power to move masses of people to act in the interest of racial justice—and because it was profoundly rooted in a love ethic.

The sixties Black Power movement shifted away from that love ethic. The emphasis was now more on power. And it is not surprising that the sexism that had always undermined the black liberation struggle intensified, that a misogynist approach to women became central as the equation of freedom with patriarchal manhood became a norm among black political leaders, almost all of whom were male. Indeed, the new militancy of masculinist black power equated love with weakness, announcing that the quintessential expression of freedom would be the willingness to coerce, do violence, terrorize, indeed utilize the weapons of domination. This was the crudest embodiment of Malcolm X's bold credo "by any means necessary."

On the positive side, Black Power movement shifted the focus of black liberation struggle from reform to revolution. This was an important political development, bringing with it a stronger anti-imperialist, global perspective. However, masculinist sexist biases in leadership led to the suppression of the love ethic. Hence progress was made even as something valuable was lost. While King had focused on loving our enemies, Malcolm called us back to ourselves, acknowledging that taking care of blackness was our central responsibility. Even though King talked about the importance of black self-love, he talked more about loving our enemies. Ultimately, neither he nor Malcolm lived long enough to fully integrate the love ethic into a vision of political decolonization that would provide a blueprint for the eradication of black self-hatred.

Black folks entering the realm of racially integrated, American life because of the success of civil rights and Black Power movement suddenly found we were grappling with an intensification of internalized racism. The deaths of these important leaders (as well as liberal white leaders who were major allies in the struggle for racial equality) ushered in tremendous feelings of hopelessness, powerlessness, and despair. Wounded in that space where we would know love, black people collectively experienced intense pain and anguish about our future. The absence of public spaces where that pain could be articulated, expressed, shared meant that it was held in—festering, suppressing the possibility that this collective grief would be reconciled in community even as ways to move beyond it and continue resistance struggle would be envisioned. Feeling as though "the world had really come to an end," in the sense that a hope had died that racial justice would become the norm, a life-threatening despair took hold in black life. We will never know to what extent the black masculinist focus on hardness and toughness served as a barrier preventing sustained public acknowledgment of the enormous grief and pain in black life. In *World as Lover, World as Self,* Joanna Macy emphasizes in her chapter on "Despair Work" that

> the refusal to feel takes a heavy toll. Not only is there an impoverishment of our emotional and sensory life . . . but this psychic numbing also impedes our capacity to process and respond to information. The energy expended in pushing down despair is diverted from more creative uses, depleting the resilience and imagination needed for fresh visions and strategies.

If black folks are to move forward in our struggle for liberation, we must confront the legacy of this unreconciled grief, for it has been the breeding ground for profound nihilistic despair. We must collectively return to a radical political vision of social change rooted in a love ethic and seek once again to convert masses of people, black and nonblack.

A culture of domination is anti-love. It requires violence to sustain itself. To choose love is to go against the prevailing values of the culture. Many people feel unable to love either themselves or others because they do not know what love is. Contemporary songs like Tina Turner's "What's Love Got To Do With It" advocate a system of exchange around desire, mirroring the economics of capitalism: the idea that love is important is mocked. In his essay "Love and Need: Is Love a Package or a Message?" Thomas Merton argues that we are taught within the framework of competitive consumer capitalism to see love as a business deal: "This concept of love assumes that the machinery of buying and selling of needs is what makes everything run. It regards life as a market and love as a variation on free enterprise." Though many folks recognize and critique the commercialization of love, they see no alternative. Not knowing how to love or even what love is, many people feel emotionally lost; others search for definitions, for ways to sustain a love ethic in a culture that negates human value and valorizes materialism.

The sales of books focusing on recovery, books that seek to teach folks ways to improve self-esteem, self-love, and our ability to be intimate in relationships, affirm that there is public awareness of a lack in most people's lives.

M. Scott Peck's self-help book *The Road Less Traveled* is enormously popular because it addresses that lack.

Peck offers a working definition for love that is useful for those of us who would like to make a love ethic the core of all human interaction. He defines love as "the will to extend one's self for the purpose of nurturing one's own or another's spiritual growth." Commenting on prevailing cultural attitudes about love, Peck writes:

Everyone in our culture desires to some extent to be loving, yet many are in fact not loving. I therefore conclude that the desire to love is not itself love. Love is as love does. Love is an act of will—namely both an intention and an action. Will also implies choice. We do not have to love. We choose to love.

His words echo Martin Luther King's declaration, "I have decided to love," which also emphasizes choice. King believed that love is "ultimately the only answer" to the problems facing this nation and the entire planet. I share that

belief and the conviction that it is in choosing love, and beginning with love as the ethical foundation for politics, that we are best positioned to transform society in ways that enhance the collective good.

It is truly amazing that King had the courage to speak as much as he did about the transformative power of love in a culture where such talk is often seen as merely sentimental. In progressive political circles, to speak of love is to guarantee that one will be dismissed or considered naive. But outside those circles there are many people who openly acknowledge that they are consumed by feelings of self-hatred, who feel worthless, who want a way out. Often they are too trapped by paralyzing despair to be able to engage effectively in any movement for social change. However, if the leaders of such movements refuse to address the anguish and pain of their lives, they will never be motivated to consider personal and political recovery. Any political movement that can effectively address these needs of the spirit in the context of liberation struggle will succeed.

In the past, most folks both learned about and tended the needs of the spirit in the context of religious experience. The institutionalization and commercialization of the church has undermined the power of religious community to transform souls, to intervene politically. Commenting on the collective sense of spiritual loss in modern society, Cornel West asserts:

There is a pervasive impoverishment of the spirit in American society, and especially among Black people. Historically, there have been cultural forces and traditions, like the church, that held cold-heartedness and mean-spiritedness at bay. However, today's impoverishment of the spirit means that this coldness and meanness is becoming more and more pervasive. The church kept these forces at bay by promoting a sense of respect for others, a sense of solidarity, a sense of meaning and value which would usher in the strength to battle against evil.

Life-sustaining political communities can provide a similar space for the renewal of the spirit. That can happen only if we address the needs of the spirit in progressive political theory and practice.

Often when Cornel West and I speak with large groups of black folks about the impoverishment of spirit in black life, the lovelessness, sharing that we can collectively recover ourselves in love, the response is overwhelming. Folks want to know how to begin the practice of loving. For me that is where education for critical consciousness has to enter. When I look at my life, searching it for a blueprint that aided me in the process of decolonization, of personal and political self-recovery, I know that it was learning the truth about how systems of domination operate that helped, learning to look both inward and outward with a critical eye. Awareness is central to the process of love as the practice of freedom. Whenever those of us who are members of exploited and oppressed groups dare to critically interrogate our locations, the identities and allegiances that inform how we live our lives, we begin the process of decolonization. If we discover in ourselves self-hatred, low self-esteem, or internalized white supremacist thinking and we face it, we can begin to heal. Acknowledging the truth of our reality, both individual and collective, is a necessary stage for personal and political growth. This is usually the most painful stage in the process of learning to love—the one many of us seek to avoid. Again, once we choose love, we instinctively possess the inner resources to confront that pain. Moving through the pain to the other side we find the joy, the freedom of spirit that a love ethic brings.

Choosing love we also choose to live in community, and that means that we do not have to change by ourselves. We can count on critical affirmation and dialogue with comrades walking a similar path. African American theologian Howard Thurman believed that we best learn love as the practice of freedom in the context of community. Commenting on this aspect of his work in the essay "Spirituality out on The Deep," Luther Smith reminds us that Thurman felt the United States was given to diverse groups of people by the universal life force as a location for the building of community. Paraphrasing Thurman,

he writes: "Truth becomes true in community. The social order hungers for a center (i.e. spirit, soul) that gives it identity, power, and purpose. America, and all cultural entities, are in search of a soul." Working within community, whether it be sharing a project with another person, or with a larger group, we are able to experience joy in struggle. That joy needs to be documented. For if we only focus on the pain, the difficulties which are surely real in any process of transformation, we only show a partial picture.

A love ethic emphasizes the importance of service to others. Within the value system of the United States any task or job that is related to "service" is devalued. Service strengthens our capacity to know compassion and deepens our insight. To serve another I cannot see them as an object, I must see their subject-hood. Sharing the teaching of Shambala warriors, Buddhist Joanna Macy writes that we need weapons of compassion and insight.

> You have to have compassion because it gives you the juice, the power, the passion to move. When you open to the pain of the world you move, you act. But that weapon is not enough. It can burn you out, so you need the other—you need insight into the radical interdependence of all phenomena. With that wisdom you know that it is not a battle between good guys and bad guys, but that the line between good and evil runs through the landscape of every human heart. With insight into our profound interrelatedness, you know that actions undertaken with pure intent have repercussions throughout the web of life, beyond what you can measure or discern.

Macy shares that compassion and insight can "sustain us as agents of wholesome change" for they are "gifts for us to claim now in the healing of our world." In part, we learn to love by giving service. This is again a dimension of what Peck means when he speaks of extending ourselves for another.

The civil rights movement had the power to transform society because the individuals who struggle alone and in community for freedom and justice wanted these gifts to be for all, not just the suffering and the oppressed. Visionary black leaders such as Septima Clark, Fannie Lou Hamer, Martin Luther King, Jr., and Howard Thurman warned against isolationism. They encouraged black people to look beyond our own circumstances and assume responsibility for the planet. This call for communion with a world beyond the self, the tribe, the race, the nation, was a constant invitation for personal expansion and growth. When masses of black folks starting thinking solely in terms of "us and them," internalizing the value system of white supremacist capitalist patriarchy, blind spots developed, the capacity for empathy needed for the building of community was diminished. To heal our wounded body politic we must reaffirm our commitment to a vision of what King referred to in the essay "Facing the Challenge of a New Age" as a genuine commitment to "freedom and justice for all." My heart is uplifted when I read King's essay; I am reminded where true liberation leads us. It leads us beyond resistance to transformation. King tells us that "the end is reconciliation, the end is redemption, the end is the creation of the beloved community." The moment we choose to love we begin to move against domination, against oppression. The moment we choose to love we begin to move towards freedom, to act in ways that liberate ourselves and others. That action is the testimony of love as the practice of freedom.

H. L. MENCKEN
Memorial Service

H. L. MENCKEN *(1880–1956) was a journalist and critic. A pungent satirist of American life, he also published a famous book,* The American Language, *which brought together American, rather than English, idioms and expressions.*

WHERE is the graveyard of dead gods? What lingering mourner waters their mounds? There was a time when Jupiter was the king of the gods, and any man who doubted his puissance was *ipso facto* a barbarian and an ignoramus. But where in all the world is there a man who worships Jupiter today? And what of Huitzilopochtli? In one year—and it is no more than five hundred years ago—50,000 youths and maidens were slain in sacrifice to him. Today, if he is remembered at all, it is only by some vagrant savage in the depths of Mexican forest. Huitzilopochtli, like many other gods, had no human father; his mother was a virtuous widow; he was born of an apparently innocent flirtation that she carried on with the sun. When he frowned, his father, the sun, stood still. When he roared with rage, earthquakes engulfed whole cities. When he thirsted he was watered with 10,000 gallons of human blood. But today, Huitzilopochtli is as magnificently forgotten as Allen G. Thurman. Once the peer of Allah, Buddha, and Wotan, he is now the peer of Richmond P. Hobson, Alton B. Parker, Adelina Patti, General Weyler, and Tom Sharkey.

Speaking of Huitzilopochtli recalls his brother Tezcatilpoca. Tezcatilpoca was almost as powerful: he consumed 25,000 virgins a year. Lead me

Mencken, H. L., "Memorial Service" from *Mencken Christomathy* by H. L. Mencken (New York: Alfred Knopf, 1949), pp. 95–98.

to his tomb: I would weep, and hang a *couronne des perles*. But who knows where it is? Or where the grave of Quitzalcoatl is? Or Xiehtecutli? Or Centeotl, that sweet one? Or Tlazolteotl, the goddess of love? Or Mictlan? Or Xipe? Or all the host of Tzitzimitles? Where are their bones? Where is the willow in which they hung their harps? In what forlorn and unheard-of Hell do they await the resurrection morn? Who enjoys their residuary estates? Or that of Dis, whom Caesar found to be the chief god of the Celts? Or that of Tarves, the bull? Or that of Moccos, the pig? Or that of Epona, the mare? Or that of Mullo, the celestial jackass? There was a time when the Irish revered all these gods, but today even the drunkest Irishman laughs at them.

But they have company in oblivion: the Hell of dead gods is as crowded as the Presbyterian Hell for babies. Damona is there, and Esus, and Drunemeton, and Silvana, and Dervones, and Adsalluta, and Deva, and Belisama, and Uxellimus, and Borvo, and Grannos, and Mogons. All mighty gods in their day, worshipped by millions, full of demands and impositions, able to bind and loose—all gods of the first class. Men labored for generations to build vast temples to them—temples with stones as large as haywagons. The business of interpreting their whims occupied thousands of priests, bishops, archbishops. To doubt them was to die, usually at the stake. Armies took to the field to defend them against infidels: villages were burned, women and children were butchered, cattle were driven off. Yet in the end they all withered and died, and today there is none so poor to do them reverence.

What has become of Sutekh, once high god of the whole Nile Valley? What has become of:

Resheph	Isis	Dagon
Anath	Ptah	Yau
Ashtoreth	Baal	Amon-Re
Nebo	Astarte	Osiris
Malek	Hadad	Molech?
Ahijah		

All these were once gods of the highest eminence. Many of them are mentioned with fear and trembling in the Old Testament. They ranked, five or six thousand years ago, with Yahweh Himself; the worst of them stood far higher than Thor. Yet they have all gone down the chute, and with them the following:

Arianrod	Iuno Lucina
Morrigu	Saturn
Govannon	Furrina
Gunfled	Cronos
Dagda	Engurra
Ogyrvan	Belus
Dea Dia	Ubilulu
U-dimmer-an-kia	Diana of Ephesus
U-sab-sib	Robigus
U-Mersi	Pluto
Tammuz	Vesta
Venus	Zer-panitu
Beltis	Merodach
Nusku	Elum
Aa	Marduk
Sin	Nin
Apsu	Persephone
Elali	Istar
Mami	Lagas
Zaraqu	Nirig
Zagaga	Nebo
Nuada Argetlam	En-Mersi
Tagd	Assur
Goibniu	Beltu
Odin	Kuski-banda
Ogma	Nin-azu
Marzin	Qarradu
Mars	Ueras

Ask the rector to lend you any good book on comparative religion: you will find them all listed. They were gods of the highest dignity—gods of civilized peoples—worshipped and believed in by millions. All were omnipotent, omniscient and immortal. And all are dead.

ALBERT CAMUS
The Absurd

ALBERT CAMUS (1913–1960), a leading French intellectual, was a political activist and an associate of Jean-Paul Sartre. He was awarded the Nobel Prize in Literature in 1957, and his philosophical concerns were often expressed in fiction. The Myth of Sisyphus *focuses on the issue of suicide, which, he says, is the ultimate philosophical problem.*

LIKE great works, deep feelings always mean more than they are conscious of saying. The regularity of an impulse or a repulsion in a soul is encountered again in habits of doing or thinking, is reproduced in consequences of which the soul itself knows nothing. Great feelings take with them their own universe, splendid or abject. They light up with their passion an exclusive world in which they recognize their climate. There is a universe of jealousy, of ambition, of selfishness, or of generosity. A universe—in other words, a metaphysic and an attitude of mind. What is true of already specialized feelings will be even more so of emotions basically as indeterminate, simultaneously as vague and as "definite," as remote and as "present" as those furnished us by beauty or aroused by absurdity.

At any street corner the feeling of absurdity can strike any man in the face. As it is, in its distressing nudity, in its light without effulgence, it is elusive. But that very difficulty deserves reflection. It is probably true that a man remains forever unknown to us and that there is in him something irreducible that escapes us. But *practically* I know men and recognize them by their behavior, by the totality of their deeds, by the consequences caused in life by their presence. Likewise, all those irrational feelings which offer no purchase to analysis. I can define them *practically*, appreciate them *practically*, by gathering together the sum of their consequences in the domain of the intelligence, by seizing and noting all their aspects, by outlining their universe. It is certain that apparently, though I have seen the same actor a hundred times, I shall not for that reason know him any better personally. Yet if I add up the heroes he has personified and if I say that I know him as little better at the hundredth character counted off, this will be felt to contain an element of truth. For this apparent paradox is also an apologue. There is a moral to it. It teaches that a man defines himself by his make-believe as well as by his sincere impulses. There is thus a lower key of feelings, inaccessible in the heart but partially disclosed by the acts they imply and the attitudes of mind they assume. It is clear that in this way I am defining a method. But it is also evident that that method is one of analysis and not of knowledge. For methods imply metaphysics; unconsciously they disclose conclusions that they often claim not to know yet. Similarly, the last pages of a book are already contained in the first pages. Such a link is inevitable. The method defined here acknowledges the feeling that all true knowledge is impossible. Solely appearances can be enumerated and the climate make itself felt.

Perhaps we shall be able to overtake that elusive feeling of absurdity in the different but closely related worlds of intelligence, of the art of living, or of art itself. The climate of absurdity is in the beginning. The end is the absurd universe and that attitude of mind which lights the world with its true colors to bring out the privileged and implacable visage which that attitude has discerned in it.

All great deeds and all great thoughts have a ridiculous beginning. Great works are often born on a street corner or in a restaurant's revolving door. So it is with absurdity. The absurd world more than others derives its nobility from that abject birth. In certain situations, replying "nothing" when asked what one is thinking about may be pretense in a man. Those who are loved are well aware of this. But if that reply is sincere, if it symbolizes that odd state of soul in which the void becomes eloquent, in which the chain of daily gestures is broken, in which the heart vainly seeks the link that will connect it again, then it is as it were the first sign of absurdity.

It happens that the stage sets collapse. Rising, streetcar, four hours in the office or the factory, meal, streetcar, four hours of work, meal, sleep, and Monday Tuesday Wednesday Thursday Friday and Saturday according to the same rhythm—this path is easily followed most of the time. But one day the "why" arises and everything begins in that weariness tinged with amazement. "Begins"—this is important. Weariness comes at the end of the acts of a mechanical life, but at the same time it inaugurates the impulse of consciousness. It awakens consciousness and provokes what follows. What follows is the gradual return into the chain or it is the definitive awakening. At the end of the awakening comes, in time, the consequence: suicide or recovery. In itself weariness has something sickening about it. Here, I must conclude that it is good. For everything begins with consciousness and nothing is worth any thing except through it. There is nothing original about these remarks. But they are obvious; that is enough for a while, during a sketchy reconnaissance in the origins of the absurd. Mere "anxiety," as Heidegger says, is at the source of everything.

Likewise and during every day of an unillustrious life time carries us. But a moment always comes when we have to carry it. We live on the future: "tomorrow," "later on," "when you have made your way," "you will understand when you are old enough." Such irrelevancies are wonderful, for, after all, it's a matter of dying. Yet a day comes when a man notices or says that he is thirty. Thus he asserts his youth. But simultaneously he situates himself in relation to time. He takes his place in it. He admits that he stands at a certain point on a curve that he acknowledges having to travel to its end. He belongs to time, and by the horror that seizes him, he recognizes his worst enemy. Tomorrow, he was longing for tomorrow, whereas everything in him ought to reject it. That revolt of the flesh is the absurd. . . .

That revolt gives life its value. Spread out over the whole length of a life, it restores its majesty to that life. To a man devoid of blinders, there is no finer sight than that of the intelligence at grips with a reality that transcends it. The sight of human pride is unequaled. No disparagement is of any use. That discipline that the mind imposes on itself, that will conjured up out of nothing, that face-to-face struggle have something exceptional about them. To impoverish that reality whose inhumanity constitutes man's majesty is tantamount to impoverishing him himself. I understand then why the doctrines that explain everything to me also debilitate me at the same time. They relieve me of the weight of my own life, and yet I must carry it alone. At this juncture, I cannot conceive that a skeptical metaphysics can be joined to an ethics of renunciation.

Consciousness and revolt, these rejections are the contrary of renunciation. Everything that is indomitable and passionate in a human heart quickens them, on the contrary, with its own life. It is essential to die unreconciled and not of one's own free will. Suicide is a repudiation. The absurd man can only drain everything to the bitter end, and deplete himself. The absurd is his extreme tension, which he maintains constantly by solitary effort, for he knows that in that consciousness and in that day-to-day revolt he gives proof of his only truth, which is defiance. . . .

But what does life mean in such a universe? Nothing else for the moment but indifference to the future and a desire to use up everything that is given. Belief in the meaning of life always implies a scale of values, a choice, our preferences. Belief in the absurd, according to our definitions, teaches the contrary. But this is worth examining.

Knowing whether or not one can live *without appeal* is all that interests me. I do not want to get out of my depth. This aspect of life being given me, can I adapt myself to it? Now, faced with this particular concern, belief in the absurd is tantamount to substituting the quantity of experiences for the quality. If I convince myself that this life has no other aspect than that of the absurd, if I feel that its whole equilibrium depends on that perpetual opposition between my conscious revolt and the darkness in which it struggles, if I admit that my freedom has no meaning except in relation to its limited fate, then I must say that what counts is not the best living but the most living. It is not up to me to wonder if this is vulgar or revolting, elegant or deplorable. Once and for all, value judgments are discarded here in favor of factual judgments. I have merely to draw the conclusions from what I can see and to risk nothing that is hypothetical. Supposing that living in this way were not honorable, then true propriety would command me to be dishonorable.

The most living; in the broadest sense, that rule means nothing. It calls for definition. It seems to begin with the fact that the notion of quantity has not been sufficiently explored. For it can account for a large share of human experience. A man's rule of conduct and his scale of values have no meaning except through the quantity and variety of experiences he has been in a position to accumulate. Now, the conditions of modern life impose on the majority of men the same quantity of experiences and consequently the same profound experience. To be sure, there must also be taken into consideration the individual's spontaneous contribution, the "given" element in him. But I cannot judge of that, and let me repeat that my rule here is to get

along with the immediate evidence. I see, then, that the individual character of a common code of ethics lies not so much in the ideal importance of its basic principles as in the norm of an experience that it is possible to measure. To stretch a point somewhat, the Greeks had the code of their leisure just as we have the code of our eight-hour day. But already many men among the most tragic cause us to foresee that a longer experience changes this table of values. They make us imagine that adventurer of the everyday who through mere quantity of experiences would break all records (I am purposely using this sports expression) and would thus win his own code of ethics. Yet let's avoid romanticism and just ask ourselves what such an attitude may mean to a man with a mind made up to take up his bet and to observe strictly what he takes to be the rules of the game.

Breaking all the records is first and foremost being faced with the world as often as possible. How can that be done without contradictions and without playing on words? For on the one hand the absurd teaches that all experiences are unimportant, and on the other it urges toward the greatest quantity of experiences. How, then, can one fail to do as so many of those men I was speaking of earlier—choose the form of life that brings us the most possible of that human matter, thereby introducing a scale of values that on the other hand one claims to reject?

But again it is the absurd and its contradictory life that reaches us. For the mistake is thinking that that quantity of experiences depends on the circumstances of our life when it depends solely on us. Here we have to be oversimple. To two men living the same number of years, the world always provides the same sum of experiences. It is up to us to be conscious of them. Being aware of one's life, one's revolt, one's freedom, and to the maximum, is living, and to the maximum. Where lucidity dominates, the scale of values becomes useless. Let's be even more simple. Let us say that the sole obstacle, the sole deficiency to be made good, is constituted by premature death. Thus it is that no depth, no emotion, no passion, and no sacrifice could render equal in the eyes of the absurd man (even if he wished it so) a conscious life of forty years and a lucidity spread over sixty years. Madness and death are his irreparables. Man does not choose. The absurd and the extra life it involves *therefore do not depend on man's will,* but on its contrary, which is death. Weighing words carefully, it is altogether a question of luck. One just has to be able to consent to this. There will never be any substitute for twenty years of life and experience.

By what is an odd inconsistency in such an alert race, the Greeks claimed that those who died young were beloved of the gods. And that is true only if you are willing to believe that entering the ridiculous world of the gods is forever losing the purest of joys, which is feeling, and feeling on this earth. The present and the succession of presents before a constantly conscious soul is the ideal of the absurd man. But the word "ideal" rings false in this connection. It is not even his vocation, but merely the third consequence of his reasoning. Having started from an anguished awareness of the inhuman, the meditation on the absurd returns at the end of its itinerary to the very heart of the passionate flames of human revolt. . . .

The preceding merely defines a way of thinking. But the point is to live.

MARY DALY

The Qualitative Leap Beyond Patriarchal Religion

MARY DALY *is a leading feminist philosopher and theologian. She is the author of a number of influential books, among them* The Church and The Second Sex *(1968);* Beyond God the Father: Toward a Philosophy of Women's Liberation *(1973);* Gyn/Ecology: The Metaethics of Radical Feminism *(1978);* Pure Lust: Elemental Feminist Philosophy *(1984);* Websters' First New Wickedary of the English Language, *conjured in cahoots with Jane Caputi (1987);* Outer Course: The Be-Dazzling Voyage *(1992);* Quintessence. . . Realizing the Archaic Future: A Radical Elemental Feminist Manifesto *(1998); and* Amazon Grace: Re-Calling the Courage to Sin Big *(2006).*

PROLEGOMENA

1. There exists a planetary sexual caste system, essentially the same in Saudi Arabia and in New York, differing only in degree.

2. This system is masked by sex role segregation, by the dual identity of women, by ideologies and myths.

3. Among the primary loci of sexist conditioning is grammar.

Daly, Mary, excerpt from her 20 page article titled "The Qualitative Leap Beyond Patriarchal Religion" which first appeared in *Quest: A Feminist Quarterly*, vol. 1, no. 4, Spring 1975. Copyright by Mary Daly. Reprinted by permission of the author.

4. The "methods" of the various "fields" are not adequate to express feminist thought. Methodolatry requires that women perform Methodicide, an act of intellectual bravery.

5. All of the major world religions function to legitimate patriarchy. This is true also of the popular cults such as the Krishna movement and the Jesus Freaks.

6. The myths and symbols of Christianity are essentially sexist. Since "God" is male, the male is God. God the Father legitimates all earthly God-fathers, including Vito Corleone, Pope Paul, President Gerald Ford, the God-fathers of medicine (e.g. the American Medical Association), of science (e.g. NASA), of the media, of psychiatry, of education, and of all the -ologies.

7. The myth of feminine evil, expressed in the story of the Fall, is reinforced by the myth of salvation/redemption by a single human being of the male sex. The idea of a unique diving incarnation in a male, the God-man of the "hypostatic union," is inherently sexist and oppressive. Christolatry is idolatry.

8. A significant and growing cognitive minority of women, radical feminists, are breaking out from under the sacred shelter of patriarchal religious myths.

9. This breaking out, facing anomy when the meaning structures of patriarchy are seen through and rejected, is a communal, political event. It is a revelatory event, a creative, political ontophany.

10. The bonding of the growing cognitive minority of women who are radical feminists, commonly called *sisterhood*, involves a process of new naming, in which words are wrenched out of their old semantic context and heard in a new semantic context. For example, the "sisterhoods" of patriarchy, such as religious congregations of women, were really mini-brotherhoods. *Sisterhood* heard with new ears is bonding for women's own liberation.

11. There is an inherent dynamic in the women's revolution in Judeo-Christian society which is Antichurch, whether or not feminists specifically concern ourselves with churches. This is so because the Judeo-Christian tradition legitimates patriarchy—the prevailing power structure and prevailing world view—which the women's revolution leaves behind.

12. The women's revolution is not only Antichurch. It is a postchristian spiritual revolution.

13. The ethos of Judeo-Christian culture is dominated by The Most Unholy Trinity: Rape, Genocide, and War. It is rapism which spawns racism. It is gynocide which spawns genocide, for sexism (rapism) is fundamental socialization to objectify "the other."

14. The women's revolution is concerned with transvaluation of values, beyond the ethics dominated by The Most Unholy Trinity.

15. The women's revolution is not merely about equality within a patriarchal society (a contradiction in terms). It is about *power* and redefining power.

16. Since Christian myths are inherently sexist, and since the women's revolution is not about "equality" but about power, there is an intrinsic dynamic in the feminist movement which goes beyond efforts to reform Christian churches. Such efforts eventually come to be recognized as comparable to a Black person's trying to reform the Ku Klux Klan.

17. Within patriarchy, power is generally understood as power *over* people, the environment, things. In the rising consciousness of women, power is experienced as *power of presence* to ourselves and to each other, as we affirm our own being against and beyond the alienated identity (non-being) bestowed upon us within patriarchy. This is experienced as *power of absence* by those who would objectify women as "the other," as magnifying mirrors.

18. The presence of women to ourselves which is *absence* to the oppressor is the essential dynamic opening up the women's revolution to human liberation. It is an invitation to men to confront non-being and hence affirm their be-ing.

19. It is unlikely that many men will accept this invitation willingly, or even be able to hear it,

since they have profound vested (though self-destructive) interest in the present social arrangements.

20. The women's movement is a new mode of relating to the self, to each other, to men, to the environment—in a word—to the cosmos. It is self-affirming, refusing objectification of the self and of the other.

21. Entrance into new feminist time/space, which is moving time/space located on the boundaries of patriarchal institutions, is active participation in ultimate reality, which is dereified, recognized as Verb, as intransitive Verb with no object to block its dynamism.

22. Entrance into radical feminist consciousness involves recognition that all male-dominated "revolutions," which do not reject the universally oppressive reality which is patriarchy, are in reality only reforms. They are "revolutions" only in the sense that they are spinnings of the wheels of the same senescent system.

23. Entrance into radical feminist consciousness implies an awareness that the women's revolution is the "final cause" (pun intended) in the radical sense that it is the cause which can move the other causes. It is the catalyst which can bring about real change, since it is the rising up of the universally and primordially objectified "Other," discrediting the myths which legitimate rapism. Rapism is by extension the objectification and destruction of all "others" and inherently tends to the destruction of the human species and of all life on this planet.

Radical feminism, the becoming of women, is very much an Otherworld Journey. It is both discovery and creation of a world other than patriarchy. Some observation reveals that patriarchy is "everywhere." Even outer space and the future have been colonized. As a rule, even the more imaginative science fiction writers (seemingly the most foretelling futurists) cannot/will not create a space and time in which women get far beyond the role of space stewardess. Nor does this situation exist simply "outside" women's minds, securely fastened into institutions which we can physically leave behind. Rather, it is also internalized, festering inside women's heads, even feminist heads.

The journey of women *becoming,* then, involves exorcism of the internalized Godfather, in his various manifestations (His name is legion). It involves dangerous encounters with these demons. Within the Christian tradition, particularly in medieval times, evil spirits have sometimes been associated with the Seven Deadly Sins, both as personifications and as causes. A "standard" and prevalent listing of the Sins is, of course, the following: pride, avarice, anger, lust, gluttony, envy, and sloth. I am contending that these have all been radically misnamed, that is, inadequately and even perversely "understood" within Christianity. These concepts have been used to victimize the oppressed, particularly women. They are particularized expressions of the overall use of "evil" to victimize women. The feminist journey involves confrontations with the demonic distortions of evil.

Why has it seemed "appropriate" in this culture that a popular book and film (*The Exorcist*) center around a Jesuit who "exorcises" a girl-child who is "possessed"? Why is there no book or film about a woman who exorcises a Jesuit? Within a culture possessed by the myth of feminine evil, the naming, describing, and theorizing about good and evil has constituted as web of deception, a Maya. The journey of women becoming is breaking through this web—a Fall into free space. It is reassuming the role of subject, as opposed to object, and naming good and evil on the basis of our own intuitive intellection. . . .

THE QUALITATIVE LEAP

Creative, living, political hope for movement beyond the gynocidal reign of the fathers will be fulfilled only if women continue to make qualitative leaps in living our transcendence. A short-circuited hope of transcendence has caused many to remain inside churches, and patriarchal religion sometimes has seemed to satisfy the hunger for transcendence. The problem has been that both the hunger and the satisfaction generated within such religions have to a great extent alienated women from our deepest aspirations. Spinning in vicious circles of false needs and false consciousness, women caught on the patriarchal wheel have not been able to experience women's own experience.

I suggest that what is required is *ludic cerebration,* the free play of intuition in our own space, giving rise to thinking that is vigorous, informed, multi-dimensional, independent, creative, tough. *Ludic cerebration* is thinking out of experience. I do not mean the experience of dredging out All That Was Wrong with Mother, or of instant intimacy in group encounters, or of waiting at the doctoral dispensary, or of self-lobotomization in order to publish, perish, and then be promoted. I mean the experience of being. *Be-ing* is the verb that says the dimensions of depth in all verbs, such as intuiting, reasoning, loving, imaging, making, acting, as well as the couraging, hoping, and playing that are always there when one is really living.

It may be that some new things happen within patriarchy, but one thing essentially stays the same: women are always marginal beings. From this vantage point of the margin it is possible to look at what is between the margins with the lucidity of The Complete Outsider. To change metaphors: The systems within the System do not appear so radically different from each other to those excluded by all. Hope for a qualitative leap lies in *us* by reason of that deviance from the "norm" which was first imposed but which can also be *chosen* on our own terms. This means that there has to be a shift from "acceptable" female deviance (characterized by triviality, diffuseness, dependence upon others for self-definition, low self-esteem, powerlessness) to deviance which may be unacceptable to others but which is acceptable to the self and *is* self-acceptance.

For women concerned with philosophical/theological questions, it seems to me, this implies the necessity of some sort of choice. One either tries to avoid "acceptable" deviance ("normal" female idiocy) by becoming accepted as a male-identified professional, or else one tries to make the qualitative leap toward self-acceptable

deviance as ludic cerebrator, questioner of everything, madwoman, and witch.

I do mean witch. The heretic who rejects the idols of patriarchy is the blasphemous creatrix of her own thoughts. She is finding her life and intends not to lose it. The witch that smolders within every woman who cared and dared enough to become a philosophically/spiritually questing feminist in the first place seems to be crying out these days: "Light my fire!" The qualitative leap, the light of those flames of spiritual imagination and cerebral fantasy can be a new dawn. . . .

WANTED: "GOD" OR "THE GODDESS"?

Feminist consciousness is experienced by a significant number of women as ontological becoming, that is, being. This process requires existential courage, courage to be and to *see,* which is both revolutionary and revelatory, revealing our participation in the ultimate reality as Verb, as intransitive Verb.

The question obviously arises of the need for anthropomorphic symbols for this reality. There is no inherent contradiction between speaking of ultimate reality as Verb and speaking of this as personal. The Verb is more personal than a mere static noun. However, if we choose to *image* the Verb in anthropomorphic symbols, we can run into a problematic phenomenon which sociologist Henri Desroche calls "crossing." "Crossing" refers to a notable tendency among oppressed groups to attempt to change or adapt the ideological tools of the oppressor, so that they can be used *against* him and *for* the oppressed. The problem here is the fact that the functioning of "crossing" does not generally move far enough outside the ideological framework it seeks to undermine. . . .

Some women religious leaders within Western culture in modern times have performed something like a "crossing" operation, notably such figures as Mary Baker Eddy and Ann Lee, in stressing the "maternal" aspect of the divinity. The result has been mixed. Eddy's "Father-Mother God" is, after all, the Christian God.

Nor does Ann Lee really move completely outside the Christian framework. . . . But it is . . . necessary to note that their theologies lack explicit relevance to the concrete problems of the oppression of women. Intellection and spirituality remain cut off from creative political movement. In earlier periods also there were women within the Christian tradition who tried to "cross" the Christian all-male God and Christ to some degree. An outstanding example was Juliana of Norwich, an English recluse and mystic who lived in the last half of the fourteenth century. Juliana's "God" and "Jesus" were—if language conveys anything—hermaphroditic constructs, with the primary identity clearly male. While there are many levels on which I could analyze Juliana's words about "our beloved Mother, Jesus (who) feeds us with himself," suffice it to say here that this hermaphroditic image is somewhat less than attractive. The "androgynous" God and Jesus present problems which occur in connection with the use of the term "androgyny" to describe the direction of women's becoming. There is something like a "liberation of the woman within" the (primarily male) God and Jesus. . . .

One fact that stands out here is that these were women whose imaginations were still partially controlled by Christian myth. My contention is that they were caught in a contradiction. . . . I am saying that there is a profound contradiction between the inherent logic of radical feminism and the inherent logic of the Christian symbol system. . . .

Both the reformers and those who leave Judaism and Christianity behind are contributing and will contribute in different ways to the process of the becoming of women. The point here is not to place value judgments upon individual persons and their efforts—and there are heroic efforts at all points of the feminist spectrum. Rather, it is to disclose an inherent logic in feminism. The courage which some women have in affirming this logic comes in part from having been on the feminist journey for quite awhile. Encouragement comes also from knowing increasing numbers of women who have chosen the route of the logical conclusion. Some

of these women have "graduated" from Christianity or religious Judaism, and some have never even been associated closely with church or synagogue, but have discovered spiritual and mythic depths in the women's movement itself. What we share is a sense of becoming in cosmic process, which I prefer to call the Verb, Being, and which some would still call "God."

For some feminists concerned with the spiritual depth of the movement, the word "God" is becoming increasingly problematic, however. This by no means indicates a movement in the direction of "atheism" or "agnosticism" or "secularism," as these terms are usually understood. Rather, the problem arises precisely because of the spiritual and mythic quality perceived in the feminist process itself. Some use expressions such as "power of being." Some reluctantly still use the word "God" while earnestly trying to divest the term of its patriarchal associations, attempting to think perhaps of the "God of the philosophers" rather than the overtly masculist and oppressive "God of the theologians." But the problem becomes increasingly troublesome, the more the "God" of the various Western philosophers is subjected to feminist analysis. "He"—"Jahweh" still often hovers behind the abstractions, stunting our own thought, giving us a sense of contrived doublethink. The word "God" just may be inherently oppressive.

Indeed, the word "Goddess" has also been problematic, but for different reasons. Some have been worried about the problem of "crossing." However, that difficulty appears more and more as a pseudo-difficulty when it is recognized that "crossing" is likely to occur only when one is trying to work *within* a sexist tradition. For example, Christian women who in their "feminist liturgies" experiment with referring to "God" as "she" and to the Trinity as "The Mother, the Daughter, and the Holy Spirit," are still working within all the boundaries of the same symbolic framework and the same power structure. Significantly, their services are at the same place and time as "the usual," and are regarded by most of the constituency of the churches as occasional variations of "business as usual."

As women who are outside the Christian church inform ourselves of evidence supporting the existence of ancient matriarchy and of evidence indicating that the Gods of patriarchy are indeed contrived, pale derivatives and reversals of the Great Goddess of an earlier period, the fear of mere "crossing" appears less appropriate and perhaps even absurd. There is also less credibility allowable to the notion that "Goddess" would function like "God" in reverse, that is, to legitimate an oppressive "female-dominated" society, if one is inclined to look seriously at evidence that matriarchal society was not structured like patriarchy, that it was non-hierarchical. . . .

Clearly, it would be inappropriate and arrogant to try to "explain" or "interpret" this experience of another person. I can only comment that many women I know are finding power of being within the self, rather than in "internalized" father images. As a philosopher, my preference has been for abstractions. Indeed I have always been annoyed and rather embarrassed by "anthropomorphic" symbols, preferring terms such as "ground and power of being" (Tillich), "beyond subjectivity and objectivity" (James), "the Encompassing" (Jaspers), or the commonly used "Ultimate Reality," or "cosmic process." More recently I have used the expression "Intransitive Verb." Despite this philosophical inclination, and also because of it, I find it impossible to ignore the realm of symbols, or to fail to recognize that many women are experiencing and participating in a remythologizing process, which is a new dawn.

It is necessary to add a few remarks about the functioning of the confusing and complex "Mary" symbol within Christianity. Through it, the power of the Great Goddess symbol is enchained, captured, used, cannibalized, tokenized, domesticated, tranquilized. In spite of this, I think that many women and at least some men, when they have heard of or imaged the "Mother of God," have, by something like a selective perception process, screened out the standardized, lobotomized, dull, derivative and dwarfed Christian reflections of a more ancient symbol; they have perceived something that might more accurately be described as the Great Goddess, and which, in

human terms, can be translated into "the strong woman who can relate because she can stand alone." A woman of Jewish background commented that "Mother of God" had always seemed strange and contradictory to her. Not having been programmed to "know" about the distinctions between the "divine" and the "human" nature of "Christ," or to "know" that the "Mother of God" is less than God, this woman had been able to hear the expression with the ears of an extraenvironmental listener. It sounded, she said, something like "infinite plus one." When this symbolic nonsense is recognized, it is more plausible simply to *think* "infinite," and to *image* something like "Great Mother," or "Goddess."

It may appear that the suffix "-ess" presents a problem, when one considers other usages of that suffix, for example, in "poetess," or in "authoress." In these cases, there is a tone of depreciation, a suggestion that women poets and authors are in a separate and "inferior" category to be judged by different standards than their male counterparts. However, the suffix does not always function in this "diminishing" way. For example, there appear to be no "diminutive" overtones suggested by the word "actress." So also it seems that the term "Goddess"— or "The Goddess"—*is not only non-diminutive*, but very strong. Indeed, it calls before the mind images of a powerful and ancient tradition before, behind, and beyond Christianity. These are multi-dimensional images of women's present and future becoming/be-ing. . . . The women's movement *is* about refusal to be merely contained as well as refusal to be mere containers. It is about saying "yes" to ourselves, which is the deepest say of saying "yes" to others. At some point in her history a woman may sincerely see ordination to the Christian priesthood as her way of saying this "yes." It is my hope that such women will *continue* their journey. Ambition to "ordination" perhaps reaches a respectable altitude for the jet age, but it does not reach very far, I think, into feminist space/time. It is my hope that these sisters will raise their ambitions and their self-respect higher, immeasurably higher, that they will one day outgrow their books of common prayer and dream less common dreams.

CHAPTER TWO

How Do I Know Whether God Exists?

One of the most discussed philosophical beliefs, one that may provide the framework for many other beliefs and determine much of your attitude toward life, is the belief (or lack of belief) in a Supreme Being, an Almighty God who not only created the universe but also still watches over it with affection and concern. To believe in God is never to feel alone or abandoned. It is a ground for lifelong optimism, the confidence that "everything will turn out for the best." It is to have a basic explanation for the way things are, especially the existence of the universe. Not to believe in God is to give up this sense of security, to lose that ground for optimism, and, for some people, this opens the way to metaphysical despair and a sense of cosmic loneliness. It is to leave the question. "Why is there something rather than nothing?" without an answer. Science might explain how things are and even how they got that way, but not even the best science can make a crack in the ultimate metaphysical question. "Why does the universe exist at all?"

Belief in God, however, is not so much an ultimate explanation as it is an inspiration. It has inspired some of the most beautiful poetry, art, and music and some of the greatest human achievements, as well as some of the bloodiest civil wars and most complex philosophies. Different societies seem to believe in God in different ways, and they believe different things about Him. They may also believe in different gods. Protracted wars have been fought over such technical theological questions as whether God, the Son, and the Holy Ghost are in fact one or three. The Old and New Testaments present significantly different portraits of God: as a wrathful and jealous God in the former and as a much more merciful and loving God in the latter. The God of the Old Testament destroys cities, has disobedient messengers swallowed by whales, and tests the faith of His believers by making them suffer (as in the story of Job). The God of the New Testament sacrifices His only son for your salvation. How are disputes about the true nature of God to be settled? How do you know what to believe in? How do you know whether God exists?

The problem is that belief in God does not seem to rest on any particular foundation. Most likely, you were raised with that belief, taught it as a child, and encouraged in it as you grew to maturity. You were taken to church or temple and naturally came to assume that the deity to which everyone referred, and to whom you yourself had often prayed, exists. But what is the evidence for that belief? How can you prove that your natural assumption is justified? A few people claim to have had God speak to them, but they are few and far between and are not always the most reliable witnesses. One popular proof of God's existence is the fact that the Bible tells us, over and over again, about God. But appealing to the Bible as evidence of God's existence presupposes just that sort of belief that is at issue, a logical fallacy often called "begging the question." Believing in God and believing that the Bible is the revealed word of God are two aspects of one and the same belief, and one cannot be used to prove the other.

You may have "felt" God's presence, but feelings, too, must be justified, because sometimes they can be misleading. Sometimes you sense danger when there is no danger, and, in the same way, it is possible to have a religious feeling without proving that the feeling refers to anything outside of you. Indeed, the very nature of God, according to many theorists and theologians, is such that God "transcends" the world and is outside of our experience. God cannot be seen or sensed as such, and that is why it is necessary to *believe in* God. If God could simply be presented to us, like a statue or a person, such a powerful notion of belief would not be necessary.

A different way of putting the same point is to say that believing in God is a matter of *faith* and not a matter of knowledge. But many believers have refused to accept the idea that this most important belief is not part of our knowledge in the strongest sense. How can our most important belief not also be the best known? Accordingly, much of the history of theology has been devoted to the project of *proving* God's existence. The idea is not to replace faith or undermine the need to believe, but rather to supplement faith and belief with a demonstration that they are indeed justified and based on knowledge of the most secure kind. The selection from Saint Augustine is one of many attempts to reconcile reason and faith, but it gives the ultimate priority to faith.

Numerous such arguments or proofs have been presented throughout the history of philosophy, but the three most popular arguments for God's existence are the **ontological, cosmological,** and **teleological** proofs. The ontological argument, originated by Saint Anselm in the twelfth century, is a deductive proof that proceeds from the premise that God is (by definition) the being greater than whom none other can be conceived, with the conclusion that God therefore *must* exist. The cosmological argument has appeared in many versions, and Saint Thomas Aquinas presents several of them in his famous "Five Ways" (of proving God's existence). They all share the inference from the existence of some imperfect, merely contingent being (for example, ourselves) to the existence of a necessary being, namely God.

The teleological argument is different in that it begins with a very complex and detailed observation: the marvelous complexity and harmony of the world. You have possibly had such an awe-filled experience, for instance, when observing the wonderful array of exotic fish in an aquarium. You may have even said at the time that the variety of life is a miraculous thing and evidence of God's great creativity. This is the essence of the teleological argument, the hypothesis that such a complex, varied, and workable world could not be the product of chance but rather must have been the creation of an intelligent, powerful creator, namely God. An analogy, suggested in a classic work by William Paley, is this: Walking along a deserted beach, you find a watch in the sand. Now, it is barely possible, but highly unlikely, that the wind and surf had pounded together pieces of sand until they happened to take the form of this intricate piece of machinery. It is much more likely that the watch was made by a watchmaker and dropped in the sand by some passerby whom you have not seen. So, too, it may be imaginable that the world as we know it came into existence quite by accident, but it seems much more plausible to assume that it was intelligently created by God.

These three arguments have met with considerable criticism, often from critics who are themselves devout. The ontological proof has been revised and updated many times using the most sophisticated techniques available in logic. The cosmological proof also gets revised with each new development in cosmology. Old inferences are discarded and new, improved steps take their place. The teleological argument was lampooned as soon as it appeared; for example, the German aphorist Lichtenberg sarcastically commented that it certainly was convenient that God put slits in cats' skin right where their eyes were, and Voltaire noted in his novel *Candide* that it was good of God to give us noses, because, how else would we wear spectacles? The most protracted and devastating criticism of the teleological argument, however, was offered by David Hume in his *Dialogues on Natural Religion,* which were so blasphemous that he dared not publish them in his own lifetime. Following Hume, however, the great German philosopher Immanuel Kant agreed that the traditional proofs don't work but suggested an alternative defense of theism by way of morality.

Many believers and philosophers, however, have rejected the entire project of trying to prove that God exists. They see nothing wrong with insisting that belief in God is a matter of faith and not knowledge. Indeed, they insist that the importance of belief in God rests on exactly that, because if we could really prove God's existence, faith would be superfluous. Perhaps the most powerful argument of this sort appeared in the mid-nineteenth century in the works of Søren Kierkegaard, a Danish philosopher who was extremely devout but also rejected the modernization of religion. In this century, the American philosopher William James also argued that what is important about religious belief is not so much its contribution to knowledge as its role in making our lives happy and fulfilled. Natalie Angier takes issue with the assumption, so prevalent in current political discussion in the United States, that everyone believes in God. She questions whether this assumption is used as a way of collapsing the separation of church and state, and so undermining the notion of a secular society. And in a short tale by John Wisdom, we see why many contemporary philosophers insist that belief in God is not the sort of belief that can be proven or disproven. Nevertheless, belief in God may be sufficiently important in our lives that questions of proof are secondary. Finally, we end with two very different selections offering alternative conceptions of God. The first is one of the most ancient religious texts, the Ṛg Veda from India, written about 1500 B.C.E. The second is a very contemporary consideration by a Christian philosopher, John Bishop, who argues that there are serious limitations to what he calls "the Omni-God."

SAINT AUGUSTINE
Faith and Reason

SAINT AUGUSTINE *(354–430), one of the most important philosophers in the Christian tradition, was born in North Africa and lived during the decline of the Roman Empire. After exploring various pagan beliefs he was converted to Christianity. In this selection, he sets up the argument that reason, although it can be an instrument of faith, must always be transcended by faith.*

AUGUSTINE

So a nature that has existence but not life or understanding, like an inanimate body, is inferior to a nature that has both existence and life but not understanding, like the souls of animals; and such a thing is in turn inferior to something that has all three, like the rational mind of a human being. Given that, do you think that you could find anything in us—that is, anything that is part of our human nature—more excellent than understanding? It is clear that we have a body, as well as a sort of life by which the body is animated and nourished; both of these we find in animals. We also have a third thing, like the head or eye of the soul, or however reason and understanding might be more aptly described; and this, animals do not have. So I ask you: can you think of anything in human nature more exalted than reason?

EVODIUS

Nothing at all.

AUGUSTINE

What if we could find something that you were certain not only exists, but is more excellent than our reason? Would you hesitate to say that this thing, whatever it is, is God?

EVODIUS

Even if I found something better than the best part of my nature, I would not immediately say that it was God. What I call "God" is not that to which my reason is inferior, but that to which nothing is superior.

AUGUSTINE

You're quite right, for God himself has enabled your reason to think so piously and correctly about him. But if you found nothing above our reason except what is eternal and unchangeable, would you hesitate to call that "God"? For you know that material objects are changeable. It is obvious that the life by which the body is animated changes from one condition to another. And reason itself is clearly changeable: sometimes it strives for the truth and sometimes it doesn't; sometimes it attains the truth and sometimes it doesn't. If reason—not by any physical organ, not by touch or taste or smell, not by the ears or eyes or any sense inferior to itself, but by itself alone—sees something eternal and unchangeable, then it should confess that it is inferior, and that the eternal and unchangeable thing is its God.

EVODIUS

If we find that to which nothing is superior, I will certainly confess that it is God.

AUGUSTINE

Good. Then it will be enough for me to show that something of this sort exists, which you can admit to be God; or if something yet higher exists, you will concede that *it* is God. Therefore, whether there is something higher or not, it will be manifest that God exists, when I with his help fulfill my promise to prove that there is something higher than reason.

SAINT ANSELM
The Ontological Argument

SAINT ANSELM *(1033–1109), archbishop of Canterbury, was one of the main opponents of the then–anti-intellectualism of the church. He is best known for his Monologion and his Proslogion, in which the ontological argument is developed.*

Truly there is a God, although the fool hath said in his heart, There is no God.

AND so, Lord, do thou, who dost give understanding to faith, give me, so far as thou knowest it to be profitable, to understand that thou art as we believe; and that thou art that which we believe. And, indeed, we believe that thou art a being than which nothing greater can be conceived. Or is there no such nature, since the fool hath said in his heart, there is no God? (Psalms xiv.I). But, at any rate, this very fool, when he hears of this being of which I speak—a being than which nothing greater can be conceived—understands what he hears, and what he understands is in his understanding; although he does not understand it to exist.

For, it is one thing for an object to be in the understanding, and another to understand that the object exists. When a painter first conceives of what he will afterwards perform, he has it in his understanding, but he does not yet understand it to be, because he has not yet performed it. But after he has made the painting, he both has it in his understanding, and he understands that it exists, because he has made it.

Hence, even the fool is convinced that something exists in the understanding, at least, than which nothing greater can be conceived. For, when he hears of this, he understands it. And whatever is understood, exists in the understanding. And assuredly that, than which nothing greater can be conceived, cannot exist in the understanding alone. For, suppose it exists in the understanding alone: then it can be conceived to exist in reality; which is greater.

Therefore, if that, than which nothing greater can be conceived, exists in the understanding alone, the very being, than which nothing greater can be conceived, is one, than which a greater can be conceived. But obviously this is impossible. Hence, there is no doubt that there exists a being, than which nothing greater can be conceived, and it exists both in the understanding and in reality.

God cannot be conceived not to exist.—God is that, than which nothing greater can be conceived.—That which can be conceived not to exist is not God.

And it assuredly exists so truly, that it cannot be conceived not to exist. For, it is possible to conceive of a being which cannot be conceived not to exist; and this is greater than one which can be conceived not to exist. Hence, if that, than which nothing greater can be conceived, can be conceived not to exist, it is not that, than which nothing greater can be conceived. But this is an irreconcilable contradiction. There is,

then, so truly a being than which nothing greater can be conceived to exist, that it cannot even be conceived not to exist; and this being thou art, O Lord, our God.

So truly, therefore, dost thou exist, O Lord, my God, that thou canst not be conceived not to exist; and rightly. For, if a mind could conceive of a being better than thee, the creature would rise above the Creator; and this is most absurd. And, indeed, whatever else there is, except thee alone, can be conceived not to exist. To thee alone, therefore, it belongs to exist more truly than all other beings, and hence in a higher degree than all others. For, whatever else exists does not exist so truly, and hence in a less degree it belongs to it to exist. Why, then, has the fool said in his heart, there is no God (Psalms xiv.I), since it is so evident, to a rational mind, that thou dost exist in the highest degree of all? Why, except that he is dull and a fool?

How the fool has said in his heart what cannot be conceived.—A thing may be conceived in two ways: (1) when the word signifying it is conceived; (2) when the thing itself is understood. As far as the word goes, God can be conceived not to exist; in reality he cannot.

But how has the fool said in his heart what he could not conceive; or how is it that he could not conceive what he said in his heart? since it is the same to say in the heart, and to conceive.

But, if really, nay, since really, he both conceived, because he said in his heart; and did not say in his heart, because he could not conceive; there is more than one way in which a thing is said in the heart or conceived. For, in one sense, an object is conceived, when the word signifying it is conceived; and in another, when the very entity, which the object is, is understood.

In the former sense, then, God can be conceived not to exist; but in the latter, not at all. For no one who understands what fire and water are can conceive fire to be water, in accordance with the nature of the facts themselves, although this is possible according to the words. So, then, no one who understands what God is can conceive that God does not exist; although he says these words in his heart, either without any, or with some foreign, signification. For, God is that than which a greater cannot be conceived. And he who thoroughly understands this, assuredly understands that this being so truly exists, that not even in concept can it be non-existent. Therefore, he who understands that God so exists, cannot conceive that he does not exist.

I thank thee, gracious Lord, I thank thee; because what I formerly believed by thy bounty, I now so understand by thine illumination, that if I were unwilling to believe that thou dost exist. I should not be able not to understand this to be true.

SAINT THOMAS AQUINAS
Whether God Exists

SAINT THOMAS AQUINAS *(1225–1274) was the architect of the most comprehensive theological structure of the Roman Catholic Church, the* Summa Theologica. *It has long been recognized as the "official" statement of orthodox Christian beliefs by many theologians. Aquinas borrowed many of his arguments from Aristotle, as can be seen in his "five ways" of demonstrating God's existence.*

OBJECTION 1. It seems that God does not exist; because if one of two contraries be infinite, the other would be altogether destroyed. But the word "God" means that He is infinite goodness. If, therefore, God existed, there would be no evil discoverable; but there is evil in the world. Therefore God does not exist.

Obj. 2. Further, it is superfluous to suppose that, what can be accounted for by a few principles has been produced by many. But it seems that everything that appears in the world can be accounted for by other principles, supposing God did not exist. For all natural things can be reduced to one principle, which is nature; and all things that happen intentionally can be reduced to one principle, which is human reason, or will. Therefore there is no need to suppose God's existence.

On the contrary, It is said in the person of God: *I am Who am* (Exod. iii. 14).

I answer that, The existence of God can be proved in five ways.

The first and more manifest way is the argument from motion. It is certain and evident to our senses that some things are in motion. Whatever is in motion is moved by another, for nothing can be in motion except it have a potentiality for that towards which it is being moved; whereas a thing moves inasmuch as it is in act. By "motion" we mean nothing else than the reduction of something from a state of potentiality into a state of actuality unless by something already in a state of actuality. Thus, that which is actually hot as fire, makes wood, which is potentially hot, to be actually hot, and thereby moves and changes it. It is not possible that the same

Saint Thomas Aquinas, "Whether God Exists" from *O Summa Theologica* (New York: Benziger Brothers, 1911) .

thing should be at once in a state of actuality and potentiality from the same point of view, but only from different points of view. What is actually hot cannot simultaneously be only potentially hot; still, it is simultaneously potentially cold. It is therefore impossible that from the same point of view and in the same way anything should be both moved and mover, or that it should move itself. Therefore, whatever is in motion must be put in motion by another. If that by which it is put in motion be itself put in motion, then this also must needs be put in motion by another, and that by another again. This cannot go on to infinity, because then there would be no first mover, and, consequently, no other mover—seeing that subsequent movers only move inasmuch as they are put in motion by the first mover; as the staff only moves because it is put in motion by the hand. Therefore it is necessary to arrive at a First Mover, put in motion by no other; and this everyone understands to be God.

The second way is from the formality of efficient causation. In the world of sense we find there is an order of efficient causation. There is no case known (neither is it, indeed, possible) in which a thing is found to be the efficient cause of itself; for so it would be prior to itself, which is impossible to go on to infinity, because in all efficient causes following in order the first is the cause of the intermediate cause, and the intermediate is the cause of the ultimate cause, whether the intermediate cause be several, or one only. To take away the cause, is to take away the effect. Therefore, if there be no first cause among efficient causes, there will be no ultimate cause, nor any intermediate. If in efficient causes it is possible to go on to infinity, there will be no first efficient cause, neither will there be an ultimate effect, nor any intermediate efficient causes; all of which is plainly false. Therefore it is necessary to put forward a First Efficient Cause, to which everyone gives the name of God.

The third way is taken from possibility and necessity, and runs thus: We find in nature things that could either exist or not exist, since they are found to be generated, and then to corrupt; and, consequently, they can exist, and then

not exist. It is impossible for these always to exist, for that which can one day cease to exist must at some time have not existed. Therefore, if everything could cease to exist, then at one time there could have been nothing in existence. If this were true, even now there would be nothing in existence, because that which does not exist only begins to exist by something already existing. Therefore, if at one time nothing was in existence, it would have been impossible for anything to have begun to exist; and thus even now nothing would be in existence—which is absurd. Therefore, not all beings are merely possible, but there must exist something the existence of which is necessary. Every necessary thing either has its necessity caused by another, or not. It is impossible to go on to infinity in necessary things which have their necessity caused by another, as has been already proved in regard to efficient causes. Therefore we cannot but postulate the existence of some being having of itself its own necessity, and not receiving it from another, but rather causing in others their necessity. This all men speak of as God.

The fourth way is taken from the gradation to be found in things. Among beings there are some more and some less good, true, noble, and the like. But "more" and "less" are predicted of different things, according as they resemble in their different ways something which is in the degree of "most," as a thing is said to be hotter according as it more nearly resembles that which is hottest; so that there is something which is truest, something best, something noblest, and, consequently, something which is uttermost being; for the truer things are, the more truly they exist. What is most complete in any genus is the cause of all in that genus; as fire, which is the most complete form of heat, is the cause whereby all things are made hot. Therefore there must also be something which is to all beings the cause of their being, goodness, and every other perfection; and this we call God.

The fifth way is taken from the governance of the world; for we see that things which lack intelligence, such as natural bodies, act for some purpose, which fact is evident from their acting always, or nearly always, in the same way, so as to obtain the best result. Hence it is plain that not fortuitously, but designedly, do they achieve their purpose. Whatever lacks intelligence cannot fulfill some purpose, unless it be directed by some being endowed with intelligence and knowledge; as the arrow is shot to its mark by the archer. Therefore some intelligent being exists by whom all natural things are ordained towards a definite purpose; and this being we call God.

Reply Obj. 1. As Augustine says: *Since God is wholly good, He would not allow any evil to exist in His works, unless His omnipotence and goodness were* *such as to bring good even out of evil.* This is part of the infinite goodness of God, that He should allow evil to exist, and out of it produce good.

Reply Obj. 2. Since nature works out its determinate end under the direction of a higher agent, whatever is done by nature must needs be traced back to God, as to its first cause. So also whatever is done designedly must also be traced back to some higher cause other than human reason or will, for these can suffer change and are defective; whereas things capable of motion and of defect must be traced back to an immovable and self-necessary first principle.

WILLIAM PALEY
The Teleological Argument

WILLIAM PALEY *(1743–1805) was an English theologian and moral philosopher. He believed that the miracles on which Christianity is based are genuine. He regarded the parts of nature as mechanisms. These form the basis of the argument from design, which he developed in his* Natural Theology.

STATE OF THE ARGUMENT

IN crossing a heath, suppose I pitched my foot against a *stone,* and were asked how the stone came to be there, I might possibly answer, that for any thing I knew to the contrary it had lain there for ever; nor would it, perhaps, be very easy to show the absurdity of this answer. But suppose I had found a watch upon the ground, and it should be inquired how the watch happened to be in that place, I should hardly think of the answer which I had before given, that for any thing I knew the watch might have always been there. Yet why should not this answer serve for the watch as well as for the stone; why is it not as admissible in the second case as in the first? For this reason, and for no other, namely, that when we come to inspect the watch, we perceive—what we could not discover in the stone—that its several parts are framed and put together for a purpose, *e.g.* that they are so formed and adjusted as to produce motion, and that motion so regulated as to point out the hour of the day; that if the different parts had been differently shaped from what they are, or placed after any other manner or in any other order than that in which they are placed, either

Paley, William, "The Teleological Argument" from *Natural Theology and the Horae Pauline,* New York: American Tract Society, 1852.

no motion at all would have been carried on in the machine, or none which would have answered the use that is now served by it. To reckon up a few of the plainest of these parts and of their offices, all tending to one result: We see a cylindrical box containing a coiled elastic spring, which, by its endeavor to relax itself, turns round the box. We next observe a flexible chain—artificially wrought for the sake of flexure—communicating the action of the spring from the box to the fusee. We then find a series of wheels, the teeth of which catch in and apply to each other, conducting the motion from the fusee to the balance and from the balance to the pointer, and at the same time, by the size and shape of those wheels, so regulating that motion as to terminate in causing an index, by an equable and measured progression, to pass over a given space in a given time. We take notice that the wheels are made of brass, in order to keep them from rust; the springs of steel, no other metal being so elastic; that over the face of the watch there is placed a glass, a material employed in no other part of the work, but in the room of which, if there had been any other than a transparent substance, the hour could not be seen without opening the case. This mechanism being observed—it requires indeed an examination of the instrument, and perhaps some previous knowledge of the subject, to perceive and understand it; but being once, as we have said, observed and understood, the inference we think is inevitable, that the watch must have had a maker—that there must have existed, at some time and at some place or other, an artificer or artificers who formed it for the purpose which we find it actually to answer, who comprehended its construction and designed its use.

I. Nor would it, I apprehend, weaken the conclusion, that we had never seen a watch made—that we had never known an artist capable of making one—that we were altogether incapable of executing such a piece of workmanship ourselves, or of understanding in what manner it was performed; all this being no more than what is true of some exquisite remains of ancient art, of some lost arts, and, to the generality of mankind, of the more curious productions of modern manufacture. Does one man in a million know how oval frames are turned? Ignorance of this kind exalts our opinion of the unseen and unknown, but raises no doubt in our minds of the existence and agency of such an artist, at some former time and in some place or other. Nor can I perceive that it varies at all the inference, whether the question arise concerning a human agent or concerning an agent of a different species, or an agent possessing in some respects a different nature.

II. Neither, secondly, would it invalidate our conclusion, that the watch sometimes went wrong, or that it seldom went exactly right. The purpose of the machinery, the design, and the designer might be evident, and in the case supposed, would be evident in whatever way we accounted for the irregularity of the movement, or whether we could account for it or not. It is not necessary that a machine be perfect, in order to show with what design it was made: still less necessary, where the only question is whether it were made with any design at all.

III. Nor, thirdly, would it bring any uncertainty into the argument, if there were a few parts of the watch, concerning which we could not discover or had not yet discovered in what manner they conduced to the general effect; or even some parts, concerning which we could not ascertain whether they conduced to that effect in any manner whatever. For, as to the first branch of the case if by the loss, or disorder, or decay of the parts in question, the movement of the watch were found in fact to be stopped, or disturbed, or retarded, no doubt would remain in our minds as to the utility or intention of these parts, although we should be unable to investigate the manner according to which, or the connection by which, the ultimate effect depended upon their action or assistance; and the more complex the machine, the more likely is this obscurity to arise. Then, as to the second thing supposed, namely, that there were parts which might be spared without prejudice to the movement of the watch, and that we had proved this by experiment, these superfluous parts, even if we were completely assured that they were such, would not vacate the reasoning which we had instituted concerning other parts. The indication of contrivance remained, with respect to them, nearly as it was before.

IV. Nor, fourthly, would any man in his senses think the existence of the watch with its various machinery accounted for, by being told that it was one out of possible combinations of material forms; that whatever he had found in the place where he found the watch, must have contained some internal configuration or other; and that this configuration might be the structure now exhibited, namely, of the works of a watch, as well as a different structure.

V. Nor, fifthly, would it yield his inquiry more satisfaction, to be answered that there existed in things a principle of order, which had disposed the parts of the watch into their present form and situation. He never knew a watch made by the principle of order; nor can he even form to himself an idea of what is meant by a principle of order, distinct from the intelligence of the watchmaker.

VI. Sixthly, he would be surprised to hear that the mechanism of the watch was no proof of contrivance, only a motive to induce the mind to think so.

VII. And not less surprised to be informed, that the watch in his hand was nothing more than the result of the laws of *metallic* nature. It is a perversion of language to assign any law as the efficient, operative cause of any thing. A law presupposes an agent; for it is only the mode according to which an agent proceeds: it implies a power; for it is the order according to which that power acts. Without this agent, without this power, which are both distinct from itself, the *law* does nothing, is nothing. The expression, "the law of metallic nature," may sound strange and harsh to a philosophic ear; but it seems quite as justifiable as some others which are more familiar to him such as "the law of vegetable nature," "the law of animal nature," or, indeed, as "the law of nature" in general, when assigned as the cause of phenomena, in exclusion of agency and power, or when it is substituted into the place of these.

VIII. Neither, lastly, would our observer be driven out of his conclusion or from his confidence in its truth, by being told that he know nothing at all about the matter. He knows enough for his argument; he knows the utility of the end; he knows the subserviency and adaptation of the means to the end. These points being known, his ignorance of other points, affect not the certainty of his reasoning. The consciousness of knowing little need not beget a distrust of that which he does know. . . .

APPLICATION OF THE ARGUMENT

Every indication of contrivance, every manifestation of design which existed in the watch, exists in the works of nature, with the difference on the side of nature of being greater and more, and that in a degree which exceeds all computation. I mean, that the contrivances of nature surpass the contrivances of art, in the complexity, subtilty, and curiosity of the mechanism; and still more, if possible, do they go beyond them in number and variety; yet, in a multitude of cases, are not less evidently mechanical, not less evidently contrivances, not less evidently accommodated to their end or suited to their office, than are the most perfect productions of human ingenuity. . . .

DAVID HUME
Why Does God Let People Suffer?

DAVID HUME *(1711–1776), a Scottish philosopher, was refused professorships at the leading universities for his "heresies." Nevertheless, he is regarded as the outstanding genius of British philosophy. In addition to writing a number of influential books, among them* A Treatise of Human Nature, An Inquiry Concerning the Principles of Morals, *and* Dialogues on Natural Religion, *Hume was a much sought-after guest in London, Edinburgh, and Paris.*

IN short, I repeat the Question: Is the World, consider'd in general, and as it appears to us in this Life, different from what a Man or such a Limited Being would, *beforehand,* expect from a very powerful, wise, and benevolent Deity? It must be strange Prejudice to assert the contrary. And from thence I conclude, that however consistent the World may be, allowing certain Suppositions and Conjectures, with the Idea of such a Deity, it can never afford us an Inference concerning his Existence. The Consistence is not absolutely deny'd, only the Inference. Conjectures, especially where Infinity is excluded from the divine Attributes, may, perhaps, be sufficient to prove a Consistence; but can never be foundations for any Inference.

There seem to be *four* Circumstances, on which depend all, or the greatest Part of the Ills, that molest sensible Creatures; and it is not impossible but all these Circumstances may be necessary and unavoidable. We know so little beyond common Life, or even of Common Life, that, with regard to the Oeconomy of a Universe, there is no Conjecture, however wild, which may not be just; nor any one, however plausible, which may not be erroneous. All that belongs to human Understanding, in this deep Ignorance and Obscurity, is to be sceptical, or at least cautious; and not to admit of any Hypothesis, whatever; much less, of any which is supported by no Appearance of Probability. Now

this I assert to be the Case with regard to all the Causes of Evil, and the Circumstances, on which it depends. None of them appear to human Reason, in the least degree, necessary or unavoidable; nor can we suppose them such, without the utmost Licence of Imagination.

The *first* Circumstance, which introduces Evil, is that Contrivance or Oeconomy of the animal Creation, by which Pains, as well as Pleasures, are employ'd to excite all Creatures to Action, and make them vigilant in the great Work of Self-preservation. Now Pleasure alone, in its various Degrees, seems to human Understanding sufficient for this Purpose. All Animals might be constantly in a State of Enjoyment; but when urg'd by any of the Necessities of Nature, such as Thirst, Hunger, Weariness; instead of Pain, they might feel a Diminution of Pleasure, by which they might be prompted to seek that Object, which is necessary to their Subsistence. Men pursue Pleasure as eagerly as they avoid Pain; at least, might have been so constituted. It seems, therefore, plainly possible to carry on the Business of Life without any Pain. Why then is any Animal ever render'd susceptible of such a Sensation? If Animals can be free from it an hour, they might enjoy a perpetual Exemption from it; and it requir'd as particular a Contrivance of their Organs to produce that Feeling, as to endow them with Sight, Hearing, or any of the Senses. Shall we conjecture, that such a

Hume, David, "Why Does God Let People Suffer?" from *The Natural History of Religion* (Oxford: Clarendon Press, 1976).

Contrivance was necessary, without any Appearance of Reason? And shall we build on that Conjecture as on the most certain Truth?

But a Capacity of Pain wou'd not alone produce Pain, were it not for the *second* Circumstance, *viz,* the conducting of the World by general Laws; and this seems no wise necessary to a very perfect Being. It is true; if every thing were conducted by particular Volitions, the Course of Nature wou'd be perpetually broken, and no man cou'd employ his Reason in the Conduct of Life. But might not other particular Volitions remedy this Inconvenience? In short, might not the Deity exterminate all Ill, wherever it were to be found; and produce all Good, without any Preparation or long Progress of Causes and Effects?

Besides, we must consider, that, according to the present Oeconomy of the World, the Course of Nature, tho' suppos'd exactly regular, yet to us appears not so, and many Events are uncertain, and many disappoint our Expectations. Health and Sickness, Calm and Tempest, with an infinite Number of other Accidents, whose Causes are unknown and variable, have a great Influence both on the Fortunes of particular Persons and on the Prosperity of public Societies: And indeed all human life, in a manner, depends on such Accidents. A Being, therefore, who knows the secret Springs of the Universe, might easily, by particular Volitions, turn all these Accidents to the Good of Mankind, and render the whole World happy, without discovering himself in any Operation. A Fleet, whose Purposes were Salutary to Society, might always meet with a fair Wind: Good Princes enjoy sound Health and long Life: Persons, born to Power and Authority, be fram'd with good Tempers and virtuous Dispositions. A few such Events as these, regularly and wisely conducted, wou'd change the Face of the World; and yet wou'd no more seem to disturb the Course of Nature or confound human Conduct, than the present Oeconomy of things, where the Causes are secret, and variable, and compounded. Some small Touches, given to *Caligula's* Brain in his Infancy, might have converted him into a *Trajan:* One Wave, a little higher than the rest, by burying *Caesar* and his Fortune in the bottom of the Ocean, might have restor'd Liberty to a considerable Part of Mankind. There may, for aught we know, be good Reasons, why Providence interposes not in this Manner; but they are unknown to us: And tho' the mere Supposition, that such Reasons exist, may be sufficient to *save* the Conclusion concerning the divine Attributes, yet surely it can never be sufficient to *establish* that Conclusion.

If every thing in the Universe be conducted by general Laws, and if Animals be render'd susceptible of Pain, it scarcely seems possible but some Ill must arise in the various Shocks of Matter, and the various Concurrence and Opposition of general Laws: But this Ill wou'd be very rare, were it not for the *third* Circumstance which I propos'd to mention, *viz,* the great Frugality, with which all Powers and Faculties are distributed to every particular Being. So well adjusted are the Organs and Capacities of all Animals, and so well fitted to their Preservation, that, as far as History or Tradition reaches, there appears not to be any single Species, which has yet been extinguish'd in the Universe. Every Animal has the requisite Endowments; but these Endowments are bestow'd with so scrupulous an Oeconomy, that any considerable Diminution must entirely destroy the Creature. Wherever one Power is encreas'd, there is a proportional Abatement in the others. Animals, which excel in Swiftness, are commonly defective in Force. Those, which possess both, are either imperfect in some of their Senses, or are oppressed with the most craving Wants. The human Species, whose chief Excellency is Reason and Sagacity, is of all others the most necessitous, and the most deficient in bodily Advantages; without Cloaths, without Arms, without Food, without Lodging, without any Convenience of Life, except what they owe to their own Skill and Industry. In short, Nature seems to have form'd an exact Calculation of the Necessities of her Creatures; and like a *rigid Master,* has afforded them little more Powers or Endowments, than what are strictly sufficient to supply those Necessities. An *indulgent Parent* wou'd have bestow'd a large Stock, in order to guard against

Accidents, and secure the Happiness and Welfare of the Creature, in the most unfortunate Concurrence of Circumstances. Every Course of Life wou'd not have been so surrounded with Precipices, that the least Departure from the true Path, by Mistake or Necessity, must involve us in Misery and Ruin. Some Reserve, some Fund wou'd have been provided to ensure Happiness; nor wou'd the Powers and the Necessities have been adjusted with so rigid an Oeconomy. The Author of Nature is inconceivably powerful: His force is suppos'd great, if not altogether inexhaustible: Nor is there any Reason, as far as we can judge, to make him observe this strict Frugality in his Dealings with his Creatures. It wou'd have been better, were his Power extremely limited, to have created fewer Animals, and to have endowed these with more Faculties for their Happiness and Preservation. A Builder is never esteem'd prudent, who undertakes a Plan, beyond what his Stock will enable him to finish.

In order to cure most of the Ills of human Life, I require not that Man should have the Wings of the Eagle, the Swiftness of the Stag, the Force of the Ox, the Arms of the Lion, the Scales of the Crocodile or Rhinoceros; much less do I demand the Sagacity of an Angel or Cherubim. I am contented to take an Encrease in one single Power or Faculty of his Soul. Let him be endow'd with a greater Propensity to Industry and Labor; a more vigorous Spring and Activity of Mind; a more constant Bent to Business and Application. Let the whole Species possess naturally an equal Diligence with that which many Individuals are able to attain by Habit and Reflection; and the most beneficial Consequences, without any Allay of Ill, is the most immediate and necessary Result of the Endowment. Almost all the moral, as well as natural Evils of human Life arise from Idleness; and were our Species, by the original Constitution of their Frame, exempt from this Vice or Infirmity, the perfect Cultivation of Land, the Improvement of Arts and Manufactures, the exact Execution of every Office and Duty, immediately follow; and Men at once may fully reach

that State of Society, which is so imperfectly attain'd by the best regulated Government. But as Industry is a Power, and the most valuable of any, Nature seems determin'd, suitably to her usual Maxims, to bestow it on men with a very sparing hand; and rather to punish him severely for his Deficiency in it, than to reward him for his Attainments. She has so contriv'd his Frame, that nothing but the most violent Necessity can oblige him to labor, and she employs all his other Wants to overcome, as least in part, the Want of Diligence, and to endow him with some Share of a Faculty, of which she has thought fit naturally to bereave him. Here our Demands may be allow'd very humble, and therefore the more reasonable. If we requir'd the Endowments of superior Penetration and Judgment, of a more delicate Taste of Beauty, of a nicer Sensibility to Benevolence and Friendship; we might be told, that we impiously pretend to break the Order of Nature, that we want to exalt Ourselves into a higher Rank of Being, that the Presents which we require, not being suitable to our State and Condition, wou'd only be pernicious to us. But it is hard; I dare to repeat it, it is hard, that being plac'd in a World so full of Wants and Necessities; where almost every Being and Element is either our Foe or refuses us their Assistance; we shou'd also have our own Temper to struggle with, and shou'd be depriv'd of that Faculty, which can alone fence against these multiply'd Evils.

The *fourth* Circumstance, whence arises the Misery and Ill of the universe, is the inaccurate Workmanship of all the Springs and Principles of the great Machine of Nature. It must be acknowledg'd, that there are few Parts of the Universe, which seem not to serve some Purpose, and whose Removal wou'd not produce a visible Defect and Disorder in the Whole. The Parts hang all together; nor can one be touch'd without affecting the rest, in a greater or less degree. But at the same time, it must be observ'd, that none of these Parts or Principles, however useful, are so accurately adjusted, as to keep precisely within those Bounds, in which their Utility consists; but they are, all of them, apt, on every Occasion, to run into the one Extreme or the other. One wou'd imagine, that this grand Production had not receiv'd the last hand of the Maker; so little finish'd is every part, and so coarse are the Strokes, with which it is executed. Thus, the Winds are requisite to convey the Vapours along the Surface of the Globe, and to assist Men in Navigation: But how oft, rising up to Tempests and Hurricanes, do they become pernicious? Rains are necessary to nourish all the Plants and Animals of the Earth: But how often are they defective? how often excessive? Heat is requisite to all Life and Vegetation; but is not always found in the due Proportion. On the Mixture and Secretion of the Humours and Juices of the Body depend the Health and Prosperity of the Animal: But the Parts perform not regularly their proper Function. What more useful than all the Passions of the Mind, Ambition, Vanity, Love, Anger? But how oft do they break their Bounds, and cause the greatest Convulsions in Society? There is nothing so advantageous in the Universe, but what frequently becomes pernicious, by its Excess or Defect; nor has Nature guarded, with the requisite Accuracy, against all Disorder or Confusion. The Irregularity is never, perhaps, so great as to destroy any Species; but is often sufficient to involve the Individuals in Ruin and Misery.

On the Concurrence, then of these *four* Circumstances does all, or the greatest Part of natural Evil depend. Were all living Creatures incapable of Pain, or were the World administer'd by particular Volitions, Evil never cou'd have found Access into the Universe: And were Animals endow'd with a large Stock of Powers and Faculties, beyond what strict Necessity requires; or were the several Springs and Principles of the Universe so accurately fram'd as to preserve always the just Temperament and Medium; there must have been very little Ill in comparison of what we feel at present. What then shall we pronounce on this Occasion? Shall we say, that these Circumstances are not necessary, and that they might easily have been alter'd in the Contrivance of the Universe? This Decision seems too presumptuous for Creatures, so blind and ignorant. Let us be more modest in our Conclusions. Let us allow, that, if the Goodness of the Deity (I mean a Goodness like the human) cou'd be establish'd on any tolerable Reasons *a priori*, these Phaenomena, however untoward, wou'd not be sufficient to subvert that Principle; but might easily, in some unknown manner, be reconcilable to it. But let us still assert, that as this Goodness is not antecedently establish'd, but must be inferr'd from the Phaenomena, there can be no Grounds for such an Inference, while there are so many Ills in the Universe, and while these Ills might so easily have been remedy'd, as far as human Understanding can be allow'd to judge on such a Subject. I am Sceptic enough to allow, that the bad Appearances, notwithstanding all my Reasonings, may be compatible with such Attributes as you suppose: But surely they can never prove these Attributes. Such a Conclusion cannot result from Scepticism; but must arise from the Phaenomena, and from our Confidence in the Reasonings, which we deduce from these Phaenomena.

Look round this Universe. What an immense Profusion of Beings, animated and organiz'd, sensible and active! You admire this prodigious Variety and Fecundity. But inspect a little more narrowly these living Existences, the only Beings worth regarding. How hostile and destructive to each other! How insufficient all of them for their own Happiness! How contemptible or odious to the Spectator! The whole presents nothing but the Idea of a blind Nature, impregnated by a great vivifying Principle, and pouring forth from her Lap, without Discernment or parental Care, her maim'd and abortive Children.

Here the *Manichoen* System occurs as a proper Hypothesis to solve the Difficulty: And no doubt, in some respects, it is very specious, and has more Probability than the common Hypothesis, by giving a plausible Account of the strange Mixture of Good and Ill, which appears in Life. But if we consider, on the other hand, the perfect Uniformity and Agreement of the Parts of the Universe, we shall not discover in it any Marks of the Combat of a malevolent with a benevolent Being. There is indeed an Opposition of Pains and Pleasures in the Feelings of sensible

Creatures: But are not all the Operations of Nature carry'd on by an Opposition of Principles, of Hot and Cold, Moist and Dry, Light and Heavy? The true Conclusion is, that the original Source of all things is entirely indifferent to all these Principles, and has no more Regard to Good above Ill than to Heat above Cold, or to Drought above Moisture, or to Light above Heavy.

There may *four* Hypotheses be fram'd concerning the first Causes of the Universe; *that* they are endow'd with perfect Goodness, *that* they have perfect Malice, *that* they are opposite and have both Goodness and Malice, *that* they have neither Goodness nor Malice. Mixt Phaenomena can never prove the two former unmixt Principles. And the Uniformity and Steadiness of general Laws seem to oppose the third. The fourth, therefore, seems by far the most probable.

IMMANUEL KANT
Proving the Existence of God by Way of Morality

IMMANUEL KANT, *the great German philosopher, denied the theoretical possibility of proving the Existence of God, but argued that it is possible to show that believing in God is rational if we can show how this belief is necessary for Morality.*

THE moral law led, in the foregoing analysis, to a practical problem which is assigned solely by pure reason and without any concurrence of sensuous incentives. It is the problem of the completeness of the first and principal part of the highest good, viz., morality; since this problem can be solved only in eternity, it led to the postulate of immortality. The same law must also lead us to affirm the possibility of the second element of the highest good, i.e., happiness proportional to that morality; it must do so just as disinterestedly as heretofore, by a purely impartial reason. This it can do on the supposition of the existence of a cause adequate to this effect, i.e., it must postulate the existence of God as necessarily belonging to the possibility of the highest good (the object of our will which is necessarily connected with moral legislation of pure reason). We proceed to exhibit this connection in a convincing manner.

Happiness is the condition of a rational being in the world. In whose whole existence everything goes according to wish and will. It thus rests on the harmony of nature with his entire end and with the essential determining ground of his will. But the moral law commands as a law of freedom through motives wholly independent

Kant, Immanuel, "Proving the Existence of God by Way of Morality" from *Critique of Pratical Reason,* 3rd Edition, translated by Beck, Lewis White, © 1993. Adapted by permission of Pearson Education, Inc., Upper Saddle River, NJ.

of nature and of its harmony with our faculty of desire (as incentives). Still, the acting rational being in the world is not at the same time the cause of the world and of nature itself. Hence there is not the slightest ground in the moral law for a necessary connection between the morality and proportionate happiness of a being which belongs to the world as one of its parts and as thus dependent on it. Nor being nature's cause, his will cannot by its own strength bring nature, as it touches on his happiness, into complete harmony with his practical principles. Nevertheless, in the practical task of pure reason, i.e., in the necessary endeavor after the highest good, such a connection is postulated as necessary: we *should* seek to further the highest good (which therefore must be at least possible). Therefore also the existence is postulated of a cause of the whole of nature, itself distinct from nature, which contains the ground of the exact coincidence of happiness with morality. This supreme cause, however, must contain the ground of the agreement of nature not merely with a law of the will of rational beings but with the idea of this law so far as they make it the supreme ground of determination of the will. Thus it contains the ground of the agreement of nature not merely

with actions moral in their form but also with their morality as the motives to such actions, i.e., with their moral intention. Therefore, the highest good is possible in the world only on the supposition of a supreme cause of nature which has a causality corresponding to the moral intention. Now a being which is capable of actions by the idea of laws is an intelligence (a rational being), and the causality of such a being according to this idea of laws is his will. Therefore, the supreme cause of nature, in so far as it must be presupposed for the highest good, is a being which is the cause (and consequently the author) of nature through understanding and will, i.e., God. As a consequence, the postulate of the possibility of a highest derived good (the best world) is at the same time the postulate of the reality of a highest original good, namely, the existence of God. Now it was our duty to promote the highest good; and it is not merely our privilege but a necessity connected with duty as a requisite to presuppose the possibility of this highest good. This presupposition is made only under the condition of the existence of God, and this condition inseparably connects this supposition with duty. Therefore, it is morally necessary to assume the existence of God.

FYODOR DOSTOEVSKY
Rebellion

FYODOR DOSTOEVSKY *(1821–1881) was one of the greatest creative writers of the nineteenth century. He was born in Russia, where he lived most of his life. Opposed to the oppressive practices of the government, he was imprisoned for a time in Siberia. His belief in the fundamental evil of human nature permeates his novels, the most famous of which are* The Brothers Karamazov *and* Crime and Punishment.

Dostoevsky, Fyodor, "Rebellion" from *The Brothers Karamazov* (New York: Macmillan, 1912).

"I MEANT to speak of the suffering of mankind generally, but we had better confine ourselves to the sufferings of the children. That reduces the scope of my argument to a tenth of what it would be. Still we'd better keep to the children, though it does weaken my case. But, in the first place, children can be loved even at close quarters, even when they are dirty, even when they are ugly (I fancy, though, children never are ugly). The second reason why I won't speak of grown-up people is that, besides being disgusting and unworthy of love, they have a compensation—they've eaten the apple and know good and evil, and they have become 'like gods.' They go on eating it still. But the children haven't eaten anything, and are so far innocent. Are you fond of children, Alyosha? I know you are, and you will understand why I prefer to speak of them. If they, too, suffer horribly on earth, they must suffer for their fathers' sins, they must be punished for their fathers, who have eaten the apple; but that reasoning is of the other world and is incomprehensible for the heart of man here on earth. The innocent must not suffer for another's sins, and especially such innocents! . . .

. . . Do you understand that, friend and brother, you pious and humble novice? Do you understand why this infamy must be and is permitted? Without it, I am told, man could not have existed on earth, for he could not have known good and evil. Why should he know that diabolical good and evil when it costs so much? Why, the whole world of knowledge is not worth that Child's prayer to 'dear, kind God'! I say nothing of the sufferings of grownup people, they have eaten the apple, damn them, and the devil take them all! But these little ones! I am making you suffer, Alyosha, you are not yourself. I'll leave off if you like."

"Never mind. I want to suffer too," muttered Alyosha.

"One picture, only one more, because it's so curious, so characteristic, and I have only just read it in some collection of Russian antiquities. I've forgotten the name. I must look it up. It was in the darkest days of serfdom at the beginning of the century, and long live the Liberator of the People! There was in those days a general of aristocratic connections, the owner of great estates, one of the those men—somewhat exceptional, I believe, even then—who, retiring from the service into a life of leisure, are convinced that they've earned absolute power over the lives of their subjects. There were such men then. So our general, settled on his property of two thousand souls, lives in pomp, and domineers over his poor neighbours as though they were dependents and buffoons. He has kennels of hundreds of hounds and nearly a hundred dog-boys—all mounted, and in uniform. One day a serf boy, a little child of eight, threw a stone in play and hurt the paw of the general's favourite hound. 'Why is my favourite dog lame?' He is told that the boy threw a stone that hurt the dog's paw. 'So you did it.' The general looked the child up and down. 'Take him.' He was taken—taken from his mother and kept shut up all night. Early that morning the general comes out on horseback, with the hounds, his dependents, dog-boys, and huntsmen, all mounted around him in full hunting parade. The servants are summoned for their edification, and in front of them all stands the mother of the child. The child is brought from the lock-up. It's a gloomy cold, foggy autumn day, a capital day for hunting. The general orders the child to be undressed; the child is stripped naked. He shivers, numb with terror, not daring to cry. . . . 'Make him run,' commands the general. 'Run! run!' shout the dog-boys. The boy runs. . . . 'At him!' yells the general, and he sets the whole pack of hounds on the child. The hounds catch him, and tear him to pieces before his mother's eyes! . . . I believe the general was afterwards declared incapable of administering his estates. Well—what did he deserve? To be shot? To be shot for the satisfaction of our moral feelings? Speak, Alyosha!"

"To be shot," murmured Alyosha, lifting his eyes to Ivan with a pale, twisted smile.

"Bravo!" cried Ivan delighted. "If even you say so . . . You're a pretty monk! So there is a little devil sitting in your heart, Alyosha Karamazov!"

"What I said was absurd, but" . . .

"That's just the point that 'but'!" cried Ivan. "Let me tell you, novice, that the absurd is only too necessary on earth. The world stands on absurdities, and perhaps nothing would have come to pass in it without them. We know what we know!" . . .

Ivan for a minute was silent, his face became all at once very sad.

"Listen! I took the case of children only to make my case clearer. Of the other tears of humanity with which the earth is soaked from its crust to its centre, I will say nothing. I have narrowed my subject on purpose. I am a bug, and I recognise in all humility that I cannot understand why the world is arranged as it is. Men are themselves to blame, I suppose; they were given paradise, they wanted freedom, and stole fire from heaven, though they knew they would become unhappy, so there is no need to pity them. With my pitiful, earthly, Euclidian understanding, all I know is that there is suffering and that there are none guilty; that cause follows effect, simply and directly; that everything flows and finds its level—but that's only Euclidian nonsense, I know that, and I can't consent to live by it! What comfort is it to me that there are none guilty and that cause follows effect simply and directly, and that I know it—I must have justice, or I will destroy myself. And not justice in some remote infinite time and space, but here on earth, and that I could see myself. I have believed in it. I want to see it, and if I am dead by then, let me rise again, for if it all happens without me, it will be too unfair. Surely I haven't suffered, simply that I, my crimes and my sufferings, may manure the soil of the future harmony for somebody else. I want to see with my own eyes the hind lie down with the lion and the victim rise up and embrace his murderer. I want to be there when every one suddenly understands what it has all been for. All the religions of the world are built on this longing, and I am a believer. But then there are the children, and what am I to do about them? That's a question I can't answer. For the hundredth time I repeat, there are numbers of questions, but I've only taken the children, because in their case

what I mean is so unanswerably clear. Listen! If all must suffer to pay for the eternal harmony, what have children to do with it, tell me, please? It's beyond all comprehension why they should suffer, and why they should pay for the harmony. Why should they, too, furnish material to enrich the soil for the harmony of the future? I understand solidarity in sin among men. I understand solidarity in retribution, too; but there can be no such solidarity with children. And if it is really true that they must share responsibility for all their fathers' crimes, such a truth is not of this world and is beyond my comprehension. Some jester will say, perhaps, that the child would have grown up and have sinned, but you see he didn't grow up, he was torn to pieces by the dogs, at eight years old. Oh, Alyosha, I am not blaspheming! I understand, of course, what an upheaval of the universe it will be, when everything in heaven and earth blends in one hymn of praise and everything that lives and has lived cries aloud: 'Thou art just, O Lord, for Thy ways are revealed.' When the mother embraces the fiend who threw her child to the dogs, and all three cry aloud with tears, 'Thou are just, O Lord!' then, of course, the crown of knowledge will be reached and all will be made clear. But what pulls me up here is that I can't accept that harmony. And while I am on earth, I make haste to take my own measures. You see, Alyosha, perhaps it really may happen that if I live to that moment, or rise again to see it, I, too, perhaps, may cry aloud with the rest, looking at the mother embracing the child's torturer, 'Thou art just, O Lord!' but I don't want to cry aloud then. While there is still time, I hasten to protect myself and so I renounce the higher harmony altogether. It's not worth the tears of that one tortured child who beat itself on the breast with its little fist and prayed in its stinking outhouse, with its unexpiated tears to 'dear, kind God'! It's not worth it, because those tears are unatoned for. They must be atoned for, or there can be no harmony. But how? How are you going to atone for them? Is it possible? By their being avenged? But what do I care for avenging them? What do I care for a hell for oppressors?

What good can hell do, since those children have already been tortured? And what becomes of harmony, if there is hell? I want to forgive. I want to embrace. I don't want more suffering. And if the sufferings of children go to swell the sum of sufferings which was necessary to pay for truth, then I protest that the truth is not worth such a price. I don't want the mother to embrace the oppressor who threw her son to the dogs! She dare not forgive him! Let her forgive him for herself, if she will, let her forgive the torturer for the immeasurable suffering of her mother's heart. But the sufferings of her tortured child she has no right to forgive; she dare not forgive the torturer, even if the child were to forgive him! And if that is so, if they dare not forgive, what becomes of harmony? Is there in the whole world a being who would have the right to forgive and could forgive? I don't want harmony. From love for humanity I don't want it. I would rather be left with the unavenged suffering. I would rather remain with my unavenged suffering and unsatisfied indignation, *even if I were*

wrong. Besides, too high a price is asked for harmony; it's beyond our means to pay so much to enter on it. And so I hasten to give back my entrance ticket, and if I am an honest man I am bound to give it back as soon as possible. And that I am doing. It's not God that I don't accept, Alyosha, only I must respectfully return Him the ticket."

"That's rebellion," murmured Alyosha, looking down.

"Rebellion? I am sorry you call it that," said Ivan earnestly. "One can hardly live in rebellion, and I want to live. Tell me yourself, I challenge you—answer. Imagine that you are creating a fabric of human destiny with the object of making men happy in the end, giving them peace and rest at last, but that it was essential and inevitable to torture to death only one tiny creature—that baby beating its breast with its fist, for instance—and to found that edifice on its unavenged tears, would you consent to be the architect on those conditions? Tell me, and tell the truth."

"No, I wouldn't consent," said Alyosha softly.

SØREN KIERKEGAARD
The Leap of Faith and the Limits of Reason

SØREN KIERKEGAARD *(1813–1855) was a Danish philosopher and theologian. Generally recognized as the father of existentialism and religious irrationalism, he believed that each individual must choose his or her own way of life. Christianity is one such choice.*

BUT what is this unknown something with which the Reason collides when inspired by its paradoxical passion, with the result of unsettling even man's knowledge of himself? It is the Unknown. It is not a human being, in so far as we know what man is; nor is it any other known thing. So let us call this unknown something: *God.* It is nothing more than a name we assign to it. The idea of demonstrating that this unknown something (God) exists, could scarcely suggest itself to the Reason. For if God does not exist it would of course be impossible to prove it; and if he does exist it would be folly to attempt it. For at the very outset, in beginning my proof, I will have presupposed it, not as doubtful but as certain (a presupposition is never doubtful, for the very reason that it is a presupposition), since otherwise I would not begin, readily understanding that the whole would be impossible if he did not exist. But if when I speak of proving God's existence I mean that I propose to prove that the Unknown, which exists, is God, then I express myself unfortunately. For in that case I do not prove anything, least of all an existence, but merely develop the content of a conception. Generally speaking, it is a difficult matter to prove that anything exists; and what is still worse for the intrepid souls who undertake the venture, the difficulty is such that fame scarcely awaits those who concern themselves with it. The entire demonstration always turns into something very different from what it assumes to be, and becomes an additional development of the consequences that flow from my having assumed that the object in question exists. Thus I always reason from existence, not toward existence, whether I move in the sphere of palpable sensible fact or in the realm of thought. I do not for example prove that a stone exists, but that some existing thing is a stone. The procedure in a court of justice does not prove that a criminal exists, but that the accused, whose existence is given, is a criminal. Whether we call existence an *accessorium* or the eternal *prius,* it is never subject to demonstration. Let us take ample time for consideration. We have no such reason for haste as have those who from concern for themselves or for God or for some other thing, must make haste to get its existence demonstrated. Under such circumstances there may indeed be need for haste, especially if the prover sincerely seeks to appreciate the danger that he himself, or the thing in question, may be nonexistent unless the proof is finished; and does

not surreptitiously entertain the thought that it exists whether he succeeds in proving it or not.

If it were proposed to prove Napoleon's existence from Napoleon's deeds, would it not be a most curious proceeding? His existence does indeed explain his deeds, but the deeds do not prove *his* existence, unless I have already understood the word "his" so as thereby to have assumed his existence. But Napoleon is only an individual, and in so far there exists no absolute relationship between him and his deeds; some other person might have performed the same deeds. Perhaps this is the reason why I cannot pass from the deeds to existence. If I call these deeds the deeds of Napoleon the proof becomes superfluous, since I have already named him; if I ignore this, I can never prove from the deeds that they are Napoleon's, but only in a purely ideal manner that such deeds are the deeds of a great general, and so forth. But between God and his works there exists an absolute relationship: God is not a name but a concept. Is this perhaps the reason that his *essentia involvit existentiam?* The works of God are such that only God can perform them. Just so, but where are the works of God? The works from which I would deduce his existence are not immediately given. The wisdom of God in nature, his goodness, his wisdom in the governance of the world—are all these manifest, perhaps, upon the very face of things? Are we not here confronted with the most terrible temptations to doubt, and is it not impossible finally to dispose of all these doubts? But from such an order of things I will surely not attempt to prove God's existence; and even if I began I would never finish, and would in addition have to live constantly in suspense, lest something terrible should suddenly happen that my bit of proof would be demolished. From what works then do I propose to derive the proof? From the works as apprehended through an ideal interpretation, i.e., such as they do not immediately reveal themselves. But in that case it is not from the works that I prove God's existence. I merely develop the ideality I have presupposed, and because of my confidence in *this* I make so bold as to defy all objections, even those that have not yet been made. In beginning my proof I presuppose the ideal interpretation, and also that I will be successful in carrying it through; but what else is this but to presuppose that God exists, so that I really begin by virtue of confidence in him?

And how does God's existence emerge from the proof? Does it follow straightaway, without any breach of continuity? Or have we not here an analogy to the behaviour of these toys, the little Cartesian dolls? As soon as I let go of the doll it stands on its head. As soon as I let it go—I must therefore let it go. So also with the proof for God's existence. As long as I keep my hold on the proof, i.e., continue to demonstrate, the existence does not come out, if for no other reason than that I am engaged in proving it; but when I let the proof go, the existence is there. But this act of letting go is surely also something; it is indeed a contribution of mine. Must not this also be taken into the account, this little moment, brief as it may be—it need not be long, for it is a *leap*. However brief this moment, if only an instantaneous now, this "now" must be included in the reckoning.

Whoever therefore attempts to demonstrate the existence of God (except in the sense of clarifying the concept), proves in lieu thereof something else, something which at times perhaps does not need proof, and in any case need none better; for the fool says in his heart that there is no God, but whoever says in his heart or to men: Wait just a little and I will prove it—what a rare man of wisdom is he! If in the moment of beginning his proof it is not absolutely undetermined whether God exists or not, he does not prove it; and if it is thus undetermined in the beginning he will never come to begin, partly from fear of failure, since God perhaps does not exist, and partly because he has nothing with which to begin.—A project of this kind would scarcely have been undertaken by the ancients. Socrates at least, who is credited with having put forth the physico-teleological proof for God's existence, did not go about it in any such manner. He always presupposes God's existence, and under this presupposition seeks to interpenetrate

nature with the ideal of purpose. Had he been asked why he pursued this method, he would doubtless have explained that he lacked the courage to venture out upon so perilous a voyage of discovery without having made sure of God's existence behind him. At the word of God he casts his net as if to catch the idea of purpose; for nature herself finds many means of frightening the inquirer, and distracts him by many a digression.

The paradoxical passion of the Reason thus comes repeatedly into collision with the Unknown, which does indeed exist, but is unknown, and in so far does not exist. The Reason cannot advance beyond this point, and yet it cannot refrain in its paradoxicalness from arriving at this limit and occupying itself therewith. It will not serve to dismiss its relation to it simply by asserting that the Unknown does not exist, since this itself involves a relationship. But what then is the Unknown, since the designation of it as God merely signifies for us that it is unknown? To say that it is the Unknown because it cannot be known, and even if it were capable of being known, it could not be expressed, does not satisfy the demands of passion, though it correctly interprets the Unknown as a limit; but a limit is precisely a torment for passion, though it also serves as an incitement. And yet the Reason can come no further, whether it risks an issue *via negationis* or *via eminentia*.

What then is the Unknown? It is the limit to which the Reason repeatedly comes, and in so far, substituting a static form of conception for the dynamic, it is the different, the absolutely different. But because it is absolutely different, there is no mark by which it could be distinguished. When qualified as absolutely different it seems on the verge of disclosure, but this is not the case; for the Reason cannot even conceive an absolute unlikeness. The Reason cannot negate itself absolutely, but uses itself for the purpose, and thus conceives only such an unlikeness within itself as it can conceive by means of itself; it cannot absolutely transcend itself, and hence conceives only such a superiority over itself as it can conceive by means of itself. Unless the Unknown (God) remains a mere limiting conception, the single idea of difference will be thrown into a state of confusion, and become many ideas of many differences. The Unknown is then in a condition of dispersion (diaspora), and the Reason may choose at pleasure from what is at hand and the imagination may suggest (the monstrous, the ludicrous, etc.).

But it is impossible to hold fast to a difference of this nature. Every time this is done it is essentially an arbitrary act, and deepest down in the heart of piety lurks the mad caprice which knows that it has itself produced its God. If no specific determination of difference can be held fast, because there is no distinguishing mark, like and unlike finally become identified with one another, thus sharing the fate of all such dialectical opposites. The unlikeness clings to the Reason and confounds it, so that the Reason no longer knows itself and quite consistently confuses itself with the unlikeness. On this point paganism has been sufficiently prolific in fantastic inventions. As for the last named supposition,

the self-irony of the Reason, I shall attempt to delineate it merely by a stroke or two, without raising any question of its being historical. There lives an individual whose appearance is precisely like that of other men; he grows up to manhood like others, he marries, he has an occupation by which he earns his livelihood, and he makes provision for the future as befits a man. For though it may be beautiful to live like the birds of the air, it is not lawful, and may lead to the sorriest of consequences: either starvation if one has enough persistence, or dependence on the bounty of others. This man is also God. How do I know? I cannot know it, for in order to know it I would have to know God, and the nature of the difference between God and man; and this I cannot know, because the Reason has reduced it to likeness with that from which it was unlike. Thus God becomes the most terrible of deceivers, because the Reason has deceived itself. The Reason has brought God as near as possible, and yet he is as far away as ever.

WILLIAM JAMES
The Will to Believe

WILLIAM JAMES *(1842–1910) was one of the greatest American philosophers. He graduated from Harvard with a medical degree but decided to teach (at Harvard) rather than practice medicine. A founder of modern pragmatism, he also established himself as one of the fathers of modern psychology with his* Principles of Psychology.

I HAVE long defended to my own students the lawfulness of voluntarily adopted faith; but as soon as they have got well imbued with the logical spirit, they have as a rule refused

to admit my contention to be lawful philosophically, even though in point of fact they were personally all the time chockfull of some faith or other themselves. I am all the while, however, so

James, William, "The Will to Believe" from *The Will to Believe and Other Essays in Popular Philosophy* (New York: Longmans & Green, 1896).

profoundly convinced that my own position is correct, that your invitation has seemed to me a good occasion to make my statements more clear. Perhaps your minds will be more open than those with which I have hitherto had to deal. I will be as little technical as I can, though I must begin by setting up some technical distinctions that will help us in the end.

Let us give the name of *hypothesis* to anything that may be proposed to our belief; and just as the electricians speak of live and dead wires, let us speak of any hypothesis as either *live* or *dead*. A live hypothesis is one which appeals as a real possibility to him to whom it is proposed. If I ask you to believe in the Mahdi, the notion makes no electric connection with your nature,—it refuses to scintillate with any credibility at all. As an hypothesis it is completely dead. To an Arab, however (even if he be not one of the Mahdi's followers), the hypothesis is among the mind's possibilities: it is alive. This shows that deadness and liveness in an hypothesis are not intrinsic properties, but relations to the individual thinker. They are measured by his willingness to act. The maximum of liveness in an hypothesis means willingness to act irrevocably. Practically, that means belief; but there is some believing tendency wherever there is willingness to act at all.

Next, let us call the decision between two hypotheses an *option*. Options may be of several kinds. They may be—1, *living* or *dead*; 2, *forced* or *avoidable*; 3, *momentous* or *trivial*; and for our purposes we may call an option a *genuine* option when it is of the forced, living, and momentous kind.

1. A living option is one in which both hypotheses are live ones. If I say to you: "Be a theosophist or be a Mohammedan," it is probably a dead option, because for you neither hypothesis is likely to be alive. But if I say, "Be an agnostic or be a Christian," it is otherwise: trained as you are, each hypothesis makes some appeal, however small, to your belief.

2. Next, if I say to you: "Choose between going out with your umbrella or without it," I do not offer you a genuine option, for it is not forced. You

can easily avoid it by not going out at all. Similarly, if I say, "Either love me or hate me," "Either call my theory true or call it false," your option is avoidable. You may remain indifferent to me, neither loving nor hating, and you may decline to offer any judgment as to my theory. But if I say, "Either accept this truth or go without it," I put on you a forced option, for there is no standing place outside of the alternative. Every dilemma based on a complete logical disjunction, with no possibility of not choosing, is an option of this forced kind. . . .

The thesis I defend is, briefly stated, this: *Our passional nature not only law fully may, but must, decide an option between propositions, whenever it is a genuine option that cannot by its nature be decided on intellectual grounds: for to say, under such circumstances, "Do not decide, but leave the question open," is itself a passional decision;—just like deciding yes or no,—and is attended with the same risk of losing the truth.* . . .

Wherever the option between losing truth and gaining it is not momentous, we can throw the chance of *gaining truth* away, and at any rate save ourselves from any chance of *believing falsehood*, by not making up our minds at all till objective evidence has come. In scientific questions, this is almost always the case; and even in human affairs in general, the need of acting is seldom so urgent that a false belief to act on is better than no belief at all. Law courts, indeed, have to decide on the best evidence attainable for the moment, because a judge's duty is to make law as well as to ascertain it, and (as a learned judge once said to me) few cases are worth spending much time over: the great thing is to have them decided on *any* acceptable principle, and got out of the way. But in our dealings with objective nature we obviously are recorders, not makers, of the truth; and decisions for the mere sake of deciding promptly and getting on to the next business would be wholly out of place. Throughout the breadth of physical nature facts are what they are quite independently of us, and seldom is there any such hurry about them that the risks of being duped by believing a premature theory need be faced. The questions here are always trivial options, the hypotheses are hardly living (at any rate not living for us spectators), the choice between believing truth or falsehood is seldom forced. The attitude of sceptical balance is therefore the absolutely wise one if we would escape mistakes. What difference, indeed, does it make to most of us whether we have or have not a theory of the Röntgen rays, whether we believe or not in mind stuff, or have a conviction about the causality of conscious states? It makes no difference. Such options are not forced on us. On every account it is better not to make them, but still keep weighing reasons *pro et contra* with an indifferent hand. . . .

But now, it will be said, these . . . cases, . . . have nothing to do with great cosmical matters, like the question of religious faith. Let us then pass on to that. Religions differ so much in their accidents that in discussing the religious question we must take it very generic and broad. What then do we now mean by the religious hypothesis? Science says things are; mortality says some things are better than other things; and religion says essentially two things.

First, she says that the best things are the more eternal things, the overlapping things, the things in the universe that throw the last stone, so to speak, and say the final word. "Perfection is eternal,"—this phrase of Charles Secrétan seems a good way of putting this first affirmation of religion, an affirmation which obviously cannot yet be verified scientifically at all.

The second affirmation of religion is that we are better off even now if we believe her first affirmation to be true.

Now, let us consider what the logical elements of this situation are *in case the religious hypothesis in both its branches be really true.* (Of course, we must admit that possibility at the outset. If we are to discuss the question at all, it must involve a living option. If for any of you religion be a hypothesis that cannot, by any living possibility be true, then you need go no farther. I speak to the "saving remnant" alone.) So proceeding, we see, first that religion offers itself as a *momentous* option. We are supposed to gain, even now, by our belief, and

to lose by our nonbelief, a certain vital good. Secondly, religion is a *forced* option, so far as that good goes. We cannot escape the issue by remaining sceptical and waiting for more light, because, although we do avoid error in that way *if religion be untrue,* we lose the good, *if it be true,* just as certainly as if we positively chose to disbelieve. It is as if a man should hesitate indefinitely to ask a certain woman to marry him because he was not perfectly sure that she would prove an angel after he brought her home. Would he not cut himself off from that particular angel-possibility as decisively as if he went and married some one else? Scepticism, then, is not avoidance of option; it is option of a certain particular kind of risk. *Better risk loss of truth than chance of error,*—that is your faith-vetoer's exact position. He is actively playing his stake as much as the believer is; he is backing the field against the religious hypothesis, just as the believer is backing the religious hypothesis against the field. To preach scepticism to us as a duty until "sufficient evidence" for religion be found, is tantamount therefore to telling us, when in presence of the religious hypothesis, that to yield to our fear of its being error is wiser and better than to yield to our hope that it may be true. It is not intellect against all passions, then; it is only intellect with one passion laying down its law. And by what, forsooth, is the supreme wisdom of this passion warranted? Dupery for dupery, what proof is there that dupery through hope is so much worse than dupery through fear? I, for one, can see no proof; and I simply refuse obedience to the scientist's command to imitate his kind of option, in a case where my own stake is important enough to give me the right to choose my own form of risk. If religion be true and the evidence for it be still insufficient, I do not wish, by putting your extinguisher upon my nature (which feels to me as if it had after all some business in this matter), to forfeit my sole chance in life of getting upon the winning side,—that chance depending, of course, on my willingness to run the risk of acting as if my passional need of taking the world religiously might be prophetic and right.

All this is on the supposition that it really may be prophetic and right, and that, even to us who are discussing the matter, religion is a live hypothesis which may be true. Now, to most of us religion comes in a still further way that makes a veto on our active faith even more illogical. The more perfect and more eternal aspect of the universe is represented in our religions as having personal form. The universe is no longer a mere *It* to us, but a *Thou*, if we are religious; and any relation that may be possible from person to person might be possible here. For instance, although in one sense we are passive portions of the universe, in another we show a curious autonomy, as if we were small active centres on our own account. We feel, too, as if the appeal of religion to us were made to our own active goodwill, as if evidence might be forever withheld from us unless we met the hypothesis halfway. To take a trivial illustration: just as a man who in a company of gentlemen made no advances, asked a warrant for every concession, and believed no one's word without proof, would cut himself off by such churlishness from all the social rewards that a more trusting spirit would earn,—so here, one who should shut himself up in snarling logicality and try to make the gods extort his recognition willy-nilly, or not get it at all, might cut himself off forever from his only opportunity of making the gods' acquaintance. This feeling, forced on us we know not whence, that by obstinately believing that there are gods (although not to do so would be so easy both for our logic and our life) we are doing the universe the deepest service we can, seems part of the living essence of the religious hypothesis. If the hypothesis *were* true in all its parts, including this one, then pure intellectualism, with its veto on our making willing advances, would be an absurdity; and some participation of our sympathetic nature would be logically required. I, therefore, for one, cannot see my way to accepting the agnostic rules for truthseeking, or wilfully agree to keep my willing nature out of the game. I cannot do so for this plain reason, that *a rule of thinking which would absolutely prevent me from acknowledging certain kinds of truth if those kinds of truth were really there, would be an irrational rule.* That for me is the long and short of the formal logic of the situation, no matter what the kinds of truth might materially be.

I confess I do not see how this logic can be escaped. But sad experience makes me fear that some of you may still shrink from radically saying with me, *in abstracto,* that we have the right to believe at our own risk any hypothesis that is live enough to tempt our will. I suspect, however, that if this is so, it is because you have got away from the abstract logical point of view altogether, and are thinking (perhaps without realizing it) of some particular religious hypothesis which for you is dead. The freedom to "believe what we will" you apply to the case of some patent superstition; and the faith you think of is the faith defined by the schoolboy when he said, "Faith is when you believe something that you know ain't true." I can only repeat that this is misapprehension. *In concreto,* the freedom to believe can only cover living options which the intellect of the individual cannot be itself resolve; and living options never seem absurdities to him who has them to consider. When I look at the religious question as it really puts itself to concrete men, and when I think of all the possibilities which both practically and theoretically it involves, then this command that we shall put a stopper on our heart, instincts, and courage, and *wait*—acting of course meanwhile more or less as if religion were *not* true—till dooms day, or till such time as our intellect and senses working together may have raked in evidence enough,—this command, I say, seems to me the queerest idol ever manufactured in the philosophic cave. Were we scholastic absolutists, there might be more excuse. If we had an infallible intellect with its objective certitudes, we might feel ourselves disloyal to such a perfect organ of knowledge in not trusting to it exclusively, in not waiting for its releasing word. But if we are empiricists, if we believe that no bell in us tolls to let us know for certain when truth is in our grasp, then it seems a piece of idle fantasticality to preach so solemnly our duty of waiting for the bell. Indeed we *may* wait if we will.—I hope you do not think that I am denying that,—but if we do so, we do so at our peril as much as if we believed. In either case we *act,* taking our life in our hands. No one of us ought to issue vetoes to the other, nor should we bandy words of abuse. We ought, on the contrary, delicately and profoundly to respect one another's mental freedom: then only shall we bring about the intellectual republic: then only shall we have that spirit of inner tolerance without which all our outer tolerance is soulless, and which is empiricism's glory; then only shall we live and let live, in speculative as well as in practical things.

NATALIE ANGIER
I'm No Believer

NATALIE ANGIER is a Pulitzer Prize winning science writer. Her work appears regularly in the New York Times. She is also the author of several books, among them Woman: An Intimate Geography *(1999).*

IN the beginning—or rather, at the end of a very lo-o-ng beginning—George W. Bush made an earnest acceptance speech and urged our nation to "rise above a house divided." He knows, he said, that "America wants reconciliation and unity," and that we all "share hopes and goals and values." After his speech he reached out, up, down and across aisles, to embrace Republicans, Democrats, Naderites, Palm Beach Buchananites, the disaffected, the disinclined.

The only problem was what President-elect Bush wanted from me and "every American." "I ask you to pray for this great nation," he said. "I ask your prayers for leaders from both parties," and for their families too, while we're at it. Whatever else I might have been inclined to think of Bush's call for comity, with his simple little request, his assumption that prayer is some sort of miracle Vicks VapoRub, it was clear that his hands were reaching for any hands but mine.

Again and again the polls proclaim the United States to be a profoundly and persistently religious nation, one in which faith remains a powerful force despite the temptations of secularism and the decline of religion's influence in most other countries of the developed world.

Every year, pollsters such as Gallup and the National Opinion Research Center ask Americans whether they believe in God, and every year the same overwhelming majority, anywhere from 92 per cent to 97 per cent, say yes. In one survey, 80 per cent professed belief in life after death. When asked how often they attend church, at least 60 per cent say once a month or more, and have said as much for the past 40 years.

Sorry Dubya, "I'm No Believer" by Natalie Angier. First published 21st January 2001 in *The Independent* on Sunday, 21st January 2001.

So who in her right mind would want to be an atheist in America today, a place where presidential candidates compete for the honour of divining "what Jesus would do," and where Senator Joseph Lieberman can declare that we shouldn't deceive ourselves into thinking that our constitutional "freedom of religion" means "freedom from religion" or "indulge the supposition that morality can be maintained without religion"?

I'll out myself. I'm an atheist. I don't believe in God, gods, godlets or any sort of higher power beyond the universe itself, which seems quite high and powerful enough to me. I don't believe in life after death, channelled chat rooms with the dead, reincarnation, telekinesis or any miracles but the miracle of life and consciousness, which again strike me as miracles in nearly obscene abundance.

I believe that the universe abides by the laws of physics, some of which are known, others of which will surely be discovered, but even if they are not, that will simply be a result, as my colleague George Johnson put it, of our brains having evolved for life on this one little planet and thus being inevitably limited. I'm convinced that the world as we see it was shaped by the again genuinely miraculous, let's even say transcendent, hand of evolution through natural selection.

I'm in the minority, even among friends and family. When I sent out a casual and non-scientific poll of my own to a wide cast of acquaintances, friends and colleagues, I was surprised, but not really, to learn that maybe 60 per cent claimed a belief in a god of some sort, including people I would have bet were unregenerate sceptics. Others just shrugged. They don't think about this stuff. It doesn't matter to them. They can't know, they won't beat themselves up trying to know and for that matter they don't care if their kids believe or not.

Rare were the respondents who considered atheism to be a significant part of their self-identities. Most called themselves "passive" atheists and said they had stopped doing battle with the big questions of life and death, meaning and eternity, pretty much when they stopped using Clearasil. To be an active atheist seems almost silly and beside the point. After all, the most famous group devoted to atheism, the American Atheists, was founded by Madalyn Murray O'Hair, an eccentric megalomaniac whose greatest claim to fame is that she and her son were kidnapped several years ago and are presumed dead.

Other atheistic groups, such as the Freedom From Religion Foundation or the Council for Secular Humanism, are more concerned with maintaining an unshakeable separation between church and state than they are with spreading any gospel of godlessness. And yet there is something to be said for a revival of pagan peevishness and outspokenness. It's not that I would presume to do something as foolish and insulting as try to convert a believer. Arguments over the question of whether God exists are ancient, recurring, sometimes stimulating but more often tedious. Arrogance and righteousness are non-denominational vices that entice the churched and unchurched alike.

Still, the current climate of religiosity can be stifling to non-believers, and it helps now and then to cry foul. For one thing, some of the numbers surrounding the deep religiousness of America, and the rarity of nonbelief, should be held to the fire of scepticism, as should sweeping statistics of any sort. Yes, Americans are comparatively more religious than Europeans, but while the vast majority of them may say generically that they believe in God, when asked what their religion is, a sizable fraction, 11 per cent, report "no religion."

What's more, in some quarters, atheism, far from being rare, is the norm. When researchers targeted members of the National Academy of Sciences, an elite coterie if ever there was one, belief in a personal god was 7 per cent, the flip of the American public at large.

Among the more irritating consequences of our flagrantly religious society is the special dispensation that mainstream religions receive. We all may talk about religion as a powerful social force, but unlike other similarly powerful institutions, religion is not to be questioned, criticised or mocked. When the singer-songwriter Sinead O'Connor ripped apart a photograph of

John Paul II to protest at what she saw as his overweening power, even the most secular humanists were outraged by her iconoclasm, and her career has never really recovered.

When conspicuous true believers such as Lieberman make the claim that religion and ethical behaviour are inextricably linked, the corollary premise is that atheists are, if not immoral, then amoral, or nihilistic misanthropes, or, worst of all, moral relativists. Believers and doubters will always be with us—and it's just possible that they need each other.

From my godless perspective, the devout remind me that it is human nature to thirst after meaning and to desire an expansion of purpose beyond the cramped Manhattan studio of self and its immediate relations.

In her brief and beautiful book *The Sacred Depths of Nature,* Ursula Goodenough, a cell biologist, articulates a sensibility that she calls "religious naturalism," a profound appreciation of the genuine workings of nature, conjoined with a commitment to preserving that natural world in all its staggering, interdependent splendour. Call it transcendent atheism: I may not believe in life after death, but what a gift it is to be alive now.

JOHN WISDOM
Gods

JOHN WISDOM *(1904–1993) was professor of philosophy at Cambridge University in England. He was both appreciative and skeptical of metaphysical arguments, which he interpreted in an often metaphorical, sometimes psychoanalytical way. In "Gods," he asks us to imagine an invisible gardener. The question is: How could the belief in such a gardener ever be confirmed?*

TWO people return to their long neglected garden and find among the weeds a few of the old plants surprisingly vigorous. One says to the other "It must be that a gardener has been coming and doing something about these plants." Upon inquiry they find that no neighbor has ever seen anyone at work in their garden. The first man says to the other "He must have worked while people slept." The other says "No, someone would have heard him and besides, anybody who cared about the plants would have kept down these weeds." The first man says "Look at the way these are arranged. There is purpose and a feeling for beauty here. I believe that someone comes, someone invisible to mortal eyes. I believe that the more carefully we look the more we shall find confirmation of this." They examine the garden ever so carefully and sometimes they come on new things suggesting the contrary and even that a malicious person has been at work. Besides examining the garden

Wisdom, John, "Gods" from *Proceedings of the Aristotelean Society,* Vol. XLV, 1944–5, p. 45. Copyright © 1944. Reprinted by courtesy of the Editor of the Aristotelian Society.

carefully they also study what happens to gardens left without attention. Each learns all the other learns about this and about the garden. Consequently, when after all this, one says "I still believe a gardener comes" while the other says "I don't" their different words now reflect no difference as to what they have found in the garden, no difference as to what they would find in the garden if they looked further, and no difference about how fast untended gardens fall into disorder. At this stage, in this context, the gardener hypothesis has ceased to be experimental; the difference between one who accepts and one who rejects it is now not a matter of the one expecting something the other does not expect. What is the difference between them? The one

says: "A gardener comes unseen and unheard. He is manifested only in his works with which we are all familiar." The other says "There is no gardener." And with this difference in what they say about the gardener goes a difference in how they feel toward the garden, in spite of the fact that neither expects anything of it which the other does not expect.

But is this the whole difference between them—that the one calls the garden by one name and feels one way toward it, while the other calls it by another name and feels in another way toward it? And if this is what the difference has become, then is it any longer appropriate to ask "Which is right?" or "Which is reasonable?"

RG VEDA

Hymn of Creation

The Rg Veda is the earliest book of Hindu scripture and one of the oldest religious texts in the world. It was written about 1500 B.C.E. and introduces the concept of Brahman, or ultimate reality, who is also introduced as a sort of "person" (purusha).

1. Non-being then existed not nor being:
    There was no air, nor sky that is beyond it.
    What was concealed? Wherein? In whose
      protection?
    And was there deep unfathomable water?

2. Death then existed not nor life immortal:
    Of neither night nor day was any token.
    By its inherent force the One breathed windless
    No other thing than that beyond existed.

3. Darkness there was at first by darkness hidden.
    Without distinctive marks, this all was water.

That which, becoming, by the void was covered.
That One by force of heat came into being.

4. Desire entered the One in the beginning:
    It was the earliest seed, of thought the product.
    The sages searching in their hearts with wisdom,
    Found out the bond of being in non-being.

5. Their ray extended light across the darkness:
    But was the One above or was it under?
    Creative force was there, and fertile power:
    Below was energy, above was impulse.

Rg Veda, "Hymn of Creation" from *Hymns from Rg Veda* (Oxford University Press, 1911).

6. Who knows for certain? Who shall here declare it?
   Whence was it born, and whence came this
      creation?
   The gods were born after this world's creation:
   Then who can know from whence it has arisen?

7. None knoweth whence creation has arisen;
   And whether he has or has not produced it:
   He who surveys it in the highest heaven,
   He only knows, or haply he may know not.

JOHN BISHOP

Can There Be Alternative Concepts of God?

JOHN BISHOP *is head of the department of Philosophy at the University of Auckland in New Zealand. He has been developing the idea of alternatives to what he calls "the Omni-God."*

1 Can it be consistent to adhere to theism, and yet to reject the belief that *omniGod* exists, where "omniGod" means a unique omnipotent, omniscient, omnibenevolent, supernatural person who is creator and sustainer of all else that exists?

On the assumptions prevailing within Philosophy of Religion, at least as practised by analytical philosophers, the answer is clearly "No." Such philosophers typically presuppose that theism virtually *by definition* requires belief that omniGod exists.

But this presupposition may be questioned, and could be overturned by articulating *an adequate alternative concept of God*, satisfying the following requirements:

(i) the concept must be genuinely distinct from the concept of omniGod;

and

(ii) the concept must be acceptable as authentically a concept *of God;* that is, belief in the existence of a God of the kind the concept specifies must be *religiously adequate* to the theistic religious tradition, in the sense that it could count at least as one viable expression of that historical tradition.

2 My aim in this paper is to contribute some philosophical prolegomena to the search for alternative concepts of God: how best should one approach the project of trying to decide whether there *are* any alternative concepts of God in the sense described?

But first let me explain why this project should be considered important. It is important, in the first place, for those who (like myself) aspire to remain within a theistic faith even though they have come to reject the reasonableness of belief in omniGod—for example, through being persuaded by the Argument from Evil—and who are nevertheless not prepared to retreat into irrationalist fideism (that is, the view that belief that omniGod exists can properly be held by faith contrary to reason). The intellectual integrity of such a position requires that there be an adequate alternative concept of God—and, moreover, an adequate alternative concept of God in whose instantiation it is reasonable to believe.

In the second place, the issue is important for the philosophical critics of theism. Someone who seeks to establish the unreasonableness of theism itself had better find out whether establishing the unreasonableness of belief in omniGod (on which so much atheistic philosophical effort has been expended) is indeed sufficient for this purpose. Such a person will need either to show that there are no adequate alternative concepts of God, or else to widen the attack on theism so that it deals not only with belief in omniGod, but also with belief in God according to each adequate alternative concept. The impatience of convinced atheists with radical theology is well known: they jealously guard the kind of God they don't believe in! They would thus gain comfort from discovering that God-concepts genuinely distinct from the concept of omniGod and yet admissible as religiously authentic are just not to be had.

3 What method should be used in tackling the question whether there are any alternative concepts of God?

At first sight, it might seem sensible to begin by conducting a grand survey of theologians and philosophers who have thought of themselves as proposing alternatives to the traditional God of theism. And the survey may also have to include a number of philosophers who have *not* so thought of themselves, but about whom it might plausibly be claimed that, for all their professed atheism, they were in fact postulating alternative concepts of God. Each concept on the list produced by such a survey would then be examined to see if it does indeed count as an adequate alternative to omniGod, satisfying the two requirements stated in Section 1 above.

In fact, however, before conducting any such survey, it is important to begin by considering the question *what the criteria are* for a putative God-concept to be religiously adequate to theistic tradition.

4 One reason why this is important is that initial clarity about the criteria for a God-concept to be religiously adequate will provide intelligent focus and thus greater efficiency to any survey, by giving us from the outset a grasp of what it takes for a proposal for an alternative concept of God to count as a serious candidate.

But there is a more important reason why an inquiry into alternative concepts of God needs to begin from a discussion of criteria of religious adequacy. For, "omniGod conservatives"—on both the theistic and the atheistic side—will surely maintain that a proper account of the criteria for a God-concept to be adequate to theism will entail that any departure from the essential features of the concept of God as omniGod will breach the criteria. Accordingly, anyone who thinks it worthwhile exploring for alternative concepts of God must be prepared to offer and defend some account of the criteria for religious adequacy of a God-concept which would at least prima facie leave it open that some God-concept genuinely distinct from the concept of omniGod might turn out to satisfy those criteria. Obviously, this has to be done at the outset: the argument which concludes that the quarry is not there to be found must first have its force significantly blunted if there is to be any point in the hunt.

Furthermore, to begin by trying to provide religious adequacy criteria which leave it open that some concept other than that of omniGod might turn out to be adequate may provide heuristics for specific candidates for an alternative concept of God. Insight into what it is for the concept of God to do the work it is supposed to do in the context of theistic religion might suggest ways of constructing a viable alternative concept of God from within the resources of theism. Lengthy surveys of historical attempts at alternative God-concepts might then prove otiose.

5 How may criteria for the religious adequacy of a God-concept be generated in such a way as to make appropriate room for the possibility of there turning out to be some adequate alternative concept or concepts of God?

Traditionally, the criteria for the religious adequacy for a God-concept have been set by means of a straightforward argument which seems to make it clear that only the concept of omniGod can be religiously adequate to theism. The concept of God has to be the concept of that which is worthy of worship. Worship requires a uniquely excellently worthy object: an object which is supremely perfect, that than which a greater cannot even be conceived. From this, the "omni-properties" of such an object have been directly inferred.

Now, of course, the proponent of the idea that there is a real possibility of there being an adequate alternative concept of God will eventually have to come to terms with this argument. And, since there would seem to be little point in trying to deny that one criterion of religious adequacy is indeed that the concept of God must be the concept of that which is worthy of worship, the traditional route from there to the conclusion that God has to be omniGod in order to be worthy of worship will have to be disputed. The would-be radical theologian will, however, start off very much on the back foot if he or she tries to take on this dispute at the outset. A better plan, I suggest, is to dig deeper and try and get at the source of the criteria for a God-concept to be religiously adequate, to see if—once we identify that source—we can find at least some additional criteria of religious adequacy which don't seem to lead quite so swiftly to the conclusion that a decently theistic God really has to be the traditional omniGod.

6 I believe that *a certain kind of* "functionalist" proposal provides the source for criteria for the religious adequacy of a God concept. I suggest that the concept of God is *the concept of something belief in whose existence plays a certain functional role* within what might be called the psychological economy of the theist. And the question whether there are any adequate alternative concepts of God then becomes the question whether belief in God according to any God-concept other than that of omniGod is fit to play this functional role.

7 Let me explain further just what kind of functionalist proposal I am here making, by distinguishing it from other kinds of functionalist proposals.

One widely current kind of functionalist proposal is the idea that some of our concepts are functional-role-concepts, in the sense that they are concepts *of* that-which-plays-a-certain-functional-role, where that role is implicitly specified by the theoretical laws of a theory or by the platitudes at the core of a body of discourse and practice. My present proposal, however, is *not* the proposal that *the content of* the concept of God be analysed in terms of that which plays a certain functional role implicitly specified by a set of theological platitudes. (This proposal would, I think, founder on the difficulty of identifying a set of genuinely platitudinous platitudes about God. Anything any given theologian offers as a theological platitude will either be so vague or ambiguous as to be useless for specifying the God-role, or else will turn out to be significantly theologically contestable. For example, many theists would take it that God's having the defining properties of omniGod is the central "platitude" of theism—yet, of course, this will be contested by anyone who thinks that it remains open whether the God of theism is indeed omniGod.)

Since I seek to leave the way open to an alternative concept of God, I resist the idea that there is such a thing as *the*, uncontested, "God-role" and that it's then a factual question what it is, if anything, which fills this role. I want to suggest that the concept of God as omniGod can have competitors—and so I want to get a grip on what these competing concepts may be understood as competing for. My proposal that *the belief that God exists* plays a certain functional role is intended to indicate what they are competing for: namely, the status of *being a specifier* of the concept of God under which belief that God exists plays the functional role which that belief plays in the psychological economy of theism. There is, so to speak, something which the belief that God exists is supposed to do for you (or, at least, for the theist), and potentially more than one specific concept of God might be such that belief in God according to that concept does that something for you. And—my proposal then is—what it is for a God-concept to be religiously adequate is for it to be such that believing that God exists according to that God-concept does that something for you, plays that functional role.

I do not exclude the possibility that, *once we have established the criteria for religious adequacy,* it may *then* be appropriate to analyse a given God-concept which meets those criteria as a functional-role concept—to hold that what it is to be God is to be that which fills "the God-role" according to that concept. The burden of my present point is to emphasise that, *while we are still seeking to develop criteria for religious adequacy,* our focus needs to be on the functional role which is played by *the belief that God exists,* or—and this is merely a terminological variant—by *the concept of God* in virtue of the role played by the belief that the concept is instantiated.

Finally—in case this isn't already obvious—I should add that what I mean here by the functional role of the belief that God exists is distinct from what a functionalist in the Philosophy of Mind would mean by that: namely, the causal role, specified in terms of actual and potential inputs, outputs and relations to other intentional states, which something has to fill in order to count as a belief with the content "God exists".

PART TWO

SCIENCE, MIND, AND NATURE

CHAPTER THREE

WHAT DOES SCIENCE TELL ME ABOUT THE WORLD?

Have you ever noticed that in your biology and chemistry classes you may get multiple-choice exams, but in your English lit or philosophy classes you are most likely to get essay exams or paper assignments? Why is that? You may think that science deals with facts and that such subjects as philosophy and literature deal with opinions and interpretations. For example, it is a fact that common table salt is composed of sodium and chlorine, whereas it is simply a matter of opinion whether there is free will. You would probably have a hard time writing an entire five-page paper on the chemical composition of table salt. And even if you think that it is a matter of fact whether there is life after death, you would be offended by a question on a philosophy exam that said, "True or false: There is life after death."

But in spite of this prevailing conception of science as being concerned only with facts, not opinions, science as it is actually practiced seems to be full of opinion and interpretation. It may surprise you to learn that scientists often disagree, not only about which of several scientific theories best explains what has been observed, but even about whether something has *been* observed. Moreover, the development of scientific theories is very seldom a process of first observing a lot of facts and then making straightforward generalizations from these observations. In this chapter, Richard Feynman, a Nobel Prize winner in physics, emphasizes the importance of imagination and guessing in science. As an example of imaginative guesswork in science, let's think about quarks. Most scientists believe that all matter is composed of curious particles (which don't really behave like particles) called quarks. The existence of quarks was first hypothesized in 1963. But no scientist has ever seen a quark. So why do they believe that quarks exist? They believe it because some ingenious scientists *invented* quarks, noticing that if quarks did exist, they could explain some other puzzling things. This turned out to be a good guess: If you believe that there are quarks, you can explain a lot. Now most scientists do believe that quarks exist. But the only evidence for the existence of quarks is that if you invent them, many complicated things become simpler and can therefore be explained. Many other things in science were "invented" in this way before they were "discovered"—gravity, molecules, genes, and the planet Neptune, to name a few. Does it still sound to you as though science deals only with facts?

Hard as it may be to believe, the institution of science is a relatively new feature of Western civilization. In the seventeenth and eighteenth centuries, what is now called "science" fell under the category of "natural philosophy." The modern use of the term "science" dates from the nineteenth century, which was also the first century in which a person could make a living by being a scientist. (It was also the century in which the term "scientist" was coined.) So although the study of nature is as old as recorded history, people have not always turned exclusively to scientists with questions about the workings of nature. In earlier times people turned to storytellers, writers, artists, religious figures, and philosophers with such questions.

But in our contemporary culture, science has achieved a particularly exalted position. It seems to us that science deals with hard facts, whereas other subjects deal with mere opinions. We have come to believe that science is objective and verifiable. We think that science has a method ("the Scientific method") for arriving at the "absolute truth."

But what is the Scientific method, and how does it differ from the methods of literature, history, or philosophy? For that matter, is there really a scientific method? How can we be so sure that what science tells us is true? During the early part of the twentieth century, a group of philosophers and scientists known as the Vienna Circle (they were working in Vienna) tried to place both philosophy and science (and with them, psychology, economics, and other fields) on a more secure base. They tried to show how we could connect all knowledge securely to the pure observation of uninterpreted facts. Anything that could not be secured in this way they claimed is meaningless. (See Chapter 6 for more about this view.) The philosophy of science that grew out of the Vienna Circle has come to be known as the "received view" and is now the classic account of how science works. It is articulated by Carl G. Hempel in his selection in this chapter.

The received view is often called "the hypothetico-deductive model" or "the deductive-nomological model." (*Nomological* means "having to do with the laws of nature.") It tries to show science to be an orderly process that moves from observation of facts to the confirmation of theories that explain those facts. Hempel focuses on questions about how a scientific theory gets confirmed by observations. He is therefore principally concerned with what makes a theory (as opposed to rival theories) true. He tries to explain what you may have had in mind a few paragraphs back if you thought that science, but not literature, deals with facts.

Karl Popper, in a piece that is also a classic, challenges Hempel's view. Instead of looking at what makes a theory *true,* he argues that the proper question concerns what makes a theory *scientific.* He argues that it is not the possibility of confirmation that makes a theory scientific, but rather the possibility of refutation. Hence, in an odd twist, he claims that the more open a theory is to being shown false, the more scientific a theory is. In developing his argument, he pays careful attention to actual theories, both those he considers scientific and those he considers pseudoscientific. Popper's view is one that many people in the scientific community have found attractive.

Hempel's view has been criticized, by both scientists and philosophers, for not reflecting the way that scientists actually work. Interestingly, the idea that to learn about how science works, we should pay attention to the way that actual scientists work, is a fairly new idea in this century. The now-classic statement of this idea is Thomas Kuhn's *The Structure of Scientific Revolutions,* part of which is reprinted in this chapter. Kuhn argues that the progress of science is not purely logical, and hence it cannot be isolated from its own historical context. Instead, it is conditioned by forces within the scientific community that he characterizes in deliberate political terms (for example, "revolution").

Evelyn Fox Keller goes at least one step beyond Kuhn. She argues that the very standards of objectivity and rationality that define traditional scientific perspective and practice are the products of unrecognized value assumptions. In particular, she argues that these standards are masculine, and she gives a psychoanalytic account of their origin. At the end of her article, she offers some suggestions about how science might be different if it were to cast away its masculinist values and become truly objective. If Keller is right, we need to rethink the cultural mechanisms that bring us both science and scientists.

Finally, two selections give us different perspectives on what science and scientists are really like. Richard Feynman gives us a feeling for how theoretical scientists think about the world. In particular, he talks about the process of guessing that was discussed at the beginning of this introduction. You might think about where the guesses come from and what makes some guesses seem better than others, in light of Kuhn's and Keller's remarks about psychological and cultural influences on scientific theory. We end the chapter with an excerpt from California philosopher Sandra Harding and her book, *Whose Science? Whose Knowledge?* Harding emphasizes the GENDER-BASED *perspectivism* of science.

CARL G. HEMPEL
The Deductive-Nomological Model of Science

CARL G. HEMPEL *(1905–1997) was one of the most influential proponents of what is now regarded as the classic view of explanation in science. Much contemporary work in philosophy of science constitutes a reaction to his view. He was for many years a professor of philosophy at Princeton University. He wrote* Aspects of Scientific Explanation *and* Philosophy of Natural Science.

EXPLANATIONS

AS was known at Galileo's time, and probably much earlier, a simple suction pump, which draws water from a well by means of a piston that can be raised in the pump barrel, will lift water no higher than about 34 feet above the surface of the well. Galileo was intrigued by this limitation and suggested an explanation for it, which was, however, unsound. After Galileo's death, his pupil Torricelli advanced a new answer. He argued that the earth is surrounded by a sea of air, which, by reason of its weight exerts pressure upon the surface below, and that this pressure upon the surface of the well forces water up the pump barrel when the piston is raised. The maximum length of 34 feet for the water column in the barrel thus reflects simply the total pressure of the atmosphere upon the surface of the well.

It is evidently impossible to determine by direct inspection or observation whether this account is correct, and Torricelli tested it indirectly. He reasoned that *if* his conjecture were true, *then* the pressure of the atmosphere should also be capable of supporting a proportionately shorter column of mercury; indeed, since the specific gravity of mercury is about 14 times that of water, the length of the mercury column should be about 34/14 feet, or slightly less than 2 1/2 feet. He checked this test implication by means of an ingeniously simple device, which

was, in effect, the mercury barometer. The well of water is replaced by an open vessel containing mercury; the barrel of the suction pump is replaced by a glass tube sealed off at one end. The tube is completely filled with mercury and closed by placing the thumb tightly over the open end. It is then inverted, the open end is submerged in the mercury well, and the thumb is withdrawn; whereupon the mercury column in the tube drops until its length is about 30 inches—just as predicted by Torricelli's hypothesis.

A further test implication of that hypothesis was noted by Pascal, who reasoned that if the mercury in Torricelli's barometer is counterbalanced by pressure of the air above the open mercury well, then its length should decrease with increasing altitude, since the weight of the air overhead becomes smaller. At Pascal's request, this implication was checked by his brother-in-law, Périer, who measured the length of the mercury column in the Torricelli barometer at the foot of the Puy-de-Dôme, a mountain some 4,800 feet high, and then carefully carried the apparatus to the top and repeated the measurement there while a control barometer was left at the bottom under the supervision of an assistant. Périer found the mercury column at the top of the mountain more than three inches shorter than at the bottom, whereas the length of the column in the control barometer had remained unchanged throughout the day. . . .

Consider . . . Périer's finding in the Puy-de-Dôme experiment, that the length of the mercury column in a Torricelli barometer decreased with increasing altitude. Torricelli's and Pascal's ideas on atmospheric pressure provided an explanation for this phenomenon; somewhat pedantically, it can be spelled out as follows:

(*a*) At any location, the pressure that the mercury column in the closed branch of the Torricelli apparatus exerts upon the mercury below equals the pressures exerted on the surface of the mercury in the open vessel by the column of air above it.

(*b*) The pressure exerted by the columns of mercury and of air are proportional to their weights; and the shorter the columns, the smaller their weights.

(*c*) As Périer carried the apparatus to the top of the mountain, the column of air above the open vessel became steadily shorter.

(*d*) (Therefore,) the mercury column in the closed vessel grew steadily shorter during the ascent.

Thus formulated, the explanation is an argument to the effect that the phenomenon to be explained, as described by the sentence *(d)*, is just what is to be expected in view of the explanatory facts cited in *(a)*, *(b)*, and *(c)*; and that, indeed, *(d)* follows deductively from the explanatory statements. The latter are of two kinds; *(a)* and *(b)* have the character of general laws expressing uniform empirical connections; whereas *(c)* describes certain particular facts. Thus, the shortening of the mercury column is here explained by showing that it occurred in accordance with certain laws of nature, as a result of certain particular circumstances. The explanation fits the phenomenon to be explained into a pattern of uniformities and shows that its occurrence was to be expected, given the specified laws and the pertinent particular circumstances.

The phenomenon to be accounted for by an explanation will henceforth also be referred to as the *explanandum phenomenon*; the sentence describing it, as the *explanandum sentence*. When the context shows which is meant, either of

them will simply be called the explanandum. The sentences specifying the explanatory information—*(a)*, *(b)*, *(c)* in our example—will be called the *explanans sentences;* jointly they will be said to form the *explanans*.

As a second example, consider the explanation of a characteristic of image formation by reflection in a spherical mirror; namely, that generally $1/u + 1/v = 2/r$, where u and v are the distances of object-point and image-point from the mirror, and r is the mirror's radius of curvature. In geometrical optics, this uniformity is explained with the help of the basic law of reflection in a plane mirror, by treating the reflection of a beam of light at any one point of a spherical mirror as a case of reflection in a plane tangential to the spherical surface. The resulting explanation can be formulated as a deductive argument whose conclusion is the explanandum sentence, and whose premises include the basic laws of reflection and of rectilinear propagation, as well as the statement that the surface of the mirror forms a segment of a sphere. . . .

The explanations just considered may be conceived, then, as deductive arguments whose conclusion is the explanandum sentence, E, and whose premiss-set, the explanans, consists of general laws, $L^1, L^2, \ldots, L^r$ and of other statements, $C^1, \ldots, C^k$, which make assertions about particular facts. The form of such arguments, which thus constitute one type of scientific explanation, can be represented by the following schema:

$$\text{(D–N)} \quad \frac{\begin{array}{l} L_1, L_2, \ldots, L_r \text{ Explanans sentences} \\[4pt] C_1, C_v, \ldots, C_k \\ \hline \end{array}}{E} \text{ Explanandum sentences}$$

Explanatory accounts of this kind will be called explanations by deductive subsumption under general laws, or *deductive-nomological explanations*. (The root of the term "nomological" is the Greek word "nomos," for law.) The laws invoked in a scientific explanation will also be called *covering laws* for the explanandum phenomenon, and the explanatory argument will be said to subsume the explanandum under those laws.

The explanandum phenomenon in a deductive-nomological explanation may be an event occurring at a particular place and time, such as the outcome of Périer's experiment. Or it may be some regularity found in nature, such as certain characteristics generally displayed by rainbows; or a uniformity expressed by an empirical law such as Galileo's or Kepler's laws. Deductive explanations of such uniformities will then invoke laws of broader scope, such as the laws of reflection and refraction, or Newton's laws of motion and of gravitation. As this use of Newton's laws illustrates, empirical laws are often explained by means of theoretical principles that refer to structures and processes underlying the uniformities in question. . . .

Some scientific explanations conform to the pattern (D–N) quite closely. This is so, particularly, when certain quantitative features of a phenomenon are explained by mathematical derivation from covering general laws, as in the case of reflection in spherical and paraboloidal mirrors. Or take the celebrated explanation, propounded by Leverrier (and independently by Adams), or peculiar irregularities in the motion of the planet Uranus, which on the current Newtonian theory could not be accounted for by the gravitational attraction of the other planets then known. Leverrier conjectured that they resulted from the gravitational pull of an as yet undetected outer planet, and he computed the position, mass, and other characteristics which that planet would have to possess to account in quantitative detail for the observed irregularities. His explanation was strikingly confirmed by the discovery, at the predicted location, of a new planet, Neptune, which had the quantitative characteristics attributed to it by Leverrier. Here again, the explanation has the character of a deductive argument whose premises include general laws—specifically, Newton's laws of gravitation and of motion—as well as statements specifying various quantitative particulars about the disturbing planet.

Not infrequently, however, deductive-nomological explanations are stated in an elliptical form: they omit mention of certain assumptions that are presupposed by the explanation but are simply taken for granted in the given context. Such explanations are sometimes expressed in the form "*E* because *C*," where *E* is the event to be explained and *C* is some antecedent or concomitant event or state of affairs. Take, for example, the statement: "The slush on the sidewalk remained liquid during the frost because it had been sprinkled with salt." This explanation does not explicitly mention any laws, but it tacitly presupposes at least one: that the freezing point of water is lowered whenever salt is dissolved in it. Indeed it is precisely by virtue of this law that the sprinkling of salt acquires the explanatory, and specifically causative, role that the elliptical because-statement ascribes to it. That statement, incidentally, is elliptical also in other respects; for example, it tacitly takes for granted, and leaves unmentioned, certain assumptions about the prevailing physical conditions, such as the temperature's not dropping to a very low point. And if nomic and other assumptions thus omitted are added to the statement that salt had been sprinkled on the slush, we obtain the premises for a deductive-nomological explanation of the fact that the slush remained liquid. . . .

As the preceding examples illustrate, corresponding general laws are always presupposed by an explanatory statement to the effect that a particular event of a certain kind, *G* (e.g., expansion of a gas under constant pressure; flow of a current in a wire loop) was *caused* by an event of another kind, *F* (e.g., heating of the gas; motion of the loop across a magnetic field). To see this, we need not enter into the complex ramifications of the notion of cause; it suffices to note that the general maxim "Same cause, same effect," when applied to such explanatory statements, yields the implied claim that whenever an event of kind *F* occurs, it is accompanied by an event of kind *G*.

To say that an explanation rests on general laws is not to say that its discovery required the discovery of the laws. The crucial new insight achieved by an explanation will sometimes lie in the discovery of some particular fact (e.g., the presence of an undetected outer planet; infectious matter adhering to the hand of examining physicians) which, by virtue of antecedently accepted general laws, accounts for the explanandum phenomenon. In other cases, such as that of the lines in the hydrogen spectrum, the explanatory achievement does lie in the discovery of a covering law (Balmer's) and eventually of an explanatory theory (such as Bohr's); in yet other cases, the major accomplishment of an explanation may lie in showing that, and exactly how, the explanandum phenomenon can be accounted for by reference to laws and data about particular facts that are already available: this is illustrated by the explanatory derivation of the reflection laws for spherical and paraboloidal mirrors from the basic law of geometrical optics in conjunction with statements about the geometrical characteristics of the mirrors.

An explanatory problem does not by itself determine what kind of discovery is required for its solution. Thus, Leverrier discovered deviations from the theoretically expected course also in the motion of the planet Mercury; and as in the case of Uranus, he tried to explain these as resulting from the gravitational pull of an as yet undetected planet, Vulcan, which would have to be a very dense and very small object between the sun and Mercury. But no such planet was found, and a satisfactory explanation was provided only much later by the general theory of relativity, which accounted for the irregularities not by reference to some disturbing particular factor, but by means of a new system of laws. . . .

THEORIES

Theories are usually introduced when previous study of a class of phenomena has revealed a system of uniformities that can be expressed in the form of empirical laws. Theories then seek to explain those regularities and, generally, to afford a deeper and more accurate understanding of the phenomena in question. To this end, a theory construes those phenomena as manifestations of

entities and processes that lie behind or beneath them, as it were. These are assumed to be governed by characteristic theoretical laws, or theoretical principles, by means of which the theory then explains the empirical uniformities that have been previously discovered, and usually also predicts "new" regularities of similar kinds. Let us consider some examples.

The Ptolemaic and Copernican systems sought to account for the observed, "apparent," motions of the heavenly bodies by means of suitable assumptions about the structure of the astronomical universe and the "actual" motions of the celestial objects. The corpuscular and the wave theories of light offered accounts of the nature of light in terms of certain underlying processes; and they explained the previously established uniformities expressed by the laws of rectilinear propagation, reflection, refraction, and diffraction as resulting from the basic laws to which the underlying processes were assumed to conform. Thus, the refraction of a beam of light passing from air into glass was explained in Huyghens' wave theory as resulting from a slowing of the light waves in the denser medium. By contrast, Newton's particle theory attributed optical refraction to a stronger attraction exerted upon the optical particles by the denser medium. Incidentally, this construal implies not only the observed bending of a beam of light: when combined with the other basic assumptions of Newton's theory, it also implies that the particles of light will be accelerated upon entering a denser medium, rather than decelerated, as the wave theory predicts. These conflicting implications were tested nearly two hundred years later by Foucault in the experiment . . . whose outcome bore out the relevant implication of the wave theory.

To mention one more example, the kinetic theory of gases offers explanations for a wide variety of empirically established regularities by construing them as macroscopic manifestations of statistical regularities in the underlying molecular and atomic phenomena.

The basic entities and processes posited by a theory, and the laws assumed to govern them, must be specified with appropriate clarity and precision; otherwise, the theory cannot serve its scientific purpose. This important point is illustrated by the neovitalistic conception of biological phenomena. Living systems, as is well known, display a variety of striking features that seem to be distinctly purposive or teleological in character. Among them are the regeneration of lost limbs in some species; the development, in other species, of normal organisms from embryos that are damaged or even cut into several pieces in an early stage of their growth; and the remarkable coordination of the many processes in a developing organism which, as though following a common plan, lead to the formation of a mature individual. According to neovitalism, such phenomena do not occur in nonliving systems and cannot be explained by means of the concepts and laws of physics and chemistry alone; rather, they are manifestations of underlying teleological agencies of a nonphysical kind, referred to as entelechies or vital forces. Their specific mode of action is usually assumed not to violate the principles of physics and chemistry, but to direct the organic processes, within the range of possibilities left open by the physico-chemical laws, in such a way that, even in the presence of disturbing factors, embryos develop into normal individuals, and adult organisms are maintained in, or returned to, a properly functioning state.

This conception may well seem to offer us a deeper understanding of the remarkable biological phenomena in question; it may give us a sense of being more familiar, more "at home" with them. But understanding in this sense is not what is wanted in science, and a conceptual system that conveys insight into the phenomena in this intuitive sense does not for that reason alone qualify as a scientific theory. The assumptions made by a scientific theory about underlying processes must be definite enough to permit the derivation of specific implications concerning the phenomena that the theory is to explain. The neovitalistic doctrine fails on this account. It does not indicate under what circumstances entelechies will go into action and specifically, in

what way they will direct biological processes: no particular aspect of embryonic development, for example, can be inferred from the doctrine, nor does it enable us to predict what biological responses will occur under specified experimental conditions. Hence, when a new striking type of "organic directiveness" is encountered, all that the neovitalist doctrine enables us to do is to make the *post factum* pronouncement: "There is another manifestation of vital forces!"; it offers us no grounds for saying: "On the basis of the theoretical assumptions, this is just what was to be expected—the theory explains it!"

This inadequacy of the neovitalistic doctrine does not stem from the circumstance that entelechies are conceived as nonmaterial agencies, which cannot be seen or felt. This becomes clear when we contrast it with the explanation of the regularities of planetary and lunar motions by means of the Newtonian theory. Both accounts invoke nonmaterial agencies: one of them vital forces; the other, gravitational ones. But Newton's theory includes specific assumptions, expressed in the law of gravitation and the laws of motion which determine *(a)* what gravitational forces each of a set of physical bodies of given masses and positions will exert upon the others, and *(b)* what changes in their velocities and, consequently, in their locations will be brought about by those forces. It is this characteristic that gives the theory its power to explain previously observed uniformities and also to yield predictions and retrodictions. Thus, the theory was used by Halley to predict that a comet he had observed in 1682 would return in 1759, and to identify it retrodictively with comets whose appearances had been recorded on six previous occasions going back to the year 1066. The theory also played a spectacular explanatory and predictive role in the discovery of the planet Neptune, on the basis of irregularities in the orbit of Uranus; and subsequently in the discovery, on the basis of irregularities in Neptune's orbit, of the planet Pluto.

Broadly speaking, then, the formulation of a theory will require the specification of two kinds of principles; let us call them internal principles and bridge principles for short. The former will characterize the basic entities and processes invoked by the theory and the laws to which they are assumed to conform. The latter will indicate how the processes envisaged by the theory are related to empirical phenomena with which we are already acquainted, and which the theory may then explain, predict, or retrodict. Let us consider some examples.

In the kinetic theory of gases, the internal principles are those that characterize the "microphenomena" at the molecular level, whereas the bridge principles connect certain aspects of the microphenomena with corresponding "macroscopic" features of a gas. . . .

Without bridge principles, . . . a theory would have no explanatory power. Without bridge principles, we may add, it would also be incapable of test. For the internal principles of a theory are concerned with the peculiar entities and processes assumed by the theory (such as the jumps of electrons from one atomic energy level to another in Bohr's theory), and they will therefore be expressed largely in terms of characteristic "theoretical concepts," which refer to those entities and processes. But the implications that permit a test of those theoretical principles will have to be expressed in terms of things and occurrences with which we are antecedently acquainted, which we already know how to observe, to measure, and to describe. In other words, while the internal principles of a theory are couched in its characteristic *theoretical terms* ("nucleus," "orbital electron," "energy level," "electron jump"), the test implications must be formulated in terms (such as "hydrogen vapor," "emission spectrum," "wavelength associated with a spectral line") which are "antecedently understood," as we might say, terms that have been introduced prior to the theory and can be used independently of it. Let us refer to them as *antecedently available* or *pretheoretical terms*. The derivation of such test implications from the internal principles of the theory evidently requires further premises that establish connections between the two sets of concepts; and this, as the preceding examples show,

is accomplished by appropriate bridge principles (connecting, for example, the energy released in an electron jump with the wavelength of the light that is emitted as a result). Without bridge principles, the internal principles of a theory would yield no test implications, and the requirement of testability would be violated.

Testability-in-principle and explanatory import, though crucially important, are nevertheless only minimal necessary conditions that a scientific theory must satisfy; a system that meets these requirements may yet afford little illumination and may lack scientific interest. . . .

In a field of inquiry in which some measure of understanding has already been achieved by the establishment of empirical laws, a good theory will deepen as well as broaden that understanding. First, such a theory offers a systematically unified account of quite diverse phenomena. It traces all of them back to the same underlying processes and presents the various empirical uniformities they exhibit as manifestations of one and the same basic laws. We noted earlier the great diversity of empirical regularities (such as those shown by free fall; the simple pendulum; the motions of the moon, the planets, comets, double stars, and artificial satellites; the tides, and so forth) that are accounted for by the basic principles of Newton's theory of gravitation and of motion. In similar fashion, the kinetic theory of gases exhibits a wide variety of empirical uniformities as manifestations of certain basic probabilistic uniformities in the random motions of the molecules. And Bohr's theory of the hydrogen atom accounts not only for the uniformity expressed by Balmer's formula, which refers to just one series of lines in the spectrum of hydrogen, but equally for analogous empirical laws representing the wavelengths of other series of lines in the same spectrum, including several series whose member lines lie in the invisible infrared or ultraviolet parts of the spectrum.

A theory will usually deepen our understanding also in a different way, namely by showing that the previously formulated empirical laws that it is meant to explain do not hold strictly and unexceptionally, but only approximately and within a certain limited range of application. Thus, Newton's theoretical account of planetary motion shows that Kepler's laws hold only approximately, and it explains why this is so: the Newtonian principles imply that the orbit of a planet moving about the sun under its gravitational influence alone would indeed be an ellipse, but that the gravitational pull exerted on it by other planets leads to departures from a strictly elliptical path. The theory gives a quantitative account of the resulting perturbations in terms of the masses and spatial distribution of the disturbing objects. Similarly, Newton's theory accounts for Galileo's law of free fall as simply one special manifestation of the basic laws for motion under gravitational attraction; but in so doing, it shows also that the law (even if applied to free fall in a vacuum) holds only approximately. One of the reasons is that in Galileo's formula the acceleration of free fall appears as a constant (twice the factor 16 in the formula "$s = 16t^2$"), whereas on Newton's inverse-square law of gravitational attraction, the force acting upon the falling body increases as its distance from the center of the earth decreases; hence, by virtue of Newton's second law of motion, its acceleration, too, increases in the course of the fall. Analogous remarks apply to the laws of geometrical optics as viewed from the vantage point of wave-theoretical optics. For example, even in a homogeneous medium, light does not move strictly in straight lines; it can bend around corners. And the laws of geometrical optics for reflection in curved mirrors and for image-formation by lenses hold only approximately and within certain limits.

It might therefore be tempting to say that theories often do not explain previously established laws, but refute them. But this would give a distorted picture of the insight afforded by a theory. After all, a theory does not simply refute the earlier empirical generalizations in its field; rather, it shows that within a certain limited range defined by qualifying conditions, the generalizations hold true in fairly close approximation. The limited range for Kepler's laws includes those cases in which the masses of the disturbing additional planets are small compared with that of the sun, or their distances from the given planet are large compared with its distance from the sun. Similarly, the theory shows that Galileo's law holds approximately for free fall over short distances.

Finally, a good theory will also broaden our knowledge and understanding by predicting and explaining phenomena that were not known when the theory was formulated. Thus, Torricelli's conception of a sea of air led to Pascal's prediction that the column of a mercury barometer would shorten with increasing height above sea level. Einstein's general theory of relativity not only accounted for the known slow rotation of the orbit of Mercury, but also predicted the bending of light in a gravitational field, a forecast subsequently borne out by astronomical measurements. Maxwell's theory of electromagnetism implied the existence of electromagnetic waves and predicted important characteristics of their propagation. Those implications, too, were later confirmed by the experimental work of Heinrich Hertz, and they provided the basis for the technology of radio transmission, among other applications.

Such striking predictive successes will of course greatly strengthen our confidence in a theory that already has given us a systematically unified explanation—and often also a correction—of previously established laws. The insight that such a theory gives us is much deeper than that afforded by empirical laws; and it is widely held, therefore, that a scientifically adequate explanation of a class of empirical phenomena can be achieved only by means of an appropriate theory. Indeed, it seems to be a remarkable fact that even if we limited ourselves to a study of the more or less directly observable or measurable aspects of our world and tried to explain these . . . by means of laws couched in terms of observables, our efforts would have only limited success. For the laws that are formulated at the observational level generally turn out to hold only approximately and within a limited range; whereas by theoretical recourse to entities and events under the familiar surface, a much more comprehensive and exact account can be achieved. It is intriguing to speculate whether simpler worlds are conceivable where all phenomena are at the observable surface, so to speak; where there occur perhaps only changes of color and of shape, within a finite range of possibilities, and strictly in accordance with some simple laws of universal form.

THOMAS KUHN
The Structure of Scientific Revolutions

THOMAS KUHN *(1922–1996) was a professor of philosophy at MIT. In 1962 he revolutionized the philosophy of science with publication of his book,* The Structure of Scientific Revolutions, *from which this selection is taken. In that book he challenged the classic view (represented by Hempel) by suggesting that we look at science as a social enterprise, rather than as a purely logical enterprise.*

IN this essay, "normal science" means research firmly based upon one or more past scientific achievements, achievements that some particular scientific community acknowledges for a time as supplying the foundation for its further practice. Today such achievements are recounted, though seldom in their original form, by science textbooks, elementary and advanced. These textbooks expound the body of accepted theory, illustrate many or all of its successful applications and compare these applications with exemplary observations and experiments. Before such books became popular early in the nineteenth century (and until even more recently in the newly matured sciences), many of the famous classics of science fulfilled a similar function. Aristotle's *Physica,* Ptolemy's *Almagest,* Newton's *Principia* and *Opticks,* Franklin's *Electricity,* Lavoisier's *Chemistry,* and Lyell's *Geology*—these and many other works served for a time implicitly to define the legitimate problems and methods of a research field for succeeding generations of practitioners. They were able to do so because they shared two essential characteristics. Their achievement was sufficiently unprecedented to attract an enduring group of adherents away from competing modes of scientific activity. Simultaneously, it was sufficiently open-ended to leave all sorts of problems for the redefined group of practitioners to resolve.

Achievements that share these two characteristics I shall henceforth refer to as 'paradigms,' a term that relates closely to 'normal science.' By choosing it, I mean to suggest that some accepted examples of actual scientific practice—examples which include law, theory, application, and instrumentation together—provide models from which spring particular coherent traditions of scientific research. These are the traditions which the historian describes under such rubrics as 'Ptolemaic astronomy' (or 'Copernican'), 'Aristotelian dynamics' (or 'Newtonian'), 'corpuscular optics' (or 'wave optics'), and so on. The study of paradigms, including many that are far more specialized than those named illustratively above, is what mainly prepares the student for membership in the particular scientific community with which he will later practice. Because he there joins men who learned the bases of their field from the same concrete models, his subsequent practice will seldom evoke overt disagreement over fundamentals. Men whose research is based on shared paradigms are committed to the same rules and standards for scientific practice. That commitment and the apparent consensus it produces are prerequisites for normal science, i.e., for the genesis and continuation of a particular research tradition. . . .

Normal science . . . is a highly cumulative enterprise, eminently successful in its aim, the steady extension of the scope and precision of scientific knowledge. In all these respects it fits with great precision the most usual image of scientific work. Yet one standard product of the scientific enterprise is missing. Normal science does not aim at novelties of fact or theory and, when successful, finds none. New and unsuspected phenomena are, however, repeatedly uncovered by scientific research and radical new theories have again and again been invented by scientists. History even suggests that the scientific enterprise has developed a uniquely powerful technique for producing surprises of this sort. If this characteristic of science is to be reconciled with what has already been said, then research under a paradigm must be a particularly effective way of inducing paradigm change. That is what fundamental novelties of fact and theory do. Produced inadvertently by a game played under one set of rules, their assimilation requires the elaboration of another set. After they have become parts of science, the enterprise, at least of those specialists in whose particular field the novelties lie, is never quite the same again.

We must now ask how changes of this sort can come about, considering first discoveries, or novelties of fact, and then inventions, or novelties

of theory. That distinction between discovery and invention or between fact and theory will, however, immediately prove to be exceedingly artificial. Its artificiality is an important clue to several of this essay's main theses. Examining selected discoveries in the rest of this section, we shall quickly find that they are not isolated events but extended episodes with a regularly recurrent structure. Discovery commences with the awareness of anomaly, i.e., with the recognition that nature has somehow violated the paradigm-induced expectations that govern normal science. It then continues with a more or less extended exploration of the area of anomaly. And it closes only when the paradigm theory has been adjusted so that the anomalous has become the expected. Assimilating a new sort of fact demands a more than additive adjustment of theory, and until that adjustment is completed—until the scientist has learned to see nature in a different way—the new fact is not quite a scientific fact at all.

To see how closely factual and theoretical novelty are intertwined in scientific discovery, examine a particularly famous example, the discovery of oxygen. At least three different men have a legitimate claim to it, and several other chemists must, in the early 1770s, have had enriched air in a laboratory vessel without knowing it. The progress of normal science, in this case of pneumatic chemistry, prepared the way to a breakthrough quite thoroughly. The earliest of the claimants to prepare a relatively pure sample of the gas was the Swedish apothecary, C.W. Scheele. We may, however, ignore his work since it was not published until oxygen's discovery had repeatedly been announced elsewhere and thus had no effect upon the historical pattern that most concerns us here. The second in time to establish a claim was the British scientist and divine, Joseph Priestley, who collected the gas released by heated red oxide of mercury as one item in prolonged normal investigation of the "airs" evolved by a large number of solid substances. In 1774 he identified the gas thus produced as nitrous oxide and in 1775, led by further tests, as common air with less than its usual quantity of phlogiston. The third claimant, Lavoisier, started the work that led him to oxygen after Priestley's experiments of 1774 and possibly as the result of a hint from Priestley. Early in 1775 Lavoisier reported that the gas obtained by heating the red oxide of mercury was "air itself entire without alteration [except that] ... it comes out more pure, more respirable." By 1777, probably with the assistance of a second hint from Priestley, Lavoisier had concluded that the gas was a distinct species, one of the two main constituents of the atmosphere, a conclusion that Priestley was never able to accept.

This pattern of discovery raises a question that can be asked about every novel phenomenon that has ever entered the consciousness of scientists. Was it Priestley or Lavoisier, if either, who first discovered oxygen? In any case, when was oxygen discovered? In that form the question could be asked even if only one claimant had existed. As a ruling about priority and date, an answer does not at all concern us. Nevertheless, an attempt to produce one will illuminate the nature of discovery, because there is no answer of the kind that is sought. Discovery is not the sort of process about which the question is appropriately asked. The fact that it is asked—the priority for oxygen has repeatedly been contested since the 1780s—is a symptom of something askew in the image of science that gives discovery so fundamental a role. Look once more at our example. Priestley's claim to the discovery of oxygen is based upon his priority in isolating a gas that was later recognized as a distinct species. But Priestley's sample was not pure, and, if holding impure oxygen in one's hand is to discover it, that had been done by everyone who ever bottled atmospheric air. Besides, if Priestley was the discoverer, when was the discovery made? In 1774 he thought he had obtained nitrous oxide, a species he already knew; in 1775 he saw the gas as dephlogisticated air, which is still not oxygen or even, for phlogistic chemists, a quite unexpected sort of gas. Lavoisier's claim may be stronger, but it presents the same problems. If we refuse the palm to

Priestley, we cannot award it to Lavoisier for the work of 1775 which led him to identify the gas as the "air itself entire." Presumably we wait for the work of 1776 and 1777 which led Lavoisier to see not merely the gas but what the gas was. Yet even this award could be questioned, for in 1777 and to the end of his life Lavoisier insisted that oxygen was an atomic "principle of acidity" and that oxygen gas was formed only when that "principle" united with caloric, the matter of heat. Shall we therefore say that oxygen had not yet been discovered in 1777? Some may be tempted to do so. But the principle of acidity was not banished from chemistry until after 1810, and caloric lingered until the 1860s. Oxygen had become a standard chemical substance before either of those dates.

Clearly we need a new vocabulary and concepts for analyzing events like the discovery of oxygen. Though undoubtedly correct, the sentence, "Oxygen was discovered," misleads by suggesting that discovering something is a single simple act assimilable to our usual (and also questionable) concept of seeing. That is why we so readily assume that discovering, like seeing or touching, should be unequivocally attributable to an individual and to a moment in time. But the latter attribution is always impossible, and the former often is as well. Ignoring Scheele, we can safely say that oxygen had not been discovered before 1774, and we would probably also say that it had been discovered by 1777 or shortly thereafter. But within those limits or others like them, any attempt to date the discovery must inevitably be arbitrary because discovering a new sort of phenomenon is necessarily a complex event, one which involves recognizing both *that* something is and *what* it is. Note, for example, that if oxygen were dephlogisticated air for us, we should insist without hesitation that Priestley had discovered it, though we would still not know quite when. But if both observation and conceptualization, fact and assimilation to theory, are inseparably linked in discovery, then discovery is a process and must take time. Only when all the relevant conceptual categories are prepared in advance, in which case the phenomenon would not be of a new sort, can discovering *that* and discovering *what* occur effortlessly, together, and in an instant.

Grant now that discovery involves an extended, though not necessarily long, process of conceptual assimilation. Can we also say that it involves a change in paradigm? To that question, no general answer can yet be given, but in this case at least, the answer must be yes. What Lavoisier announced in his papers from 1777 on was not so much the discovery of oxygen as the oxygen theory of combustion. That theory was the keystone for a reformulation of chemistry so vast that it is usually called the chemical revolution. Indeed, if the discovery of oxygen had not been an intimate part of the emergence of a new paradigm for chemistry, the question of priority from which we began would never have seemed so important. In this case as in others, the value placed upon a new phenomenon and thus upon its discoverer varies with our estimate of the extent to which the phenomenon violated paradigm-induced anticipations. Notice, however, since it will be important later, that the discovery of oxygen was not by itself the cause of the change in chemical theory. Long before he played any part in the discovery of the new gas, Lavoisier was convinced both that something was wrong with the phlogiston theory and that burning bodies absorbed some part of the atmosphere. That much he had recorded in a sealed note deposited with the Secretary of the French Academy in 1772. What the work on oxygen did was to give much additional form and structure to Lavoisier's earlier sense that something was amiss. It told him a thing he was already prepared to discover—the nature of the substance that combustion removes from the atmosphere. That advance awareness of difficulties must be a significant part of what enabled Lavoisier to see in experiments like Priestley's a gas that Priestley had been unable to see there himself. Conversely, the fact that a major paradigm revision was needed to see what Lavoisier saw must be the principal reason why Priestley was, to the end of his long life, unable to see it. . . .

To a greater or lesser extent (corresponding to the continuum from the shocking to the anticipated result), the characteristics common to the . . . example above are characteristic of all discoveries from which new sorts of phenomena emerge. Those characteristics include: the previous awareness of anomaly, the gradual and simultaneous emergence of both observational and conceptual recognition, and the consequent change of paradigm categories and procedures often accompanied by resistance. There is even evidence that these same characteristics are built into the nature of the perceptual process itself. In a psychological experiment that deserves to be far better known outside the trade, Bruner and Postman asked experimental subjects to identify on short and controlled exposure a series of playing cards. Many of the cards were normal, but some were made anomalous, e.g., a red six of spades and a black four of hearts. Each experimental run was constituted by the display of a single card to a single subject in a series of gradually increased exposures. After each exposure the subject was asked what he had seen, and the run was terminated by two successive correct identifications.

Even on the shortest exposures many subjects identified most of the cards, and after a small increase all the subjects identified them all. For the normal cards these identifications were usually correct, but the anomalous cards were almost always identified, without apparent hesitation or puzzlement, as normal. The black four of hearts might, for example, be identified as the four of either spades or hearts. Without any awareness of trouble, it was immediately fitted to one of the conceptual categories prepared by prior experience. One would not even like to say that the subjects had seen something different from what they identified. With a further increase of exposure to the anomalous cards, subjects did begin to hesitate and to display awareness of anomaly. Exposed, for example, to the red six of spades, some would say: That's the six of spades, but there's something wrong with it—the black has a red border. Further increase of exposure resulted in still more hesitation and confusion until finally, and sometimes quite suddenly, most subjects would produce the correct identification without hesitation. Moreover, after doing this with two or three of the anomalous cards, they would have little further difficulty with the others. A few subjects, however, were never able to make the requisite adjustment of their categories. Even at forty times the average exposure required to recognize normal cards for what they were, more than 10 percent of the anomalous cards were not correctly identified. And the subjects who then failed often experienced acute personal distress. One of the exclaimed: "I can't make the suit out, whatever it is. It didn't even look like a card that time. I don't know what color it is now or whether it's a spade or a heart. I'm not even sure now what a spade looks like. My God!" In the next section we shall occasionally see scientists behaving this way too.

Either as a metaphor or because it reflects the nature of the mind, that psychological experiment provides a wonderfully simple and cogent schema for the process of scientific discovery. In science, as in the playing card experiment, novelty emerges only with difficulty, manifested by resistance, against a background provided by expectation. Initially, only the anticipated and usual are experienced even under circumstances where anomaly is later to be observed. Further acquaintance, however, does result in awareness of something wrong or does relate the effect to something that has gone wrong before. That awareness of anomaly opens a period in which conceptual categories are adjusted until the initially anomalous has become the anticipated. At this point the discovery has been completed. I have already urged that that process or one very much like it is involved in the emergence of all fundamental scientific novelties. Let me now point out that, recognizing the process, we can at last begin to see why normal science, a pursuit not directed to novelties and tending at first to suppress them, should nevertheless be so effective in causing them to arise.

In the development of any science, the first received paradigm is usually felt to account quite successfully for most of the observations and experiments easily accessible to that science's practitioners. Further development, therefore, ordinarily calls for the construction of elaborate equipment, the development of an esoteric vocabulary and skills, and a refinement of concepts that increasingly lessens their resemblance to their usual common-sense prototypes. That professionalization leads, on the one hand, to an immense restriction of the scientist's vision and to a considerable resistance to paradigm change. The science has become increasingly rigid. On the other hand, within those areas to which the paradigm directs the attention of the group, normal science leads to a detail of information and to a precision of the observation-theory match that could be achieved in no other way. Furthermore that detail and precision-of-match have a value that transcends their not always very high intrinsic interest. Without the special apparatus that is constructed mainly for anticipated functions, the results that lead ultimately to novelty could not occur. And even when the apparatus exists, novelty ordinarily emerges only for the man who, knowing *with precision* what he should expect, is able to recognize that something has gone wrong. Anomaly appears only against the background provided by the paradigm. The more precise and far-reaching that paradigm is, the more sensitive an indicator it provides of anomaly and hence of an occasion for paradigm change. In the normal mode of discovery, even resistance to change has a use that will be explored more fully in the next section. By ensuring that the paradigm will not be too easily surrendered, resistance guarantees that scientists will not be lightly distracted and that the anomalies that lead to paradigm change will penetrate existing knowledge to the core. The very fact that a significant scientific novelty so often emerges simultaneously from several laboratories is an index both to the strongly traditional nature of normal science and to the completeness with which that traditional pursuit prepares the way for its own change. . . .

If awareness of anomaly plays a role in the emergence of new sorts of phenomena, it should surprise no one that a similar but more profound awareness is prerequisite to all acceptable changes of theory. On this point historical evidence is, I think, entirely unequivocal. The state of Ptolemaic astronomy was a scandal before Copernicus' announcement. Galileo's contributions to the study of motion depended closely upon difficulties discovered in Aristotle's theory by scholastic critics. Newton's new theory of light and color originated in the discovery that none of the existing pre-paradigm theories would account for the length of the spectrum, and the wave theory that replaced Newton's was announced in the midst of growing concern about anomalies in the relation of diffraction and polarization effects to Newton's theory. Thermodynamics was born from the collision of two existing nineteenth-century physical theories, and quantum mechanics from a variety of difficulties surrounding black-body radiation, specific heats, and the photo-electric effect. Furthermore, in all these cases except that of Newton the awareness of anomaly had lasted so long and penetrated so deep that one can appropriately describe the fields affected by it as in a state of growing crisis. Because it demands large-scale paradigm destruction and major shifts in the problems and techniques of normal science, the emergence of new theories is generally preceded by a period of pronounced professional insecurity. As one might expect, that insecurity is generated by the persistent failure of the puzzles of normal science to come out as they should. Failure of existing rules is the prelude to a search for new ones. . . .

Philosophers of science have repeatedly demonstrated that more than one theoretical construction can always be placed upon a given collection of data. History of science indicates that, particularly in the early developmental stages of a new paradigm, it is not even very difficult to invent such alternates. But that invention of alternates is just what scientists seldom undertake except during the pre-paradigm stage of their science's development and at very special occasions during its subsequent evolution. So long as the tools a paradigm supplies continue to prove capable of solving the problems it defines,

science moves fastest and penetrates most deeply through confident employment of those tools. The reason is clear. As in manufacture so in science—retooling is an extravagance to be reserved for the occasion that demands it. The significance of crises is the indication they provide that an occasion for retooling has arrived. . . .

How, then, do scientists respond to the awareness of an anomaly in the fit between theory and nature? What has just been said indicates that even a discrepancy unaccountably larger than that experienced in other applications of the theory need not draw any very profound response. There are always some discrepancies. Even the most stubborn ones usually respond at last to normal practice. Very often scientists are willing to wait, particularly if there are many problems available in other parts of the field. . . . [D]uring the sixty years after Newton's original computation, the predicted motion of the moon's perigee remained only half of that observed. As Europe's best mathematical physicists continued to wrestle unsuccessfully with the well-known discrepancy, there were occasional proposals for a modification of Newton's inverse square law. But no one took these proposals very seriously, and in practice this patience with a major anomaly proved justified. Clairaut in 1750 was able to show that only the mathematics of the application had been wrong and that Newtonian theory could stand as before. Even in cases where no mere mistake seems quite possible (perhaps because the mathematics involved is simpler or of a familiar and elsewhere successful sort), persistent and recognized anomaly does not always induce crisis. No one seriously questioned Newtonian theory because of the long-recognized discrepancies between predictions from that theory and both the speed of sound and the little motion of Mercury. The first discrepancy was ultimately and quite unexpectedly resolved by experiments on heat undertaken for a very different purpose; the second vanished with the general theory of relativity after a crisis that it had had no role in creating. Apparently neither had seemed sufficiently fundamental to evoke the malaise that goes with crises. They could be recognized as counterinstances and still be set aside for later work.

It follows that if an anomaly is to evoke crisis, it must usually be more than just an anomaly. There are always difficulties somewhere in the paradigm-nature fit; most of them are set right sooner or later, often by processes that could not have been foreseen. The scientist who pauses to examine every anomaly he notes will seldom get significant work done. We therefore have to ask what it is that makes an anomaly seem worth concerted scrutiny, and to that question there is probably no fully general answer. The cases we have already examined are characteristic but scarcely prescriptive. Sometimes an anomaly will clearly call into question explicit and fundamental generalizations of the paradigm, as the problem of ether drag did for those who accepted Maxwell's theory. Or, as in the Copernican revolution, an anomaly without apparent fundamental import may evoke crisis if the applications that it inhibits have a particular practical importance, in this case for calendar design and astrology. Or, as in eighteenth-century chemistry, the development of normal science may transform an anomaly that had previously been only a vexation into a source of crisis: the problem of weight relations had a very different status after the evolution of pneumatic-chemical techniques. Presumably there are still other circumstances that can make an anomaly particularly pressing, and ordinarily several of these will combine. We have already noted, for example, that one source of the crisis that confronted Copernicus was the mere length of time during which astronomers had wrestled unsuccessfully with the reduction of the residual discrepancies in Ptolemy's system.

When, for these reasons or others like them, an anomaly comes to seem more than just another puzzle of normal science, the transition to crisis and to extraordinary science has begun. The anomaly itself now comes to be more generally recognized as such by the profession. More and more attention is devoted to it by more and more of the field's most eminent men.

If it still continues to resist, as it usually does not, many of them may come to view its resolution as *the* subject matter of their discipline. For them the field will no longer look quite the same as it had earlier. Part of its different appearance results simply from the new fixation point of scientific scrutiny. An even more important source of change is the divergent nature of the numerous partial solutions that concerted attention to the problem has made available. The early attacks upon the resistant problem will have followed the paradigm rules quite closely. But with continuing resistance, more and more of the attacks upon it will have involved some minor or not so minor articulation of the paradigm, no two of them quite alike, each partially successful, but none sufficiently so to be accepted as paradigm by the group. Through this proliferation of divergent articulations (more and more frequently they will come to be described as *ad hoc* adjustments), the rules of normal science become increasingly blurred. Though there still is a paradigm, few practitioners prove to be entirely agreed about what it is. Even formerly standard solutions of solved problems are called in question. . . .

Confronted with anomaly or with crisis, scientists take a different attitude toward existing paradigms, and the nature of their research changes accordingly. The proliferation of competing articulations, the willingness to try anything, the expression of explicit discontent, the recourse to philosophy and to debate over fundamentals, all these are symptoms of a transition from normal to extraordinary research. It is upon their existence more than upon that of revolutions that the notion of normal science depends. . . .

In learning a paradigm the scientist acquires theory, methods, and standards together, usually in an inextricable mixture. Therefore, when paradigms change, there are usually significant shifts in the criteria determining the legitimacy both of problems and of proposed solutions.

That observation returns us to the point from which this section began, for it provides our first explicit indication of why the choice between competing paradigms regularly raises questions that cannot be resolved by the criteria of normal science. To the extent, as significant as it is incomplete, the two scientific schools disagree about what is a problem and what a solution, they will inevitably talk through each other when debating the relative merits of their respective paradigms. In the partially circular arguments that regularly result, each paradigm will be shown to satisfy more or less the criteria that it dictates for itself and to fall short of a few of those dictated by its opponent. There are other reasons, too, for the incompleteness of logical contact that consistently characterizes paradigm debates. For example, since no paradigm ever solves all the problems it defines and since no two paradigms leave all the same problems unsolved, paradigm debates always involve the question: Which problems is it more significant to have solved? Like the issue of competing standards, that question of values can be answered only in terms of criteria that lie outside of normal science altogether, and it is that recourse to external criteria that most obviously makes paradigm debates revolutionary.

KARL POPPER
Science: Conjectures and Refutations

KARL POPPER *(1902–1994), with a background in psychology, physics, and mathematics, was a professor at Canterbury University College in New Zealand until 1945, when he became reader in logic and scientific method at the London School of Economics. His first book,* The Logic of Scientific Discovery, *was a major response to the school of thought known as logical positivism. His work has been unusually influential among scientists.*

WHEN I received the list of participants in this course and realized that I had been asked to speak to philosophical colleagues I thought, after some hesitation and consultation, that you would probably prefer me to speak about those problems which interest me most, and about those developments with which I am most intimately acquainted. I therefore decided to do what I have never done before: to give you a report on my own work in the philosophy of science, since the autumn of 1919 when I first began to grapple with the problem, *'When should a theory be ranked as scientific?'* or *'Is there a criterion for the scientific character or status of a theory?'*

The problem which troubled me at the time was neither, "When is a theory true?" nor, "When is a theory acceptable?" My problem was different. *I wished to distinguish between science and pseudo-science;* knowing very well that science often errs, and that pseudo-science may happen to stumble on the truth.

I knew, of course, the most widely accepted answer to my problem: that science is distinguished from pseudo-science—or from "metaphysics"—by its *empirical method*, which is essentially *inductive*, proceeding from observation or experiment. But this did not satisfy me. On the contrary, I often formulated my problem as one of distinguishing between a genuinely empirical method and a non-empirical or even a pseudo-empirical method—that is to say, a method which, although it appeals to observation and experiment, nevertheless does not come up to scientific standards. The latter method may be exemplified by astrology, with its stupendous mass of empirical evidence based on observation—on horoscopes and on biographies.

But as it was not the example of astrology which led me to my problem I should perhaps briefly describe the atmosphere in which my problem arose and the examples by which it was stimulated. After the collapse of the Austrian Empire there had been a revolution in Austria: the air was full of revolutionary slogans and ideas, and new and often wild theories. Among the theories which interested me, Einstein's theory of relativity was no doubt by far the most important. Three others were Marx's theory of history, Freud's psycho-analysis, and Alfred Adler's so-called "individual psychology."

There was a lot of popular nonsense talked about these theories, and especially about relativity (as still happens even today), but I was fortunate in those who introduced me to the study of this theory. We all—the small circle of students to which I belonged—were thrilled with the result of Eddington's eclipse observations which in 1919 brought the first important confirmation of Einstein's theory of gravitation. It was a great experience for us, and one which had a lasting influence on my intellectual development.

The three other theories I have mentioned were also widely discussed among students at that time. I myself happened to come into personal contact with Alfred Adler, and even to cooperate with him in his social work among the children and young people in the working-class districts of Vienna where he had established social guidance clinics.

It was during the summer of 1919 that I began to feel more and more dissatisfied with these three theories—the Marxist theory of history, psycho-analysis, and individual psychology; and I began to feel dubious about their claims to scientific status. My problem perhaps first took the simple form, "What is wrong with Marxism, psychoanalysis, and individual psychology? Why are they so different from physical theories, from Newton's theory, and especially from the theory of relativity?"

To make this contrast clear I should explain that few of us at the time would have said that we believed in the *truth* of Einstein's theory of gravitation. This shows that it was not my doubting the *truth* of those other three theories which bothered me, but something else. Yet neither was it that I merely felt mathematical physics to be more *exact* than the sociological or psychological type of theory. Thus what worried me was neither the problem of truth, at that stage at least, nor the problem of exactness or measurability. It was rather that I felt that these other three theories, though posing as sciences, had in fact more in common with primitive myths than with science; that they resembled astrology rather than astronomy.

I found that those of my friends who were admirers of Marx, Freud, and Adler, were impressed by a number of points common to these theories, and especially by their apparent *explanatory power*. These theories appeared to be able to explain practically everything that happened within the fields to which they referred. The study of any of them seemed to have the effect of an intellectual conversion or revelation, opening your eyes to a new truth hidden from those not yet initiated. Once your eyes were thus opened you saw confirming instances everywhere: the world was full of *verifications* of the theory. Whatever happened always confirmed it. Thus its truth appeared manifest; and unbelievers were clearly people who did not want to see the manifest truth; who refused to see it, either because it was against their class interest, or because of their repressions which were still "unanalysed" and crying aloud for treatment.

The most characteristic element in this situation seemed to me the incessant stream of confirmations, of observations which "verified" the theories in question; and this point was constantly emphasized by their adherents. A Marxist could not open a newspaper without finding on every page confirming evidence for his interpretation of history; not only in the news but also in its presentation—which revealed the class bias of the paper—and especially of course in what the paper did *not* say. The Freudian analysts emphasized that their theories were constantly verified by their "clinical observations." As for Adler, I was much impressed by a personal experience. Once, in 1919, I reported to him a case which tome did not seem particularly Adlerian, but which he found no difficulty in analysing in terms of his theory of inferiority feelings, although he had not even seen the child. Slightly shocked, I asked him how he could be so sure. "Because of my thousandfold experience," he replied; whereupon I could not help saying: "And with this new case, I suppose, your experience has become thousand-and-one-fold."

What I had in mind was that his previous observations may not have been much sounder than this new one; that each in its turn had been interpreted in the light of "previous experience," and at the same time counted as additional confirmation. What, I asked myself, did it confirm? No more than that a case could be interpreted in the light of the theory. But this meant very little, I reflected, since every conceivable case could be interpreted in the light of Adler's theory, or equally Freud's. I may illustrate this by two very different examples of human behaviour: that of a man who pushes a child into the water with the intention of drowning it; and that of a man who sacrifices his life in an attempt to save the child. Each of these two cases can be explained with equal ease in Freudian and in Adlerian terms. According to Freud the first man suffered from repression (say, of some component of his Oedipus complex), while the second man had achieved sublimation. According to Adler the

first man suffered from feelings of inferiority (producing perhaps the need to prove to himself that he dared to commit some crime), and so did the second man (whose need was to prove to himself that he dared to rescue the child). I could not think of any human behaviour which could not be interpreted in terms of either theory. It was precisely this fact—that they always fitted, that they were always confirmed—which in the eyes of their admirers constituted the strongest argument in favour of these theories. It began to dawn on me that this apparent strength was in fact their weakness.

With Einstein's theory the situation was strikingly different. Take one typical instance—Einstein's prediction, just then confirmed by the findings of Eddington's expedition. Einstein's gravitational theory had led to the result that light must be attracted by heavy bodies (such as the sun), precisely as material bodies were attracted. As a consequence it could be calculated that light from a distant fixed star whose apparent position was close to the sun would reach the earth from such a direction that the star would seem to be slightly shifted away from the sun; or, in other words that stars close to the sun would look as if they had moved a little away from the sun, and from one another. This is a thing which cannot normally be observed since such stars are rendered invisible in daytime by the sun's overwhelming brightness; but during an eclipse it is possible to take photographs of them. If the same constellation is photographed at night one can measure the distances on the two photographs, and check the predicted effect.

Now the impressive thing about this case is the *risk* involved in a prediction of this kind. If observation shows that the predicted effect is definitely absent, then the theory is simply refuted. The theory is *incompatible with certain possible results of observation*—in fact with results which everybody before Einstein would have expected. This is quite different from the situation I have previously described, when it turned out that the theories in question were compatible with the most divergent human behaviour, so that it was practically impossible to describe any human behaviour that might not be claimed to be a verification of these theories.

These considerations led me in the winter of 1919–20 to conclusions which I may now reformulate as follows:

(1) It is easy to obtain confirmations, or verifications, for nearly every theory—if we look for confirmations.

(2) Confirmations should count only if they are the result of *risky predictions;* that is to say, if, unenlightened by the theory in question, we should have expected an event which was incompatible with the theory—an event which would have refuted the theory.

(3) Every "good" scientific theory is a prohibition: it forbids certain things to happen. The more a theory forbids, the better it is.

(4) A theory which is not refutable by any conceivable event is nonscientific. Irrefutability is not a virtue of a theory (as people often think) but a vice.

(5) Every genuine *test* of a theory is an attempt to falsify it, or to refute it. Testability is falsifiability; but there are degrees of testability: some theories are more testable, more exposed to refutation, than others; they take, as it were, greater risks.

(6) Confirming evidence should not count *except when it is the result of a genuine test of the theory;* and this means that it can be presented as a serious but unsuccessful attempt to falsify the theory. (I now speak in such cases of "corroborating evidence.")

(7) Some genuinely testable theories, when found to be false, are still upheld by their admirers—for example by introducing *ad hoc* some auxiliary assumption, or by reinterpreting the theory *ad hoc* in such a way that it escapes refutation. Such a procedure is always possible, but it rescues the theory from refutation only at the price of destroying, or at least lowering, its scientific status. (I later described such a rescuing operation as a "*conventionalist twist*" or a "*conventionalist stratagem.*")

One can sum up all this by saying that *the criterion of the scientific status of a theory is its falsifiability, or refutability, or testability.*

I may perhaps exemplify this with the help of the various theories so far mentioned. Einstein's theory of gravitation clearly satisfied the criterion of falsifiability. Even if our measuring instruments at the time did not allow us to pronounce on the results of the tests with complete assurance, there was clearly a possibility of refuting the theory.

Astrology did not pass the test. Astrologers were greatly impressed, and misled, by what they believed to be confirming evidence—so much so that they were quite unimpressed by any unfavourable evidence. Moreover, by making their interpretations and prophecies sufficiently vague they were able to explain away anything that might have been a refutation of the theory had the theory and the prophecies been more precise. In order to escape falsification they destroyed the testability of their theory. It is a typical soothsayer's trick to predict things so vaguely that the predictions can hardly fail: that they become irrefutable.

The Marxist theory of history, in spite of the serious efforts of some of its founders and followers, ultimately adopted this soothsaying practice. In some of its earlier formulations (for example in Marx's analysis of the character of the "coming social revolution") their predictions were testable, and in fact falsified. Yet instead of accepting the refutations the followers of Marx reinterpreted both the theory and the evidence in order to make them agree. In this way they rescued the theory from refutation; but they did so at the price of adopting a device which made it irrefutable. They thus gave a "conventional twist" to the theory; and by this stratagem they destroyed its much advertised claim to scientific status.

The two psycho-analytic theories were in a different class. They were simply nontestable, irrefutable. There was no conceivable human behaviour which could contradict them. This does not mean that Freud and Adler were not seeing certain things correctly: I personally do not doubt that much of what they say is of considerable importance, and may well play its part one day in a psychological science which is testable.

But it does mean that those "clinical observations" which analysts naively believe confirm their theory cannot do this any more than the daily confirmations which astrologers find in their practice. And as for Freud's epic of the Ego, the Super-ego, and the Id, no substantially stronger claim to scientific status can be made for it than for Homer's collected stories from Olympus. These theories describe some facts, but in the manner of myths. They contain most interesting psychological suggestions, but not in a testable form.

At the same time I realized that such myths may be developed, and become testable; that historically speaking all—or very nearly all—scientific theories originate from myths, and that a myth may contain important anticipations of scientific theories. Examples are Empedocles' theory of evolution by trial and error, or Parmenides' myth of the unchanging block universe in which nothing ever happens and which, if we add another dimension, becomes Einstein's block universe (in which, too, nothing ever happens, since everything is, four-dimensionally speaking, determined and laid down from the beginning). I thus felt that if a theory is found to be nonscientific, or "metaphysical" (as we might say), it is not thereby found to be unimportant, or insignificant, or "meaningless", or "nonsensical." But it cannot claim to be backed by empirical evidence in the scientific sense—although it may easily be, in some genetic sense, the "result of observation."

(There were a great many other theories of this pre-scientific or pseudo-scientific character, some of them, unfortunately, as influential as the Marxist interpretation of history; for example, the racialist interpretation of history—another of those impressive and all-explanatory theories which act upon weak minds like revelations.)

Thus the problem which I tried to solve by proposing the criterion of falsifiability was neither a problem of meaningfulness or significance, nor a problem of truth or acceptability. It was the problem of drawing a line (as well as this can be done) between the statements, or systems of statements, of the empirical sciences, and all other statements—whether they are of a religious or of a metaphysical character, or simply pseudo-scientific. Years later—it must have been in 1928 or 1929—I called this first problem of mine the *"problem of demarcation."* The criterion of falsifiability is a solution to this problem of demarcation, for it says that statements or systems of statements, in order to be ranked as scientific, must be capable of conflicting with possible, or conceivable, observations.

•   •   •

The belief that science proceeds from observation to theory is still so widely and so firmly held that my denial of it is often met with incredulity. I have even been suspected of being insincere—of denying what nobody in his senses can doubt.

But in fact the belief that we can start with pure observations alone, without anything in the nature of a theory, is absurd: as may be illustrated by the story of the man who dedicated his life to natural science, wrote down everything he could observe, and bequeathed his priceless collection of observations to the Royal Society to be used as inductive evidence. This story should show us that though beetles may profitably be collected, observations may not.

Twenty-five years ago I tried to bring home the same point to a group of physics students in Vienna by beginning a lecture with the following instructions: "Take pencil and paper; carefully observe, and write down what you have observed!" They asked, of course, *what* I wanted them to observe. Clearly the instruction, "Observe!" is absurd. (It is not even idiomatic, unless the object of the transitive verb can be taken as understood.) Observation is always selective. It needs a chosen object, a definite task, an interest, a point of view, a problem. And its description presupposes a descriptive language, with property words; it presupposes similarity and classification, which in its turn presupposes interests, points of view, and problems. "A hungry animal," writes Kaltz, "divides the environment into edible and inedible things. An animal in flight sees roads to escape and hiding places. . . . Generally speaking, objects change . . . according to the needs of the animal." We may add that objects can be classified, and can become similar or dissimilar, *only* in this way—by being related to needs and interests. This rule applies not only to animals but also to scientists. For the animal a point of view is provided by its needs, the task of the moment, and its expectations; for the scientist by his theoretical interests, the special problem under investigation, his conjectures and anticipations, and the theories which he accepts as a kind of background: his frame of reference, his "horizon of expectations."

The problem "Which comes first, the hypothesis *(H)* or the observation *(O),*" is soluble: as is the problem, "Which comes first, the hen *(H)* or the egg *(O)*." The reply to the latter is, "An earlier kind of hypothesis." It is quite true that any particular hypothesis we choose will have been preceded by observations—the observations, for example, which it is designed to explain. But these observations, in their turn, presupposed the adoption of a frame of reference: a frame of expectations: a frame of theories. If they were significant, if they created a need for explanation and thus gave rise to the invention of a hypothesis, it was because they could not be explained within the old theoretical framework, the old horizon of expectations. There is no danger here of an infinite regress. Going back to more and more primitive theories and myths we shall in the end find unconscious, *inborn* expectations.

The theory of inborn *ideas* is absurd, I think; but every organism has inborn *reactions* or *responses;* and among them, responses adapted to impending events. These responses we may describe as "expectations" without implying that these "expectations" are conscious. The newborn baby "expects," in this sense, to be fed (and, one could even argue, to be protected and loved). In view of the close relation between expectation and knowledge we may even speak in quite a reasonable sense of "inborn knowledge." This "knowledge" is not, however, *valid a priori;* an inborn expectation, no matter how strong and

specific, may be mistaken. (The newborn child may be abandoned, and starve.)

Thus we are born with expectations; with "knowledge" which, although not *valid a priori,* is *psychologically or genetically a priori,* i.e. prior to all observational experience. One of the most important of these expectations is the expectation of finding a regularity. It is connected with an inborn propensity to look out for regularities, or with a *need* to *find* regularities, as we may see from the pleasure of the child who satisfies this need.

. . . genetically speaking the pseudo-scientific attitude is more primitive than, and prior to, the scientific attitude: it is a prescientific attitude. And this primitivity or priority also has its logical aspect. For the critical attitude is not so much opposed to the dogmatic attitude as superimposed upon it: criticism must be directed against existing and influential beliefs in need of critical revision—in other words, dogmatic beliefs. A critical attitude needs for its raw material, as it were, theories or beliefs which are held more or less dogmatically.

Thus science must begin with myths, and with the criticism of myths; neither with the collection of observations, nor with the invention of experiments, but with the critical discussion of myths, and of magical techniques and practices. The scientific tradition is distinguished from the prescientific tradition in having two layers. Like the latter, it passes on its theories; but it also passes on a critical attitude toward them. The theories are passed on, not as dogmas, but rather with the challenge to discuss them to improve upon them. This tradition is Hellenic: it may be traced back to Thales, founder of the first *school* (I do not mean "of the first *philosophical* school," but simply "of the first school") which was not mainly concerned with the preservation of a dogma.

The critical attitude, the tradition of free discussion of theories with the aim of discovering their weak spots so that they may be improved upon, is the attitude of reasonableness, or rationality. It makes far-reaching use of both verbal argument and observation—of observation in the interest of argument, however. The Greeks' discovery of the critical method gave rise at first to the mistaken hope that it would lead to the solution of all the great old problems; that it would establish certainty; that it would help to *prove* our theories, to *justify* them. But this hope was a residue of the dogmatic way of thinking; in fact nothing can be justified or proved (outside of mathematics and logic). The demand for rational proofs in science indicates a failure to keep distinct the broad realm of rationality and the narrow realm of rational certainty: it is an untenable, an unreasonable demand. . . .

Assume that we have deliberately made it our task to live in this unknown world of ours; to adjust ourselves to it as well as we can; to take advantage of the opportunities we can find in it; and to explain it, *if* possible (we need not assume that it is), and as far as possible, with the help of laws and explanatory theories. *If we have made this our task, then there is no more rational procedure than the method of trial and error—of conjecture and refutation:* of boldly proposing theories; of trying our best to show that these are erroneous; and of accepting them tentatively if our critical efforts are unsuccessful.

From the point of view here developed all laws, all theories, remain essentially tentative, or conjectural, or hypothetical, even when we feel unable to doubt them any longer. Before a theory has been refuted we can never know in what way it may have to be modified. That the sun will always rise and set within twenty-four hours is still proverbial as a law "established by induction beyond reasonable doubt." It is odd that this example is still in use, though it may have served well enough in the days of Aristotle and Pytheas of Massalia—the great traveller who for centuries was called a liar because of his tales of Thule, the land of the frozen sea and the *midnight sun.*

The method of trial and error is not, of course, simply identical with the method of conjecture and refutation. The method of trial and error is applied not only by Einstein but, in a more dogmatic fashion, by the amoeba also. The difference lies not so much in the trials as in a critical and constructive attitude towards errors;

errors which the scientist consciously and cautiously tries to uncover in order to refute his theories with searching arguments, including appeals to the most severe experimental tests which his theories and his ingenuity permit him to design.

The critical attitude may be described as the conscious attempt to make our theories, our conjectures, suffer in our stead in the struggle for the survival of the fittest. It gives us a chance to survive the elimination of an inadequate hypothesis—when a more dogmatic attitude would eliminate it by eliminating us. (There is a touching story of an Indian community which disappeared because of its belief in the holiness of life, including that of tigers.) We thus obtain the fittest theory within our reach by the elimination of those which are less fit. (By 'fitness' I do not mean merely 'usefulness' but truth. . . .) I do not think that this procedure is irrational or in need of any further rational justification.

. . . From what I have said it is obvious that there was a close link between the two problems which interested me at the time: demarcation, and induction or scientific method. It was easy to see that the method of science is criticism, i.e. attempted falsifications. Yet it took me a few years to notice that the two problems—of demarcation and of induction—were in a sense one.

Why, I asked, do so many scientists believe in induction? I found they did so because they believed natural science to be characterized by the inductive method—by a method starting from, and relying upon, long sequences of observations and experiments. They believed that the difference between genuine science and metaphysical or pseudo-scientific speculation depended solely upon whether or not the inductive method was employed. They believed (to put it in my own terminology) that only the inductive method could provide a satisfactory *criterion of demarcation.*

I recently came across an interesting formulation of this belief in a remarkable philosophical book by a great physicist—Max Born's *Natural Philosophy of Cause and Chance.* He writes: "Induction allows us to generalize a number of observations into a general rule: that night follows day and day follows night. . . . But while everyday life has no definite criterion for the validity of an induction, . . . science has worked out a code, or rule of craft, for its application." Born nowhere reveals the contents of this inductive code (which as his wording shows, contains a "definite criterion for the validity of an induction"); but he stresses that "there is no logical argument" for its acceptance: "it is a question of faith"; and he is therefore "willing to call induction a metaphysical principle." But why does he believe that such a code of valid inductive rules must exist? This becomes clear when he speaks of the "vast communities of people ignorant of, or rejecting, the rule of science, among them the members of anti-vaccination societies and believers in astrology. It is useless to argue with them; I cannot compel them to accept the same criteria of valid induction in which I believe: the code of scientific rules." This makes it quite clear that *'valid induction' was here meant to serve as a criterion of demarcation between science and pseudo-science.*

But it is obvious that this rule or craft of "valid induction" is not even metaphysical: it simply does not exist. No rule can ever guarantee that a generalization inferred from true observations, however often repeated, is true. (Born himself does not believe in the truth of Newtonian physics, in spite of its success, although he believes

that it is based on induction.) And the success of science is not based upon luck, ingenuity, and the purely deductive rules of critical argument.

I may summarize some of my conclusions as follows:

(1) Induction, i.e. inference based on many observations, is a myth. It is neither a psychological fact, nor a fact of ordinary life, nor one of scientific procedure.

(2) The actual procedure of science is to operate with conjectures: to jump to conclusion—often after one single observation (as noticed for example by Hume and Born).

(3) Repeated observations and experiments function in science as *tests* of our conjectures or hypotheses, i.e. as attempted refutations.

(4) The mistaken belief in induction is fortified by the need for a criterion of demarcation which, it is traditionally but wrongly believed, only the inductive method can provide.

(5) The conception of such an inductive method, like the criterion of verifiability, implies a faulty demarcation.

(6) None of this is altered in the least if we say that induction makes theories only probable rather than certain. . . .

EVELYN FOX KELLER
Feminism and Science

EVELYN FOX KELLER *(1936–) was trained in physics and wrote a biography of the Nobel Prize–winning biologist Barbara McClintock. She has been a pioneer in bringing feminist perspectives to the study of science. She is a professor of history and philosophy of science in the Program of Science, Technology and Society at MIT. Her many books include* Reflections on Gender and Science *(1985) and* Making Sense of Life *(2002).*

Keller, Evelyn Fox, "Feminism and Science" from *Journal of Women in Culture and Society,* vol. 7, no. 3, 1982. Reprinted by permission of The University of Chicago Press.

IN recent years, a new critique of science has begun to emerge from a number of feminist writings. The lens of feminist politics brings into focus certain masculinist distortions of the scientific enterprise, creating, for those of us who are scientists, a potential dilemma. Is there a conflict between our commitment to feminism and our commitment to science? As both a feminist and a scientist, I am more familiar than I might wish with the nervousness and defensiveness that such a potential conflict evokes. As scientists, we have very real difficulties in thinking about the kinds of issues that, as feminists, we have been raising. These difficulties may, however, ultimately be productive. My purpose in the present essay is to explore the implications of recent feminist criticism of science for the relationship between science and feminism. Do these criticisms imply conflict? If they do, how necessary is that conflict? I will argue that those elements of feminist criticism that seem to conflict most with at least conventional conceptions of science may, in fact, carry a liberating potential for science. It could therefore benefit scientists to attend closely to feminist criticism. I will suggest that we might even use feminist thought to illuminate and clarify part of the substructure of science (which may have been historically conditioned into distortion) in order to preserve the things that science has taught us, in order to be more objective. But first it is necessary to review the various criticisms that feminists have articulated.

The range of their critique is broad. Though they all claim that science embodies a strong androcentric bias, the meanings attached to this charge vary widely. It is convenient to represent the differences in meaning by a spectrum that parallels the political range characteristic of feminism as a whole. I label this spectrum from right to left, beginning somewhere left of center with what might be called the liberal position. From the liberal critique, charges of androcentricity emerge that are relatively easy to correct. The more radical critique calls for correspondingly more radical changes; it requires a reexamination of the underlying assumptions of scientific theory

and method for the presence of male bias. The difference between these positions is, however, often obscured by a knee-jerk reaction that leads many scientists to regard all such criticism as a unit—as a challenge to the neutrality of science. One of the points I wish to emphasize here is that the range of meanings attributed to the claim of androcentric bias reflects very different levels of challenge, some of which even the most conservative scientists ought to be able to accept.

First, in what I have called the liberal critique, is the charge that is essentially one of unfair employment practices. It proceeds from the observation that almost all scientists are men. This criticism is liberal in the sense that it in no way conflicts either with traditional conceptions of science or with current liberal, egalitarian politics. It is, in fact, a purely political criticism, and one that can be supported by all of us who are in favor of equal opportunity. According to this point of view, science itself would in no way be affected by the presence or absence of women.

A slightly more radical criticism continues from this and argues that the predominance of men in the sciences has led to a bias in the choice and definition of problems with which scientists have concerned themselves. This argument is most frequently and most easily made in regard to the health sciences. It is claimed, for example, that contraception has not been given the scientific attention its human importance warrants and that, furthermore, the attention it has been given has been focused primarily on contraceptive techniques to be used by women. In a related complaint, feminists argue that menstrual cramps, a serious problem for many women, have never been taken seriously by the medical profession. Presumably, had the concerns of medical research been articulated by women, these particular imbalances would not have arisen. Similar biases in sciences remote from the subject of women's bodies are more difficult to locate—they may, however, exist. Even so, this kind of criticism does not touch our conception of what science is, nor our confidence in the neutrality of science. It may be true that in some areas we have ignored certain problems, but our definition of science does not include the choice of problem—that, we can readily agree, has always been influenced by social forces. We remain, therefore, in the liberal domain.

Continuing to the left, we next find claims of bias in the actual design and interpretation of experiments. For example, it is pointed out that virtually all of the animal-learning research on rats has been performed with male rats. Though a simple explanation is offered—namely, that female rats have a four-day cycle that complicates experiments—the criticism is hardly vitiated by the explanation. The implicit assumption is, of course, that the male rat represents the species. There exist many other, often similar, examples in psychology. Examples from the biological sciences are somewhat more difficult to find, though one suspects that they exist. An area in which this suspicion is particularly strong is that of sex research. Here the influence of heavily invested preconceptions seems all but inevitable. In fact, although the existence of such preconceptions has been well documented historically, a convincing case for the existence of a corresponding bias in either the design or interpretation of experiments has yet to be made. That this is so can, I think, be taken as testimony to the effectiveness of the standards of objectivity operating.

But evidence for bias in the interpretation of observations and experiments is very easy to find in the more socially oriented sciences. The area of primatology is a familiar target. Over the past fifteen years women working in the field have undertaken an extensive reexamination of theoretical concepts, often using essentially the same methodological tools. These efforts have resulted in some radically different formulations. The range of difference frequently reflects the powerful influence of ordinary language in biasing our theoretical formulations. A great deal of very interesting work analyzing such distortions has been done. Though I cannot begin to do justice to that work here, let me offer, as a single example, the following description of a single-male troop of animals that Jane Lancaster provides as a substitute for the familiar concept of "harem": "For a female, males are a resource in her environment which she may use to further the survival of herself and her offspring. If environmental conditions are such that the male role can be minimal, a one-male group is likely. Only one male is necessary for a group of females if his only role is to impregnate them."

These critiques, which maintain that a substantive effect on scientific theory results from the predominance of men in the field, are almost exclusively aimed at the "softer," even the "softest," sciences. Thus they can still be accommodated within the traditional framework by the simple argument that the critiques, if justified, merely reflect the fact that these subjects are not sufficiently scientific. Presumably, fair-minded (or scientifically minded) scientists can and should join forces with the feminists in attempting to identify the presence of bias—equally offensive, if for different reasons, to both scientists and feminists—in order to make these "soft" sciences more rigorous.

It is much more difficult to deal with the truly radical critique that attempts to locate androcentric bias even in the "hard" sciences, indeed in scientific ideology itself. This range of criticism takes us out of the liberal domain and requires us to question the very assumptions of objectivity and rationality that underlie the scientific enterprise. To challenge the truth and necessity of the conclusions of natural science on the grounds that they too reflect the judgment of men is to take the Galilean credo and turn in on its head. It is not true that "the conclusions of natural science are true and necessary, and the judgment of man has nothing to do with them"; it is the judgment of woman that they have nothing to do with.

The impetus behind this radical move is twofold. First, it is supported by the experience of feminist scholars in other fields of inquiry. Over and over, feminists have found it necessary, in seeking to reinstate women as agents and as subjects, to question the very canons of their fields. They have turned their attention, accordingly, to the operation of patriarchal bias on ever deeper levels of social structure, even of language and thought.

But the possibility of extending the feminist critique into the foundations of scientific thought is created by recent developments in the history and philosophy of science itself. As long as the course of scientific thought was judged to be exclusively determined by its own logical and empirical necessities, there could be no place for any signature, male or otherwise, in that system of knowledge. Furthermore, any suggestion of gender differences in our thinking about the world could argue only too readily for the further exclusion of women from science. But as the philosophical and historical inadequacies of the classical conception of science have become more evident, and as historians and sociologists have begun to identify the ways in which the development of scientific knowledge has been shaped by its particular social and political context, our understanding of science as a social process has grown. This understanding is a necessary prerequisite, both politically and intellectually, for a feminist theoretic in science.

Joining feminist thought to other social studies of science brings the promise of radically new insights, but it also adds to the existing intellectual danger a political threat. The intellectual danger resides in viewing science as pure social product; science then dissolves into ideology and objectivity loses all intrinsic meaning. In the resulting cultural relativism, any emancipatory function of modern science is negated, and the arbitration of truth recedes into the political domain. Against this background, the temptation arises for feminists to abandon their claim for representation in scientific culture and, in its place, to invite a return to a purely "female" subjectivity, leaving rationality and objectivity in the male domain, dismissed as products of a purely male consciousness. . . .

Many authors have addressed the problems raised by total relativism; here I wish merely to mention some of the special problems added by its feminist variant. They are several. In important respects, feminist relativism is just the kind of radical move that transforms the political spectrum into a circle. By rejecting objectivity as a masculine ideal, it simultaneously lends its voice to an enemy chorus and dooms women to residing outside of the realpolitik modern culture; it exacerbates the very problem it wishes to solve. It also nullifies the radical potential of feminist criticism for our understanding of science. As I see it, the task of a feminist theoretic in science is twofold: to distinguish that which is parochial from that which is universal in the scientific impulse, reclaiming for women what has historically been denied to them; and to legitimate those elements of scientific culture that have been denied precisely because they are defined as female.

It is important to recognize that the framework inviting what might be called the nihilist retreat is in fact provided by the very ideology of objectivity we wish to escape. This is the ideology that asserts an opposition between (male) objectivity and (female) subjectivity and denies the possibility of mediation between the two. A first step, therefore, in extending the feminist critique to the foundations of scientific thought is to reconceptualize objectivity as a dialectical process so as to allow for the possibility of distinguishing the objective effort from the objectivist illusion.

Rather than abandon the quintessential human effort to understand the world in rational terms, we need to refine that effort. To do this, we need to add to the familiar methods of rational and empirical inquiry the additional process of critical self-reflection. Following Piaget's injunction, we need to "become conscious of self." In this way we can become conscious of the features of the scientific project that belie its claim to universality.

The ideological ingredients of particular concern to feminists are found where objectivity is linked with autonomy and masculinity, and in turn, the goals of science with power and domination. The linking of objectivity with social and political autonomy has been examined by many authors and shown to serve a variety of important political functions. The implications of joining objectivity with masculinity are less well understood. This conjunction also serves critical political functions. But an understanding of the sociopolitical meaning of the entire constellation requires an examination of the psychological processes through which these connections become internalized and perpetuated. Here psychoanalysis offers us an invaluable perspective, and it is to the exploitation of that perspective that much of my own work has been directed. In an earlier paper, . . . [I sought] to understand the ways in which our earliest experiences—experiences in large part determined by the socially structured relationships that form the context of our developmental processes—help to shape our conception of the world and our characteristic orientation to it. . . . In brief, I argued the following: Our early maternal environment, coupled with the cultural definition of masculine (that which can never appear feminine) and of autonomy (that which can never be compromised by dependency) leads to the association of female with the pleasures and dangers of merging, and of male with the comfort and loneliness of separateness. The boy's internal anxiety about both self and gender is echoed by the more widespread cultural anxiety, thereby encouraging postures of autonomy and masculinity, which can, indeed may, be designed to defend against that anxiety and the longing that generates it. Finally, for all of us, our sense of reality is carved out of the same developmental matrix. As Piaget and others have emphasized, the capacity for cognitive distinction between self and other (objectivity) evolves concurrently and interdependently with the development of psychic autonomy; our cognitive ideals thereby become subject to the same psychological influences as our emotional and gender ideals. Along with autonomy, the very act of separating subject from object—objectivity itself—comes to be associated with masculinity. The combined psychological and cultural pressures lead all three ideals—affective, gender, and cognitive—to a mutually reinforcing process of exaggeration and rigidification. The net result is the entrenchment of an objectivist ideology and a correlative devaluation of (female) subjectivity.

This analysis leaves out many things. Above all it omits discussion of the psychological meanings of power and domination.

In his work *The Domination of Nature* William Leiss observes, "The necessary correlate of domination is the consciousness of subordination in those who must obey the will of another; thus properly speaking only other men can be the objects of domination." (Or women, we might add.) Leiss infers from this observation that it is not the domination of physical nature we should worry about but the use of our knowledge of physical nature as an instrument for the domination of human nature. He therefore sees the need for correctives, not in science but in its uses. This is his point of departure from other authors of the Frankfurt school, who assume the very logic of science to be the logic of domination. I agree with Leiss's basic observation but draw a somewhat different inference. I suggest that the impulse toward domination does find expression in the goals (and even in the theories and practice) of modern science, and argue that where it finds such expression the impulse needs to be acknowledged as projection. In short, I argue that not only in the denial of interaction between subject and other but also in the access of domination to the goals of scientific knowledge, one finds the intrusion of a self we begin to recognize as partaking in the cultural construct of masculinity.

The value of consciousness is that it enables us to make choices—both as individuals and as scientists. Control and domination are in fact intrinsic neither to selfhood (i.e., autonomy) nor to scientific knowledge. I want to suggest, rather, that the particular emphasis western science has placed on these functions of knowledge is twin to the objectivist ideal. Knowledge in general, and scientific knowledge in particular, serves two gods: power and transcendence. It aspires alternately to mastery over and union with nature. Sexuality serves the same two gods, aspiring to domination and ecstatic communion—in short, aggression and eros. And it is hardly a new insight to say that power, control, and domination are fueled largely by aggression, while union satisfies a more purely erotic impulse.

To see the emphasis on power and control so prevalent in the rhetoric of western science as projection of a specifically male consciousness requires no great leap of the imagination. Indeed, that perception has become a commonplace. Above all, it is invited by the rhetoric that conjoins the domination of nature with the insistent image of nature as female, nowhere more familiar than in the writings of Francis Bacon. For Bacon, knowledge and power are one, and the promise of science is expressed as "leading to you Nature with all her children to bind her to your service and make her your slave," by means that do not "merely exert a gentle guidance over nature's course; they have the power to conquer and subdue her, to shake her to her foundations." In the context of the Baconian vision, Bruno Bettelheim's conclusion appears inescapable: "Only with phallic psychology did aggressive manipulation of nature become possible...."

The presence of contrasting themes, of a dialectic between aggressive and erotic impulses, can be seen both within the work of individual scientists and, even more dramatically, in the juxtaposed writings of different scientists. Francis Bacon provides us with one model; there are many others. For an especially striking contrast, consider a contemporary scientist who insists on the importance of "letting the material speak to you," of allowing it to "tell you what to do next"—one who chastises other scientists for attempting to "impose an answer" on what they see. For this scientist, discovery is facilitated by becoming "part of the system," rather than remaining outside; one must have a "feeling for the organism." It is true that the author of these remarks is not only from a different epoch and a different field (Bacon himself was not actually a scientist by most standards), she is also a woman. It is also true that there are many reasons, some of which I have already suggested, for thinking that gender (itself constructed in an ideological context) actually does make a difference in scientific inquiry. Nevertheless, my point here is that neither science nor individuals are totally bound by ideology. In fact, it is not difficult to find similar sentiments expressed by male scientists. Consider, for example, the following remarks: "I have often had cause to feel that my hands are cleverer than my head. That is a crude way of characterizing the dialectics of experimentation. When it is going well, it is like a quiet conversation with Nature." The difference between conceptions of science as "dominating" and as "conversing with" nature may not be a difference primarily between epochs, nor between the sexes. Rather it can be seen as representing a dual theme played out in the work of all scientists, in all ages. But the two poles of this dialectic do not appear with equal weight in the history of science. What we therefore need to attend to is the evolutionary process that selects one theme as dominant.

Elsewhere I have argued for the importance of a different selection process. In part, scientists are themselves selected by the emotional appeal of particular (stereotypic) images of science. Here I am arguing for the importance of selection within scientific thought—first of preferred methodologies and aims, and finally of preferred theories. The two processes are not unrelated. While stereotypes are not binding (i.e., they do not describe all or perhaps any individuals), and this fact creates the possibility for an ongoing contest within science, the first selection process undoubtedly influences the outcome of the second. That is, individuals drawn by particular ideology will tend to select themes consistent with that ideology.

One example in which this process is played out on a theoretical level is in the fate of interactionist theories in the history of biology. Consider the contest that has raged throughout this century between organismic and particulate views of cellular organization—between what might be described as hierarchical and nonhierarchical theories. Whether the debate is over the primacy of the nucleus or the cell as a whole, the genome or the cytoplasm, the proponents of hierarchy have won out. One geneticist has described the conflict in explicitly political terms:

Two concepts of genetic mechanisms have persisted side by side throughout the growth of modern genetics, but the emphasis has been very strongly in favor of one of these.... The first of these we will designate as the "Master Molecule" concept. . . . This is in essence the Theory of the Gene, interpreted to suggest a totalitarian government. . . . The second concept we will designate as the "Steady State" concept. By this term . . . we envision a dynamic self-perpetuating organization of a variety of molecular species which owes its specific properties not to the characteristic of any one kind of molecule, but to the functional interrelationships of these molecular species.

Soon after these remarks, the debate between "master molecules" and dynamic interactionism was foreclosed by the synthesis provided by DNA and the "central dogma." With the success of the new molecular biology such "steady state" (or egalitarian) theories lost interest for almost all geneticists. But today, the same conflict shows signs of reemerging—in genetics, in theories of the immune system, and in theories of development.

I suggest that method and theory may constitute a natural continuum, despite Popperian claims to the contrary, and that the same processes of selection may bear equally and simultaneously on both the means and aims of science and the actual theoretical descriptions that emerge. I suggest this in part because of the recurrent and striking consonance that can be seen in the way scientists work, the relation they take to their object of study, and the theoretical orientation they favor. To pursue the example cited earlier, the same scientist who allowed herself to become "part of the system," whose investigations were guided by a "feeling for the organism," developed a paradigm that diverged as radically from the dominant paradigm of her field as did her methodological style.

In lieu of the linear hierarchy described by the central dogma of molecular biology, in which DNA encodes and transmits all instruction for the unfolding of a living cell, her research yielded a view of the DNA in delicate interaction with the cellular environment—an organismic view. For more important than the genome as such (i.e., the DNA) is the "overall organism." As she sees it, the genome functions "only in respect to the environment in which it is found." In this work the program encoded by the DNA is itself subject to change. No longer is a master control to be found in a single component of the cell; rather, control resides in the complex interactions of the entire system. When first presented, the work underlying this vision was not understood, and it was poorly received. Today much of that work is undergoing a renaissance, although it is important to say that her full vision remains too radical for most biologists to accept.

This example suggests that we need not rely on our imagination for a vision of what a different science—a science less restrained by the impulse to dominate—might be like. Rather, we need only look to the thematic pluralism in the history of our own science as it has evolved. Many other examples can be found, but we lack an adequate understanding of the full range of influences that lead to the acceptance or rejection not only of particular theories but of different theoretical orientations. What I am suggesting is that if certain theoretical interpretations have been selected against, it is precisely in this process of selection that ideology in general, and a masculinist ideology in particular, can be found to effect its influence. The task this implies for a radical feminist critique of science is, then, first a historical one, but finally a transformative one. In the historical effort, feminists can bring a whole new range of sensitivities, leading to an equally new consciousness of the potentialities lying latent in the scientific project.

RICHARD FEYNMAN
Seeking New Laws of Nature

RICHARD FEYNMAN *(1918–1988) was a professor of physics at California Institute of Technology. In 1945 he was declared mentally deficient for service in the U.S. Army. In 1965 he won the Nobel Prize in physics. He was also well known for his abilities with the bongo drums.*

WHAT I want to talk about in this lecture is not, strictly speaking, the character of physical law. One might imagine at least that one is talking about nature when one is talking about the character of physical law; but I do not want to talk about nature, but rather about how we stand relative to nature now. I want to tell you . . . what there is to guess, and how one goes about guessing. Someone suggested that it would be ideal if, as I went along, I would slowly explain how to guess a law, and then end by creating a new law for you. I do not know whether I shall be able to do that. . . .

In general we look for a new law by the following process. First we guess it. Then we compute the consequences of the guess to see what would be implied if this law that we guessed is right. Then we compare the result of the computation to nature with experiment or experience, compare it directly with observation, to see if it works. If it disagrees with experiment it is wrong. In that simple statement is the key to science. It does not make any difference how beautiful your guess is. It does not make any difference how smart you are, who made the guess, or what his name is—if it disagrees with experiment it is wrong. That is all there is to it. It is true that one has to check a little to make sure that it is wrong, because whoever did the experiment may have reported incorrectly, or there may have been some feature in the experiment that was not noticed, some dirt or something; or

the man who computed the consequences, even though it may have been the one who made the guesses, could have made some mistake in the analysis. These are obvious remarks, so when I say if it disagrees with experiment it is wrong, I mean after the experiment has been checked, the calculations have been checked, and the thing has been rubbed back and forth a few times to make sure that the consequences are logical consequences from the guess, and that in fact it disagrees with a very carefully checked experiment.

This will give you a somewhat wrong impression of science. It suggests that we keep on guessing possibilities and comparing them with experiment, and this is to put experiment into a rather weak position. In fact experimenters have a certain individual character. They like to do experiments even if nobody has guessed yet, and they very often do their experiments in a region in which people know the theorist has not made any guesses. For instance, we may know a great many laws, but do not know whether they really work at high energy, because it is just a good guess that they work at high energy. Experimenters have tried experiments at higher energy, and in fact every once in a while experiment produces trouble; that is, it produces a discovery that one of the things we thought right is wrong. In this way experiment can produce unexpected results, and that starts us guessing again. One instance of an unexpected result is the mu meson and its neutrino, which was not guessed by anybody at all before it was discovered, and even today nobody yet has any method of guessing by which this would be a natural result.

You can see, of course, that with this method we can attempt to disprove any definite theory. If we have a definite theory, a real guess, from which we can conveniently compute consequences which can be compared with experiment, then in principle we can get rid of any theory. There is always the possibility of proving any definite theory wrong; but notice that we can never prove it right. Suppose that you invent a good guess, calculate the consequences, and discover every time that the consequences you have calculated agree with experiment. The theory is then right? No, it is simply not proved wrong. In the future you could compute a wider range of consequences, there could be a wider range of experiments, and you might then discover that the thing is wrong. That is why laws like Newton's laws for the motion of planets last such a long time. He guessed the law of gravitation, calculated all kinds of consequences for the system and so on, compared them with experiment—and it took several hundred years before the slight error of the motion of Mercury was observed. During all that time the theory had not been proved wrong, and could be taken temporarily to be right. But it could never be proved right, because tomorrow's experiment might succeed in proving wrong what you thought was right. We never are definitely right, we can only be sure we are wrong. However, it is rather remarkable how we can have some ideas which will last so long.

One of the ways of stopping science would be only to do experiments in the region where you know the law. But experimenters search most diligently, and with the greatest effort, in exactly those places where it seems most likely that we can prove our theories wrong. In other words we are trying to prove ourselves wrong as quickly as possible, because only in that way can we find progress. For example, today among ordinary low energy phenomena we do not know where to look for trouble, we think everything is all right, and so there is no particular big programme looking for trouble in nuclear reactions, or in

super-conductivity. In these lectures I am concentrating on discovering fundamental laws. The whole range of physics, which is interesting, includes also an understanding at another level of these phenomena like super-conductivity and nuclear reactions, in terms of the fundamental laws. But I am talking now about discovering trouble, something wrong with fundamental laws, and since among low energy phenomena nobody knows where to look, all the experiments today in this field of finding out a new law, are of high energy.

Another thing I must point out is that you cannot prove a vague theory wrong. If the guess that you make is poorly expressed and rather vague, and the method that you use for figuring out the consequences is a little vague—you are not sure, and you say, "I think everything's right because it's all due to so and so, and such and such do this and that more or less, and I can sort of explain how this works . . . ," then you see that this theory is good, because it cannot be proved wrong! Also if the process of computing the consequences is indefinite, then with a little skill any experimental results can be made to look like the expected consequences. You are probably familiar with that in other fields. "A" hates his mother. The reason is, of course, because she did not caress him or love him enough when he was a child. But if you investigate you find out that as a matter of fact she did love him very much, and everything was all right. Well then, it was because she was over-indulgent when he was a child! By having a vague theory it is possible to get either result. The cure for this one is the following. If it were possible to state exactly, ahead of time, how much love is not enough, and how much love is over-indulgent, then there would be a perfectly legitimate theory against which you could make tests. It is usually said when this is pointed out, "When you are dealing with psychological matters things can't be defined so precisely." Yes, but then you cannot claim to know anything about it.

You will be horrified to hear that we have examples in physics of exactly the same kind. We have these approximate symmetries, which work something like this. You have an approximate symmetry, so you calculate a set of consequences supposing it to be perfect. When compared with experiment, it does not agree. Of course—the symmetry you are supposed to expect is approximate, so if the agreement is pretty good you say, "Nice!," while if the agreement is very poor you say, "Well, this particular thing must be especially sensitive to the failure of the symmetry." Now you may laugh, but we have to make progress in that way. When a subject is first new, and these particles are new to us, this jockeying around, this "feeling" way of guessing at the results, is the beginning of any science. The same thing is true of the symmetry proposition in physics as is true of psychology, so do not laugh too hard. It is necessary in the beginning to be very careful. It is easy to fall into the deep end by this kind of vague theory. It is hard to prove it wrong, and it takes a certain skill and experience not to walk off the plank in the game. . . .

Because I am a theoretical physicist, and more delighted with this end of the problem, I want now to concentrate on how to make the guesses.

As I said before, it is not of any importance where the guess comes from; it is only important that it should agree with experiment, and that it should be as definite as possible. "Then," you say, "that is very simple. You set up a machine, a great computing machine, which has a random wheel in it that makes a succession of guesses, and each time it guesses a hypothesis about how nature should work it computes immediately the consequences, and makes a comparison with a list of experimental results it has at the other end." In other words, guessing is a dumb man's job. Actually it is quite the opposite, and I will try to explain why.

The first problem is how to start. You say, "Well I'd start off with all the known principles." But all the principles that are known are inconsistent with each other, so something has to be removed. We get a lot of letters from people insisting that we ought to make holes in our guesses. You see, you make a hole, to make room for a new guess. Somebody says, "You know, you people always say that space is continuous. How do you know when

you get to a small enough dimension that there really are enough points in between, that it isn't just a lot of dots separated by little distances?" Or they say, "You know those quantum mechanical amplitudes you told me about, they're so complicated and absurd, what makes you think those are right? Maybe they aren't right." Such remarks are obvious and are perfectly clear to anybody who is working on this problem. It does not do any good to point this out. The problem is not only what might be wrong but what, precisely, might be substituted in place of it. In the case of the continuous space, suppose the precise proposition is that space really consists of a series of dots, and that the space between them does not mean anything, and that the dots are in a cubic array. Then we can prove immediately that this is wrong. It does not work. The problem is not just to say something might be wrong, but to replace it by something—and that is not so easy. As soon as any really definite idea is substituted it becomes almost immediately apparent that it does not work.

The second difficulty is that there is an infinite number of possibilities of these simple types. It is something like this. You are sitting working very hard, you have worked for a long time trying to open a safe. Then some Joe comes along who knows nothing about what you are doing, except that you are trying to open the safe. He says "Why don't you try the combination 10:20:30?" Maybe you know already that the middle number is 32, not 20. Maybe you know as a matter of fact that it is a five-digit combination. . . . So please do not send me any letters trying to tell me how the thing is going to work. I read them—I always read them to make sure that I have not already thought of what is suggested—but it takes too long to answer them, because they are usually in the class "try 10:20:30." As usual, nature's imagination far surpasses our own, as we have seen from the other theories which are subtle and deep. To get such a subtle and deep guess is not so easy. One must be really clever to guess, and it is not possible to do it blindly by machine.

I want to discuss now the art of guessing nature's laws. It is an art. How is it done? One way you might suggest is to look at history to see how the other guys did it. So we look at history.

We must start with Newton. He had a situation where he had incomplete knowledge, and he was able to guess the laws by putting together ideas which were all relatively close to experiment; there was not a great distance between the observations and the tests. That was the first way, but today it does not work so well.

The next guy who did something great was Maxwell, who obtained the laws of electricity and magnetism. What he did was this. He put together all the laws of electricity, due to Faraday and other people who came before him, and he looked at them and realized that they were mathematically inconsistent. In order to straighten it out he had to add one term to an equation. He did this by inventing for himself a model of idler wheels and gears and so on in space. He found what the new law was—but nobody paid much attention because they did not believe in the idler wheels. We do not believe in the idler wheels today, but the equations that he obtained were correct. So the logic may be wrong but the answer is right.

In the case of relativity the discovery was completely different. There was an accumulation of paradoxes; the known laws gave inconsistent results. This was a new kind of thinking, a thinking in terms of discussing the possible symmetries of laws. It was especially difficult, because for the first time it was realized how long something like Newton's laws could seem right, and still ultimately be wrong. Also it was difficult to accept that ordinary ideas of time and space, which seemed so instinctive, could be wrong.

Quantum mechanics was discovered in two independent ways—which is a lesson. There again, and even more so, an enormous number of paradoxes were discovered experimentally, things that absolutely could not be explained in any way by what was known. It was not that the knowledge was incomplete, but that the knowledge was too complete. Your prediction was that this should happen—it did not. The two different routes were one by Schrödinger, who guessed the equation, the other by Heisenberg, who argued that you must analyze what is measurable. These two different philosophical methods led to the same discovery in the end.

More recently, the discovery of the laws of the weak decay I spoke of, when a neutron disintegrates into a proton, an electron and an antineutrino—which are still only partly known—add up to a somewhat different situation. This time it was a case of incomplete knowledge, and only the equation was guessed. The special difficulty this time was that the experiments were all wrong. How can you guess the right answer if, when you calculate the result, it disagrees with experiment? You need courage to say the experiments must be wrong. I will explain where that courage comes from later.

Today we have no paradoxes—maybe. We have this infinity that comes in when we put all the laws together, but the people sweeping the dirt under the rug are so clever that one sometimes thinks this is not a serious paradox. Again, the fact that we have found all these particles does not tell us anything except that our knowledge is incomplete. I am sure that history does not repeat itself in physics, as you can tell from looking at the examples I have given. The reason is this. Any schemes—such as "think of symmetry laws," or "put the information in mathematical form," or "guess equations"—are known to everybody now, and they are all tried all the time. When you are struck, the answer cannot be one of these, because you will have tried these right away. There must be another way next time. Each time we get into this log-jam of too much trouble, too many problems, it is because the methods that we are using are just like the ones we have used before. The next scheme, the new discovery, is going to be made in a completely different way. So history does not help us much. . . .

It is not unscientific to make a guess, although many people who are not in science think it is. Some years ago I had a conversation with a layman about flying saucers— because I am scientific I know all about flying saucers! I said "I don't think there are flying saucers." So my antagonist said, "Is it impossible that there are flying saucers? Can you prove that there are flying saucers? Can you prove that it's impossible?" "No," I said, "I can't prove it's impossible. It's just very unlikely." At that he said, "You are very unscientific. If you can't prove it impossible then how can you say that it's unlikely?" But that is the way that *is* scientific. It is scientific only to say what is more likely and what is less likely, and not to be proving all the time the possible and impossible. To define what I mean, I might have said to him, "Listen, I mean that from my knowledge of the world that I see around me, I think, that it is much more likely that the reports of flying saucers are the results of the known irrational characteristics of terrestrial intelligence than of the unknown rational efforts of extraterrestrial intelligence." It is just more likely, that is all. It is a good guess. And we always try to guess the most likely explanation, keeping in the back of the mind the fact that if it does not work we must discuss the other possibilities. . . .

That reminds me of another point, that the philosophy or ideas around a theory may change enormously when there are very tiny changes in the theory. For instance, Newton's ideas about space and time agreed with experiment very well, but in order to get the correct motion of the orbit of Mercury, which was a tiny, tiny difference, the difference in the character of the theory needed was enormous. The reason is that Newton's laws were so simple and so perfect, and they produced definite results. In order to get something that would produce a slightly different result it had to be completely different. In stating a new law you cannot make imperfections on a perfect thing; you have to have another perfect thing. So the difference in philosophical ideas between Newton's and Einstein's theories of gravitation are enormous.

What are these philosophies? They are really tricky ways to compute consequences quickly. A philosophy, which is sometimes called an understanding of the law, is simply a way that a person hold the laws in his mind in order to guess quickly at consequences. Some people have said, and it is true in cases like Maxwell's equations, "Never mind the philosophy, never mind anything of this kind, just guess the equations. The problem is only to compute the answers so that they agree with experiment, and it is not necessary to have a philosophy, or argument, or words, about the equation." That is good in the sense

that if you only guess the equation you are not prejudicing yourself, and you will guess better. On the other hand, maybe the philosophy helps you to guess. It is very hard to say.

For those people who insist that the only thing that is important is that the theory agrees with experiment, I would like to imagine a discussion between a Mayan astronomer and his student. The Mayans were able to calculate with great precision predictions, for example, for eclipses and for the position of the moon in the sky, the position of Venus, etc. It was all done by arithmetic. They counted a certain number and subtracted some numbers, and so on. There was no discussion of what the moon was. There was no discussion even of the idea that it went around. They just calculated the time when there would be an eclipse, or when the moon would rise at the full, and so on. Suppose that a young man went to the astronomer and said, "I have an idea. Maybe those things are going around, and there are balls of something like rocks out there, and we could calculate how they move in a completely different way from just calculating what time they appear in the sky." "Yes," says the astronomer, "and how accurately can you predict eclipses?" He says, "I haven't developed the thing very far yet." Then says the astronomer, "Well, we can calculate eclipses more accurately than you can with your model, so you must not pay any attention to your idea because obviously the mathematical scheme is better." There is a very strong tendency, when someone comes up with an idea and says, "Let's suppose that the world is this way," for people to say to him, "What would you get for the answer to such and such a problem?" And he says, "I haven't developed it far enough." And they say, "Well, we have already developed it much further, and we can get the answers very accurately." So it is a problem whether or not to worry about philosophies behind ideas.

Another way of working, of course, is to guess new principles. In Einstein's theory of gravitation he guessed, on top of all the other principles, the principle that corresponded to the idea that the forces are always proportional to the masses. He guessed the principle that if you are in an accelerating car you cannot distinguish that from being in a gravitational field, and by adding that principle to all the other principles, he was able to deduce the correct laws of gravitation.

That outlines a number of possible ways of guessing. I would now like to come to some other points about the final result. First of all, when we are all finished, and we have a mathematical theory by which we can compute consequences, what can we do? It really is an amazing thing. In order to figure out what an atom is going to do in a given situation we make up rules with marks on paper, carry them into a machine which has switches that open and close in some complicated way, and the result will tell us what the atom is going to do! If the way that these switches open and close were some kind of model of the atom, if we thought that the atom had switches in it, then I would say that I understood more or less what is going on. I find it quite amazing that it is possible to predict what will happen by mathematics, which is simply following rules which really have nothing to do with what is going on in the original thing. The closing and opening of switches in a computer is quite different from what is happening in nature.

One of the most important things in this "guess—compute consequences—compare with experiment" business is to know when you are right. It is possible to know when you are right way ahead of checking all the consequences. You can recognize truth by its beauty and simplicity. It is always easy when you have made a guess, and done two or three little calculations to make sure that it is not obviously wrong, to know that it is right—at least if you have any experience—because usually what happens is that more comes out than goes in. Your guess is, in fact, that something is very simple. If you cannot see immediately that it is wrong, and it is simpler than it was before, then it is right. The inexperienced, and crackpots, and people like that, make guesses that are simple, but you can immediately see that they are wrong, so that does not count. Others, the inexperienced students, make guesses that are very complicated, and it sort of looks as if it is all right, but I know it is not true because the truth always turns out to be simpler than you thought.

What we need is imagination, but imagination in a terrible straitjacket. We have to find a new view of the world that has to agree with everything that is known, but disagree in its predictions somewhere, otherwise it is not interesting. And in that disagreement it must agree with nature. If you can find any other view of the world which agrees over the entire range where things have already been observed, but disagrees somewhere else, you have made a great discovery. It is very nearly impossible, but not quite, to find any theory which agrees with experiments over the entire range in which all theories have been checked, and yet gives different consequences in some other range, even a theory whose different consequences do not turn out to agree with nature. A new idea is extremely difficult to think of. It takes a fantastic imagination.

What of the future of this adventure? What will happen ultimately? We are going along guessing the laws; how many laws are we going to have to guess? I do not know. Some of my colleagues say that this fundamental aspect of our science will go on; but I think there will certainly not be perpetual novelty, say for a thousand years. This thing cannot keep on going so that we are always going to discover more and more new laws. If we do, it will become boring that there are so many levels one underneath the other. It seems to me that what can happen in the future is either that all the laws become known—that is, if you had enough laws you could compute consequences and they would always agree with experiment, which would be the end of the line—or it may happen that the experiments get harder and harder to make, more and more expensive, so you get 99.9 per cent of the phenomena, but there is always some phenomenon which has just been discovered, which is very hard to measure, and which disagrees; and as soon as you have the explanation of that one there is always another one, and it gets slower and slower and more and more uninteresting. That is another way it may end. But I think it has to end in one way or another.

We are very lucky to live in an age in which we are still making discoveries. It is like the discovery of America—you only discover it once. The age in which we live is the age in which we are discovering the fundamental laws of nature, and that day will never come again. It is very exciting, it is marvellous, but this excitement will have to go. Of course in the future there will be other interests. There will be the interest of the connection of one level of phenomena to another—phenomena in biology and so on, or, if you are talking about exploration, exploring other planets, but there will not still be the same things that we are doing now.

Another thing that will happen is that ultimately, if it turns out that all is known, or it gets very dull, the vigorous philosophy and the careful attention to all these things that I have been talking about will gradually disappear. The philosophers who are always on the outside making stupid remarks will be able to close in, because we cannot push them away by saying, "If you were right we would be able to guess all the rest of the laws," because when the laws are all there they will have an explanation for them. For instance, there are always explanations about why the world is three-dimensional. Well, there is only one world, and it is hard to tell if that explanation is right or not, so that if everything were known there would be some explanation about why those were the right laws. But that explanation would be in a frame that we cannot criticize by arguing that type of reasoning will not permit us to go further. There will be a degeneration of ideas, just like the degeneration that great explorers feel is occurring when tourists begin moving in on a territory.

In this age people are experiencing a delight, the tremendous delight that you get when you guess how nature will work in a new situation never seen before. From experiments and information in a certain range you can guess what is going to happen in a region where no one has ever explored before. It is a little different from regular exploration in that there are enough clues on the land discovered to guess what the land that has not been discovered is going to look like. These guesses, incidentally, are often very different from what you have already seen—they take a lot of thought.

What is it about nature that lets this happen, that it is possible to guess from one part what the rest is going to do? That is an unscientific question: I do not know how to answer it, and therefore I am going to give an unscientific answer. I think it is because nature has a simplicity and therefore a great beauty.

SANDRA HARDING

An Epistemological Problem for Feminism

SANDRA HARDING *is a philosopher who teaches at the University of California (Los Angeles). Her book* Whose Science? Whose Knowledge? *argues for tying science and scientific research to the needs of all the world's peoples. This excerpt is from a series of essays on feminist epistemology and the philosophy of science.*

Harding, Sandra, "An Epistemological Problem for Feminism" from Garry and Pearsal, ed. *Women, Knowledge, and Reality,* pp. 190–192. Copyright © 1996. Reproduced by permission of Routledge, Inc., part of The Taylor & Francis Group, LLC.

FEMINISM is a political movement for social change. Viewed from the perspective of the assumptions of science's self-understanding, "feminist knowledge," "feminist science," and "feminist philosophy of science" should be contradictions in terms. Scientific knowledge-seeking is supposed to be value-neutral, objective, dispassionate, and disinterested. It is supposed to be protected from political interests by the norms of science. These norms are said to include commitments to, and well-tested sociological and logical methods for, maintaining rigid separations between the goals of "special-interest" political movements (as feminism is often perceived) and the conduct of scientific research. Of course, few people familiar with the history or practices of science really believe these sociological and logical norms have ever been effective. Nevertheless, for better or worse, appeal to these norms serves as a resource to justify whatever social relations and logical habits the scientific community in fact practices.

However, some social scientists and biologists have made claims that clearly have been produced through research guided by feminist concerns. Many of these claims appear more plausible (better supported, more reliable, less false, more likely to be confirmed by evidence, etc.) than the beliefs they would replace. These claims appear to increase the objectivity of our understandings of nature and social life. I alluded to some of these claims earlier—the ones about the evolutionary importance of gathering activities and of female activities more generally, about the social construction of families and of sexualities, and so forth. (While one need not find any particular claim more plausible than the beliefs it would replace, one must find *some* such feminist-inspired claim or other more plausible, less false, more likely to be confirmed by evidence, etc. in order to enter the discourse of this essay. It is the justification of this kind of claim that is at issue. If you cannot find *any* scientific claim generated by feminist-inspired research to be reasonable, then do not waste your time reading further!)

These claims raise fundamental epistemological questions. How can politicized inquiry be increasing the objectivity of our explanations and understandings? On what grounds should these claims be justified? What are the accounts of the processes of objective inquiry that will explain the apparently bizarre phenomenon of politically guided research producing more adequate explanations, less biased results of inquiry? An examination of the reports of this research reveals two main justificational strategies. Each of these responses to the epistemological questions has its virtues and its problems. Each also reveals more clearly than have other critiques the problems in the "parental discourse" on which each draws.

FEMINIST EMPIRICISM

The argument here is that it is social biases—sexism and androcentrism—that are responsible for the false claims that have been made in biology and the social sciences. Sexism and androcentrism are prejudices that arise from false beliefs (ones that originate in superstition, custom, ignorance, or miseducation) and from hostile attitudes. They enter research particularly at the stage of the identification of scientific problems, but also in the design of research and the collection and interpretation of evidence. Researchers can eliminate sexism and androcentrism by stricter adherence to the existing methodological norms of inquiry. It is "bad science" that is responsible for the sexist and androcentric results of research. Movements for social liberation "make it possible for people to see the world in an enlarged perspective because they remove the covers and blinders that obscure knowledge and observation" (Millman and Kanter). Thus the women's movement creates the opportunity for such an enlarged perspective. Furthermore, the women's movement creates more women scientists and more feminist scientists (both male and female feminists) who are more likely than are sexists to notice androcentric biases. These considerations explain how it is that this kind of politically guided research can produce less biased results.

This epistemology has great strengths. Its appeal is obvious: many of the claims emerging from feminist research in biology and the social sciences are capable of accumulating better empirical support than the claims they replace. This research better meets the overt standards of "good science" than do the purportedly gender-blind studies. Should not the weight of this empirical support be valued more highly than the ideal of "value-neutrality" that was advanced, we are told, only in order to increase empirical support for hypotheses? It is not that all feminist claims are automatically preferable because they are feminist; rather, when the results of such research show good empirical support, the fact that they were produced through politically guided research should not count against them. Moreover, feminist empiricism leaves intact empiricist understandings of the principles of scientific inquiry that are *de rigeur* for most practicing natural and social scientists. It appears to challenge only the incomplete way empiricism has been practiced, not the norms of empiricism themselves: science bereft of feminist guidance does not rigorously enough adhere to its own norms. Furthermore, one can appeal to historical precedents to increase the plausibility of this kind of claim. After all, wasn't it the bourgeois revolution of the fifteenth to seventeenth centuries that made it possible for early modern thinkers to see the world in an enlarged perspective, because this great social revolution from feudalism to modernism removed the covers and blinders that obscured earlier knowledge-seeking and observation? Wasn't the proletarian revolution of the late nineteenth and early twentieth centuries responsible for yet one more leap in the objectivity of knowledge claims as it permitted an understanding of the effects of class relations on social relations and on our beliefs? Doesn't the post-1960s deconstruction of European and U.S. colonialism have positive effects on the growth of scientific knowledge? From this perspective, the contemporary women's movement is bringing about the most recent of these revolutions, each of which moves us yet closer to achieving the goals of the creators of science.

CHAPTER FOUR

WHICH SHOULD I BELIEVE: DARWIN OR GENESIS?

In July 1925, a young teacher named John Scopes was brought to trial in Dayton, Tennessee, in one of the most celebrated court cases of the century. Assisting the prosecution was William Jennings Bryan, who had run for the presidency in 1896 and who is still regarded by many as the greatest orator in this country's history. Defending Scopes was Clarence Darrow, the most famous criminal lawyer of his generation. Reporters swarmed from all over the country to the small southern town, and the trial soon became the showcase for a national debate. What was at issue was not a shocking murder or a scandalous political crime, but rather whether Scopes would be permitted to teach Charles Darwin's theory of evolution in the Tennessee public schools.

It will surprise many of you to learn that the debate over teaching evolutionary theory in the public schools has been going on for so long. Philosophers have been interested in the controversy for a number of reasons. It raises issues about the nature of science and about the relationship between science and religion. It also forces us to think about the responsibilities of public education.

Many religions have accounts of creation. You are probably already familiar with at least one of the creation accounts in the Bible. In some religions in India, the sky, the air, and the earth were understood as gods created by Aditi, a female goddess. In the Hindu religion, Brahma created himself along with other gods and men; he placed a golden egg into the ocean, and out of the egg hatched Brahma himself, who then divided into two to create the heavens and the earth. Religious liberals often take such accounts as metaphorical, or even as mythical. But a literal reading of scriptural or other accounts of creation will usually be incompatible with Darwin's evolutionary account. This incompatibility has fueled a continuing controversy between religious conservatives who are committed to a literal reading of creation stories and those who are committed to evolutionary theory. To understand this controversy, we must first see why scientists are so wedded to evolutionary accounts.

Nature seems to embody purpose. Animals have two eyes because two is the minimum number to enable them to see depth, and therefore to judge distance. Giraffes' long necks enable them to eat the leaves from the tall trees in their natural habitat. The delicate balance of hormones in your body enables it to adjust to changes in your environment, in everything from digestion to reproduction, and helps you to get around in the world. How could such delicate and complicated mechanisms arise by mere chance? Evolutionary theory offers the following kind of explanation. Among members of an animal population, there will be small individual differences. (The mechanisms of genetic mutation were not known in Darwin's time, but they obviously provide an explanation of how such differences can arise.) Some of these differences will be advantageous to the organism, either because it will be better equipped to survive and reproduce or because its social structure will be better equipped (as with bees). Other differences will make either the individual organism or the social structure less likely to survive and reproduce. The differences that are advantageous will be genetically transmitted more often because the organisms that have those differences will survive and reproduce more; the differences that are not advantageous will be transmitted less often. Over the course of millions of years, species will therefore evolve in the direction of increasing adaptation to their environment. In the simplest cases, giraffes with longer necks will eat better, and hence reproduce more often, than short-necked giraffes; consequently, giraffes as a species will gradually become longer necked. In a more complicated way, the same account explains the origin of two eyes instead of one, and of complex hormonal and metabolic pathways to deal with complicated interactions between an organism and its environment. The result of all this theorizing is that the *purpose* in nature gets explained without supposing that there is a creator who is arranging for his or her purpose to be met.

Evolutionary theory is not the only theory that works in this way. There are countless others. For example, in a "properly working" free capitalistic market, just the right amount of copper will be mined to serve the needs of the population. Nobody in the government needs to decide how much copper to mine; indeed, if anybody tries to, he or she will almost certainly do worse than if nobody thinks about it. It is as though there is an "invisible hand" guiding the individual decisions that people make for it to turn out that just the right amount of copper is produced. But market theory explains how the free market and the so-called law of supply and demand bring this about without guidance or control by any outside force.

Even though such explanations allow us to avoid the assumption of outside forces, such as God, they do not require us to do so. Economists can consistently believe that God directs the day-to-day workings of the market; undoubtedly some do. Similarly, some biologists believe that God directs the day-to-day workings of evolution. Others believe that at creation, God set in motion the initial laws of nature, including the mechanisms of evolution, and left them to run by themselves for all of time. Others do not believe in God at all. Evolutionary theory does not require that we choose between these kinds of alternatives. The conflict enters when we look at the details of some religious creation accounts.

For example, both of the creation stories from Genesis that are in this chapter describe the creation all at once of fully developed species. Moreover, they describe this creation in a time frame of several thousand years, rather than the many millions of years required by the Darwinian account of creation. It is not the religious viewpoint in general that is incompatible with the evolutionary point of view, but rather the details of particular literal interpretations of religious doctrines.

One focus for the tension between these frameworks is in the teaching in school (usually high school) of accounts of creation. Many conservative religious figures who take creation accounts literally nevertheless believe that it is on the basis of *faith*, not evidence, that such accounts are to be accepted. Other scientific creationists believe that the literal biblical account of creation is backed by scientific evidence and that the creationist account should thus be taught in science classes as an alternative to the evolutionary account. This has sparked a brisk debate on what exactly counts as science and what doesn't. Some of that debate is reproduced in this chapter.

The book of Genesis contains the Judeo-Christian creation accounts that most of the current controversy centers around. Notice that in Chapters 1 and 2 of Genesis there are actually *two* stories of creation that differ from one another, particularly in the order of creation that is given. Thus, it is inaccurate to speak simply of *the* biblical account. Rather one must speak of the account of Chapter 1 or the account of Chapter 2.

About the middle of the nineteenth century, several biologists arrived independently at the notion of an evolutionary theory to explain the origin of biological adaptation. Darwin became the best known of these. Between 1831 and 1836 he traveled around the world on the ship *The Beagle;* in the course of that voyage he made many of the observations that gave a richness of detail to his theoretical account. In 1859 he published *The Origin of Species,* the book that launched evolutionary theory. Later, in 1871, *The Descent of Man* was published. In it he responded to a number of critics, revised his views on a number of points, and expanded his account to talk in greater detail about the origin of humans. The selection here is from that book.

Because the U.S. Constitution establishes a clear separation between religion and government, the courts have prohibited the teaching of religious views in public schools. But many advocates of a literal reading of the biblical account have argued not on religious but on scientific grounds. They claim that evolutionary theory is itself bad science and that an unbiased, truly scientific look at the evidence will favor creationist views. Among their charges are that evolutionary theory is circular and not subject to the experimental method, that it stands against God and hence itself embodies a religious viewpoint, that it violates well-accepted scientific doctrine, and that it is not as well supported as creationism by the fossil record. Duane T. Gish, perhaps the primary contemporary spokesperson for creationist science, wrote the article included in this chapter, in which all of these claims are spelled out and defined.

In his article, Philip Kitcher responds to Gish's charges, discussing in detail the issue of the fossil record and some of the particulars of the empirical claims of creationist science. Next, Michael Ruse, an established critic of creationism, shocked many of his colleagues in a 1993 address to a scientific meeting by suggesting that evolutionary theory, like creationism, is based on articles of faith (articles which he believes are superior to creationists' articles of faith). He went on to suggest that scientists have been afraid to speak this truth in public for fear that it will be misappropriated by courts and school systems in order to put creationism in the public school curriculum. His address also illustrates the less formal style that philosophers sometimes adopt when they are giving talks.

We include in this chapter a selection from Texas philosopher Cory Juhl, who argues a sophisticated version of the complexity theory that is often used in the Intelligent Design "argument against evolution." Finally, Daniel Dennett issues a challenge to the defenders of Creation Science and Intelligent Design: show me the evidence.

THE BIBLE

Genesis

The book of Genesis is the opening book of the Old Testament of THE BIBLE. The word genesis, means "beginning." Most religious scholars believe that the accounts recorded in Genesis were compiled by a number of different people.

CHAPTER 1

IN the beginning God created the heaven and the earth.

2 And the earth was without form, and void; and darkness *was* upon the face of the deep. And the Spirit of God moved upon the face of the waters.

3 And God said, Let there be light: and there was light.

4 And God saw the light, that *it was* good: and God divided the light from the darkness.

5 And God called the light Day, and the darkness he called Night. And the evening and the morning were the first day.

6 And God said, Let there be a firmament in the midst of the waters, and let it divide the waters from the waters.

7 And God made the firmament, and divided the waters which *were* under the firmament from the waters which *were* above firmament: and it was so.

8 And God called the firmament Heaven. And the evening and the morning were the second day.

9 And God said, Let the waters under the heaven be gathered together unto one place, and let the dry *land* appear: and it was so.

10 And God called the dry *land* Earth; and the gathering together of the waters called he Seas: and God saw that *it was* good.

11 And God said, Let the earth bring forth grass, the herb yielding seed, *and* the fruit tree yielding fruit after his kind, whose seed *is* in itself, upon the earth: and it was so.

12 And the earth brought forth grass, *and* herb yielding seed after his kind, and the tree yielding fruit, whose seed *was* in itself, after his kind: and God saw *it was* good.

13 And the evening and the morning were the third day.

14 And God said, Let there be lights in the firmament of the heaven to divide the day from the night; and let them be for signs, and for seasons, and for days, and years:

15 And let them be for lights in the firmament of the heaven to give light upon the earth: and it was so.

16 And God made two great lights; the greater light to rule the day, and the lesser light to rule the night: *he made* the stars also.

17 And God set them in the firmament of the heaven to give light upon the earth,

18 And to rule over the day and over the night, and to divide the light from the darkness: and God saw that *it was* good.

19 And the evening and the morning were the fourth day.

20 And God said, Let the waters bring forth abundantly the moving creature that hath life, and fowl *that* may fly above the earth in the open firmament of heaven.

21 And God created great whales, and every living creature that moveth, which the waters brought forth abundantly, after their kind, and every winged fowl after his kind: and God saw that *it was* good.

22 And God blessed them, saying, Be fruitful, and multiply, and fill the waters in the seas, and let fowl multiply in the earth.

23 And the evening and the morning were the fifth day.

24 And God said, Let the earth bring forth the living creature after his kind, cattle, and creeping thing, and beast of the earth after his kind: and it was so.

25 And God made the beast of the earth after his kind, and cattle after their kind, and every thing that creepeth upon the earth after his kind: and God saw that *it was* good.

26 And God said, Let us make man in our image, after our likeness: and let them have dominion over the fish of the sea, and over the fowl of the air, and over the cattle, and over all the earth, and over every creeping thing that creepeth upon the earth.

27 So God created man in his *own* image, in the image of God created he him; male and female created he them.

28 And God blessed them, and God said unto them, Be fruitful, and multiply, and replenish the earth, and subdue it: and have dominion over the fish of the sea, and over the fowl of the air, and over every living thing that moveth upon the earth.

29 And God said, Behold, I have given you every herb bearing seed, which *is* upon the face of all the earth, and every tree, in the which *is* the fruit of a tree yielding seed; to you it shall be for meat.

30 And to every beast of the earth, and to every fowl of the air, and to every thing that creepeth upon the earth, wherein *there is* life, *I have given* every green herb for meat: and it was so.

31 And God saw every thing that he had made, and, behold, *it was* very good. And the evening and the morning were the sixth day.

CHAPTER 2

Thus the heavens and the earth were finished, and all the host of them.

2 And on the seventh day God ended his work which he had made; and he rested on the seventh day from all his work which he had made.

3 And God blessed the seventh day, and sanctified it: because that in it he had rested from all his work which God created and made.

4 These *are* the generations of the heavens and of the earth when they were created, in the day that the LORD God made the earth and the heavens

5 And every plant of the field before it was in the earth, and every herb of the field before it grew: for the LORD God had not caused it to rain upon the earth, and *there was* not a man to till the ground.

6 But there went up a mist from the earth, and watered the whole face of the ground.

7 And the LORD God formed man *of* the dust of the ground, and breathed into his nostrils the breath of life; and man became a living soul.

8 And the LORD God planted a garden eastward in Eden; and there he put the man whom he had formed.

9 And out of the ground made the LORD God to grow every tree that is pleasant to sight, and good for food; the tree of life also in the midst of the garden, and the tree of knowledge of good and evil.

10 And a river went out of Eden to water the garden; and from thence it was parted, and became into four heads.

11 The name of the first *is* Pí-son: that *is* it which compasseth the whole land of Haí-i-lah, where *there* is gold;

12 And the gold of that land *is* good: there *is* bdellium and the onyx stone.

13 And the name of the second river *is* Gíhon: the same *is* it that compasseth the whole land of E-thi-ó-pi-a.

14 And the name of the third river *is* Hid'-de-kel: that *is* it which goeth toward the east of Assyria. And the fourth river *is* Eu-phrá-tes.

15 And the LORD God took the man, and put him into the garden of Eden to dress it and keep it.

16 And the LORD God commanded the man, saying, Of every tree of the garden thou mayest freely eat:

17 But of the tree of the knowledge of good and evil, thou shalt not eat of it: for in the day that thou eatest thereof thou shalt surely die.

18 And the LORD God said, *It is* not good that the man should be alone; I will make him an help meet for him.

19 And out of the ground the LORD God formed every beast of the field, and every fowl of the air; and brought *them* unto Adam to see what he would call them: and whatsoever Adam called every living creature, that *was* the name thereof.

20 And Adam gave names to all cattle, and to the fowl of the air, and to every beast of the field; but for Adam there was not found an help meet for him.

21 And the LORD God caused a deep sleep to fall upon Adam, and he slept: and he took

one of his ribs, and closed up the flesh instead thereof;

22 And the rib which the LORD God had taken from man, made he a woman, and brought her unto the man.

23 And Adam said, This *is* now bone of my bones, and flesh of my flesh: she shall be called Woman, because she was taken out of Man.

24 Therefore shall a man leave his father and his mother, and shall cleave unto his wife: and they shall be one flesh.

25 And they were both naked, the man and his wife, and were not ashamed.

CHARLES DARWIN
The Descent of Man

CHARLES DARWIN *(1809–1882) was an English naturalist whose theory of evolution formed the basis for modern evolutionary theory. He suffered most of his life from poor health; he was a reclusive man who shied away from the controversy that raged even then over the conflict between evolutionary theory and some religious doctrines.*

NATURAL Selection.—We have now seen that man is variable in body and mind; and that the variations are induced, either directly or indirectly, by the same general causes, and obey the same general laws, as with the lower animals. Man has spread widely over the face of the earth, and must have been exposed, during his incessant migrations, to the most diversified conditions. The inhabitants of Tierra del Fuego, the Cape of Good Hope, and Tasmania in the one hemisphere, and of the Arctic regions in the other, must have passed through many climates, and changed their habits many times, before they reached their present homes. The early progenitors of man must also have tended, like all other animals, to have increased beyond their means of subsistence; they must, therefore, occasionally have been exposed to a struggle for existence, and consequently to the rigid law of natural selection. Beneficial variations of all kinds will thus, either occasionally or habitually, have been preserved and injurious ones eliminated. I do not refer to strongly marked deviations of structure, which occur only at long intervals of time, but to mere individual differences. We

Darwin, Charles, "The Descent of Man" from *The Descent of Man*, A. L. Burt Publishers, 1874.

know, for instance, that the muscles of our hands and feet, which determine our powers of movement, are liable, like those of the lower animals, to incessant variability. If then the progenitors of man inhabiting any district, especially one undergoing some change in its conditions, were divided into two equal bodies, the one-half which included all the individuals best adapted by their powers of movement for gaining subsistence, or for defending themselves, would on an average survive in greater numbers, and procreate more offspring than the other and less well endowed half.

Man in the rudest state in which he now exists is the most dominant animal that has ever appeared on this earth. He has spread more widely than any other highly organized form: and all others have yielded before him. He manifestly owes this immense superiority to his intellectual faculties, to his social habits, which lead him to aid and defend his fellows, and to his corporeal structure. The supreme importance of these characters has been proved by the final arbitrament of the battle for life. Through his powers of intellect, articulate language has been evolved; and on this his wonderful advancement has mainly depended. As Mr. Chauncey Wright remarks: "a psychological analysis of the faculty of language shows, that even the smallest proficiency in it might require more brain power than the greatest proficiency in any other direction." He has invented and is able to use various weapons, tools, traps, etc., with which he defends himself, kills or catches prey, and otherwise obtains food. He has made rafts or canoes for fishing or crossing over to neighboring fertile islands. He has discovered the art of making fire, by which hard and stringy roots can be rendered innocuous. This discovery of fire, probably the greatest ever made by man, excepting language, dates from before the dawn of history. These several inventions, by which man in the rudest state has become so preeminent, are the direct results of the development of his powers of observation, memory, curiosity, imagination, and reason. I cannot, therefore, understand how it is that Mr. Wallace maintains, that "natural selection could only have endowed the savage with a brain a little superior to that of an ape."

Although the intellectual powers and social habits of man are of paramount importance to him, we must not underrate the importance of his bodily structure, to which subject the remainder of this chapter will be devoted. . . .

If it be an advantage to man to stand firmly on his feet and to have his hands and arms free, of which, from his preeminent success in the battle of life, there can be no doubt, then I can see no reason why it should not have been advantageous to the progenitors of man to have become more and more erect or bipedal. They would thus have been better able to defend themselves with stones or clubs, to attack their prey, or otherwise to obtain food. The best built individuals would in the long run have succeeded best and survived in larger numbers. If the gorilla and a few allied forms had become extinct, it might have been argued, with great force and apparent truth, that an animal could not have been gradually converted from a quadruped into a biped, as all the individuals in an intermediate condition would have been miserably ill-fitted for progression. But we know (and this is well worthy of reflection) that the anthropomorphous apes are now actually in an intermediate condition; and no one doubts that they are on the whole well adapted for their conditions of life. Thus the gorilla runs with a sidelong shambling gait, but more commonly progresses by resting on its bent hands. The long-armed apes occasionally use their arms like crutches, swinging their bodies forward between them, and some kinds of Hylobates, without having been taught, can walk or run upright with tolerable quickness; yet they move awkwardly and much less securely than man. We see, in short, in existing monkeys a manner of progression intermediate between that of a quadruped and a biped; but, as an unprejudiced judge insists, the anthropomorphous apes approach in structure more nearly to the bipedal than to the quadrupedal type.

As the progenitors of man became more and more erect, with their hands and arms more and more modified for prehension and other purposes, with their feet and legs at the same time transformed for firm support and progression, endless other changes of structure would have become necessary. The pelvis would have to be broadened, the spine peculiarly curved, and the head fixed in an altered position, all of which changes have been attained by man. . . .

The free use of the arms and hands, partly the cause and partly the result of man's erect position, appears to have led in an indirect manner to other modifications of structure. The early male forefathers of man were, as previously stated, probably furnished with great canine teeth; but as they gradually acquired the habit of using stones, clubs, or other weapons for fighting with their enemies or rivals they would use their jaws and teeth less and less. In this case the jaws, together with the teeth, would become reduced in size, as we may feel almost sure from innumerable analogous cases. In a future chapter we shall meet with a closely parallel case in the reduction or complete disappearance of the canine teeth in male ruminants, apparently in relation with the development of their horns; and in horses in relation to their habits of fighting with their incisor teeth and hoofs. . . .

Another most conspicuous difference between man and the lower animals is the nakedness of his skin. Whales and porpoises (Cetacea), dugongs (Sirenia) and the hippopotamus are naked; and this may be advantageous to them for gliding through the water; nor would it be injurious to them from the loss of warmth, as the species which inhabit the colder regions are protected by a thick layer of blubber, serving the same purposes as the fur of seals and otters. Elephants and rhinoceroses are almost hairless; and as certain extinct species, which formerly lived under an Arctic climate, were covered with long wool or hair, it would almost appear as if the existing species of both genera had lost their hairy covering from exposure to heat. This appears the more probable, as the elephants in India which live on elevated and cool districts are more hairy than those on the lowlands. May we then infer that man became divested of hair

from having aboriginally inhabited some tropical land? That the hair is chiefly retained in the male sex on the chest and face, and in both sexes at the junction of all four limbs with the trunk, favors this inference—on the assumption that the hair was lost before man became erect; for the parts which now retain most hair would then have been most protected from the heat of the sun. The crown of the head, however, offers a curious exception, for at all times it must have been one of the most exposed parts, yet is thickly clothed with hair. The fact, however, that the other members of the order of Primates, to which man belongs, although inhabiting various hot regions, are well clothed with hair, generally thickest on the upper surface, is opposed to the supposition that man became naked through the action of the sun. Mr. Belt believes that within the tropics it is an advantage to man to be destitute of hair, as he is thus enabled to free himself of the multitude of ticks (acari) and other parasites, with which he is often infested, and which sometimes cause ulceration. But whether this evil is of sufficient magnitude to have led to the denudation of his body through natural selection, may be doubted, since none of the many quadrupeds inhabiting the tropics have, as far as I know, acquired any specialized means of relief. The view which seems to me the most probable is that man, or rather primarily woman, became divested of hair for ornamental purposes, as we shall see under Sexual Selection; and, according to this belief, it is not surprising that man should differ so greatly in hairiness from all other Primates, for characters, gained through sexual selection, often differ to an extraordinary degree in closely related forms. . . .

I have now endeavored to show that some of the most distinctive characters of man have in all probability been acquired, either directly, or more commonly indirectly, through natural selection. We should bear in mind that modifications in structure or constitution which do not serve to adapt an organism to its habits of life, to the food which it consumes, or passively to the surrounding conditions, cannot have been thus acquired. We must not, however, be too confident in deciding what modifications are of service to each being; we should remember how little we know about the use of many parts, or what changes in the blood or tissues may serve to fit an organism for a new climate or new kinds of food. Nor must we forget the principle of correlation, by which, as Isidore Geoffroy has shown in the case of man, many strange deviations of structure are tied together. Independently of correlation, a change in one part often leads, through the increased or decreased use of other parts, to other changes of a quite unexpected nature. It is also well to reflect on such facts, as the wonderful growth of galls on plants caused by the poison of an insect, and on the remarkable changes of color in the plumage of parrots when fed on certain fishes, or inoculated with the poison of toads; for we can thus see that the fluids of the system, if altered for some special purpose, might induce other changes. We should especially bear in mind that modifications acquired and continually used during past ages for some useful purpose, would probably become firmly fixed, and might be long inherited.

Thus a large yet undefined extension may safely be given of natural selection; but I now admit, after reading the essay by Nägeli on plants, and the remarks by various authors with respect to animals, more especially those recently made by Prof. Broca, that in the earlier editions of my "Origin of Species" I perhaps attributed too much to the action of natural selection or the survival of the fittest. I have altered the fifth edition of the "Origin" so as to confine my remarks to adaptive changes of structure; but I am convinced, from the light gained during even the last few years, that very many structures which now appear to us as useless, will hereafter be proved to be useful, and will therefore come within the range of natural selection. Nevertheless, I did not formerly consider sufficiently the existence of structures, which, as far as we can at present judge, are neither beneficial nor injurious; and this I believe to be one of the greatest oversights as yet detected in my work. I may be permitted to say, as some excuse, that I had two distinct objects in view; firstly, to show that

species had not been separately created, and secondly, that natural selection had been the chief agent of change, though largely aided by the inherited effects of habit, and slightly by the direct action of the surrounding conditions. I was not, however, able to annul the influence of my former belief, then almost universal, that each species had been purposely created; and this led to my tacit assumption that every detail of structure, excepting rudiments, was of some special though unrecognized, service. Any one with this assumption in his mind would naturally extend too far the action of natural selection, either during past or present times. Some of those who admit the principle of evolution, but reject natural selection, seem to forget, when criticizing my book, that I had the above two objects in view; hence, if I have erred in giving to natural selection great power, which I am very far from admitting, or in having exaggerated its power, which is in itself probable, I have at least, as I hope, done good service in aiding to overthrow the dogma of separate creations. . . .

Conclusion.—In this chapter we have seen that as man at the present day is liable, like every other animal, to multiform individual differences or slight variations, so no doubt were the early progenitors of man; the variations being formerly induced by the same general causes, and governed by the same general and complex laws as at present. As all animals tend to multiply beyond their means of subsistence, so it must have been with the progenitors of man; and this would inevitably lead to a struggle for existence and to natural selection. The latter process would be greatly aided by the inherited effects of the increased use of parts, and these two processes would incessantly react on each other. It appears, also, as we shall hereafter see, that various unimportant characters have been acquired by man through sexual selection. An unexplained residuum of change must be left to the assumed uniform action of those unknown agencies, which occasionally induce strongly marked and abrupt deviations of structure in our domestic productions.

Judging from the habits of savages and of the greater number of the Quadrumana, primeval men, and even their ape-like progenitors, probably lived in society. With strictly social animals, natural selection sometimes acts on the individual, through the preservation of variations which are beneficial to the community. A community which includes a large number of well-endowed individuals increases in number, and is victorious over other less favored ones; even although each separate member gains no advantage over the others of the same community. Associated insects have thus acquired many remarkable structures, which are of little or no service to the individual, such as the pollen-collecting apparatus, or the sting of the worker-bee, or the great jaws of soldier-ants. With the higher social animals, I am not aware that any structure has been modified solely for the good of the community, though some are of secondary service to it. For instance, the horns of ruminants and the great canine teeth of baboons appear to have been acquired by the males as weapons for sexual strife, but they are used in defense of the herd or troop. In regard to certain mental powers the case, as we shall see in the fifth chapter, is wholly different; for these faculties have been chiefly, or even exclusively, gained for the benefit of the community, and the individuals thereof have at the same time gained an advantage indirectly.

It has often been objected to such views as the foregoing, that man is one of the most helpless and defenseless creatures in the world; and that during his early and less well developed condition he would have been still more helpless. The Duke of Argyll, for instance, insists that "the human frame has diverged from the structure of brutes in the direction of greater physical helplessness and weakness. That is to say, it is a divergence which of all others it is most impossible to ascribe to mere natural selection." He adduces the naked and unprotected state of the body, the absence of great teeth or claws for defense, the small strength and speed of man, and his slight power of discovering food or of avoiding danger by smell. To these deficiencies there might be added one still more serious, namely, that he cannot climb quickly and so escape from enemies. The loss of hair would not have been a great injury to the inhabitants of a warm country. For we know that the unclothed Fuegians can exist under a wretched climate. When we compare the defenseless state of man with that of apes we must remember that the great canine teeth with which the latter are provided are possessed in their full development by the males alone, and are chiefly used by them for fighting with the rivals; yet the females, which are not thus provided, manage to survive.

In regard to bodily size or strength, we do not know whether man is descended from some small species, like the chimpanzee, or from one as powerful as the gorilla; and, therefore, we cannot say whether man has become larger and stronger, or smaller and weaker than his ancestors. We should, however, bear in mind that an animal possessing great size, strength, and ferocity, and which, like the gorilla, could defend itself from all enemies, would not perhaps have become social: and this would most effectually have checked the acquirement of the higher mental qualities, such as sympathy and the love of his fellows. Hence it might have been an immense advantage to man to have sprung from some comparatively weak creature.

The small strength and speed of man, his want of natural weapons, etc., are more than counterbalanced, firstly, by his intellectual powers, through which he has formed for himself weapons, tools, etc., though still remaining in a barbarous state, and secondly, by his social qualities which lead him to give and receive aid from his fellow-men. No country in the world abounds in a greater degree with dangerous beasts than Southern Africa; no country presents more fearful physical hardships than the Arctic regions; yet one of the puniest of races, that of the Bushmen, maintains itself in Southern Africa, as do the dwarfed Esquimaux in the Arctic regions. The ancestors of man were, no doubt, inferior in intellect, and probably in social disposition to the lowest existing savages; but it is quite conceivable that they might have existed, or even flourished, if they had advanced in intellect, while gradually losing their brute-like powers, such as that of climbing trees, etc.

But these ancestors would not have been exposed to any special danger, even if far more helpless and defenseless than any existing savages, had they inhabited some warm continent or large island, such as Australia, New Guinea, or Borneo, which is now the home of the orang. And natural selection arising from the competition of tribe with tribe in some such large area as one of these, together with the inherited effects of habit, would, under favorable conditions, have sufficed to raise man to his present high position on the organic scale.

DUANE T. GISH
Creationist Science and Education

DUANE T. GISH (b. 1921) received his Ph.D. in biochemistry from the University of California. He has been a National Institute of Health fellow and has held a number of research positions. He is currently senior vice president of the Institute for Creation Research, founded by Henry Morris, in El Cajon, California.

IT is commonly believed that the theory of evolution is the only scientific explanation of origins and that the theory of special creation is based solely on religious beliefs. It is further widely accepted that the theory of evolution is supported by such a vast body of scientific evidence, while encountering so few contradictions, that evolution should be accepted as an established fact. As a consequence, it is maintained by many educators that the theory of evolution should be accepted as an established fact. As a consequence, it is maintained by many educators that the theory of evolution should be included in science textbooks as the sole explanation for origins but that the theory of special creation, if taught at all, must be restricted to social science courses.

As a matter of fact, neither evolution nor creation qualifies as a scientific theory. Furthermore, it is become increasingly apparent that there are a number of irresolvable contradictions between evolution theory and the facts of science, and that the mechanism postulated for the evolutionary process could account for no more than trivial changes.

It would be well at this point to define what we mean by creation and evolution. By *Creation* we are referring to the theory that the universe and all life forms came into existence by the direct creative acts of a Creator external to and independent of the natural universe. It is postulated that the basic plant and animal kinds were separately created, and that any variation or speciation that has occurred since creation has been limited within the circumscribed boundaries of these created kinds. It is further postulated that the earth has suffered at least one great worldwide catastrophic event or flood which would account for the mass death, destruction, and extinction found on such a monumental scale in geological deposits.

"Creationist Science and Education" by Dr. Duane T. Gish as it appeared in *Philosophy and Contemporary Issues* edited by J. Barra and M. Goldinger, pp. 458–470. © 1984. Institute for Creation Research.

By *Evolution* we are referring to the General Theory of Evolution. This is the theory that all living things have arisen by naturalistic, mechanistic processes from a single primeval cell, which in turn had arisen by similar processes from a dead, inanimate world. This evolutionary process is postulated to have occurred over a period of many hundreds of millions of years. It is further postulated that all major geological formations can be explained by present processes acting essentially at present rates without resort to any world-wide catastrophe(s).

Creation has not been observed by human witnesses. Since creation would have involved unique, unrepeatable historical events, creation is not subject to the experimental method. Furthermore, creation as a theory is non-falsifiable. That is, it is impossible to conceive an experiment that could disprove the possibility of creation. Creation thus does not fulfill the criteria of a scientific theory. That does not say anything about its ultimate validity, of course. Furthermore, creation theory can be used to correlate and explain data, particularly that available from the fossil record, and is thus subject to test in the same manner that other alleged historical events are subject to test—by comparison with historical evidence.

Evolution theory also fails to meet the criteria of a scientific theory. Evolution has never been witnessed by human observers; evolution is not subject to the experimental method; and as formulated by present-day evolutionists, it has become non-falsifiable.

It is obvious that no one has ever witnessed the type of evolutionary changes postulated by the general theory of evolution. No one, for example, witnessed the origin of the universe or the origin of life. No one has ever seen a fish evolve into an amphibian, nor has anyone observed an ape evolve into a man. No one, as a matter of fact, has ever witnessed a significant evolutionary change of any kind.

The example of the peppered moth in England has been cited by such authorities as H. B. D. Kettlewell and Sir Gavin De Beer as the most striking evolutionary change ever witnessed by man. Prior to the industrial revolution in England, the peppered moth, *Biston betularia,* consisted predominantly of a light-colored variety, with a dark-colored form comprising a small minority of the population. This was so because predators (birds) could more easily detect the dark-colored variety as these moths rested during the day on light-covered rocks. With the onset of the industrial revolution and resultant air pollution, the tree trunks and rocks became progressively darker. As a consequence, the dark-colored variety of moths became more and more difficult to detect, while the light-colored variety ultimately became an easy prey. Birds, therefore, began eating more light-colored than dark-colored moths, and today over 95% of the peppered moths in the industrial areas of England are of the darker-colored variety.

Although, as noted above, this shift in populations of peppered moths has been described as the most striking example of evolution ever observed by man, it is obvious that no significant evolutionary change of any kind has occurred among these peppered moths, certainly not the type required to substantiate the general theory of evolution. For however the populations may have shifted in their proportions of the light and dark forms, all of the moths remained from beginning to end peppered moths, *Biston betularia.* It seems evident, then, that if this example is the most striking example of evolution witnessed by man, no real evolution of any kind has ever been observed.

The world-famous evolutionist, Theodosis Dobzhansky, while endeavoring to proclaim his faith in evolution, admitted that no real evolutionary change has ever been observed by man when he said, ". . . the occurrence of the evolution of life in the history of the earth is established about as well as events *not witnessed by human observers can be.*" It can be said with certainty, then, that evolution in the present world has never been observed. It remains as far outside the pale of human observation as the origin of the universe or the origin of life. Evolution has been *postulated* but *never observed.*

Since evolution cannot be observed, it is not amenable to the methods of experimental science.

This has been acknowledged by Dobzhansky when he stated, "These evolutionary happenings are unique, unrepeatable, and irreversible. It is as impossible to turn a land vertebrate into a fish as it is to effect the reverse transformation. The applicability of the experimental method to the study of such unique historical processes is severely restricted before all else by the time intervals involved, which far exceed the lifetime of any human experimenter. And yet it is just such *impossibility* that is demanded by antievolutionists when they ask for 'proofs' of evolution which they would magnanimously accept as satisfactory."

Please note that Dobzhansky has said that the applicability of the experimental method to the study of evolution is an impossibility! It is obvious, then, that evolution fails to qualify as a scientific theory, for it is certain that a theory that cannot be subjected to experimental test is not a scientific theory.

Furthermore, modern evolution theory has become so plastic, it is non-falsifiable. It can be used to prove anything and everything. Thus, Murray Eden, a professor at Massachusetts Institute of Technology and an evolutionist, has said, with reference to the falsifiability of evolution theory, "This cannot be done in evolution, taking it in its broad sense, and this is really all I meant when I called it tautologous in the first place. It can, indeed, explain anything. You may be ingenious or not in proposing a mechanism which looks plausible to human beings and mechanisms which are consistent with other mechanisms which you have discovered, but it is still an unfalsifiable theory."

Paul Ehrlich and L. C. Birch, biologists at Stanford University and the University of Sydney, respectively, have said, "Our theory of evolution has become . . . one which cannot be refuted by any possible observations. Every conceivable observation can be fitted into it. It is thus 'outside of empirical science' but not necessarily false. No one can think of ways in which to test it. Ideas, either without basis or based on a few laboratory experiments carried out in extremely simplified systems, have attained currency far beyond their validity. They have become

part of an evolutionary dogma accepted by most of us as part of our training."

Some evolutionists have been candid enough to admit that evolution is really no more scientific than is creation. In an article in which he states his conviction that the modern neo-Darwinian theory of evolution is based on axioms, Harris says ". . . the axiomatic nature of the neo-Darwinian theory places the debate between evolutionists and creationists in a new perspective. Evolutionists have often challenged creationists to provide experimental proof that species have been fashioned *de novo*. Creationists have often demanded that evolutionists show how chance mutations can lead to adaptability, or to explain why natural selection allows apparently detrimental organs to persist. We may now recognize that either challenge is fair. If the neo-Darwinian theory is axiomatic, it is not valid for creationists to demand proof of the axioms, and it is not valid for evolutionists to dismiss special creation as unproved so long as it is stated as an axiom."

In his introduction to a 1971 edition of Charles Darwin's *Origin of Species,* Matthews states, "In accepting evolution as a fact, how many biologists pause to reflect that science is built upon theories that have been proved by experiment to be correct, or remember that the theory of animal evolution has never been thus proved? . . . The fact of evolution is the backbone of biology, and biology is thus in the peculiar position of being a science founded on an unproved theory—is it then a science or a faith? Belief in the theory of evolution is thus exactly parallel to belief in creation—both are concepts which believers know to be true but neither, up to the present, has been capable of proof."

It can be seen from the above discussion, taken from the scientific literature published by leading evolutionary authorities, that evolution has never been observed and is outside the limits of experimental science. Evolution theory is, therefore, no more scientific than creation theory. That does not make it necessarily false, and it can be tested in the same way that creation theory can be tested—by its ability to correlate and explain historical data, that is, the fossil record. Furthermore, since evolution is supposed to have occurred by processes still operating today, the theory must not contradict natural laws.

Evolutionists protest, of course, that these weaknesses of evolution as a theory are not necessarily due to weaknesses of the theory, per se, but are inherent in the very nature of the evolutionary process. It is claimed that the evolutionary process is so slow that it simply cannot be observed during the lifetime of a human experimenter, or, as a matter of fact, during the combined observations of all recorded human experience. Thus, as noted above, Dobzhansky is incensed that creationists should demand that evolution be subjected to the experimental method before any consideration could be given to evolution as an established process.

It must be emphasized, however, that it is for precisely this reason that evolutionists insist that creation must be excluded from science textbooks or, for that matter, from the whole realm of science, as a viable alternative evolution. They insist that creation must be excluded from possible consideration as a scientific explanation for origins because creation theory cannot be tested by the experimental method. It is evident, however, that this is a characteristic that it shares in common with evolution theory. Thus, if creation must be excluded from science texts and discussions, then evolution must likewise be excluded.

Evolutionists insist that, in any case, the teaching of the creation model would constitute the teaching of religion because creation requires a Creator. The teaching about the creation model and the scientific evidence supporting it, however, can be done without reference to any religious literature. Furthermore, belief in evolution is as intrinsically religious as is belief in creation.

If creation must be excluded from science in general and from science textbooks and science classrooms in particular because it involves the supernatural, it is obvious that theistic evolution must be excluded for exactly the same reason. Thus the only theory that can be taught according to this reasoning, and in fact, the only theory that is being taught in almost all public schools

and universities and in the texts they use, is a purely mechanistic, naturalistic, and thus atheistic, theory of evolution. But atheism, the antithesis of theism, is itself a religious belief.

The late Sir Julian Huxley, British evolutionist and biologist, has said that "Gods are peripheral phenomena produced by evolution." What Huxley meant was that the idea of God merely evolved as man evolved from lower animals. Huxley desired to establish a humanistic religion based on evolution. Humanism has been defined as "the belief that man shapes his own destiny. It is a constructive philosophy, a *non-theistic religion,* a way of life." This same publication quotes Huxley as saying. "I use the word 'Humanist' to mean someone who believes that man is just as much a natural phenomenon as an animal or plant; that his body, mind, and soul were not supernaturally created but are products of *evolution,* and that he is not under the control or guidance of any supernatural being or beings, but has to rely on himself and his own powers." The inseparable link between this non-theistic humanistic religion and belief in evolution is evident.

George Gaylord Simpson, Professor of Vertebrate Paleontology at Harvard University until his retirement and one of the world's best-known evolutionists, has said that the Christian faith, which he calls the "higher superstition" (in contrast to the "lower superstition" of pagan tribes of South America and Africa) is intellectually unacceptable. Simpson concludes his book, *Life of the Past,* with what Sir Julian Huxley has called "a splendid assertion of evolutionist view of man." "Man," Simpson writes, "stands alone in the universe, a unique product of a long, unconscious, impersonal, material process with unique understanding and potentialities. These he owes to no one but himself, and it is to himself that he is responsible. He is not the creature of uncontrollable and undeterminable forces, but his own master. He can and must decide and manage his own destiny."

Thus, according to Simpson, man is alone in the Universe (there is no God), he is the result of an impersonal, unconscious process (no one directed his origin or creation), and he is his own master and must manage his own destiny (there is no God to determine man's destiny). That, according to Simpson and Huxley, is the evolutionist's view of man. That this is the philosophy held by most biologists has been recently emphasized by Dobzhansky. In his review of Monod's book, *Chance and Necessity,* Dobzhansky said, "He has stated with admirable clarity, and eloquence often verging on pathos, the mechanistic materialist philosophy shared by most of the present 'establishment' in the biological science."

No doubt a majority of the scientific community embraces the mechanistic materialistic philosophy of Simpson, Huxley, and Monod. Many of these men are highly intelligent, and they have woven the fabric of evolution theory in an ingenious fashion. They have then combined this evolution theory with humanistic philosophy and have clothed the whole with the term "science." The product, a non-theistic religion, with evolutionary philosophy as its creed under the guise of "science," is being taught in most public schools, colleges and universities of the United States. It has become our unofficial state-sanctioned religion.

Furthermore, a growing number of scientists are becoming convinced that there are basic contradictions between evolution theory and empirical scientific data as well as known scientific laws. On the other hand, these scientists believe special creation provides an excellent model for explaining the correlating data related to origins which is free of such contradictions. Even some evolutionists are beginning to realize that the formulations of modern evolution theory are really incapable of explaining anything and that an adequate scientific theory of evolution, if ever attainable, must await the discovery of as yet unknown natural laws.

The core of modern evolution theory, known as the neo-Darwinian theory of evolution, or the modern synthetic theory, is the hypothesis that the evolutionary process has occurred through natural selection of random mutational changes in the genetic material, selection being in accordance with alterations in the environment. Natural selection, itself, is not a chance process, but the material it must act on, mutant genes, is produced by random, chance processes.

It is an astounding fact that while at the time Darwin popularized it, the concept of natural selection seemed to explain so much, today there is a growing realization that the presently accepted concept of natural selection really explains nothing. It is a mere tautology, that is, it involves circular reasoning.

In modern theory, natural selection is defined in terms of differential reproduction. In fact, according to Lewontin, differential reproduction *is* natural selection. When it is asked, what survives, the answer is, the fittest. But when it is asked, what are the fittest, the answer is, those that survive! Natural selection thus collapses into a tautology, devoid of explanatory value. It is not possible to explain *why* some varieties live to reproduce more offspring—it is only known that they do.

In discussing Richard Levins' concept of fitness set analysis, Hamilton stated, "This criticism amounts to restating what I think is the admission of most evolutionists, that we do not yet know what natural selection maximizes." Now if evolutionists do not know what natural selection maximizes, they do not know what natural selection selects.

In a review of the thinking in French scientific circles, it was stated, "Even if they do not publicly take a definite stand, almost all French specialists hold today strong mental reservations as to the validity of natural selection." Creationists maintain that indeed natural selection could not result in increased complexity or convert a plant or animal into another basic kind. It can only act to eliminate the unfit.

Macbeth has recently published an especially incisive criticism of evolution theory and of the concept of natural selection as used by evolutionists. He points out that although evolutionists have abandoned classical Darwinism, the modern synthetic theory they have proposed as a substitute is equally inadequate to explain progressive change as a result of natural selection, and, as a matter of fact, they cannot even define natural selection in non-tautological terms. Inadequacies of the present theory and failure of the fossil record to substantiate predictions based on the theory leave macro-evolution, and even micro-evolution, intractable mysteries according to Macbeth. Macbeth suggests that no theory at all may be preferable to the present theory of evolution.

Using Macbeth's work as the starting point for his own investigation of modern evolution theory, Bethell, a graduate of Oxford with a major in philosophy, has expressed his complete dissatisfaction with the present formulations of evolution theory and natural selection from the viewpoint of the philosophy of science. Both Macbeth and Bethell present excellent reviews of the thinking of leading evolutionists concerning the relationship of natural selection to evolution theory. While both are highly critical, neither profess to be creationists.

According to modern evolutionary theory, ultimately all of the evolution is due to mutations. Mutations are random changes in the genes or chromosomes which are highly ordered structures. Any process that occurs by random chance events is subject to the laws of probability.

It is possible to estimate mutation rates. It is also possible to estimate how many favorable mutations would be required to bring about certain evolutionary changes. Assuming that these mutations were produced in a random, chance manner, as is true in the neo-Darwinian interpretation of evolution, it is possible to calculate how long such an evolutionary process would have required to convert an amoeba into a man. When this is done, according to a group of mathematicians, all of whom are evolutionists, the answer turns out to be billions of times longer than the assumed five billion years of earth history!

One of these mathematicians, Murray Eden, stated, "It is our contention that if 'random' is given a serious and crucial interpretation from a probabilistic point of view, the randomness postulate is highly implausible and that an *adequate*

scientific theory of evolution must await the discovery and elucidation of new natural laws—physical, physicochemical, and biological." What Eden and these mathematicians are saying is that the modern neo-Darwinian theory of evolution is totally inadequate to explain more than trivial change and thus we simply have no basis at present for attempting to explain how evolution may have occurred. As a matter of fact, based on the assumption that the evolutionary process was dependent upon random chance processes, we can simply state that evolution would have been impossible.

Furthermore, evolution theory contradicts one of the most firmly established laws known to science, the Second Law of Thermodynamics. The obvious contradiction between evolution and the Second Law of Thermodynamics becomes evident when we compare the definition of this Law and its consequences by several scientists (all of whom, as far as we know, accept evolutionary philosophy) with the definition of evolution by Sir Julian Huxley, biologist and one of the best-known spokesmen for evolution theory.

There is a general natural tendency of all observed systems to go from order to disorder, reflecting dissipation of energy available for future transformations—the law of increasing entropy.

All real processes go with an increase of entropy. The entropy also measures the randomness, or lack of orderliness of the system: the greater the randomness, the greater the entropy.

Another way of stating the second law then is: "The universe is constantly getting more disorderly!" Viewed that way, we can see the second law all about us. We have to work hard to straighten a room, but left to itself it becomes a mess again very quickly and very easily. Even if we never enter it, it becomes dusty and musty. How difficult to maintain houses, and machinery, and our own bodies in perfect working order: how easy to let them deteriorate. In fact, all we have to do is nothing, and everything deteriorates, collapses, breaks down, wears out, all by itself—and that is what the second law is all about.

Now compare these definitions or consequences of the Second Law of Thermodynamics to the theory of evolution as defined by Huxley:

Evolution in the extended sense can be defined as a directional and essentially irreversible process occurring in time, which in its course gives rise to an increase of variety and an increasingly high level of organization in its products. Our present knowledge indeed forces us to the view that the whole of reality is evolution—a single process of self-transformation.

There is a natural tendency, then, for all observed natural systems to go from order to disorder, towards increasing randomness. This is true throughout the entire known universe, both at the micro and macro levels. This tendency is so invariant that it has never been observed to fail. It is a natural law—the Second Law of Thermodynamics.

On the other hand, according to the general theory of evolution, as defined by Huxley, there is a general tendency of natural systems to go from disorder to order, towards an ever higher and higher level of complexity. This tendency supposedly operates in every corner of the universe, both at the micro and macro levels. As a consequence, it is believed, particles have evolved into people.

It is difficult to understand how a discerning person could fail to see the basic contradiction between these two processes. It seems apparent that both cannot be true, but no modern scientist would dare challenge the validity of the Second Law of Thermodynamics.

The usual, but exceedingly naive, answer given by evolutionists to this dilemma is that the Second Law of Thermodynamics applies only to closed systems. If the system is open to an external source of energy, it is asserted, complexity can be generated and maintained within this system at the expense of the energy supplied to it from the outside.

Thus, our solar system is an open system, and energy is supplied to the earth from the sun. The decrease in entropy, or increase in order, on the earth during the evolutionary process, it is said, has been more than compensated by the increase in entropy, or decrease in order, on the sun. The overall result has been a net decrease in order, so the Second Law of Thermodynamics has not been violated, we are told.

An open system and an adequate external source of energy are necessary *but not sufficient* conditions, however, for order to be generated and maintained, since raw, undirected, uncontrolled energy is destructive, not constructive. For example, without the protective layer of ozone in the upper atmosphere which absorbs most of the ultraviolet light coming from the sun, life on earth would be impossible. Bacterial cells exposed to such radiation die within seconds. This is because ultraviolet light, or irradiation of any kind, breaks chemical bonds and thus randomizes and destroys the highly complex structures found in biologically active macromolecules, such as proteins and DNA. Biological activity of these vitally important molecules is destroyed and death rapidly follows.

That much more than merely an external energy source is required to form complex molecules and systems from simpler ones is evident from the following statement by Simpson and Beck:

... the simple expenditure of energy is not sufficient to develop and maintain order. A bull in a china shop performs work, but he neither creates nor maintains organization. The work needed is *particular* work; it must follow specifications; it requires information on how to proceed.

Thus a green plant, utilizing the highly complex photosynthetic system it possesses, can trap light energy from the sun and convert this light energy into chemical energy. A series of other complex systems within the green plant allows the utilization of this energy to build up complex molecules and systems from simple starting material. Of equal importance is the fact that the green plant possesses a system for directing, maintaining, and replicating these complex energy conversion mechanisms—an incredibly complex genetic system. Without the genetic system, no specifications on how to proceed would exist, chaos would result, and life would be impossible.

For complexity to be generated within a system, then, four conditions must be met:

1. The system must be an open system.

2. An adequate external energy source must be available.

3. The system must possess energy conversion mechanisms.

4. A control mechanism must exist within the system for directing, maintaining, and replicating these energy conversion mechanisms.

The seemingly irresolvable dilemma, from an evolutionary point of view, is, how such complex energy conversion mechanisms and genetic systems arose in the *absence* of such systems, when there is a general natural tendency to go from order to disorder, a tendency so universal it can be stated as a natural law, the Second Law of Thermodynamics. Simply stated, machines are required to build machines, and something or somebody must operate the machinery.

The creationist thus opposes the wholly unscientific evolutionary hypothesis that the natural universe with all of its incredible complexity, was capable of generating itself, and maintains that there must exist, external to the natural universe, a Creator, or supernatural Agent, who was responsible for introducing, or creating, the high degree of order found within this natural universe. While creationism is extra-scientific, it is not antiscientific, as is the evolutionary hypothesis which contradicts one of the most well-established laws of science.

Finally, but of utmost significance, is the fact that the fossil record is actually hostile to the evolution model, but conforms remarkably well to predictions based on the creation model. Complex forms of life appear abruptly in the fossil record in the so-called Cambrian sedimentary deposits or rocks. Although these animals, which include such highly complex and diverse forms of life as brachiopods, trilobites, worms, jellyfish, sponges, sea urchins, and sea cucumbers, as well as other crustaceans and molluscs, supposedly required about two to three billion years to evolve, not a single ancestor for any of these animals can be found anywhere on the face of the earth. George Gaylord Simpson has characterized the absence of Precambrian fossils as "the major mystery of the history of life." This fact of the fossil record, incomprehensible in the light of the evolution model, is exactly as predicted on the basis of the creation model.

The remainder of the fossil record reveals a remarkable absence of the many transitional forms demanded by the theory of evolution. Gaps between all higher categories of plants and animals, which creationists believe constituted the created kinds, are systematic. For example, Simpson has admitted that "Gaps among known orders, classes, and phyla are systematic and almost always large." Richard B. Goldschmidt, well-known geneticist and a rabid evolutionist, acknowledged that "practically all orders or families known appear suddenly and without any apparent transitions." E. J. H. Corner, Cambridge University botanist and an evolutionist, stated, ". . . I still think, to the unprejudiced, the fossil record of plants is in favor of special creation."

Recently, the well-known evolutionary paleontologist, David B. Kitts, stated,

Despite the bright promise that paleontology provides a means of "seeing" evolution, it has presented some nasty difficulties for evolutionists the most notorious of which is the presence of "gaps" in the fossil record. *Evolution requires intermediate forms between species and paleontology does not provide them.* . . .

Lord Solly Zuckerman, for many years the head of the Department of Anatomy at the University of Birmingham, was first knighted and then later raised to the peerage as recognition of his distinguished career as a research scientist. After over 15 years of research on the subject, with a team that rarely included less than four scientists, Lord Zuckerman concluded that *Australopithecus* did not walk upright, he was not intermediate between ape and man, but that he was merely an anthropoid ape. *Australopithecus* (Louis Leakey's "Nutcracker Man," and Donald Johanson's "Lucy") is an extinct apelike creature that almost all evolutionists believe walked erect and showed many characteristics intermediate between ape and man. Lord Zuckerman, although not a creationist, believes there is very little, if any, science in the search for man's fossil ancestry. Lord Zuckerman states his conviction, based on a life-time of investigation, that if man has evolved from an ape-like creature he did so without leaving any trace of the transformation in the fossil record. This directly contradicts the popular idea that paleontologists have found numerous evidences of ape-like ancestors for man, but rather suggests they have found none at all.

The explosive appearance of highly complex forms of life in Cambrian and other rocks with the absence of required ancestors, and the abrupt appearance of each major plant and animal kind without apparent transitional forms are the facts of greatest importance derivable for a study of the fossil record. These facts are highly contradictory to predictions based on the evolution model, but are just as predicted on the basis of the creation model of origins.

The facts described above are some of the reasons why creationists maintain that, on the basis of available scientific evidence, the creation model is not only a viable alternative to the evolution model, but is actually a far superior model. Furthermore, after more than a century of effort to establish Darwinian evolution, even some evolutionists are beginning to express doubts. This is evidently true, for example, of Pierre P. Grassé one of the most distinguished of French scientists. In his review of Grassé's book, *L'Evolution du Vivant,* Dobzhansky states, "The book of Pierre P. Grassé is a frontal attack on all kinds of 'Darwinism.' Its purpose is 'to destroy the myth of evolution as a simple, understood, and explained phenomenon,' and to show that evolution is a mystery about which little is, and perhaps can be, known. Now, one can disagree with Grassé but not ignore him. He is the most distinguished of French zoologists, the editor of the 28 volumes of 'Traite de Zoologie,' author of

numerous original investigations, and expresident of the Academie des Sciences. His knowledge of the living world is encyclopedic. . . ." In the closing sentence of his review, Dobzhansky says, "The sentence with which Grassé ends his book is disturbing: 'It is possible that in this domain biology, impotent, yields the floor to metaphysics.'"

Grassé thus closes his book with the statement that biology is powerless to explain the origin of living things and that it may possibly have to yield to metaphysics (supernatural creation of some kind).

In his Presidential Address to the Linnaean Society of London, "A Little on Lungfishes," Errol White said, "But whatever ideas authorities may have on the subject, the lungfishes, like every other major group of fishes I know, have their origin firmly based in *nothing.* . . ." He then said, "I have often said how little I should like to have to prove organic evolution in a court of law." He closed his address by saying, "We still do not know the mechanics of evolution in spite of the over-confident claims in some quarters, nor are we likely to make further progress in this by the classical methods of paleontology or biology: and we shall certainly not advance matters by jumping up and down shrilling 'Darwin is God and I, So-and-so, am his prophet'— the recent researches of workers like Dean and Hinshelwood (1964) already suggest the possibility of incipient cracks in the seemingly monolithic walls of the Neo-Darwinian Jericho." White thus seems to be suggesting that the modern neo-Darwinian theory of evolution is in danger of crashing down just as did the walls of Jericho!

Thus, today we have a most astounding situation. Evolution has never been observed by human witnesses. Evolution cannot be subjected to the experimental method. The most sacred tenet of Darwinism—natural selection—in modern formulation is incapable of explaining anything. Furthermore, even some evolutionists are conceding that the mechanism of evolution proposed by evolutionary biologists could account for no more than trivial change in the time believed to have been available, and that an adequate scientific theory of evolution, based on present knowledge, seems impossible. Finally, the major features of the fossil record accord in an amazing fashion with the predictions based on special creation, but contradict the most fundamental predictions generated by the theory of evolution. And yet the demand is unceasing that evolution theory be accepted as the only scientific explanation for origins, even as an established fact, while excluding creation as a mere religious concept!

This rigid indoctrination in evolutionary dogma, with the exclusion of the competing concept of special creation, results in young people being indoctrinated in a non-theistic, naturalistic, humanistic religious philosophy in the guise of science. Science is perverted, academic freedom is denied, the educational process suffers, and constitutional guarantees of religious freedom are violated.

This unhealthy situation could be corrected by presenting students with the two competing models for origins, the creation model and the evolution model, with all supporting evidence for each model. This would permit an evaluation of the students of the strengths and weaknesses of each model. This is the course true education should pursue rather than following the present process of brain-washing students in evolutionary philosophy.

PHILIP KITCHER
Against Creationism

PHILIP KITCHER *(b. 1947) teaches philosophy at Columbia University. In addition to a book on sociobiology, he is author of* Abusing Science, *the book on evolutionary theory from which this selection is excerpted.*

BEFORE turning to "scientific" Creationism itself—that is, the theory peddled by the Institute for Creation Research and advertised by the Moral Majority—it is important to distinguish two other forms that a belief in special creation might take. The central idea of strict Creationism is that all kinds of organisms presently existing, and perhaps some more, were formed on the earth in a single event. Some people hold this view purely as an article of religious faith, making no claim that it is a part of science supported by scientific evidence. Such people accept strict Creationism because its central doctrine follows from two other beliefs that they hold: (i) The Bible is to be read literally; (ii) When the Bible is read literally, it says that all kinds of organisms were formed on earth in a single event. I disagree with this view, because I do not believe it is possible, let alone reasonable, to read the Bible literally. (Nor do I think that Christians and Jews are compelled, as sincere believers, to read the Bible literally.) However, I have no intention of criticizing Creationism insofar as it is held as an explicitly religious belief, a belief that is recognized as running counter to the scientific evidence.

There is another way to be a Creationist. One might offer Creationism as a scientific theory: Life did not evolve over millions of years; rather all forms were created at one time by a particular Creator. Although pure versions of Creationism were no longer in vogue among scientists by the end of the eighteenth century, they had flourished earlier (in the writings of Thomas Burnet, William Whiston, and others). Moreover, *variants* of Creationism were supported by a number of eminent nineteenth-century scientists— William Buckland, Adam Sedgwick, and Louis Agassiz, for example. These creationists trusted that their theories would accord with the Bible, interpreted in what they saw as a correct way. However, that fact does not affect the scientific status of those theories. Even postulating an unobserved Creator need be no more unscientific than postulating unobservable particles. What matters is the character of the proposals and the ways in which they are articulated and defended. The great scientific Creationists of the eighteenth and nineteenth centuries offered problem-solving strategies for many of the questions addressed by evolutionary theory. They struggled hard to explain the observed distribution of fossils. Sedgwick, Buckland, and others practiced genuine science. They stuck their necks out and volunteered information about the catastrophes that they invoked to explain biological and geological findings. Because their theories offered definite proposals, those theories were refutable. Indeed, the theories actually achieved refutation. In 1831, in his presidential address to the Geological Society, Adam Sedgwick publicly announced that his own variant of Creationism had been refuted:

> Having been myself a believer, and, to the best of my power, a propagator of what I now regard as a philosophic heresy . . . I think it right, as one of my last acts before I quit this Chair, thus publicly to read my recantation.
>
> We ought, indeed, to have paused before we first adopted the diluvian theory, and referred all our old superficial gravel to the action of the Mosaic Flood. For of man, and the works of his hands, we have not yet found a single trace among the remnants of a former world entombed in these ancient deposits. In classing together distant unknown formations under one name; in giving them a simultaneous origin, and in determining their date, not by the organic remains we had discovered, but by those we expected hypothetically hereafter to discover, in them; we have given one more example of the passion with which the mind fastens upon general conclusions, and of the readiness with which it leaves the consideration of unconnected truths. . . .

Since they want Creationism taught in public schools, contemporary Creationists cannot present their view as based on religious faith. On the other hand, the doctrine is too dear to be subjected to the possibility of outright defeat. What is wanted, then, is a version of Creationism that is not vulnerable to refutation, but that appears to enjoy the objective status that can only be conferred by evidential support. This is an impossible demand. A theory cannot drink at the well of evidential support without running the risk of being poisoned by future data. What emerges from the conflict of goals is the pseudoscience promulgated by the Institute for Creation Research. It is vaguely suggested that the central Creationist idea could be used to solve some problems. But the details are never given, the links to nature never forged. Oddly, "scientific" Creationism fails to be a science not because of what it says (or, in its "public school" editions, very carefully omits) about a Divine Creator, but because of what it does not say about the natural world. The theory has no infrastructure, no ways of articulating its vague central idea, so that specific features of living forms can receive detailed explanations.

Despite my best efforts, I have found only two problem-solving strategies in the writing of "scientific" Creationists. Most of the literature is negative. . . . The positive proposals of Creation "science" are remarkably skimpy. Even *Scientific Creationism* (the work that is intended to enable teachers to present the "creation model") spends far more pages attacking evolutionary theory than in developing Creationist account. Nevertheless, there are passages where a positive doctrine seems to flicker among the criticisms.

Similarly, the much earlier book *The Genesis Flood*, mixes attempts at constructing Creation "science" with its explicit Biblical interpretation. Because of the uniformly negative character of most other Creationist writings, my evaluation of the positive theory presented by "scientific" Creationists will be based primarily on these two works. The two problem-solving strategies of "scientific" Creationism are the attempt to use Flood Geology to answer questions about the ordering of fossils and an appeal to a mix of "design" and historical narrative to account for the properties, relationships, and distributions of organisms. I shall document my remarks about pseudoscience by taking a closer look at how these explanatory vehicles operate.

ROOM AT THE TOP FOR THE UPWARDLY MOBILE?

Creationists recognize that the fossil record is ordered. All over the earth we find a regular succession of organisms through the rock strata. At the lowest levels, we find only small marine invertebrates. As we move up, other groups of animals are encountered: Fish join the marine invertebrates; then come the amphibians, reptiles, and, finally, the mammals and birds. Of course, within each of these groups there is also an order. The first reptiles diversify, giving rise at later times to several different groups, some of which, like the dinosaurs, die out, while others of which, like the snakes, turtles, lizards, and crocodilians, persist to the present. Even without evolutionary assumptions, it is possible to offer a simple explanation of this order. The different strata all contain remains of the distinctive organisms that were alive at the time at which those strata were deposited, and the order reflects the fact that different groups of animals have existed at different times. In other words, the animals who have inhabited the earth were not all contemporaries.

Although this simple explanation makes no commitment to the *evolution* of organisms, Creationists cannot accept it. For they believe that all the animals that have ever existed were formed in one original event of Creation. Nor can they abandon this belief without forswearing the theological payoff of their "science." So how are they to explain the order of the fossil record? Some antievolutionists of the late nineteenth century ascended to new levels of ad hoc explanation with two transparent ruses: (i) The Devil placed the fossils in the rocks to deceive us; (ii) God put the fossils there to test us. Contemporary Creationists are more subtle. They invoke the Flood. They hypothesize a worldwide, cataclysmic deluge, which destroyed virtually all the animals of the earth and deposited almost all the fossil-bearing rocks, thereby producing the fossil record.

Here is an outline of their major ideas. The primeval earth was a very pleasant place, consisting of land masses divided by "narrow seas." It was surrounded by a canopy of water vapor, producing a "greenhouse effect." In the Flood, water came from two directions; primitive waters inside the earth burst through the crust, and, at the same time, the vapor canopy was broken up to cause torrential rain. Some humans and animals escaped in boats (including, presumably, Noah, his family, and a pair of [land] animals of every kind). Others, less lucky, were drowned or destroyed, and some of them were engulfed by mud and other debris that were later deposited as sediments. (The latter animals are the ones that became fossilized.) Finally, the Flood came to an end, partly as the result of evaporation, partly because mountains erupted, producing basins in which the residual waters were entrapped. At this point, the remaining animals dispersed, bred, multiplied, and spread themselves over the new earth.

The attempt to explain geological formations by reference to the Flood is not new. Contemporary Creationists are heirs to a long tradition, begun by Thomas Burnet (whose *Sacred Theory of the Earth* was published in 1681). The idea of invoking a *single* cataclysm (and a single period of Creation) had been abandoned by the wiser geologists by the end of the eighteenth century, at which time the enterprise appeared hopeless. Nineteenth-century   Catastrophists—Cuvier,

Buckland, Sedgwick, and their followers—preferred to think of Noah's Flood as the last in a series of catastrophes. But "scientific" Creationists will have none of these newfangled compromises. So their account is vexed by all the questions that arose for their illustrious predecessors—as well as other questions inspired by the discoveries of the past 150 years. Here are just a few. How exactly did the land reemerge? (In traditional terms, how was "the pond drained"?) Did *all* kinds of land animals go on Noah's ship? If so, why are there so many kinds that are unrecorded in "post-Deluge" strata? How were the domestic economies managed during the voyage of the Ark? Obviously, the *mechanisms* of the whole episode could stand considerably more description. Creationists sometimes admit the point; Morris exhorts teachers to prepare geology students who can help with the task of working out the details. However, neither he nor any other Creationist I have read seems to have any definite conception of where or how to begin this Herculean task. . . .

To see why Flood Geology deserves an obituary, let us watch it in action. The most ambitious attempt at detailed problem solving is presented by Henry Morris. Morris is very emphatic that Flood Geology accounts for the order of the fossils. After announcing fourteen "obvious predictions" of his story, he concludes, "Now there is no question that all of the above predictions from the cataclysmic model are explicitly confirmed in the geologic column. The general order from simple to complex in the fossil record in the geologic column, considered by evolution, is thus likewise predicted by the rival model, only with more precision and detail. But it is the exceptions that are inimical to the evolution model." Bold words. Before we take up the large claims made for Flood Geology, let us consider the swipes at the evolutionary account. First, the "general order from simple to complex" in the fossil record is not considered "the main proof" of evolution. Evolutionary theory rests on its ability to subsume a vast number of diverse phenomena—including the *details* of biogeography, adaptive characteristics, relationships among

organisms, and the sequence of fossils—under a single type of historical reasoning. To say that "the general order from simple to complex" in the fossil record is the primary evidence for evolution is like saying that the fact that most bodies tend to fall is the primary evidence for Newtonian theory. Second, those "inimical exceptions" are our old friends, the overthrusts, the cave drawings—and, of course, Paluxy. As I have already pointed out, these are not genuine problems for evolutionary theory.

How exactly does Morris propose to "predict" the order of the fossils from his model? Let us look at some of his "predictions" and their justifications:

• • •

3. In general, animals living at the lowest elevations would tend to be buried at the lowest elevations, and so on, with elevations in the strata thus representing elevations of habitat or ecological zones.

4. Marine invertebrates would normally be found in the bottom rock of any local geologic column, since they live on the sea bottom.

5. Marine vertebrates (fishes) would be found in higher rocks than the bottom-dwelling invertebrates. They live at higher elevations and also could escape burial longer.

6. Amphibians and reptiles would tend to be found at still higher elevations, in the commingled sediments at the interface between land and water. . . .

9. In the marine strata where invertebrates were fossilized, these would tend locally to be sorted hydrodynamically into assemblages of similar size and shape. Furthermore, as the turbulently upwelling waters and sediments settled back down, the simpler animals, more nearly spherical or streamlined in shape, would tend to settle out first because of lower hydraulic drag. Thus each kind of marine invertebrate would tend to appear in its simplest form at the lowest elevation, and so on.

10. Mammals and birds would be found in general at higher elevations than reptiles and amphibians, both because of their habitat and because of their greater mobility. However, few birds would be found at all, only occasional exhausted birds being trapped and buried in sediments.

It is hard to know where to start. Morris appears to have three possible explanatory factors: (1) *habitat* (lower dwelling animals were deposited first), (2) *hydraulic characteristics* (the order of deposition depends on the animal's resistance to the downward waters), (3) *mobility* (more mobile animals will be deposited later). The passages I have quoted juggle these three methods so as to obtain the desired results.

Now, for all the extravagant claims about "prediction" with "more precision and detail," the account Morris offers is extremely vague. Puzzles begin to appear in large numbers when we start to consider the details of the fossil record. Why are bottom-dwelling marine invertebrates found at *all* levels of the strata? Why are some very delicate marine invertebrates, which would have been likely to sink more slowly, found at the very lowest levels? Why are all the "modern" fishes (the *teleostean* fishes, which, on the standard account, emerged only in the age of dinosaurs and became spectacularly successful as the reign of the dinosaurs came to its end) found only in Morris's "late Flood" deposits? Why do these particular fishes not occur, as other fishes do, at lower levels? Why are whales and dolphins only found at high levels, while marine reptiles of similar size are found only much lower? Why do lumbering creatures like ground sloths appear only in Morris's post-Flood deposits, while much more agile mammals (such as the ancestors of contemporary carnivores and ungulates) appear much lower? Why are the *flying* reptiles found "in the commingled sediments at the interface between land and water"? Why were not *most* of the birds "exhausted," since perching places would have been hard to find in the raging Deluge? The sequence of questions could go on and on.

Morris does not consider the particularities. So the idea that we get *more* detail from his account is simply bluster. In fact, given that the problems raised for evolutionary theory are spurious—the "inimical exceptions" do not present any difficulty—the question we must ask is whether Flood Geology can *emulate* the ability of evolutionary theory to explain the fossil record. There are two ways in which Creationists might elaborate their proposals. One would be to acknowledge that the account so far given is programmatic and incomplete and to face up to the task of working out the details. The second would be to deny that there are residual questions for "scientific" Creationism to answer.

In the spirit of Morris's exhortation to young paleontologists, Creationists might concede that Flood Geology is only a "sketch." However, it is hardly a matter of adding a bit of detail to the main lines of the account. Problems are everywhere, solutions nowhere. What were the mechanics of the Flood? How were the animals preserved? Why are the details of the fossil ordering as we find them to be? It is reasonable to wonder what Flood Geology does have going for it that inspires people to work further on it. Wonderment increases when we realize that Creationists have abandoned the position of the most enlightened nineteenth-century Catastrophists. . . .

Here is a different "theory sketch" about the history of life on earth. For a very long time, the earth has been a laboratory for clever aliens who live in outer space. Periodically, they have "seeded" our planet with living organisms. In the beginning, they were only able to produce rather simple terrestrial organisms. So they started off with some marine invertebrates. After a while, they came for a visit to see how things were going. At this time, a dreadful thing happened. Something about the alien spacecraft caused a cataclysm on the earth; volcanoes erupted, there were massive earthquakes, enormous tidal waves, and so forth. Perhaps the spacecraft emitted some peculiar type of radiation that triggered all these unfortunate events. In any case, all the first crop of organisms were destroyed and buried in the cataclysm. The whole experiment was spoiled. However, since they understood the moral of Kipling's "If," the aliens decided to try again. Their technology had now improved, and they were able to manufacture more complicated animals. Some of those that had not performed well on the first round were dropped from the cast. The experiment went very well again—until they came to take another look. Once again, their presence led to disaster, and they were forced to start over from scratch. So it has gone for a number of trials. (How many would you like?) The aliens are very persevering. They still have not figured out what it is about their presence that makes the earth go into convulsions. But their technology is clearly improving by leaps and bounds. After all, last time they made us.

My brief acquaintance with the "theory sketch" of the last paragraph has not yet led to a deep attachment. (It took me about ten minutes to make it up.) So I shall not exhort others to join me in working out the details. However, I do want to suggest that, *from a scientific point of view,* my silly proposal is no worse than Morris's Flood Geology. It would not be difficult to mimic the "fourteen predictions." ("What evolutionists call *trends* are really the aliens' progress in fine tuning already workable designs." Notice, too, that my theory, like Morris's vague account of Flood Geology, has plenty of "wiggle room.") The point of the comparison should be obvious. There is utterly no reason to take either my proposal or Flood Geology seriously—or to exhort promising students to waste their careers in the pursuit of such obvious folly.

The second way in which the Creationists can respond to questions about the details is even worse. Instead of taking the problems of detail seriously, they can contend that we can never know how the Flood worked. All that can be done is to lay down some general considerations, which hold "as a rule," and suggest that, given some unknowable distribution of upwelling waters, torrential rains, and trapped animals, everything sorted out as it did. So, for example, the questions I have raised about teleostean fishes, whales, flying reptiles, and giant sloths can just be ducked. These are "the exceptional cases."

Some passages suggest that, when push comes to shove, Morris and his fellow Creationists will slide in this direction:

14. All the above predictions would be expected statistically but, because of the cataclysmic nature of the phenomena, would also admit of many exceptions in every case. In other words, the cataclysmic model predicts the general order and character of the deposits but also allows for occasional exceptions.

In other localities, and perhaps somewhat later in the period of the rising waters of the Flood, in general, land animals and plants would be expected to be caught in the sediments and buried; and this, of course, is exactly what the strata show. Of course, this would be only a general rule and there would be many exceptions, as currents would be intermingling from all directions, particularly as the lands became increasingly submerged and more and more amphibians, reptiles and mammals were overtaken by the waters.

The remarkable point about these passages is not the *number* of qualifying phrases, but their *variable strength.* Are there "many exceptions in every case" or are the exceptions "occasional"? I do not know what Morris or Whitcomb intend. Yet one thing is clear. Such passages can be used to maintain that the anomalies I have mentioned are not genuine problems for Flood Geology. Morris and Whitcomb have carefully provided an all-purpose escape clause. So while (alleged) exceptions are "inimical" to evolutionary theory—they would mean refutation—exceptions, even hordes of exceptions, in no way weaken the case for Creation "science." For Creation "scientists" data has only one function; it is a potential source of problems for evolution. Counterexamples to the "theory" of Creation "science" do not count.

To see how severe the anomalies are, let us look at one example in more detail. Fossils of teleostean fishes (this class comprises just about all contemporary types from sardines to swordfish) are found only from late Triassic times (roughly 200 million years ago), and they show increasing abundance in the fossil record. Now recall that a leading principle of Flood Geology is that "animals living at the lowest elevations would tend to be buried at the lowest elevations."

Overlooking such niceties as the fact that some teleosteans are deep-sea fish, let us ask what accounts for their success in resisting the Flood. Were they hydraulically special, less "streamlined" than other fish? No, as a group, there is more variation of shape *within* the teleosteans than there is between teleosteans and the groups of fish that were buried beneath them. So, perhaps the answer is that they found room at the top because they were upwardly mobile? But this explanation loses its attractiveness when we realize that the teleosts "range from speedy swimmers to slow swimmers to almost sedentary forms, from dwellers in the open ocean to bottom-living types to lake and river fishes." Yet all these lucky teleostean fishes managed to resist the flood waters for a long time, while large numbers of speedy fish are buried beneath them.

By considering this one example, I hope to have explained what lies behind my charge that Flood Geology faces serious anomalies. But my principal purpose is to illustrate the impotence of the idea that worrisome details can be written off as "exceptional cases." Were *all* the teleosts exceptional? Was there no single unlucky sardine, salmon, or swordfish who was buried in the early deposits? Is it enough to remind ourselves that there are bound to be exceptions "because of the cataclysmic nature of the phenomena"? The case of the teleosts is only one among many. Ground sloths, flying reptiles, whales, trilobites, and a host of other creatures prove similarly embarrassing. . . .

Writing in 1961, Whitcomb and Morris made it clear what their last resort would be if the difficult questions began to threaten: "It is because the Bible itself teaches us these things that we are fully justified in appealing to *the power of God*, whether or not He used means amenable to our scientific understanding, for the gathering of two of every kind of animal into the Ark and for the care and preservation of those animals in the Ark during the 371 days of the Flood." Today, "scientific" Creationists have pledged themselves to argue on the scientific evidence. So this last refuge is—officially, at least—out of bounds.

The second major biological problem-solving strategy offered by Creationism attempts to answer questions about adaptation, relationships among organisms, and biogeographical distribution. . . .

The basic idea is straightforward. When we recognize a characteristic of an organism as unmodified, the Creationist explanation of its presence will be to show how the feature manifests the Creator's design. The account of similarities among distinct "basic kinds" will identify the similar needs of organisms of those distinct kinds. Here are some sample "explanations." Bats have wings because the Creator endowed them with wings, and He did so because they need to fly. Chimps and humans have similar hemoglobins (and other biological molecules) because the Creator gave them similar molecules from the start, and He did so because their physiological requirements are similar. Some (perfectly palatable) butterflies mimic unpalatable butterflies of the same region because the Creator saw that they had to have some defense against predators. To each according to his need.

If one wants to believe in Creationism, the picture can easily lull critical faculties. Yet, if we think about it, it is bizarre. Surely we should not imagine the Creator contemplating a wingless bat, recognizing that it would be defective, and so equipping it with the wings it needs. Rather, if we take the idea of a single creative event seriously, we must view it as the origination of an entire system of kinds of organisms, *whose needs themselves arise in large measure from the character of the system.* Why were bats created at all? Why were any defenses against predation needed? Why did the Creator form this system of organisms, with their interrelated needs, needs that are met in such diverse and complicated ways?

Invocation of the word "design," or the passing reference to the satisfaction of "need," explains nothing. The needs are not given in advance of the design of structures to accommodate them, but are themselves encompassed in the design. Nor do we achieve any understanding of the adaptations and relationships of organisms until we see, at least in outline, what the Grand Plan of

Creation might have been. This point has been clear at least since the seventeenth century. At the beginning of the *Discourse on Metaphysics,* Leibniz gave a beautiful exposition of it. He recognized that unless there are independent criteria of design, then praise of the Creator's design is worthless: "In saying, therefore, that things are not good according to any standard of goodness, but simply by the will of God, it seems to me that one destroys, without realizing it, all the love of God and all his glory; for why praise him for what he has done, if he would be equally praiseworthy in doing the contrary?" For Leibniz, to invoke "design" without saying what counts as good design is not only vacuous but blasphemous. Later in the same work, Leibniz developed the theme with a striking analogy. *Any* world can be conceived as regular ("designed") just as *any* array of points can be joined by a curve with some algebraic formula.

Why are contemporary Creationists silent about the Design? Because things did not go so well for their predecessors who tried to show how each kind of organism had been separately created with a special design. They found it hard to reconcile the observed features of some organisms with the attributes of the Creator. Contemporary Creationists have learned from these heroic—but fruitless—efforts.

So we encounter the strategy exemplified by Morris: Talk generally about design, pattern, purpose, and beauty in nature. There are many examples of adaptations that can be used—the wings of bats or "the amazing circulatory system," for example. But what happens if we press some more difficult cases? Well, if there seems to be no design or purpose to a feature (and if its presence cannot be understood as a modification of ancestral characters), one can always point out that some parts of the Creator's plan may be too vast for human understanding. *We* do not see what the design is, but there *is* design, nonetheless.

Since no plan of design has been specified, Creationists have available another all-purpose escape clause. But it is precisely this feature of Creation "science" that impugns its scientific credentials. To mumble that "the ways of the Creator are many and mysterious" may excuse one from identifying design in unlikely places. It is not to do science.

To provide scientific explanations, a Creationist would have to identify the plan implemented in the Creation. The trouble is that there are countless examples of properties of organisms that are hard to integrate into a coherent theory of design. There are two main types of difficulty, stemming from the frequent tinkerings of evolution and the equally common nastiness of nature. Let us begin with evolutionary tinkering. Structures already present are modified to answer to the organism's current needs. The result may be clumsy and inefficient, but it gets the job done. A beautiful example is the case of the Panda's thumb. Although they belong to the order Carnivora, giant pandas subsist on a diet of bamboo. In adapting to this diet they needed a means to grasp the shoots. Like other carnivores, they lack an opposable thumb. Instead, a bone in the wrist has become extended to serve as part of a device for grasping it. It does not work well. Any competent engineer who wanted to design a giant panda could have done better. But it works well enough.

It is easy to multiply examples. Orchids have evolved complicated structures that discourage self-fertilization. These baroque contraptions are readily understood if we understand them as built out of the means available. Ruminants have acquired very complicated stomachs and a special digestive routine. These characteristics have enabled them to break down the cellulose layers that encase valuable proteins in many grasses. Their inner life could have been so much simpler had they been given the right enzymes from the start.

The second class of cases covers those in which, to put it bluntly, nature's ways are rather repulsive. There is nothing intrinsically beautiful about the scavenging of vultures, the copulatory behavior of the female praying mantis (who tries to bite off the head of the "lucky" male), or the ways in which some insects paralyze their prey. Let me describe one example in more detail. Some animals practice *coprophagy.* They produce feces that they eat. Rabbits, for example, devour their morning droppings. From an evolutionary perspective, the phenomenon is understood. Rabbits have solved the problem of breaking down cellulose by secreting bacteria toward the end of their intestinal tracts. Since the cellulose breakdown occurs at the end of the tract, much valuable protein and many valuable bacteria are liable to be lost in the feces. Hence the morning feces are eaten, the protein is metabolized, and the supply of bacteria is kept up. Creationists ought to find such phenomena puzzling. Surely an all-powerful, all-loving Creator, who *separately designed* each kind of living thing, could have found some less repugnant (and, I might add, more efficient) way to get the job done. (These examples are, of course, far less problematic for those who believe simply that the Creator set the universe in motion billions of years ago and that contemporary organisms are the latest product of the laws and conditions instituted in that original creative event.)

So far, I have concentrated on Creationist resources for answering questions about the characteristics of organisms and the similarities and differences among kinds of organisms. Let us now take a brief look at Creationist biogeography. Discussions of the distribution of animals are not extensive, but the following passage lays down the ground rules of the enterprise: "If the Flood was geographically universal, then all the air-breathers of the animal kingdom which were not in the Ark perished; and present-day animal distribution must be explained on the basis of migrations from the mountains of Ararat." One's first response is surely to ask: Why only one Ark? Why Ararat? (Why not New Jersey?) Of course, we know the answers to these questions. But what *scientific* evidence is there for supposing that there was just one vehicle for preserving land animals during the Deluge and that the subsequent radiation began from Mount Ararat? Creationists tie their hands behind their backs when they approach problems of biogeography with such gratuitous assumptions. There are obvious difficulties posed by the existence of peculiar groups of animals in

particular places. The most striking example is the presence of marsupials as the dominant mammals of Australia. Given that all the land animals reemerged at the same place at the same time, why did Australia become a stronghold for marsupial mammals?

Whitcomb and Morris consider precisely this question. Much of their discussion is directed against claims made by one of their evangelical rivals, a geologist who advocated only a "local flood." However, they do indicate the main lines of their answer. In essence, they propose to accelerate the migration of organisms described in a standard evolutionary account. Here is the standard explanation of how the marsupials came to dominate Australia.

One central hypothesis is *placental chauvinism:* Marsupials are competitively inferior to the recent eutherian (placental) mammals. This hypothesis is confirmed by evidence of the consequences of introducing eutherian competitors into marsupial populations. It is usually suggested that the marsupials arose in North America about 130 million years ago and that they were able to compete successfully with the *early* eutherian mammals. The marsupials radiated extensively, established themselves in South America and crossed over to Australia by way of Antarctica. (Australia, Antarctica, and South America become separated about 70 million years ago.) Their eutherian contemporaries did not reach Australia, so that the marsupials were able to diversify and attain their modern forms without competition from eutherians. Other marsupial strongholds (for example, South America) became vulnerable when new continental connections (the Isthmus of Panama) made it possible for the highly successful *recent* eutherians to invade. But Australia was sufficiently isolated, and a rich marsupial fauna developed there.

What Creationists propose to do is to squash something like this sequence of events into less than 100 centuries. Here, then, is the scenario. Noah's Ark lands on Mount Ararat. Out come the animals. They begin to compete for resources. Because they are inferior competitors, the poor marsupials are forced to disperse ever more widely. Spreading southward, they eventually manage to reach Australia. By the time the placentals have given chase, the land connection with Australia is severed. The marsupials are safe in their stronghold.

This is an exciting story, worthy of the best cowboy tradition. The trouble is that it has the marsupials arising in the wrong place, going by the wrong route, and competing with the wrong animals. Apart from that, the pace is just a bit too quick. If Creationists are going to explain fossil findings that, by their own lights, are post-Flood, they had better suppose that the marsupials reached Australia by travelling through Europe, North America, and South America. If they are going to insist that *contemporary* kinds of eutherian mammals emerged form the Ark, then they will have to explain why competition was not so severe that the marsupials were completely vanquished. Waiving these difficulties, let us consider the rate of the migration. When we think of marsupials, we naturally think of kangaroos—so we have the vision of successive generations of kangaroos hopping toward Australia. But kangaroos are relatively speedy. Some marsupials—wombats, koalas, and marsupial moles, for example—move very slowly. Koalas are sedentary animals, and it is difficult to coax them out of the eucalyptus trees on which they feed. Wombats, like marsupial moles, construct elaborate burrows, in which they spend their time and carry on their social relations. The idea of *any* of these animals engaging in a hectic dash around the globe is patently absurd. (On the evolutionary account, of course, they are all descendants of ancestral marsupials who had millions of years to reach their destination.)

Next we must face the question of why all the lucky refugees were *marsupials.* Surely, large numbers of animals would have found it prudent to disperse widely from the Ark. Why is it that the marsupials, almost *alone* among the mammals, were able to find the land connection to Australia and scurry across before other mammals in need of *Lebensraum* [Ed.-room for living] could catch up with them? And what about the

conveniently disappearing land connection itself? Creationists seem to assume very rapid movements of land masses. Unlike orthodox geologists, who have independent evidence for slow separation of the continents, they maintain that, in a matter of centuries, a land connection that would support a full-scale exodus of marsupials presented an insuperable barrier to the pursuing eutherians. Indeed, if the marsupials were really *driven* across by eutherian competition, then we would expect the competition to be snapping at their heels—otherwise would not the wombat have stopped to dig a burrow, the koala have settled in a convenient tree? In that case, the bridge would have to be cut *very* quickly.

Once again, when the Creationist story is pressed for details, anomalies appear in droves. . . . What constraints govern hypotheses about past land connections? Since the Creationists have forsworn the apparatus of modern geology, their claims about the past relations of land masses seem invulnerable to independent checks. No worries about mechanisms for rapid land subsidence need perturb them, for they may always appeal to the after effects of the great cataclysm. Anything goes.

When Whitcomb and Morris wrote *The Genesis Flood* in 1961, Creationist strategy was somewhat different from that currently in vogue. Those were halcyon days, when Creationists did not mind admitting their reliance on unfathomable supernatural mechanisms. Perhaps they even hoped that a version of Creationism, explicitly based on the Genesis account, might find its place in science education. The following passage is far less guarded than more recent statements:

> The more we study the fascinating story of animal distribution around the earth, the more convinced we have become that this vast river of variegated life forms, moving ever outward from the Asiatic mainland, across the continents and seas, has not been a chance and haphazard phenomenon. Instead, *we see the hand of God guiding and directing these creatures in ways that man, with all his ingenuity, has never been able to fathom,* in order that the great commission to the postdiluvian animal kingdom might be carried out,

and "that they may breed abundantly in the earth, and be fruitful, and multiply upon the earth" (Gen. 8:17).

There is the all-purpose escape clause. If the way in which the animals might have managed to leave the Ark and distribute themselves around the globe boggles your mind, do not tax yourself. They were guided, directed in ways that we are not able to understand.

Morris's subsequent writings take a different line about biogeographical questions. The subject is not discussed. Hence it is impossible to be sure that current Creationists would involve the actions of the Creator to help out when the going gets tough. Nevertheless, this is one more instance of the phenomenon that we have seen repeatedly. The alleged rival to evolutionary theory provides no definite problem-solving strategies that can be applied to give detailed answers to specific questions. . . .

Creation "science" is spurious science. To treat it as science we would have to overlook its intolerable vagueness. We would have to abandon large parts of well-established sciences (physics, chemistry, and geology, as well as evolutionary biology, are all candidates for revision). We would have to trade careful technical procedures for blind guesses, unified theories for motley collections of special techniques. Exceptional cases, whose careful pursuit has so often led to important turnings in the history of science, would be dismissed with a wave of the hand. Nor would there be any gains. There is not a single scientific question to which Creationism provides its own detailed problem solution. In short, Creationism could take a place among the sciences only if the substance and methods of contemporary science were mutilated to make room for a scientifically worthless doctrine. What price Creationism?

MICHAEL RUSE
Is Evolutionary Theory a Secular Religion?

MICHAEL RUSE *(b. 1940) teaches Philosophy at Florida State University. He has written many books on evolutionary theory, and served as an expert witness at the Arkansas creation/evolution trial in 1981. His most recent book is* Darwin and Design: Does Evolution Have a Purpose? *(2003). This selection is a transcript from a talk he delivered to the American Association for the Advancement of Science in 1993. In the wake of this talk, which has been circulated widely among opponents of evolutionary theory, he was accused of having "given away the store" by conceding too much to creationists.*

EUGENIE SCOTT

Our next speaker is Dr. Michael Ruse, from the Department of Philosophy at the University of Guelph in Ontario. I thought I saw him a little earlier today. Michael, hello. Michael is actually doing a couple of sessions

today, he's been a very busy fellow. And we're very pleased that he was
able to make ours as well.

Michael Ruse is a philosopher of science, particularly of the evolutionary
sciences. He's almost a person who needs no introduction in this context.
He's the author of several books on Darwinism and evolutionary theory,
including an analysis of scientific creationism entitled *But Is It Science?*
No. I don't think I've spoiled the plot. I mean, I would recommend that
you read this book, it's really quite good. But that is his conclusion. He'll
be speaking today about "Nonliteralist Antievolution." Michael?

Would you like some more light?

[THE SPEAKER'S PODIUM IS DARK.]

RUSE

It's the first time I've actually sort of given a lecture literally in the dark, as
opposed to just metaphorically. Actually, the title of my book *But Is It
Science?: The Evolution-Creation Controversy,* is intended very much to
raise the question about both evolution and creationism, and, in a way,
that's the theme of what I want to say today. . . . I am going to throw out
one or two ideas, which, in the words of Father Huddleston, who of course
got them from somewhere else, "I trust they're not to your comfort."

[THE MICROPHONE IS MOVED CLOSER TO RUSE]

God, not only am I in the dark, I've got this bloody great thing sticking in
my face too! Even if you can see me, I can't see you anymore. Talk about
non-intelligent design going on here. I was intending to come along,
when I was asked to participate in this colloquium, I was intending to
come along and talk about the book by the California lawyer Phillip
Johnson, the title of the book I'm glad to say has thankfully escaped me
just at the moment. *Darwin on Trial,* okay. What happened was I was
asked to review Phillip Johnson's book a couple of years ago, and it was
an exercise in what not to do, from my point of view, what not to do if
you're a book reviewer. Namely, if you write such a critical review of a
book, the editor who has commissioned the review might look at your
review and say, obviously that book is so lousy I don't think it's worth
talking about in our journal. And that's what happened to my review of
Phillip Johnson. It became a non-review, not I think in any sense because
it was being censored, but simply because the editor, the book review
editor, said, well frankly, I've got a lot more interesting books that we
could talk about, so we'll just drop it.

In fact, when I read Phillip Johnson's book, I mean, at one level, it's a very
impressively put together piece of work. Phillip Johnson is certainly I
think a very good lawyer, he's got a good legal mind, and he does a good
slick job of packaging. I think that when you look, when you dig down
underneath, you do start to see many of the same sorts of themes and the
ideas coming across which have been expressed—perhaps more crudely,
let's put it—by some of the friends who have been mentioned earlier,
people like Duane Gish and Henry Morris. Like everybody who reads a

book who's written anything themselves, I looked up my own name in the index first, and then went to the passages which refer to me, and thank God, I am—it's not just Stephen Jay Gould who's being referred to these days—but there were a couple of comments about me— regretfully in footnotes. And I was able to satisfy myself quite readily that in fact Phillip Johnson was playing much the same trick that everybody else was. I was quoted as putting forward some fairly hard-line social Darwinian views, in East Germany, of all places, a country which as you know no longer exists. And, in fact, fortunately the comments I had in fact made in what was East Germany in those days were taken down and in fact are printed. And I went and I checked, and, I must say, not to my—to my great relief, anyway—I was saying the exact opposite of what Phillip Johnson was saying. I mean, I'm much given to contradiction, but, thank God, this was one of those—thank God, well, thank Darwin, anyhow, as we've just heard, this wasn't one of those occasions.

So, I was intending, as I say, to come along and talk about Phillip Johnson. What happened between then and now, on the way, was that a few months ago I was invited to participate by some evangelicals in what was a sort of weekend session that they'd got, and Phillip Johnson and I were put face to face. And as I always find when I meet creationists or non-evolutionists or critics or whatever, I find it a lot easier to hate them in print than I do in person. And in fact I found—I must confess—I found Phillip Johnson to be a very congenial person, with a fund of very funny stories about Supreme Court justices, some of which may even be true, unlike his scientific claims. We did debate, and in fact I thought that we had, as others said afterwards, both evolutionists and non-evolutionists, I thought that we had what was really quite, and I want to be quite fair about this, I thought we had a really quite constructive interchange. Because basically we didn't talk so much about creationism. We certainly didn't so much talk about his particular arguments in his book, or arguments that I've put forward in *Darwinism Defended,* or these sorts of things.

But we did talk much more about the whole question of metaphysics, the whole question of philosophical bases. And what Johnson was arguing was that, at a certain level, the kind of position of a person like myself, an evolutionist, is metaphysically based at some level, just as much as the kind of position of let us say somebody, some creationist, someone like Gish or somebody like that. And to a certain extent, I must confess, in the ten years since I performed, or I appeared, in the creationism trial in Arkansas, I must say that I've been coming to this kind of position myself. And, in fact, when I first thought of putting together my collection *But Is It Science?,* I think Eugenie was right, I was inclined to say, well, yes, creationism is not science and evolution is, and that's the end of it, and you know just trying to prove that.

Now I'm starting to feel—I'm no more of a creationist now than I ever was, and I'm no less of an evolutionist now that I ever was—but I'm inclined to think that we should move our debate now onto another level, or move on. And instead of just sort of, just—I mean I realize that when one is dealing with people, say, at the school level, or these sorts of things, certain sorts of arguments are appropriate. But those of us who are academics, or for other reasons pulling back and trying to think about these things, I think that we should recognize, both historically and perhaps philosophically, certainly that the science side has certain metaphysical assumptions built into doing science, which—it may not be a good thing to admit in a court of law—but I think that in honesty that we should recognize, and that we should be thinking about some of these sorts of things. [Ed.—see articles by Hempel, Popper, and Keller in ch. 3.]

Certainly, I think that philosophers like myself have been much more sensitized to these things, over the last ten years, by trends and winds and whatever the right metaphor is, in the philosophy of science. That we've become aware, thanks to Marxists and to feminists, criticisms—the criticisms of historians and sociologists and others—that science is a much more idealistic, in the a priori sense, enterprise, than one would have got from reading the logical positivists, or even the great philosophers. The people like Popper and Hempel and Nagel, of the 1950s and 1960s, which was when my generation entered the field and started to grow up.

Certainly, historically, that if you look at, say, evolutionary theory, and of course this was brought out I think rather nicely by the talk just before me, it's certainly been the case that evolution has functioned, if not as a religion as such, certainly with elements akin to a secular religion. Those of us who teach philosophy of religion always say there's no way of defining religion by a neat, necessary and sufficient condition. The best that you can do is list a number of characteristics, [all of which some religions have, and none of which all religions have.] And certainly, there's no doubt about it, that in the past, and I think also in the present, for many evolutionists, evolution has functioned as something with elements which are, let us say, akin to being a secular religion.

I think, for instance, of the most famous family in the history of evolution, namely, the Huxleys. I think of Thomas Henry Huxley, the grandfather, and of Julian Huxley, the grandson. Certainly, if you read Thomas Henry Huxley, when he's in full flight, there's no question but that for Huxley at some very important level, evolution and science generally, but certainly evolution in particular, is functioning a bit as a kind of secular religion. Interestingly, Huxley—and I've gone through his own lectures, I've gone through two complete sets of lecture notes that Huxley gave to his students—Huxley never talked about evolution when he was actually teaching. He kept evolution for affairs like this, and when he was talking at a much more popular sort of level. Certainly, though, as I say, for Thomas Henry Huxley, I don't think there's any question but that evolution functioned, at a level, as a kind of secular religion.

And there's no question whatsoever that for Julian Huxley, when you read *Evolution, the Modern Synthesis,* that Julian Huxley saw evolution as a kind of progressive thing upwards. I think Julian Huxley was certainly an atheist, but he was at the same time a kind of neovitalist, and he bound this up with his science. If you look both at his printed stuff, and if you go down to Rice University which has got all his private papers, again and again in the letters, it comes through very strongly that for Julian Huxley evolution was functioning as a kind of secular religion.

I think that this—and I'm not saying this now particularly in a critical sense, I'm just saying this in a matter-of-fact sense—I think that today also, for more than one eminent evolutionist, evolution in a way functions as a kind of secular religion. And let me just mention my friend Edward O. Wilson. Certainly, I think that if you look at some of the stuff which caused some much controversy in the 1970s, what is interesting is not so much the fact that Wilson was talking about trying to include humans in the evolutionary scenario. Everybody was doing that. It was not so much even the fact that he was using what is now called sexist language, like "Man," because I went to look at Richard Lewontin's book, which he published the year before Wilson, and in the index it says "Homo sapiens, see 'Man' "—so, I mean, we were all committing that sort of mistake, as it is now judged. But certainly, if you look for instance in *On Human Nature*, Wilson is quite categorical about wanting to see evolution as the new myth, and all sorts of language like this. That for him, at some level, it's functioning as a kind of metaphysical system.

So, as I say, historically I think, however we're going to deal with creationism, or new creationism, or these sorts of things, whether you think that . . . what I've just been saying means that we'd better put our house in order, or whatever, I think at least we must recognize the historical facts. . . . I think that we should also look at evolution and science, in particular, biology, . . . a lot more critically—and I don't say negatively, please understand that—I think a lot more critically than we were doing ten years ago. Sensitized, I say, by the work of the social constructivists and others, historians, sociologists, and these sorts of people.

And it seems to me very clear that at some very basic level, evolution as a scientific theory makes a commitment to a kind of naturalism, namely, that at some level one is going to exclude miracles and these sorts of things, come what may. Now, you might say, does this mean it's just a religious assumption, does this mean it's irrational to do something like this? I would argue very strongly that it's not. At a certain pragmatic level, the proof of the pudding is in the eating. And that if certain things do work, you keep going with this, and that you don't change in midstream, and so on and so forth. I think that one can in fact defend a scientific and naturalistic approach, even if one recognizes that this does include metaphysical assumption [about] the regularity of nature, or something of this nature.

So as I say, I think that one can defend [this assumption] as reasonable, but I don't think it helps matters by denying that one is making it. And I think that once one has made such an assumption, one has perfect powers to turn to, say, creation science, which claims to be naturalistic also, and point out that it's wrong. I think one has every right to show that evolutionary theory in various forms certainly seems to be the most reasonable position, once one has taken a naturalistic position. So I'm not coming here and saying, give up evolution, or anything like that.

But I am coming here and saying, I think . . . philosophically that one should be sensitive to what I think history shows, namely, that evolution, just as much as religion—or at least, leave "just as much," let me leave that phrase—evolution, akin to religion, involves making certain *a priori* or metaphysical assumptions, which at some level cannot be proven empirically. I guess we all knew that, but I think that we're all much more sensitive to these facts now. And I think that the way to deal with creationism . . . is not to deny these facts, but to recognize them, and to see where we can go, as we move on from there.

Well, I've been very short, but that was my message, and I think it's an important one.

EUGENIE SCOTT

Any questions?

[THERE IS A MOMENTARY SILENCE.]

RUSE

State of shock! Yes, Ed Manier. [Manier is on the faculty of Notre Dame University.]

MANIER

Well, congratulations. I mean, you took less time than Bill Clinton. I think—maybe not quite. But you made a remark about Stephen Gould. I earlier made a remark about Stephen Gould. I think there is perhaps some sense in which you and Stephen disagree, either scientifically or metaphysically. I wonder if you could comment on that.

RUSE

That we agree or disagree?

MANIER

That you disagree. I'm always more interested in disagreement.

RUSE

Certainly I think that Steve Gould and I, we certainly disagree about the nature of evolution, there's no question about that. At some level, I'm a hard-line Darwinian. That means, you know, I'm somewhere to the right of Archdeacon Paley when it comes to design. I mean, when I look, even at you. Ed, when I look even at you, I'm already speculating why you've got a bald head, and, you know, why this makes you sexually attractive, and so on. So, I mean, yeah—whereas I think that Gould falls very much into the other, much more Germanic Naturphilosophie tradition, which stresses form over function. I don't think there's any question about that. And at a certain level, I'd be inclined to say that these are, if you like, metaphysical assumptions, paradigms, or something like that, *a priori* constraints that we're putting on the ways that we're looking at the world and all those sorts of things. Certainly, at that level, we do differ.

Where else do we differ? Gould says that he thinks that science is simply, you know, disinterested reflection of reality, then again we differ also. But of course the thing is that Gould, although he denies being a Marxist or anything like this, certainly if you look at Gould's work, for instance, when he's praising stuff, even apart from when he's criticizing stuff, I think that Gould—as much as anybody, more than most—has long been sensitive to the fact that science involves a kind of metaphysical assumption. I use the word "metaphysical" because I don't look on the word "metaphysical" as a dirty word. Like I don't look upon "teleology" as a dirty word. He may, you know, he may very ardently say don't call me a metaphysician, but I suspect that we agree, whatever we call the terms. I mean, the trouble is, metaphysics, you know, people think of metaphysics and Scottish idealists and Hegelians and all those sorts of things. So he may not want to use my language. But I suspect that about the nature of science—I suspect, but ask him—I suspect that we don't differ there. But we do differ about how we want to cash it out in the actual evolutionary realm.

MANIER

Well, if I could just pursue that, for just a minute, he may very well be more of a Naturphilosoph than you. And perhaps, although I suspect that you deny this in almost every context, more of a Romantic than you. But I'm wondering—

RUSE

How can you say that about me? After the things you said last night over drinks, but go on—

MANIER

You made reference to my baldness, and I'm sensitive about that.

RUSE

I was trying to give it an adaptive function. It's okay, I don't think it's a mistake. I mean, you know, I think God designed it that way. Go on.

MANIER

But you say that about everything.

RUSE

That's right. I'm somewhere to the right of Archdeacon Paley on this, I really am.

MANIER

Well, pardon me if I'm not flattered. What I'm curious about is the extent to which your talk suggests a strategy to the National Society of Science Teachers to have something like a pluralistic approach to these issues. That is, it's one thing to be snide about them—

RUSE

Yes. I think that's a point well taken. The trouble is, you know, Ed, I mean, everybody, I mean, the trouble is, we're balancing, we're trying to juggle so many balls in the air.

On the one hand, we're trying to do some philosophy. Another ball is trying to be science educators, both at the university level, but more particularly, at the schools level. At another level, we've got the actual political facts, of how do you fight school boards, and that sort of thing. At another level you've got the legal questions of, you know, your laws are different from my laws, for instance. Up in Canada we don't have a Constitution in that sort of way. Or at least, we've got a Constitution which has a weasel clause, you know, "in a democratic and fair society" which means that it can all be altered, if they want to, and it often is.

So, I mean you've got all of these sorts of issues, and I'm very sensitive to the fact that if a philosopher tries out, say, ideas and thinks those sorts of things, people might well say, well I hope to God you don't say this outside in public, because we're going to run into problems with the third or fourth ball, and I'm very sensitive to that.

And, to a certain extent, I think I personally have for many years used, to a certain extent, self-censorship, you know just basically not talking too much on these sorts of lines. But at the same time, I'm not sure that the way forward is by simply not thinking about things philosophically or responding to ideas, or saying, well gosh, I find what the social constructivists are saying very interesting, but, by God, I'd better not believe or accept any of this—because it's going to get us into trouble at the school board level. I mean, that's a tension. But I think that somehow, it seems to me, well, maybe two wrongs don't make a right, or do make a right. But I just don't want to do that.

As I hope I said right at the end, I don't come here preaching creationism or preaching, you know, some message of negativism: folks give up, modern philosophy of science is now showing that science is just as much a religion as creation science, so frankly folks there's nothing that you could do, and if I could go back ten years to Arkansas I'd just reverse everything. I think that you can do it. I mean I think you can't do it in just a gung-ho, straightforward, neo-Popperian way: here we've got science on the one side, here we've got religion on the other side. Evolution falls on the science side, creationism falls on the other side, and, you know, never the twain shall meet. I think you've got to go at different ways, things like, as I mentioned, pragmatism, for instance. Taking some sort of coherence theory of truth, or something like that. I still think that one can certainly exclude creation science on those grounds. Now, whether or not—how that fits in with your laws—one has to ask the lawyers, those sorts of things. I certainly think that's something that you can do.

[APPLAUSE]

EUGENIE SCOTT

Wait a minute, just—

RUSE

Before you start applauding, she's going to cut off all of my buttons, and drum me out of the society.

SCOTT

Not a bit, but he's not done yet. I'm going to take my chairman's prerogative, to ask a question, if I may. I wonder whether it might be useful to distinguish between the naturalism or materialism that is necessary to perform science as we do it in the twentieth century, as opposed to the Baconian approach, etc., and distinguish that from philosophical attitudes that we as individuals may or may not have regarding materialism or naturalism. And perhaps some of this confusion that we find at the practical level, at the school board level, and in dealing with people [like] Johnson, is that Johnson, for example, does confuse these two things. He assumes that if you are a scientist then you therefore are a philosophical materialist, in addition to being a practical materialist, in the operation of your work.

RUSE

Oh yes, I think that point is well taken. I think to sort of redress some of the rather flip comments I made, I think that's absolutely true. Let me end certainly by saying that although I got on quite well with Johnson at the personal level, I still think that his book is a slippery piece of work. And you're absolutely right that he, like any lawyer, is out to win. That's the name of the game in law. And certainly he can get points by shifting back and forth on meanings of naturalism, or if he can get a report on what Ed Manier and I were doing, and then sort of take it out of context, I've no reason to think that he wouldn't do that sort of thing. Don't misunderstand me. I'm not saying, I'm not denying the power or the importance of the sort of thing he's doing, or the importance of combatting that sort of thing.

What I am saying, nevertheless, and I will sit down now, is . . . that I as a philosopher of science am worried about what I think were fairly crude neo-positivistic attitudes that I had about science, even as much as ten years ago, when I was fighting in Arkansas. This doesn't mean to say that I don't want to stand up for evolution, I certainly do. But I do think that philosophy of science, history of science, moves on, and I think it's incumbent upon us who take this particular creationism-evolution debate seriously, to be sensitive to these facts, and not simply put our heads in the sand, and say, well, if we take this sort of stuff seriously, we're in deep trouble. Perhaps we are. But I don't think that the solution is just by simply ignoring them.

EUGENIE SCOTT

Now you can applaud, he's done.

CORY JUHL

On the "Fine-Tuning" Argument

Philosopher Cory Juhl teaches philosophy at the University of Texas and works in philosophy of science and philosophy of language.

AS Paul Davies notes in *The Mind of God*, there appear to be a large number of surprising "coincidences" in the structure of physical laws. For instance, he notes that in 1913 the Harvard biochemist Lawrence Henderson pointed out how remarkable was the "fit" of the earth's environment to life, and in the 1960s astronomer Fred Hoyle was struck by the fact that the reactions that made life possible were "a lucky fluke." It seems that the fundamental constants of physics, such as the gravitational constant and dozens of others, seem "finely tuned" to allow for life as we know it. According to the fine-tuning argument, the surprising way in which the various constants "fit together" strongly suggests that an intelligent being was involved in the production of our universe. The reasoning is straightforward. Of all the combinations of values that the constants might have taken, their values are distributed in just the right way to yield a universe that can produce life as we know it. If there is a God who wants life as we know it to arise, this is not

surprising. If there is no God, the probability that such a combination would come in to being spontaneously, or accidentally, is infinitesimally small. Since these hypotheses exhaust the class of possible explanations, we should infer that God (or at least some extremely powerful intelligent being) "fine-tuned" the universe and its laws.

A number of responses have been given to this argument. One common response made by a number of physicists is that, granting the prior improbability of any single universe being "fine-tuned," it may be that there are an enormous number of universes, whose fundamental constant values vary randomly across the collection. Given enough such universes, it is not surprising that some universe should be fine-tuned. Furthermore, intelligent observers will be around asking such questions only in fine-tuned universes, so it should not be surprising that we (intelligent observers) find ourselves in a universe of this sort. Fine-tuning advocates have responded that such a "many-universes" response

Juhl, Cory, "The Fine-Tuning Argument." Used by permission of the author.

seems ad hoc, since, they claim, there is no independent motivation (aside from theism-avoidance) for positing such worlds. Whether the "many-universes" hypothesis can be independently supported is an interesting open question.

Another response to the fine-tuning argument raises concerns about our assignments of prior probabilities to the various "universe production" scenarios. Unlike types of events that are produced regularly within our universe, we are only able to observe one universe. For example, it seems possible, for all we know, that there is a "law of universe production" that guarantees that only fine-tuned universes are ever produced. In the absence of further relevant data, which data seems impossible in principle to gather (that is, data about other universes), we simply have no justification for thinking that universes like ours are probable or improbable.

A common reaction to the proposal of a "law of universe production" that necessarily yields fine-tuned universes like ours is that "this just pushes the question back," as to why such an improbable law obtains. However, a *tu quoque* is possible here: why should a God of just the sort theists propose exist? The arguments are reminiscent of those pertaining to the cosmological argument discussed earlier. As to our ability to know prior probabilities, advocates of fine-tuning will insist that on any reasonable assignment of prior probabilities to various possible universes, fine-tuned universes will turn out to have an extremely low probability. Just as we make our best guesses on the basis of what we know in other more familiar cases, we should make our best guess in this case, which is without a doubt the conjecture that there is an Intelligent Designer.

Whether this is our best guess, though, remains questionable. In order to see why, we can consider any hypothesis as to the probability that God would produce a universe of any given type. Given any hypothesis of this sort, there is an atheistic hypothesis (involving, say, a law of universe production) that yields universes of any given type with exactly the same probability. In a nutshell, given any theistic hypothesis about the probabilities of various types of universes, there is an "equivalent" atheistic hypothesis that assigns exactly the same probabilities to the creation of exactly the same types of universes. So the question becomes, is it obvious that in general we should prefer theistic hypotheses of that sort over atheistic hypotheses of the same sort? Opinions will differ, but it is far from clear that of any such pair of analogous pairs of hypotheses, the theistic hypotheses are intrinsically more plausible.

DANIEL C. DENNETT
Show Me the Science

DANIEL C. DENNETT *is Distinguished Arts and Science Professor and Director of Cognitive Studies at Tufts University and the author of* Darwin's Dangerous Idea, Consciousness Explained, *and many other books.*

PRESIDENT Bush, announcing this month that he was in favor of teaching about "intelligent design" in the schools, said, "I think that part of education is to expose people to different schools of thought." A couple of weeks later, Senator Bill Frist of Tennessee, the Republican leader, made the same point. Teaching both intelligent design and evolution "doesn't force any particular theory on anyone," Mr. Frist said. "I think in a pluralistic society that is the fairest way to go about education and training people for the future."

Is "intelligent design" a legitimate school of scientific thought? Is there something to it, or have these people been taken in by one of the most ingenious hoaxes in the history of science? Wouldn't such a hoax be impossible? No. Here's how it has been done.

First, imagine how easy it would be for a determined band of naysayers to shake the world's confidence in quantum physics—how weird it is!—or Einsteinian relativity. In spite of a century of instruction and popularization by physicists, few people ever really get their heads around the concepts involved. Most people eventually cobble together a justification for accepting the assurances of the experts: "Well, they pretty much agree with one another, and they claim that it is their understanding of these strange topics that allows them to harness atomic energy, and to make transistors and lasers, which certainly do work. . . ."

Fortunately for physicists, there is no powerful motivation for such a band of mischief-makers to form. They don't have to spend much time persuading people that quantum physics and Einsteinian relativity really have been established beyond all reasonable doubt.

With evolution, however, it is different. The fundamental scientific idea of evolution by natural selection is not just mind-boggling; natural selection, by executing God's traditional task of designing and creating all creatures great and small, also seems to deny one of the best reasons we have for believing in God. So there is plenty of motivation for resisting the assurances of the biologists. Nobody is immune to wishful thinking. It takes

scientific discipline to protect ourselves from our own credulity, but we've also found ingenious ways to fool ourselves and others. Some of the methods used to exploit these urges are easy to analyze; others take a little more unpacking.

A creationist pamphlet sent to me some years ago had an amusing page in it, purporting to be part of a simple questionnaire:

Test Two

> Do you know of any building that didn't have a builder? [YES] [NO]
>
> Do you know of any painting that didn't have a painter? [YES] [NO]
>
> Do you know of any car that didn't have a maker? [YES] [NO]
>
> If you answered YES for any of the above, give details:

Take that, you Darwinians! The presumed embarrassment of the test-taker when faced with this task perfectly expresses the incredulity many people feel when they confront Darwin's great idea. It seems obvious, doesn't it, that there couldn't be any designs without designers, any such creations without a creator.

Well, yes—until you look at what contemporary biology has demonstrated beyond all reasonable doubt: that natural selection—the process in which reproducing entities must compete for finite resources and thereby engage in a tournament of blind trial and error from which improvements automatically emerge—has the power to generate breathtakingly ingenious designs.

Take the development of the eye, which has been one of the favorite challenges of creationists. How on earth, they ask, could that engineering marvel be produced by a series of small, unplanned steps? Only an intelligent designer could have created such a brilliant arrangement of a shape-shifting lens, an aperture-adjusting iris, a light-sensitive image surface of exquisite sensitivity, all housed in a sphere that can shift its aim in a hundredth of a second and send megabytes of information to the visual cortex every second for years on end.

But as we learn more and more about the history of the genes involved, and how they work—all the way back to their predecessor genes in the sightless bacteria from which multicelled animals evolved more than a half-billion years ago—we can begin to tell the story of how photosensitive spots gradually turned into light-sensitive craters that could detect the rough direction from which light came, and then gradually acquired their lenses, improving their information-gathering capacities all the while.

We can't yet say what all the details of this process were, but real eyes representative of all the intermediate stages can be found, dotted around the animal kingdom, and we have detailed computer models to demonstrate that the creative process works just as the theory says.

All it takes is a rare accident that gives one lucky animal a mutation that improves its vision over that of its siblings; if this helps it have more offspring than its rivals, this gives evolution an opportunity to raise the bar and ratchet up the design of the eye by one mindless step. And since these lucky improvements accumulate—this was Darwin's insight—eyes can automatically get better and better and better, without any intelligent designer.

Brilliant as the design of the eye is, it betrays its origin with a tell-tale flaw: the retina is inside out. The nerve fibers that carry the signals from the eye's rods and cones (which sense light and color) lie on top of them, and have to plunge through a large hole in the retina to get to the brain, creating the blind spot. No intelligent designer would put such a clumsy arrangement in a camcorder, and this is just one of hundreds of accidents frozen in evolutionary history that confirm the mindlessness of the historical process.

If you still find Test Two compelling, a sort of cognitive illusion that you can feel even as you discount it, you are like just about everybody else in the world; the idea that natural selection has the power to generate such sophisticated designs is deeply counterintuitive. Francis Crick, one of the discoverers of DNA, once jokingly credited his colleague Leslie Orgel with "Orgel's Second

Rule": Evolution is cleverer than you are. Evolutionary biologists are often startled by the power of natural selection to "discover" an "ingenious" solution to a design problem posed in the lab.

This observation lets us address a slightly more sophisticated version of the cognitive illusion presented by Test Two. When evolutionists like Crick marvel at the cleverness of the process of natural selection they are not acknowledging intelligent design. The designs found in nature are nothing short of brilliant, but the process of design that generates them is utterly lacking in intelligence of its own.

Intelligent design advocates, however, exploit the ambiguity between process and product that is built into the word "design." For them, the presence of a finished product (a fully evolved eye, for instance) is evidence of an intelligent design process. But this tempting conclusion is just what evolutionary biology has shown to be mistaken.

Yes, eyes are for seeing, but these and all the other purposes in the natural world can be generated by processes that are themselves without purposes and without intelligence. This is hard to understand, but so is the idea that colored objects in the world are composed of atoms that are not themselves colored, and that heat is not made of tiny hot things.

The focus on intelligent design has, paradoxically, obscured something else: genuine scientific controversies about evolution that abound. In just about every field there are challenges to one established theory or another. The legitimate way to stir up such a storm is to come up with an alternative theory that makes a prediction that is crisply denied by the reigning theory—but that turns out to be true, or that explains something that has been baffling defenders of the status quo, or that unifies two distant theories at the cost of some element of the currently accepted view.

To date, the proponents of intelligent design have not produced anything like that. No experiments with results that challenge any mainstream biological understanding. No observations from the fossil record or genomics or biogeography or comparative anatomy that undermine standard evolutionary thinking.

Instead, the proponents of intelligent design use a ploy that works something like this. First you misuse or misdescribe some scientist's work. Then you get an angry rebuttal. Then, instead of dealing forthrightly with the charges leveled, you cite the rebuttal as evidence that there is a "controversy" to teach.

Note that the trick is content-free. You can use it on any topic. "Smith's work in geology supports my argument that the earth is flat," you say, misrepresenting Smith's work. When Smith responds with a denunciation of your misuse of her work, you respond, saying something like: "See what a controversy we have here? Professor Smith and I are locked in a titanic scientific debate. We should teach the controversy in the classrooms." And here is the delicious part: you can often exploit the very technicality of the issues to your own advantage, counting on most of us to miss the point in all the difficult details.

William Dembski, one of the most vocal supporters of intelligent design, notes that he provoked Thomas Schneider, a biologist, into a response that Dr. Dembski characterizes as "some hair-splitting that could only look ridiculous to outsider observers." What looks to scientists—and is—a knockout objection by Dr. Schneider is portrayed to most everyone else as ridiculous hair-splitting.

In short, no science. Indeed, no intelligent design hypothesis has even been ventured as a rival explanation of any biological phenomenon. This might seem surprising to people who think that intelligent design competes directly with the hypothesis of non-intelligent design by natural selection. But saying, as intelligent design proponents do, "You haven't explained everything yet," is not a competing hypothesis. Evolutionary biology certainly hasn't explained everything that perplexes biologists. But intelligent design hasn't yet tried to explain anything.

To formulate a competing hypothesis, you have to get down in the trenches and offer details that have testable implications. So far,

intelligent design proponents have conveniently sidestepped that requirement, claiming that they have no specifics in mind about who or what the intelligent designer might be.

To see this shortcoming in relief, consider an imaginary hypothesis of intelligent design that could explain the emergence of human beings on this planet:

About six million years ago, intelligent genetic engineers from another galaxy visited Earth and decided that it would be a more interesting planet if there was a language-using, religion-forming species on it, so they sequestered some primates and genetically re-engineered them to give them the language instinct, and enlarged frontal lobes for planning and reflection. It worked.

If some version of this hypothesis were true, it could explain how and why human beings differ from their nearest relatives, and it would disconfirm the competing evolutionary hypotheses that are being pursued.

We'd still have the problem of how these intelligent genetic engineers came to exist on their home planet, but we can safely ignore that complication for the time being, since there is not the slightest shred of evidence in favor of this hypothesis.

But here is something the intelligent design community is reluctant to discuss: no other intelligent-design hypothesis has anything more going for it. In fact, my farfetched hypothesis has the advantage of being testable in principle: we could compare the human and chimpanzee genomes, looking for unmistakable signs of tampering by these genetic engineers from another galaxy. Finding some sort of user's manual neatly embedded in the apparently functionless "junk DNA" that makes up most of the human genome would be a Nobel Prize-winning coup for the intelligent design gang, but if they are looking at all, they haven't come up with anything to report.

It's worth pointing out that there are plenty of substantive scientific controversies in biology that are not yet in the textbooks or the classrooms. The scientific participants in these arguments vie for acceptance among the relevant expert communities in peer-reviewed journals, and the writers and editors of textbooks grapple with judgments about which findings have risen to the level of acceptance—not yet truth—to make them worth serious consideration by undergraduates and high school students.

So get in line, intelligent designers. Get in line behind the hypothesis that life started on Mars and was blown here by a cosmic impact. Get in line behind the aquatic ape hypothesis, the gestural origin of language hypothesis and the theory that singing came before language, to mention just a few of the enticing hypotheses that are actively defended but still insufficiently supported by hard facts.

The Discovery Institute, the conservative organization that has helped to put intelligent design on the map, complains that its members face hostility from the established scientific journals. But establishment hostility is not the real hurdle to intelligent design. If intelligent design were a scientific idea whose time had come, young scientists would be dashing around their labs, vying to win the Nobel Prizes that surely are in store for anybody who can overturn any significant proposition of contemporary evolutionary biology.

Remember cold fusion? The establishment was incredibly hostile to that hypothesis, but scientists around the world rushed to their labs in the effort to explore the idea, in hopes of sharing in the glory if it turned out to be true.

Instead of spending more than $1 million a year on publishing books and articles for non-scientists and on other public relations efforts, the Discovery Institute should finance its own peer-reviewed electronic journal. This way, the organization could live up to its self-professed image: the doughty defenders of brave iconoclasts bucking the establishment.

For now, though, the theory they are promoting is exactly what George Gilder, a long-time affiliate of the Discovery Institute, has said it is: "Intelligent design itself does not have any content."

Since there is no content, there is no "controversy" to teach about in biology class. But here is a good topic for a high school course on current events and politics: Is intelligent design a hoax? And if so, how was it perpetrated?

CHAPTER FIVE

How Is My Mind Connected to My Body?

Anybody who can read this book, or even this sentence, can think. It is tempting to conclude, as Descartes did in his *Second Meditation,* that anybody who can read this book, or even this sentence, has a mind. In addition, most of us are quite certain that we have a body, although Descartes attempted to doubt even this. But the question of what the relationship is between our minds and our bodies is one of the most enduring and puzzling in philosophy. It is also one of the most immediate, because it has direct consequences for our views about what and who we are.

Descartes believed that the mind and the body are distinct substances. He was therefore a **dualist,** a person who believes that there are two fundamentally different kinds of "stuff" (mental and physical) in the universe. The dualist is faced with the difficult problem of explaining what the relationship is between these two fundamentally different kinds of stuff. The usual view is this. Let's say there is a song playing on the radio (a physical event). You hear the song, and that causes you to remember or think of a summer friend (a mental event). Your remembering in turn causes you to write your friend a letter (a physical event). Here, a physical event (the playing of the song) causes a mental event (the remembering), which causes a physical event (the writing). Here's another example: You hit your thumb with a hammer (physical event), which causes pain (mental event), which in turn causes you to scream and hop up and down (physical event). The view that mental and physical events interact in this way is called **interactionism.** Dualistic interactionism represents most people's commonsense view about the relationship between the mental and the physical.

Unfortunately, there are two very difficult problems that an interactionist dualist must solve. The first is the problem of what it is that makes your mind yours and not someone else's. Is it perhaps located in your body? But if so, what makes it move when your body moves? Is it glued, stapled, or tied to your brain? If so, how do you attach a nonphysical substance to a physical one? Perhaps it is not located in space at all. (How could a nonphysical substance be located in space anyway?) But if it's not, how exactly did the broken bone in your thumb cause a pain in *your* mind and not in your brother's mind? How did the pain in your mind cause *your* body to hop and not Mick Jagger's?

Related to this problem, and even more vexing, is the question of giving a clear and exact account of how any nonphysical substance could cause changes in a physical substance, or vice versa. How exactly would a nonphysical substance cause molecules of a transmitter substance to be released from the cells of the brain? (This is the mechanism for the transmission of signals in the brain.) Most people regard with suspicion a claim that a nonphysical mind has moved some dice or a table. They should regard with equal suspicion a claim that a nonphysical mind has moved an arm or a toe.

It is these problems that have led some philosophers and quite a few scientists to the odd view that mind and brain do not interact as we might have thought. The most common of these views is **epiphenomenalism.** According to this view, mental events are epiphenomena, which are literally phenomena *outside* the rest of the person. Epiphenomenalists believe that physical events can cause mental events but that mental events never affect physical events. What you think, believe, and desire is merely a symptom of what is going on in your brain; it never actually makes a difference in what you *do.* Your mind is merely a window into your brain: It observes what happens in the brain and reacts accordingly, but it can never affect the workings of the brain (or the body). Epiphenomenalism must then explain how our ordinary view, that mental events do cause physical events, can be so badly mistaken. It must also give some explanation of how it could be that a physical event could cause a nonphysical event.

One attractive way of dealing with these problems is to deny that they are problems at all. This is what Gilbert Ryle, the famous **behaviorist,** does in his selection, from his book *The Concept of Mind.* In a later part of that book, he argues that our talk of mental states and events is really just talk about behavior, not, as it pretends, talk about inner events that cause us to do what we do.

In response to these problems, most contemporary philosophers have adopted some form of **physicalism,** the view that there are not separate mental and physical things in the universe, but rather that everything is physical. Much of the current philosophical debate about the mind/body problem presupposes a framework of physicalism. One early form of physicalism is known as the **identity theory.** The identity theory claimed that each mental event—for example, wanting to eat dinner—could be identified with a very specific, purely physical event—for example, firing of neurons number 87 and 163. This requires that each time a "wanting to eat dinner" takes place, a firing of neurons 87 and 163 takes place, because wanting to eat dinner *is* the firing of those two neurons. The identity theory, in this crude form, has now largely been discredited by the observation that dogs and extraterrestrials could both want to eat dinner, but might not have any neurons at all (in the case of extraterrestrials), much less neurons number 87 and 163. Different organisms, with very different physical structures, can all have nonphysical things such as beliefs and desires.

Thus, much current physicalism rejects the identity theory and tries to explain how mental events could be physical but not definable in terms of neurophysiological states. Eliminative materialists take a radical view, claiming that the language of biological science is a privileged scientific way of describing human beings. Because mental states like belief and desire can't be defined in that language, talk of such mental states must be radically defective and should be eliminated in favor of vocabulary that *can* be explained in purely biological terms. They conclude that people do not really have beliefs and desires; the view that we have beliefs and desires is, they go on to claim, an outmoded theory, a **folk-psychology,** that, like other defective theories, should be discarded with the advance of physical science.

Most people are not willing to accept the conclusion that we do not really have beliefs, desires, or other mental states. The problem then becomes how to explain beliefs and desires as genuine physical states of a person, while still rejecting the notion that they can be defined neurophysiologically. **Functionalism** is the view to which most modern physicalists have turned. It is the view that mental events are defined in terms of what they cause and what they affect, which includes both physical events and other mental events. Thus, different things (a person, a dog, an extraterrestrial, a computer) could have the same mental events by having (physically) different things going on inside that are related causally or functionally (that is, in terms of what their function is) in the ways characteristic of those mental events. The pain in your foot may be signals in the thalamus in your brain. In a dog, the pain in its foot may have to do with some other part of its brain. A spaceman may not have a thalamus but could still have a pain in his foot. In each being, whatever state is caused by dropping a hammer on its toe and causing it to hop up and down and scream is pain. In this view, it is not possible to "reduce" psychological terms such as "believe" or "want" to biological terms. But even though mental terms cannot be reduced to physical terms and so we must still have a psychological vocabulary, that does not mean that there is mental stuff in the universe. There is only mental talk about physical stuff. William Lycan argues for a particularly appealing form of functionalism and for the consequent view that machines could come to have the same moral and social properties and relationships that humans now have.

By way of contrast, John R. Searle, in a now-classic argument against functionalism, launches a deep and provocative critique of the approach taken by Lycan and others. He argues with some flair that any approach that ignores the actual biological stuff of an organism (the "wetware") cannot genuinely explain that organism. If Searle is right, then it is not possible for a computer really to think or to have feelings. The best that a computer could do is to behave as *though* it has thoughts and feelings. If so, then the project of understanding our conscious mental lives in the functionalist terms of the causal roles that our mental states occupy is hopelessly mistaken.

Elizabeth V. Spelman in her selection offers an entirely different analysis of the mind/body problem, claiming that philosophers have been influenced systematically by unrecognized political and social views (specifically, gender views) in their conceptions of the relationship between mind and body. She argues that our entire conception of the mind (or soul) serves a view of humans that deprecates women and nondominant races. In raising this issue she places under scrutiny the very process by which philosophers have traditionally addressed philosophical issues.

Finally, Francisco Varela and his coauthors agree with Spelman that our difficulties with the mind-body problem have been created by the very structure in which we have conceived of the problem. But in contrast to Spelman, Varela et al. argue that Buddhist conceptions of the self provide a way for seeing ourselves as simultaneously physical and spiritual—as "embodied minds."

The mind/body problem offers philosophical terrain that is both treacherous and rewarding. The problems it poses are particularly pressing because they are so closely tied to a great deal of current scientific work and because they are so frightfully misunderstood. For example, a neuroscientist (a scientist who studies brain function) may have discovered a physiological basis for some phenomenon such as depression. She may then go on to conclude that psychologists (Freud, for example) who have hypothesized a psychological origin for depression have thereby been shown to be wrong. Nothing could be further from the truth. Differing physiological and psychological explanations for the same phenomenon are exactly what one would expect if physicalism is true.

Another subtler mistake is this: A neuroscientist may, at the end of a long career, come to despair of ever being able to define some psychological state, such as the state of understanding, in biological terms. She may conclude that understanding is not a biological phenomenon. This is how many neuroscientists come oddly to be epiphenomenalists. Again the conclusion rests on a confusion. As both functionalism and eliminative materialism make clear, physicalism does not suggest that one can reduce the psychological to the physical or define psychological terms in biological (or any other physical) terms. So the inability to define understanding, or any other mental phenomenon, in biological terms does not show that there is anything nonphysical about understanding, or any other mental phenomenon. It is possible to be physicalist and still to believe strongly in the need for psychological theories. All these are areas in which philosophers have much by way of clarification to contribute to their scientific friends.

RENÉ DESCARTES
Mind as Distinct from Body

RENÉ DESCARTES *(1596–1650) was born in Britanny, France. He went to college at the age of eight and was finished at the age of sixteen, having studied logic, philosophy, and mathematics. He did important work in mathematics and science in addition to his revolutionary work in philosophy. Descartes was in the habit of spending long morning hours reflecting in bed. But when he entered the service of Sweden's Queen Christina in 1649, he was expected to begin teaching her in the library at 5 A.M. Unaccustomed to such rigors, and to the Swedish winter, he took fever and died early in 1650.*

MEDITATIONS ON THE FIRST PHILOSOPHY IN WHICH THE EXISTENCE OF GOD AND THE DISTINCTION BETWEEN MIND AND BODY ARE DEMONSTRATED

Meditation I.

Of the Things which May Be Brought within the Sphere of the Doubtful. It is now some years since I detected how many were the false beliefs that I had from my earliest youth admitted as true, and how doubtful was everything I had since constructed on this basis; and from that time I was convinced that I must once for all seriously undertake to rid myself of all the opinions which I had formerly accepted, and commence to build anew from the foundation, if I wanted to establish any firm and permanent structure in the sciences. But as this enterprise appeared to be a very great one, I waited until I had attained an age so mature that I could not hope that at any later date I should be better fitted to execute my design. This reason caused me to delay so long that I should feel that I was doing wrong were I to occupy in deliberation the time that yet remains to me for action. Today, then, since very opportunely for the plan I have in view I have delivered my mind from every care [and am happily agitated by no passions]

and since I have procured for myself an assured leisure in a peaceable retirement, I shall at last seriously and freely address myself to the general upheaval of all my former opinions.

Now for this object it is not necessary that I should show that all of these are false—I shall perhaps never arrive at this end. But inasmuch as reason already persuades me that I ought no less carefully to withhold my assent from matters which are not entirely certain and indubitable than from those which appear to me manifestly to be false, if I am able to find in each one some reason to doubt, this will suffice to justify my rejecting the whole. And for that end it will not be requisite that I should examine each in particular, which would be an endless undertaking; for owing to the fact that the destruction of the foundations of necessity brings with it the downfall of the rest of the edifice, I shall only in the first place attack those principles upon which all my former opinions rested.

All that up to the present time I have accepted as most true and certain I have learned either from the senses or through the senses; but it is sometimes proved to me that these senses are deceptive, and it is wiser not to trust entirely to any thing by which we have once been deceived.

But it may be that although the senses some-times deceive us concerning things which are

"Mind as Distinct From Body," from *Meditations* by Rene Descartes, translated by Haldane and Ross (Cambridge University Press, 1911)

hardly perceptible, or very far away, there are yet many others to be met with as to which we cannot reasonably have any doubt, although we recognise them by their means. For example, there is the fact that I am here, seated by the fire, attired in a dressing gown, having this paper in my hands and other similar matters. And how could I deny that these hands and this body are mine, were it not perhaps that I compare myself to certain persons, devoid of sense, whose cerebella are so troubled and clouded by the violent vapours of black bile, that they constantly assure us that they think they are kings when they are really quite poor, or that they are clothed in purple when they are really without covering, or who imagine that they have an earthenware head or are nothing but pumpkins or are made of glass. But they are mad, and I should not be any the less insane were I to follow examples so extravagant.

At the same time I must remember that I am a man, and that consequently I am in the habit of sleeping, and in my dreams representing to myself the same things or sometimes even less probable things, than do those who are insane in their waking moments. How often has it happened to me that in the night I dreamt that I found myself in this particular place, that I was dressed and seated near the fire, whilst in reality I was lying undressed in bed! At this moment it does indeed seem to me that it is with eyes awake that I am looking at this paper; that this head which I move is not asleep, that it is deliberately and of set purpose that I extend my hand and perceive it; what happens in sleep does not appear so clear nor so distinct as does all this. But in thinking over this I remind myself that on many occasions I have in sleep been deceived by similar illusions, and in dwelling carefully on this reflection I see so manifestly that there are no certain indications by which we may clearly distinguish wakefulness from sleep that I am lost in astonishment. And my astonishment is such that it is almost capable of persuading me that I now dream.

Now let us assume that we are asleep and that all these particulars, e.g. that we open our eyes, shake our head, extend our hands, and so on, are but false delusions; and let us reflect that possibly neither our hands nor our whole body are such as they appear to us to be. At the same time we must at least confess that the things which are represented to us in sleep are like painted representations which can only have been formed as the counterparts of something real and true, and that in this way those general things at least, i.e. eyes, a head, hands, and a whole body, are not imaginary things, but things really existent. For, as a matter of fact, painters, even when they study with the greatest skill to represent sirens and satyrs by forms the most strange and extraordinary, cannot give them natures which are entirely new, but merely make a certain medley of the members of different animals; or if their imagination is extravagant enough to invent something so novel that nothing similar has ever before been seen, and that then their work represents a thing purely fictitious and absolutely false, it is certain all the same that the colours of which this is composed are necessarily real. And for the same reason, although these general things, to wit, [a body], eyes, a head, hands, and such like, may be imaginary, we are bound at the same time to confess that there are at least some other objects yet more simple and more universal, which are real and true; and of these just in the same way as with certain real colours, all these images of things which dwell in our thoughts, whether true and real or false and fantastic, are formed.

To such a class of things pertains corporeal nature in general, and its extension, the figure of extended things, their quantity or magnitude and number, as also the place in which they are, the time which measures their duration, and so on.

That is possibly why our reasoning is not unjust when we conclude from this that Physics, Astronomy, Medicine and all other sciences which have as their end the consideration of composite things, are very dubious and uncertain; but that Arithmetic, Geometry and other sciences of that kind which only treat of things that are very simple and very general, without taking great trouble to ascertain whether they are actually existent or not, contain some measure of certainty and an element of the indubitable. For whether I am awake or asleep, two and three together always form five, and the square can never have more than four sides, and it does not seem possible that truths so clear and apparent can be suspected of any falsity [or uncertainty].

Nevertheless I have long had fixed in my mind that belief that an all-powerful God existed by whom I have been created such as I am. But how do I know that He has not brought it to pass that there is no earth, no heaven, no extended body, no magnitude, no place, and that nevertheless [I possess the perceptions of all these things and that] they seem to me to exist just exactly as I now see them? And, besides, as I sometimes imagine that others deceive themselves in the things which they think they know best, how do I know that I am not deceived every time that I add two and three, or count the sides of a square, or judge of things yet simpler, if anything simpler can be imagined? But possibly God has not desired that I should be thus deceived, for He is said to be supremely good. If, however, it is contrary to His goodness to have made me such that I constantly deceive myself, it would also appear to be contrary to His goodness to permit me to be sometimes deceived, and nevertheless I cannot doubt that He does permit this.

There may indeed be those who would prefer to deny the existence of a God so powerful, rather than believe that all other things are uncertain. But let us not oppose them for the present, and grant that all that is here said of a God is a fable; nevertheless in whatever way they suppose that I have arrived at the state of being that I have reached—whether they attribute it to fate or to accident, or make out that it is by a continual succession of antecedents, or by some other method—since to err and deceive oneself is a defect, it is clear that the greater will be the probability of my being so imperfect as to deceive myself ever, as is the Author to whom they assign my origin the less powerful. To these reasons I have certainly nothing to reply, but at the end I feel constrained to confess that there is nothing in all that I formerly believed to be true,

of which I cannot in some measure doubt, and that not merely through want of thought or through levity, but for reasons which are very powerful and maturely considered; so that henceforth I ought not the less carefully to refrain from giving credence to these opinions than to that which is manifestly false, if I desire to arrive at any certainty [in the sciences].

But it is not sufficient to have made these remarks, we must also be careful to keep them in mind. For these ancient and commonly held opinions still revert frequently to my mind, long and familiar custom having given them the right to occupy my mind against my inclination and rendered them almost masters of my belief; nor will I ever lose the habit of deferring to them or of placing my confidence in them, so long as I consider them as they really are, i.e. opinions in some measure doubtful, as I have just shown, and at the same time highly probable, so that there is much more reason to believe in than to deny them. That is why I consider that I shall not be acting amiss, if, taking of set purpose a contrary belief, I allow myself to be deceived, and for a certain time pretend that all these opinions are entirely false and imaginary, until at last, having thus balanced my former prejudices with my latter [so that they cannot divert my opinions more to one side than to the other], my judgment will no longer be dominated by bad usage or turned away from the right knowledge of the truth. For I am assured that there can be neither peril nor error in this course, and that I cannot at present yield too much to distrust, since I am not considering the question of action, but only of knowledge.

I shall then suppose, not that God who is supremely good and the fountain of truth, but some evil genius not less powerful than deceitful, has employed his whole energies in deceiving me; I shall consider that the heavens, the earth, colours, figures, sound, and all other external things are nought but the illusions and dreams of which this genius has availed himself in order to lay traps for my credulity; I shall consider myself as having no hands, no eyes, no flesh, no blood, nor any senses, yet falsely believing myself to possess all these things; I shall remain obstinately attached to this idea, and if by this means it is not in my power to arrive at the knowledge of any truth, I may at least do what is in my power [i.e. suspend my judgment], and with firm purpose avoid giving credence to any false thing, or being imposed upon by this arch deceiver, however powerful and deceptive he may be. But this task is a laborious one, and insensibly a certain lassitude leads me into the course of my ordinary life. And just as a captive who in sleep enjoys an imaginary liberty, when he begins to suspect that his liberty is but a dream, fears to awaken, and conspires with these agreeable illusions that the deception may be prolonged, so insensibly of my own accord I fall back into my former opinions, and I dread awakening from this slumber, lest the laborious wakefulness which would follow the tranquillity of this repose should have to be spent not in daylight, but in the excessive darkness of the difficulties which have just been discussed.

Meditation II.

Of the Nature of the Human Mind; and that It Is More Easily Known than the Body. The Meditation of yesterday filled my mind with so many doubts that it is no longer in my power to forget them. And yet I do not see in what manner I can resolve them; and, just as if I had all of a sudden fallen into very deep water, I am so disconcerted that I can neither make certain of setting my feet on the bottom, nor can I swim and so support myself on the surface. I shall nevertheless make an effort and follow anew the same path as that on which I yesterday entered, i.e. I shall proceed by setting aside all that in which the least doubt could be supposed to exist, just as if I had discovered that it was absolutely false; and I shall ever follow in this road until I have met with something which is certain, or at least, if I can do nothing else, until I have learned for certain that there is nothing in the world that is certain. Archimedes, in order that he might draw the terrestrial globe out of its place, and transport it elsewhere, demanded only

that one point should be fixed and immoveable; in the same way I shall have the right to conceive high hopes if I am happy enough to discover one thing only which is certain and indubitable.

I suppose, then, that all the things that I see are false; I persuade myself that nothing has ever existed of all that my fallacious memory represents to me. I consider that I possess no senses; I imagine that body, figure, extension, movement and place are but the fictions of my mind. What, then, can be esteemed as true? Perhaps nothing at all, unless that there is nothing in the world that is certain.

But how can I know there is not something different from those things that I have just considered, of which one cannot have the slightest doubt? Is there not some God, or some other being by whatever name we call it, who puts these reflections into my mind? That is not necessary, for is it not possible that I am capable of producing them myself? I myself, am I not at least something? But I have already denied that I had senses and body. Yet I hesitate, for what follows from that? Am I so dependent on body and senses that I cannot exist without these? But I was persuaded that there was nothing in all the world, that there was no heaven, no earth, that there were no minds, nor any bodies: was I not then likewise persuaded that I did not exist? Not at all; of a surety I myself did exist since I persuaded myself of something [or merely because I thought of something]. But there is some deceiver or other, very powerful and very cunning, who ever employs his ingenuity in deceiving me. Then without doubt I exist also if he deceives me, and let him deceive me as much as he will, he can never cause me to be nothing so long as I think that I am something. So that after having reflected well and carefully examined all things, we must come to the definite conclusion that this proposition: I am, I exist, is necessarily true each time that I pronounce it, or that I mentally conceive it.

But I do not yet know clearly enough what I am, I who am certain that I am; and hence I must be careful to see that I do not imprudently take some other object in place of myself, and thus that I do not go astray in respect of this knowledge that I hold to be the most certain and most evident of all that I have formerly learned. That is why I shall now consider anew what I believed myself to be before I embarked upon these last reflections; and of my former opinions I shall withdraw all that might even in a small degree be invalidated by the reasons which I have just brought forward, in order that there may be nothing at all left beyond what is absolutely certain and indubitable.

GILBERT RYLE
The Concept of Mind

GILBERT RYLE *(1900–1976) was for many years a professor of philosophy at Oxford. His book,* The Concept of Mind, *from which this selection is taken, was a highly influential statement of philosophical behaviorism.*

THE OFFICIAL DOCTRINE

THERE is a doctrine about the nature and place of minds which is so prevalent among theorists and even among laymen that it deserves to be described as the official theory. Most philosophers, psychologists and religious teachers subscribe, with minor reservations, to its main articles and, although they admit certain theoretical difficulties in it, they tend to assume that these can be overcome without serious modifications being made to the architecture of the theory. It will be argued here that the central principles of the doctrine are unsound and conflict with the whole body of what we know about minds when we are not speculating about them.

The official doctrine, which hails chiefly from Descartes, is something like this. With the doubtful exceptions of idiots and infants in arms, every human being has both a body and a mind. His body and his mind are ordinarily harnessed together, but after the death of the body his mind may continue to exist and function.

Human bodies are in space and are subject to the mechanical laws which govern all other bodies in space. Bodily processes and states can be inspected by external observers. So a man's bodily life is as much a public affair as are the lives of animals and reptiles and even as the careers of trees, crystals and planets.

But minds are not in space, nor are their operations subject to mechanical laws. The workings of one mind are not witnessable by other observers; its career is private. Only I can take direct cognisance of the states and processes of my own mind. A person therefore lives through two collateral histories, one consisting of what happens in and to his body, the other consisting of what happens in and to his mind. The first is public, the second private. The events in the first history are events in the physical world, those in the second are events in the mental world.

It has been disputed whether a person does or can directly monitor all or only some of the episodes of his own private history; but, according to the official doctrine, of at least some of these episodes he has direct and unchallengeable cognisance. In consciousness, self-consciousness and introspection he is directly and authentically apprised of the present states and operations of his mind. He may have great or small uncertainties about concurrent and adjacent episodes in the physical world, but he can have none about at least part of what is momentarily occupying his mind.

It is customary to express this bifurcation of his two lives and of his two worlds by saying that the things and events which belong to the physical world, including his own body, are external, while the workings of his own mind are internal. This antithesis of outer and inner is of course meant to be construed as a metaphor, since minds, not being in space, could not be described as being spatially inside anything else, or as having things going on spatially inside themselves. But relapses from this good intention are common and theorists are found speculating how stimuli, the physical sources of which are yards or miles outside a person's skin, can generate mental responses inside his skull, or how decisions framed inside his cranium can set going movements of his extremities.

Even when 'inner' and 'outer' are construed as metaphors, the problem how a person's mind and body influence one another is notoriously charged with theoretical difficulties. What the mind wills, the legs, arms and the tongue execute; what affects the ear and the eye has something to do with what the mind perceives; grimaces and smiles betray the mind's moods and bodily castigations lead, it is hoped, to moral improvement. But the actual transactions between the episodes of the private history and those of the public history remain mysterious, since by definition they can belong to neither series. They could not be reported among the happenings described in a person's autobiography of his inner life, but nor could they be reported among those described in some one

else's biography of that person's overt career. They can be inspected neither by introspection nor by laboratory experiment. They are theoretical shuttlecocks which are forever being bandied from the physiologist back to the psychologist and from the psychologist back to the physiologist.

Underlying this partly metaphorical representation of the bifurcation of a person's two lives there is a seemingly more profound and philosophical assumption. It is assumed that there are two different kinds of existence or status. What exists or happens may have the status of physical existence, or it may have the status of mental existence. Somewhat as the faces of coins are either heads or tails, or somewhat as living creatures are either male or female, so, it is supposed, some existing is physical existing, other existing is mental existing. It is a necessary feature of what has physical existence that it is in space and time, it is a necessary feature of what has mental existence that it is in time but not in space. What has physical existence is composed of matter, or else is a function of matter; what has mental existence consists of consciousness, or else is a function of consciousness.

There is thus a polar opposition between mind and matter, an opposition which is often brought out as follows. Material objects are situated in a common field, known as "space," and what happens to one body in one part of space is mechanically connected with what happens to the other bodies in other parts of space. But mental happenings occur in insulated fields, known as "minds," and there is, apart maybe from telepathy, no direct causal connection between what happens in one mind and what happens in another. Only through the medium of the public physical world can the mind of one person make a difference to the mind of another. The mind is its own place and in his inner life each of us lives the life of a ghostly Robinson Crusoe. People can see, hear and jolt one another's bodies, but they are irremediably blind and deaf to the workings of one another's minds and inoperative upon them.

What sort of knowledge can be secured of the workings of a mind? On the one side, according to the official theory, a person has direct knowledge of the best imaginable kind of the working of his own mind. Mental states and processes are (or are normally) conscious states and processes, and the consciousness which irradiates them can engender no illusions and leaves the door open for no doubts. A person's present thinkings, feelings and willings, his perceivings, rememberings and imaginings are intrinsically "phosphorescent"; their existence and their nature are inevitably betrayed to their owner. The inner life is a stream of consciousness of such a sort that it would be absurd to suggest that the mind whose life is that stream might be unaware of what is passing down it.

True, the evidence adduced recently by Freud seems to show that there exist channels tributary to this stream, which run hidden from their owner. People are actuated by impulses the existence of which they vigorously disavow; some of their thoughts differ from the thoughts which they acknowledge; and some of the actions which they think they will to perform they do not really will. They are thoroughly gulled by some of their own hypocrisies and they successfully ignore facts about their mental lives which on the official theory ought to be patent to them. Holders of the official theory tend, however, to maintain that anyhow in normal circumstances a person must be directly and authentically seized of the present state and working of his own mind.

Besides being currently supplied with these alleged immediate data of consciousness, a person is also generally supposed to be able to exercise from time to time a special kind of perception, namely inner perception, or introspection. He can take a (non-optical) "look" at what is passing in his mind. Not only can he view and scrutinize a flower through his sense of sight and listen to and discriminate the notes of a bell through his sense of hearing; he can also reflectively or introspectively watch, without any bodily organ of sense, the current episodes of his inner life. This self-observation is also commonly supposed to be immune from illusion, confusion or doubt. A mind's reports of its own affairs have a certainty superior to the best that is possessed by its reports of matters in the physical world. Sense-perceptions can, but consciousness and introspection cannot, be mistaken or confused.

On the other side, one person has no direct access of any sort to the events of the inner life of another. He cannot do better than make problematic inferences from the observed behaviour of the other person's body to the states of mind which, by analogy from his own conduct, he supposes to be signalised by that behaviour. Direct access to the workings of a mind is the privilege of that mind itself; in default of such privileged access, the workings of one mind are inevitably occult to everyone else. For the supposed arguments from bodily movements similar to their own to mental workings similar to their own would lack any possibility of observational corroboration. Not unnaturally, therefore, an adherent of the official theory finds it difficult to resist this consequence of his premisses, that he has no good reason to believe that there do exist minds other than his own. Even if he prefers to believe that to other human bodies there are harnessed minds not unlike his own, he cannot claim to be able to discover their individual characteristics, or the particular things that they undergo and do. Absolute solitude is on this showing the ineluctable destiny of the soul. Only our bodies can meet.

As a necessary corollary of this general scheme there is implicitly prescribed a special way of construing our ordinary concepts of mental powers and operations. The verbs, nouns and adjectives, with which in ordinary life we describe the wits, characters and higher-grade performances of the people with whom we have to do, are required to be construed as signifying special episodes in their secret histories, or else as signifying tendencies for such episodes to occur. When someone is described as knowing, believing or guessing something, as hoping, dreading, intending or shirking something, as designing this or being amused at that, these verbs are supposed to denote the occurrence of specific modifications in his (to us) occult stream of consciousness. Only his own privileged access to this stream in direct awareness and introspection could provide authentic testimony that these mental-conduct verbs were correctly or incorrectly applied. The onlooker, be he teacher, critic, biographer or friend, can never assure himself that his comments have any vestige of truth. Yet it was just because we do in fact all know how to make such comments, make them with general correctness and correct them when they turn out to be confused or mistaken, that philosophers found it necessary to construct their theories of the nature and place of minds. Finding mental-conduct concepts being regularly and effectively used, they properly sought to fix their logical geography. But the logical geography officially recommended would entail that there could be no regular or effective use of these mental-conduct concepts in our descriptions of, and prescriptions for, other people's minds.

THE ABSURDITY OF THE OFFICIAL DOCTRINE

Such in outline is the official theory. I shall often speak of it, with deliberate abusiveness, as "the dogma of the Ghost in the Machine." I hope to prove that it is entirely false, and false not in detail but in principle. It is not merely an assemblage of particular mistakes. It is one big mistake and a mistake of a special kind. It is, namely, a category-mistake. It represents the facts of mental life as if they belonged to one logical type or category (or range of types or categories), when they actually belong to another. The dogma is therefore a philosopher's myth. In attempting to explode the myth I shall probably be taken to be denying well-known facts about the mental life of human beings, and my plea that I aim at doing nothing more than rectify the logic of mental-conduct concepts will probably be disallowed as mere subterfuge.

I must first indicate what is meant by the phrase 'Category-mistake.' This I do in a series of illustrations.

A foreigner visiting Oxford or Cambridge for the first time is shown a number of colleges, libraries, playing fields, museums, scientific departments and administrative offices. He then asks "But where is the University? I have seen where the members of the Colleges live, where the Registrar works, where the scientists experiment and the rest. But I have not yet seen the University in which reside and work the members of your University." It has then to be explained to him that the University is not another collateral institution, some ulterior counterpart to the colleges, laboratories and offices which he has seen. The University is just the way in which all that he has already seen is organized. When they are seen and when their coordination is understood, the University has been seen. His mistake lay in his innocent assumption that it was correct to speak of Christ Church, the Bodleian Library, the Ashmolean Museum *and* the University, to speak, that is, as if 'the University' stood for an extra member of the class of which these other units are members. He was mistakenly allocating the University to the same category as that to which the other institutions belong. The same mistake would be made by a child witnessing the march-past of a division, who, having had pointed out to him such and such battalions, batteries, squadrons, etc., asked when the division was going to appear. He would be supposing that a division was a counterpart to the units already seen, partly similar to them and partly unlike them. He would be shown his mistake by being told that in watching the battalions, batteries and squadrons marching past he had been watching the division marching past. The march-past was not a parade of battalions, batteries, squadrons *and* a division; it was a parade of the battalions, batteries and squadrons *of* a division.

One more illustration. A foreigner watching his first game of cricket learns what are the functions of the bowlers, the batsmen, the fielders, the umpires and the scorers. He then says "But there is no one left on the field to contribute the famous element of team-spirit. I see who does the bowling, the batting and the wicket-keeping; but I do not see whose role it is to exercise *esprit de corps*." Once more, it would have to be explained that he was looking for the wrong type of thing. Team-spirit is not another cricketing-operation supplementary to all of the other special tasks. It is, roughly, the keenness with which each of the special tasks is performed, and performing a task keenly is not performing two tasks. Certainly exhibiting team-spirit is not the same thing as bowling or catching, but nor is it a third thing such that we can say that the bowler first bowls *and* then exhibits team-spirit or that a fielder is at a given moment *either* catching *or* displaying *esprit de corps.*

These illustrations of category-mistakes have a common feature which must be noticed. The mistakes were made by people who did not know how to wield the concepts *University, division* and *team-spirit.* Their puzzles arose from inability to use certain items in the English vocabulary.

The theoretically interesting category-mistakes are those made by people who are perfectly competent to apply concepts, at least in the situations with which they are familiar, but are still liable in their abstract thinking to allocate those concepts to logical types to which they do not belong. An instance of a mistake of this sort would be the following story. A student of politics has learned the main differences between the British, the French and the American Constitutions, and has learned also the differences and connections between the Cabinet, Parliament, the various Ministries, the Judicature and the Church of England. But he still becomes embarrassed when asked questions about the connections between the church of England, the Home Office and the British Constitution. For while the Church and the Home Office are institutions, the British Constitution is not another institution in the same sense of that noun. So inter-institutional relations which can be asserted or denied to hold between the Church and the Home Office cannot be asserted or denied to hold between either of them and the British Constitution. 'The British Constitution' is not a term of the same logical type as 'the Home Office' and 'the Church of England'. In a partially similar way, John Doe may be a relative, a friend, an enemy or a stranger to Richard Roe;

but he cannot be any of these things to the Average Taxpayer. He knows how to talk sense in certain sorts of discussions about the Average Taxpayer, but he is baffled to say why he could not come across him in the street as he can come across Richard Roe.

It is pertinent to our main subject to notice that, so long as the student of politics continues to think of the British Constitution as a counterpart to the other institutions, he will tend to describe it as a mysteriously occult institution; and so long as John Doe continues to think of the Average Taxpayer as a fellow-citizen, he will tend to think of him as an elusive insubstantial man, a ghost who is everywhere yet nowhere.

My destructive purpose is to show that a family of radical category-mistakes is the source of the double-life theory. The representation of a person as a ghost mysteriously ensconced in a machine derives from this argument. Because, as is true, a person's thinking, feeling and purposive doing cannot be described solely in the idioms of physics, chemistry and physiology, therefore they must be described in counterpart idioms. As the human body is a complex organised unit, so the human mind must be another complex organised unit, though one made of a different sort of stuff and with a different sort of structure. Or, again, as the human body, like any other parcel of matter, is a field of causes and effects, so the mind must be another field of causes and effects, though not (Heaven be praised) mechanical causes and effects.

THE ORIGIN OF THE CATEGORY-MISTAKE

One of the chief intellectual origins of what I have yet to prove to be the Cartesian category-mistake seems to be this. When Galileo showed that his methods of scientific discovery were competent to provide a mechanical theory which should cover every occupant of space, Descartes found in himself two conflicting motives. As a man of scientific genius he could not but endorse the claims of mechanics, yet as a religious and moral man he could not accept, as Hobbes accepted, the discouraging rider to those claims, namely that human nature differs only in degree of complexity from clockwork. The mental could not be just a variety of the mechanical.

He and subsequent philosophers naturally but erroneously availed themselves of the following escape-route. Since mental-conduct words are not to be construed as signifying the occurrence of non-mechanical processes; since mechanical laws explain movements in space as the effects of other movements in space, other laws must explain some of the non-spatial workings of minds as the effects of other non-spatial workings of minds. The difference between the human behaviours which we describe as intelligent and those which we describe as unintelligent must be a difference in their causation; so, while some movements of human tongues and limbs are the effects of mechanical causes, others must be the effects of non-mechanical causes, i.e. some issue from movements of particles of matter, others from workings of the mind.

The differences between the physical and the mental were thus represented as differences inside the common framework of the categories of "thing," "stuff," "attribute," "state," "process," "change," "cause" and "effect." Minds are things, but different sorts of things from bodies; mental processes are causes and effects, but different sorts of causes and effects from bodily movements. And so on. Somewhat as the foreigner expected the University to be an extra edifice, rather like a college but also considerably different, so the repudiators of mechanism represented minds as extra centres of causal processes, rather like machines but also considerably different from them. Their theory was a para-mechanical hypothesis.

That this assumption was at the heart of the doctrine is shown by the fact that there was from the beginning felt to be a major theoretical difficulty in explaining how minds can influence and be influenced by bodies. How can a mental process, such as willing, cause spatial movements like the movements of the tongue? How can a physical change in the optic nerve have among its effects a mind's perception of a flash of light?

This notorious crux by itself shows the logical mould into which Descartes pressed his theory of the mind. It was the self-same mould into which he and Galileo set their mechanics. Still unwittingly adhering to the grammar of mechanics, he tried to avert disaster by describing minds in what was merely an obverse vocabulary. The workings of minds had to be described by the mere negatives of the specific descriptions given to bodies; they are not in space, they are not motions, they are not modifications of matter, they are not accessible to public observation. Minds are not bits of clockwork, they are just bits of not-clockwork.

As thus represented, minds are not merely ghosts harnessed to machines, they are themselves just spectral machines. Though the human body is an engine, it is not quite an ordinary engine, since some of its workings are governed by another engine inside it—this interior governor-engine being one of a very special sort. It is invisible, inaudible and it has not size or weight. It cannot be taken to bits and the laws it obeys are not those known to ordinary engineers. Nothing is known of how it governs the bodily engine.

A second major crux points to the same moral. Since, according to the doctrine, minds belong to the same category as bodies and since bodies are rigidly governed by mechanical laws, it seemed to many theorists to follow that minds must be similarly governed by rigid non-mechanical laws. The physical world is a deterministic system, so the mental world must be a deterministic system. Bodies cannot help the modifications that they undergo, so minds cannot help pursuing the careers fixed for them. *Responsibility, choice, merit* and *demerit* are therefore inapplicable concepts— unless the compromise solution is adopted of saying that the laws governing mental processes, unlike those governing physical processes, have the congenial attribute of being only rather rigid. The problem of the Freedom of the Will was the problem of how to reconcile the hypothesis that minds are to be described in terms drawn from the categories of mechanics with the knowledge that higher-grade human conduct is not of a piece with the behaviour of machines.

It is an historical curiosity that it was not noticed that the entire argument was broken-backed. Theorists correctly assumed that any sane man could already recognise the differences between, say, rational and non-rational utterances or between purposive and automatic behaviour. Else there would have been nothing requiring to be salved from mechanism. Yet the explanation given presupposed that one person could in principle never recognise the difference between the rational and the irrational utterances issuing from other human bodies, since he could never get access to the postulated immaterial causes of some of their utterances. Save for the doubtful exception of himself, he could never tell the difference between a man and a Robot. It would have to be conceded, for example, that, for all that we can tell, the inner lives of persons who are classed as idiots or lunatics are as rational as those of anyone else. Perhaps only their overt behaviour is disappointing; that is to say, perhaps "idiots" are not really idiotic, or "lunatics" lunatic. Perhaps, too, some of those who are classed as sane are really idiots. According to the theory, external observers could never know how the overt behaviour of others is correlated with their mental powers and processes and so they could never know or even plausibly conjecture whether their applications of mental-conduct concepts to these other people were correct or incorrect. It would then be hazardous or impossible for a man to claim sanity or logical consistency even for himself, since he would be debarred from comparing his own performances with those of others. In short, our characterisations of persons and their performances as intelligent, prudent and virtuous or as stupid, hypocritical and cowardly could never have been made, so the problem of providing a special causal hypothesis to serve as the basis of such diagnoses would never have arisen. The question, "How do persons differ from machines?" arose just because everyone already knew how to apply mental-conduct concepts before the new causal hypothesis was introduced. This causal hypothesis could not therefore be the source of the criteria used in those applications. Nor, of course, has the causal hypothesis in any degree improved our handling of those criteria. We still distinguish good from bad arithmetic, politic from impolitic conduct and fertile from infertile imaginations in the ways in which Descartes himself distinguished them before and after he speculated how the applicability of these criteria was compatible with the principle of mechanical causation.

He had mistaken the logic of his problem. Instead of asking by what criteria intelligent behaviour is actually distinguished from non-intelligent behaviour, he asked "Given that the principle of mechanical causation does not tell us the difference, what other causal principle will it tell us?" He realised that the problem was not one of mechanics and assumed that it must therefore be one of some counterpart to mechanics. Not unnaturally psychology is often cast for just this role.

When two terms belong to the same category, it is proper to construct conjunctive propositions embodying them. Thus a purchaser may say that he bought a left-hand glove and a right-hand glove, but not that he bought a left-hand glove, a right-hand glove and a pair of gloves. "She came home in a flood of tears and a sedan-chair" is a well-known joke based on the absurdity of conjoining terms of different types. It would have been equally ridiculous to construct the disjunction "She came home either in a flood of tears or else in a sedan-chair." Now the dogma of the Ghost in the Machine does just this. It maintains that there exist both bodies and minds; that there occur physical processes and mental processes; that there are mechanical causes of corporeal movements. I shall argue that these and other analogous conjunctions are absurd; but, it must be noticed, the argument will not show that either of the illegitimately conjoined propositions is absurd in itself. I am not, for example, denying that there occur mental processes. Doing long division is a mental process and so is making a joke. But I am saying that the phrase "there occur mental processes" does not mean the same sort of thing as "there occur physical processes," and, therefore, that it makes no sense to conjoin or disjoin the two.

If my argument is successful, there will follow some interesting consequences. First, the hallowed contrast between Mind and Matter will be dissipated, but dissipated not by either of the equally hallowed absorptions of Mind by Matter or of Matter by Mind, but in quite a different way. For the seeming contrast of the two will be shown to be as illegitimate as would be the contrast of "she came home in a flood of tears" and "she came home in a sedan-chair." The belief that there is a polar opposition between Mind and Matter is the belief that they are terms of the same logical type.

It will also follow that both Idealism and Materialism are answers to an improper question. The "reduction" of the material world to mental states and processes, as well as the "reduction" of mental states and processes to physical states and processes, presuppose the legitimacy of the disjunction "Either there exist minds or there exist bodies (but not both)." It would be like saying, "Either she bought a left-hand and a right-hand glove or she bought a pair of gloves (but not both)."

It is perfectly proper to say, in one logical tone of voice, that there exist minds and to say, in another logical tone of voice, that there exist bodies. But these expressions do not indicate two different species of existence, for 'existence' is not a generic world like 'coloured' or 'sexed'. They indicate two different senses of 'exist', somewhat as 'rising' has different senses in 'the tide is rising', 'hopes are rising', and 'the average age of death is rising'. A man would be thought to be making a poor joke who said that three things are now rising, namely the tide, hopes and the average age of death. It would be just as good or bad a joke to say that there exist prime numbers and Wednesdays and public opinions and navies; or that there exist both minds and bodies. In the succeeding chapters I try to prove that the official theory does rest on a batch of category-mistakes by showing that logically absurd corollaries follow from it. The exhibition of these absurdities will have the constructive effect of bringing out part of the correct logic of mental-conduct concepts.

WILLIAM LYCAN
Robots and Minds

WILLIAM LYCAN *(b. 1945) teaches philosophy at the University of North Carolina at Chapel Hill. He is one of the principal proponents of a view that he calls "homunctionalism," which sees mental capacities as constituted of committees of committees of committees (etc.) of progressively more and more stupid submental capacities. He is author of* Consciousness *(1987) and* Consciousness and Experience *(1996).*

ARTIFICIAL Intelligence (AI) is, very crudely, the science of getting machines to perform jobs that normally require intelligence and judgment. Researchers at any number of AI labs have designed machines that prove mathematical theorems, play chess, sort mail, guide missiles, assemble auto engines, diagnose illnesses, read stories and other written texts, and converse with people in a rudimentary way. This is, we might say, intelligent behavior.

But what is this "intelligence"? As a first pass, I suggest that intelligence of the sort I am talking about is a kind of flexibility, a responsiveness to contingencies. A dull or stupid machine must have just the right kind of raw materials presented to it in just the right way, or it is useless: the electric can-opener must have an appropriately sized can fixed under its drive wheel *just so*, in order to operate at all. Humans (most of us, anyway) are not like that. We deal with the unforeseen. We take what comes and make the best of it, even though we may have had no idea what it would be. We play the ball from whatever lie we are given, and at whatever angle to the green; we read and understand texts we have never seen before; we find our way back to Chapel Hill after getting totally lost in downtown Durham (or downtown Washington, D.C., or downtown Lima, Peru).

Our pursuit of our goals is guided while in progress by our ongoing perception and handling of interim developments. Moreover, we can pursue any number of different goals at the same time, and balance them against each other. We are sensitive to contingencies, both external and internal, that have a very complex and unsystematic structure.

It is almost irresistible to speak of *information* here, even if the term were not as trendy as it is. An intelligent creature, I want to say, is an *information-sensitive* creature, one that not only *registers* information through receptors such as sense-organs but somehow stores and manages and finally uses that information. Higher animals are intelligent beings in this sense, and so are we, even though virtually nothing is known about how we organize or manage the vast, seething profusion of information that comes our way. And there is one sort of machine that is information-sensitive also: the digital computer. A computer *is* a machine specifically designed to be fed complexes of information, to store them, manage them, and produce appropriate theoretical or practical conclusions on demand. Thus, if artificial intelligence is what one is looking for, it is no accident that one looks to the computer.

Yet a computer has two limitations in common with machines of less elite and grandiose sorts, both of them already signalled in the characterization I have just given. First, a (present-day) computer must be *fed* information, and the choice of what information to feed and in what form is up to a human programmer or operator. (For that matter, a present-day computer must be plugged into an electrical outlet and have its switch turned to ON, but this is a very minor contingency given the availability of nuclear power-packs.) Second, the *appropriateness* and effectiveness of a computer's output depends entirely on what the programmer or operator had in mind and goes on to make of it. A computer has intelligence in the sense I have defined, but has no judgment, since it has no goals and purposes of its own and no internal sense of appropriateness, relevance, or proportion.

For essentially these reasons—that computers are intelligent in my minimal sense, and that they are nevertheless limited in the two ways I have mentioned—AI theorists, philosophers and intelligent laymen have inevitably compared computers to human minds, but at the same time debated both technical and philosophical questions raised by this comparison. The questions break down into three main groups or types:

(A) Questions of the form, "Will a computer ever be able to do *X*?," where *X* is something that intelligent humans can do. (B) Questions of the form, "Given that a computer can or could do *X*, have we any reason to think that it does *X* in the same way that humans do *X*?" (C) Questions of the form, "Given that some futuristic supercomputer were able to do *X, Y, Z,* . . . , for some arbitrarily large range and variety of human activities, would that show that the computer had property *P?*," where *P* is some feature held to be centrally, vitally characteristic of human minds, such as thought, consciousness, feeling, sensation, emotion, creativity, or freedom of the will.

Questions of type A are empirical questions and cannot be settled without decades, perhaps centuries of further research—compare ancient and mediaeval speculations on the questions of whether a machine could ever fly. Questions of type B are brutely empirical too, and their answers are unavailable to AI researchers *per se,* lying squarely in the domain of cognitive psychology, a science or alleged science barely into its infancy. Questions of type C are philosophical and conceptual, and so I shall essay to answer them all at one stroke.

Let us begin by supposing that all questions types A and B have been settled affirmatively—that one day we might be confronted by a much-improved version of Hal, the soft-spoken computer in Kubrick's *2001* (younger readers may substitute *Star Wars'* C3PO or whatever subsequent cinematic robot is the most lovable). Let us call this more versatile machine "Harry." Harry (let us say) is humanoid in form—he is a miracle of miniaturization and has lifelike plastic skin—and he can converse intelligently on all sorts of subjects, play golf *and* the viola, write passable poetry, control his occasional nervousness pretty well, make love, prove mathematical theorems (of course), show envy when outdone, throw gin bottles at annoying children, etc., etc. We may suppose he fools people into thinking is human. Now the question is, is Harry really a *person?* Does he have thoughts, feelings, and so on? Is he actually conscious, or is he just a mindless walking hardware store whose movements are astoundingly *like* those of a person?

Plainly his acquaintances would tend from the first to see him as a person, even if they were aware of his dubious antecedents. I think it is a plain psychological fact, if nothing more, that we could not help treating him as a person, unless we resolutely made up our minds, on principle, not to give him the time of day. But how could we really tell that he is conscious?

Well, how do we really tell that any humanoid creature is conscious? How do you tell that I am conscious, and how do I tell that you are? Surely we tell, and decisively, on the basis of our standard behavioral tests for mental states. We know that a human being has such-and-such mental states when it behaves, to speak very generally, in the ways we take to be appropriate to organisms which are in those states. (The point is of course an epistemological one only, no metaphysical implications intended or tolerated.) We know for practical purposes that a creature has a mind when it fulfills all the right criteria. And by hypothesis, Harry fulfills all our behavioral criteria with a vengeance; moreover, he does so *in the right way* (cf. questions of type B): the processing that stands causally behind his behavior is just like ours. It follows that we are at least *prima facie* justified in believing him to be conscious.

We haven't *proved* that he is conscious, of course—any more than you have proved that I am conscious. An organism's merely behaving in a certain way is no logical guarantee of sentience; from my point of view it is at least imaginable, a bare logical possibility, that my wife, my daughter and my chairman are not conscious, even though I have excellent, overwhelming behavioral reason to think that they are. But for that matter, our "standard behavioral tests" for mental states yield practical or moral certainty only so long as the situation is not palpably extraordinary or bizarre. A human chauvinist—in this case, someone who denies that Harry has thoughts and feelings, joys and sorrows—thinks precisely that Harry is as bizarre as they come. But *what is bizarre about him?* There are quite a few chauvinist answers to this, but what they boil down to, and given our hypothesized facts all they could boil down to, are two differences between Harry and ourselves: his *origin* (a laboratory is not a proper mother), and the *chemical composition of his anatomy,* if his creator has used silicon instead of carbon, for example. To exclude him from our community for either or both of *those* reasons seems to me to be a clear case of racial or ethnic prejudice (literally) and nothing more. I see no obvious way in which either a creature's origin or its sub-neuroanatomical chemical composition should matter to its psychological processes or any aspect of its mentality.

My argument can be reinforced by a thought-experiment. Imagine that we take a normal human being, Henrietta, and begin gradually replacing parts of her with synthetic materials—first a few prosthetic limbs, then a few synthetic arteries, then some neural fibers, and so forth. Suppose that the surgeons who perform the successive operations (particularly the neurosurgeons) are so clever and skillful that Henrietta survives in fine style: her intelligence, personality, perceptual acuity, poetic abilities, etc., remain just as they were before. But after the replacement process has eventually gone on to completion, Henrietta will have become an artifact—at least, her body will then be nothing but a collection of artifacts. Did she lose consciousness at some point during the sequence of operations, despite her continuing to behave and respond normally? When? It is hard to imagine that there is some privileged portion of the human nervous system that is for some reason indispensable, even though kidneys, lungs, heart, and any given bit of brain could in principle be replaced by a prosthesis (for *what* reason?); and it is also hard to imagine that there is some *pro*portion of the nervous system such that removal of more than that proportion causes loss of consciousness or sentience despite perfect maintenance of all intelligent capacities.

If this quick but totally compelling defense of Harry and Henrietta's personhood is correct, then the two, and their ilk, will have not only mental lives like ours, but *moral* lives like ours, and moral rights and privileges accordingly. Just as origin and physical constitution fail to affect psychological personhood, if a creature's internal organization is sufficiently like ours, so do they fail to affect moral personhood. We do not discriminate against a person who has a wooden leg, or a mechanical kidney, or a nuclear heart regulator; no more should we deny any human or civil right to Harry or Henrietta on grounds of their origin or physical makeup, which they cannot help.

But this happy egalitarianism raises a more immediate question: *In real life,* we shall soon be faced with medium-grade machines, which have some intelligence and are not "mere" machines like refrigerators or typewriters but which fall far short of flawless human simulators like Harry. For AI researchers may well build machines which will appear to have some familiar mental capacities but not others. The most obvious example is that of a sensor or perception, which picks up information from its immediate environment, records it, and stores it in memory for future printout. (We already have at least crude machines of this kind. When they become versatile and sophisticated enough, it will be quite natural to say that they see or hear and that they remember.) But the possibility of "specialist" machines of this kind raises an unforeseen contingency: There is an enormous and many-dimensional range of possible being in between our current "mere" machines and our fully developed, flawless human simulators; we have not even begun to think of all the infinitely possible variations on this theme. And once we do begin to think of these hard cases, we will be at a loss as to where to draw the "personhood" line between them. How complex, eclectic and impressive must a machine be, and in what respects, before we award it the accolade of personhood and/or of consciousness? There is, to say the least, no clear answer to be had *a priori*, Descartes' notorious view of animals to the contrary notwithstanding.

This typical philosophical question would be no more than an amusing bon-bon, were it not for the attending moral conundrum: What moral rights would an intermediate or marginally intelligent machine have? Adolescent machines of this sort will confront us much sooner than will any good human simulators, for they are easier to design and construct; more to the moral point, they will be designed mainly as *labor-saving devices,* as servants who will work for free, and servants of this kind are (literally) made to be exploited. If they are intelligent to any degree, we should have qualms in proportion.

I suggest that this moral problem, which may become a real and pressing one, is parallel to the current debate over animal rights. Luckily I have never wanted to cook and eat my IBM portable.

Suppose I am right about the irrelevance of biochemical constitution to psychology; and suppose I was also right about the coalescing of the notions *computation, information, intelligence.* Then our mentalized theory of computation suggests in turn a computational theory of mentality, and a computational picture of the place of human beings in the world. In fact, philosophy aside, that picture has already begun to get a grip on people's thinking—as witness the filtering down of computer jargon into contemporary casual speech—and that grip is not going to loosen. Computer science is the defining technology of our time, and in this sense the computer is the natural cultural successor to the steam engine, the clock, the spindle and the potter's wheel. Predictably, an articulate computational theory of the mind has also gained credence among professional psychologists and philosophers. I have been trying to support it here and elsewhere; I shall say no more about it for now, save to note again its near-indispensability in accounting for intentionality (noted), and to address the ubiquitous question of computer creativity and freedom.

Soft Determinism or Libertarianism may be true of humans. But many people have far more rigidly deterministic intuitions about computers. Computers, after all, (let us all say it together:) "only do what they are told/programmed to do," they have no spontaneity and no freedom of choice. But human beings choose all the time, and the ensuing states of the world often depend entirely on these choices. Thus the "computer analogy" ultimately fails.

The alleged failure of course depends on what we think freedom really is. As a Soft Determinist, I think that to have freedom of choice in acting is (roughly) for one's action to proceed out of one's own desires, deliberation, will and intention, rather than being compelled or coerced by external forces regardless of my desires or will. As before, free actions are not

uncaused actions. My free actions are those that *I* cause, i.e., that are caused by my own mental processes rather than by something pressing on me from the outside. I have argued elsewhere that I am free in that my beliefs, desires, deliberations and intentions are all functional or computational states and processes within me which do interact in characteristic ways to produce my behavior. Note now that the same response vindicates our skilled human-simulating machines from the charge of puppethood. The word "robot" is often used as a veritable synonym for "puppet," so it may seem that Harry and Henrietta are paradigm cases of *un*free mechanisms which "only do what they are programmed to do." This is a slander—for two reasons.

First, even an ordinary computer, let alone a fabulously sophisticated machine like Harry, is in a way unpredictable. You are at its mercy. You *think* you know what it is going to do: you know what it should do, what it is supposed to do, but there is no guarantee—and it may do something *awful* or at any rate something that you could not have predicted and could not figure out if you tried with both hands. This practical sort of unpredictability would be multiplied a thousandfold in the case of a machine as complex as the human brain, and it is notably characteristic of *people*.

The unpredictability has several sources. (i) Plain old physical defects, as when Harry's circuits have been damaged by trauma, stress, heat, or the like. (ii) Bugs in one or more of his programs. (I have heard that once upon a time, somewhere, a program was written that had not a single bug in it, but this is probably an urban folk tale.) (iii) Randomizers, quantum-driven or otherwise; elements of Harry's behavior may be *genuinely,* physically random. (iv) Learning and analogy mechanisms; if Harry is equipped with these as he inevitably would be, then his behavior-patterns will be modified in response to his experiential input from the world, which would be neither controlled nor even observed by us. We don't know where he's been. (v) The relativity of reliability to goal-description. This last needs a bit of explanation.

People often say things like, "A computer just crunches binary numbers; provided it isn't broken, it just chugs on mindlessly through whatever flipflop settings are predetermined by its electronic makeup." But such remarks ignore the multilevelled character of real computer programming. At any given time, a computer is running *each of any number of* programs, depending on how it is described and on the level of functional organization that interest us. True, it is always crunching binary numbers, but in crunching them it is also doing any number of more esoteric things. And (more to the point) what counts as a mindless, algorithmic procedure at a very low level of organization may constitute, at a higher level, a hazardous do-or-die heuristic that might either succeed brilliantly or (more likely) fail and leave its objective unfulfilled.

As a second defense, remember that Harry too has beliefs, desires and intentions (provided my original argument is sound). If this is so, then his behavior normally proceeds out of his own mental processes rather than being externally compelled; and so he satisfies the definition of freedom-of-action formulated above. In most cases it will be appropriate to say that Harry could have done other than what he did do (but in fact chose after some ratiocination to do what he did, instead). Harry acts in the same sense as that in which we act, though one might continue to quarrel over what sense that is.

Probably the most popular remaining reason for doubt about machine consciousness has to do with—you guessed it—the raw qualitative character of experience. Could a mere bloodless runner-of-programs have states that *feel to it* in any of the various dramatic ways in which our mental states feel to us?

The latter question is usually asked rhetorically, expecting a resounding answer "NO!!" But I do not hear it rhetorically, for I do not see why the negative answer is supposed to be at all obvious, even for machines as opposed to biologic humans. Of course there is an incongruity *from our human point of view* between human feeling and printed circuitry or silicon pathways; that is to be expected, since we are considering those high-tech items from an external, third-person perspective and at the same time comparing them to our own first-person feels. But argumentatively, that *Gestalt* phenomenon counts for no more in the present case than it did in that of human consciousness, *viz.*, for nothing, especially if my original argument about Harry was successful in showing that biochemical constitution is irrelevant to psychology. What matters to mentality is not the stuff of which one is made, but the complex way in which that stuff is organized. If after years of close friendship we were to open Harry up to find that he is stuffed with microelectronic gadgets instead of protoplasm, we would be taken aback—no question. But our *Gestalt* clash on the occasion would do nothing *at all* to show that Harry does not have his own rich inner qualitative life. If an objector wants to insist that computation alone cannot provide consciousness with its qualitative character, the objector will have to take the initiative and come up with a further, substantive argument to show why not. We have already seen that such arguments have failed wretchedly for the case of humans; I see no reason to suspect that they would work any better for the case of robots. We must await further developments. But at the present stage of inquiry I see no compelling feel-based objection to the hypothesis of machine consciousness.

JOHN R. SEARLE
The Myth of the Computer

JOHN R. SEARLE *(b. 1932) teaches philosophy at the University of California, Berkeley. He has done important work in philosophy of language and more recently has become an influential critic of the view that computers can tell us something important about the mind. He is author of* Mind, Language and Society *(1998), and numerous other books.*

OUR ordinary ways of talking about ourselves and other people, of justifying our behavior and explaining that of others, express a certain conception of human life that is so close to us, so much a part of common sense that we can hardly see it. It is a conception according to which each person has (or perhaps *is*) a mind; the contents of the mind—beliefs, fears, hopes, motives, desires, etc.—cause and therefore explain our actions; and the continuity of our minds is the source of our individuality and identity as persons.

In the past couple of centuries we have also become convinced that this commonsense psychology is grounded in the brain, that these mental states and events are somehow, we are not quite sure how, going on in the neurophysiological processes of the brain. So this leaves us with two levels at which we can describe and explain human beings: a level of commonsense psychology, which seems to work well enough in practice but which is not scientific; and a level of neurophysiology, which is certainly scientific but which even the most advanced specialists know very little about.

But couldn't there be a third possibility, a science of human beings that was not introspective commonsense psychology but was not neurophysiology either? This has been the great dream of the human sciences in the twentieth century, but so far all of the efforts have been, in varying degrees, failures. The most spectacular failure was behaviorism, but in my intellectual lifetime I have lived through exaggerated hopes placed on and disappointed by games theory, cybernetics, information theory, generative grammar, structuralism, and Freudian psychology, among others. Indeed it has become something of a scandal of twentieth-century intellectual life that we lack a science of the human mind and human behavior, that the methods of the natural sciences have produced such meager results when applied to human beings.

The latest candidate or family of candidates to fill the gap is called cognitive science, a collection of related investigations into the human mind involving psychology, philosophy, linguistics, anthropology, and artificial intelligence. Cognitive science is really the name of a family of research projects and not a theory, but many of its practitioners think that the heart of cognitive science is a theory of the mind based on artificial intelligence (AI). According to this theory minds just are computer programs of certain kinds. The main ideological aim of Hofstadter and Dennett's book is to advance this theory. . . .

The theory, which is fairly widely held in cognitive science, can be summarized in three propositions.

1. *Mind as Program.*
   What we call minds are simply very complex digital computer programs. Mental states are simply computer states and mental processes are computational processes. Any system whatever that had the right program, with the right input

and output, would have to have mental states and processes in the same literal sense that you and I do, because that is all there is to mental states and processes, that is all that you and I have. The programs in question are "self-updating" or "self-designing" "systems of representations."

2. *The Irrelevance of the Neurophysiology of the Brain.* In the study of the mind actual biological facts about actual human and animal brains are irrelevant because the mind is an "abstract sort of thing" and human brains just happen to be among the indefinitely large number of kinds of computers that can have minds. Our minds happen to be embodied in our brains, but there is no essential connection between the mind and the brain. Any other computer with the right program would also have a mind. Theses 1 and 2 are summarized in the introduction where the author speaks of "the emerging view of the mind as software or program—as an abstract sort of thing whose identity is independent of any particular physical embodiment."

3. *The Turing Test as the Criterion of the Mental.* The conclusive proof of the presence of mental states and capacities is the ability of a system to pass the Turing test, the test devised by Alan Turing and described in his article in [Hofstadter and Dennett's] book. If a system can convince a competent expert that it has mental states then it really has those mental states. If, for example, a machine could "converse" with a native Chinese speaker in such a way as to convince the speaker that it understood Chinese then it would literally understand Chinese.

The three theses are neatly lumped together when one of the editors writes, "Minds exist in brains and may come to exist in programmed machines. If and when such machines come about, their causal powers will derive not from the substances they are made of, but from their design and the programs that run in them. And the way we will know they have those causal powers is by talking to them and listening carefully to what they have to say."

We might call this collection of theses "strong artificial intelligence" (strong AI).* These theses are certainly not obviously true and they are seldom explicitly stated and defended.

Let us inquire first into how plausible it is to suppose that specific biochemical powers of the brain are really irrelevant to the mind. It is an amazing fact, by the way, that in twenty-seven pieces about the mind the editors have not seen fit to include any whose primary aim is to tell us how the brain actually works, and this omission obviously derives from their conviction that since "mind is an abstract sort of thing" the specific neurophysiology of the brain is incidental. This idea derives part of its appeal from the editors' keeping their discussion at a very abstract general level about "consciousness" and "mind" and "soul," but if you consider specific mental states and processes—being thirsty, wanting to go to the bathroom, worrying about your income tax, trying to solve math puzzles, feeling depressed, recalling the French word for "butterfly"—then it seems at least a little odd to think that the brain is so irrelevant.

Take thirst, where we actually know a little bit about how it works. Kidney secretions of renin synthesize a substance called angiotensin. This substance goes into the hypothalamus and triggers a series of neuron firings. As far as we know these neuron firings are a very large part of the cause of thirst. Now obviously there is more to be said, for example about the relations of the hypothalamic responses to the rest of the brain, about other things going on in the hypothalamus, and about the possible distinctions between the *feeling* of thirst and the *urge* to drink. Let us suppose we have filled out the story with the rest of the biochemical causal account of thirst.

Now these theses of the mind as program and the irrelevance of the brain would tell us that what matters about this story is not the specific

---

*"Strong" to distinguish the position form "weak" or "cautious" AI, which holds that the computer is simply a very useful tool in the study of the mind, not that the appropriately programmed computer literally has a mind.

biochemical properties of the angiotensin or the hypothalamus but only the formal computer programs that the whole sequence instantiates. Well, let's try that out as a hypothesis and see how it works. A computer can simulate the formal properties of the sequence of chemical and electrical phenomena in the production of thirst just as much as it can simulate the formal properties of anything else—we can simulate thirst just as we can simulate hurricanes, rainstorms, five-alarm fires, internal combustion engines, photosynthesis, lactation, or the flow of currency in a depressed economy. But no one in his right mind thinks that a computer simulation of a five-alarm fire will burn down the neighborhood, or that a computer simulation of an internal combustion engine will power a car or that computer simulation of lactation and photosynthesis will produce milk and sugar. To my amazement, however, I have found that a large number of people suppose that computer simulations of mental phenomena, whether at the level of brain processes or not, literally produce mental phenomena.

Again, let's try it out. Let's program our favorite PDP-10 computer with the formal program that simulates thirst. We can even program it to print out at the end "Boy, am I thirsty!" or "Won't someone please give me a drink?" etc. Now would anyone suppose that we thereby have even the slightest reason to suppose that the computer is literally thirsty? Or that any simulation of any other mental phenomena, such as understanding stories, feeling depressed, or worrying about itemized deductions, must therefore produce the real thing? The answer, alas, is that a large number of people are committed to an ideology that requires them to believe just that. So let us carry the story a step further.

The PDP-10 is powered by electricity and perhaps its electricity properties can reproduce some of the actual causal powers of the electrochemical features of the brain in producing mental states. We certainly couldn't rule out that eventuality *a priori*. But remember: the thesis of strong AI is that the mind is "independent of *any* particular embodiment" because the mind is

just a program and the program can be run on a computer made of anything whatever provided it is stable enough and complex enough to carry the program. The actual physical computer could be an ant colony (one of their examples), a collection of beer cans, streams of toilet paper with small stones placed on the squares, men sitting on high stools with green eye shades—anything you like.

So let us imagine our thirst-simulating program running on a computer made entirely of old beer cans, millions (or billions) of old beer cans that are rigged up to levers and powered by windmills. We can imagine that the program simulates the neuron firings at the synapses by having beer cans bang into each other, thus achieving a strict correspondence between neuron firings and beer-can bangings. At the end of the sequence a beer can pops up on which is written "I am thirsty." Now, to repeat the question, does anyone suppose that this Rube Goldberg apparatus is literally thirsty in the sense in which you and I are?

Notice that the thesis of Hofstadter and Dennett is not that *for all we know* the collection of beer cans might be thirsty but rather that if it has the right program with the right input and output it *must* be thirsty (or understand Proust or worry about its income tax or have any other mental state) because that is all the mind is, a certain kind of computer program, and any computer made of anything at all running the right program would have to have the appropriate mental states.

I believe that everything we have learned about human and animal biology suggests that what we call "mental" phenomena are as much a part of our biological natural history as any other biological phenomena, as much a part of biology as digestion, lactation, or the secretion of bile. Much of the implausibility of the strong AI thesis derives from its resolute opposition to biology; the mind is not a concrete biological phenomenon but "an abstract sort of thing."

Still, in calling attention to the implausibility of supposing that the specific causal powers of brains are irrelevant to minds I have not yet fully exposed the preposterousness of the strong AI position, held by Hofstadter and Dennett, so let us press on and examine a bit more closely the thesis of mind as program.

Digital computer programs by definition consist of sets of purely formal operations on formally specified symbols. The ideal computer does such things as print a zero on the tape, move one square to the left, erase a 1, move back to the right, etc. It is common to describe this as "symbol manipulation" or, to use the term favored by Hofstadter and Dennett, the whole system is a "self-updating representational system"; but these terms are at least a bit misleading since as far as the computer is concerned the symbols *don't symbolize* anything or *represent* anything. They are just formal counters.

The computer attaches no meaning, interpretation, or content to the formal symbols; and qua computer it couldn't because if we tried to give the computer an interpretation of its symbols we could only give it more uninterpreted symbols. The interpretation of the symbols is entirely up to the programmers and users of the computer. For example, on my pocket calculator if I print "3 × 3 =," the calculator will print "9" but it has no idea that "3" means 3 or that "9" means 9 or that anything means anything. We might put this point by saying that the computer has a syntax but no semantics. The computer manipulates formal symbols but attaches no meaning to them, and this simple observation will enable us to refute the thesis of mind as program.

Suppose that we write a computer program to simulate the understanding of Chinese so that, for example, if the computer is asked questions in Chinese the program enables it to give answers in Chinese; if asked to summarize stories in Chinese it can give such summaries; if asked questions about the stories it has been given it will answer such questions.

Now suppose that I, who understand no Chinese at all and can't even distinguish Chinese symbols from some other kinds of symbols, am locked in a room with a number of cardboard boxes full of Chinese symbols. Suppose that I am given a book of rules in English that instruct me how to match these Chinese symbols with each other. The rules say such things as that the "squiggle-squiggle" sign is to be followed by the "squoggle-squoggle" sign. Suppose that people outside the room pass in more Chinese symbols and that following the instructions book I pass Chinese symbols back to them. Suppose that unknown to me the people who pass me the symbols call them "questions," and the book of instructions that I work from they call "the program"; the symbols I give back to them they call "answers to the questions" and me they call "the computer." Suppose that after a while the programmers get so good at writing the programs and I get so good at manipulating the symbols that my answers are indistinguishable from those of native Chinese speakers. I can pass the Turing test for understanding Chinese. But all the same I still don't understand a word of Chinese and neither does any other digital computer because all the computer has is what I have: a formal program that attaches no meaning, interpretation, or content to any of the symbols.

What this simple argument shows is that no formal program by itself is sufficient for understanding, because it would always be possible in principle for an agent to go through the steps in the program and still not have the relevant understanding. And what works for Chinese would also work for other mental phenomena. I could, for example, go through the steps of the thirst-simulating program without feeling thirsty. The argument also, *en passant,* refutes the Turing test because it shows that a system, namely me, could pass the Turing test without having the appropriate mental states. . . .

The rest of what they have to say is mostly a repetition of points made by other authors and already answered by me. Specifically, they endorse the "systems reply" to the Chinese room argument, according to which the man in the room does not understand Chinese, but the system of which he is a part—including the instruction book, the Chinese symbols, etc.—really does understand Chinese. Adherents of this view believe, to my constant amazement, that though the man fails to understand, the *room* does understand Chinese. The obvious objection to this is that the system has no way of attaching meaning to the uninterpreted Chinese symbols, any more than the man did in the first place. The system, like the man, has a syntax but no semantics. And you can see this by simply imagining that the man internalizes the whole system. Suppose he has a super memory and a super intelligence so that he memorizes the instruction book and does all the calculations in his head. To get rid of the room, we can even suppose he works outdoors. Now since the man doesn't understand Chinese, and since there's nothing in the system that is not in the man, there is no way the system could understand Chinese. As near as I can tell Hofstadter and Dennett's only reply to this is to observe that no normal human being could perform such a feat of memory. This is of course quite true, but also quite irrelevant to the point, which, to repeat, is that from syntax alone you don't get semantics. . . .

The details of how the brain works are immensely complicated and largely unknown, but some of the general principles of the relations between brain functioning and computer programs can be stated quite simply. First, we know that brain processes cause mental phenomena. Mental states are caused by and realized in the structure of the brain. From this it follows that any system that produced mental states would have to have powers equivalent to those of the brain. Such a system might use a different chemistry, but whatever its chemistry it would have to be able to cause what the brain causes. We know from the Chinese room argument that digital computer programs by themselves are never sufficient to produce mental states. Now since brains do produce minds, and since programs by themselves can't produce minds, it follows that the way the brain does it can't be simply instantiating a computer program. (Everything, by the way, instantiates some program or other, and brains are no exception. So in that trivial sense brains, like everything else, are digital computers.) And it also follows that if you wanted to build a machine to produce mental states, a thinking machine, you couldn't do it

solely in virtue of the fact that your machine ran a certain kind of computer program. The thinking machine couldn't work solely in virtue of being a digital computer but would have to duplicate the specific causal powers of the brain.

A lot of the nonsense talked about computers nowadays stems from the relative rarity and hence mystery. As computers and robots become more common, as common as telephones, washing machines, and forklift trucks, it seems likely that this aura will disappear and people will take computers for what they are, namely useful machines. In the meantime one has to try to avoid certain recurring mistakes that keep cropping up in Hofstadter and Dennett's book as well as in other current discussions.

The first is the idea that somehow computer achievements pose some sort of threat or challenge to human beings. But the fact, for example, that a calculator can outperform even the best mathematician is no more significant or threatening than the fact that a steam shovel can outperform the best human digger. (An oddity of artificial intelligence, by the way, is the slowness of the programmers in devising a program that can beat the very best chess players. From the point of view of games theory, chess is a trivial game since each side has perfect information about the other's position and possible moves, and one has to assume that computer programs will soon be able to outperform any human chess player.)

A second fallacy is the idea that there might be some special human experience beyond computer simulation because of its special humanity. We are sometimes told that computers couldn't simulate feeling depressed or falling in love or having a sense of humor. But as far as simulation is concerned you can program your computer to print out "I am depressed," "I love Sally," or "Ha, ha," as easily as you can program it to print out "$3 \times 3 = 9$." The real mistake is to suppose that simulation is duplication, and that mistake is the same regardless of what mental states we are talking about. A third mistake, basic to all the others, is the idea that if a computer can simulate having a certain mental state then we have the same grounds for supposing it really has that mental state as we have for supposing that human beings have that state. But we know from the Chinese room argument as well as from biology that this simple-minded behaviorism of the Turing test is mistaken.

Until computers and robots become as common as cars and until people are able to program and use them as easily as they now drive cars we are likely to continue to suffer from a certain mythological conception of digital computers. [Hofstadter & Dennett's] book is very much a part of the present mythological era of the computer.

ELIZABETH V. SPELMAN
Woman as Body

ELIZABETH V. SPELMAN *(b. 1945) teaches philosophy at Smith College. She has written widely in ancient philosophy and in feminist philosophy and is author of* Fruits of Sorrow: Framing Our Attention to Suffering *(1998). The selection here is a revised version of an earlier paper.*

―――

and what
pure happiness to know
all our high-toned questions
breed in a lively animal.

—ADRIENNE RICH
"Two Songs"

W HAT philosophers have had to say about women typically has been nasty, brutish and short. A page or two of quotations from those considered among the great philosophers (Aristotle, Hume, and Nietzsche, for example) constitutes a veritable litany of contempt [Ed. see Chapter 15]. Because philosophers have not said much about women, and, when they have, it has usually been in short essays or chatty addenda which have not been considered to be part of the central body of their work, it is tempting to regard their expressed views about women as asystemic: their remarks on women are unofficial asides which are unrelated to the heart of their philosophical doctrines. After all, it might be thought, how could one's view about something as unimportant as women have anything to do with one's views about something as important as the nature of knowledge, truth, reality, freedom? Moreover—and this is the philosopher's move par excellence—wouldn't it be charitable to

Spelman, Elizabeth, "Woman as Body," from *Feminist Studies*, Vol. 8, No. 1 (1982) pp. 109–131. Used by permission of the publisher, Feminist Studies, Inc. c/o Women's Studies Program, University of Maryland, College Park, MD 20742.

consider those opinions about women as coming merely from the *heart,* which all too easily responds to the tenor of the times, while philosopher "proper" comes from the *mind,* which resonates not with the times but with the truth?

Part of the intellectual legacy from philosophy "proper," that is, the issues that philosophers have addressed which are thought to be the serious province of philosophy, is the soul/body or mind/body distinction (differences among the various formulations are not crucial to this essay). However, this part of philosophy might have not merely accidental connections to attitudes about women. For when one recalls that the Western philosophical tradition has not been noted for its celebration of the body, and that women's nature and women's lives have long been associated with the body and bodily functions, then a question is suggested. What connection might there be between attitudes toward the body and attitudes toward women? . . .

PLATO'S LESSONS ABOUT THE SOUL AND THE BODY

Plato's dialogues are filled with lessons about knowledge, reality, and goodness, and most of the lessons carry with them strong praise for the soul and strong indictments against the body. According to Plato, the body, with its deceptive senses, keeps us from real knowledge; it rivets us in a world of material things which is far removed from the world of reality; and it tempts us away from the virtuous life. It is in and through the soul, if at all, that we shall have knowledge, be in touch with reality, and lead a life of virtue. Only the soul can truly know, for only the soul can ascend to the real world, the world of the Forms or Ideas. That world is the perfect model to which imperfect, particular things we find in matter merely approximate. It is a world which, like the soul, is invisible, unchanging, not subject to decay, eternal. To be good, one's soul must know the Good, that is, the Form of Goodness, and this is impossible while one is dragged down by the demands and temptations of bodily life. Hence, bodily death is

nothing to be feared: immortality of the soul not only is possible, but greatly to be desired, because when one is released from the body one finally can get down to the real business of life, for this real business of life is the business of the soul. Indeed, Socrates describes his own commitment, while still on earth, to encouraging his fellow Athenians to pay attention to the real business of life:

> [I have spent] all my time going about trying to persuade you, young and old, to make your first and chief concern not for your bodies nor for your possessions, but for the highest welfare of your souls.

Plato also tells us about the nature of beauty. Beauty has nothing essentially to do with the body or with the world of material things. *Real* beauty cannot "take the form of a face, or of hands, or of anything that is of the flesh." Yes, there are beautiful things, but they only are entitled to be described that way because they "partake in" the form of Beauty, which itself is not found in the material world. Real beauty has characteristics which merely beautiful *things* cannot have; real beauty

> is an everlasting loveliness which neither comes nor goes, which neither flowers nor fades, for such beauty is the same on every hand, the same then as now, here as there, this way as that way, the same to every worshipper as it is to every other.

Because it is only the soul that can know the Forms, those eternal and unchanging denizens of Reality, only the soul can know real Beauty; our changing, decaying bodies only can put us in touch with changing, decaying pieces of the material world.

Plato also examines love. His famous discussion of love in the *Symposium* [Ed. see the selection in Chapter 9.] ends up being a celebration of the soul over the body. Attraction to and appreciation for the beauty of another's body is but a vulgar fixation unless one can use such appreciation as a stepping stone to understanding Beauty itself. One can begin to learn about Beauty, while one is still embodied, when one notices that this body is beautiful, that that body is beautiful, and so on, and then one begins to realize that Beauty itself is something beyond any particular beautiful body or thing. The kind of love between people that is to be valued is not the attraction of one body for another, but the attraction of one soul for another. There is pro-creation of the spirit as well as of the flesh. All that bodies in unison can create are more bodies—the children women bear—which are mortal, subject to change and decay. But souls in unison can create "something lovelier and less mortal than human seed," for spiritual lovers "conceive and bear the things of the spirit," that is, "wisdom and all her sister virtues." Hence, spiritual love between men is preferable to phys-ical love between men and women. At the same time, physical love between men is ruled out, on the ground that "enjoyment of the flesh by flesh" is "wanton shame," while desire of soul for soul is at the heart of a relationship that "reverences, aye and worships, chastity and manhood, great-ness and wisdom." The potential for harm in sexual relations is very great—harm not so much to one's body or physique, but to one's soul. Young men especially shouldn't get caught up with older men in affairs that threaten their "spiritual development," for such development is "assuredly and ever will be of supreme value in the sight of gods and men alike."

So, then, one has no hope of understanding the nature of knowledge, reality, goodness, love, or beauty unless one recognizes the distinction between soul and body; and one has no hope of attaining any of these unless one works hard on freeing the soul from the lazy, vulgar, beguiling body. A philosopher is someone who is commit-ted to doing just that, and that is why philoso-phers go willingly unto death; it is, after all, only the death of their bodies, and finally, once their souls are released from their bodies, these philo-sophical desiderata are within reach. . . .

The division among parts of the soul is inti-mately tied to one other central and famous aspect of Plato's philosophy that hasn't been mentioned so far: Plato's political views. His dis-cussion of the parts of the soul and their proper relation to one another is integral to his view about the best way to set up a state. The rational part of the soul ought to rule the soul and ought to be attended by the spirited part in keeping watch over the unruly appetitive part; just so, there ought to be rulers of the state (the small minority in whom reason is dominant), who, with the aid of high-spirited guardians of order, watch over the multitudes (whose appetites need to be kept under control).

What we learn from Plato, then, about knowledge, reality, goodness, beauty, love, and statehood, is phrased in terms of a distinction between soul and body, or alternatively and roughly equivalently, in terms of a distinction between the rational and irrational. And the body, or the irrational part of the soul, is seen as an enormous and annoying obstacle to the pos-session of these desiderata. If the body gets the upper hand over the soul, or if the irrational part of the soul over powers the rational part, one can't have knowledge, one can't see beauty, one will be far from the highest form of love, and the state will be in utter chaos. So the soul/body dis-tinction, or the distinction between the rational and irrational parts of the soul, is a highly charged distinction. An inquiry into the distinc-tion is no mild metaphysical musing. It is quite clear that the distinction is heavily value-laden. Even if Plato hadn't told us outright that the soul is more valuable than the body, and the rational part of the soul is more important than the irrational part, that message rings out in page after page of his dialogues. The soul/body distinction, then, is integral to the rest of Plato's views, and the higher worth of the soul is integral to that distinction.

PLATO'S VIEW OF THE SOUL AND BODY, AND HIS ATTITUDE TOWARD WOMEN

Plato, and anyone else who conceives of the soul as something unobservable, cannot of course speak as if we could point to the soul, or hold it up for direct observation. At one point, Plato says no mere mortal can really understand the nature of the soul, but one perhaps could tell what it resembles. So it is not surprising to find

Plato using many metaphors and analogies to describe what the soul is *like,* in order to describe relations between parts of the soul. For example, thinking, a function of the soul, is described by analogy to talking. The parts of the soul are likened to a team of harnessed, winged horses and their charioteer. The body's relation to the soul is such that we are to think of the body vis-à-vis the soul as a tomb, a grave or prison, or as barnacles or rocks holding down the soul. Plato compares the lowest or bodylike part of the soul to a brood of beasts.

But Plato's task is not only to tell us what the soul is like, not only to provide us with ways of getting a fix on the differences between souls and bodies, or differences between parts of the soul. As we've seen, he also wants to convince us that the soul is much more important than the body, and that it is to our peril that we let ourselves be beckoned by the rumblings of the body at the expense of harkening to the call of the soul. And he means to convince us of this by holding up for our inspection the silly and sordid lives of those who pay too much attention to their bodies and do not care enough for their soul; he wants to remind us of how unruly, how without direction, are the lives of those in whom the lower part of the soul holds sway over the higher part. Because he can't *point* to an adulterated soul, he points instead to those embodied beings whose lives are in such bad shape that we can be sure that their souls are adulterated. And whose lives exemplify the proper soul/body relationship gone haywire? The lives of women (or sometimes the lives of children, slaves and brutes).

For example, how are we to know when the body has the upper hand over the soul, or when the lower part of the soul has managed to smother the higher part? We presumably can't see such conflict, so what do such conflicts translate into, in terms of actual human lives? Well, says Plato, look at the lives of women. It is women who get hysterical at the thought of death; obviously, their emotions have overpowered their reason, and they can't control themselves. The worst possible model for young men could be "a woman, young or old or wrangling with her husband, defying heaven, loudly boasting, fortunate

in her own conceit, or involved in misfortune or possessed by grief and lamentation—still less a woman that is sick, in love, or in labor. . . ."

Moreover, Plato on many occasions points to women to illustrate the improper way to pursue the things for which philosophers are constantly to be searching. For example, Plato wants to explain how important and also how difficult the attainment of real knowledge is. He wants us to realize that not just anyone can have knowledge, there is a vital distinction between those who really have knowledge and those who merely think they do. Think, for example, about the question of health. If we don't make a distinction between those who know what health is, and those who merely have unfounded and confused opinions about what health is, then "in the matter of good or bad health . . . any woman or child—or animal, for that matter—knows what is wholesome for it and is capable of curing itself." The implication is clear: if any old opinion were to count as real knowledge, then we'd have to say that women, children, and maybe even animals have knowledge. But surely *they* don't have knowledge! And why not? For one thing, because they don't recognize the difference between the material, changing world of appearance, and the invisible, eternal world of Reality. In matters of beauty, for example, they are so taken by the physical aspects of things that they assume that they can see and touch what is beautiful; they don't realize that what one knows when one has knowledge of real Beauty cannot be something that is seen or touched. Plato offers us, then, as an example of the failure to distinguish between Beauty itself, on the one hand, and beautiful things, on the other, "boys and women when they see bright-colored things." They don't realize that it is not through one's senses that one knows about beauty or anything else, for real beauty is eternal and invisible and unchangeable and can only be known through the soul.

So the message is that in matters of knowledge, reality, and beauty, don't follow the example of women. They are mistaken about those things. In matters of love, women's lives serve as negative examples also. Those men who are drawn by "vulgar" love, that is, love of body for body, "turn to women as the object of their love, and raise a family"; those men drawn by a more "heavenly" kind of love, that is, love of soul for soul, turn to other men. But there are strong sanctions against physical love between men: such physical unions, especially between older and younger men, are "unmanly." The older man isn't strong enough to resist his lust (as in woman, the irrational part of the soul has overtaken the rational part), and the younger man, "the impersonator of the female," is reproached for this "likeness to the model." The problem with physical love between men, then, is that men are acting like women.

To summarize the argument so far: the soul/body distinction is integral to the rest of Plato's views; integral to the soul/body distinction is the higher worth and importance of the soul in comparison to the body; finally, Plato tries to persuade his readers that it is to one's peril that one does not pay proper attention to one's soul—for if one doesn't, one will end up acting and living as if one were a woman. We know, Plato says, about lives dictated by the demands and needs and inducements of the body instead of the soul. Such lives surely are not good models for those who want to understand and undertake a life devoted to the nurturance of the best part of us: our souls.

To anyone at all familiar with Plato's official and oft-reported views about women, the above recitation of misogynistic remarks may be quite surprising. Accounts of Plato's views about women usually are based on what he says in book 5 of the *Republic*. In that dialogue, Plato startled his contemporaries, when as part of his proposal for the constitution of an ideal state, he suggested that

> there is no pursuit of the administrators of a state that belongs to woman because she is a woman or to a man because he is a man. But the natural capacities are distributed alike among both creatures, and women naturally share in all pursuits and men in all. . . .

Well now, what are we to make of this apparent double message in Plato about women? What are we to do with the fact that on the one hand, when Plato explicitly confronts the question of women's nature, in the *Republic*, he seems to affirm the equality of men and women; while on the other hand, the dialogues are riddled with misogynistic remarks? . . .

The contradictory sides of Plato's views about women are tied to the distinction he makes between soul and body and the lessons he hopes to teach his readers about their relative values. When preaching about the overwhelming importance of the soul, he can't but regard the kind of body one has as of no final significance, so there is no way for him to assess differentially the lives of women and men; but when making gloomy pronouncements about the worth of the body, he points an accusing finger at a class of people with a certain kind of body—women—because he regards them, as a class, as embodying the very traits he wishes no one to have. In this way, women constitute a deviant class in Plato's philosophy, in the sense that he points to their lives as the kinds of lives that are not acceptable philosophically: they are just the kind of lives no one, especially philosophers, ought to live. . . .

In summary, Plato does not merely embrace a distinction between soul and body; for all the good and hopeful and desirable possibilities for human life (now and in an afterlife) are aligned with the soul, while the rather seedy and undesirable liabilities of human life are aligned with the body (alternatively, the alignment is with the higher or lower parts of the soul). There is a highly polished moral gloss to the soul/body distinction in Plato. One of his favorite devices for bringing this moral gloss to a high luster is holding up, for our contempt and ridicule, the lives of women. This is one of the ways he tries to make clear that it makes no small difference whether you lead a soul-directed or a bodily directed life.

FEMINISM AND "SOMATOPHOBIA"

There are a number of reasons why feminists should be aware of the legacy of the soul/body distinction. It is not just that the distinction has been wound up with the depreciation and degradation of women, although, as has just been shown, examining a philosopher's view of the distinction may give us a direct route to his views about women.

First of all, as the soul or mind or reason is extolled, and the body or passion is denounced by comparison, it is not just women who are both relegated to the bodily or passionate sphere of existence and then chastised for belonging to that sphere. Slaves, free laborers, children, and animals are put in "their place" on almost the same grounds as women are. The images of women, slaves, laborers, children, and animals are almost interchangeable. For example, we find Plato holding that the best born and best educated should have control over "children, women and slaves . . . and the base rabble of those who are free in name," because it is in these groups that we find "the mob of motley appetites and pleasures and pains." As we saw above, Plato lumps together women, children, and animals as ignoramuses. (For Aristotle, there is little difference between a slave and an animal, because both "with their bodies attend to the needs of life." A common way of denigrating a member of any one of these groups is to compare that member to a member of one of the other groups—women are thought to have slavish or childish appetites, slaves are said to be brutish. Recall too, that Plato's way of ridiculing male homosexuals was to say that they imitated women. It is no wonder that the images and insults are almost interchangeable, for there is a central descriptive thread holding together the images of all these groups. The members of these groups lack, for all intents and purposes, mind or the power of reason; even the humans among them are not considered fully human.

It is important for feminists to see to what extent the images and arguments used to denigrate women are similar to those used to denigrate one group of men vis-à-vis another, children vis-à-vis adults, animals vis-à-vis humans, and even—though I have not discussed it here—the natural world vis-à-vis man's will (yes, man's will). For to see this is part of understanding how the oppression of women occurs in the context of, and is related to, other forms of oppression or exploitation.

There is a second reason why feminists should be aware of the legacy of the soul/body distinction. Some feminists have quite happily adopted both the soul/body distinction and relative value attached to soul and to body. But in doing so, they may be adopting a position inimical to what on a more conscious level they are arguing for.

For all her magisterial insight into the way in which the image of woman as body has been foisted upon and used against us, Simone de Beauvoir can't resist the temptation to say that woman's emancipation will come when woman, like man, is freed from this association with—according to the male wisdom of the centuries—the less important aspect of human existence. According to *The Second Sex*, women's demand is "not that they be exalted in their femininity; they wish that in themselves, as in humanity in general, transcendence may prevail over immanence." But in de Beauvior's own terms, for "transcendence" to prevail over "immanence" is for the spirit or mind to prevail over matter or body, for reason to prevail over passion and desire. This means not only that the old images of women as mired in the world of "immanence"—the world of nature and physical existence—will go away. It will also happen that women won't lead lives given over mainly to their "natural" functions: "the pain of childbirth is on the way out"; "artificial insemination is on the way in." Although de Beauvoir doesn't explicitly say it, her directions for women are to find means of leaving the world of immanence and joining the men in the realm of transcendence. Men have said, de Beauvoir reminds us, that to be human is to have mind prevail over body; and no matter what disagreements she has elsewhere with men's perceptions and priorities, de Beauvoir here seems to agree with them. . . .

. . . [I]n *The Feminine Mystique*, [Betty] Friedan remarks on the absence, in women's lives, of "the world of thought and ideas, the life of the mind and spirit." She wants women to be "culturally" as well as "biologically" creative—she wants us to think about spending our lives "mastering the secrets of the atoms, or the stars, composing symphonies, pioneering a new concept in government or society." And she associates "mental activity" with the "professions of highest value to society." Friedan thus seems to believe that men have done the more important things, the mental things; women have been relegated in the past to the less important human tasks involving bodily functions, and their liberation will come when they are allowed and encouraged to do the more important things in life.

Friedan's analysis relies on our old friend, the mind/body distinction, and Friedan, no less than Plato or de Beauvoir, quite happily assumes that mental activities are more valuable than bodily ones. Her solution to what she referred to as the "problem that has no name" is for women to leave (though not entirely) women's sphere and "ascend" into man's. Certainly there is much pleasure and value in the "mental activities" she extolls. But we can see the residue of her own negative attitude about tasks associated with the body: the bodily aspects of our existence must be attended to, the "liberated" woman, who is on the ascendant, can't be bothered with them. There is yet another group of people to whom these tasks will devolve: servants. Woman's liberation—and of course it is no secret that by "woman," Friedan could only have meant middle-class white women—seems to require woman's dissociation and separation from those who will perform the bodily tasks which the liberated woman has left behind in pursuit of "higher," mental activity. So we find Friedan quoting, without comment, Elizabeth Cady Stanton:

I now understood the practical difficulties most women had to contend with in the isolated household and the impossibility of women's best development if in contact the chief part of her life with servants and children. . . .

Friedan at times seems to chide those women who could afford to have servants but don't: the women pretend there's a "servant problem" when there isn't, or insist on doing their own menial work. The implication is that women could find servants to do the "menial work," if they wanted to, and that it would be desirable for them to do

so. But what difference is there between the place assigned to women by men and the place assigned to some women (or men) by Friedan herself? . . .

What I have tried to do here is bring attention to the fact that various versions of women's liberation may themselves rest on the very same assumptions that have informed the deprecation and degradation of women, and other groups which, of course, include women. Those assumptions are that we must distinguish between soul and body, and that the physical part of our existence is to be devalued in comparison to the mental. Of course, these two assumptions alone don't mean that women or other groups have to be degraded; it's these two assumptions, along with the further assumption that woman is body, or is bound to her body, or is meant to take care of the bodily aspects of life, that have so deeply contributed to the degradation and oppression of women. And so perhaps feminists would like to keep the first two assumptions (about the difference between mind and body, and the relative worth of each of them) and somehow or other get rid of the last—in fact, that is what most of the feminists previously discussed have tried to do. Nothing that has been said so far has amounted to an argument against those first two assumptions: it hasn't been shown that there is no foundation for the assumptions that the mind and body are distinct and that the body is to be valued less than the mind.

There is a feminist thinker, however, who has taken it upon herself to chip away directly at the second assumption and to a certain extent at the first. Both in her poetry, and explicitly in her recent book, *Of Woman Born*, Adrienne Rich has begun to show us why use of the mind/body distinction does not give us appropriate descriptions of human experience; and she has begun to remind us of the distance we keep from ourselves when we try to keep a distance from our bodies. She does this in the process of trying to redefine the dimensions of the experience of childbirth, as she tries to show us why childbirth and motherhood need not mean what they have meant under patriarchy.

We are reminded by Rich that it is possible to be alienated from our bodies not only by pretending or wishing they weren't there, but also by being "incarcerated" in them. The institution of motherhood has done the latter in its insistence on seeing woman only or mainly as a reproductive machine. Defined as flesh by flesh-loathers, woman enters the most "fleshly" of her experiences with that same attitude of flesh-loathing—surely "physical self-hatred and suspicion of one's own body" is scarcely a favorable emotion with which to enter an intense physical experience.

But Rich insists that we don't have to experience childbirth in that way—we don't have to experience it as "torture rack"; but neither do we have to mystify it as a "peak experience." The experience of childbirth can be viewed as a way of recognizing the integrity of our experience, because pain itself is not usefully catalogued as something just our minds or just our bodies experience. . . . The point of "natural childbirth" should be thought of not as enduring pain, but as having an active physical experience—a distinction we recognize as crucial for understanding, for example, the pleasure in athletics.

Rich recognizes that feminists have not wanted to accept patriarchal versions of female biology, of what having a female body means. It has seemed to feminists, she implies, that we must either accept that view of being female, which is, essentially, to be a body, or deny that view and insist that we are "disembodied spirits." It perhaps is natural to see our alternatives that way:

> We have been perceived for too many centuries as pure Nature, exploited and raped like the earth and the solar system; small wonder if we not try to become Culture: pure spirit, mind.

But we don't *have* to do that, Rich reminds us; we can appeal to the physical without denying what is called "mind." We can come to regard our physicality as "resource, rather than a destiny":

> In order to live a fully human life we require not only *control* of our bodies (though control is a prerequisite); we must touch the unity and resonance of our physicality, our bond with the natural order, the corporeal ground of our intelligence.

Rich doesn't deny that we will have to start thinking about our lives in new ways; she even implies that we'll have to start thinking about thinking in new ways. Maybe it will give such a project a small boost to point out that philosophers for their part still squabble about mind/body dualism; the legacy of dualism is strong, but not unchallenged by any means. And in any event, . . . one can hardly put the blame for sexism (or any other form of oppression) on dualism itself. Indeed, the mind/body distinction can be put to progressive political ends, for example, to assert equality between human beings in the face of physical differences between them. There is nothing intrinsically sexist or otherwise oppressive about dualism, that is, about the belief that there are minds and there are bodies and that they are distinct kinds of things. But historically, the story dualists tell often ends up being a highly politicized one; although the story may be different at different historical moments, often it is said not only that there are minds (or souls) and bodies, but also that one is meant to rule and control the other. And the stage is thereby set for the soul/body distinction, now highly politicized and hierarchically ordered, to be used in a variety of ways in connection with repressive theories of the self, as well as oppressive theories of social and political relations. Among the tasks facing feminists is to think about the criteria for an adequate theory of self. Part of the value of Rich's work is that it points to the necessity of such an undertaking, and it is no criticism of her to say that she does no more than remind us of some of the questions that need to be raised.

A FINAL NOTE ABOUT THE SIGNIFICANCE OF SOMATOPHOBIA IN FEMINIST THEORY

In the history of political philosophy, the grounds given for the inferiority of women to men often are quite similar to those given for the inferiority of slaves to masters, children to fathers, animals to humans. In Plato, for example, all such subordinate groups are guilty by association with one another and each group is guilty by association with the bodily. In their eagerness to end the stereotypical association of woman and body, feminists such as de Beauvoir, Friedan, Firestone, and Daly have overlooked the significance of the connections—in theory and in practice—between the derogation and oppression of women on the basis of our sexual identity and the derogation and oppression of other groups on the basis of, for example, skin color and class membership. It is as if in their eagerness to assign women a new place in the scheme of things, these feminist theorists have by implication wanted to dissociate women from other subordinate groups. One problem with this, of course, is that those other subordinate groups include women.

What is especially significant about Rich's recent work is that in contrast to these other theorists she both challenges the received tradition about the insignificance and indignity of bodily life and bodily tasks and explicitly focuses on racism as well as sexism as essential factors in women's oppression. I believe that it is not merely a coincidence that someone who attends to the first also attends to the second. Rich pauses not just to recognize the significance attached to the female body, but also to reevaluate that significance. "Flesh-loathing" is loathing of flesh by some particular group under some particular circumstances—the loathing of women's flesh by men, but also the loathing of black flesh by whites. (Here I begin to extrapolate from Rich, but I believe with some warrant.) After all, bodies are always particular bodies—they are male or female bodies (our deep confusion when we can't categorize a body in either way supports and does not belie the general point); but they are black or brown or biscuit or yellow or red bodies as well. We cannot seriously attend to the social significance attached to embodiment without recognizing this. I believe that it is Rich's recognition of this that distinguishes her work in crucial ways from that of most other major white feminists. Although the topic of feminism, sexism, and racism deserves a much fuller treatment, it is important to point out in the context of the present paper that not only does Rich challenge an assumption about the nature of the bodily that has been used to oppress women, but, unlike other feminists who do not challenge this assumption, she takes on the question of the ways in which sexism and racism interlock. Somatophobia historically has been symptomatic not only of sexism, but also of racism, so it is perhaps not surprising that someone who has examined that connection between flesh-loathing and sexism would undertake an examination of racism.

FRANCISCO VARELA, EVAN THOMPSON, AND ELEANOR ROSCH
The Embodied Mind

FRANCISCO VARELA *(1946–2001) was director of research at the Centre National de Recherche Scientifique and professor of cognitive science and epistemology at the École Polytechnique in Paris.* EVAN THOMPSON *(b. 1962) is the author of* Colour Vision. ELEANOR ROSCH *is professor of psychology at the University of California, Berkeley.*

Varela, Francisco, et al., "The Embodied Mind," from *Cognitive Science and Human Experience* (MIT Press, 1991)

EVEN in *The Crisis,* Husserl insisted that phenomenology is the study of essences. Thus the analysis of the life-world that he undertook there was not anthropological or historical; it was philosophical. But if all theoretical activity presupposes the life-world, what, then, of phenomenology? It is a distinctly theoretical pursuit; indeed, Husserl claimed it is the very highest form of theory. But then phenomenology too must presuppose the life-world, even as it attempts to explicate it. Thus Husserl was being haunted by the untraversed steps of the fundamental circularity.

Husserl recognized some of this circularity and tried to deal with it in an interesting way. He argued that the life-world was really a set of sedimented, background *preunderstandings* or (roughly speaking) assumptions, which the phenomenologist could make explicit and treat as a system of beliefs. In other words, Husserl tried to break out of the circle by treating the background as consisting essentially of representations. Once the life-world is construed in this way, however, Husserl's claim (indeed, the central claim of phenomenology) that the life-world is always prior to science becomes unstable. If the background consists of representations, what is to prevent scientific knowledge from permeating the background and contributing to its tacit store of beliefs? And if such permeation is possible, then what happens to the priority of phenomenology?

Husserl must have recognized these problems because he argued both that the life-world is prior to science and that our Western tradition is unique because our life-world is permeated by science. The task of the phenomenologist was to move back from an analysis of our scientifically permeated life-world to the "original" or "pregiven" life-world. But Husserl held on to the idea that this original life-world could be exhaustively accounted for by tracing it back to the essential structures of consciousness. He thus embraced the peculiar thought that the phenomenologist could stand both inside and outside of the life-world: he stood inside because all theory presupposed the life-world, and yet he stood outside because phenomenology alone could trace the genesis of the life-world in consciousness. Indeed, phenomenology was the highest form of theory for Husserl precisely because it was capable of such a peculiar contortion.

Given this peculiar contortion, it is not surprising that Husserl's pure phenomenology was not (as he hoped it would be) cultivated and improved on from one generation to the next, unlike other methodological discoveries such as the methods for statistical inference. Indeed, it has been the headache of later commentators to find out just exactly how his method of "phenomenological reduction" is to proceed.

But there is a deeper reason for the failure of the Husserlian project that we wish to emphasize here: Husserl's turn toward experience and "the things themselves" was entirely *theoretical,* or, to make the point the other way around, it completely lacked any *pragmatic* dimension. It is hardly surprising, therefore, that it could not overcome the rift between science and experience, for science, unlike phenomenological reflection, has a life beyond theory. Thus although Husserl's turn toward a phenomenological analysis of experience seemed radical, it was, in fact, quite within the mainstream of Western philosophy. . . .

Within our Western tradition, phenomenology was and still is *the* philosophy of human experience, the only extant edifice of thought that addresses these issues head-on. But above all, it was and still is philosophy as theoretical reflection. In most of the Western tradition since the Greeks, philosophy has been the discipline that seeks to find the truth, including the truth about the mind, purely by means of abstract, theoretical reasoning. Even philosophers who critique or problematize reason do so only be means of arguments, demonstration, and—especially in our so-called postmodern era—linguistic exhibitions (i.e., by means of abstract thought). Merleau-Ponty's critique of science and phenomenology, that they are theoretical activities after the fact, can equally be applied to most of Western philosophy as theoretical reflection. In this way, the loss of faith in reason so rampant in current thought becomes simultaneously a loss of faith in philosophy.

But if we turn away from reason, if reason is no longer taken as the method for knowing the mind, what can be used instead? One alternative is *un*reason, and, in the form of psychoanalytic theory, it has probably come to have more influence on our Western folk conception of the mind than any other single cultural factor. People—certainly middle-class North Americans and Europeans—have come to believe that they have an unconscious that is developmentally and symbolically primitive. They believe that both dreams and much of their waking life—motives, fantasies, preferences, aversions, emotions, behaviors, and pathological symptoms—are explainable by means of this unconscious. Thus, in the folk view, to know the mind "from the inside" is to use some version of psychoanalytic method to delve into the unconscious.

This "folk psychoanalytic" view is subject to the same critique that Merleau-Ponty made of science and phenomenology. The psychoanalytic method works within an individual's conceptual system. Whether an individual is commenting on a free association or using mathematical logic, having an ordinary waking conversation or dealing with the highly convoluted symbolic language of dreams, that person is knowing the mind and commenting on it in an after-the-fact fashion. The "professional" psychoanalyst knows, however, that he has to work within an individual's conceptual system and that a method that no theory can substitute for is required to go beyond this stage. What we find particularly interesting about psychoanalysis is that despite its great differences from cognitive science—despite the fact that it deals with phenomena of mind that are quite different from the normal subject matter of cognitive science and studies them by patently different methods—we see some of the same stages of evolution that we identify in cognitive science mirrored in psychoanalytic theory. . . .

A NON-WESTERN PHILOSOPHICAL TRADITION

At this point, a bold step needs to be taken . . . : we need to enlarge our horizon to encompass non-Western traditions of reflection upon experience. If philosophy in the West no longer occupies a privileged, foundational position with respect to other cultural activities such as science or art, then a full appreciation of philosophy and its importance for human experience requires that we examine the role of philosophy in cultures other than our own. In our culture, cognitive science has caused great excitement among philosophers (and the public at large) because it has enabled them to see their tradition in a new light. Were we to entertain the idea that there is no hard-and-fast distinction between science and philosophy then philosophers such as Descartes, Locke, Leibniz, Hume, Kant, and Husserl would take on a new significance: they could be seen, among other things, as protocognitive scientists. (Or as Jerry Fodor puts it, "In intellectual history, everything happens twice, first as philosophy and then as cognitive science.") Might this not also be the case for philosophical traditions with which we are less familiar?

In this book we will focus on one such tradition, that which derives from the Buddhist method of examining experience called *mindfulness meditation*. We believe that the Buddhist doctrines of no-self and of nondualism that grew out of this method have a significant contribution to make in a dialogue with cognitive science: (1) The no-self doctrine contributes to understanding the fragmentation of self portrayed in cognitivism and connectionism. (2) Buddhist nondualism, particularly as it is presented in the Madhyamika (which literally means "middle way") philosophy of Nagarjuna, may be juxtaposed with the entre deux of Merleau-Ponty and with the more recent ideas of cognition as enaction.

It is our contention that the rediscovery of Asian philosophy, particularly of the Buddhist tradition, is a second renaissance in the cultural history of the West, with the potential to be equally important as the rediscovery of Greek thought in the European renaissance. Our Western histories of philosophy, which ignore Indian thought, are artificial, since India and Greece share with us an Indo-European linguistic heritage as well as many cultural and philosophical preoccupations. . . .

EXAMINING EXPERIENCE WITH A METHOD: MINDFULNESS/AWARENESS

There are many human activities of body and mind, both Buddhist and non-Buddhist. The word *meditation* in its general usage in modern America has a number of different prominent folk meanings: (1) a state of concentration in which consciousness is focused on only one object; (2) a state of relaxation that is psychologically and medically beneficial; (3) a dissociated state in which trance phenomena can occur; and (4) a mystical state in which higher realities or religious objects are experienced. These are all altered states of consciousness; the meditator is doing something to get away from his usual mundane, unconcentrated, unrelaxed, nondissociated, lower state of reality.

Buddhist mindfulness/awareness practice is intended to be just the opposite of these. Its purpose is to become mindful, to experience what one's mind is doing as it does it, to be present with one's mind. What relevance does this have for cognitive science? We believe that if cognitive science is to include human experience, it must have some method for exploring and knowing what human experience is. It is for this reason that we are focusing on the Buddhist tradition of mindfulness meditation.

To get a sense of what mindfulness meditation is, one must first realize the extent to which people are normally not mindful. Usually one notices the tendency of the mind to wander only when one is attempting to accomplish some mental task and the wandering interferes. Or perhaps one realizes that one has just finished an anticipated pleasurable activity without noticing it. In fact, body and mind are seldom closely coordinated. In the Buddhist sense, we are not present. . . .

The purpose of calming the mind in Buddhism is not be become absorbed but to render the mind able to be present with itself long enough to gain insight into its own nature and functioning. (There are many traditional analogies for this process. For example, to be able to see painting on the wall of a dark cave, one needs a good light protected from the wind.) . . . Typically mindfulness/awareness is trained by means of formal periods of sitting meditation. The purpose of such periods is to simplify the situation to the bare minimum. The body is put into an upright posture and held still. Some simple object, often the breath, is used as the focus of alert attention. Each time the meditator realizes that his mind is wandering unmindfully, he is to acknowledge nonjudgmentally that wandering (there are various instructions as to how this is to be done) and bring the mind back to its object.

Breathing is one of the most simple, basic, ever-present bodily activities. Yet beginning meditators are generally astonished at how difficult it is to be mindful of even so uncomplex an object. Meditators discover that mind and body are not coordinated. The body is sitting, but the mind is seized constantly by thoughts, feelings, inner conversations, daydreams, fantasies, sleepiness, opinions, theories, judgments about thoughts and feelings, judgments about judgments—a never-ending torrent of disconnected mental events that the meditators do not even realize are occurring except at those brief instants when they remember what they are doing. Even when they attempt to return to their object of mindfulness, the breath, they may discover that they are only thinking about the breath rather than being mindful of the breath.

Eventually, it begins to dawn on the meditators that there is an actual difference between being present and not being present. In daily life they also begin to have instants of waking up to the realization that they are not present and of flashing back for a moment to be present—not to the breath, in this case, but to whatever is going on. Thus the first great discovery of mindfulness meditation tends to be not some encompassing insight into the nature of mind but the piercing realization of just how disconnected humans normally are from their very experience. Even the simplest or most pleasurable of daily activities—walking, eating, conversing, driving, reading, waiting, thinking, making love, planning, gardening, drinking, remembering, going to a therapist, writing, dozing, emoting, sightseeing—all pass rapidly in a blur of abstract commentary as the mind hastens to its next mental occupation. The meditator now discovers that the abstract attitude which Heidegger and Merleau-Ponty ascribe to science and philosophy is actually the attitude of everyday life when one is not mindful. This abstract attitude is the spacesuit, the padding of habits and preconceptions, the armor with which one habitually distances oneself from one's experience.

From the point of view of mindfulness/awareness meditation, humans are not trapped forever in the abstract attitude. The dissociation of mind from body, of awareness from experience, is the result of habit, and these habits can be broken. As the meditator again and again interrupts the flow of discursive thought and returns to be present with his breath or daily activity, there is a gradual taming of the mind's restlessness. One begins to be able to see the restlessness as such and to become patient with it, rather than becoming automatically lost in it. Eventually meditators report periods of a more panoramic perspective. This is called awareness. At this point the breath is no longer needed as a focus. In one traditional analogy, mindfulness is likened to the individual words of a sentence, whereas awareness is the grammar that encompasses the entire sentence. . . .

THE ROLE OF REFLECTION IN THE ANALYSIS OF EXPERIENCE

If the results of mindfulness/awareness practice are to bring one closer to one's ordinary experience rather than further from it, what can be the role of reflection? One of our popular cultural images of Buddhism is that the intellect is destroyed. In fact, study and contemplation play a major role in all Buddhist schools. The spontaneous action, much dramatized in the popular image of the Zen master, is not contradictory to the use of reflection as a mode of learning. How can this be?

This question brings us to the methodological heart of the interaction between mindfulness/awareness meditation, phenomenology, and cognitive science. What we are suggesting is a change in the nature of reflection from an abstract, disembodied activity to an embodied (mindful), open-ended reflection. By *embodied*, we mean reflection in which body and mind have been brought together. What this formulation intends to convey is that reflection is not just *on* experience, but reflection *is* a form of experience itself—and that reflective form of experience can be performed with mindfulness/awareness. When reflection is done in that way, it can cut the chain of habitual thought patterns and preconceptions such that it can be an open-ended reflection, open to possibilities other than those contained on one's current representations of the life space. We call this form of reflection *mindful, open-ended reflection.*

In our usual training and practice as Western scientists and philosophers, we obviously proceed differently. We ask, "What is Mind?", "What is Body?" and proceed to reflect theoretically and to investigate scientifically. This procedure gives rise to a gamut of claims, experiments, and results on various facets of cognitive abilities. But in the course of these investigations we often forget just who is asking this question and how it is asked. By not including ourselves in the reflection, we pursue only a partial reflection, and our question becomes disembodied; it attempts to express, in the words of the philosopher Thomas Nagel, a "view from nowhere." It is ironic that it is just this attempt to have a disembodied view from nowhere that leads to having a view from a very specific, theoretically confined, preconceptually entrapped somewhere.

The phenomenological tradition, from Husserl on, complained bitterly about this lack of self-included reflection but was able to offer in its place only a project of theoretical reflection *on* experience. The other extreme is to include the self but abandon reflection altogether in favor of a naive, subjective impulsivity. Mindfulness/awareness is neither of these; it works directly with, and so expresses, our basic embodiment.

Let us see how the difference in the theoretical and the mindfulness traditions of reflection manifest in an actual issue—the so-called mind-body problem. From Descartes on, the guiding question in Western philosophy has been whether body and mind are one or two distinct substances (properties, levels of description, etc.) and what the ontological relation between them is. We have already seen the simple, experiential, pragmatic approach taken in mindfulness/awareness meditation. It is a matter of simple experience that our mind and body can be dissociated, that the mind can wander, that we can be unaware of where we are and what our body or mind are doing. But this situation, this habit of mindlessness, can be changed. Body and mind can be brought together. We can develop habits in which body and mind are fully coordinated. The result is a mastery that is not only known to the individual meditator himself but that is visible to others—we easily recognize by its precision and grace a gesture that is animated by full awareness. We typically associate such mindfulness with the actions of an expert such as an athlete or musician.

We are suggesting that Descartes's conclusion that he was a thinking thing was the product of his question, and that question was a product of specific practices—those of disembodied, unmindful reflection. Husserlian phenomenology, though it embraced experience in a radical way, nonetheless continued the tradition by reflecting only upon the essential structures of thought. And even though it has recently become quite fashionable to criticize or "deconstruct" this stand-point of the *cogito*, philosophers still do not depart from the basic *practice* responsible for it.

Theoretical reflection need not be mindless and disembodied. The basic assertion of this progressive approach to human experience is that the mind-body relation or modality is not simply fixed and given but can be fundamentally changed. Many people would acknowledge the obvious truth of this conviction. Western philosophy does not deny this truth so much as ignore it. . . .

In summary it is because reflection in our culture has been severed from its bodily life that the mind-body problem has become a central topic for abstract reflection. Cartesian dualism is not so much one competing solution as it is the formulation of this problem. Reflection is taken to be distinctively mental, and so the problem arises of how it could ever be linked to bodily life. Although contemporary discussions of this problem have become quite sophisticated—largely because of the development of cognitive science—they have nevertheless not departed from the essentially Cartesian problematic of trying to understand how two seemingly distinct things are related. (Whether these things are substances, properties, or merely levels of description rarely makes a difference to the basic structure of the discussion.)

From the standpoint of a mindful, open-ended reflection the mind-body question need not be, What is the ontological relation between body and mind, regardless of anyone's experience?—but rather, What are the relations of body and mind in actual experience (the mindfulness aspect), and how do these relations develop, what forms can they take (the open-ended aspect)? As the Japanese philosopher Yasuo Yussa remarks, "One starts from the experiential assumption that the mind-body modality changes through the training of the mind and body by means of cultivation (*Shugyo*) or training (*Kelko*). Only after assuming this experiential ground does one ask what the mind-body relation is. That is, the mind-body issue is not simply a theoretical speculation but it is originally a practical, lived experience (*taiken*), involving the mustering of one's whole mind and body. The theoretical is only a reflection on this lived experience."

We may notice that his viewpoint is resonant with pragmatism, a view in philosophy that is having a modern revival. The body and mind relation is known in terms of what it can do. When one takes the more abstract attitude in philosophy or science, one might think that questions about the body-mind relation can be answered only after one first satisfactorily determines what is body and what is mind in isolation and abstraction. In the pragmatic, open-ended reflection, however, these questions are not separate from "the mustering of one's whole mind and body." Such involvement prevents the question, What is mind? from becoming disembodied. When we include in our reflection on a question the asker of the question and the process of asking itself (recall the fundamental circularity), then the question receives a new life and meaning.

Perhaps the closest discipline familiar to Westerners that verges on a pragmatic, open-ended view toward knowledge is psychoanalysis. We have in mind not so much the content of psychoanalytic theory but rather the idea that the very conception of mind and of the subject who is undergoing analysis is understood to change as the web of representations in which the self is entangled is slowly penetrated through analysis. What we believe traditional psychoanalytic methods lack, however, is the mindfulness/awareness component of reflection. . . .

In conclusion, we have argued that it is necessary to have a disciplined perspective on human experience that can enlarge the domain of cognitive science to include direct experience. We suggest such a perspective already exists in the form of mindfulness/awareness meditation. Mindfulness/awareness practice, phenomenological philosophy, and science are human activities; each is an expression of our human embodiment. Naturally, Buddhist doctrine, Western phenomenology, and science are each heir to numerous doctrinal disputes and conflicting claims. Each, however, insofar as it is a form of experimentation, is open to everyone and may be examined with the methods of each of the others. Thus, we believe that mindfulness/ awareness meditation can provide a natural bridge between cognitive science and human experience. Particularly impressive to us is the convergence that we have discovered among some of the main themes of Buddhist doctrine, phenomenology, and cognitive science—themes concerning the self and the relation between subject and object. It is to these themes that we now turn in our journey of discovery.

PART THREE

THINKING
AND KNOWING

CHAPTER SIX

WHAT DO I KNOW?

Right now, you think that you are reading a book. In fact, you *know* that you are. Surely nothing could be more obvious than that. Of course, to philosophers, nothing is obvious. Indeed, the nature and extent of our knowledge have been central concerns of philosophy since Plato. Plato provided a basis for what is usually referred to as **epistemology,** or the theory of knowledge, by suggesting that knowledge must be distinguished from mere belief. A belief can fall short of knowledge in two ways: (1) A belief can be false, or (2) it can be based on insufficient evidence. Your little sister might believe that Santa Claus exists. After all, everyone tells her that Santa Claus puts presents under the tree; she sees Santa at the mall and on television; she leaves cookies and milk for Santa on Christmas Eve, and they are gone on Christmas morning. In spite of all this evidence, she still doesn't *know* that Santa exists. Why not? Because, in fact, he doesn't. (You might also think that her evidence isn't very good, but compare the evidence that she has for Santa Claus to the evidence that you have for the existence of Eddie Murphy. Is there such a big difference?) Because your sister's belief isn't true, it isn't a case of knowledge. On the other hand, truth alone isn't enough to guarantee that a belief is knowledge. Suppose I tell you that I believe that Oprah Winfrey bakes pies on Thursdays and that I believe this because she reminds me of my friend Naomi, and Naomi bakes pies on Thursdays. Suppose that, just by coincidence, Oprah Winfrey does bake pies on Thursdays. My belief, then, is true, but given the weakness of my evidence, we should not count my belief as a case of knowledge. Knowledge requires real, hard evidence, something more than quirky associations, random hunches, or mere coincidences. If Oprah's cook, Rosie, had told me that Oprah bakes pies on Thursdays, then not only would my belief be true, but also it would be based on good evidence.

Whereas many philosophers have devoted their attention to determining just how much evidence is required for knowledge, others have argued for the extreme position that we have no knowledge at all. The position is called **skepticism.** Descartes, as you will see when you read the selection from *Meditations,* entertained some alarming skeptical possibilities. Although you think that you are reading right now, maybe you are really snuggled under your covers, fast asleep and merely dreaming that you are reading. It wouldn't be a terribly interesting dream, but haven't you sometimes had dreams that are quite mundane? An even more extreme, and perhaps less plausible, possibility is that there is an all-powerful Evil Demon, or Genius, whose greatest pleasure comes from deceiving mere mortals. Right now, by his ingenious methods, he is making you think that you are reading a philosophy book, but in fact you aren't.

Needless to say, skepticism is a position that most philosophers have tried to avoid, usually by dismissing it as nothing more than a source of irritation. Other philosophers, although disliking skepticism's conclusions, think that it cannot simply be ignored. They have attempted to show that skeptical arguments rest on impossible suppositions. Many philosophers, defending common sense, would argue that we can be certain of many things. You can be certain that you are enrolled in a philosophy course, for example. If a friend were to challenge your belief that you are, you could respond by taking her to class. If that were not enough, you could ask her to call the registrar. If she remains doubtful, that is her problem. You have done everything that you possibly could to prove that you are enrolled, and that is enough. Lewis Carroll provides some fictional reinforcements for the skeptics' arsenal.

Recall that knowledge (supposing now that we do have some) requires belief and evidence. Many of the beliefs that we have are about what philosophers have called the "external world," the world of tables and chairs, peanut butter and jelly. The evidence that we have for beliefs about the external world is evidence that we get through our senses. Sally believes that she is eating a peanut butter and jelly sandwich. Why? Because she sees the sandwich; she experiences its quintessentially American taste; she feels the stickiness on the roof of her mouth; she hears the smacking of her lips as they cope with the sticky mess between them; she inhales that characteristic peanut smell. All this sensory evidence contributes to Sally's belief.

The case of Sally and her sandwich is a very ordinary case of perception, the sort of perception that leads to knowledge. It is not so obvious, however, how we should understand exactly what goes on, even in a simple case such as this. We might agree that perception gives us knowledge but disagree as to what perception gives us knowledge *of*. If we asked Sally to describe her sandwich, she would say it is roughly five inches square, about an inch thick, is of various colors (white, purple, and brown), and so on. But some philosophers, Bertrand Russell among them, might say that Sally has failed to answer our question. She hasn't described the sandwich, but has rather described how the sandwich *appears* to her. Physics, the science that tells us how the world really is, would describe the sandwich as a cloud of colorless molecules. It is nonsensical to suppose, so the reasoning goes, that something could be both colorless and white, purple, and brown. Thus, color is not a quality of the sandwich itself, but rather a quality of the *appearance* of the sandwich. What Sally sees, then, is not the real, underlying sandwich. Instead she sees her *sense datum* of the sandwich. A sense datum is a mental representation of an externally existing object. Images, smells, tactile sensations, sounds, and tastes are all sense data corresponding to a particular sense organ. A visual sense datum, then, is a two-dimensional visual image.

The claim that we directly perceive sense data and only indirectly perceive physical objects, although supported by contemporary science, has its origins in the work of

John Locke. He noticed that some qualities of an object seem to be dependent on our perception of it, whereas others seem more to be "in" the object itself. How Sally's sandwich tastes to her seems clearly to have much to do with Sally. If she has just brushed her teeth, it will taste one way to her. If she has just indulged her habit of lemon sucking, it will taste another way. The chemical composition of the sandwich, on the other hand, will not be affected by Sally's prelunch activities. On the basis of considerations like these, Locke concluded that we must distinguish between two different kinds of qualities, the ones that are had by objects themselves and the ones that are had by our *ideas* (Locke's word for sense data) of objects. We directly perceive the latter qualities but not the former ones. Locke thus arrived at a conclusion similar to that suggested by Russell, but for different reasons.

It might have occurred to you that the sort of reasoning used by Russell and Locke seems to lead us right back to skepticism. After all, if Sally never perceives her sandwich, but only her ideas or sense data of it, then how can she ever know what her sandwich really is? Of course, in ordinary life, the true nature of her sandwich may not be of much concern to Sally. She just wants to finish her lunch. But as you are probably now well aware, philosophers, although they do get hungry, are seldom content to let ordinary life get in their way. So troubled was Bishop George Berkeley by what he took to be the skeptical consequences of Locke's reasoning that he argued that there are no physical objects at all! Although that sounds like a crazy way to avoid skepticism, you will see when you read Berkeley's selection that his arguments are very persuasive.

In her contribution to this chapter, Lorraine Code draws our attention to the fact that traditional philosophical discussions of knowledge have a peculiarly abstract idea of what a knower is. Indeed, these discussions assume only that knowers have beliefs, that they are capable of gaining evidence for and against their beliefs, and thus that they have cognitive abilities. But it has not occurred to most philosophers that, for example, the sex of the knower might make a difference in how we understand what knowledge is and under what conditions someone might have it. So Code presents some interesting reasons why we should reconsider the relationship between theories of knowledge and philosophers' assumptions about knowers. In reflecting on Code's essay, you might want to think about whether features of a person's identity other than sex might be equally relevant to developing theories of knowledge. Might not the race of the knower, or her socioeconomic status, be significant as well?

But before we enter into our worries about skepticism, we have begun the chapter with the most enthusiastic portrayal of the nature of knowledge from Plato's dialogue, *The Republic*. Plato presents us with the idea of nothing less than absolute knowledge, which can be gained by looking at reality itself, rather than the mere "shadows" of reality that surround us. It is against the background of Plato's stark image that much of skepticism is motivated.

PLATO

The Myth of the Cave

PLATO *(427–347 B.C.), in Book VII of his classic* Republic, *offers us one of the most striking and enduring images in the history of Western philosophy. It is a parable about education and its immense impact on those who acquire it. He asks us to imagine prisoners in a cave who see only the shadows of things on the wall. He then asks us to imagine how it would seem to one who turns towards the sunlight and sees things as they really are. That is how dazzling true knowledge is, and the person who gains it would be utterly unwilling to return to an ignorant state, no matter the ridicule he or she suffered from his or her still unenlightened peers. (*The Republic *is a dialogue, and the short replies to Socrates are by his friend Glaucon.)*

NEXT, I said, compare the effect of education and the lack of it upon our human nature to a situation like this: imagine men to be living in an underground cave-like dwelling place, which has a way up to the light along its whole width, but the entrance is a long way up. The men have been there from childhood, with their neck and legs in fetters, so that they remain in the same place and can only see ahead of them, as their bonds prevent them turning their heads. Light is provided by a fire burning some way behind and above them. Between the fire and the prisoners, some way behind them and on a higher ground, there is a path across the cave and along this a low wall has been built, like the screen at a puppet show in front of the performers who show their puppets above it.

I see it.

See then also men carrying along that wall, so that they overtop it, all kinds of artifacts, statues of men, reproductions of other animals in stone or wood fashioned in all sorts of ways, and, as is likely, some of the carriers are talking while others are silent.

This is a strange picture, and strange prisoners.

They are like us, I said. Do you think, in the first place, that such men could see anything of themselves and each other except the shadows which the fire casts upon the wall of the cave in front of them?

How could they, if they have to keep their heads still throughout life?

And is not the same true of the objects carried along the wall?

Quite.

If they could converse with one another, do you not think that they would consider these shadows to be the real things?

Necessarily.

What if their prison had an echo which reached them from in front of them? Whenever one of the carriers passing behind the wall spoke, would they not think that it was the shadow passing in front of them which was talking? Do you agree?

By Zeus I do.

Altogether then, I said, such men would believe the truth to be nothing else than the shadows of the artifacts?

They must believe that.

Consider then what deliverance from their bonds and the curing of their ignorance would be if something like this naturally happened to them. Whenever one of them was freed, had to stand up suddenly, turn his head, walk, and look

Plato, "The Myth of the Cave," from *The Republic;* VII, 514–518.

up toward the light, doing all that would give him pain, the flash of the fire would make it impossible for him to see the objects of which he had earlier seen the shadows. What do you think he would say if he was told that what he saw then was foolishness, that he was now somewhat closer to reality and turned to things that existed more fully, that he saw more correctly? If one then pointed to each of the objects passing by, asked him what each was, and forced him to answer, do you not think he would be at a loss and believe that the things which he saw earlier were truer than the things now pointed out to him?

Much truer.

If one then compelled him to look at the fire itself, his eyes would hurt, he would turn round and flee toward those things which he could see, and think that they were in fact clearer than those now shown to him.

Quite so.

And if one were to drag him thence by force up the rough and steep path, and did not let him go before he was dragged into the sunlight, would he not be in physical pain and angry as he was dragged along? When he came into the light, with the sunlight filling his eyes, he would not be able to see a single one of the things which are now said to be true.

Not at once, certainly.

I think he would need time to get adjusted before he could see things in the world above; at first he would see shadows most easily, then reflections of men and other things in water, then the things themselves. After this he would see objects in the sky and the sky itself more easily at night, the light of the stars and the moon more easily than the sun and the light of the sun during the day.

Of course.

Then, at last, he would be able to see the sun, not images of it in water or in some alien place, but the sun itself in its own place, and be able to contemplate it.

That must be so.

After this he would reflect that it is the sun which provides the seasons and the years, which governs everything in the visible world, and is also in some way the cause of those other things which he used to see.

Clearly that would be the next stage.

What then? As he reminds himself of his first dwelling place, of the wisdom there and of his fellow prisoners, would he not reckon himself happy for the change, and pity them?

Surely.

And if the men below had praise and honours from each other, and prizes for the man who saw most clearly the shadows that passed before them, and who could best remember which usually came earlier and which later, and which came together and thus could most ably prophesy the future, do you think our man would desire those rewards and envy those who were honoured and held power among the prisoners, or would he feel, as Homer put it, that he certainly wished to be "serf to another man without possessions upon the earth" and go through any suffering, rather than share their opinions and live as they do?

Quite so, he said, I think he would rather suffer anything.

Reflect on this too, I said. If this man went down into the cave again and sat down in the same seat, would his eyes not be filled with darkness, coming suddenly out of the sunlight?

They certainly would.

And if he had to contend again with those who had remained prisoners in recognizing those shadows while his sight was affected and his eyes had not settled down—and the time for this adjustment would not be short—would he not be ridiculed? Would it not be said that he had returned from his upward journey with his eyesight spoiled, and that it was not worthwhile even to attempt to travel upward? As for the man who tried to free them and lead them upward, if they could somehow lay their hands on him and kill him, they would do so.

They certainly would.

This whole image, my dear Glaucon, I said, must be related to what we said before. The realm of the visible should be compared to the prison dwelling, and the fire inside it to the power of the sun. If you interpret the upward journey and the contemplation of things above as the upward journey of the soul to the intelligible realm, you will grasp what I surmise since you were keen to hear it. Whether it is true or not only the god knows, but this is how I see it, namely that in the intelligible world the Form of the Good is the last to be seen, and with difficulty; when seen it must be reckoned to be for all the cause of all that is right and beautiful, to have produced in the visible world both light and the fount of light, while in the intelligible world it is itself that which produces and controls truth and intelligence, and he who is to act intelligently in public or in private must see it.

I share your thought as far as I am able.

Come then, share with me this thought also: do not be surprised that those who have reached this point are unwilling to occupy themselves with human affairs, and that their souls are always pressing upward to spend their time there, for this is natural if things are as our parable indicates.

That is very likely.

Further, I said, do you think it at all surprising that anyone coming to the evils of human life from the contemplation of the divine behaves awkwardly and appears very ridiculous while his eyes are still dazzled and before he is sufficiently adjusted to the darkness around him, if he is compelled to contend in court or some other place about the shadows of justice or the objects of which they are shadows, and to carry through the contest about these in the way these things are understood by those who have never seen Justice itself?

That is not surprising at all. . . .

Education . . . then is the art of doing this very thing, this turning around, the knowledge of how the soul can most easily and most effectively be turned around; it is not the art of putting the capacity of sight into the soul; the soul possesses that already but it is not turned the right way or looking where it should. This is what education has to deal with.

That seems likely.

RENÉ DESCARTES
Meditation

RENÉ DESCARTES *(1596–1650) was born in Brittany, France. He went to college from the ages of eight to sixteen, studying logic, philosophy, and mathematics. He did important work in mathematics and science in addition to his revolutionary work in philosophy. His* Meditations, *from which this selection is taken, was published in 1641.*

FIRST of all, because I know that all things which I apprehend clearly and distinctly can be created by God as I apprehend them, it suffices that I am able to apprehend one thing apart from another clearly and distinctly in order to be certain that the one is different from the other, since they may be made to exist in separation at least by the omnipotence

"Meditation 1" from *Meditations* by René Descartes, translated by Haldane and Ross (Cambridge University Press, 1911).

of God; and it does not signify by what power this separation is made in order to compel me to judge them to be different: and, therefore, just because I know certainly that I exist, and that meanwhile I do not remark that any other thing necessarily pertains to my nature or essence, excepting that I am a thinking thing, I rightly conclude that my essence consists solely in the fact that I am a thinking thing [or a substance whose whole essence or nature is to think]. And although possibly (or rather certainly, as I shall say in a moment) I possess a body with which I am very intimately conjoined, yet because, on the one side, I have a clear and distinct idea of myself inasmuch as I am only a thinking and unextended thing, and as, on the other, I possess a distinct idea of body, inasmuch as it is only an extended and unthinking thing, it is certain that this I [that is to say, my soul by which I am what I am], is entirely and absolutely distinct from my body, and can exist without it.

I further find in myself faculties employing modes of thinking peculiar to themselves, to wit, the faculties of imagination and feeling, without which I can easily conceive myself clearly and distinctly as a complete being; while, on the other hand, they cannot be so conceived apart from me, that is without an intelligent substance in which they reside, for [in the notion we have of these faculties, or, to use the language of the Schools] in their formal concept, some kind of intellection is comprised, from which I infer that they are distinct from me as its modes are from a thing. I observe also in me some other faculties such as that of change of position, the assumption of different figures and such like, which cannot be conceived, any more than can the preceding, apart from some substance to which they are attached, and consequently cannot exist without it; but it is very clear that these faculties, if it be true that they exist, must be attached to some corporeal or extended substance, and not to an intelligent substance, since in the clear and distinct conception of these there is some sort of extension found to be present, but no intellection at all. There is certainly further in me a certain passive faculty of perception, that

is, of receiving and recognising the ideas of sensible things, but this would be useless to me [and I could in no way avail myself of it], if there were not either in me or in some other thing another active faculty capable of forming and producing these ideas. But this active faculty cannot exist in me [inasmuch as I am a thing that thinks] seeing that it does not presuppose thought, and also that those ideas are often produced in me without my contributing in any way to the same, and often even against my will; it is thus necessarily the case that the faculty resides in some substance different from me in which all the reality which is objectively in the ideas that are produced by this faculty is formally or eminently contained, as I remarked before. And this substance is either a body, that is, a corporeal nature in which there is contained formally [and really] all that which is objectively [and by representation] in those ideas, or it is God Himself, or some other creature more noble than body in which that same is contained eminently. But, since God is no deceiver, it is very manifest that He does not communicate to me these ideas immediately and by Himself, nor yet by the intervention of some creature in which their reality is not formally, but only eminently, contained. For since He has given me no faculty to recognise that this is the case, but, on the other hand, a very great inclination to believe [that they are sent to me or] that they are conveyed to me by corporeal objects, I do not see how He could be defended from the accusation of deceit if these ideas were produced by causes other than corporeal objects. Hence we must allow that corporeal things exist. However, they are perhaps not exactly what we perceive by the senses, since this comprehension by the senses is in many instances very obscure and confused; but we must at least admit that all things which I conceive in them clearly and distinctly, that is to say, all things which, speaking generally, are comprehended in the object of pure mathematics, are truly to be recognised as external objects.

As to other things, however, which are either particular only, as, for example, that the sun is of such and such a figure, etc., or which are less clearly and distinctly conceived, such as light, sound, pain and the like, it is certain that although they are very dubious and uncertain, yet on the sole ground that God is not a deceiver and that consequently He has not permitted any falsity to exist in my opinion which He has not likewise given me the faculty of correcting, I may assuredly hope to conclude that I have within me the means of arriving at the truth even here. And first of all there is no doubt that in all things which nature teaches me there is some truth contained; for by nature, considered in general, I now understand no other thing than either God Himself or else the order and disposition which God has established in created things; and by my nature in particular I understand no other thing than the complexus of all the things which God has given me.

But there is nothing which this nature teaches me more expressly [nor more sensibly] than that I have a body which is adversely affected when I feel pain, which has need of food or drink when I experience the feelings of hunger and thirst, and so on; nor can I doubt there being some truth in all this. . . .

In order to begin this examination, then, I here say, in the first place, that there is a great difference between mind and body, inasmuch as body is by nature always divisible, and the mind is entirely indivisible. For, as a matter of fact, when I consider the mind, that is to say, myself inasmuch as I am only a thinking thing, I cannot distinguish in myself any parts, but apprehend myself to be clearly one and entire; and although the whole mind seems to be united to the whole body, yet if a foot, or an arm, or some other part, is separated from my body, I am aware that nothing has been taken away from my mind. And the faculties of willing, feeling, conceiving, etc. cannot be properly speaking said to be its parts, for it is one and the same mind which employs itself in willing and in feeling and understanding. But it is quite otherwise with corporeal or extended objects, for there is not one of these imaginable by me which my mind cannot easily divide into parts, and which consequently I do not recognise as being divisible; this would

be sufficient to teach me that the mind or soul of man is entirely different from the body, if I had not already learned it from other sources.

I further notice that the mind does not receive the impressions from all parts of the body immediately, but only from the brain, or perhaps even from one of its smallest parts, to wit, from that in which the common sense is said to reside, which, whenever it is disposed in the same particular way, conveys the same thing to the mind, although meanwhile the other portions of the body may be differently disposed, as is testified by innumerable experiments which it is unnecessary here to recount.

I notice, also, that the nature of body is such that none of its parts can be moved by another part a little way off which cannot also be moved in the same way by each one of the parts which are between the two, although this more remote part does not act at all. As, for example, in the cord *A B C D* (which is in tension) if we pull the last part *D*, the first part *A* will not be moved in any way differently from what would be the case if one of the intervening parts *B* or *C* were pulled, and the last part *D* were to remain unmoved. And in the same way, when I feel pain in my foot, my knowledge of physics teaches me that this sensation is communicated by means of nerves dispersed through the foot, which, being extended like cords from there to the brain, when they are contracted in the foot, at the same time contract the inmost portions of the brain which is their extremity and place of origin, and then excite a certain movement which nature has established in order to cause the mind to be affected by a sensation of pain represented as existing in the foot. But because these nerves must pass through the tibia, the thigh, the loins, the back and the neck, in order to reach from the leg to the brain, it may happen that although their extremities which are in the foot are not affected, but only certain ones of their intervening parts [which pass by the loins or the neck] this action will excite the same movement in the brain that might have been excited there by a hurt received in the foot, in consequence of which the mind will necessarily feel in the foot the same pain as if it had received a hurt. And the same holds good of all the other perceptions of our senses.

I notice finally that since each of the movements which are in the portion of the brain by which the mind is immediately affected brings about one particular sensation only, we cannot under the circumstances imagine anything more likely than that this movement, amongst all the sensations which it is capable of impressing on it, causes mind to be affected by that one which is best fitted and most generally useful for the conservation of the human body when it is in health. But experience makes us aware that all the feelings with which nature inspires us are such as I have just spoken of; and there is therefore nothing in them which does not give testimony to the power and goodness of the God [who has produced them]. Thus, for example, when the nerves which are in the feet are violently or more than usually moved, their movement, passing through the medulla of the spine to the inmost parts of the brain, gives a sign to the mind which makes it feel somewhat, to wit, pain, as though in the foot, by which the mind is excited to do its utmost to remove the cause of the evil as dangerous and hurtful to the foot. It is true that God could have constituted the nature of man in such a way that this same movement in the brain would have conveyed something quite different to the mind; for example, it might have produced consciousness of itself either in so far as it is in the brain, or as it is in the foot, or as it is in some other place between the foot and the brain, or it might finally have produced consciousness of anything else whatsoever; but none of all this would have contributed so well to the conservation of the

body. Similarly, when we desire to drink, a certain dryness of the throat is produced which moves its nerves, and by their means the internal portions of the brain; and this movement causes in the mind the sensation of thirst, because in this case there is nothing more useful to us than to become aware that we have need to drink for the conservation of our health; and the same holds good in other instances.

From this it is quite clear that, notwithstanding the supreme goodness of God, the nature of man, inasmuch as it is composed of mind and body, cannot be otherwise than sometimes a source of deception. For if there is any cause which excites, not in the foot but in some part of the nerves which are extended between the foot and the brain, or even in the brain itself, the same movement which usually is produced when the foot is detrimentally affected, pain will be experienced as though it were in the foot, and the sense will thus naturally be deceived; for since the same movement in the brain is capable of causing but one sensation in the mind, and this sensation is much more frequently excited by a cause which hurts the foot than by another existing in some other quarter, it is reasonable that it should convey to the mind pain in the foot rather than in any other part of the body. And although the parchedness of the throat does not always proceed, as it usually does, from the fact that drinking is necessary for the health of the body, but sometimes comes from quite a different cause, as is the case with dropsical patients, it is yet much better that it should mislead on this occasion than if, on the other hand, it were always to deceive us when the body is in good health; and so on in similar cases. . . .

LEWIS CARROLL
Through the Looking Glass

LEWIS CARROLL *(1832–1898), whose real name was Charles Lutwidge Dodgson, was an English mathematician and logician. His mother died when he went away to college, and he became increasingly drawn to the company of children, especially little girls. He was afflicted with a stammer, which made him uncomfortable in the company of adults. His books* Alice in Wonderland *and* Through the Looking Glass *are two of the great children's books in English. He also published mathematical works.*

AFTER a pause, Alice began, "Well—were *both* very unpleasant characters—" Here she checked herself in some alarm, at hearing something that sounded to her like the puffing of a large steam-engine in the wood near them, though she feared it was more likely to be a wild beast. "Are there any lion or tigers about here?" she asked timidly.

"It's only the Red King snoring," said Tweedledee.

"Come and look at him!" the brothers cried, and they each took one of Alice's hands, and led her up to where the King was sleeping.

"Isn't he a *lovely* sight?" said Tweedledum.

Alice couldn't say honestly that he was. He had a tall red night-cap on, with a tassel, and he was lying crumpled up into a sort of untidy heap, and snoring loud—"fit to snore his head off!" as Tweedledum remarked.

"I'm afraid he'll catch cold with lying on the damp grass," said Alice, who was a very thoughtful little girl.

"He's dreaming now," said Tweedledee: "and what do you think he's dreaming about?"

Alice said "Nobody can guess that."

"Why, about *you!*" Tweedledee exclaimed, clapping his hands triumphantly. "And if he left off dreaming about you, where do you suppose you'd be?"

"Where I am now, of course," said Alice.

"Not you!" Tweedledee retorted contemptuously. "You'd be nowhere. Why, you're only a sort of thing in his dream!"

"If that there King was to wake" added Tweedledum, "You'd go out—bang!—just like a candle!"

"I shouldn't!" Alice exclaimed indignantly. "Besides, if *I'm* only a sort of thing in his dream, what are *you*, I should like to know?"

"Ditto," said Tweedledum

"Ditto, ditto!" cried Tweedledee.

He shouted this so loud that Alice couldn't help saying "Hush! You'll be waking him, I'm afraid, if you make so much noise."

"Well, it's no use *your* talking about waking him," said Tweedledum, "when you're only one of the things in his dream. You know very well you're not real."

"I *am* real!" said Alice, and began to cry.

"You won't make yourself a bit realler by crying," Tweedledee remarked: "there's nothing to cry about."

"If I wasn't real," Alice said—half-laughing through her tears, it all seemed so ridiculous—"I shouldn't be able to cry."

"I hope you don't suppose those are *real* tears?" Tweedledum interrupted in a tone of great contempt.

BERTRAND RUSSELL
Appearance and Reality

BERTRAND RUSSELL *(1872–1970) was one of the greatest philosophers of this century. He wrote an enormous number of philosophical books and articles, from* Principia Mathematica *(with Alfred North Whitehead) to some notorious polemics in favor of "free love" and atheism. Like Hume, he was too controversial for most universities, and a famous court case prevented him from teaching at City College of New York. He did, however, win the Nobel Prize for Literature in 1950. At the age of eighty-nine, he was jailed for protesting against nuclear arms.*

IN daily life, we assume as certain many things which, on a closer scrutiny, are found to be so full of apparent contradictions that only a great amount of thought enables us to know what it is that we really may believe. In the search for certainty, it is natural to begin with our present experiences, and in some sense, no doubt, knowledge is to be derived from them. But any statement as to what it is that our immediate experiences make us know is very likely to be wrong. It seems to me that I am now sitting in a chair, at a table of a certain shape, on which I see sheets of paper with writing or print. By turning my head I see out of the window buildings and clouds and the sun. I believe that the sun is about ninety-three million miles from the earth; that it is a hot globe many times bigger than the earth; that, owing to the earth's rotation, it rises every morning, and will continue to do so for an indefinite time in the future. I believe that, if any other normal person comes into my room he will see the same chairs and tables and books and papers as I see, and that the table which I see is the same as the table which I feel pressing against my arm. All this seems to be so evident as to be hardly worth stating, except in answer to a man who doubts whether I know anything. Yet all this may be reasonably doubted, and all of it requires much careful discussion before we can be sure that we have stated it in a form that is wholly true.

To make our difficulties plain, let us concentrate attention on the table. To the eye it is oblong, brown and shiny, to the touch it is smooth and cool and hard; when I tap it, it gives out a wooden sound. Any one else who sees and feels and hears the table will agree with this description, so that it might seem as if no difficulty would arise; but as soon as we try to be more precise our troubles begin. Although I believe that the table is "really" of the same colour all over, the parts that reflect the light look much brighter than the other parts, and some parts look white because of reflected light. I know that, if I move, the parts that reflect the light will be different, so that the apparent distribution of colours on the table will change. It follows that if several people are looking at the table at the same moment, no two of them will see exactly the same distribution of colours, because no two can see it from exactly the same point of view, and any change in the point of view makes some change in the way the light is reflected.

For most practical purposes these differences are unimportant, but to the painter they are all-important: the painter has to unlearn the habit of thinking that things seem to have the colour which common sense says they "really" have, and to learn the habit of seeing things as they appear. Here we have already the beginning of one of the distinctions that cause most trouble in philosophy—the distinction between "appearance" and "reality," between what things seem to be and what they are. The painter wants to know what things seem to be, the practical man and the philosopher want to know what they are; but the philosopher's wish to know this is stronger than the practical man's, and is more troubled by knowledge as to the difficulties of answering the question.

To return to the table. It is evident from what we have found, that there is no colour which preeminently appears to be *the* colour of the table, or even of any one particular part of the table—it appears to be of different colours from different points of view, and there is no reason for regarding some of these as more really its colour than others. And we know that even from a given point of view the colour will seem different by artificial light, or to a colourblind man, or to a man wearing blue spectacles, while in the dark there will be no colour at all, though to touch and hearing the table will be unchanged. This colour is not something which is inherent in the table, but something depending upon the table and the spectator and the way the light falls on the table. When, in ordinary life, we speak of *the* colour of the table, we only mean the sort of colour which it will seem to have to a normal spectator from an ordinary point of view under usual conditions of light. But the other colours which appear under other conditions have just as good a right to be considered real; and therefore, to avoid favouritism, we are compelled to deny that, in itself, the table has any one particular colour.

The same thing applies to the texture. With the naked eye one can see the grain, but otherwise the table looks smooth and even. If we look at it through a microscope, we should see roughnesses and hills and valleys, and all sorts of differences that are imperceptible to the naked eye. Which of these is the "real" table? We are naturally tempted to say that what we see through the microscope is more real, but that in turn would be changed by a still more powerful microscope. If, then, we cannot trust what we see with the naked eye, why should we trust what we see through a microscope? Thus, again, the confidence in our sense with which we began deserts us.

The *shape* of the table is no better. We are all in the habit of judging as to the "real" shapes of things, and we do this so unreflectingly that we come to think we actually see the real shapes. But, in fact, as we all have to learn if we try to draw, a given thing looks different in shape from every different point of view. If our table is "really" rectangular, it will look, from almost all points of view, as if it had two acute angles and two obtuse angles. If opposite sides are parallel, they will look as if they converged to a point away from the spectator; if they are of equal length, they will look as if the nearer side were longer. All these things are not commonly noticed in looking at a table, because experience has taught us to construct the "real" shape from the apparent shape, and the "real" shape is what we see; it is something inferred from what we see. And what we see is constantly changing in shape as we move about the room; so that here again the senses seem not to give us the truth about the table itself, but only about the appearance of the table.

Similar difficulties arise when we consider the sense of touch. It is true that the table always gives us a sensation of hardness, and we feel that it resists pressure. But the sensation we obtain depends upon how hard we press the table and also upon what part of the body we press with; thus the various sensations due to various pressures or various parts of the body cannot be supposed to reveal *directly* any definite property of the table, but at most to be *signs* of some property which perhaps *causes* all the sensations, but is not actually apparent in any of them. And the same applies still more obviously to the sounds which can be elicited by rapping the table.

Thus it becomes evident that the real table, if there is one, is not the same as what we immediately experienced by sight or touch or hearing. The real table, if there is one, is not *immediately* known to us at all, but must be an inference from what is immediately known. Hence, two very difficult questions at once arise; namely (1) Is there a real table at all? (2) If so, what sort of object can it be?

JOHN LOCKE
Where Our Ideas Come From

JOHN LOCKE *(1632–1704) taught philosophy at Oxford until he earned his medical degree. He devoted considerable time to politics, and his two* Treatises on Government *were highly influential in establishing the theoretical grounds of the U.S. Constitution. Not only is he the founder of modern political liberalism, but also his* Essay Concerning Human Understanding *initiated what has come to be known as British empiricism.*

SOME FARTHER CONSIDERATIONS CONCERNING OUR SIMPLE IDEAS OF SENSATION

1 *Positive ideas from privative causes.*— Concerning the simple ideas of sensation it is to be considered, that whatsoever is so constituted in nature as to be able by affecting our senses to cause any perception in the mind, doth thereby produce in the understanding a simple idea; which, whatever be the external cause of it, when it comes to be taken notice of by our discerning faculty, it is by the mind looked on and considered there to be a real positive idea in the understanding, as much as any other whatsoever; though perhaps the cause of it be but a privation in the subject.

2 Thus the ideas of heat and cold, light and darkness, white and black, motion and rest, are equally clear and positive ideas in the mind; though perhaps some of the causes which produce them are barely privations in those subjects from whence our senses derive those ideas. These the understanding, in its view of them, considers all as distinct positive ideas without taking notice of the causes that produce them; which is an inquiry not belonging to the ideas as it is in the understanding, but to the nature of the things existing without us. These are two very different things, and carefully to be distinguished; it being one thing to perceive and know the idea of white or black, and quite another to examine what kind of particles they must be, and how ranged in the superficies, to make any object appear white or black.

3 A painter or dyer who never inquired into their causes, hath the ideas of white and black and other colours as clearly, perfectly, and distinctly in his understanding, and perhaps more distinctly than the philosopher who hath busied himself in considering their natures, and thinks he knows how far either of them is in its cause positive or privative; and the idea of black is no less positive in his mind than that of white, however the cause of that colour in the external object may be only a privation.

4 If it were the design of my present undertaking to inquire into the natural causes and manner of perception, I should offer this as a reason why a privative cause might, in some cases at least, produce a positive idea, viz., that all sensation being produced in us only by different degrees and modes of motion in our animal spirits, variously agitated by external objects, the abatement of any former motion must as necessarily produce a new sensation as the variation or increase of it; and so introduce a new idea, which depends only on a different motion of the animal spirits in that organ.

5 But whether this be so or not I will not here determine, but appeal to every one's own experience, whether the shadow of a man, though it consists of nothing but the absence of light (and the more the absence of light is, the more discernible is the shadow), does not, when a man

Locke, John, "Where Our Ideas Come From," from *Essays Concerning Human Understanding,* book II, Ch. 8, sect. 1–17, ed. Mary Whiton Calkins, The Open Court Philosophical Company, 1933.

looks on it, cause as clear and positive an idea in his mind as a man himself, though covered over with clear sunshine! And the picture of a shadow is a positive thing. Indeed, we have negative names, [which stand not directly for positive ideas, but for their absence, such as *insipid, silence, nihil, &c.,* which words denote positive ideas, *v. g., taste, sound, being,* with a signification of their absence.]

6 *Positive ideas from privative causes.*—And thus one may truly be said to see darkness. For, supposing a hole perfectly dark, from whence no light is reflected, it is certain one may see the figure of it, or it may be painted; or whether the ink I write with make any other idea, is a question. The privative causes I have here assigned of positive ideas are according to the common opinion; but, in truth, it will be hard to determine whether there be really any ideas from a privative cause, till it be determined whether rest be any more a privation than motion.

7 *Ideas in the mind, qualities in bodies.*—To discover the nature of our ideas the better, and to discourse of them intelligibly, it will be convenient to distinguish them, as they are ideas or perceptions in our minds, and as they are modifications of matter in the bodies that use such perceptions in us; that so we may not think (as perhaps usually is done) that they are exactly the images and resemblances of something inherent in the subject; most of those of sensation being in the mind no more the likeness of something existing without us than the names that stand for them are the likeness of our ideas, which yet upon hearing they are apt to excite in us.

8 Whatsoever the mind perceives in itself, or is the immediate object of perception, thought, or understanding, that I call "ideal"; and the power to produce any idea in our mind, I call "quality" of the subject wherein that power is. Thus a snowball having the power to produce in us the ideas of white, cold, and round, the powers to produce those ideas in us as they are in the snowball, I call "qualities"; and as they are sensations or perceptions in our understanding, I call them "ideas"; which ideas, if I speak of them sometimes as in the things themselves, I would

be understood to mean those qualities in the objects which produce them in us.

9 *Primary qualities.*—[Qualities thus considered in bodies are, First, such as are utterly inseparable from the body, in what estate soever it be;] and such as, in all the alterations and changes it suffers, all the force can be used upon it, it constantly keeps; and such as sense constantly finds in every particle of matter which has bulk enough to be perceived, and the mind finds inseparable from every particle of matter, though less than to make itself singly be perceived by our senses: *v. g.,* take a grain of wheat, divide it into two parts, each part has still solidity, extension, figure, and mobility; divide it again, and it retains still the same qualities: and so divide it on till the parts become insensible, they must retain still each of them all those qualities. For, division (which is all that a mill or pestle or any other body does upon another, in reducing it to insensible parts) can never take away either solidity, extension, figure, or mobility from any body, but only makes two or more distinct separate masses of matter of that which was but one before; all which distinct masses reckoned as so many distinct bodies, after division, make a certain number. [These I call *original* or *primary* qualities of body, which I think we may observe to produce simple ideas in us, viz., solidity, extension, figure, motion or rest, and number.]

10 *Secondary qualities.*—Secondly. Such qualities, which in truth are nothing in the objects themselves, but powers to produce various sensations in us by their primary qualities, i.e., by the bulk, figure, texture, and motion of their insensible parts, as colours, sounds, tastes, &c., these I call *secondary* qualities. [To these might be added a third sort, which are allowed to be barely powers, though they are as much real qualities in the subject as those which I, to comply with the common way of speaking, call qualities, but, for distinction, *secondary* qualities. For, the power in fire to produce a new colour or consistency in wax or clay, by its primary qualities, is as much a quality in fire as the power it has to produce in me a new idea or sensation of

warmth or burning, which I felt not before, by the same primary qualities, viz., the bulk, texture, and motion of its insensible parts.]

11 [*How primary qualities produce their ideas.*—The next thing to be considered is, how bodies produce ideas in us; and that is manifestly by impulse, the only way which we can conceive bodies to operate in.]

12 If, then, external objects be not united to our minds when they produce ideas therein, and yet we perceive these original qualities in such of them as singly fall under our senses, it is evident that some motion must be thence continued by our nerves, or animal spirits, by some parts of our bodies, to the brains or the seat of sensation, there to produce in our minds the particular ideas we have of them. And since the extension, figure, number, and motion of bodies of an observable bigness, may be perceived at a distance by the sight, it is evident some singly imperceptible bodies must come from them to the eyes, and thereby convey to the brain some motion which produces these ideas which we have of them in us.

13 *How secondary.*—After the same manner that the ideas of these original qualities are produced in us, we may conceive that the ideas of secondary qualities are also produced, viz., by the operation of insensible particles on our senses. For it being manifest that there are bodies, and good store of bodies, each whereof are so small that we cannot by any of our senses discover either their bulk, figure, or motion (as is evident in the particles of the air and water, and other extremely smaller than those, perhaps as much smaller than the particles of air or water as the particles of air or water are smaller than peas or hailstones): let us suppose at present that the different motions and figures, bulk and number, of such particles, effecting several organs of our senses, produce in us those different sensations which we have from the colours and smells of bodies, *v. g.,* that a violet, by the impulse of such insensible particles of matter of peculiar figures and bulks, and in different degrees and modifications of their motions, causes the ideas of the blue colour and sweet scent of that flower to be produced in our minds; it being

no more impossible to conceive that God should annex such ideas to such motions, with which they have no similitude, than that he should annex the idea of pain to the motion of a piece of steel dividing our flesh, with which the idea hath no resemblance.

14 What I have said concerning colours and smells may be understood also of tastes and sounds, and other the like sensible qualities; which, whatever reality we by mistake attribute to them, are in truth nothing in the objects themselves, but powers to produce various sensations in us, and depend on those primary qualities, viz., bulk, figure, texture, and motion of parts [as I have said].

15 *Ideas of primary qualities are resemblances; of secondary, not.*—From whence I think it is easy to draw this observation, that the ideas of primary qualities of bodies are resemblances of them, and their patterns do really exist in the bodies themselves; but the ideas produced in us by these secondary qualities have no resemblance of them at all. There is nothing like our ideas existing in the bodies themselves. They are, in the bodies we denominate from them, only a power to produce those sensations in us; and what is sweet, blue, or warm in idea, is but the certain bulk, figure, and motion of the insensible parts in the bodies themselves, which we call so.

16 Flame is denominated *hot* and *light;* snow, *white* and *cold;* and manna *white* and *sweet,* from the ideas they produce in us, which qualities are commonly thought to be the same in those bodies that those ideas are in us, the one the perfect resemblance of the other, as they are in a mirror; and it would by most men be judged very extravagant, if one should say otherwise. And yet he that will consider that the same fire that at one distance produces in us the sensation of warmth, does at a nearer approach produce in us the far different sensation of pain, ought to be-think himself what reason he has to say, that this idea of warmth which produced in him the same way is not in the fire. Why is whiteness and coldness in snow and pain not, when it produces the one and the other idea in us, and can

do neither but by the bulk, figure, number, and motion of its solid parts?

17 The particular bulk, number, figure, and motion of the parts of fire or snow are really in them, whether any one's senses perceive them or no; and therefore they may be called *real* qualities, because they really exist in those bodies. But light, heat, whiteness, or coldness, are no more really in them than sickness or pain is in manna. Take away the sensation of them; let not the eyes see light or colours, nor the ears hear sounds; let the palate not taste, nor the nose smell; and all colours, tastes, odours, and sounds, as they are such particular ideas, vanish and cease, and are reduced to their causes, *i.e.,* bulk, figure, and motion of parts.

GEORGE BERKELEY
To Be Is to Be Perceived

GEORGE BERKELEY *(1685–1753) was born, raised, and educated in Ireland. He wrote virtually all the works that made him famous before he was twenty-eight. Unlike his fellow empiricists Locke and Hume, he focused most of his philosophical attention on a single issue—perception. His most famous work is his* Treatise Concerning the Principles of Human Knowledge.

1 It is evident to any one who takes a survey of the *objects of human knowledge,* that they are either *ideas* actually imprinted on the senses; or else such as are perceived by attending to the passions and operations of the mind; or lastly, *ideas* formed by help of memory and imagination—either compounding, dividing, or barely representing those originally perceived in the aforesaid ways. By sight I have the ideas of light and colours, with their several degrees and variations. By touch I perceive hard and soft, heat and cold, motion and resistance; and of all these more and less either as to quantity or degree. Smelling furnishes me with odours; the palate with tastes; the hearing conveys sounds to the mind in all their variety of tone and composition.

And as several of these are observed to accompany each other, they come to be marked by one name, and so to be reputed as one *thing.* Thus, for example, a certain colour, taste, smell, figure and consistence having been observed to go together; are accounted one distinct thing, signified by the name apple; other collections of ideas constitute a stone, a tree, a book, and the like sensible things; which as they are pleasing or disagreeable excite the passion of love, hatred, joy, grief, and so forth.

2 But, besides all that endless variety of ideas or objects of knowledge, there is likewise Something which knows or perceives them; and exercises divers operations, as willing, imagining, remembering, about them. This perceiving, active being is what I call *mind, spirit, soul,* or *myself.* By which words I do not denote any one of my ideas, but a thing entirely distinct from them, wherein they exist, or, which is the same

Berkeley, George, "To Be Is to Be Perceived," from *Berkeley's Complete Works,* Volume I, Part I, Sec. 1–23, ed. A. C. Fraser, Oxford: Clarendon Press, 1901.

thing, whereby they are perceived; for the existence of an idea consists in being perceived.

3 That neither our thoughts, nor passions, nor ideas formed by the imagination, exist without the mind is what everybody will allow. And to me it seems no less evident that the various sensations or ideas imprinted on the Sense, however blended or combined together (that is, whatever objects they compose), cannot exist otherwise than in a mind perceiving them. I think an intuitive knowledge may be obtained of this, by any one that shall attend to what is meant by the term *exist* when applied to sensible things. The table I write on I say exists; that is, I see and feel it: and if I were out of my study I should say it existed; meaning thereby that if I was in my study I might perceive it, or that some other spirit actually does perceive it. There was an odour, that is, it was smelt; there was a sound, that is, it was heard; a colour or figure, and it was perceived by sight or touch. This is all that I can understand by these and the like expressions. For as to what is said of the *absolute* existence of unthinking things, without any relation to their being perceived, that is to me perfectly unintelligible. Their *esse* is *percipi;* nor is it possible they should have any existence out of the minds or thinking things which perceive them.

4 It is indeed an opinion strangely prevailing amongst men, that houses, mountains, rivers, and in a word all sensible objects, have an existence, natural or real, distinct from their being perceived by the understanding. But, with how great an assurance and acquiescence soever this Principle may be entertained in the world, yet whoever shall find in his heart to call it in question may, if I mistake not, perceive it to involve a manifest contradiction. For, what are the forementioned objects but the things we perceive by sense? and what do we perceive besides our own ideas or sensations? and is it not plainly repugnant that any one of these, or any combination of them, should exist unperceived?

5 If we thoroughly examine this tenet it will, perhaps, be found at bottom to depend on the doctrine of *abstract ideas*. For can there be a nicer strain of abstraction than to distinguish the existence of sensible objects from their being perceived, so as to conceive them existing unperceived? Light and colours, heat and cold, extension and figures—in a word the things we see and feel—what are they but so many sensations, notions, ideas, or impressions on the sense? and is it possible to separate, even in thought, any of these from perception? For my part, I might as easily divide a thing from itself. I may, indeed, divide in my thoughts, or conceive apart from each other, those things which perhaps I never perceived by sense so divided. Thus, I imagine the trunk of a human body without the limbs, or conceive the smell of a rose without thinking on the rose itself. So far, I will not deny, I can abstract; if that may properly be called *abstraction* which extends only to the conceiving separately such objects as it is possible may really exist or be actually perceived asunder. But my conceiving or imagining power does not extend beyond the possibility of real existence or perception. Hence, as it is impossible for me to see or feel anything without an actual sensation of that thing, so is it impossible for me to conceive in my thoughts any sensible thing or object distinct from the sensation or perception of it. [In truth, the object and the sensation are the same thing, and cannot therefore be abstracted from each other.]

6 Some truths there are so near and obvious to the mind that a man need only open his eyes to see them. Such I take this important one to be, viz. that all the choir of heaven and furniture of the earth, in a word all those bodies which compose the mighty frame of the world, have not any subsistence without a mind; that their *being* is to be perceived or known; that consequently so long as they are not actually perceived by me, or do not exist in my mind, or that of any other created spirit, they must either have not existence at all, or else subsist in the mind of some Eternal Spirit: it being perfectly unintelligible, and involving all the absurdity of abstraction, to attribute to any single part of them an existence independent of a spirit. To be convinced of which, the reader need only reflect, and try to separate in his own thoughts the *being* of a sensible thing from its *being perceived*.

7 From what has been said it is evident there is not any other Substance than *Spirit,* or that which perceives. But, for the fuller proof of this point, let it be considered the sensible qualities are colour, figure, motion, smell, taste, and such like, that is, the ideas perceived by sense. Now, for an idea to exist in an unperceiving thing is a manifest contradiction; for to have an idea is all one as to perceive: that therefore wherein colour, figure, and the like qualities exist must perceive them. Hence it is clear there can be no unthinking substance or *substratum* of those ideas.

8 But, say you, though the ideas themselves do not exist without the mind, yet there may be things like them, whereof they are copies or resemblances; which things exist without the mind, in an unthinking substance. I answer, an idea can be like nothing but an idea; a colour or figure can be like nothing but another colour or figure. If we look but ever so little into our thoughts, we shall find it impossible for us to conceive a likeness except only between our ideas. Again, I ask whether those supposed *originals,* or external things, of which our ideas are the pictures or representations, be themselves perceivable or no? If they are, then *they* are ideas, and we have gained our point; but if you say they are not, I appeal to any one whether it be sense to assert a colour is like something which is invisible; hard or soft, like something which is intangible; and so of the rest.

9 Some there are who make a distinction betwixt *primary* and *secondary* qualities. By the former they mean extension, figure, motion, rest, solidity or impenetrability, and number; by the latter they denote all other sensible qualities, as colours, sounds, tastes, and so forth. The ideas we have of these last they acknowledge not to be the resemblances of anything existing without the mind, or unperceived; but they will have our ideas of the *primary qualities* to be patterns or images of things which exist without the mind, in an unthinking substance which they call Matter. By Matter, therefore, we are to understand an inert, senseless substance, in which extension, figure, and motion do actually subsist. But it is

evident, from what we have already shewn, that extension, figure, and motion are only ideas existing in the mind, and that an idea can be like nothing but another idea; and that consequently neither they nor the archetypes can exist in an unperceiving substance. Hence, it is plain that the very notion of what is called *Matter* or *corporeal substance,* involves a contradiction in it. Insomuch that I should not think it necessary to spend more time in exposing its absurdity. But, because the tenet of the existence of Matter seems to have taken so deep a root in the minds of philosophers, and draws after it so many ill consequences, I choose rather to be thought prolix and tedious than omit anything that might conduce to the full discovery and extirpation of that prejudice.

10 They who assert that figure, motion, and the rest of the primary or original qualities do exist without the mind, in unthinking substances, do at the same time acknowledge that colours, sounds, heat, cold, and suchlike secondary qualities, do not; which they tell us are sensations, existing in the mind alone, that depend on and are occasioned by the different size, texture, and motion of the minute particles of matter. This they take for an undoubted truth, which they can demonstrate beyond all exception. Now, if it be certain that those *original* qualities are inseparably united with the other sensible qualities, and not, even in thought, capable of being abstracted from them, it plainly follows that *they* exist only in the mind. But I desire any one to reflect, and try whether he can, by an abstraction of thought, conceive the extension and motion of a body without all other sensible qualities. For my own part, I see evidently that it is not in my power to frame an idea of a body extended and moving, but I must withal give it some colour or other sensible quality, which is acknowledged to exist only in the mind. In short, extension, figure, and motion, abstracted from all other qualities, are inconceivable. Where therefore the other sensible qualities are, there must these be also, to wit, in the mind and nowhere else. . . .

14 I shall farther add, that, after the same manner as modern philosophers prove certain sensible qualities to have no existence in Matter, or without the mind, the same thing may be likewise proved of all other sensible qualities whatsoever. Thus, for instance, it is said that heat and cold are affections only of the mind, and not at all patterns of real beings, existing in the corporeal substances which excite them; for that the same body which appears cold to one hand seems warm to another. Now, why may we not as well argue that figure and extension are not patterns or resemblances of qualities existing in Matter; because to the same eye at different stations, or eyes of a different texture at the same station, they appear various and cannot therefore be the images of anything settled and determinate without the mind? Again, it is proved that sweetness is not really in the sapid thing; because the thing remaining unaltered the sweetness is changed into bitter, as in case of a fever or otherwise vitiated palate. Is it not as reasonable to say that motion is not without the mind; since if the succession of ideas in the mind become swifter, the motion, it is acknowledged, shall appear slower, without any alteration in any external object?

15 In short, let any one consider those arguments which are thought manifestly to prove that colours and tastes exist only in the mind, and he shall find they may with equal force be brought to prove the same thing of extension, figure, and motion. Though it must be confessed this method of arguing does not so much prove that there is no extension or colour in an outward object, as that we do not know by sense which is the true extension or colour of the object. But the arguments foregoing plainly shew it to be impossible that any colour or extension at all, or other sensible quality whatsoever, should exist in an unthinking subject without the mind, or in truth that there should be any such thing as an outward object.

16 But let us examine a little the received opinion. It is said extension is a *mode* or *accident* of Matter, and that Matter is the *substratum* that supports it. Now I desire that you would explain to me what is meant by Matter's *supporting* extension. Say you, I have no idea of Matter; and therefore cannot explain it. I answer, though you have no positive, yet, if you have any meaning at all, you must at least have a relative idea of Matter; though you know not what it is, yet you must be supposed to know what relation it bears to accidents, and what is meant by its supporting them. It is evident *support* cannot here be taken in its usual or literal sense, as when we say that pillars support a building. In what sense therefore must it be taken? For my part, I am not able to discover any sense at all that can be applicable to it.

17 If we inquire into what the most accurate philosophers declare themselves to mean by *material substance*, we shall find them acknowledge they have no other meaning annexed to those sounds but the idea of Being in general, together with the relative notion of its supporting accidents. The general idea of Being appeareth to me the most abstract and incomprehensible of all other; and as for its supporting accidents, this, as we have just now observed, cannot be understood in the common sense of those words: it must therefore be taken in some other sense, but what that is they do not explain. So that when I consider the two parts or branches which make the signification of the words *material substance*, I am convinced there is no distinct meaning annexed to them. But why should we trouble ourselves any farther, in discussing this material *substratum* or support of figure and motion and other sensible qualities? Does it not suppose they have an existence without the mind? And is not this a direct repugnancy, and altogether inconceivable?

18 But, though it were possible that solid, figured, moveable substances may exist without the mind, corresponding to the ideas we have of bodies, yet how is it possible for us to know this? Either we must know it by Sense or by Reason. As for our senses, by them we have the knowledge only of our sensations, ideas, or those things that are immediately perceived by sense, call them what you will: but they do not inform us that things exist without the mind, or unperceived, like to those which are perceived. This

the materialists themselves acknowledge.—It remains therefore that if we have any knowledge at all of external things, it must be by reason inferring their existence from what is immediately perceived by sense. But (I do not see) what reason can induce us to believe the existence of bodies without the mind, from what we perceive, since the very patrons of Matter themselves do not pretend there is any necessary connexion betwixt them and our ideas? I say it is granted on all hands (and what happens in dreams, frensies, and the like, puts it beyond dispute) that it is possible we might be affected with all the ideas we have now, though no bodies existed without resembling them. Hence it is evident the supposition of external bodies is not necessary for the producing our ideas; since it is granted they are produced sometimes, and might possibly be produced always, in the same order we see them in at present without their concurrence.

19 But, though we might possibly have all our sensations without them, yet perhaps it may be thought easier to conceive and explain the manner of their production, by supposing external bodies, in their likeness rather than otherwise; and so it might be at least probable there are such things as bodies that excite their ideas in our minds. But neither can this be said. For, though we give the materialists their external bodies, they by their own confession are never the nearer knowing how our ideas are produced; since they own themselves unable to comprehend in what manner body can act upon spirit, or how it is possible it should imprint any idea in the mind. Hence it is evident the production of ideas or sensations in our minds, can be no reason why we should suppose Matter or corporeal substances; since that is acknowledged to remain equally inexplicable with or without this supposition. If therefore it were possible for bodies to exist without the mind, yet to hold they do so must needs be a very precarious opinion; since it is to suppose, without any reason at all, that God has created innumerable beings that are entirely useless, and serve to no manner of purpose.

20 In short, if there were external bodies, it is impossible we should ever come to know it; and if there were not, we might have the very same reasons to think there were that we have now. Suppose—what no one can deny possible—an intelligence, without the help of external bodies, to be affected with the same train of sensations or ideas that you are, imprinted in the same order and with like vividness in his mind. I ask whether that intelligence hath not all the reason to believe the existence of Corporeal Substances, represented by his ideas, and exciting them in his mind, that you can possibly have for believing the same thing? Of this there can be no question. Which one consideration were enough to make any reasonable person suspect the strength of whatever arguments he may think himself to have, for the existence of bodies without the mind. . . .

23 But, say you, surely there is nothing easier than for me to imagine trees, for instance, in a park, or books existing in a closet, and nobody by to perceive them. I answer, you may so, there is no difficulty in it. But what is all this, I beseech you, more than framing in your mind certain ideas which you call *books* and *trees,* and at the same time omitting to frame the idea of any one that may perceive them? But do not you yourself perceive or think of them all the while? This therefore is nothing to the purpose: it only shews you have the power of imagining, or forming ideas in your mind; but it does not shew that you can conceive it possible the objects of your thoughts may exist without the mind. To make out this, it is necessary that you conceive them existing unconceived or unthought of; which is a manifest repugnancy. When we do our utmost to conceive the existence of external bodies, we are all the while only contemplating our own ideas. But the mind, taking no notice of itself, is deluded to think it can and does conceive bodies existing unthought of, or without the mind, though at the same time they are apprehended by, or exist in, itself. A little attention will discover to any one the truth and evidence of what is here said, and make it unnecessary to insist on any other proofs against the existence of *material substance.*

LORRAINE CODE
What Can She Know?

LORRAINE CODE *teaches philosophy at York University. She is the author, most recently, of* Rhetorical Spaces: Essays on (Gendered) Locations *(1995) and* What Can She Know? *(1991) from which the following selection is taken.*

A question that focuses on the knower, as the title of this chapter does, claims that there are good reasons for asking who that knower is. Uncontroversial as such a suggestion would be in ordinary conversations about knowledge, academic philosophers commonly treat "the knower" as a featureless abstraction. Sometimes, indeed, she or he is merely a place holder in the proposition "S knows that p." Epistemological analyses of the proposition tend to focus on the "knowing that," to determine conditions under which a knowledge claim can legitimately be made. Once discerned, it is believed, such conditions will hold across all possible utterances of the proposition. Indeed, throughout the history of modern philosophy the central "problem of knowledge" has been to determine necessary and sufficient conditions for the possibility and justification of knowledge claims. Philosophers have sought ways of establishing a relation of correspondence between knowledge and "reality" and/or ways of establishing the coherence of particular knowledge claims within systems of already-established truths. They have proposed methodologies for arriving at truth, and criteria for determining the validity of claims to the effect that "S knows that p." Such endeavors are guided by the putatively self-evident principle that truth once discerned, knowledge once established, claim their status *as* truth and knowledge by virtue of a grounding in or coherence within a permanent, objective, ahistorical, and circumstantially neutral framework or set of standards.

The question "Who is S?" is regarded neither as legitimate nor as relevant in these endeavors. As inquirers into the nature and conditions of human knowledge, epistemologists commonly work from the assumption that they need concern themselves only with knowledge claims that meet certain standards of *purity.* . . .

The only thing that is clear about S from the standard proposition "S knows that p" is that S is a (would-be) knower. Although the question "Who is S?" rarely arises, certain assumptions about S as knower permeate epistemological inquiry. Of special importance for my argument is the assumption that knowers are self-sufficient and solitary individuals, at least in their knowledge-seeking activities. This belief derives from a long and venerable heritage, with its roots in Descartes's quest for a basis of perfect certainty on which to establish his knowledge. The central aim of Descartes's endeavors is captured in this claim: "I shall have the right to conceive high hopes if I am happy enough to discover one thing only which is certain and indubitable." That "one thing," Descartes believed, would stand as the fixed pivotal, Archimedean point on which all the rest of his knowledge would turn. Because of its systematic relation to that point, his knowledge would be certain and indubitable.

Most significant for this discussion is Descartes's conviction that his quest will be conducted in a private, introspective examination of the contents of his own mind. It is true that, in the last section of the *Discourse on the Method,* Descartes acknowledges the benefit "others may receive from the communication of [his] reflection," and he states his belief that combining "the lives and labours of many" is essential to progress in scientific knowledge. It is also true that this individualistically described act of knowing exercises the aspect of the soul that is common to and alike in all knowers: namely, the faculty of reason. Yet his claim that knowledge seeking is an introspective activity of an individual mind accords no relevance either to a knower's embodiment or to his (or her) intersubjective relations. For each knower, the Cartesian route to knowledge is through private, abstract thought, through the efforts of reason unaided either by the senses or by consultation with other knowers. It is this individualistic, self-reliant, private aspect of Descartes's philosophy that has been influenced in shaping subsequent epistemological ideals.

Reason is conceived as autonomous in the Cartesian project in two ways, then. Not only is the quest for certain knowledge an independent one, undertaken separately by each rational being, but it is a journey of reason alone, unassisted by the senses. For Descartes believed that sensory experiences had the effect of distracting reason from its proper course.

The custom of formulating knowledge claims in the "S knows that p" formula is not itself of Cartesian origin. The point of claiming Cartesian inspiration for an assumption implicit in the formulation is that the knower who is commonly presumed to be the subject of that proposition is modeled, in significant respects, on the Cartesian pure inquirer. For epistemological purposes, all knowers are believed to be alike with respect both to their cognitive capacities and to their methods of achieving knowledge. In the empiricist tradition this assumption is apparent in the belief that simple, basic observational data can provide the foundation of knowledge just because perception is invariant from observer to observer, in standard observation

conditions. In fact, a common way of filling the places in the "S knows that p" proposition is with substitutions such as "Peter knows that the door is open" or "John knows that the book is red." It does not matter who John or Peter is.

Such knowledge claims carry implicit beliefs not only about would-be knowers but also about the knowledge that is amenable to philosophical analysis. Although (Cartesian) rationalists and empiricists differ with respect to what kinds of claim count as foundational, they endorse similar assumptions about the relation of foundational claims to the rest of a body of knowledge. With "S knows that p" propositions, the belief is that such propositions stand as paradigms for knowledge in general. Epistemologists assume that knowledge is analyzable into prepositional "simples" whose truth can be demonstrated by establishing relations of correspondence to reality, or coherence within a system of known truths. These relatively simple knowledge claims (i.e., John knows that the book is red) could indeed be made by most "normal" people who know the language and are familiar with the objects named. Knowers would seem to be quite self-sufficient in acquiring such knowledge. Moreover, no one would claim to know "a little" that the book is red or to be in the process of acquiring knowledge about the openness of the door. Nor would anyone be likely to maintain that S knows better than W does that the door is open or that the book is red. Granting such examples paradigmatic status creates the mistaken assumption that all knowledge worthy of the name will be like this. . . .

In proposing that the sex of the knower is epistemologically significant, I am claiming that the scope of epistemological inquiry has been too narrowly defined. . . . There are numerous questions to be asked about knowledge whose answers matter to people who are concerned to know well. Among them are questions that bear not just on criteria of evidence, justification, and warrantability, but on the "nature" of cognitive agents: questions about their character; their material, historical, cultural circumstances; their interests in the inquiry at issue. These are questions about how credibility is established, about connections between knowledge and power, about the place of knowledge in ethical and aesthetic judgments, and about political agendas and the responsibilities of knowers. I am claiming that all of these questions are epistemologically significant. . . .

Although it has rarely been spelled out prior to the development of feminist critiques, it has long been tacitly assumed that S is male. Nor could S be just any man, the apparently infinite substitutability of the "S" term notwithstanding. The S who could count as a model, paradigmatic knower has most commonly—if always tacitly—been an adult (but not *old*), white, reasonably affluent (latterly middle-class) educated man of status, property, and publicly acceptable accomplishments. In theory of knowledge he has been allowed to stand for all men. This assumption does not merely derive from habit or coincidence, but is a manifestation of engrained philosophical convictions. Not only has it been taken for granted that knowers properly so-called are male, but when male philosophers have paused to note this fact, as some indeed have done, they have argued that things are as they should be. Reason may be alike in all men, but it would be a mistake to believe that "man," in this respect, "embraces woman." Women have been judged incapable, for many reasons, of achieving knowledge worthy of the name. It is no exaggeration to say that anyone who wanted to *count* as a knower has commonly had to be male.

In the *Politics,* Aristotle observes: "The freeman rules over the slave after another manner from that in which the male rules over the female, or the man over the child; although the parts of the soul are present in all of them, they are present in different degrees. For the slave has no deliberative faculty at all; the woman has, but it is without authority, and the child has, but it is immature." Aristotle's assumption that a woman will naturally be ruled by a man connects directly with his contention that a woman's deliberative faculty is "without authority." Even if a woman could, in her sequestered, domestic position, acquire deliberative skills, she would remain reliant on her husband for her sources of knowledge and information. She must be ruled by a man because, in the social structure of the *polis,* she enjoys neither the autonomy nor the freedom to put into visible practice the results of the deliberations she may engage in, in private. If she can claim no authority for her rational, deliberative endeavors, then her chances of gaining recognition as a knowledgeable citizen are seriously limited, whatever she may do.

Aristotle is just one of a long line of western thinkers to declare the limitations of women's cognitive capacities. Rousseau maintains that young men and women should be educated quite differently because of women's inferiority in reason and their propensity to be dragged down by their sensual natures. For Kierkegaard, women are merely aesthetic beings: men alone can attain the (higher) ethical and religious levels of existence. And for Nietzsche, the Apollonian (intellectual) domain is the male preserve, whereas women are Dionysian (sensuous) creatures. Nineteenth-century philosopher and linguist Wilhelm von Humboldt, who writes at length about women's knowledge, sums up the central features of this line of thought as follows: "A sense of truth exists in [women] quite literally as a sense: . . . their nature also contains a lack or a failing of analytic capacity which draws a strict line of demarcation between ego and world; therefore, they will not come as close to the ultimate investigation of truth as man." The implication is that women's knowledge, if ever the products of their projects deserve that label, is inherently and inevitably *subjective*—in the most idiosyncratic sense—by contrast with the best of men's knowledge.

Objectivity, quite precisely construed, is commonly regarded as a defining feature of knowledge per se. So if women's knowledge is declared to be *naturally* subjective, then a clear answer emerges to my question. The answer is that if the would-be knower is female, then her sex is indeed epistemologically significant, for it disqualifies her as a knower in the fullest sense of that term. Such disqualifications will operate differently for women of different classes, races, ages, and allegiances, but in every circumstance they will operate asymmetrically for women and for men. Just what is to be made of these points—how their epistemological significance is to be construed—is the subject of this book.

The presuppositions I have just cited claim more than the rather simple fact that many kinds of knowledge and skill have, historically, been inaccessible to women on a purely practical level. It is true, historically speaking, that even women who were the racial and social "equals" of standard male knowers were only rarely able to become learned. The thinkers I have cited (and others like them) claim to find a rationale for this state of affairs through appeals to dubious "facts" about women's natural incapacity for rational thought. Yet deeper questions still need to be asked: Is there knowledge that is, quite simply, inaccessible to members of the female, or the male, sex? Are there kinds of knowledge that only men, or only woman, can acquire? Is the sex of the knower crucially determining in this respect, across all other specificities? The answers to these questions should not address only the *practical* possibilities that have existed for members of either sex. Such practical possibilities are the constructs of complex social arrangements that are themselves constructed out of historically specific choices, and are, as such, open to challenge and change.

Knowledge, as it achieves credence and authoritative status at any point in the history of the male-dominated mainstream, is commonly held to be a product of the individual efforts of human knowers. References to Pythagoras's theorem, Copernicus's revolution, and Newtonian and Einsteinian physics signal an epistemic community's attribution of pathbreaking contributions to certain of its individual members. The implication is that *that* person, single-handedly, has effected a leap of progress in a particular field of inquiry. In less publicly spectacular ways, other cognitive agents are represented as contributors to the growth and stability of public knowledge.

Now any contention that such contributions are the results of independent endeavor is highly contestable. . . . A complex of historical and other sociocultural factors produces the conditions that make "individual" achievement possible, and "individuals" themselves are socially constituted. The claim that individual *men* are the creators of the authoritative . . . landmarks of western intellectual life is particularly interesting for the fact that the contributions—both practical and substantive—of their lovers, wives, children, servants, neighbors, friends, and colleagues rarely figure in analyses of their work.

The historical attribution of such achievements to specific cognitive agents does, nonetheless, accord a significance to individual efforts which raises questions pertinent to my project. It poses the problem, in another guise, of whether aspects of human specificity could, in fact, constitute conditions for the existence of knowledge or determine the kinds of knowledge that a knower can achieve. It would seem that such incidental physical attributes as height, weight, or hair color would not count among factors that would determine a person's capacities to know (though the arguments that skin color *does* count are too familiar). It is not necessary to consider how much Archimedes weighed when he made his famous discovery, nor is there any doubt that a thinner or a fatter person could have reached the same conclusion. But in cultures in which sex differences figure prominently in virtually every mode of human interaction, being female or male is far more fundamental to the construction of subjectivity than are such attributes as size or hair color. So the question is whether femaleness or maleness are the kinds of subjective factor (i.e., factors about the circumstances of a knowing subject) that are constitutive of the form and content of knowledge. Attempts to answer this question are complicated by the fact that sex/gender, then, always risks abstraction and is limited in its scope by the abstracting process. Further, the question seems to imply that sex and gender are themselves constants, thus obscuring the processes of *their* sociocultural construction. Hence the formulation of adequately nuanced answers is problematic and necessarily partial.

Even if it should emerge that gender-related factors play a crucial role in the construction of knowledge, then, the inquiry into the epistemological significance of the sex of the knower would not be complete. The task would remain of considering whether a distinction between "natural" and socialized capacity can retain any validity. The equally pressing question as to how the hitherto devalued products of *women's* cognitive projects can gain acknowledgment as "knowledge" would need to be addressed so as to uproot entrenched prejudices about knowledge, epistemology, and women. "The epistemological project" will look quite different once its tacit underpinnings are revealed. . . .

Feminist philosophy simply did not exist until philosophers learned to perceive the near-total absence of women in philosophical writings from the very beginning of western philosophy, to stop assuming that "man" could be read as a generic term. Explicit denigrations of women, which became the focus of philosophical writing in the early years of the contemporary women's movement, were more readily perceptible. The authors of derogatory views about women in classical texts clearly needed power to be able to utter their pronouncements with impunity: a power they claimed from a "received" discourse that represented women's nature in such a way that women undoubtedly merited the negative judgments that Aristotle or Nietzsche made about them. Women are now in a position to recognize and refuse these overt manifestations of contempt.

CHAPTER SEVEN

DOES LANGUAGE MAKE ME THINK THE WAY I DO?

In what ways are taking a test, calling a friend, and buying a sandwich similar to one another? One important way is that they all involve language. Whenever we write or speak, we use language. Whenever we make a promise or ask a question, we use language. Because we spend a good deal of our lives writing or speaking, language is an important part of much that we do.

In fact, language may be even more pervasive than the preceding paragraph leads us to believe. Anything that involves communication requires a medium for communication. It has been claimed that any medium for communication involves a language. According to this view, then, there is a language (or languages) of art, as well as a language (or languages) of love. If we extend the notion of a language this far, then almost any exchange that is embedded in social interaction can be seen as involving language. Short of sitting quietly alone on a mountaintop looking at a beautiful sunset, it looks as though nearly everything involves language.

But wait a minute. Might it be that even sitting alone on a mountaintop involves the use of language? There are two ways in which it might. First, what are you doing while you are sitting on the mountaintop? Are you thinking about something? Suppose, unlikely as it may seem, that you are thinking about whether the U.S. economy is healthy. Now try to have the same thoughts without using words. Can you do it? Most people experience their thoughts as "using" words. Words may be involved in this way in most of our thinking.

A second way in which language is pervasive is that, even if much of our mental and emotional life could be carried on without any direct use of language, language may be involved in the formation, acquisition, and meaning of the very concepts that we employ when we think, feel, perceive, or desire. For example, language does not seem to be involved when we feel angry. But learning what it is to feel angry requires things like having your mother, when you are a child, point to someone who is shouting and say, "Why is he so angry?" It may be that this (linguistic) background is part of what makes your feeling a feeling of anger. In addition, feeling angry may also involve having certain beliefs, for example, the belief that you have been insulted or unjustly deprived. So unless you are sitting on that mountaintop in a coma (actually you would have to be lying down), as long as you are thinking, believing, or perceiving, it appears that language may be involved in what you are doing.

But despite the fact that language is probably the most pervasive human activity, or perhaps *because* of that fact, we do not think much about language. Language itself, because it is everywhere, is not noticed. It is part of the background. Moreover, we do not think about it because we see it as an instrument, not as a thing in itself. For example, a beginning painter trying to paint a landscape will focus on the color of the sky and the configuration of the mountains and trees. She will not typically be thinking about the composition of the paint itself or about the fiber content of the canvas. But experienced painters know that an understanding of the *medium* of expression (in this case, of the paint, brushes, and canvas) is crucial in expressing oneself well. The medium imposes hidden constraints on what we can and cannot do. Until we understand those constraints, we will be bound by them without knowing that we are.

So it is with language. To understand the constraints that language places on what we think or feel, and on how we do it, we must somehow be able to think about language itself. But if we can think only by means of language, then in thinking about language we will be using language! This may place us in a vicious circle from which we cannot escape. This is just one of the many complications and difficulties that go along with the philosophical study of language.

Jonathan Swift, in the selection from *Gulliver's Travels,* starts off by claiming ironically that language is an irritating and misleading nuisance. Instead of using words, we should just carry around the things that our words name (because nouns are the only important words anyway). Swift suggests a view of language that was articulated by Saint Augustine, in the fourth century A.D., in a famous passage from his *Confessions*. Wittgenstein begins his excerpt in this chapter by considering this "primitive" picture of language, according to which words are simply names. (This is a view of language that he himself had held earlier but that he gave up.) He argues that we understand the meaning of an expression by understanding its *use* and that expressions have many more uses than simply that of naming. He also rejects the Socratic method of trying to understand a concept by trying to *define* it. Instead, he argues that most concepts (his example is the concept of a game) do not have neat definitions, but instead work by picking out a range of things that resemble one another loosely. We discover these associations by looking carefully at how expressions are used by actual people. Wittgenstein's view of language strikes at the heart of traditional philosophical method.

It is tempting to think that first we have thoughts and that our language simply reports, or expresses, these thoughts. Many of the authors of this chapter argue, in one way or another, against that simple picture. Whorf, for example, argues that our language creates the conceptual scheme within which we think. As a result of his work in anthropology, he formulated what is now referred to as the "Whorf hypothesis," namely, that our conceptual scheme is determined by our language. If so, people whose language is sufficiently different from ours could not have the same thoughts that we have in our language. Conversely, beings whose conceptual schemes are sufficiently different from ours could not share our language. As Wittgenstein put it, "If a lion could speak, we could not understand him."

Steven Pinker, a linguist, brings a mass of current research in linguistics to bear on these issues. He argues forcefully not only that the Whorf hypothesis is clearly false, but also that it was foolish for anybody to have it in the first place. Instead, he claims, all (biologically normal) humans have a built-in "language of thought"—"mentalese," it has been dubbed. This language of thought, and not our cultural environment, determines both our concepts and the structure of all human languages.

Stephanie Ross, in her selection, discusses the extent to which language can be put to (dangerous) political uses. She focuses on the sexist use of language and argues that the wrongness of sexist language does not lie only in the fact that it expresses false claims. More important, sexist language actually hurts women. The metaphors used to describe women (for example, "dog," "cow," "shrew") reveal attitudes that are destructive of equality and trust. Her method is therefore in accord with Wittgenstein's claim that we understand language not by trying to isolate its content, but rather by looking at the use to which it is put.

Lewis Carroll, whose children's books are brimming with philosophical interest, brings us full circle to another "primitive" view of language, but one that, unlike Swift's, takes account of the intimate connection between language and thought. If Swift (and Augustine) claim that the meaning of words is tied directly to what they name and is therefore fixed rigidly. Humpty Dumpty claims that the meaning of words is not constrained at all: Words mean whatever he wants them to mean. Thus, Carroll plays counterpoint to Swift.

As you read these selections, you might think about whether or how the structure of your language places constraints on what and how you can think, feel, believe, and desire.

JONATHAN SWIFT
Getting Rid of Words

JONATHAN SWIFT *(1667–1745), Irish author, journalist, and clergyman, was one of the foremost satirists of all time. He finished* Gulliver's Travels, *from which this selection is taken, in 1725. In 1729 he published a grimly satirical "letter" in which a civic-minded citizen proposes that the poor would contribute more to society if their children were used as food.*

WE next went to the school of language, where three professors sat in consultation upon improving that of their own country.

The first project was to shorten discourse, by cutting polysyllables into one, and leaving out verbs and participles, because, in reality, all things imaginable are but nouns.

The other project was a scheme for entirely abolishing all words whatsoever, and this was urged as a great advantage in point of health as well as brevity. For it is plain that every word we speak is in some degree a diminution of our lungs by corrosion, and consequently, contributes to the shortening of our lives. An expedient was therefore offered, that, since words are only names for things, it would be more convenient for all men to carry about them such things as were necessary to express a particular business they are to discourse on. And this invention would certainly have taken place, to the great ease as well as health of the subject, if the women, in conjunction with the vulgar and illiterate, had not threatened to raise a rebellion, unless they might be allowed the liberty to speak with their tongues, after the manner of their forefathers; such constant irreconcilable enemies to science are the common people. However, many of the most learned and wise adhere to the new scheme of expressing themselves by things, which has only this inconvenience attending it, that if a man's business be very great, and of various kinds, he must be obliged, in proportion, to carry a greater bundle of things upon his back, unless he can afford one or two strong servants to attend him. I have often beheld two of these sages almost sinking under the weight of their packs, like pedlars among us; who, when they met in the street, would lay down their loads, open their sacks, and hold conversation for an hour together, then put up their implements, help each other to resume their bundles, and take their leave.

But for short conversations, a man may carry implements in his pockets, and under his arms, enough to supply him: and in his house he cannot be at a loss. Therefore the room where company meet who practise this art is full of all things, ready at hand, requisite to furnish matter for this kind of artificial converse.

Another great advantage proposed by this invention was, that it would serve as a universal language, to be understood in all civilised nations, whose goods and utensils are generally of the same kind, or nearly resembling, so that their uses might easily be comprehended. And thus ambassadors would be qualified to treat with foreign princes, or ministers of state, to whose tongues they were utter strangers.

LUDWIG WITTGENSTEIN
Meaning as Use

LUDWIG WITTGENSTEIN *(1889–1951) was born in Austria. He studied engineering, logic, and philosophy. He was a soldier, an architect, a third-grade teacher, and finally a professor of philosophy. He was a troubled man, and his work was nearly as misunderstood as it was influential. His* Philosophical Investigations, *from which this selection is taken, is an ordered series of aphoristic remarks on language, mind, and the conduct of philosophy. The remarks reprinted here have been reordered so as to focus his views on language.*

1 "When they (my elders) named some object and accordingly moved towards something, I saw this and I grasped that the thing was called by the sound they uttered when they meant to point it out. Their intention was shewn by their bodily movements, as it were the natural language of all peoples: the expression of the face, the play of the eyes, the movement of other parts of the body, and the tone of voice which expresses our state of mind in seeking, having, rejecting, or avoiding something. Thus, as I heard words repeatedly used in their proper places in various sentences, I gradually learnt to understand what objects they signified; and after I had trained my mouth to form these signs, I used them to express my own desires." (Augustine, *Confessions*)

These words, it seems to me, give us a particular picture of the essence of human language. It is this: the individual words in language name objects—sentences are combinations of such names.—In this picture of language we find the roots of the following idea: Every word has a meaning. This meaning is correlated with the word. It is the object for which the word stands.

Augustine does not speak of there being any difference between kinds of word. If you describe the learning of language in this way you are, I believe, thinking primarily of nouns like "table," "chair," "bread," and of people's name, and only secondarily of the names of certain actions and properties; and of the remaining kinds of word as something that will take care of itself.

Now think of the following use of language: I send someone shopping. I give him a slip marked "five red apples." He takes the slip to the shopkeeper, who opens the drawer marked "apples"; then he looks up the word "red" in a table and finds a colour sample opposite it; then he says the series of cardinal numbers—I assume that he knows them by heart—up to the word "five" and for each number he takes an apple of the same colour as the sample out of the drawer.—It is in this and similar ways that one operates with words.—"But how does he know where and how he is to look up the word 'red' and what he is to do with the word 'five'?"—Well, I assume that he *acts* as I have described. Explanations come to an end somewhere.—But what is the meaning of the word "five"?—No such thing was in question here, only how the word "five" is used.

2 That philosophical concept of meaning has its place in a primitive idea of the way language functions. But one can also say that it is the idea of language more primitive than ours.

Let us imagine a language for which the description given by Augustine is right. The language is meant to serve for communication between a builder A and an assistant B. A is building with building stones: there are blocks, pillars, slabs and beams. B has to pass the stones, and that in the order in which A needs them. For this purpose they use a language consisting of the words "block," "pillar," "slab," "beam." A calls them out;—B brings the stone which he has learnt to bring at such-and-such a call.—Conceive this as a complete primitive language.

3 Augustine, we might say, does describe a system of communication; only not everything that we call language is this system. And one has to say this in many cases where the question arises "Is this an appropriate description or not?" The answer is "Yes, it is appropriate, but only for this narrowly circumscribed region, not for the whole of what you were claiming to describe."

It is as if someone were to say: "A game consists in moving objects about on a surface according to certain rules . . ."—and we replied: You seem to be thinking of board games, but there are others. You can make your definition correct by expressly restricting it to those games.

4 Imagine a script in which the letters were used to stand for sounds, and also as signs of emphasis and punctuation. (A script can be conceived as a language for describing sound-patterns.) Now imagine someone interpreting that script as if there were simply a correspondence of letters to sounds and as if the letters had not also completely different functions. Augustine's conception of language is like such an over-simple conception of the script.

5 If we look at the example in #1, we may perhaps get an inkling how much this general notion of the meaning of a word surrounds the working of language with a haze which makes clear vision impossible. It disperses the fog to study the phenomena of language in primitive kinds of application in which one can command a clear view of the aim and functioning of the words.

A child uses such primitive forms of language when it learns to talk. Here the teaching of language is not explanation, but training.

6 We could imagine that the language of #2 was the *whole* language of A and B; even the whole language of a tribe. The children are brought up to perform *these* actions, to use *these* words as they do so, and to react in *this* way to the words of others.

An important part of the training will consist in the teacher's pointing to the objects, directing the child's attention to them, and at the same time uttering a word; for instance, the word "slab" as he points to that shape. (I do not want to call this "ostensive definition," because the child cannot as yet *ask* what the name is. I will call it "ostensive teaching of words."—I say that it will form an important part of the training, because it is so with human beings; not because it could not be imagined otherwise.) This ostensive teaching of words can be said to establish an association between the word and the thing. But what does this mean? Well, it may mean various things; but one very likely thinks first of all that a picture of the object comes before the child's mind when it hears the word. But now, if this does happen—is it the purpose of the word?—Yes, it *may* be the purpose.—I can imagine such a use of words (of series of sounds). (Uttering a word is like striking a note on the keyboard of the imagination.) But in the language of #2 it is *not* the purpose of the words to evoke images. (It may, of course, be discovered that that helps to attain the actual purpose.)

But if the ostensive teaching has this effect,—am I to say that it effects an understanding of the word? Don't you understand the call "Slab!" if you act upon it in such-and-such a way?—Doubtless the ostensive teaching helped to bring this about; but only together with a particular training. With different training the same ostensive teaching of these words would have effected a quite different understanding.

"I set the brake up by connecting up rod and lever."—Yes, given the whole of the rest of the mechanism. Only in conjunction with that is it a brake-lever, and separated from its support it is not even a lever; it may be anything, or nothing.

7 In the practice of the use of language (2) one party calls out the words, the other acts on them. In instruction in the language the following process will occur; the learner *names* the objects; that is, he utters the word when the teacher points to the stone.—And there will be this still simpler exercise: the pupil repeats the words after the teacher—both of these being processes resembling language.

We can also think of the whole process of using words in (2) as one of those games by means of which children learn their native language. I will call these games "language-games" and will sometimes speak of a primitive language as a language-game.

And the processes of naming the stones and of repeating words after someone might also be called language-games. Think of much of the use of words in games like ring-a-ring-a-roses.

I shall also call the whole, consisting of language and the actions into which it is woven, the "language-game."

8 Let us now look at an expansion of language (2). Besides the four words "block," "pillar," etc., let it contain a series of words used as the shopkeeper in (1) used the numerals (it can be the series of letters of the alphabet); further, let there be two words, which may as well be "there" and "this" (because this roughly indicates their purpose), that are used in connexion with a pointing gesture; and finally a number of colour samples. A gives an order like: "d—slab—there." At the same time he shews the assistant a colour sample, and when he says "there" he points to a place on the building site. From the stock of slabs B takes one for each letter of the alphabet up to "d," of the same colour as the sample, and brings them to the place indicated by A.—On other occasions A gives the order "this—there." At "this" he point to a building stone. And so on.

9 When a child learns this language, it has to learn the series of 'numerals' a, b, c, . . . by heart. And it has to learn their use.—Will this training include ostensive teaching of the words?—Well, people will, for example, point to slabs and count: "a, b, c slabs."—Something more like the ostensive teaching of the words "block," "pillar," etc. would be the ostensive teaching of numerals that serve not to count but to refer to groups of objects that can be taken in at a glance. Children do learn the use of the first five or six cardinal numerals in this way.

Are "there" and "this" also taught ostensively?—Imagine how one might perhaps teach their use. One will point to places and things—but in this case the pointing occurs in the *use* of the words too and not merely in learning the use.

10 Now what do the words of this language *signify?*—What is supposed to shew what they signify, if not the kind of use they have? And we have already described that. So we are asking for the expression "This word signifies *this*" to be made part of the description. In other words the description ought to take the form: "The word . . . signifies. . . ."

Of course, one can reduce the description of the use of the word "slab" to the statement that this word signifies this object. This will be done when, for example, it is merely a matter of removing the mistaken idea that the word "slab" refers to the shape of building-stone that we in fact call a "block"—but the kind of "*referring*" this is, that is to say the use of these words for the rest, is already known.

Equally one can say that the signs "a," "b," etc. signify numbers; when for example this removes the mistaken idea that "a," "b," "c," play the part actually played in language by "block," "slab," "pillar." And one can also say that "c" means this number and not that one; when for example this serves to explain that the letters are to be used in the order a, b, c, d, etc. and not in the order a, b, d, c.

But assimilating the descriptions of the uses of words in this way cannot make the uses themselves any more like one another. For, as we see, they are absolutely unlike.

11 Think of the tools in a tool-box: there is a hammer, pliers, a saw, a screwdriver, a rule, a glue-pot, glue, nails and screws.—The functions of words are as diverse as the functions of these objects. (And in both cases there are similarities.)

Of course, what confuses us is the uniform appearance of words when we hear them spoken or meet them in script and print. For their *application* is not presented to us so clearly, especially when we are doing philosophy!

12 It is like looking into the cabin of a locomotive. We see handles all looking more or less alike. (Naturally, since they are all supposed to be handled.) But one is the handle of a crank which can be moved continuously (it regulates the opening of a valve); another is the handle of a switch, which has only two effective positions, it is either off or on; a third is the handle of a brake-lever, the harder one pulls on it, the harder it brakes; a fourth, the handle of a pump: it has an effect only so long as it is moved to and fro.

13 When we say: "Every word in language signifies something" we have so far said *nothing whatever;* unless we have explained exactly *what* distinction we wish to make. (It might be, of course, that we wanted to distinguish the words of language (8) from words "without meaning" such as occur in Lewis Carroll's poems, or words like "Lilliburlero" in songs.)

14 Imagine someone's saying: "*All* tools serve to modify something. Thus the hammer modifies the position of the nail, the saw the shape of the board, and so on."—And what is modified by the rule, the glue-pot, the nails?—"Our knowledge of a thing's length, the temperature of the glue, and the solidity of the box."—Would anything be gained by this assimilation of expressions?

15 The word "to signify" is perhaps used in the most straightforward way when the object signified is marked with the sign. Suppose that the tools A uses in building bear certain marks. When A shews his assistant such a mark, he brings the tool that has that mark on it.

It is in this and more or less similar ways that a name means and is given to a thing.—It will often prove useful in philosophy to say to ourselves: naming something is like attaching a label to a thing.

16 What about the colour samples that A shews to B: are they part of the *language?* Well, it is as you please. They do not belong among the words; yet when I say to someone: "Pronounce the word 'the,'" you will count the second "the" as part of the sentence. Yet it has a role just like that of a colour-sample in language-game (8); that is, it is a sample of what the other is meant to say.

It is most natural, and causes least confusion, to reckon the samples among the instruments of the language.

(Remark on the reflexive pronoun "*this* sentence.")

17 It will be possible to say: In language (8) we have different *kinds of word.* For the functions of the word "slab" and the word "block" are more alike than those of "slab" and "d." But how we group words into kinds will depend on the aim of the classification,—and on our own inclination.

Think of the different points of view from which one can classify tools or chess-men. . . .

23 But how many kinds of sentence are there? Say assertion, question, and command?— There are *countless* kinds: countless different kinds of use of what we call "symbols," "words," "sentences." And this multiplicity is not something fixed, given once for all; but new types of language, new language-games, as we may say, come into existence, and others become obsolete and get forgotten. (We can get a *rough picture* of this from the changes in mathematics.)

Here the term "language-*game*" is meant to bring into prominence the fact that the *speaking* of a language is part of an activity, or of a form of life.

Review the multiplicity of language-games in the following examples, and in others:

Giving orders, and obeying them

Describing the appearance of an object, or giving its
    measurements

Constructing an object from a description (a drawing)

Reporting an event

Speculating about an event

Forming and testing a hypothesis

Presenting the results of an experiment in tables and
    diagrams

Making up a story; and reading it

Play-acting

Singing catches

Guessing riddles

Making a joke; telling it

Solving a problem in practical arithmetic

Translating from one language into another

Asking, thanking, cursing, greeting, praying

It is interesting to compare the multiplicity of the tools in language and of the ways they are used, the multiplicity of kinds of word and sentence, with what logicians have said about the structure of language.

27 "We name things and then we can talk about them: can refer to them in talk."—As if what we did next were given with the mere act of naming. As if there were only one thing called "talking about a thing." Whereas in fact we do the most various things with our sentences. Think of exclamations alone, with their completely different functions.

Water!

Away!

Ow!

Help!

Fine!

No!

Are you inclined still to call these words "names of objects"?

In languages (2) and (8) there was no such thing as asking something's name. This, with its correlate, ostensive definition, is, we might say, a language-game on its own. That is really to say: we are brought up, trained, to ask: "What is that called?"—upon which the name is given. And there is also a language-game of inventing a name for something, and hence of saying, "This is . . ." and then using the new name. (Thus, for example, children give names to their dolls and then talk about them and to them. Think in this connexion how singular is the use of a person's name to *call* him!) . . .

32 Someone coming into a strange country will sometimes learn the language of the inhabitants from ostensive definition that they give him; and he will often have to *guess* the meaning of these definitions; and will guess sometimes right, sometimes wrong.

And now, I think, we can say: Augustine describes the learning of human language as if the child came into a strange country and did not understand the language of the country; that is, as if it already had a language, only not this one. Or again: as if the child could already *think*, only not yet speak. And "think" would here mean something like "talk to itself." . . .

37 What is the relation between name and thing named?—Well, what *is* it? Look at language-game (2) or at another one: there you can see the sort of thing this relation consists in. This relation may also consist, among many other things, in the fact that hearing the name calls before our mind the picture of what is named; and it also consists among other things, in the name's being written on the thing named or being pronounced when that thing is pointed at.

38 But what, for example, is the word "this" the name of in language-game (8) or the word "that" in the ostensive definition "that is called . . ."?—If you do not want to produce confusion you will do best not to call these words names at all.—Yet, strange to say, the word "this" has been called the only *genuine* name; so that anything else we call a name was one only in an inexact, approximate sense.

This queer conception springs from a tendency to sublime the logic of our language—as one might put it. The proper answer to it is: we call very different things "names"; the word "name" is used to characterize many different kinds of use of a word, related to one another in many different ways;—but the kind of use that "this" has is not among them.

It is quite true that, in giving an ostensive definition for instance, we often point to the object named and say the name. And similarly, in giving an ostensive definition for instance, we say the word "this" while pointing to a thing. And also the word "this" and a name that it is defined by means of the demonstrative expression "that is N" (or "That is called 'N'"). But do we also give the definitions: "That is called 'this,'" or "this is called 'this'"?

This is connected with the conception of naming as, so to speak, an occult process. Naming appears as a *queer* connexion of a word with an object.—And you really get such a queer connexion when the philosopher tries to bring out *the* relation between name and thing by staring at an object in front of him and repeating a name or even the word "this" innumerable times. For philosophical problems arise when language *goes on holiday*. And *here* we may indeed fancy naming to be some remarkable act of mind, as it were a baptism of an object. And we can also say the word "this" *to* the object, as it were *address* the object as "this"—a queer use of this word, which doubtless only occurs in doing philosophy. . . .

410 "I" is not the name of a person, nor "here" of a place, and "this" is not a name. But they are connected with names. Names are explained by means of them. It is also true that it is characteristic of physics not to use these words.

65 Here we come up against the great question that lies behind all these considerations.—For someone might object against me: "You take the easy way out! You talk about all sorts of language-games, but have nowhere said what the essence of a language-game, and hence of language, is: what is common to all these activities, and what makes them into language or parts of language. So you let yourself off the very part of the investigation that once gave you yourself most headache, the part about the *general form of propositions* and of language."

And this is true.—Instead of producing something common to all that we call language, I am saying that these phenomena have no one thing in common which makes us use the same word for all,—but that they are *related* to one another in many different ways. And it is because of this relationship, or these relationships, that we call them all "language." I will try to explain this.

66 Consider for example the proceeding that we call "games." I mean board-games, card-games, ball-games, Olympic games, and so on.

What is common to them all?—Don't say: "There *must* be something common, or they would not be called 'games'"—but *look and see* whether there is anything common to all.—For if you look at them you will not see something that is common to *all*, but similarities, relationships, and a whole series of them at that. To repeat: don't think, but look!—Look for example at board-games, with their multifarious relationships. Now pass to card-games; here you find many correspondences with the first group, but many common features drop out, and others appear. When we pass next to ball-games, much that is common is retained, but much is lost.—Are they all "amusing"? Compare chess with noughts and crosses. Or is there always winning and losing, or competition between players? Think of patience. In ball-games there is winning and losing; but when a child throws his ball at the wall and catches it again, this feature has disappeared. Look at the parts played by skill and luck; and at the difference between skill in chess and skill in tennis. Think now of games like ring-a-ring-a-roses; here is the element of amusement, but how many other characteristic features have disappeared! And we can go through the many, many other groups of games in the same way; can see how similarities crop up and disappear.

And the result of this examination is: we see a complicated network of similarities overlapping and criss-crossing: sometimes overall similarities, sometimes similarities of detail.

67 I can think of no better expression to characterize these similarities than "family resemblances"; for the various resemblances between members of a family: build, features, colour of eyes, gait, temperament, etc. etc. overlap and criss-cross in the same way.—And I shall say: "games" form a family.

And for instance the kinds of number form a family in the same way. Why do we call something a "number"? Well, perhaps because it has a—direct—relationship with several things that have hitherto been called number; and this can be said to give it an indirect relationship to other things we call the same name. And we extend our concept of number as in spinning a thread we twist fibre on fibre. And the strength of the thread does not reside in the fact that some one fibre runs through its whole length, but in the overlapping of many fibres.

But if someone wished to say: "There is something common to all these constructions—namely the disjunction of all their common properties"—I should reply: Now you are only playing with words. One might as well say: "Something runs through the whole thread—namely the continuous overlapping of those fibres."

241 "So you are saying that human agreement decides what is true and what is false?"—It is what human beings *say* that is true and false; and they agree in the *language* they use. That is not agreement in opinions but in form of life.

242 If language is to be a means of communication there must be agreement not only in definitions but also (queer as this may sound) in judgments. This seems to abolish logic, but does not do so.—It is one thing to describe methods of measurement, and another to obtain and state results of measurement. But what we call "measuring" is partly determined by a certain constancy in results of measurements. . . .

350 One cannot guess how a word functions. One has to *look at* its use and learn from that.

But the difficulty is to remove the prejudice which stands in the way of doing this. It is not a *stupid* prejudice. . . .

383 We are not analysing a phenomenon (e.g. thought) but a concept (e.g. that of thinking), and therefore the use of a word. So it may look as if what we were doing were Nominalism. Nominalists make the mistake of interpreting all words as *names*, and so of not really describing their use, but only, so to speak, giving a paper draft on such a description. . . .

309 What is your aim in philosophy?—To shew the fly the way out of the flybottle.

BENJAMIN WHORF
Language, Thought, and Reality

BENJAMIN WHORF *(1897–1941) studied chemical engineering at MIT. He worked for his entire career as a fire prevention engineer for a Hartford insurance company, and he pursued his work in anthropology and linguistics on the side, refusing a number of academic positions. He originally became interested in linguistics through his interest in religion.*

Human beings do not live in the objective world alone, not alone in the world of social activity as ordinarily understood, but are very much at the mercy of the particular language which has become the medium of expression for their society. It is quite an illusion to imagine that one adjusts to reality essentially without the use of language and that language is merely an incidental means of solving specific problems of communication or reflection. The fact of the matter is that the "real world" is to a large extent unconsciously built up on the language habits of the group. . . . We see and hear and otherwise experience very largely as we do because the language habits of our community predispose certain choices of interpretation.

—EDWARD SAPIR

THERE will probably be general assent to the proposition that an accepted pattern of using words is often prior to certain lines of thinking and forms of behavior, but he who assents often sees in such a statement nothing more than a platitudinous recognition of the hypnotic power of philosophical and learned terminology on the one hand or of catchwords, slogans, and rallying cries on the other. To see only thus far is to miss the point of one of the important interconnections which Sapir saw between language, culture, and psychology, and succinctly expressed in the introductory quotation. It is not so much in these special uses of language as in its constant ways of arranging data and its most ordinary everyday analysis of phenomena that we need to recognize the influence it has on other activities, cultural and personal. . . .

Every normal person in the world, past infancy in years, can and does talk. By virtue of that fact, every person—civilized or uncivilized—carries through life certain naive but deeply rooted ideas about talking and its relation to thinking. Because of their firm connection with speech habits that have become unconscious and automatic, these notions tend to be rather intolerant of opposition. They are by no means entirely personal and haphazard; their basis is definitely systematic, so that we are justified in calling them a system of natural logic—a term that seems to me preferable to the term common sense, often used for the same thing.

According to natural logic, the fact that every person has talked fluently since infancy makes every man his own authority on the process by which he formulates and communicates. He has merely to consult a common substratum of logic or reason which he and everyone else are supposed to possess. Natural logic says that talking is merely an incidental process concerned strictly with communication, not with formulation of ideas. Talking, or the uses of language, is supposed only to "express" what is essentially already formulated nonlinguistically. Formulation is an independent process, called thought or thinking, and is supposed to be largely indifferent to the nature of particular languages. Languages have grammars, which are assumed to be merely norms of conventional and social correctness, but the use of language is supposed to be guided not so much by them as by correct, rational, or intelligent *thinking*.

Thought, in this view, does not depend on grammar but on laws of logic or reason which are supposed to be the same for all observers of the universe—to represent a rationale in the universe that can be "found" independently by all intelligent observers, whether they speak Chinese or Choctaw. In our own culture, the formulations of mathematics and of formal logic have acquired the reputation of dealing with this order of things: i.e., with the realm and laws of pure thought. Natural logic holds that different languages are essentially parallel methods for expressing this one-and-the-same rationale of thought and, hence, differ really in but minor ways which may seem important only because they are seen at close range. It holds that mathematics, symbolic logic, philosophy, and so on are systems contracted with language which deal directly with this realm of thought, not that they are themselves specialized extensions of language. The attitude of natural logic is well shown in an old quip about a German grammarian who devoted his whole life to the study of the dative case. From the point of view of natural logic, the dative case and grammar in general are an extremely minor issue. A different attitude is said to have been held by the ancient Arabians: Two princes, so the story goes, quarreled over the honor of putting on the shoes of the most learned grammarian of the realm; whereupon their father, the caliph, is said to have remarked

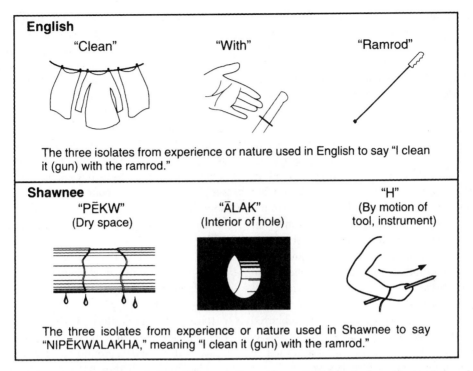

English

"Clean"   "With"   "Ramrod"

The three isolates from experience or nature used in English to say "I clean it (gun) with the ramrod."

Shawnee

"PĒKW"   "ĀLAK"   "H"
(Dry space)   (Interior of hole) (By motion of tool, instrument)

The three isolates from experience or nature used in Shawnee to say "NIPĒKWALAKHA," meaning "I clean it (gun) with the ramrod."

Languages dissect nature differently. The different isolates of meaning (thoughts) used by English and Shawnee in reporting the same experience, that of cleaning a gun by running the ramrod through it. The pronouns "I" and "it" are not shown by symbols, as they have the same meaning in each language. In Shawnee *ni-* equals "I"; *-a* equals "it."

that it was the glory of his kingdom that great grammarians were honored even above kings.

The familiar saying that the exception proves the rule contains a good deal of wisdom, though from the standpoint of formal logic it became an absurdity as soon as "prove" no longer meant "put on trial." The old saw began to be profound psychology from the time it ceased to have standing in logic. What it might well suggest to us today is that, if a rule has absolutely no exceptions, it is not recognised as a rule or as anything else; it is then part of the background of experience of which we tend to remain unconscious. Never having experienced anything in contrast to it, we cannot isolate it and formulate it as a rule until we so enlarge our experience and expand our base of reference that we encounter an interruption of its regularity. The situation is somewhat analogous to that of not missing the

water till the well runs dry, or not realizing that we need air till we are choking.

For instance, if a race of people had the physiological defect of being able to see only the color blue, they would hardly be able to formulate the rule that they saw only blue. The term blue would convey no meaning to them, their language would lack color terms, and their words denoting their various sensations of blue would answer to, and translate, our words "light, dark, white, black," and so on, not our word "blue." In order to formulate the rule or norm of seeing only blue, they would need exceptional moments in which they saw other colors. The phenomenon of gravitation forms a rule without exceptions: needless to say, the untutored person is utterly unaware of any law of gravitation, for it would never enter his head to conceive of a universe in which bodies behaved otherwise than they do at the earth's surface. Like the color blue with our hypothetical race, the law of gravitation is a part of the untutored individual's background, not something he isolates from that background. The law could not be formulated until bodies that always fell were seen in terms of a wider astronomical world in which bodies moved in orbits or went this way and that.

Similarly, whenever we turn our heads, the image of the scene passes across our retinas exactly as it would if the scene turned around us. But this effect is background, and we do not recognize it; we do not see a room turn around us but are conscious only of having turned our heads in a stationary room. If we observe critically while turning the head or eyes quickly, we shall see, no motion it is true, yet a blurring of the scene between two clear views. Normally we are quite unconscious of this continual blurring but seem to be looking about in an unblurred world. Whenever we walk past a tree or house, its image on the retina changes just as if the tree or house were turning on an axis; yet we do not see trees or houses turn as we travel about at ordinary speeds. Sometimes ill-fitting glasses will reveal queer movements in the scene as we look about, but normally we do not see the relative motion of the environment when we move; our psychic makeup is somehow adjusted to disregard whole realms of phenomena that are so all-pervasive as to be irrelevant to our daily lives and needs.

Natural logic contains two fallacies: First, it does not see that the phenomena of a language are to its own speakers largely of a background character and so are outside the critical consciousness and control of the speaker who is expanding natural logic. Hence, when anyone, as a natural logician, is talking about reason, logic, and the laws of correct thinking, he is apt to be simply marching in step with purely grammatical facts that have somewhat of a background character in his own language or family of languages but are by no means universal in all languages and in no sense a common substratum of reason. Second, natural logic confuses agreement about subject matter, attained through use

of language, with knowledge of the linguistic process by which agreement is attained: i.e., with the province of the despised (and to its notion superfluous) grammarian. Two fluent speakers, of English let us say, quickly reach a point of assent about the subject matter of their speech; they agree about what their language refers to. One of them, A, can give directions that will be carried out by the other, B, to A's complete satisfaction. Because they thus understand each other so perfectly, A and B, as natural logicians, suppose they must of course know how it is all done. They think, e.g., that it is simply a matter of choosing words to express thoughts. If you ask A to explain how he got B's agreement so readily, he will simply repeat to you, with more or less elaboration or abbreviation, what he said to B. He has no notion of the process involved. The amazingly complex system of linguistic patterns and classifications, which A and B must have in common before they can adjust to each other at all, is all background to A and B. . . .

The situation here is not unlike that in any other field of science. All real scientists have their eyes primarily on background phenomena that cut very little ice, as such, in our daily lives; and yet their studies have a way of bringing out a close relation between these unsuspected realms of fact and such decidedly foreground activities as transporting goods, preparing food, treating the sick, or growing potatoes, which in time may become very much modified, simply because of pure scientific investigation in no way concerned with these brute matters themselves. Linguistics presents a quite similar case; the background phenomena with which it deals are involved in all our foreground activities of talking and of reaching agreement, in all reasoning and arguing of cases, in all law, arbitration, conciliation, contracts, treaties, public opinion, weighing of scientific theories, formulation of scientific results. Whenever agreement or assent is arrived at in human affairs, and whether or not mathematics or other specialized symbolisms are made part of the procedure, *this agreement is reached by linguistic processes, or else it is not reached.*

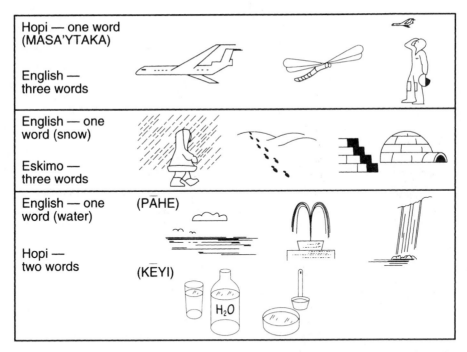

Languages classify items of experience differently. The class corresponding to one word and one thought in language A may be regarded by language B as two or more classes corresponding to two or more words and thoughts.

As we have seen, an overt knowledge of the linguistic processes by which agreement is attained is not necessary to reaching some sort of agreement, but it is certainly no bar thereto; the more complicated and difficult the matter, the more such knowledge is a distinct aid, till the point may be reached—I suspect the modern world has arrived at it—when the knowledge becomes not only an aid but a necessity. The situation may be likened to that of navigation. Every boat that sails is in the lap of planetary forces; yet a boy can pilot his small craft around a harbor without benefit of geography, astronomy, mathematics, or international politics. To the captain of an ocean liner, however, some knowledge of all these subjects is essential.

When linguists became able to examine critically and scientifically a large number of languages of widely different patterns, their base of reference was expanded; they experienced an interruption of phenomena hitherto held universal, and a whole new order of significances came into their ken. It was found that the background linguistic system (in other words, the grammar) of each language is not merely a reproducing instrument for voicing ideas but rather is itself the shaper of ideas, the program and guide for the individual's mental activity, for his analysis of impressions, for his synthesis of his mental stock in trade. Formulation of ideas is not an independent process, strictly rational in the old sense, but is part of a particular grammar, and differs, from slightly to greatly, between different grammars. We dissect nature along lines laid down by our native languages. The categories and types that we isolate from the world of phenomena we do not find there because they stare every observer in the face; on the contrary, the world is presented in a kaleidoscopic flux of impressions which has to be organized by our minds—and this means largely by the linguistic systems in our minds. We cut nature up,

Objective field	Speaker (Sender)	Hearer (Receiver)	Handling of topic, Running of third person
Situation 1a			English: "He is running" Hopi: "WARI" (running, statement of fact)
Situation 1b Objective field blank Devoid of running			English: "He ran" Hopi: "WARI" (running, statement of fact)
Situation 2			English: "He is running" Hopi: "WARI" (running, statement of fact)
Situation 3 Objective field blank			English: "He ran" Hopi: "ERA WARI" (running, statement of fact from memory)
Situation 4 Objective field blank			English: "He will run" Hopi: "WARIKNI" (running, statement of expectation)
Situation 5 Objective field blank			English: "He runs" (e.g., on the track team) Hopi: "WARIKNGWE" (running, statement of law)

Contrast between a "temporal" language (English) and a "timeless" language (Hopi). What are to English differences of time are to Hopi differences in the kind of validity.

organize it into concepts, and ascribe significances as we do, largely because we are parties to an agreement to organize it this way—an agreement that holds throughout our speech community and is codified in the patterns of our language. The agreement is, of course, an implicit and unstated one, *but its terms are absolutely obligatory;* we cannot talk at all except by subscribing to the organization and classification of data which the agreement decrees.

This fact is very significant for modern science, for it means that no individual is free to describe nature with absolute impartiality but is constrained to certain modes of interpretation even while he thinks himself most free. The person most nearly free in such respects would be a linguist familiar with very many widely different linguistic systems. As yet no linguist is in any such position. We are thus introduced to a new principle of relativity, which holds that all observers are not led by the same physical evidence to the same picture of the universe, unless their linguistic backgrounds are similar, or can in some way be calibrated.

This rather startling conclusion is not so apparent if we compare only our modern European languages, with perhaps Latin and Greek thrown in for good measure. Among these tongues there is a unanimity of major pattern which at first seems to bear out natural logic. But this unanimity exists only because these tongues are all Indo-European dialects cut to the same basic plan, being historically transmitted from what was long ago one speech community; because the modern dialects have long shared in building up a common culture; and because much of this culture, on the more intellectual side, is derived from the linguistic backgrounds of Latin and Greek. Thus this group of languages satisfies the special case of the clause beginning "unless" in the statement of the linguistic relativity principle at the end of the preceding paragraph. From this condition follows the unanimity of description of the world in the community of modern scientists. But it must be emphasized that "all modern Indo-European-speaking observers" is not the same thing as "all observers." That modern Chinese or Turkish scientists describe the world in the same terms as Western scientists means, of course, only that they have taken over bodily the entire Western system of rationalizations, not that they have corroborated that system from their native posts of observation.

When Semitic, Chinese, Tibetan, or African languages are contrasted with our own, the divergence in analysis of the world becomes more apparent; and, when we bring in the native languages of the Americas, where speech communities for many millenniums have gone their ways independently of each other and of the Old World, the fact that languages dissect nature in many different ways becomes patent. The relativity of all conceptual systems, ours included, and their dependence upon language stand revealed. That American Indians speaking only their native tongues are never called upon to act

as scientific observers is in no wise to the point. To exclude the evidence which their languages offer as to what the human mind can do is like expecting botanists to study nothing but food plants and hothouse roses and then tell us what the plant world is like!

Let us consider a few examples. In English we divide most of our words into two classes, which have different grammatical and logical properties. Class 1 we call nouns, e.g., 'house, man'; class 2, verbs, e.g., 'hit, run.' Many words of one class can act secondarily as of the other class, e.g., 'a hit, a run,' or 'to man (the boat),' but, on the primary level, the division between the classes is absolute. Our language thus gives us a bipolar division of nature. But nature herself is not thus polarized. If it be said that 'strike, turn, run,' are verbs because they denote temporary or short-lasting events, i.e., actions, why then is 'fist' a noun? It also is a temporary event. Why are 'lightning, spark, wave, eddy, pulsation, flame, storm, phase, cycle, spasm, noise, emotion' nouns? They are temporary events. If 'man' and 'house' are nouns because they are long-lasting and stable events, i.e., things, what then are 'keep, adhere, extend, project, continue, persist, grow, dwell,' and so on doing among the verbs? If it be objected that 'possess, adhere' are verbs because they are stable relationships rather than stable precepts, why then should 'equilibrium, pressure, current, peace, group, nation, society, tribe, sister,' or any kinship term be among the nouns? It will be found that an 'event' to us means 'what our language classes as a verb' or something analogized therefrom. And it will be found that is not possible to define 'event, thing, object, relationship,' and so on, from nature, but that to define them always involves a circuitous return to the grammatical categories of the definer's language.

In the Hopi language, 'lightning, wave, flame, meteor, puff of smoke, pulsation' are verbs. 'Cloud' and 'storm' are at about the lower limit of duration for nouns. Hopi, you see, actually has a classification of events (or linguistic isolates) by duration type, something strange to our modes of thought. On the other hand, in Nootka, a language of Vancouver Island, all words seem to us to be verbs, but really there are no classes 1 and 2; we have, as it were, a monistic view of nature that gives us only one class of word for all kinds of events. 'A house occurs', or 'it houses' is the way of saying 'house,' exactly like 'a flame occurs' or 'it burns.' These terms seem to us like verbs because they are inflected for durational and temporal nuances, so that the suffixes of the word for house event make it mean long-lasting house, temporary house, future house, house that used to be, what started out to be a house, and so on.

Hopi has one noun that covers every thing or being that flies, with the exception of birds, which class is denoted by another noun. The former noun may be said to denote the class (*FC – B*)—flying class minus bird. The Hopi actually call insect, airplane, and aviator all by the same word, and feel no difficulty about it. The situation, of course, decides any possible confusion among very disparate members of a broad linguistic class, such as this class (*FC – B*). This class seems to us too large and inclusive, but so would our class "snow" to an Eskimo. We have the same word for falling snow, snow on the ground, snow packed hard like ice, slushy snow, wind-driven flying snow—whatever the situation may be. To an Eskimo, this all-inclusive word would be almost unthinkable; he would say that falling snow, slushy snow, and so on, are sensuously and operationally different, different things to contend with; he uses different words for them and for other kinds of snow. The Aztecs go even farther than we in the opposite direction, with 'cold,' 'ice,' and 'snow' all represented by the same basic word with different terminations; 'ice' is the noun form; 'cold,' the adjectival form; and for 'snow,' 'ice mist.'

What surprises most is to find that various grand generalizations of the Western world, such as time, velocity, and matter, are not essential to the construction of a consistent picture of the universe. The psychic experiences that we class under these headings are, of course, not destroyed; rather, categories derived from other kinds of experiences take over the rulership of the cosmology and seem to function just as well. Hopi may be called a timeless language. It recognizes psychological time, which is much like Bergson's "duration," but this "time" is quite unlike the mathematical time, *T*, used by our physicists. Among the peculiar properties of Hopi time are that it varies with each observer, does not permit of simultaneity, and has zero dimensions; i.e., it cannot be given a number greater than one. The Hopi do not say, "I stayed five days," but "I left on the fifth day." A word referring to this kind of time, like the word day, can have no plural. The puzzle picture will give mental exercise to anyone who would like to figure out how the Hopi verb gets along without tenses. Actually, the only practical use of our tenses, in one-verb sentences, is to distinguish among five typical situations, which are symbolized in the picture. The timeless Hopi verb does not distinguish between the present, past, and future of the event itself but must always indicate what type of validity the speaker intends the statement to have: (a) report of an event (situations 1, 2, 3, in the picture); (b) expectation of an event (situation 4); (c) generalization or law about events (situation 5). Situation 1, where the speaker and listener are in contact with the same objective field, is divided by our language into the two conditions, 1*a* and 1*b*, which it calls present and past, respectively. This division is unnecessary for a language which assures one that the statement is a report.

Hopi grammar, by means of its forms called aspects and modes, also makes it easy to distinguish among momentary, continued, and repeated occurrences, and to indicate the actual sequence of reported events. Thus the universe can be described without recourse to a concept of dimensional time. How would a physics constructed along these lines work, with no *T* (time) in its equations? Perfectly, as far as I can see, though of course it would require different ideology and perhaps different mathematics. Of course (velocity) would have to go too. The Hopi language has no word really equivalent to our 'speed' or 'rapid.' What translates these terms is usually a word meaning intense or very, accompanying any verb of motion. Here is a clue to the nature of our new physics. We may have to introduce a new term I, intensity. Every thing and event will have an I, whether we regard the thing or event as moving or as just enduring or being. Perhaps the I of an electric charge will turn out to be its voltage, or potential. We shall use clocks to measure some intensities, or, rather, some *relative* intensities, for the absolute intensity of anything will be meaningless. Our old friend acceleration will still be there but doubtless under a new name. We shall perhaps call it V, meaning not velocity but variation. Perhaps all growths and accumulations will be regarded as Vs. We should not have the concept of rate in the temporal sense, since, like velocity, rate introduces a mathematical and linguistic time. Of course we know that all measurements are ratios, but the measurements of intensities made by comparison with the standard intensity of a clock or a planet we do not treat as ratios, any more than we so treat a distance made by comparison with a yardstick.

A scientist from another culture that used time and velocity would have great difficulty in getting us to understand these concepts. We should talk about the intensity of a chemical reaction; he would speak of its velocity or its rate, which words we should at first think were simply words for intensity in his language. Likewise, he at first would think that intensity was simply our own word for velocity. At first we should agree, later we should begin to disagree, and it might dawn upon both sides that different systems of rationalization were being used. He would find it very hard to make us understand what he really meant by velocity of a chemical reaction. We should have no words that would fit. He would try to explain it by likening it to a running horse, to the difference between a good horse and a lazy horse. We should try to show him, with a superior laugh, that his analogy also was a matter of different intensities, aside from

which there was little similarity between a horse and a chemical reaction in a beaker. We should point out that a running horse is moving relative to the ground, whereas the material in the beaker is at rest.

One significant contribution to science from the linguistic point of view may be the greater development of our sense of perspective. We shall no longer be able to see a few recent dialects of the Indo-European family, and the rationalizing techniques elaborated from their patterns, as the apex of the evolution of the human mind, nor their present wide spread as due to any survival from fitness or to anything but a few events of history—events that could be called fortunate only from the parochial point of view of the favored parties. They, and our own thought processes with them, can no longer be envisioned as spanning the gamut of reason and knowledge but only as one constellation in a galactic expanse. A fair realization of the incredible degree of diversity of linguistic systems that ranges over the globe leaves one with an inescapable feeling that the human spirit is inconceivably old; that the few thousand years of history covered by our written records are no more than the thickness of a pencil mark on the scale that measures our past experience on this planet; that the events of these recent millenniums spell nothing in any evolutionary wise, that the race has taken no sudden spurt, achieved no commanding synthesis during recent millenniums, but has only played a little with a few of the linguistic formulations and views of nature bequeathed from an inexpressible long past. Yet neither this feeling nor the sense of precarious dependence of all we know upon linguistic tools which themselves are largely unknown need be discouraging to science but should, rather, foster that humility which accompanies the true scientific spirit, and thus forbid that arrogance of the mind which hinders real scientific curiosity and detachment.

STEVEN PINKER

The Language Instinct

STEVEN PINKER, *a linguist by training, is a professor in the Department of Brain and Cognitive Sciences at MIT. He has won awards for his work in visual cognition and in child language acquisition and for his teaching at MIT. His 1994 book,* The Language Instinct, *from which this selection is taken, is a lively and readable overview of contemporary linguistics from the perspective of cognitive science. In it he argues that language is an innate human instinct, rather than a cultural artifact. His most recent book is* The Blank Slate *(2002).*

THE year 1984 has come and gone, and it is losing its connotation of the totalitarian nightmare of George Orwell's 1949 novel. But relief may be premature. In an appendix to *Nineteen Eighty-four,* Orwell wrote of an even more ominous date. In 1984, the infidel Winston Smith had to be converted with imprisonment, degradation, drugs, and torture; by 2050, there would be no Winston Smiths. For in that year the ultimate technology for thought control would be in place: the language Newspeak.

The purpose of Newspeak was not only to provide a medium of expression for the world-view and mental habits proper to the devotees of Ingsoc [English Socialism], but to make all other modes of thought impossible. It was intended that when Newspeak had been adopted once and for all and Oldspeak forgotten, a heretical thought—that is, a thought diverging from the principles of Ingsoc—should be literally unthinkable, at least so far as thought is dependent on words. Its vocabulary was so constructed as to give exact and often very subtle expression to every meaning that a Party member could properly wish to express, while excluding all other meaning and also the possibility of arriving at them by indirect methods. This was done partly by the invention of new words, but chiefly by eliminating undesirable words and by stripping such words as remained of unorthodox meanings, and so far as

possible of all secondary meanings whatever. To give a single example. The word *free* still existed in Newspeak, but it could only be used in such statements as "This dog is free from lice" or "This field is free from weeds." It could not be used in its old sense of "politically free" or "intellectually free," since political and intellectual freedom no longer existed even as concepts, and were therefore of necessity nameless.

... A person growing up with Newspeak as his sole language would no more know that *equal* had once had the secondary meaning of "politically equal," or that *free* had once meant "intellectually free," than, for instance, a person who had never heard of chess would be aware of the secondary meanings attaching to *queen* and *rook.* There would be many crimes and errors which it would be beyond his power to commit, simply because they were nameless and therefore unimaginable.

But there is a straw of hope for human freedom: Orwell's caveat "at least so far as thought is dependent on words." Note his equivocation: at the end of the first paragraph, a concept is unimaginable and therefore nameless; at the end of the second, a concept is nameless and therefore unimaginable. *Is* thought dependent on words? Do people literally think in English, Cherokee, Kivunjo, or, by 2050, Newspeak? Or are our thoughts couched in some silent medium of the brain—a language of thought, or "mentalese"—and merely clothed in words whenever we need to communicate them to a listener? No question could be more central to understanding the language instinct.

In much of our social and political discourse, people simply assume that words determine thoughts. Inspired by Orwell's essay "Politics and the English Language," pundits accuse governments of manipulating our minds with euphemisms like *pacification* (bombing), *revenue enhancement* (taxes), and *nonretention* (firing). Philosophers argue that since animals lack language, they must also lack consciousness— Wittgenstein wrote, "A dog could not have the thought 'perhaps it will rain tomorrow'"—and therefore they do not possess the rights of conscious beings. Some feminists blame sexist thinking on sexist language, like the use of *he* to refer to a generic person. Inevitably, reform movements have sprung up. Many replacements for *he* have been suggested over the years, including *E, hesh, po, tey, co, jhe, ve, xe, he'er, thon,* and *na.* The most extreme of these movements is General Semantics, begun in 1933 by the engineer Count Alfred Korzybski and popularized in long-time best-sellers by his disciples Stuart Chase and S. I. Hayakawa. (This is the same Hayakawa who later achieved notoriety as the protest-defying college president and snoozing U.S. senator.) General Semantics lays the blame for human folly on insidious "semantic damage" to thought perpetrated by the structure of language. Keeping a forty-year-old in prison for a theft he committed as a teenager assumes that the forty-year-old John and the eighteen-year-old John are "the same person," a cruel logical error that would be avoided if we referred to them not as *John* but as *John 1972* and *John 1994,* respectively. The verb *to be* is a particular source of illogic, because it identifies individuals with abstractions, as in *Mary is a woman,* and licenses evasions of responsibility, like Ronald Reagan's famous nonconfession *Mistakes were made.* One faction seeks to eradicate the verb altogether.

And supposedly there is a scientific basis for these assumptions: the famous Sapir-Whorf hypothesis of linguistic determinism, stating that people's thoughts are determined by the categories made available by their language, and its weaker version, linguistic relativity, stating that differences among languages cause differences in the thoughts of their speakers. People who remember little else from their college education can rattle off the factoids: the languages that carve the spectrum into color words at different places, the fundamentally different Hopi concept of time, the dozens of Eskimo words for snow. The implication is heavy: the foundational categories of reality are not "in" the world but are imposed by one's culture (and hence can be challenged, perhaps accounting for the perennial appeal of the hypothesis to undergraduate sensibilities).

But it is wrong, all wrong. The idea that thought is the same thing as language is an example of what can be called a conventional absurdity: a statement that goes against all common sense but that everyone believes because they dimly recall having heard it somewhere and because it is so pregnant with implications. (The "fact" that we use only five percent of our brains, that lemmings commit mass suicide, that the *Boy Scout Manual* annually outsells all other books, and that we can be coerced into buying by subliminal messages are other examples.) Think about it. We have all had the experience of uttering or writing a sentence, then stopping and realizing that it wasn't exactly what we meant to say. To have that feeling, there has to be a "what we meant to say" that is different from what we said. Sometimes it is not easy to find *any* words that properly convey a thought. When we hear or read, we usually remember the gist, not the exact words, so there has to be such a thing as a gist that is not the same as a bunch of words. And if thoughts depended on words, how could a new word ever be coined? How could a child learn a word to begin with? How could translation from one language to another be possible?

The discussions that assume that language determines thought carry on only by a collective suspension of disbelief. A dog, Bertrand Russell noted, may not be able to tell you that its parents were honest though poor, but can anyone really conclude from this that the dog is *unconscious?* (Out cold? A zombie?) A graduate student once argued with me using the following deliciously backwards logic: Language must affect thought, because if it didn't, we would have no reason to fight sexist usage (apparently, the fact that it is offensive is not reason enough). As for government euphemism, it is contemptible not because it is a form of mind control but because it is a form of lying (Orwell was quite clear about this in his masterpiece essay). For example, "revenue enhancement" has a much broader meaning than "taxes," and listeners naturally assume that if a politician had meant "taxes," he would have said "taxes." Once a euphemism is pointed out, people are not so brain washed that they have trouble understanding the deception. The National Council of Teachers of English annually lampoons government doublespeak in a widely reproduced press release, and calling attention to euphemism is a popular form of humor, like the speech from the irate pet store customer in *Monty Python's Flying Circus:*

> This parrot is no more. It has ceased to be. It's expired and gone to meet its maker. This is a late parrot. It's a stiff. Bereft of life, it rests in peace. If you hadn't nailed it to the perch, it would be pushing up the daisies. It's rung down the curtain and joined the choir invisible. This is an ex-parrot.

As we shall see in this chapter, there is no scientific evidence that languages dramatically shape their speakers' ways of thinking. But I want to do more than review the unintentionally comical history of attempts to prove that they do. The idea that language shapes thinking seemed plausible when scientists were in the dark about how thinking works or even how to study it. Now that cognitive scientists know to think about thinking, there is less of a temptation to equate it with language just because words are more palpable than thoughts. By understanding *why* linguistic determinism is wrong, we will be in a better position to understand how language itself works when we turn to it in the next chapters.

• • •

The linguistic determinism hypothesis is closely linked to the names Edward Sapir and Benjamin Lee Whorf. Sapir, a brilliant linguist, was a student of the anthropologist Franz Boas. Boas and his students (who also include Ruth Benedict and Margaret Mead) were important intellectual figures in this century, because they argued that nonindustrial peoples were not primitive savages but had systems of language, knowledge, and culture as complex and valid in their world view as our own. In his study of Native American languages Sapir noted that speakers of different languages have to pay attention to different aspects of reality simply to put words together into grammatical sentences. For example, when English speakers decide whether or not to put *-ed* unto the end of a verb, they must pay attention to tense, the relative time of occurrence of the event they are referring to and the moment of speaking. Wintu speakers need not bother with tense, but when they decide which suffix to put on their verbs, they must pay attention to whether the knowledge they are conveying was learned through direct observation or by hearsay.

Sapir's interesting observation was soon taken much farther. Whorf was an inspector for the Hartford Fire Insurance Company and an amateur scholar of Native American languages, which led him to take courses from Sapir at Yale. In a much-quoted passage, he wrote:

> We dissect nature along lines laid down by our native languages. The categories and types that we isolate from the world of phenomena we do not find there because they stare every observer in the face; on the contrary, the world is presented in a kaleidoscopic flux of impressions which has to be organized by our minds—and this means largely by the linguistic systems in our minds. We cut nature up, organize it into concepts, and ascribe significances as we do, largely because we are parties to an agreement to organize it in this way—an agreement that holds throughout our speech community and is codified in the patterns of our language. The agreement is, of course, an implicit and unstated one, *but its terms are absolutely obligatory;* we cannot talk at all

except by subscribing to the organization and classification of data which the agreement decrees.

What led Whorf to this radical position? He wrote that the idea first occurred to him in his work as a fire prevention engineer when he was struck by how language led workers to misconstrue dangerous situations. For example, one worker caused a serious explosion by tossing a cigarette into an "empty" drum that in fact was full of gasoline vapor. Another lit a blowtorch near a "pool of water" that was really a basin of decomposing tannery waste, which, far from being "watery," was releasing inflammable gases. Whorf's studies of American languages strengthened his conviction. For example, in Apache, *It is a dripping spring* must be expressed "As water, or springs, whiteness moves downward." "How utterly unlike our way of thinking!" he wrote.

But the more you examine Whorf's arguments, the less sense they make. Take the story about the worker and the "empty" drum. The seeds of disaster supposedly lay in the semantics of *empty,* which, Whorf claimed, means both "without its usual contents" and "null and void, empty, inert." The hapless worker, his conception of reality molded by his linguistic categories, did not distinguish between the "drained" and "inert" senses, hence, flick . . . boom! But wait. Gasoline vapor is invisible. A drum with nothing but vapor in it looks just like a drum with nothing in it at all. Surely this walking catastrophe was fooled by his eyes, not by the English language.

The example of whiteness moving downward is supposed to show that the Apache mind does not cut up events into distinct objects and actions. Whorf presented many such examples from Native American languages. The Apache equivalent of *The boat is grounded on the beach* is "It is on the beach pointwise as an event of canoe motion." *He invites people to a feast* becomes "He, or somebody, goes for eaters of cooked food." *He cleans a gun with a ramrod* is translated as "He directs a hollow moving dry spot by movement of tool." All this, to be sure, is utterly unlike our way

of talking. But do we know that it is utterly unlike our way of thinking?

As soon as Whorf's articles appeared, the psycholinguists Eric Lenneberg and Roger Brown pointed out two non sequiturs in his argument. First, Whorf did not actually study any Apaches; it is not clear that he ever met one. His assertions about Apache psychology are based entirely on Apache grammar—making his argument circular. Apaches speak differently, so they must think differently. How do we know that they think differently? Just listen to the way they speak!

Second, Whorf rendered the sentences as clumsy, word-for-word translations, designed to make the literal meanings seem as odd as possible. But looking at the actual glosses that Whorf provided, I could, with equal grammatical justification, render the first sentence as the mundane "Clear stuff—water—is falling." Turning the tables, I could take the English sentence "He walks" and render it "As solitary masculinity, leggedness proceeds." Brown illustrates how strange the German mind must be, according to Whorf's logic, by reproducing Mark Twain's own translation of a speech he delivered in flawless German to the Vienna Press Club:

> I am indeed the truest friend of the German language—and not only now, but from long since—yes, before twenty years already. . . . I would only some changes effect. I would only the language method—the luxurious, elaborate construction compress, the eternal parenthesis suppress, do away with, annihilate; the introduction of more than thirteen subjects in one sentence forbid; the verb so far to the front pull that one it without a telescope discover can. With one word, my gentlemen, I would your beloved language simplify so that, my gentlemen, when you her for prayer need, One her yonder-up understands.
>
> . . . I might gladly the separable verb also a little bit reform. I might none do let what Schiller did: he has the whole history of the Thirty Years' War between the two members of a separate verb inpushed. That has even Germany itself aroused, and one has Schiller the permission refused the History of the Hundred Years' War to compose—God be it

thanked! After all these reforms established be will, will the German language the noblest and the prettiest on the world be.

Among Whorf's "kaleidoscopic flux of impressions," color is surely the most eye-catching. He noted that we see objects in different hues, depending on the wavelengths of the light they reflect, but that physicists tell us that wavelength is a continuous dimension with nothing delineating red, yellow, green, blue, and so on. Languages differ in their inventory of color words: Latin lacks generic "gray" and "brown"; Navajo collapses blue and green into one word; Russian has distinct words for dark blue and sky blue; Shona speakers use one word for the yellower greens and the greener yellows, and a different one for the bluer greens and the nonpurplish blues. You can fill in the rest of the argument. It is language that puts the frets in the spectrum; Julius Caesar would not know shale from Shinola.

But although physicists see no basis for color boundaries, physiologists do. Eyes do not register wavelength the way a thermometer registers temperature. They contain three kinds of cones, each with a different pigment, and the cones are wired to neurons in a way that makes the neurons respond best to red patches against a green background or vice versa, blue against yellow, black against white. No matter how influential language might be, it would seem preposterous to a physiologist that it could reach down into the retina and rewire the ganglion cells.

Indeed, humans the world over (and babies and monkeys, for that matter) color their perceptual worlds using the same palette, and this constrains the vocabularies they develop. Although languages may disagree about the wrappers in the sixty-four crayon box—the burnt umbers, the turquoises, the fuchsias—they agree much more on the wrappers in the eight-crayon box—the fire-engine reds, grass greens, lemon yellows. Speakers of different languages unanimously pick these shades as the best examples of their color words, as long as the language has a color word in that general part of the spectrum. And where languages do differ in their color words, they differ predictably, not according to

the idiosyncratic tastes of some word-coiner. Languages are organized a bit like the Crayola product line, the fancier ones adding colors to the more basic ones. If a language has only two color words, they are for black and white (usually encompassing dark and light, respectively). If it has three, they are for black, white, and red; if four, black, white, red, and either yellow or green. Five adds in both yellow and green; six, blue; seven, brown; more than seven, purple, pink, orange, or gray. But the clinching experiment was carried out in the New Guinea highlands with the Grand Valley Dani, a people speaking one of the black-and-white languages. The psychologist Eleanor Rosch found that the Dani were quicker at learning a new color category that was based on fire-engine red than a category based on an off-red. The way we see colors determines how we learn words for them, not vice versa.

The fundamentally different Hopi concept of time is one of the more startling claims about how minds can vary. Whorf wrote that the Hopi language contains "no words, grammatical forms, constructions, or expressions that refer directly to what we call 'time,' or to past, or future, or to enduring or lasting." He suggested, too that the Hopi had "no general notion or intuition of time as a smooth flowing continuum in which everything in the universe proceeds at equal rate, out of a future, through a present, into a past." According to Whorf, they did not conceptualize events as being like points, or lengths of time like days as countable things. Rather, they seemed to focus on change and process itself, and on psychological distinctions between presently known, mythical, and conjecturally distant. The Hopi also had little interest in "exact sequences, dating, calendars, chronology."

What, then, are we to make of the following sentence translated from Hopi?

> Then indeed, the following day, quite early in the morning at the hour when people pray to the sun, around that time then he woke up the girl again.

Perhaps the Hopi are not as oblivious to time as Whorf made them out to be. In his extensive study of the Hopi, the anthropologist Ekkehart Malotki, who reported this sentence, also showed that Hopi speech contains tense, metaphors for time, units of time (including days, numbers of days, parts of the day, yesterday and tomorrow, days of the week, weeks, months, lunar phases, seasons, and the year), ways to quantify units of time, and words like "ancient," "quick," "long time," and "finished." Their culture keeps records with sophisticated methods of dating, including a horizon-based sun calendar, exact ceremonial day sequences, knotted calendar strings, notched calendar sticks, and several devices for timekeeping using the principle of the sundial. No one is really sure how Whorf came up with his outlandish claims, but his limited, badly analyzed sample of Hopi speech and his longtime leanings toward mysticism must have contributed.

Speaking of anthropological canards, no discussion of language and thought would be complete without the Great Eskimo Vocabulary Hoax. Contrary to popular belief, the Eskimos do not have more words for snow than do speakers of English. They do not have four hundred words for snow, as it has been claimed in print, or two hundred, or one hundred, or forty-eight, or even nine. One dictionary puts the figure at two. Counting generously, experts can come up with about a dozen, but by such standards English would not be far behind, with *snow, sleet, slush, blizzard, avalanche, hail, hard-pack, powder, flurry, dusting,* and a coinage of Boston's WBZ-TV meteorologist Bruce Schwoegler, *snizzling.*

Where did the myth come from? Not from anyone who has actually studied the Yupik and Inuit-Inupiaq families of polysynthetic languages spoken from Siberia to Greenland. The anthropologist Laura Martin has documented how the story grew like an urban legend, exaggerated with each retelling. In 1912 Boas casually mentioned that Eskimos used four unrelated word roots for snow. Whorf embellished the count to seven and implied that there were more. His article was widely reprinted, then cited in textbooks and popular books on language, which led to successively inflated estimates in other textbooks, articles, and newspaper columns of Amazing Facts.

The linguist Geoffrey Pullum, who popularized Martin's article in his essay "The Great Eskimo Vocabulary Hoax," speculates about why the story got so out of control: "The alleged lexical extravagance of the Eskimos comports so well with the many other facets of their polysynthetic perversity; rubbing noses; lending their wives to strangers; eating raw seal blubber; throwing Grandma out to be eaten by polar bears." It is an ironic twist. Linguistic relativity came out of the Boas school, as part of a campaign to show that nonliterate cultures were as complex and sophisticated as European ones. But the supposedly mind-broadening anecdotes owe their appeal to a patronizing willingness to treat other cultures' psychologies as weird and exotic compared to our own. As Pullum notes,

Among the many depressing things about this credulous transmission and elaboration of a false claim is that even if there *were* a large number of roots for different snow types in some Arctic language, this would *not*, objectively, be intellectually interesting; it would be a most mundane and unremarkable fact. Horse-breeders have various names for breeds, sizes, and ages of horses; botanists have names for leaf shapes; interior decorators have names for shades of mauve; printers have many different names for fonts (Carlson, Garamond, Helvetica, Times Roman, and so on), naturally enough. . . . Would anyone think of writing about printers the same kind of slop we find written about Eskimos in bad linguistics textbooks? Take [the following] random textbook . . . , with its earnest assertion "It is quite obvious that in the culture of the Eskimos . . . snow is of great enough importance to split up the conceptual sphere that corresponds to one word and one thought in English into several distinct classes. . . ." Imagine reading: "It is quite obvious that in the culture of printers . . . fonts are of great enough importance to split up the conceptual sphere that corresponds to one word and one thought among non-printers into several distinct classes. . . ." Utterly boring, even if true. Only the link to those legendary, promiscuous, blubber-gnawing hunters of the icepacks could permit something this trite to be presented to us for contemplation.

If the anthropological anecdotes are bunk, what about controlled studies? The thirty-five years of research from the psychology laboratory is distinguished by how little it has shown. Most of the experiments have tested banal "weak" versions of the Whorfian hypothesis, namely that words can have some effect on memory or categorization. Some of these experiments have actually worked, but that is hardly surprising. In a typical experiment, subjects have to commit paint chips to memory and are tested with a multiple-choice procedure. In some of these studies, the subjects show slightly better memory for colors that have readily available names in their language. But even colors are remembered by verbal labels alone. All it shows is that subjects remembered the chips in two forms, a nonverbal visual image and a verbal label, presumably because two kinds of memory, each one fallible, are better than one. In another type of experiment subjects have to say which two out of three color chips go together; they often put the ones together that have the same name in their language. Again, no surprise. I can imagine the subjects thinking to themselves, "Now how on earth does this guy expect me to pick two chips to put together? He didn't give me any hints, and they're all pretty similar. Well, I'd probably call those two 'green' and that one 'blue,' and that seems as good a reason to put them together as any." In these experiments, language is, technically speaking, influencing a form of thought in some way, but so what? It is hardly an example of incommensurable world views, or of concepts that are nameless and therefore unimaginable, or of dissecting nature along lines laid down by our native languages according to terms that are absolutely obligatory.

The only really dramatic finding comes from the linguist and now Swarthmore College president Alfred Bloom in his book *The Linguistic Shaping of Thought*. English grammar, says Bloom, provides its speakers with the subjunctive construction: *If John were to go to the hospital,*

he would meet Mary. The subjunctive is used to express "counterfactual" situations, events that are known to be false but entertained as hypotheticals. (Anyone familiar with Yiddish knows a better example, the ultimate riposte to someone reasoning from improbable premises: *Az der bubbe vot gehat baytzim vot zie geven mein zayde,* "If my grandmother had balls, she'd be my grandfather.") Chinese, in contrast, lacks a subjunctive and any other simple grammatical construction that directly expresses a counterfactual. The thought must be expressed circuitously, something like "If John is going to the hospital . . . but he is not going to the hospital . . . but if he is going, he meets Mary."

Bloom wrote stories containing sequences of implications from a counterfactual premise and gave them to Chinese and American students. For example, one story said, in outline, "Bier was an eighteenth-century European philosopher. There was some contact between the West and China at that time, but very few works of Chinese philosophy had been translated. Bier could not read Chinese, but if he had been able to read Chinese, he would have discovered B; what would have most influenced him would have been C; once influenced by that Chinese perspective, Bier would then have done D," and so on. The subjects were then asked to check off whether B, C, and D actually occurred. The American students gave the correct answer, no, ninety-eight percent of the time; the Chinese students gave the correct answer only seven percent of the time! Bloom concluded that the Chinese language renders its speakers unable to entertain hypothetical false worlds without great mental effort. (As far as I know, no one has tested the converse prediction on speakers of Yiddish.)

The cognitive psychologists Terry Au, Yohtaro Takano, and Lisa Liu were not exactly enchanted by these tales of the concreteness of the Oriental mind. Each one identified serious flaws in Bloom's experiments. One problem was that his stories were written in stilted Chinese. Another was that some of the science stories turned out, upon careful rereading, to be genuinely ambiguous. Chinese college students tend to have more science training than American students, and thus they were *better* at detecting the ambiguities that Bloom himself missed. When these flaws were fixed, the differences vanished.

• • •

We have met deaf children who lack a language and soon invent one. Even more pertinent are the deaf adults occasionally discovered who lack any form of language whatsoever—no sign language, no writing, no lip reading, no speech. In her recent book *A Man Without Words*, Susan Schaller tells the story of Ildefonso, a twenty-seven-year-old illegal immigrant from a small Mexican village whom she met while working as a sign language interpreter in Los Angeles. Ildefonso's animated eyes conveyed an unmistakable intelligence and curiosity, and Schaller became his volunteer teacher and companion. He soon showed her that he had a full grasp of number: he learned to do addition on paper in three minutes and had little trouble understanding the base-ten logic behind two-digit numbers. In an epiphany reminiscent of the story of Helen Keller, Ildefonso grasped the principle of naming when Schaller tried to teach him the sign for "cat." A dam burst, and he demanded to be shown the signs for all the objects he was familiar with. Soon he was able to convey to Schaller parts of his life story: how as a child he had begged his desperately poor parents to send him to school, the kinds of crops he had picked in different states, his evasions of immigration authorities. He led Schaller to other languageless adults in forgotten corners of society. Despite their isolation from the verbal world, they displayed many abstract forms of thinking, like rebuilding broken locks, handling money, playing card games, and entertaining each other with long pantomimed narratives.

Our knowledge of the mental life of Ildefonso and other languageless adults must remain impressionistic for ethical reasons: when they surface, the first priority is to teach them language, not to study how they manage without it.

But there are other languageless beings who have been studied experimentally, and volumes have been written about how they reason about space, time, objects, number, rate, causality, and categories. Let me recount three ingenious examples. One involves babies, who cannot think in words because they have not yet learned any. One involves monkeys, who cannot think in words because they are incapable of learning them. The third involves human adults, who, whether or not they think in words, claim their best thinking is done without them.

The developmental psychologist Karen Wynn has recently shown that five-month-old babies can do a simple form of mental arithmetic. She used a technique common in infant perception research. Show a baby a bunch of objects long enough, and the baby gets bored and looks away; change the scene, and if the baby notices the difference, he or she will regain interest. The methodology has shown that babies as young as five days old are sensitive to number. In one experiment, an experimenter bores a baby with an object, then occludes the object with an opaque screen. When the screen is removed, if the same object is present, the babies look for a little while, then get bored again. But if, through invisible subterfuge, two or three objects have ended up there, the surprised babies stare longer.

In Wynn's experiment, the babies were shown a rubber Mickey Mouse doll on a stage until their little eyes wandered. Then a screen came up, and a prancing hand visibly reached out from behind a curtain and placed a second Mickey Mouse behind the screen. When the screen was removed, if there were two Mickey Mouses visible (something the babies had never actually seen), the babies looked for only a few moments. But if there was only one doll, the babies were captivated—even though this was exactly the scene that had bored them before the screen was put in place. Wynn also tested a second group of babies, and this time, after the screen came up to obscure a *pair* of dolls, a hand visibly reached behind the screen and removed one of them. If the screen fell to reveal a single Mickey, the babies looked briefly; if it revealed the old scene with two, the babies had more trouble tearing themselves away. The babies must have been keeping track of how many dolls were behind the screen, updating their counts as dolls were added or subtracted. If the number inexplicably departed from what they expected, they scrutinized the scene, as if searching for some explanation. . . .

What sense, then, can we make of the suggestion that images, numbers, kinship relations, or logic can be represented in the brain without being couched in words? In the first half of this century, philosophers had an answer: none. Reifying thoughts as things in the head was a logical error, they said. A picture or family tree or number in the head would require a little man, a homunculus, to look at it. And what would be inside *his* head—even smaller pictures, with an even smaller man looking at them? But the argument was unsound. It took Alan Turing, the brilliant British mathematician and philosopher, to make the idea of a mental representation scientifically respectable. Turing described a hypothetical machine that could be said to engage in reasoning. In fact this simple device, named Turing Machine in his honor, is powerful enough to solve any problem that any computer, past, present, or future, can solve. And it clearly uses an internal symbolic representation—a kind of mentalese—without requiring a little man or any occult processes. . . .

Remember that a representation does not have to look like English or any other language; it just has to use symbols to represent concepts, and arrangements of symbols to represent the logical relations among them, according to some consistent scheme. But though internal representations in an English speaker's mind don't *have* to look like English, they *could*, in principle, look like English—or like whatever language the person happens to speak. So here is the question: Do they in fact? For example, if we know that Socrates is a man, is it because we have neural patterns that correspond one-to-one to the English words *Socrates, is, a,* and *man,* and groups of neurons in the brain that correspond to the subject of an English sentence, the verb,

and the object, laid out in that order? Or do we use some other code for representing concepts and their relations in our heads, a language of thought or mentalese that is not the same as any of the world's languages? We can answer this question by seeing whether English sentences embody the information that a processor would need to perform valid sequences of reasoning—without requiring any fully intelligent homunculus inside doing the "understanding."

The answer is a clear no. English (or any other language people speak) is hopelessly unsuited to serve as our internal medium of computation. . . .

People do not think in English or Chinese or Apache; they think in a language of thought. This language of thought probably looks a bit like all these languages; presumably it has symbols for concepts, and arrangements of symbols that correspond to who did what to whom. . . . But compared with any given language, mentalese must be richer in some ways and simpler in others. It must be richer, for example, in that several concept symbols must correspond to a given English word like *stool* or *stud.* There must be extra paraphernalia that differentiate logically distinct kinds of concepts . . . and that link different symbols that refer to the same thing. . . . On the other hand, mentalese must be simpler than spoken languages; conversation-specific words and constructions (like *a* and *the*) are absent, and information about pronouncing words, or even ordering them, is unnecessary. Now, it could be that English speakers think in some kind of simplified and annotated quasi-English, with the design I have just described, and that Apache speakers think in a simplified and annotated quasi-Apache. But to get these languages of thought to subserve reasoning properly, they would have to look much more like each other than either one does to its spoken counterpart, and it is likely that they are the same: a universal mentalese.

Knowing a language, then, is knowing how to translate mentalese into strings of words and vice versa. People without a language would still have mentalese, and babies and many nonhuman animals presumably have simpler dialects. Indeed, if babies did not have a mentalese to translate to and from English, it is not clear how learning English could take place, or even what learning English would mean.

So where does all this leave Newspeak? Here are my predictions for the year 2050. First, since mental life goes on independently of particular languages, concepts of freedom and equality will be thinkable even if they are nameless. Second, since there are far more concepts than there are words, and listeners must always charitably fill in what the speaker leaves unsaid, existing words will quickly gain new senses, perhaps even regain their original senses. Third, since children are not content to reproduce any old input from adults but create a complex grammar than can go beyond it, they would creolize Newspeak into a natural language, possibly in a single generation. The twenty-first-century toddler may be Winston Smith's revenge.

STEPHANIE ROSS
How Words Hurt

STEPHANIE ROSS *teaches philosophy at the University of Missouri in St. Louis. She does work in feminist theory and in aesthetics.*

AN old nursery rhyme assures us that "Sticks and stones may break my bones/But names can never hurt me." Yet many philosophers claim that words *can* hurt. They argue that ordinary language is sexist and that sexist language oppresses women. For example, Elizabeth Beardsley has drawn attention to referential genderization (RG) which occurs "whenever a speaker who is saying something about human beings must make distinctions based on sex on pain of saying something linguistically incorrect." She claims that RG increases sexual distinctions, and thereby "helps to provide a conceptual framework useful for rationalizing sex-based discriminatory treatment." Robert Baker claims that

any movement dedicated to breaking the bonds of female servitude must destroy our ways of identifying and hence of conceiving of women. . . . Contemporary feminists should advocate the utilization of neutral proper names and the elimination of gender from our language.

I believe these claims are sound, but to my knowledge no philosopher has provided a satisfactory account of *how* words hurt. Certainly words can be used to taunt and defame, to voice threats and instill fear, to express discriminatory edits and tyrannical decrees. Yet none of these possibilities explains the particular charge that our ordinary, everyday ways of talking about women are sexist and oppressive. Some writers

Ross, Stephanie, "How Words Hurt," from *How Words Hurt: Attitudes, Metaphor and Oppression* from Mary Vetterling-Braggin, ed., *Sexist Language* (Totowa, NJ: Rowman & Littlefield, 1981).

suggest that the oppressive aspects of ordinary language are etymological: certain words have roots which are denigrating and offensive to women. Yet most of us are unaware of the etymologies of the words we use. How can historical facts of which both speakers and listeners are unaware transform their words into vehicles of oppression?

In this paper I shall offer an account of how words can hurt. I shall begin by sketching a theory which doesn't work—the theory of etymological oppression. I shall argue that the ancient roots of ordinary English words cannot—by themselves—make those words oppressive. Then I shall turn to a closely related phenomenon which does perpetuate sexism in language. This is the phenomenon of metaphoric identification. . . . Briefly, I claim that metaphors often express attitude, and that the metaphors implicit in sexist language express attitudes of contempt and disdain towards women. . . . I shall also point out a structural similarity which makes metaphor an apt vehicle for the expression of attitude. Thus I hope to show that the nursery rhyme with which I opened is mistaken. Words can hurt, and one way they do is by conveying denigrating or demeaning attitudes.

ETYMOLOGICAL ECHOES?

In an angry article in the *New York Times*, Barbara Lawrence traces the etymology of the verb *to fuck* to the German *ficken* meaning "to strike," to the Latin *fustis,* meaning "a staff or cudgel," and to Celtic *buc,* meaning "a point, hence, to pierce." She goes on to discuss the etymology of the verb *to screw* and to point out what a painful and mutilating activity screwing is:

> Consider what a screw actually does to the wood it penetrates. . . . The verb, besides its explicit imagery, has antecedent associations to "write on," "scratch," "scarify," and so forth—a revealing fusion of a mechanical or painful action with an obviously denigrated object.

Lawrence suggests that these two words oppress women because of the brutal and denigrating imagery implicit in their etymology. While I

agree that both words are offensive, I believe that neither one oppresses in virtue of its etymology. And of the two, only "screw" offends by virtue of its associated imagery. . . . In the next section I shall show that the facts cited by Lawrence are relevant to a different sort of explanation of how words hurt. . . .

METAPHORICAL IDENTIFICATION

Return to Lawrence's two examples, "fuck" and "screw." We agree that both these words are insulting and that both are classed as impolite. In addition, I have argued that "fuck" does not offend women because of its etymological ties to "ficken," "fustis," and "buc." Most speakers are unaware of these ties. They find the term offensive because they know it is classed as offensive by their fellow speakers. I believe the offensiveness of "screw" can be explained quite differently, and this is shown even in Lawrence's summary reference to its "revealing fusion of a mechanical or painful action with an obviously denigrated object." The difference here is that most of us are aware of these aspects of screws. Even if we haven't given much thought to screwing as a method of fastening (as opposed to nailing or glueing) we can immediately acknowledge the correctness of Lawrence's claims. A screw is hard and sharp; wood by contrast is soft and yielding; force is applied to make a screw penetrate wood; a screw can be unscrewed and reused but wood—wherever a screw has been embedded in it—is destroyed forever. Once we marshal these everyday facts about screws and screwing, their ramifications become clear. When the verb *to screw* is used to describe sexual intercourse, it carries with it images of dominance and destruction. The woman's role in intercourse is similar to that of wood destroyed by the screw which enters it. Additional echoes are carried by a further use of the verb *to screw* in financial contexts. To screw someone in this sense is to wring her dry, to practice extortion.

Metaphor is the device at work here. The use of the verb *to screw* to describe sexual intercourse invites us to view this latter activity in terms drawn from carpentry and mechanics. As noted above, many facts about screws and screwing are applicable to the new realm as well. And this is just what we should expect of an apt metaphor. But "screwing" is not a fresh, new label for intercourse. This use of the term is accepted, though deemed coarse and impolite. Thus we are dealing here with a dead metaphor—an established use of the word "screw" which has additional depth and resonance because it associates the two realms of sex and mechanics. The central claim I want to make in this paper is that metaphors of this sort are our primary vehicles for conveying attitudes. The offensiveness of the verb *to screw* is rooted in the attitude it conveys toward the female role in intercourse, and this attitude can be specified by attending to the details of the metaphor. None of the claims I shall make are tied to any one theory of metaphor. While there is much debate about the nature of metaphorical truth, the paraphrasability of metaphors, and so on, I shall skirt these issues. I trust that my positive claims about metaphor will apply to any reasonable account of that trope.

The relation between sexism and metaphor has been charted ably by Robert Baker in his article "'Pricks' and 'Chicks': A Plea for 'Persons.'" I want to expand on his work by showing in detail how metaphors can serve to express attitudes. But let me first outline Baker's position. Baker claims that the way in which we identify something reflects our conception of it. This claim is not controversial. It may even be tautological on some reading of "concept." However, the identifications Baker focuses on throughout his paper are metaphorical ones. This enlivens things because metaphors are not finitely paraphrasable. Since their implications can be spun out at length, the identifications they convey are comparably complex.

To establish his claim, Baker first considers racial identifications. He compares the differing conceptions of blacks conveyed by the four labels "Negro," "colored," "Afro-American," and "black." In the course of his discussion, he imagines the remarks "Where did that girl get to?" and "Who is the new boy that Lou hired to help out at the filling stations?" voiced by white Southerners, and then comments:

> If the persons the terms apply to are adult Afro-Americans, then 'girl' and 'boy' are metaphorical identifications. The fact that the metaphorical identifications in question are standard in the language reflects that certain characteristics of the objects properly classified as boys and girls (for example, immaturity, inability to take care of themselves, need for guidance) are generally held by those who use the identifications to be properly attributable to Afro-Americans.

Baker's acknowledgment that these metaphors are standard usage is important, for it establishes that the metaphors in question are dead metaphors. The Southerners who use them do not first think long and hard about race relations, then consciously construct metaphors which reveal the situation. Rather, they use the terms "boy" and "girl" because these are common currency. Probably few speakers spell out the implications of these terms for themselves as Baker has in the passage quoted above. Nonetheless, these implications are available—at least potentially—to any competent speaker. They resonate in each metaphorical use of the terms "boy" and "girl" quite unlike the supposed echoes of "buc," "fustis," and "ficken" resonating in each use of "fuck."

This is the important difference between Baker's account of the offensiveness of certain idioms and the account I proposed and rejected in Part I of this paper—the implications of dead metaphors are known or accessible to their speakers, while etymological details often are not. To see this, note that dead metaphors are those which have become trite and commonplace. Tenor and vehicle have been associated so frequently that their juxtaposition no longer seems fresh or illuminating. Given this long and public liaison, it follows that neither tenor nor vehicle can be entirely mysterious unless the metaphor was consistently misunderstood. (One obvious exception to this claim is the use of metaphor in scientific theories. Here the subject matter is indeed arcane and the presence of metaphor signals that our understanding is not yet complete. However, these cases needn't concern us here since our problem is ordinary language and its power to offend and oppress.) Finally, these comments about metaphor apply equally to metaphorical identifications. These are simply cases where instead of a full statement of the metaphor ("A is B") the name or description of the vehicle replaces that of the tenor ("B is o" replaces "A is f").

Baker takes the account of metaphorical identification which emerges from his discussion of racism and applies it to a second area, that of sexism. He argues that many of our ways of identifying women involve (dead) metaphors which insult and belittle. Among the categories of metaphorical identification he points out are animal terms ("chick," "fox"), toy terms ("doll"), juvenile terms ("babe," "kid," "sis") as well as more explicitly sexual and/or anatomical terms. I believe Baker is right about the force of these terms, though I grant there are certain cases which his account does not explain. For example, his theory does not apply to terms (like "fuck") which offend because we class them as offensive. Nor does it apply to terms which offend by excluding women from consideration. Examples here include general labels like "chairman" and "fireman" as well as the personal pronouns "he" and "his" when used to agree with an antecedent of unspecified gender ("everyone," "someone"). Neither of these examples offends in virtue of metaphorical implications. (However, in keeping with Baker's program we can explain both by reference to a second figure of speech: synecdoche. Both wrongly take part of humanity—the male sex—and use it to stand for the whole. The resulting idioms make it all too easy for women to be overlooked.)

ATTITUDE AND METAPHOR

Despite these lacunae, Baker's account fits a sizable number of cases of sexism in language. However, Baker calls our attention to the relation between metaphor and sexism without explaining how this relation fosters the oppression of women. I believe this is a fact in need of explanation. In what follows, I shall extend Baker's program by proposing an account of how metaphorical identifications oppress and offend. I suggest that metaphors often express attitudes. In particular, I suggest that the metaphorical identifications which Baker discusses express contemptuous and disdainful attitudes towards women. To justify this claim, I shall present three sorts of evidence. First, I shall present and discuss a single example, drawn from a novel of Willa Cather. Rather than argue in the abstract that metaphors can express attitudes, I shall examine a particular passage and argue that the best interpretation of it accords with my theory. Next, I shall offer some evidence drawn from social psychology. I shall examine the methods social psychologists employ to test for attitudes and point out the central role played by metaphor. Finally, I shall offer a more abstract argument for my claim, based on "structural" resemblances between attitude and metaphor.

Consider the following passages from *The Professor's House:*

> He loved his family, he would make any sacrifice for them, but just now he couldn't live with them. He must be alone. That was more necessary to him than anything had ever been, more necessary than his marriage had been in his vehement youth. He could not live with his family again—not even with Lillian. Especially not with Lillian! Her nature was intense and positive; it was like a chiselled surface, a die, a stamp upon which he could not be beaten out any longer. If her character were reduced to an heraldic device, it would be a hand (a beautiful hand) holding flaming arrows—the shafts of her violent loves and hates, her clear-cut ambition.

In these lines Willa Cather details the reactions of her protagonist, Professor Godfrey St. Peter, to the news that his family is returning early from a European tour. That passage tells us a good deal about St. Peter's temperament, loyalties, and needs, his early attachments and his current desires. But my interest is in the Professor's description of his wife, Lillian. Just what is revealed by the simile comparing her nature to a sharp metallic die, or the metaphor imagining her character as a heraldic device? What do we learn about the professor in learning that *these* are his thoughts?

For a start, we do not learn about the Professor's beliefs. At least not in any straightforward sense. One might object that St. Peter expresses at least the belief that Lillian's character can be represented by a heraldic device of such and such a sort. But little follows from this concession. The Professor uses figurative language to talk about his wife. His beliefs about Lillian herself are of primary interest, not his beliefs about the suitability of various metaphors. And his endorsement of a particular trope does little to reveal his literal beliefs about his wife. This is so in part because metaphors aren't readily paraphrased; also because we rarely resort to metaphor to formulate and communicate our literal (pedestrian) beliefs. Thus, although the Professor's description is revealing, it doesn't reveal his beliefs about Lillian.

Nor does it reveal particular emotions he feels toward Lillian. Granted, the tone of the entire passage is hysterical, and its general topic seems to be love. But neither love nor hysteria characterizes St. Peter's portrait of Lillian. Although the opening sentence of the passage assures us that St. Peter loves his family, his portrait reveals love's absence, or its aftermath. (He remarks later, "Surely the saddest thing in the world is falling out of love—if once one has ever fallen in.") Similarly, although St. Peter seems hysterical and overwrought in this passage, these emotions do not carry over to his description of Lillian. She is not the object of his hysteria. Instead she receives a knowing, considered assessment.

What, then, does the Professor's description convey? I suggest it expresses his attitude toward Lillian. It reveals, first, the Professor's admiration for his wife. The words "intense," "positive," "flaming," and "violent" attest to her strength, while the mention of a heraldic device connotes nobility, privilege, and respect. The assessment is not entirely admiring, however, for many of St. Peter's terms come from the vocabularies of war and technology. Here Lillian is characterized as strong in a more pejorative sense—strength as hardness. The metaphors of the die and stamp suggest unyielding resistance, insistent repetition. St. Peter pictures himself weary, beaten, obliterated by her stamp. The mention of a chiselled surface provides further reinforcement, not only with the immediate image of cold stone and hard edges, but also in its muted suggestion of struggle, of an adversary relationship. (Compare chiselling stone with casting bronze, building clay.) In all these metaphors Lillian is portrayed as awesome, strong, stubborn, and dangerous. The final conceit suggests more specific criticisms of her character—the violence of her emotions and the transparence of her ambition.

The two figures of speech St. Peter employs to describe Lillian are thus immensely effective. They convey his admiration and awe, his distaste and defeat. I claim that these features indicate the Professor's attitude towards his wife. What do I mean by an attitude? Examples might include admiration, approval, dislike and disdain. Attitudes are intentional states (in Brentano's sense). Thus they are object directed; all attitudes are attitudes toward or attitudes about something or other. In addition, attitudes involve beliefs about their objects and convey evaluation of them. If I admire Jane because she is intelligent, capable, and sympathetic, then Jane is the object of my attitude, and my attitude is grounded in my beliefs about her character. Since intelligence, competence, and sympathy are traits we prize, my attitude conveys a favorable evaluation of Jane. Some of my beliefs about Jane might be mistaken. If so, my attitude is misplaced or inappropriate. Attitudes themselves are not classed as true or false. In sum, if we imagine a continuum of psychological states, attitudes occupy an intermediate ground between judgment and belief, on the one hand, and emotions and moods, on the other. Like emotions, attitudes are object-directed, non-propositional and evaluative. Yet attitudes are less visceral than emotions, less partisan, and less closely tied to distinctive behavioral manifestations. Returning to our example, the Professor's attitude towards Lillian is not conveyed by the bare factual claim that he takes her loves and hates to be violent. Thus it is not merely a belief or judgment about his wife. Nor is it a violent state which has overwhelmed him. The reflective mood of his extended metaphorical description indicates that he is not in the throes of a ravaging emotion. His psychological state lies between these poles.

My claim that metaphors express attitudes must be qualified in several respects. First, I do not claim that *all* metaphors serve this function, nor that they do so in all contexts. I would certainly be at a loss to determine the attitude conveyed by "The camel is the ship of the desert!" My claim is that sometimes metaphors express attitudes. And second, even in those cases where metaphors do convey attitude, I do not claim that we can always specify just which attitude is being expressed. The example discussed above is a case in point. The Professor's attitude towards Lillian is a complex attitude for which we have no standard name. It is not plain awe or unalloyed admiration. Despite our inability to name his attitude, I believe it is correct and illuminating to classify it as such. Finally, attitudes, like emotions and beliefs, can be unconscious. There may well be cases where someone has an attitude, expresses it in various ways (including metaphorical identifications of the attitude-object) yet doesn't know that this is so. Thus we are not always the best authorities about the attitudes we hold, reveal, express. Note that this accords with the claims made in Part I of this paper about knowledge and oppression. We do not always know when we are being oppressed; we can in fact become unwitting collaborators in our own oppression. (I do not, by the way, claim that the attitude St. Peter expresses toward his wife Lillian is a sexist one; it is simply a negative attitude, directed towards a woman.) . . .

INTENTIONAL TRANSCENDENCE

My concluding argument for this connection between metaphor and attitude appeals to what I shall (loosely) call structural considerations. I claim that there is an isomorphism between metaphor on the one hand and attitude on the other which makes metaphor a particularly apt vehicle for the expression of attitude. This isomorphism has to do with the logical structure of attitude and metaphor: in particular, with their irreducibility to belief and to literal talk, respectively. I shall call this shared trait intentional transcendence.

Consider one of the central questions about metaphors—their paraphrasability. Can the significance of a metaphor be completely spelled out? In the article "Aesthetic Problems of Modern Philosophy," Stanley Cavell argues that metaphors are paraphrasable. To prove his point, he proposes the following paraphrase of the metaphor "Juliet is the sun":

> Romeo means that Juliet is the warmth of his world; that his day begins with her; that only in her nourishment can he grow. And his declaration suggests that the moon, which other lovers use as emblems of their love, is merely her reflected light, and dead in comparison; and so on.

Cavell's "and so on" is crucial here. He qualifies his claim by noting that metaphors are paraphrasable in a manner "marked by its concluding sense of 'and so on.'" Thus Romeo does not mean that Juliet is like the sun in four respects and four respect only. His metaphor has further significance, further ramifications to be drawn out. For instance, that Juliet is the center of his universe. This richness is what some call the pregnancy of metaphor; it is what I mean by the phrase "intentional transcendence." A number of other writers call attention to this trait. For example, Max Black distinguishes a class of interaction metaphors which cannot be replaced by literal translations without loss of cognitive content. Philip Wheelwright distinguishes two forms of metaphor, one of which—diaphor—creates new meaning through presentational juxtaposition. Nelson Goodman's metaphorical account of metaphor (as the transfer of a schema to an alien realm, where the immigrant sometimes effects new organization and new associations) gives a picture of paraphrase which helps to explain its richness. Alan Tormey's subjunctive theory of metaphor also supports this view. Relations between tenor and vehicle can be spun out indefinitely because we can explore countless crannies of the possible world in which the counterfactual holds.

Consider now intentional transcendence in the psychological realm. Just as metaphors resist collapse into a finite set of literal sentences, so attitudes resist collapse into a finite set of grounding beliefs. All attitudes are belief-dependent. For example, to have an attitude of admiration towards Lauren Bacall, I must hold a number of factual beliefs about her (e.g. that she is the blonde actress in "To Have and Have Not," that she also appears in "Key Largo," that she was Bogart's wife). Such beliefs establish that my attitude is directed towards the proper object. There aren't any particular beliefs about Bacall such that I need to hold *those* beliefs in order to have an attitude directed towards her. I simply must have some collection of beliefs about her, some of which are accurate. [If all my beliefs about Bacall were false and applied instead to Ginger Rogers—e.g. "She's the brassy redheaded actress who danced with Fred Astaire"—then my attitude is not an attitude towards Lauren Bacall at all. It is an attitude towards Ginger Rogers about whom I have (at least) this false belief: that her name is Lauren Bacall.]

This dependence of attitude upon belief has been ably documented in the literature. Though some collection of Bacall-beliefs must be present in order to direct my admiration, these beliefs do not constitute my attitude. This is so because many of Bacall's detractors might hold the very same beliefs logically involved in my attitude. In addition to the beliefs which direct my attitude towards the appropriate object (in this case, Bacall) I hold additional beliefs which determine which attitude it is. Thus, if I think Bacall acts well, is beautiful and intelligent, then my attitude is one of admiration. If I think her a cheap brassy blonde with no acting skills, my attitude is instead one of disdain. Note that my admiration for Bacall does not reduce to this further set of beliefs about her. First, because other people might admire her without holding these particular beliefs. And second, because some might hold these same beliefs without admiring her. Nor can we reduce admiration to holding a preponderance of favorable beliefs, nor even to the single belief that its object is admirable. It is always possible to hold such beliefs about a person (object) yet not admire that person (object).

My point about these attitudes is this: they are no more reducible to the cluster of beliefs which ground them than metaphors are reducible to the set of sentences which provide a paraphrase. To proclaim Bacall stunning, quick, and talented is not yet to admire her; to cite ten ways in which Juliet resembles the sun is not yet to exhaust Shakespeare's metaphor. Thus metaphors and attitudes alike have a sort of intentional transcendence which accords them both richness and mystery. And this structural similarity suggests why metaphorical language might express attitudes more effectively than literal talk *or* wordless gestures. . . .

. . . If correct, my analysis explains not only how metaphorical language can hurt and offend, but also how it can flatter, comfort and soothe. It does so by conveying the various attitudes which are essential to our evaluations, enthusiasms, prejudices, and passions.

LEWIS CARROLL
Humpty Dumpty

LEWIS CARROLL *(1832–1898), whose real name was Charles Lutwidge Dodgson, was an English mathematician and logician. His mother died when he went away to college, and he became increasingly drawn to the company of children, especially little girls. He was afflicted with a stammer, which made him uncomfortable in the company of adults. His books* Alice in Wonderland *and* Through the Looking Glass *are two of the great children's books in English. He also published mathematical works.*

HOWEVER, the egg only got larger and larger, and more and more human: when she had come within a few yards of it, she saw that it had eyes and a nose and mouth; and, when she had come close to it, she saw clearly that it was HUMPTY DUMPTY himself. "It can't be anybody else!" she said to herself. "I'm as certain of it, as if his name were written all over his face!"

It might have been written a hundred times, easily, on that enormous face. Humpty Dumpty was sitting, with his legs crossed like a Turk, on the top of a high wall—such a narrow one that Alice quite wondered how he could keep his balance—and, as his eyes were steadily fixed in the opposite direction, and he didn't take the least notice of her, she thought he must be a stuffed figure, after all.

"And how exactly like an egg he is!" she said aloud, standing with her hands ready to catch him, for she was every moment expecting him to fall. . . .

"Don't stand chattering to yourself like that," Humpty Dumpty said, looking at her for the first time, "but tell me your name and your business."

"My *name* is Alice, but"

"It's a stupid name enough!" Humpty Dumpty interrupted impatiently. "What does it mean?"

"*Must* a name mean something?" Alice asked doubtfully.

"Of course it must," Humpty Dumpty said with a short laugh: "*my* name means the shape I am—and a good handsome shape it is, too. With a name like yours, you might be any shape, almost."

"Why do you sit out here all alone?" said Alice, not wishing to begin an argument.

"Why, because there's nobody with me!" cried Humpty Dumpty. "Did you think I didn't know the answer to *that?* Ask another." . . .

"What a beautiful belt you've got on!" Alice suddenly remarked. . . . "At least," she corrected herself on second thoughts, "a beautiful cravat, I should have said—no, a belt, I mean—I beg your pardon!" she added in dismay, for Humpty Dumpty looked thoroughly offended, and she began to wish she hadn't chosen that subject. "If only I knew," she thought to herself, "which was neck and which was waist!"

Evidently Humpty Dumpty was very angry, though he said nothing for a minute or two. When he *did* speak again, it was in a deep growl.

"It is a—*most—provoking*—thing," he said at last, "when a person doesn't know a cravat from a belt!"

"I know it's very ignorant of me," Alice said, in so humble a tone that Humpty Dumpty relented.

"It's a cravat, child, and a beautiful one, as you say. It's a present from the White King and Queen. There now!"

Carroll, Lewis, "Humpty Dumpty," from *Through the Looking Glass,* New York: Heritge Press, 1941.

"Is it really?" said Alice, quite pleased to find that she *had* chosen a good subject, after all.

"They gave it to me," Humpty Dumpty continued thoughtfully, as he crossed one knee over the other and clasped his hand round it, "they gave it to me—for an un-birthday present."

"I beg your pardon?" Alice said with a puzzled air.

"I'm not offended," said Humpty Dumpty.

"I mean, what *is* an un-birthday present?"

"A present given when it isn't your birthday, of course."

Alice considered a little. "I like birthday presents best," she said at last.

"You don't know what you're talking about!" cried Humpty Dumpty. "How many days are there in a year?"

"Three hundred and sixty-five," said Alice.

"And how many birthdays have you?"

"One."

"And if you take one from three hundred and sixty-five, what remains?"

"Three hundred and sixty-four, of course."

Humpty Dumpty looked doubtful. "I'd rather see that done on paper," he said.

Alice couldn't help smiling as she took out her memorandum-book, and worked the sum for him:

365

−1

364

. . . "[T]hat shows that there are three hundred and sixty-four days when you might get un-birthday presents"

"Certainly," said Alice.

"And only *one* for birthday presents, you know. There's glory for you!"

"I don't know what you mean by 'glory,'" Alice said.

Humpty Dumpty smiled contemptuously. "Of course you don't—till I tell you. I meant 'there's a nice knock-down argument for you!'"

"But 'glory' doesn't mean 'a nice knock-down argument,'" Alice objected.

"When *I* use a word," Humpty Dumpty said, in rather a scornful tone, "it means just what I choose it to mean—neither more nor less."

"The question is," said Alice, "whether you *can* make words mean so many different things."

"The question is," said Humpty Dumpty, "which is to be master—that's all."

Alice was too much puzzled to say anything; so after a minute Humpty Dumpty began again. "They've a temper, some of them—particularly verbs: they're the proudest—adjectives you can do anything with but not verbs—however, *I* can manage the whole lot of them! Impenetrability! That's what *I* say!"

"Would you tell me, please," said Alice, "what that means?"

"Now you talk like a reasonable child," said Humpty Dumpty, looking very much pleased. "I meant by 'impenetrability' that we've had enough of that subject, and it would be just as well if you'd mention what you mean to do next, as I suppose you don't mean to stop here all the rest of your life."

"That's a great deal to make one word mean," Alice said in a thoughtful tone.

"When I make a word do a lot of work like that," said Humpty Dumpty, "I always pay it extra."

"Oh!" said Alice. She was too much puzzled to make any other remark.

"Ah, you should see 'em come round me of a Saturday night," Humpty Dumpty went on, wagging his head gravely from side to side, "for to get their wages, you know."

(Alice didn't venture to ask what he paid them with; and so you see I can't tell *you*.)

PART FOUR

THE DILEMMAS
OF PERSONHOOD

CHAPTER EIGHT

WHO AM I?

Y ou have heard your mother tell the story a thousand times. One day, when you were very little, just past your second birthday, your parents went to visit Aunt Helen. You sat in the back seat, apparently asleep. Next to you your mother had placed a box of cupcakes, Aunt Helen's favorites. Having arrived, your mother went to get you and the cupcakes out of the car. At that point she discovered only you in the back seat, because you had managed in some way to consume every one of the cupcakes. Cooing and gurgling, you peered out from behind a mask of chocolate and crumbs.

Underlying stories such as this one is an assumption that only a philosopher would question seriously, namely, that there is such a thing as personal (or self) identity. Personal identity is what accounts for the fact that we all have childhoods, that once we were small, not very knowledgeable or emotionally complex, whereas now we are grown and full of complex thoughts, feelings, and beliefs. Philosophers' attempts to account for our persistence through time and through change fall into roughly three categories. First, there are those who explain personal identity in mentalistic terms. Our identity through time is considered to be a function of the continuity of our thoughts, beliefs, and feelings (sometimes referred to jointly as our "personality" or "character"). Second, there are those who explain personal identity in terms of the continuity of our bodies. Although the body that you have now is larger than the one you had when you were two years old, their "spatio-temporal" continuity provides the basis for your identity through time. Finally, some philosophers argue that personal identity is just an illusion. In fact, we don't persist through time and change.

The earliest and most familiar version of the view that personal identity can be explained in mentalistic terms has its origin in the religious belief in the existence of the soul. Although philosophers since Descartes have tended to substitute the term "mind" for "soul," the underlying idea is basically the same: What now makes you the same person as the one who overindulged in cupcakes many years ago is the persistence of your soul. This view has what many people consider the added advantage of allowing for the possibility of continued existence past the death of the body.

In the dialogue by John Perry, Sam Miller is a passionate advocate of what we will call the *Soul Theory*. He finds a formidable opponent, however, in Gretchen Weirob, who insists that her identity is a function of nothing more than the identity of her (live) body. We will call that view the *Body Theory*. Weirob is concerned to persuade Miller not so much that his belief in the existence of the soul is misguided, but rather that the soul, even if it exists, cannot be responsible for personal identity.

Although the soul has fallen into disrepute as a means for explaining personal identity, philosophers have been reluctant to abandon the spirit of the Soul Theory. That is, many philosophers would like to account for personal identity in terms that acknowledge our special human uniqueness. Our rich mental life distinguishes us from other animals, and we are all psychologically distinct from one another. Surely, then, our self-identity must be intimately tied to our mental characteristics. John Locke is a famous advocate of the view, usually called the *Memory Theory,* that personal identity is based on self-consciousness, in particular, on memories about one's former experiences. Just as you cannot think my thoughts and I cannot think yours, so, too, you cannot remember my experiences and I cannot remember yours. This unique relationship that each of us has to his or her former experiences guarantees the link between what are sometimes called "stages" of a person. Suppose that you are now remembering the day you learned to ride a bicycle. Because you *now* are remembering the experience as one that happened to you *then,* you are self-identical to the person who had that experience. One difficulty with the Memory Theory is that we forget many of our experiences. You don't, for example, remember eating the cupcakes when you were two. You probably don't remember what you had for lunch on July 25, 1997, nor what the first word of this chapter is. Locke needs to specify precisely how we are to explain the connection between our present selves and those forgotten stages of our former selves.

Another difficulty with the Memory Theory is that our memories are not always accurate. For example, you swear that you left the sponge in the sink; you remember doing so very clearly. When you later find it in the refrigerator, you realize that you only *seemed* to remember leaving it in the sink. Your memory was merely apparent, not genuine. Similarly, we have all heard of people who believe that they are Abraham Lincoln, Jesus Christ, even Janis Joplin. What seem to them to be real memories cannot be. Yet, if it is only genuine memories that guarantee the link between the stages of a person, we need to determine which memories are the genuine ones. Unfortunately, the most obvious way to distinguish genuine from apparent memories is by pointing out that a genuine memory is a memory of an experience actually had by the rememberer. The person who is having the memory must be the same as the person who had the experience. But in distinguishing genuine from apparent memory in this way we have presupposed the existence of a persisting, self-identical person. We cannot use the concept of memory to explain personal identity if the only way to explain memory is by appealing to the concept of personal identity. As attractive as the Memory Theory might initially seem to be, it leaves us with this discouragingly large problem.

This problem, sometimes referred to as the "problem of circularity," is alluded to in the selection by Meredith W. Michaels. Much of the contemporary debate over personal identity centers around an attempt to avoid the circularity problem. That is, philosophers want to provide a noncircular way of distinguishing between genuine and apparent memories. The *Brain Theory,* discussed by Michaels, is one such attempt. Basically, the Brain Theory argues that "whither my brain goes, there go I." As you will see, the Brain Theory and its principal rival, the Body Theory, encourage some bizarre speculations about the results of imagined "brain transplants" (alternatively called "body transplants"). Justin Leiber's story provides a glimpse into a future where such practices are an ordinary part of life. Although stories like his appear fanciful, they provoke us to consider just what we think *is* responsible for our identity through time.

Long ago, David Hume came to the conclusion that nothing is responsible for our identity through time because, strictly speaking, it is only a "fiction." If we look inward in the hopes of finding a source of identity, all we find is an array of disconnected and distinct "perceptions" (that is, ideas). Our desire to forge them into a coherent, temporally continuous whole is so strong that we simply invent one and call it a "self." Hume's argument is a masterpiece of philosophical gymnastics, so beware.

Simone de Beauvoir was the first philosopher to develop a systematic account of the conceptual relationships that constitute our understanding of gendered identity. In her groundbreaking book, *The Second Sex,* she argued that gender is a socially constructed phenomenon. A person is not born a woman or a man, but rather learns to become one through specific social practices—practices that create a specifically gendered consciousness. According to de Beauvoir, "one is not born, but becomes a woman."

The idea of duplicating a person has been around for a long time. Science fiction is full of replicants and clones. But reality is catching up with fiction. The cloned sheep Dolly was born to much media fanfare in 1997. Since then, clone-watchers have raced to predict when the first cloned human will appear. Maybe he or she already has. Given its science fictional history, cloning is prone to considerable misunderstanding, both with regard to how it is done and to its implications for personal identity. What relation does a clone have to the person from whom she was cloned? To other clones from the same person? What are the moral dangers of cloning? Under what circumstances, if any, is it morally justifiable to clone a human being? Is reproductive cloning a defensible solution to infertility? The selection on cloning in this chapter is aimed at clarifying some of the confusion attendant upon cloning human beings. Robert Wachbroit gives us a philosophical consideration of the relationship between cloning and other reproductive practices.

The problem of personal identity is particularly troubling because it appears so clear that we do indeed persist through time. Surely, it is absurd to suppose that the person who began reading this chapter only a few minutes ago no longer exists. Aren't you that very same person? Of course you are. But if it is so obvious that one and the same person is born, lives a life, and eventually dies, why is it so difficult for philosophers to explain personal identity? The problem of personal identity is a paradigm case of the tension between the appeal of ordinary experience and the demands of philosophy.

JOHN PERRY
The First Night

JOHN PERRY *teaches philosophy at Stanford University. He specializes in philosophy of language and metaphysics. Among his publications are* Identity, Personal Identity, and the Self *(2002) and* A Dialogue on Personal Identity and Immortality *(1978), from which this selection is taken.*

THIS is a record of conversations of Gretchen Weirob, a teacher of philosophy at a small midwestern college, and two of her friends. The conversations took place in her hospital room on the three nights before she died from injuries sustained in a motorcycle accident. Sam Miller is a chaplain and a longtime friend of Weirob's; Dave Cohen is a former student of hers.

COHEN

I can hardly believe what you say, Gretchen. You are lucid and do not appear to be in great pain. And yet you say things are hopeless?

WEIROB

These devices can keep me alive for another day or two at most. Some of my vital organs have been injured beyond anything the doctors know how to repair, apart from certain rather radical measures I have rejected. I am not in much pain. But as I understand it that is not a particularly good sign. My brain was uninjured and I guess that's why I am as lucid as I ever am. The whole situation is a bit depressing, I fear. But here's Sam Miller. Perhaps he will know how to cheer me up.

MILLER

Good evening, Gretchen. Hello, Dave. I guess there's not much point in beating around the bush, Gretchen; the medics tell me you're a goner. Is there anything I can do to help?

WEIROB

Crimenetley, Sam! You deal with the dying every day. Don't you have anything more comforting to say than "Sorry to hear you're a goner"?

MILLER

Well, to tell you the truth, I'm a little at a loss for what to say to you. Most people I deal with are believers like I am. We talk of the prospects for survival. I give assurance that God, who is just and merciful, would not permit such a travesty as that our short life on this earth should be the end of things. But you and I have talked about religious and philosophical issues for years. I have never been able to find in you the least inclination to believe in God; indeed, it's a rare day when you are sure that your friends have minds or that you can see your own hand in front of your face, or that there is any reason to believe that the sun will rise tomorrow. How can I hope to comfort you with the prospect of life after death, when I know you will regard it as having no probability whatsoever?

WEIROB

I would not require so much to be comforted, Sam. Even the possibility of something quite improbable can be comforting, in certain situations. When we used to play tennis, I beat you no more than one time in twenty. But this was enough to establish the possibility of beating you on any given occasion, and by focusing merely on the possibility I remained eager to play. Entombed in a secure prison, thinking our situation quite hopeless, we may find unutterable joy in the information that there is, after all, the slimmest possibility of escape. Hope provides comfort and hope does not always require probability. But we must believe that what we hope for is at least possible. So I will set an easier task for you. Simply persuade me that my survival after the death of this body, is *possible,* and I promise to be comforted. Whether you succeed or not, your attempts will be a diversion, for you know I like to talk philosophy more than anything else.

MILLER

But what is possibility, if not reasonable probability?

WEIROB

I do not mean possible in the sense of likely, or even in the sense of conforming to the known laws of physics or biology. I mean possible only in the weakest sense—of being conceivable, given the unavoidable facts. Within the next couple of days, this body will die. It will be buried and it will rot away. I ask that, given these facts, you explain to me how it even makes *sense* to talk of me continuing to exist. Just explain to me what it is I am to *imagine,* when I imagine surviving, that is consistent with these facts, and I shall be comforted.

MILLER

But then what is there to do? There are many conceptions of immortality, of survival past the grave, which all seem to make good sense. Surely not the possibility, but only the probability can be doubted. Take your choice! Christians believe in life, with a body, in some Hereafter—the details vary, of course, from sect to sect. There is the Greek idea of the body as a prison, from which we escape at death—so that we have continued life without a body. Then there are conceptions in which, so to speak, we merge with the flow of being—

WEIROB

I must cut short your lesson in comparative religion. Survival means surviving, no more, no less. I have no doubts that I shall merge with being; plants will take root in my remains, and the chemicals that I am will continue to make their contribution to life. I am enough of an ecologist to be comforted. But survival, if it is anything, must offer comforts of a different sort, the comforts of *anticipation.* Survival means that tomorrow, or sometime in the future, there will be someone who will experience, who will see and touch and smell—or at the very least, think and reason and remember. And this person will be *me.* This person will be related to me in such a way that it is correct for me to anticipate, to look forward to, those future experiences. And I am related to her in such a way that it will be right for her to remember what I have thought and done, to feel remorse for what I have done wrong, and pride in what I have done right. And the only relation that supports anticipation and memory in this way, is simply *identity.* For it is never correct to anticipate, as happening to oneself, what will happen to someone else, is it? Or to remember, as one's own thoughts and deeds, what someone else did? So, don't give me merger with being, or some such nonsense. Give me identity, or let's talk about baseball or fishing—but I'm sorry to get so emotional. I react strongly when words which mean one thing are used for another—when one talks about survival, but does not mean to say that the same person will continue to exist. It's such a sham!

MILLER

I'm sorry. I was just trying to stay in touch with the times, if you want to know the truth, for when I read modern theology or talk to my students who have studied Eastern religions, the notion of survival simply as continued existence of the same person seems out of date. Merger with Being! Merger with Being! That's all I hear. My own beliefs are quite simple, if somewhat vague. I think you will live again—with or without a body, I don't know—I draw comfort from my belief that you and I will be together again, after I also die. We will communicate, somehow. We will continue to grow spiritually. That's what I believe, as surely as I believe that I am sitting here. For I don't know how God could be excused, if this small sample of life is all that we are allotted; I don't know why He should have created us, if these few years of toil and torment are the end of it—

WEIROB

Remember our deal, Sam. You don't have to convince me that survival is probable, for we both agree you would not get to first base. You have only to convince me that it is possible. The only condition is that it be real survival we are talking about, not some up-to-date ersatz survival, which simply amounts to what any ordinary person would call totally ceasing to exist.

MILLER

I guess I just miss the problem, then. Of course, it's possible. You just continue to exist after your body dies. What's to be defended or explained? You want details? Okay. Two people meet a thousand years from now, in a place that may or may not be part of this physical universe. I am one and you are the other. So you must have survived. Surely you can imagine that. What else is there to say?

WEIROB

But in a few days *I* will quit breathing, *I* will be put into a coffin, *I* will be buried. And in a few months or a few years *I* will be reduced to so much humus. That, I take it, is obvious, is given. How then can you say that I am one of these persons a thousand years from now? Suppose I took this box of Kleenex and lit fire to it. It is reduced to ashes and I smash the ashes and flush them down the john. Then I say to you, go home and on the shelf will be *that very box of Kleenex*. It has survived! Wouldn't that be absurd? What sense could you make if it? And yet that is just what you say to me. I will rot away. And then, a thousand years later, there I will be. What sense does that make?

MILLER

There could be an *identical* box of Kleenex at your home, one just like it in every respect. And, in this sense, there is no difficulty in there being someone identical to you in the Hereafter, though your body has rotted away.

WEIROB

You are playing with words again. There could be an *exactly similar* box of Kleenex on my shelf. We sometimes use "identical" to mean "exactly similar," as when we speak of "identical twins." But I am using "identical" in a way in which *identity* is the condition of memory and correct anticipation. If I am told that tomorrow, though I will be dead, someone else that looks and sounds and thinks just like me will be alive—would that be comforting? Could I correctly *anticipate* having her experiences? Would it make sense for me to fear her pains and look forward to her pleasures? Would it be right for her to feel remorse at the harsh way I am treating you? Of course not. Similarity, however exact, is not identity. I use identity to mean there is but one thing. If I am to survive, there must be one person who lies in this bed now, and who talks to someone in your Hereafter ten or a thousand years from now. After all, what comfort could there be in the notion of a heavenly imposter, walking around getting credit for the few good things I have done?

MILLER

I'm sorry. I see that I was simply confused. Here is what I should have said. If
you were merely a live human body—as the Kleenex box is merely
cardboard and glue in a certain arrangement—then the death of your
body would be the end of you. But surely you are more than that,
fundamentally more than that. What is fundamentally you is not your
body, but your soul or self or mind.

WEIROB

Do you mean these words, "soul," "self," or "mind" to come to the same thing?

MILLER

Perhaps distinctions could be made, but I shall not pursue them now. I mean
the nonphysical and nonmaterial aspects of you, your consciousness. It is
this that I get at with these words, and I don't think any further
distinction is relevant.

WEIROB

Consciousness? I am conscious, for a while yet. I see, I hear, I think, I
remember. But "to be conscious"—that is a verb. What is the subject of
the verb, the thing which is conscious? Isn't it just this body, the same
object that is overweight, injured, and lying in bed?—and which will be
buried and not be conscious in a day or a week at the most?

MILLER

As you are a philosopher, I would expect you to be less muddled about these
issues. Did Descartes not draw a clear distinction between the body and
the mind, between that which is overweight, and that which is
conscious? Your mind or soul is immaterial, lodged in your body while
you are on earth. The two are intimately related but not identical. Now
clearly, what concerns us in survival is your mind or soul. It is this which
must be identical to the person before me now, and to the one I expect to
see in a thousand years in heaven.

WEIROB

So I am not really this body, but a soul or mind or spirit? And this soul cannot
be seen or felt or touched or smelt? That is implied, I take it, by the fact
that it is immaterial?

MILLER

That's right. Your soul sees and smells, but cannot be seen or smelt.

WEIROB

Let me see if I understand you. You would admit that I am the very same
person with whom you had lunch last week at Dorsey's?

MILLER

Of course you are.

WEIROB

Now when you say I am the same person, if I understand you, that is not a
    remark about this body you see and could touch and I fear can smell.
    Rather it is a remark about a soul, which you cannot see or touch or
    smell. The fact that the same body that now lies in front of you on the
    bed was across the table from you at Dorsey's—that would not mean that
    the same *person* was present on both occasions, if the same soul were not.
    And if, through some strange turn of events, the same soul were present
    on both occasions, but lodged in different bodies, then it *would* be the
    same person. Is that right?

MILLER

You have understood me perfectly. But surely, you understood all of this before!

WEIROB

But wait. I can repeat it, but I'm not sure I understand it. If you cannot see or
    touch or in any way perceive my soul, what makes you think the one you
    are confronted with now *is* the very same soul you were confronted with
    at Dorsey's?

MILLER

But I just explained. To say it is the same soul and to say it is the same person,
    are the same. And, of course, you are the same person you were before.
    Who else would you be if not yourself? You *were* Gretchen Weirob, and
    you *are* Gretchen Weirob.

WEIROB

But how do you know you are talking to Gretchen Weirob at all, and not
    someone else, say Barbara Walters or even Mark Spitz!

MILLER

Well, it's just obvious. I can see who I am talking to.

WEIROB

But all you can see is my body. You can see, perhaps, that the same body
    is before you now that was before you last week at Dorsey's. But you
    have just said that Gretchen Weirob is not a body but a soul. In
    judging that the same person is before you now as was before you
    then, you must be making a judgment about souls—which, you said,
    cannot be seen or touched or smelt or tasted. And so, I repeat, how
    do you know?

MILLER

Well, I *can* see that it is the same body before me now that was across the table
at Dorsey's. And I know that the same soul is connected with the body
now that was connected with it before. That's how I know it's you. I see
no difficulty in the matter.

WEIROB

You reason on the principle, "Same body, same self."

MILLER

Yes.

WEIROB

And would you reason conversely also? If there were in this bed Barbara
Walters' body—that is, the body you see every night on the news—
would you infer that it was not me, Gretchen Weirob, in the bed?

MILLER

Of course I would. How would you have come by Barbara Walters' body?

WEIROB

But then merely extend this principle to Heaven, and you will see that your
conception of survival is without sense. Surely this very body, which will
be buried and as I must so often repeat, *rot away*, will not be in your
Hereafter. Different body, different person. Or do you claim that a body
can rot away on earth, and then still wind up somewhere else? Must I
bring up the Kleenex box again?

MILLER

No, I do not claim that. But I also do not extend a principle, found reliable on
earth, to such a different situation as is represented by the Hereafter.
That a correlation between bodies and souls has been found on earth
does not make it inconceivable or impossible that they should separate.
Principles found to work in one circumstance may not be assumed to
work in vastly altered circumstances. January and snow go together here,
and one would be a fool to expect otherwise. But the principle does not
apply in southern California.

WEIROB

So the principle, "same body, same soul," is a well-confirmed regularity, not
something you know "a priori."

MILLER

By "a priori" you philosophers mean something which can be known without
observing what actually goes on in the world—as I can know that two

plus two equals four just by thinking about numbers, and that no bachelors are married, just by thinking about the meaning of "bachelor"?

WEIROB

Yes.

MILLER

Then you are right. If it was part of the meaning of "same body" that wherever we have the same body we have the same soul, it would have to obtain universally, in Heaven as well as on earth. But I just claim it is a generalization we know by observation on earth, and it need not automatically extend to Heaven.

WEIROB

But where do you get this principle? It simply amounts to a correlation between being confronted with the same body and being confronted with the same soul. To establish such a correlation in the first place, surely one must have some *other* means of judging sameness of soul. You do not have such a means; your principle is without foundation; either you really do not know the person before you now is Gretchen Weirob, the very same person you lunched with at Dorsey's, or what you do know has nothing to do with sameness of some immaterial soul.

MILLER

Hold on, hold on. You know I can't follow you when you start spitting out arguments like that. Now what is this terrible fallacy I'm supposed to have committed?

WEIROB

I'm sorry. I get carried away. Here—by way of a peace offering—have one of the chocolates Dave brought.

MILLER

Very tasty. Thank you.

WEIROB

Now why did you choose that one?

MILLER

Because it had a certain swirl on the top which shows that it is a caramel.

WEIROB

That is, a certain sort of swirl is correlated with a certain type of filling—the swirls with caramel, the rosettes with orange, and so forth.

MILLER

Yes. When you put it that way, I see an analogy. Just as I judged that the filling
would be the same in this piece as in the last piece that I ate with such a
swirl, so I judge that the soul with which I am conversing is the same as
the last soul with which I conversed when sitting across from that body.
We see the outer wrapping and infer what is inside.

WEIROB

But how did you come to realize that swirls of that sort and caramel insides
were so associated?

MILLER

Why, from eating a great many of them over the years. Whenever I bit into a
candy with that sort of swirl, it was filled with caramel.

WEIROB

Could you have established the correlation had you never been allowed to bite
into a candy and never seen what happened when someone else bit into
one? You could have formed the hypothesis, "same swirl, same filling."
But could you have ever established it?

MILLER

It seems not.

WEIROB

So your inference, in a particular case, to the identity of filling from the
identity of swirl would be groundless?

MILLER

Yes, it would. I think I see what is coming.

WEIROB

I'm sure you do. Since you can never, so to speak, bite into my soul, can never
see or touch it, you have no way of testing your hypothesis that sameness
of body means sameness of self.

MILLER

I dare say you are right. But now I'm a bit lost. What is supposed to follow
from all of this?

WEIROB

If, as you claim, identity of persons consisted in identity of immaterial
unobservable souls, then judgments of personal identity of the sort we

make every day whenever we greet a friend or avoid a pest are really judgments about such souls.

MILLER

Right.

WEIROB

But if such judgments were really about souls, they would all be groundless and without foundation. For we have no direct method of observing sameness of soul, and so—and this is the point made by the candy example—we can have no indirect method either.

MILLER

That seems fair.

WEIROB

But our judgments about persons are not simply groundless and silly, so we must not be judging of immaterial souls after all.

MILLER

Your reasoning has some force. But I suspect the problem lies in my defense of my position, and not the position itself. Look here—there *is* a way to test the hypothesis of a correlation after all. When I entered the room, I expected you to react just as you did—argumentatively and skeptically. Had the person with this body reacted completely differently perhaps I would have been forced to conclude it was not you. For example, had she complained about not being able to appear on the six o'clock news, and missing Harry Reasoner, and so forth, I might eventually have been persuaded it was Barbara Walters, and not you. Similarity of psychological characteristics—a person's attitudes, beliefs, memories, prejudices, and the like—is observable. These are correlated with identity of body on the one side, and of course with sameness of soul on the other. So the correlation between body and soul can be established after all by this intermediate link.

WEIROB

And how do you know that?

MILLER

Know what?

WEIROB

That where we have sameness of psychological characteristics, we have sameness of soul.

MILLER

Well, now you are really being just silly. The soul or mind is just that which is responsible for one's character, memory, belief. These are aspects of the mind, just as one's height, weight, and appearance are aspects of the body.

WEIROB

Let me grant for the sake of argument that belief, character, memory, and so forth are states of mind. That is, I suppose, I grant that what one thinks and feels is due to the states one's mind is in at that time. And I shall even grant that a mind is an immaterial thing—though I harbor the gravest doubts that this is so. I do not see how it follows that similarity of such traits requires, or is evidence to the slightest degree, for identity of the mind or soul. Let me explain my point with an analogy. If we were to walk out of this room, down past the mill and out towards Wilbur, what would we see?

MILLER

We would come to the Blue River, among other things.

WEIROB

And how would you recognize the Blue River? I mean, of course if you left from here, you would scarcely expect to hit the Platte or Niobrara. But suppose you were actually lost, and came across the Blue River in your wandering, just at that point where an old dam partly blocks the flow. Couldn't you recognize it?

MILLER

Yes, I'm sure as soon as I saw that part of the river I would again know where I was.

WEIROB

And how would you recognize it?

MILLER

Well, the turgid brownness of the water, the sluggish flow, the filth washed up on the banks, and such.

WEIROB

In a word, the states of the water which makes up the river at the time you see it.

MILLER

Right.

WEIROB

If you saw blue clean water, with bass jumping, you would know it wasn't the Blue River.

MILLER

Of course.

WEIROB

So you expect, each time you see the Blue, to see the water, which makes it up, in similar states—not always exactly the same, for sometimes it's a little dirtier, but by and large similar.

MILLER

Yes, but what do you intend to make of this?

WEIROB

Each time you see the Blue, it consists of *different* water. The water that was in it a month ago may be in Tuttle Creek Reservoir or in the Mississippi or in the Gulf of Mexico by now. So the *similarity* of states of water, by which you judge the sameness of river, does not require *identity* of the water which is in those states at these various times.

MILLER

And?

WEIROB

And so just because you judge as to personal identity by reference to similarity of states of mind, it does not follow that the mind, or soul, is the same in each case. My point is this. For all you know, the immaterial soul which you think is lodged in my body might change from day to day, from hour to hour, from minute to minute, replaced each time by another soul psychologically similar. You cannot see it or touch it, so how would you know?

MILLER

Are you saying I don't really know who you are?

WEIROB

Not at all. *You* are the one who say personal identity consists in sameness of this immaterial, unobservable, invisible, untouchable soul. I merely point out that *if* it did consist in that, you *would* have no idea who I am. Sameness of body would not necessarily mean sameness of person. Sameness of psychological characteristics would not necessarily mean sameness of person. I am saying that if you do know who I am then you are wrong that personal identity consists in sameness of immaterial soul.

MILLER

I see. But wait. I believe my problem is that I simply forgot a main tenet of my theory. The correlation can be established in my own case. I know that *my* soul and my body are intimately and consistently found together. From this one case I can generalize, at least as concerns life in this world, that sameness of body is a reliable sign of sameness of soul. This leaves me free to regard it as intelligible, in the case of death, that the link between the particular soul and the particular body it has been joined with is broken.

WEIROB

This would be quite an extrapolation, wouldn't it, from one case directly observed, to a couple of billion in which only the body is observed? For I take it that we are in the habit of assuming, for every person now on earth, as well as those who have already come and gone, that the principle "one body, one soul" is in effect.

MILLER

This does not seem an insurmountable obstacle. Since there is nothing special about my case, I assume the arrangement I find in it applies universally until given some reason to believe otherwise. And I never have been.

WEIROB

Let's let that pass. I have another problem that is more serious. How is it that you know in your own case that there is a single soul which has been so consistently connected with your body?

MILLER

Now you really cannot be serious, Gretchen. How can I doubt that I am the same person I was? Is there anything more clear and distinct, less susceptible to doubt? How do you expect me to prove anything to you, when you are capable of denying my own continued existence from second to second? Without knowledge of our identity, everything we think and do would be senseless. How could I think if I did not suppose that the person who begins my thought is the one who completes it? When I act, do I not assume that the person who forms the intention is the very one who performs the action?

WEIROB

But I grant that a single *person* has been associated with your body since you were born. The question is whether one immaterial soul has been so associated—or more precisely, whether you are in a position to know it. You believe that a judgment that one and the same person has had your body all these many years is a judgment that one and the same immaterial soul has been lodged in it. I say that such judgments concerning the soul are totally mysterious, and that if our knowledge of sameness of persons consisted in knowledge of sameness of immaterial soul, it too would be totally mysterious. To point out, as you do, that it is not mysterious, but perhaps the most secure knowledge we have, the foundation of all reason and action, is simply to make the point that it cannot consist of knowledge of identity of an immaterial soul.

MILLER

You have simply asserted, and not established, that my judgment that a single soul has been lodged in my body these many years is mysterious.

WEIROB

Well, consider these possibilities. One is that a single soul, one and the same, has been with this body I call mine since it was born. The other is that one soul was associated with it until five years ago and then another, psychologically similar, inheriting all the old memories and beliefs, took over. A third hypothesis is that every five years a new soul takes over. A fourth is that every five minutes a new soul takes over. The most radical is that there is a constant flow of souls through this body, each psychologically similar to the preceding, as there is a constant flow of water molecules down the Blue. What evidence do I have that the first hypothesis, the "single soul hypothesis" is true, and not one of the others? Because I am the same person I was five minutes or five years ago? But the issue in question is simply whether from sameness or person, which isn't in doubt, we can infer sameness of soul. Sameness of body? But how do I establish a stable relationship between soul and body? Sameness of thoughts and sensations? But they are in constant flux. By the nature of the case, if the soul cannot be observed it cannot be observed to be the same. Indeed, no sense has ever been assigned to the phrase "same soul." Nor could any sense be attached to it! One would have to say what a single soul looked like or felt like, how an encounter with a single soul at different times differed from encounters with different souls. But this can hardly be done, since a soul according to your conception doesn't look or feel like *anything* at all. And so of course "souls" can afford no principle of identity. And so they cannot be used to bridge the gulf between my existence now and my existence in the hereafter.

MILLER

Do you doubt the existence of your own soul?

WEIROB

I haven't based my argument on there being no immaterial souls of the sort you describe, but merely on their total irrelevance to questions of personal identity, and so to questions of personal survival. I do indeed harbor grave doubts whether there are any immaterial souls of the sort to which you appeal. Can we have a notion of a soul unless we have a notion of the *same* soul? But I hope you do not think that means I doubt my own existence. I think I lie here, overweight and conscious. I think you can see me, not just some outer wrapping, for I think I am just a live human body. But that is not the basis of my argument. I give you these souls. I merely observe that they can by their nature provide no principle of personal identity.

MILLER

I admit I have no answer.

I'm afraid I do not comfort you, though I have perhaps provided you with some entertainment. Emerson said that a little philosophy turns one away from religion, but that deeper understanding brings one back. I know no one who has thought so long and hard about philosophy as you have. Will it never lead you back to a religious frame of mind?

WEIROB

My former husband used to say that a little philosophy turns one away from religion, and more philosophy makes one a pain in the neck. Perhaps he was closer to the truth than Emerson.

MILLER

Perhaps he was. But perhaps by tomorrow night I will have come up with a better argument.

WEIROB

I hope I live to hear it.

JOHN LOCKE
Of Identity and Diversity

JOHN LOCKE *(1632–1704) taught philosophy at Oxford until he earned his medical degree. He devoted considerable time to politics, and his two* Treatises on Government *were highly influential in establishing the theoretical grounds of the U.S. Constitution. Not only is he the founder of modern political liberalism, but also his* Essay Concerning Human Understanding *initiated what has come to be known as British empiricism.*

Locke, John, "Of Identity and Diversity," from *Essays Concerning Human Understanding,* Book 2, ed. Mary Whiton Calkins, The Open Court Philosphical Company, Book II, Ch. 27, 1905.

PERSONAL identity.—To find wherein personal identity consists, we must consider what "person" stands for; which I think, is a thinking intelligent being, that has reason and reflection, and can consider itself as itself, the same thinking thing, in different times and places; which it does only by that consciousness which is inseparable from thinking, and it seems to me essential to it: it being impossible for any one to perceive, without perceiving that he does perceive. When we see, hear, smell, taste, feel, meditate, or will any thing, we know that we do so. Thus it is always as to our present sensations and perceptions: and by this every one is to himself that which he calls "self;" it not being considered, in this case, whether the same self be continued in the same or diverse substances. For since consciousness always accompanies thinking, and it is that that makes every one to be what he calls "self," and thereby distinguishes himself from all other thinking things; in this alone consists personal identity, *i.e.,* the sameness of a rational being: and as far as this consciousness can be extended backwards to any past action or thought, so far reaches the identity of that person; it is the same self now it was then; and it is by the same self with this present one that now reflects on it, that that action was done.

Consciousness makes personal identity.—But it is farther inquired, whether it be the same identical substance? This, few would think they had reason to doubt of, if these perceptions, with their consciousness, always remained present in the mind, whereby the same thinking thing would be always consciously present, and, as would be thought, evidently the same to itself. But that which seems to make the difficulty is this, that this consciousness being interrupted always by forgetfulness, there being no moment of our lives wherein we have the whole train of all our past actions before our eyes in one view: but even the best memories losing the sight of one part whilst they are viewing another; and we sometimes, and that the greatest part of our lives, not reflecting on our past selves, being intent on our present thoughts, and, in sound sleep, having no thoughts at all, or at least, none with that consciousness which remarks our waking thoughts: I say, in all these cases, our consciousness being interrupted, and we losing the sight of our past selves, doubts are raised whether we are the same thinking thing, *i.e.,* the same substance, or no? which, however reasonable or unreasonable, concerns not personal identity at all: the question being, what makes the same person? and not, whether it be the same identical substance which always thinks in the same person? which in this case matters not at all; different substances, by the same consciousness (where they do partake in it), being united into one person, as well as different bodies by the same life are united into one animal, whose identity is preserved, in that change of substance, by the unity of one continued life. For it being the same consciousness that makes a man be himself to himself, personal identity depends on that only, whether it be annexed solely to one individual substance, or can be continued in a succession of several substances. For as far as any intelligent being can repeat the idea of any past action with the same consciousness it had of it at first, and with the same consciousness it has of any present action; so far it is the same personal self. For it is by the consciousness it has of its present thoughts and actions that it is self to itself now, and so will be the same self, as far as the same consciousness can extend to actions past or to come; and would be by distance of time, or change of substance, no more two persons than a man be two men, by wearing other clothes today than he did yesterday, with a long or short sleep between: the same consciousness uniting those distant actions into the same person, whatever substance contributed to their production.

Personal identity in change of substances.—That is so, we have some kind of evidence in our very bodies, all whose particles—whilst vitally united to this same thinking conscious self, so that we feel when they are touched, and are affected by and conscious of good or harm that happens to them—are a part of ourselves; *i.e.,* of our thinking conscious self. Thus the limbs of his body is to every one a part of himself: he sympathises and is concerned for them. Cut off a hand and thereby separate it from that consciousness he had of its heat, cold, and other affections, and it is then no longer a part of that which is himself, any more than the remotest part of matter. Thus we see the substance, whereof personal self consisted at one time, may be varied at another, without the change of personal identity; there being no question about the same person, though the limbs, which but now were a part of it, be cut off.

Whether in the change of thinking substances.— But the question is, Whether, if the same substance which thinks be changed, it can be the same person, or remaining the same, it can be different persons?

And to this I answer, First, This can be no question at all to those who place thought in a purely material, animal constitution, void of an immaterial substance. For, whether their supposition be true or no, it is plain they conceive personal identity preserved in something else than identity of substance; as animal identity is preserved in identity of life, and not of substance. And therefore those who place thinking in an immaterial substance only, before they can come to deal with these men, must show why personal identity cannot be preserved in the change of immaterial substances, or variety of particular immaterial substances, as well as animal identity is preserved in the change of material substances, or variety of particular bodies: unless they will say, it is one immaterial spirit that makes the same life in brutes, as it is one immaterial spirit that makes the same person in men, which the Cartesians at least will not admit, for fear of making brutes thinking things too.

But next, as to the first part of the question, Whether, if the same thinking substance (supposing immaterial substances only to think) be changed, it can be the same person? I answer, That cannot be resolved but by those who know what kind of substances they are that do think, and whether the consciousness of past actions can be transferred from one thinking substance to another. I grant, were the same consciousness the same individual action, it could not; but it being but a present representation of a past action, why it may not be possible that *that* may be represented to the mind to have been *which* really never was, will remain to be shown. And therefore how far the consciousness of past actions is annexed to any individual agent, so that another cannot possibly have it, will be hard for us to determine, till we know what kind of action it is that cannot be done without a reflex act of perception accompanying it, and how performed by thinking substances who cannot think without being conscious of it. But that which we call "the same consciousness" not being the same individual act, why one intellectual substance may not have represented to it as done by itself what it never did, and was perhaps done by some other agent; why, I say, such a representation may not possibly be without reality of matter of fact, as well as several representations in dreams are, which yet, whilst dreaming, we take for true, will be difficult to conclude from the nature of things. And that it never is so, will by us (till we have clearer views of the nature of thinking substances) be best resolved into the goodness of God, who, as far as the happiness or misery of any of his sensible creatures is concerned in it, will not by a fatal error of theirs transfer from one to another that consciousness which draws reward or punishment with it. How far this may be an argument against those who would place thinking in a system of fleeting animal spirits, I leave to be considered. But yet, to return to the question before us, it must be allowed, that if the same consciousness (which, as has been shown, is quite a different thing from the same numerical figure or motion in the body) can be transferred from one thinking substance to another, it will be possible that two thinking substances may make but one person. For the same consciousness being preserved, whether in the same or different substances, the personal identity is preserved.

As to the second part of the question, Whether, the same immaterial substance remaining, there may be two distinct persons? Which question seems to me to be built on this,

Whether the same immaterial being, being conscious of the action of its past duration, may be wholly stripped of all the consciousness of its past existence, and lose it beyond the power of ever retrieving it again; and so, as it were, beginning a new account from a new period, have a consciousness that cannot reach beyond this new state? All those who hold preexistence are evidently of this mind, since they allow the soul to have no remaining consciousness of what it did in that pre-existent state, either wholly separate from body, or informing any other body; and if they should not, it is plain experience would be against them. So that personal identity reaching no farther than consciousness reaches, a pre-existent spirit not having continued so many ages in a state of silence, must needs make different persons. Suppose a Christian, Platonist, or a Pythagorean, should, upon God's having ended all his works of creation the seventh day, think his soul hath existed ever since; and should imagine it has revolved in several human bodies, as I once met with one who was persuaded his had been the soul of Socrates: (how reasonably I will not dispute: this I know, that in the post he filled, which was no inconsiderable one, he passed for a very rational man; and the press has shown that he wanted not parts or learning:) would any one say, that he, being not conscious of any of Socrates's actions or thoughts, could be the same person with Socrates? Let any one reflect upon himself, and conclude, that he has in himself immaterial spirit, which is that which thinks in him, and in the constant change of his body keeps him the same; and is that which he calls himself: let him also suppose it to be the same soul that was in Nestor or Thersites, at the siege of Troy, (for souls being, as far as we know any thing of them, in their nature indifferent to any parcel of matter, the supposition has no apparent absurdity in it), which it may have been as well as it is now the soul of any other man: but he now having no consciousness of any of the actions either of Nestor or Thersites, does or can he conceive himself the same person with either of them? Can he be concerned in either of their actions? attribute them to himself, or think them his own, more than the actions of any other man that ever existed? So that this consciousness not reaching to any of the actions of either of those men, he is no more one self with either of them, than if the soul or immaterial spirit that now informs him had been created and began to exist when it began to inform his present body, though it were never so true that the same spirit that informed Nestor's or Thersites's body were numerically the same that now informs his. For this would no more make him the same person with Nestor, than if some of the particles of matter that were once a part of Nestor were now a part of this man; the same immaterial substance, without the same consciousness, no more making the same person by being united to any body, makes the same person. But let him once find himself conscious of any of the actions of Nestor, he then finds himself the same person with Nestor.

And thus we may be able, without any difficulty, to conceive the same person at the resurrection, though in a body not exactly in make or parts the same which he had here, the same consciousness going along with the soul that inhabits it. But yet the soul alone, in the change of bodies, would scarce to any one, but to him that makes the soul the man, be enough to make the same man. For, should the soul of a prince, carrying with it the consciousness of the prince's past life, enter and inform the body of a cobbler, as soon as deserted by his own soul, every one sees he would be the same person with the prince, accountable only for the prince's actions: but who would say it was the same man? The body too goes to the making of the man, and would, I guess, to every body determine the man in this case, wherein the soul, with all its princely thoughts about it, would not make another man; but he would be the same cobbler to every one besides himself. I know that, in the ordinary way of speaking, the same person and the same man stand for one and the same thing. And, indeed, every one will always have a liberty to speak as he pleases, and to apply what articulate sounds to what ideas he thinks fit, and change them as often as he pleases. But yet, when we will inquire what makes the same spirit, man, or person, we must fix the ideas of spirit, man, or person in our minds; and having resolved with ourselves what we mean by them, it will not be hard to determine in either of them, or the like, when it is the same and when not.

Consciousness makes the same person.—But though the same immaterial substance or soul does not alone, wherever it be, and in whatsoever state, make the same man; yet it is plain, consciousness, as far as ever it can be extended, should it be to ages past, unites existences and actions, very remote in time, into the same person, as well as it does the existences and actions of the immediately preceding moment: so that whatever has the consciousness of present and past actions is the same person to whom they both belong. Had I the same consciousness that I saw the ark and Noah's flood, as that I saw an overflowing of the Thames last winter, or as that I write now, I could no more doubt that I who write this now, that saw the Thames overflowed last winter, and that viewed the flood at the general deluge, was the same self, place that self in what substance you please, than that I who write this am the same myself now whilst I write (whether I consist of all the same substance, material or immaterial, or no) that I was yesterday. For, as to this point of being the same self, it matters not whether this present self be made up of the same or other substances, I being as much concerned and as justly accountable for any action was done a thousand years since appropriated to me now by this self-consciousness, as I am for what I did the last moment.

Self depends on consciousness.—Self is that conscious thinking thing (whatever substance made up of, whether spiritual or material, simple or compounded, it matters not) which is sensible or conscious of pleasure and pain, capable of happiness or misery, and so is concerned for itself, as far as that consciousness extends. Thus every one finds, that whilst comprehended under that consciousness, the little finger is as much a part of himself as what is most so. Upon separation of this little finger, should this consciousness go along with the little finger, and leave the rest of the body, it is evident the little finger would be the person, the same person; and self then would have nothing to do with the rest of the body. As in this case it is the consciousness that goes along with the substance, when one part is separate from another, which makes the same person, and constitutes this inseparable self, so it is in reference to substances remote in time. That with which the consciousness of this present thinking thing can join itself makes the same person, and is one self with it, and with nothing else; and so attributes to itself and owns all the actions of that thing as its own, as far as that consciousness reaches, and no farther; as every one who reflects will perceive. . . .

This may show us wherein personal identity consists, not in the identity of substance but, as I have said, in the identity of consciousness; wherein if Socrates and the present mayor of Queinborough agree, they are the same person. If the same Socrates waking and sleeping do not partake of the same consciousness, Socrates waking and sleeping is not the same person; and to punish Socrates waking for what sleeping Socrates thought, and waking Socrates was never conscious of, would be no more of right than to punish one twin for what his brother-twin did, whereof he knew nothing, because their outsides were so like that they could not be distinguished; for such twins have been seen.

DAVID HUME

Of Personal Identity

DAVID HUME *(1711–1776), a Scottish philosopher, was refused professorships at the leading universities for his "heresies." Nevertheless, he is regarded as the outstanding genius of British philosophy. He wrote a number of influential books, among them* A Treatise of Human Nature, An Inquiry Concerning the Principles of Morals, *and* Dialogues on Natural Religion.

THERE are some philosophers, who imagine we are every moment intimately conscious of what we call our *Self;* that we feel its existence and its continuance in existence; and are certain, beyond the evidence of a demonstration, both of its perfect identity and simplicity. The strongest sensation, the most violent passion, say they, instead of distracting us from this view, only fix it the more intensely, and make us consider their influence on *self* either by their pain or pleasure. To attempt a farther proof of this were to weaken its evidence; since no proof can be deriv'd from any fact, of which we are so intimately conscious; nor is there any thing, of which we can be certain, if we doubt of this.

Unluckily all these positive assertions are contrary to that very experience, which is pleaded for them, nor have we any idea of *self,* after the manner it is here explain'd. For from what impression cou'd this idea be deriv'd? This question 'tis impossible to answer without a manifest contradiction and absurdity; and yet 'tis a question, which must necessarily be answer'd, if we wou'd have the idea of self pass for clear and intelligible. It must be some one impression, that gives rise to every real idea. But self or person is not any one impression, but that to which our several impressions and ideas are suppos'd to have a reference. If any impression gives rise to the idea of self, that impression must continue invariably the same, thro' the whole course of our lives; since self is suppos'd to exist after that manner. But there is no impression constant and invariable. Pain and pleasure, grief and joy, passions and sensations succeed each other, and never all exist at the same time. It cannot, therefore, be from any of these impressions, or from any other, that the idea of self is deriv'd; and consequently there is no such idea.

But farther, what must become of all our particular perceptions upon this hypothesis? All these are different, and distinguishable, and separable from each other, and may be separately consider'd, and may exist separately, and have no need of any thing to support their existence. After what manner, therefore, do they belong to self; and how are they connected with it? For my part, when I enter most intimately into what I call *myself,* I always stumble on some particular perception or other, of heat or cold, light or shade, love or hatred, pain or pleasure. I never can catch *myself* at any time without a perception, and never can observe any thing but the perception. When my perceptions are remov'd for any time, as by sound sleep; so long am I insensible of *myself,* and may truly be said not to exist. And were all my perceptions remov'd by death, and cou'd I neither think, nor feel, nor see, nor love, nor hate after the dissolution of my body, I shou'd be entirely annihilated, nor do I conceive what is farther requisite to make me a

Hume, David, "Of Personal Identity," from *A Treatise of Human Nature,* ed. Shelby-Brigge, Book 1, part IV, Section VI. Oxford: Clarendon Press, 1888, reprinted 1897.

perfect non-entity. If any one upon serious and unprejudic'd reflection, thinks he has a different notion of *himself*, I must confess I can reason no longer with him. All I can allow him is, that he may be in the right as well as I, and that we are essentially different in this particular. He may, perhaps, perceive something simple and continu'd, which he calls *himself*; tho' I am certain there is no such principle in me.

But setting aside some metaphysicians of this kind, I may venture to affirm of the rest of mankind, that they are nothing but a bundle or collection of different perceptions, which succeed each other with an inconceivable rapidity, and are in a perpetual flux and movement. Our eyes cannot turn in their sockets without varying our perceptions. Our thought is still more variable than our sight; and all our other senses and faculties contribute to this change; nor is there any single power of the soul, which remains unalterably the same, perhaps for one moment. The mind is a kind of theatre, where several perceptions successively make their appearance; pass, repass, glide away, and mingle in an infinite variety of postures and situations. There is properly no *simplicity* in it at one time, nor *identity* in different; whatever natural propension we may have to imagine that simplicity and identity. The comparison of the theatre must not mislead us. They are the successive perceptions only, that constitute the mind; nor have we the most distant notion of the place, where these scenes are represented, or of the materials, of which it is compos'd.

What then gives us so great a propension to ascribe an identity to these successive perceptions, and to suppose ourselves possest of an invariable and uninterrupted existence thro' the whole course of our lives?...

... 'Tis evident, that the identity, which we attribute to the human mind, however perfect we may imagine it to be, is not able to run the several different perceptions into one, and make them lose their characters of distinction and difference, which are essential to them. 'Tis still true, that every distinct perception, which enters into the composition of the mind, is a distinct existence, and is different, and distinguishable, and separable from every other perception, either contemporary or successive. But, as, notwithstanding this distinction and separability, we suppose the whole train of perceptions to be united by identity, a question naturally arises concerning this relation of identity; whether it be something that really binds our several perceptions together, or only associates their ideas in the imagination. That is, in other words, whether in pronouncing concerning the identity of a person, we observe some real bond among his perceptions, or only feel one among the ideas we form of them. This question we might easily decide, if we wou'd recollect what has been already prov'd at large, that the understanding never observes any real connexion among objects, and that even the union of cause and effect, when strictly examin'd, resolves itself into a customary association of ideas. For from thence it evidently follows, that identity is nothing really belonging to these different perceptions, and uniting them together; but is merely a quality, which we attribute to them, because of the union of their ideas in the imagination, when we reflect upon them. Now the only qualities, which can give ideas an union in the imagination, are these relations above-mention'd. These are the uniting principles in the ideal world, and without them every distinct object is separable by the mind, and may be separately consider'd, and appears not to have any more connexion with any other object, than if disjoin'd by the greatest difference and remoteness. 'Tis, therefore, on some of these three relations of resemblance, contiguity and causation, that identity depends; and as the very essence of these relations consists in their producing an easy transition of ideas; it follows, that our notions of personal identity, proceed entirely from the smooth and uninterrupted progress of the thought along a train of connected ideas, according to the principles above-explain'd.

The only question, therefore, which remains, is, by what relations this uninterrupted progress of our thought is produc'd, when we consider the successive existence of a mind or thinking person. And here 'tis evident we must confine ourselves to resemblance and causation, and must drop contiguity, which has little or no influence in the present case.

To begin with *resemblance;* suppose we cou'd see clearly into the breast of another, and observe that succession of perceptions, which constitutes his mind or thinking principle, and suppose that he always preserves the memory of a considerable part of past perceptions; 'tis evident that nothing cou'd more contribute to the bestowing a relation on this succession amidst all its variations. For what is the memory but a faculty, by which we raise up the images of past perceptions? And as an image necessarily resembles its object, must not the frequent placing of these resembling perceptions in the chain of thought, convey the imagination more easily from one link to another, and make the whole seem like the continuance of one object? In this particular, then, the memory not only discovers the identity, but also contributes to its production, by producing the relation of resemblance among the perceptions. The case is the same whether we consider ourselves or others.

As to *causation;* we may observe, that the true idea of the human mind, is to consider it as a system of different perceptions or different existences, which are link'd together by the relation of cause and effect, and mutually produce, destroy, influence, and modify each other. Our impressions give rise to their correspondent ideas; and these ideas in their turn produce other impressions. One thought chases another, and draws after it a third, by which it is expell'd in its turn. In this respect, I cannot compare the soul more properly to any thing than to a republic or commonwealth, in which the several members are united by the reciprocal ties of government and subordination, and give rise to other persons, who propagate the same republic in the incessant changes of its parts. And as the same individual republic may not only change its members, but also its laws and constitutions; in like manner the same person may vary his character and disposition, as well as his impressions and ideas, without losing his identity. Whatever changes he endures, his several parts are still

connected by the relation of causation. And in this view our identity with regard to the passions serves to corroborate that with regard to the imagination, by the making our distant perceptions influence each other, and by giving us a present concern for our past or future pains or pleasures.

As memory alone acquaints us with the continuance and extent of this succession of perceptions, 'tis to be consider'd, upon that account chiefly, as the source of personal identity. Had we no memory, we never shou'd have any notion of causation, nor consequently of that chain of causes and effects, which constitute our self or person. But having once acquir'd this notion of causation from the memory, we can extend the same chain of causes, and consequently the identity of our persons beyond our memory, and can comprehend times, and circumstances, and actions, which we have entirely forgot, but suppose in general to have existed. For how few of our past actions are there, of which we have any memory? Who can tell me, for instance, what were his thoughts and actions on the first of *January* 1715, the 12th of *March* 1719, and the 3d of *August* 1733? Or will he affirm, because he has entirely forgot the incidents of these days, that the present self is not the same person with the self of that time; and by that means overturn all the most establish'd notions of personal identity? In this view, therefore, memory does not so much *produce* as *discover* personal identity, by shewing us the relation of cause and effect among our different perceptions. 'Twill be incumbent on those, who affirm that memory produces entirely our personal identity, to give a reason why we can thus extend our identity beyond our memory.

The whole of this doctrine leads us to a conclusion, which is of great importance in the present affair, *viz.* that all the nice and subtile questions concerning personal identity can never possibly be decided, and are to be regarded rather as grammatical than as philosophical difficulties. Identity depends on the relations of ideas; and these relations produce identity, by means of that easy transition they occasion.

But as the relations, and the easiness of the transition may diminish by insensible degrees, we have no just standard, by which we can decide any dispute concerning the time, when they acquire or lose a title to the name of identity. All the disputes concerning the identity of connected objects are merely verbal, except so far as the relation of parts gives rise to some fiction or imaginary principle of union, as we have already observ'd.

MEREDITH W. MICHAELS
Persons, Brains, and Bodies

MEREDITH MICHAELS *(b. 1950) teaches Philosophy at Smith College. Her work focuses on issues in reproductive ethics and feminist epistemology. Her most recent book is* Fetal Subjects/Feminist Positions *(1999) (with Lynn Morgan).*

ONE night, after a serious bout with the library, you and your best friend Wanda Bagg (or Walter, if you prefer) decide to indulge yourselves at the College Haven. Before you can stop her, Wanda steps out in front of a steamroller that happens to be moving down Main Street. Wanda is crushed. Witnessing the horror of the accident, you have a stroke. Fortunately, Dr. Hagendaas, the famous neurosurgeon who has been visiting the campus, is also on the way to the College Haven. Taking charge, he rushes you and Wanda to the Health Center, where he performs a "body transplant." He takes Wanda's brain, which miraculously escaped the impact of the steamroller, and puts it in the place of yours, which was, of course, severely damaged by the stroke. After several days, the following battle ensues. Wanda's parents claim that they are under no obligation to continue paying tuition. After all, Wanda was killed by a steamroller. Your parents claim that they are under no obligation to continue paying tuition; after all, you died of a stroke. It is clear, then, that a basic question is in need of an answer, who is the person lying in bed in the Health Center? Is it Wanda? Is it you? Is it someone else altogether? For the sake of discussion, let us call the person lying in the bed Schwanda. What reasons do we have for believing that Schwanda is Wanda? Given that one's self-consciousness, one's thoughts, beliefs and feelings are all mental phenomena, we might naturally conclude that a person goes wherever her brain goes (on the assumption that our mental characteristics are more likely "located" in the brain than in, say, our smallest left toe). Schwanda will remember having set off for the College Haven with you; she will remember receiving the college acceptance letter addressed, "Dear Wanda, We are happy to inform you that . . .";

she'll remember being hugged by Wanda's mother on the afternoon of her first day of school. That is, Schwanda will *believe* that she's Wanda.

Nevertheless, the fact that Schwanda believes herself to be Wanda does not in itself guarantee that she is. Do we have any basis for insisting that Schwanda is Wanda and not someone who is *deluded* into thinking that she's Wanda? How can we determine whether Schwanda's Wanda memories are genuine and not merely apparent? As we came to realize in our discussion of Locke's Memory Theory, it is not legitimate at this point to appeal to the self-identity of Schwanda and Wanda, since that is precisely what we're trying to determine. In other words, in attempting to establish that Schwanda's Wanda memories are genuine memories, we cannot argue that they are genuine on the grounds that Schwanda *is* Wanda.

Perhaps it is possible to stop short of circularity. Why couldn't we say that Schwanda's Wanda memories are genuine because the *brain* that is remembering is the same as the brain that had the original experiences. Thus, the experiences are preserved in the very organ that underwent them. Though there is an initial plausibility to this response, it fails to solve our problem. Suppose that Schwanda is Wanda—remembering the experience of learning to ride a bicycle. Though the brain in question is indeed the same, it is nonetheless clear to all of us that brains alone do not learn to ride bicycles, or, indeed, do brains alone remember having done so. *People* learn to ride bicycles and *people* remember having done so. And the question we are trying to answer is whether Schwanda (who is remembering) is the same person as Wanda (who did the bicycling). The appeal to the fact that the same brain is involved in each event does not provide us with a way out of the Lockean circle.

It is at this point that philosophers begin to reconsider the Aristotelian position . . . that self-identity is essentially *bodily* identity. If the Body Theory of Personal Identity is true, then the person lying in bed at the Health Center is you, deluded into believing that you are Wanda. That is, Schwanda is self-identical to you.

You might wonder, at this point, whether there are any positive reasons for endorsing the Body Theory, or whether it is simply a place to which one retreats only in defeat? The following case is designed to persuade you that there is at least *some* plausibility to the Body Theory. Suppose that an evil scientist, Dr. Nefarious, has selected you as his prime subject for a horrible experiment. You are dragged into his office. He says, "Tomorrow at 5:00, you will be subjected to the most terrible tortures. Your nails will be pulled out one by one. Rats will be caged round head. Burning oil will drip slowly on your back. The remainder I leave as a surprise."

Are you worried about what will happen to you at 5:00 tomorrow? If you have any sense, you are. You think of the excruciating pain and suffering you will undergo and would surely do just about anything to avoid it. But now, Dr. Nefarious says, "Tomorrow at 4:55, I will use my Dememorizer to erase your memory of this conversation." Are you still anxious about what is going to happen to you tomorrow at 5:00? Surely you are. After all the fact that you won't, between 4:55 and 5:00, be anticipating your torture doesn't entail that the torture itself will be any less painful. When you forget that your Calculus professor told the class there would be a test on Friday, you aren't thereby spared the experience of taking the test (in fact, in that case the experience is made worse by your not having had the opportunity to anticipate it).

Now, Dr. Nefarious says, "Tomorrow at 4:57, I will use my Dememorizer to erase *all* of your memories." Are you still anxious about what will happen tomorrow at 5:00? Isn't it natural to describe the situation as one in which you will undergo horrible torture, though you won't know who you are or why this is happening to you? *You* will still experience *your* fingernails being pulled out, *your* back being burned, *your* face being eaten up by rats. Surely, those experiences are ones you would like to avoid.

Finally, Dr. Nefarious says to you, "Tomorrow at 4:58, I am going to use my Rememorizer to implant in your brain all of Ronald Reagan's memories." Though this may not please you for personal or political reasons, the relevant question remains this: are you still worried about what is going to happen tomorrow at 5:00? Isn't it again perfectly natural to describe the situation as one in which you will undergo horrible torture, all the while believing that you are Ronald Reagan. Do you not *now* remain concerned that *you* will experience excruciating pain and intolerable suffering? Look at your fingernails while you consider your answer to this question.

What this story demonstrates is not the conclusive superiority of the Body Theory over the Memory (or Brain) Theory, but rather the importance of our bodies to our self-identity. This is something that tends to get lost in the traditional conceptions of personal identity. Furthermore, returning to the case of Schwanda, we can now see that it is not altogether preposterous to argue that Schwanda is indeed you, deluded into believing that she is Wanda. In other words, anyone who wishes to dismiss that possibility must also dismiss the possibility that the person who undergoes the torture is indeed you, deluded into believing that you are Ronald Reagan.

While it is true that we tend to identify ourselves with and by our thoughts, beliefs, inclinations and feelings, our discussion of the Body Theory should remind us that there are reasons for believing that our bodies are, at the very least, important to who we are. Some philosophers would argue that our bodies *are* who we are, that self-identity *is* bodily identity.

In considering these admittedly fanciful problem cases, we have seen that we lack a concept of self-identity that allows us to predict when we would or wouldn't persist through time. This might suggest to us that our concept of self-identity is not an all-or-nothing one, that, in fact, our concept is one which admits of degrees. If so, we are no longer talking about identity *per se*, which is an all-or-nothing concept, but rather about some other relation of psychological and physical connectedness. Nevertheless, we can now see first, that the answer to the question "Who ought to pay Schwanda's tuition?" will depend upon which theory of personal identity we are inclined to endorse and second, that the answer may not be as clear and unequivocal as we would like it to be.

JUSTIN LEIBER
How to Build a Person

JUSTIN LEIBER, *a professor of philosophy at the University of Houston, also writes science fiction. This selection is from his novel* Beyond Rejection.

WORMS began his spiel: "People often think that it ought to be simple enough to just *manufacture* an adult human body, like building a house or a helicopter. You'd think that, well, we know what chemicals are involved, and how they go together, how they form cells according to DNA templates, and how the cells form organ systems

Leiber, Justin, "How to Build a Person," from *Beyond Rejection* by Justin Leiber (New York: Random House, 1980).

regulated by chemical messengers, hormones, and the like. So we ought to be able to build a fully functional human body right up from scratch."

Worms moved so that he blocked their view of the jogger. He brought his drained coffee cup down for emphasis.

"And, of course, we could build a human body up from scratch, theoretically, anyhow. But no one ever has. In fact, no one has ever even started to. De Reinzie manufactured the first fully functional human cell—muscle tissue—in the middle of the last century, about 2062 or so. And shortly after that the major varieties were cooked up. And even then it wasn't really manufactured from scratch. De Reinzie, like all the rest, built some basic DNA templates from actual carbon, oxygen, hydrogen, and so on, or rather from simple sugars and alcohols. *But then he grew the rest from these.* That's growth, not manufacture. And nobody's come closer to building an organ than a lab that made a millimeter of stomach wall for several million credits a couple of decades ago.

"I don't want to bother you with the mathematics," he continued, looking away from Terry. "But my old professor at Tech used to estimate that it would take all the scientific and manufacturing talent of Earth and the rest of the Federation something like fifty years and a googol credits to build a single human hand.

"You can imagine what it would take to make something like that," he said, moving out of their line of vision and gesturing at the jogging figure. He took the clipboard that hung next to the treadmill's controls and scanned the sheets on it.

"This body had been blank for three years. It has a running-time age of thirty-one years, though of course Sally Cadmus—that's the person involved—was born over thirty-four years ago. What with demand, of course, three years is a long time for a body to remain out of action. She's in good health, fine musculature for a spacer—says Sally was an asteroid miner here. Seems the body spent two years frozen in a Holmann orbit. We've had it for four months and we're preparing it now. You might see her walking around any day now.

"But Sally Cadmus won't. Her last tape was just the obligatory one made on reaching majority and she left no instructions for implantation. I trust, people, that all your tapes are updated." He gave them the family doctor look and went on, moving closer and dropping his voice.

"I have my mind taped every six months, just to be safe. After all, the tape is *you*—your individual software, or program, including memory store. Everything that makes you *you.*" He walked up to the aide who had brought the beautiful young man.

"You—for instance—Ms. Pedersen, when did you have your last tape job?"

The aide, a gaunt red-haired woman in her mid-thirties, snatched her arm from around her young man and glared at Austin Worms.

"What business—"

"Oh, I wouldn't really expect you to say in front of other people." He grinned at the others as Pedersen subsided. "But that's the whole point, you see. Maybe she has been renewing her tape yearly, which is what our profession recommends as an absolute minimum. But a lot of people neglect this elementary precaution because they are so appalled by the thought of severe bodily injury. They just let things slide. And because the topic is so personal, no one knows, no one asks, no one reminds them until the once-in-half-a-million accident happens—truly irreparable body damage or total destruction.

"And then you find that the person hasn't taped for twenty years. Which means. . . ."

He surveyed the group to let it sink in. Then he saw the beautiful girl-child. Terry had been hiding her, no doubt. A classic blond-haired, blue-eyed girl in her mid-teens. She was looking straight into his eyes. Or *through* them. Something . . . He went on.

"Which means if he or she is lucky and there's estate money, you've got someone who has to face all the ordinary problems of rejection that come in trying to match a young mind with what is almost certain to be a middle-aged body. But also the implant has all those problems multiplied by another. The implant has to deal with a world that is *twenty years in the future.* And a 'career' that is meaningless because he lacks the memory and skills that his old mind picked up over that twenty years.

"More likely, you'll get the real blowout. You'll get massive rejection, psychosis and premature essential senility, and death. Real, final mind death."

"But you would still have the person's tape, their software, as you call it," said Ms. Pedersen. "Couldn't you just try again, with another blank body?" She still had her hands off her young man.

"Two problems. First"—he stuck his index finger in the air—"you got to realize how very difficult it is for a mind and a body to make a match, even with all the help us somaticians and psycheticians can provide, the best that modern biopsychological engineering can put together. Even with a really creative harmonizer to get in there and make the structure jell. Being reborn is very hard work indeed.

"And the failure rate under ordinary circumstances—tapes up-to-date, good stable mind, decent recipient body—is about twenty percent. And we know that it jumps to ninety-five percent if there's a second time around. It's nearly that bad the first time if you got someone whose tapes are twenty years out of date. The person may get through the first few days all right but he can't pull himself into reality. Everything he knows was lost twenty years ago. No friends, no career, everything out of shape. Then the mind will reject its new body just as it rejects the new world it has woken up to. So you don't have much of a chance. Unless, of course, you're the rare nympher or still rarer leaper.

"Second, the Government underwrites the cost of the first implantation. Of course, they don't pay for a fancy body—a nympher body, that is. You'd pay more than two million credits for one of those beauties. You get what's available and you are lucky if you get it within a year or two. What the Government underwrites is the basic operation and tuning job. That alone costs one and a half million or so. Enough to pay my salary for a hundred years. Enough to send the half-dozen or so of you on the Cunard

Line Uranium Jubilee All-Planets Tour in first class."

Austin had been moving over to the treadmill control console while speaking. As he finished, his audience noticed a large structure descending from the ceiling just over the jogging figure, Sally Cadmus's body. It looked like a cross between the upper half of a large mummy and a comfortably stuffed armchair. Austin glided over to the treadmill. The audience watched the structure open like an ancient iron maiden. Some noticed that the jogging figure was slowing down.

Austin arrived just in time to complete a flurry of adjustments on the jogger's control package before the structure folded itself around. Two practiced blows on the back of the jogger's thighs brought the legs out of contact with the slowing treadmill.

"It's a lucky thing that implantation is so risky and the sort of accident that calls for it so rare," he said as the structure ascended behind him. "Otherwise, the Kellog-Murphy Law, which underwrites the first implantation, would bankrupt the Government."

"Where is the body going?" asked the blond-haired youngster. Austin could see now that she was probably no more than ten or eleven years old. Something about her posture had made him think she was older.

"Normally it would go into a kind of artificial hibernation—low temperature and vital activity. But this body will be implanted tomorrow, so we'll keep it at a normal level of biological function." He had given the body an additional four cc.'s of glucose-saline plasma beyond the program. That was to compensate for the extra jogging. He hadn't done the official calculations. It wasn't that such mathematics was more than a minor chore. If you had asked him to explain, he would have said that the official calculation would have called for half again as much plasma. But he sensed that the body got more than usual from every cc. of water, from every molecule of sugar. Perhaps it was something in the sweat smell, the color and feel of the skin, the resilience of the musculature. But Austin knew.

The somatic aides would have said that Austin Worms was the best ghoul in the Solar System, a zombie's best friend. And they would have meant what they said even if they went on to joke.

Austin had vomited for the first and only time in his life when he learned the origin of the slang terms "ghoul" and "vampire."

The sounds of Terry's tour group faded as they moved up the hall to the psychetician laboratory. But Austin did not return to Bruhler's *The Central Equations of the Abstract Theory of Mind.* He had been puzzled by what the eleven-year-old blond girl had said to him before sauntering off to catch up with the rest of the tour. She had said, "I bet that mind is gonna be in for a real shock when it wakes up with that thing on its backside." He wondered how she could know that it wasn't just part of the crazy-quilt system of tubes and wires that the jogger had on her back.

"I'm Candy Darling," she had added as she left the room. Now he knew who she was. You never knew what to expect in a harmonizer.

• • •

Psycheticians take care of minds. That's why they are sometimes called vampires. Somaticians are called ghouls because they take care of bodies.

—I.F. + S.C. Operation Logbook, Append. II, Press Releases

Germaine Means grinned wolfishly at them. "I am a psychetician. What Terry would call a vampire. Call me Germaine if that does not appeal."

They were seated facing a blackboard at one end of a large room which was otherwise filled with data cabinets, office cubicles, and computer consoles. The woman who addressed them wore severe and plain overalls. When she had first come to the Norbert Wiener Research Hospital— NWRH—the director had suggested that the chief psychetician might dress more suitably. That director had retired early.

"As you know from what Austin Worms told you, we think of the individual human mind as an abstract pattern of memory, skill, and experience that has been impressed on the physical hardware of the brain. Think of it this way: when you get a computer factory-fresh, it is like a blanked human brain. The computer has no subroutines, just as the brain has no skills. The computer has no data arrays to call on, just as the blanked brain has no memories.

"What we do here is try to implant the pattern of memory, skill, and experience that is all that is left of a person into a blanked brain. It is not easy because brains are not manufactured. You have to grow them. And a unique personality has to be part of this growth and development. So each brain is different. So no software mind fits any hardware brain perfectly. Except the brain that it grew up with.

"For instance," Germaine Means continued, softening her tone so she would not alert Ms. Pedersen's boyfriend, who was dozing in a well-padded chair, his elegant legs thrust straight out in full display, tights to sandals. "For instance, when pressure is applied to this person's foot, his brain knows how to interpret the nervous impulses from his foot." She suited her action to her words.

"His yelp indicated that his brain recognizes that considerable pressure has been applied to the toes of his left foot. If, however, we implanted another mind, it would not interpret the nervous impulses correctly—it might feel the impulses as a stomachache."

The young man was on his feet, bristling. He moved toward Germaine, who had turned away to pick up what looked like a pair of goggles with some mirrors and gears on top. As he reached her, she turned to face him and pushed the goggles into his hands.

"Yes, thank you for volunteering. Put them on." Not knowing what else to do, he did.

"I want you to look at that blond-haired girl who just sat down over there." She held his arm lightly as he turned and his balance wavered. He appeared to be looking through the goggles at a point several degrees to the right of Candy Darling.

"Now I want you to point at her with your right hand—quick!" The young man's arm shot out, the finger also pointing several degrees to the right of the girl. He began moving his finger to the left, but Germaine pulled his hand down to his side, outside the field of vision that the goggles allowed him.

"Try it again, quick," she said. This time the finger was not as far off. On the fifth try his finger pointed directly to Candy Darling, though he continued to look to her right.

"Now off with the goggles. Look at her again. Point quick!" Germaine grabbed his hand the instant he pointed. Though he was not looking directly at Candy Darling, he was pointing several degrees *to the left* of her. He looked baffled.

Germaine Means chalked a head and goggles on the blackboard, seen as if you were looking down at them from the ceiling. She drew another head to the left of the line of sight of the goggled head and chalked "15°" in to indicate the angle.

"What happened is a simple example of tuning. The prisms in the goggles bend the light so that when his eyes told him he was looking straight at her, his eyes were in fact pointed fifteen degrees to her right. The muscles and nerves of his hand were tuned to point where his eyes were actually pointed—so he pointed fifteen degrees to the right.

"But then his eyes saw his hand going off to the right, so he began to compensate. In a couple of minutes—five tries—his motor coordination compensates so that he points to where his eyes tell him she is—he adjusted to pointing fifteen degrees *to the left* from usual. When I took the goggles off, his arm was still tuned to compensate, so he pointed off to the left until he readjusted."

She picked up the goggles. "Now, a human can adjust to that distortion in a few minutes. But I could calibrate these so that they would turn the whole room upside down. If you then walked around and tried to do things, you would find it difficult. Very difficult. But if you kept the goggles on, the whole room would turn right side up after a day or two. Everything would seem normal because your system would have retuned itself.

"What do you think will happen if you then take the goggles off?"

Candy Darling giggled. Ms. Pedersen said, "Oh, I see. Your mind would have adjusted to turning the, ah, messages from your eyes upside down, so when you took the goggles off—"

"Precisely," said Germaine, "everything would look upside down to you until you readjusted to having the goggles off—and it happens the same way. You stumble around for a day or so and then everything snaps right side up again. And the stumbling-around part is important. If you are confined to a chair with your head fixed in position, your mind and body can't tune themselves.

"Now I want you to imagine what happens when we implant a mind into a blanked brain. *Almost everything will be out of tune*. The messages from your eyes won't simply be inverted, they'll be scrambled in countless ways. Same thing with your ears, nose, tongue—and with the whole nerve net covering your body. And that's just incoming messages. Your mind will have even more problems when it tries to tell the body to do something. Your mind will try to get your lips to say 'water,' and Sol knows what sound will come out.

"And what's worse is that whatever sound does come out, your new ears won't be able to give your mind an accurate version of it."

Germaine smiled at them and glanced at her watch. Terry stood up.

"Terry will be wanting to take you on. Let me wrap this up by saying that it is a very simple thing to play someone's mind tape into a prepared brain. The great problem is in getting the rearranged brain, the cerebral cortex, speaking strictly, to be tuned into the rest of the system. As Austin Worms may have told you, we start an implant operation tomorrow. The initial tape-in will take days and days. Even months, if you count all the therapy. Questions?"

"Just one," said Ms. Pedersen. "I can understand how difficult it is for a mind to survive implantation. And, of course, I know it is illegal to implant a mind that is over eighty-five. But couldn't a person—if you call a mind a person—live forever bypassing through body after body?"

"Okay, that's a tough one to explain even if we had a lot of time and you knew a lot of mathematics. Until this century it was believed that senility was a by-product of the physical breakdown of the body. Today we know that a human mind can have roughly one hundred years of experiences before it reaches essential senility, however young the body it occupies. As you know, a few successful leapers have survived implantation after a fifty-year wait. So a leaper might, in theory, still be functioning a thousand years from now. But such an individual's mind will not be able to encompass any more lived experience than you. When all there is of you is a tape in storage, you aren't really alive."

After they had filed out, Germaine Means noticed that the blond-haired girl had remained.

"Hi, I'm Candy Darling," she cried. "I hope you don't mind. I thought it would be fun to sneak in on the standard tour. Get the smell of the place."

"Where's your VAT?"

• • •

Austin Worms declared that basic physical meshing procedures were complete.

—I. F. + S. C. Operation Logbook
Gxxhdt.
Etaoin shrdlu. Mmm.
Anti-M.
Away mooncow Taddy-fair fine. Fine again, take. Away, along, alas, alung the orbit-run, from swerve of space to wormhole wiggle, brings us. Start now. Wake.

So hear I am now coming out of nothing like Eros out of Death, knowing only that I was Ismael Forth—stately, muscled well—taping in, and knowing that I don't know when I'm waking or where, or where-in. And hoping that it is a dream. But it isn't. Oh, no, it isn't. With that goggling piece of munster cheese oumphowing on my eyelids.

And seemingly up through endless levels and configurations that had no words and now no memories. Wake.

"Helow, I'm Candy Darlinz."

"I am Ismael returned" was what I started to reply. After the third attempt it came out better.

And the munster cheese had become a blond-haired young girl with piercing blue eyes.

"Your primary implantation was finished yesterday, finally. Everyone thinks you're a success. Your body is a pip. You're in the Norbert Wiener Research Hospital in Houston. You have two estates clear through probate. Your friend Peter Strawson has covered your affairs. It's the first week of April, 2112. You're alive."

She stood up and touched my hand. "You start therapy tomorrow. Now sleep."

I was already drifting off by the time she had closed the door behind her. I couldn't even get myself worked up by what I was noticing. My nipples felt as big as grapes. I went out as I worked my way down past the belly button.

The next day I discovered that I had not only lost a penis. I had gained a meter-long prehensile tail. It was hate at first sense.

I had worked my way to consciousness in slow stages. I had endless flight dreams—walking, running, staggering on, away from some nameless horror. And brief flashes of sexuality that featured performances by my (former) body.

I really liked my old body. One of my biggest problems, as Dr. Germaine Means was soon to tell me. I could picture clearly how it had looked in the mirrors as I did my stretch and tone work. Just a hair over six foot four. Two hundred and five pounds, well-defined muscles, and just enough fat to be comfortable. A mat of curly red chest hair that made it easy to decide to have my facial hair wiped permanently. It felt good to be a confident even slightly clumsy giant, looking down on a world of little people.

Oh, I wasn't a real body builder or anything like that. Just enough exercise to look good—and attractive. I hadn't in fact been all that good at physical sports. But I had liked my body. It was also a help in the public relations work that I did for IBO.

I was still lying on my back. I felt shrunk. Shrunk. As the warm, muzzy flush of sleep faded, my right hand moved up over my ribs. Ribs. They were thin and they stuck out, as if the skin were sprayed over the bare cage. I felt like a skeleton until I got to the lumps. Bags. Growths.

Sacks. Even then part of me realized that they were not at all large for a woman, while most of me felt that they were as big as cantaloupes.

You may have imagined it as a kind of erotic dream. There you are in the hospital bed. You reach and there they are. Apt to the hands, the hardening nipples nestled between index and middle fingers. (Doubtless some men have felt this warm reverie with their hands on real flesh. The women may have felt pinch and itch rather than the imagined sensual flush. I know whereof I speak. I now know a lot of sexuality is like that. Perhaps heterosexuality continues as well as it does because of ignorance: each partner is free to invent the feeling of the other.)

But I was quite unable to feel erotic about my new acquisitions. Both ways. My fingers, as I felt them, felt pathology. Two dead cancerous mounds. And from the inside—so to speak—I felt that my flesh had swollen. The sheet made the nipples feel raw. A strange feeling of separation, as if the breast were disconnected, nerveless jelly—and then two points of sensitivity some inches in front of my chest. Dead spots. Rejection. I learned a lot about these.

As my hand moved down I was prepared for the swerve of hip. I couldn't feel a penis and I did not expect to find one. I did not call it "gash." Though that term is found occasionally in space-marine slang and often among the small number of male homosexuals of the extreme S&M type (Secretary & Master). I first learned the term a few days later from Dr. Means. She said that traditional male-male pornography revealed typical male illusions about female bodies: a "rich source of information about body-image pathologies." She was certainly right in pointing out that "gash" was how I felt about it. At first.

I was not only scrawny, I was almost hairless. I felt *really* naked, naked and defenseless as a baby. Though my skin was several shades less fair—and I passed a scar. I was almost relieved to feel the curly groin hair. Gone. Sticklike legs. But I *did* feel something between my thighs. And knees. And ankles, by Sol.

At first I thought it was some sort of tube to take my body wastes. But as I felt down between my legs I could tell that it wasn't covering those areas. It was attached at the end of my spine—or rather it had become the end of my spine, stretching down to my feet. It was my flesh. I didn't quite intend it—at that point I can't say that I intended anything I was so shook—but the damned thing flipped up from the bottom of the bed like a snake, throwing the sheet over my face.

I screamed my head off.

"Cut it off " was what I said after they had given me enough betaorthoamine to stop me flailing about. I said this several times to Dr. Germaine Means, who had directed the rest of them out of the room.

"Look, Sally—I'll call you that until you select a name yourself—we are not going to cut your tail off. By our calculations such a move would make terminal rejection almost certain. You would die. Several thousand nerves connect your brain with your prehensile tail. A sizable portion of your brain monitors and directs your tail—that part of your brain needs exercise and integration like any other component. We taped the pattern of your mind into your present brain. They *have to* learn to live together or you get rejection. In brief, you will die."

Dr. Means continued to read me the riot act. I would have to learn to love my new body—she practically gushed with praise for it—my new sex, my new tail. I would have to do a lot of exercise and tests. And I would have to talk to a lot of people about how I felt. And I should feel pleased as pisque to have an extra hand.

My new body broke into a cold sweat when I realized that I had—truly—no choice. I wasn't poor, assuming what I had heard yesterday was true. But I certainly couldn't afford an implant, let alone a desirable body. What I had, of course, came free under the Kellog-Murphy Bill.

After a while she left. I stared at the wall numbly. A nurse brought a tray with scrambled eggs and toast. I ignored both nurse and tray. The thin-lipped mouth salivated. Let it suffer.

SIMONE DE BEAUVOIR
I Am a Woman

SIMONE DE BEAUVOIR *(1908–1986) was a French philosopher best known for her extensive contributions to the development of feminist thought. She was a lifelong companion of Jean-Paul Sartre, and her philosophical roots are in the existentialist tradition. Her book* The Second Sex, *from which the following selection is taken, is a classic of feminist philosophy.*

FOR a long time I have hesitated to write a book on woman. The subject is irritating, especially to women; and it is not new. Enough ink has been spilled in the quarreling over feminism, now practically over, and perhaps we should say no more about it. It is still talked about, however, for the voluminous nonsense uttered during the last century seems to have done little to illuminate the problem. After all, is there a problem? And if so, what is it? Are there women, really? Most assuredly the theory of the eternal feminine still has its adherents who will whisper in your ear: "Even in Russia women still are *women*"; and other erudite persons—sometimes the very same—say with a sigh: "Woman is losing her way, woman is lost." One wonders if women still exist, if they will always exist, whether or not it is desirable that they should, what place they occupy in this world, what their place should be. "What has become of women?" was asked recently in an ephemeral magazine.

But first we must ask: what is a woman? *Tota mulier in utero,*" says one, "woman is a womb." But in speaking of certain women, connoisseurs declare that they are not women, although they are equipped with a uterus like the rest. All agree in recognizing the fact that females exist in the human species; today as always they make up about one half of humanity. And yet we are told that femininity is in danger; we are exhorted to be women, remain women, become women. It would appear, then, that every female human being is not necessarily a woman; to be so considered she must share in that mysterious and threatened reality known as femininity. Is this attribute something secreted by the ovaries? Or is it a Platonic essence, a product of the philosophic imagination? Is a rustling petticoat enough to bring it down to earth? Although some women try zealously to incarnate this essence, it is hardly patentable. It is frequently described in vague and dazzling terms that seem to have been borrowed from the vocabulary of the seers, and indeed in the times of St. Thomas it was considered an essence as certainly defined as the somniferous virtue of the poppy.

But conceptualism has lost ground. The biological and social sciences no longer admit the existence of unchangeable fixed entities that determine given characteristics, such as those ascribed to woman, the Jew, or the Negro. Science regards any characteristic as a reaction dependent in part upon a *situation.* If today femininity no longer exists, then it never existed. But does the word *woman,* then, have no specific content? This is stoutly affirmed by those who hold to the philosophy of the enlightenment, of rationalism, of nominalism; women, to them, are merely the human beings arbitrarily designated by the word *woman.* Many American women particularly are prepared to think that there is no longer any place for woman as such; if a backward individual still takes herself for a woman, her friends advise her to be psychoanalyzed and thus get rid of this obsession. In regard to a work, *Modern Woman: The Lost Sex,* which in other respects has its irritating features, Dorothy Parker has written: "I cannot be just to books which treat of woman as woman. . . . My idea is that all of us, men as well as women, should be regarded as human beings." But nominalism is a rather inadequate doctrine, and the antifemininists have had no trouble in showing that women simply *are not* men. Surely woman is, like man, a human being; but such a declaration is abstract. The fact is that every concrete human being is always a singular, separate individual. To decline to accept such notions as the eternal feminine, the black soul, the Jewish character, is not to deny that Jews, Negroes, women exist today— this denial does not represent a liberation for those concerned, but rather a flight from reality. Some years ago a well-known woman writer refused to permit her portrait to appear in a series of photographs especially devoted to women writers; she wished to be counted among the men. But in order to gain this privilege she made use of her husband's influence! Women who assert that they are men lay claim none the less to masculine consideration and respect. I recall also a young Trotskyite standing on a platform at a boisterous meeting and getting ready to use her fists, in spite of her evident fragility. She was denying her feminine weakness; but it was for love of a militant male whose equal she wished to be. The attitude of defiance of many American women proves that they are haunted by a sense of their femininity. In truth, to go for a walk with one's eyes open is enough to demonstrate that humanity is divided into two classes of individuals whose clothes, faces, bodies, smiles, gaits, interests, and occupations are manifestly different. Perhaps these differences are superficial, perhaps they are destined to disappear. What is certain is that right now they do most obviously exist.

If her functioning as a female is not enough to define woman, if we decline also to explain her through "the eternal feminine," and if nevertheless we admit, provisionally, that women do exist, then we must face the question: what is a woman?

To state the question is, to me, to suggest, at once, a preliminary answer. The fact that I ask it is in itself significant. A man would never get the notion of writing a book on the peculiar situation of the human male. But if I wish to define myself, I must first of all say: "I am a woman"; on this truth must be based all further discussion. A man never begins by presenting himself as an individual of a certain sex; it goes without saying that he is a man. The terms *masculine* and *feminine* are used symmetrically only as a matter of form, as on legal papers. In actuality the relation of the two sexes is not quite like that of two electrical poles, for man represents both the positive and the neutral, as is indicated by the common use of *man* to designate human beings in general; whereas woman represents only the negative, defined by limiting criteria, without reciprocity. In the midst of an abstract discussion it is vexing to hear a man say: "You think thus and so because you are a woman"; but I know that my only defense is to reply: "I think thus and so because it is true," thereby removing my subjective self from the argument. It would be out of the question to reply: "And you think the contrary because you are a man," for it is understood that the fact of being a man is no peculiarity. A man is in the right in being a man; it is the woman who is in the wrong. It amounts to this: just as for the ancients there was an absolute vertical with reference to which the oblique was defined, so there is an absolute human type, the masculine. Woman has ovaries, a uterus; these peculiarities imprison her in her subjectivity, circumscribe her within the limits of her own nature. It is often said that she thinks with her glands. Man superbly ignores the fact that his anatomy also includes glands, such as the testicles, and that they secrete hormones. He thinks of his body as a direct and normal connection with the world, which he believes he apprehends objectively, whereas he regards the body of woman as a hindrance, a prison, weighed down by everything peculiar to it. "The female is a female by virtue of a certain *lack* of qualities," said Aristotle; "we should regard the female nature as afflicted with a natural defectiveness." And St. Thomas for his part pronounced woman to be an "imperfect man," an "incidental" being. This is symbolized in Genesis where Eve is depicted as made from what Bossuet called "a supernumerary bone" of Adam.

Thus humanity is male and man defines woman not in herself but as relative to him; she is not regarded as an autonomous being. Michelet writes: "Woman, the relative being. . . ." And Benda is most positive in his *Rapport d'Uriel:* "The body of man makes sense in itself quite apart from that of woman, whereas the latter seems wanting in significance by itself. . . . Man can think of himself without woman. She cannot think of herself without man." And she is simply what man decrees; thus she is called "the sex," by which is meant that she appears essentially to the male as a sexual being. For him she is sex—absolute sex, no less. She is defined and differentiated with reference to man and not he with reference to her; she is the incidental, the inessential as opposed to the essential. He is the Subject, he is the Absolute—she is the Other.

The category of the *Other* is as primordial as consciousness itself. In the most primitive societies, in the most ancient mythologies, one finds the expression of a duality—that of the Self and the Other. This duality was not originally attached to the division of the sexes; it was not dependent upon any empirical facts. It is revealed in such works as that of Granet on Chinese thought and those of Dumzéil on the East Indies and Rome. The feminine element was at first no more involved in such pairs as Varuna-Mitra, Uranus-Zeus, Sun-Moon, and Day-Night than it was in the contrasts between Good and Evil, lucky and unlucky auspices, right and left, God and Lucifer. Otherness is a fundamental category of human thought.

Thus it is that no group ever sets itself up as the One without at once setting up the Other over against itself. If three travelers chance to occupy the same compartment, that is enough to make vaguely hostile "others" out of all the rest of the passengers on the train. In small-town eyes all persons not belonging to the village are "strangers" and suspect; to the native of a country all who inhabit other countries are "foreigners"; Jews are "different" for the anti-Semite, Negroes are "inferior" for American racists, aborigines are "natives" for colonists, proletarians are the "lower class" for the privileged. . . .

. . . The native traveling abroad is shocked to find himself in turn regarded as a "stranger" by the natives of neighboring countries. As a matter of fact, wars, festivals, trading, treaties, and contests among tribes, nations, and classes tend to deprive the concept *Other* of its absolute sense and to make manifest its relativity; willy-nilly, individuals and groups are forced to realize the reciprocity of their relations. How is it, then, that this reciprocity has not been recognized between the sexes, that one of the contrasting terms is set up as the sole essential, denying any relativity in regard to its correlative and defining the latter as pure otherness? Why is it that women do not dispute male sovereignty? No subject will readily volunteer to become the object, the inessential; it is not the Other who, in defining himself as the Other, establishes the One. The Other is posed as such by the One in defining himself as the One. But if the Other is not to regain the status of being the One, he must be submissive enough to accept this alien point of view. Whence comes this submission in the case of woman? . . .

History has shown us that men have always kept in their hands all concrete powers; since the earliest days of the patriarchate they have thought best to keep woman in a state of dependence; their codes of law have been set up against her; and thus she has been definitely established as the Other. This arrangement suited the economic interests of the males; but it conformed also to their ontological and moral pretensions. Once the subject seeks to assert himself, the Other, who limits and denies him, is none the less a necessity to him: he attains himself only through that reality which he is not, which is something other than himself. That is why man's life is never abundance and quietude; it is dearth and activity, it is struggle. Before him, man encounters Nature; he has some hold upon her, he endeavors to mold her to his desire. But she cannot fill his needs. Either she appears simply as a purely impersonal opposition, she is an obstacle and remains a stranger; or she submits passively to man's will and permits assimilation, so that he takes possession of her only through consuming her—that is, through destroying her. In both cases he remains alone; he is alone when he touches a stone, alone when he devours a fruit. There can be no presence of an other unless the other is also present in and for himself: which is to say that true alterity—otherness—is that of a consciousness separate from mine and substantially identical with mine.

It is the existence of other men that tears each man out of his immanence and enables him to fulfill the truth of his being, to complete himself through transcendence, through escape toward some objective, through enterprise. But this liberty not my own, while assuring mine, also conflicts with it: there is the tragedy of the unfortunate human consciousness; each separate conscious being aspires to set himself up alone as sovereign subject. Each tries to fulfill himself by reducing the other to slavery. But the slave, though he works and fears, senses himself somehow as the essential; and, by a dialectical inversion, it is the master who seems to be the inessential. It is possible to rise above this conflict if each individual freely recognizes the other, each regarding himself and the other simultaneously as object and as subject in a reciprocal manner. But friendship and generosity, which alone permit in actuality this recognition of free beings, are not facile virtues; they are assuredly man's highest achievement, and through that achievement he is to be found in his true nature. But this true nature is that of a struggle unceasingly begun, unceasingly abolished; it requires man to outdo himself at every moment. We might put it in other words and say that man attains an authentically moral attitude when he renounces *mere being* to assume his position as

an existent; through this transformation also he renounces all possession, for possession is one way of seeking mere being; but the transformation through which he attains true wisdom is never done, it is necessary to make it without ceasing, it demands a constant tension. And so, quite unable to fulfill himself in solitude, man is incessantly in danger in his relations with his fellows: his life is a difficult enterprise with success never assured.

But he does not like difficulty; he is afraid of danger. He aspires in contradictory fashion both to life and to repose, to existence and to merely being; he knows full well that "trouble of spirit" is the price of development, that his distance from the object is the price of his nearness to himself; but he dreams of quiet in disquiet and of an opaque plenitude that nevertheless would be endowed with consciousness. This dream incarnated is precisely woman; she is the wished-for intermediary between nature, the stranger to man, and the fellow being who is too closely identical. She opposes him with neither the hostile silence of nature nor the hard requirement of a reciprocal relation; through a unique privilege she is a conscious being and yet it seems possible to possess her in the flesh. Thanks to her, there is a means for escaping that implacable dialectic of master and slave which has its source in the reciprocity that exists between free beings.

We have seen that there were not at first free women whom the males had enslaved nor were there even castes based on sex. To regard woman simply as a slave is a mistake; there were women among the slaves, to be sure, but there have always been free women—that is, women of religious and social dignity. They accepted man's sovereignty and he did not feel menaced by a revolt that could make of him in turn the object. Woman thus seems to be the inessential who never goes back to being the essential, to be the absolute Other, without reciprocity. This conviction is dear to the male, and every creation myth has expressed it, among others the legend of Genesis, which, through Christianity, has been kept alive in Western civilization. Eve was not fashioned at the same time as the man; she was not fabricated from a different substance, nor of the same clay as was used to model Adam: she was taken from the flank of the first male. Not even her birth was independent; God did not spontaneously choose to create her as an end in herself and in order to be worshipped directly by her in return for it. She was destined by Him for man; it was to rescue Adam from loneliness that He gave her to him, in her mate was her origin and her purpose; she was his complement on the order of the inessential. Thus she appeared in the guise of privileged prey. She was nature elevated to transparency of consciousness; she was a conscious being, but naturally submissive. And therein lies the wondrous hope that man has often put in woman: he hopes to fulfill himself as a being by carnally possessing a being, but at the same time confirming his sense of freedom through the docility of a free person. No man would consent to be a woman, but every man wants women to exist. "Thank God for having created woman." "Nature is good since she has given women to men." In such expressions man once more asserts with naïve arrogance that his presence in this world is an ineluctable fact and a right, that of woman a mere accident—but a very happy accident. Appearing as the Other, woman appears at the same time as an abundance of being in contrast to that existence the nothingness of which man senses in himself; the Other, being regarded as the object in the eyes of the subject, is regarded as *en soi;* therefore as a being. In woman is incarnated in positive form the lack that the existent carries in his heart, and it is in seeking to be made whole through her that man hopes to attain self-realization. . . .

. . . Perhaps the myth of woman will some day be extinguished; the more women assert themselves as human beings, the more the marvelous quality of the Other will die out in them. But today it still exists in the heart of every man.

A myth always implies a subject who projects his hopes and his fears toward a sky of transcendence. Women do not set themselves up as Subject and hence have erected no virile myth in which their projects are reflected; they have no religion or poetry of their own: they still dream through the dreams of men. Gods made by males are the gods they worship. Men have shaped for their own exaltation great virile figures: Hercules, Prometheus, Parsifal; woman has only a secondary part to play in the destiny of these heroes. No doubt there are conventional figures of man caught in his relations to woman: the father, the seducer, the husband, the jealous lover, the good son, the wayward son; but they have all been established by men, and they lack the dignity of myth, being hardly more than clichés. Whereas woman is defined exclusively in her relation to man. The asymmetry of the categories—male and female—is made manifest in the unilateral form of sexual myths. We sometimes say "the sex" to designate woman; she is the flesh, its delights and dangers. The truth that for woman man is sex and carnality has never been proclaimed because there is no one to proclaim it. Representation of the world, like the world itself, is the work of men; they describe it from their own point of view, which they confuse with absolute truth.

It is always difficult to describe a myth; it cannot be grasped or encompassed; it haunts the human consciousness without ever appearing before it in fixed form. The myth is so various, so contradictory, that at first its unity is not discerned: Delilah and Judith, Aspasia and Lucretia, Pandora and Athena—woman is at once Eve and the Virgin Mary. She is an idol, a servant, the source of life, a power of darkness; she is the elemental silence of truth, she is artifice, gossip, and falsehood; she is healing presence and sorceress; she is man's prey, his downfall, she is everything that he is not and that he longs for, his negation and his *raison d'être.* . . .

Man seeks in woman the Other as Nature and as his fellow being. But we know what ambivalent feelings Nature inspires in man. He exploits her, but she crushes him, he is born of her and dies in her; she is the source of his being and the realm that he subjugates to his will; Nature is a vein of gross material in which the soul is imprisoned, and she is the supreme reality; she is contingence and Idea, the finite and the whole; she is what opposes the Spirit, and the Spirit itself. Now ally, now enemy, she appears as the dark chaos from whence life wells up, as this life itself, and as the over-yonder toward which life tends. Woman sums up nature as Mother, Wife, and Idea; these forms now mingle and now conflict and each of them wears a double visage. . . .

This, then, is the reason why woman has a double and deceptive visage: she is all that man desires and all that he does not attain. She is the good mediatrix between propitious Nature and man; and she is the temptation of unconquered Nature, counter to all goodness. She incarnates all moral values, from good to evil, and their opposites; she is the substance of action and whatever is an obstacle to it, she is man's grasp on the world and his frustration; as such she is the source and origin of all man's reflection on his existence and of whatever expression he is able to give to it; and yet she works to divert him from himself, to make him sink down in silence and in death. She is servant and companion, but he expects her also to be his audience and critic and to confirm him in his sense of being; but she opposes him with her indifference, even with her mockery and laughter. He projects upon her what he desires and what he fears, what he loves and what he hates. And if it is so difficult to say anything specific about her, that is because man seeks the whole of himself in her and because she is All. She is All, that is, on the plane of the inessential; she is all the Other. And, as the other, she is other than herself, other than what is expected of her. Being all, she is never quite *this* which she should be; she is everlasting deception, the very deception of that existence which is never successfully attained nor fully reconciled with the totality of existents.

ROBERT WACHBROIT
Genetic Encores
The Ethics of Human Cloning

ROBERT WACHBROIT *teaches at the University of Maryland School of Medicine, is a Senior Research Fellow at the Kennedy Institute of Ethics at Georgetown University, and a research scholar at the Institute for Philosophy and Public Policy. He has written numerous articles in the areas of philosophy of science, philosophy of medicine, and medical ethics.*

THE successful cloning of an adult sheep, announced in Scotland this past February, is one of the most dramatic recent examples of a scientific discovery becoming a public issue. During the last few months, various commentators—scientists and theologians, physicians and legal experts, talk-radio hosts and editorial writers—have been busily responding to

Wachbroit, Robert, "Genetic Encores: The Ethics of Human Cloning" by Robert Wachbroit, from *Report from the Institute for Philosophy and Public Policy* (Fall 1997). Reprinted by permission of the author.

the news, some calming fears, other raising alarms about the prospect of cloning a human being. At the request of the President, the National Bioethics Advisory Commission (NBAC) held hearings and prepared a report on the religious, ethical, and legal issues surrounding human cloning. While declining to call for a permanent ban on the practice, the Commission recommended a moratorium on efforts to clone human beings, and emphasized the importance of further public deliberation on the subject.

An interesting tension is at work in the NBAC report. Commission members were well aware of "the widespread public discomfort, even revulsion, about cloning human beings." Perhaps recalling the images of Dolly the ewe that were featured on the covers of national news magazines, they noted that "the impact of these most recent developments on our national psyche has been quite remarkable." Accordingly, they felt that one of their tasks was to articulate, as fully and sympathetically as possible, the range of concerns that the prospect of human cloning had elicited.

Yet it seems clear that some of these concerns, at least, are based on false beliefs about genetic influence and the nature of the individuals that would be produced through cloning. Consider, for instance, the fear that a clone would not be an "individual" but merely a "carbon copy" of someone else—an automaton of the sort familiar from science fiction. As many scientists have pointed out, a clone would not in fact be an identical *copy,* but more like a delayed identical *twin.* And just as identical twins are two separate people—biologically, psychologically, morally and legally, though not genetically—so, too, a clone would be a separate person from her non-contemporaneous twin. To think otherwise is to embrace a belief in genetic determinism—the view that genes determine everything about us, and that environmental factors or the random events in human development are insignificant.

The overwhelming scientific consensus is that genetic determinism is false. In coming to understand the ways in which genes operate,

biologists have also become aware of the myriad ways in which the environment affects their "expression." The genetic contribution to the simplest physical traits, such as height and hair color, is significantly mediated by environmental factors (and possibly by stochastic events as well). And the genetic contribution to the traits we value most deeply, from intelligence to compassion, is conceded by even the most enthusiastic genetic researchers to be limited and indirect.

It is difficult to gauge the extent to which "repugnance" toward cloning generally rests on a belief in genetic determinism. Hoping to account for the fact that people "instinctively recoil" from the prospect of cloning, James Q. Wilson wrote, "There is a natural sentiment that is offended by the mental picture of identical babies being produced in some biological factory." Which raises the question: once people learn that this picture is mere science fiction, does the offense that cloning presents to "natural sentiment" attenuate, or even disappear? Jean Bethke Elshtain cited the nightmare scenarios of "the man and woman on the street," who imagine a future populated by "a veritable army of Hitlers, ruthless and remorseless bigots who kept reproducing themselves until they had finished what the historic Hitler failed to do: annihilate us." What happens, though, to the "pity and terror" evoked by the topic of cloning when such scenarios are deprived (as they deserve to be) of all credibility?

Richard Lewontin has argued that the critics' fears—or at least, those fears that merit consideration in formulating public policy—dissolve once genetic determinism is refuted. He criticizes the NBAC report for excessive deference to opponents of human cloning, and calls for greater public education on the scientific issues. (The Commission in fact makes the same recommendation, but Lewontin seems unimpressed.) Yet even if a public education campaign succeeded in eliminating the most egregious misconceptions about genetic influence, that wouldn't settle the matter. People might continue to express concerns about the interests and rights of human clones, about the social and moral consequences of the cloning process, and about the possible motivations for creating children in this way.

One set of ethical concerns about human clones involves the risks and uncertainties associated with the current state of cloning technology. This technology has not yet been tested with human subjects, and scientists cannot rule out the possibility of mutation or other biological damage. Accordingly, the NBAC report concluded that "at this time, it is morally unacceptable for anyone in the public or private sector, whether in a research or clinical setting, to attempt to create a child using somatic cell nuclear transfer cloning." Such efforts, it said, would pose "unacceptable risks to the fetus and/or potential child."

The ethical issues of greatest importance in the cloning debate, however, do not involve possible failures of cloning technology, but rather the consequences of its success. Assuming that scientists were able to clone human beings without incurring the risks mentioned above, what concerns might there be about the welfare of clones?

Some opponents of cloning believe that such individuals would be wronged in morally significant ways. Many of these wrongs involve the denial of what Joel Feinberg has called "the right to an open future." For example, a child might be constantly compared to the adult from whom he was cloned, and thereby burdened with oppressive expectations. Even worse, the parents might actually limit the child's opportunities for growth and development: a child cloned from a basketball player, for instance, might be denied any educational opportunities that were not in line with a career in basketball. Finally, regardless of his parents' conduct or attitudes, a child might be burdened by the *thought* that he is a copy and not an "original." The child's sense of self-worth or individuality or dignity, so some have argued, would thus be difficult to sustain.

How should we respond to these concerns? On the one hand, the existence of a right to an open future has a strong intuitive appeal. We are troubled by parents who radically constrict their children's possibilities for growth and development. Obviously, we would condemn a cloning parent for crushing a child with oppressive expectations, just as we might condemn fundamentalist parents for utterly isolating their children from the modern world, or the parents of twins for inflicting matching wardrobes and rhyming names. But this is not enough to sustain an objection to cloning itself. Unless the claim is that cloned parents cannot help but be oppressive, we would have cause to say they had wronged their children only because of their subsequent, and avoidable, sins of bad parenting— not because they had chosen to create the child in the first place. (The possible reasons for making this choice will be discussed below.)

We must also remember that children are often born in the midst of all sorts of hopes and expectations; the idea that there is a special burden associated with the thought "There is someone who is genetically just like me" is necessarily speculative. Moreover, given the falsity of genetic determinism, any conclusions a child might draw from observing the person from whom he was cloned would be uncertain at best. His knowledge of his future would differ only in degree from what many children already know once they begin to learn parts of their family's (medical) history. Some of us knew that we would be bald, or to what diseases we might be susceptible. To be sure, the cloned individual might know more about what he or she could become. But because our knowledge of the effect of environment on development is so incomplete, the clone would certainly be in for some surprises.

Finally, even if we were convinced that clones are likely to suffer particular burdens, that would not be enough to show that it is wrong to create them. The child of a poor family can be expected to suffer specific hardships and burdens, but we don't thereby conclude that such children shouldn't be born. Despite the hardships, poor children can experience parental love and many of the joys of being alive: the deprivations of poverty, however painful, are not decisive. More generally, no one's life is entirely free of some difficulties or burdens. In order for these considerations to have decisive weight, we have to be able to say that life doesn't offer any compensating benefits. Concerns expressed about the welfare of human clones do not appear to justify such a bleak assessment. Most such children can be expected to have lives well worth living; many of the imagined harms are no worse than those faced by children acceptably produced by more conventional means. If there is something deeply objectionable about cloning, it is more likely to be found by examining implications of the cloning process itself, or the reasons people might have for availing themselves of it.

Human cloning falls conceptually between two other technologies. At one end we have the assisted reproductive technologies, such as in vitro fertilization, whose primary purpose is to enable couples to produce a child with whom they have a biological connection. At the other end we have the emerging technologies of genetic engineering—specifically, gene transplantation technologies—whose primary purpose is to produce a child that has certain traits. Many proponents of cloning see it as part of the first technology: cloning is just another way of providing a couple with a biological child they might otherwise be unable to have. Since this goal and these other technologies are acceptable, cloning should be acceptable as well. On the other hand, many opponents of cloning see it as part of the second technology: even though cloning is a transplantation of an entire nucleus and not of specific genes, it is nevertheless an attempt to produce a child with certain traits. The deep misgivings we may have about the genetic manipulation of offspring should apply to cloning as well.

The debate cannot be resolved, however, simply by determining which technology to assimilate cloning to. For example, some opponents of human cloning see it as continuous with assisted reproductive technologies; but since they find those technologies objectionable as well, the assimilation does not indicate approval. Rather than argue for grouping cloning with one technology or another, I wish to suggest that we can best understand the significance of the cloning process by comparing it with these other technologies, and thus broadening the debate.

To see what can be learned from such a comparative approach, let us consider a central argument that has been made against cloning—that it undermines the structure of the family by making identities and lineages unclear. On the one hand, the relationship between an adult and the child cloned from her could be described as that between a parent and offspring. Indeed, some commentators have called cloning "asexual reproduction," which clearly suggests that cloning is a way of generating *descendants*. The clone, on this view, has only one biological parent. On the other hand, from the point of view of genetics, the clone is a *sibling*, so that cloning is more accurately described as "delayed twinning" rather than as asexual reproduction. The clone, on this view, has two biological parents, not one—they are the same parents as those of the person from whom that individual was cloned.

Cloning thus results in ambiguities. Is the clone an offspring or a sibling? Does the clone have one biological parent or two? The moral significance of these ambiguities lies in the fact that in many societies, including our own, lineage identifies responsibilities. Typically, the parent, not the sibling, is responsible for the child. But if no one is unambiguously the parent, so the worry might go, who is responsible for the clone? Insofar as social identity is based on biological ties, won't this identity be blurred or confounded?

Some assisted reproductive technologies have raised similar questions about lineage and identity. An anonymous sperm donor is thought to have no parental obligations towards his biological child. A surrogate mother may be required to relinquish all parental claims to the child she bears. In these cases, the social and legal determination of "who is the parent" may appear to proceed in defiance of profound biological facts, and to subvert attachments that we as a society are ordinarily committed to upholding. Thus, while the *aim* of assisted reproductive technologies is to allow people to produce or raise a child to whom they are biologically connected, such technologies may also involve the creation of social ties that are permitted to override biological ones.

In the case of cloning, however, ambiguous lineages would seem to be less problematic, precisely because no one is being asked to relinquish a claim on a child to whom he or she might otherwise acknowledge a biological connection. What, then, are the critics afraid of? It does not seem plausible that someone would have herself cloned and then hand the child over to her parents, saying, "You take care of her! She's *your* daughter!" Nor is it likely that, if the cloned individual did raise the child, she would suddenly refuse to pay for college on the grounds that this was not a sister's responsibility. Of course, policymakers should address any confusion in the social or legal assignment of responsibility resulting from cloning. But there are reasons to think that this would be *less* difficult than in the case of other reproductive technologies.

Similarly, when we compare cloning with genetic engineering, cloning may prove to be the less troubling of the two technologies. This is true even though the dark futures to which they are often alleged to lead are broadly alike. For example, a recent *Washington Post* article examined fears that the development of genetic enhancement technologies might "create a market in preferred physical traits." The reporter asked, "Might it lead to a society of DNA haves and have-nots, and the creation of a new underclass of people unable to keep up with the genetically fortified Joneses?" Similarly, a member of the National Bioethics Advisory Commission expressed concern that cloning might become "almost a preferred practice," taking its place "on the continuum of providing the best for your child." As a consequence, parents who chose to "play the lottery of old-fashioned reproduction would be considered irresponsible."

Such fears, however, seem more warranted with respect to genetic engineering than cloning. By offering some people—in all probability, members of the upper classes—the opportunity to acquire desired traits through genetic manipulation, genetic engineering could bring about a biological reinforcement (or accentuation) of existing social divisions. It is hard enough already for disadvantaged children to compete with their more affluent counterparts, given the material resources and intellectual opportunities that are often available only to children of privilege. This unfairness would almost certainly be compounded if genetic manipulation came into the picture. In contrast, cloning does not bring about "improvements" in the genome: it is, rather, a way of *duplicating* the genome—with all its imperfections. It wouldn't enable certain groups of people to keep getting better and better along some valued dimension.

To some critics, admittedly, this difference will not seem terribly important. Theologian Gilbert Meilaender, Jr., objects to cloning on the grounds that children created through this technology would be "designed as a product" rather than "welcomed as a gift." The fact that the design process would be more selective and nuanced in the case of genetic engineering would, from this perspective, have no moral significance. To the extent that this objection reflects a concern about the commodification of human life, we can address it in part when we consider people's reasons for engaging in cloning.

This final area of contention in the cloning debate is as much psychological as it is scientific or philosophical. If human cloning technology were safe and widely available, what use would people make of it? What reasons would they have to engage in cloning?

In its report to the President, the Commission imagined a few situations in which people might avail themselves of cloning. In one scenario, a husband and wife who wish to have children are both carriers of a lethal recessive gene:

Rather than risk the one in four chance of conceiving a child who will suffer a short and painful existence, the couple considers the alternatives: to forgo rearing children; to adopt; to use prenatal diagnosis and selective abortion; to use donor gametes free of the recessive trait; or to use the cells of one of the adults and attempt to clone a child. To avoid donor gametes and selective abortion, while maintaining a genetic tie to their child, they opt for cloning. In another scenario, the parents of a terminally ill child are told that only a bone marrow transplant can save the child's life. "With no other donor available, the parents attempt to clone a human being from the cells of the dying child. If successful, the new child will be a perfect match for bone marrow transplant, and can be used as a donor without significant risk or discomfort. The net result: two healthy children, loved by their parents, who happen [sic] to be identical twins of different ages."

The Commission was particularly impressed by the second example. That scenario, said the NBAC report, "makes what is probably the strongest possible case for cloning a human being, as it demonstrates how this technology could be used for lifesaving purposes." Indeed, the report suggests that it would be a "tragedy" to allow "the sick child to die because of a moral or political objection to such cloning." Nevertheless, we should note that many people would be morally uneasy about the use of a minor as a donor, regardless of whether the child were a result of cloning. Even if this unease is justifiably overridden by other concerns, the "transplant scenario" may not present a more compelling case for cloning than that of the infertile couple desperately seeking a biological child.

Most critics, in fact, decline to engage the specifics of such tragic (and presumably rare) situations. Instead, they bolster their case by imagining very different scenarios. Potential users of the technology, they suggest, are narcissists or control freaks—people who will regard their children not as free, original selves but as products intended to meet more or less rigid specifications. Even if such people are not genetic determinists, their recourse to cloning will indicate a desire to exert all possible influence over the "kind" of child they produce.

The critics' alarm at this prospect has in part to do, as we have seen, with concerns about the psychological burdens such a desire would impose on the clone. But it also reflects a broader concern about the values expressed, and promoted, by a society's reproductive policies. Critics argue that a society that enables people to clone themselves thereby endorses the most narcissistic reason for having children—to perpetuate oneself through a genetic encore. The demonstrable falsity of genetic determinism may detract little, if at all, from the strength of this motive. Whether or not clones will have a grievance against their parents for producing them with this motivation, the societal indulgence of that motivation is improper and harmful.

It can be argued, however, that the critics have simply misunderstood the social meaning of a policy that would permit people to clone themselves even in the absence of the heartrending exigencies described in the NBAC report. This country has developed a strong commitment to reproductive autonomy. (This commitment emerged in response to the dismal history of eugenics—the very history that is sometimes invoked to support restrictions on cloning.) With the exception of practices that risk coercion and exploitation—notably baby-selling and commercial surrogacy—we do not interfere with people's freedom to create and acquire children by almost any means, for almost any reason. This policy does not reflect a dogmatic libertarianism. Rather, it recognizes the extraordinary personal importance and private character of reproductive decisions, even those with significant social repercussions.

Our willingness to sustain such a policy also reflects a recognition of the moral complexities of parenting. For example, we know that the motives people have for bringing a child into the world do not necessarily determine the manner in which they raise him. Even when parents start out as narcissists, the experience of childrearing will sometimes transform their initial impulses, making them caring, respectful, and even self-sacrificing. Seeing their child grow and develop, they learn that she is not merely an extension of themselves. Of course, some parents never make this discovery; others, having done so, never forgive their children for it. The pace and extent of moral development among parents (no less than among children) is infinitely variable. Still, we are justified in saying that those who engage in cloning will not, by virtue of this fact, be immune to the transformative effects of parenthood—even if it is the case (and it won't always be) that they begin with more problematic motives than those of parents who engage in the "genetic lottery."

Moreover, the nature of parental motivation is itself more complex than the critics often allow. Though we can agree that narcissism is a vice not to be encouraged, we lack a clear notion of where pride in one's children ends and narcissism begins. When, for example, is it unseemly to bask in the reflected glory of a child's achievements? Imagine a champion gymnast who takes delight in her daughter's athletic prowess. Now imagine that the child was actually cloned from one of the gymnast's somatic cells. Would we have to revise our moral assessment of her pleasure in her daughter's success? Or suppose a man wanted to be cloned and to give his child opportunities he himself had never enjoyed. And suppose that, rightly or wrongly, the man took the child's success as a measure of his own untapped

potential—an indication of the flourishing life he might have had. Is *this* sentiment blamable? And is it all that different from what many natural parents feel?

Until recently, there were few ethical, social, or legal discussions about human cloning via nuclear transplantation, since the scientific consensus was that such a procedure was not biologically possible. With the appearance of Dolly, the situation has changed. But although it now seems more likely that human cloning will become feasible, we may doubt that the practice will come into widespread use.

I suspect it will not, but my reasons will not offer much comfort to the critics of cloning. While the technology for nuclear transplantation advances, other technologies—notably the technology of genetic engineering—will be progressing as well. Human genetic engineering will be applicable to a wide variety of traits; it will be more powerful than cloning, and hence more attractive to more people. It will also, as I have suggested, raise more troubling questions than the prospect of cloning has thus far.

CHAPTER NINE

Why Are My Emotions Important to Me?

What was your latest passion? When did you last get angry, or feel love, or find yourself envious or jealous? What was the significance of that emotion? Was it an unwelcome intrusion into an otherwise calm and enjoyable day? Or did your emotion actually define your day, perhaps even (as with love) define your life for months or years to come? Was this a familiar emotion to you—do you get angry or fall in love often—or did it seem out of character, a strange reaction that does not represent your real personality? Was it annoying and embarrassing, or did it feel right and good, perhaps even refreshing or elevating? What is the significance of your emotions in your life? Are they disruptions or punctuations? Are they just moments of excitement, or do they have some more significant meaning? How are we to understand emotion, and how do our emotions fit into our lives? We often warn one another against emotion, against becoming "emotional." Indeed, becoming emotional is often viewed as a sign of weakness, poor character, or temporary irrationality. "Let's be reasonable" often means "Let's not get carried away by our emotions," and a familiar line in a popular movie counsels us, "Don't get mad, get even."

Twenty-five hundred years of emphasis on reason as the subject matter of philosophy and the core of human nature has tended to minimize the importance of emotions in human life. It is true that a person who is all emotion and is never rational is a monster, but a person who is all rationality and without emotion is also a monster, a mere automaton, a walking computer and not a human being. One of the great horror films, *Invasion of the Body Snatchers,* portrays aliens as humanoids without emotion. It is our emotions, as well as our reason, that make us human.

Emotions have had a confused place in the history of philosophy. On the one hand, they are acknowledged to be vital, important, and essential to life. Aristotle insisted that the good life consists of having the right emotions as well as having reason and doing the right things. Christian philosophers have long insisted that love and those emotions associated with faith are among the most important things in life. On the other hand, philosophers have recognized that the emotions can be dangerous.

Ancient philosophers likened love and anger to madness, and the famed storyteller Aesop insisted that "emotions should be the slaves, not the masters, of reason." Accordingly, the view that emotions are important and necessary has always been balanced by the view that emotions are subhuman, our more bestial aspect and the "lowest" part of the soul. In more modern times, both popular and scientific views of emotions have reduced them to primitive physical reactions and have opposed them to reason and intelligence. Thus, Descartes and most of his contemporaries referred to the emotions as "animal spirits," and William James more recently defined emotion in terms of physiological ("visceral") reaction. In such a view, emotions typically emerge as unlearned, instinctual, perhaps even stupid if not destructive, and, in any case, disruptive and intrusive in our otherwise rational lives.

Obviously our emotions occupy an ambiguous place in our conception of ourselves. They are not within our direct control, but neither are they alien to us. Our emotions are different from reasoning and thinking as such, but they are clearly affected by our reasoning, and they affect our thinking in turn. Our emotions are in some sense "in the mind," but like perceptions and unlike a pain or a stomachache, they are about people and situations in the world. They obviously involve our bodies, but they also involve thought and awareness. They are essential to being a good person, but they also contribute to selfishness, evil, and insanity.

Aristotle long ago recognized that emotions are not just feeling but also perceptions: They involve seeing the world in a certain way. Emotions also involve motives; they urge us to action. His view—augmented by the Stoic philosophers in subsequent generations—was that emotions already include certain aspects of reason; they are learned and can be learned well or badly. They can be smart or foolish, noble or embarrassing.

One particularly ingenious theory of emotion as something more than mere feeling is Book II of David Hume's *Treatise of Human Nature*. A passion, Hume suggested, is a complex mix of impressions (sensations or feelings) and ideas. Pride, for example, involves not just a pleasant feeling but also a set of ideas about one's *self*. Hume opposed passion and reason, but in an unusual and provocative twist of the usual philosophical championing of reason, he announced that "reason is and ought to be the slave of the passions." Showing a great deal of sympathy for David Hume, contemporary philosopher Annette Baier makes the point that emotions are essential for things that we care about. A very different view of emotions was developed by the French existentialist Jean-Paul Sartre. Emotions, he suggested, are "magical transformations of the world." Like Aristotle, he recognized the perception-like nature of emotion, but Sartre added another unusual twist. Emotions are purposive, he argued; they have an end in mind. He believed that we get afraid or angry or resentful in order to accomplish something, usually to escape from or deny an unpleasant situation.

Understanding emotions in general is perhaps not as personally rewarding as understanding specific emotions. Anger is a particularly misunderstood emotion. It is often thought to be irrational and dangerous, even a sin. We often talk about it as if it were a fluid that fills us up and makes us "hot," occasionally "bursting" or "exploding." Robert Solomon suggests a very different way of thinking about anger.

Love, by contrast, is an emotion that is almost universally and uncritically praised, but the price of that adulation is that love is an emotion that is rarely scrutinized. In Plato's *Symposium,* a half dozen of Socrates's friends give speeches on the topic of "love and its virtues." One of those speeches is a fantastic tale of the origins of love told by the comic playwright Aristophanes. Another (related by Socrates) is a lesson from the muse Diotima. Following Aristophanes, Robert Solomon offers a theory of love understood as a form of shared identity.

ARISTOTLE

On Anger

ARISTOTLE *(384–322 B.C.) was a biologist as well as a great philosopher and wrote widely on topics in virtually every other science, from astronomy and physics to psychology. The following excerpt is taken from his book on rhetoric, in which he discusses the uses of emotion in moving the public to action.*

WE shall define an emotion as that which leads one's condition to become so transformed that his judgment is affected, and which is accompanied by pleasure and pain. Examples of emotions include anger, pity, fear, and the like, as well as the opposites of these. We will need with each of these emotions to investigate three particulars; in investigating anger, for instance, we will ask what the temperament is of angry people, with whom they most often become angry, and at what sort of things. To grasp one or two but not all three of these conditions would make it impossible to induce anger in one's audience. The same is true with the other emotions. So, just as we listed propositions in what we said earlier, let us do this again in analyzing these emotions in the same way.

Let anger be defined as a distressed desire for conspicuous vengeance in return for a conspicuous and unjustifiable contempt of one's person or friends. If this indeed defines anger, then the anger of the angry person is necessarily always directed towards someone in particular, e.g., Cleon, but not towards all of humanity; also of necessity is that this individual has done or intended to do something to him or one of his friends, and that accompanying every outburst of anger is a certain pleasure derived from the hope for revenge. I say "pleasure" because it is pleasant to contemplate achieving one's goals; and no one attempts to achieve what seems to be impossible for himself, so the angry man attempts to achieve what is possible for himself. The poet spoke correctly when he said that anger,

Much sweeter than dripping honey,
Swells in men's hearts.

Pleasure follows upon anger for this reason and because the mind is consumed with thoughts of vengeance; like dreams, the visions then conjured up create pleasure.

Slighting is the implementing of an opinion about what one considers to be worthless; for we think both the good and the bad to be worthy of attention (as well as what is potentially good or bad), but we do not consider whatever is of little or no account to be worthy of attention.

There are three forms of slighting—scorn, spite, and insolence. One slights what he scorns, for whatever one thinks to be worthy of nothing he scorns, and he slights what is worthy of nothing. Then one who is spiteful is also scornful, for spite involves the interference in another's wishes, not to achieve anything for oneself, but only to make sure that the other achieves nothing. Since he achieves nothing for himself, he slights the other. It is evident that the other does not intend to harm him; if he did, it would then be a matter of fear, not of slighting. It is evident also that he does not intend to help him to any appreciable degree, for there would then be an attempt at creating a friendship.

Aristotle, "On Anger," trans. Jon Solomon, from *Rhetoric*, 1378a–1380a4, tr. Jon Solomon.

To act insolently constitutes a form of slighting, for insolence involves doing and saying things that produce shame for the person to whom these things are done or said—so that something else might happen to him (other than what has already happened), but for the other's pleasure. If it were done in retaliation, then this would not be insolence, but sheer vengeance. The insolent person derives pleasure from this because he sees others suffer and thus considers himself quite superior. The young and the rich often derive pleasure from such insolence, for they consider themselves superior when acting insolently. Dishonor is an act of insolence, and the one who dishonors is one who slights, since that which is worthy of nothing—of neither good or bad—has no honor. For this reason the angered Achilles says,

> He has dishonored me; he has himself taken and keeps my prize.

and,

> I am without honor, as if some foreigner.

and shows that he is angered for this very reason. Some think it fitting that they be esteemed by those of lesser birth, ability, nobility, or whatever quality in which one is generally superior to another; for example, the rich man considers himself worthy of esteem from a poor man where wealth is concerned, as does the rhetorician from one who is inarticulate, the ruler from the governed, and even the hopeful ruler from those he hopes to rule. So it is said,

> The anger of divine kings is mighty,

and,

> But he holds his anger for another day;

the cause of their vexation is their superior station, and still others feel anger at those from whom they expect the proper care, for example, from those for whom he—either acting by himself or *via* his agents or friends—has done or is doing willful or willed service.

It is now evident from these analyses what the temperament is of angered people, at whom they become angered, and for what reasons. They become angry when they are in distress, for one in distress desires something. If someone should in any manner stand in one's way, for instance, if one should directly prevent a thirsty man from drinking (or even if it is done indirectly, he will appear to be doing the same thing), or if someone opposes, fails to assist, or in some other way annoys a distressed person, he will become angry at any of those individuals. For this reason the sick, the poor, those at war, the lover, and anyone with an unsatisfied desire, are prone to anger and irascibility, particularly against those who make light of their present distress. Examples include the ill person angry at those making light of his illness, the poor man angry at those making light of his poverty, the warrior angry at those making light of his struggle, the lover at those making light of his love and so forth, for each person is predisposed towards his own kind of anger caused by his own sort of distress. He will also anger if he should happen to receive the opposite of what he expected, for the unexpected creates a greater bitterness just as it can create the greater joy if one attains his desires contrary to his expectations. From these observations the hours, periods, moods, and ages most conducive to anger become apparent, as do the places and occasions; and the more intense or numerous these conditions are, the more conducive to anger they become.

We have now seen what sort of temperament belongs to people predisposed to anger. They become angry at those who laugh, scoff, and jeer at them—all acts of insolence—and at those doing them harm in manners which represent an attitude of insolence. This harm cannot be either retaliatory or beneficial to the doers, for then it would not seem to be an act of insolence. They also become angry at those who malign them or scorn matters they take greatly to heart; zealous philosophers and those concerned with their appearance, to cite just two of many examples, anger at those who scorn philosophy and those who scorn their appearance, respectively. Such anger becomes increasingly severe if the angered individuals suspect that this ability or quality does not belong or appear to belong to them, for they do not mind the ridicule when they feel thoroughly superior in those abilities or qualities at which others scoff. Anger is also directed at their friends more often than at others, since better treatment is expected from them, and also at those who normally give honor to take thought of them, but then cease to act in this way; the angry individuals here assume they are being scorned, for otherwise they would be treated in the same way as usual. They also become angry at those who fail to repay or inadequately repay acts of kindness and at inferiors who work against them, for any such people appear to have a scornful attitude; in the latter example the angered individuals are opposed by those who consider them inferior and in the former they have offered kindness to those who consider them inferior.

They especially anger at those of no account who slight them, since we suggested that an anger resulting from a slight was directed towards those who have no right to slight another, and it is one's inferiors who have no right to do so. They also become angry at their friends who fail to speak well of them or who fail to treat them well, or especially when they do the opposite, or when they do not understand their needs (just as Antiphon's Plexippus failed to understand Meleager's needs). It is a sign of contempt to fail to perceive the needs of a friend, since we do not forget those who are on our mind. One also angers at those who celebrate or act quite cheerfully in his misfortunes; either action is a sign of enmity or slight. One also feels anger against those who show no concern for the pains

they have given him, which explains why one becomes angry with messengers who bring bad news. One also feels anger at those who listen to talk about him or ogle at his weaknesses, for it is as if they are slighters or enemies; friends would sympathize, since everyone is pained to focus on his own weaknesses. In addition, one angers at those who slight him in the presence of five classes of people—those who envy him, those he admires, those by whom he wishes to be admired, those whom he respects, and those who respect him. When people slight him in the presence of these, they incite him to an even greater anger. One also feels anger at those who slight those whom it would be a disgrace not to defend—parents, children, wives, subordinates—or to those who do not return a favor (since such a slight is an impropriety), or to those who pretend not to know about a matter he feels to be of importance, since this is an act of scorn. And one feels anger toward those beneficent to others, but not to him as well, for it is again an act of scorn to deem everyone else worthy of treatment he is not deemed worthy to receive. Forgetfulness, even of something so insignificant as a name, also produces anger, since forgetfulness as well seems to be a sign of slight and since forgetfulness derives from neglect, which is a slight.

We have now established simultaneously at whom one becomes angry, the temperament of the angry person, and the causes for his anger. It is clear that in his speech the orator must create in his audience a temperament suitable for anger and establish his adversaries as those to be held liable for what makes his audience anger and as the sort of men at whom they should be angry.

RENÉ DESCARTES

The Passions of the Soul

RENÉ DESCARTES *(1596–1650) is, among many other things, the father of Cartesian dualism, which holds that the mind and the body are separate "substances." This raises the difficult question of how they interact, but it raises specific problems for the analysis of emotion. Emotions, more than any other psychic phenomena, seem to be both of the mind and of the body. In the following excerpt, Descartes tried to solve such problems with his theory of "animal spirits," which are of the body but move the soul as well.*

OF THE PASSIONS IN GENERAL, AND INCIDENTALLY OF THE WHOLE NATURE OF MAN

THAT *What in Respect of a Subject Is Passion, Is in Some Other Regard Always Action.* There is nothing in which the defective nature of the sciences which we have received from the ancients appears more clearly than in what they have written on the passions; for, although this is a matter which has at all times been the object of much investigation, and though it would appear to be one of the most difficult, inasmuch as since every one has experience of the passions within himself, there is not necessity to borrow one's observations from elsewhere in order to discover their nature; yet that which the ancients have taught regarding them is both so slight, and for the most part so far from credible, that I am unable to entertain any hope of approximation to the truth excepting by shunning the paths which they have followed. This is why I shall be here obliged to write just as though I were treating of a matter which no one had ever touched on before me; and, to begin with, I consider that all that which occurs or that happens anew, is by the philosophers, generally speaking, termed a passion, in as far as the subject to which it occurs is concerned, and an action in respect of him who causes it to occur. Thus although the agent and the recipient are frequently very different, the action and the passion are always one and the same thing, although having different names, because of the two diverse subjects to which it may be related.

What the Functions of the Soul Are. After having thus considered all the functions which pertain to the body alone, it is easy to recognise that there is nothing in us which we ought to attribute to our soul excepting our thoughts, which are mainly of two sorts, the one being the actions of the soul, and the other its passions. Those which I call its actions are all our desires, because we find by experience that they proceed directly from our soul, and appear to depend on it alone: while, on the other hand, we may usually term one's passions all those kinds of perception or forms of knowledge which are found in us, because it is often not our soul which makes them what they are, and because it always receives them from the things which are represented by them. . . .

Of the Perceptions. Our perceptions are also of two sorts, and the one have the soul as a cause and the other the body. Those which have the soul as a cause are the perceptions of our desires, and of all the imaginations or other thoughts which depend on them. For it is certain that we cannot desire anything without perceiving by the same means that we desire it; and, although in regard to our

Descartes, René, "The Passions of the Soul," from *The Philosphical Works of Descartes*, Volume 1, trans. Elizabeth S. Haldane and F. R. T. Ross (Cambridge University Press, 1967). Reprinted by permission of Cambridge University Press.

soul it is an action to desire something, we may say that it is also one of its passions to perceive that it desires. Yet because this perception and this will are really one and the same thing, the more noble always supplies the denomination, and thus we are not in the habit of calling it a passion, but only an action. . . .

That the Imaginations Which only Depend on the Fortuitous Movements of the Spirits, May Be Passions Just as Truly as the Perceptions Which Depend on the Nerves. It remains for us to notice here that all the same things which the soul perceives by the intermission of the nerves, may also be represented by the fortuitous course of the animal spirits, without there being any other difference excepting that the impressions which come into the brain by the nerves are usually more lively or definite than those excited there by the spirits, which caused me to say [previously] that the former resemble the shadow or picture of the latter. We must also notice that it sometimes happens that this picture is so similar to the thing which it represents that we may be mistaken therein regarding the perceptions which relate to objects which are outside us, or at least those which relate to certain parts of our body, but that we cannot be so deceived regarding the passions, inasmuch as they are so close to, and so entirely within our soul, that it is impossible for it to feel them without their being actually such as it feels them to be. Thus often when we sleep, and sometimes even when we are awake, we imagine certain things so forcibly, that we think we see them before us or feel them in our body although they do not exist at all; but although we may be asleep, or dream, we cannot feel sad or moved by any other passion without its being very true that the soul actually has the passion within it.

The Definition of the Passions of the Soul. After having considered in what the passions of the soul differ from all its other thoughts, it seems to me that we may define them generally as the perceptions, feelings, or emotions of the soul which we relate specially to it, and which are caused, maintained, and fortified by some movement of the spirits.

Explanation of the First Part of This Definition. We may call them perceptions when we make use of this word generally to signify all the thoughts which are not actions of the soul, or desires, but not when the term is used only to signify clear cognition; for experience shows us that those who are the most agitated by their passions, are not those who know them best; and that they are of the number of perceptions which the close alliance which exists between the soul and the body, renders confused and obscure. We may also call them feelings because they are received into the soul in the same way as are the objects of our outside senses, and are not otherwise known by it; but we can yet more accurately call them emotions of the soul, not only because the name may be attributed to all the changes which occur in it—that is, in all the diverse thoughts which come to it, but more especially because of all the kinds of thought which it may have, there are no others which so powerfully agitate and disturb it as do these passions.

Explanation of the Second Part. I add that they particularly relate to the soul, in order to distinguish them from the other feelings which are related, the one to outside objects such as scents, sounds, and colours; the others to our body such as hunger, thirst, and pain. I also add that they are caused, maintained, and fortified by some movement of the spirits, in order to distinguish them from our desires, which we may call emotions of the soul which relate to it, but which are used by itself; and also in order to explain their ultimate and most proximate cause, which plainly distinguishes them from the other feelings.

How the Soul and the Body Act on One Another. Let us then conceive here that the soul has its principal seat in the little gland which exists in the middle of the brain, from whence it radiates forth through all the remainder of the body by means of the animal spirits, nerves, and even the blood, which, participating in the impressions of the spirits, can carry them by the arteries into all the members. . . . Let us here add that the small gland which is the main seat of the soul is so suspended between the cavities which contain the spirits that it can be moved by them in as many different ways as there are sensible diversities in the object, but that it may also be moved in diverse ways by the soul, whose nature is such that it receives in itself as many diverse impressions, that is to say, that it possesses as many diverse perceptions as there are diverse movements in this gland. Reciprocally, likewise, the machine of the body is so formed that from the simple fact that this gland is diversely moved by the soul, or by such other cause, whatever it is, it thrusts the spirits which surround it towards the pores of the brain, which conduct them by the nerves into the muscles, by which means it causes them to move the limbs. . . .

How One and the Same Cause May Excite Different Passions in Different Men.   The same impression which a terrifying object makes on the gland, and which causes fear in certain men, may excite in others courage and confidence; the reason of this is that all brains are not constituted in the same way, and that the same movement of the gland which in some excites fear, in others causes the spirits to enter into the pores of the brain which conduct them partly into the nerves which serve to move the hands for purposes of self-defense, and partly into those which agitate and drive the blood towards the heart in the manner requisite to produce the spirits proper for the continuance of this defense, and to retain the desire of it.

The Principal Effect of the Passions.   For it is requisite to notice that the principal effect of all the passions in men is that they incite and dispose their soul to desire those things for which they prepare their body, so that the feeling of fear incites it to desire to fly, that of courage to desire to fight, and so on.

What Is the Power of the Soul in Reference to Its Passions?   Our passions cannot likewise be directly excited or removed by the action of our will, but they can be so indirectly by the representation of things which are usually united to the passions which we desire to have, and which are contrary to those which we desire to set aside. Thus, in order to excite courage in oneself and remove fear, it is not sufficient to have the will to do so, but we must also apply ourselves to consider the reasons, the objects or examples which persuade us that the peril is not great; that there is always more security in defense than in flight; that we should have the glory and joy of having vanquished, while we could expect nothing but regret and shame for having fled, and so on.

The Reason Which Prevents the Soul From Being Able Wholly to Control Its Passion.   And there is a special reason which prevents the soul from being able at once to change or arrest its passions, which has caused me to say in defining them that they are not only caused, but are also maintained and strengthened by some particular movement of the spirits. This reason is that they are nearly all accompanied by some commotion which takes place in the heart, and in consequence also in the whole of the blood and the animal spirits, so that until this commotion has subsided, they remain present to our thought in the same manner as sensible objects are present there while they act upon the organs or our senses. And as the soul, in rendering itself very attentive to some other thing, may prevent itself from hearing a slight noise or feeling a slight pain, but cannot prevent itself in the same way from hearing thunder or feeling the fire which burns the hand, it may similarly easily get the better of the lesser passions, but not the most violent and strongest, excepting after the commotion of the blood and spirits is appeased. The most that the will can do while this commotion is in its full strength is not to yield to its effects and to restrain many of the movements to which it disposes the body. For example, if anger causes us to lift our hand to strike, the will can usually hold it back; if fear incites our legs to flee, the will can arrest them, and so on in other similar cases.

DAVID HUME
On Pride

DAVID HUME *(1711–1776) was one of the few philosophers of the Enlightenment who would argue that "reason is and ought to be the slave of the passions." Placing emotions in such an elevated position, he spent a significant proportion of his philosophy trying to analyze them and show how they are constructed out of combinations of "impressions and ideas"—the two basic components of his theory of mind. What follows is his analysis of pride from his* Treatise of Human Nature, *with some comments on love and hate.*

OF THE PASSIONS
Division of the Subject

A S all the perceptions of the mind may be divided into *impressions* and *ideas,* so the impressions admit of another division into *original* and *secondary.* This division of the impressions is the same with that which I formerly made use of when I distinguish'd them into impressions of *sensation* and *reflexion.* Original impressions or impressions of sensation are such as without any antecedent perception arise in the soul, from the constitution of the body, from the animal spirits, or from the application of objects to the external organs. Secondary, or reflective impressions are such as proceed from some of these original ones, either immediately or by the interposition of its idea. Of the first kind are all the impressions of the senses, and all bodily pains and pleasures: Of the second are the passions, and other emotions resembling them.

'Tis certain, that the mind, in its perceptions, must begin somewhere; and that since the impressions precede their correspondent ideas, there must be some impressions, which without any introduction make their appearance in the soul. As these depend upon natural and physical causes, the examination of them wou'd lead me too far from my present subject, into the sciences of anatomy and natural philosophy. For this reason I shall here confine myself to those other impressions, which I have call'd secondary and reflective, as arising either from the original impressions, or from their ideas. Bodily pains and pleasures are the source of many passions, both when felt and consider'd by the mind; but arise originally in the soul, or in the body, whichever you please to call it; without any preceding thought or perception. A fit of the gout produces a long train of passions, as grief, hope, fear; but is not deriv'd immediately from any affection or idea.

The reflective impressions may be divided into two kinds, *viz.* the *calm* and the *violent.* Of the first kind is the sense of beauty and deformity in action, composition, and external objects. Of the second are the passions of love and hatred, grief and joy, pride and humility. This division is far from being exact. The raptures of poetry and music frequently rise to the greatest height; while those other impressions properly called *passions,* may decay into so soft an emotion, as to become, in a manner, imperceptible. But as in general the passions are more violent than the emotions arising from beauty and deformity, these impressions have been commonly distinguish'd from each other. The subject of the human mind being so copious and various, I shall here take advantage of this vulgar

Hume, David, "On Pride," from *Treatise of Human Nature,* ed. Selby-Bigge, Book 2, part 2, sec. 2–3, Oxford: Clarendon Press, 1888.

and specious division, that I may proceed with the greater order; and having said all I thought necessary concerning our ideas, shall now explain these violent emotions or passions, their nature, origin, causes, and effects.

When we take a survey of the passions, there occurs a division of them into *direct* and *indirect*. By direct passions I understand such as arise immediately from good or evil, from pain or pleasure. By indirect such as proceed from the same principles, but by the conjunction of other qualities. This distinction I cannot at present justify or explain any farther. I can only observe in general, that under the indirect passions I comprehend pride, humility, ambition, vanity, love, hatred, envy, pity, malice, generosity, with their dependents. And under the direct passions, desire, aversion, grief, joy, hope, fear, despair and security. I shall begin with the former.

Of Pride and Humility; Their Objects and Causes

The passions of *pride* and *humility* being simple and uniform impressions, 'tis impossible we can ever, by a multitude of words, give a just definition of them, or indeed of any of the passions. The utmost we can pretend to is a description of them, by an enumeration of such circumstances, as attend them: But as these words, *pride* and *humility,* are of general use, and the impressions they represent the most common of any, every one, of himself, will be able to form a just idea of them, without any danger of mistake. For which reason, not to lose time upon preliminaries, I shall immediately enter upon the examination of these passions.

'Tis evident, that pride and humility, tho' directly contrary, have yet the same OBJECT. This object is self, or that succession of related ideas and impressions, of which we have an intimate memory and consciousness. Here the view always fixes when we are actuated by either of these passions. According as our idea of ourself is more or less advantageous, we feel either of those opposite affections, and are elated by pride, or dejected with humility. What ever other objects may be comprehended by the mind, they are always consider'd with a view to ourselves; otherwise they wou'd never be able either to excite these passions, or produce the smallest encrease or diminution of them. When self enters not into the consideration, there is no room either for pride or humility.

But tho' that connected succession of perceptions, which we call *self,* be always the object of these two passions, 'tis impossible it can be their CAUSE, or be sufficient alone to excite them. For as these passions are directly contrary, and have the same object in common; were their object also their cause; it cou'd never produce any degree of the one passion, but at the same time it must excite an equal degree of the other; which opposition and contrariety must destroy both. 'Tis impossible a man can at the same time be both proud and humble; and where he has different reasons for these passions, as frequently happens, the passions either take place alternately; or if they encounter, the one annihilates the other, as far as its strength goes, and the remainder only of that, which is superior, continues to operate upon the mind. But in the present case neither of the passions cou'd ever become superior; because supposing it to be the view only of ourself, which excited them, that being perfectly indifferent to either, must produce both in the very same proportion; or in other words, can produce neither. To excite any passion, and at the same time raise an equal share of its antagonist, is immediately to undo what was done, and must leave the mind at last perfectly calm and indifferent.

We must, therefore, make a distinction betwixt the cause and the object of these passions; betwixt that idea, which excites them, and that to which they direct their view, when excited. Pride and humility, being once rais'd, immediately turn our attention to ourself, and regard that as their ultimate and final object; but there is something farther requisite in order to raise them: Something, which is peculiar to one of the passions, and produces not both in the very same degree. The first idea, that is presented to the mind, is that of the cause or productive principle. This excites the passion, connected with it; and the passion, when excited, turns our view to another idea, which is that of self. Here then is a passion plac'd betwixt two ideas, of which the one produces it, and the other is produc'd by it. The first idea, therefore, represents the *cause*, the second the *object* of the passion.

To begin with the causes of pride and humility; we may observe, that their most obvious and remarkable property is the vast variety of *subjects*, on which they may be plac'd. Every valuable quality of the mind, whether of the imagination, judgment, memory or disposition; wit, good-sense, learning, courage, justice, integrity; all these are the causes of pride; and their opposites of humility. Nor are these passions confin'd to the mind, but extend their view to the body likewise. A man may be proud of his beauty, strength, agility, good mien, address in dancing, riding, fencing, and of his dexterity in any manual business or manufacture. But this is not all. The passion looking farther, comprehends whatever objects are in the least ally'd or related to us. Our country, family, children, relations, riches, houses, gardens, horses, dogs, cloaths; any of these may become a cause either of pride or humility.

From the consideration of these causes, it appears necessary we shou'd make a new distinction in the causes of the passion, betwixt that *quality*, which operates, and the *subject*, on which it is plac'd. A man, for instance, is vain of a beautiful house, which belongs to him, or which he has himself built and contriv'd. Here the object of the passion is himself, and the cause is the beautiful house: Which cause again is sub-divided into two parts, *viz.* the quality, which operates upon the passion, and the subject, in which the quality inheres. The quality is the beauty, and the subject is the house, consider'd as his property or contrivance. Both these parts are essential, nor is the distinction vain and chimerical. Beauty, consider'd merely as such, unless plac'd upon something related to us, never produces any pride or vanity; and the strongest relation alone, without beauty, or something else in its place, has little influence on that passion. . . .

Having thus in a manner suppos'd two properties of the causes of these affections, *viz.* that the *qualities* produce a separate pain or pleasure, and that the *subjects*, on which the qualities are plac'd, are related to self; I proceed to examine the passions themselves, in order to find something in them, correspondent to the suppos'd properties of their causes. *First,* I find, that the peculiar object of pride and humility is determin'd by an original and natural instinct, and that 'tis absolutely impossible, from the primary constitution of the mind, that these passions shou'd ever look beyond self, or that individual person, of whose actions and sentiments each of us is intimately conscious. Here at last the view always rests, when we are actuated by either of these passions; nor can we, in that situation of mind, ever lose sight of this object. For this I pretend not to give any reason; but consider such a peculiar direction of the thought as an original quality.

The *second* quality, which I discover in these passions, and which I likewise consider as an original quality, is their sensations, or the peculiar emotions they excite in the soul, and which constitute their very being and essence. Thus pride is a pleasant sensation, and humility a painful; and upon the removal of the pleasure and pain, there is in reality no pride nor humility. Of this our very feeling convinces us; and beyond our feeling, 'tis here in vain to reason or dispute. . . .

What I have said of pride is equally true of humility. The sensation of humility is uneasy, as that of pride is agreeable; for which reason the separate sensation, arising from the causes, must be revers'd, while the relation to self continues the same. Tho' pride and humility are directly contrary in their effects, and in their sensations, they have notwithstanding the same object; so that 'tis requisite only to change the relation of impressions, without making any change upon that of ideas. Accordingly we find, that a beautiful house, belonging to ourselves, produces pride; and that the same house, still belonging to ourselves, produces humility, when by any accident its beauty is chang'd into deformity, and thereby the sensations of pleasure, which corresponded to pride, is transform'd into pain, which is related to humility. The double relation between the ideas and impressions subsists in both cases, and produces an easy transition from the one emotion to the other.

OF LOVE AND HATRED
Of the Objects and Causes of Love and Hatred

'Tis altogether impossible to give any definition of the passions of *love* and *hatred;* and that because they produce merely a simple impression, without any mixture or composition. 'Twou'd be as unnecessary to attempt any description of them, drawn from their nature, origin, causes and objects; and that both because these are the subjects of our present enquiry, and because these passions of themselves are sufficiently known from our common feeling and experience. This we have already observ'd concerning pride and humility, and here repeat it concerning love and hatred; and indeed there is so great a resemblance betwixt these two sets of passions, that we shall be oblig'd to begin with a kind of abridgment of our reasonings concerning the former, in order to explain the latter.

As the immediate *object* of pride and humility is self or that identical person, of whose thoughts, actions, and sensations we are intimately conscious; so the *object* of love and hatred is some other person, of whose thoughts, actions, and sensations we are not conscious. This is sufficiently evident from experience. Our love and hatred are always directed to some sensible being external to us; and when we talk of *self-love,* 'tis not in a proper sense, nor has the sensation it produces any thing in common with that tender emotion, which is excited by a friend or mistress. 'Tis the same case with hatred. We may be mortified by our own faults and follies; but never feel any anger or hatred, except from the injuries of others.

But tho' the object of love and hatred be always some other person, 'tis plain that the object is not, properly speaking, the *cause* of these passions, or alone sufficient to excite them. For since love and hatred are directly contrary in their sensation, and have the same object in common, if that object were also their cause, it wou'd produce these opposite passions in an equal degree; and as they must, from the very first moment, destroy each other, none of them wou'd ever be able to make its appearance. There must, therefore, be some cause different from the object.

If we consider the causes of love and hatred, we shall find they are very much diversify'd, and have not many things in common. The virtue, knowledge, wit, good sense, good humour of any person, produce love and esteem; as the opposite qualities, hatred and contempt. The same passions arise from bodily accomplishments, such as beauty, force, swiftness, dexterity; and from their contraries; as likewise from the external advantages and disadvantages of family, possessions, cloaths, nation and climate. There is not one of these objects, but what by its different qualities may produce love and esteem, or hatred and contempt. . . .

'Twou'd be tedious to trace the passions of love and hatred, thro' all the observations which we have form'd concerning pride and humility, and which are equally applicable to both sets of passions. 'Twill be sufficient to *remark* in general, that the object of love and hatred is evidently some thinking person; and that the sensation of the former passion is always agreeable, and of the latter uneasy.

WILLIAM JAMES
What Is an Emotion?

WILLIAM JAMES *(1842–1910) was one of America's greatest philosopher–psychologists and wrote what for many years was the classic textbook of psychology. He had a special interest in emotions, and his analysis of emotion still dominates much of current thinking in psychology. What follows is taken from his 1884 essay "What Is an Emotion?"*

THE physiologists who, during the past few years, have been so industriously exploring the functions of the brain, have limited their attempts at explanation to its cognitive and volitional performances. Dividing the brain into sensorial and motor centres, they have found their division to be exactly paralleled by the analysis made by empirical psychology, of the perceptive and volitional parts of the mind into their simplest elements. But the *aesthetic* sphere of the mind, its longings, its pleasures and pains, and its emotions, have been . . . ignored.

And yet it is even now certain that of two things concerning the emotions, one must be true. Either separate and special centres, affected to them alone, are their brain-seat, or else they correspond to processes occurring in the motor and sensory centres, already assigned, or in others like them, not yet mapped out. If the former be the case we must deny the current view, and hold the cortex to be something more than the surface of "projection" for every sensitive spot and every muscle in the body. If the latter be the case, we must ask whether the emotional "process" in the sensory or motor centre be an altogether peculiar one, or whether it resembles the ordinary perceptive processes of which those centres are already recognized to be the seat. The purpose of the following pages is to show that the last alternative comes nearest to the truth, and that the emotional brain-processes not only resemble the ordinary sensorial brain-processes, but in very truth *are* nothing but such processes variously combined. . . .

I should say first of all that the only emotions I propose expressly to consider here are those that have a distinct bodily expression. That there are feelings of pleasure and displeasure, of interest and excitements, bound up with mental operations, but having no obvious bodily expression for their consequence, would, I suppose, be held true by most readers. Certain arrangements of sounds, of lines, of colours, are agreeable, and others the reverse, without the degree of the feeling being sufficient to quicken the pulse or breathing, or to prompt to movements of either the body or the face. Certain sequences of ideas charm us as much as others tire us. It is a real intellectual delight to get a problem solved, and a real intellectual torment to have to leave it unfinished. . . .

Our natural way of thinking about [the] standard emotions is that the mental perception of some fact excites the mental affection called the emotion, and that this latter state of mind gives rise to the bodily expression. My thesis on the contrary is that *the bodily changes follow directly the* PERCEPTION *of the exciting fact, and that our feeling of the same changes as they occur* IS *the emotion.* Common sense says, we lose our fortune, we are sorry and weep; we meet a bear, are frightened and run; we are insulted by a rival, are angry and strike. The hypothesis here to be defended says that this order of sequence is

James, William, "What Is an Emotion?" from *Journal of Philosophy*, 1884.

incorrect, that the one mental state is not imme-diately induced by the other, that the bodily manifestations must first be interposed between, and that the more rational statement is that we feel sorry because we cry, angry because we strike, afraid because we tremble, and not that we cry, strike, or tremble, because we are sorry, angry, or fearful, as the case may be. Without the bodily states following on the perception, the latter would be purely cognitive in form, pale, colourless, destitute of emotional warmth. We might then see the bear, and judge it best to run, receive the insult and deem it right to strike, but we could not actually *feel* afraid or angry.

Stated in this crude way, the hypothesis is pretty sure to meet with immediate disbelief. And yet neither many nor farfetched considera-tions are required to mitigate its paradoxical character, and possibly to produce conviction of its truth.

To begin with, readers . . . do not need to be reminded that the nervous system of every living thing is but a bundle of predispositions to react in particular ways upon the contact of particular features of the environment. As surely as the hermit-crab's abdomen presupposes the exis-tence of empty whelk-shells somewhere to be found, so surely do the hound's olfactories imply the existence, on the one hand, of deer's or foxes' feet, and on the other, the tendency to follow up their tracks. The neural machinery is but a hyphen between determinate arrangements of matter outside the body and determinate im-pulses to inhibition or discharge within its or-gans. When the hen sees a white oval object on the ground, she cannot leave it; she must keep upon it and return to it, until at last its transfor-mation into a little mass of moving chirping down elicits from her machinery an entirely new set of performances. The love of man for woman, or of the human mother for her babe, our wrath at snakes and our fear of precipices, may all be described similarly, as instances of the way in which peculiarly conformed pieces of the world's furniture will fatally call forth most par-ticular mental and bodily reactions, in advance of, and often in direct opposition to, the verdict of our deliberate reason concerning them. The labours of Darwin and his successors are only just beginning to reveal the universal parasitism of each special creature upon other special things, and the way in which each creature brings the signature of its special relations stamped on its nervous system with it upon the scene.

Every living creature is in fact a sort of lock, whose wards and springs presuppose special forms of key,—which keys however are not born attached to the locks, but are sure to be found in the world near by as life goes on. And the locks are indifferent to any but their own keys. The egg fails to fascinate the hound, the bird does not fear the precipice, the snake waxes not wroth at his kind, the deer cares nothing for the woman or the human babe. . . .

Now among these nervous anticipations are of course to be reckoned the emotions, so far as these may be called forth directly by the percep-tion of certain facts. In advance of all experience of elephants no child can but be frightened if he suddenly find one trumpeting and charging upon him. No woman can see a handsome little naked baby without delight, no man in the wilderness see a human form in the distance without excitement and curiosity. I said I should consider these emotions only so far as they have bodily movements of some sort for their accom-paniments. But my first point is to show that their bodily accompaniments are much more farreaching and complicated than we ordinarily suppose. . . . [N]ot only the heart, but the entire circulatory system, forms a sort of sounding-board, which every change of our consciousness, however slight, may make reverberate. Hardly a sensation comes to us without sending waves of alternate constriction and dilation down the arteries of our arms. The blood-vessels of the ab-domen act reciprocally with those of the more outward parts. The bladder and bowels, the glands of the mouth, throat, and skin, and the liver, are known to be affected gravely in certain severe emotions, and are unquestionably affected tran-siently when the emotions are of a lighter sort. That the heart-beats and rhythm of breathing play a leading part in all emotions whatsoever, is a matter too notorious for proof. And what is really equally prominent, but less likely to be admitted until special attention is drawn to the fact, is the continuous co-operation of the voluntary muscles in our emotional states. Even when no change of outward attitude is produced, their inward tension alters to suit each varying mood, and is felt as a difference of tone or of strain. In depression the flexors tend to prevail; in elation or belligerent excitement the extensors take the lead. And the various permutations and combinations of which these organic activities are susceptible, make it abstractly possible that no shade of emotion, however slight, should be without a bodily reverberation as unique, when taken in its totality, as is the mental mood itself.

The immense number of parts modified in each emotion is what makes it so difficult for us to reproduce in cold blood the total and integral expression of any one of them. We may catch the trick with the voluntary muscles, but fail with the skin, glands, heart, and other viscera. Just as an artificially imitated sneeze lacks something of the reality, so the attempt to imitate an emotion in the absence of its normal instigating cause is apt to be rather "hollow."

The next thing to be noticed is this, that every one of the bodily changes, whatsoever it be, is *felt*, acutely or obscurely, the moment it occurs. If the reader has never paid attention to this matter, he will be both interested and astonished to learn how many different local bodily feelings he can detect in himself as characteristic of his various emotional moods. It would be perhaps too much to expect him to arrest the tide of any strong gust of passion for the sake of any such curious analysis as this; but he can observe more tranquil states, and that may be assumed here to be true of the greater which is shown to be true of the less. Our whole cubic capacity is sensibly alive; and each morsel of it contributes its pulsations of feeling, dim or sharp, pleasant, painful, or dubious, to that sense of personality that every one of us unfailingly carries with him. It is surprising what little items give accent to

these complexes of sensibility. When worried by any slight trouble, one may find that the focus of one's bodily consciousness is the contraction, often quite inconsiderable, of the eyes and brows. When momentarily embarrassed, it is something in the pharynx that compels either a swallow, a clearing of the throat, or a slight cough; and so on for as many more instances as might be named. Our concern here being with the general view rather than with the details, I will not linger to discuss these but, assuming the point admitted that every change that occurs must be felt, I will pass on.

I now proceed to urge the vital point of my whole theory, which is this. If we fancy some strong emotion, and then try to abstract from our consciousness of it all the feelings of its characteristic bodily symptoms, we find we have nothing left behind, no "mind-stuff" out of which the emotion can be constituted, and that a cold and neutral state of intellectual perception is all that remains. It is true, that although most people, when asked, say that their introspection verifies this statement, some persist in saying theirs does not. Many cannot be made to understand the question. When you beg them to imagine away every feeling of laughter and of tendency to laugh from their consciousness of the ludicrousness of an object, and then to tell you what the feeling of its ludicrousness would be like, whether it be anything more than the perception that the object belongs to the class "funny," they persist in replying that the thing proposed is a physical impossibility, and that they always *must* laugh, if they see a funny object. Of course the task proposed is not the practical one of seeing a ludicrous object and annihilating one's tendency to laugh. It is the purely speculative one of subtracting certain elements of feeling from an emotional state supposed to exist in its fullness, and saying what the residual elements are. I cannot help thinking that all who rightly apprehend this problem will agree with the proposition above laid down. What kind of an emotion of fear would be left, if the feelings neither of quickened heart-beats nor of shallow breathing, neither of trembling lips nor of weakened limbs, neither of goose-flesh nor of visceral stirrings, were present, it is quite impossible to think. Can one fancy the state of rage and picture no ebullition of it in the chest, no flushing of the face, no dilation of the nostrils, no clenching of the teeth, no impulse to vigorous action, but in their stead limp muscles, calm breathing, and a placid face? The present writer, for one, certainly cannot. The rage is as completely evaporated as the sensation of its socalled manifestations, and the only thing that can possibly be supposed to take its place is some cold-blooded and dispassionate judicial sentence, confined entirely to the intellectual realm, to the effect that a certain person or persons merit chastisement for their sins. In like manner of grief: what would it be without its tears, its sobs, its suffocation of the heart, its pang in the breastbone? A feelingless cognition that certain circumstances are deplorable, and nothing more. Every passion in turn tells the same story. A purely disembodied human emotion is a nonentity. I do not say that it is a contradiction in the nature of things, or that pure spirits are necessarily condemned to cold intellectual lives; but I say that for *us*, emotion dissociated from all bodily feeling is inconceivable. The more closely I scrutinise my states, the more persuaded I become, that whatever moods, affections, and passions I have, are in very truth constituted by, and made up of, those bodily changes we ordinarily call their expression or consequence; and the more it seems to me that if I were to become corporeally anaesthetic, I should be excluded from the life of the affections, harsh and tender alike, and drag out an existence of merely cognitive or intellectual form. Such an existence, although it seems to have been the ideal of ancient sages, is too apathetic to be keenly sought after by those born after the revival of the worship of sensibility, a few generations ago. . . .

If our theory be true, a necessary corollary of it ought to be that any voluntary arousal of the so-called manifestations of a special emotion ought to give us the emotion itself. Of course in the majority of emotions, this test is inapplicable; for many of the manifestations are in organs over which we have no volitional control. Still, within the limits in which it can be verified, experience fully corroborates this test. Everyone knows how panic is increased by flight, and how giving way to the symptoms of grief or anger increases those passions themselves. Each fit of sobbing makes the sorrow more acute, and calls forth another fit stronger still, until at last repose only ensues with lassitude and with the apparent exhaustion of the machinery. In rage, it is notorious how we "work ourselves up" to a climax by repeated outbreaks of expression. Refuse to express a passion, and it dies. Count ten before venting your anger, and its occasion seems ridiculous. Whistling to keep up courage is no mere figure of speech. On the other hand, sit all day in a moping posture, sigh, and reply to everything with a dismal voice, and your melancholy lingers. There is no more valuable precept in moral education than this, as all who have experience know: if we wish to conquer undesirable emotional tendencies in ourselves, we must assiduously, and in the first instance cold-bloodedly, go through the *outward motions* of those contrary dispositions we prefer to cultivate. The reward of persistency will infallibly come, in the fading out of the sullenness or depression, and the advent of real cheerfulness and kindliness in their stead. Smooth the brow, brighten the eye, contract the dorsal rather than the ventral aspect of the frame, and speak in a major key, pass the genial compliment, and your heart must be frigid indeed if it does not gradually thaw!

The only exceptions to this are apparent, not real. The great emotional expressiveness and mobility of certain persons often lead us to say "They would feel more if they talked less." And in another class of persons, the explosive energy with which passion manifests itself on critical occasions, seems correlated with the way in which they bottle it up during the intervals. But these are only eccentric types of character, and within each type the law of the last paragraph prevails. The sentimentalist is so constructed that "gushing" is his or her normal mode of expression. Putting a stopper on the "gush" will only to a limited extent cause more "real" activities to take its place; in the main it will simply produce listlessness. On the other hand the ponderous and bilious "slumbering volcano," let him repress the expression of his passions as

he will, will find them expire if they get no vent at all; whilst if the rare occasions multiply which he deems worthy of their outbreak, he will find them grow in intensity as life proceeds.

ANNETTE BAIER
Feelings That Matter

ANNETTE BAIER *was professor of philosophy at the University of Pittsburgh and is now retired in her native New Zealand. She is the author of several books on Hume and on the emotions.*

EMOTIONS AND THE IMPORTANT

WE all accept the idea that emotions are reactions to matters of apparent importance to us, fear to danger, surprise to the unexpected, outrage to insult, disgust to what will make us sick, envy of the more favored, gratitude for benefactors, hate for enemies, love for friends, and so on. And sometimes the felt emotion can precede knowledge of precisely what the danger, the insult, the nauseating substance, and so on is. Emotion then plays the role of alerting us to something important to us—a danger, or an insult. As I prepare this paper, a young man on trial for stabbing his mother to death in the family home (just down the road from where I live), whose defense is insanity, claims memory loss for the time of the murder, but says he knows he must have done it, since, quite apart from the overwhelming physical evidence, he has "the guilty sort of feeling, like I have done something" (*Otago Daily Times*, Aug. 29, 2001). This is a rare and doubtless pathological

case, but emotions can on occasion play the role of showing us that something important has occurred, before we become clear what exactly it is.

In such cases emotions alert us to important matters, good or ill. And the emotion itself may at least help constitute the good or the ill. Descartes says all the good or ill of this life depend on the passions. Hume, and many other writers about human passions, have divided them into the pleasant and the unpleasant, on the one hand those that respond to, alert us to, or constitute goods, on the other hand, ills. There are some purely unpleasant emotions, such as boredom, grief, and guilt, and some purely pleasant ones, such as relief and joy. But as Hume (and Kant) knew, gratitude, although occasioned by what is a good to us, may be itself unpleasant for a proud person to have to feel, and anger, response to a perceived injury, can be invigorating and releasing, not altogether unenjoyable. Hume would explain such cases by saying that the pleasure of receiving help is mixed with the pain of humility, of needing the help, the pain of being injured with the satisfaction of incipient aggression to the injurer. There surely can be mixed feelings evoked by one event or situation. But some individual emotions, or at any rate states for which we have a single name, while they have a distinctive phenomenological feel, seem to have an essentially mixed hedonic tone—nostalgia, for example. And some, I shall suggest, are neutral in hedonic tone, neither pleasant nor unpleasant. Surprise and interest seem of this hedonically neutral sort, at any rate unless boredom is the worst evil. I want to direct attention on an emotion very close to interest, perhaps a variant of it.

Consider this case: a person receives a long-distance phone call from a close relative. When she answers the phone the first words her caller says, after greeting her, are "Are you sitting down?" At once she knows that the message to come is of importance, and she feels an appropriate emotional disturbance. As she finds a chair and seats herself, she may reply, "Why? Has someone died?" But she may not jump to that conclusion, and the news may be momentous but good, say that a son listed missing in action has after many years been found safe and well. She certainly feels strongly while awaiting the news that is about to be given her. She will go on, once the news is broken to her, to feel joy or sorrow, but the first feeling seems neither joy nor distress. Interest, concern, anticipation and nervousness, yes, but more than that, some sort of shock, and intent seriousness. For what she now anticipates is no ordinary good or bad news, unlikely to cause her to need support. Nor is uncertainty alone enough to explain the emotion she feels even before the big news is given her. But what name has this emotion, felt as important, simply as such? Interest seems not quite right, since one can be interested in quite trivial news, or relayed gossip, which one could with no danger receive while on one's feet. Concern in its older sense, of what regards one, would be close, but in its contemporary English sense it is too close to anxiety for the hedonically neutral emotion I am after.

In the case I have sketched, the opening question creates drama, and until the momen-

tous news is given there will be uncertainty. Hume noted that uncertainty itself intensifies an emotion, as does a mixture of contrary emotions from simultaneous different causes. His example of mixture, the man who gets, at one time, news both of the loss of a lawsuit, and of the birth of his son, resulting in an alternation of extreme joy with extreme distress (Treatise 441–2), can be adapted for my purpose. Suppose this man is waiting for news both of his lawsuit and of the delivery of his child. On Hume's view, the uncertainty will make both fear of losing at court and hope of a safe delivery especially violent. Suppose a messenger appears, so he at once knows that one of the uncertainties is about to be ended, but not which or how. He will feel this so far nameless emotion, no doubt along with his fear and his hope, and considerable impatience. But in this case he will likely tell from his messenger's face whether that person is the bearer of good or bad tidings, so it is unlike my telephone call case, in which no fear or hope precedes the call. My adaptation of Hume's example will not be a pure case of an emotion reserved for the important, as such, as distinct from the important threat, loss, insult, enmity, or for the important joy, victory, honor, friendship. And pure cases of a feeling reserved for the important may be quite rare.

WHAT REALLY MATTERS

I have said that it is our emotions, or lack of them, that will speak the truth about if and how much something matters to us. It may be objected that emotion too can surely be wrong about that. Fears can be exaggerated, even sometimes self-fulfilling, anger-crippling, envy-unbased, pride-vain and silly. (Buddhists supposedly recognize 84,000 dysfunctional emotions, and as many antidotes.) In cases like these, the danger, the insult, the cause of envy, the honor or accomplishment in which foolish pride is taken, is not important enough to justify the person's felt emotion. Or we may later find our earlier mild reactions too muted. Thought and reflection, perhaps after discussion with others, may correct what the initial emotion got wrong. If there is a special feeling, gravity, or chalance, which is directed specifically on what matters to a person, can it not also be wrong, and need correction?

This postulated feeling that something is of great importance to us, and its antithesis, will usually be among the most thought-mediated and reflective of our emotions. Indeed it will typically come into play when other earlier emotions are self-criticised. One may later shrug off the accomplishment in which one earlier felt exaggerated pride. Or one may feel, on reflection, that a past insult should have angered one more than it did at the time. How much trust should we put in our feelings about what matters? The relative who phones to tell someone of the safe return of a lost son, or the finding of his corpse, will have no doubt that the news matters to her hearer, and is surely right about that. Many beliefs, memories of earlier communicated anguish, and sympathy, all feed into her request that her hearer seat herself. And the hearer infers from that request that something momentous is about to be revealed. The emotion she feels as she awaits the news is inference-based, and imbued with trust concerning how well her caller can judge what will matter to her. Then when she gets the good (or bad) news, let us suppose that her son is found and safe, its impact will be mediated by all her past anxiety.

What matters to a person stays in the mind, and memory preserves what relates to that with particular tenacity, as experts on improving one's memory are well aware. What is of little concern to us we tend to forget quickly. (How many of your past shoulder shrugs can you recall?) What stays in the memory, and keeps resurfacing to the forefront of attention, is what mattered and matters. But it is said that memory can lie, and so, it might be suggested, can our feelings about what is and is not of importance, which affect what memory retains. Of course any emotion based on a false belief or unsound inference can be in that derivative sense false. If the caller who asks her hearer to be seated before she continues goes on to tell her a joke so funny that she might have fallen over laughing, the feeling of chalance will have

been misplaced. Jokes, however good, are not occasions for that. But if there is no mistaken factual belief, nor faulty inference, can the feeling itself mislead us? Can we not attribute, on the strength of it, too much importance to something, exaggerate or underrate how much it matters?

Were there such a thing as objective mattering, God's mattering, and were that reliably communicated to us, then our personal findings of importance could be said to be correct or incorrect in comparison with the divine standard. But for non-theists, the most we can expect is that criticism of personal findings of relative importance may come from later feelings, and from spokespersons for cultural priorities. We may grant the adolescent that he does not care about tidiness, but try to get him to care. In our rhetoric with him we may well say things like, "You are wrong to think tidiness does not matter—it matters to us who live with you." In my childhood there was a nasty little song which ran: "Don't care was made to care. Don't care was hung. Don't care was put in a pot, and boiled till he was done." This indicates how we try to change what matters to a person, when we do. We work on what already matters to them—in this case whether or not one gets to be hanged and boiled. We do manipulate, as best we can, other people's feelings about what matters. But that does not really establish that the changed feelings are more correct, in any other sense than more politically correct, than what they superseded. We can change our mind, or, if I am right, our heart, about how much something mattered, but that is what it will be, a change. We update our priorities, but the later ones, even when better informed, need not be any wiser than the earlier. Wisdom is a good sense of what matters more than what, but it takes it to discern it. Our criterion of relative wisdom will keep up with our changes of mind about what matters most. We will disapprove of too frequent reversals or fluctuations in our evaluations of what matters. Vanessa Bell is reported to have refused to go to social occasions at which formal dress was expected, since such grand parties "changed one's values" in unwanted ways. There is a kind of integrity in not having one's version of what matters to one change too easily with change of scene, or of company.

To appreciate the sense in which a person's feelings about what matters to him at a particular time are the final word on that, consider a person who faces a driving test, on his birthday, and refuses any celebration until the test is behind him. He may seem, to those close to him, to be taking the matter unduly seriously. They assure him that he is well prepared for the test, that he is a good driver, so has no need to worry. He may reply, "I admit I am a little nervous. Passing this test is very important to me." Should there be thought to be any real chance that he might fail, we might to tell him that it was not the end of the world if this happened. But it might be the end of his world, the world he wants to continue in. For if the birthday he refuses yet to celebrate is his 84th, and if failure to pass this particular test would mean the end of his driving life, we might have to agree with him that the test was a serious matter. His mobility and independence would be at stake. We would still try to point out that reduced versions of these undisputed goods might still be available to him, but we would not be correcting or challenging his feeling that such goods matter very much. Aging may bring new things into a serious light—renewing one's driving license in one's eighties cannot be taken as lightheartedly as it might have been earlier, for the experienced driver.

But the older person's sense that mobility and independence matter is continuous with the toddler's and the adolescent's valuing of them. It does not take the wisdom of age to discern their value, merely to realise more vividly how temporary our hold on them may be. Should our man fail the test, his life will be seriously the worse, however stoically he adapts to his reduced style of life.

For most of us the question will not be if anything matters, but rather how much various things, that may compete for our attention, matter. The relative strength of our reflective feelings about them, what I have called our feelings of chalance, what we give weight to, and what we shrug off, will decide that. This subjective feeling, or its absence, will not settle what if anything really matters, only what matters to us, now. And as Descartes wrote, "What is it to us that someone should make out that the perception whose truth we are so firmly convinced of may appear false to God or some angel, so that it is, absolutely speaking, false?" (A. T VII, 145, tr. Cottingham). What matters to us is what we and those we can be in touch with take to matter. My concern here has been our every-day feelings about what matters, and our communication of such feelings. I offer for your attention what we accept or reject as having weight, what we, not Atlas or Sisyphus, let alone Zeus or Jehovah, shoulder or shrug off.

JEAN-PAUL SARTRE
Emotions as Transformations of the World

JEAN-PAUL SARTRE *(1905–1980), a philosopher, novelist, playwright, and political activist, wrote his essay on the emotions just before he began his monumental existentialist*

Sartre, Jean-Paul, "Emotions as Transformations of the World," from *The Emotions: Outline of a Theory,* tr. Bernard Frechtman, Philosophical Library, New York, (1971) pp. 50–52, 58, 60–62, 73–75, 77. Used by permission of Philosophical Library, New York.

treatise, Being and Nothingness. *He was reacting against such theories as that of James, and in place of a physiological theory he urged a "phenomenological" view, a study of emotions in terms of the person's own experience. Such a view, he argues, leads us to the conclusion that emotions are a mode of intentional and purposive behavior, a "magical transformation of the world."*

PERHAPS what will help us in our investigation is a preliminary observation which may serve as a general criticism of all the theories of emotion which we have encountered. . . . For most psychologists everything takes place as if the consciousness *of* the emotion were first a reflective consciousness, that is, as if the first form of the emotion as a fact of consciousness were to appear to us as a modification of our psychic being or, to use everyday language, to be first perceived as a *state of consciousness.* And certainly it is always possible to take consciousness of emotion as the affective structure of consciousness, to say, "I'm angry, I'm afraid, etc." But fear is not originally consciousness of being afraid, any more than the perception of this book is consciousness *of* perceiving the book. Emotional consciousness is, at first, unreflective, and on this plane it can be conscious of itself only on the non-positional mode. Emotional consciousness is, at first, consciousness *of* the world. It is not even necessary to bring up the whole theory in order clearly to understand this principle. A few simple observations may suffice, and it is remarkable that the psychologists of emotion have never thought of making them. It is evident, in effect, that the man who is afraid is afraid *of* something. Even if it is a matter of one of those indefinite anxieties which one experiences in the dark, in a sinister and deserted passageway, etc., one is afraid *of* certain aspects of the night, of the world. And doubtless, all psychologists have noted that emotion is set in motion by a perception, a representation-signal, etc. But it seems that for them the emotion then withdraws from the object in order to be absorbed into itself. Not much reflection is needed to understand that, on the contrary, the emotion returns to the object at every moment and is fed there. For example,

flight in a state of fear is described as if the object were not, before anything else, a flight *from* a certain object, as if the object fled did not remain present in the flight itself, as its theme, its reason for being, *that from which one flees.* And how can one talk about anger, in which one strikes, injures, and threatens, without mentioning the person who represents the objective unity of these insults, threats, and blows? In short, the affected subject and the affective object are bound in an indissoluble synthesis. Emotion is a certain way of apprehending the world. . . . The subject who seeks the solution of a practical problem is outside in the world; he perceives the world every moment through his acts. If he fails in his attempts, if he gets irritated, his very irritation is still a way in which the world appears to him. And, between the action which miscarries and the anger, it is not necessary for the subject to reflect back upon his behaviour, to intercalate a reflexive consciousness. There can be a continuous passage from the unreflective consciousness "world-acted" (action) to the unreflective consciousness "world-hateful" (anger). The second is a transformation of the other.

At present, we can conceive of what an emotion is. It is a transformation of the world. When the paths traced out become too difficult, or when we see no path, we can no longer live in so urgent and difficult a world. All the ways are barred. However, we must act. So we try to change the world, that is, to live as if the connection between things and their potentialities were not ruled by deterministic processes, but by magic. Let it be clearly understood that this is not a game; we are driven against a wall, and we throw ourselves into this new attitude with all the strength we can muster. Let it also be understood that this attempt is not conscious of being such, for it would then be the object of a reflection. Before anything else, it is the seizure of new connections and new exigencies.

But the emotive behavior is not on the same plane as the other behaviors; it is not *effective*. Its end is not really to act upon the object as such through the agency of particular means. It seeks by itself to confer upon the object, and without modifying it in its actual structure, another quality, a lesser existence, or a lesser presence (or a greater existence, etc.). In short, in emotion it is the body which, directed by consciousness, changes its relations with the world in order that the world may change its qualities. If emotion is a joke, it is a joke we believe in. A simple example will make this emotive structure clear: I extend my hand to take a bunch of grapes. I can't get it; it's beyond my reach. I shrug my shoulders, I let my hand drop, I mumble, "They're too green," and I move on. All these gestures, these words, this behavior are not seized upon for their own sake. We are dealing with a little comedy which I am playing *under* the bunch of grapes, through which I confer upon the grapes the characteristic of being "too green" which can serve as a substitute for the behavior which I am unable to keep up. At first, they presented themselves as "having to be picked." But this urgent quality very soon becomes unbearable because the potentiality cannot be realized. This unbearable tension becomes, in turn, a motive for foisting upon the grapes the new quality "too green," which will resolve the conflict and eliminate the tension. Only I cannot confer this quality on the grapes chemically. I cannot act upon the bunch in the ordinary ways. So I seize upon this sourness of the too-green grapes by acting disgusted. I magically confer upon the grapes the quality I desire. Here the comedy is only half sincere. But let the situation be more urgent, let the incantatory behavior be carried out with seriousness; there we have emotion. . . .

True emotion is . . . accompanied by belief. The qualities conferred upon objects are taken as true qualities. Exactly what is meant by that? Roughly this: the emotion is undergone. One cannot abandon it at will; it exhausts itself, but

we cannot stop it. Besides, the behavior which boils down to itself alone does nothing else than sketch upon the object the emotional quality which we confer upon it. A flight which would simply be a journey would not be enough to establish the object as being horrible. Or rather it would confer upon it the formal quality of *horrible,* but not the matter of this quality. In order for us truly to grasp the horrible, it is not only necessary to mimic it; we must be spellbound, flooded by our own emotion; the formal frame of the behavior must be filled with something opaque and heavy which serves as matter. We understand in this situation the role of purely physiological phenomena: they represent the *seriousness* of the emotion; they are phenomena of belief. They should certainly not be separated from behavior. At first, they present a certain analogy with it. The hyper-tension of fear or sadness, the vaso-constrictions, the respiratory difficulties, symbolize quite well a behavior which aims at denying the world or discharging it of its affective potential by denying it. It is then impossible to draw exactly a borderline between the pure difficulties and the behavior. They finally enter with the behavior into a total synthetic form and cannot be studied by themselves; to have considered them in isolation is precisely the error of the peripheric theory. And yet they are not reducible to behavior; one can stop himself from fleeing, but not from trembling. I can, by a violent effort, raise myself from my chair, turn my thought from the disaster which is crushing me, and get down to work; my hands will remain icy. Therefore, the emotion must be considered not simply as being enacted; it is not a matter of pure demeanor. It is the demeanor of a body which is in a certain state; the state alone would not provoke the demeanor; the demeanor without the state is comedy; but the emotion appears in a highly disturbed body which retains a certain behavior. The disturbance can survive the behavior, but the behavior constitutes the form and signification of the disturbance. On the other hand, without this disturbance, the behavior would be pure signification, an affective scheme. We are really dealing with a synthetic form; *in order to believe* in magical behavior it is necessary to be highly disturbed.

Thus the origin of emotion is a spontaneous and lived degradation of consciousness in the face of the world. What it cannot endure in one way it tries to grasp in another by going to sleep, by approaching the consciousness of sleep, dream, and hysteria. And the disturbance of the body is nothing other than the lived belief of consciousness, insofar as it is seen from the outside.

ROBERT C. SOLOMON
Anger as a Way of Engaging the World

ROBERT C. SOLOMON *(b. 1942) teaches philosophy at the University of Texas, and is the author of* The Passions.

ANGER has a well-deserved reputation as the most explosive and most dangerous emotion. Thus it is usually the first example of a "negative" emotion. It is also one of the emotions that seem most obviously beyond our control, and such expressions as "losing one's temper" and "going ballistic" make this amply clear. In the current research on the physiological basis of emotions, anger, together with fear, form the paradigmatic and most often studied "basic" emotions. As current theorists use the term, a basic emotion is one that is essentially neurological-hormonal-muscular in nature, trans-cultural and universal, and it is originally a product of evolution rather than of learning or culture. Basic emotions have distinctive "hard-wired" expressions (especially facial expressions) as well as characteristic autonomic nervous system responses (heart beating harder, sweating, more sensitive skin responses, etc.) Anger displays characteristic autonomic nervous system responses: the heart beats faster, one tends to get red in the face, the muscles of the body tense and the brow furrows and teeth clench, all of this spontaneous and not a product of thinking or deliberation. One sees similar responses in animals, with appropriate anatomical differences. (Think of the peculiar tail movement of an angry cat, or the growling of a dog whose territory has just been invaded.)

But is this all that anger is? Of course, I accept the neurological and clinical evidence, such as it is. But I think that an emotion is a much more cognitively and value-rich phenomenon. It necessarily involves feeling and judgment as well. But no one worries about brief bursts of anger. It is protracted anger tending toward hatred and manifested in schemes of retaliation and vengeance that we fear. It is the hostile judgmental nature of anger, even stripped of hatred and vengeance, that the Christian tradition warns us against and considers sinful. Buddhists, too, consider anger among the worst "agitations," disturbing any possible tranquility or satisfaction with one's life. What is missing from the basic emotions model of anger, are feelings

"Anger as a Way of Engaging the World" by Robert C. Solomon. It is adapted from a forthcoming book, *True to Our Feelings,* to be published by Oxford University Press next year.

and judgments, anger's "cognitive" aspects. The cognitive aspects of anger include what philosophers call *intentionality,* the fact that anger is about the world, an engagement in the world. In anger, I judge that another person or a situation or a thing has frustrated or offended me, gotten in the way of my goals or projects, or actually gone out of the way to insult or humiliate me. Thus the President gets angry at the Senator who leads a move to block a favorite project, or worse, he gets angry at the journalist who questions his ability to lead. One does not understand the anger if one only understands the neurology. One understands the anger only if one grasps what the anger is about, the relation between the angry person and the world or aspect of the world at which he is angry. And in cases of long-term anger, for instance, in partisan bickering, the evidence for the neurological activity discussed by the basic emotions theorists may be only occasional and a brief dramatic issue (for instance, when one of the partisans "loses his temper").

Why do we get angry? Perhaps the simplest cause of anger is simple frustration, finding one's goals or projects blocked or more difficult than one expected. More complex is offense, when it is not just a matter of frustration but someone is *to blame* for the blockage or interference. It is with this in mind that we might best appreciate how *judgmental* anger is. I think it is judgmental in two somewhat different senses. First, like all emotions (I will argue) it is constituted or structured by judgments, ways of perceiving, conceiving of, and evaluating ("appraising") the world. But, second, anger is distinctive among emotions in setting up a scenario that involves a particularly judgmental stance towards the world. Lewis Carroll, in *Alice in Wonderland,* suggests, "I'll be judge, I'll be jury, Said cunning old fury." This is a brilliant analysis of anger. Anger, in addition to being structured by judgments, is a literally judgmental emotion. The offended subject turns the tables on the offender, thus saving face (at least as far as the subject is concerned). The subject casts him- or herself in the superior role of judge or magistrate, and jury as well.

Thus the phenomenology of anger involves a sort of courtroom scenario (a "kangaroo court," one might argue, in which judgments are peremptory, there is no defense, and few people ever get a fair trial). I have suggested that emotions are strategies, and the strategic advantage of this set-up should be obvious. Emerging from a situation in which one has been hurt, offended or humiliated, one repositions oneself as nevertheless superior, even as righteous. It is a powerful psychological position. It is also presumptuous, which is why Christian tradition rightly warns against it.

Emotions are typically contrasted with reason and being reasonable. In our ordinary way of talking, "don't get emotional about it" typically means, "don't be angry" or "be reasonable." But, to ask a basic question, aren't there times when it is perfectly right to get angry, to get emotional? Or more pointedly, aren't there occasions when what is perfectly reasonable is to get angry? A friend of mine was brutally cut off from tenure at the University, despite a remarkable collection of published writings, excellent teaching, and devoted service to the institution. The problem, of course, was politics. He had just rubbed someone in power the wrong way. I was appalled when my friend failed to get angry, accepting his humiliation and forced change of life as "just one of those things." And so, I got angry on his behalf, but I also got angry (mixed with sympathy) *at him.* It seemed to me that not only did he have a perfect right to be angry but that he *ought* to have been angry. The emotion was both rational and, in my view, somewhat obligatory. You don't let administrators get away with institutional murder. On a larger scale, one of the main teachings of modern feminism was that it was OK for women to get angry; in fact, women *ought to* get angry, for there was a lot to be angry about. Their anger was *righteous* anger, and not irrational at all.

Many people will reject this. They will say, "No. Anger is *never* the best strategy." And I will admit that this answer has much to recommend it. There is considerable virtue in my friend's response. But first, I want to argue to the contrary and suggest at least that anger can be a reasonable and rational response to adversity. But I also want to see just what even this negative answer has to offer our understanding of anger. The idea that anger is always wrong is codified, most straightforwardly, in the heptalog of "deadly" or "mortal" sins, compiled by the Pope Gregory the Great in the eighth century. It is an idea that pervades a good deal of Christian and other religious thought (e.g., Buddhism), and it can rightly be juxtaposed against earlier religious traditions which tended to sanctify or celebrate anger, for example, in the wrathful God of the Hebrew Bible or the destructive Shiva of ancient Hinduism. So, too, Socrates and Plato turned from the warrior wrath and vengeful justice of the Homeric heroes to a more "civilized" conception of justice in which vengeance played no role. So the idea that anger is best avoided is an age-old idea with impressive philosophical credentials. Nevertheless, let's take a look at why this long-reviled emotion has such a hold on us, why it is so often appealing and even reasonable.

Let me start by repeating what the detractors of anger and its would-be defenders agree upon, the idea that anger is a way of engaging the world. On the one hand, this is obvious. We get angry *at* someone, *about* something. We do not just "get angry," the way we might get a fever or a headache or a pain in the chest. This *aboutness* feature of anger, its *intentionality* means that anger is "directed toward" someone or some situation, that is an engagement with the world means that a description or an understanding of anger involves an account of the world, or, more accurately, a person's relationship with other people in the world. To be sure, the anger may also involve symptoms that look a lot like having a fever or getting a pain in the chest. But these alone are not anger. Anger requires an "object," an engagement with the world. So the first question is whether the anger is rightly aimed—has it picked out the right object (the offender), and whether the anger is warranted by the situation. (The person targeted may in fact be the offender, but the offense is so minor that it does not warrant the anger.) If both the object is right

and the seriousness of the accusation is warranted, then the anger is rational and reasonable. (It is possible that future evidence and considerations may throw the original judgment into question, but then we would say that "given what he knew at the time" or "given what then seemed to be the case," his anger was rational and reasonable.)

But I suggested that anger can also be a *strategy*. So there is an additional consideration, beyond accuracy and fairness, that governs the rationality of anger. Namely, Does getting angry serve one's ultimate ends? Getting angry at one's boss may be right and even righteous, but it is only rarely rational. Getting angry at one's professor before she has graded your exam may be right and righteous, but it is usually not a rational strategy. Thus anger is rational depending on whether or not it fits into a person's longer-term interests. What follows is that some modes of engagement, some strategies, are better than others. Some are foolish. Some are stupid and unwarranted. John's frustration because he cannot solve a puzzle—for instance, he cannot prove a mathematical conjecture that has long evaded the best mathematicians, is foolish. John's anger at Sally for insulting him in public because she failed to mention that he was the best lover in the world at a testimonial dinner is most likely enormously stupid and inappropriate. Getting angry at a merely imagined slight is almost always both a bad strategy and, when expressed, it may be a moral injustice. But sometimes, it seems more foolish *not* to get angry. After being humiliated in public, getting turned down for a promotion which one clearly deserved, being repeatedly punched or pushed by a stranger while simply standing in line, one has a right to get angry, whether or not there are other avenues of expression or recourse. (The traditional wisdom, "Don't get mad, get even," neglects to point out that getting mad is the first step as well as the ongoing motivation to getting even.) Thus Aristotle insisted, in line with the Homeric heroes, that there are times when one would be a fool *not* to get angry. And even in the New Testament, anger is not so much extinguished as delegated to a loving God, who can be trusted to manage it much more fairly and effectively.

Granted that there are better and worse ways of dealing with anger, we need to understand the attractions and the warrant of anger if we are to know how to deal with it. And the first thing to say is that there are reasons—sometimes *good* reasons—for anger. Even if anger is not the best strategy, it may be right to get angry. What's more, it is not as if we always get angry against our better natures, or to our own dismay. The second thing to say is that we sometimes *enjoy* getting angry. Anger feels good. It can even feel cleansing, as at the climax of Camus's wonderfully perplexing existential novel, *The Stranger,* where he describes himself as "ready to start life all over again." But how can such a negative emotion feel good? Well, if it transforms a situation in which we have been humbled or humiliated into one in which we are the righteous accuser, it is easy to see how it might feel good even in the absence of external expression. And if the anger is effectively expressed, without serious consequences (for example, getting hit back or punished), it may indeed be extremely satisfying. But, then, is anger really a "negative" emotion?

If the idea is that there are better ways to deal with the world than getting angry, that's fine. But that only makes anger a less good strategy, not a "negative emotion." It may well be that getting angry (or getting angry without adequate means of expressing it) is bad for your health, and in that sense is on a par with overworking, over-worrying, or over-indulging. But that does not make anger a "negative emotion." It may be that getting angry makes one feel bad,

in part due, no doubt, to centuries of moral conditioning that say getting angry is sinful. But anger at least sometimes feels good and right, and this is not necessarily due to any fatal flaw in character or misunderstanding of the nature of the cosmos. It is also true that anger expressed often invites anger in retaliation, and the results of this (in your boss, in your professor) may be disastrous. But it does not follow that anger is a "negative emotion," only that anger is not always the best strategy.

Instead of dismissing anger wholesale, across the board, here is a better strategy. Let us distinguish between anger in its cruder or more vulgar forms, including its more crude and vulgar forms of expression, and refined anger and more refined forms of expression. Picasso's *Guernica* is such an expression, and the anger that inspired it thereby becomes more refined as well. Baudelaire's poetry could, with no imagination whatsoever, be alternatively expressed in crude barnyard language, betraying emotions equally crude. Instead of talking about the "irrationality" of emotion (which as most people use the term means an absence of rationality rather than a poor strategy or a strategy gone awry), we would do much better to explore such seemingly aesthetic as well as moral evaluations, crude versus refined, appropriate versus inappropriate, idiotic as opposed to insightful, sensitive, and intelligent. Our emotions are as complex as our engagements with the world and other people. They define and determine our engagements with the world, and they can be as elegant or as ugly as we make them.

PLATO
Two Speeches on Love

PLATO'S Symposium *consists of a half dozen or so speeches about love. Aristophanes, who had spoofed Socrates in his play* Clouds, *is paid in kind by Plato, who has him give an unbelievable but utterly charming speech about the origins of love in the tragic splitting of our original selves. Then Socrates gives us his own speech, much of which consists of a report from the muse Diotima, who presents a highly idealized (and extremely influential) portrait of love and immortality. (You will notice that some of Plato's views about sexual orientation are rather liberal.) Socrates' view makes eros out to be something very sophisticated and philosophical, unlike the bodily lust that characterized the concept among most Greeks of the time. Indeed, the true lover turns out to be the philosopher, who longs for Beauty itself.*

ARISTOPHANES' SPEECH

FIRST you must learn what Human Nature was in the beginning and what has happened to it since, because long ago our nature was not what it is now, but very different. . . . The shape of each human being was completely round, with back and sides in a circle; they had four hands each, as many legs as hands, and two faces, exactly alike, on a rounded neck. Between the two faces, which were on opposite sides, was one head with four ears. There were two sets of sexual organs, and everything else was the way you'd imagine it from what I've told you. They walked upright, as we do now, whatever direction they wanted. And whenever they set out to run fast, they thrust out all their eight limbs, the ones they had then, and spun rapidly, the way gymnasts do cartwheels, by bringing their legs around straight. . . .

In strength and power, therefore, they were terrible, and they had great ambitions. They made an attempt on the gods, and Homer's story about Ephialtes and Otos was originally about them: how they tried to make an ascent to heaven so as to attack the gods. Then Zeus and the other gods met in council to discuss what to do, and they were sore perplexed. They couldn't wipe out the human race with thunderbolts and kill them all off, as they had the giants, because that would wipe out the worship they receive, along with the sacrifices we humans give them. On the other hand, they couldn't let them run riot. At last, after great effort, Zeus had an idea.

"I think I have a plan," he said, "that would allow human beings to exist and stop their misbehaving: they will give up being wicked when they lose their strength. So I shall now cut each of them in two. At one stroke they will lose their strength and also become more profitable to us, owing to the increase in their number. They shall walk upright on two legs. But if I find they still run riot and do not keep the peace," he said, "I will cut them in two again, and they'll have to make their way on one leg, hopping." So saying, he cut those human beings in two, the way people cut sorb-apples before they dry them or the way they cut eggs with hairs. . . .

Now, since their natural form had been cut in two, each one longed for its own other half, and so they would throw their arms about each

Plato, "Aristophanes' Speech on Love," from *Plato's Symposium* by Plato, translated by Alexander Nehamas and Paul Woodruff (Hackett Publishing Company, 1989). Used by permission of Hackett Publishing other, weaving themselves together, wanting to grow together. In that condition they would die from hunger and general idleness, because they would not do anything apart from each other. Whenever one of the halves died and one was left, the one that was left still sought another and wove itself together with that. Sometimes the half he met came from a woman, as we'd call her now, sometimes it came from a man; either way, they kept on dying.

. . . This, then, is the source of our desire to love each other. Love is born into every human being; it calls back the halves of our original nature together, it tries to make one out of two and heal the wound of human nature.

Each of us, then, is a "matching half" of a human whole, because each was sliced like a flatfish, two out of one, and each of us is always seeking the half that matches him. . . . And so, when a person meets the half that is his very own, whatever his orientation, . . . then something wonderful happens: the two are struck from their senses by love, by a sense of belonging to one another, and by desire, and they don't want to be separated from one another, not even for a moment.

These are the people who finish out their lives together and still cannot say what it is they want from one another. No one would think it is the intimacy of sex—that mere sex is the reason each lover takes so great and deep a joy in being with the other. It's obvious that the soul of every lover longs for something else; his soul cannot say what it is, but like an oracle it has a sense of what it wants, and like an oracle it hides behind a riddle. Suppose two lovers are lying together and Hephaestus stands over them with his mending tools, asking, "What is it you human beings really want from each other?" And suppose they're perplexed, and he asks them again: "Is this your heart's desire, then—for the two of you to become parts of the same whole, as near as can be, and never to separate, day or night? Because if that's your desire, I'd like to weld you together and join you into something that is naturally whole, so that the two of you are made into one. Then the two of you would share one

life, as long as you lived, because you would be one being, and by the same token, when you died, you would be one and not two in Hades, having died a single death. Look at your love, and see if this is what you desire: wouldn't this be all the good fortune you could want?"

Surely you can see that no one who received such an offer would turn it down; no one would find anything else that he wanted. Instead, everyone would think he'd found out at last what he had always wanted: to come together and melt together with the one he loves, so that one person emerged from two. Why should this be so? It's because, as I said, we used to be complete wholes in our original nature, and now "Love" is the name of our pursuit of wholeness, for our desire to be complete. . . .

If we are to give due praise to the god who can give us this blessing, then, we must praise Love. Love does the best that can be done for the time being: he draws us towards what belongs to us. But for the future, Love promises the greatest hope of all: If we treat the gods with due reverence, he will restore to us our original nature, and by healing us, he will make us blessed and happy.

DIOTIMA'S SPEECH

"When Aphrodite was born, the gods held a celebration. Poros the son of Metis, was there among them. When they had feasted, Penia came begging, as poverty does when there's a party, and stayed by the gates. Now Poros got drunk on nectar (there was no wine yet, you see) and, feeling drowsy, went into the garden of Zeus, where he fell asleep. Then Penia schemed up a plan to relieve her lack of resources: she would get a child from Poros. So she lay beside him and got pregnant with Love. That is why Love was born to follow Aphrodite and serve her: because he was conceived on the day of her birth. And that's why he is also by nature a lover of beauty, because Aphrodite herself is especially beautiful."

"As the son of Poros and Penia, his lot in life is set to be like theirs. In the first place, he is always poor, and he's far from being delicate and beautiful (as ordinary people think he is); instead, he is tough and shriveled and shoeless and homeless, always lying on the dirt without a bed, sleeping at gates and in roadsides under the sky, having his mother's nature, always living with Need. But on his father's side he is a schemer after the beautiful and the good; he is brave, impetuous, and intense, an awesome hunter, always weaving snares, resourceful in his pursuit of intelligence, a lover of wisdom through all his life, a genius with enchantments, potions, and clever pleadings."

"He is by nature neither immortal nor mortal. But now he springs to life when he gets his way; now he dies—all in the very same day. Because he is his father's son, however, he keeps coming back to life, but then anything he finds his way to always slips away, and for this reason Love is never completely without resources, nor is he ever rich."

"He is in between wisdom and ignorance as well. In fact, you see, none of the gods loves wisdom or wants to become wise—for they are wise—and no one else who is wise already loves wisdom; on the other hand, no one who is ignorant will love wisdom either or want to become wise. For what's especially difficult about being ignorant is that you are content with yourself, even though you're neither beautiful and good nor intelligent. If you don't think you need anything, of course you won't want what you don't think you need."

"In that case, Diotima, who are the people who love wisdom, if they are neither wise nor ignorant?"

"That's obvious," she said. "A child could tell you. Those who love wisdom fall in between those two extremes. And Love is one of them, because he is in love with what is beautiful, and wisdom is extremely beautiful. It follows that Love must be a lover of wisdom and, as such, is in between being wise and being ignorant. This, too, comes to him from his parentage, from a father who is wise and resourceful and a mother who is not wise and lacks resource. My dear Socrates, that, then, is the nature of the Spirit called Love. Considering what you thought about Love, it's no surprise that you were led into thinking of Love as you did. On the basis of what you say, I conclude that you thought Love was being loved, rather than being a lover. I think that's why Love struck you as beautiful in every way: because it is what is really beautiful and graceful that deserves to be loved, and this is perfect and highly blessed; but being a lover takes a different form, which I have just described. . . ."

"All of us are pregnant, Socrates, both in body and in soul, and, as soon as we come to a certain age, we naturally desire to give birth. Now no one can possibly give birth in anything ugly; only in something beautiful. That's because when a man and a woman come together in order to give birth, this is a godly affair. Pregnancy, reproduction—this is an immortal thing for a mortal animal to do, and it cannot occur in anything that is out of harmony, but ugliness is out of harmony with all that is godly. Beauty, however is in harmony with the divine. Therefore the goddess who presides at childbirth—she's called Moira or Eileithuia—is really Beauty. That's why, whenever pregnant animals or persons draw near to beauty, they become gentle and joyfully disposed and give birth and reproduce; but near ugliness they are foul faced and draw back in pain; they turn away and shrink back and do not reproduce, and because they hold on to what they carry inside them, the labor is painful. This is the source of the great excitement about beauty that comes to anyone who is pregnant and already teeming with life: beauty releases them from their great pain. You see, Socrates," she said, "what Love wants is not beauty, as you think it is."

"Well, what is it, then?"

"Reproduction and birth in beauty. . . . Now why reproduction? It's because reproduction goes on forever; it is what mortals have in place of immortality. A lover must desire immortality along with the good, if what we agreed earlier was right, that Love wants to possess the good forever. It follows from our argument that Love must desire immortality. . . . Now, some people are pregnant in body, and for this reason turn more to women and pursue love in that way, providing themselves, through childbirth, with immortality and remembrance and happiness, as they think, for all time to come; while others are pregnant in soul—because there surely are those who are even more pregnant in their souls than in their bodies, and these are pregnant with what is fitting for a soul to bear and bring to birth. And what is fitting? Wisdom and the rest of virtue. . . . A lover who goes about this matter correctly must begin in his youth to devote himself to beautiful bodies. First, if the leader leads aright, he should love one body and beget beautiful ideas there; then he should realize that the beauty of any one body is brother to the beauty of any other and that if he is to pursue beauty of form he'd be very foolish not to think that the beauty of all bodies is one and the same. When he grasps this, he must become a lover of all beautiful bodies, and he must think that this wild gaping after just one body is a small thing and despise it.

"After this he must think that the beauty of people's souls is more valuable than the beauty of their bodies, so that if someone is decent in his soul, even though he is scarcely blooming in his body, our lover must be content to love and care for him and to seek to give birth to such ideas as will make young men better. The result is that our lover will be forced to gaze at the beauty of activities and laws and to see that all this is akin to itself, with the result that he will think that the beauty of bodies is a thing of no importance. After customs he must move on to various kinds of knowledge. The result is that he will see the beauty of knowledge and be looking mainly not at beauty in a single example—as a servant would who favored the beauty of a little boy or a man or a single custom (being a slave, of course, he's low and small-minded)—but the lover is turned to the great sea of beauty, and, gazing upon this, he gives birth to many gloriously beautiful ideas and theories, in unstinting love of wisdom, until, having grown and been strengthened there, he catches sight of such knowledge, and it is the knowledge of such beauty. . . . "

ROBERT C. SOLOMON
What Love Is

ROBERT C. SOLOMON *(b. 1942) is a philosopher at the University of Texas who writes about emotions. The following is taken from his 1981 book,* Love: Emotion, Myth and Metaphor.

THE question, What is love? is neither a request for a confession nor an excuse to start moralizing. It is not an invitation to amuse us with some *bon mot* ("Love is the key that opens up the doors of happiness") or to impress us with an author's sensitivity. And love is much more than a "feeling." When a novelist wants us to appreciate his character's emotions, he does not just describe sweaty palms and a moment of panic; he instead describes a *world*,

Solomon, Robert C., "What Love Is," from *Love: Emotion, Myth and Metaphors* (New York: Doubleday, 1981). Used by permission.

the world as it is experienced—in anger, or in envy, or in love. Theorizing about emotion, too, is like describing an exotic world. It is a kind of conceptual anthropology—identifying a peculiar list of characters—heroes, villains, knaves or lovers—understanding a special set of rules and roles—rituals, fantasies, myths, slogans and fears. But these are not merely empirical observations on the fate of a feeling; none of this will make any sense to anyone who has not [had the emotion]. Love can be understood only "from the inside," as a language can be understood only by someone who speaks it, as a world can be known only by someone who has—even if vicariously—*lived* in it.

To analyze an emotion by looking at the world it defines allows us to cut through the inarticulateness of mere "feelings" and do away once and for all with the idea that emotions in general and love in particular are "ineffable" or beyond description. This might make some sense if describing an emotion were describing something "inside of us." It is not easy, for example, to describe how one feels when nauseous; even describing something so specific as a migraine headache falls back on clumsy metaphors ("as if my head's in a vise," "as if someone were driving a nail through my skull"). But once we see that every emotion defines a world for itself, we can then describe in some detail what that world involves, with its many variations, describe its dimensions and its dynamics. The world defined by love—or what we shall call the *loveworld*—is a world woven around a single relationship with all else pushed to the periphery. To understand love is to understand the specifics of this relationship and the world woven around it.

Love has been so misunderstood both because so often it has been taken to be *other-worldly* rather than one world of emotion among others, and because it has sometimes been taken to be a "mere emotion"—just a feeling and not a world at all. Because of this, perhaps it would be best to illustrate the theory that every emotion is a world by beginning with a less problematic emotion, namely, *anger*. Anger too defines its world. It is a world in which one

defines oneself in the role of "the offended" and defines someone else (or perhaps a group or an institution) as "the offender." The world of anger is very much a courtroom world, a world filled with blame and emotional litigation. It is a world in which everyone else tends to become a co-defendant, a friend of the court, a witness or at least part of the courtroom audience. (But when you're *very* angry, there are no innocent bystanders.) Writes Lewis Carroll in *Alice in Wonderland:* "'I'll be judge, I'll be jury,' said cunning old Fury." It is a world in which one does indeed define oneself as judge and jury, compete with a grim righteousness, with "justice"—one's own vengeance—as the only legitimate concern. It is a *magical* world, which can change a lackadaisical unfocused morning into a piercing, all-consuming day, an orgy of vindictive self-righteousness and excitement. At the slightest provocation it can change an awkward and defensive situation into an aggressive confrontation. To describe the world of anger is therefore to describe its fantasies, for example, the urge to kill, though rarely is this taken seriously or to its logical conclusion. It has its illusions too, for instance, the tendency to exaggerate the importance of some petty grievance to the level of cosmic injustice; in anger we sometimes talk as if "man's inhumanity to man" is perfectly manifested in some minor slight at the office yesterday. It is a world with a certain fragility; a single laugh can explode the whole pretense of angry self-righteousness. And it is a world with a purpose—for when do we feel more self-righteous than in anger? Getting angry in an otherwise awkward situation may be a way of saving face or providing a quick ego boost; "having a bad temper" may be not so much a "character trait" as an emotional strategy, a way of *using* emotion as a means of controlling other people. To describe anger, in other words, is to describe the way the world is structured—and why—by a person who is angry.

The world of love—the loveworld—can be similarly described as a theatrical scenario, not as a courtroom but rather as "courtly," a romantic drama defined by its sense of elegance (badly interpreted as "spiritual"), in which we also take up a certain role—"the lover"—and cast another person into a complementary role—"the beloved." But where anger casts two antagonistic characters, romantic love sets up an idea of unity, absolute complementary and total mutual support and affection. It is the *rest* of the world that may be the antagonist. [The Russian novelist] Boris Pasternak describes the loveworld beautifully—the world as Adam and Eve, naked, surrounded by chaos.

It is a world we know well, of course—the world of *Casablanca, Romeo and Juliet* and a thousand stories and novels. It is a world in which we narrow our vision and our cares to that single duality, all else becoming trifles, obstacles or interruptions. It is a magical world, in which an ordinary evening is transformed into the turning point of a lifetime, the metamorphosis of one's self into a curious kind of double being. It may seem like a sense of "discovery"; in fact it is a step in a long search, a process of creation. . . .

Like every emotional world, the loveworld has its essential rules and rituals, its basic structures and internal dynamics. Some of these rules and structures are so obvious that it is embarrassing to have to spell them out, for example, the fact that the loveworld (typically) includes two people, instead of only one (as in shame) or three (as in jealousy) or indeed an entire class of people (as in national mourning or revolutionary resentment). Or the fact that the loveworld involves extremely "positive" feelings about the person loved, perhaps even the uncritical evaluation that he or she is "the most wonderful person in the world." Or the fact that the loveworld is held together by the mutual desire to be together (to touch, be touched, to caress and make love) no less essentially than the world of Newton and Einstein is held together by the forces of electromagnetism and gravity. Such features are so obvious to us that we fail to think of them as the structures of love; we take them for granted and, when asked to talk about love, consider them not even worth mentioning. Having thus ignored the obvious, love becomes a mystery. But other seemingly equally "obvious" features of love may

not be part of the structure of the loveworld at all—for example, the comforting equation between love and trust. Here, indeed, there is some room for "mystery" in love, not the emotion itself but its essential lack of predictability, the fascination with the unknown and the attraction that comes not with trust but with vulnerability, sometimes even suspicion and doubt. . . .

THE "OBJECT" OF LOVE

Talking about the loveworld is not only a way to avoid the hopeless conception of love as a feeling; it is also a way of rejecting an insidious view of love—and emotions in general—which many philosophers have come to accept as "obvious," particularly in this century. The view simply stated, is that love is an attitude *toward* someone, a feeling directed *at* a person, instead of a shared world. The view is often disguised by a piece of professional jargon—an impressive work, "intentionality." It is said that emotions are "intentional," which is a way of saying that they are "about" something. What an emotion is "about" is called its "intentional object" or, simply, its "object." Thus shame is an emotion which is "about" someone else. The language comes from the medieval scholastics, by way of an Austrian philosopher named Franz Brentano, one of whose students in Vienna was the young Sigmund Freud. Thus Freud talks all the time about the "object" of love, not without some discomfort, for though the conception fits his general theories perfectly, he nonetheless sensed correctly that some considerable conceptual damage was being done to the emotion thereby.

The idea—though not the terminology—of "intentionality" and "intentional objects" was introduced into British philosophy by the Scottish philosopher David Hume. He analyzed a number of emotions in terms of the "objects" with which they were "naturally associated," for example pride and humility, which both took as their "objects" oneself, and hatred and love, which both took as their objects another person. But we can already see what is going to be wrong with this familiar type of analysis. First of all, all such talk about "objects" leaves out the crucial fact that, in love at least, it is the other as a "subject" that is essential. To be in love (even unrequited) is [to wish] to be looked *at,* not just to look. Thus it is the eyes, not the body (nor the soul), that present the so-called "beloved," not as object but as subject, not first as beautiful or lovable but always as (potentially) *loving.* It's the eyes that have it, nothing else. . . .

Love is not just an attitude directed toward another person: it is an emotion which, [one hopes], is *shared with* him or her. . . . [A]ny account of love that begins with the idea of an "object" of love is probably going to miss the main point of the emotion, namely, that it is not an emotion "about" another person so much as, in our terms, a world we share. . . .

One obvious misunderstanding is this: the Christian view of love is not alone in teaching us that love is essentially *selfless.* Proponents of romantic love have argued that too. The idea is that love is thoroughly "about" another person, so that any degree of self-love is incompatible with "true" selfless love. But this is impossible. There is no emotion without self-involvement, and no love that is not also "about" oneself. The other side is just as confused, however; La Rochefoucauld, for example, insists that "all love is self-love." But to be self-involved is not yet to be selfish, nor does self-involvement in any way exclude a total concern for the other person as well. The practical consequence of this confusion, in turn, is the readiness with which we can be made to feel guilty at the slightest suggestion that our love is not "pure" but turns on "selfish" motives, and it renders unaskable what is in fact a most intelligible question—namely, "What am I getting out of this?"—to which the answer may well be, "Not enough to make it worth while." But then, love is not just what one "gets out of it" either.

• • •

So what is love? It is, in a phrase, an emotion through which we create for ourselves a little world—the loveworld, in which we play the roles of lovers and, quite literally, create our selves as well. . . . Even so-called "unrequited" love is shared love and shared identity, if only from one side and thereby woefully incomplete. Of course, occasionally an imagined identity may be far preferable to the actuality, but even when this is the case unrequited love represents at most a hint toward a process and not the process as such. Unrequited love is still love, but love in the sense that a sprout from an acorn is already an oak, no more. . . .

In love we transform ourselves and one another, but the key to this emotion is the understanding that the transformation of selves is not merely reciprocal, a swap of favors like "I'll cook you dinner if you'll wash the car." The self transformed in love is a shared self, and therefore by its very nature at odds with, even contradictory to, the individual autonomous selves that each of us had before. Sometimes our new shared self may be a transformation of a self that I (perhaps we) shared before. Possibly all love is to some extent the transposition of seemingly "natural" bonds which have somehow been abandoned or destroyed, and therefore the less than novel transformation of a self that has always been shared, in one way or another. But the bonds of love are always, to some extent, "unnatural," and our shared identity is always, in some way, uncomfortable. Aristophanes' delightful allegory about the double creatures cleft in two and seeking their other halves is charming but false. Love is never so neat and tidy, antigen and antibody forming the perfect fit. The Christian concept of a couple sanctified as a "union" before God is reassuring, as if one thereby receives some special guarantee, an outside bond of sorts, which will keep two otherwise aimless souls together. But the warranty doesn't apply. What is so special about romantic love, and what makes it so peculiar to our and similar societies, is the fact that it is entirely based on the idea of individuality and freedom, and this means, first of all, that the presupposition of love is a strong sense of individual identity and autonomy which exactly contradicts the ideal of "union" and "yearning to be one" that some of our literature has celebrated so one-sidedly. And, second, the freedom that is built into the loveworld includes not just the freedom to come together but the freedom to go as well. Thus love and the loveworld are always in a state of tension, always changing, dynamic, tenuous and explosive.

. . . To understand love is to understand this tension, this dialectic between individuality and the shared ideal. To think that love is to be found at the ends of the spectrum—in that first enthusiastic "discovery" of a shared togetherness or at the end of the road, after a lifetime together—is to miss the loveworld almost entirely, for it is neither an initial flush of feeling nor the retrospective congratulations of old age but a struggle for unity and identity. And it is this struggle—neither the ideal of togetherness nor the contrary demand for individual autonomy and identity alone—that defines the dynamics of that convulsive and tenuous world we call romantic love.

CHAPTER TEN

How Should I Feel
about Abortion
and Embryo Research?

The issues of abortion and embryo research are as controversial within philosophy as they are outside of philosophy. In thinking about them, we are forced to assess our views about sex, about reproduction, about the beginning of human life, about preventing and treating disease, about killing, about responsibility, about sexual equality, and about religion. Philosophy may not resolve the question whether abortion is morally right or wrong, or whether using human embryos for research is ever justified, but philosophy can help to shed light on why these questions provoke so much disagreement, and hence why it is difficult to formulate consistent public policy in these areas.

When considering abortion as a philosophical topic, it is helpful to begin by considering what women actually think about when they are trying to decide whether or not to have an abortion. Obviously, the factors that a woman considers will depend upon her particular circumstances. Sometimes, the pregnancy itself presents difficulties. A teenager may think that being pregnant would create serious personal and social difficulties for her. A woman about to set off on an arduous archeological expedition may decide that being pregnant would interfere with her work. Sometimes, the pregnancy itself is not so much a problem; rather, the problem is the child that will be its result. A student may feel that having a child at this point would seriously jeopardize her chances of finishing school. A mother of two children may conclude that having another child would impair her emotional and financial ability to care for her existing ones. It is important for us to bear in mind that actual abortion decisions are made in the context of a woman's ongoing and invariably complex life. When philosophers abstract the problem of abortion from that context, it may take on different dimensions. Susan Tracy begins this chapter with a stark reminder of the dangers, both physical and emotional, of illegal abortion. Her poem recounts her experience of an unwanted pregnancy shortly before the 1972 Supreme Court decision *Roe v. Wade* that legalized abortion.

Most opposition to abortion is based on the claim that human life begins at conception and thus that a human embryo or fetus is a person like any other and so has a right to life. Although there is disagreement among philosophers as to all that a right to life involves, we can assume that at the very least it guarantees that one not be killed unjustifiably. Unwarranted or unjustified killing is murder. Murder is not permissible. Those opposed to abortion typically believe that the killing of an innocent embryo is unwarranted. If so, they conclude, abortion is murder and hence is impermissible. When the problem of abortion is framed in this way, it appears that those who wish to defend the practice of abortion against this conclusion are forced to argue that personhood does not begin at conception, but rather at some later stage in pregnancy or at birth. The question of exactly when human life, or personhood, begins is not a straightforward one. (You may want to look at Chapter 8 for more on this topic.) In pushing the abortion issue into this murky territory, those opposed to abortion are replacing one difficult question (is abortion morally justifiable?) with another one (when does human life or personhood begin?). Judith Jarvis Thomson argues that those concerned with establishing the permissibility of abortion need not become entangled in the issue of fetal personhood. For the sake of argument, she grants those opposed to abortion their major premise, namely, that the fetus is a person. She then proceeds to argue that, even if the fetus is a person, it does not follow that the woman is required to carry it to term. The woman's right to control over her own body outweighs the rights of the fetus. She draws analogies between the sacrifices that pregnant women must make to keep fetuses alive and other situations in which one person's life depends on the willingness of another to act on his or her behalf. In doing so, she hopes to set abortion in a context that displays clearly what she takes to be the central moral issue that it raises: Does a woman have an *obligation* to maintain, for the sake of the fetus, an unwanted pregnancy to term? (Chapters 13 and 15 supply useful background for the issue of obligation.) Thomson's example of the unconscious violinist who requires the use of your kidneys to stay alive has become legendary. It is up to you to decide whether you take it, or any of the other analogies, to be persuasive.

Sidney Callahan believes that new visualization technologies prove that the fetus should be granted the same value as any other human life. She argues that we see fetal life in the context of what she calls "ecological consciousness of caretaking," according to which we recognize the interdependence of all life, past, present, and future. If we think in this way, we can more readily accept our responsibility for protecting the unborn.

Alice Walker's polemic paints a stark picture of the factors that limit black women's procreative agency. The exercise of nearly limitless power by white men over the planet and its people leaves black women particularly vulnerable to the ravages of regulated reproduction, environmental pollution, and economic discrimination. She suggests a remedy for the historical legacy of racism in regard to reproduction.

As you can see, abortion raises a variety of troubling and challenging questions. First, it raises ethical questions, such as those addressed by Judith Thomson: Is abortion always wrong? Is it always right? Or is it sometimes right and sometimes wrong? Do embryos and fetuses have rights? Second, it raises what are called metaethical questions. What is the most reasonable way to think about abortion? Is it best seen as a conflict between the woman's right to have control over her body and the fetus' right to life? Or does the language of rights distort the issue? Does it leave out some essential features of the difficulties and dilemmas women confront when deciding whether to have an abortion? What relationship does abortion have to other reproductive practices and choices?

The technological advances that enable us to "see" embryonic and fetal development have proceeded alongside others that enable scientists to manipulate embryonic cells for reproductive and medical purposes. Most controversial of these is human cloning. In this chapter, we focus on what is referred to as *therapeutic cloning* (*reproductive cloning* is addressed in Chapter 6), which is the use of embryonic stem cells in the treatment of diseases. Such stem calls are derived from a *blastocyst*, a very young embryo that contains 200 to 250 cells and is shaped like a hollow sphere. The stem cells of a blastocyst ultimately develop into a person or animal. Medical researchers are interested in using stem cells to repair or replace damaged body tissues because stem cells are less likely than other foreign cells to be rejected by the immune system when they are implanted in the body. Embryonic stem cells have the capacity to develop into every type of tissue found in an adult. Therapeutic cloning thus has the potential to provide organs for transplant, and to replace cells damaged by disease or injury. The selections on therapeutic cloning in this chapter are designed to help you understand why therapeutic cloning raises many of the same moral issues as does abortion. Because the practice requires scientists to use human embryos for research, the question arises whether embryos fall under the same guidelines as human subjects. According to those guidelines, some forms of experimentation are allowed as long as a subject consents to them. Others are not allowed at all. Since embryos cannot give consent, and since no embryo used for experimentation survives intact, it is not clear whether they can or should be viewed as human subjects. Is it morally acceptable to use frozen embryos that would be discarded anyway? What about creating embryos for the purpose of medical experimentation? The National Institutes of Health claims both that human embryos should be treated with "profound respect," and that some research on them is humane because it promises to benefit people suffering from disease or injury. Daniel Callahan subjects this claim to scrutiny, and asks us to consider it in relation to a woman's right to terminate a pregnancy. The right to abortion is typically grounded on the right of a woman to have control over her own body. What bearing, if any, does this have on the use of embryos for medical purposes? Dena Davis explores in more detail the importance of distinguishing, for moral purposes, between the two cases. Mahowald and Mahowald introduce what they take to be another important distinction, namely, that between biological and philosophical definitions of human life and death.

One of the arguments over abortion has to do with the question whether or not the fetus is aware of pain. In response to this controversy, Senator Sam Brownback has suggested legislation to consider the "feelings" of the fetus.

Whatever you ultimately decide about the morality of abortion and therapeutic cloning, it is clear that scientific developments in the study of the human embryo have complicated our understanding of human life. While no moral conclusion can legitimately be drawn from science alone, as you can see from considering these issues, scientific knowledge and moral beliefs are mutually influential.

SUSAN TRACY

The Abortion

SUSAN TRACY *(b. 1947) teaches American studies at Hampshire College. She is the author of* In the Master's Eye: Representations of Women, Blacks and Poor Whites in Antebellum Southern Literature *(1996).*

I.
The respectable school doctor was stunned,
When I confirmed that
The stomachaches and vomit and pain was not
    an ulcer.

Finally, he assured me in his understanding way
That the college
Was very good about
Girls like me.
They would not expel me.
And the Catholic relief charities
In Northampton
Would see that The Baby
Was placed.

"There will be no baby."
I told the doctor blankly
"There will be no baby
To be placed."

II.
The abortion was arranged
In a faraway city
Quite illegally of course.
Because unlike today
Those were the days
When men owned women's bodies.
That good doctor was calming.
He said I would be dancing
That evening.
But he was wrong.
It was not at all
"Like having a tooth pulled."

III.
The ride home was too long.
We were very quiet and
I didn't feel like dancing.
But when the pain started creeping up my legs
Strangling all conscious thought
And the blood started pouring out from deep
    inside me,
And I crossed over into that cold, blank darkness
I finally felt the rage
Of a woman betrayed.

IV.
I am still not sure
How I got into that white room.
But there I was,
Back in the stirrups again.
And a kind doctor was there.
He said I had been very foolish
To have had an illegal abortion.
And didn't I know
That I almost died.
And what would my parents think.
And why didn't I use contraceptives
In the first place.
And he would see me in the morning
To discuss "my case."

V.
My head was spinning
And I felt cold with nausea and fright.
It was not the time for a debate.
So I could not remind him
That contraceptives were illegal

Tracy, Susan, "The Abortion," from Marlene Fried, *From Abortion to Reproductive Freedom* (South End Press, 1990). Reprinted by permission of the author.

For single girls like me.
And although abortions were illegal, too,
My parents could better live
With an unknown abortion
Than with a "bastard" who shared their name.

This story is true.
It happened long ago
In those days
When men owned women's bodies.

JUDITH JARVIS THOMSON
A Defense of Abortion

JUDITH JARVIS THOMSON *is a philosophy professor at MIT. She has worked extensively on ethics and metaphysics. Among her many writings is her book* The Realm of Rights *(1990).*

MOST opposition to abortion relies on the premise that the fetus is a human being, a person, from the moment of conception. The premise is argued for, but, as I think, not well. Take, for example, the most common argument. We are asked to notice that the development of a human being from conception through birth into childhood is continuous; then it is said that to draw a line, to choose a point in this development and say "before this point the thing is not a person, after this point it is a person" is to make an arbitrary choice, a choice for which in the nature of things no good reason can be given. It is concluded that the fetus is, or anyway that we had better say it is, a person from the moment of conception. But this conclusion does not follow. Similar things might be said about the development of an acorn into an oak tree, and it does not follow that acorns are oak trees, or that we had better say they are. Arguments of this form are sometimes called "slippery slope arguments"—the phrase is perhaps self-explanatory—and it is dismaying that opponents of abortion rely on them so heavily and uncritically.

I am inclined to agree, however, that the prospects for "drawing a line" in the development of the fetus look dim. I am inclined to think also that we shall probably have to agree that the fetus has already become a human person well before birth. Indeed, it comes as a surprise when one first learns how early in its life it begins to acquire human characteristics. By the tenth week, for example, it already has a face, arms and legs, fingers and toes; it has internal organs, and brain activity is detectable. On the other hand, I think that the premise is false, that the fetus is not a person from the moment of conception. A newly fertilized ovum, a newly implanted clump of cells, is no more a person that an acorn is an oak tree. But I shall not discuss any of this. For it seems to me to be of great interest to ask what happens if, for the sake of argument, we allow the premise. How, precisely,

Thompson, Judith Jarvis, "A Defense of Abortion," from *Philosophy and Public Affairs*, Vol. 1, no. 1 (Blackwell Publishing). Reprinted by permission of Blackwell Publishing.

are we supposed to get from there to the conclusion that abortion is morally impermissible? Opponents of abortion commonly spend most of their time establishing that the fetus is a person, and hardly any time explaining the step from there to the impermissibility of abortion. Perhaps they think the step too simple and obvious to require much comment. Or perhaps instead they are simply being economical in argument. Many of those who defend abortion rely on the premise that the fetus is not a person, but only a bit of tissue that will become a person at birth; and why pay out more arguments than you have to? Whatever the explanation, I suggest that the step they take is neither easy nor obvious, that it calls for closer examination than it is commonly given, and that when we do give it this closer examination we shall feel inclined to reject it.

I propose, then, that we grant that the fetus is a person from the moment of conception. How does the argument go from here? Something like this, I take it. Every person has a right to life. So the fetus has a right to life. No doubt the mother has a right to decide what shall happen in and to her body; everyone would grant that. But surely a person's right to life is stronger and more stringent than the mother's right to decide what happens in and to her body, and so outweighs it. So the fetus may not be killed; an abortion may not be performed.

It sounds plausible. But now let me ask you to imagine this. You wake up in the morning and find yourself back to back in bed with an unconscious violinist. A famous unconscious violinist. He has been found to have a fatal kidney ailment, and the Society of Music Lovers has canvassed all the available medical records and found that you alone have the right blood type to help. They have therefore kidnapped you, and last night the violinist's circulatory system was plugged into yours, so that your kidneys can be used to extract poisons from his blood as well as your own. The director of the hospital now tells you, "Look, we're sorry the Society of Music Lovers did this to you—we would never have permitted it if we had known. But still, they did it, and the violinist now is plugged into you. To

unplug you would be to kill him. But never mind, it's only for nine months. By then he will have recovered from his ailment, and can safely be unplugged from you." Is it morally incumbent on you to accede to this situation? No doubt it would be very nice of you if you did, a great kindness. But do you *have* to accede to it? What if it were not nine months, but nine years? Or longer still? What if the director of the hospital says, "Tough luck, I agree, but you've now got to stay in bed, with the violinist plugged into you, for the rest of your life. Because remember this. All persons have a right to life, and violinists are persons. Granted you have a right to decide what happened in and to your body, but a person's right to life outweighs your right to decide what happens in and to your body. So you cannot ever be unplugged from him." I imagine you would regard this as outrageous, which suggests that something really is wrong with that plausible-sounding argument I mentioned a moment ago.

In this case, of course, you were kidnapped; you didn't volunteer for the operation that plugged the violinist into your kidneys. Can those who oppose abortion on the ground I mentioned make an exception for a pregnancy due to rape? Certainly. They can say that persons have a right to life only if they didn't come into existence because of rape; or they can say that all persons have a right to life, but that some have less of a right to life than others, in particular, that those who came into existence because of rape have less. But these statements have a rather unpleasant sound. Surely the question of whether you have a right to life at all, or how much of it you have, shouldn't turn on the question of whether or not you are the product of a rape. And in fact the people who oppose abortion on the ground I mentioned do not make this distinction, and hence do not make an exception in case of rape.

Nor do they make an exception for a case in which the mother has to spend the nine months of her pregnancy in bed. They would agree that would be a great pity, and hard on the mother; but all the same, all persons have a right to life, the fetus is a person, and so on. I suspect, in fact, that they would not make an exception for a case in which, miraculously enough, the pregnancy went on for nine years, or even the rest of the mother's life.

Some won't even make an exception for a case in which continuation of the pregnancy is likely to shorten the mother's life; they regard abortion as impermissible even to save the mother's life. Such cases are nowadays very rare, and many opponents of abortion do not accept this extreme view. All the same, it is a good place to begin: a number of points of interest come out in respect to it.

1. Let us call the view that abortion is impermissible even to save the mother's life "the extreme view." I want to suggest first that it does not issue from the argument I mentioned earlier without the addition of some fairly powerful premises. Suppose a woman has become pregnant, and now learns that she has a cardiac condition such that she will die if she carries the baby to term. What may be done for her? The fetus, being a person, has a right to life, but as the mother is a person too, so has she a right to life. Presumably they have an equal right to life. How is it supposed to come out that an abortion may not be performed? If mother and child have an equal right to life, shouldn't we perhaps flip a coin? Or should we add to the mother's right to life her right to decide what happens in and to her body, which everybody seems to be ready to grant—the sum of her rights now outweighing the fetus' right to life?

   The most familiar argument here is the following. We are told that performing the abortion would be directly killing the child, whereas doing nothing would not be killing the mother, but only letting her die. Moreover in killing the child, one would be killing an innocent person, for the child has committed no crime, and is not aiming at his mother's death. And then there are a variety of ways in which this might be continued. (1) But as directly killing an innocent person is always and absolutely impermissible, an abortion may not be performed. Or, (2) as directly killing an inno-

cent person is murder, and murder is always and absolutely impermissible, an abortion may not be performed. Or, (3) as one's duty to refrain from directly killing an innocent person is more stringent than one's duty to keep a person from dying, an abortion may not be performed. Or, (4) if one's only options are directly killing an innocent person or letting a person die, one must prefer letting the person die, and thus an abortion may not be performed.

Some people seem to have thought that these are not further premises which must be added if the conclusion is to be reached, but that they follow from the very fact that an innocent person has a right to life. But this seems to me to be a mistake, and perhaps the simplest way to show this is to bring out that while we must certainly grant that innocent persons have a right to life, the theses in (1) through (4) are all false. Take (2), for example. If directly killing an innocent person is murder, and thus is impermissible, then the mother's directly killing the innocent person inside her is murder, and thus is impermissible. But it cannot seriously be thought to be murder if the mother performs an abortion on herself to save her life. It cannot seriously be said that she *must* refrain, that she *must* sit passively by and wait for her death. Let us look again at the case of you and the violinist. There you are, in bed with the violinist, and the director of the hospital says to you, "It's all most distressing, and I deeply sympathize, but you see this is putting an additional strain on your kidneys, and you'll be dead within the month. But you *have* to stay where you are all the same. Because unplugging you would be directly killing an innocent violinist, and that's murder, and that's impermissible." If anything in the world is true, it is that you do not commit murder, you do not do what is impermissible, if you reach around to your back and unplug yourself from that violinist to save your life.

The main focus of attention in writing on abortion has been on what a third party may or may not do in answer to a request from a woman for an abortion. This is in a way understandable. Things being as they are, there isn't much a woman can safely do to abort herself. So the question asked is what a third party may do, and what the mother may do, if it is mentioned at all, is deduced, almost as an afterthought, from what it is concluded that third parties may do. But it seems to me that to treat the matter in this way is to refuse to grant to the mother that very status of person which is so firmly insisted on for the fetus. For we cannot simply read off what a person may do from what a third party may do. Suppose you find yourself trapped in a tiny house with a growing child. I mean a very tiny house and in a few minutes you'll be crushed to death. The child on the other hand won't be crushed to death; if nothing is done to stop him from growing he'll be hurt, but in the end he'll simply burst open the house and walk out a free man. Now I could well understand it if a bystander were to say, "There's nothing we can do for you. We cannot choose between your life and his, we cannot be the ones to decide who is to live, we cannot intervene." But it cannot be concluded that you too can do nothing, that you cannot attack it to save your life. However innocent the child may be, you do not have to wait passively while it crushes you to death. Perhaps a pregnant woman is vaguely felt to have the status of house, to which we don't allow the right of self-defense. But if the woman houses the child, it should be remembered that she is a person who houses it.

I should perhaps stop to say explicitly that I am not claiming that people have a right to do anything whatever to save their lives. I think, rather, that there are drastic limits to the right to self-defense. If someone threatens you with death unless you torture someone else to death, I think you have not the right, even to save your life, to do so. But the case under consideration here is very different. In our case there are only two people involved, one whose life is threatened, and one who threatens it. Both are innocent: the one who threatens does not threaten because of any fault. For this reason we may feel that we bystanders cannot intervene. But the person threatened can.

In sum, a woman surely can defend her life against the threat to it posed by the unborn child,

even if doing so involves its death. And this shows not merely that the theses in (1) through (4) are false; it shows also that the extreme view of abortion is false, and so we need not canvass any other possible ways of arriving at it from the argument I mentioned at the outset.

2. The extreme view could of course be weakened to say that while abortion is permissible to save the mother's life, it may not be performed by a third party, but only by the mother herself. But this cannot be right either. For what we have to keep in mind is that the mother and the unborn child are not like two tenants in a small house which has, by an unfortunate mistake, been rented to both: the mother *owns* the house. The fact that she does adds to the the offensiveness of deducing that the mother can do nothing from the supposition that third parties can do nothing. But it does more than this: it casts a bright light on the supposition that third parties can do nothing. Certainly it lets us see that a third party who says "I cannot choose between you" is fooling himself if he thinks this is impartiality. If Jones has found and fastened on a certain coat, which he needs to keep him from freezing, but which Smith also needs to keep him from freezing, then it is not impartiality that says "I cannot choose between you" when Smith owns the coat. Women have said again and again "This body is *my* body!" and they have reason to feel angry, reason to feel that it has been like shouting into the wind. Smith, after all, is hardly likely to bless us if we say to him, "Of course it's your coat, anybody would grant that it is. But no one may choose between you and Jones who is to have it."

We should really ask what it is that says "no one may choose" in the face of the fact that the body that houses the child is the mother's body. It may be simply a failure to appreciate this fact. But it may be something more interesting, namely the sense that one has a right to refuse to lay hands on people, even where it would be just and fair to do so, even where justice seems to require that somebody do so. Thus justice might call for somebody to get Smith's coat back from Jones, and yet you have a right to refuse to be the one to lay hands on Jones, a right to refuse to do physical violence to him. This, I think, must be granted. But then what should be said is not "no one may choose," but only "*I* cannot choose," and indeed not even this, but "*I* will not *act*," leaving it open that somebody else can or should, and in particular that anyone in a position of authority, with the job of securing people's rights, both can and should. So this is no difficulty. I have not been arguing that any given third party must accede to the mother's request that he perform an abortion to save her life, but only that he may.

I suppose that in some views of human life the mother's body is only on loan to her, the loan not being one which gives her any prior claim to it. One who held this view might well think it impartiality to say "I cannot choose." But I shall simply ignore this possibility. My own view is that if a human being has any just, prior claim to anything at all, he has a just, prior claim to his own body. And perhaps this needn't be argued for here anyway, since, as I mentioned, the arguments against abortion we are looking at do grant that the woman has a right to decide what happens in and to her body.

But although they do grant it, I have tried to show that they do not take seriously what is done in granting it. I suggest the same thing will reappear even more clearly when we turn away from cases in which the mother's life is at stake, and attend, as I propose we now do, to the vastly more common cases in which a woman wants an abortion for some less weighty reason than preserving her own life.

3. Where the mother's life is not at stake, the argument I mentioned at the outset seems to have a much stronger pull. "Everyone has a right to life, so the unborn person has a right to life." And isn't the child's right to life weightier than anything other than the mother's own right to life, which she might put forward as ground for an abortion?

This argument treats the right to life as if it were unproblematic. It is not, and this seems to me to be precisely the source of the mistake.

For we should now, at long last, ask what it comes to, to have a right to life. In some views having a right to life includes having a right to be given at least the bare minimum one needs for continued life. But suppose that what in fact *is* the bare minimum a man needs for continued life is something he has no right at all to be given? If I am sick unto death, and the only thing that will save my life is the touch of Henry Fonda's cool hand on my fevered brow, then all the same, I have no right to be given the touch of Henry Fonda's cool hand on my fevered brow. It would be frightfully nice of him to fly in from the West Coast to provide it. It would be less nice, though no doubt well meant, if my friends flew out to the West Coast and carried Henry Fonda back with them. But I have no right at all against anybody that he should do this for me. Or again, to return to the story I told earlier, the fact that for continued life that violinist needs the continued use of your kidneys does not establish that he has a right to be given the continued use of your kidneys. He certainly has no right against you that *you* should give him continued use of your kidneys. For nobody has any right to use your kidneys unless you give him such a right; and nobody has the right against you that you shall give him the right—if you do allow him to go on using your kidneys, this is a kindness on your part, and not something he can claim from you as his due. Nor has he any right against anybody else that *they* should give him continued use of your kidneys. Certainly he had no right against the Society of Music Lovers that they should plug him into you in the first place. And if you now start to unplug yourself, having learned that you will otherwise have to spend nine years in bed with him, there is nobody in the world who must try to prevent you, in order to see to it that he is given something he has a right to be given.

Some people are rather stricter about the right to life. In their view, it does not include the right to be given anything, but amounts to, and only to, the right not to be killed by anybody. But here a related difficulty arises. If everybody is to refrain from killing that violinist, then everybody must refrain from doing a great many different sorts of things. Everybody must refrain from slitting his throat, everybody must refrain from shooting him—and everybody must refrain from unplugging you from him. But does he have a right against everybody that they shall refrain from unplugging you from him? To refrain from doing this is to allow him to continue to use your kidneys. It could be argued that he has a right against us that *we* should allow him to continue to use your kidneys. That is, while he had no right against us that we should give him the use of your kidneys, it might be argued that he anyway has a right against us that we shall not now intervene and deprive him of the use of your kidneys. I shall come back to third-party interventions later. But certainly the violinist has no right against you that *you* shall allow him to continue to use your kidneys. As I said, if you do allow him to use them, it is a kindness on your part, and not something you owe him.

This difficulty I point out here is not peculiar to the right to life. It reappears in connection with all the other natural rights; and it is something which an adequate account of rights must deal with. For present purposes it is enough just to draw attention to it. But I would stress that I am not arguing that people do not have a right to life—quite to the contrary, it seems to me that the primary control we must place on the acceptability of an account of rights is that it should turn out in that account to be a truth that all persons have a right to life. I am arguing only that having a right to life does not guarantee having either a right to be given the use of or a right to be allowed continued use of another person's body—even if one needs it for life itself. So the right to life will not serve the opponents of abortion in the very simple and clear way in which they seem to have thought it would.

4. There is another way to bring out the difficulty. In the most ordinary sort of case, to deprive someone of what he has a right to is to treat him unjustly. Suppose a boy and his small brother are jointly given a box of chocolates for Christmas. If the older boy takes the box and refuses to give his brother any of the chocolates, he is unjust to

him, for the brother has been given a right to half of them. But suppose that, having learned that otherwise it means nine years in bed with that violinist, you unplug yourself from him. You surely are not being unjust to him, for you gave him no right to use your kidneys, and no one else can have given him any such right. But we have to notice that in unplugging yourself, you are killing him; and violinists, like everybody else, have a right to life, and thus in the view we were considering just now, the right not to be killed. So here you do what he supposedly has a right you shall not do, but you do not act unjustly to him in doing it.

The emendation which may be made at this point is this: the right to life consists not in the right not to be killed, but rather in the right not to be killed unjustly. This runs a risk of circularity, but never mind: it would enable us to square the fact that the violinist has a right to life with the fact that you do not act unjustly toward him in unplugging yourself, thereby killing him. For if you do not kill him unjustly, you do not violate his right to life, and so it is no wonder you do him no injustice.

But if this emendation is accepted, the gap in the argument against abortion stares us plainly in the face: it is by no means enough to show that the fetus is a person, and to remind us that all persons have a right to life—we need to be shown also that killing the fetus violates its right to life, i.e., that abortion is unjust killing. And is it?

I suppose we may take it as a datum that in a case of pregnancy due to rape the mother has not given the unborn person a right to the use of her body for food and shelter. Indeed, in what pregnancy could it be supposed that the mother has given the unborn person such a right? It is not as if there were unborn persons drifting about the world, to whom a woman who wants a child says "I invite you in."

But it might be argued that there are other ways one can have acquired a right to the use of another person's body than by having been invited to use it by that person. Suppose a woman voluntarily indulges in intercourse, knowing of the chance it will issue in pregnancy, and then she does become pregnant; is she not in part responsible for the presence, in fact the very existence, of the unborn person inside her? No doubt she did not invite it in. But doesn't her partial responsibility for its being there itself give it a right to the use of her body? If so, then her aborting it would be more like the boy's taking away the chocolates, and less like your unplugging yourself from the violinist—doing so would be depriving it of what it does have a right to, and thus would be doing in an injustice.

And then, too, it might be asked whether or not she can kill it even to save her own life: If she voluntarily called it into existence, how can she now kill it, even in self-defense?

The first thing to be said about this is that it is something new. Opponents of abortion have been so concerned to make out the independence of the fetus, in order to establish that it has a right to life, just as its mother does, that they have tended to overlook the possible support they might gain from making out that the fetus is *dependent* on the mother, in order to establish that she has a special kind of responsibility for it, a responsibility that gives it rights against her which are not possessed by any independent person—such as an ailing violinist who is a stranger to her.

On the other hand, this argument would give the unborn person a right to its mother's body only if her pregnancy resulted from a voluntary act, undertaken in full knowledge of the chance a pregnancy might result from it. It would leave out entirely the unborn person whose existence is due to rape. Pending the availability of some further argument, then, we would be left with the conclusion that unborn persons whose existence is due to rape have no right to the use of their mothers' bodies, and thus that aborting them is not depriving them of anything they have a right to and hence is not unjust killing.

And we should also notice that it is not at all plain that this argument really does go even as far as it purports to. For there are cases and cases, and the details make a difference. If the room is stuffy, and I therefore open a window to air it, and a burglar climbs in, it would be absurd to say, "Ah, now he can stay, she's given him a right to the use of her house—for she is partially responsible for his presence there, having voluntarily done what enabled him to get in, in full knowledge that there are such things as burglars, and that burglars burgle." It would be still more absurd to say this if I had had bars installed outside my windows, precisely to prevent burglars from getting in, and a burglar got in only because of a defect in the bars. It remains equally absurd if we imagine it is not a burglar who climbs in, but an innocent person who blunders or falls in. Again suppose it were like this: people-seeds drift about in the air like pollen, and if you open your windows, one may drift in and take root in your carpets or upholstery. You don't want children, so you fix up your windows with fine mesh screens, the very best you can buy. As can happen, however, and on very, very rare occasions does happen, one of the screens is defective; and a seed drifts in and takes root. Does the person-plant who now develops have a right to the use of your house? Surely not—despite the fact that you voluntarily opened your windows, you knowingly kept carpets and upholstered furniture, and you knew that screens were sometimes defective. Someone may argue that you are responsible for its rooting, that it does have a right to your house, because after all you *could* have lived out your life with bare floors and furniture, or with sealed windows and doors. But this won't do—for by the same token anyone can avoid a pregnancy due to rape by having a hysterectomy, or anyway by never leaving home without a (reliable!) army.

It seems to me that the argument we are looking at can establish at most that there are *some* cases in which the unborn person has a right to the use of its mother's body, and therefore *some* cases in which abortion is unjust killing. There is room for much discussion and argument as to precisely which, if any. But I think we should sidestep this issue and leave it open, for at any rate the argument certainly does not establish that all abortion is unjust killing.

5. There is room for yet another argument here, however. We surely must all grant that there

may be cases in which it would be morally indecent to detach a person from your body at the
cost of his life. Suppose you learn that what the
violinist needs is not nine years of your life, but
only one hour: all you need do to save his life is
to spend one hour in that bed with him. Suppose also that letting him use your kidneys for
that one hour would not affect your health in
the slightest. Admittedly you were kidnapped.
Admittedly you did not give anyone permission
to plug him into you. Nevertheless it seems to
me plain you *ought* to allow him to use your
kidneys for that hour—it would be indecent to
refuse.

Again, suppose pregnancy lasted only an
hour, and constituted no threat to life or health.
And suppose that a woman becomes pregnant as
a result of rape. Admittedly she did not voluntarily do anything to bring about the existence
of a child. Admittedly she did nothing at all
which would give the unborn person a right to
the use of her body. All the same it might well
be said, as in the newly emended violinist story,
that she *ought* to allow it to remain for that
hour—that it would be indecent in her to refuse.

Now some people are inclined to use the
term "right" in such a way that it follows from
the fact that you ought to allow a person to use
your body for the hour he needs, that he has a
right to use your body for the hour he needs
even though he has not been given that right by
any person or act. They may say that it follows
also that if you refuse, you act unjustly toward
him. This use of the term is perhaps so common
that it cannot be called wrong; nevertheless it
seems to me to be an unfortunate loosening of
what we would do better to keep a tight rein on.
Suppose that box of chocolates I mentioned earlier had not been given to both boys jointly, but
was given only to the older boy. There he sits,
stolidly eating his way through the box, his
small brother watching enviously. Here we are
likely to say "You ought not to be so mean.
You ought to give your brother some of those
chocolates." My own view is that it just does not
follow from the truth of this that the brother
has any right to any of the chocolates. If the boy

refuses to give his brother any, he is greedy,
stingy, callous—but not unjust. I suppose that
the people I have in mind will say it does follow
that the brother has a right to some of the
chocolates, and thus that the boy does act unjustly if he refuses to give his brother any. But
the effect of saying this is to obscure what we
should keep distinct, namely the difference between the boy's refusal in this case and the boy's
refusal in the earlier case, in which the box was
given to both boys jointly, and in which the
small brother thus had what was from any point
of view clear title to half.

A further objection to so using the term
"right" that from the fact that A ought to do a
thing for B, it follows that B has a right against
A that A do it for him, is that it is going to
make the question of whether or not a man has
a right to a thing turn on how easy it is to provide him with it; and this seems not merely
unfortunate, but morally unacceptable. Take the
case of Henry Fonda again. I said earlier that I
had no right to the touch of his cool hand on
my fevered brow, even though I needed it to
save my life. I said it would be frightfully nice of
him to fly in from the West Coast to provide me
with it, but that I had no right against him that
he should do so. But suppose he has only to
walk across the room, place a hand briefly on my
brow—and lo, my life is saved. Then surely he
ought to do it, it would be indecent to refuse. Is
it to be said "Ah, well, it follows that in this case
she has a right to the touch of his hand on her
brow, and so it would be an injustice in him to
refuse?" So that I have a right to it when it is
easy for him to provide it, though no right when
it's hard? It's rather a shocking idea that anyone's rights should fade away and disappear as it
gets harder and harder to accord them to him.

So my own view is that even though you
ought to let the violinist use your kidneys for
the one hour he needs, we should not conclude
that he has a right to do so—we should say
that if you refuse, you are, like the boy who
owns all the chocolates and will give none away,
self-centered and callous, indecent in fact, not
unjust. And similarly, that even supposing a case

in which a woman pregnant due to rape ought to allow the unborn person to use her body for the hour he needs, we should not conclude that he has a right to do so; we should conclude that she is self-centered, callous, indecent, but not unjust, if she refuses. The complaints are no less grave; they are just different. However, there is no need to insist on this point. If anyone does wish to deduce "he has a right" from "you ought," then all the same he must surely grant that there are cases in which it is not morally required of you that you allow that violinist to use your kidneys, and in which he does not have a right to use them, and in which you do not do him an injustice if you refuse. And so also for mother and unborn child. Except in such cases as the unborn person has a right to demand it—and we were leaving open the possibility that there may be such cases—nobody is morally *required* to make large sacrifices, of health, of all other interests and concerns, of all other duties and commitments, for nine years, or even for nine months, in order to keep another person alive.

6. We have in fact to distinguish between two kinds of Samaritan: the Good Samaritan and what we might call the Minimally Decent Samaritan. The story of the Good Samaritan, you will remember, goes like this:

A certain man went down from Jerusalem to Jericho, and fell among thieves, which stripped him of his raiment, and wounded him, and departed, leaving him half dead.

And by chance there came down a certain priest that way; and when he saw him, he pasĪsed by on the other side.

And likewise a Levite, when he was at the place, came and looked on him, and passed on the other side.

But a certain Samaritan, as he journeyed, came where he was; and when he saw him he had compassion on him.

And went to him, and bound up his wounds, pouring in oil and wine, and set him on his own beast, and brought him to an inn, and took care of him.

And on the morrow, when he departed, he took out two pence, and gave them to the host, and said unto him. "Take care of him; and whatsoever thou spendest more, when I come again, I will repay thee."

(Luke 10:30–35)

The Good Samaritan went out of his way, at some cost to himself, to help one in need of it. We are not told what the options were, that is, whether or not the priest and the Levite could have helped by doing less than the Good Samaritan did, but assuming they could have, then the fact they did nothing at all shows they were not even Minimally Decent Samaritans, not because they were not Samaritans, but because they were not even minimally decent. These things are a matter of degree, of course, but there is a difference, and it comes out perhaps most clearly in the story of Kitty Genovese, who, as you will remember, was murdered while thirty-eight people watched or listened, and did nothing at all to help her. A Good Samaritan would have rushed out to give direct assistance against the murderer. Or perhaps we had better allow that it would have been a Splendid Samaritan who did this, on the ground that it would have involved a risk of death for himself. But the thirty-eight not only did not do this, they did not even trouble to pick up a phone to call the police. Minimally Decent Samaritanism would call for doing at least that, and their not having done it was monstrous.

After telling the story of the Good Samaritan, Jesus said "Go, and do thou likewise." Perhaps he meant that we are morally required to act as the Good Samaritan did. Perhaps he was urging people to do more than is morally required of them. At all events it seems plain that it was not morally required of any of the thirty-eight that he rush out to give direct assistance at the risk of his own life, and that it is not morally required of anyone that he give long stretches of life—nine years or nine months—to sustaining the life of a person who has no special right (we were leaving open the possibility of this) to demand it.

Indeed, with one rather striking class of exceptions, no one in any country in the world is *legally* required to do anywhere near as much as this for anyone else. The class of exceptions is obvious. My main concern here is not the state of the law in respect to abortion, but it is worth drawing attention to the fact that in no state in this country is any man compelled by law to be even a Minimally Decent Samaritan to any person; there is no law under which charges could be brought against the thirty-eight who stood by while Kitty Genovese died. By contrast, in most states in this country women are compelled by law to be not merely Minimally Decent Samaritans to unborn persons inside them. This doesn't by itself settle anything one way or the other, because it may well be argued that there should be laws in this country—as there are in many European countries—compelling at least Minimally Decent Samaritanism. But it does show that there is a gross injustice in the existing state of the law. And it shows also that the groups currently working against liberalization of abortion laws, in fact working toward having it declared unconstitutional for a state to permit abortion, had better start working for the adoption of Good Samaritan laws generally, or earn the charge that they are acting in bad faith.

I should think, myself, that Minimally Decent Samaritan laws would be one thing, Good Samaritan laws quite another, and in fact highly improper. But we are not here concerned with the law. What we should ask is not whether anybody should be compelled by laws to be a Good Samaritan, but whether we must accede to a situation in which somebody is being compelled—by nature, perhaps—to be a Good Samaritan. We have, in other words, to look now at third-party interventions. I have been arguing that no person is morally required to make large sacrifices to sustain the life of another who has no right to demand them, and this even where the sacrifices do not include life itself; we are not morally required to be Good Samaritans or anyway Very Good Samaritans to one another. But what if a man cannot extricate himself from such a situation? What if he

appeals to us to extricate him? It seems to me plain that there are cases in which we can, cases in which a Good Samaritan would extricate him. There you are, you were kidnapped, and nine years in bed with that violinist lie ahead of you. You have your own life to lead. You are sorry, but you simply cannot see giving up so much of your life to the sustaining of his. You cannot extricate yourself, and ask us to do so. I should have thought that—in light of his having no right to the use of your body—it was obvious that we do not have to accede to your being forced to give up so much. We can do what you ask. There is no injustice to the violinist in our doing so.

7. Following the lead of the opponents of abortion, I have throughout been speaking of the fetus merely as a person, and what I have been asking is whether or not the argument we began with, which proceeds only from the fetus' being a person, really does establish its conclusion. I have argued that it does not.

But of course there are arguments and arguments, and it may be said that I have simply fastened on the wrong one. It may be said that what is important is not merely the fact that the fetus is a person, but that it is a person for whom the woman has a special kind of responsibility issuing from the fact that she is its mother. And it might be argued that all my analogies are therefore irrelevant—for you do not have that special kind of responsibility for that violinist, Henry Fonda does not have that special kind of responsibility for me. And our attention might be drawn to the fact that men and women both *are* compelled by law to provide support for their children.

I have in effect dealt (briefly) with this argument in section 4 above; but a (still briefer) recapitulation now may be in order. Surely we do not have any such "special responsibility" for a person unless we have assumed it, explicitly or implicitly. If a set of parents do not try to prevent pregnancy, do not obtain an abortion, and then at the time of birth of the child do not put it out for adoption, but rather take it home with them, then they have assumed responsibility for it, they have given it rights, and they cannot *now* withdraw support from it at the cost of its life because they now find it difficult to go on providing for it. But if they have taken all reasonable precautions against having a child, they do not simply by virtue of their biological relationship to the child who comes into existence have a special responsibility for it. They may wish to assume responsibility for it, or they may not wish to. And I am suggesting that if assuming responsibility for it would require large sacrifices, then they may refuse. A Good Samaritan would not refuse—or anyway, a Splendid Samaritan, if the sacrifices that had to be made were enormous. But then so would a Good Samaritan assume responsibility for that violinist; so would Henry Fonda, if he is a Good Samaritan, fly in from the West Coast and assume responsibility for me.

8. My argument will be found unsatisfactory on two counts by many of those who want to regard abortion as morally permissible. First, while I do argue that abortion is not impermissible, I do not argue that it is always permissible. There may well be cases in which carrying the child to term requires only Minimally Decent Samaritanism of the mother, and this is a standard we must not fall below. I am inclined to think it a merit of my account precisely that it does *not* give a general yes or a general no. It allows for and supports our sense that, for example, a sick and desperately frightened fourteen-year-old schoolgirl, pregnant due to rape, may *of course* choose abortion, and that any law which rules this out is an insane law. And it also allows for and supports our sense that in other cases resort to abortion is even positively indecent. It would be indecent in the woman to request an abortion, and indecent in a doctor to perform it, if she is in her seventh month, and wants the abortion just to avoid the nuisance of postponing a trip abroad. The very fact that the arguments I have been drawing attention to

treat all cases of abortion, or even all cases of abortion in which the mother's life is not at stake, as morally on a par ought to have made them suspect at the outset.

Secondly, while I am arguing for the permissibility of abortion in some cases, I am not arguing for the right to secure the death of the unborn child. It is easy to confuse these two things in that up to a certain point in the life of the fetus it is not able to survive outside the mother's body hence removing it from her body guarantees its death. But they are importantly different. I have argued that you are not morally required to spend nine months in bed, sustaining the life of that violinist; but to say this is by no means to say that if, when you unplug yourself, there is a miracle and he survives, you then have a right to turn round and slit his throat. You may detach yourself even if this costs him his life; you have no right to be guaranteed his death, by some other means, if unplugging yourself does not kill him. There are some people who will feel dissatisfied by this feature of my argument. A woman may be utterly devastated by the thought of a child, a bit of herself, put out for adoption and never seen or heard of again. She may therefore want not merely that the child be detached from her, but more, that it die. Some opponents of abortion are inclined to regard this as beneath contempt—thereby showing insensitivity to what is surely a powerful source of despair. All the same, I agree that the desire for the child's death is not one which anybody may gratify, should it turn out to be possible to detach the child alive.

At this place, however, it should be remembered that we have only been pretending throughout that the fetus is a human being from the moment of conception. A very early abortion is surely not the killing of a person, and so is not dealt with by anything I have said here.

ALICE WALKER

Right to Life

What Can the White Man Say to the Black Woman?

ALICE WALKER *is a poet, essayist, and novelist, perhaps most famous for her novel*
The Color Purple *(1982). Her most recent books are* Anything We Love Can Be Saved:
A Writer's Activism *(1997) and* By the Light of My Father's Smile *(1998).*

———

What is of use in these words I offer in memory and recognition of our common mother. And to my daughter.

W HAT can the white man say to the
black woman?
    For four hundred years he ruled
over the black woman's womb.

Let us be clear. In the barracoons and along
the slave shipping coasts of Africa, for more
than twenty generations, it was he who dashed
our babies' brains out against the rocks.

*What can the white man say to the black
woman?*

For four hundred years he determined which
black woman's children would live or die.

Let it be remembered. It was he who placed
our children on the auction block in cities all
across the eastern half of what is now the United
States, and listened to and watched them beg for
their mothers' arms, before being sold to the
highest bidder and dragged away.

What can the white man say to the black woman?

We remember that Fannie Lou Hamer, a poor
sharecropper on a Mississippi plantation, was one
of twenty-one children; and that on plantations
across the South black women often had twelve,
fifteen, twenty children. Like their enslaved
mothers and grandmothers before them, these
black women were sacrificed to the profit the
white man could make from harnessing their bodies and their children's bodies to the cotton gin.

*What can the white man say to the black
woman?*

We see him lined up on Saturday nights, century after century, to make the black mother,
who must sell her body to feed her children, go
down on her knees to him.

Let us take note:

He has not cared for a single one of the dark
children in his midst, over hundreds of years.

Where are the children of the Cherokee, my
great grandmother's people?

Gone.

Where are the children of the Blackfoot?

Gone.

Where are the children of the Lakota?

Gone.

Of the Cheyenne?

Of the Chippewa?

Of the Iroquois?

Of the Sioux?

Of the Mandinka?

Of the Ibo?

Of the Ashanti?

Where are the children of the "Slave Coast"
and Wounded Knee?

We do not forget the forced sterilization
and forced starvations on the reservations,
here as in South Africa. Nor do we forget the

smallpox-infested blankets Indian children were given by the Great White Fathers of the United States government.

What has the white man to say to the black woman?

When we have children you do everything in your power to make them feel unwanted from the moment they are born. You send them to fight and kill other dark mothers' children around the world. You shove them onto public highways into the path of oncoming cars. You shove their heads through plate glass windows. You string them up and you string them out.

What has the white man to say to the black woman?

From the beginning, you have treated all dark children with absolute hatred.

Thirty million African children died on the way to the Americas, where nothing awaited them but endless toil and the crack of a bull-whip. They died of a lack of food, of lack of movement in the holds of ships. Of lack of friends and relatives. They died of depression, bewilderment and fear.

What has the white man to say to the black woman?

Let us look around us: Let us look at the world the white man has made for the black woman and her children.

It is a world in which the black woman is still forced to provide cheap labor, in the form of children, for the factories and on the assembly lines of the white man.

It is a world into which the white man dumps every foul, person-annulling drug he smuggles into creation.

It is a world where many of our babies die at birth, or later of malnutrition, and where many more grow up to live lives of such misery they are forced to choose death by their own hands.

What has the white man to say to the black woman, and to all women and children everywhere?

Let us consider the depletion of the ozone; let us consider homelessness and the nuclear peril; let us consider the destruction of the rain forests—in the name of the almighty hamburger. Let us consider the poisoned apples and the poisoned water and the poisoned air and the poisoned earth.

And that all of our children, because of the white man's assault on the planet, have a possibility of death by cancer in their almost immediate future.

What has the white, male lawgiver to say to any of us? To those of us who love life too much to willingly bring more children into a world saturated with death?

Abortion, for many women, is more than an experience of suffering beyond anything most men will ever know; it is an act of mercy, and an act of self-defense.

To make abortion illegal again is to sentence millions of women and children to miserable lives and even more miserable deaths.

Given his history, in relation to us, I think the white man should be ashamed to attempt to speak for the unborn children of the black woman. To force us to have children for him to ridicule, drug and turn into killers and homeless wanderers is a testament to his hypocrisy.

What can the white man say to the black woman?

Only one thing that the black woman might hear.

Yes, indeed, the white man can say, Your children have a right to life. Therefore I will call back from the dead those 30 million who were tossed overboard during the centuries of the slave trade. And the other millions who died in my cotton fields and hanging from my trees.

I will recall all those who died of broken hearts and broken spirits, under the insult of segregation.

I will raise up all the mothers who died exhausted after birthing twenty-one children to work sunup to sundown on my plantation. I will restore to full health all those who perished for lack of food, shelter, sunlight, and love; and from my inability to see them as human beings.

But I will go even further.

I will tell you, black woman, that I wish to be forgiven the sins I commit daily against you and your children. For I know that until I treat your children with love, I can never be trusted by my own. Nor can I respect myself.

And I will free your children from insultingly high infant mortality rates, short life spans, horrible housing, lack of food, rampant ill health. I will liberate them from the ghetto. I will open wide the doors of all the schools and hospitals and businesses of society to your children. I will look at your children and see not a threat but a joy.

I will remove myself as an obstacle in the path that your children, against all odds, are making toward the light. I will not assassinate them for dreaming dreams and offering new visions of how to live. I will cease trying to lead your children, for I can see I have never understood where I was going. I will agree to sit quietly for a century or so, and meditate on this.

This is what the white man can say to the black woman.

We are listening.

SIDNEY CALLAHAN

The Moral Duty to the Unborn and Its Significance

SIDNEY CALLAHAN *is Distinguished Professor of Theology and Religious Studies at St. John's University. She is the author of many books and articles, among them* Abortion: Understanding Differences *(1984) (with Daniel Callahan) and* Parents Forever: You and Your Adult Children *(1996).*

Although we invent medical and legal definitions to devalue and dehumanize prenatal life, although we declare it non-living, non-viable, non-human, or a non-person, from the moment of our conception we are never anything less than human life with a human face that will manifest itself in due time.

How can we teach our children to value and respect human life while through the example of hundreds of thousands of abortions each year we show them that human life has value only if wanted, planned and not inconvenient?

—NATHANIEL DAVIS

There is much more to abortion than abortion. It has numbed, as if with Novocaine, a respect for life in American society. . . . [O]nce killing of any kind is legal, it becomes easier, with time, for the harvest of death to increase. And once anything is legal, most people believe that it is moral. . . . My reason for opposing abortion—in addition to a desire to stop the mass killing—is that it is anesthetizing the society.

—NAT HENTOFF

Callahan, Sidney, "The Moral Duty to the Unborn and Its Significance," from *The Silent Subject* edited by Brad Stern (Praeger Press, Westport, 1996), pp. 43–49. Reproduced with permission of Greenwood Publishing Group, Inc., Westport, CT.

THE unborn are not without influence. Our society is shaped by the story we tell ourselves about life before birth. Conflicts and questions mar present accounts. What kind of entity is a developing human organism? Do we have any moral obligations to it?

Beliefs about embryonic and fetal life will necessarily apply to one's personal prenatal history as well as form general attitudes toward having children. Every image, schema, concept, or idea we hold about the unborn subtly but powerfully affects our perspectives on the nature and worth of a human being.

As we envision the relationships of the unborn with mother, father, grandparents, extended families and larger communities, we create prototypical patterns of human connections—or lack of them.

Today science and technology have allowed us to see that famous series of photographs, or the even more amazing movie, detailing the incredible journey from conception to birth. A new human life can be observed as it progresses from a zygote to a fully developed nine-month-old fetus barely indistinguishable from a newborn. Once seen, these images can arouse the same kind of awe and expanded perspectives as did the first pictures of earth taken from the moon's surface.

Of course, reactions of wonder can always be muted. The dynamic development from conception to birth can be dismissed as "merely" another biological process which has little importance compared to the intelligent decision making and self-conscious rationality characteristic of normal adults. For some observers of the human condition, only the possession of fully rational capacities counts as an adequate criterion for human status; only self-governing persons should be accorded moral equality or human rights.

By contrast, all forms of human life that are "immature," "unformed" or "prerational" will be seen as being embedded in a natural world that is subject to human dominion and constructive interpretation. For many, the meaning and value of natural processes depend solely upon the meaning and value given them by the deliberations of rational human beings. *Ergo*, if the legal community and polity decide that an embryo is to be valued as a human being only if it receives its mother's emotional investment and affirmation of its existence, then so be it.

Such a view of the contingent value of fetal development assails the foundational moral belief that certain values and realities exist whether or not humans recognize them. Reality can be defined as that which exists despite what humans might or might not wish to be so. Dynamic growth, development and irreversible one-way trajectories through time characterize all of reality and human life as we know it.

Each human embryo possesses its own eon worth of evolutionary genetic heritage, with its own incredibly complex program for dynamic development. This potentiality of the individual springs from its membership in the human species, which itself emerged from the evolutionary developmental processes of selection taking millions of years. The dynamics of embryonic development are still not fully understood. But consider, in one telling example, the fact that at one point in human development brain cells in the fetus are created and migrate to their positions at the rate of 250,000 cells a minute.

Even after birth each human being is still shaped by processes of its unique genetic program. Innate fixed patterns of ordered development interact with novel environmental influences. An adult body maintains its pattern through time because the information in the genetic program regulates the continual replacements of matter and energy from the environment. When the genetic program runs its course, then adult bodies die and disintegrate. The fetal body and an adult body share genetic continuity in maintenance operations.

If we could rerun a moving picture taken of every person now alive, we could go back day by day, minute by minute, to that moment when a particular sperm meets and joins with a specific egg. This is true despite the fact that no one can remember either encounter or all those stages of infancy and childhood that are experienced before the development of self-consciousness and continuous memory. The rational decision-making self emerges too late and functions too sporadically to be the marker and criterion of human value. Besides, as we now understand the brain's operations, we can see that many of the adult human being's most vital operations operate without conscious awareness.

In the end, it is impossible to deny that fetal life needs only time and nurture to develop its future potential. If we protect helpless immature newborns then why not the fetus? Indeed, the journey from conceptus to newborn does not seem nearly as immense as the change that takes place between a 6 pound newborn and a 6 foot, 180 pound adult male in the peak of his powers.

When the embryo's developmental processes through time and its future potential are denied as an independent objective reality with intrinsic value, then other kinds of human potential lose their moral claim. If only the present achieved status of a human life is taken into moral account, then society is going to suffer. Permitting the destruction of fetal life because of its immature dependent status and lack of development sets a chilling precedent.

Once future potential no longer counts then those who have power, strength, health and achieved status need no longer be committed to the future potential of newborns, children, women, the ill or oppressed minorities. After all, schooling, healing professions, reform movements like feminism and altruistic parental care-taking are based on the moral injunction to fulfill human potential and keep faith with the future.

But, some say, doesn't the minuscule size of the human embryo make a difference in our evaluation of it? Embryos would be invisible without sophisticated ultrasound technologies and other like marvels which allow us to be aware of their functioning. But why should size be seen as a relevant guide to importance once we have learned that the whole universe right after the Big Bang was smaller than a zygote? Power and vast potentialities are released in microevents as we know from the effects of splitting the atom

and epidemics caused by infectious viruses. As we become more scientifically educated, we realize that what is visible to the naked eye is not the measure of objective reality. It takes almost eight weeks before a fetus looks like a baby in miniature, but the programmed information which informs the dynamic developmental process is present after the initial microevent. Something real happens, a human life begins.

Perceived size, in any case, depends upon the framework that exists. If one thinks of the expanded universe with its vast reaches of space and billions of stars, then even a fully grown adult person on our small planet resembles but a speck of dust. In the same way, a long life of ninety plus years would seem but a nanosecond compared to the life and death of stars.

Numbers and scale need not numb our powers of appreciation. The number of human embryos of Homo sapiens who have ever been conceived or been born would seem minute compared to the millions upon millions of existing stars. When people worry over the proportion of (probably) normal embryos which are lost before birth, the so-called wastage problem, they are not fully cognizant of the vast numbers of entities that emerge and then die in the known universe.

If we decided that the survival rate of embryos must mean that they could not have value, what do we make of the thousands of infants and children who die before reaching maturity? Earth has always been a place of death and extinction arising from plagues, floods, fires and other natural and manmade disasters. Human beings have always died before their time, but this does not mean that they have no value and can just as well be destroyed. Indeed, in the midst of so much death every instance of human life can be seen as being even more meaningful and valuable.

Once we withdraw value from the human embryo because of its size or immaturity or the fact that so many human embryos die before birth, we are logically drawn on to diminishing the value of all humankind. Within the framework of the universe, every finite human life exists as but a microevent for a moment. Are we to despair and conclude that human life is meaningless? Is it really the case that "We are to the gods as flies to wanton boys, they kill us for their sport." Never.

Happily, a new ecological consciousness of the value and interdependence of all forms of life is emerging. Human beings not only depend on the environment for sustenance but also, through their common genetic heritage, are biologically connected with other species. Instead of praising humanity's dominion and sovereignty over the world, we now are given new models to emulate, such as befriending the world and cooperating with its ecosystem. Many ecofeminists have held up the image of mothering the earth and nurturing the environment. At the very least, careless persons and policies must desist from selfishly exploiting natural resources and arrogantly destroying other forms of life.

As the newly dawning ecological consciousness of caretaking begins to affirm that all life is interdependent in a larger ecosystem, will we not have to reconsider human responses to fetal life? If we are to mother the earth and nurture life, we will have to give up modes of unilateral control. Our civilization must heed Erik Erikson's urging to carefully reflect on the relationship between the will to master totally, in any form, and the will to destroy.

In the interests of survival, cooperation, and human flourishing, a new ecological consciousness encourages us to have a sense of solidarity with all the members of the human family, as well as with other species sharing the environment. This new view of caretaking makes us concerned about our responsibilities to the future potential of those now alive as well as for those future generations of our kind who will inherit the earth. We're forced into asking new questions about what is private and what is public; where does individual liberty end and justice for all begin?

At this point we find disturbing inconsistencies in American polity. Certain species, such as eagles and their nesteggs, are protected from destruction while fetal life can be aborted and killed on demand. In some towns, such as my own, a tree cannot be cut down without permission from a local commission, while a nearby abortion clinic freely extinguishes fetal life by the thousands year after year. The killing of a developing fetal life is supposedly justified in order to grant a woman her autonomy, privacy and right to totally control her reproductive capacity.

Here two kinds of power can be discerned. One kind of power follows the logic of domination and insists on unilateral control by repression, coercion and destruction to achieve a willed outcome. Another type of power is actualizing power or the power to create, engender and bring existing potential to fruition and fulfillment.

Both of these forms of power spring from the evolved capacities of the human species for using foresight, planning, and taking the role of another. Human beings are able either to nurture or destroy in unique ways because of their intense rational and emotional capacities. The human capacity for empathic understanding of the needs of others can be used either to lovingly care for them or to manipulate and even torture others for one's own ends.

In exercises of actualizing power, persons who identify with their own prenatal past can empathize with fetal life; in solidarity they will act to protect immature but potential development and well-being. Following the logic of domination, however, adult persons will feel free to kill or selectively destroy a fetus which is not wanted, planned for, or does not measure up to some acceptable criteria, including gender.

Women have been enjoined to think of abortion as a sacrament or a rite of passage. In this message exalting the autonomous will, a woman must be courageous enough to destroy a fetus which threatens her own individual development of self. To grow strong, the individual must choose self before others and break free from any bonds which may entrap. Fetal life may be recognized as a necessary human sacrifice or be discounted by being labeled a "parasite" or "tissue."

Such a permissive view of abortion affirms that an individual may define reality (I decide whether a truly human life has begun) as well as determine morality (only my emotional investment and choice create any moral claim upon me). If a society takes this route of absolutizing individual autonomy and choice, even to the point of self-definitions of reality and moral obligations, then other moral claims must fall.

Can it be that only freely willed and consciously contracted relationships can create moral obligations? If so, then all moral responsibilities in relationships which we have not entered into with informed consent will be endangered. Our parents, siblings, neighbors and compatriots would have no claim upon us.

Such a constricted view of moral responsibility appears both unconvincing and unworthy of human life. Indeed, no one has ever given informed consent to be born into earth's ecosystem, yet we can have obligations to care for the earth and the environment out of gratitude for sustaining our life. Surely we have other bonds and moral obligations that we have not chosen. Life is full of unexpected encounters and unplanned events that demand a moral response. Think of the obligations we would have to rescue someone with whom we had been in an automobile accident. So, too, obligations to care for an unborn life may exist even if we did not plan the conception. Of course, the obligation to a woman's unborn fetus would be strengthened by the sharing of kinship ties and the complete, if temporary, dependence upon the mother for the preservation of life.

If we as a human community abandon the completely helpless powerless unborn life, then actualizing nurturing power once more gives way to the logic of domination. Already under the rule of the marketplace and the jungle's law of survival of the fittest, there are calls for selective infanticide as a parent's right. Infanticide, we should remember, was approved of as a respectable practice in ancient Roman society, for any reason whatsoever, even to increase the family fortune. Modern abortion can be seen as a resurgence of one of the oldest of human customs, selectively killing unwanted offspring.

Once human life has been deemed expendable and it is exploited at will, it becomes difficult to stop the process. Suicide rates have climbed at the same alarming rates in the decades since abortion has become a routine way of solving the stressful problems of unwanted pregnancy. Everywhere in our society we see violence and abuse of the powerless by the more powerful and dominant.

It seems puzzling that so many advocates of abortion as a tragic necessity still believe that a destructive and violent solution permitted in one stage of the human life cycle will not generalize to other stressful situations in life. If a child only exists on its parent's sufferance and by choice, its claim to inalienable rights and dignity are more fragile. The commandment against killing has always supported the moral rule against using another person as a means to an end. Breaking both of these cultural taboos by allowing the killing of the unborn pollutes our moral ecosystem. Women, children, the aged, the ill and the impaired will suffer the consequences.

The unborn human being has value because it is a member of the human family and shares in the heritage of the human species. The human status and human potential of the dependent embryo deserve respect and protection.

Current struggles over the treatment of the unborn exemplify a larger cultural conflict between the logic of domination and the exercise of nurturing actualizing power. This moral strife will hardly remain confined to the abortion controversy, but will spread to other domains and other human relationships.

Is human life a gift which we accept gratefully? Do we have moral obligations to mother the earth, nurture the immature and protect dependent lives? A vision of human bonding and the value of all the living urges us to answer yes. A yes to the unborn is both an assertion of justice and an affirmation of hope for humankind.

DENA S. DAVIS

Stem Cells, Cloning, and Abortion

Making Careful Distinctions

DENA S. DAVIS *teaches at the Cleveland-Marshall College of Law and is legal consultant to the Committee on Bioethics of the American Academy of Pediatrics. Her most recent book is* Genetics Dilemmas: Reproductive Technology, Parental Choices, and Children's Futures *(2001).*

THE current controversy over federal funding for research involving stem cells derived from very early embryos is situated between two other equally difficult issues: abortion and cloning. As Laurie Zoloth says, talk about stem cells is "directly proximate" to the abortion debate. Nonetheless, a settled position in favor of abortion rights does not necessarily lead to support for research that involves the death of embryos. Nor should opposition to reproductive cloning necessarily entail opposition to therapeutic cloning. There are important ways in which our attitudes toward research with embryonic stem cells ought to be entwined with our thinking about abortion and cloning, but there are also some very important distinctions which are getting lost in the noisy debate.

With regard to abortion, it is important to remember that the embryos from which stem cells are derived have never been and will never be within a woman's body. I have noticed recently that a lot of acquaintances, when we are talking about stem cells, say, "Well, of course I'm pro-choice," as if that settles the question of how they feel about stem cell research. But think about the most common reasons people give for being pro-choice: women have the right to decide what to do with their bodies; women can compete effectively in the workplace only if they can reliably control their fertility; only the individual woman can decide if she wants to be a parent; making abortion illegal risks women's lives; unwanted children are less likely to fare well. All of these arguments are compatible with the belief that an embryo has some moral status, even quite weighty moral status, just not weighty enough to overbalance the woman's right to make that choice. Judith Jarvis Thomson, in a famous and influential article, has shown that even imagining the embryo as having the same moral status as an adult human being, does not entail that a woman is required to function as that person's life support system for nine months. Thus, legally at least, Ronald Green is not correct when he says that if an embryo were regarded as a woman's moral equivalent from the point of fertilization, a woman's interests could be overridden if they clashed with the moral claims of the embryo or fetus. Laurence Tribe reminds us that

> There is . . . only one place in the law where a really significant and intimate sacrifice has been required of anyone in order to save another: the law of abortion. If you woke up with [Thomson's] hypothetical violinist attached to you, the law—and, probably, the views of morality held by most people—would permit you to free yourself of him. When the law

"Stem Cells, Cloning, and Abortion" by Dena Davis, from *American Journal Of Bioethics*, 2:1 (Winter, 2002), pp. 47–49. Reproduced by permission of Taylor & Francis Group, LLC., http://www.taylorandfrancis.com.

prohibits a woman from freeing herself of the fetus that is inside her, the law appears to work a harsh discrimination against women *even if fetuses count as persons.*

Thus, even a woman who would never have an abortion herself can be pro-choice, supporting each woman's right to make that decision for herself.

Tribe joins legal scholar Guido Calabresi in making the intriguing suggestion that the Supreme Court, when deciding *Roe v. Wade*, unnecessarily insulted people for whom fetal personhood is a bedrock of their faith. The Court could have said, "Even if the fetus *is* a person, the Constitution forbids compelling a woman to carry it for nine months and become a mother."

But when the embryo is *outside* the woman's body, frozen in a pipette somewhere, none of these arguments apply. A person could be firmly pro-choice, out of concern for women's liberty and well-being, and still oppose the destruction of extracorporeal embryos. At the same time, as we have seen in Congress, even some staunch pro-lifers have come out in favor of stem cell research, finding that the prospective benefits for people now struggling with diseases such as diabetes and multiple sclerosis, to name just a few, outweigh the moral claims of very early, unimplanted embryos that would, in most scenarios, be discarded. Thus, thinking clearly and well about stem cell research requires us to give up slogans and knee-jerk reactions.

On the other end of the spectrum, stem cell research calls up the specter of cloning, with all the visceral reactions that word engenders. It is true that Advanced Cell Technology, a Massachusetts biotech company, is trying to use "therapeutic cloning" to derive stem cells. The process, if perfected, would go something like this: Jane needs a new liver, but cadaveric livers are scarce and never perfectly matched. So, a scientist takes cells from Jane's cheek and inserts the DNA into a donor egg that has had the DNA sucked out of it. The egg is coaxed to divide and grow, and, when it is perhaps 32-cells old, it is destroyed. Stem cells are taken from it

and are used to grow a new kidney that will, of course, have Jane's genetic blueprint and which Jane's body will not reject. The basic technique, somatic cell nuclear transfer, is the same as the process used to create Dolly.

What are the reasons people commonly give for being opposed to cloning of humans? Some objections are based on ignorance, such as the notion that cloning will enable us to "copy" 100 Hitlers or Mother Teresas, full-blown adults with the personalities and characters of their models. (This is the false image of cloning depicted in popular films such as *The Sixth Day*.) However, as Leon Kass reminds us, "cloning is not Xeroxing." Here are some other, more thoughtful reasons: concern for children brought up in the "shadow" of the parent, dead sibling, or beloved relative from whom they were cloned; suspicion that parents who choose cloning will do so from narcissistic motives; fear that cloning children "to order" will result in thinking of children more as commodities and less as precious gifts. Kass again: "Through cloning, we can work our wants and wills on the very identity of our children, exercising control as never before." Finally, the huge number of miscarriages and malformed births necessary to produce one Dolly should tell us that we are a very long way from safely using cloning to reproduce human beings.

But when the issue at stake is *therapeutic* (rather than reproductive) cloning, none of these reasons applies. The embryos created through this process will be destroyed within the first few days of their creation in order to retrieve their stem cells to begin the process of producing a new organ. People who believe that the embryo from the moment of conception is fully protectable human life will probably find it consistent to oppose therapeutic cloning. Although these embryos are not conceived in the usual way, they do carry the full component of potential "humanhood." But for everyone else, it is difficult to see the objections to therapeutic cloning. Certainly the fears and concerns raised by reproductive cloning cannot reasonably be used to oppose therapeutic cloning. Ralph Potter, a scholar of ethics, once proposed a system of thinking about ethics in which various "boxes" enclosed important questions. One of the questions was: *What do you fear?* The fears (legitimate and otherwise) that prompt people to oppose abortion and reproductive cloning are not necessarily relevant to stem cell research.

THE PRESIDENT'S COUNCIL ON BIOETHICS (PCBE)
The Moral Status of the Embryo

THE PRESIDENT'S COUNCIL ON BIOETHICS *was created by President George W. Bush in November 2001. The Executive Order stated that the goal of the council is "to undertake fundamental inquiry into the human and moral significance" of developments in biotechnology. The PCBE is further charged to "provide a forum for a national discussion of bioethical issues" and to "facilitate a greater understanding" of them. The PCBE replaces the National Bioethics Advisory Commission created by President Clinton in 1996.*

APPENDIX A: Typology of the Moral Status of the Embryo (The following staff-prepared typology of views about the moral status of the human embryo is for members' discussion purposes only and does not purport to be definitive or exhaustive.)

a. Embryos are cells, no different from other cells in the body. All types of embryos should be available for use in biomedical research.

b. Embryos are not nothing, but they are certainly not the moral equivalent of the later stage fetus or of post-birth human beings: Therefore, possible medical benefits for the living do justify the use of all types of embryos for research—both those created via IVF and those created via cloning.

c. Embryos are not nothing, but they are not the moral equivalent of the later stage fetus or of post-birth human beings: Given this, possible medical benefits for the living do justify the use of embryos for reproductive purposes through IVF but left unused, but do not justify the creation of cloned or IVF embryos solely for research and destruction or the added danger of opening the door to human reproductive cloning.

d. Embryos are not nothing, but they are not the moral equivalent of the later stage fetus or of post-birth human beings: Nevertheless, possible medical benefits for the living do not justify the use of any embryos for research and destruction or the added danger of opening the door to human reproductive cloning. Embryos created through IVF that are left over in clinics should be left to "die naturally" or be adopted.

e. Embryos are the moral equivalent of both the later stage fetus and all living human beings. They are what human beings should look like—what human beings are—at that stage of development. They should not be used for research in any way, and couples that use IVF should not create embryos that they do not intend to implant with the goal of pregnancy.

1. The states that have enacted legislation banning human cloning are California, Louisiana, Michigan, Missouri, Rhode Island, and Virginia.

DANIEL CALLAHAN

The Puzzle of Profound Respect

Human Embryo Research

DANIEL CALLAHAN *was a cofounder in 1969 of the Hastings Center, a research institute for problems in biomedical and environmental ethics, and a Senior Fellow at the Harvard Medical School. He has written thirty-six books, most recently* The Research Imperative: What Price Better Health? *(2003).*

IN 1979 the Ethics Advisory Board of the (then) Department of Health, Education and Welfare declared that the human embryo is "entitled to profound respect; but this respect does not necessarily encompass the full legal and moral rights attributed to persons." That position has always seemed to me sensible, opening the way for early abortions and reflecting the judgment of many religions and cultures that early human life is not the same as more developed life.

Yet though I have argued such a position myself for many years (beginning with *Abortion: Law, Choice, and Morality* in 1970), I have always felt a nagging uneasiness at trying to rationalize the killing of something for which I claim to have a "profound respect." What in the world can that kind of respect mean? An odd form of esteem—at once high-minded and altogether

lethal. Of course the answer to that puzzle is simple enough: the diminished status of the embryo provides a justification for abortion, which seems desirable in some circumstances, while the wafting incense of "profound respect" at least makes me feel a little better about it all.

I have wondered for twenty-five years whether this is profound wisdom or profound self-deception. How does one tell?

Now we as a society are asked to take a further step down that strange road of respect. The Human Embryo Research Panel of the National Institutes of Health has reaffirmed both a respect for embryos and the acceptability under some circumstances of carrying out research on them, including the creation of some embryos for research purposes only. Such research has been the goal of some investigators for many years and only the political opposition of the

Callahan, Daniel, "The Puzzle of Profound Respect: Human Embryo Research," from *The Hastings Center Report*, Jan./Feb. 1995, Vol. 25, No. 1. Reprinted by permission of the author.

Reagan and Bush administrations and the likely resistance of Congress has stood in its way. The new Congress is no less likely to be resistant.

The report of the Human Embryo Research Panel is worthy of much praise, considerable astonishment, some puzzlement, and outright amusement. The praise is for its careful analysis of the moral status of the embryo, the astonishment for its utterly uncritical blessing of research, the puzzlement because of its unwitting challenge to the 1973 *Roe v. Wade* decision on abortion, and the amusement over its straight-faced pretension that it has taken no particular religious or philosophical position on the status of the embryo.

To repeat, the panel deserves praise for the care with which it analyzed the moral status of the preimplantation embryo. No other group has done nearly so well in working its way through that moral thicket. The position it finally takes, that the emergence of the primitive streak (around fourteen days after fertilization) represents "a major milestone in embryonic development," has much to commend it biologically. It is a major milestone—but then so are many other points in embryonic and fetal development. Why should this one be singled out as particularly important for decisions on research limits? The panel's twofold answer is that (a) no single criterion for personhood can withstand criticism, while (b) a "pluralistic approach," stressing "a variety of distinct, intersecting, and mutually supporting considerations" can be serviceable for public policy purposes. "The pluralistic approach," the report states, "accords some moral weight to the preimplantation embryo, but does not rule out well justified research." In other words, the report seems to be saying, if your aim is to do research, then a "pluralistic approach" will give you the leeway to do it but within reasonable limits.

That is a plausible argument, but there is also a problem lurking here. How are we to go about establishing some kind of moral proportionality between the claims of research (which the report at one point calls a "duty"), and that of the "moral weight" of the embryo? Some

astonishment is in order at this point. Though the report sets up a clear moral tension between those two goods, it is utterly silent on how research claims and possibilities should be evaluated for their moral weight and benefit. It is no less silent on how, even with that information in hand, a moral calculus is to be constructed to do the necessary balancing. The section on "ethical considerations" is exclusively devoted to the moral status of the human embryo, with not a word devoted to the moral status of proposed research or the criteria necessary for establishing some kind of proportionality.

What a free ride this is for the researchers, whose claims of potential benefits are treated with the kind of deference and credulity not seen since the days when the golden calf was worshipped. But of course for modern medicine research is the golden calf, questioned only at one's own risk. Duly reverential, the panel satisfied itself with simply listing all the research possibilities, including the improvement and increased safety of IVF, the creation of cell lines that might someday be useful for bone marrow transplantation, repair of spinal cord injuries, skin replacement and, naturally, the hint of a greater understanding of cancer.

Was not a little skepticism in order here? Did not anyone recall that a deference to the requirements of research was once taken to be a self-evident justification for experimentation on human subjects without their consent? Could not anyone have thought to ask how the possibilities of increased knowledge through embryo research compare with the myriad other possibilities of research that can also be pursued without the use of embryos? If, as the report notes, the developmental potentialities of the preimplantation embryo are still uncertain—nature disposes of a high proportion of them—how does that compare with the odds of success from potentially fruitful lines of research? What is the scientific mortality rate of ideas about promising approaches to understanding cancer? What is the appropriate moral method for comparing these potentialities? There is no hint of an answer, but then there is no hint of a question either.

The report notes that four countries already allow embryo research and that it has been going on for some years in private laboratories in this country. Yet not a single actual benefit derived so far from that research is cited to back the claims of great potential benefits from having even more of it. There is, oddly, no mention of any results whatever from that research, other than the oblique suggestion that it would be much improved if government funds could be brought to bear. Would it be unfair to conclude that either there have been no notable research benefits so far and thus the subject was finessed, or that the panel just forgot to ask? In any case, we are asked to bet on the future benefits. I wonder what odds the bookies in Las Vegas would give on this one.

Still another question about the research claims can be asked: if the research needs are so great, and the likely benefits so significant, why not draw the line much later in gestation—at the point, say, of viability, as *Roe v. Wade* did, rather than at fourteen days? Why not allow late embryo and early fetal research? The report says that the appearance of the primitive streak is an important dividing line. But since it also states that the personhood and value of the fetus increase over time, it needs to tell us why that line is crucial when research at a later stage could presumably tell us more. The precise logical connection is never actually made but merely assumed, as if the job is done simply by setting the research potentialities side by side with a particular view of the preimplantation embryo.

That omission sets the stage for some further puzzlement, the other side of the line-drawing coin, so to speak: if the emergence of the primitive streak is such a decisive event, why then should it not be used to set a limit on abortion as well? The report, to be sure, manages very neatly to stay as far away from the abortion issue as possible, no doubt for reasons of political prudence. But what if some Supreme Court case in the future forced a reopening of *Roe v. Wade*, and the justices had to return to the question of where to draw a line between permissible and impermissible abortions? Some justice, needing

little imagination, might well find this report interesting and suggestive.

Why, she might wonder, is it not acceptable to carry out medically enlightening and socially useful research on an embryo after fourteen days, but perfectly acceptable to kill a fetus for any reason a woman privately deems permissible up to twenty-four weeks? I am reminded here of a recently posed puzzle of cosmology: how can it be that the universe itself may only be eight to twelve billion years old but that individual stars may be older than that? Something comparable would seem to be going on with efforts to draw a bright and early line on embryo research but hardly any at all on abortion, no less lethal than the research. Why should our "profound respect" for the preimplantation embryo turn out to be far more demanding when research is in question than the respect due a fetus at a more advanced stage of gestation? Ironically, because the panel itself chose to use a developmental criterion for personhood, it sets itself up for just this line of questioning—and there is nothing in the report to even hint at how the panel would respond.

If astonishment and puzzlement are in order with the report, so also is just a touch of amusement. The report states that the panel "was not called upon to decide" which of the many views of the moral status of the preimplantation embryo "is correct"; and it went on to add that its deliberations were conducted "in terms that were independent of a particular religious or philosophical perspective." A bemused smile is in order when reading that statement. The report has in fact adopted a particular philosophical viewpoint on the purpose of law, on the imperative of scientific research, and on the moral status of the fetus. If the panel did not notice that, just about everyone else will.

I believe that the panel failed to come even close to making a persuasive case for preimplantation embryo research. It failed to tell us why there is a duty to carry out research that requires such techniques, and it failed to persuasively explain how such research is compatible with its expressed respect for the moral status of the fetus. It is one thing to be willing to swallow one's worry about the moral status of the fetus in order to allow women to have abortions (as I still would), but still another to do so to justify embryo research. I suspect that the only way successfully to make the case for embryo research is not, as this panel tried to do, by showing that research needs to take precedence over the respect it says is due the embryo. Instead, it is better and more honestly done by simply stripping preimplantation embryos of any value at all. If we look under the rhetoric of respect, that seems to me the actual meaning of what the panel has done.

At best, the kind of respect it would accord embryos is to them as a class, not as individual embryos. Those embryos that stand in the way of research are to be sacrificed—as nice a case of the ends justifying the means as can be found.

Research that stays within moral limits is worthy of respect. Research that restlessly seeks to find a way around them, holding out some supposedly higher goods, is not. If there can be such a thing as modern idolatry, that is it. Can not the research community find a Moses to go after that golden calf?

MARY B. MAHOWALD AND ANTHONY P. MAHOWALD
Embryonic Stem Cell Retrieval and a Possible Ethical Bypass

MARY B. MAHOWALD *is a professor at the University of Chicago School of Medicine. She writes extensively about social ethics and medicine. One of her recent books is* Genes, Women, and Equality *(2000)*.

ANTHONY P. MAHOWALD *is the Louis Block Professor of Molecular Genetics and Cell Biology at the University of Chicago.*

WITTGENSTEIN'S famous description of philosophy as a "battle against the bewitchment of our intelligence by means of language" is clearly pertinent to the work of bioethicists. In the context of embryo research, the term *pre-embryo* bewitches some people into thinking of an organism that is not yet an embryo; others realize that the term more accurately refers to the preimplantation embryo, in which the embryo as well as extraembryonic material are contained.

Possibly the most bewitching use of language in discussions of embryos arises from failure to distinguish between biological and philosophical definitions. The term *person*, for example, is a philosophical, religious, and legal designation subject to myriad interpretations and interminable controversy. In contrast, the terms *human* and *life* are biologically definable solely on grounds of criteria that distinguish between human and nonhuman and between living and nonliving. As Jane Maienschein observes, "we risk making bad policies" if we don't utilize definitions "that make scientific sense." Acknowledging that a developing embryo is human and living makes biological sense without implying that the embryo is a person who, as such, has a right to life. To be credible, the link between these biological and philosophical or religious definitions must be defended, not assumed.

Religious traditions ... illustrate the undefended assumption of a coincidence between "human life" and "personhood." While incorporating their new knowledge of biological development, [some religious analyses] allow that human embryos may have some moral status even if they are not persons. However, neither adequately addresses the fact that living human embryos are directly killed (cf. *destroyed*) through the procedure by which stem cells are retrieved from them.

Even if human embryos are not considered persons, many people balk at the thought of deliberately extinguishing their potential to become, indisputably, persons. As a society we generally oppose killing innocent people even when we know they are dying or irreversibly comatose, but we permit people to die if prolonging their lives through medical technology does not benefit them.

Embryos in a petri dish are more likely to die than become indisputably persons by being born—even if they are transferred to a woman's body for gestation. The great majority are nonviable, which means that they will die within a short time (the onset of which may be delayed through freezing) no matter what efforts are made to sustain their development. Since death is certain for thousands of in vitro embryos that would otherwise be discarded, shouldn't the same standard by which hospital patients are legally and morally allowed to die be acceptable for them? No such standard is needed for those who have no moral qualms about the issue; for others, however, it offers a means of bypassing the dilemma posed by embryonic stem cell research.

"The same standard" assumes a distinction between "killing" and "allowing to die." Legal statutes permit the latter in some cases but not the former. Some ethicists have disputed the moral relevance of this distinction, but many have upheld it. It remains true that embryos need not be killed in order to obtain stem cells. Instead, the embryos may be allowed to die before retrieving their stem cells, just as vital organs and tissues are routinely removed from patients who have died so that their organs may be used for research or transplantation. Consent for retrieval and use of the stem cells is obtainable from those whose eggs and sperm generated the embryos.

Retrieving stem cells directly from living embryos may be a more efficient method for researchers than retrieval after allowing them to die. A comparison, however, with retrieval of vital organs from born donors is again relevant: we don't remove them from those who are alive even if they are dying, because killing them (rather than allowing them to die) is as wrong as killing those who are not yet dying. We do, however, attempt to preserve organs for successful transplantation by continuing mechanical supports in those pronounced dead.

Death implies the inability of an organism to continue existing as such. The death of an embryo may therefore be defined as its inability to continue existing as an embryo. Trophoblastic cells that surround early embryos are indispensable to their further development. Allowing these cells to separate from the cell mass of an embryo in a petri dish is thus equivalent to allowing the embryo to die. If stem cells are then retrieved from the embryos that have expired, the retrieval is morally analogous to retrieval of vital organs from those who are newly deceased.

Embryos in a petri dish may be killed by deliberately discarding them into the lab sink or adding a lethal compound to the medium surrounding them in the petri dish. Alternatively, they may be allowed to die in a respectful or disrespectful manner. Just as some people are allowed to die in a morally reprehensible way (e.g., when death is probably avoidable without extraordinary interventions), allowing embryos to die may be wrong if their probability of survival is high without extraordinary interventions. Since this is not the case, embryos may be allowed to die in a respectful manner; they may even be buried with an accompanying ritual, just as born humans are sometimes allowed to die and be buried with appropriate rituals.

There seems, then, to be an ethical bypass to the dilemma faced by those who wish to avoid the direct killing of nascent human life while supporting the therapeutic possibilities of stem cell research. Regardless of whether developing embryos are deemed persons, respect for human life in its earliest stages is compatible with research on stem cells obtained from human embryos so long as the cells are retrieved from embryos that have been allowed, respectfully, to die.

SENATOR SAM BROWNBACK
The Feelings of the Unborn

SAM BROWNBACK *is a United States Senator from the state of Kansas.*

MR. BROWNBACK. Mr. President, I rise today to introduce the bipartisan Unborn Child Pain Awareness Act, and I am joined by 22 original cosponsors.

Unborn children can experience pain, and they can certainly respond to touch from outside the womb. Any woman who has been blessed with carrying a baby in the second trimester can tell you this.

I remember my own children kicking and squirming inside of my wife's womb. And my wife certainly remembers feeling their kicks. That unborn child is very much alive. All along, women have been able to feel the child inside of them, but now, science is telling us what the child inside of his or her mother can feel.

Many among us are unaware of the scientific, medical fact that unborn children can feel, but it is true. Not only can they feel, but their ability to experience pain is heightened. The highest density of pain receptors per square inch of skin in human development occurs in utero from 20 to 30 weeks gestation.

An expert report on fetal development, prepared for the Partial Birth Abortion Ban trials, notes that while unborn children are obviously incapable of verbal expressions, we know that they can experience pain based upon anatomical, functional, physiological and behavioral indicators that are correlated with pain in children and adults.

Unborn children can experience pain. This is why unborn children are often administered anesthesia during in utero surgeries.

Think about the pain that unborn children can experience, and then think about the more gruesome abortion procedures. Of course, we have heard about Partial Birth Abortion, but

Statement by Senator Sam Brownback from the *Congressional Record,* May 20, 2004.

also consider the D&E abortion. During this procedure, commonly performed after 20 weeks—when there is medical evidence that the child can experience severe pain—the child is torn apart limb from limb. Think about how that must feel to a young human.

We would never allow a dog to be treated this way. Yet, the creature we are talking about is a young, unborn child.

Fortunately, the issue of pain experienced by unborn children has been covered by the news media during the ongoing Partial Birth Abortion Ban trials. Take for instance an April 7, 2004 Associated Press news article covering the trials. And I quote: "A type of abortion banned under a new federal law would cause 'severe and excruciating' pain to 20-week-old fetuses, a medical expert testified yesterday. . . . 'I believe the fetus is conscious,' said Dr. Kanwaljeet 'Sonny' Anand, a pediatrician at the University of Arkansas for Medical Sciences. . . . said yesterday that fetuses show increased heart rate, blood flow, and hormone levels in response to pain. 'The physiological responses have been very clearly studied,' he said. The fetus cannot talk . . . so this is the best evidence we can get.'"

Today I introduce a bill that would require those who perform abortions on unborn children 20 weeks after fertilization to inform the woman seeking an abortion of the medical evidence that the unborn child feels pain: (a.) Through a verbal statement given by the abortion provider, and also (b.) by providing a brochure—developed by the Department of Health and Human Services—that goes into more detail than the verbal statement on the medical evidence of pain experienced by an unborn child 20 weeks after fertilization.

The bill would also ensure that the woman, if she chooses to continue with the abortion procedure after being given the medical information, has the option of choosing anesthesia for the child, so that the unborn child's pain is less severe.

Women should not be kept in the dark; women have the right to know what their unborn child experiences during an abortion. After being presented with the medical and scientific information on the development of the unborn child 20 weeks after fertilization, the woman is more aware of the pain experienced by the child during an abortion procedure, and able—at the very least—to make an informed decision. It is simply not fair to keep women in the dark.

Unborn children do not have a voice, but they are young members of the human family. It is time to look at the unborn child, and recognize that it is really a young human, who can feel pain and should be treated with care.

I urge my colleagues to support and pass this important piece of legislation.

CHAPTER ELEVEN

WHAT IS THE
MEANING OF DEATH?

It may have struck you that many of the topics that philosophers find interesting (the nature of knowledge, the relationship between the mind and the body, the nature of justice, and so on) aren't ones that people generally worry much about. Although people may have views about, for example, whether a particular law is just, they usually don't spend much time trying to understand the nature of justice itself. That task gets left to the philosopher. But it seems that most people do, at various times in their lives, wonder about the nature of death. What is death? What is it like to be dead? Does that question make sense? Why do we usually consider death to be a bad thing, a thing to be avoided? Is it ever reasonable to prefer death over life? Is there "life" after death? If so, what is it like?

In his paper "Death," Thomas Nagel tries to figure out just what is so bad about death, given that death is the end of conscious existence. How can something be bad for me if I don't even exist? If you have trouble settling this question and those above, if they present you with endless opportunity for speculation, it is partly because each of them is connected not only to one another, but also to a host of other questions that resist easy answers. For example, take the question that Nagel sidesteps, namely, whether there is "life" after death. When someone poses that question, she is usually wondering if, after the death of her body, anything is left of the person who once "inhabited" it. After all, the corpse rots away under the earth, or succumbs to the flames of the crematorium. Where, then, is the person who once was? As you can see, how you answer this question will depend in part on your views about the relationship between the mind and the body (see Chapter 5). For example, if you have been persuaded that a person is a purely physical being and that the notion of an immaterial mind or soul is nonsensical, then you will likely dismiss the idea that a person could survive the death of her body. You can see, too, that underlying this last claim are assumptions about the nature of persons. Thus, any view about life after death will have as a counterpart some view about personal identity (see Chapter 8). Very often, concerns about the afterlife can be seen as concerns about what it is that gives life meaning. Some people think that, without some promise of life beyond that on earth, our lives here are meaningless and without any real purpose.

Shades of this view can be found in Plato's *Phaedo*, in which Socrates makes explicit his position on the question of the afterlife. He thought that the physical body is a mere impediment, something that we have to live with, so to speak, while we are stationed in the material world. To him, the *real* world was purely immaterial. Our embodied life, if lived properly (you will see what Socrates thought about the life well lived), is a process of moving closer and closer to reality. In and of itself, our embodied life means nothing. Chuang-Tzu offers another ancient view of death that contrasts in interesting ways with that of Socrates.

The mysteries of death and the afterlife thus provide wide room for philosophical speculation. But there is as well a set of distinctly ethical questions about death and dying that warrants careful attention. Simply put, the most central of such questions is whether it is ever permissible to cause someone to die or even to let someone die. Surely, few people endorse cold-blooded murder. But what about "pulling the plug" in the case of an elderly patient who is in a coma, with no chance of gaining consciousness? Or what about administering a lethal dose of morphine to a terminally ill cancer patient in intractable pain? Immediately, a number of ancillary questions arise. Is there a difference between killing and letting someone die? What role do the desires of the afflicted person play in the decision to "let nature take its course" or to help nature along its way? The Greek word *euthanasia*, which taken literally means "good death," is often used to refer to cases such as these.

Patricia Mann examines the ways in which our cultural expectations about death are likely to be transformed by the legalization of assisted suicide. She argues that the morality of end-of-life decisions must be understood, not simply as relevant to the one who is dying, but as embedded in a web of interconnected relationships. Thus, she concludes, the philosophical framework of individual autonomy and rights is inadequate to the task of determining the morality of assisted suicide.

James Rachels proposes that it is a distinction without a difference. He agrees that "active euthanasia" and "passive euthanasia" are legally different, but by spelling out for us some of the consequences of trying to maintain such a distinction, he argues that there is no moral basis to it. In her response to Rachels' argument, Bonnie Steinbock claims to the contrary that the distinction between active and passive euthanasia can be supported in cases in which the patient refuses treatment and in cases in which the purpose of failing to treat a patient is not the termination of life, but rather the reduction of pain.

PLATO
The Death of Socrates

PLATO *(427–347 B.C.) was born into a family of considerable wealth and power. In Athens he came under the influence of Socrates and turned his attention to philosophy. After Socrates was condemned to death for corrupting the minds of the youth of Athens, Plato took it upon himself to continue Socrates' work. In the selection here from the* Phaedo, *Socrates, who always serves as Plato's spokesman in his dialogues, discusses his view of death with Cebes.*

YOU realize, he said, that when a man dies, the visible part, the body, which exists in the visible world, which we call the corpse, for which it would be natural to dissolve, fall apart and be blown away, does not immediately suffer any of these things but remains for a fair time, in fact, quite a long time if the man dies with his body in a suitable condition and at a favourable season? If the body is emaciated or embalmed, as in Egypt, it remains almost whole for a remarkable length of time, and even if the body decays, some part of it, namely bones and sinews and the like are nevertheless, one might say, deathless. Is that not so?—Yes.

Will the soul, the invisible part which makes its way to a region of the same kind, noble and pure and invisible, to Hades in fact, to the good and wise god whither, god willing, my soul must soon be going—will the soul, being of this kind and nature, be scattered and destroyed on leaving the body, as the majority of men say? Far from it, my dear Cebes and Simmias, but what happens is much more like this: if it is pure when it leaves the body and drags nothing bodily with it, as it had no willing association with the body in life, but avoided it and gathered itself together by itself and always practices this, which is no other than practicing philosophy in the right way, in fact, training to die easily. Or is this not training for death?

It surely is.

A soul in this state makes its way to the invisible, which is like itself, the divine and immortal and wise, and arriving there it can be happy, having rid itself of confusion, ignorance, fear violent desires and the other human ills and, as is said of the initiates, truly spend the rest of time with the gods. Shall we say this, Cebes, or something different?

This, by Zeus, said Cebes.

But I think if the soul is polluted and impure when it leaves the body, having always been associated with it and served it, bewitched by physical desires and pleasures to the point at which nothing seems to exist for it but the physical, which one can touch and see or eat and drink or make use of for sexual enjoyment, and if that soul is accustomed to hate and fear and avoid that which is dim and invisible to the eyes but intelligible and to be grasped by philosophy—do you think such a soul will escape pure and by itself?

Impossible, he said.

I think it is permeated by the physical, which constant intercourse and association with the body, as well as considerable practice, has cause to become ingrained in it.

Quite so.

We must believe, my friend, that this bodily element is heavy, ponderous, earthy and visible. Through it, such a soul has become heavy, and is

Plato, "The Death of Socrates," from *Phaedo* (New York: Heritage Press).

dragged back to the visible region in fear of the unseen, which is called Hades. It wanders, as we are told, around graves and monuments, where shadowy phantoms, images that such souls produce, have been seen, souls that have not been freed and purified but share in the visible, and are therefore seen.

That is likely, Socrates.

It is indeed, Cebes. Moreover, these are not the souls of good but of inferior men, which are forced to wander there, paying the penalty for their previous bad upbringing. They wander until their longing for that which accompanies them, the physical, again imprisons them in a body, and they are then, as is likely, bound to such characters as they have practiced in their life.

What kind of characters do you say these are, Socrates?

Those, for example, who have carelessly practiced gluttony, violence and drunkenness are likely to join a company of donkeys or of similar animals. Do you not think so?

Very likely.

Those who have esteemed injustice highly, and tyranny and plunder will join the tribes of wolves and hawks and kites, or where else shall we say that they go?

Certainly to those, said Cebes.

And clearly, the destination of the others will depend on the way in which they have behaved.

Clearly, of course.

The happiest of these, who will also have the best destination, are those who have practised popular and social virtue which they call moderation and justice by habit and practice, without philosophy or understanding.

How are they the happiest?

Because it is likely that they will again join a social and gentle group, either of bees or wasps or ants, and then again the same kind of human group, and so be moderate men.

That is likely.

No one may join the company of the gods who has not practised philosophy and is not completely pure when he departs from life, no one but the lover of learning. It is for this reason, my friends Simmias and Cebes, that those who

practise philosophy in the right way keep away from all bodily passions, master them and do not surrender themselves to them; it is not at all for fear of wasting their substance and of poverty, which the majority and the money-lovers fear, nor for fear of dishonour and ill repute, like the ambitious and lovers of honours, that they keep away from them.

That would not be natural for them, Socrates, said Cebes.

By Zeus, no, he said. Those who care for their own soul and do not live for the service of their body dismiss all these things. They do not travel the same road as those who do not know where they are going but, believing that nothing should be done contrary to philosophy and their deliverance and purification, they turn to this and follow wherever philosophy leads.

How so, Socrates?

I will tell you, he said. The lovers of learning know that when philosophy gets hold of their soul, it is imprisoned in and clinging to the body, and that it is forced to examine other things through it as though a cage and not by itself, and that it wallows in every kind of ignorance. Philosophy sees that the worst feature of this imprisonment is that it is due to desires, so that the prisoner is contributing to his own incarceration. As I say, the lovers of learning know that philosophy gets hold of their soul when it is in that state, then gently encourages it and tries to free it by showing them that investigation through the eyes is full of deceit, as is that through the ears and the other senses. Philosophy then persuades the soul to withdraw from the senses in so far as it is not compelled to use them and bids the soul to gather itself together by itself, to trust only itself and whatever reality, existing by itself, the soul by itself understands, and not to consider as true whatever it examines by other means, for this is different in different circumstances and is sensible and visible, whereas what the soul itself sees is intelligible and invisible. The philosopher thinks that this deliverance must not be opposed and so keeps away from pleasures and desires and pains as far as he can; he reflects that violent pleasure or pain or passion does not cause merely such evils as one might expect, such as one suffers when one has been sick or extravagant through desire, but the greatest and most extreme evil, though one does not reflect on this.

What is that, Socrates? asked Cebes.

What the soul of every man, when it feels violent pleasure or pain in connection with some object, inevitably believes at the same time that what causes such feelings must be very real true, which it is not. Such objects are mostly visible, are they not?

Certainly.

And such an experience ties the soul to the body most completely.

How so?

Because every pleasure and every pain provides, as it were, another nail to rivet the soul to the body and to weld them together. It makes the soul corporeal, so that it believes that truth is what the body says it is. As it shares the beliefs and delights of the body, I think it inevitably comes to share its ways and manner of life and is unable ever to reach Hades in a pure state; it is always full of body when it departs, so that it soon falls back into another body and grows with it as if it had been sewn into it. Because of this, it can have no part in the company of the divine, the pure and uniform.

What you say is very true, Socrates, said Cebes.

This is why genuine lovers of learning are moderate and brave, or do you think it is for the reasons the majority says they are?

I certainly do not.

Indeed no. This is how the soul of a philosopher would reason: it would not think that while philosophy must free it, it should while being freed surrender itself to pleasures and pains and imprison itself again, thus labouring in vain like Penelope at her web. The soul of the philosopher achieves a calm from such emotions; it follows reason and ever stays with it contemplating the true, the divine, which is not the object of opinion. Nurtured by this, it believes that one should live in this manner as long as one is alive and, after death, arrive at what is akin and of the same kind, and escape from human evils.

CHUANG-TZU

A Taoist on Death

CHUANG-TZU *(fourth century B.C.) was a Taoist philosopher who believed that we must understand our true natures and our place in nature as a whole.*

CHUANG-TZU'S wife died. When Hui Tzu went to convey his condolences, he found Chuang-Tzu sitting with his legs sprawled out, pounding on a tub and *singing*. "You lived with her, she brought up your children and grew old," said Hui Tzu. "It should be enough simply not to weep at her death. But pounding on a tub and singing—this is going too far, isn't it?"

Chuang-Tzu, "A Taoist on Death," from *Death and Philosophy,* translated by Roger Ames. Reprinted by permission of the author.

Chuang-Tzu said, "You're wrong. When she first died, do you think I didn't grieve like anyone else? But I looked back to her beginning and the time before she was born. Not only the time before she was born, but the time before she had a body. Not only the time before she had a body, but the time before she had a spirit. In the midst of the jumble of wonder and mystery a change took place and she had a spirit. Another change and she had a body. Another change and she was born. Now there's been another change and she's dead. It's just like the progression of the four seasons, spring, summer, fall, winter.

"Now she's going to lie down peacefully in a vast room. If I were to follow after her bawling and sobbing, it would show that I don't understand anything about fate. So I stopped."

THOMAS NAGEL

Death

THOMAS NAGEL *teaches philosophy at New York University. He has published widely in epistemology and moral philosophy. Among his recent publications are* Mortal Questions *(1991) and* The Last Word *(1996).*

IF death is the unequivocal and permanent end of our existence, the question arises whether it is a bad thing to die.

There is conspicuous disagreement about the matter: some people think death is dreadful; others have no objection to death *per se,* though they hope their own will be neither premature nor painful. Those in the former category tend to think those in the latter are blind to the obvious, while the latter suppose the former to be prey to some sort of confusion. On the one hand it can be said that life is all we have and the loss of it is the greatest loss we can sustain. On the other hand it may be objected that death deprives this supposed loss of its subject, and that if we realize that death is not an unimaginable condition of the persisting person, but a mere blank, we will see that it can have no value whatever, positive or negative.

Since I want to leave aside the question whether we are, or might be, immortal in some form, I shall simply use the word "death" and its cognates in this discussion to mean *permanent* death, unsupplemented by any form of conscious survival. I want to ask whether death is in itself an evil; and how great an evil, and of what kind, it might be. The question should be of interest even to those who believe in some form of immortality, for one's attitude toward immortality must depend in part on one's attitude toward death.

If death is an evil at all, it cannot be because of its positive features, but only because of what it deprives us of. I shall try to deal with the difficulties surrounding the natural view that death is an evil because it brings to an end all the goods that life contains. We need not give an account of these goods here, except to observe that some of them, like perception, desire, activity, and thought, are so general as to be constitutive of human life. They are widely regarded as formidable benefits in themselves, despite the fact that they are conditions of misery as well as of happiness, and that a sufficient quantity of more particular evils can perhaps outweigh them. That is what is meant, I think, by the allegation that it is good simply to be alive, even if one is undergoing terrible experiences. The situation is roughly this: There are elements which, if added to one's experience, make life better; there are other elements which, if added to one's experience, make life worse. But what remains when these are set aside is not merely *neutral:* it is emphatically positive. Therefore life is worth living even when the bad elements of experience are plentiful, and the good ones too meager to outweigh the bad ones on their own. The additional positive weight is supplied by experience itself, rather than by one of its contents.

I shall not discuss the value that one person's life or death may have for others, or its objective value, but only the value it has for the person who is its subject. That seems to me the primary case, and the case which presents the greatest difficulties.

Let me add only two observations. First, the value of life and its contents does not attach to mere organic survival: almost everyone would be indifferent (other things equal) between immediate death and immediate coma followed by death and immediate coma followed by death twenty years later without reawakening. And second, like most goods, this can be multiplied by time: more is better than less. The added quantities need not be temporally continuous (though continuity has its social advantages). People are attracted to the possibility of long-term suspended animation or freezing, followed by the resumption of conscious life, because they can regard it from within simply as a *continuation* of their present life. If these techniques are ever perfected, what from outside appeared as a

dormant interval of three hundred years could be experienced by the subject as nothing more than a sharp discontinuity in the character of his experiences. I do not deny, of course, that this has its own disadvantages. Family and friends may have died in the meantime; the language may have changed; the comforts of social, geographical, and cultural familiarity would be lacking. Nevertheless these inconveniences would not obliterate the basic advantage of continued, though discontinuous, existence.

If we turn from what is good about life to what is bad about death, the case is completely different. Essentially, though there may be problems about their specification, what we find desirable in life are certain states, conditions, or types of activity. It is *being* alive, *doing* certain things, having certain experiences, that we consider good. But if death is an evil, it is the *loss of life*, rather than the state of being dead, or nonexistent, or unconscious, that is objectionable. This asymmetry is important. If it is good to be alive, that advantage can be attributed to a person at each point of his life. It is a good of which Bach had more than Schubert, simply because he lived longer. Death, however, is not an evil of which Shakespeare has so far received a larger portion than Proust. If death is a disadvantage, it is not easy to say when a man suffers it.

There are two other indications that we do not object to death merely because it involves long periods of nonexistence. First, as has been mentioned, most of us would not regard the *temporary* suspension of life, even for substantial intervals, as in itself a misfortune. If it ever happens that people can be frozen without reduction of the conscious lifespan, it will be inappropriate to pity those who are temporarily out of circulation. Second, none of us existed before we were born (or conceived), but few regard that as a misfortune. I shall have more to say about this later.

The point that death is not regarded as an unfortunate *state* enables us to refute a curious but very common suggestion about the origin of the fear of death. It is often said that those who object to death have made the mistake of trying to imagine what it is like to *be* dead. It is alleged that the failure to realize that this task is logi-cally impossible (for the banal reason that there is nothing to imagine) leads to the conviction that death is a mysterious and therefore terrify-ing prospective *state*. But this diagnosis is evi-dently false, for it is just as impossible to imagine being dead (though it is easy enough to imagine oneself, from the outside, in either of those con-ditions). Yet people who are averse to death are not usually averse to unconsciousness (so long as it does not entail a substantial cut in the total duration of waking life).

If we are to make sense of the view that to die is bad, it must be on the ground that life is a good and death is the corresponding deprivation or loss, bad not because of any positive features but because of the desirability of what it re-moves. We must now turn to the serious difficul-ties which this hypothesis raises, difficulties about loss and privation in general, and about death in particular.

Essentially, there are three types of problems. First, doubt may be raised whether *anything* can be bad for a man without being positively un-pleasant to him: specifically, it may be doubted that there are any evils which consist merely in the deprivation or absence of possible goods, and which do not depend on someone's *minding* that deprivation. Second, there are special diffi-culties, in the case of death, about how the sup-posed misfortune is to be assigned to a subject at all. There is doubt both as to *who* its subject is, and as to *when* he undergoes it. So long as a per-son exists, he has not yet died, and once he has died, he no longer exists; so there seems to be no time when death, if it is a misfortune, can be as-cribed to its unfortunate subject. The third type of difficulty concerns the asymmetry, mentioned above, between our attitudes to posthumous and prenatal nonexistence. How can the former be bad if the latter is not?

It should be recognized that if these are valid objections to counting death as an evil, they will apply to many other supposed evils as well. The first type of objection is expressed in general form by the common remark that what you don't know can't hurt you. It means that even if a man

is betrayed by his friends, ridiculed behind his back, and despised by people who treat him po-litely to his face, none of it can be counted as a misfortune for him so long as he does not suffer as a result. It means that a man is not injured if his wishes are ignored by the executor of his will, or if, after death, the belief becomes current that all the literary works on which his fame rests were really written by his brother, who died in Mexico at the age of 28. It seems to me worth asking what assumptions about good and evil lead to these drastic restrictions.

All the questions have something to do with time. There certainly are goods and evils of a simple kind (including some pleasures and pains) which a person possesses at a given time simply in virtue of his condition at that time. But this is not true of all the things we regard as good or bad for a man. Often we need to know his history to tell whether something is a misfor-tune or not; this applies to ills like deterioration, deprivation, and damage. Sometimes his experi-ential *state* is relatively unimportant—as in the case of a man who wastes his life in the cheerful pursuit of a method of communicating with asparagus plants. Someone who holds that all goods and evils must be temporally assignable states of the person may of course try to bring difficult cases into line by pointing to the plea-sure or pain that more complicated goods and evils cause. Loss, betrayal, deception, and ridicule are on this view bad because people suf-fer when they learn of them. But it should be asked how our ideas of human value would have to be constituted to accommodate these cases directly instead. One advantage of such an account might be that it would enable us to explain *why* the discovery of these misfortunes causes suffering—in a way that makes it reason-able. For the natural view is that the discovery of betrayal makes us unhappy because it is bad to be betrayed—not that betrayal is bad because its discovery makes us unhappy.

It therefore seems to me worth exploring the position that most good and ill fortune has as its subject a person identified by his history and his possibilities, rather than merely by his categorical state of the moment—and that while this subject can be exactly located in a sequence of places and times, the same is not necessarily true of the goods and ills that befall him.

These ideas can be illustrated by an example of deprivation whose severity approaches that of death. Suppose an intelligent person receives a brain injury that reduces him to the mental condition of a contented infant, and that such desires as remain to him can be satisfied by a custodian, so that he is free from care. Such a development would be widely regarded as a severe misfortune, not only for his friends and relations, or for society, but also, and primarily, for the person himself. This does not mean that a contented infant is unfortunate. The intelligent adult who has been *reduced* to this condition is the subject of the misfortune. He is the one we pity, though of course he does not mind his condition—there is some doubt, in fact, whether he can be said to exist any longer.

The view that such a man has suffered a misfortune is open to the same objections which have been raised in regard to death. He does not mind his condition. It is in fact the same condition he was in at the age of three months, except that he is bigger. If we did not pity him then, why pity him now; in any case, who is there to pity? The intelligent adult has disappeared, and for a creature like the one before us, happiness consists in a full stomach and dry diaper.

If these objections are invalid, it must be because they rest on a mistaken assumption about the temporal relation between the subject of a misfortune and the circumstances which constitute it. If, instead of concentrating exclusively on the oversized baby before us, we consider the person he was, and the person he *could* be now, then his reduction to this state and the cancellation of his natural adult development constitute a perfectly intelligible catastrophe.

This case should convince us that it is arbitrary to restrict the goods and evils that can befall a man to nonrelational properties ascribable to him at particular times. As it stands, that restriction excludes not only such cases of gross degeneration, but also a good deal of what is important about success and failure, and other features of a life that have the character of processes. I believe we can go further, however. There are good and evils which are irreducibly relational; they are features of the relations between a person, with spatial and temporal boundaries of the usual sort, and circumstances which may not coincide with him either in space or in time. A man's life includes much that does not take place within the boundaries of his life. These boundaries are commonly crossed by the misfortunes of being deceived, or despised, or betrayed. (If this is correct, there is a simple account of what is wrong with breaking a deathbed promise. It is an injury to the dead man. For certain purposes it is possible to regard time as just another type of distance.) The case of mental degeneration shows us an evil that depends on a contrast between the reality and the possible alternatives. A man is the subject of good and evil as much because he has hopes which may or may not be fulfilled, or possibilities which may or may not be realized, as because of his capacity to suffer and enjoy. If death is an evil, it must be accounted for in these terms, and the impossibility of locating it within life should not trouble us.

When a man dies we are left with his corpse, and while a corpse can suffer the kind of mishap that may occur to an article of furniture, it is not a suitable object for pity. The man, however, is. He has lost his life, and if he had not died, he would have continued to live it, and to possess whatever good there is in living. If we apply to death the account suggested for the case of dementia, we shall say that although the spatial and temporal locations of the individual who suffered the loss are clear enough, the misfortune itself cannot be so easily located. One must be content just to state that his life is over and there will never be any more of it. That *fact* rather than his past or present condition, constitutes his misfortune, if it is one. Nevertheless if there is a loss, someone must suffer it, and *he* must have existence and specific spatial and temporal location even if the loss itself does not. The fact that Beethoven had no children may have been a cause of regret to him, or a sad thing for the world, but it cannot be described as a misfortune for the children that he never had. All of us, I believe, are fortunate to have been born. But unless good and ill can be assigned to an embryo, or even to an unconnected pair of gametes, it cannot be said that not to be born is a misfortune. (That is a factor to be considered in deciding whether abortion and contraception are akin to murder.)

This approach also provides a solution to the problem of temporal asymmetry, pointed out by Lucretius. He observed that no one finds it disturbing to contemplate the eternity preceding his own birth, and he took this to show that it must be irrational to fear death, since death is simply the mirror image of the prior abyss. That is not true, however, and the difference between the two explains why it is reasonable to regard them differently. It is true that both the time before a man's birth and the time after his death are times when he does not exist. But the time after his death is time of which his death deprives him. It is time in which, had he not died then, he would be alive. Therefore any death entails the loss of *some* life that its victim would have led had he not died at that or any earlier point. We know perfectly well what it would be for him to have had it instead of losing it, and there is no difficulty in identifying the loser.

But we cannot say that the time prior to a man's birth is time in which he would have lived had he been born not then but earlier. For aside from the brief margin permitted by premature labor, he *could* not have been born earlier: anyone born substantially earlier than he was would have been someone else. Therefore the time prior to his birth is not time in which his subsequent birth prevents him from living. His birth, when it occurs, does not entail the loss to him of any life whatever.

The direction of time is crucial in assigning possibilities to people or other individuals. Distinct possible lives of a single person can diverge from a common beginning, but they cannot converge to a common conclusion from diverse beginnings. (The latter would represent not a set of different possible lives of one individual, whose lives have identical conclusions.) Given an identifiable individual, countless possibilities for his continued existence are imaginable, and we can clearly conceive of what it would be for him to go on existing indefinitely. However inevitable it is that this will not come about, its possibility is still that of the continuation of a good for him, if life is the good we take it to be.

We are left, therefore, with the question whether the nonrealization of this possibility is in every case a misfortune or whether it depends on what can naturally be hoped for. This seems to me the most serious difficulty with the view that death is always an evil. Even if we can dispose of the objections against admitting misfortune that is not experienced, or cannot be assigned to a definite time in the person's life, we still have to set some limits on *how* possible a possibility must be for its nonrealization to be a misfortune (or good fortune, should the possibility be a bad one). The death of Keats at 24 is generally regarded as tragic; that of Tolstoy at 82 is not. Although they will both be dead forever, Keats' death deprived him of many years of life which were allowed to Tolstoy; so in a clear sense Keats' loss was greater (though not in the sense standardly employed in mathematical comparison between infinite quantities). However, this does not prove that Tolstoy's loss was insignificant. Perhaps we record an objection only to evils which are gratuitously added to the inevitable; the fact it is worse to die at 24 than at 82 does not imply that it is not a terrible thing to die at 82, or even at 806. The question is whether we can regard as a misfortune any limitation, like mortality, that is normal to the species. Blindness or near-blindness is not a misfortune for a mole, nor would it be for a man, if that were the natural condition of the human race.

The trouble is that life familiarizes us with the goods of which death deprives us. We are already able to appreciate them, as a mole is not able to appreciate vision. If we put aside doubts about their status as goods and grant that their quantity is in part a function of their duration, the question remains whether death, no matter when it occurs, can be said to deprive its victim of what is in the relevant sense a possible continuation of life.

The situation is an ambiguous one. Observed from without, human beings obviously have a natural lifespan and cannot live much longer than a hundred years. A man's sense of his own experience, on the other hand, does not embody this idea of a natural limit. His existence defines for him an essentially open-ended possible future, containing the usual mixture of goods and evils that he has found so tolerable in the past. Having been gratuitously introduced to the world by a collection of natural, historical, and social accidents, he finds himself the subject of a *life* with an indeterminate and not essentially limited future. Viewed in this way, death, no matter how inevitable, is an abrupt cancellation of indefinitely extensive possible goods. Normality seems to have nothing to do with it, for the fact that we will all inevitably die in a few score years cannot by itself imply that it would not be good to live longer. Suppose that we were all inevitably going to die in *agony*—physical agony lasting six months. Would inevitability make *that* prospect any less unpleasant? And why should it be different for a deprivation? If the normal lifespan were a thousand years, death at 80 would be a tragedy. As things are, it may just be a more widespread tragedy. If there is no limit to the amount of life that it would be good to have, then it may be that a bad end is in store for us all.

JAMES RACHELS
Active and Passive Euthanasia

JAMES RACHELS *teaches philosophy at the University of Alabama. His work focuses on ethics, particularly ethical issues in biomedicine. Among his recent books are* Can Ethics Provide Answers? *(1996) and* Ethical Theory *(1998).*

THE distinction between active and passive euthanasia is thought to be crucial for medical ethics. The idea is that it is permissible, at least in some cases, to withhold treatment and allow a patient to die, but it is never permissible to take any direct action designed to kill the patient. This doctrine seems to be accepted by most doctors, and it is endorsed in a statement adopted by the House of Delegates of the American Medical Association of December 4, 1973:

The intentional termination of the life of one human being by another—mercy killing—is contrary to that for which the medical profession stands and is contrary to the policy of the American Medical Association.

The cessation of the employment of extraordinary means to prolong the life of the body when there is irrefutable evidence that biological death is imminent is the decision of the patient and/or his immediate family. The advice and judgment of the physician should be freely available to the patient and/or his immediate family.

Rachels, James, "Active and Passive Euthanasia," from *The New England Journal of Medicine* (Vol. 292, 1975), pp. 78–80. Copyright © 1975 Massachusetts Medical Society. All rights reserved.

However, a strong case can be made against this doctrine. In what follows I will set out some of the relevant arguments, and urge doctors to reconsider their views on this matter.

To begin with a familiar type of situation, a patient who is dying of incurable cancer of the throat is in terrible pain, which can no longer be satisfactorily alleviated. He is certain to die within a few days, even if present treatment is continued, but he does not want to go on living for those days since the pain is unbearable. So he asks the doctor for an end to it, and his family joins in the request.

Suppose the doctor agrees to withhold treatment, as the conventional doctrine says he may. The justification for his doing so is that the patient is in terrible agony, and since he is going to die anyway, it would be wrong to prolong his suffering needlessly. But now notice this. If one simply withholds treatment, it may take the patient longer to die, and so he may suffer more than he would if more direct action were taken and a lethal injection given. This fact provides strong reason for thinking that, once the initial decision not to prolong his agony has been made, active euthanasia is actually preferable to passive euthanasia, rather than the reverse. To say otherwise is to endorse the option that leads to more suffering rather than less, and is contrary to the humanitarian impulse that prompts the decision to prolong his life in the first place.

Part of my point is that the process of being "allowed to die" can be relatively slow and painful, whereas being given a lethal injection is relatively quick and painless. Let me give a different sort of example. In the United States about one in 600 babies is born with Down's syndrome. Most of these babies are otherwise healthy—that is, with only the usual pediatric care, they will proceed to an otherwise normal infancy. Some, however, are born with congenital defects such as intestinal obstructions that require operations if they are to live. Sometimes, the parents and the doctor will decide not to operate, and let the infant die. Anthony Shaw describes what happens then:

When surgery is denied [the doctor] must try to keep the infant from suffering while natural forces sap the baby's life away. As a surgeon whose natural inclination is to use the scalpel to fight off death, standing by and watching a salvageable baby die is the most emotionally exhausting experience I know. It is easy at a conference, in a theoretical discussion to decide that such infants should be allowed to die. It is altogether different to stand by in the nursery and watch as dehydration and infection wither a tiny being over hours and days. This is a terrible ordeal for me and the hospital staff—much more so than for the parents who never set foot in the nursery.

I can understand why some people are opposed to all euthanasia, and insist that such infants must be allowed to live. I think I can also understand why other people favor destroying these babies quickly and painlessly. But why should anyone favor letting "dehydration and infection wither a tiny being over hours and days"? The doctrine that says that a baby may be allowed to dehydrate and wither, but may not be given an injection that would end its life without suffering, seems so patently cruel as to require no further refutation. The strong language is not intended to offend, but only to put the point in the clearest possible way.

My second argument is that the conventional doctrine leads to decisions concerning life and death made on irrelevant grounds.

Consider again the case of the infants with Down's syndrome who need operations for congenital defects unrelated to the syndrome to live. Sometimes, there is no operation, and the baby dies, but when there is no such defect, the baby lives on. Now, an operation such as that to remove an intestinal obstruction is not prohibitively difficult. The reason why such operations are not performed in these cases is, clearly, that the child has Down's syndrome and the parents and the doctor judge that because of that fact it is better for the child to die.

But notice that this situation is absurd, no matter what view one takes of the lives and potentials of such babies. If the life of such an infant is worth preserving what does it matter if it needs a simple operation? Or, if one thinks it better that such a baby should not live on, what difference does it make that it happens to have an unobstructed intestinal tract? In either case, the matter of life and death is being decided on irrelevant grounds. It is the Down's syndrome, and not the intestines, that is the issue. The matter should be decided, if at all, on that basis, and not be allowed to depend on the essentially irrelevant question of whether the intestinal tract is blocked.

What makes this situation possible, of course, is the idea that when there is an intestinal blockage, one can "let the baby die," but when there is no such defect there is nothing that can be done, for one must not "kill" it. The fact that this idea leads to such results as deciding life or death on irrelevant grounds is another good reason why the doctrine would be rejected.

One reason why so many people think there is an important moral difference between active and passive euthanasia is that they think killing someone is morally worse than letting someone die. But is it? Is killing, in itself, worse than letting die? To investigate this issue, two cases may be considered that are exactly alike except that one involves killing whereas the other involves letting someone die. Then, it can be asked whether this difference makes any difference to the moral assessments. It is important that the cases be exactly alike, except for this one difference, since otherwise one cannot be confident that it is this difference and not some other that accounts for any variation in the assessments of the two cases. So, let us consider this pair of cases:

In the first, Smith stands to gain a large inheritance if anything should happen to his six-year-old cousin. One evening while the child is taking his bath, Smith sneaks into the bathroom and drowns the child, and then arranges things so that it will look like an accident.

In the second, Jones also stands to gain if anything should happen to his six-year-old cousin. Like Smith, Jones sneaks in planning to drown the child in his bath. However, just as he enters the bathroom Jones sees the child slip and hit his head and fall face down in the water. Jones is delighted; he stands by, ready to push the child's head back under if it is necessary. But it is not necessary. With only a little thrashing about, the child drowns all by himself "accidentally," as Jones watches and does nothing.

Now Smith killed the child, whereas Jones "merely" let the child die. That is the only difference between them. Did either man behave better, from a moral point of view? If the difference between killing and letting die were in itself a morally important matter, one should say that Jones's behavior was less reprehensible than Smith's. But does one really want to say that? I think not. In the first place, both men acted from the same motive, personal gain, and both had exactly the same end in view when they acted. It may be inferred from Smith's conduct that he is a bad man, although that judgment may be withdrawn or modified if certain further facts are learned about him—for example that he is mentally deranged. But would not the very same thing be inferred about Jones from his conduct? And would not the same further considerations also be relevant to any modification of this judgment? Moreover, suppose Jones pleaded, in his own defense. "After all, I didn't do anything except just stand there and watch the child drown. I didn't kill him; I only let him die." Again, if letting die were in itself less bad than killing, this defense should have at least some weight. But it does not. Such a "defense" can only be regarded as a grotesque perversion of moral reasoning. Morally speaking, it is no defense at all.

Now, it may be pointed out, quite properly, that the cases of euthanasia with which doctors are concerned are not like this at all. They do not involve personal gain or the destruction of normal healthy children. Doctors are concerned only with cases in which the patient's life is of no further use to him, or in which the patient's life has become or will soon become a terrible burden. However, the point is the same in these cases; the bare difference between killing and letting die does not, in itself, make a moral difference. If a doctor lets a patient die, for humane reasons, he is in the same moral position as if he had given the patient a lethal injection for humane reasons. If his decision was wrong—if, for example, the patient's illness was in fact curable—the decision would be equally regrettable no matter which method was used to carry it out. And if the doctor's decision was the right one, the method used is not in itself important.

The AMA policy statement isolates the crucial issue very well: the crucial issue is "the intentional termination of the life of one human being by another." But after identifying this issue, and forbidding "mercy killing," the statement goes on to deny that the cessation of treatment is the intentional termination of a life. This is where the mistake comes in, for what is the cessation of treatment, in these circumstances, if it is not "the intentional termination of life of one human being by another"? Of course it is exactly that, and if it were not, there would be no point to it.

Many people will find this judgment hard to accept. One reason, I think, is that it is very easy to conflate the question of whether killing is, in itself, worse than letting die, with the very different question of whether most actual cases of killing are more reprehensible than most actual cases of letting die. Most actual cases of killing are clearly terrible (think, for example, of all the murders reported in the newspapers), and one hears of such cases every day. On the other hand, one hardly ever hears of a case of letting die, except for the actions of doctors who are motivated by humanitarian reasons. So one learns to think of killing in a much worse light than of letting die. But this does not mean that there is something about killing that makes it in itself worse then letting die, for it is not the bare difference between killing and letting die that makes the difference in these cases. Rather, the other factors—the murderer's motivation—account for different reactions to the different cases.

I have argued that killing is not in itself any worse than letting die; if my contention is right, it follows that active euthanasia is not any worse than passive euthanasia. What arguments can be given on the other side? The most common, I believe, is the following:

The important difference between active and passive euthanasia is that, in passive euthanasia, the doctor does not do anything to bring about the patient's death. The doctor does nothing, and the patient dies of whatever ills already afflict him. In active euthanasia, however, the doctor does something to bring about the patient's death: he kills him. The doctor who gives the patient with cancer a lethal injection has himself caused his patient's death; whereas if he merely ceases treatment, the cancer is the cause of the death.

A number of points need to be made here. The first is that it is not exactly correct to say that in passive euthanasia the doctor does nothing, for he does do one thing that is very important: he lets the patient die. "Letting someone die" is certainly different, in some respects, from other types if action—mainly in that it is a kind of action that one may perform by way of not performing certain other actions. For example, one may let a patient die by way of not giving medication, just as one may insult someone by way of not shaking his hand. But for any purpose of moral assessment, it is a type of action nonetheless. The decision to let a patient die is subject to moral appraisal: it may be assessed as wise or unwise, compassionate or sadistic, right or wrong. If a doctor deliberately lets a patient die who was suffering from a routinely curable illness, the doctor would certainly be to blame if he had needlessly killed the patient. Charges against him would be appropriate. If so, it would be no defense at all for him to insist that he didn't "do anything." He would have done something very serious indeed, for he let his patent die.

Fixing the cause of death may be very important from a legal point of view, for it may determine whether criminal charges are brought against the doctor. But I do not think that this notion can be used to show a moral difference between active and passive euthanasia. The reason why it is considered bad to be the cause of someone's death is that death is regarded as a great evil—and so it is. However, if it has been decided that euthanasia—even passive euthanasia—is desirable in a given case, it has also been decided that in this instance death is no greater an evil than the patient's continued existence. And if this is true, the usual reason for not wanting to be the cause of someone's death simply does not apply.

Finally, doctors may think that all of this is only of academic interest—the sort of thing that philosophers may worry about but that has no practical bearing on their own work. After all, doctors must be concerned about the legal consequences of what they do, and active euthanasia is clearly forbidden by the law. But even so, doctors should also be concerned with the fact that the law is forcing upon them a moral doctrine that may be indefensible, and has a considerable effect on their practices. Of course, most doctors are not now in the position of being coerced in this matter, for they do not regard themselves as merely going along with what the law requires. Rather, in statements such as the AMA policy

statement that I have quoted they are endorsing this doctrine as a central point of medical ethics. In that statement, active euthanasia is condemned not merely as illegal but as "contrary to that for which the medical profession stands," whereas passive euthanasia is approved. However, the preceding considerations suggest that there is really no moral difference between the two, considered in themselves (there may be important moral difference in some cases in their *consequences*, but, as I pointed out, these differences may make active euthanasia, and not passive euthanasia, the morally preferable option). So, whereas doctors may have to discriminate between active and passive euthanasia to satisfy the law, they should not do any more than that. In particular, they should not give the distinction any added authority and weight by writing it into official statements of medical ethics.

BONNIE STEINBOCK
The Intentional Termination of Life

BONNIE STEINBOCK *teaches philosophy at the State University of New York at Albany. She has published widely on ethical issues at the beginning and end of life. Among her books are* Life Before Birth: The Moral and Legal Status of Embryos and Fetuses *(1992) and* Killing and Letting Die *(1994).*

ACCORDING to James Rachels and Michael Tooley, a common mistake in medical ethics is the belief that there is a moral difference between active and passive euthanasia. This is a mistake, they argue, because the rationale underlying the distinction between active and passive euthanasia is the idea that there is a significant moral difference between intentionally killing and intentionally letting die. "This idea," Tooley says, "is admittedly very common. But I believe that it can be shown to reflect either confused thinking, or a moral

Steinbock, Bonnie, reprinted from *Social Science & Medicine,* Vol. 6, 1979, pp. 59–64. Steinbock: "The Intentional Termination of Life," with permission of Elsevier Science.

point of view unrelated to the interests of individuals." Whether the belief that there is a significant moral difference (between intentionally killing and intentionally letting die) is mistaken is not my concern here. For it is far from clear that this distinction is not the basis of the doctrine of the American Medical Association which Rachels attacks. And if the killing/letting die distinction is not the basis of the AMA doctrine, then arguments showing that the distinction has no moral force do not, in themselves, reveal in the doctrine's adherents either "confused thinking" or "a moral point of view unrelated to the interest of individuals." Indeed, as we examine the AMA doctrine, I think it will become clear that it appeals to and makes use of a number of overlapping distinctions, which may have moral significance in particular cases, such as the distinction between intending and foreseeing, or between ordinary and extraordinary care. Let us then turn to the statement, from the House of Delegates of the American Medical Association, which Rachels cites:

> The intentional termination of the life of one human being by another—mercy-killing—is contrary to that for which the medical profession stands and is contrary to the policy of the American Medical Association.
>
> The cessation of the employment of extraordinary means to prolong the life of the body when there is irrefutable evidence that biological death is imminent is the decision of the patient and/or his immediate family. The advice and judgment of the physician should be freely available to the patient and/or his immediate family.

Rachels attacks this statement because he believes that it contains a moral distinction between active and passive euthanasia. . . .

I intend to show that the AMA statement does not imply support of the active/passive euthanasia distinction. In forbidding the intentional termination of life, the statement rejects both active and passive euthanasia. It does allow for ". . . the cessation of the employment of extraordinary means . . ." to prolong life. The mistake Rachels and Tooley make is in identifying the

cessation of life-prolonging treatment with passive euthanasia or intentionally letting die. If it were right to equate the two, then the AMA statement would be self-contradictory, for it would begin by condemning, and end by allowing the intentional termination of life. But if the cessation of life-prolonging treatment is not always or necessarily passive euthanasia, then there is no confusion and no contradiction. Why does Rachels think that the cessation of life-prolonging treatment is in the intentional termination of life? He says:

> The AMA policy statement isolates the crucial issue very well; the crucial issue is "the intentional termination of the life of one human being by another." But after identifying this issue, and forbidding "mercy-killing," the statement goes on to deny that the cessation of treatment is the intentional termination of a life. This is where the mistake comes in, for what is the cessation of treatment, in these circumstances, if it is not "the intentional termination of the life of one human being by another"? Of course it is exactly that, and if it were not, there would be no point to it.

However, there *can* be a point (to the cessation of life-prolonging treatment) other than an endeavor to bring about the patient's death, and so the blanket identification of cessation of treatment with the intentional termination of a life is inaccurate. There are at least two situations in which the termination of life-prolonging treatment cannot be identified with the intentional termination of the life of one human being by another.

The first situation concerns the patient's right to refuse treatment. Both Tooley and Rachels give the example of a patient dying of an incurable disease, accompanied by unrelievable pain, who wants to end the treatment which cannot cure him but can only prolong his miserable existence. Why, they ask, may a doctor accede to the patient's request to stop treatment, but not provide a patient in a similar situation with a lethal dose? The answer lies in the patient's right to refuse treatment. In general, a competent adult has the right to refuse treatment, even where such treatment is necessary to prolong life. Indeed, the right to refuse treatment has been upheld even when the patient's reason for refusing treatment is generally agreed to be inadequate. This right can be over-ridden (if, for example, the patient has dependent children) but, in general, no one may legally compel you to undergo treatment to which you have not consented. "Historically, surgical intrusion has always been considered a technical battery upon the person and one to be excused or justified by consent of the patient or justified by necessity created by the circumstances of the moment. . . ."

At this point, it might be objected that if one has the right to refuse life-prolonging treatment, then consistency demands that one have the right to decide to end his life and to obtain help in doing so. The idea is that the right to refuse treatment somehow implies a right to voluntary euthanasia, and we need to see why someone might think this. The right to refuse treatment has been considered by legal writers as an example of the right to privacy or, better, the right to bodily self-determination. You have the right to decide what happens to your own body, and the right to refuse treatment is an instance of that more general right. But if you have the right to determine what happens to your body, then should you not have the right to choose to end your life, and even a right to get help in doing so?

However, it is important to see that the right to refuse treatment is not the same as nor does it entail, a right to voluntary euthanasia, even if both can be derived from the right to bodily self-determination. The right to refuse treatment is not itself a "right to die"; that one may choose to exercise this right or even at the risk of death or even *in order to die,* is irrelevant. The purpose of the right to refuse medical treatment is not to give persons a right to decide whether to live or die, but to protect them from the unwanted inferences of others. Perhaps we ought to interpret the right to bodily self-determination more broadly so as to include a right to die: but this would be a substantial extension of our present understanding of the right to bodily self-determination, and not a consequence of it.

Should we recognize a right to voluntary euthanasia, we would have to agree that people have the right not merely to be left alone, but also the right to be killed. I leave to one side that substantive moral issue. My claim is simply that there can be a reason for terminating life-prolonging treatment other than "to bring about the patient's death."

The second case in which termination of treatment cannot be identified with intentional termination of life is where continued treatment has little chance of improving the patient's condition and brings greater discomfort than relief.

The question here is what treatment is appropriate to the particular case. A cancer specialist describes it in this way:

> My general rule is to administer therapy as long as a patient responds well and has the potential for a reasonably good quality of life. But when all feasible therapies have been administered and a patient shows signs of rapid deterioration, the continuation of therapy can cause more discomfort than the cancer. From that time I recommend surgery, radiotherapy, or chemotherapy only as a means of relieving pain. But if a patient's condition should once again stabilize after the withdrawal of active therapy and if it should appear that he could still gain some good time, I would immediately reinstitute active therapy. The decision to cease anticancer treatment is never irrevocable, and often the desire to live will push a patient to try for another remission, or even a few more days of life.

The decision here to cease anticancer treatment cannot be construed as a decision that the patient die, or as the intentional termination of life. It is a decision to provide the most appropriate treatment for that patient at that time. Rachels suggests that the point of the cessation of treatment is the intentional termination of life. But here the point of discontinuing treatment is not to bring about the patient's death but to avoid treatment that will cause more discomfort than the cancer and has little hope of benefiting the patient. Treatment that meets this description is often called "extraordinary." The concept is flexible, and what might be considered "extraordinary" in one situation might be ordinary in another. The use of a respirator to sustain a patient through a severe bout with a respiratory disease would be considered ordinary; its use to sustain the life of a severely brain damaged person in an irreversible coma would be considered extraordinary.

Contrasted with extraordinary treatment is ordinary treatment, the care a doctor would normally be expected to provide. Failure to provide ordinary care constitutes neglect, and can even be construed as the intentional infliction of harm, where there is a legal obligation to provide care. The importance of the ordinary/extraordinary care distinction lies partly in its connection to the doctor's intention. The withholding of extraordinary care should be seen as a decision not to inflict painful treatment on a patient without reasonable hope of success. The withholding of ordinary care, by contrast, must be seen as neglect. Thus, one doctor says, "We have to draw a distinction between ordinary and extraordinary means. We never withdraw what's needed to make a baby comfortable, we would never withdraw the care a parent would provide. We never kill a baby. . . . But we may decide certain heroic intervention is not worthwhile."

We should keep in mind the ordinary/extraordinary care distinction when considering an example given by both Tooley and Rachels to show the irrationality of the active/passive distinction with regard to infanticide. The example is this: a child is born with Down's syndrome and also has an intestinal obstruction which requires corrective surgery. If the surgery is not performed the infant will starve to death, since it cannot take food orally. This may take days or even weeks, as dehydration and infection set in. Commenting on this situation, Rachels says:

> I can understand why some people are opposed to all euthanasia, and insist that such infants must be allowed to live. I think I can also understand why other people favor destroying these babies quickly and painlessly. But why should anyone favor letting "dehydration and infection wither a tiny being over hours and days"? The doctrine that says that a baby may be allowed to dehydrate and wither, but may

not be given an injection that would end its life without suffering, seems so patently cruel as to require no further refutation.

Such a doctrine perhaps does not need further refutation; but this is not the AMA doctrine. For the AMA statement criticized by Rachels allows only for the cessation of extraordinary means to prolong life when death is imminent. Neither of these conditions is satisfied in this example. Death is not imminent in this situation, any more than it would be if a normal child had an attack of appendicitis. Neither the corrective surgery to remove the intestinal obstruction, nor the intravenous feeding required to keep the infant alive until such surgery is performed, can be regarded as extraordinary means, for neither is particularly expensive, nor does either place an overwhelming burden on the patient or others. (The continued existence of the child might be thought to place an overwhelming burden on its parents, but that has nothing to do with the characterization of the means to prolong its life as extraordinary. If it had, then *feeding* a severely defective child who required a great deal of care could be regarded as extraordinary.) The chances of success if the operation is undertaken are quite good, though there is always a risk in operating on infants. Though the Down's syndrome will not be alleviated, the child will proceed to an otherwise normal infancy.

It cannot be argued that the treatment is withheld for the infant's sake, unless one is prepared to argue that all mentally retarded babies are better off dead. This is particularly implausible in the case of Down's syndrome babies who generally do not suffer and are capable of giving and receiving love, of learning and playing, to varying degrees.

In a film on this subject entitled, "Who Should Survive?", a doctor defended a decision not to operate, saying that since the parents did not consent to the operation, the doctors' hands were tied. As we have seen, surgical intrusion requires consent, and in the case of infants, consent would normally come from the parents. But, as their legal guardians, parents are required to provide medical care for their children, and failure to do so can constitute criminal neglect or even homicide. In general, courts have been understandably reluctant to recognize a parental right to terminate life-prolonging treatment. Although prosecution is unlikely, physicians who comply with invalid instructions from the parents and permit the infant's death could be liable for aiding and abetting, failure to report child neglect, or even homicide. So it is not true that, in this situation, doctors are legally bound to do as the parents wish.

To sum up, I think that Rachels is right to regard the decision not to operate in the Down's syndrome example as the intentional termination of life. But there is no reason to believe that either the law or the AMA would regard it otherwise. Certainly the decision to withhold treatment is not justified by the AMA statement. That such infants have been allowed to die cannot be denied; but this, I think, is the result of doctors misunderstanding the law and the AMA position.

Withholding treatment in this case is the intentional termination of life because the infant is deliberately allowed to die; that is the point of not operating. But there are other cases in which that is not the point. If the point is to avoid inflicting painful treatment on a patient with little or no reasonable hope of success, this is not the intentional termination of life. The permissibility of such withholding of treatment, then, would have no implications for the permissibility of euthanasia, active or passive.

. . . Someone might say: Even if the withholding of treatment is not the intentional termination of life, does that make a difference, morally speaking? If life-prolonging treatment may be withheld, for the sake of the child, may not an easy death be provided, for the sake of the child, as well? The unoperated child with spina bifida may take months or even years to die. Distressed by the spectacle of children "lying around, waiting to die," one doctor has written, "It is time that society and medicine stopped perpetuating the fiction that withholding treatment is ethically different from terminating a life. It is time that society began to discuss mechanisms by which we can alleviate the pain and suffering for those individuals whom we cannot help."

I do not deny that there may be cases in which death is in the best interests of the patient. In such cases, a quick and painless death may be the best thing. However, I do not think that, once active or vigorous treatment is stopped, a quick death is always preferable to a lingering one. We must be cautious about attributing to defective children *our* distress at seeing them linger. Waiting for them to die may be tough on parents, doctors and nurses—it isn't necessarily tough on the child. The decision not to operate need not mean a decision to neglect, and it may be possible to make the remaining months of the child's life comfortable, pleasant and filled with love. If this alternative is possible, surely it is more decent and humane than killing the child. In such a situation, withholding treatment, foreseeing the child's death, is not ethically equivalent to killing the child, and we cannot move from the permissibility of the former to that of the latter. I am worried that there will be a tendency to do precisely that if active euthanasia is regarded as morally equivalent to the withholding of life-prolonging treatment.

PATRICIA MANN
Meanings of Death

PATRICIA MANN *is the author of* Micro-Politics: Agency in a Postfeminist Era *(1994).*

WE philosophers are always trying to get a grip on death, and always failing. Anthropologists and social historians are likely to do better than philosophers in their efforts to characterize death, insofar as they can investigate the many faces of death in different cultural contexts: Death in battle may be heroic; death in youth may be tragic; death in old age benign. In different times and different cultures death means very different things, as is clear when we read of suttee, the Hindu widow's immolation of herself on her husband's funeral pyre, or of seppuku, the suicidal disembowelling done by Japanese for infractions of honor.

Yet all these so-called meanings of death are more precisely identified as different social practices and associations surrounding death. Death itself is an event that exceeds our human capacity to wrest meaning from occurrences in the world. Strangely in our world and of it, death is also elusively yet absolutely not of our world. As when we speak of God, we speak of death in self-consciously metaphoric ways. We speak of a loved one's dying in terms of their "leaving us," "passing," or "passing away." But when we say they have left us, we mean only that they are no longer capable of interacting with us in daily physical interactions. We didn't really see them leave, and we have no real idea of where they have gone, even if we believe in heaven and the immortality of the soul. And they do not fully leave us, remaining present in our memories, or in books or letters they have written or in sweaters they have knitted or in projects they have begun for us to finish.

Similarly, when we say someone has passed away, we experience their physical absence, but we don't experience their actual passing to another place, whether to nothingness or some spiritual realm. The event of death is one that we only understand from the side of the living. A person who dies passes out of our culture, but it's not clear how they go, or where. We have no physical, temporal, or conceptual grasp upon where they are going, and so there is also no obvious border between our world and death. As Jacques Derrida remarks, "The crossing of a border always announces itself according to the movement of a certain step—and of the step that crosses a line. . . . Consequently, where the figure of the step is refused to intuition, where the identity or indivisibility of a line is compromised . . . the crossing of the line—becomes a *problem*." For this reason, Derrida designates the boundary that is death as an "aporia," a site of interminable confusion. So long as we live, we see only life and living, and so we speak necessarily with metaphors and elliptical partiality of our experience of another person's death and passage from life.

While it is impossible to speak about death as a destination in any literal sense, it might seem obvious that we can speak of it as a cessation of our human agency or efficacy in the world. From the perspective of materialism, we as human agents simply cease to exist. But what does that mean? It turns out that we also require metaphors to express an end of our worldly agency. To the Greek philosopher Epicurus, for example, death is a matter of ceasing to experience pleasure and pain; whereas Socrates in the *Apology* suggests that death may be a dreamless sleep. I am not sure these notions of a cessation of our human agency are any more imaginable, however, than is a deathly destination beyond life. I do not know what it would be to experience an end of pleasure and pain. And while I often fail to remember dreaming, it is only when I awake from sleep that I experience my dreamless sleep. I cannot imagine the dreamless sleep of death because I cannot imagine failing to wake up from sleep. Quite generally, I cannot understand the end of my experience, except as another experience. So these references to the end of my experience of agency leave me with a sense of interminable confusion, or in Derrida's terms, aporia.

The philosopher Emmanuel Levinas argues that Epicurus misunderstands the whole paradox of death, insofar as he "effaces our unique relationship with death," which involves precisely our inability as living agents to experience the nothingness of this future state. Levinas suggests that death announces itself in suffering, in "an experience of the passivity of the subject which until then had been active." But even this is not quite right, he points out, insofar as a subject who experiences passivity still experiences the alternative possibility of initiative and activity. So finally, he posits, "the unknown of death signifies that the [subject] . . . is in relationship with mystery." In fact, Levinas's philosophical project involves emphasizing the radical alterity or mystery of other persons. So, the almost tangible mystery of death provides a metaphoric pathway to the otherness or mystery of other persons.

For Martin Heidegger, on the other hand, death provides a unique possibility for self-conscious reflection upon one's individual life. According to Heidegger, a human subject (Dasein) exists fundamentally as a "potentiality-for-Being" in the world. "It is essential to the basic constitution of Dasein that there is constantly something still to be settled . . . something still outstanding in one's potentiality-for-Being." In death, of course, our human potentiality comes to an abrupt and absolute end. In anticipating death, or Being-towards-death, Heidegger believes we discover in a primordial way our potentiality-for-Being, insofar as we attempt to

imagine an end of our potentiality. In anticipating death, we must imagine an impossible wholeness of Dasein insofar as nothing is left outstanding; we imagine a heady freedom from human entanglements insofar as nothing remains to be settled. Death, Heidegger emphasizes, is the only worldly phenomenon which is nonrelational, and so very much our own, our "ownmost possibility." So, in properly confronting the fact that we will die, we have access to a more authentic knowledge of ourselves as individuals.

Both Levinas and Heidegger offer accounts of our living agency in relation to dying. Dying itself remains beyond. Death for these philosophers illuminates aspects of living, but they have no more access to death itself than do non-philosophers. And so it seems that they can tell us little about our relationship to death when we are actually dying. Philosophers are limited by their commitment to the articulable; insofar as death is finally an inarticulable aspect of experience, they have no obvious recommendations about how we should reckon with dying.

Religions and other self-consciously spiritual narratives offer a more literal relationship with death, insofar as they see death as a continuation of life. Or rather, not seeing at all, they counsel faith that death is a continuation of life. In positing an immortal soul, religions within the Judeo-Christian tradition, for example, offer various narratives of how our human agency can, in some mysterious sense, continue after death. These narratives counsel both a responsibility to live well prior to death, and then when death beckons, a responsibility to die well, in God's hands. Insofar as these narratives require faith in God and an afterlife, they posit a culture on either side of the border of death, to utilize one of Derrida's metaphors. Religions offer comfort in the face of death insofar as they accept our human inability to imagine our own end, and offer a narrative of how life continues after death. Religions prepare us to face death by denying its most fearful and unimaginable implications, an absolute end to our human agency.

Philosophers and theologians, alike, in our Western cultural tradition have assumed that people will have a passive relationship with their own deaths, dying of natural causes or perhaps at the hands of another in battle. While not unthinkable, suicide has remained an exceptional, highly dramatic personal statement. With recent proposals that we legalize assisted suicide, we must envision the normalization of a very much more active relationship with our own deaths. Given the inarticulability of the experience of death, we may wonder what it will mean for individuals to actively choose it.

Given Heidegger and Levinas's belief that death illuminates aspects of our life prior to death, we may ask how proposals for legalizing assisted suicide illuminate the lives we are leading today prior to death. While I am not opposed to legalizing assisted suicide, I believe that we have not yet begun to grapple with important social implications of such a policy decision. Advocates of assisted suicide currently emphasize the value of an autonomous choice at the end of one's life, while opponents are concerned with categories of individuals—the poor, the disabled, minorities—who may be coerced rather than autonomous in their "choice" of assisted suicide. By contrast, I will suggest that the very notion of an autonomous choice at the end of one's life is problematic and misleading. We need a more complicated framework for evaluating the agency of dying individuals today, as well as for tracking changes in agency if assisted suicide becomes an option.

The much debated issue of assisted suicide corresponds with a rather paradoxical social situation in our late twentieth century. On the one hand, a combination of social and technological forces have combined to give individuals an unprecedented sense of control over their physical narratives. When we are hungry we may nonchalantly satisfy our hunger with fruits from Peru or condiments from India. When it becomes very hot, we move from one air conditioned environment to another. When we experience allergies, we take medications that eliminate our symptoms. We utilize contraception of various sorts so that sexual interactions cease to be organically related to reproduction. When a hip, knee, or shoulder joint fails, we replace it. We even replace such basic organs as kidneys and hearts. It seems consistent with this extraordinary level of control over our physical options that we would also exercise greater control over the time and place of our death. It is in this spirit that six contemporary moral philosophers have referred to an individual's death as "the final act of life's drama," in a recent amici curiae brief submitted to the Supreme Court in support of a constitutional right to assisted suicide.

On the other hand, many people are discovering that it can be difficult to retain any sense at all of personal control over the end of one's life within a high-powered medical context. Medical technology has developed amazing resources for dealing with the failure of various bodily functions and organs; and the institutional commitment to life-saving treatment of the medically ill tends to move into high gear as patients become sicker and nearer death. The medical technology for curing bodily ills is on a continuum with the technology for extending life through deferring systemic bodily failures. A high-minded medical commitment to preserving individual lives can sometimes today lead to a tortuous standoff between powerful medical technologies capable of deferring immediate death and a bodily self whose physical resources have dwindled to the point where the continuation of life seems futile. Yet the dying individual may experience herself as caught up in a force field of medical technology, and she may be frustrated in efforts to extricate herself. Indeed, she may experience intolerable pain and seek help in dying more quickly, to no avail. As legal philosopher Ronald Dworkin declares, these are situations we all dread today, and he believes that individuals require the right to assisted suicide in order to properly exercise self-determination in the face of a medical establishment which often seems implacably and impersonally committed to the extension of life.

As one of the foremost public intellectuals addressing this issue today, Ronald Dworkin brings the philosophical resources of our liberal democratic tradition to bear on this problem in a clear, incisive manner in his book *Life's Dominion*. Assisted suicide involves an effort to restore to individuals a conscious relationship to their own process of dying and death. Assisted suicide is defended as an extension of the individual autonomy or self-determination we seek to enact throughout our lives. As Dworkin explains it, we act in the course of our lives in response to various convictions about what makes life worth living, and these convictions about how to live tend to color our views about when and how we should die. An aggressive medical establishment may treat our bodily ills while disregarding these personal views about how and when we should die. Our sense of personal autonomy may be compromised in such instances, and assisted suicide is proposed as a means of restoring a sense of control to individuals nearing the end of their life. It is thus envisioned as a logical extension of our individual freedom to pursue our lives as we please, so long as we do not harm others. Poignantly, if also a little oddly, assisted suicide is viewed as a way of making our individual death a meaningful concluding act in our own individual life.

In the Philosophers' Brief, Dworkin joins with five other contemporary moral philosophers to argue that assisted suicide should be added to the list of controversial personal decisions protected by the Fourteenth Amendment's due process clause. Over the last thirty years, the Supreme Court has concluded that a number of socially contested personal decisions (from contraception and abortion to the right to request removal of a feeding tube) are constitutionally protected as aspects of the "ordered liberty" mentioned in the due process clause.

The Supreme Court very recently responded to this and other arguments by ruling that there are not currently sufficient grounds to conclude that such a constitutional right to assisted suicide exists. But while they did not deny the right of states to make assisted suicide illegal, they also did not prohibit states from legalizing it. Oregon voters approved an assisted suicide policy by referendum in 1994, but it never went into effect due to constitutional challenges upheld by

a federal court. Oregon voted again on an assisted suicide referendum in November 1997, rejecting a repeal measure. We may be sure that "the earnest and profound debate on the morality, legality, and practicality of physician-assisted suicide" encouraged by Justice Rehnquist and others in the recent Supreme Court decisions will take place over the next few years in many state legislatures and popular referenda. It is appropriate to consider the philosophical adequacy of arguments for and against the legalization of assisted suicide at this point.

Many theorists have pointed out dangers in legalizing assisted suicide, as effectively giving a social sanction to a form of killing people. Instead of enhancing individual autonomy, such a policy might result in various pressures for particular sorts of people to "choose" to die. While these results are not intended by the proponents of assisted suicide, philosopher Richard Doerflinger maintains that they are inherent in the policy. The idea is that once assisted suicide becomes a legal option, individuals who are very sick or very old will become vulnerable to various sorts of pressures by those caring for them. Those with limited economic resources may feel great pressure from either healthcare organizations or from relatives to simply call it quits, insofar as efforts to preserve their life and care for them are likely to be very expensive. Even those with substantial economic resources may feel pressure from families to free them from the psychologically draining aspects of tending a dying person. In addition, the families of wealthy patients may be impatient to claim their portions of the patient's estate. For a variety of reasons then, there are grounds to fear that laws intended to increase the autonomy of individuals at the end of their lives may, in fact, make them vulnerable to new forms of social coercion.

Proponents of assisted suicide respond to these concerns by arguing that legal safeguards are capable of protecting dying individuals from these pressures. Indeed, Ronald Dworkin makes a persuasive case that laws allowing assisted suicide can be written so as to include various features encouraging other sorts of patient options that are often in short supply today. Improved forms of pain control and hospice care can be mandated as legal alternatives to assisted suicide, and may thereby become more available than they currently are.

Yet it is not clear why laws encouraging various sorts of ameliorative care at the end of life should be linked with laws allowing assisted suicide. It will be beneficial if the debate over assisted suicide promotes greater patient welfare by encouraging greater attention to various sorts of ameliorative care at the end of life. But one would hope that improved forms of pain control as well as hospice facilities will become available regardless of policy decisions about assisted suicide. Moreover, one suspects that the mere existence of palliative care and pain medication does not really address what Richard Doerflinger has referred to as the "loose cannon" social consequences of legalizing assisted suicide, although it is difficult to articulate these consequences within a paradigm of patient autonomy.

I assigned Ronald Dworkin's *Life's Dominion* in an upper-level philosophy seminar recently, and it inspired some very interesting discussions. Indeed, as we analyzed Dworkin's very reasonable examination of how and why individuals might want to bring their life to a close through assisted suicide, Heather, one of my students, burst into tears, saying, "It just doesn't work like that." Her grandmother had died recently, and Heather was certain, in a way that she could not articulate, that there was something very much missing from Dworkin's apparently judicious discussion of individual choices at the end of one's life.

As we addressed Heather's experience, as well as the experiences of other students in the class, what was missing from Dworkin's analysis became more evident. Dworkin's defense of assisted suicide refers exclusively to issues of the individual patient's agency at the end of his or her life. In the context of the autonomy framework, the agency of others, whether family or doctors, is seen only as a potential problem insofar as it threatens to impinge upon the sick individual's agency.

However, as we discussed situations of death and dying in the context of our own families and friends, we noticed a rather more complicated and dynamic quality of interpersonal agency in these situations. In fact, little about a dying person's situation supports a sense of their autonomy, in any but the most formal sense. A dying person's sense of agency is fundamentally bound up with their relationships to other family members or friends. Perhaps a dying woman wants to remain alive long enough to see a grandchild graduate. Or perhaps she has come to a point where she cannot accept being a burden on family and friends any longer. In addition, the wishes of family and friends inevitably affect the dying person's sense of their own agency. A spouse's desire that the dying person continue to live may be an overriding concern. By contrast, the recent death of a spouse may mean that the patient feels little further reason to live. All these relationships, and many more, impact immediately and inevitably on a sick person's agency in the face of death.

The discussion of assisted suicide has centered on notions of individual autonomy and self-determination, as the values ideally characterizing an individual's decision to seek an end of his or her life. And criticisms of assisted suicide have focussed on social and political reasons why various groups of people—the poor, the disabled, minorities—are not likely to be allowed to exercise an autonomous choice. I want to suggest that the whole notion of an autonomous choice at the end of one's life is problematic and misleading. I believe that we need a richer framework for understanding the agency of dying individuals. . . .

Because of our idealization of individual autonomy as a basic perspective of liberal individualism, we rarely notice the complex social motivations of individual actions. But end-of-life situations provide a particularly powerful demonstration of the inadequacy of self-referential notions of individual agency and the need for a more socially nuanced conception of individual actions and choices. . . .

. . . A politics of liberal individualism highlights the value of autonomy, or lack of interference from others, insofar as our desiring agency, our individual appetites and desires, are likely to place us in conflict with others. . . .

. . . But in order to fully comprehend individual agency, we must recognize the three potential dimensions of any individual action. Individual agency may be comprised of self-referential desires, of other-directed feelings of responsibility, as well as by expectations of recognition and reward that are directed toward others while also referring to oneself. One is empowered when one has agency involving all three dimensions. But, quite typically, these dimensions are distributed among different individuals within a situation, often in accord with prevailing power relations. We care about the desires of the dominant person, and we offer them recognition and rewards. The subordinate person's agency, by contrast, involves primarily the dimension of responsibility. Servants, slaves, minimum wage workers, women in traditional roles may have important duties and responsibilities, but they receive relatively little recognition and reward for them, and people rarely inquire after their desires.

An important consequence of this distribution of the dimensions of agency is that we can only understand the agency of particular individuals insofar as we understand their relationships with other individuals. The binary opposition of self and other . . . no longer makes sense; each of the dimensions of agency are about self-other relations in constitutive but different ways. Whether we act out of desires, or out of a sense of responsibility, or with an expectation of recognition and reward, we are acting in relation to relevant others. Autonomy, understood as freedom from interference of others, ceases to be a meaningful value, insofar as it ignores the fabric of relationships, good and bad, within which our actions necessarily occur. (We could, of course, still use a notion of autonomy to refer to situations in which we were free from overt forms of physical or mental coercion. But we would have to be very careful not to let this slip back into a vision of being free from the influence of others.)

My three-dimensional social theory of agency relations allows us to discuss the situation of sick or dying individuals in terms of the various relationships that affect their senses of living and dying. And it enables us to consider how these relationships will be affected by legalizing assisted suicide.

We may begin by reassessing the end-of-life situation that, as Ronald Dworkin points out, many people most dread. Suppose we become very ill, perhaps unto death, and we are in the care of a highly respected doctor at a major medical institution. The agency of this doctor is quite clear. Everything in her medical training and practice promote in her a strong desire, compounded by a sense of medical duty via the Hippocratic oath, to find a method of returning us to health. Moreover, her recognition and rewards in the world of medicine are based upon her reputation for overcoming the forces of disease and physical decline. The hospital stands behind her in this. The agency of our doctor is well-defined in terms of her commitment to the care and maintenance of life.

As a patient, we are often less certain of our goals, and almost always less certain of how to go about achieving them. As we experience bodily decline, it is common to be ambivalent and confused about our own desires. And even if we have a firm commitment either to fighting for life to the very end, or alternatively, a commitment to die with dignity while we still have all of our faculties about us, we are likely to require a great deal of help in accomplishing either goal. We also may have a strong sense of responsibility, quite apart from our desires, to either continue living, or to die as rapidly as possible. But here, too, we may be conflicted, and we will require aid in accomplishing our goals. Expectations of recognition and reward may add to our sense of anxiety and ambivalence. We may be horrified at the thought of losing our mental and physical capacities and being remembered in that way. We may thus desire to die as quickly as possible, but at the same time we may not want to be remembered as having made the cowardly choice of killing ourselves. There is no end to our possible conflicts about living and dying at this stage of our lives.

Our physical situation makes us extremely dependent upon others, in a society in which dependency is not recognized as a basic and constant human reality. Only children are acknowledged as legitimately dependent, and so we may feel like children when we are ill. Our society also emphasizes the value of having clearly articulated goals, on a daily as well as longer-range basis. But with death approaching, we must establish a very different sort of relationship with our future. As Levinas observed, our relationship to death is a relationship with mystery. And as Derrida said, death is fundamentally confusing and paradoxical. Our sense of being out of control at the end of our life has as much to do with our extreme dependency and with our sense of uncertainty in relation to the approach of our death as it does with an aggressive medical establishment denying our wishes.

The potential appeal of assisted suicide to dying individuals in our society is almost too clear. As a dying person, we are, as Levinas pointed out, experiencing a final form of passivity. Our agency is waning, objectively and painfully. We confront mystery, uncertainty, aporia. Yet our culture teaches us that mature adults are supposed to struggle against all forms of uncertainty and dependency. Accordingly, in choosing suicide, we marshall our waning powers aggressively in order to put an end to uncertainty and dependency in the only way possible. We may congratulate ourselves upon seizing back, not just from an overwhelming medical establishment, but from God him- or herself, the power of death. We refuse the fundamental and continuing fact of human potentiality and hope in order to control the moment and the site of our final breaths of life. As Heidegger would point out, however, we seek to create a final act which we can never experience as a final act, insofar as our human subjectivity ends when its potentiality ends.

Let's examine the other agency relations surrounding such a death. In the first place, if we are asking assistance in this suicide, there is at least one medical doctor involved. If assisted suicide becomes legal, some doctors will no doubt assert their continuing commitment to the Hippocratic oath and refuse to participate in it. But many doctors will adjust their practices, and gradually their values, as well. Initially, some will simply desire to help patients in this final act, and some will feel it part of their medical responsibility to do so, regardless of their personal desires. Insofar as assisted suicide is a cost-efficient means of death, doctors are also likely to be rewarded by healthcare companies for participating in it. As institutional expectations and rewards increasingly favor assisted suicide, expectations and rewards within the medical profession itself will gradually shift to reflect this. Medical students will learn about assisted suicide as an important patient option from the beginning of their training. We may expect that a growing proportion of doctors will find themselves sympathetic to this practice, and will find themselves comfortable with recommending it to their patients.

Families will also be affected by the legalization of assisted suicide. Familial agency in the context of a dying loved one is likely to be as confused and conflicted as that of the patient. Family members may want a loved one to remain alive as long as possible, while also harboring secret desires to be done with this painful process. Many people today are ashamed of such secret desires, regarding the very thought of hastening a loved one's death as wrongful and blameworthy. But if assisted suicide becomes legal, such desires will cease to be wrongful in such an obvious way. If patients themselves may decide to put an end to this painful process of dying, then it is not blameworthy for relatives of such a patient to inquire whether he or she may be thinking along these lines, and to offer sympathetic support for the idea.

As dying individuals begin to articulate their desires to be done with the painful process of suffering and decline, relatives will participate in the dialogue, adding their own perspectives on the option of assisted suicide. They may quite reasonably desire to get on with their lives, and in this new context of considering assisted suicide, they may experience these desires more strongly. Where they once felt great responsibility to put up with the pains and inconveniences of an extended process of dying, they may no longer feel it necessary to hide their impatience with the process. And they may even find themselves emphasizing their competing responsibilities to healthy children and spouses. Where they would once have felt ashamed to feel these things, and may even now be surprised to hear themselves saying them, they may come to feel free to have them recognized. Once assisted suicide ceases to be illegal, its many advantages to busy relatives will become readily apparent. More than merely an acceptable form of ending, relatives and friends may come to see it as a preferred or praiseworthy form of death. They will become comfortable with considering the merits of assisted suicide in relation to their loved ones because it will be designated a socially good end.

Managed-care organizations will also be involved. If dying sooner is more cost-efficient, their profit-based concerns will make them prefer patients to choose assisted suicide, and their sense of responsibility to shareholders will reinforce this preference. Economic interests may still seem crass in relation to dying patients, and yet we are already accustomed to recognizing them in the context of treatment, as well as in all other contexts of daily life. When we legalize assisted suicide, it too becomes a part of daily life. Everyone is allowed to have and to express their own interests in relation to acts of assisted suicide, once it is viewed as an accepted patient alternative, as an established, approved ending.

The appeal of assisted suicide to relatives and friends and to healthcare organizations is easy to comprehend. In legalizing assisted suicide, we will be legalizing a method of death which will be very much more convenient as well as more cost-effective than current methods of dying. In our society, where almost everyone is pressed for time, and many are pressed for money, individual notions of agency and the fabric of social agency relations may evolve very quickly to reflect its conveniences and cost efficiency. The agency of medical doctors is likely to remain more conflicted, insofar as healing remains their primary role. Many doctors may find it difficult to change hats and aid people in dying. But as doctors come to be employed primarily by managed-care organizations, they will inevitably come to reflect the efficiency concerns of their employers.

Now let us consider the dynamic fabric of agency relations surrounding a dying person in a society where assisted suicide has become an accepted practice. Patients may still have the legal right to exercise options for aggressive treatment, or for transferral to a hospice, as well as for assisted suicide. But those who are dying will be aware—sometimes keenly, sometimes dimly—of the wishes of their family and friends, their doctors and managed care organizations, as well as the general cultural expectations for one in their circumstances. Some relatives may speak frankly and not necessarily unkindly about their burdensome work or family obligations and their inability to devote much more time to caring for the ill person. They may gently propose assisted suicide as the best solution for everyone at this point (as children today sometimes gently propose to elderly parents that it would be appropriate to enter a nursing home). Other relatives may say they desire the patient to live as long as possible, while at the same time making clear that they deem it the responsibility of the patient to choose assisted suicide to relieve them of this ordeal of dying. It will be legitimate for families to have and express these feelings.

Some doctors may enthusiastically recommend assisted suicide in a variety of circumstances, while others may evince desires to keep fighting for the patient's life. All, however, will be operating within a framework of managed care organizations' holding medical doctors responsible for making reasonable decisions about when to encourage the patient to give up. Healthcare providers will surely create guidelines and rules about when it ceases to be rational to treat illnesses, and when hospice care or assisted suicide become the appropriate choices. Of course, wealthy patients will retain the right to pay for further aggressive care, and rules designating the limits of rational treatment will be most stringent in the health plans of the most impoverished.

Assisted suicide will offer all patients a way to escape overwhelming and unpleasant feelings of dependency and uncertainty as they experience serious bodily and, perhaps, mental decline. And the undeniable convenience of avoiding a lingering, painful, indeterminate period of dying will have great advantages for the friends and relatives of almost everyone. In a society where an ever larger portion of our population is becoming elderly, the cost efficiency of cutting short a potentially extended process of dying is readily apparent and desirable. A lingering death may come to seem an extravagance, a frivolous indulgence. If you doubt that our views on death could change so rapidly, remember, or try to remember, how strong the expectations were for even highly educated women to become fulltime homemakers during the '50s and '60s. And consider how rapidly we have come to consider it somewhat indulgent and eccentric for such a woman to decide today to give up work and remain at home fulltime caring for her children and house. We can be relatively certain that our views of dying will change quite radically if and when assisted suicide is legalized. . . .

I have suggested the inadequacy of the philosophical framework currently taken as the basis for discussing the advantages as well as the dangers of legalizing assisted suicide. I do not believe that individual autonomy is any sort of possibility for dying patients, regardless of the social policies that surround death in a society, insofar as our individual agency in this situation is necessarily intertwined with that of various relevant others. I do acknowledge that an ideal of autonomy and a fear of its opposite, dependency, play a large role in the current debate about assisted suicide. But rather than misrepresenting the capabilities of a policy of assisted suicide to guarantee autonomy, I believe we need to confront the qualities of dependency and relatedness that are inevitable in this situation. By means of my three-dimensional theory of agency relations, I

have attempted to show the dynamic ways in which we will all be likely to adjust to the option of assisted suicide as a preferred end-of-life option. My theory of social agency relations does not deny individual choice; rather it explains the qualitative complexity of individual choice, as well as its dynamic social process of evolving. . . .

In legalizing assisted suicide, we will be ushering in a whole new set of relationships between dying individuals and their friends, relatives, and healthcare providers. Various end-of-life rituals may develop around this new process of dying. Surely the ultimate mystery surrounding death will remain; the abyss between life and death will not be altered by our new practices of assisted suicide. But insofar as we accept assisted suicide, we will believe that there is a moment when the element of hope and potentiality that philosophers identify with human life is properly extinguished by those who might continue to live with hope and potentiality somewhat longer.

My analysis does not indicate whether assisted suicide is an appropriate social option at this time within our culture. As the elderly make up a growing proportion of our populace, the costs and inconveniences of the dying process are already growing astronomically. Assisted suicide is a very efficient way of dying. Perhaps the Supreme Court will reverse its recent holding in *Washington v. Glucksberg* and find it a constitutionally sanctioned liberty interest within the next few years. If so, assisted suicide may become a ubiquitous form of death within the next quarter of a century. That may be a good thing, or it may not. Insofar as it is clear that our agency relations with relatives, friends, medical caregivers, and institutional providers will be transformed, it will be important to evaluate the quality of the new relationships, something I cannot do here. What I hope to have done, however, is shift the grounds of evaluation away from an illusory goal of autonomy, and towards the new social relations that will develop if we legalize assisted suicide.

CHAPTER TWELVE

How Should I Respond to War or Terrorism?

Since the Civil War in the mid-nineteenth century, North Americans have never had to fight a war on their own soil. Despite our successful involvement in two World Wars, a forty year "cold war" with the Soviet Union, and numerous incursions into various "trouble spots" around the globe (for instance, the Philippines at the turn of the last century, Vietnam and Iraq more recently), North Americans have been spared the anxiety, devastation and trauma of living in the midst of war.

In addition, much of the world has suffered and struggled with sporadic terrorism, and some parts with sustained and systematic terrorism (for instance, by both sides in Northern Ireland, by the Basque Liberation Front in Spain, and by the Hutus in Rwanda). While there have been occasional terrorist attacks within the United States, they have been viewed as the isolated work of foreigners or crackpots. But on September 11, 2001, that changed, and the shock was so great that it was widely agreed (at least in the United States) that "the world has changed forever." Whether or not history will bear this out, or whether Americans just got a taste of the horror that many of the world's people have lived through for much of their lives, it is clear that we all now face an important set of questions to which we were blissfully oblivious before. How should we think about terrorism? Who is a terrorist? How do we deal with terrorism? And behind these questions is a very old set of questions, which Americans like everyone else have had to deal with from time to time: How should we think about war? When is it worth the cost in terms of trauma and death to fight a war? Is there such a thing as a "just war" or are all wars immoral and unjustified because of the horrendous human cost?

In the ancient world, perhaps, such questions were not so prevalent. Aggressive nations waged wars in their own self-interest, and the nations attacked were forced to fight for their own survival. Pacifism, insofar as it was an acknowledged view at all, was clearly marginal. But with the advent of Christianity and some other world religions (notably Buddhism), the question whether war was ever right and justifiable moved to center stage. The founder of Christianity, in particular, taught that one should "turn the other cheek," and violence was to be avoided. But it was not as if the Christian church was immune from either the dangers of being attacked by others or the temptations of war, and so there was an essential conflict between the desirability of pacifism on the one hand and the necessity of violence on the other. Saint Thomas Aquinas, a respected spokesman for the Catholic Church in the thirteenth century at a time when it was a hugely powerful political institution, formulated his conception of a "just war" in relation to this tension. According to him, a just war is one whose cause could be defended even against a background of pacifism. Determining whether a war is just, however, is not a straightforward process, so it is no surprise that the concept of a just war remains a highly contentious one. It was hotly debated, for example, during the American involvement in Vietnam, and it is being hotly debated again regarding American involvement in the Middle East.

When is military action warranted? Sometimes this is understood as a question of means: for example, when a country considers how long it should hold out for a diplomatic solution to a conflict. Sometimes, it is understood as a question of prudence: for example, when a country considers the risks and costs involved in military action given its limited resources. But to ask whether military action is warranted can also be a fundamentally ethical question. Even if victory could be quick and inexpensive (which is rarely the case), would it be *right* to go to war? That is the question that must be faced by the citizens of what is now the most powerful nation in the world.

But September 11 drove home another, even more complex set of questions. War is straightforward in one sense: it involves a more or less direct confrontation between or among nations. We say "more or less" because some wars are fought "by proxy." The United States never waged war against the Soviet Union directly but it did wage war against nations that it took to be under the same umbrella of communism as the Soviet Union. That is what happened in the case of Vietnam, which was also complicated by the fact that war was never officially declared and thus lacked the legal status that so clearly defined the combatants in World War II. This new war, the "War on Terror," lacks not only the legal status of a declaration of war but a clear opponent. There is no nation with which we are at war, and terrorists can now be found in virtually every corner of the globe and in every society, including in our own. What's more, wars are usually fought and won or lost with the surrender of one side or the other, even if they last thirty or a hundred years. But there is no one to surrender in the war against terrorism, nor is it at all likely that the religious conflicts and miserable living conditions that spawn terrorism around the world will soon be resolved. Thus, we are confronted with a new set of ethical questions. How much should a free society compromise its commitments to the freedom of its citizens for the sake of routing out terrorism? When is a nation justified in attacking or otherwise interfering with the sovereignty of another nation when terrorists have made their home there? What counts as "sponsorship" of terrorism by a state (when, presumably, there are few provable links between the terrorists and the state)? And to what extent is the War on Terrorism a preventative war and to what extent is it taking revenge for past terrorist actions? These are difficult but now unavoidable questions.

The following readings begin with Saint Thomas Aquinas on the idea of a "Just War" and Hannah Arendt, who discusses the important distinctions between "power, strength, force, authority, and violence" (the words indicating "the means by which man rules over man") from her *On Violence* (1970). Then there is President George W. Bush's "Address to the Nation" on the evening of September 11th, expressing the nation's outrage and initiating the War on Terrorism. In "The Experiments of Gandhi," John Dear discusses the strategy of nonviolence adopted by the great Indian leader Mahatma Gandhi and later adapted to the civil rights movement by Martin Luther King, Jr. Richard Falk, who is well-known for his long rejection of military solutions to political problems, expresses his misgivings about the pacifist position. Richard Deats, a member of the Fellowship of Reconciliation, warns that "In War Truth Is the First Casualty." War and terrorism involve more than killing. Claudia Card unpacks the meaning of a "war" on terrorism by exploring the relationship between terrorist acts and domestic battering. Finally, Mumia Abu-Jamal considers the question "who is a terrorist?" and suggests that this question does not always have a clear answer.

SAINT THOMAS AQUINAS

Whether It Is Always Sinful to Wage War

SAINT THOMAS AQUINAS *(1225–1274) was the most influential Christian thinker of medieval Europe. He was born in Italy and spent much of his life teaching in Paris. Because Christianity was from its inception a largely pacifist religion and war was considered sinful, the question of when to use violence was always a difficult and important question. In the following excerpt, Aquinas gives us what has become one of the most influential answers to the question of what constitutes a "just war."*

OBJECTION 1: It would seem that it is always sinful to wage war. Because punishment is not inflicted except for sin. Now those who wage war are threatened by Our Lord with punishment, according to Mt. 26:52: "All that take the sword shall perish with the sword." Therefore all wars are unlawful.

Objection 2: Further, whatever is contrary to a Divine precept is a sin. But war is contrary to a Divine precept, for it is written (Mt. 5:39): "But I say to you not to resist evil"; and (Rm. 12:19): "Not revenging yourselves, my dearly beloved, but give place unto wrath." Therefore war is always sinful.

Objection 3: Further, nothing, except sin, is contrary to an act of virtue. But war is contrary to peace. Therefore war is always a sin.

Objection 4: Further, the exercise of a lawful thing is itself lawful, as is evident in scientific exercises. But warlike exercises which take place in tournaments are forbidden by the Church, since those who are slain in these trials are deprived of ecclesiastical burial. Therefore it seems that war is a sin in itself.

On the contrary, Augustine says in a sermon on the son of the centurion [*Ep. ad Marcel. cxxxviii]: "If the Christian Religion forbade war altogether, those who sought salutary advice in the Gospel would rather have been counseled to cast aside their arms, and to give up soldiering altogether. On the contrary, they were told: 'Do violence to no man . . . and be content with your pay' [*Lk. 3:14]. If he commanded them to be content with their pay, he did not forbid soldiering."

I answer that, In order for a war to be just, three things are necessary.

First, the authority of the sovereign by whose command the war is to be waged. For it is not the business of a private individual to declare war, because he can seek for redress of his rights from the tribunal of his superior. Moreover it is not the business of a private individual to summon together the people, which has to be done in wartime. And as the care of the common weal is committed to those who are in authority, it is their business to watch over the common weal of the city, kingdom or province subject to them. And just as it is lawful for them to have recourse to the sword in defending that common weal against internal disturbances, when they punish evil-doers, according to the words of the Apostle (Rm. 13:4): "He beareth not the sword in vain: for he is God's minister, an avenger to execute wrath upon him that doth evil"; so too, it is their business to have recourse to the sword of war in defending the common weal against external enemies. Hence it is said to those who are in authority (Ps. 81:4): "Rescue the poor: and deliver the needy out of the hand of the sinner"; and for this reason Augustine says (Contra

Aquinas, Saint Thomas, "Whether It Is Always Sinful to Wage War," from "The Just War."

Faust. xxii, 75): "The natural order conducive to peace among mortals demands that the power to declare and counsel war should be in the hands of those who hold the supreme authority."

Secondly, a just cause is required, namely that those who are attacked, should be attacked because they deserve it on account of some fault. Wherefore Augustine says (Questions. in Hept., qu. x, super Jos.): "A just war is wont to be described as one that avenges wrongs, when a nation or state has to be punished, for refusing to make amends for the wrongs inflicted by its subjects, or to restore what it has seized unjustly."

Thirdly, it is necessary that the belligerents should have a rightful intention, so that they intend the advancement of good, or the avoidance of evil. Hence Augustine says (De Verb. Dom. [*The words quoted are to be found not in St. Augustine's works, but Can. Apud. Caus. xxiii, qu. 1]): "True religion looks upon as peaceful those wars that are waged not for motives of aggrandizement, or cruelty, but with the object of securing peace, of punishing evil-doers, and of uplifting the good." For it may happen that the war is declared by the legitimate authority, and for a just cause, and yet be rendered unlawful through a wicked intention. Hence Augustine says (Contra Faust. xxii, 74): "The passion for inflicting harm, the cruel thirst for vengeance, an unpacific and relentless spirit, the fever of revolt, the lust of power, and such like things, all these are rightly condemned in war."

Reply to Objection 1: As Augustine says (Contra Faust. xxii, 70): "To take the sword is to arm oneself in order to take the life of anyone, without the command or permission of superior or lawful authority." On the other hand, to have recourse to the sword (as a private person) by the authority of the sovereign or judge, or (as a public person) through zeal for justice, and by the authority, so to speak, of God, is not to "take the sword," but to use it as commissioned by another, wherefore it does not deserve punishment. And yet even those who make sinful use of the sword are not always slain with the sword, yet they always perish with their own sword, because, unless they repent, they are punished eternally for their sinful use of the sword.

Reply to Objection 2: Such like precepts, as Augustine observes (De Serm. Dom. in Monte i, 19), should always be borne in readiness of mind, so that we be ready to obey them, and, if necessary, to refrain from resistance or self-defense. Nevertheless it is necessary sometimes for a man to act otherwise for the common good, or for the good of those with whom he is fighting. Hence Augustine says (Ep. ad Marcellin. cxxxviii): "Those whom we have to punish with a kindly severity, it is necessary to handle in many ways against their will. For when we are stripping a man of the lawlessness of sin, it is good for him to be vanquished, since nothing is more hopeless than the happiness of sinners, whence arises a guilty impunity, and an evil will, like an internal enemy."

Reply to Objection 3: Those who wage war justly aim at peace, and so they are not opposed to peace, except to the evil peace, which Our Lord "came not to send upon earth" (Mt. 10:34). Hence Augustine says (Ep. ad Bonif. clxxxix): "We do not seek peace in order to be at war, but we go to war that we may have peace. Be peaceful, therefore, in warring, so that you may vanquish those whom you war against, and bring them to the prosperity of peace."

Reply to Objection 4: Manly exercises in warlike feats of arms are not all forbidden, but those which are inordinate and perilous, and end in slaying or plundering. In olden times warlike exercises presented no such danger, and hence they were called "exercises of arms" or "bloodless wars," as Jerome states in an epistle.

HANNAH ARENDT
Power and Violence

HANNAH ARENDT *(1906–1975) was one of the most important political philosophers of the twentieth century. To escape Nazi persecution, she came to the United States from Germany in 1941. Active in intellectual life, she wrote a number of highly influential books, among them* The Origins of Totalitarianism *(1951),* On Revolution *(1963),* Eichmann in Jerusalem *(1963), and* On Violence *(1970), from which this selection is taken.*

IT is, I think, a rather sad reflection on the present state of political science that our terminology does not distinguish among such key words as "power," "strength," "force," "authority," and, finally, "violence"—all of which refer to distinct, different phenomena and would hardly exist unless they did. To use them as synonyms not only indicates a certain deafness to linguistic meanings, which would be serious enough, but it has also resulted in a kind of blindness to the realities they correspond to. In such a situation it is always tempting to introduce new definitions, but—though I shall briefly yield to temptation—what is involved is not simply a matter of careless speech. Behind the apparent confusion is a firm conviction in whose light all distinctions would be, at best, of minor importance: the conviction that the most crucial political issue is, and always has been, the question of Who rules Whom? Power, strength, force, authority, violence—these are but words to indicate the means by which man rules over man; they are held to be synonyms because they have the same function. It is only after one ceases to reduce public affairs to the business of dominion that the original data in the realm of human affairs will appear, or, rather, reappear, in their authentic diversity.

These data, in our context, may be enumerated as follows:

Power corresponds to the human ability not just to act but to act in concert. Power is never the property of an individual; it belongs to a group and remains in existence only so long as the group keeps together. When we say of somebody that he is "in power" we actually refer to his being empowered by a certain number of people to act in their name. The moment the group, from which the power originated to begin with, disappears, "his power" also vanishes. In current usage, when we speak of a "powerful man" or a "powerful personality," we already use the word "power" metaphorically; what we refer to without metaphor is "strength."

Strength unequivocally designates something in the singular, an individual entity; it is the property inherent in an object or person and belongs to its character, which may prove itself in relation to other things or persons, but is essentially independent of them. The strength of even the strongest individual can always be overpowered by the many, who often will combine for no other purpose than to ruin strength precisely because of its peculiar independence. The almost instinctive hostility of the many toward the one has always, from Plato to Nietzsche, been ascribed to resentment, to the envy of the weak for the strong, but this psychological interpretation misses the point. It is in the nature of a group and its power to turn against independence, the property of individual strength.

Force, which we often use in daily speech as a synonym for violence, especially if violence serves as a means of coercion, should be reserved, in terminological language, for the "forces of nature" or the "force of circumstances," that is, to indicate the energy released by physical or social movements.

Authority, relating to the most elusive of these phenomena and therefore, as a term, most frequently abused, can be vested in persons—there is such a thing as personal authority, as, for instance, in the relation between parent and child, between teacher and pupil—or it can be vested in offices, as, for instance, in the Roman senate or in the hierarchical offices of the Church (a priest can grant valid absolution even though he is drunk). Its hallmark is unquestioning recognition by those who are asked to obey; neither coercion nor persuasion is needed. (A father can lose his authority either by beating his child or by starting to argue with him, that is, either by behaving to him like a tyrant or by treating him as an equal.) To remain in authority requires respect for the person or the office. The greatest enemy of authority, therefore, is contempt, and the surest way to undermine it is laughter.

Violence, finally, as I have said, is distinguished by its instrumental character. Phenomenologically, it is close to strength, since the implements of violence, like all other tools, are designed and used for the purpose of multiplying natural strength until, in the last stage of their development, they can substitute for it.

It is perhaps not superfluous to add that these distinctions, though by no means arbitrary, hardly ever correspond to watertight compartments in the real world, from which nevertheless they are drawn. Thus institutionalized power in organized communities often appears in the guise of authority, demanding instant, unquestioning recognition; no society could function without it. (A small, and still isolated, incident in New York shows what can happen if authentic authority in social relations has broken down to the point where it cannot work any longer even in its derivative, purely functional form. A minor mishap in the subway system—the doors on a train failed to operate—turned into a

serious shutdown on the line lasting four hours and involving more than fifty thousand passengers, because when the transit authorities asked the passengers to leave the defective train, they simply refused.) Moreover, nothing, as we shall see, is more common than the combination of violence and power, nothing less frequent than to find them in their pure and therefore extreme form. From this, it does not follow that authority, power, and violence are all the same.

Still it must be admitted that it is particularly tempting to think of power in terms of command and obedience, and hence to equate power with violence, in a discussion of what actually is only one of power's special cases—namely, the power of government. Since in foreign relations as well as domestic affairs violence appears as a last resort to keep the power structure intact against individual challengers—the foreign enemy, the native criminal—it looks indeed as though violence were the prerequisite of power and power nothing but a facade, the velvet glove which either conceals the iron hand or will turn out to belong to a paper tiger. On closer inspection, though, this notion loses much of its plausibility. For our purpose, the gap between theory and reality is perhaps best illustrated by the phenomenon of revolution.

Since the beginning of the century theoreticians of revolution have told us that the chances of revolution have significantly decreased in proportion to the increased destructive capacities of weapons at the unique disposition of governments. The history of the last seventy years, with its extraordinary record of successful and unsuccessful revolutions, tells a different story. Were people mad who even tried against such overwhelming odds? And, leaving out instances of full success, how can even a temporary success be explained? The fact is that the gap between state-owned means of violence and what people can muster by themselves—from beer bottles to Molotov cocktails and guns—has always been so enormous that technical improvements make hardly any difference. Textbook instructions on "how to make a revolution" in a step-by-step progression from dissent to conspiracy, from resistance to armed uprising, are all based on the mistaken notion that revolutions are "made." In a contest of violence against violence the superiority of the government has always been absolute; but this superiority lasts only as long as the power structure of the government is intact, that is, as long as commands are obeyed and the army or police forces are prepared to use their weapons. When this is no longer the case, the situation changes abruptly. Not only is the rebellion not put down, but the arms themselves change hands—sometimes, as in the Hungarian revolution, within a few hours. (We should know about such things after all these years of futile fighting in Vietnam, where for a long time, before getting massive Russian aid, the National Liberation Front fought us with weapons that were made in the United States.) Only after this has happened, when the disintegration of the government in power has permitted the rebels to arm themselves, can one speak of an "armed uprising," which often does not take place at all or occurs when it is no longer necessary. Where commands are no longer obeyed, the means of violence are of no use; and the question of this obedience is not decided by the command-obedience relation but by opinion, and, of course, by the number of those who share it. Everything depends on the power behind the violence. The sudden dramatic breakdown of power that ushers in revolutions reveals in a flash how civil obedience—to laws, to rulers, to institutions—is but the outward manifestation of support and consent.

Where power has disintegrated, revolutions are possible but not necessary. We know of many instances when utterly impotent regimes were permitted to continue in existence for long periods of time—either because there was no one to test their strength and reveal their weakness or because they were lucky enough not to be engaged in war and suffer defeat. Disintegration often becomes manifest only in direct confrontation; and even then, when power is already in the street, some group of men prepared for such an eventuality is needed to pick it up and assume responsibility. We have recently witnessed how it did not take more than the relatively harmless, essentially nonviolent French students' rebellion to reveal the vulnerability of the whole political system, which rapidly disintegrated before the astonished eyes of the young rebels. Unknowingly they had tested it; they intended only to challenge the ossified university system, and down came the system of governmental power, together with that of the huge party bureaucracies. It was a textbook case of a revolutionary situation that did not develop into a revolution because there was nobody, least of all the students, prepared to seize power and the responsibility that goes with it.

No government exclusively based on the means of violence has ever existed. Even the totalitarian ruler, whose chief instrument of rule is torture, needs a power basis—the secret police and its net of informers. Only the development of robot soldiers, which, as previously mentioned, would eliminate the human factor completely and, conceivably, permit one man with a push button to destroy whomever he pleased, could change this fundamental ascendancy of power over violence. Even the most despotic domination we know of, the rule of master over slaves, who always outnumbered him, did not rest on superior means of coercion as such, but on a superior organization of power—that is, on the organized solidarity of the masters. Single men without others to support them never have enough power to use violence successfully. Hence, in domestic affairs, violence functions as the last resort of power against criminals or rebels—that is, against single individuals who, as it were, refuse to be overpowered by the consensus of the majority. And as for actual warfare, we have seen in Vietnam how an enormous superiority in the means of violence can become helpless if confronted with an ill-equipped but well-organized opponent who is much more powerful. This lesson, to be sure, was there to be learned from the history of guerrilla warfare, which is at least as old as the defeat in Spain of Napoleon's still-unvanquished army.

To switch for a moment to conceptual language: Power is indeed of the essence of all government, but violence is not. Violence is by nature instrumental; like all means, it always stands in need of guidance and justification through the end it pursues. And what needs justification by something else cannot be the essence of anything. The end of war—end taken in its twofold meaning—is peace or victory; but to the question And what is the end of peace? there is no answer. Peace is an absolute, even though in recorded history periods of warfare have nearly always outlasted periods of peace. Power is in the same category; it is, as they say, "an end in itself." (This, of course, is not to deny that governments pursue policies and employ their power to achieve prescribed goals. But the power structure itself precedes and outlasts all aims, so that power, far from being the means to an end, is actually the very condition enabling a group of people to think and act in terms of the means-end category.) And since government is essentially organized and institutionalized power, the current question What is the end of government? does not make much sense either. The answer will be either question-begging—to enable men to live together—or dangerously utopian—to promote happiness or to realize a classless society or some other nonpolitical ideal, which if tried out in earnest cannot but end in some kind of tyranny.

Power needs no justification, being inherent in the very existence of political communities; what it does need is legitimacy. The common treatment of these two words as synonyms is no less misleading and confusing than the current equation of obedience and support. Power springs up whenever people get together and act in concert, but it derives its legitimacy from the initial getting together rather than from any action that then may follow. Legitimacy, when challenged, bases itself on an appeal to the past, while justification relates to an end that lies in the future. Violence can be justifiable, but it never will be legitimate. Its justification loses in plausibility the farther its intended end recedes into the future. No one questions the use of violence in self-defense, because the danger is not only clear but also present, and the end justifying the means is immediate.

Power and violence, though they are distinct phenomena, usually appear together. Wherever they are combined, power, we have found, is the primary and predominant factor. The situation, however, is entirely different when we deal with them in their pure states—as, for instance, with foreign invasion and occupation. We saw that the current equation of violence with power rests on government's being understood as domination of man over man by means of violence. If a foreign conqueror is confronted by an impotent government and by a nation unused to the exercise of political power, it is easy for him to achieve such domination. In all other cases the difficulties are great indeed, and the occupying invader will try immediately to find a native power base to support his dominion.

Violence, we must remember, does not depend on numbers or opinions, but on implements, and the implements of violence, as I mentioned before, like all other tools, increase and multiply human strength. Those who oppose violence with mere power will soon find that they are confronted not by men but by men's artifacts, whose inhumanity and destructive effectiveness increase in proportion to the distance separating the opponents. Violence can always destroy power; out of the barrel of a gun grows the most effective command, resulting in the most instant and perfect obedience. What never can grow out of it is power.

In a head-on clash between violence and power, the outcome is hardly in doubt. If Gandhi's enormously powerful and successful strategy of nonviolent resistance had met with a different enemy—Stalin's Russia, Hitler's Germany, even prewar Japan, instead of England—the outcome would not have been decolonization, but massacre and submission. However, England in India had good reasons for [its] restraint. Rule by sheer violence comes into play where power is being lost; it was the shrinking power of European imperialism that became manifest in the alternative between decolonization and massacre. To substitute violence for power can bring victory, but the price is very high; for it is not only paid by the vanquished, it is also paid by the victor in terms of his own power. This is especially true when the victor happens to enjoy domestically the blessings of constitutional government. Henry Steele Commager is entirely right: "If we subvert world order and destroy world peace we must inevitably subvert and destroy our own political institutions first." The recent gas attack on the campus at Berkeley, where not just tear gas but also another gas, "outlawed by the Geneva Convention and used by the Army to flush out guerrillas in Vietnam," was laid down while gas-masked Guardsmen stopped anybody and everybody "from fleeing the gassed area," is an excellent example of this "back-lash" phenomenon. It has often been said that impotence breeds violence, and psychologically this is quite true, at least of persons possessing natural strength, moral or physical. Politically speaking, the point is that loss of power becomes a temptation to substitute violence for power—in 1968 during the Democratic convention in Chicago we could watch this process on television and that violence itself results in impotence. Where violence is no longer backed and restrained by power, the well-known reversal in reckoning with means and ends has taken place. The means, the means of destruction, now determine the end—with the consequence that the end will be the destruction of all power.

Nowhere is the self-defeating factor in the victory of violence over power more evident than in the use of terror to maintain domination, about whose weird successes and eventual failures we know perhaps more than any generation before us. Terror is not the same as violence; it is, rather, the form of government that comes into being when violence, having destroyed all power, does not abdicate but, on the contrary, remains in full control. It has often been noticed that the effectiveness of terror depends almost entirely on the degree of social atomization. Every kind of organized opposition must disappear before the full force of terror can be let loose. This atomization—an outrageously pale, academic word for the horror it implies—is maintained and intensified through the ubiquity of the informer, who can be literally omnipresent because he no longer is merely a professional agent in the pay of the police but potentially every person one comes into contact with. The decisive difference between totalitarian domination, based on terror, and tyrannies and dictatorships, established by violence, is that the former turns not only against its enemies but against its friends and supporters as well, being afraid of all power, even the power of its friends. The climax of terror is reached when the police state begins to devour its own children, when yesterday's executioner becomes today's victim. And this is also the moment when power disappears entirely.

To sum up: politically speaking, it is insufficient to say that power and violence are not the same. Power and violence are opposites; where the one rules absolutely, the other is absent. Violence appears where power is in jeopardy, but left to its own course it ends in power's disappearance. This implies that it is not correct to think of the opposite of violence as nonviolence; to speak of nonviolent power is actually redundant. Violence can destroy power; it is utterly incapable of creating it. Hegel's and Marx's great trust in the dialectial "power of negation," by virtue of which opposites do not destroy but smoothly develop into each other because contradictions promote and do not paralyze development, rests on a much older philosophical prejudice: that evil is no more than a privative modus of the good, that good can come out of evil; that, in short, evil is but a temporary manifestation of a still-hidden good. Such time-honored opinions have become dangerous. They are shared by many who have never heard of Hegel or Marx, for the simple reason that they inspire hope and dispel fear—a treacherous hope used to dispel legitimate fear. By this, I do not mean to equate violence with evil; I only want to stress that violence cannot be derived from its opposite, which is power, and that in order to understand it for what it is, we shall have to examine its roots and nature.

GEORGE W. BUSH
Address to the Nation, September 11, 2001

GEORGE W. BUSH *(b. 1946) was President of the United States during the terrorist attacks on New York and Washington on September 11, 2001. This is the speech he delivered to the American people the night of the attacks, launching a campaign of "war against terrorism."*

THE PRESIDENT: Good evening. Today, our fellow citizens, our way of life, our very freedom came under attack in a series of deliberate and deadly terrorist acts. The victims were in airplanes, or in their offices; secretaries, businessmen and women, military and federal workers; moms and dads, friends and neighbors. Thousands of lives were suddenly ended by evil, despicable acts of terror.

The pictures of airplanes flying into buildings, fires burning, huge structures collapsing, have filled us with disbelief, terrible sadness, and a quiet, unyielding anger. These acts of mass murder were intended to frighten our nation into chaos and retreat. But they have failed; our country is strong.

A great people has been moved to defend a great nation. Terrorist attacks can shake the foundations of our biggest buildings, but they cannot touch the foundation of America. These acts shattered steel, but they cannot dent the steel of American resolve.

America was targeted for attack because we're the brightest beacon for freedom and opportunity in the world. And no one will keep that light from shining.

Today, our nation saw evil, the very worst of human nature. And we responded with the best of America—with the daring of our rescue workers, with the caring for strangers and neighbors who came to give blood and help in any way they could.

Immediately following the first attack, I implemented our government's emergency response plans. Our military is powerful, and it's prepared. Our emergency teams are working in New York City and Washington, D.C., to help with local rescue efforts.

Our first priority is to get help to those who have been injured, and to take every precaution to protect our citizens at home and around the world from further attacks.

The functions of our government continue without interruption. Federal agencies in Washington which had to be evacuated today are reopening for essential personnel tonight, and will be open for business tomorrow. Our financial institutions remain strong, and the American economy will be open for business, as well.

The search is underway for those who are behind these evil acts. I've directed the full resources of our intelligence and law enforcement communities to find those responsible and to bring them to justice. We will make no distinction between the terrorists who committed these acts and those who harbor them.

I appreciate so very much the members of Congress who have joined me in strongly condemning these attacks. And on behalf of the American people, I thank the many world leaders who have called to offer their condolences and assistance.

America and our friends and allies join with all those who want peace and security in the world, and we stand together to win the war against terrorism. Tonight, I ask for your prayers for all those who grieve, for the children whose

Bush, George W., "Address to the Nation, September 11, 2001."

worlds have been shattered, for all whose sense of safety and security has been threatened. And I pray they will be comforted by a power greater than any of us, spoken through the ages in Psalm 23: "Even though I walk through the valley of the shadow of death, I fear no evil, for You are with me."

This is a day when all Americans from every walk of life unite in our resolve for justice and peace. America has stood down enemies before, and we will do so this time. None of us will ever forget this day. Yet, we go forward to defend freedom and all that is good and just in our world.

Thank you. Good night, and God bless America.

JOHN DEAR
The Experiments of Gandhi
Nonviolence in the Nuclear Age

JOHN DEAR *is a Jesuit priest who has served as head of the Fellowship of Reconciliation, a nonviolence organization. He has lived and worked in El Salvador, Guatemala, and Northern Ireland. He has frequently been arrested, and served nine months in prison for civil disobedience at a U.S. Air Force base in North Carolina. Among his many writings are* The God of Peace: Toward a Theology of Nonviolence *(1997). The following essay was written in 1988.*

JANUARY 30, 1988 marks the fortieth anniversary of the assassination of Mohandas Gandhi. He died shortly after World War II, after the atomic bombings of Hiroshima and Nagasaki, after India's independence and civil war. He was killed at a prayer service.

Forty years later, the nuclear arms race has soared to astronomical numbers; while millions of dollars are spent daily on weapons, over 45,000 people die of starvation every day.

What has become of Gandhi's experiments in truth, his rediscovery of nonviolence as the personal and public method for positive social change? What does Gandhi's nonviolent resistance and truth force mean for North Americans, forty years after his death?

Gandhi never achieved political office. He sought solidarity with the poorest of the poor, and in this powerlessness he found the power of love and truth. "My message is my life," he wrote, and his life was a never-ending series of experiments in truth and nonviolence. "My greatest weapon is prayer," he maintained, and through his steadfast faith and study of the

Dear, John, "The Experiments of Ghandi: Nonviolent in the Nuclear Age," from Dear, John, "In War Truth Is the First Casualty" from *Fellowship of Reconciliation,* 2001. Used by permission of *Fellowship,* the magazine of the Fellowship of Reconciliation (www.forusa.org).

Bhagavad Gita and the Sermon on the Mount, he was able to move mountains. "Truth is God," he realized, and in truth, he found a way to liberation and resistance, the way of nonviolence.

But nonviolence was never simply a tactic. For Gandhi, "nonviolence is a matter of the heart." From his inner unity, through years of discipline and renunciation, Gandhi found the ability to suffer for justice's sake, to refuse to harm others, to go to prison for peace. For his friends in the independence movement, he wrote an essay, "How to Enjoy Jail." Such an essay came as a fruit of inner freedom already realized. Gandhi's nonviolence starts from within and moves outward.

His nonviolence and truth-seeking gave him the strength to claim in all humility, "I have ceased for over forty years to hate anybody. I hold myself to be incapable of hating any being on earth." His willingness to lay down his life for suffering humanity gave birth to tremendous new life in himself and for those around him. With great care and discipline, he discovered new truths, and his discoveries were open to all. "I have not the shadow of a doubt that any man or woman can achieve what I have, if he or she would make the same effort and cultivate the same hope and faith."

Gandhi's sense of experimentation in truth continued through to the last day of his life. He was constantly growing, seeking new ways to pursue the truth of nonviolence in his own heart and therefore in his world. The world of North America has much to learn from Gandhi's experiments. As we race ahead in the mad rush of violence, his message of nonviolence waits calmly to be heard and undertaken anew. Several points may apply to our own North American context as we remember and ponder his life.

Faith was the center of life for Gandhi. Gandhi believed in God, in truth. "What I want to achieve, what I have been striving and pining to achieve these thirty years," he wrote in his autobiography, "is self-realization, to see God face to face. I live and move and have my being in pursuit of this goal. All that I do by way of speaking and writing, and all my ventures in the political field, are directed to this same end." Gandhi saw the face of God in the poorest peasant and in the struggle of nonviolent resistance and love in the public realm. He sought to uncover truth at every turn and found that justice and nonviolence spring from the journey in truth. "You may be sent to the gallows, or put to torture, but if you have truth in you, you will experience an inner joy. Truth, for Gandhi, is the essence of life.

Nonviolence is the essence of truth; one cannot seek truth, Gandhi discovered, and still continue to participate in violence and injustice, within one's heart and in the world. Nonviolence is the power of the powerless, the power of God, the only power that overcomes evil, including the evil of the bomb. "Nonviolence is the greatest and most active force in the world. . . . One person who can express nonviolence in life exercises a force superior to all the forces of brutality. . . . Nonviolence cannot be preached. It has to be practiced," he insisted. "If we remain nonviolent, hatred will die as everything does, from disuse."

Gandhi's nonviolence began with prayer, solitude and fasting. By avoiding power in all its forms of violence and control, and by renouncing his desire for immediate results, Gandhi discovered that one could be reduced to zero. From this ground zero of emptiness, the compassionate love of God—nonviolence—can grow. At this point, Gandhi wrote, the individual becomes "irresistible" and one's nonviolence becomes "all-pervasive."

Gandhi's experiments in truth revealed that the mandate of the Sermon on the Mount—to love one's enemies—is of critical importance. In all of Gandhi's public uses of nonviolence, he always manifested a desire for reconciliation, friendship, with his opponent. In South Africa, he showed deep respect for General Smuts and the two adversaries became fast friends. In India, Gandhi struggled to win over Jinnah, his Muslim opponent, through nonviolent love. His satyagraha campaigns began in a community of love and resistance and endeavored to extend that beloved community as far and wide as possible. When in prison, Gandhi befriended his jailers.

Gandhi always taught that "noncooperation with evil is as much a duty as cooperation with good." In order to seek God's kingdom first, Gandhi believed one must dissociate one's self from every form of evil, within and without. His noncooperation campaigns put into public practice the teachings of Jesus: "When someone strikes you on one cheek, turn and offer the other." His willingness to suffer for justice's sake (his apparent cooperation with violence) actually was a total noncooperation with violence. The violence ended there, in Gandhi's own person, as Jesus showed, and Gandhi's noncooperation with evil, his nonviolent resistance, led to the presence of new life and love.

Gandhi learned nonviolence, he confessed, from his wife, Kasturbai. "I learnt the lesson of nonviolence from my wife, when I tried to bend her to my will." Gandhi wrote. "Her determined resistance to my will, on the one hand, and her quiet submission to the suffering my stupidity involved, on the other, ultimately made me ashamed of myself and cured me of my stupidity." Kasturbai taught Mohandas that nonviolence includes feminism, the practice of the equality of the sexes. Gandhi became an advocate of women's rights and maintained that if the world was to make any progress, sexism must be banned and forgotten.

Gandhi always tried to stand with the outcasts of society and to speak up for the rights of the marginalized. In India, such solidarity primarily meant taking the radical, scandalizing public stand on behalf of the so-called "untouchables." Gandhi called them harijans, or "children of God" and begged his fellow Indians to banish untouchability from their hearts and lives. His message needs to be proclaimed in every part of the world today, including North America. Such solidarity might mean touching the lives of the marginalized in our own society: gays and lesbians, people of color, illegal aliens, the elderly, the mentally handicapped and AIDS victims.

Gandhi also developed a practical, constructive program to rid India and the world of poverty and injustice. He lived with the poor and taught ways to improve their lives, while always advocating voluntary poverty and simplicity of life. He tried to improve the environment and public sanitation, and to encourage the personal responsibility of daily work through the spinning wheel. Gandhi's motto was: "Recall the face of the poorest and the most helpless person whom you have seen and ask yourself if the step you contemplate is going to be of any use to that person. Will he or she be able to gain anything by it?"

In our own day and age, Gandhi's lessons of nonviolent resistance are more essential than ever. Perhaps, the primary lesson we need to relearn from Gandhi is to choose every day for the rest of our lives, with the gift of our lives, the truth of nonviolence over the lie of nuclear violence. Gandhi's path to nonviolence—the way of the cross—is an invitation to resist the nuclear arms race at its roots, within each of us. The spiritual power of nonviolent love when sought through prayer, fasting and discipline, will mean the reversal of the arms race. Such nonviolent love will lead to noncooperation and loving disobedience, and possibly imprisonment and death for some.

But Gandhi believed that there is no such thing as defeat for the person seeking the truth of nonviolence. When one accepts love and nonviolence in one's empty heart, then the doors of life are opened. Suffering can be accepted willingly and transformed into a gift of love that will bear fruit in humanity. Arrest and imprisonment for nonviolent resistance become doorways to freedom. Death becomes the door to resurrection. Gandhi's nonviolent resistance is based in hope, in a vision like the dream of Martin Luther King, Jr. of a new life, a new age, a new world without weapons or fear, in which all will be treated as one, as brothers and sisters, everyone a child of God.

In his autobiographical essay, "Pilgrimage to Nonviolence," Martin Luther King, Jr. tells how he "came upon the life and teachings of Mahatma Gandhi" and "became deeply fascinated." He wrote:

"Gandhi was probably the first person in history to lift the love ethic of Jesus above mere interaction between individuals to a powerful and effective social force on a large scale. For Gandhi love was a potent instrument for social and collective transformation. It was in this Gandhian emphasis on love and nonviolence that I discovered the method for social reform that I had been seeking for so many months. . . . I came to feel that this was the only morally and practically sound method open to oppressed people in their struggle for freedom."

Hours before he was assassinated, Gandhi was asked by a North American journalist how he would meet the atomic bomb with nonviolence. Gandhi replied: "I will not go underground. I will not go into shelter. I will come out in the open and let the pilot see I have not a trace of ill-will against him. The pilot will not see our faces from his great height, I know. But the longing in our hearts—that he will not come to harm—would reach up to him and his eyes would be opened."

Ultimately, Gandhi's message of nonviolence for North Americans today is a call to resist the nuclear arms race. "We have to make truth and nonviolence not matters for mere individual practice but for practice by groups and communities and nations," Gandhi wrote. "That, at any rate, is my dream. I shall live and die in trying to realize it."

Gandhi's life pursuit of the reign of truth and love led him to nonviolent resistance in a variety of campaigns. He and his colleagues resisted the violence and death in untouchability, sexism, racism, war, colonization, religious division and the nuclear arms race. His participation in the struggle resulted in imprisonment, beatings, and eventually, assassination. But Gandhi had pledged his life to seek justice and peace without the use of violence; he willingly accepted the punishment meted out to him. He had long ago offered to sacrifice his life for peace and justice. He went to jail smiling. He was killed while offering a sign of peace. These acts of resistance done in this spirit of nonviolence epitomized the message of Gandhi.

One of Gandhi's associates, Asha Devi, was asked by a BBC interviewer: "Don't you think that Gandhi was a bit unrealistic, that he failed to reckon with the limits of our capacities?" With joy, Asha Devi responded, "There are no limits to our capacities."

RICHARD FALK
Defining a Just War

RICHARD FALK *(b. 1930) is Albert C. Milbank Professor of International Law and Practice at the Center for International Studies, Princeton University. He has written widely on the nature and justification of war. Here he responds to the terrorist attacks on New York and Washington, D.C., in September of 2001.*

Falk, Richard, "Defining a Just War," reprinted with permission from the October 29, 2001, issue of *The Nation*. For subscription information, call 1-800-333-8536. Portions of each week's *Nation* magazine can be accessed at http://www.thenation.com.

I have never since my childhood supported a shooting war in which the United States was involved, although in retrospect I think the NATO war in Kosovo achieved beneficial results. The war in Afghanistan against apocalyptic terrorism qualifies in my understanding as the first truly just war since World War II. But the justice of the cause and of the limited ends is in danger of being negated by the injustice of improper means and excessive ends. Unlike World War II and prior just wars, this one can be won only if tactics adhere to legal and moral constraints on the means used to conduct it, and to limited ends.

The perpetrators of the September 11 attack cannot be reliably neutralized by nonviolent or diplomatic means; a response that includes military action is essential to diminish the threat of repetition, to inflict punishment and to restore a sense of security at home and abroad. The extremist political vision held by Osama bin Laden, which can usefully be labeled "apocalyptic terrorism," places this persisting threat well outside any framework of potential reconciliation or even negotiation for several reasons: Its genocidal intent is directed generically against Americans and Jews; its proclaimed goal is waging an unconditional civilizational war—Islam against the West—without drawing any distinction between civilian and military targets; it has demonstrated a capacity and willingness to inflict massive and traumatizing damage on our country and a tactical ingenuity and ability to carry out its missions of destruction by reliance on the suicidal devotion of its adherents.

There are three types of responses to the attack, each of which contains some merit and enjoys some support. None of them are adequate, however.

I. Antiwar/Pacifist Approach   The pacifist position opposing even limited military action overlooks the nature of the threat and is thus irrelevant to meeting the central challenge of restoring some sense of security among our citizenry and in the world generally.

Also, in the current setting, unlike in the civil rights movement and the interventionist conflicts of the cold war era (especially Vietnam), antiwar and pacifist stands possess little or no cultural resonance with the overwhelming majority of Americans. It may be that at later stages of the war this assessment will prove to have been premature, and even now Quaker, Christian, Gandhian and Buddhist forms of pacifism offer a profound critique of wars. These critiques should be seriously heeded, since they lend weight to the view that the use of force should be marginal and kept to an absolute minimum. Certainly the spiritually motivated pacifist witness can be both inspirational and instructive, and help to mitigate and interrogate militarist postures.

Another form of antiwar advocacy rests on a critique of the United States as an imperialist superpower or empire. This view also seems dangerously inappropriate in addressing the challenge posed by the massive crime against humanity committed on September 11. Whatever the global role of the United States—and it is certainly responsible for much global suffering and injustice, giving rise to widespread resentment that at its inner core fuels the terrorist impulse—it cannot be addressed so long as this movement of global terrorism is at large and prepared to carry on with its demonic work. These longer-term concerns—which include finding ways to promote Palestinian self-determination, the internationalization of Jerusalem and a more equitable distribution of the benefits of global economic growth and development—must be addressed. Of course, much of the responsibility for the failure to do so lies with the corruption and repressive policies of governments, especially in the Middle East, outside the orbit of US influence. A distinction needs to be drawn as persuasively as possible between inherently desirable lines of foreign policy reform and retreating in the face of terrorism.

II. Legalist/UN Approach   International treaties that deal with terrorism on civil aircraft call for cooperation in apprehending suspects and allow for their subsequent indictment and prosecution by national courts. Such laws could in theory be invoked to capture Osama bin Laden and his leading associates and charge them with international crimes, including crimes against humanity. A tribunal could be constituted under the authority of the United Nations, and a fair trial could then be held that would avoid war and the ensuing pain, destruction and associated costs. The narrative of apocalyptic terrorism could be laid before the world as the crimes of Nazism were bared at Nuremberg.

But this course is unlikely to deal effectively with the overall threat. A public prosecution would give bin Laden and associates a platform to rally further support among a large constituency of sympathizers, and conviction and punishment would certainly be viewed as a kind of legal martyrdom. It would be impossible to persuade the United States government to empower such a tribunal unless it was authorized to impose capital punishment, and it is doubtful that several of the permanent members of the Security Council could be persuaded to allow death sentences. Beyond this, the evidence linking bin Laden to the September 11 attacks and other instances of global terrorism may well be insufficient to produce an assured conviction in an impartial legal tribunal, particularly if conspiracy was not among the criminal offenses that could be charged. European and other foreign governments are unlikely to be willing to treat conspiracy as a capital crime. And it strains the imagination to suppose that the Bush Administration would relinquish control over bin Laden to an international tribunal. On a more general level, it also seems highly improbable that the US government can be persuaded to rely on the collective security mechanisms of the UN even to the unsatisfactory degree permitted during the Gulf War. To be sure, the UN Security Council has provided a vague antiterrorist mandate as well as an endorsement of a US right of response, but such legitimizing gestures are no more than that. For better and worse, the United States is relying on its claimed right of self-defense, and Washington seems certain to insist on full operational control over the means and ends of the war that is now under way. Such a reliance is worrisome, given past US behavior and the somewhat militaristic character of both the leadership in Washington and the broader societal orientation in America toward the use of overwhelming force against the nation's enemies.

Yet at this stage it is unreasonable to expect the US government to rely on the UN to fulfill its defensive needs. The UN lacks the capability, authority and will to respond to the kind of threat to global security posed by this new form of terrorist world war. The UN was established to deal with wars among states, while a transnational actor that cannot be definitively linked to a state is behind the attacks on the United States. Al Qaeda's relationship to the Taliban regime in Afghanistan is contingent, with Al Qaeda being more the sponsor of the state rather than the other way around.

Undoubtedly, the world would be safer and more secure with a stronger UN that had the support of the leading states in the world. The United States has for years acted more to obstruct than to foster such a transformation. Surely the long-term effects of this crisis should involve a new surge of support for a reformed UN that would have independent means of financing its operations, with its own peacekeeping and enforcement capabilities backed up by an international criminal court. Such a transformed UN would generate confidence that it could and would uphold its charter in an evenhanded manner that treats people equally. But it would be foolish to pretend that the UN today, even if it were to enjoy a far higher level of US support than it does, could mount an effective response to the September 11 attacks.

III. Militarist Approach Unlike pacifism and legalism, militarism poses a practical danger of immense proportions. Excessive reliance on the military will backfire badly, further imperiling the security of Americans and others, spreading war and destruction far afield, as well as emboldening the government to act at home in ways that weaken US democracy. So far the Bush Administration has shown some understanding of these dangers, going slowly in its reliance on military action and moving relatively cautiously to bolster its powers over those it views as suspicious or dangerous, so as to avoid the perception of waging a cultural war against Islam. The White House has itself repeatedly stressed that this conflict is unlike previous wars, that nonmilitary means are also important, that victory will come in a different way and that major battlefield encounters are unlikely to occur.

Such reassurances, however, are not altogether convincing. The President's current rhetoric seems to reflect Secretary of State Colin Powell's more prudent approach, which emphasizes diplomacy and nonmilitary tactics, and restricts military action to Al Qaeda and the Taliban regime. Even here, there is room for dangerous expansion, depending on how the Al Qaeda network is defined. Some maximalists implicate twenty or more countries as supporters of terrorism. Defense Secretary Donald Rumsfeld, his deputy Paul Wolfowitz and others are definitely beating the drums for a far wider war; they seem to regard the attacks as an occasion to implement their own vision of a new world, one that proposes to rid the world of "evil" and advances its own apocalyptic vision. This vision seeks the destruction of such organizations as Hezbollah and Hamas, which have only minimal links to Al Qaeda and transnational terror, and which have agendas limited mainly to Palestinian rights of self-determination and the future of Jerusalem. These organizations, while legally responsible for terrorist operations within their sphere of concerns, but also subject to terrorist provocations, have not shown any intention of pursuing bin Laden's apocalyptic undertaking. Including such groups on the US target list will surely undermine the depth and breadth of international support and engender dangerous reactions throughout the Islamic world, and possibly in the West as well.

Beyond this, there is speculation that there will be a second stage of response that will include a series of countries regarded as hostile to the United States, who are in possession of weapons of mass destruction but are not currently related to global terrorism in any significant fashion. These include Iraq, Libya and possibly even Syria, Iran and Sudan. To expand war objectives in this way would be full of risks, require massive military strikes inflicting much destruction and suffering, and would create a new wave of retaliatory violence directed against the United States and Americans throughout the world. If military goals overshoot, either by becoming part of a design to destroy Israel's enemies or to solve the problem of proliferation of weapons of mass destruction, the war against global terrorism will be lost, and badly.

Just as the pacifist fallacy involves unrealistic exclusion of military force from an acceptable response, the militarist fallacy involves an excessive reliance on military force in a manner that magnifies the threat it is trying to diminish or eliminate. It also expands the zone of violence in particularly dangerous ways that are almost certain to intensify and inflame anti-Americanism. It should be kept in mind that war occasions deep suffering, and recourse to international force should be both a last resort and on as limited a scale as possible.

But there is a fourth response, which has gained support among foreign policy analysts and probably a majority of Americans.

IV. Limiting Means and Ends Unlike in major wars of the past, the response to this challenge of apocalyptic terrorism can be effective only if it is also widely perceived as legitimate. And legitimacy can be attained only if the role of military force is marginal to the overall conduct of the war and the relevant frameworks of moral, legal and religious restraint are scrupulously respected.

Excessive use of force in pursuing the perpetrators of September 11 will fan the flames of Islamic militancy and give credence to calls for holy war. What lent the WTC/Pentagon attack its quality of sinister originality was the ability of a fanatical political movement to take advantage of the complex fragility and vulnerability of advanced technology. Now that this vulnerability has been exposed to the world, it is impossible to insure that other extremists will not commit similar acts—even if Osama bin Laden is eliminated.

The only way to wage this war effectively is to make sure that force is used within relevant frameworks of restraint. Excessive force can take several forms, like the pursuit of political movements remote from the WTC attack, especially if such military action is seen as indirectly doing the dirty work of eliminating threats to Israel's occupation of Palestinian territories and Jerusalem. Excessiveness would also be attributed to efforts to destroy and restructure regimes, other than the Taliban, that are hostile to the United States but not significantly connected with either the attack or Al Qaeda.

The second, closely related problem of successfully framing a response is related to the US manner of waging war: The US temperament has tended to approach war as a matter of confronting evil. In such a view, victory can be achieved only by the total defeat of the other, and with it, the triumph of good.

In the current setting, goals have not been clarified, and US leaders have used grandiose language about ending terrorism and destroying the global terrorist network. The idea of good against evil has been a consistent part of the process of public mobilization, with the implicit message that nothing less than a total victory is acceptable. What are realistic ends? Or put differently, what ends can be reconciled with a commitment to achieve an effective response? What is needed is extremely selective uses of force, especially in relation to the Taliban, combined with criminal law enforcement operations—cutting off sources of finance, destroying terrorist cells, using policing techniques abetted, to the extent necessary, by paramilitary capabilities.

Also troubling is the Bush Administration's ingrained disdain for multilateralism and its determination to achieve security for the United States by military means—particularly missile defense and space weaponization. This unilateralism has so far been masked by a frantic effort to forge a global coalition, but there is every indication that the US government will insist on complete operational control over the war and will not be willing to accept procedures of accountability within the UN framework.

The Administration has often said that many of the actions in this war will not be made known to the public. But an excessive emphasis on secrecy in the conduct of military operations is likely to make the uses of force more difficult to justify to those who are skeptical about US motives and goals, thus undercutting the legitimacy of the war.

In building a global coalition for cooperative action, especially with respect to law enforcement in countries where Al Qaeda operates, the US government has struck a number of Faustian bargains. It may be necessary to enter into arrangements with governments that are themselves responsible for terrorist policies and brutal repression, such as Russia in Chechnya and India in Kashmir. But the cost of doing so is to weaken claims that a common antiterrorist front is the foundation of this alliance. For some governments the war against apocalyptic terrorism is an opportunity to proceed with their own repressive policies free from censure and interference. The US government should weigh the cost of writing blank checks against the importance of distinguishing its means and ends from the megaterrorist ethos that animated the September 11 attacks. There are some difficult choices ahead, including the extent to which Afghan opposition forces, particularly the Northern Alliance, should be supported in view of their own dubious human rights record.

How, then, should legitimacy be pursued in the current context? The first set of requirements is essentially political: to disclose goals that seem reasonably connected with the attack and with the threat posed by those who planned, funded and carried it out. In this regard, the destruction of both the Taliban regime and the Al Qaeda network, including the apprehension and prosecution of Osama bin Laden and any associates connected with this and past terrorist crimes, are appropriate goals. In each instance, further specification is necessary. With respect to the Taliban, its relation to Al Qaeda is established and intimate enough to attribute primary responsibility, and the case is strengthened to the degree that its governing policies are so oppressive as to give the international community the strongest possible grounds for humanitarian intervention. We must make a distinction between those individuals and entities that have been actively engaged in the perpetration of the visionary program of international, apocalyptic terrorism uniquely Al Qaeda's and those who have used funds or training to advance more traditional goals relating to grievances associated with the governance of a particular country and have limited their targets largely to the authorities in their countries, like the ETA in Spain and the IRA in Ireland and Britain.

Legitimacy with respect to the use of force in international settings derives from the mutually reinforcing traditions of the "just war" doctrine, international law and the ideas of restraint embedded in the great religions of the world. The essential norms are rather abstract in character, and lend themselves to debate and diverse interpretation. The most important ideas are:

• the principle of discrimination: force must be directed at a military target, with damage to civilians and civilian society being incidental;

• the principle of proportionality: force must not be greater than that needed to achieve an acceptable military result and must not be greater than the provoking cause;

• the principle of humanity: force must not be directed even against enemy personnel if they are subject to capture, wounded or under control (as with prisoners of war);

• the principle of necessity: force should be used only if nonviolent means to achieve military goals are unavailable.

These abstract guidelines for the use of force do not give much operational direction. In each situation we must ask: Do the claims to use force seem reasonable in terms of the ends being pursued, including the obligation to confine civilian damage as much as possible? Such assessments depend on interpretation, but they allow for debate and justification, and clear instances of violative behavior could be quickly identified. The justice of the cause and of the limited ends will be negated by the injustice of improper means and excessive ends. Only the vigilance of an active citizenry, alert to this delicate balance, has much hope of helping this new war to end in a true victory.

RICHARD DEATS
In War Truth Is the First Casualty

RICHARD DEATS *is editor of the magazine of the Fellowship of Reconciliation, an international interfaith organization that works to find peaceful means for resolving conflict. He is the author of* Martin Luther King, Jr.: Spirit-led Prophet *(1999).*

Deats, Richard, "In War Truth Is the First Casualty," from "Ghandi's Nonviolent Resistance in the Nuclear Age," from *Fellowship of Reconciliation,* 2001. Used by permission of *Fellowship,* the magazine of the Fellowship of Reconciliation (www.forusa.org).

SAMUEL Johnson had it right: truth is the first casualty in war. Because war is a life and death matter, advocates for each side are inclined to listen to those sources that show that their side is in mortal danger and is only defending itself, that their side is more fair and humane, and that their side has a conscience unlike the brutes and animals on the other side. Evidence that shows the other side to have legitimate grievances or to have suffered terribly is discounted as propaganda—or at the very least not to be nearly as significant as the grievances and suffering of the favored side. In the peacemaking work of the Fellowship of Reconciliation in the Middle East, the FOR and me in particular are denounced as "apologists for murder" whose sympathies lie with "the Arab purveyors of terror."

For the record I have a Jewish daughter, son-in-law and eleven grandchildren who live in Jerusalem. I worry about their safety and pray for them every day. And it is precisely because I care about them and their future that I favor policies that in the long run will create a Middle East where everyone shall sit under their vine and fig tree and none shall make them afraid. Everyone means just that—every one. Policies that favor one side at the expense of the other will in the long run fail. Extremists on both sides have created fear and hate that poison the atmosphere and have set the agenda for unending violence. Gandhi had it absolutely right: an eye for an eye leaves the world blind. Partisans on both sides refuse to acknowledge that the consequences of all the killings and the destruction destroy the future. Instead of the justification of each act of violence (or counter violence), we need to favor those actions that break the cycle of violence. As Dr. King said, our choice is nonviolence or nonexistence.

The FOR interfaith delegations, unlike many groups that go to the Middle East, do not go to meet with just one side. Our branches there include Jews, Muslims and Christians. We meet with human rights groups that document Palestinian and Israeli abuses. We go to Palestinian villages as well as to Jewish settlements. We meet with and support Israeli and Palestinian groups working for a peaceful, nonviolent resolution of the conflict. These groups are a minority and receive very little press coverage but they are courageous and steadfast in their work and witness. Rather than being ignored and marginalized they should be listened to and helped.

Suicide bombers are reprehensible and the cult of martyrdom that envelopes them is a sickness. Violent Palestinian groups such as Islamic Jihad not only desecrate true Islam but destroy the likelihood of peaceful coexistence. The corruption and ineffectiveness of Arafat's government and its links with terrorists betray the needs and aspirations of the Palestinian people.

But to demonize Arafat as the source of all evil is wrong-headed and dishonest. Sharon's brutal policies have not led to the peace and security he promised. He has one answer to problems: more military force. The reoccupation of the West Bank and the building of a wall throughout the land in the long run will only increase the desperation and hopelessness on which terrorism feeds. People that recoil at suicide bombers should also recoil at state terrorism that uses tanks and warplanes to kill and destroy. Collective punishment by whatever means is abhorrent.

The occupation and the settlements do not increase Israel's security; they only prolong the agony and suffering of all. Although most Israelis recognize this, the settlers are able to influence government policies and expenditures far beyond their numbers. By denying the Palestinians any hope of their own viable state, the ever expanding settlements (ever since Oslo!) assure continuing strife.

Barak's offer was not rejected "because Arafat doesn't want peace." It was rejected because it did not offer a viable state. It was a state that left borders and security firmly under Israeli military and civilian control for an indefinite future. Territorial continuity was undermined by Israeli settlements, by-pass roads and road blocs, even as settlement building continued under Barak. No nation would accept such a deal. Further negotiations at Taba held promise but Sharon's provocation by going to the Temple Mount with a thousand armed police and military was like gasoline thrown on smoldering ashes. It thrust him into the limelight as the fearless general who would smash the Palestinians into submission. Sharon's subsequent defeat of Barak in the election stopped negotiations dead in their tracks.

FOR is accused of being pro-Palestinian. Yes we are. And we are pro-Israeli and pro-human. To criticize disastrous policies is an act of responsibility and caring.

Whose side is God on? God is on the side of those who suffer.

CLAUDIA CARD

Questions Regarding a War on Terrorism

CLAUDIA CARD *teaches philosophy at the University of Wisconsin, Madison. She has made many significant contributions to feminist philosophy, including* The Unnatural Lottery: Character and Moral Luck *(1996) and* The Atrocity Paradigm: A Theory of Evil *(2002).*

Unlike some critics, I do not have great moral difficulty in identifying as terrorist and as evil the bombing attacks on the World Trade Center on September 11, 2001. Regardless of perpetrators' grievances and their understandings of their religious commitments or aspirations, mass killing of unarmed civilians targeted deliberately as such and without warning is evil. On Carl Wellman's widely received view of terrorism as political violence with two targets, one direct (but secondary target) who suffers immediate harm and the other an indirect (but primary) target to whom a message is sent by way of that harm, the attacks were also terrorist if their larger intent was to manipulate the United States government politically. . . . No one has yet publicly claimed responsibility for the attacks or offered an official explanation. And so we can only infer the larger intent. But evidence shows the attacks, including the surprise element, to have been planned. This was no ordinary wrong. If evils are intolerable harms that were reasonably foreseeable (if not planned) and produced by culpable wrongdoing, these events appear to be paradigmatic evils.

Philosophically less clear is whether the response of a war on terrorism is not also an evil. Without resolving that question I mention issues that make it unclear and suggest a way to address particular cases. More importantly, in drawing on an analogy with terrorism in the home, I suggest an alternative, preferable response that would make such a determination unnecessary.

Some may regard the expression "war on terrorism" as metaphorical, like the expressions "war on drugs" or "war on crime." Yet "war" here

Card, Claudia, "Questions Regarding a War on Terrorism," from *Hypatia*, Vol. 18, No. 1 (Winter 2003), pp. 164–169. Reprinted by permission of the author and Indiana University Press.

confers an appearance of legitimacy, conveys that lesser means were tried and exhausted, and dignifies the original attack as an act of war, rather than simply an atrocious crime. How metaphorical is it, one may wonder, when military forces are deployed to carry out the war? Despite the dropping of food and supplies for civilians, U.S. armed forces have inflicted intolerable harm, including much death, on people in Afganistan, including many unarmed women and children. Whether that is evil depends on whether those intolerable harms were reasonably foreseeable and perpetrated through culpable wrongdoing.

Whether war can be a legitimate response to attacks carried out by persons unauthorized by any state raises philosophical issues about the meaning of war and questions about the justice of a military force response, whatever we call it. Is war on terrorism within the bounds of what justice permits as a response to the attacks of 9/11? What are the boundaries, the limits, of a "war on terrorism"? In particular, how is the scope of this war's opponents limited?

Appropriate responses to 9/11, in my view, would include global hunts (with international cooperation) for responsible survivors, those complicit in the planning and support of the attacks, including the provision of training, financial backing, and safe harbors. Persons apprehended would ideally then be tried by international tribunals, treated as (suspected) criminal agents, charged with crimes against humanity for targeting victims on the basis of their (perceived) identity as Americans, American sympathizers, or as capitalists. Universal jurisdiction applies for crimes against humanity. Still, an international court would be more appropriate, as those killed in the World Trade Center represented many nations. The deed threatens security globally. Although suspects may try to avoid being taken alive, pursuers can aim to take them alive and try them. If war is declared rather than a hunt for responsible individuals, who has the opportunity for a fair trial?

War, according to *Merriam Webster's Collegiate Dictionary Tenth Edition,* is "a state of usually open and declared armed hostile conflict between states or nations" (s.v. "war"). Internationally accepted rules of war have evolved to regulate wars *with* or *between* opponents. What guidelines regulate wars *on* or *against* such "opponents" as terrorism or drugs? By tradition, a just war must be declared by appropriate authorities. A major point of this requirement is to give fair notice to opponents. On whom is a war on "terrorism" declared? Who is given fair notice? In wars between states, heads of state can negotiate for peace. Who among the opponents in a war on terrorism has authority to negotiate for peace? If peace is not negotiable, how must such a war end? What is to prevent it from becoming a war of extermination?

According to just war theory, a principle of discrimination between combatants and noncombatants holds that it is unjust to target civilians directly. It is unjust to kill civilians simply for the sake of demoralizing one's opponent, for example. Such a policy violates Immanuel Kant's principle that humanity in anyone's person must never be treated merely as a means but must be treated always at the same time as an end. Modern warfare makes it nearly impossible to use weapons such as bombs against combatants without risking lives of noncombatants. Still, the principle of discrimination is not empty as long as it rules out deliberately targeting civilians when risking their lives is not a consequence of using weapons against combatants. But whom is it unjust to target directly in a war on terrorism?

Members of nations at war who wear a military uniform are identifiable as combatants; those who do not are presumed civilians. Guerilla warfare, of course, complicates this distinction, as guerilla combatants wear no uniform. Wars against opponents who are not nations raise more complications. What corresponds to "civilian" in the party to a war that is not a nation or state? What must one's relationship to acts of terrorism be in order for one to count as a terrorist?

"Terrorists" is not a well-defined group. "Terrorist" is not an identity, like British or French. To identify someone as a terrorist is to render a judgment on them, not simply to make a discovery. Not all terrorists have common goals, belong to a unified organization, or have the same opponents. There are terrorists within the United States who are U.S. citizens and not immigrants, legal or illegal. The Ku Klux Klan is one of the most infamous of terrorist organizations, and the era of lynching is one of the most infamous episodes of domestic terrorism in U.S. history.

Other domestic terrorists are less widely or publicly acknowledged as such. The reigning stereotype of a terrorist is one who, in seeking attention for national or international political causes, carries out destructive acts against public institutions or in public places. This stereotype ignores not only state terrorism, as Jonathan Glover, Emma Goldman, and others have pointed out, but it also ignores the terrorism of violence in the home. Such violence in the home functions to maintain dominance (usually patriarchal) and thereby can be acknowledged as political. A truly global war on terrorism would include among its targets perpetrators of domestic partner abuse, elder abuse, child abuse, and rape. President Bush has not yet recognized such perpetrators as terrorists. They do not appear to be among his targets. But for those who would support a war on terrorism, it should be an interesting question whether war would be an appropriate response to terrorists in the home.

If the United States is justified in conducting a war on international terrorists, should feminists declare war on terrorism in the home? Should battered women (and likewise battered children and battered elders) regard themselves as existing in a state of nature—as though laws, courts, and governments did not exist—with respect to batterers? After years of stalking and battering by her former husband, against whom the law either would not or could not protect her and her children, Francine Hughes poured gasoline over her batterer one night and ignited it while he slept. If killing without capture and trial is clearly an appropriate response to international terrorists, should Francine Hughes even have been put on trial for murder?

It will be objected that feminists and victims of battery are not in positions of authority to undertake such matters as declaring war. Yet why is the issue of authority important, if not as part of a broader understanding of rules defining conditions under which fighting is fair? Have not such rules been abandoned already, if opponents are not sufficiently well-defined that one can identify who has authority to negotiate for peace? Is the real objection that the victims of terrorism in the home are usually female and that war is not an appropriate response for females?

When terrorists disregard fairness, victims face a difficult question: to what extent ought one to be fair even to those who disregard fairness themselves? Domestic criminals often enough blatantly disregard fairness. Yet the state offers them a trial. Trials are reassuring to others not accused in a particular case, as they might one day be mistakenly identified as criminals, in which case a fair trial would give them the opportunity to rebut the charge. Striking back without trial, on the assumption that those who are unfair to others do not deserve fairness, ignores the possibility that retaliators might be mistaken in their judgments about those identified as criminal (mistaken either about what was done or about who did it). The same point applies to international terrorism. Without trials by international tribunals, what assurance do citizens of the world have that they will not be mistakenly identified as terrorists and summarily dispatched? Some arguments analogous to these were offered in support of the International Tribunal at Nuremberg against those who advocated simply shooting those identified by the Allies as Axis leaders at the end of World War II.

It was unfortunate but nevertheless right to try Francine Hughes and to make public the facts that led her to the deed. A trial is the right way to determine whether her response was justified, and if so, to clear her name. It would have been morally right to acquit her, even without the insanity defense, given her history of having exhausted less desperate methods of self-defense. She should never have been left in the position of having to defend herself by extreme means. The man she killed is the person who, ideally, should have had to stand trial.

If a nation declares a war on terrorism, rather than on another nation, it takes matters into its own hands in a manner that is in some respects analogous to what Francine Hughes did. It steps outside the bounds and processes of law—in this case, international law. Of course, Francine Hughes appears not to have warned her opponent, who was asleep and therefore unable to try to escape. A state may warn terrorists by declaring war. But if "terrorist" is not well-defined (and the reader may notice by now that I have not really defined it; it is currently a hotly contested concept, which is part of the point), who knows that they are being warned? If everyone in a territory that includes terrorists is warned, of what value is the warning when many inhabitants who are not terrorists have no means of escape or self-defense?

If it was right for the state of Michigan to try Francine Hughes for murder (which as stated above, I believe it was), then perhaps it would also be right, and for similar reasons, for an international tribunal to try, for crimes against humanity, the leaders of nations who declare and perpetrate war on terrorists, when those nations kill masses of unarmed civilians. Such a trial may be the right way to determine whether the war was justified, and if so, to clear the names of nations who wage it. Such a trial should also offer some reassurance to others who might one day be wrongly identified as terrorists. It would consider, for example, whether less drastic but appropriate responses had been exhausted by any nation that wages a war allegedly on terrorism in which it kills masses of unarmed civilians who have no means of escape.

Would it not make better sense, however, for an international team to capture and try, in an international court, those initially accused of international terrorism and or of being complicit in it, just as it would have made better sense to capture and try the batterer of Francine Hughes?

MUMIA ABU-JAMAL
War Against Terror or War to Govern the World?

MUMIA ABU-JAMAL, *a former radio journalist in Philadelphia, known as "the voice of the voiceless," has spent over 20 years on death row for murdering a police officer, a crime he maintains he did not commit. He remains active in a variety of political causes. His most recent book is* Live from Death Row *(1995).*

Abu-Jamal, Mumia, "War Against Terror or War to Govern the World?" by Mumia Abu-Jamal from *Labyrinth,* Winter 2001.

I T is helpful sometimes, in times of great and confusing events, to consider simple things, which can shed light on things that are far more complex.

The events of 9/11, and in turn the resultant aerial bombardment of Afghanistan by American military, is now the opening act of what promises to be a global military campaign that threatens to be waged in Iraq, perhaps Iran, Somalia, and even the far Philippines.

We are told that this war will be waged for years, perhaps for decades, in far-flung areas of the earth. It is, in Bush Administration terms, a "war against terrorism," a "war against evil," and a "clash of civilizations." (Of course, the royal "we" are the perfect good; "they" are the eternal evil.)

One wonders, when is a "terrorist," not a terrorist?

The late Pakistani scholar, Eqbal Ahmad, points to how history and circumstance can change characterizations:

Until the 1930s and 1940s, the Jewish underground in Palestine was described as "terrorist." Then something happened: around 1942, as news of the Holocaust was spreading, a certain liberal sympathy with the Jewish people began to emerge in the Western world. By 1944, the terrorists of Palestine, who were Zionists, suddenly began being described as "freedom fighters." If you look in history books you can find at least two Israeli prime ministers, including Menachem Begin, appearing in "Wanted" posters saying, TERRORISTS, REWARD [this much]. The highest reward I have seen offered was 100,000 British pounds for the head of Menachem Begin, the terrorist (Yitzhak Shamir is the other)

The terrorism of yesterday has become the nationalism of today.

The interests and objectives of the US, and its Western partners, have less to do with terrorism, than with making the world quiescent and calm in the face of a neo-colonialist, corporate capitalism.

What is at stake is not democracy, for if this was so why does the West support regimes, like the Saudis or the Emirates, that don't even have a pretense of a democratic form of government? What is at stake is western control over resources, like oil, or natural gas.

What is at stake is hegemony, or the continued dominance over the emerging world by the industrial, corporate West, under the flag of globalism.

What is globalized is the use of force to suppress local, national and regional movements seeking liberation or autonomy. What is globalized is the media machinery of the wealthy elites to justify an inequitable status quo. What is globalized is terror, on a world scale, to protect the system.

CHAPTER THIRTEEN

HOW DOES RACISM
AFFECT MY LIFE?

A man is running down a country road. Two policemen in a cruiser pull up next to him and yell at him to stop. "Who are you? What are you doing here?" one of the policemen asks him. "My name is Bob Smith," he replies. "I'm jogging." "Do you live around here?" the other policeman asks him. "Yes, I live on Maple Street," the man responds. "Show us your ID," the police demand, getting out of the car. "But I don't have any. I'm just out jogging!" the man says. "Where do you work, then?" "At Pratt Paper Company. I'm an account executive." "What's the name of the company president then?" "Brenda Schwartz, of course. But why are you asking me these questions?"

Beginning with Plato, there has been a tendency in Western philosophy to assume that a person's real identity is quite independent of the social and political circumstances in which he or she lives (see Chapter 8). This notion of what we might think of as a "context free" identity underlies much of traditional ethics as well (see Chapter 15). That is, your race, gender, and class status aren't thought to be important in attempting to discover whether your actions are morally good or whether you are a good person. In this chapter, you will have the opportunity to explore the extent to which race actually does figure in the identities and in the moral lives of people who live in a racist society—namely, all of us.

Is the story about Bob puzzling? Why, indeed, are the policemen so suspicious and so lacking in trust? Suppose we add to the story the fact that Bob is black and the policemen are white. Suddenly, the story becomes less puzzling. And yet, in order to understand why something like this might happen, it is necessary to explore carefully the variety of ways in which racism manifests itself in our society. The fact that the policemen stop a black man who is running down the road may well be a function of their having a stereotypical notion that a black person who is running must be trying not to get caught for doing something wrong. Furthermore, if the community in which Bob is running is largely white, his mere presence may be considered grounds for suspicion. The fact that the policemen are inclined to believe that Bob is lying about his employment indicates their tendency to think that blacks can't be account executives. Indeed, in our society it is the case that black people are less likely than white people to be jogging down country roads in middle-class communities. It is also less likely that they will be account executives. So, the racism of our society does make Bob an anomaly. This may explain the responses of the policemen, but does it justify them?

The readings in this chapter are designed to address the ways in which particular practices, attitudes, and institutions serve to perpetuate racism and thereby define the context within which white people and people of color negotiate their individual identities and their relationships with one another. The essay by Jean-Paul Sartre focuses on anti-Semitism. While anti-Semitism may be properly understood as discrimination on the basis of ethnicity rather than race, Sartre's analysis of anti-Semitism provides an account of the psychological mechanisms involved in the sort of thinking that underlies the hatefulness of discrimination in a more general sense. For Sartre, the overtly anti-Semitic person is driven by a passionate hatred of Jews that serves to buttress his own self-esteem. Such a person attempts to overcome his own mediocrity by constructing another group of people as essentially inferior to him. Laurence Thomas discusses the significance of his own role as a black professor. Why should race or gender matter if the most important thing a professor does is to convey knowledge to his or her students? Thomas raises these questions in the context of current arguments about the legitimacy of affirmative action policies designed to correct the effects of discrimination against women and racial minorities. He argues that diversity within an academic institution provides the basis for wider intellectual affirmation, a prerequisite to success within such an environment. Hence, affirmative action is one step in countering the racism and sexism that have prevented racial minorities and women, respectively, from thriving either as faculty or as students.

W.E.B. DuBois was an American who embraced Africa as his true home and became known as "the Father of Pan-Africanism." He wrote movingly of the "two souls" that tormented African-Americans in his most famous book, *The Souls of Black Folk*, published in 1903. Anthony Appiah approaches the issue of race from a very different perspective. Appiah is particularly concerned to distinguish between "metaphysical" and "ethical" identity, and so to show how race, gender, and ethnicity figure in the construction of one's sense of self and sense of other. Elizabeth V. Spelman then argues that, given the power that white people have exercised over black people, there is the danger that the experiences, beliefs, and behavior of white people will continue to serve as the standard by which everyone is judged. Thus, even at a very basic level—namely, that of the body—those whose bodies are different from those of white people will be seen as deviant or inferior. For Spelman, it is particularly important to look at the way in which sexism and racism together ensure that black women, given that they are neither white nor male, will doubly fall short of the white male standard.

JEAN-PAUL SARTRE
Anti-Semite and Jew

JEAN-PAUL SARTRE *(1905–1980) was a leader of the existentialist movement. He wrote numerous books, essays, and plays, including* No Exit, Nausea, Existentialism and Humanism, *and* The Wall. *In 1964, he turned down the Nobel Prize for Literature.*

I F the Jew did not exist, the anti-Semite would invent him. . . . Anti-Semitism is a free and total choice of oneself, a comprehensive attitude that one adopts not only toward Jews but toward men in general, toward history and society; it is at one and the same time a passion and a conception of the world. . . . [O]rdinarily hate and anger have a *provocation:* I hate someone who has made me suffer, someone who condemns or insults me. . . . [A]nti-Semitic passion could not have such a character. It precedes the facts that are supposed to call it forth: it seeks them out to nourish itself upon them; it must even interpret them in a special way so that they may become truly offensive. Indeed, if you so much as mention a Jew to an anti-Semite, he will show all the signs of a lively irritation. If we recall that we must always *consent* to anger before it can manifest itself and that, as is indicated so accurately by the French idiom, we "put ourselves" into anger, we shall have to agree that the anti-Semite has *chosen* to live on the plane of passion. It is not unusual for people to elect to live a life of passion rather than one of reason. But ordinarily they love the *objects* of passion: women, glory, power, money. Since the anti-Semite has chosen hate, we are forced to conclude that it is the *state* of passion that he loves. . . .

How can one choose to reason falsely? Is it because of a longing for impenetrability? The rational man groans as he gropes for the truth; he knows that his reasoning is no more than tentative, that other considerations may supervene to cast doubt on it. He never sees very clearly where he is going; he is "open"; he may even appear to be hesitant. But there are people who are attracted by the durability of a stone. They wish to be massive and impenetrable; they wish not to change. Where, indeed, would change take them? We have here a basic fear of oneself and of truth. What frightens them is not the content of truth, of which they have no conception, but the form itself of truth, that thing of indefinite approximation. It is as if their own existence were in continual suspension. But they wish to exist all at once and right away. They do not want any acquired opinions; they want them to be innate. Since they are afraid of reasoning, they wish to lead the kind of life wherein reasoning and research play only a subordinate role, wherein one seeks only what he has already found, wherein one becomes only what he already was. This is nothing but passion. . . .

If then, as we have been able to observe, the anti-Semite is impervious to reason and to experience, it is not because his conviction is strong. Rather his conviction is strong because he has chosen first of all to be impervious.

He has chosen also to be terrifying. People are afraid of irritating him. No one knows to what lengths the aberrations of his passion will carry him—but he knows, for this passion is not provoked by something external. He has it well in hand; it is obedient to his will: now he lets go the reins and now he pulls back on them. He is not afraid of himself, but he sees in the eyes of

Sartre, Jean-Paul, "Anti-Semite and Jew," from *Anti-Semite and Jew,* translated by George J. Becker. Used by permission of Random House, Inc.

others a disquieting image—his own—and he makes his words and gestures conform to it. Having this external model, he is under no necessity to look for his personality within himself. He has chosen to find his being entirely outside himself, never to look within, to be nothing save the fear he inspires in others. What he flees even more than Reason is his intimate awareness of himself. . . .

. . . The anti-Semite has no illusions about what he is. He considers himself an average man, modestly average, basically mediocre. There is no example of an anti-Semite's claiming individual superiority over the Jews. But you must not think that he is ashamed of his mediocrity; he takes pleasure in it; I will even assert that he has chosen it. This man fears every kind of solitariness, that of the genius as much as that of the murderer; he is the man of the crowd. However small his stature, he takes every precaution to make it smaller, lest he stand out from the herd and find himself face to face with himself. He has made himself an anti-Semite because that is something one cannot be alone. The phrase, "I hate the Jews," is one that is uttered in chorus; in pronouncing it, one attaches himself to a tradition and to a community—the tradition and community of the mediocre.

We must remember that a man is not necessarily humble or even modest because he has consented to mediocrity. On the contrary, there is a passionate pride among the mediocre, and anti-Semitism is an attempt to give value to mediocrity as such, to create an elite of the ordinary. To the anti-Semite, intelligence is Jewish; he can thus disdain it in all tranquillity, like all the other virtues which the Jew possesses. They are so many ersatz attributes that the Jew cultivates in place of that balanced mediocrity which he will never have. . . .

Thus I would call anti-Semitism a poor man's snobbery. . . . Anti-Semitism is *not* merely the joy of hating; it brings positive pleasures too. By treating the Jew as an inferior and pernicious being, I affirm at the same time that I belong to the elite. This elite, in contrast to those of modern times which are based on merit or labor, closely resembles an aristocracy of birth. There is nothing I have to do to merit my superiority, and neither can I lose it. It is given once and for all. It is a *thing*. . . .

We begin to perceive the meaning of the anti-Semite's choice of himself. He chooses the irremediable out of fear of being free; he chooses mediocrity out of fear of being alone, and out of pride he makes of his irremediable mediocrity a rigid aristocracy. To this end he finds the existence of the Jew absolutely necessary. Otherwise to whom would he be superior? Indeed, it is vis-à-vis the Jew and the Jew alone that the anti-Semite realizes that he has rights. If by some miracles all the Jews were exterminated as he wishes, he would find himself nothing but a concierge or a shopkeeper in a strongly hierarchical society in which the quality of "true Frenchman" would be at a low valuation, because everyone would possess it. He would lose his sense of rights over the country because no one would any longer contest them, and that profound equality which brings him close to the nobleman and the man of wealth would disappear all of a sudden, for it is primarily negative. His frustrations, which he has attributed to the disloyal competition of the Jew, would have to be imputed to some other cause, lest he be forced to look within himself. He would run the risk of falling into bitterness, into a melancholy hatred of the privileged classes. Thus the anti-Semite is in the unhappy position of having a vital need for the very enemy he wishes to destroy.

LAURENCE THOMAS
What Good Am I?

LAURENCE THOMAS *teaches philosophy at Syracuse University and writes in the areas of social philosophy and moral psychology. His most recent book is* Sexual Orientation and Human Rights *(1999).*

WHAT good am I as a black professor? The raging debate over affirmative action surely invites me to ask this searching question of myself, just as it must invite those belonging to other so-called suspect categories to ask it of themselves. If knowledge is color-blind, why should it matter whether the face in front of the classroom is a European white, a Hispanic, an Asian, and so on? Why should it matter whether the person is female or male?

One of the most well-known arguments for affirmative action is the role-model argument. It is also the argument that I think is the least satisfactory—not because women and minorities do not need role models—everyone does—but because as the argument is often presented, it comes dangerously close to implying that about the only thing a black, for instance, can teach a white is how not to be a racist. Well, I think better of myself than that. And I hope that all women and minorities feel the same about themselves. It is a credit to the authors of this volume that they do not make much of this argument.

But even if the role-model argument were acceptable in some version or the other, affirmative action would still seem unsavory, as the implicit assumption about those hired as affirmative action appointments is that they are less qualified than those who are not. For, so the argument goes, the practice would be unnecessary if, in the first place, affirmative action appointees were the most qualified for the position, since they would be hired by virtue of their merits. I call this the counterfactual argument from qualifications.

Now, while I do not want to say much about it, this argument has always struck me as extremely odd. In a morally perfect world, it is no doubt true that if women and minorities were the most qualified they would be hired by virtue of their merits. But this truth tells me nothing about how things are in this world. It does not show that biases built up over decades and centuries do not operate in the favor of, say, white males over nonwhite males. It is as if one argues against feeding the starving simply on the grounds that in a morally perfect world starvation would not exist. Perhaps it would not. But this is no argument against feeding the starving now.

It would be one thing if those who advance the counterfactual argument from qualifications addressed the issue of built-up biases that operate against women and minorities. Then I could perhaps suppose that they are arguing in good faith. But for them to ignore these built-up biases in the name of an ideal world is sheer hypocrisy. It is to confuse what the ideal should be with the steps that should be taken to get there. Sometimes the steps are very simple or, in any case, purely procedural: instead of *A,* do *B;* or perform a series of well-defined steps that guarantee the outcome. Not so with nonbiased hiring, however, since what is involved is a change in attitude and feelings—not even merely a change in belief. After all, it is possible to believe something quite sincerely and yet not have the emotional wherewithal to act in accordance with that belief. It is this reality regarding sexism and racism that I believe is not fully appreciated in this volume.

The philosophical debate over affirmative action has stalled . . . because so many who oppose it, and some who do not, are unwilling to acknowledge the fact that sincere belief in equality does not entail a corresponding change in attitude and feelings in day-to-day interactions with women and minorities. Specifically, sincere belief does not eradicate residual and, thus, unintentional sexist and racist attitudes. So, joviality among minorities may be taken by whites as the absence of intellectual depth or sincerity on the part of those minorities, since such behavior is presumed to be uncommon among high-minded intellectual whites. Similarly, it is a liability for academic women to be too fashionable in their attire, since fashionably attired women are often taken by men as aiming to be seductive.

Lest there be any misunderstanding, nothing I have said entails that unqualified women and minorities should be hired. I take it to be obvious, though, that whether someone is the best qualified is often a judgment call. On the other hand, what I have as much as said is that there are built-up biases in the hiring process that disfavor women and minorities and need to be corrected. I think of it as rather on the order of correcting for unfavorable moral head winds. It is possible to be committed to gender and racial equality and yet live a life in which residual, and thus unintentional, sexism and racism operate to varying degrees of explicitness.

I want to return now to the question with which I began this essay: What good am I as a black professor? I want to answer this question because, insofar as our aim is a just society, I think it is extremely important to see the way in which it does matter that the person in front of the class is not always a white male, notwithstanding the truth that knowledge, itself, is color-blind.

Teaching is not just about transmitting knowledge. If it were, then students could simply read books and professors could simply pass out tapes or lecture notes. Like it or not, teachers are the object of intense emotions and feelings on the part of students solicitous of faculty approval and affirmation. Thus, teaching is very much about intellectual affirmation; and there can be no such affirmation of the student by the mentor in the absence of deep trust between them, be the setting elementary or graduate school. Without this trust, a mentor's practice will ring empty; constructive criticism will seem mean-spirited; and advice will be poorly received, if sought after at all. A student needs to be confident that he can make a mistake before the professor without being regarded as stupid in the professor's eyes and that the professor is interested in seeing beyond his weaknesses to his strengths. Otherwise, the student's interactions with the professor will be plagued by uncertainty; and that uncertainty will fuel the self-doubts of the student.

Now, the position that I should like to defend, however, is not that only women can trust women, only minorities can trust minorities, and only whites can trust whites. That surely is not what we want. Still, it must be acknowledged, first of all, that racism and sexism have very often been a bar to such trust between mentor and student, when the professor has been a white male and the student has been either a woman or a member of a minority group. Of course, trust between mentor and student is not easy to come by in any case. This, though, is compatible with women and minorities having even greater problems if the professor is a white male.

Sometimes a woman professor will be necessary if a woman student is to feel the trust of a mentor that makes intellectual affirmation possible; sometimes a minority professor will be necessary for a minority student; indeed, sometimes a white professor will be necessary for a white student. (Suppose the white student is from a very sexist and racist part of the United States, and it takes a white professor to undo the student's biases.)

Significantly, though, in an academy where there is gender and racial diversity among the faculty, that diversity alone gives a woman or minority student the hope that intellectual affirmation is possible. This is so even if the student's mentor should turn out to be a white male. For part of what secures our conviction that we are living in a just society is not merely that we experience justice, but that we see justice around us. A diverse faculty serves precisely this end in terms of women and minority students believing that it is possible for them to have an intellectually affirming mentor relationship with a faculty member regardless of the faculty's gender or race.

Naturally, there are some women and minority students who will achieve no matter what the environment. Harriet Jacobs and Frederick Douglass were slaves who went on to accomplish more than many of us will who have never seen the chains of slavery. Neither, though, would have thought their success a reason to leave slavery intact. Likewise, the fact that there are some women and minorities who will prevail in spite of the obstacles is no reason to leave the status quo in place.

There is another part of the argument. Where there is intellectual affirmation, there is also gratitude. When a student finds that affirmation in a faculty member, a bond is formed, anchored in the student's gratitude, that can weather almost anything. Without such ties there could be no "ole boy" network—a factor that is not about racism, but a kind of social interaction running its emotional course. When women and minority faculty play an intellectually affirming role in the lives of white male students, such faculty undermine a nonracist and nonsexist pattern of emotional feelings that has unwittingly served the sexist and racist end of passing the intellectual mantle from white male to white male. For what we want, surely, is not just blacks passing the mantle to blacks, women to women, and white males to white males, but a world in which it is possible for all to see one another as proper recipients of the intellectual mantle. Nothing serves this end better than the gratitude between mentor and student that often enough ranges over differences between gender and race or both.

Ideally, my discussion of trust, intellectual affirmation, and gratitude should have been supplemented with a discussion of nonverbal behavior. For it seems to me that what has been ignored by all of the authors is the way in which judgments are communicated not simply by what is said but by a vast array of nonverbal behavior. Again, a verbal and sincere commitment to equality, without the relevant change in emotions and feelings, will invariably leave nonverbal behavior intact. Mere voice intonation and flow of speech can be a dead give-away that the listener does not expect much of substance to come from the speaker. Anyone who doubts this should just remind her or himself that it is a commonplace to remark to someone over the phone that he sounds tired or "down" or distracted, where the basis for this judgment, obviously, can only be how the individual sounds. One can get the clear sense that one called at the wrong time just by the way in which the other person responds or gets involved in the conversation. So, ironically, there is a sense in which it can be easier to convince ourselves that we are committed to gender and racial equality than it is to convince a woman or a minority person; for the latter see and experience our nonverbal behavior in a way that we ourselves do not. Specifically, it so often happens that a woman or minority can see that a person's nonverbal behavior belies their verbal support of gender and racial equality in faculty hiring—an interruption here, or an all too quick dismissal or a remark there. And this is to say nothing of the ways in which the oppressor often seems to know better than the victim how the victim is affected by the oppression that permeates her or his life, an arrogance that is communicated in a myriad of ways. . . .

Before moving on let me consider an objection to my views. No doubt some will balk at the very idea of women and minority faculty intellectually affirming white male students. But this is just so much nonsense on the part of those balking. For I have drawn attention to a most powerful force in the lives of all individuals, namely trust and gratitude; and I have indicated that just as those feelings have unwittingly served racist and sexist ends, they can serve ends that are morally laudable. Furthermore, I have rejected the idea, often implicit in the role-model argument, that women and minority faculty are only good for their own kind. What is more, the position I have advocated is not one of subservience in the least, as I have spoken of an affirming role that underwrites an often unshakable debt of gratitude.

So, to return to the question with which I began this essay: I matter as a black professor and so do women and minority faculty generally, because collectively, if not in each individual case, we represent the hope, sometimes in a very personal way, that the university is an environment where the trust that gives rise to intellectual affirmation and the accompanying gratitude is possible for all, and between all peoples. Nothing short of the reality of diversity can permanently anchor this hope for ourselves and posterity.

. . . I do not advocate the representation of given viewpoints or the position that the ethnic and gender composition of faculty members should be proportional to their numbers in society. The former is absurd because it is a mistake to insist that points of view are either gender- or color-coded. The latter is absurd because it would actually entail getting rid of some faculty, since the percentage of Jews in the academy far exceeds their percentage in the population. If one day this should come to be true of blacks or Hispanics, they in turn would be fair game.

. . . [However], the continued absence of any diversity whatsoever draws attention to itself. My earlier remarks about nonverbal behavior taken in conjunction with my observations about trust, affirmation, and gratitude are especially apropos here. The complete absence of diversity tells departments more about themselves than no doubt they are prepared to acknowledge.

I would like to conclude with a concrete illustration of the way in which trust and gratitude can make a difference in the academy. As everyone knows, being cited affirmatively is an important indication of professional success.

Now, who gets cited is not just a matter of what is true and good. On the contrary, students generally cite the works of their mentors and the work of others introduced to them by their mentors; and, on the other hand, mentors generally cite the work of those students of theirs for whom they have provided considerable intellectual affirmation. Sexism and racism have often been obstacles to faculty believing that women and minorities can be proper objects of full intellectual affirmation. It has also contributed to the absence of women and minority faculty which, in turn, has made it well-nigh impossible for white male students to feel an intellectual debt of gratitude to women and minority faculty. Their presence in the academy cannot help but bring about a change with regard to so simple a matter as patterns of citation, the professional ripple effect of which will be significant beyond many of our wildest dreams.

If social justice were just a matter of saying or writing the correct words, then equality would have long ago been a *fait accompli* in the academy. For I barely know anyone who is a faculty member who has not bemoaned the absence of minorities and women in the academy, albeit to varying degrees. So, I conclude with a very direct question: Is it really possible that so many faculty could be so concerned that women and minorities should flourish in the academy, and yet so few do? You will have to forgive me for not believing that it is. For as any good Kantian knows, one cannot consistently will an end without also willing the means to that end. Onora O'Neill writes: "Willing, after all, is not just a matter of wishing that something were the case, but involves committing oneself to doing something to bring that situation about when opportunity is there and recognized. Kant expressed this point by insisting that rationality requires that whoever wills some end wills the necessary means insofar as these are available." If Kant is right, then much hand-wringing talk about social equality for women and minorities can only be judged insincere.

W.E.B. DuBois

The Souls of Black Folk

W.E.B. DuBois *(William Edward Burghardt DuBois) was born in 1868 in Massachusetts but died in self-imposed exile in Africa in 1963. He was an early champion of Black nationalism and Pan-Africanism. He went to Fisk College and then Harvard University, but even then was keenly sensitive to racial prejudice. (He later wrote "I was in Harvard but not of it.") He received his Ph.D. at the University of Berlin in Germany and began writing on the African Slave Trade. In Africa he became famous for his attacks on foreign imperialism and earned the title "Father of Pan-Africanism."*

OF OUR SPIRITUAL STRIVINGS

BETWEEN me and the other world there is ever an unasked question: unasked by some through feelings of delicacy; by others through the difficulty of rightly framing it. All, nevertheless, flutter round it. They approach me in a half-hesitant sort of way, eye me curiously or compassionately, and then, instead of saying directly, How does it feel to be a problem? they say, I know an excellent colored man in my town; or, I fought at Mechanicsville; or, Do not these Southern outrages make your blood boil? At these I smile, or am interested, or reduce the boiling to a simmer, as the occasion may require. To the real question, How does it feel to be a problem? I answer seldom a word.

And yet, being a problem is a strange experience,—peculiar even for one who has never been anything else, save perhaps in babyhood and in Europe. It is in the early days of rollicking boyhood that the revelation first bursts upon one, all in a day, as it were. I remember well when the shadow swept across me. I was a little thing, away up in the hills of New England, where the dark Housatonic winds between Hoosac and Taghkanic to the sea. In a wee wooden schoolhouse, something put it into the boys' and girls' heads to buy gorgeous visiting-cards—ten cents a package—and exchange. The exchange was merry, till one girl, a tall newcomer, refused my card,—refused it peremptorily, with a glance. Then it dawned upon me with a certain suddenness that I was different from the others; or like, mayhap, in heart and life and longing, but shut out from their world by a vast veil. I had thereafter no desire to tear down that veil, to creep through; I held all beyond it in common contempt, and lived above it in a region of blue sky and great wandering shadows. That sky was bluest when I could beat my mates at examination-time, or beat them at a foot-race, or even beat their stringy heads. Alas, with the years all this fine contempt began to fade; for the worlds I longed for, and all their dazzling opportunities, were theirs, not mine. But they should not keep these prizes, I said; some, all, I would wrest from them. Just how I would do it I could never decide: by reading law, by healing the sick, by telling the wonderful tales that swam in my head,—some way. With other black boys the strife was not so fiercely sunny: their youth shrunk into tasteless sycophancy, or into silent hatred of the pale world about them and mocking distrust of everything white; or wasted itself in a bitter cry, Why did God make me an outcast and a stranger in mine own house? The shades of the prison-house closed round about us all: walls strait and stubborn to the whitest, but

DuBois, W.E.B., "The Souls of Black Folk," Essay 1 from *Of Our Spiritual Strivings* (A. C. McClurg: Chicago, 1903).

relentlessly narrow, tall, and unscalable to sons of night who must plod darkly on in resignation, or beat unavailing palms against the stone, or steadily, half hopelessly, watch the streak of blue above.

After the Egyptian and Indian, the Greek and Roman, the Teuton and Mongolian, the Negro is a sort of seventh son, born with a veil, and gifted with second-sight in this American world,—a world which yields him no true self-consciousness, but only lets him see himself through the revelation of the other world. It is a peculiar sensation, this double-consciousness, this sense of always looking at one's self through the eyes of others, of measuring one's soul by the tape of a world that looks on in amused contempt and pity. One ever feels his two-ness,—an American, a Negro; two souls, two thoughts, two unreconciled strivings; two warring ideals in one dark body, whose dogged strength alone keeps it from being torn asunder.

The history of the American Negro is the history of this strife,—this longing to attain self-conscious manhood, to merge his double self into a better and truer self. In this merging he wishes neither of the older selves to be lost. He would not Africanize America, for America has too much to teach the world and Africa. He would not bleach his Negro soul in a flood of white Americanism, for he knows that Negro blood has a message for the world. He simply wishes to make it possible for a man to be both a Negro and an American, without being cursed and spit upon by his fellows, without having the doors of Opportunity closed roughly in his face.

This, then, is the end of his striving: to be a co-worker in the kingdom of culture, to escape both death and isolation, to husband and use his best powers and his latent genius. These powers of body and mind have in the past been strangely wasted, dispersed, or forgotten. The shadow of a mighty Negro past flits through the tale of Ethiopia the Shadowy and of Egypt the Sphinx. Throughout history, the powers of single black men flash here and there like falling stars, and die sometimes before the world has

rightly gauged their brightness. Here in America, in the few days since Emancipation, the black man's turning hither and thither in hesitant and doubtful striving has often made his very strength to lose effectiveness, to seem like absence of power, like weakness. And yet it is not weakness,—it is the contradiction of double aims. The double-aimed struggle of the black artisan—on the one hand to escape white contempt for a nation of mere hewers of wood and drawers of water, and on the other hand to plough and nail and dig for a poverty-stricken horde—could only result in making him a poor craftsman, for he had but half a heart in either cause. By the poverty and ignorance of his people, the Negro minister or doctor was tempted toward quackery and demagogy; and by the criticism of the other world, toward ideals that made him ashamed of his lowly tasks. The would-be black *savant* was confronted by the paradox that the knowledge his people needed was a twice-told tale to his white neighbors, while the knowledge which would teach the white world was Greek to his own flesh and blood. The innate love of harmony and beauty that set the ruder souls of his people a-dancing and a-singing raised but confusion and doubt in the soul of the black artist; for the beauty revealed to him was the soul-beauty of a race which his larger audience despised, and he could not articulate the message of another people. This waste of double aims, this seeking to satisfy two unreconciled ideals, has wrought sad havoc with the courage and faith and deeds of ten thousand thousand people,—has sent them often wooing false gods and invoking false means of salvation, and at times has even seemed about to make them ashamed of themselves.

Away back in the days of bondage they thought to see in one divine event the end of all doubt and disappointment; few men ever worshipped Freedom with half such unquestioning faith as did the American Negro for two centuries. To him, so far as he thought and dreamed, slavery was indeed the sum of all villainies, the cause of all sorrow, the root of all prejudice; Emancipation was the key to a promised land of sweeter beauty than ever stretched before the eyes of wearied Israelites. In song and exhortation swelled one refrain—Liberty; in his tears and curses the God he implored had Freedom in his right hand. At last it came,—suddenly, fearfully, like a dream. With one wild carnival of blood and passion came the message in his own plaintive cadences:—

"Shout, O children!
Shout, you're free!
For God has bought your liberty!"

Years have passed away since then,—ten, twenty, forty; forty years of national life, forty years of renewal and development, and yet the swarthy spectra site in its accustomed seat at the Nation's feast. In vain do we cry to this our vastest social problem:—

"Take any shape but that, and my firm nerves
Shall never tremble!"

The Nation has not yet found peace from its sins; the freedman has not yet found in freedom his promised land. Whatever of good may have come in these years of change, the shadow of a deep disappointment rests upon the Negro people,—a disappointment all the more bitter because the unattained ideal was unbounded save by the simple ignorance of a lowly people.

The first decade was merely a prolongation of the vain search for freedom, the boon that seemed ever barely to elude their grasp,—like a tantalizing will-o'-the-wisp, maddening and misleading the headless host. The holocaust of war, the terrors of the Ku-Klux Klan, the lies of carpet-baggers, the disorganization of industry, and the contradictory advice of friends and foes, left the bewildered serf with no new watchword beyond the old cry for freedom. As the time flew, however, he began to grasp a new idea. The ideal of liberty demanded for its attainment powerful means, and these the Fifteenth Amendment gave him. The ballot, which before he had looked upon as a visible sign of freedom, he now regarded as the chief means of gaining and perfecting the liberty with which war had partially endowed him. And why not? Had not votes made war and emancipated millions? Had not votes enfranchised the freedmen? Was anything impossible to a power that had done all this? A million black men started with renewed zeal to vote themselves into the kingdom. So the decade flew away, the revolution of 1876 came, and left the half-free serf weary, wondering, but still inspired. Slowly but steadily, in the following years, a new vision began gradually to replace the dream of political power,—a powerful movement, the rise of another ideal to guide the unguided, another pillar of fire by night after a clouded day. It was the ideal of "book-learning"; the curiosity, born of compulsory ignorance, to know and test the power of the cabalistic letters of the white man, the longing to know. Here at last seemed to have been discovered the mountain path to Canaan; longer than the highway of Emancipation and law, steep and rugged, but straight, leading to heights high enough to overlook life.

Up the new path the advance guard toiled, slowly, heavily, doggedly; only those who have watched and guided the faltering feet, the misty minds, the dull understandings, of the dark pupils of these schools know how faithfully, how piteously, this people strove to learn. It was weary work. The cold statistician wrote down the inches of progress here and there, noted also where here and there a foot had slipped or some one had fallen. To the tired climbers, the horizon was ever dark, the mists were often cold, the Canaan was always dim and far away. If, however, the vistas disclosed as yet no goal, no resting-place, little but flattery and criticism, the journey at least gave leisure for reflection and self-examination; it changed the child of Emancipation to the youth with dawning self-consciousness, self-realization, self-respect. In those sombre forests of his striving his own soul rose before him, and he saw himself,—darkly as through a veil; and yet he saw in himself some faint revelation of his power, of his mission. He began to have a dim feeling that, to attain his place in the world, he must by himself, and not another. For the first time he sought to analyze the burden he bore upon his back, that dead-weight of social degradation partially masked behind a half-named Negro problem. He felt his poverty; without a cent, without a home, without land, tools, or savings, he had entered into competition with rich, landed, skilled neighbors. To be a poor man is hard, but to be a poor race in a land of dollars is the very bottom of hardships. He felt the weight of his ignorance,—not simply of letters, but of life, of business, of the humanities; the accumulated sloth and shirking and awkwardness of decades and centuries shackled his hands and feet. Nor was his burden all poverty and ignorance. The red stain of bastardy, which two centuries of systematic legal defilement of Negro women had stamped upon his race, meant not only the loss of ancient African chastity, but also the hereditary weight of a mass of corruption from white adulterers, threatening almost the obliteration of the Negro home.

A people thus handicapped ought not to be asked to race with the world, but rather allowed to give all its time and thought to its own social problems. But alas! while sociologists gleefully count his bastards and his prostitutes, the very soul of the toiling, sweating black man is darkened by the shadow of a vast despair. Men call the shadow prejudice, and learnedly explain it as the natural defence of culture against barbarism, learning against ignorance, purity against crime, the "higher" against the "lower" races. To which the Negro cries Amen! and swears that to so much of this strange prejudice as is founded on just homage to civilization, culture, righteousness, and progress, he humbly bows and meekly does obeisance. But before that nameless prejudice that leaps beyond all this he stands helpless, dismayed, and well-nigh speechless; before that personal disrespect and mockery, the ridicule and systematic humiliation, the distortion of fact and wanton license of fancy, the cynical ignoring of the better and the boisterous welcoming of the worse, the all-pervading desire to inculcate disdain for everything black, from Toussaint to the devil,—before this there rises a sickening despair that would disarm and discourage any nation

save that black host to whom "discouragement" is an unwritten word.

But the facing of so vast a prejudice could not but bring the inevitable self-questioning, self-disparagement, and lowering of ideals which ever accompany repression and breed in an atmosphere of contempt and hate. Whisperings and portents came borne upon the four winds; Lo! we are diseased and dying, cried the dark hosts; we cannot write, our voting is vain; what need of education, since we must always cook and serve? And the Nation echoed and enforced this self-criticism, saying: Be content to be servants, and nothing more; what need of higher culture for half-men? Away with the black man's ballot, by force or fraud,—and behold the suicide of a race! Nevertheless, out of the evil came something of good,—the more careful adjustment of education to real life, the clearer perception of the Negroes' social responsibilities, and the sobering realization of the meaning of progress.

So dawned the time of *Sturm und Drang:* storm and stress to-day rocks our little boat on the mad waters of the world-sea; there is within and without the sound of conflict, the burning of body and rending of soul; inspiration strives with doubt, and faith with vain questionings. The bright ideals of the past,—physical freedom, political power, the training of brains and the training of hands,—all these in turn have waxed and waned, until even the last grows dim and overcast. Are they all wrong,—all false? No, not that, but each alone was over-simple and incomplete,—the dreams of a credulous race-childhood, or the fond imaginings of the other world which does not know and does not want to know our power. To be really true, all these ideals must be melted and welded into one. The training of the schools we need to-day more than ever,—the training of deft hands, quick eyes and ears, and above all the broader, deeper, higher culture of gifted minds and pure hearts. The power of the ballot we need in sheer self-defence,—else what shall save us from a second slavery? Freedom, too, the long-sought, we still seek,—the freedom of life and limb, the freedom to work and think, the freedom to love and aspire. Work, culture, liberty,—all these we need, not singly but together, not successively but together, each growing and aiding each, and all striving toward that vaster ideal that swims before the Negro people, the ideal of human brotherhood, gained through the unifying ideal of Race; the ideal of fostering and developing the traits and talents of the Negro, not in opposition to or contempt for other races, but rather in large conformity to the greater ideals of the American Republic, in order that some day on American soil two world-races may give each to each those characteristics both so sadly lack. We the darker ones come even now not altogether empty-handed: there are to-day no truer exponents of the pure human spirit of the Declaration of Independence than the American Negroes; there is no true American music but the wild sweet melodies of the Negro slave; the American fairy tales and folk-lore are Indian and African; and, all in all, we black men seem the sole oasis of simple faith and reverence in a dusty desert of dollars and smartness. Will America be poorer if she replace her brutal dyspeptic blundering with light-hearted but determined Negro humility? or her coarse and cruel wit with loving jovial good-humor? or her vulgar music with the soul of the Sorrow Songs?

Merely a concrete test of the underlying principles of the great republic is the Negro Problem, and the spiritual striving of the freedmen's sons is the travail of souls whose burden is almost beyond the measure of their strength, but who bear it in the names of an historic race, in the name of this land of their fathers' fathers, and in the name of human opportunity.

ANTHONY APPIAH
"But Would That Still Be Me?"

ANTHONY APPIAH *is a professor of philosophy and Afro-American studies at Harvard University. He has published widely on the relations among philosophy, ethnicity, and race. His books include* In My Father's House: Africa in the Philosophy of Culture *(1992) and* Globalization and Its Discontents *(1998).*

I F you had asked most Anglo-American philosophers twenty-five years ago what conditions someone had to meet in order to be (identical with) me, they would, no doubt, have taken this (correctly) to be a conceptual question, and (incorrectly) inferred that is was to be answered a priori by reflection in the properties whose presence would have led them to say that an imagined entity was Anthony Appiah. Since there are hardly any properties of persons whose absence we cannot intelligibly imagine, it was tempting to conclude that there was something odd about the very question.

. . . Some believe not only that this is a question about real essences, but that we know its answer: that the real essence of a person is the

Appiah, Anthony, "But Would That Still Be Me?" from *The Journal Of Philosophy*, LXXXVII, No. 10 (October 1990). Reprinted by permission of The Journal of Philosophy, Inc. and the author.

chromosomal structure produced by the coition of his actual parents, a thesis that is the biological fleshing out of the metaphysical doctrine of the necessity of origins. . . . [It] seems to me that there is an important set of questions that recent theorizing [about personal identity] has left to one side, a set of questions that can also be raised by asking, about a possible individual, "But would that still be me?" I want to argue that there is a sense of this question which is best answered in the "old-fashioned" conceptual way; and to get at what I have in mind, nothing could provide a better starting point than questions about "race," ethnicity, gender, and sex.

Consider, for the purposes of an initial example, the possibility that I might have been born a girl. Someone convinced of the chromosomal account of individual identity and convinced, too, that what it is to be biologically female or male is to have the appropriate chromosomal structure, will argue that this is only an apparent possibility. A female person could have been born to my parents when I was, if a different sperm and egg had met: but she would not have been me. It will be false, in this view, that I could have been born a woman.

I am prepared to concede all this for the purposes of argument; but there is a different question I might want to consider about a different possibility. Might I not, without any genetic modification, have been raised as a girl? This sort of thing certainly can happen; as when, for example, surgeons engaged in male circumcision remove the whole penis in error: rather than face a child with what—in our society—is bound to be the trauma of growing into a man without a penis, surgeons will often, in such circumstance, remove the testes from the abdomen, construct a facsimile of the female external genitalia, and ask the parents to bring the child back for hormone therapy in time to manage a facsimile of female puberty. If the good doctor who circumcised me had made such a mistake, could not I—this very metaphysical individual here—have been raised with a feminine (social) gender even though, on the chromosomal essentialist view, I was still of the male (biological) sex?

My claim in this paper is that, while there may be a sense of the question, "Would that have been me?" under which the answer to this question is "yes," there is another, intelligible reading under which it could, surely, be "no."

To get at that reading, consider the—admittedly, very different—possibility that I might seek to have a sex change prior to which I could consider our guiding question about the possible future social female this metaphysical individual would then become. "Would that still be me?" I could ask. Now it seems to me that I can give either of two answers here, and that which answer I should give depends in large part on how central my being-a-man—my social masculinity and, perhaps, my possession of the biological appurtenances of maleness—is, as would ordinarily say, to my identity. And it is in exploring this sense of the term "identity" that we can come to learn why it is that there is a sense to this question—I shall call it the ethical sense—in which I may choose to answer it in the negative.

To say that I may choose is to speak loosely. The issue is not really a matter of choice. What answer I should give to the question understood this way depends on how central my being-a-man is to my identity, not on how central I choose to make it. Transsexuals will surely answer in the affirmative; they often say that they were always of the "other" sex all along. For the chromosomal essentialist, this will be false. But a transsexual might . . . come to conclude that what he or she really had in mind was the different thought that his or her real identity, in the sense of the term I am now trying to explore, was that of the sex into which he or she was not born. And if I were a transsexual convinced of this I would say, contemplating the feminine person that I might become, "Yes, that would be me; in fact it would be the real me, the one I have always really been all along."

But what I am actually inclined to say is: "No. A sex-change operation would make of the (metaphysical) person a different (ethical) person." And so there is a sense in which she would not be me.

As many people think of them, sex (female and male, the biological statuses) and gender (masculine and feminine, the social roles) provide the sharpest models for a distinction between the metaphysical notion of identity . . . and the notion of identity—the ethical notion—that I am seeking to explore. I say "as many people think of them" because the real world is full of complications. Not every human being is XX or XY. And there are people who are XY in whom the indifferent gonad was not prompted to form the characteristic male external genitalia; people whom it seems to me odd to regard as "really" biological males. Just as it would be odd to treat an XX person with male external genitalia, produced as the result of a burst of testosterone from a maternal tumor, as "really" biologically female. Once you have an inkling of how messy the real world of the biology of the reproductive organs is, you are likely, if you are wise, to give up the idea that there are just two biological sexes into which all human beings must fall. And this is important because most people do not make the distinctions (or know the facts) necessary to appreciate this, and thus have thoughts about what it is to be a man or a woman which involve concepts that essentially presuppose falsehoods about how people biologically are. Before someone has made a sex-gender conceptual distinction we cannot always say whether what these thoughts were about was one or the other: there are, so to speak, thoughts that no one who *had* made these distinctions could have.

But the general point can be made in cases far from the biological hard cases: if you consider a straightforward case of an XY biological infant, born with standard male internal and external genitalia, who is assigned a feminine gender as the result of early loss of his gonads, it is clear that such a person can agree to a . . . "metaphysical" identification as a biological male and insist on the centrality to her of her feminine-gender identity, on being, so to speak, ethically a woman. But before I say more about what this means, it will help to have a couple of rather different cases before us.

Take next, then, so-called "racial" identity. Here the biological situation is much worse than

in the case of sex. No coherent system of biological classification of people—no classification, that is, that serves explanatory purposes central to biological theory—corresponds to the folk-theoretical classifications of people into Caucasian, Negro, and such. This is not, of course, to deny that there are differences in morphology among humans: people's skins do differ in color. But these sorts of distinctions are not—as those who, believe in races apparently suppose—markers of deeper biologically-based racial essences, correlating closely with most (or even many) important biological (let alone nonbiological) properties. I announce this rather than argue for it, because it is hardly a piece of biological news, being part of a mainstream consensus in human biology. This means that here we cannot make use of an analog of the systematic sex-gender distinction: the underlying biology does not deliver something that we can use, like the sex chromosomes, as a biological essence for the Caucasian or the Negro.

But this does not mean that people cannot have ethical identities tied up with being, say, Euro- or African- or Asian-American; what it does mean, given that such identities often presuppose falsehood about the underlying biology, is that, once the facts are in, a different theoretical account of those identities is required. From an external point of view, we can construct an account of what it is that people take to be grounds for assigning people to these racial categories. We can note that they are supposed to be asymmetrically based on descent: that "whites" in America are supposed to have no non-"white" ancestry, but that "blacks" and Asians may have non-"black" and non-Asian ancestry. But from the point of view of people whose ethical identity is at stake, it is not going to be enough simply to remark how others classify them. And to see this we can return to our guiding question.

Let us suppose that an American of African descent could be offered the possibility of losing all the morphological markers that are associated in this society with that descent. Her skin is lightened, her hair straightened, her lips thinned: she has, in short, all the services of Michael Jackson's cosmetic surgeon and more. Surely, in contemplating this possibility, she could ask herself whether, once these changes had occurred, the resulting ethical person "would still be me." And, so far as I can see, almost everyone who does contemplate this question in our society is likely to judge that, whether or not these changes are desirable, the answer here must be "yes."

I am asserting here, therefore, a contrast between our attitudes to (ethical) gender and (ethical) "race." I suggest that we standardly hold it open to people to believe that the replacement of the characteristic morphology of their sex with a (facsimile) of that of the other (major) one would produce someone other than themselves, a new ethical person; while the replacement of the characteristic morphology of their sex with a (facsimile) of that of the other (major) one would produce someone other than themselves, a new ethical person; while the replacement of the characteristic morphology of their ethical "race" by that of another would not leave them free to disclaim the new person. "Racial" ethical identities are for us—and that means something like, us in the modern West—apparently less conceptually central to who one is than gender ethical identities.

That this is so does not entail that being-an-African-American cannot be an *important* ethical identity: it is a reflection, rather, of the fact that ethical identity is not a matter of morphology, that skin and hair and so on are simply signs for it. Such an identity is, as we ordinarily understand it, exactly a matter of descent: and nothing you do to change your appearance or behavior can change the past fact that your ancestors were of some particular origin. Nevertheless, even for those for whom being-African-American is an important aspect of their ethical identity, what matters to them is almost always not the unqualified fact of that descent, but rather something that they suppose to go with it: the experience of a life as a member of a group of people who experience themselves as—and are held by others to be—a community in virtue of

their mutual recognition—and their recognition by others—as people of a common descent.

It is a reasonable question how such "racial" identities differ from those we call "ethnic." What matters about the identity of, say, Irish-Americans—which was conceived of racially in the nineteenth century in North America—is that it, like an African-American identity, involves experiences of community in virtue of a mutual recognition of a common descent. What differentiates Irish-American from African-American identity, as understood in these United States, is that it is largely recognized nowadays that what flows from this common descent is a matter of a shared culture. People of Irish-American descent adopted and raised outside Irish-American culture are still, perhaps, to be thought of as Irish-Americans; but they have a choice about whether this fact, once they are aware of it, should be central to their ethical identities, and their taking it as central would involve them in adopting certain cultural practices. Someone who refuses to do anything with the fact of their Irish-American descent—who fails to acknowledge it in any of their projects—is not generally held to be inauthentic; is not held to be unfaithful to something about herself to which she ought to respond. So far as I can see, by contrast, African-Americans who respond in this way fall into two categories, depending on whether or not their visible morphology permits them to "pass," permits them, that is, to act in society without their African ancestry's being noticed.

If they cannot pass, they will often be thought of as inauthentic, as refusing to acknowledge something about themselves that they ought to acknowledge, though they will not be thought to be dishonest, since their morphology reveals the fact that is being denied. If they can pass, they will be thought of by many, as being not merely inauthentic but dishonest. And while they may have prudential reasons for concealing the fact of their (partial) African descent, this will be held by many to amount to inauthenticity, especially if they adopt cultural styles associated with "white" people.

Now, so far as I can see, these differences between the identities that we think of as "racial" and those which we think of as "ethnic" cannot be made intelligible without adverting to certain (false) beliefs. Someone who conceals the fact of an African ancestry in his social life quite generally is held to be inauthentic, because there is still around in the culture the idea that being (partially) descended from black people makes you "really" black—in ways that have ethical consequences—while being descended from Irish stock merely correlates roughly with a certain cultural identity. If "races" were biologically real, this would, perhaps, begin to be a possible distinction; though it would require further argument to persuade me that ethical consequences flowed from membership in races. But since they are not, this distinction seems, as I say, to require a distinction that someone apprised of the facts should just give up.

That "race" and gender have interestingly different relations to metaphysical identity would not obscure the fact that as ethical identities they have a central importance for us. What this means is, presumably, something like this: that for us, in our society, being-of-a-certain-gender and being-of-a-certain-race are for many people facts that are centrally implicated in the construction of life plans. To ignore one's race and one's gender in thinking about the ethical project of composing a life for oneself requires, in many minds, a kind of ignoring of social reality which amounts to attempting to fool oneself; and that is part of what is involved in the thought that passing for the "wrong" gender or race involves a certain inauthenticity.

We construct ethical identities—woman, man, African-American, "white"—in ways that depend crucially on false beliefs about metaphysical identities; something like each of them could be reconstructed out of other materials. But if we were to live in a society that did not institutionalize those false metaphysical beliefs, it is unclear that the project of reconstruction would be an attractive one. In a truly nonsexist, nonracist society, gender, the ethical identity constructed on the base of sexual differences, would at least be radically differently configured, and might, like "race," entirely wither away; ethnic identities, by contrast—and this is something an African-American identity could become—seem likely to persist so long as there are human cultures and subcultures, which is likely to mean as long as people are raised in families.

ELIZABETH V. SPELMAN
The Erasure of Black Women

ELIZABETH V. SPELMAN *teaches philosophy at Smith College. She is the author of* Inessential Woman: Problems of Exclusion in Feminist Thought *(1988) and most recently of* Fruits of Sorrow: Framing Our Attention to Suffering *(1997).*

Spelman, Elizabeth, "The Erasure of Black Women," from *Quest: A Feminist Quarterly*, Vol. 5, No. 4, 1982. Reprinted by permission of the author.

RECENT feminist theory has not totally ignored white racism, though white feminists have paid much less attention to it than have black feminists. Nor have white feminists explicitly enunciated and espoused positions of white superiority. Yet much of feminist theory has reflected and contributed to what Adrienne Rich has called "white solipsism":

> to think, imagine, and speak as if whiteness described the world. not the consciously held belief that one race is inherently superior to all others, but a tunnel-vision which simply does not see nonwhite experience or existence as precious or significant, unless in spasmodic, impotent guilt-reflexes, which have little or no long-term, continuing momentum or political usefulness.

In this essay, I shall focus on what I take to be instances and sustaining sources of such solipsism in recent theoretical works by, or of interest to, feminists—in particular, certain ways of comparing sexism and racism, and some well-ingrained habits of thought about the source of women's oppression and the possibility of our liberation. . . . To begin, I will examine some recent prominent claims to the effect that sexism is more fundamental than racism. . . . Before turning to the evidence that has been given in behalf of that claim, we need to ask what it means to say that sexism is more fundamental than racism. It has meant or might mean several different though related things.

• It is harder to eradicate sexism than it is to eradicate racism.

• There might be sexism without racism but not racism without sexism: any social and political changes which eradicate sexism will have eradicated racism, but social and political changes which eradicate racism will not have eradicated sexism.

• Sexism is the first form of oppression learned by children.

• Sexism is historically prior to racism.

• Sexism is the cause of racism.

• Sexism is used to justify racism.

In the process of comparing racism and sexism, Richard Wasserstrom describes ways in which women and blacks have been stereotypically conceived of as less fully developed than white men. "Men and women are taught to see men as independent, capable, and powerful; men and women are taught to see women as dependent, limited in abilities, and passive. . . ." But who is taught to see black men as "independent, capable, and powerful," and by whom are they taught? Are black men taught that? Black women? White men? White women? Similarly, who is taught to see black women as "dependent, limited in abilities, and passive"? If this stereotype is so prevalent, why then have black women had to defend themselves against the images of matriarch and whore?

Wasserstrom continues:

> As is true for race, it is also a significant social fact that to be a female is to be an entity or creature viewed as different from the standard, fully developed person who is male as well as white. **But to be female, as opposed to being black,** is not to be conceived of as simply a creature of less worth. That is one important thing that differentiates sexism from racism: the ideology of sex, as opposed to the ideology of race, is a good deal more complex and confusing. **Women are both put on a pedestal** and deemed not fully developed persons. (emphasis mine)

In this brief for the view that sexism is a "deeper phenomenon" than racism, Wasserstrom leaves no room for the black woman. For a black woman cannot be "female, as opposed to being black"; she is female *and* black. Since Wasserstrom's argument proceeds from the assumption that one is either female or black, it cannot be an argument that applies to black women. Moreover, we cannot generate a composite image of the black woman from the above, since the description of women as being put on a pedestal, or being dependent, never generally applied to black women in the United States and was never meant to apply to them.

Wasserstrom's argument about the priority of sexism over racism has an odd result, which stems from the erasure of black women in his analysis.

He wishes to claim that in this society sex is a more fundamental fact about people than race. Yet his description of woman does not apply to the black woman, which implies that being black is a more fundamental fact about her than being a woman. I am not saying that Wasserstrom actually believes this is true, but that paradoxically the terms of his theory force him into that position. . . .

ADDITIVE ANALYSES

. . . [S]EXISM and racism do not have different "objects" in the case of black women. Moreover, it is highly misleading to say, without further explanation, that black women experience sexism and racism. For to say merely that suggests that black women experience one form of oppression, as blacks—the same thing black men experience—and that they experience another form of oppression, as women—the same thing white women experience. But this way of describing and analyzing black women's experience seems to me to be inadequate. For while it is true that images and institutions that are described as sexist affect both black and white women, they are affected in different ways, depending upon the extent to which they are affected by other forms of oppression.

For example, . . . it will not do to say that women are oppressed by the image of the "feminine" woman as fair, delicate, and in need of support and protection by men. While all women are oppressed by the use of that image, we are not oppressed in the same ways. As Linda Brent puts it so succinctly, "That which commands admiration in the white woman only hastens the degradation of the female slave." More specifically, as Angela Davis reminds us, "the alleged benefits of the ideology of femininity did not accrue" to the black female slave—she was expected to toil in the fields for just as long and hard as the black male was.

Reflection on the experience of black women also shows that it is not as if one form of oppression is merely piled upon another. As Barbara Smith has remarked, the effect of multiple oppression "is not merely arithmetic." Such an

"additive" analysis informs, for example, Gerda Lerner's remark about the nature of the oppression of black women under slavery: "Their work and duties were the same as that of the men, while childbearing and rearing fell upon them as an added burden." But, as Angela Davis has pointed out, the mother-housewife role (even the words seem inappropriate) doesn't have the same *meaning* for women who experience racism as it does for those who are not so oppressed:

> . . . In the infinite anguish of ministering to the needs of the men and children around her (who were not necessarily members of her immediate family), she was performing the **only** labor of the slave community which could not be directly and immediately claimed by the oppressor. . . . Even as she was suffering from her unique oppression as female, she was thrust by the force of circumstances into the center of the slave community.

The meaning and the oppressive nature of the "housewife" role has to be understood in relation to the roles against which it is contrasted. The work of mate/mother/nurturer has a different meaning depending on whether it is contrasted to work which has high social value and ensures economic independence, or to labor which is forced, degrading and unpaid. All of these factors are left out in a simple additive analysis. How one form of oppression (e.g., sexism) is experienced, is influenced by and influences how another form (i.e., racism) is experienced. So it would be quite misleading to say simply that black women and white women both are oppressed as *women,* and that a black woman's oppression as a black is thus separable from her oppression as a woman because she shares the latter but not the former with the white woman. An additive analysis treats the oppression of a black woman in a sexist and racist society as if it were a *further* burden than her oppression in a sexist but non-racist society, when, in fact, it is a *different* burden. As the article by Davis among others, shows, to ignore the difference is to deny or obscure the particular reality of the black woman's experience.

If sexism and racism must be seen as interlocking, and not as piled upon each other, serious problems arise for the claim that one of them is more fundamental than the other. As we saw, one meaning of the claim that sexism is more fundamental than racism is that sexism causes racism: racism would not exist if sexism did not, while sexism could and would continue to exist even in the absence of racism. In this connection, racism is sometimes seen as something which is both derivative from sexism and in the service of it: racism keeps women from uniting in alliance against sexism. This view has been articulated by Mary Daly in *Beyond God the Father*. According to Daly, sexism is "root and paradigm" of other forms of oppression such as racism. Racism is a "deformity *within* patriarchy. . . . It is most unlikely that racism will be eradicated as long as sexism prevails."

Daly's theory relies on an additive analysis, and we can see again why such an analysis fails to describe adequately black women's experience. Daly's analysis makes it look simply as if both black and white women experience sexism, while black women also experience racism. Black women should realize, Daly says, that they must see what they have in common with white women—shared sexist oppression—and see that black and white women are "pawns in the racial struggle, which is basically not the struggle that will set them free as *women*." The additive analysis obscures the differences between black and white women's struggles. Insofar as she is oppressed by racism in a sexist context and sexism in a racist context, the black woman's struggle cannot be compartmentalized into two struggles—one as a black and one as a woman. But that way of speaking about her struggle is required by a theory which insists not only that sexism and racism are distinct but that one might be eradicated before the other. Daly rightly points out that the black woman's struggle can easily be, and has usually been, subordinated to the black man's struggle in antiracist organizations. But she does not point out that the black woman's struggle can easily be, and usually has been, subordinated to the white woman's struggle in anti-sexist organizations.

Daly's line of thought also promotes the idea that, were it not for racism, there would be no important differences between black and white women. Since sexism is the fundamental form of oppression, and racism works in its service, the only significant differences between black and white women are differences which men have created and which are the source of antagonism between women. What is really crucial about us is our sex; racial distinctions are one of the many products of sexism, of patriarchy's attempt to keep women from uniting. It is through our shared sexual identity that we are oppressed together; it is through our shared sexual identity that we shall be liberated together.

A serious problem in thinking or speaking this way, however, is that it seems to deny or ignore the positive aspects of "racial" identities. It ignores the fact that being black is a source of pride, as well as an occasion for being oppressed. It suggests that once racism is eliminated (1), black women no longer need be concerned about or interested in their blackness—as if the only reason for paying attention to one's blackness is that it is the source of pain and sorrow and agony. But that is racism pure and simple, if it assumes that there is nothing positive about having a black history and identity. . . .

RACISM AND SOMATOPHOBIA

. . . [F]EMINIST theorists as politically diverse as Simone de Beauvoir, Betty Friedan and Shulamith Firestone have described the conditions of women's liberation in terms which suggest that the identification of woman with her body has been the source of our oppression, and that, hence, the source of our liberation lies in sundering that connection. For example, de Beauvoir introduces *The Second Sex* with the comment that woman has been regarded as "womb"; woman is thought of as planted firmly in the world of "immanence," that is, the physical world of nature, her life defined by the dictates of their "biologic fate." In contrast, men live in the world of "transcendence," actively using their minds to create "values, mores, religions," the world of culture as opposed to the world of nature. Among Friedan's central messages is that women should be allowed and encouraged to be "culturally" as well as "biologically" creative, because the former activities, which are "mental," are of "highest value to society" in comparison to child-bearing and rearing—"mastering the secrets of atoms, or the stars, composing symphonies, pioneering a new concept in government or society." . . .

I bring up the presence of somatophobia in the work of Firestone and others because I think it is a force that contributes to white solipsism in feminist thought, in at least three related ways.

First, insofar as feminists do not examine somatophobia, but actually accept it and embrace it in prescriptions for women's liberation, we will not be examining what often has been an important element in racist thinking. For the superiority of men to women is not the only hierarchical relationship that has been linked to the superiority of the mind to the body. Certain kinds, or "races," of people have been held to be more body-like than others, and this has been meant as more animal-like and less god-like.

For example, in *The White Man's Burden*, Winthrop Jordan describes ways in which white Englishmen portrayed black Africans as beastly, dirty, highly sexed beings. Lillian Smith tells us in *Killers of the Dream* how closely run together were her lessons about the evil of the body and the evil of blacks.

Derogatory stereotypes of blacks versus whites (as well as of manual workers versus intellectuals) have been very similar to the derogatory stereotypes of women versus men. Indeed, the grounds on which Plato ridiculed women were so similar to those on which he ridiculed slaves, beasts and children that he typically ridiculed them in one breath. He also thought it sufficient ridicule of one such group to accuse it of being like another (women are like slaves, slaves are like children, etc.). Aristotle's defense of his claim about the inferiority of women to men in the *Politics* is almost the same as his defense of the view that some people are meant to be slaves. (Aristotle did not identify what he called the natural class of slaves by skin color, but he says that identifying that class would be much easier if there were readily available physical characteristics by which one could do that.)

Neither in women nor in slaves does the rational element work the way it ought to. Hence women and slaves are, though in different ways, to attend to the physical needs of the men/masters/intellectuals. . . .

So we need to examine and understand somatophobia and look for it in our own thinking, for the idea that the work of the body and for the body has no part in real human dignity has been part of racist as well as sexist ideology. That is, oppressive stereotypes of "inferior races" and of women have typically involved images of their lives as determined by basic bodily functions (sex, reproduction, appetite, secretions and excretions) and as given over to attending to the bodily functions of others (feeding, washing, cleaning, doing the "dirty work"). Superior groups, we have been told from Plato on down, have better things to do with their lives. As Hannah Arendt has pointed out, the position of women and slaves has been directly tied to the notion that their lives are to be devoted to taking care of bodily functions. It certainly does not follow from the presence of somatophobia in a person's writings that she or he is a racist or a sexist. But somatophobia historically has been symptomatic of sexist and racist (as well as classist) attitudes.

Human groups know that the work of the body and for the body is necessary for human existence, and they make provisions for that fact. And so even when a group views its liberation in terms of being free of association with, or responsibility for, bodily tasks, explicitly or implicitly, its own liberation may be predicated on the oppression of other groups—those assigned to do the body work. For example, if feminists decide that women are not going to be relegated to doing such work, who do we think is going to do it? Have we attended to the role that racism (and classism) historically has played in settling that question?

Finally, if one thinks—as de Beauvoir, Friedan and Firestone do—that the liberation of women requires abstracting the notion of woman from the notion of woman's body, then one perhaps also will think that the liberation of blacks requires abstracting the notion of a black person from the notion of a black body. Since the body is thought to be the culprit (or anyway certain aspects of the body are thought to be the culprits), the solution may seem to be: keep the person and leave the occasion for oppression behind. Keep the woman, somehow, but leave behind her woman's body; keep the black person but leave the blackness behind. . . .

Once the concept of woman is divorced from the concept of woman's body, conceptual room is made for the idea of a woman who is no particular historical woman—she has no color, no accent, no particular characteristics that require having a body. She is somehow all and only woman; that is her only identifying feature. And so it will seem inappropriate or beside the point to think of women in terms of any physical characteristics, especially if it has been in the name of such characteristics that oppression has been rationalized. . . .

RICH ON EMBODIMENT

. . . Adrienne Rich is perhaps the only well-known white feminist to have noted "white solipsism" in feminist theorizing and activity. I think it is no coincidence that she also noticed and attended to the strong strain of somatophobia in feminist theory. . . .

. . . Both de Beauvoir and Firestone wanted to break it by insisting that women need be no more connected—in thought or deed—with the body than men have been. De Beauvoir and Firestone more or less are in agreement, with the patriarchal cultural history they otherwise question, that embodiment is a drag. Rich, however, insists that the negative connection between woman and body be broken along other lines. She asks us to think about whether what she calls "flesh-loathing" is the only attitude it is possible to have toward our bodies. Just as she explicitly distinguishes between motherhood as experience and motherhood as institution, so she implicitly asks us to distinguish between embodiment as experience and embodiment as institution. Flesh-loathing is part of the well-entrenched beliefs, habits and practices epitomized in the treatment of pregnancy as a

disease. But we need not experience our flesh, our body, as loathsome. . . . I think it is not a psychological or historical accident that having reflected so thoroughly on flesh-loathing. Rich focused on the failure of white women to see black women's experience as different from their own. For looking at embodiment is one way (though not the only one) of coming to note and understand the *particularity* of experience. Without bodies we could not have personal histories, for without them we would not live at a particular time nor in a particular place. Moreover, without them we could not be identified as woman or man, black or white. This is not to say that reference to publicly observable bodily characteristics settles the question of whether someone is woman or man, black or white; nor is it to say that being woman or man, black or white, just means having certain bodily characteristics. But different meanings are attached to having those characteristics, in different places and at different times and by different people, and those differences make a huge difference in the kinds of lives we lead or experiences we have. Women's oppression has been linked to the meanings assigned to having a woman's body by male oppressors. Blacks' oppression has been linked to the meanings assigned to having a black body by white oppressors. We cannot hope to understand the meaning of a person's experiences, including her experiences of oppression, without first thinking of her as embodied, and second thinking about the particular meanings assigned to that embodiment. If, because of somatophobia, we think and write as if we are not embodied, or as if we would be better off if we were not embodied, we are likely to ignore the ways in which different forms of embodiment are correlated with different kinds of experience. . . . Rich does not run away from the fact that women have bodies, nor does she wish that women's bodies were not so different from men's. That healthy regard for the ground of our differences from men is logically connected—though of course does not ensure—to a healthy regard for the ground of the differences between black women and white women. . . .

PART FIVE

LIVING A GOOD LIFE

CHAPTER FOURTEEN

WHY SHOULDN'T I BE SELFISH?

Only this morning, no doubt, you had to face up to a basic moral question. Perhaps something you wanted was just sitting there, unguarded, and you could have walked off with it without fear of getting caught. Or maybe someone asked you a question, and you could have lied—much to your advantage. Or possibly you made a promise to a friend, who seems to have forgotten about it, and you wondered if you should remind him or not. Every day, we find ourselves choosing between our own interests and the interests of others, between our personal desires and the promises we have made or principles we ought to obey. But why should you concern yourself with others and obey principles that are not to your own advantage? In short, why shouldn't you be selfish, as Ntozake Shange argues (ironically) in her poem, "get it & feel good"?

Daily observation and perhaps logic seem to show us that all of our actions are self-interested, if not actually selfish. We seem to do what we want, whenever we can, and when we don't, it is because we can't, because someone or something prevents us, because we want something else even more, or because we are afraid of the consequences—which we fear even more than we want what we want. But if we can get what we want, and there is nothing that we want or fear more, the argument goes, we will surely do whatever will get us what we want. This tempting generalization soon becomes the thesis that "everyone is selfish" or more philosophically, "everyone is an egoist." We hesitate, however, because the thesis seems so crude and unflattering and because of an admittedly small cluster of actions and agents that seem not to be motivated by self-interest at all, examples of altruism that seem to have nothing to do with selfishness. Occasionally we find ourselves making a small sacrifice, performing an act of seemingly pure generosity, or obeying a rule despite the fact that it is not in our interest and there is virtually no chance of our getting caught for any such transgression. And we occasionally meet people and we read about saints who consistently behave with little regard for their own interests, apparently altruists, all the time.

Nevertheless, we are still tempted (or tormented) by that generalization. Ever since Plato (and no doubt before) the same question has plagued philosophers: "Why not be selfish?" The most obvious answers do not seem to work. For instance, "because it is unfair to others" will not be very effective with someone who readily admits that he or she doesn't really care about anyone else, and "because it will make you unhappy," although perhaps true, only rejects selfishness by an appeal to selfishness, so the egoistic thesis remains unchallenged.

In Plato's *Republic,* Glaucon (one of Socrates' several interlocutors) argues that we would all be selfish if we could get away with it, and he introduces the myth of the "ring of Gyges" to make the point. The ring in question supposedly rendered its wearer invisible, and if a man were invisible, Glaucon suggests, he could get away with anything. Indeed, Glaucon argues that if a person could get away with doing whatever he wanted and did not do so, people would think him a fool rather than a saint. Selfishness is the natural order of things, and there is no good reason—except fear of getting caught and suffering the consequences—why we do not all act selfishly all the time.

One of the arguments for the necessity of egoism is the argument from human nature, the argument that all of us are "naturally" selfish. One specific argument for the universality of **egoism** goes back to ancient times: that all of us naturally seek and enjoy pleasure, dislike and avoid pain. All our actions, accordingly, are aimed at this end, which is called hedonism, the pursuit of pleasure. Two thousand years ago, the Greek philosopher Epicurus defended this thesis, and he was so persuasive that we still call people who enjoy the good things in life "Epicureans." It is worth noting, however, that Epicurus did not defend the pursuit of every pleasure without qualification; he knew that some pleasures are better and more durable than others and urged us to seek the "higher" pleasures. Nevertheless, the argument that we act for the sake of our own pleasure (and to avoid pain) provides a powerful argument for egoism. It is argued that whatever people seem to be doing—going boating, studying for an exam, opening a can of Pepsi, helping a friend with a problem—they are really acting toward one goal: obtaining pleasure and avoiding pain. You want to go boating because of the pleasure you get out of boating. You study not just to learn but also to obtain pleasure—from the learning itself, but also from the confidence that you will do well in the exam or that you are doing what you are supposed to be doing on a Wednesday night and may well be rewarded. You want a Pepsi, but you really want the satisfaction, the quenching of thirst, and the uplifting feeling. You help a friend because it gives you pleasure to do so—or because you predict the pain of guilt if you don't. It seems, then, that people satisfy their own hedonistic interests. This gives us a way of understanding the behavior of saints and ourselves in our "best" moments: It may seem that we are acting unselfishly, but in fact we are working for the good feeling that comes from having done the right thing. Alternatively, we are just trying to avoid the painful feelings of guilt or shame, not to mention punishment and the verbal abuse of our neighbors, that follow obviously selfish and inconsiderate behavior.

The argument for universal egoism has recently received an even more sophisticated formulation in the theory of evolution and genetics. Perhaps selfishness is built right into our genes as a matter of evolutionary survival, for how long could an individual or even a species exist if it did not take care of itself? Saints, perhaps, are rare exceptions, as are the admirable inspirations of generosity that we experience ourselves.

But self-interest, it is argued, is built right into our basic nature, and although we might find exceptions to it, there is no avoiding the conclusion that we are all basically selfish, however altruistic our ideals. Against this, it is argued that cooperation and fellow feeling are also essential parts of human nature. The urge to help a fellow creature in trouble is just as strong and just as "natural" as the urge to satisfy one's own desires—indeed, that urge is one of our most natural desires. In this view, purely selfish actions become the exceptions, not sainthood and spontaneous generosity. Such controversies about the natural origins of selfishness go back to early interpretations of Genesis, but the modern argument becomes exquisitely subtle and scientific (represented here by Richard Dawkins). It is nothing less than an argument about our basic nature and what we can and should expect of ourselves. But even if selfishness is not "natural" as such, it may be argued that selfishness is essential to thriving. So argues the Russian immigrant philosopher Ayn Rand: We *ought* to be selfish, and what we call "altruism" is a form of pathetic self-destructiveness. But here we might start questioning the soundness of the distinction itself. Are all acts of altruism self-destructive? Philosopher Tara Smith argues on the basis of individual rights that the welfare state—altruism institutionalized—is illegitimate. James Rachels, taking up a similar concern, examines the underlying soundness of the Randian argument for self-interest.

One argument for the universality of selfishness is derived from logical considerations alone. It is argued, first, that people always do what they want to do barring obstacles and interference with their actions. If a man trips and falls on the way to the supermarket, we do not assume that he wanted to trip and fall, but if he succeeds in going to the market, we will not be easily persuaded that he did not want to do just that. Of course, our fellow may have gone to the market not because he enjoys shopping but rather because he desired some sausage meat for lunch, which he very much wanted. Or he may have gone to the market to get food for the cat and to stop her meowing—which annoyed him enormously. But we can assume that when a person completes an action without interference, he or she has satisfied his or her own desire—whether that desire involves pleasure and pain, keeping a promise, or proving one's sainthood.

But if every action involves the satisfaction of one's own desire, then it is tempting to conclude that every act is at least self-interested, if not selfish. This gives us a more cynical explanation of saints and our own generous impulses: Whatever the motives of our actions, the saints or we are satisfying desires, and so the actions are selfish. We might object here to the word *selfish* and insist on saving it for just those self-interested actions that also interfere with other people. Thus, buying a sausage and sharing it because one is both hungry and desirous of company is not selfish, but pushing everyone else out of the way to eat the whole sausage oneself would be. Nevertheless, in the sense that seems to count, all actions are selfish; it is just that some are obnoxiously so and others are quite acceptable to the rest of us (because they do not interfere with our own selfish desires). But if this is so, if there is a distinction to be made between those "selfish" actions that harm and those that help other people, we should suspect the true force of this "logical" argument. Perhaps the satisfaction of desire is irrelevant to the question of selfishness.

Against the view that all our actions are selfish, philosophers ever since Plato have vigorously argued (1) that at least some of our actions are not selfish but rather honestly based on generosity, charity, or moral principles; and (2) that we *ought* to act unselfishly. Even the ancient author Epicurus, whose name is almost synonymous with a life of self-indulgent pleasure, argued for moderation in the pursuit of pleasure and peace of mind. But the seventeenth century English philosopher Thomas Hobbes argued that people are basically selfish by nature, and he is followed by a selection from the Scottish economist Adam Smith (in whose name selfishness is often defended), who argues that concern for others, not only self-interest, is built right into our human natures. Next Oxford evolutionist Richard Dawkins argues a similar thesis on the level of the gene. Then follows the debate between Ayn Rand, Tara Smith, and James Rachels. Most philosophers now reject the psychological and logical arguments that make all actions out to be selfish, and most also agree with the ethical thesis that we ought to act unselfishly, at least some of the time. Finally, Jim Holt discusses the limits of altruism.

NTOZAKE SHANGE

get it & feel good

NTOZAKE SHANGE *is a poet, novelist, playwright, and educator. Her most famous work is her play* For Colored Girls Who Have Considered Suicide When the Rainbow Is Enuf. *Her plays have been produced both on Broadway and in regional theater across the world. She has received the Obie Award and the Outer Critics Circle Award.*

you cd just take what
he's got for you
i mean what's available
cd add up in the long run
if it's music/take it
say he's got good
dishwashing techniques
he cd be a marvelous
masseur/take it
whatever good there is to
get/get it & feel good

say there's an electrical
wiring fanatic/he cd
come in handy some day
suppose they know how to tend plants
if you want somebody
with guts/you cd go to a rodeo
a prize fight/or a gang war might be up
    your alley
there's somebody out there
with something you want/
not alla it/but a lil
bit from here & there can
add up in the long run

whatever good there is to get
get it & feel good
this one's got kisses
that one can lay
linoleum
this one likes wine

that one fries butter fish
real good
this one is a anarcho-musicologist
this one wants pushkin to rise again
& that one has had it with the past tense/
whatever good there is to get/
get it & feel good
this one cd make music
roll around the small of
yr back & that one jumps
up & down in the gardens
it cd be yrs
there really is enuf to get
by with in this world but
you have to know what yr looking
for/whatever good there is to get
get it & feel good
you have to know what
they will give up easily
what's available is not always
all that's possible
but there's so much fluctuation
in the market these days
you have to be
particular

whatever good there is to get
get it & feel good
whatever good there is to get
get it & feel good/get it & feel good
snatch it & feel good
grab it & feel good

steal it & feel good	you cd
borrow it & feel good	oh yeah
reach it & feel good	& feel good.

PLATO

The Ring of Gyges

PLATO's *(427–347 B.C.) Republic is a blueprint for what would be, in Plato's opinion, the ideal society. Its central theme is justice, and the challenge with which Plato begins is the problem of the immoralist—the man who thinks that there is no reason not to be selfish and pursue one's own interests. Socrates' interlocutor Glaucon argues this thesis by using the myth of the "ring of Gyges," which makes its wearer invisible and allows him to get away with anything.*

GLAUCON (TO SOCRATES)

I have never yet heard the superiority of justice to injustice maintained by anyone in a satisfactory way. I want to hear justice praised in respect of itself; then I shall be satisfied, and you are the person from whom I think that I am most likely to hear this; and therefore I will praise the unjust life to the utmost of my power and my manner of speaking will indicate the manner in which I desire to hear you too praising justice and censuring injustice. Will you say whether you approve of my proposal?

SOCRATES

Indeed I do; nor can I imagine any theme about which a man of sense would oftener wish to converse.

GLAUCON

I am delighted to hear you say so, and shall begin by speaking, as I proposed, of the nature and origin of justice.

They say that to do injustice is, by nature, good; to suffer injustice, evil; but that there is more evil in the latter than good in the former. And so when men have both done and suffered injustice and have had

Plato, "The Ring of Gynges," from *Republic*, Book 2, trans. Benjamin Jowett, New York: Heritage Press.

experience of both, any who are not able to avoid the one and obtain the other, think that they had better agree among themselves to have neither; hence they began to establish laws and mutual convenants; and that which was ordained by law was termed by them lawful and just. This, it is claimed, is the origin and nature of justice;—it is a mean or compromise, between the best of all, which is to do injustice and not be punished, and the worst of all, which is to suffer injustice without the power of retaliation; and justice, being at a middle point between the two, is tolerated not as a good but as the lesser evil, and honored where men are too feeble to do injustice. For no man who is worthy to be called a man would ever submit to such an agreement with another if he had the power to be unjust; he would be mad if he did. Such is the received account Socrates, of the nature of justice, and the circumstances which bring it into being.

Now that those who practise justice do so involuntarily and because they have not the power to be unjust will best appear if we imagine something of this kind: having given to both the just and the unjust power to do what they will, let us watch and see whither desire will lead them; then we shall discover in the very act the just and unjust man to be proceeding along the same road, following their interest, which all creatures instinctively pursue as their good; the force of law is required to compel them to pay respect to equality. The liberty which we are supposing may be most completely given to them in the form of such a power as is said to have been possessed by Gyges, the ancestor of Croesus the Lydian. According to the tradition, Gyges was a shepherd in the service of the reigning king of Lydia; there was a great storm, and an earthquake made an opening in the earth at the place where he was feeding his flock. Amazed at the sight, he descended into the opening, where, among other marvels which form part of the story, he beheld a hollow brazen horse, having doors, at which he stooping and looking in saw a dead body of stature, as appeared to him, more than human; he took from the corpse a gold ring that was on the hand, but nothing else, and so reascended. Now the shepherds met together, according to custom, that they might send their monthly report about the flocks to the king; into their assembly he came having the ring on his finger, and as he was sitting among them he chanced to turn the collet of the ring to the inside of his hand, when instantly he became invisible to the rest of the company and they began to speak of him as if he were no longer present. He was astonished at this, and again touching the ring he turned the collet outwards and reappeared; when he perceived this, he made several trials of the ring, and always with the same result—when he turned the collet inwards he became invisible, when outwards he was visible. Whereupon he contrived to be chosen one of the messengers who were sent to the court; where as soon as he arrived he seduced the queen, and with her help conspired against the king and slew him, and took the kingdom. Suppose now that there were two such magic rings, and the just put on one of them and the unjust the other; no man can be imagined to be of such an iron nature that he would stand fast in justice.

No man would keep his hands off what was not his own when he could safely take what he liked out of the market, or go into houses and lie with any one at his pleasure, or kill or release from prison whom he would, and in all respects be like a god among men. Then the actions of the just would be as the actions of the unjust; they would both tend to the same goal. And this we may truly affirm to be a great proof that a man is just, not willingly or because he thinks that justice is any good to him individually, but of necessity; for wherever anyone thinks that he can safely be unjust, there he is unjust. For all men believe in their hearts that injustice is far more profitable to the individual than justice and he who argues as I have been supposing will say that they are right. If you could imagine anyone obtaining this power of becoming invisible, and never doing any wrong or touching what was another's, he would be thought by the lookers-on to be an unhappy man and a fool, although they would praise him to one another's faces, and keep up appearances with one another from a fear that they too might suffer injustice. Enough of this.

Now, if we are to form a real judgement of the two lives in these respects, we must set apart the extremes of justice and injustice; there is no other way; and how is the contrast to be effected? I answer: Let the unjust man be entirely unjust, and the just man entirely just; nothing is to be taken away from either of them, and both are to be perfectly furnished for the work of their respective lives. First, let the unjust be like other distinguished masters of craft; like the skillful pilot or physician, who knows intuitively what is possible or impossible in his art and keeps within those limits, and who, if he fails at any point, is able to recover himself. So let the unjust man attempt to do the right sort of wrongs, and let him escape detection if he is to be pronounced a master of injustice. To be found out is a sign of incompetence; for the height of injustice is to be deemed just when you are not. Therefore I say that in the perfectly unjust man we must assume the most perfect injustice; there is to be no deduction, but we must allow him, while doing the most unjust acts, to have acquired the greatest reputation for justice. If he has taken a false step he must be able to recover himself; he must be one who can speak with effect, if any of his deeds come to light, and who can force his way where force is required, by his courage and strength and command of wealth and friends. And at his side let us place the just man in his nobleness and simplicity, wishing, as Aeschylus says, to be and not to seem good. There must be no seeming, for if he seems to be just he will be honoured and rewarded, and then we shall not know whether he is just for the sake of justice or for the sake of honours and rewards; therefore, let him be clothed in justice only, and have no other covering; and he must be imagined in a state of life the opposite of the former. Let him be the best of men, and let him be reputed the worst; then he will have been put to the test and we shall see whether his justice is proof against evil reputation and its consequences. And let him continue thus to the hour of death; being just and seeming to be unjust. When both have reached the uttermost extreme, the one of justice and the other of injustice, let judgement be given which of them is the happier of the two.

SOCRATES

Heavens! my dear Glaucon . . . how energetically you polish them up for the decision, first one and then the other, as if they were two statues.

EPICURUS

The Pursuit of Pleasure

EPICURUS (ca. 342–270 B.C.) was a Greek philosopher who argued that the good life consists of pleasure. He is still regarded as one of the most articulate spokespersons for hedonism. His insistence on pleasure, however, is hardly of the "beer and pizza" variety, as the following selection from his Menocceus *makes clear.*

LET no one when young delay to study philosophy, nor when he is old grow weary of his study. For no one can come too early or too late to secure the health of his soul. And the man who says that the age for philosophy has either not yet come or has gone by is like the man who says that the age for happiness is not yet come to him, or has passed away. Wherefore both when young and old a man must study philosophy, that as he grows old he may be young in blessings through the grateful recollection of what has been, and that in youth he may be old as well, since he will know no fear of what is to come. We must then meditate on the things that make our happiness, seeing that when that is with us we have all, but when it is absent we do all to win it.

The things which I used unceasingly to commend to you, these do and practise, considering them to be the first principles of the good life. First of all believe that god is a being immortal and blessed, even as the common idea of a god is engraved on men's minds, and do not assign to him anything alien to his immortality or ill-suited to his blessedness: but believe about him everything that can uphold his blessedness and immortality. . . .

Become accustomed to the belief that death is nothing to us. For all good and evil consists in sensation, but death is deprivation of sensation. And therefore a right understanding that death is nothing to us makes the mortality of life enjoyable, not because it adds to it an infinite span of time, but because it takes away the craving for immortality. For there is nothing terrible in life for the man who has truly comprehended that there is nothing terrible in not living. So that the man speaks but idly who says that he fears death not because it will be painful when it comes, but because it is painful in anticipation. For that which gives no trouble when it comes, is but an empty pain in anticipation. So death, the most

Epicurus, "The Pursuit of Pleasure," from *Epicurus: The Extant Remains* (1926) edited by Cyril Bailey. Reprinted by permission of Oxford University Press.

terrifying of ills, is nothing to us, since so long as we exist death is not with us; but when death comes, then we do not exist. It does not then concern either the living or the dead, since for the former it is not, and the latter are no more.

But the many at one moment shun death as the greatest of evils, at another yearn for it as a respite from the evils in life. But the wise man neither seeks to escape life nor fears the cessation of life, for neither does life offend him nor does the absence of life seem to be any evil. And just as with food he does not seek simply the larger share and nothing else, but rather the most pleasant, so he seeks to enjoy not the longest period of time, but the most pleasant.

And he who counsels the young man to live well, but the old man to make a good end, is foolish, not merely because of the desirability of life, but also because it is the same training which teaches to live well and to die well. Yet much worse still is the man who says it is good not to be born, but

once born make haste to pass the gates of Death. (Theognis, 427)

For if he says this from conviction why does he not pass away out of life? For it is open to him to do so, if he had firmly made up his mind to this. But if he speaks in jest, his words are idle among men who cannot receive them.

We must then bear in mind that the future is neither ours, nor yet wholly not ours, so that we may not altogether expect it as sure to come, nor abandon hope of it, as if it will certainly not come.

We must consider that of desires some are natural, others vain, and of the natural some are necessary and others merely natural; and of the necessary some are necessary for happiness, others for the repose of the body, and others for very life. The right understanding of these facts enables us to refer all choice and avoidance to the health of the body and the soul's freedom from disturbance, since this is the aim of the life of blessedness. For it is to obtain this end that we always act, namely, to avoid pain and fear. And when this is once secured for us, all the tempest of the soul is dispersed, since the living creature has not to wander as though in search of

something that is missing, and to look for some other thing by which he can fulfil the good of the soul and the good of the body. For it is then that we have need of pleasure, when we feel pain owing to the absence of pleasure; but when we do not feel pain, we no longer need pleasure. And for this cause we call pleasure the beginning and end of the blessed life. For we recognize pleasure as the first good innate in us, and from pleasure we begin every act of choice and avoidance, and to pleasure we return again, using the feeling as the standard by which we judge every good.

And since pleasure is the first good and natural to us, for this very reason we do not choose every pleasure, but sometimes we pass over many pleasures, when greater discomfort accrues to us as the result of them: and similarly we think many pains better than pleasures, since a greater pleasure comes to us when we have endured pains for a long time. Every pleasure then because of its natural kinship to us is good, yet not every pleasure is to be chosen: even as every pain also is an evil, yet not all are always of a nature to be avoided. Yet by a scale of comparison and by the consideration of advantages and disadvantages we must form our judgement on all these matters. For the good on certain occasions we treat as bad, and conversely the bad as good.

And again independence of desire we think a great good—not that we may at all times enjoy but a few things, but that, if we do not possess many, we may enjoy the few in the genuine persuasion that those have the sweetest pleasure in luxury who least need it, and that all that is natural is easy to be obtained, but that which is superfluous is hard. And so plain savours bring us a pleasure equal to a luxurious diet, when all the pain due to want is removed; and bread and water produce the highest pleasure, when one who needs them puts them to his lips. To grow accustomed therefore to simple and not luxurious diet gives us health to the full, and makes a man alert for the needful employments of life, and when after long intervals we approach luxuries, disposes us better towards them, and fits us to be fearless of fortune.

When, therefore, we maintain that pleasure is the end, we do not mean the pleasures of profligates and those that consist in sensuality, as is supposed by some who are either ignorant or disagree with us or do not understand, but freedom from pain in the body and from trouble in the mind. For it is not continuous drinkings and revellings, nor the satisfaction of lusts, nor the enjoyment of fish and other luxuries of the wealthy table, which produce a pleasant life, but sober reasoning, searching out the motives for all choice and avoidance, and banishing mere opinions, to which are due the greatest disturbance of the spirit.

Of all this the beginning and the greatest good is prudence. Wherefore prudence is a more precious thing even than philosophy: for from prudence are sprung all the other virtues, and it teaches us that it is not possible to live pleasantly without living prudently and honourably and justly, nor, again, to live a life of prudence, honour, and justice without living pleasantly. For the virtues are by nature bound up with the pleasant life, and the pleasant life is inseparable from them. For indeed who, think you, is a better man than he who holds reverent opinions concerning the gods, and is at all times free from fear of death, and has reasoned out the end ordained by nature? He understands that the limit of good things is easy to fulfil and easy to attain, whereas the course of ills is either short in time or slight in pain: he laughs at destiny, whom some have introduced as the mistress of all things. He

thinks that with us lies the chief power in determining events, some of which happen by necessity and some by chance, and some are within our control; for while necessity cannot be called to account, he sees that chance is inconstant, but that which is in our control is subject to no master, and to it are naturally attached praise and blame. For, indeed, it were better to follow the myths about the gods than to become a slave to the destiny of the natural philosophers: for the former suggests a hope of placating the gods by worship, whereas the latter involves a necessity which knows no placation. As to chance, he does not regard it as a god as most men do (for in god's acts there is no disorder), nor as an uncertain cause of all things: for he does not believe that good and evil are given by chance to man for the framing of a blessed life, but that opportunities for great good and great evil are afforded by it. He therefore thinks it better to be unfortunate in reasonable action than to prosper in unreason. For it is better in a man's actions that what is well chosen should fail, rather than that what is ill chosen should be successful owing to chance.

Meditate therefore on these things and things akin to them night and day by yourself, and with a companion like to yourself, and never shall you be disturbed waking or asleep, but you shall live like a god among men. For a man who lives among immortal blessings is not like to a mortal being.

THOMAS HOBBES
People Are Selfish

THOMAS HOBBES *(1588–1679) was an English philosopher famous for his work in political theory. He saw the fate of ancient Athens to be a warning against the excesses of*

Hobbes, Thomas, "People Are Selfish," from *Leviathan* by Thomas Hobbes (New York: Hafner, 1926).

democracy. His most famous work is Leviathan *(1651), in which, among other things, he suggests, at least, that all people are selfish by nature.*

IT may seem strange to some man, that has not well weighed these things; that nature should thus dissociate, and render men apt to invade, and destroy one another: and he may therefore, not trusting to this inference, made from the passions, desire perhaps to have the same confirmed by experience. Let him therefore consider with himself, when taking a journey, he arms himself, and seeks to go well accompanied; when going to sleep, he locks his doors; when even in his house he locks his chests; and this when he knows there be laws, and public officers, armed, to revenge all injuries shall be done him; what opinion he has of his fellow subjects, when he rides armed; of his fellow citizens, when he locks his doors; and of his children, and servants, when he locks his chests. Does he not there as much accuse mankind by his actions, as I do by my words? But neither of us accuse man's nature in it. The desires, and other passions of man, are in themselves no sin. No more are the actions, that proceed from those passions, till they know a law that forbids them: which till laws be made they cannot know: nor can any law be made, till they have agreed upon the person that shall make it.

It may peradventure be thought, there was never such a time, nor condition of war as this; and I believe it was never generally so, over all the world: but there are many places, where they live so now. For the savage people in many places of America, except the government of small families, the concord whereof dependeth on natural lust, have no government at all; and live at this day in that brutish manner, as I said before. Howsoever, it may be perceived what manner of life there would be, where there were no common power to fear, by the manner of life, which men that have formerly lived under a peaceful government, use to degenerate into, in civil war.

But though there had never been any time, wherein particular men were in a condition of war one against another; yet in all times, kings, and persons of sovereign authority, because of their independency, are in continual jealousies, and in the state and posture of gladiators; having their weapons pointing, and their eyes fixed on one another; that is, their forts, garrisons, and guns upon the frontiers of their kingdoms; and continual spies upon their neighbours; which is a posture of war. But because they uphold thereby, the industry of their subjects; there does not follow from it, that misery, which accompanies the liberty of particular men.

To this war of every man, against every man, this also is consequent; that nothing can be unjust. The notions of right and wrong, justice and injustice have there no place. Where there is no common power, there is no law: where no law, no injustice. Force, and fraud, are in war the two cardinal virtues. Justice, and injustice are none of the faculties neither of the body, nor mind. If they were, they might be in a man that were alone in the world, as well as his senses, and passions. They are qualities, that relate to men in society, not in solitude. It is consequent also to the same condition, that there be no propriety, no dominion, no *mine* and *thine* distinct; but only that to be every man's, that he can get: and for so long, as he can keep it. And thus much for the ill condition, which man by mere nature is actually placed in; though with a possibility to come out of it, consisting partly in the passions, partly in his reason. . . .

ADAM SMITH
Compassion

ADAM SMITH (1723–1790) is often called "the father of free enterprise." He is best known for his groundbreaking work in economics, The Wealth of Nations. *But before he wrote that book, which is often cited as a justification of pure self-interest, he wrote* A Theory of the Moral Sentiments, *from which this selection is taken. Here, he argues that people are not essentially selfish. They are naturally sympathetic to others and concerned for their well-being.*

HOW selfish soever man may be supposed, there are evidently some principles in his nature, which interest him in the fortune of others, and render their happiness necessary to him, though he derives nothing from it except the pleasure of seeing it. Of this kind is pity or compassion, the emotion which we feel for the misery of others, when we either see it, or are made to conceive it in a very lively manner. That we often derive sorrow from the sorrow of others, is a matter of fact too obvious to require any instances to prove it; for this sentiment, like all the other original passions of human nature, is by no means confined to the virtuous and humane, though they perhaps may feel it with the most exquisite sensibility. The greatest ruffian, the most hardened violator of the laws of society, is not altogether without it.

As we have no immediate experience of what other men feel, we can form no idea of the manner in which they are affected, but by conceiving what we ourselves should feel in the like situation. Though our brother is upon the rack, as long as we ourselves are at our ease, our senses will never inform us of what he suffers. They never did, and never can, carry us beyond our own person, and it is by the imagination only that we can form any conception of what are his sensations. Neither can that faculty help us to this any other way, than by representing to us what would be our own, if we were in his case. It is the impressions of our own senses only, not those of his, which our imaginations copy. By the imagination we place ourselves in his situation, we conceive ourselves enduring all the same torments, we enter as it were into his body, and become in some measure the same person with him, and thence form some idea of his sensations, and even feel something which, though weaker in degree, is not altogether unlike them. His agonies, when they are thus brought home to ourselves, when we have thus adopted and made them our own, begin at last to affect us, and we then tremble and shudder at the thought of what he feels. For as to be in pain or distress of any kind excites the most excessive sorrow, so to conceive or to imagine that we are in it, excites some degree of the same emotion, in proportion to the vivacity or dullness of the conception.

That this is the source of our fellow-feeling for the misery of others, that it is by changing places in fancy with the sufferer, that we come either to conceive or to be affected by what he feels, may be demonstrated by many obvious observations, if it should not be thought sufficiently evident of itself. When we see a stroke aimed and just ready to fall upon the leg or arm of another person, we naturally shrink and draw back our own leg or our own arm; and when it does fall, we feel it in some measure, and are hurt by it as well as the sufferer. The mob, when they are gazing at a dancer on the slack rope, naturally writhe and twist and balance their own bodies, as they see him do, and as they feel that they themselves

Smith, Adam, "Compassion," from *Theory of the Moral Sentiments.*

must do if in his situation. Persons of delicate fibres and a weak constitution of body complain, that in looking on the sores and ulcers which are exposed by beggars in the streets, they are apt to feel an itching or uneasy sensation in the correspondent part of their own bodies. The horror which they conceive at the misery of those wretches affects that particular part in themselves more than any other; because that horror arises from conceiving what they themselves would suffer, if they really were the wretches whom they are looking upon, and if that particular part in themselves was actually affected in the same miserable manner. The very force of this conception is sufficient, in their feeble frames, to produce that itching or uneasy sensation complained of. Men of the most robust make, observe that in looking upon sore eyes they often feel a very sensible soreness in their own, which proceeds from the same reason; that organ being in the strongest man more delicate, than any other part of the body is in the weakest.

Neither is it those circumstances only, which create pain or sorrow, that call forth our fellow-feeling. Whatever is the passion which arises from any object in the person principally concerned, an analogous emotion springs up, at the thought of his situation, in the breast of every attentive spectator. Our joy for the deliverance of those heroes of tragedy of romance who interest us, is as sincere as our grief for their distress, and our fellow-feeling with their misery is not more real than that with their happiness. We enter into their gratitude towards those faithful friends who did not desert them in their difficulties; and we heartily go along with their resentment against those perfidious traitors who injured, abandoned, or deceived them. In every passion of which the mind of man is susceptible, the emotions of the bystander always correspond to what, by bringing the case home to himself, he imagines should be the sentiments of the sufferer.

Pity and compassion are words appropriated to signify our fellow-feeling with the sorrow of others. Sympathy, though its meaning was, perhaps, originally the same, may now, however, without much impropriety, be made use of to denote our fellow-feeling with any passion whatever.

RICHARD DAWKINS
The Selfish Gene

RICHARD DAWKINS *is a British biologist and the author of* The Selfish Gene, *an excerpt from which is reproduced here.*

THIS chapter is mostly about the much-misunderstood topic of aggression. We shall continue to treat the individual as a selfish machine, programmed to do whatever is best for his genes as a whole. This is the language of convenience. At the end of the chapter we return to the language of single genes.

To a survival machine, another survival machine (which is not its own child or another close relative) is a part of its environment, like a rock or a river or a lump of food. It is something that gets in the way, or something that can be exploited. It differs from a rock or a river in one important respect: it is inclined to hit back. This is because it too is a machine which holds its immortal genes in trust for the future, and it too will stop at nothing to preserve them. Natural selection favours genes which control their survival machines in such a way that they make the best use of their environment. This includes making the best use of other survival machines, both of the same and of different species.

In some cases survival machines seem to impinge rather little on each others' lives. For instance moles and blackbirds do not eat each other, mate with each other, or compete with each other for living space. Even so, we must not treat them as completely insulated. They may compete for something, perhaps earthworms. This does not mean you will ever see a mole and a blackbird engaged in a tug of war over a worm; indeed a blackbird may never set eyes on a mole in its life. But if you wiped out the population of moles, the effect on blackbirds might be dramatic, although I could not hazard a guess as to what the details might be, nor by what tortuously indirect routes the influence might travel.

Survival machines of different species influence each other in a variety of ways. They may be predators or prey, parasites or hosts, competitors for some scarce resource. They may be exploited in special ways, as for instance when bees are used as pollen carriers by flowers.

Survival machines of the same species tend to impinge on each others' lives more directly. This is for many reasons. One is that half the population of one's own species may be potential mates, and potentially hard-working and exploitable parents to one's children. Another reason is that members of the same species, being very similar to each other, being machines for preserving genes in the same kind of place, with the same kind of way of life, are particularly direct competitors for all the resources necessary for life. To a blackbird, a mole may be a competitor, but it is not nearly so important a competitor as another blackbird. Moles and blackbirds may compete for worms, but blackbirds and blackbirds compete with each other for worms *and* for everything else. If they are members of the same sex, they may also compete for mating partners. For reasons which we shall see, it is usually the males who compete with each other for females. This means that a male might benefit his own genes if he does something detrimental to another male with whom he is competing.

The logical policy for a survival machine might therefore seem to be to murder its rivals, and then, preferably, to eat them. Although murder and cannibalism do occur in nature, they are not as common as a naive interpretation of the selfish gene theory might predict. Indeed Konrad Lorenz, in *On Aggression,* stresses the restrained and gentlemanly nature of animal fighting. For him the notable thing about animal fights is that they are formal tournaments, played according to rules like those of boxing or fencing. Animals fight with gloved fists and blunted foils. Threat and bluff take the place of deadly earnest. Gestures of surrender are recognized by victors, who then refrain from dealing the killing blow or bite which our naive theory might predict.

This interpretation of animal aggression as being restrained and formal can be disputed. In particular, it is certainly wrong to condemn poor old *Homo sapiens* as the only species to kill his own kind, the only inheritor of the mark of Cain, and similar melodramatic charges. Whether a naturalist stresses the violence or the restraint of animal aggression depends partly on the kinds of animals he is used to watching, and partly on his evolutionary preconceptions— Lorenz is, after all, a "good of the species" man. Even if it has been exaggerated, the gloved fist view of animal fights seems to have at least some truth. Superficially this looks like a form of altruism. The selfish gene theory must face up to the difficult task of explaining it. Why is it that animals do not go all out to kill rival members of their species at every possible opportunity?

The general answer to this is that there are costs as well as benefits resulting from outright pugnacity, and not only the obvious costs in time and energy. For instance, suppose that *B* and *C* are both my rivals, and I happen to meet *B*. It might seem sensible for me as a selfish individual to try to kill him. But wait. *C* is also my rival, and *C* is also *B*'s rival. By killing *B*, I am potentially doing a good turn to *C* by removing one of his rivals. I might have done better to let *B* live, because he might then have competed or fought with *C*, thereby benefiting me indirectly. The moral of this simple hypothetical example is that there is no obvious merit in indiscriminately trying to kill rivals. In a large and complex system of rivalries, removing one rival from the scene does not necessarily do any good: other rivals may be more likely to benefit from his death than oneself. This is the kind of hard lesson that has been learned by pest-control officers. You have a serious agricultural pest, you discover a good way to exterminate it and you gleefully do so, only to find that another pest benefits from the extermination even more than human agriculture does, and you end up worse off than you were before.

On the other hand, it might seem a good plan to kill, or at least fight with, certain particular rivals in a discriminating way. If *B* is an elephant seal in possession of a large harem full of females, and if I, another elephant seal, can acquire his harem by killing him, I might be well advised to attempt to do so. But there are costs and risks even in selective pugnacity. It is to *B*'s advantage to fight back, to defend his valuable property. If I start a fight, I am just as likely to end up dead as he is. Perhaps even more so. He holds a valuable resource, that is why I want to fight him. But why does he hold it? Perhaps he won it in combat. He has probably beaten off other challengers before me. He is probably a good fighter. Even if I win the fight and gain the harem, I may be so badly mauled in the process that I cannot enjoy the benefits. Also, fighting uses up time and energy. These might be better conserved for the time being. If I concentrate on feeding and on keeping out of trouble for a time, I shall grow bigger and stronger. I'll fight him for the harem in the end, but I

may have a better chance of winning eventually if I wait, rather than rush in now.

This subjective soliloquy is just a way of pointing out that the decision whether or not to fight should ideally be preceded by a complex, if unconscious, "cost-benefit" calculation. The potential benefits are not all stacked up on the side of fighting, although undoubtedly some of them are. Similarly, during a fight, each tactical decision over whether to escalate the fight or cool it has costs and benefits which could, in principle, be analyzed. This has long been realized by ethologists in a vague sort of way, but it has taken J. Maynard Smith, not normally regarded as an ethologist, to express the idea forcefully and clearly. In collaboration with G. R. Price and G. A. Parker, he uses the branch of mathematics known as Game Theory. Their elegant ideas can be expressed in words without mathematical symbols, albeit at some cost in rigour.

The essential concept Maynard Smith introduces is that of the *evolutionarily stable strategy,* an idea which he traces back to W. D. Hamilton and R. H. MacArthur. A "strategy" is a preprogrammed behavioural policy. An example of a strategy is: "Attack opponent; if he flees pursue him; if he retaliates run away." It is important to realize that we are not thinking of the strategy as being consciously worked out by the individual. Remember that we are picturing the animal as a robot survival machine with a preprogrammed computer controlling the muscles. To write the strategy out as a set of simple instructions in English is just a convenient way for us to think about it. By some unspecified mechanism, the animal behaves as if he were following these instructions.

An evolutionarily stable strategy or ESS is defined as a strategy which, if most members of a population adopt it, cannot be bettered by an alternative strategy. It is a subtle and important idea. Another way of putting it is to say that the best strategy for an individual depends on what the majority of the population are doing. Since the rest of the population consists of individuals, each one trying to maximize his *own* success, the only strategy that persists will be one which, once evolved, cannot be bettered by any deviant individual. Following a major environmental change there may be a brief period of evolutionary instability, perhaps even oscillation in the population. But once an ESS is achieved it will stay: selection will penalize deviation from it.

AYN RAND
The Virtue of Selfishness

AYN RAND *(1905–1982) was immensely popular in the 1950s for her novels* The Fountainhead *and* Atlas Shrugged, *in which she argued for individualism and "the virtue of selfishness" against the reigning ethic of "altruism."*

IN popular usage, the word "selfishness" is a synonym of evil; the image it conjures is of a murderous brute who tramples over piles of corpses to achieve his own ends, who cares for no living being and pursues nothing but the gratification of the mindless whims of any immediate moment.

Yet the exact meaning and dictionary definition of the word "selfishness" is: *concern with one's own interests.*

This concept does *not* include a moral evaluation; it does not tell us whether concern with one's own interests is good or evil; nor does it tell us what constitutes man's actual interests. It is the task of ethics to answer such questions.

The ethics of altruism has created the image of the brute, as its answer, in order to make men accept two inhuman tenets: (a) that any concern with one's own interests is evil, regardless of what these interests might be, and (b) that the brute's activities are *in fact* to one's own interest (which altruism enjoins man to renounce for the sake of his neighbors).

For a view of the nature of altruism, its consequences and the enormity of the moral corruption it perpetrates, I shall refer you to *Atlas Shrugged*—or to any of today's newspaper headlines. What concerns us here is altruism's *default* in the field of ethical theory.

There are two moral questions which altruism lumps together into one "package-deal": (1) What are values? (2) Who should be the beneficiary of values? Altruism substitutes the second for the first; it evades the task of defining a code of moral values, thus leaving man, in fact, without moral guidance.

Altruism declares that any action taken for the benefit of others is good, and any action taken for one's own benefit is evil. Thus the *beneficiary* of an action is the only criterion of moral value—and so long as that beneficiary is anybody other than oneself, anything goes.

Hence the appalling immorality, the chronic injustice, the grotesque double standards, the insoluble conflicts and contradictions that have characterized human relationships and human societies throughout history, under all the variants of the altruist ethics.

Observe the indecency of what passes for moral judgments today. An industrialist who produces a fortune, and a gangster who robs a bank are regarded as equally immoral, since they both sought wealth for their own "selfish" benefit. A young man who gives up his career in order to support his parents and never rises beyond the rank of grocery clerk is regarded as morally superior to the young man who endures an excruciating struggle and achieves his personal ambition. A dictator is regarded as moral, since the unspeakable atrocities he committed were intended to benefit "the people," not himself.

Observe what this beneficiary-criterion of morality does to a man's life. The first thing he learns is that morality is his enemy: he has nothing to gain from it, he can only lose; self-inflicted loss, self-inflicted pain and the gray, debilitating pall of an incomprehensible duty is all that he can expect. He may hope that others might occasionally sacrifice themselves for his benefit, as he grudgingly sacrifices himself for theirs, but he knows that the relationship will bring mutual resentment, not pleasure—and that, morally, their pursuit of values will be like an exchange of unwanted, unchosen Christmas presents, which neither is morally permitted to buy for himself. Apart from such times as he manages to perform some act of self-sacrifice, he possesses no moral significance: morality takes no cognizance of him and has nothing to say to him for guidance in the crucial issues of his life; it is only his own personal, private, "selfish" life and, as such, it is regarded either as evil or, at best, *amoral*.

Since nature does not provide man with an automatic form of survival, since he has to support his life by his own effort, the doctrine that concern with one's own interests is evil means that man's desire to live is evil—that man's life, as such, is evil. No doctrine could be more evil than that.

Yet that is the meaning of altruism, implicit in such examples as the equation of an industrialist with a robber. There is a fundamental moral difference between a man who sees his self-interest in production and a man who sees it in robbery. The evil of a robber does *not* lie in the fact that he pursues his own interests, but in *what* he regards

as to his own interest; *not* in the fact that he pursues his values, but in *what* he chose to value; *not* in the fact that he wants to live, but in the fact that he wants to live on a subhuman level (see "The Objectivist Ethics").

If it is true that what I mean by "selfishness" is not what is meant conventionally, then *this* is one of the worst indictments of altruism: it means that altruism *permits no concept* of a self-respecting, self-supporting man—a man who supports his life by his own effort and neither sacrifices himself nor others. It means that altruism permits no view of men except as sacrificial animals and profiteers-on-sacrifice, as victims and parasites—that it permits no concept of a benevolent coexistence among men—that it permits no concept of *justice.*

If you wonder about the reasons behind the ugly mixture of cynicism and guilt in which most men spend their lives, these are the reasons: cynicism, because they neither practice nor accept the altruist morality—guilt, because they dare not reject it.

To rebel against so devastating an evil, one has to rebel against its basic premise. To redeem both man and morality, it is the concept of "*selfishness*" that one has to redeem.

The first step is to assert *man's right to a moral existence*—that is: to recognize his need of a moral code to guide the course and the fulfillment of his own life.

For a brief outline of the nature and the validation of a rational morality, see my lecture on "The Objectivist Ethics" which follows. The reasons why man needs a moral code will tell you that the purpose of morality is to define man's proper values and interests, that *concern with his own interests* is the essence of a moral existence, and that *man must be the beneficiary of his own moral actions.*

Since all values have to be gained and/or kept by men's actions, any breach between actor and beneficiary necessitates an injustice: the sacrifice of some men to others, of the actors to the nonactors, of the moral to the immoral. Nothing could ever justify such a breach, and no one ever has.

The choice of the beneficiary of moral values is merely a preliminary or introductory issue in the field of morality. It is not a substitute for morality nor a criterion of moral value, as altruism has made it. Neither is it a moral *primary;* it has to be derived from and validated by the fundamental premises of a moral system.

The Objectivist ethics holds that the actor must always be the beneficiary of his action and that man must act for his own *rational* self-interest. But his right to do so is derived from his nature as man and from the function of moral values in human life—and, therefore, is applicable *only* in the context of a rational, objectively demonstrated and validated code of moral principles which define and determine his actual self-interest. It is not a license "to do as he pleases" and it is not applicable to the altruists' image of a "selfish" brute nor to any man motivated by irrational emotions, feelings, urges, wishes or whims.

This is said as a warning against the kind of "Nietzschean egoists" who, in fact, are a product of the altruist morality and represent the other side of the altruist coin: the men who believe that any action, regardless of its nature, is good if it is intended for one's own benefit. Just as the satisfaction of the irrational desires of others is *not* a criterion of moral value, neither is the satisfaction of one's own irrational desires. Morality is not a contest of whims.

TARA SMITH
Individual Rights, Welfare Rights

TARA SMITH *teaches philosophy at the University of Texas and works mainly on social and political philosophy. In the following piece, she uses the legitimacy of individual rights to attack what she calls "welfare rights" (the right of a needy person to public assistance, for example) as illegitimate.*

ONCE one understands that genuine rights cannot conflict with one another, the problem with welfare rights is obvious. Recognition of welfare rights would precipitate conflicts, necessitating the violation of the very freedom that is to be safeguarded by rights. Fulfilling the welfare rights of one person would require infringing on the liberty rights of others. Others' freedom would have to be invaded in order to satisfy welfare rightholders' needs. Fulfillment of the "right" to employment or health care, for instance, could be assured only by encroaching on others' freedom to run their businesses or spend their money as they choose. Requiring a company owner to employ someone or requiring a worker to finance others' health care compels that person to act against her will in the same way that an outlaw compels his victim to act against her will in the holdup. The person obligated to fulfill others' welfare rights is made, on pain of physical force, to surrender something that is hers.

Smith, Tara, "Individual Rights, Welfare Rights," from *Moral Rights and Political Freedom* (Rowman & Littlefield, 1995), pp. 199–202. Reprinted by permission of The Rowman & Littlefield Publishing Group.

If individuals are truly entitled to freedom of action, this invasion of their freedom cannot be abided. Sanctioning such a breach would defeat the purpose of recognizing rights. No one may have a right to infringe on rights. Such a right would completely unravel the protective fabric that rights provide. Yet this is precisely what recognition of welfare rights would do.

Property rights protect an owner's exclusive authority to control the use of particular goods. If a person's property may be seized in order to fulfill another person's welfare right, however, this authority is lost. Property rights would be fair game, open to others' appropriation. As such, they would no longer qualify as rights; they would no longer provide decisive moral protection.

There is simply no conceivable way to respect both liberty rights and welfare rights as rights, to treat both as having equal stature. One type of claim must yield to the other. If rights are to retain any usefulness, then when a practical dispute erupts, one right must hold sway. Which should it be? Neither of the alternatives could honor both claims as rights. For if property rights are given priority over welfare rights, we would not recognize welfare rights at all, since any welfare right requires violation of property rights. Thus an advocate of welfare rights must demand priority for welfare rights (since this is the only posture from which welfare rights can gain any respect). In that case, though, property rights would be obliterated.

Lest one be tempted to brush aside this problem on the notion that property rights are comparatively insignificant (that they pale beside certain other rights), it is important to realize that any violation of a property right also is an assault on the right to life. This is because, as we saw earlier, property rights are a necessary corollary of the right to life. This, in turn, again reflects the fact that strictly, individuals possess a single broad right to freedom of action. And freedom is indivisible.

The freedom that a person might exercise to lead her life as she chooses (e.g., by pursuing a career in theater, playing tennis, or publicly expressing her political opinions) or the freedom that a person might exercise to acquire property (by earning a paycheck, building a boat, or buying a computer) is the same freedom that is violated when another person (or government) forcibly prevents her from hiring whom she chooses or forces her to surrender her time or income to others. Just as individuals do not possess diverse rights, we do not possess diverse freedoms. Freedom is the general condition marked by the absence of others' use of force against a person. Consequently, a breach of any authentic right is an obstruction of a person's freedom. It prevents the victim from leading her life as she wishes. Whether the gun-wielding outlaw demands Valerie's wallet, her silence, her profession of devotion to Allah, her attendance at a political rally, or her ongoing submission to his commands, he is obstructing Valerie's authority to direct her own actions.

One person could not, then, respect another person's one right (such as to life or to liberty) while violating another of her rights (such as the right to property). Genuine rights all stand or fall together. By infringing on any specific right, the violator disrupts one particular use of the freedom to which his victim is entitled.

The central and inescapable barrier to recognition of welfare rights is that welfare rights could be satisfied only at the expense of other rights. Since money doesn't grow on trees—since jobs, services, and all the other objects of welfare rights are produced by individuals' efforts—to maintain that some are entitled to these things because of their failure to have acquired them without resorting to force is to declare some individuals the serfs of others. Some individuals' freedom will be sacrificed so that others can have these goods. This plainly contradicts the conviction that we should respect *all* individuals as ends in themselves. It retracts the recognition that each person is entitled to her own life. It abandons the reverence for individuals' freedom that respect for rights is meant to uphold.

JAMES RACHELS
Ethical Egoism

JAMES RACHELS *teaches philosophy at the University of Alabama and writes widely on both theoretical and practical ethical issues. In this selection, he considers the merits of psychological egoism—and raises some doubts about it.*

———

The achievement of his own happiness is man's highest moral purpose.

—AYN RAND
The Virtue of Selfishness (1961)

EACH year millions of people die of malnutrition and related health problems. A common pattern among children in poor countries is death from dehydration caused by diarrhea brought on by malnutrition. James Grant, executive director of the United Nations Children's Fund (UNICEF), estimates that about 15,000 children die in this way *every day*. That comes to 5,475,000 children annually. Even if his estimate is too high, the number that die is staggering.

For those of us in the affluent countries, this poses an acute moral problem. We spend money on ourselves, not only for the necessities of life but for innumerable luxuries—for fine automobiles, fancy clothes, stereos, sports, movies, and so on. In our country, even people with modest incomes enjoy such things. The problem is that we *could* forgo our luxuries and give the money for famine relief instead. The fact that we don't suggests that we regard our luxuries as more important than feeding the hungry.

Why do we allow people to starve to death when we could save them? Very few of us actually believe our luxuries are that important. Most of us, if asked the question directly, would probably be a bit embarrassed, and we would say that we probably should do more for famine relief. The explanation of why we do not is, at least in part,

that we hardly ever think of the problem. Living our own comfortable lives, we are effectively insulated from it. The starving people are dying at some distance from us; we do not see them and we can avoid even thinking of them. When we do think of them, it is only abstractly, as bloodless statistics. Unfortunately for the starving, statistics do not have much power to motivate action.

But leaving aside the question of *why* we behave as we do, what is our *duty*? What *should* we do? We might think of this as the "common-sense" view of the matter: morality requires that we balance our own interests against the interests of others. It is understandable, of course, that we look out for our own interests, and no one can be faulted for attending to his own basic needs. But at the same time the needs of others are also important, and when we can help others—especially at little cost to ourselves—we should do so. Suppose you are thinking of spending ten dollars on a trip to the movies, when you are reminded that ten dollars could buy food for a starving child. Thus you could do a great service for the child at little cost to yourself. Common-sense morality would say, then, that you should give the money for famine relief rather than spending it on the movies.

This way of thinking involves a general assumption about our moral duties: it is assumed

James, Rachels, "Ethical Egoism," from *Elements of Moral Psychology*. Reprinted by permission of The McGraw-Hill Companies.

that we have moral duties *to other people*—and not merely duties that we create, such as by making a promise or incurring a debt. We have "natural" duties to others *simply because they are people who could be helped or harmed by our actions.* If a certain action would benefit (or harm) other people, then that is a reason why we should (or should not) do that action. The common-sense assumption is that other people's interests *count,* for their own sakes, from a moral point of view.

But one person's common sense is another person's naive platitude. Some thinkers have maintained that, in fact, we have no "natural" duties to other people. *Ethical Egoism* is the idea that each person ought to pursue his or her own self-interest exclusively. It is different from Psychological Egoism, which is a theory of human nature concerned with how people *do* behave—Psychological Egoism says that people do in fact always pursue their own interests. Ethical Egoism, by contrast, is a normative theory—that is, a theory about how we *ought* to behave. Regardless of how we do behave, Ethical Egoism says we have no moral duty except to do what is best for ourselves.

It is a challenging theory. It contradicts some of our deepest moral beliefs—beliefs held by most of us, at any rate—but it is not easy to refute. We will examine the most important arguments for and against it. If it turns out to be true, then of course that is immensely important. But even if it turns out to be false, there is still much to be learned from examining it—we may, for example, gain some insight into the reasons why we *do* have obligations to other people.

But before looking at the arguments, we should be a little clearer about exactly what this theory says and what it does not say. In the first place, Ethical Egoism does not say that one should promote one's own interests *as well as* the interests of others. That would be an ordinary, unexceptional view. Ethical Egoism is the radical view that one's *only* duty is to promote one's own interests. According to Ethical Egoism, there is only one ultimate principle of conduct, the principle of self-interest, and this principle sums up *all* of one's natural duties and obligations.

However, Ethical Egoism does not say that you should *avoid* actions that help others, either. It may very well be that in many instances your interests coincide with the interests of others, so that in helping yourself you will be aiding others willy-nilly. Or it may happen that aiding others is an effective *means* for creating some benefit for yourself. Ethical Egoism does not forbid such actions; in fact, it may demand them. The theory insists only that in such cases the benefit to others is not what makes the act right. What makes the act right is, rather, the fact that it is to one's own advantage.

Finally, Ethical Egoism does not imply that in pursuing one's interests one ought always to do what one wants to do, or what gives one the most pleasure in the short run. Someone may want to do something that is not good for himself or that will eventually cause himself more grief than pleasure—he may want to drink a lot or smoke cigarettes or take drugs or waste his best years at the race track. Ethical Egoism would frown on all this, regardless of the momentary pleasure it affords. It says that a person ought to do what *really is* to his or her own best advantage, *over the long run.* It endorses selfishness, but it doesn't endorse foolishness.

THREE ARGUMENTS IN FAVOR OF ETHICAL EGOISM

What reasons can be advanced to support this doctrine? Why should anyone think it is true? Unfortunately, the theory is asserted more often than it is argued for. Many of its supporters apparently think its truth is self-evident, so that arguments are not needed. When it *is* argued for, three lines of reasoning are most commonly used.

1 The first argument has several variations, each suggesting the same general point:

a. Each of us is intimately familiar with our own individual wants and needs. Moreover, each of us is uniquely placed to pursue those wants and needs effectively. At the same time, we know the desires and needs of other people only imperfectly, and we are not well situated to pursue them. Therefore, it is reasonable to believe that if we set out to be "our brother's keeper," we would often bungle the job and end up doing more mischief than good.

b. At the same time, the policy of "looking out for others" is an offensive intrusion into other people's privacy; it is essentially a policy of minding other people's business.

c. Making other people the object of one's "charity" is degrading to them; it robs them of their individual dignity and self-respect. The offer of charity says, in effect, that they are not competent to care for themselves; and the statement is self-fulfilling—they cease to be self-reliant and become passively dependent on others. That is why the recipients of "charity" are so often resentful rather than appreciative.

What this adds up to is that the policy of "looking out for others" is self-defeating. If we want to promote the best interests of everyone alike, we should *not* adopt so-called altruistic policies of behavior. On the contrary, if each person looks after his or her *own* interests, it is more likely that everyone will be better off, in terms of both physical and emotional well-being. . . .

Of course no one favors bungling, butting in, or depriving people of their self-respect. But is this really what we are doing when we feed hungry children? Is the starving child in Ethiopia really harmed when we "intrude" into "her business" by supplying food? It hardly seems likely. Yet we can set this point aside, for considered as an argument for Ethical Egoism, this way of thinking has an even more serious defect.

The trouble is that it isn't really an argument *for Ethical Egoism* at all. The argument concludes that we should adopt certain policies of action; and on the surface they appear to be egoistic policies. However, the *reason* it is said we should adopt those policies is decidedly *un*egoistic. The reason is one that to an egoist shouldn't matter. It is said that we should adopt those policies because doing so will promote the "betterment of society"—but according to Ethical Egoism, that is something we should

not be concerned about. Spelled out fully, with everything laid on the table, the argument says:

(1) We ought to do whatever will promote the best interests of everyone alike.

(2) The interests of everyone will best be promoted if each of us adopts the policy of pursuing our own interests exclusively.

(3) Therefore, each of us should adopt the policy of pursuing our own interests exclusively.

If we accept this reasoning, then we are not ethical egoists at all. Even though we might end up *behaving* like egoists, our ultimate principle is one of beneficence—we are doing what we think will help everyone, not merely what we think will benefit ourselves. Rather than being egoists, we turn out to be altruists with a peculiar view of what in fact promotes the general welfare.

2 The second argument was put forward with some force by Ayn Rand, a writer little heeded by professional philosophers but who nevertheless was enormously popular on college campuses during the 1960s and 1970s. Ethical Egoism, in her view, is the only ethical philosophy that respects the integrity of the individual human life. She regarded the ethics of "altruism" as a totally destructive idea, both in society as a whole and in the lives of individuals taken in by it. Altruism, to her way of thinking, leads to a denial of the value of the individual. It says to a person: *your* life is merely something that may be sacrificed. "If a man accepts the ethics of altruism," she writes, "his first concern is not how to live his life, but how to sacrifice it." Moreover, those who would *promote* this idea are beneath contempt—they are parasites who, rather than working to build and sustain their own lives, leech off those who do. Again, she writes:

Parasites, moochers, looters, brutes and thugs can be of no value to a human being—nor can he gain any benefit from living in a society geared to *their* needs, demands and protections, a society that treats him as a sacrificial animal and penalizes him for his virtues in order to reward *them* for their vices, which means: a society based on the ethics of altruism.

By "sacrificing one's life" Rand does not necessarily mean anything so dramatic as dying. A person's life consists (in part) of projects undertaken and goods earned and created. To demand that a person abandon his projects or give up his goods is also a clear effort to "sacrifice his life." Furthermore, throughout her writings Rand also suggests that there is a *metaphysical* basis for egoistic ethics. Somehow, it is the only ethics that takes seriously the *reality* of the individual person. She bemoans "the enormity of the extent to which altruism erodes men's capacity to grasp . . . the value of an individual life; it reveals a mind from which the reality of a human being has been wiped out."

What, then, of the starving people? It might be argued, in response, that Ethical Egoism "reveals a mind from which the reality of a human being has been wiped out"—namely, the human being who is starving. Rand quotes with approval the evasive answer given by one of her followers: "Once, when Barbara Brandon was asked by a student: 'What will happen to the poor . . . ?'—she answered: 'If *you* want to help them, you will not be stopped.'"

All these remarks are, I think, part of one continuous argument that can be summarized like this:

(1) A person has only one life to live. If we place any value on the individual—that is, if the individual has any moral worth—then we must agree that this life is of supreme importance. After all, it is all one has, and all one is.

(2) The ethics of altruism regards the life of the individual as something one must be ready to sacrifice for the good of others.

(3) Therefore, the ethics of altruism does not take seriously the value of the human individual.

(4) Ethical Egoism, which allows each person to view his or her own life as being of ultimate value, *does* take the human individual seriously—in fact, it is the only philosophy that does so.

(5) Thus, Ethical Egoism is the philosophy that ought to be accepted.

The problem with this argument, as you may already have noticed, is that it relies on picturing the alternatives in such an extreme way. "The ethics of altruism" is taken to be such an extreme philosophy that *nobody*, with the possible exception of certain monks, would find it congenial. As Ayn Rand presents it, altruism implies that one's own interests have *no* value, and that *any* demand by others calls for sacrificing them. If that is the alternative, then any other view, including Ethical Egoism, will look good by comparison. But this is hardly a fair picture of the choices. What we called the common-sense view stands somewhere between the two extremes. It says that one's own interests and the interests of others are both important and must be balanced against one another. Sometimes, when the balancing is done, it will turn out that one should act in the interests of others; other times, it will turn out that one should take care of oneself. So even if the Randian argument refutes the extreme "ethics of altruism," it does not follow that one must accept the other extreme of Ethical Egoism.

3 The third line of reasoning takes a somewhat different approach. Ethical Egoism is usually presented as a *revisionist* moral philosophy, that is, as a philosophy that says our common-sense moral views are mistaken and need to be changed. It is possible, however, to interpret Ethical Egoism in a much less radical way, as a theory that *accepts* common-sense morality and offers a surprising account of its basis.

The less radical interpretation goes as follows. In everyday life, we assume that we are obliged to obey certain rules. We must avoid doing harm to others, speak the truth, keep our promises, and so on. At first glance, these duties appear to be very different from one another. They appear to have little in common. Yet from a theoretical point of view, we may wonder whether there is not some hidden *unity* underlying the hodge-podge of separate duties. Perhaps there is some small number of fundamental principles that explain all the rest, just as in physics there are basic principles that bring together and explain diverse phenomena. From a theoretical point of view, the smaller the number of basic principles, the better. Best of all would be *one* fundamental principle, from which all the rest could be derived. Ethical Egoism, then, would be the theory that all our duties are ultimately derived from the one fundamental principle of self-interest.

Taken in this way, Ethical Egoism is not such a radical doctrine. It does not challenge common-sense morality; it only tries to explain and systematize it. And it does a surprisingly successful job. It can provide plausible explanations of the duties mentioned above, and more:

a. If we make a habit of doing things that are harmful to other people, people will not be reluctant to do things that will harm *us*. We will be shunned and despised; others will not have us as friends and will not do us favors when we need them. If our offenses against others are serious enough, we may even end up in jail. Thus it is to our own advantage to avoid harming others.

b. If we lie to other people, we will suffer all the ill effects of a bad reputation. People will distrust us and avoid doing business with us. We will often need for people to be honest with us, but we can hardly expect them to feel much of an obligation to be honest with us if they know we have not been honest with them. Thus it is to our own advantage to be truthful.

c. It is to our own advantage to be able to enter into mutually beneficial arrangements with other people. To benefit from those arrangements, we need to be able to rely on others to keep their parts of the bargains we make with them—we need to be able to rely on them to keep their promises to us. But we can hardly expect others to keep their promises to us if we are not willing to keep our promises to them. Therefore, from the point of view of self-interest, we should keep our promises.

Pursuing this line of reasoning, Thomas Hobbes suggested that the principle of Ethical Egoism leads to nothing less than the Golden Rule: we should "do unto others" *because* if we do, others will be more likely to "do unto us."

Does this argument succeed in establishing Ethical Egoism as a viable theory of morality? It is, in my opinion at least, the best try. But there are two serious objections to it. In the first place, the argument does not prove quite as much as it needs to prove. At best, it shows only that *as a general rule* it is to one's own advantage to avoid harming others. It does not show that this is *always* so. And it could not show that, for even though it may usually be to one's advantage to avoid harming others, sometimes it is not. Sometimes one might even *gain* from treating another person badly. In that case, the obligation not to harm the other person could *not* be derived from the principle of Ethical Egoism. Thus it appears that not all our moral obligations can be explained as derivable from self-interest.

JIM HOLT
The Life of the Saint

JIM HOLT *also writes for the "Critics" column for* The New Yorker *and other New York and Web publications.*

Jim, Holt, "The Life of the Saint," from *The New Yorker*, Aug. 13, 2001. Used by permission of the author.

SUPPOSE you wish to achieve excellence in life, but you have no real talent for anything in particular. You are not smart enough to be a great scientist or creative enough to be a great artist; you do not possess the native shrewdness to be a distinguished statesman or the exquisite taste (and inherited wealth) to be a legendary hedonist. Are you then doomed to mediocrity? There is a school of thought that says no. The idea is that even if you are not clever or beautiful or talented, you can still, through sheer force of will, be very, very good. You can go beyond the norms of everyday morality—being kind to people, not telling lies, giving the odd dollar to Oxfam—and devote all your energies to feeding the hungry and succoring the afflicted. In other words, you can become a moral saint.

Is it a wise idea to strive to be as good and self-sacrificing as possible? Is "moral sainthood"—a coinage of the philosopher Susan Wolf—a form of human excellence one should aspire to? Is it, indeed, something each of us has a *duty* to aspire to?

Philosophers, over the past couple of thousand years, have offered two reasons for aiming at the heights of moral goodness: to improve the world and to perfect one's self. These reasons do not sit together very well, since one of them is directed outward and the other is directed inward. Can you really perfect your own self by forgetting it in the service of others? There are grounds, in fact, for thinking that being as good as possible is neither good for the world nor good for one's soul.

Start with the soul part. Do those who devote their lives to the service of others tend to have beautiful, Socrates-like personalities? Well, no. Unnaturally developed moral virtues—patience, charity in thought as well as in deed, a constant concern with alleviating the suffering of others—tend to crowd out the nonmoral virtues, like humor, intellectual curiosity, and dash. Susan Wolf has distinguished two kinds of moral saint: the Loving Saint, whose happiness lies wholly and exclusively in helping others; and the Rational Saint, who is made happy by the same things as the rest of us—friends, family, material comforts, art, books, sports, sex—but who sacrifices his happiness out of a sense of duty. The Loving Saint, blind to so much of what life offers, has a soul that is strangely barren. The Rational Saint, who must continually suppress or deny his strongest desires, has a soul that is soured by frustration.

Suppose you see a little girl drowning in a shallow pool of water. Wouldn't you feel duty-bound to rescue her—never mind that jumping in the water means ruining your two-hundred-dollar shoes? Unfortunately, there are many children throughout the world in a situation analogous to that of the drowning girl. They are dying of starvation or of easily prevented maladies like diarrhea; and, owing to the existence of a network of overseas relief organizations, it is within your power to save them. Indeed, the estimated cost of rescuing one child in this way has been put at about two hundred dollars. All you have to do is call a toll-free number with your credit card in hand. Is there an important distinction between failing to do this and walking away from the drowning child? And, if there is not, can you in good conscience stop at just two hundred dollars? Don't your ethical convictions compel you to save as many children as your bank account permits?

In the past several years, philosophers like Peter Singer, of Princeton, and Peter Unger, of New York University, have used such simple but intuitively powerful "rescue cases" to argue for an inconvenient conclusion: we rich Westerners should be giving away most of our money to international relief efforts. Doing so is not praiseworthy; it is *required* by the ethical principles we all implicitly share. Singer himself has said that he gives away a fifth of his income, and wonders whether that is enough. How could it be? Even if a middle-class American family were already giving up four-fifths of its household income to Oxfam, an incremental donation of two hundred dollars would still save yet another child dying for lack of food or medical care, at the cost of relatively little distress to the giver.

As for the occasional sybaritic indulgence, forget it. What's a bottle of Dom Perignon compared to a child's life?

If *that's* what morality asks of me, you might say, to hell with it. And Simon Blackburn, a philosopher at Cambridge, would probably sympathize with you. In "Being Good," he argues that this kind of overdemandingness threatens to undermine ethics itself. "The center of ethics must be occupied by things we can *reasonably* demand of each other," he writes. Our duty to help others cannot be infinite. The moral principles we adopt must not reduce us to slaves of the impersonal good. It may be praiseworthy to give away all your money in order to save starving children abroad, or to quit your Park Avenue medical practice and join Doctors Without Borders, or to invite the homeless to crash in your apartment, but it is not obligatory.

These conclusions of Blackburn's are comforting, and in line with those arrived at by the narrator of Hornby's novel. Yet how are we to resist those rescue-case arguments? Blackburn does not dwell on the matter, but one line of response goes something like this. Singer is an avowed utilitarian. In its purest form, utilitarianism says that we should seek to act in a way that brings about the greatest happiness in the world. Now, one test of an ethical principle is that it be "universalizable." We ask what the world would be like if everybody acted on this principle. What if everyone devoted himself to the happiness of others? Then, on average, everyone would be less happy, because everyone would be subordinating his own happiness to the needs of others. And if everyone gave all his money to Oxfam, the resulting contraction in consumer demand would cause the world economy to collapse, leading to enormous suffering. So these principles of doing good, you might think, are collectively self-defeating.

The universalization test suggests a way of quantifying our duty to help others. Perhaps the minimum sacrifice morality requires of us is simply our "fair share": the amount that, if everyone supplied it, would result in the most happiness and the least suffering in the world.

This principle makes each individual's charitable burden quite reasonable: if you have already donated a modest sum to famine relief and done a little light ladling in the soup kitchen down at your local church, you can go ahead and pop that tin of sevruga in good conscience. (Well, not entirely good conscience, because now we have to worry about the sturgeon.) Any do-gooding you engage in beyond your fair share would be what ethicists call supererogatory—commendable to perform but not blameworthy to omit.

And suppose we do go beyond the call of duty. Even if we succeed in achieving some immediate good, there is no telling what the remoter consequences of our altruism will be. All we know is that these consequences will extend far into the future, beyond the purview of our will. Owing to the contingent and chaotic nature of cause and effect, the balance of good over evil involves something like a random walk, with unforeseen reversals at every stage. (Consider the doctor who successfully delivered the fourth child of Klara and Alois Hitler after the couple's first three infants had tragically sickened and died.) It is the unknowability of the distant effects of our actions that led G. E. Moore to say, in his "Principia Ethica," that "no sufficient reason has ever yet been found for considering one action more right or more wrong than another." Moore's conclusion, as it happens, had a liberating effect on Vanessa Bell and the Bloomsbury circle, who looked to him as their sage. Under his influence, the Bloomsburies decided that the virtues of self—the kind of virtues that go together with a "rich and beautiful life," as the narrator of "How to Be Good" puts it—were more important than the old Victorian virtues of charity and self-sacrifice.

Once you venture outside Bloomsbury, of course, you may encounter extraordinary circumstances in which it is possible to do extraordinary good. Think of the "good Germans" who risked their lives to aid Jews during the Final Solution, or of the sole member of Lieutenant Calley's platoon who conspicuously lowered his rifle instead of shooting the peasants at My Lai. What does it take to be good in such extreme situations? Skill can certainly help, as the examples of Oskar Schindler and Raoul Wallenberg show, but it is not always necessary. Is good will ever enough? Not unless it is combined with some other hard-to-define quality of character, which, waving our hands, we call "nerve" or "heart." Whatever this quality is, it is one that most seemingly good-willed people lack, which is why they become silent accomplices when great evils are being committed. In ordinary circumstances, of course, there remains the Oxfam option; yet even here there is no fixed proportion between the will to do good and the good one actually does. The widow's mite, for all the benevolence behind it, is null compared with the face-saving millions given to charities by the heartless capitalist.

So exceptional goodness always seems to require special qualifications: either great savoir faire or great bravery plus exposure to extreme circumstances that call for moral heroism. If you happen to be short on both counts, you're probably out of the running. Sainthood, it turns out, is one of those career prospects—like making millions in mail order—that seem to be open to everyone but pan out for only the fortunate few.

Beyond the necessary technical and organizational skills, achieving great altruistic feats seems to require a sort of demonic creativity. Florence Nightingale, who dedicated her life to the care of the war wounded, did an enormous amount of good (although her reforms, by reducing the human cost of war, might have made future wars more likely). But Nightingale, as Strachey pointed out to shocked Edwardians, was not a sweet, self-abnegating angel of mercy; she was an angry, acerbic, sarcastic, and self-important woman of stern and indomitable will. She had, you could say, an artist's temperament. Evelyn Waugh once observed, "Humility is not a virtue propitious to the artist. It is often pride, emulation, avarice, malice—all the odious qualities—which drive a man to complete, elaborate, refine, destroy, renew his work until he has made something that gratifies his pride and envy and greed. And in doing so he enriches the world more than the generous and good, though he may lose his own soul in the process. That is the paradox of artistic achievement." It may also be the paradox of altruistic achievement. If you want to be a saint, forget about being an angel.

CHAPTER FIFTEEN

CAN THERE BE SEXUAL EQUALITY?

Story: Driving the truck to work one day, Sandy noticed somebody by the side of the road with a flat tire. Sandy stopped and got out to help fix the flat. Because neither of them had a jack, Sandy had to hold up the rear end of the car while the owner replaced the tire. When they were done, Sandy reminded herself to buy a new jack on her way home.

Story: Sandy was putting the finishing touches on the pie when the kids rushed in the door. "What's for dinner? We're starved." "Wash your hands, kids, and set the table," Sandy replied. "We'll be eating as soon as Mom gets home from work."

It is a rare person indeed who would read either of these stories without experiencing a "gender jolt" at the end of them. No matter what your views are about sexual equality, it is nevertheless true that we tend to make certain associations when it comes to gender. Even if your father does the cooking every night, you probably assumed that the person putting the finishing touches on the pie was a woman. Similarly, even if your mother is a body builder who rides a Harley, you probably assumed that the person holding up the rear of the car was a man.

One of the questions of concern to philosophers is whether these characteristic associations are rooted in fundamental, irreversible differences between women and men, or whether they are a function of changeable social practices. Look around the world. How many women are truck drivers? Heads of large corporations? CIA agents? Roofing contractors? How many men are elementary school teachers? Are staying at home with their children? Are secretaries? Nurses? It is important to notice two things. First, men and women tend to occupy different roles in our culture. Second, the roles that women occupy tend to be subordinate to those of men. (This doesn't mean that women have no power, nor does it mean that all men have power. There are other factors, such as class and race, that affect the distribution of power.)

Some of the differences between men and women, their reproductive capacities, for example, are clearly not the result of social practices. Women have uteruses; for the time being, at least, men do not. To what extent do the physical differences between men and women determine their social roles (sometimes called "gender roles")? Should physical differences determine gender roles? You will see that Plato hedges on an answer to this question. In the selection from *The Republic*, Socrates discusses with Glaucon the education and training necessary for those who are going to rule Socrates' ideal city. Socrates makes it quite clear that education, more than any other single thing, determines what a person will be equipped to do. If men and women are educated in the same way, then they will be able to perform the same functions. The fact that women bear children, for example, does not entail that they should raise them. Rather, the raising of children should be done by those trained to do so, be they men or women. In principle, then, both men and women are capable of ruling the city as well. It is clear, however, that Socrates believes men to be naturally superior to women. Although there will be some men who are exceeded by women at performing a task, there will always be men who are better at it than any woman could be (except, he suggests, when making pancakes and jam). It is difficult to see how he can reconcile the view that men are naturally superior with the view that our capabilities are a result of education and training.

According to Mill, he can't. Confusions such as that of Socrates are the result of taking facts about the way things are as equivalent to facts about the way things must be. Suppose that you are in the hospital for a week, and during that week you never encounter a male nurse. Are you entitled to conclude that men can't, by nature, be nurses? Or that women, by nature, are suited to nursing? Mill provides us with some reasons for questioning inferences like these. Was Socrates making such an inference when he claimed that men are naturally superior to women? If so, he finds himself in notable philosophical company. As you can see from the selections by Aristotle and Kant, philosophers' remarks about women tend to reinforce stereotypical associations. It is claimed that women are more emotional than men, are physically weaker than men, have a tendency to lie and to talk too much, and are lazier and more shameless than men.

Marilyn Frye looks to those elements of our social relations that reinforce sexual inequality. According to Frye, sexism is the result of a particular social system of "sex-marking." She asks us to think about the variety of ways in which sex differences are reinforced by clothing and by manners of walking and speaking. In Frye's view, however, the reinforcement of sex differences is not life-enhancing. Rather it serves to maintain a system in which one group of people is subordinate to another. By continuing to emphasize the importance of sex differences, we further reinforce the relationship of domination and subordination whose purpose it serves.

Natalie Angier takes up a contemporary version of the problem raised by Mill, namely whether there are any inherent differences between male and female nature. In arguing that there are, several authors appeal to the "new science" of evolutionary psychology, which is based on a Darwinian explanation for the relative pickiness of females when it comes to selecting sexual partners. Because the female has to bear (and care for?) her offspring, she can reproduce far less often than the male. (See Chapter 4 for further discussion of Darwin's views.) Hence, on this Darwinian account, the female has to assess both the genetic suitability of her potential mates, and the degree to which they appear likely to provide for their offspring. For obvious reasons feminists have been suspicious of anything that looks like biological determinism since, as we can see from the opening selections in this chapter, it has been used as a rationale for depriving women of political, economic, and moral status. So it is not surprising that contemporary feminists have viewed evolutionary psychology as yet another attempt to keep women in their degraded place. Angier reviews the evidence that has been marshaled to support the tenets of the Darwinian view. Her aim is to show that there are alternative, highly plausible explanations for the allegedly supporting phenomena. Thus the observed differences between (some) men and (some) women cannot be used to establish a hardwired difference between males and females.

Finally, Sarah McCarry writes an entertaining essay on how one joins the feminist revolution.

In thinking about the question of sexual equality, it is important to consider just what *are* the sources of social inequalities. In addition, it is important to reflect on how, ideally, you think things should be, and how you think we might best achieve those ends. You can begin by thinking about the ways in which you are affected by the importance that our society attaches to sex differences. If you think that you aren't affected, then remember the two stories with which we began.

PLATO

The Equality of Women

PLATO *(427–347 B.C.) was born into a family of considerable wealth and power. In Athens he came under the influence of Socrates and turned his attention to philosophy. After Socrates was condemned to death for corrupting the minds of the youth of Athens, Plato took it upon himself to continue Socrates' work. In this selection from* The Republic, *Socrates, who serves as Plato's spokesman in the dialogue, discusses his views about sexual equality with Glaucon.*

WELL, I replied, I suppose that I must retrace my steps and say what I perhaps ought to have said before in the proper place. The part of the men has been played out, and now properly enough comes the turn of the women. Of them I will proceed to speak, and the more readily since I am invited by you.

For men born and educated like our citizens, the only way, in my opinion, of arriving at a right conclusion about the possession and use of women and children is to follow the path on which we originally started, when we said that the men were to be the guardians and watchdogs of the herd.

True.

Let us further suppose the birth and education of our women to be subject to similar or nearly similar regulations; then we shall see whether the result accords with our design.

What do you mean?

What I mean may be put into the form of a question, I said: Are dogs divided into hes and shes, or do they both share equally in hunting and in keeping watch and in the other duties of dogs? or do we entrust to the males the entire and exclusive care of the flocks, while we leave the females at home, under the idea that the bearing and suckling their puppies is labour enough for them?

No, he said, they share alike; the only difference between them is that the males are stronger and the females weaker.

But can you use different animals for the same purpose, unless they are bred and fed in the same way?

You cannot.

Then, if women are to have the same duties as men, they must have the same nurture and education?

Yes.

The education which was assigned to the men was music and gymnastic. Yes.

Then women must be taught music and gymnastic and also the art of war, which they must practise like the men?

That is the inference, I suppose.

I should rather expect, I said, that several of our proposals, if they are carried out, being unusual, may appear ridiculous.

No doubt of it.

Yes, and the most ridiculous thing of all will be the sight of women naked in the palaestra, exercising with the men, especially when they are no longer young; they certainly will not be a vision of beauty, any more than the enthusiastic old men who in spite of wrinkles and ugliness continue to frequent the gymnasia.

Yes, indeed, he said: according to present notions the proposal would be thought ridiculous.

Plato, "The Equality of Women," from *The Republic,* translated Benjamin Jowett, New York: Heritage Press, 1944.

But then, I said, as we have determined to speak our minds, we must not fear the jests of the wits which will be directed against this sort of innovation; how they will talk of women's attainments both in music and gymnastic, and above all about their wearing armour and riding upon horseback!

Very true, he replied.

Yet having begun we must go forward to the rough places of the law; at the same time begging of these gentlemen for once in their life to be serious. Not long ago, as we shall remind them, the Hellenes were of the opinion, which is still generally received among the barbarians, that the sight of a naked man was ridiculous and improper; and when first the Cretans and then the Lacedaemonians introduced the custom, the wits of that day might equally have ridiculed the innovation.

No doubt.

But when experience showed that to let all things be uncovered was far better than to cover them up, and the ludicrous effect to the outward eye vanished before the better principle which reason asserted, then the man was perceived to be a fool who directs the shafts of his ridicule at any other sight but that of folly and vice, or seriously inclines to weigh the beautiful by any other standard but that of the good.

Very true, he replied.

First, then, whether the question is to be put in jest or in earnest, let us come to an understanding about the nature of woman: Is she capable of sharing either wholly or partially in the actions of men, or not at all? And is the art of war one of those arts in which she can or can not share? That will be the best way of commencing the enquiry, and will probably lead to the fairest conclusion.

That will be much the best way.

Shall we take the other side first and begin by arguing against ourselves; in this manner the adversary's position will not be undefended.

Why not? he said.

Then let us put a speech into the mouths of our opponents. They will say: "Socrates and Glaucon, no adversary need convict you, for you yourselves, at the first foundation of the State, admitted the principle that everybody was to do the one work suited to his own nature." And certainly, if I am not mistaken, such an admission was made by us. "And do not the natures of men and women differ very much indeed?" And we shall reply: Of course they do. Then we shall be asked, "Whether the tasks assigned to men and to women should not be different, and such as are agreeable to their different natures?" Certainly they should. "But if so, have you not fallen into a serious inconsistency in saying that men and women, whose natures are so entirely different, ought to perform the same actions?"— What defence will you make for us, my good Sir, against any one who offers these objections?

That is not an easy question to answer when asked suddenly; and I shall and I do beg of you to draw out the case on our side.

These are the objections, Glaucon, and there are many others of a like kind, which I foresaw long ago; they made me afraid and reluctant to take in hand any law about the possession and nurture of women and children.

By Zeus, he said, the problem to be solved is anything but easy.

Why yes, I said, but the fact is that when a man is out of his depth, whether he has fallen into a little swimming bath or into mid-ocean, he has to swim all the same.

Very true.

And must not we swim and try to reach the shore: we will hope that Arion's dolphin or some other miraculous help may save us?

I suppose so, he said.

Well then, let us see if any way of escape can be found. We acknowledged—did we not? that different natures ought to have different pursuits, and that men's and women's natures are different. And now what are we saying?—that different natures ought to have the same pursuits,—this is the inconsistency which is charged upon us.

Precisely.

Verily, Glaucon, I said, glorious is the power of the art of contradiction!

Why do you say so?

Because I think that many a man falls into the practice against his will. When he thinks that he is reasoning he is really disputing, just because he cannot define and divide, and so know that of which he is speaking; and he will pursue a merely verbal opposition in the spirit of contention and not of fair discussion.

Yes, he replied, such is very often the case; but what has that to do with us and our argument?

A great deal; for there is certainly a danger of our getting unintentionally into a verbal opposition.

In what way?

Why, we valiantly and pugnaciously insist upon the verbal truth, that different natures ought to have different pursuits, but we never considered at all what was the meaning of sameness or difference of nature, or why we distinguished them when we assigned different pursuits to different natures and the same to the same natures.

Why, no, he said, that was never considered by us.

I said: Suppose that by way of illustration we were to ask the question whether there is not an opposition in nature between bald men and hairy men; and if this is admitted by us, then, if bald men are cobblers, we should forbid the hairy men to be cobblers, and conversely?

Yes, I said, a jest; and why? because we never meant when we constructed the State, that the opposition of natures should extend to every difference, but only to those differences which affected the pursuit in which the individual is engaged; we should have argued, for example, that a physician and one who is in mind a physician may be said to have the same nature.

True.

Whereas the physician and the carpenter have different natures?

Certainly.

And if, I said, the male and female sex appear to differ in their fitness for any art or pursuit, we should say that such pursuit or art ought to be assigned to one or the other of them; but if the difference consists only in women bearing and men begetting children, this does not amount to a proof that a woman differs from a man in respect to the sort of education she should receive; and we shall therefore continue to maintain that our guardians and their wives ought to have the same pursuits.

Very true, he said.

Next, we shall ask our opponent how, in reference to any of the pursuits or arts of civic life, the nature of a woman differs from that of a man?

That will be quite fair.

And perhaps he, like yourself, will reply that to give a sufficient answer on the instant is not easy; but after a little reflection there is no difficulty.

Yes, perhaps.

Suppose then that we invite him to accompany us in the argument, and then we may hope to show him that there is nothing peculiar in the constitution of women which would affect them in the administration of the State.

By all means.

Let us say to him: Come now, and we will ask you a question:—when you spoke of a nature gifted or not gifted in any respect, did you mean to say that one man will acquire a thing easily, another with difficulty; a little learning will lead the one to discover a great deal; whereas the other, after much study and application, no sooner learns than he forgets; or again, did you mean, that the one has a body which is a good servant to his mind, while the body of the other is a hindrance to him?—would not these be the sort of differences which distinguish the man gifted by nature from the one who is ungifted?

No one will deny that.

And can you mention any pursuit of mankind in which the male sex has not all these gifts and qualities in a higher degree than the female? Need I waste time in speaking of the art of weaving, and the management of pancakes and preserves, in which womankind does really appear to be great, and in which for her to be beaten by a man is of all things the most absurd?

You are quite right, he replied, in maintaining the general inferiority of the female sex: although many women are in many things superior to many men, yet on the whole what you say is true.

And if so, my friend, I said, there is no special faculty of administration in a state which a woman has because she is a woman, or which a man has by virtue of his sex, but the gifts of nature are alike diffused in both; all the pursuits of men are the pursuits of women also, but in all of them a woman is inferior to a man.

Very true.

Then are we to impose all our enactments on men and none of them on women?

That will never do.

One woman has a gift of healing, another not; one is a musician, and another has no music in her nature?

Very true.

And one woman has a turn for gymnastic and military exercises, and another is unwarlike and hates gymnastics?

Certainly.

And one woman is a philosopher, and another is an enemy of philosophy; one has spirit, and another is without spirit?

That is also true.

Then one woman will have the temper of a guardian, and another not. Was not the selection of the male guardians determined by differences of this sort?

Yes.

Men and women alike possess the qualities which make a guardian; they differ only in their comparative strength or weakness.

Obviously.

And those women who have such qualities are to be selected as the companions and colleagues of men who have similar qualities and whom they resemble in capacity and in character?

Very true.

And ought not the same natures to have the same pursuits?

They ought.

Then, as we were saying before, there is nothing unnatural in assigning music and gymnastic to the wives of the guardians—to that point we come round again.

Certainly not.

The law which we then enacted was agreeable to nature, and therefore not an impossibility or mere aspiration; and the contrary practice, which prevails at present, is in reality a violation of nature.

That appears to be true.

We had to consider, first, whether our proposals were possible, and secondly whether they were the most beneficial?

Yes.

And the possibility has been acknowledged?

Yes.

The very great benefit has next to be established?

Quite so.

You will admit that the same education which makes a man a good guardian will make a woman a good guardian; for their original nature is the same?

Yes.

I should like to ask you a question.

What is it?

Would you say that all men are equal in excellence, or is one man better than another?

The latter.

And in the commonwealth which we were founding do you conceive the guardians who have been brought up on our model system to be more perfect men, or the cobblers whose education has been cobbling?

What a ridiculous question!

You have answered me, I replied: Well, and may we not further say that our guardians are the best of our citizens?

By far the best.

And will not their wives be the best women?

Yes, by far the best.

And can there be anything better for the interests of the State than that the men and women of a State should be as good as possible?

There can be nothing better.

And this is what the arts of music and gymnastic, when present in such manner as we have described, will accomplish?

Certainly.

Then we have made an enactment not only possible but in the highest degree beneficial to the State?

True.

Then let the wives of our guardians strip, for their virtue will be their robe, and let them share in the toils of war and the defence of their country; only in the distribution of labours the lighter are assigned to the women, who are the weaker natures, but in other respects their duties are to be the same. And as for the man who laughs at naked women exercising their bodies from the best of motives, in his laughter he is plucking *A fruit of unripe wisdom*, and he himself is ignorant of what he is laughing at, or what he is about;—for that is, and ever will be, the best of sayings, *That the useful is the noble and the hurtful is the base.*

Very true.

ARISTOTLE
The Inequality of Women

ARISTOTLE *(384–322 B.C.) was for eighteen years a student of Plato. After Plato's death, he turned to the study of biology. In addition to his biological studies, Aristotle virtually created the sciences of logic and linguistics. He developed extravagant theories in physics and made significant contributions to metaphysics, ethics, politics, and aesthetics.*

WOMAN is more compassionate than man, more easily moved to tears. At the same time, she is more jealous, more querulous, more apt to scold and to strike. She is, furthermore, more prone to despondency and less hopeful than man, more devoid of shame or self-respect, more false of speech, more deceptive and of more retentive memory. She is also more wakeful, more shrinking, more difficult to rouse to action, and she requires a smaller amount of nutriment.

IMMANUEL KANT
The Inequality of Women

IMMANUEL KANT *(1724–1804) was probably the greatest philosopher since Plato and Aristotle. He lived his entire life in East Prussia. He was a professor at the University in Königsberg for over thirty years. He never married, and his neighbors said that his*

Aristotle, "The Inequality of Women," from *The History of Animals,* 9.1, 60868.

Kant, Immanuel, "The Inequality of Women," from *Lectures On Ethics,* translated by Lois Infield, New York: Harper and Row, 1963.

habits were so regular that they could set their watches by him. His philosophical system was embodied in three volumes, The Critique of Pure Reason, The Critique of Practical Reason, *and* The Critique of Judgment.

THE person who is as silent as a mute goes to one extreme; the person who is loquacious goes to the opposite. Both tendencies are weaknesses. Men are liable to the first, women to the second. Someone has said that women are talkative because the training of infants is their special charge, and their talkativeness soon teaches a child to speak, because they can chatter to it all day long. If men had the care of the children they would take much longer to learn to talk. However that may be, we dislike anyone who will not speak: he annoys us; his silence betrays his pride. On the other hand, loquaciousness in men is contemptible and contrary to the strength of the male. All this by the way, we shall now pass to more weighty matters.

JOHN STUART MILL
The Subjection of Women

JOHN STUART MILL *(1806–1873) was one of the documented geniuses of modern history. By the age of ten, he had accomplished more than most scholars do in a lifetime. He is best known for his moral and political writings, particularly* On Liberty *and* Utilitarianism.

NEITHER does it avail anything to say that the *nature* of the two sexes adapts them to their present functions and position, and renders these appropriate to them. Standing on the ground of common sense and the constitution of the human mind, I deny that any one knows, or can know, the nature of the two sexes, as long as they have only been seen in their present relation to one another. If men had ever been found in society without women, or women without men, or if there had been a society of men and women in which the women were not under the control of the men, something might have been positively known about the mental and moral differences which may be inherent in the nature of each. What is now called the nature of women is an eminently artificial thing—the result of forced repression in some directions, unnatural stimulation in others. It may be asserted without scruple, that no other class of dependents have had their character so entirely distorted from its natural proportions by their relation with their masters; for, if conquered and slave races have been, in some respects, more forcibly repressed, whatever in them has not been crushed down by an iron heel has generally been let alone, and if left with any liberty of development, it has developed itself according to its own

Mill, John Stuart "The Subjection of Women," from *The Subjection of Women*, D. Appleton and Company, 1869.

laws; but in the case of women, a hot-house and stove cultivation has always been carried on of some of the capabilities of their nature, for the benefit and pleasure of their masters. Then, because certain products of the general vital force sprout luxuriantly and reach a great development in this heated atmosphere and under this active nurture and watering, while other shoots from the same root, which are left outside in the wintry air, with ice purposely heaped all around them, have a stunted growth, and some are burnt off with fire and disappear; men, with that inability to recognize their own work which distinguishes the unanalytic mind, indolently believe that the tree grows of itself in the way they have made it grow, and that it would die if one half of it were not kept in a vapour bath and the other half in the snow.

Of all difficulties which impede the progress of thought, and the formation of well-grounded opinions on life and social arrangements, the greatest is now the unspeakable ignorance and inattention of mankind in respect to the influences which form human character. Whatever any portion of the human species now are, or seem to be, such, it is supposed, they have a natural tendency to be: even when the most elementary knowledge of the circumstances in which they have been placed, clearly points out the causes that made them what they are. . . . Because the Greeks cheated the Turks, and the Turks only plundered the Greeks, there are persons who think that the Turks are naturally more sincere: and because women, as is often said, care nothing about politics except their personalities, it is supposed that the general good is naturally less interesting to women than to men. History, which is now so much better understood than formerly, teaches another lesson: if only by showing the extraordinary susceptibility of human nature to external influences, and the extreme variableness of those of its manifestations which are supposed to be most universal and uniform. But in history, as in travelling, men usually see only what they already had in their own minds; and few learn much from history, who do not bring much with them to its study.

Hence, in regard to that most difficult question, what are the natural differences between the two sexes—a subject on which it is impossible in the present state of society to obtain complete and correct knowledge—while almost everybody dogmatizes upon it, almost all neglect and make light of the only means by which any partial insight can be obtained into it. This is, an analytic study of the most important department of psychology, the laws of the influence of circumstances on character. For, however great and apparently ineradicable the moral and intellectual differences between men and women might be, the evidence of their being natural differences could only be negative. Those only could be inferred to be natural which could not possibly be artificial—the residuum, after deducting every characteristic of either sex which can admit of being explained from education or external circumstances. The profoundest knowledge of the laws of the formation of character is indispensable to entitle any one to affirm even that there is any difference, much more what the difference is, between the two sexes considered as moral and rational beings; and since no one, as yet, has that knowledge (for there is hardly any subject which, in proportion to its importance, has been so little studied), no one is thus far entitled to any positive opinion on the subject. Conjectures are all that can at present be made; conjectures more or less probable, according as more or less authorized by such knowledge as we yet have of the laws of psychology, as applied to the formation of character.

Even the preliminary knowledge, what the differences between the sexes now are, apart from all question as to how they are made what they are, is still in the crudest and most incomplete state. Medical practitioners and physiologists have ascertained, to some extent, the differences in bodily constitution; and this is an important element to the psychologist: but hardly any medical practitioner is a psychologist. Respecting the mental characteristics of women; their observations are of no more worth than those of common men. It is a subject on which nothing final can be known, so long as those who alone can really know it, women themselves, have given but little testimony, and that little, mostly suborned. It is easy to know stupid women. Stupidity is much the same all the world over. A stupid person's notions and feelings may confidently be inferred from those which prevail in the circle by which the person is surrounded. Not so with those whose opinions and feelings are an emanation from their own nature and faculties. It is only a man here and there who has any tolerable knowledge of the character even of the women of his own family. I do not mean, of their capabilities; these nobody knows, not even themselves, because most of them have never been called out. I mean their actually existing thoughts and feelings. Many a man thinks he perfectly understands women, because he has had amatory relations with several, perhaps with many of them. If he is a good observer, and his experience extends to quality as well as quantity, he may have learnt something of one narrow department of their nature—an important department, no doubt. But of all the rest of it, few persons are generally more ignorant, because there are few from whom it is so carefully hidden. The most favorable case which a man can generally have for studying the character of a woman, is that of his own wife: for the opportunities are greater, and the cases of complete sympathy not so unspeakably rare. And in fact, this is the source from which any knowledge worth having on the subject has, I believe, generally come. But most men have not had the opportunity of studying in this way more than a single case: accordingly one can, to an almost laughable degree, infer what a man's wife is like, from his opinions about women in general. To make even this one case yield any results, the woman must be worth knowing, and the man not only a competent judge, but of a character so sympathetic in itself, and so well adapted to hers, that he can either read her mind by sympathetic intuition, or has nothing in himself which makes her shy of disclosing it. Hardly anything, I believe, can be more rare than this conjunction. It often happens that there is the most complete unity of

feeling and community of interests as to all external things, yet the one has as little admission into the internal life of the other as if they were common acquaintance. Even with true affection, authority on the one side and subordination on the other prevent perfect confidence. Though nothing may be intentionally withheld, much is not shown. In the analogous relation of parent and child, the corresponding phenomenon must have been in the observation of every one. As between father and son, how many are the cases in which the father, in spite of real affection on both sides, obviously to all the world does not know, nor suspect, parts of the son's character familiar to his companions and equals. The truth is, that the position of looking up to another is extremely unpropitious to complete sincerity and openness with him. The fear of losing ground in his opinion or in his feelings is so strong, that even in an upright character, there is an unconscious tendency to show only the best side, or the side which, though not the best, is that which he most likes to see: and it may be confidently said that thorough knowledge of one another hardly ever exists, but between persons who, besides being intimates, are equals. How much more true, then, must all this be, when the one is not only under the authority of the other, but has it inculcated on her as a duty to reckon everything else subordinate to his comfort and pleasure, and to let him neither see nor feel anything coming from her, except what is agreeable to him. All these difficulties stand in the way of a man's obtaining any thorough knowledge even of the one woman whom alone, in general, he has sufficient opportunity of studying. When we further consider that to understand one woman necessarily is not to understand any other woman; that even if he could study many women of one rank, or of one country, he would not thereby understand women of other ranks or countries; and even if he did, they are still only the women of a single period of history; we may safely assert that the knowledge which men can acquire of women, even as they have been and are, without reference to what they might be, is wretchedly imperfect and superficial, and always will be so, until women themselves have told all that they have to tell.

And this time has not come; nor will it come otherwise than gradually. It is but of yesterday that women have either been qualified by literary accomplishments, or permitted by society, to tell anything to the general public. As yet very few of them dare tell anything, which men, on whom their literary success depends, are unwilling to hear. Let us remember in which manner, up to a very recent time, the expression, even by a male author, of uncustomary opinions, or what are deemed eccentric feelings, usually was, and in some degree still is, received; and we may form some faint conception under what impediments a woman, who is brought up to think custom and opinion her sovereign rule, attempts to express in books anything drawn from the depths of her own nature. The greatest woman who has left writings behind her sufficient to give her an eminent rank in the literature of her country, thought it necessary to prefix as a motto to her boldest work, "A man dares to have an opinion; a woman must submit to it." The greater part of what women write about women is mere sycophancy to men. In the case of unmarried women, much of it seems only intended to increase their chance of a husband. Many, both married and unmarried, overstep the mark, and inculcate a servility beyond what is desired or relished by any man, except the very vulgarest. But this is not so often the case as, even at a quite late period, it still was. Literary women are becoming more freespoken, and more willing to express their real sentiments. Unfortunately, in this country especially, they are themselves such artificial products, that their sentiments are compounded of a small element of individual observation and consciousness, and a very large one of acquired associations. This will be less and less the case, but it will remain true to a great extent, as long as social institutions do not admit the same free development of originality in women which is possible to men. When that time comes, and not before, we shall see, and not merely hear, as much as it is necessary to know of the nature of women, and the adaptation of other things to it.

I have dwelt so much on the difficulties which at present obstruct any real knowledge by men of the true nature of women, because in this as in so many other things "opinio copiae inter maximas causas inopiae est"; and there is little chance of reasonable thinking on the matter, while people flatter themselves that they perfectly understand a subject of which most men know absolutely nothing, and of which it is at present impossible that any man, or all men taken together, should have knowledge which can qualify them to lay down the law to women as to what is, or is not, their vocation. Happily, no such knowledge is necessary for any practical purpose connected with the position of women in relation to society and life. For, according to all the principles involved in modern society, the question rests with women themselves—to be decided by their own experience, and by the use of their own faculties. There are no means of finding what either one person or many can do, but by trying—and no means by which any one else can discover for them what it is for their happiness to do or leave undone.

One thing we may be certain of—that what is contrary to women's nature to do, they never will be made to do by simply giving their nature free play. The anxiety of mankind to interfere in behalf of nature, for fear lest nature should not succeed in effecting its purpose, is an altogether unnecessary solicitude. What women by nature cannot do, it is quite superfluous to forbid them from doing. What they can do, but not so well as the men who are their competitors, competition suffices to exclude them from; since nobody asks for protective duties and bounties in favour of women; it is only asked that the present bounties and protective duties in favour of men should be recalled. If women have a greater natural inclination for some things than for others, there is no need of laws or social inculcation to make the majority of them do the former in preference to the latter. Whatever women's services are most wanted for, the free play of competition will hold out the strongest inducements to them to undertake. And, as the words imply, they are most wanted for the things for which they are most fit; by the apportionment of which to them, the collective faculties of the two sexes can be applied on the whole with the greatest sum of valuable result.

The general opinion of men is supposed to be, that the natural vocation of a woman is that of a wife and mother. I say, is supposed to be, because, judging from acts—from the whole of the present constitution of society—one might infer that their opinion was the direct contrary. They might be supposed to think that the alleged natural vocation of women was of all things the most repugnant to their nature; insomuch that if they are free to do anything else—if any other means of living, or occupation of their time and faculties, is open, which has any chance of appearing desirable to them—there will not be enough of them who will be willing to accept the condition said to be natural to them. If this is the real opinion of men in general, it would be well that it should be spoken out. I should like to hear somebody openly enunciating the doctrine (it is already implied in much that is written on the subject) "It is necessary to society that women should marry and produce children. They will not do so unless they are compelled. Therefore it is necessary to compel them." The merits of the case would then be clearly defined. It would be exactly that of the slaveholders of South Carolina and Louisiana. "It is necessary that cotton and sugar should be grown. White men cannot produce them. Negroes will not, for any wages which we choose to give. *Ergo* they must be compelled." An illustration still closer to the point is that of impressment. Sailors must absolutely be had to defend the country. It often happens that they will not voluntarily enlist. Therefore there must be the power of forcing them. How often has this logic been used! and, but for one flaw in it, without doubt it would have been successful up to this day. But it is open to the retort—First pay the sailors the honest value of their labour. When you have made it as well worth their while to serve you, as to work for other employers, you

will have no more difficulty than others have in obtaining their services. To this there is no logical answer except "I will not": and as people are now not only ashamed, but are not desirous, to rob the labourer of his hire, impressment is no longer advocated. Those who attempt to force women into marriage by closing all other doors against them, lay themselves open to a similar retort. If they mean what they say, their opinion must evidently be, that men do not render the married condition so desirable to women, as to induce them to accept it for its own recommendations. It is not a sign of one's thinking the boon one offers very attractive, when one allows only Hobson's choice, "that or none." And here, I believe, is the clue to the feelings of those men, who have a real antipathy to the equal freedom of women. I believe they are afraid, not lest women should be unwilling to marry, for I do not think that any one in reality has that apprehension; but lest they should insist that marriage should be on equal conditions; lest all women of spirit and capacity should prefer doing almost anything else, not in their own eyes degrading, rather than marry, when marrying is giving themselves a master, and a master too of all their earthly possessions. And truly, if this consequence were necessarily incident to marriage, I think that the apprehension would be very well founded. I agree in thinking it probable that few women, capable of anything else, would, unless under an irresistible *entrainement*, rendering them for the time insensible to anything but itself, choose such a lot, when any other means were open to them of filling a conventionally honourable place in life: and if men are determined that the law of marriage shall be a law of despotism, they are quite right, in point of mere policy, in leaving to women only Hobson's choice. But, in that case, all that has been done in the modern world to relax the chain on the minds of women, has been a mistake. They never should have been allowed to receive a literary education. Women who read, much more women who write, are, in the existing constitution of things, a contradiction and a disturbing element: and it was wrong to bring women up with any acquirements but those of an odalisque, or of a domestic servant. . . .

When we consider how vast is the number of men, in any great country, who are little higher than brutes, and that this never prevents them from being able, through the law of marriage, to obtain a victim, the breadth and depth of human misery caused in this shape alone by the abuse of the institution swells to something appalling. Yet these are only the extreme cases. They are the lowest abysses, but there is a sad succession of depth after depth before reaching them. In domestic as in political tyranny, the case of absolute monsters chiefly illustrates the institution by showing that there is scarcely any horror which may not occur under it if the despot pleases, and thus setting in a strong light what must be the terrible frequency of things only a little less atrocious. Absolute fiends are as rare as angels, perhaps rarer: ferocious savages, with occasional touches of humanity, are, however, very frequent: and in the wide interval which separates these from any worthy representatives of the human species, how many are the forms and gradations of animalism and selfishness, often under an outward varnish of civilization and even cultivation, living at peace with the law, maintaining a creditable appearance to all who are not under their power, yet sufficient often to make the lives of all who are so, a torment and a burthen to them! It would be tiresome to repeat the commonplaces about the unfitness of men in general for power, which, after the political discussions of centuries, every one knows by heart, were it not that hardly any one thinks of applying these maxims to the case in which above all others they are applicable, that of power, not placed in the hands of a man here and there, but offered to every adult male, down to the basest and most ferocious. . . . I know that there is another side to the question. I grant that the wife, if she cannot effectually resist, can at least retaliate; she, too, can make the man's life extremely uncomfortable, and by that power is able to carry many points which she ought, and many which she ought not, to prevail in. But this instrument of self-protection—

which may be called the power of the scold, or the shrewish sanction—has the fatal defect, that it avails most against the least tyrannical superiors, and in favor of the least deserving dependants. It is the weapon of irritable and self-willed women; of those who would make the worst use of power if they themselves had it, and who generally turn this power to a bad use. The amiable cannot use such an instrument, the high-minded disdain it. And on the other hand, the husbands against whom it is used most effectively are the gentler and more inoffensive; those who cannot be induced, even by provocation, to resort to any very harsh exercise of authority. The wife's power of being disagreeable generally only establishes a counter-tyranny, and makes victims in their turn chiefly of those husbands who are least inclined to be tyrants. . . .

With regard to the fitness of women, not only to participate in elections, but themselves to hold offices or practise professions involving important public responsibilities; I have already observed that this consideration is not essential to the practical question in dispute: since any woman, who succeeds in an open profession, proves by that very fact that she is qualified for it. And in the case of public offices, if the political system of the country is such as to exclude unfit men, it will equally exclude unfit women: while if it is not, there is no additional evil in the fact that the unfit persons whom it admits may be either women or men. As long therefore as it is acknowledged that even a few women may be fit for these duties, the laws which shut the door on those exceptions cannot be justified by any opinion which can be held respecting the capacities of women in general. But, though this last consideration is not essential, it is far from being irrelevant. An unprejudiced view of it gives additional strength to the arguments against the disabilities of women, and reinforces them by high consideration of practical utility.

Let us at first make entire abstraction of all psychological considerations tending to show, that any of the mental differences supposed to exist between women and men are but the natural effect of the differences in their education and circumstances, and indicate no radical difference, far less radical inferiority, of nature. Let us consider women only as they already are, or as they are known to have been; and the capacities which they have already practically shown. What they have done, that at least, if nothing else, it is proved that they can do. When we consider how sedulously they are all trained away from, instead of being trained towards, any of the occupations or objects reserved for men, it is evident that I am taking a very humble ground for them, when I rest their case on what they have actually achieved. For, in this case, negative evidence is worth little, while any positive evidence is conclusive. It cannot be inferred to be impossible that a woman should be a Homer, or an Aristotle, or a Michelangelo, or a Beethoven, because no woman has yet actually produced works comparable to theirs in any of those lines of excellence. This negative fact at most leaves the question uncertain, and open to psychological discussion. But it is quite certain that a woman can be a Queen Elizabeth, or a Deborah, or a Joan of Arc, since this is not inference, but fact. Now it is a curious consideration, that the only things which the existing law excludes women from doing, are the things which they have proved that they are able to do. There is no law to prevent a woman from having written all the plays of Shakespeare, or composed all the operas of Mozart. But Queen Elizabeth or Queen Victoria, had they not inherited the throne, could not have been entrusted with the smallest of the political duties, of which the former showed herself equal to the greateest.

If anything conclusive could be inferred from experience, without psychological analysis, it would be that the things which women are not allowed to do are the very ones for which they are peculiarly qualified; since their vocation for government has made its way, and become conspicuous, through the very few opportunites which have been given; while in the lines of distinction which apparently were freely open to them, they have by no means so eminently distinguished themselves. We know how small a number of reigning queens history presents, in comparison with that of kings. Of this smaller number a far larger proportion have shown talents for rule; though many of them have occupied the throne in difficult periods. It is remarkable, too, that they have, in a great number of instances, been distinguished by merits the most opposite to the imaginary and conventional character of women; they have been as much remarked for the firmness and vigour of their rule, as for its intelligence. When, to queens and empresses, we add regents, and viceroy's of provinces, the list of women who have been eminent rulers of mankind swells to a great length. . . .

. . . Exactly where and in proportion as women's capacities for government have been tried, in that proportion have they been found adequate.

This fact is in accordance with the best general conclusion which the world's imperfect experience seems as yet to suggest, concerning the peculiar tendencies and aptitudes characteristic of women, as women have hitherto been. I do not say, as they will continue to be; for, as I have already said more than once, I consider it presumption in any one to pretend to decide what women are or are not, can or cannot be, by natural constitution. They have always hitherto been kept, as far as regards spontaneous development, in so unnatural a state, that their nature cannot but have been greatly distorted and disguised; and no one can safely pronounce that if women's nature were left to choose its direction as freely as men's, and if no articficial bent were attempted to be given to it except that required by the conditions of human society, and given to both sexes alike, there would be any material difference, or perhaps any difference at all, in the character and capacities which would unfold themselves. . . . [E]ven the least contestable of the differences which now exist, are such as may very well have been produced merely by circumstances, without any difference of natural capacity.

MARILYN FRYE
Sexism

MARILYN FRYE *is a professor of philosophy at Michigan State University. Her extensive contributions to feminist thought are collected in* The Politics of Reality *(1983), from which the following selection is taken, and more recently in* Willful Virgin *(1994).*

THE first philosophical project I undertook as a feminist was that of trying to say carefully and persuasively what sexism is, and what it is for someone, some institution or some act to be sexist. This project was pressed on me with considerable urgency because, like most women coming to a feminist perception of themselves and the world, I was seeing sexism everywhere and trying to make it perceptible to others. I would point out, complain and criticize, but most frequently my friends and colleagues would not see that what I declared to be sexist was sexist, or at all objectionable.

As the critic and as the initiator of the topic, I was the one on whom the burden of proof fell—it was I who had to explain and convince. Teaching philosophy had already taught me that people cannot be persuaded of things they are not ready to be persuaded of; there are certain complexes of will and prior experience which will inevitably block persuasion, no matter the merits of the case presented. I knew that even if I could explain fully and clearly what I was saying when I called something sexist, I would not necessarily be able to convince various others of the correctness of this claim. But what troubled me enormously was that I could not explain it in any way which satisfied *me*. It is this sort of moral and intellectual frustration which, in my case at least, always generates philosophy.

The following was the product of my first attempt to state clearly and explicitly what sexism is:

The term "sexist" in its core and perhaps most fundamental meaning is a term which characterizes anything whatever which creates, constitutes, promotes or exploits any irrelevant or impertinent marking of the distinction between the sexes.

When I composed this statement, I was thinking of the myriads of instances in which persons of the two sexes are treated differently, or behave differently, but where nothing in the real differences between females and males justifies or explains the difference of treatment or behavior. I was thinking, for instance, of the tracking of boys into Shop and girls into Home Ec, where one can see nothing about boys or girls considered in themselves which seems to connect essentially with the distinction between wrenches and eggbeaters. I was thinking also of sex discrimination in employment—cases where someone otherwise apparently qualified for a job is not hired because she is a woman. But when I tried to put this definition of "sexist" to use, it did not stand the test.

Consider this case: If a company is hiring a supervisor who will supervise a group of male workers who have always worked for male supervisors, it can scarcely be denied that the sex of a candidate for the job is relevant to the candidate's prospects of moving smoothly and successfully into an effective working relation-ship with the supervisees (though the point is usually exaggerated by those looking for excuses not to hire women). Relevance is an intrasys-tematic thing. The patterns of behavior, attitude and custom within which a process goes on determine what is relevant to what in matters of describing, predicting or evaluating. In the case at hand, the workers' attitudes and the sur-rounding customs of the culture make a differ-ence to how they interact with their supervisor and, in particular, *make* the sex of the supervisor a relevant factor in predicting how things will work out. So then, if the company hires a man, in preference to a more experienced and knowl-edgeable woman, can we explain our objection to the decision by saying it involved distinguish-ing on the basis of sex when sex is irrelevant to the ability to do the job? No: sex is relevant here.

So, what did I mean to say about "sexist?" I was thinking that in a case of a candidate for a super-visory job, the reproductive capacity of the candi-date has nothing to do with that person's knowing what needs to be done and being able to give properly timed, clear and correct directions. What I was picturing was a situation purified of all sex-ist perception and reaction. But, of course, *if* the whole context were not sexist, sex would not be an issue in such a job situation; indeed, it might go entirely unnoticed. It is precisely the fact that the sex of the candidate *is* relevant that is the salient symptom of the sexism of the situation.

I had failed, in that first essay, fully to grasp or understand that the locus of sexism is primarily in the system or framework, not in the particular act. It is not accurate to say that what is going on in cases of sexism is that distinctions are made on the basis of sex when sex is irrelevant; what is wrong in cases of sexism is, in the first place, that sex *is* relevant; and then that the making of dis-tinctions on the basis of sex reinforces the pat-terns which make it relevant.

In sexist cultural/economic systems, sex is always relevant. To understand what sexism is, then, we have to step back and take a larger view.

Sex-identification intrudes into every mo-ment of our lives and discourse, no matter what the supposedly primary focus or topic of the mo-ment is. Elaborate, systematic, ubiquitous and redundant marking of a distinction between the two sexes of humans and most animals is cus-tomary and obligatory. One *never* can ignore it.

Examples of sex-marking behavior patterns abound. A couple enters a restaurant; the head-waiter or hostess addresses the man and does not address the woman. The physician addresses the man by surname and honorific (Mr. Baxter, Rev. Jones) and addresses the woman by given name (Nancy, Gloria). You congratulate your friend—a hug, a slap on the back, shaking hands, kissing; one of the things which deter-mines which of these you do is your friend's sex. In everything one does one has two complete repertoires of behavior, one for interactions with women and one for interactions with men. Greeting, story-telling, order-giving and order-receiving, negotiating, gesturing deference or dominance, encouraging, challenging, asking for information: one does all of these things differ-ently depending upon whether the relevant oth-ers are male or female.

That this is so has been confirmed in socio-logical and socio-linguistic research, but it is just as easily confirmed in one's own experience. To discover the differences in how you greet a woman and how you greet a man, for instance, just observe yourself, paying attention to the fol-lowing sorts of things: frequency and duration of eye contact, frequency and type of touch, tone and pitch of voice, physical distance maintained between bodies, how and whether you smile, use of slang or swear words, whether your body dips into a shadow curtsy or bow. That I have two repertoires for handling introductions to people was vividly confirmed for me when a student introduced me to his friend, Pat, and I really could not tell what sex Pat was. For a moment I was stopped cold, completely incapable of action. I felt myself helplessly caught between two paths—the one I would take if Pat were female and the one I would take if Pat were male. Of course the paralysis does not last. One is rescued by one's ingenuity and good will; one can invent a way to behave as one says "How do you do?" to a human being. But the habitual ways are not for humans: they are one way for women and another for men. . . .

In order to behave "appropriately" toward women and men, we have to know which of the people we encounter are women and which are men. But if you strip humans of most of their cultural trappings, it is not always that easy to tell without close inspection which are female, which are male. The tangible and visible physical differences between the sexes are not particularly sharp or numerous and in the physical dimensions we associate with "sex differences," the range of individual variation is very great. The differences between the sexes could easily be, and sometimes are, obscured by bodily decoration, hair removal and the like. So the requirement of knowing everyone's sex in every situation and under almost all observational conditions generates a requirement that we all let others know our sex in every situation. And we do. We announce our sexes in a thousand ways. We deck ourselves from head to toe with garments and decorations which serve like badges and buttons to announce our sexes. For every type of occasion there are distinct clothes, gear and accessories, hairdos, cosmetics and scents, labeled as "ladies'" or "men's" and labeling us as females or males, and most of the time most of us choose, use, wear or bear the paraphernalia associated with our sex. It goes below the skin as well. There are different styles of gait, gesture, posture, speech, humor, taste and even of perception, interest and attention that we learn as we grow up to be women or to be men and that label and announce us as women or as men. It begins early in life: even infants in arms are color coded.

That we wear and bear signs of our sexes, and that this is absolutely compulsory, is made clearest in the relatively rare cases when we do not do so, or not enough. Responses ranging from critical to indignant to hostile meet mothers whose babies are not adequately coded; one of the most agitated criticisms of the sixties' hippies was that "you can't tell the boys from the girls." The requirement of sex-announcement is laden,

indeed, with all the urgency of the taboo against homosexuality. One appears heterosexual by informing people of one's sex *very* emphatically and *very* unambiguously, and lesbians and homosexuals who wish *not* to pass as heterosexual generally can accomplish this just by cultivating ambiguous sex-indicators in clothes, behavior and style. The power of this ambiguity to generate unease and punitive responses in others mirrors and demonstrates the rigidity and urgency of this strange social rule that we all be and assertively act "feminine" or "masculine" (and not both)—that we flap a full array of sex-signals at all times.

The intense demand for marking and for asserting what sex each person is adds up to a strenuous requirement that there *be* two distinct and sharply dimorphic sexes. But, in reality, there are not. There are people who fit on a biological spectrum between two not-so-sharply defined poles. In about 5 percent of live births, possibly more, the babies are in some degree and way not perfect exemplars of male and female. There are individuals with chromosome patterns other than XX or XY and individuals whose external genitalia at birth exhibit some degree of ambiguity. There are people who are chromosomally "normal" who are at the far ends of the normal spectra of secondary sex characteristics—height, musculature, hairiness, body density, distribution of fat, breast size, etc.—whose overall appearance fits the norm of people whose chromosomal sex is the opposite of theirs.

These variations notwithstanding, persons (mainly men, of course) with the power to do so actually *construct* a world in which men are men and women are women and there is nothing in between and nothing ambiguous; they do it by chemically and/or surgically altering people whose bodies are indeterminate or ambiguous with respect to sex. Newborns with "imperfectly formed" genitals are immediately "corrected" by chemical or surgical means, children and adolescents are given hormone "therapies" if their bodies seem not to be developing according to what physicians and others declare to be the norm for what has been declared to be that individual's sex.

Persons with authority recommend and supply cosmetics and cosmetic regimens, diets, exercises and all manner of clothing to revise or disguise the too-hairy lip, the too-large breast, the too-slender shoulders, the too-large feet, the too-great or too-slight stature. Individuals whose bodies do not fit the picture of exactly two sharply dimorphic sexes are often enough quite willing to be altered or veiled for the obvious reason that the world punishes them severely for their failure to be the "facts" which would verify the doctrine of two sexes. The demand that the world be a world in which there are exactly two sexes is inexorable, and we are all compelled to answer to it emphatically, unconditionally, repetitiously and unambiguously.

Even being physically "normal" for one's assigned sex is not enough. One must *be* female or male, actively. Again, the costumes and performances. Pressed to acting feminine or masculine, one colludes (co-lude: play along) with the doctors and counselors in the creation of a world in which the apparent dimorphism of the sexes is so extreme that one can only think there is a great gulf between female and male, that the two are, essentially and fundamentally and naturally, utterly different. One helps to create a world in which it seems to us that we *could* never mistake a woman for a man or a man for a woman. We never need worry.

Along with all the making, marking and announcing of sex-distinction goes a strong and visceral feeling or attitude to the effect that sex-distinction is the most important thing in the world: that it would be the end of the world if it were not maintained, clear and sharp and rigid; that a sex-dualism which is rooted in the nature of the beast is absolutely crucial and fundamental to all aspects of human life, human society and human economy. . . .

It is a general and obvious principle of information theory that when it is very, very important that certain information be conveyed, the suitable strategy is redundancy. If a message *must* get through, one sends it repeatedly and by as many means or media as one has at one's command. On the other end, as a receiver of information, if one receives the same information over and over, conveyed by every medium one knows, another message comes through as well, and implicitly: the message that this information is very, very important. The enormous frequency with which information about people's sexes is conveyed conveys implicitly the message that this topic is enormously important. I suspect that this is the single topic on which we most frequently receive information from others throughout our entire lives. If I am right, it would go part way to explaining why we end up with an almost irresistible impression, unarticulated, that the matter of people's sexes is the most important and most fundamental topic in the world.

We exchange sex-identification information, along with the implicit message that it is very important, in a variety of circumstances in which there really is no concrete or experientially obvious point in having the information. There are reasons, as this discussion has shown, why you should want to know whether the person filling your water glass or your tooth is male or female and why that person wants to know what you are, but those reasons are woven invisibly into the fabric of social structure and they do not have to do with the bare mechanics of things being filled. Furthermore, the same culture which drives us to this constant information exchange also simultaneously enforces a strong blanket rule requiring that the simplest and most nearly definitive physical manifestations of sex difference be hidden from view in all but the most private and intimate circumstances. The double message of sex-distinction and its pre-eminent importance is conveyed, in fact, in part *by* devices which systematically and deliberately cover up and hide from view the few physical things which do (to a fair extent) distinguish two sexes of humans. The messages are overwhelmingly dissociated from the concrete facts they supposedly pertain to, and from matrices of concrete and sensible reasons and consequences. . . .

If one is made to feel that a thing is of prime importance, but common sensory experience does not connect it with things of obvious concrete and practical importance, then there is mystery, and with that a strong tendency to the construction of mystical or metaphysical conceptions of its importance. If it is important, but not of mundane importance, it must be of transcendent importance. All the more so if it is *very* important.

This matter of our sexes must be very profound indeed if it must, on pain of shame and ostracism, be covered up and must, on pain of shame and ostracism, be boldly advertised by every means and medium one can devise.

There is one more point about redundancy that is worth making here. If there is one thing more effective in making one believe a thing than receiving the message repetitively, it is rehearsing it repetitively. Advertisers, preachers, teachers, all of us in the brainwashing professions, make use of this apparently physical fact of human psychology routinely. The redundancy of sex-marking and sex-announcing serves not only to make the topic seem transcendently important, but to make the sex-duality it advertises seem transcendently and unquestionably *true*. . . .

Sex-marking and sex-announcing are equally compulsory for males and females; but that is as far as equality goes in this matter. The meaning and import of this behavior is profoundly different for women and for men.

Imagine—A colony of humans established a civilization hundreds of years ago on a distant planet. It has evolved, as civilizations will. Its language is a descendant of English.

The language has personal pronouns marking the child/adult distinction, and its adult personal pronouns mark the distinction between straight and curly public hair. At puberty each person assumes distinguishing clothing styles and manners so others can tell what type she or he is without the closer scrutiny which would generally be considered indecent. People with straight pubic hair adopt a style which is modest and self-effacing and clothes which are fragile and confining; people with curly public hair adopt a style which is expansive and prepossessing and clothes which are sturdy and comfortable.

People whose pubic hair is neither clearly straight nor clearly curly alter their hair chemically in order to be clearly one or the other. Since those with curly pubic hair have higher status and economic advantages, those with ambiguous pubic hair are told to make it straight, for life will be easier for a low-status person whose category might be doubted than for a high-status person whose category might be doubted.

It is taboo to eat or drink in the same room with any person of the same pubic hair type as oneself. Compulsory heterogourmandism, it is called by social critics, though most people think it is just natural human desire to eat with one's pubic-hair opposite. A logical consequence of this habit, or taboo, is the limitation to dining only singly or in pairs—a taboo against banquetism, or, as the slang expression goes, against the group gulp.

Whatever features an individual male person has which tend to his social and economic disadvantage (his age, race, class, height, etc.), one feature which never tends to his disadvantage in the society at large is his maleness. The case for females is the mirror image of this. Whatever features an individual female person has which tend to her social and economic advantage (her age, race, etc.), one feature which always tends to her disadvantage is her femaleness. Therefore, when a male's sex-category is the thing about him that gets first and most repeated notice, the thing about him that is being framed and emphasized and given primacy is a feature which in general is an asset to him. When a female's sex-category is the thing about her that gets first and most repeated notice, the thing about her that is being framed and emphasized and given primacy is a feature which in general is a liability to her. Manifestations of this divergence in the meaning and consequences of sex-announcement can be very concrete.

Walking down the street in the evening in a town or city exposes one to some risk of assault. For males the risk is less; for females the risk is greater. If one announces oneself male, one is presumed by potential assailants to be more rather than less likely to defend oneself or be able to evade the assault and, if the male-announcement is strong and unambiguous, to be a non-candidate for sexual assault. If one announces oneself female, one is presumed by potential assailants to be less rather than more likely to defend oneself or to evade the assault and, if the female-announcement is strong and unambiguous, to be a prime candidate for sexual assault. Both the man and the woman "announce" their sex through style of gait, clothing, hair style, etc., but they are not equally or identically affected by announcing their sex. The male's announcement tends toward his protection or safety, and the female's announcement tends toward her victimization. It could not be more immediate or concrete; the meaning of the sex-identification could not be more different.

The sex-marking behavioral repertoires are such that in the behavior of almost all people of both sexes addressing or responding to males (especially within their own culture/race) generally is done in a manner which suggests basic respect, while addressing or responding to females is done in a manner that suggests the females' inferiority (condescending tones, presumptions of ignorance, overfamiliarity, sexual aggression, etc.). So, when one approaches an ordinary well-socialized person in such cultures, if one is male, one's own behavioral announcement of maleness tends to evoke supportive and beneficial response and if one is female, one's own behavioral announcement of femaleness tends to evoke degrading and detrimental response.

The details of the sex-announcing behaviors also contribute to the reduction of women and the elevation of men. The case is most obvious in the matter of clothing. As feminists have been saying for two hundred years or so, ladies' clothing is generally restrictive, binding, burdening and frail; it threatens to fall apart and/or to uncover something that is supposed to be covered if you bend, reach, kick, punch or run. It typically does not protect effectively against hazards in the environment, nor permit the wearer to protect herself against the hazards of the human environment. Men's clothing is generally the opposite of

all this—sturdy, suitably protective, permitting movement and locomotion. The details of feminine manners and postures also serve to bind and restrict. To be feminine is to take up little space, to defer to others, to be silent or affirming of others, etc. It is not necessary here to survey all this, for it has been done many times and in illuminating detail in feminist writings. My point here is that though both men and women must behave in sex-announcing ways, the behavior which announces femaleness is in itself both physically and socially binding and limiting as the behavior which announces maleness is not.

The sex-correlated variations in our behavior tend systematically to the benefit of males and the detriment of females. The male, announcing his sex in sex-identifying behavior and dress, is both announcing and acting on his membership in a dominant caste—dominant within his subculture and to a fair extent across subcultures as well. The female, announcing her sex, is both announcing and acting on her membership in the subordinated caste. She is obliged to inform others constantly and in every sort of situation that she is to be treated as inferior, without authority, assaultable. She cannot move or speak within the usual cultural norms without engaging in self-deprecation. The male cannot move or speak without engaging in self-aggrandizement. Constant sex-identification both defines and maintains the caste boundary without which there could not be a dominance-subordination structure. . . .

The cultural and economic structures which create and enforce elaborate and rigid patterns of sex-making and sex-announcing behavior, that is, create gender as we know it, mold us as dominators and subordinates (I do not say "mold our minds" or "mold our personalities"). They construct two classes of animals, the masculine and the feminine, where another constellation of forces might have constructed three or five categories, and not necessarily hierarchically related. Or such a spectrum of sorts that we would not experience them as "sorts" at all.

The term "sexist" characterizes cultural and economic structures which create and enforce the elaborate and rigid patterns of sex-marking and sex-announcing which divide the species, along lines of sex, into dominators and subordinates. Individual acts and practices are sexist which reinforce and support those structures, either as culture or as shapes taken on by the enculturated animals. Resistance to sexism is that which undermines those structures by social and political action and by projects of reconstruction and revision of ourselves.

NATALIE ANGIER

Monogamy vs. Promiscuity: Putting Evolutionary Psychology on the Couch

NATALIE ANGIER *is a Pulitzer Prize winning science writer. Her work appears regularly in the* New York Times. *She is also the author of several books, among them* Woman: An Intimate Geography *(1999) in which this essay (in a longer form) appears.*

HERE is a little ditty, sometimes attributed to William James, sometimes to Dorothy Parker.

Hoggamus, higgamus, Men are polygamous
Higgamus, hoggamus, Women monogamous.

Lately, that idea has found new fodder and new fans, through the explosive growth of a field known as evolutionary psychology. Evolutionary psychology professes to have discovered the fundamental modules of human nature, most notably the essential nature of man and of woman. Now, it makes sense to be curious about the evolutionary roots of human behaviour. It's reasonable to attempt to understand our impulses and actions by applying Darwinian logic to the problem. We're animals. We're not above the rude little prods and jests of natural selection. But evolutionary psychology, as it has been disseminated across mainstream consciousness, is a cranky and despotic Cyclops, its single eye glaring through an overwhelmingly masculinist lens. I say "masculinist" rather than male because the view of male behaviour promulgated by hard-core evolutionary psychologists is as narrow and inflexible as their view of womanhood. I'm not going to explain to men what they really want or how they should behave. If a fellow chooses to tell himself that his yen for the fetching young secretary in his office and his concomitant disgruntlement with his ageing wife's housekeeping lacunae make perfect Darwinian sense, who am I to argue with him? I'm only going to propose here that the hard-core evolutionary psychologists have got a lot about women wrong, and that we want more and deserve better than the cartoons handed down for popular consumption.

The cardinal premises of evolutionary psychology of interest to our discussion are as follows: 1) Men are more promiscuous and less sexually reserved than women; 2) Women are inherently more interested in a stable relationship than men; 3) Women are naturally attracted to high-status men with resources; 4) Men are naturally attracted to youth and beauty; 5) Our core preferences and desires were hammered out long, long ago, a hundred thousand years ago or more, in the legendary environment of evolutionary adaptation, or EEA, also known as the ancestral environment, also known as the Stone Age, and they have not changed appreciably since then, nor are they likely to change in the future.

In sum: higgamus, hoggamus, Pygmalionus, Playboy magazine, eternitas. Amen.

Hard-core evolutionary psychology (evo-psycho) types go to extremes to promote their theses, and to argue in favour of the yawning chasm that separates the innate desires of women and men. They declare ringing confirmation for their theories even in the face of feeble data.

For example: Among the cardinal principles of the evo-psycho set is that men are innately more promiscuous than women, and that men are much more accepting of casual, even anonymous sex than women are. Men can't help themselves, they say.

When a female friend of mine questioned Robert Wright, the author of *The Moral Animal* and one of the prime popularisers of this position, about some of his unshakable convictions in the male-female contrariety, he opened his eyes wide, stared at her, and said, manfully, "You don't know what it's like." And she replied, "You don't know what it's like for us, either." David Buss, of the University of Michigan, another evolutionary psychologist of the unerring Nicene Creed, has said that asking a man not to lust after a pretty young woman is like telling a carnivore not to like meat.

At the same time, they recognise that the overwhelming majority of men and women get married, and they have much to say about the differences between innate mate preferences among men and women. Men look for the hallmarks of youth, such as smooth skin, full lips and perky breasts; they want a mate who has a long child-bearing career ahead of her. Men also want women who are virginal and who seem as though they'll be faithful and not make cuckolds of them. The sexy-vampy types are fine for a Saturday-night romp, but when it comes to choosing a marital partner, men want the earmarks of modesty and fidelity.

Women want a provider, the theory goes. They want a man who seems rich, stable and ambitious. They want to know that they and their children will be cared for. They want a man who can take charge, maybe dominate them just a little, enough to reassure them that the man is genotypically, phenotypically eternally a king. Women's innate preference for a well-to-do man continues to this day, the evolutionary psychologists insist, even among financially independent and professionally successful women who don't need the man as a provider. It was adaptive in the past to look for the most resourceful man, they say, and adaptations can't be willed away in a generation or two of cultural change.

And what of the evidence for these male-female verities? For the difference in promiscuity quotas, the hard-cores love to raise the example of the differences between gay men and lesbians. Homosexuals are seen as a revealing population because they supposedly can behave according to the innermost impulses of their sex, untempered by the need to adjust to the demands and wishes of the opposite sex, as heterosexuals theoretically are. What do we see in our ideal study group? Just look at how gay men carry on! They are perfectly happy to have hundreds, thousands of sexual partners, to have sex in bathhouses, in bathrooms, on Clapham Common. By contrast, lesbians are sexually sedate. They don't cruise sex clubs. They couple up and stay coupled, and they like cuddling and hugging more than they do serious, genitally-based sex. There's a phenomenon called "lesbian bed death," in which some lesbian couples, after an initial flurry of heated passion, settle into a near sexless relationship, measuring their encounters by the month rather than by the day or week.

In the hard-core rendering of inherent male-female discrepancies in promiscuity, gay men are offered up as true men, real men, deep men, men unfettered, men set free to be men, while lesbians are real women, ultra-women, acting out every woman's fantasy of love and commitment without the fuss and slop of sex. Interestingly, though, in other theoretical instances, gay men and lesbians are not considered real men and real women, but the opposite: gay men are feminine men, halfway between men and women, while lesbians are posited as mannish women.

Thus, in brain studies that purport to find the origins of sexual orientation, gay men are said to have hypothalamic nuclei that are smaller than a straight man's and closer in size to a woman's, and thus they are attracted to men. Their brains are posited as being so incompletely masculinised that they are said to be comparatively poor at maths, girlish rather than boyish in their native talents. Lesbians are said to have relatively good visuo-spatial abilities, more like a man's than a woman's.

Young boys who like to play with dolls and tea-sets are thought to be at risk of growing up into homosexual men; young girls who take tomboyishness to extremes are said to have a higher-than-average likelihood of ending up as lesbians. And so gay men are sissy boys in some contexts, and Stone Age manly men in others, while lesbians are battering rams one day and flower into the softest, most divested of feminine gals the next.

On the question of mate preferences, evopsychos rely on surveys, most of them compiled by David Buss. His surveys are celebrated by some, derided by others, but, in any event, they are ambitious—performed in 37 countries, he says, on various continents and among a reasonable sampling of cultures and subcultures. His surveys, and others aspiring to them, consistently find that men rate youth and beauty as important traits in a mate, while women give comparatively greater weight to ambitiousness and financial success.

Surveys show that surveys never lie. Lest you think that women's mate preferences change with their mounting economic clout, surveys assure us not. Surveys of female medical students, according to John Marshall Townsend, of Syracuse University, indicate that they hope to marry men with an earning power and social status at least equal to, and preferably greater than, their own.

What does it mean if surveys show that women want a man who earns a living wage? It means that men can earn a living wage better, even now, than women can. Men still own and operate most of what can be claimed and controlled. They make up less than 50 per cent of the world's population, but they own somewhere between 88 and 95 per cent of the world's wealth—the currency, the minerals, the timber, the gold, the stocks, the amber fields of grain. In her superb book, *Why So Slow?*, Virginia Valian, a professor of psychology at Hunter College, lays out the extent of lingering economic discrepancies between men and women in the US. In 1978, there were two women heading Fortune 1,000 companies; in 1994, there were still two; in 1996, the number had jumped all the way to four. In 1985, 2 per cent of the Fortune 1,000's senior-level executives were women; by 1992, that number had hardly budged, to 3 per cent.

A 1990 salary and compensation survey of 799 major companies showed that, of the highest-paid officers and directors, less than 0.5 per cent were women. Ask, and he shall receive. In the US, the possession of a bachelor's degree adds $28,000 to a man's salary, but only $9,000 to a woman's. A degree from a high-prestige school contributes $11,500 to a man's income, but subtracts $2,400 from a woman's—yes, subtracts, though no one knows why. The most successful women in the world are more precariously positioned than comparable men. In Hollywood, the careers and asking price of actresses and female directors are easily derailed by the occasional flop, even when the women are superstars such as Sharon Stone and Barbra Streisand, while actors such as Kevin Costner and Sylvester Stallone can appear in dog after dog and still command the salary of plutocrats.

If women continue to worry that they need a man's money to persist because the playing field remains about as level as the surface of Mars—or Venus, if you prefer—then we can't conclude anything about innate preferences. If women continue to suffer from bag-lady syndrome even as they become prosperous, if they see their wealth as still provisional, still capsizable, and if they still hope to find a man with a dependable income to supplement their own, then we can credit women with intelligence and acumen, for inequities abound and find new and startling permutations even in the most economically advanced countries and among the most highly skilled populations of women.

There's another reason that smart, professional women might respond on surveys that they'd like a mate of their socio-economic status or better. Smart, professional women are smart enough to know that men can be tender of ego—is it genetic?—and that it hurts a man to earn less money than his wife, and that resentment is a noxious chemical in a marriage. "A woman who is more successful than her mate threatens his position in the male hierarchy," Elizabeth Cashdan, of the University of Utah, has written. If women could be persuaded that men don't mind their being high achievers, were in fact pleased and proud to be affiliated with them, we might predict that women would stop caring about the particulars of their mates' income.

The anthropologist Sarah Blaffer Hrdy writes that "when female status and access to resources do not depend on her mate's status, women will likely use a range of criteria, not primarily or even necessarily prestige and wealth, for male selection." She describes a *New York Times* story written by Donatella Lorch in 1996, called "Bride Wore White, Groom Hopes For Parole." The story is about women from a wide range of professions—bankers, judges, teachers, journalists—who marry male prisoners. The allure of the men is not their income, for you can't earn much when you make licence plates for a living. Instead, it is the men's gratitude that proves irresistible. The men are happy to have the love of these women, these smart, free women, and they focus all their thoughts, attention and energy on their wives. The women also like the fact that

their husbands' fidelity is guaranteed; the longer the inmates' sentences are, the more attractive the men become.

Do women love older men? Do women find grey hair and wrinkles attractive on men—as attractive, that is, as a fine, full head of pigmented hair and a vigorous, firm complexion? The evolutionary psychologists suggest yes. They believe that women look for signs of maturity in men because a mature man is likely to be a comparatively wealthy and resourceful man.

Of course, the thesis can't be taken too far. Desmond Morris once expressed his surprise that baldness wasn't considered a particularly attractive state. One might predict, he said, that since baldness comes with age and a man's status generally rises with age, the bald head, gleaming in the midday sun of the veldt or the fishbelly glow of a fluorescent office light, would lure the attention of every woman on the prowl for her alpha mate. But no, he admitted there was no evidence that baldness was adaptive, nor that women admired rather than merely accepted a thinning hairline.

Nevertheless, the legend of the sexy older man persists, particularly among older men. The older male moguls in Hollywood can't stop casting older male actors in roles that have them flinging about on the wide screen like elephants in must, and the age gap between the men and their female co-stars gapes ever wider. Jack Nicholson, Clint Eastwood, Robert De Niro, Al Pacino, Woody Allen: no matter to what extenuated proportions their cartilaginous features grow, the men are portrayed as sexy, comely, frisky, desirable, to women 25, 30 years their junior, to women who are themselves considered "mature" for being older than, oh, 30.

Do women find older men innately attractive? Is it the men's alpha status? Or could it be something less complimentary to the male, something like the following: that an older man is appealing not because he is powerful, but because in his maturity he has lost some of his power, has become less marketable and desirable and potentially more grateful and gracious, more likely to make a younger woman feel that there is a balance of power in the relationship? The rude little calculation is simple: He is male, I am female—advantage, man. He is older, I am younger—advantage, woman. By the same token, a woman may place little value on a man's appearance because she values something else far more: room to breathe. Who can breathe in the presence of a handsome young man, whose ego, if expressed as a vapour, would fill Biosphere II? Not even, I'm afraid, a beautiful young woman.

In the end, what is important to question, and to hold to the fire of alternative interpretation, is the immutability and adaptive logic of the discrepancy, its basis in our genome rather than in the ecological circumstances in which a genome manages to express itself. Evolutionary psychologists insist on the innate discordance between the strength of the male and the female sex drive. They admit that many non-human female primates gallivant about rather more than we might have predicted before primatologists began observing their behaviour in the field—more, far more, than is necessary for the sake of production. Nonetheless, the credo of the coy female persists.

"Amid the great variety of social structure in (ape) species, the basic theme . . . stands out, at least in minimal form: males seem very eager for sex and work hard to find it; females work less hard," Robert Wright says in *The Moral Animal.* "This isn't to say the females don't like sex. They love it, and may initiate it. And, intriguingly, the females of the species most closely related to humans—chimpanzees and bonobos—seem particularly amenable to a wild sex life, including a variety of partners. Still, female apes don't do what male apes do: search high and low, risking life and limb, to find sex, and to find as much of it, with as many different partners, as possible; it has a way of finding them." In fact, female chimpanzees do search high and low and risk life and limb to find sex with partners other than the partners who have a way of finding them. As we have seen, DNA studies of chimpanzees in the Gombe reserve, Tanzania, show that half the offspring in the group of closely scrutinised chimpanzees turned out not to be the offspring of the resident males.

The females of the group didn't rely on sex 'finding' its way to them; they proactively left the local environs under such conditions of secrecy that not even their vigilant human observers knew they had gone, and became impregnated by outside males. They did so even at the risk of life and limb—their own, and those of their offspring. Male chimpanzees try to control the movements of the females. They'll scream at them and hit them if they think the females aren't listening. They may even kill an infant they think is not their own. We don't know why the females take such risks to philander, but they do, and to say that female chimpanzees "work less hard" than males do at finding sex is not supported by the data.

Evo-psychos pull us back and forth until we might want to sue for whiplash. On the one hand, we are told that women have a lower sex-drive than men do. On the other hand, we are told that the madonna/whore dichotomy is a universal stereotype. In every culture, there is a tendency among both men and women to adjudge women as either chaste or trampy. The chaste ones are accorded esteem. The trampy ones are consigned to the basement, a notch or two below goats in social status. A woman can't sleep around without risking terrible retribution, to her reputation, to her prospects, to her life. "Can anyone find a single culture in which women with unrestrained sexual appetites aren't viewed as more aberrant than comparably libidinous men?" Wright asks rhetorically.

Women are said to have lower sex-drives than men, yet they are universally punished if they display evidence to the contrary.

Nor is their sex drive ever low enough.

No, there is still just enough of a lingering female infidelity impulse that cultures everywhere have had to gird against it by articulating a rigid dichotomy, still enough to justify infibulation, purdah, claustration. Men have the naturally higher sex drive, yet all the laws, customs, punishments, shame, strictures, mystiques, and anti-mystiques are aimed at that tepid, sleepy, hypoactive creature the female libido. "It seems premature to attribute the relative lack of female interest in sexual variety to women's biological nature alone in the face of overwhelming evidence that women are consistently beaten for promiscuity and adultery," Barbara Smuts has written. "If female sexuality is muted compared to that of men, then why must men the world over go to extreme lengths to control and contain it?" Why, indeed. Consider a brief evolutionary apologia for President Clinton's adulteries that appeared in the *New Yorker*, written by the cognitive psychologist Steven Pinker, of the Massachusetts Institute of Technology. "Most human drives have ancient Darwinian rationales," Pinker wrote. "A prehistoric man who slept with 50 women could have sired 50 children, and would have been more likely to have descendants who inherited his tastes. A woman who slept with 50 men would have no more descendants than a woman who slept with one. Thus, men should seek quantity in sexual partners; women, quality." And isn't it so, he says, everywhere and always so? "In our society, most young men tell researchers that they would like eight sexual partners in the next two years; most women say that they would like one." Yet would a man find the prospect of a string of partners so appealing if the following rules were applied: that no matter how much he may like a particular woman and be pleased by her performance and want to sleep with her again, he will have no say in the matter, will be dependent on her mood and good graces for all future contact; that each act of casual sex will cheapen his status and make him increasingly less attractive to other women; and that society will not wink at his randiness, but, rather, sneer at him and think him pathetic, sullied, smaller than life? Until men are subjected to the same threat of censure as women are, and until they are given the lower hand in a so-called casual encounter, it is hard to insist with such self-satisfaction that, hey, it's natural, men like a lot of sex with a lot of people, and women don't.

Consider Pinker's philandering caveman who slept with 50 women. Just how good a reproductive strategy is this chronic, random shooting of the gun? A woman is fertile only

two or three days a month. Her ovulation is concealed. The man doesn't know when she's fertile. She might be in the early stages of pregnancy when he gets to her; she might still be lactating and thus not ovulating. Moreover, even if our hypothetical Don Juan hits a day on which a woman is ovulating, his sperm has only a 20 per cent chance of fertilising her egg; human reproduction is complicated, and most eggs and sperm are not up to the demands of proper fusion. Even if conception occurs, the resulting embryo has a 25 to 30 per cent chance of miscarrying.

In sum, fleeting sex has a remarkably small probability of yielding a baby, and because the man is beating and running, he isn't able to prevent any of his one-night stands from turning around and mating with other men. The poor fellow. He has to mate with so many scores of women for his wham-bam strategy to pay off. And where are all these women to be found, anyway? Population density during that purportedly all-powerful psyche-shaper the "ancestral environment" was quite low, and long-distance travel dangerous and difficult.

There were alternatives to wantonness, as a number of theorists have emphasised.

If, for example, a man were to spend a bit more time with one woman rather than dashing breathlessly from sheet to sheet, if he were to feel compelled to engage in what animal behaviourists call mate-guarding, he might be better off, reproductively speaking, than the wild Lothario, both because the odds of his getting the woman during her fertile time would increase and because he'd be monopolising her energy and keeping her from the advances of other sperm-bearers. It takes the average couple about four months, or 120 days, of regular sexual intercourse to become pregnant. That number of days is approximately equal to the number of partners our hypothetical libertine needs to sleep with to have one of them result in a "fertility unit," that is a baby.

The two strategies, then, shake out about the same. A man can sleep with a lot of women—the quantitative approach—or he can sleep with one woman for months at a time, and be madly in love with her—the qualitative tactic.

Now, it's possible that these two reproductive strategies are distributed in discrete packets among the male population, with the result that some men are born philanderers and can never attach, while others are born romantics and perpetually in love with love; but it's also possible that men teeter back and forth from one impulse to the other, suffering an internal struggle between the desire to bond and the desire to retreat, their needs and desires difficult to understand, paradoxical, fickle, treacherous, and glorious.

We don't have to argue that men and women are exactly the same, or that humans are meta-evolutionary beings, removed from nature and slaves to culture, to reject the perpetually regurgitated model of the coy female and the ardent male. Conflicts of interest are always among us, and the outcomes of those conflicts are interesting, more interesting by far than what the ultra-evolutionary psychology line has handed us. Patricia Gowaty, of the University of Georgia, sees conflict between males and females as inevitable and pervasive. She calls it sexual dialectics. "Human mating systems are characterised by conflict from start to finish," she says. The thesis is that females and males vie for control over the means of reproduction. Those means are the female body, for there is as yet no such beast as the parthenogenetic man.

Women are under selective pressure to maintain control over their reproduction, to choose with whom they will mate and with whom they will not—to exercise female choice. If they make bad mating decisions, they will have less viable offspring than if they are clever in their choices. Men are under selective pressure to make sure they're chosen or, barring that, to subvert female choice and coerce the female to mate against her will. "But once you have this basic dialectic set in motion, it's going to be constant push-me, pull-you," Gowaty says. "That dynamism cannot possibly result in a unitary response, the caricatured coy woman and ardent man. Instead, there are going to be some coy, reluctantly mating males and some ardent females, and any number of variations in between.

"A female will choose to mate with a male whom she believes, consciously or otherwise, will confer some advantage on her and her offspring. Some theorists talk about the 'good genes' model of mate selection, the idea that a female looks for a male who exhibits signs of having a superior genotype. The 'good genes' model leads to oversimplified notions that there is a 'best male' out there, a top-of-the-line hunk whom all females would prefer to mate with if they had the wherewithal. But in the viability model, a female brings her own genetic complement to the equation, with the result that what looks good genetically to one woman might be a clash of colours for another." Maybe the man's immune system doesn't complement her own, for example, Gowaty proposes. There's evidence that the search for immune variation is one of the subtle factors driving mate selection, which may be why we care about how our lovers smell; immune molecules may be volatilised and released in sweat, hair, the oil on our skin. We are each of us a chemistry set, and each of us has a distinctive mix of reagents. "What pleases me might not please somebody else," Gowaty says. "There is no one-brand great male out there. We're not all programmed to look for the alpha male and only willing to mate with the little guy because we can't do any better. Some women might find it exciting to be with the little guy. He might be a fabulous lover. She might like him for all the subliminal reasons of chemistry that we find hard to articulate. But the propaganda gives us a picture of the right man and the ideal woman, and the effect of the propaganda is insidious. It becomes self-reinforcing.

People who don't fit the model think, "I'm weird, I'll have to change my behaviour." It is this danger, that the ostensible "discoveries" of evolutionary psychology will be used as propaganda, that makes the enterprise so disturbing. Variation and flexibility are the key themes that get set aside in the breathless dissemination of evolutionary psychology. Females vary. So, too, do males. Primatologist Barbara Smuts has studied olive baboons, and she has seen males pursuing all sorts of mating strategies. "There are some whose primary strategy is dominating other males, and being able to gain access to more females because of their fighting ability," she says. "Then there is the type of male who avoids competition and cultivates long-term relationships with females and their infants. These are the nice, affiliative guys. There's a third type, who focuses on sexual relationships. He's the consorter. He's not around females when they're pregnant or lactating, but when they're in oestrus, he knows how to relate to them in a way that decreases the females' motivation to go after other guys. The strategy that a male pursues is not related to status or age: a high-status male can be an affiliative male, while a male who's low in the hierarchy may stake his future on his fighting power. Instead, the differences in mating strategy seem to be born largely of temperament, of innate differences in personality and physiology. And as far as we can tell, no one reproductive strategy has advantages over the others." Women are said to need an investing male (or more than one, if they can get it). We think we know the reason why. Human babies are difficult and time-consuming to raise. Chimpanzee females may be able to provision their offspring on their own, but women cannot. Stone Age mothers needed husbands to bring home the bison. Yet the age-old assumption that male parental investment lies at the heart of human evolution is now open to serious question. Men in traditional foraging cultures do not necessarily invest resources in their offspring. Hadza men of Tanzania hunt, but they share the bounty of that hunting widely, politically, strategically. They don't deliver it straight to the mouths of their progeny. Women rely on their senior female kin to help get their children fed. The men are often away hunting, in quest of big game. The women gather.

There is a division of labour by sex. But in hunting, the men are not engaging in the most calorically productive enterprise.

In many cases, they would be better off gathering, or combining an occasional hunt with the trapping of small prey. The big hunt, though, is a big opportunity to win status and allies. The women and their children in a hunter-gatherer society clearly benefit from the meat that hunters bring back to the group. But they benefit as a group, not as a collection of nuclear family units, each beholden to the father's personal pound of wildeburger.

This is a startling revelation, which up-ends many of our presumptions about the origins of marriage and what women want from men and what men want from women. It opens the door to a whole range of new questions.

For example, Nicholas Blurton Jones, of the University of California at Los Angeles, and others have proposed that marriage developed as an extension of men's efforts at mate-guarding. Just as male baboons demand exclusivity during peak oestrus, so a man might attempt to claim access to a woman and keep other men away from her. The invention of lethal weapons of war very likely upped the ante for male-male competition relatively early in human evolution. When armed men fight, they can kill with far greater ease than the males of other species can. If fighting for access to other females resulted in too high a cost too often, then the average archaic male wouldn't have wanted to get into such contests terribly often.

In other words, the bed-hopper, who tried to spread his seed quantitatively, might not have survived long enough to have many successful hits, for each effort at wooing a fertile female would have pushed him smack up against a thicket of other suitors' spear tips. The cost of philandering becomes ludicrously high. The man might be better off trying to claim rights to one woman at a time. Regular sex with a fertile woman is at least likely to yield offspring at comparatively little risk to his life, particularly if sexual access to the woman is formalised through a public ceremony—a wedding.

Looked at from this perspective, we must wonder why an ancestral woman bothered to get married, particularly if she and her female relatives did most of the work of keeping the family fed from year to year. Perhaps, Blurton Jones suggests, to limit the degree to which she was harassed. Chronic male harassment can be a terrible problem for a female, he says, and if a woman has to forage to feed herself and her dependent young, the cost of harassment to her efficiency may be too high to bear. Better to agree to a ritualised bond with a male, and to benefit from whatever hands-off policy that marriage may bring, than to spend all of her time locked in one sexual dialectic or another.

Thus, marriage may have arisen as a multifaceted social pact: between man and woman, between male and male, and between the couple and the tribe. It is a reasonable solution to a series of cultural challenges that arose in concert with the expansion of the human neocortex. But its roots may not be what we think they are, nor may our contemporary mating behaviours stem from the pressures of an ancestral environment as it is commonly portrayed, in which a woman needed a mate to help feed and clothe her young. Instead, our "deep" feelings about marriage may be more pragmatic, more contextual, and, dare I say it, more egalitarian than we give them credit for being.

If marriage is a social compact, a mutual bid between man and woman to contrive a reasonably stable and agreeable micro-habitat in a community of shrewd and well-armed cohorts, then we can understand why, despite rhetoric to the contrary, men are as eager to marry as women are—sometimes, it seems, even more so. Are not men the ones who gain most in health and happiness from being married? A raft of epidemiological studies have shown that marriage adds more years to the life of a man than it does to that of a woman. Why should that be, if men are so "naturally" ill-suited to matrimony? What do women want? None of us can speak for all women, or for more than one woman, really, but we can hazard a mad guess that a desire for emotional parity is widespread and profound. It doesn't go away, although it often hibernates under duress, and it may be perverted by the restrictions of habitat or culture into something that looks like its opposite. The impulse for liberty is congenital. It is the ultimate manifestation of selfishness, which is why we can count on its endurance.

SARAH MCCARRY
Selling Out

SARAH MCCARRY *is a writer and self-described "half-hearted anarchist" whose fiction won second place in* Seventeen *magazine's annual fiction contest.*

Your revolution starts in your house. It started the day you noticed feminism wasn't such a bad word, the day you started working at a women's shelter, the day you started composting.

YOUR friend Serene has cable. Once every six months when you are both tipsy and there's nothing else to do, you wacth television for hours on end, your chins gradually slackening toward your chests: a captive audience. As you watch, you find the commercials deeply disorienting and frequently disturbing, perhaps because you see them so rarely. People in commercials are adamant and clean and perpetually in motion. The technology presented in commercials bewilders you, as does the prevalence of high-powered executives and mascara and small, gyrating children in brightly colored ensembles. The women fascinate you most of all. They wear suits and tote cell phones pagers portfolios laptops *purpose* and they drive very nice cars. They are skinny and their hair shines brightly in the sun. They are entitled to various small pleasures: luxurious pantyhose, upgraded long distance, expensive running shoes and diamonds, because they work hard. As do you. Men frequently fall at their feet, the feet of these women who are as likely to sprout wings and float about in their excellently designed undergarments as they are to confidently give important business presentations. Obviously women have come a very long way.

It occurs to you one afternoon, in a fit of blistering insight, that these luscious women in the throes of hip new-adulthood, these confident women who want you to purchase kicky heels sporty automobiles investment portfolios gym memberships slinky underwear because you deserve them, these women are supposed to be *you.* Even on your most groomed days you do not resemble these women with their enormous white teeth. When it rains your hair gets fuzzy and makeup makes you feel sticky. You are forever getting dirty or falling down or bruising yourself. But the women on television are tantalizing, so within the reach of the possible for you. They are sleek, like horses. They have *careers.*

Look at these women! They are glorious; they are everything you are not; they gleam. They are movers and and shakers in this big new world of hyperspeed Internet connections and online trading, a force to be reckoned with. These women can do anything and it shouldn't be such a stretch for you to be just like them, for you to join the ranks of the entitled. These women are a far cry from the detergent-toting, box-dinner-serving, beaming matrons that populated advertisements the last time you watched television regularly. These women are strong and independent and can apply liquid blush in their sleep. These women look right at you with their big bright eyes.

Tonight on television there's a video of a girl singing. The video features her wiggling her miniature hips around and groping herself and dancing with the heads of various boys wedged between her legs. Her pink-and-white hair wafts atop her head like a giant tuft of cotton candy, and her concave belly is coated with glitter. You can't change the channel. It's like slowing down to watch a car wreck on the freeway—you can't help yourselves. The girl singer's eyes are blue as mouthwash and she's talking about flirting and how great it is for her to playfully express her budding sexuality onscreen and in her music. Truthfully, there is nothing playful about her. She freaks the hell out of you, she's terrifying. And here she is talking about how great it is to be a *girl* with her flaming pink oilslick of a mouth. This is feminism for the new millennium, all right. Go fuck 'em girls! But be sure you look like me!

You see smaller versions of the girl singer everywhere you go. They saunter, twitching their tiny malnourished bottoms, rolling their eyes, the younger and more glittery siblings of the briefcase-and-career television women. These girls have an entire industry devoted to them: books and magazines written about the perils of girlhood, whole store aisles pink gadgetry dedicated to their empowerment. They have more disposable income than you do. If they are properly consumerized they will grow up just like the television women, and then they will he happy. They will still be hipless and white and they'll be rich, too, and that's all a girl needs these days. That's what a girl deserves.

If you were to go to the mall you could buy a *Girls Kick Ass* bumper sticker and put it on your car. You could buy the Barbie for President 2000 doll (default blonde, also available in brunette and African American in order of marketing demographic), who is a role model for young women everywhere. You could buy nail polish called *Great Fuck* and T-shirts that read *Bitch Princess Diva Goddess Flirt.* It's a whole empire of self-assertion at your fingertips—Mastercard or Visa? Your very own girlpower revolution, sponsored by Nike and assembled by women and children in countries you will never have to think about.

You get into a conversation with a girl who's ecstatic because didn't you know there's a female CEO now? A female CEO of a very important and powerful company that makes billions and billions of dollars? Isn't that *exciting?* Women are everywhere! They really are! They're earning and earning, buying and buying, just like the good old boys have been doing as long as capitalism's been around. This system works very well for girls like you; maybe you can't apply eyeliner to save your life, but you're white and you grew up with money so everything will still work out for you in the end. You have so many economic opportunities you can't live long enough to use them all. Who needs feminism when you, too, can head your very own company in a few years? You can open factories in developing countries and provide economic advancement for the underprivileged masses by paying them three cents an hour. The new economy isn't just for old white guys anymore, it's for white girls too!

You start to wonder where exactly it was that everyone missed the boat. You see pictures from the Democratic convention featuring famous feminists, your mother's heroines, drinking champagne with one-man economic superpowers. How marvelous the world will be, say the feminists, now that we make seventy-two cents to every boy dollar! Who needs welfare reform? Your entire generation of empowered women is now a target audience. Time to celebrate.

For a minute you get excited and think, *Hell yeah!* Those are feminists! The Democrats invited *feminists!* But it's not a very long minute. Outside the Democratic convention, a few of your friends and hundreds of people you don't know are shouting and carrying signs and being pissed off because they know and you know that feminism has never been about good girls joining forces with the good old boys. Inside is not really where the feminists belong, not inside convention centers and not inside malls or ads or girlpower-soundbites.

The new economy may view women in a variety of roles, but the new economy is not about feminism. The new economy is about money, and all the money in the world won't buy you a revolution. You're a hot commodity, you're wanted by marketers, you are supposed to *believe* in your entitlement. You want, you need, you deserve, and the more you buy the less you think, the less you pay attention to what's really going on, to who's being bought. The less you notice what's being sold.

But you are not a *girl,* and you are not afraid to be a feminist, either, you are not afraid to shout and be pissed yourself. You know better than to think empowerment can be found between the housewares aisle and electronics, you know all the bumper stickers in the world don't make up a community. Your revolution starts in your house. It started the day you noticed feminism wasn't such a bad word, the day you started working at a women's shelter, the day you started composting. Your revolution started with the little things, sometimes with just doing nothing; because not consuming is the most useful sort of inactivity you can think of.

Your revolution happens at the houses of your friends who make you vegan brownies and then go wheatpasting on campus and ride their bikes home. Your revolution happens in books and in letters and at two in the morning. Your revolution happens with big realizations and small actions, when you get out of the house and into the street, when your friends hitchhike to Philadelphia to protest on national TV, when people you don't know boycott Wal-Mart. Your revolution will happen when the girls on television realize they're all alone up there, that a skinny white world is not a very interesting one, that some things you can't buy and revolution is one of them.

Next time, you'll just turn off the TV.

CHAPTER SIXTEEN

WHAT IS THE RIGHT THING FOR ME TO DO?

You once told your friend, "If you ever need me, I'll come right over," but now you've got to study for an exam you have in an hour, and you promised you'd call your mother this morning, and you're exhausted, and now it's obvious that you aren't going to have time to do everything. What is the right thing for you to do? See your friend, who seems to be in trouble? Study for your exam? Call your mom? Take a short nap? This happens to be an especially bad day for you, but you face similar decisions all the time, and you know that, once in a while, it gets much worse. A friend of yours once had to decide whether to turn in his brother, who had committed a serious crime, to the police. Deciding whether to study, sleep, call your mother, or visit your friend is nothing by comparison. But the basic questions are the same: What is the right thing to do, and how do you decide what that is? This is the subject matter of ethics.

The field of ethics is concerned with the question: "What should one do?" but in a very special sense. There are a great many contexts in which we ask for guidance in getting what we want or achieving our goals, but these tend to be prudential concerns and not yet ethical. So, too, it is important in almost any public context to know what the law is—for example, whether in a certain country one drives on the right or left side of the road or whether in a particular park it is permissible to walk your dog without a leash. But such legal questions are not ethics either, although one would naturally expect some connection (sometimes troublesome) between the law and ethical concerns. One way of delineating ethics in particular is by reference to the questions, "What *ought* I to do? What is the *right* thing to do?" The right thing to do is usually in our own prudential interests, and it is usually within the law if not also specified by law. But what characterizes this special word *ought* is the existence of a set of rules or expectations that goes beyond the interests of any individual and constitutes a powerful force in our lives quite apart from the question of whether they are bound by law or not.

A familiar example is that one should not lie to one's friends. It may or may not be to your advantage to tell the truth, but in general (at least when you are not signing a contract or testifying in court) lying is not illegal. But lying to your friends is clearly unethical, or we might even say that it is immoral. The realm of ethics and morality includes a great many actions that deceive, hurt, or endanger the well-being of others or society as a whole, not only lying but also cheating, stealing, killing, and a large number of related wrongdoings. Some of these are crimes, but not all are. "Honor thy father and mother" is considered by most people to be a central rule of morality, but (at least in our country) there is no law against dishonoring or embarrassing one's parents. What makes these the province of ethics and morality is that they are such basic concerns of all of us. The problem of ethical (or moral) philosophy is exactly what does define this set of basic concerns and, even more challenging, how these basic rules can be justified.

Imagine a person (you may not have to look far) who refused to do what she ought to do and demanded of you, "Why should I be moral?" What would you say? You might respond, "It is in your interests to be moral," but being moral is in fact not always in our interests and, even if it is, we would want to make some distinction between those who do the right thing because it is right and others who do it just because it happens to be to their advantage. (Knowing that a friend keeps his promises gives you a very different kind of confidence than knowing that he keeps his promises only when it is convenient.) One might insist that we should be moral because God wishes it (and will punish us if we aren't), but the temporal delay between moral transgression and divine punishment is such that many people either don't really believe it or are willing to take the chance on a huge dose of confession and repentance later. Ethics and morality have also been justified on the basis that they serve the overall interests and well-being of society, but then the serious question arises of whether the most basic rules might in fact differ from society to society depending on their various needs and customs. In response to the possibility of such relativism (that is, the variance of the most basic rules of morality from one culture to another), some philosophers have defended universal principles of morality on the grounds that they satisfy the demands of human reason and thus apply everywhere regardless of the particular conditions or customs of a culture.

The following selections provide a spectrum of very different views of the nature and justification of morality. The foremost example of a moral code in our culture is the Ten Commandments in the Old Testament, coupled with the ethical precepts presented by Jesus, for instance, in the Sermon on the Mount. The basis and justification of that code, needless to say, are its divine origins. Selections from Confucius and the Koran follow. But there are other codes and other ways of justifying them. Aristotle, who wrote the most detailed manual of contemporary ethics in ancient Athens, justifies that code—whose ultimate goal is happiness—by appeal to a conception of human nature. Immanuel Kant, by way of contrast, justifies moral principles as the product of "pure practical reason" whose primary concern is duty and whose focus is not the consequences of our actions (including personal happiness) so much as the notion of a "good will," that is, good intentions based on the demands of the moral law. John Stuart Mill takes a very different approach to ethics; its primary concern is the happiness of all individuals—the common good, or what he calls "the greatest good of the greatest number."

Not every author takes the desirability of morality for granted, however. The German philosopher Friedrich Nietzsche believed that morality is basically a sham, a deceit that protects the weak and incompetent from the strong and creative. A. J. Ayer declares ethics to be nothing but an expression of emotion, and Simone de Beauvoir argues for the centrality of freedom in ethics. Jonathan Bennett offers us a shocking example of moral choice based on Mark Twain's classic American novel, *Huckleberry Finn*. Claudia Card raises the question of a feminist view of ethics. Finally, the whole question of "the right moral theory" is the cause of concern for Robert Kane as he tackles the problem of moral relativism.

THE BIBLE

The Ten Commandments and the Sermon on the Mount

THE BIBLE *has been the most influential source of Western morality. What follows from the King James version are the Ten Commandments and the Sermon on the Mount.*

AND God spake all these words, saying,

2 I *am* the LORD thy God, which have brought thee out of the land of Egypt, out of the house of bondage.

3 Thou shalt have no other gods before me.

4 Thou shalt not make unto thee any graven image, or any likeness *of any thing* that *is* in heaven above, or that *is* in the earth beneath, or that *is* in the water under the earth;.

5 Thou shalt not bow down thyself to them, nor serve them: for I the LORD thy God *am* a jealous God, visiting the iniquity of the fathers upon the children unto the third and fourth *generation* of them that hate me;

6 And shewing mercy unto thousands of them that love me, and keep my commandments.

7 Thou shalt not take the name of the LORD thy God in vain; for the LORD will not hold him guiltless that taketh his name in vain.

8 Remember the sabbath day, to keep it holy.

9 Six days shalt thou labour, and do all thy work:

10 But the seventh day *is* the sabbath of the LORD thy God: *in it* thou shalt not do any work, thou, nor thy son, nor thy daughter, thy manservant, nor thy maidservant, nor thy cattle, nor thy stranger that is within thy gates:

11 For *in* six days the LORD made heaven and earth, the sea, and all that in them *is,* and rested the seventh day: wherefore the LORD blessed the sabbath day, and hallowed it.

12 Honour thy father and thy mother: that thy days may be long upon the land which the LORD thy God giveth thee.

13 Thou shalt not kill.

14 Thou shalt not commit adultery.

15 Thou shalt not steal.

16 Thou shalt not bear false witness against thy neighbour.

17 Thou shalt not covet thy neighbour's house, thou shalt not covet thy neighbour's wife, nor his manservant, nor his maidservant, nor his ox, nor his ass, nor any thing that *is* thy neighbour's.

18 And all the people saw the thunderings, and the lightnings, and the noise of the trumpet, and the mountain smoking: and when the people saw *it,* they removed, and stood afar off. . . .

• • •

And seeing the multitudes, [Jesus] went up into a mountain: and when he was set, his disciples came unto him:

2 And he opened his mouth, and taught them, saying,

3 Blessed *are* the poor in spirit: for theirs is the kingdom of heaven.

4 Blessed *are* they that mourn: for they shall be comforted.

Bible, "The Ten Commandments and The Sermon on the Mount." The Ten Commandments, Exodus: 20, and The Sermon on the Mount, Matthew: 5–7.

5 Blessed *are* the meek: for they shall inherit the earth.

6 Blessed *are* they which do hunger and thirst after righteousness: for they shall be filled.

7 Blessed *are* the merciful: for they shall obtain mercy.

8 Blessed *are* the pure in heart: for they shall see God.

9 Blessed *are* the peacemakers: for they shall be called the children of God.

10 Blessed *are* they which are persecuted for righteousness' sake: for theirs is the kingdom of heaven.

11 Blessed are ye, when *men* shall revile you, and persecute *you,* and shall say all manner of evil against you falsely, for my sake.

12 Rejoice, and be exceeding glad: for great *is* your reward in heaven: for so persecuted they the prophets which were before you.

13 Ye are the salt of the earth: but if the salt have lost his savour, wherewith shall it be salted? it is thenceforth good for nothing, but to be cast out, and to be trodden under foot of men.

14 Ye are the light of the world. A city that is set on an hill cannot be hid.

15 Neither do men light a candle, and put it under a bushel, but on a candlestick; and it giveth light unto all that are in the house.

16 Let your light so shine before men, that they may see your good works, and glorify your Father which is in heaven.

17 Think not that I am come to destroy the law, or the prophets: I am not come to destroy, but to fulfil.

18 For verily I say unto you, Till heaven and earth pass, one jot or one tittle shall in no wise pass from the law, till all be fulfilled.

19 Whosoever therefore shall break one of these least commandments, and shall teach men so, he shall be called the least in the kingdom of heaven: but whosoever shall do and teach *them,* the same shall be called great in the kingdom of heaven.

20 For I say unto you, That except your righteousness shall exceed *the righteousness* of the scribes and Pharisees, ye shall in no case enter into the kingdom of heaven.

21 Ye have heard that it was said by them of old time, Thou shalt not kill; and whosoever shall kill shall be in danger of the judgment:

22 But I say unto you, That whosoever is angry with his brother without a cause shall be in danger of the judgment: and whosoever shall say to his brother, Raca, shall be in danger of the council: but whosoever shall say, Thou fool shall be in danger of hell fire.

23 Therefore if thou bring thy gift to the altar, and there rememberest that thy brother hath ought against thee;

24 Leave there thy gift before the altar, and go thy way; first be reconciled to thy brother, and then come and offer thy gift.

25 Agree with thine adversary quickly, whiles thou art in the way with him; lest at any time the adversary deliver thee to the judge, and the judge deliver thee to the officer, and thou be cast into prison.

26 Verily I say unto thee, Thou shalt by no means come out thence, till thou hast paid the uttermost farthing.

27 Ye have heard that it was said by them of old time, Thou shalt not commit adultery:

28 But I say unto you, That whosoever looketh on a woman to lust after her hath committed adultery with her already in his heart.

29 And if thy right eye offend thee, pluck it out, and cast *it* from thee: for it is profitable for thee that one of thy members should perish, and not *that* thy whole body should be cast into hell.

30 And if thy right hand offend thee, cut it off, and cast *it* from thee: for it is profitable for thee that one of thy members should perish, and not *that* thy whole body should be cast into hell.

31 It hath been said, Whosoever shall put away his wife, let him give her a writing of divorcement:

32 But I say unto you, That whosoever shall put away his wife, saving for the cause of fornication, causeth her to commit adultery: and whosoever shall marry her that is divorced committeth adultery.

33 Again, ye have heard that it hath been said by them of old time, Thou shalt not

forswear thyself, but shalt perform unto the Lord thine oaths:

34 But I say unto you, Swear not at all; neither by heaven; for it is God's throne:

35 Nor by the earth; for it is his footstool: neither by Jerusalem; for it is the city of the great King.

36 Neither shalt thou swear by thy head, because thou canst not make one hair white or black.

37 But let your communication be, Yea, yea; Nay, nay: for whatsoever is more than these cometh of evil.

38 Ye have heard that it hath been said, An eye for an eye, and a tooth for a tooth:

39 But I say unto you, That ye resist not evil: but whosoever shall smite thee on thy right cheek, turn to him the other also.

40 And if any man will sue thee at the law, and take away thy coat, let him have *thy* cloak also.

41 And whosoever shall compel thee to go a mile, go with him twain.

42 Give to him that asketh thee, and from him that would borrow of thee turn not thou away.

43 Ye have heard that it hath been said, Thou shalt love thy neighbour, and hate thine enemy.

44 But I say unto you, Love your enemies, bless them that curse you, do good to them that hate you, and pray for them which despitefully use you, and persecute you;

45 That ye may be the children of your Father which is in heaven: for he maketh his sun to rise on the evil and on the good, and sendeth rain on the just and on the unjust.

46 For if ye love them which love you, what reward have ye? do not even the publicans the same?

47 And if ye salute your brethren only, what do ye more *than others?* do not even the publicans so?

48 Be ye therefore perfect, even as your Father which is in heaven is perfect.

• • •

Judge not, that ye be not judged.

2 For with what judgment ye judge, ye shall be judged: and with what measure ye mete, it shall be measured to you again.

3 And why beholdest thou the mote that is in thy brother's eye, but considerest not the beam that is in thine own eye?

4 Or how wilt thou say to thy brother, Let me pull out the mote out of thine eye; and, behold, a beam *is* in thine own eye?

5 Thou hypocrite, first cast out the beam out of thine own eye; and then shalt thou see clearly to cast out the mote out of thy brother's eye.

6 Give not that which is holy unto the dogs, neither cast ye your pearls before swine, lest they trample them under their feet, and turn again and rend you.

7 Ask, and it shall be given you; seek, and ye shall find; knock, and it shall be opened unto you:

8 For every one that asketh receiveth; and he that seeketh findeth; and to him that knocketh it shall be opened.

9 Or what man is there of you, whom if his son ask bread, will he give him a stone?

10 Or if he ask a fish, will he give him a serpent?

11 If ye then, being evil, know how to give good gifts unto your children, how much more shall your Father which is in heaven give good things to them that ask him?

12 Therefore all things whatsoever ye would that men should do to you, do ye even so to them: for this is the law and the prophets.

13 Enter ye in at the strait gate: for wide *is* the gate, and broad *is* the way, that leadeth to destruction, and many there be which go in thereat:

14 Because strait *is* the gate, and narrow *is* the way, which leadeth unto life, and few there be that find it.

15 Beware of false prophets, which come to you in sheep's clothing, but inwardly they are ravening wolves.

16 Ye shall know them by their fruits. Do men gather grapes of thorns, or figs of thistles?

17 Even so every good tree bringeth forth good fruit; but a corrupt tree bringeth forth evil fruit.

18 A good tree cannot bring forth evil fruit, neither *can* a corrupt tree bring forth good fruit.

19 Every tree that bringeth not forth good fruit is hewn down, and cast into the fire.

20 Wherefore by their fruits ye shall know them.

21 Not every one that saith unto me, Lord, Lord, shall enter into the kingdom of heaven; but he that doeth the will of my Father which is in heaven.

22 Many will say to me in that day, Lord, Lord, have we not prophesied in thy name? and in thy name have cast out devils? and in thy name done many wonderful works?

23 And then will I profess unto them, I never knew you: depart from me, ye that work iniquity.

24 Therefore whosoever heareth these sayings of mine, and doeth them, I will liken him unto a wise man, which built his house upon a rock:

25 And the rain descended, and the floods came, and the winds blew, and beat upon that house; and it fell not: for it was founded upon a rock.

26 And every one that heareth these sayings of mine, and doeth them not, shall be likened unto a foolish man, which built his house upon the sand:

27 And the rain descended, and the floods came, and the winds blew, and beat upon that house; and it fell: and great was the fall of it.

28 And it came to pass, when Jesus had ended these sayings, the people were astonished at his doctrine:

29 For he taught them as *one* having authority, and not as the scribes.

CONFUCIUS
The Analects

CONFUCIUS *(551–479 B.C.) was a famous Chinese poet and teacher. Self-educated, he sought to effect social change by holding a political office but was unable to secure such a position. Instead, he acquired a small group of dedicated students and spent his life teaching them his philosophical beliefs.*

BOOK I

8 The Master said, If a gentleman is frivolous, he will lose the respect of his inferiors and lack firm ground upon which to build up his education. First and foremost he must learn to be faithful to his superiors, to keep promises, to refuse the friendship of all who are not like him. And if he finds he has made a mistake, then he must not be afraid of admitting the fact and amending his ways.

BOOK II

6 Mêng Wu Po asked about the treatment of parents. The Master said, Behave in such a way

that your father and mother have no anxiety about you, except concerning your health.

BOOK VI

25 Once when Yen Hui and Tzu-lu were waiting upon him the Master said, Suppose each of you were to tell his wish. Tzu-lu said, I should like to have carriages and horses, clothes and fur rugs, share them with my friends and feel no annoyance if they were returned to me the worse for wear. Yen Hui said, I should like never to boast of my good qualities nor make a fuss about the trouble I take on behalf of others. Tzu-lu said, A thing I should like is to hear the Master's wish. The Master said, In dealing with the aged, to be of comfort to them; in dealing with friends, to be of good faith with them; in dealing with the young, to cherish them.

BOOK IX

24 The Master said, First and foremost, be faithful to your superiors, keep all promises, refuse the friendship of all who are not like you; and if you have made a mistake, do not be afraid of admitting the fact and amending your ways.

BOOK XVII

6 Tzu-chang asked Master K'ung about Goodness. Master K'ung said, He who could put the Five into practice everywhere under Heaven would be Good. Tzu-chang begged to hear what these were. The Master said, Courtesy, breadth, good faith, diligence and clemency. "He who is courteous is not scorned, he who is broad wins the multitude, he who is of good faith is trusted by the people, he who is diligent succeeds in all he undertakes, he who is clement can get service from the people."

8 The Master said, Yu, have you ever been told of the Six Sayings about the Six Degenerations? Tzu-lu replied, No, never. (The Master said) Come, then; I will tell you. Love of Goodness without love of learning degenerates into silliness. Love of wisdom without love of learning degenerates into utter lack of principle. Love of keeping promises without love of learning degenerates into villainy. Love of uprightness without love of learning degenerates into harshness. Love of courage without love of learning degenerates into turbulence. Love of courage without love of learning degenerates into mere recklessness.

THE KORAN
The Unjust

THE KORAN, *or Qur'an, is the sacred scripture of Islam. It chronicles the revelations of God to the prophet Mohammed. Originally the Koran was memorized by followers, and segments were used in prayer. It is hailed by Muslims to be the ultimate authority on all ethical and spiritual matters.*

———

In the Name of Allah, the Compassionate, the Merciful

Koran, The, "The Unjust," from *the Koran.*

WOE to the unjust who, when others measure for them, exact in full, but when they measure or weight for others, defraud them!

Do such men think that they will not be raised to life upon a fateful day, the day when all mankind will stand before the Lord of the Creation?

Truly, the record of the sinners is in Sidjeen. Would that you knew what Sidjeen is! It is a sealed book.

Woe on that day to the disbelievers who deny the Last Judgment! None denies it except the transgressors, the evil-doers who, when Our revelations are recited to them, cry: "Fables of the ancients!"

No! Their own deeds have cast a veil over their hearts.

No! On that day a barrier shall be set between them and their Lord. They shall burn in Hell, and a voice will say to them: "This is the scourge that you denied!"

But the record of the righteous shall be in Illiyun.

Would that you knew what Illiyun is! It is a sealed book, seen only by those who are closest to Allah.

The righteous shall surely dwell in bliss. Reclining upon soft couches they will gaze around them: and in their faces you shall mark the glow of joy. They shall drink of a pure wine, securely sealed, whose very dregs are musk (for this let all men emulously strive); a wine tempered with the waters of Tasnim, a spring at which the favoured will refresh themselves.

The evil-doers scoff at the faithful and wink at one another as they pass by them. When they meet their own folk they speak of them with jests and when they see them they say: "These are erring men!" Yet they were not sent to be their guardians.

But on that day the faithful will mock the unbelievers as they recline upon their couches and gaze around them.

Shall not the unbelievers be rewarded according to their deeds?

ARISTOTLE
Happiness and the Good Life

ARISTOTLE's *(384–322 B.C.) Nicomachean Ethics was both a sociological summary of Athenian ethics in the fourth century B.C. and the classic philosophical theory of ethics. In the selection from Book I that follows, he argues his "teleological" view of ethics—that is, the idea that all human behavior is purposive and that the ultimate purpose of all our actions is happiness.*

BOOK I

1 Every art and every kind of inquiry, and likewise every act and purpose, seems to aim at some good; and so it has been well said that the good is that at which everything aims. But a difference is observable among these aims or ends. What is aimed at is sometimes the exercise of a faculty, sometimes a certain result

Aristotle, "Happiness and the Good Life," from "The Goal of Human Activity" in *Nichomachean Ethics*, translated Peters (8th ed.), 1901, Book 1, sec. I–X.

beyond that exercise. And where there is an end beyond that act, there the result is better than the exercise of the faculty. Now since there are many kinds of actions and many arts and sciences, it follows that there are many ends also; *e.g.* health is the end of medicine, ships of shipbuilding, victory of the art of war, and wealth of economy. But when several of these are subordinated to some one art or science,—as the making of bridles and other trappings to the art of horsemanship, and this in turn, along with all else that the soldier does, to the art of war, and so on,—then the end of the master art is always more desired than the end of the subordinate arts, since these are pursued for its sake. And this is equally true whether the end in view be the mere exercise of a faculty or something beyond that, as in the above instances.

2 If then in what we do there be some end which we wish for on its own account, choosing all the others as means to this, but not every end without exception as a means to something else (for so we should go on *ad infinitum,* and desire would be left void and objectless),—this evidently will be the good or the best of all things. And surely from a practical point of view it much concerns us to know this good; for then, like archers shooting at a definite mark, we shall be more likely to attain what we want. . . . Though this good is the same for the individual and the state, yet the good of the state seems a grander and more perfect thing both to attain and to secure; and glad as one would be to do this service for a single individual, to do it for a people and for a number of states is nobler and more divine.

This then is the aim of the present inquiry, which is a sort of political inquiry.

3 We must be content if we can attain to so much precision in our statement as the subject before us admits of; for the same degree of accuracy is no more to be expected in all kinds of reasoning than in all kinds of handicraft. Now the things that are noble and just (with which Politics deals) are so various and so uncertain, that some think these are merely conventional and not natural distinctions. There is a similar

uncertainty also about what is good, because good things often do people harm: men have before now been ruined by wealth, and have lost their lives through courage. Our subject, then, and our data being of this nature, we must be content if we can indicate the truth roughly and in outline, and if, in dealing with matters that are not amenable to immutable laws, and reasoning from premises that are but probable, we can arrive at probable conclusions. The reader, on his part, should take each of my statements in the same spirit; for it is the mark of an educated man to require, in each kind of inquiry, just so much exactness as the subject admits of: it is equally absurd to accept probable reasoning from a mathematician, and to demand scientific proof from an orator.

But each man can form a judgment about what he knows, and is called "a good judge" of that—of any special matter when he has received a special education therein, "a good judge" (without any qualifying epithet) when he has received a universal education. And hence a young man is not qualified to be a student of Politics; for he lacks experience of the affairs of life, which form the data and the subject-matter of Politics. Further, since he is apt to be swayed by his feelings, he will derive no benefit from a study whose aim is not speculative but practical. But in this respect young in character counts the same as young in years; for the young man's disqualification is not a matter of time, but is due to the fact that feeling rules his life and directs all his desires. Men of this character turn the knowledge they get to no account in practice, as we see with those we call incontinent; but those who direct their desires and actions by reason will gain much profit from the knowledge of these matters. . . .

4 Since . . . all knowledge and all purpose aims at some good, what is this which we say is the aim of Politics; or, in other words, what is the highest of all realizable goods? As to its name, I suppose nearly all men are agreed; for the masses and the men of culture alike declare that it is happiness, and hold that to "live well" or to "do well" is the same as to be "happy." But they

differ as to what this happiness is, and the masses do not give the same account of it as the philosophers. The former take it to be something palpable and plain, as pleasure or wealth or fame; one man holds it to be this, and another that, and often the same man is of different minds at different times—after sickness it is health, and in poverty it is wealth; while when they are impressed with the consciousness of their ignorance, they admire most those who say grand things that are above their comprehension. Some philosophers, on the other hand, have thought that, beside these several good things, there is an "absolute" good which is the cause of their goodness. As it would hardly be worth while to review all the opinions that have been held, we will confine ourselves to those which are most popular, or which seem to have some foundation in reason. . . .

5 It seems that men not unreasonably take their notions of the good or happiness from the lives actually led, and that the masses who are the least refined suppose it to be pleasure, which is the reason why they aim at nothing higher than the life of enjoyment. For the most conspicuous kinds of life are three: this life of enjoyment, the life of the statesman, and thirdly, the contemplative life. The mass of men show themselves utterly slavish in their preference for the life of brute beasts, but their views receive consideration because many of those in high places have the tastes of Sardanapalus. Men of refinement with a practical turn prefer honour; for I suppose we may say that honour is the aim of the statesman's life. But this seems too superficial to be the good we are seeking; for it appears to depend upon those who give rather than upon those who receive it; while we have a presentiment that the good is something that is peculiarly a man's own and can scarce be taken away from him. Moreover, these men seem to pursue honour in order that they may be assured of their own excellence,—at least, they wish to be honoured by men of sense, and by those who know them, and on the ground of their virtue or excellence. It is plain, then, that in their view, at any rate, virtue or excellence is better than

honour; and perhaps we should take this to be the end of the statesman's life, rather than honour. But virtue or excellence also appears too incomplete to be what we want; for it seems that a man might have virtue and yet be asleep or be inactive all his life, and, moreover, might meet with the greatest disasters and misfortunes; and no one would maintain that such a man is happy, except for argument's sake. But we will not dwell on these matters now, for they are sufficiently discussed in the popular treatises. The third kind of life is the life of contemplation: we will treat of it further on. As for the money-making life, it is something quite contrary to nature; and wealth evidently is not the good of which we are in search, for it is merely useful as a means to something else. So we might rather take pleasure and virtue or excellence to be ends than wealth; for they are chosen on their own account. But it seems that not even they are the end, though much breath has been wasted in attempts to show that they are. . . .

7 Leaving these matters, then, let us return once more to the question, what this good can be of which we are in search. It seems to be different in different kinds of action and in different arts,—one thing in medicine and another in war, and so on. What then is the good in each of these cases? Surely that for the sake of which all else is done. And that in medicine is health, in war is victory, in building is a house,—a different thing in each different case, but always, in whatever we do and in whatever we choose, the end. For it is always for the sake of the end that all else is done. If then there be one end of all that man does, this end will be the realizable good,—or these ends, if there be more than one.

By this generalization our argument is brought to the same point as before. This point we must try to explain more clearly. We see that there are many ends. But some of these are chosen only as means, as wealth, flutes, and the whole class of instruments. And so it is plain that not all ends are final. But the best of all things must, we conceive, be something final. If then there be only one final end, this will be what we are seeking,—or if there be more than one, then the most final of them. Now that which is pursued as an end in itself is more final than that which is pursued as means to something else, and that which is never chosen as means than that which is chosen both as an end in itself and as means, and that is strictly final which is always chosen as an end in itself and never as means.

Happiness seems more than anything else to answer to this description: for we always choose it for itself, and never for the sake of something else; while honour and pleasure and reason, and all virtue or excellence, we choose partly indeed for themselves (for, apart from any result, we should choose each of them), but partly also for the sake of happiness, supposing that they will help to make us happy. But no one chooses happiness for the sake of these things, or as a means to anything else at all. We seem to be led to the same conclusion when we start from the notion of self-sufficiency. The final good is thought to be self-sufficing [or all-sufficing]. In applying this term we do not regard a man as an individual leading a solitary life, but we also take account of parents, children, wife, and, in short, friends and fellow-citizens generally, since man is naturally a social being. Some limit must indeed be set to this; for if you go on to parents and descendants and friends of friends, you will never come to a stop. But this we will consider further on: for the present we will take self-sufficing to mean what by itself makes life desirable and in want of nothing. And happiness is believed to answer to this description. And further, happiness is believed to be the most desirable thing in the world, and that not merely as one among other good things: if it were merely one among other good things [so that other things could be added to it], it is plain that the addition of the least of other goods must make it more desirable; for the addition becomes a surplus of good, and of two goods the greater is always more desirable. Thus it seems that happiness is something final and self-sufficing, and is the end of all that man does.

But perhaps the reader thinks that though no one will dispute the statement that happiness is the best thing in the world, yet a still more precise definition of it is needed. This will best be gained, I think, by asking, What is the function of man? For as the goodness and the excellence of a piper or a sculptor, or the practiser of any art, and generally of those who have any function or business to do, lies in that function, so man's good would seem to lie in his function, if he has one. But can we suppose that, while a carpenter and a cobbler has a function and a business of his own, man has no business and no function assigned him by nature? Nay, surely as his several members, eye and hand and foot, plainly have each his own function, so we must suppose that man also has some function over and above all these.

What then is it? Life evidently he has in common even with the plants, but we want that which is peculiar to him. We must exclude, therefore, the life of mere nutrition and growth. Next to this comes the life of sense; but this too he plainly shares with horses and cattle and all kinds of animals. There remains then the life whereby he acts—the life of his rational nature, with its two sides or divisions, one rational as obeying reason, the other rational as having and exercising reason. But as this expression is ambiguous, we must be understood to mean thereby the life that consists in the exercise [not the mere possession] of the faculties; for this seems to be more properly entitled to the name.

The function of man, then, is exercise of his vital faculties [or soul] on one side in obedience to reason, and on the other side with reason. But what is called the function of a man of any profession and the function of a man who is good in that profession are, generically the same, *e.g.* of a harper and of a good harper; and this holds in all cases without exception, only that in the case of the latter his superior excellence at his work is added; for we say a harper's function is to harp, and a good harper's to harp well. Man's function then being, as we say, a kind of life—that is to say, exercise of his faculties and action of various kinds with reason—the good man's function is to do this well and beautifully [or nobly]. But the function of anything is done well when it is done in accordance with the proper excellence of that thing. If this be so the result is that the good of man is exercise of his faculties in accordance with excellence or virtue, or, if there be more than one, in accordance with the best and most complete virtue. But there must also be a full term of years for this exercise; for one swallow or one fine day does not make a spring, nor does one day or any small space of time make a blessed or happy man.

This, then, may be taken as a rough outline of the good; for this, I think, is the proper method,—first to sketch the outline, and then to fill in the details. But it would seem that, the outline once fairly drawn, any one can carry on the work and fit in the several items which time reveals to us or helps us to find. And this indeed is the way in which the arts and sciences have grown; for it requires no extraordinary genius to fill up the gaps. We must bear in mind, however, what was said above, and not demand the same degree of accuracy in all branches of study, but in each case so much as the subject-matter admits of and as is proper to that kind of inquiry. The carpenter and the geometer both look for the right angle, but in different ways: the former only wants such an approximation to it as his work requires, but the latter wants to know what constitutes a right angle, or what is its special quality; his aim is to find out the truth. And so in other cases we must follow the same course, lest we spend more time on what is immaterial than on the real business in hand. . . .

8 . . . Now, good things have been divided into three classes, external goods on the one hand, and on the other goods of the soul and goods of the body; and the goods of the soul are commonly said to be goods in the fullest sense, and more good than any other. But "actions and exercises of the vital faculties may be said to be of the soul." So our account is confirmed by this opinion, which is both of long standing and approved by all who busy themselves with philosophy. But, indeed, we secure the support of this opinion by the mere statement that certain actions and exercises are the end; for this implies that it is to be ranked among the goods of the soul, and not among external goods. Our account, again, is in harmony with the common saying that the happy man lives well and does well; for we may say that happiness, according to us, is living well and doing well. And, indeed, all the characteristics that men expect to find in happiness seem to belong to happiness as we define it. Some hold it to be virtue or excellence, some prudence, others a kind of wisdom; others, again, held it to be all or some of these, with the addition of pleasure, either as an ingredient or as a necessary accompaniment; and some even include external prosperity in their account of it. Now, some of these views have the support of many voices and of old authority; others have few voices, but those of weight; but it is probable that neither the one side nor the other is entirely wrong, but that in some one point at least, if not in most, they are both right.

First, then, the view that happiness is excellence or a kind of excellence harmonizes with our account; for "exercise of faculties in accordance with excellence" belongs to excellence. But I think we may say that it makes no small difference whether the good be conceived as the mere possession of something, or as its use—as a mere habit or trained faculty, or as the exercise of that faculty. For the habit or faculty may be present, and yet issue in no good result, as when a man is asleep, or in any other way hindered from his function; but with its exercise this is not possible for it must show itself in acts and in good acts. And as at the Olympic games it is not the fairest and strongest who receive the crown, but those who contend (for among these are the victors), so in life, too, the winners are those who not only have all the excellences, but manifest these in deed.

And, further, the life of these men is in itself pleasant. For pleasure is an affection of the soul, and each man takes pleasure in that which he is said to love,—he who loves horses in horses, he who loves sight-seeing in sight-seeing, and in the same way he who loves justice in acts of justice, and generally the lover of excellence or virtue in virtuous acts or the manifestation of excellence. And while with most men there is a perpetual conflict between the several things in which they find pleasure, since these are not naturally pleasant, those who love what is noble take pleasure in that which is naturally pleasant. For the manifestations of excellence are naturally pleasant, so that they are both pleasant to them and pleasant in themselves. Their life, then, does not need pleasure to be added to it as an appendage, but contains pleasure in itself.

Indeed, in addition to what we have said, a man is not good at all unless he takes pleasure in noble deeds. No one would call a man just who did not take pleasure in doing justice, nor generous who took no pleasure in acts of generosity, and so on. If this be so, the manifestations of excellence will be pleasant in themselves. But they are also both good and noble, and that in the highest degree—at least, if the good man's judgment about them is right, for this is his judgment. Happiness, then, is at once the best and noblest and pleasantest thing in the world, and these are not separated.

For all these characteristics are united in the best exercises of our faculties; and these, or some one of them that is better than all the others, we identify with happiness.

But nevertheless happiness plainly requires external goods too, as we said; for it is impossible, or at least not easy, to act nobly without some furniture of fortune. There are many things that can only be done through instruments, so to speak, such as friends and wealth and political influence: and there are some things whose absence takes the bloom off our happiness, as good birth, the blessing of children, personal beauty; for a man is not very likely to be happy if he is very ugly in person, or of low birth, or alone in the world, or childless, and perhaps still less if he has worthless children or friends, or has lost good ones that he had. As we said, then, happiness seems to stand in need of this kind of prosperity; and so some identify it with good fortune, just as others identify it with excellence.

9 This has led people to ask whether happiness is attained by learning, or the formation of habits, or any other kind of training, or comes by some divine dispensation or even by chance. Well, if the Gods do give gifts to men, happiness is likely to be among the number, more likely, indeed, than anything else, in proportion as it is better than all other human things. This belongs more properly to another branch of inquiry; but we may say that even if it is not heaven-sent, but comes as a consequence of virtue or some kind of learning or training, still it seems to be one of the most divine things in the world; for the prize and aim of virtue would appear to be better than anything else and something divine and blessed. Again, if it is thus acquired it will be widely accessible; for it will then be in the power of all except those who have lost the capacity for excellence to acquire it by study and diligence. And if it be better that men should attain happiness in this way rather than by chance, it is reasonable to suppose that it is so, since in the sphere of nature all things are arranged in the best possible way, and likewise in the sphere of art, and of each mode of causation, and most of all in the sphere of the noblest mode of causation. And indeed it would be too absurd to leave what is noblest and fairest to the dispensation of chance.

But our definition itself clears up the difficulty; for happiness was defined as a certain kind of exercise of the vital faculties in accordance with excellence or virtue. And of the remaining goods [other than happiness itself], some must be present as necessary conditions, while others are useful instruments to happiness. And this agrees with what we said at starting. We then laid down that the end of the art political is the best of all ends; but the chief business of that art is to make the citizens of a certain character—that is, good and apt to do what is noble. It is not without reason, then, that we do not call an ox, or a horse, or any brute happy; for none of them is able to share in this kind of activity. For the same reason also a child is not happy; he is as yet, because of his age, unable to do such things. If we ever call a child happy, it is because we hope he will do them. For, as we said, happiness requires not only perfect excellence or virtue, but also a full term of years for its exercise. For our circumstances are liable to many changes and to all sorts of chances, and it is possible that he who is now most prosperous will in his old age meet with great disasters, as is told of Priam in the tales of Troy; and a man who is thus used by fortune and comes to a miserable end cannot be called happy.

BOOK II

1 VIRTUE, then, being of two kinds, intellectual and moral, intellectual virtue in the main owes both its birth and its growth to teaching (for which reason it requires experience and time), while moral virtue comes about as a result of habit, whence also its name (h'uikh') is one that is formed by a slight variation from the word euoz (habit). From this it is also plain that none of the moral virtues arises in us by nature; for nothing that exists by nature can form a habit contrary to its nature. For instance the stone which by nature moves downwards cannot be habituated to move upwards, not even if one tries to train it by throwing it up ten thousand times; nor can fire be habituated to move downwards, nor can anything else that by nature behaves in one way be trained to behave in another. Neither by nature, then, nor contrary to nature do the virtues arise in us; rather we are adapted by nature to receive them, and are made perfect by habit.

Again, of all the things that come to us by nature we first acquire the potentiality and later exhibit the activity (this is plain in the case of the senses; for it was not by often seeing or often hearing that we got these senses, but on the contrary we had them before we used them, and did not come to have them by using them); but the virtues we get by first exercising them, as also happens in the case of the arts as well. For the things we have to learn before we can do them, we learn by doing them, *e.g.* men become builders by building and lyre-players by playing the lyre; so too we become just by doing just acts, temperate by doing temperate acts, brave by doing brave acts. . . .

Again, it is from the same causes and by the same means that every virtue is both produced and destroyed, and similarly every art; for it is from playing the lyre that both good and bad lyre-players are produced. And the corresponding statement is true of builders and of all the rest; men will be good or bad builders as a result of building well or badly. For if this were not so, there would have been no need of a teacher, but all men would have been born good or bad at their craft. This, then, is the case with the virtues also; by doing the acts that we do in our transactions with other men we become just or unjust, and by doing the acts that we do in the presence of danger, and being habituated to feel fear or confidence, we become brave or cowardly. The same is true of appetites and feelings of anger; some men become temperate and good-tempered, others self-indulgent and irascible, by behaving in one way or the other in the appropriate circumstances. Thus, in one word, states of character arise out of like activities. This is why the activities we exhibit must be of a certain kind; it is because the states of character correspond to the differences between these. It makes no small difference, then, whether we form habits of one kind or of another from our very youth; it makes a very great difference, or rather *all* the difference. . . .

6 We must, however, not only describe virtue as a state of character, but also say what sort of state it is. We may remark, then, that every virtue or excellence both brings into good condition the thing of which it is the excellence and makes the work of that thing be done well; *e.g.* the excellence of the eye makes both the eye and its work good; for it is by the excellence of the eye that we see well. Similarly the excellence of the horse makes a horse both good in itself and good at running and at carrying its rider and at awaiting the attack of the enemy. Therefore, if this is true in every case, the virtue of man also will be the state of character which makes a man good and which makes him do his own work well.

How this is to happen we have stated already, but it will be made plain also by the following consideration of the specific nature of virtue. In everything that is continuous and divisible it is possible to take more, less, or an equal amount, and that either in terms of the thing itself or relatively to us; and the equal is an intermediate between excess and defect. By the intermediate in the object I mean that which is equidistant from each of the extremes, which is one and the same for all men; by the intermediate relatively to us that which is neither too much nor too little—and this is not one, nor the same for all. For instance, if ten is many and two is few, six is the intermediate, taken in terms of the object; for it exceeds and is exceeded by an equal amount; this is intermediate according to arithmetical proportion. But the intermediate relatively to us is not to be taken so; if ten pounds are too much for a particular person to eat and two too little, it does not follow that the trainer will order six pounds; for this also is perhaps too much for the person who is to take it, or too little—too little for Milo [a famous wrestler], too much for the beginner in athletic exercises. The same is true of running and wrestling. Thus a master of any art avoids excess and defect, but seeks the intermediate and chooses this—the intermediate not in the object but relatively to us.

If it is thus, then, that every art does its work well—by looking to the intermediate and judging its works by this standard (so that we often say of good works of art that it is not possible either to take away or to add anything, implying that excess and defect destroy the goodness of works of art, while the mean preserves it; and good artists, as we say, look to this in their work), and if, further, virtue is more exact and better than any art, as nature also is, then virtue must have the quality of aiming at the intermediate. I mean moral virtue; for it is this that is concerned with passions and actions, and in these there is excess, defect, and the intermediate. For instance, both fear and confidence and appetite and anger and pity and in general pleasure and pain may be felt both too much and too little, and in both cases not well; but to feel them at the right times, with reference to the right objects, towards the right people, with the right motive, and in the right way, is what is both intermediate and best, and this is characteristic of virtue. Similarly with regard to actions also there is excess, defect, and the intermediate. Now virtue is concerned with passions and actions, in which excess is a form of failure, and so is defect, while the intermediate is praised and is a form of success; and being praised and being successful are both characteristics of virtue. Therefore virtue is a kind of mean, since, as we have seen, it aims at what is intermediate. . . .

Virtue, then, is a state of character concerned with choice, lying in a mean, *i.e.* the mean relative to us, this being determined by a rational principle, and by that principle by which the man of practical wisdom would determine it. Now it is a mean between two vices, that which depends on excess and that which depends on defect; and again it is a mean because the vices respectively fall short of or exceed what is right in both passions and actions, while virtue both finds and chooses that which is intermediate. . . .

IMMANUEL KANT
Foundations of the Metaphysics of Morals

IMMANUEL KANT *(1724–1804), the great German philosopher, wrote his short*
Foundations of the Metaphysics of Morals *as an anticipation of the more elaborate
arguments in his* Critique of Practical Reason *(1788). In both books, he defends morality
and moral principles as the product of practical reason, not feelings or "inclinations." Kant
describes morality as concerning "a good will" rather than the consequences of an action or
any other matters of good fortune that are not matters of intention. The principle of
practical reason is called "the categorical imperative."*

NOTHING can possibly be conceived in the world, or even out of it, which can be called good without qualification, except a *good will*. Intelligence, wit, judgment, and other talents of the mind, however they may be named, or courage, resolution, perseverance, as qualities of temperament, are undoubtedly good and desirable in many respects; but these gifts of nature may also become extremely bad and mischievous if the will which is to make use of them, and which, therefore, constitutes what is called *character*, is not good. It is the same with the *gifts of fortune*. Power, riches, honor, even health, and the general well-being and contentment with one's condition which is called *happiness*, inspire pride, and often presumption, if there is not a good will to correct the influence of these on the mind, and with this also to rectify the whole principle of acting, and adapt it to its end. The sight of a being who is not adorned with a single feature of a pure and good will, enjoying unbroken prosperity, can never give pleasure to an impartial rational spectator. Thus a good will appears to constitute the indispensable condition even of being worthy of happiness.

There are even some qualities which are of service to this good will itself, and may facilitate its action, yet which have no intrinsic unconditional value, but always presuppose a good will, and this qualifies the esteem that we justly have for them, and does not permit us to regard them as absolutely good. Moderation in the affections and passions, self-control, and calm deliberation are not only good in many respects, but even seem to constitute part of the intrinsic worth of the person; but they are far from deserving to be called good without qualification, although they have been so unconditionally praised by the ancients. For without the principles of a good will, they may become extremely bad; and the coolness of a villain not only makes him far more dangerous, but also directly makes him more abominable in our eyes than he would have been without it.

A good will is good not because of what it performs or effects, not by its aptness for the attainment of some proposed end, but simply by virtue of the volition—that is, it is good in itself, and considered by itself is to be esteemed much higher than all that can be brought about by it in favor of any inclination, nay, even of the sum-total of all inclinations. Even if it should happen that, owing to special disfavor of fortune, or the niggardly provision of a stepmotherly nature, this will should wholly lack power to accomplish its purpose, if with its greatest efforts it should yet achieve nothing, and there should remain only the good will (not, to be sure, a mere wish, but

Kant, Immanuel, *Foundations of the Metaphysics of Morals*, translated Abbott, Sec. 1, pp. 393–395;
sec. 2, pp. 412–434.

the summoning of all means in our power), then, like a jewel, it would still shine by its own light, as a thing which has its whole value in itself. Its usefulness or fruitlessness can neither add to nor take away anything from this value. It would be, as it were, only the setting to enable us to handle it the more conveniently in common commerce, or to attract to it the attention of those who are not yet connoisseurs, but not to recommend it to true connoisseurs, or to determine its value. . . .

Everything in nature works according to laws. Rational beings alone have the faculty of acting according *to the conception* of laws, that is according to principles, *i.e.* have a *will.* Since the deduction of actions from principles requires *reason,* the will is nothing but practical reason. If reason infallibly determines the will, then the actions of such a being which are recognized as objectively necessary are subjectively necessary also, *i.e.* the will is a faculty to choose *that only* which reason independent of inclination recognizes as practically necessary, *i.e.* as good. But if reason of itself does not sufficiently determine the will, if the latter is subject also to subjective conditions (particular impulses) which do not always coincide with the objective conditions; in a word, if the will does not in *itself* completely accord with reason (which is actually the case with men), then the actions which objectively are recognized as necessary are subjectively contingent, and the determination of such a will according to objective laws is *obligation,* that is to say, the relation of the objective laws to a will that is not thoroughly good is conceived as the determination of the will of a rational being by principles of reason, but which the will from its nature does not of necessity follow.

The conception of an objective principle, in so far as it is obligatory for a will, is called a command (of reason), and the formula of the command is called an Imperative. . . .

Now all *imperatives* command either *hypothetically* or *categorically.* The former represent the practical necessity of a possible action as means to something else that is willed (or at least which one might possibly will). The categorical imperative would be that which represented an action as necessary of itself without reference to another end, *i.e.* as objectively necessary.

Since every practical law represents a possible action as good, and on this account, for a subject who is practically determinable by reason, necessary, all imperatives are formulae determining an action which is necessary according to the principle of a will good in some respects. If now the action is good only as a means to *something else,* then the imperative is *hypothetical;* if it is conceived as good in itself and consequently as being necessarily the principle of a will which of itself conforms to reason, then it is *categorical.* . . .

When I conceive a hypothetical imperative, in general I do not know beforehand what it will contain until I am given the condition. But when I conceive a categorical imperative, I know at once what it contains. For as the imperative contains besides the law only the necessity that the maxims shall conform to this law, while the law contains no conditions restricting it, there remains nothing but the general statement that the maxim of the action should conform to a universal law, and it is this conformity alone that the imperative properly represents as necessary.

There is . . . but one categorical imperative, namely, this: *Act only on that maxim whereby thou canst at the same time will that it should become a universal law.*

Now if all imperatives of duty can be deduced from this one imperative as from their principle, then, although it should remain undecided whether what is called duty is not merely a vain notion, yet at least we shall be able to show what we understand by it and what this notion means.

Since the universality of the law according to which effects are produced constitutes what is properly called *nature* in the most general sense (as to form), that is the existence of things so far as it is determined by general laws, the imperative of duty may be expressed thus: *Act as if the maxim of thy action were to become by thy will a universal law of nature.*

We will now enumerate a few duties, adopting the usual division of them into duties to ourselves and to others, and into perfect and imperfect duties.

1. A man reduced to despair by a series of misfortunes feels wearied of life, but is still so far in possession of his reason that he can ask himself whether it would not be contrary to his duty to himself to take his own life. Now he inquires whether the maxim of his action could become a universal law of nature. His maxim is: From self-love I adopt it as a principle to shorten my life when its longer duration is likely to bring more evil than satisfaction. It is asked then simply whether this principle founded on self-love can become a universal law of nature. Now we see at once that a system of nature of which it should be a law to destroy life by means of the very feeling whose special nature it is to impel to the improvement of life would contradict itself, and therefore could not exist as a system of nature; hence that maxim cannot possibly exist as a universal law of nature, and consequently would be wholly inconsistent with the supreme principle of all duty.

2. Another finds himself forced by necessity to borrow money. He knows that he will not be able to repay it, but sees also that nothing will be lent to him, unless he promises stoutly to repay it in a definite time. He desires to make this promise, but he has still so much conscience as to ask himself: Is it not unlawful and inconsistent with duty to get out of a difficulty in this way? Suppose, however, that he resolves to do so, then the maxim of his action would be expressed thus: When I think myself in want of money. I will borrow money and promise to repay it, although I know that I never can do so. Now this principle of self-love or of one's own advantage may perhaps be consistent with my whole future welfare; but the question now is. Is it right? I change then the suggestion of self-love into a universal law, and state the question thus: How would it be if my maxim were a universal law? Then I see at once that it could never hold as a universal law of nature, but would necessarily contradict itself. For supposing it to be a universal law that everyone when he thinks himself in a difficulty should be able to promise whatever he pleases, with the purpose of not keeping his promise, the promise itself would become impossible, as well as the

end that one might have in view in it, since no one would consider that anything was promised to him, but would ridicule all such statements as vain pretences.

3. A third finds in himself a talent which with the help of some culture might make him a useful man in many respects. But he finds himself in comfortable circumstances, and prefers to indulge in pleasure rather than to take pains in enlarging and improving his happy natural capacities. He asks, however, whether his maxim of neglect of his natural gifts, besides agreeing with his inclination to indulgence, agrees also with what is called duty. He sees then that a system of nature could indeed subsist with such a universal law although men (like the South Sea islanders) should let their talents rest, and resolve to devote their lives merely to idleness, amusement, and propagation of their species—in a word, to enjoyment; but he cannot possibly *will* that this should be a universal law of nature, or be implanted in us as such by a natural instinct. For, as a rational being, he necessarily wills that his faculties be developed, since they serve him, and have been given him, for all sorts of possible purposes.

4. A fourth, who is in prosperity, while he sees that others have to contend with great wretchedness and that he could help them, thinks: What concern is it of mine? Let everyone be as happy as Heaven pleases, or as he can make himself; I will take nothing from him nor even envy him, only I do not wish to contribute anything to his welfare or to his assistance in distress! Now no doubt if such a mode of thinking were a universal law, the human race might very well subsist, and doubtless even better than in a state in which everyone talks of sympathy and good will, or even takes care occasionally to put it into practice, but, on the other side, also cheats when he can, betrays the rights of men, or otherwise violates them. But although it is possible that a universal law of nature might exist in accordance with that maxim, it is impossible to *will* that such a principle should have the universal validity of a law of nature. For a will which resolved this would contradict itself, inasmuch as many

cases might occur in which one would have need of the love and sympathy of others, and in which, by such a law of nature, sprung from his own will, he would deprive himself of all hope of the aid he desires. . . .

We have thus established at least this much, that if duty is a conception which is to have any import and real legislative authority for our actions, it can only be expressed in categorical, and not at all in hypothetical imperatives. We have also, which is of great importance, exhibited clearly and definitely for every practical application the content of the categorical imperative, which must contain the principle of all duty if there is such a thing at all. We have not yet, however, advanced so far as to prove *à priori* that there actually is such an imperative, that there is a practical law which commands absolutely of itself, and without any other impulse, and that the following of this law is duty. . . .

Now I say: man and generally any rational being *exists* as an end in himself, *not merely as a means* to be arbitrarily used by this or that will, but in all his actions, whether they concern himself or other rational beings, must be always regarded at the same time as an end. All objects of the inclinations have only a conditional worth; for if the inclinations and the wants founded on them did not exist, then their object would be without value. But the inclinations themselves being sources of want are so far from having an absolute worth for which they should be desired, that, on the contrary, it must be the universal wish of every rational being to be wholly free from them. Thus the worth of any object which is *to be acquired* by our action is always conditional. Beings whose existence depends not on our will but on nature's, have nevertheless, if they are not rational beings, only a relative value as means, and are therefore called *things;* rational beings, on the contrary, are called *persons,* because their very nature points them out as ends in themselves, that is as something which must not be used merely as means, and so far therefore restricts freedom of action (and is an object of respect). These, therefore, are not merely subjective

ends whose existence has a worth for *us* as an effort of our action, but *objective ends,* that is things whose existence is an end in itself: an end moreover for which no other can be substituted, which they should subserve *merely* as means, for otherwise nothing whatever would possess *absolute worth;* but if all worth were conditioned and therefore contingent, then there would be no supreme practical principle of reason whatever.

If then there is a supreme practical principle or, in respect of the human will, a categorical imperative, it must be one which, being drawn from the conception of that which is necessarily an end for everyone because it is *an end in itself,* constitutes an *objective* principle of will, and can therefore serve as a universal practical law. The foundation of this principle is: *rational nature exists as an end in itself.* Man necessarily conceives his own existence as being so: so far then this is a *subjective* principle of human actions. But every other rational being regards its existence similarly, just on the same rational principle, that holds for me: so that it is at the same time an objective principle, from which as a supreme practical law all laws of the will must be capable of being deduced. Accordingly the practical imperative will be as follows: *So act as to treat humanity, whether in thine own person or in that of any other, in every case as an end withal, never as means only.* . . .

The conception of every rational being as one which must consider itself as giving all the maxims of its will universal laws, so as to judge itself and its actions from this point of view—this conception leads to another which depends on it and is very fruitful, namely, that of a *kingdom of ends.*

By a *kingdom* I understand the union of different rational beings in a system by common laws. Now since it is by laws that ends are determined as regards their universal validity, hence, if we abstract from the personal differences of rational beings, and likewise from all the content of their private ends, we shall be able to conceive all ends combined in a systematic whole (including both rational beings as ends in themselves, and also the special ends which each may propose to himself), that is to say, we can conceive a kingdom of ends, which on the preceding principles is possible.

JOHN STUART MILL
Utilitarianism

JOHN STUART MILL *(1806–1873) was the most famous proponent of*
"utilitarianism"—a movement started by Jeremy Bentham in the late eighteenth century.
Here Mill defines utilitarianism as the ethics that prescribes doing "the greatest good for the
greatest number," and he argues that all of our ethical thinking presupposes this principle.

THE creed which accepts [utility] as the foundation of morals, or the Greatest Happiness Principle, holds that actions are right in proportion as they tend to promote happiness, wrong as they tend to produce the reverse of happiness. By happiness is intended pleasure, and the absence of pain; by unhappiness, pain, and the privation of pleasure. To give a clear view of the moral standard set up by the theory, much more requires to be said; in particular, what things it includes in the ideas of pain and pleasure; and to what extent this is left an open question. But these supplementary explanations do not affect the theory of life on which this theory of morality is grounded— namely, that pleasure, and freedom from pain, are the only things desirable as ends; and that all desirable things (which are as numerous in the utilitarian as in any other scheme) are desirable either for the pleasure inherent in themselves, or as means to the promotion of pleasure and the prevention of pain.

Now, such a theory of life excites in many minds, and among them in some of the most estimable in feeling and purpose, inveterate dislike. To suppose that life has (as they express it) no higher end than pleasure—no better and nobler object of desire and pursuit—they designate as utterly mean and grovelling; as a doctrine worthy only of swine, to whom the followers of Epicurus were, at a very early period, contemptuously likened; and modern holders of the doctrine are occasionally made the subject of equally polite comparisons by its German, French, and English assailants.

When thus attacked, the Epicureans have always answered, that it is not they, but their accusers, who represent human nature in a degrading light; since the accusation supposes human beings to be capable of no pleasures except those of which swine are capable. If this supposition were true, the charge could not be gainsaid, but would then be no longer an imputation; for if the sources of pleasure were precisely the same to human beings and to swine, the rule of life which is good enough for the one would be good enough for the other. The comparison of the Epicurean life to that of beasts is felt as degrading, precisely because a beast's pleasures do not satisfy a human being's conceptions of happiness. Human beings have faculties more elevated than the animal appetites, and when once made conscious of them, do not regard anything as happiness which does not include their gratification. I do not, indeed, consider the Epicureans to have been by any means faultless in drawing out their scheme of consequences from the utilitarian principle. To do this in any sufficient manner, many Stoic, as well as Christian elements require to be included. But there is no known Epicurean theory of life which does not assign to the pleasures of the intellect, of the feelings and imagination, and of the moral sentiments, a much higher value as pleasures than to those of mere sensation. It must be admitted, however, that utilitarian writers in general have placed the superiority of mental over bodily

Mill, John Stuart, "Utilitarianism," from *Utilitarianism* by John Stuart Mill, London, NY: Longman, 1907.

pleasures chiefly in the greater permanency, safety, uncostliness, etc., of the former—that is, in their circumstantial advantages rather than in their intrinsic nature. And on all these points utilitarians have fully proved their case; but they might have taken the other, and, as it may be called, higher ground, with entire consistency. It is quite compatible with the principle of utility to recognize the fact, that some *kinds* of pleasure are more desirable and more valuable than others. It would be absurd that while, in estimating all other things, quality is considered as well as quantity, the estimation of pleasures should be supposed to depend on quantity alone.

If I am asked, what I mean by difference of quality in pleasures, or what makes one pleasure more valuable than another, merely as a pleasure, except its being greater in amount, there is but one possible answer. Of two pleasures, if there be one to which all or almost all who have experience of both give a decided preference, irrespective of any feeling of moral obligation to prefer it, that is the more desirable pleasure. If one of the two is, by those who are competently acquainted with both, placed so far above the other that they prefer it, even though knowing it to be attended with a greater amount of discontent, and would not resign it for any quantity of the other pleasure which their nature is capable of, we are justified in ascribing to the preferred enjoyment a superiority in quality, so far outweighing quantity as to render it, in comparison, of small account.

Now it is an unquestionable fact that those who are equally acquainted with, and equally capable of appreciating and enjoying, both, do give a most marked preference to the manner of existence which employs their higher faculties. Few human creatures would consent to be changed into any of the lower animals, for a promise of the fullest allowance of a beast's pleasures; no intelligent human being would consent to be a fool, no instructed person would be an ignoramus, no person of feeling and conscience would be selfish and base, even though they should be persuaded that the fool, the dunce, or the rascal is better satisfied with his lot than they are with theirs. They would not resign what they possess more than he for the most complete satisfaction of all the desires which they have in common with him. If they ever fancy they would, it is only in cases of unhappiness so extreme, that to escape from it they would exchange their lot for almost any other, however undesirable in their own eyes. A being of higher faculties requires more to make him happy, is capable probably of more acute suffering, and certainly accessible to it at more points, than one of an inferior type; but in spite of these liabilities, he can never really wish to sink into what he feels to be a lower grade of existence. We may give what explanation we please of this unwillingness; we may attribute it to pride, a name which is given indiscriminately to some of the most and to some of the least estimable feelings of which mankind are capable: we may refer it to the love of liberty and personal independence, an appeal to which was with the Stoics one of the most effective means for the inculcation of it; to the love of power, or to the love of excitement, both of which do really enter into and contribute to it: but its most appropriate appellation is a sense of dignity, which all human beings possess in one form or other, and in some, though by no means in exact, proportion to their higher faculties, and which is so essential a part of the happiness of those in whom it is strong, that nothing which conflicts with it could be, otherwise than momentarily, an object of desire to them. Whoever supposes that this preference takes place at a sacrifice of happiness—that the superior being, in anything like equal circumstances, is not happier than the inferior—confounds the two very different ideas, of happiness, and content. It is indisputable that the being whose capacities of enjoyment are low, has the greatest chance of having them fully satisfied; and a highly endowed being will always feel that any happiness which he can look for, as the world is constituted, is imperfect. But he can learn to bear its imperfections, if they are at all bearable; and they will not make him envy the being who is indeed unconscious of the imperfections, but only because he feels not at all the good which those imperfections qualify. It is better to be a human being dissatisfied than a pig satisfied; better to be Socrates dissatisfied than a fool satisfied. And if the fool, or the pig, are of a different opinion, it is because they only know their own side of the question. The other party to the comparison knows both sides.

It may be objected, that many who are capable of the higher pleasures, occasionally, under the influence of temptation, postpone them to the lower. But this is quite compatible with a full appreciation of the intrinsic superiority of the higher. Men often, from infirmity of character, make their election for the nearer good, though they know it to be the less valuable; and this no less when the choice is between two bodily pleasures, than when it is between bodily and mental. They pursue sensual indulgences to the injury of health, though perfectly aware that health is the greater good. It may be further objected, that many who begin with youthful enthusiasm for everything noble, as they advance in years sink into indolence and selfishness. But I do not believe that those who undergo this very common change, voluntarily choose the lower description of pleasures in preference to the higher. I believe that before they devote themselves exclusively to the one, they have already become incapable of the other. Capacity for the nobler feelings is in most natures a very tender plant, easily killed, not only by hostile influences, but by mere want of substance; and in the majority of young persons it speedily dies away if the occupations to which their position in life has devoted them, and the society into which it has thrown them, are not favorable to keeping that higher capacity in exercise. Men lose their high aspirations as they lose their intellectual tastes, because they have not time or opportunity for indulging them; and they addict themselves to inferior pleasures, not because they deliberately prefer them, but because they are either the only ones to which they have access, or the only ones which they are any longer capable of enjoying. It may be questioned whether any one who has remained equally susceptible to both classes of pleasures, ever

knowingly and calmly preferred the lower, though many, in all ages, have broken down in an ineffectual attempt to combine both.

From this verdict of the only competent judges, I apprehend there can be no appeal. On a question which is the best worth having of two pleasures, or which of two modes of existence is the most grateful to the feelings, apart from its moral attributes and from its consequences, the judgment of those who are qualified by knowledge of both, or, if they differ, that of the majority among them, must be admitted as final. And there needs be the less hesitation to accept this judgment respecting the quality of pleasures, since there is no other tribunal to be referred to even on the question of quantity. What means are there of determining which is the acutest of two pains, or the intensest of two pleasurable sensations, except the general suffrage of those who are familiar with both? Neither pains nor pleasures are homogeneous, and pain is always heterogeneous with pleasure. What is there to decide whether a particular pleasure is worth purchasing at the cost of a particular pain, except the feelings and judgment of the experienced? When, therefore, those feelings and judgment declare the pleasures derived from the higher faculties to be preferable. *In kind,* apart from the question of intensity, to those of which the animal nature, disjoined from the higher faculties, is susceptible, they are entitled on this subject to the same regard.

I have dwelt on this point, as being a necessary part of a perfectly just conception of Utility or Happiness, considered as the directive rule of human conduct. But it is by no means an indispensable condition to the acceptance of the utilitarian standard; for that standard is not the agent's own greatest happiness, but the greatest amount of happiness altogether; and if it may possibly be doubted whether a noble character is always the happier for its nobleness, there can be no doubt that it makes other people happier, and that the world in general is immensely a gainer by it. Utilitarianism, therefore, could only attain its end by the general cultivation of nobleness of character, even if each individual were only benefited by the nobleness of others, and his own, so far as happiness is concerned, were a sheer deduction from the benefit. But the bare enunciation of such an absurdity as this last, renders refutation superfluous.

According to the Greatest Happiness Principle, as above explained, the ultimate end, with reference to and for the sake of which all other things are desirable (whether we are considering our own good or that of other people), is an existence exempt as far as possible from pain, and as rich as possible in enjoyments, both in point of quantity and quality; the test of quality, and the rule for measuring it against quantity, being the preference felt by those who in their opportunities of experience, to which must be added their habits of self-consciousness and self-observation, are best furnished with the means of comparison. This, being, according to the utilitarian opinion, the end of human action, is necessarily also the standard of morality; which may accordingly be defined, the rules and precepts for human conduct, by the observance of which an existence such as has been described might be, to the greatest extent possible, secured to all mankind; and not to them only, but, so far as the nature of things admits, to the whole sentient creation. . . .

. . . I must again repeat, what the assailants of utilitarianism seldom have the justice to acknowledge, that the happiness which forms the utilitarian standard of what is right in conduct, is not the agent's own happiness, but that of all concerned. As between his own happiness and that of others, utilitarianism requires him to be as strictly impartial as a disinterested and benevolent spectator. In the golden rule of Jesus of Nazareth, we read the complete spirit of the ethics of utility. To do as you would be done by, and to love your neighbour as yourself, constitute the ideal perfection of utilitarian morality.

FRIEDRICH NIETZSCHE
The Natural History of Morals

FRIEDRICH NIETZSCHE *(1844–1900) was a German philosopher who spent most of his life traveling in northern Italy and Switzerland toward the end of the nineteenth century. He was a harsh critic of Christianity and Judeo-Christian morality and argued that, contrary to their own protestations of piety, both religion and morality are in fact products of the resentment of the weak and a rejection of the ancient virtue of nobility. The following excerpt is from his book,* Beyond Good and Evil.

THE moral sentiment in Europe at present is perhaps as subtle, belated, diverse, sensitive, and refined, as the "Science of Morals" belonging thereto is recent, initial, awkward, and coarse-fingered:—an interesting contrast, which sometimes becomes incarnate and obvious in the very person of a moralist. . . . One ought to avow with the utmost fairness *what* is still necessary here . . . as preparation for a *theory of types* of morality. To be

Nietzsche, Friedrich, "The Natural History of Morals," from *Beyond Good and Evil* by Friedrich Nietzsche, translated Helen Zimmern. Allen & Unwin.

sure, people have not hitherto been so modest. All the philosophers, with a pedantic and ridiculous seriousness, demanded of themselves something very much higher, more pretentious, and ceremonious, when they concerned themselves with morality as a science: they wanted to *give a basis* to morality—and every philosopher hitherto has believed that he has given it a basis; morality itself, however, has been regarded as something "given." How far from their awkward pride was the seemingly insignificant problem— left in dust and decay—of a description of forms of morality. . . . They did not even come in sight of the real problems of morals—problems which only disclose themselves by a comparison of *many* kinds of morality. . . .

Apart from the value of such assertions as "there is a categorical imperative in us," one can always ask: What does such an assertion indicate about him who makes it? There are systems of morals which are meant to justify their author in the eyes of other people; other systems of morals are meant to tranquillise him, and make him self-satisfied; with other systems he wants to crucify and humble himself: with others he wishes to take revenge; with others to conceal himself; with others to glorify himself and gain superiority and distinction:—this system of morals helps its author to forget, that system makes him, or something of him, forgotten; many a moralist would like to exercise power and creative arbitrariness over mankind; many another, perhaps, Kant especially, gives us to understand by his morals that "what is estimable in me, is that I know how to obey—and with you it *shall* not be otherwise than with me!" In short, systems of morals are only *a sign-language of the emotions.*

. . . Every system of morals is a sort of tyranny against "nature" and also against "reason"; that is, however, no objection, unless one should again decree by some system of morals, that all kinds of tyranny and unreasonableness are unlawful. What is essential and invaluable in every system of morals, is that it is a long constraint. . . . The essential thing "in heaven and in earth" is that there should be long *obedience* in the same direction; there thereby results, and has always

resulted in the long run, something which has made life worth living; for instance, virtue, art, music, dancing, reason, spirituality—anything whatever that is transfiguring, refined, foolish, or divine. The long bondage of the spirit, the distrustful constraint in the communicability of ideas, the discipline which the thinker imposed on himself to think in accordance with the rules of a church or a court, or conformable to Aristotelian premises, the persistent spiritual will to interpret everything that happened according to a Christian scheme, and in every occurrence to rediscover and justify the Christian God:—all this violence, arbitrariness, severity, dreadfulness, and unreasonableness, has proved itself the disciplinary means whereby the European spirit has attained its strength, its remorseless curiosity and subtle mobility; granted also that much irrecoverable strength and spirit had to be stifled, suffocated, and spoiled in the process (for here, as everywhere, "nature" shows herself as she is, in all her extravagant and *indifferent* magnificence, which is shocking, but nevertheless noble). . . . [T]his tyranny, this arbitrariness, this severe and magnificent stupidity, has *educated* the spirit. . . .

In a tour through the many finer and coarser moralities which have hitherto prevailed or still prevail on the earth. I found certain traits recurring regularly together, and connected with one another, until finally two primary types revealed themselves to me, and a radical distinction was brought to light. There is *master-morality* and *slave-morality;*—I would at once add, however, that in all higher and mixed civilizations, there are also attempts at the reconciliation of the two moralities: but one finds still oftener the confusion and mutual misunderstanding of them, indeed, sometimes their close juxtaposition— even in the same man, within one soul. The distinctions of moral values have either originated in a ruling caste, pleasantly conscious of being different from the ruled—or among the ruled class, the slaves and dependents of all sorts. In the first case, when it is the rulers who determine the conception "good," it is the exalted, proud disposition which is regarded as the distinguishing feature, and that which determines the order of rank. The noble type of man separates from himself the beings in whom the opposite of this exalted, proud disposition displays itself: he despises them. Let it at once be noted that in this first kind of morality the antithesis "good" and "bad" means practically the same as "noble" and "despicable":—the antithesis "good" and "*evil*" is of a different origin. The cowardly, the timid, the insignificant, and those thinking merely of narrow utility are despised; moreover, also, the distrustful, with their constrained glances, the self-abasing, the dog-like kind of men who let themselves be abused, the mendicant flatterers, and above all the liars:—it is a fundamental belief of all aristocrats that the common people are untruthful. "We truthful ones"—the nobility in ancient Greece called themselves.

It is obvious that everywhere the designations of moral value were at first applied to *men* and were only derivatively and at a later period applied to *actions;* it is a gross mistake, therefore, when historians of morals start questions like, "Why have sympathetic actions been praised?" The noble type of man regards *himself* as a determiner of values; he does not require to be approved of; he passes the judgment: "What is injurious to me is injurious in itself": he knows that it is he himself only who confers honour on things; he is a *creator of values.* He honours whatever he recognizes in himself: such morality is self-glorification. In the foreground there is the feeling of plentitude, of power, which seeks to overflow, the happiness of high tension, the consciousness of a wealth which would fain give and bestow!—the noble man also helps the unfortunate, but not—or scarcely—out of pity, but rather from an impulse generated by the superabundance of power. The noble man honours in himself the powerful one, him also who has power over himself, who knows how to speak and how to keep silence, who takes pleasure in subjecting himself to severity and hardness, and has reverence for all that is severe and hard. "Wotan placed a hard heart in my breast," says an old Scandinavian Saga: it is thus rightly expressed from the soul of a proud Viking. Such a type of man is even proud of *not* being made for

sympathy; the hero of the Saga therefore adds warningly: "He who has not a hard heart when young, will never have one."

The noble and brave who think thus are the furthest removed from the morality which sees precisely in sympathy, or in acting for the good of others, or in *désintéressement,* the characteristic of the moral; faith in oneself, pride in oneself, a radical enmity and irony towards "selflessness," belong as definitely to noble morality, as do a careless scorn and precaution in presence of sympathy and the "warm heart."—It is the powerful who *know* how to honour, it is their art, their domain for invention. The profound reverence for age and for tradition—all law rests on this double reverence,—the belief and prejudice in favour of ancestors and unfavourable to newcomers, is typical in the morality of the powerful: and if, reversely, men of "modern ideas" believe almost instinctively in "progress" and the "future," and are more and more lacking in respect for old age, the ignoble origin of these "ideas" has complacently betrayed itself thereby.

A morality of the ruling class, however, is more especially foreign and irritating to present day taste in the sternness of its principle that one has duties only to one's equals; that one may act towards beings of a lower rank, towards all that is foreign, just as seems good to one, or "as the heart desires," and in any case "beyond good and evil": it is here that sympathy and similar sentiments can have a place. The ability and obligation to exercise prolonged gratitude and prolonged revenge—both only within the circle of equals,—artfulness in retaliation, *raffinement* of the idea in friendship, a certain necessity to have enemies (as outlets for the emotions of envy, quarrelsomeness, arrogance—in fact, in order to be a good *friend*): all these are typical characteristics of the noble morality, which, as has been pointed out, is not the morality of "modern ideas," and is therefore at present difficult to realise, and also to unearth and disclose.

It is otherwise with the second type of morality, *slave-morality.* Supposing that the abused, the oppressed, the suffering, the unemancipated, the weary, and those uncertain of themselves, should moralise, what will be the common element in their moral estimates? Probably a pessimistic suspicion with regard to the entire situation of man will find expression, perhaps a condemnation of man, together with his situation. The slave has an unfavourable eye for the virtues of the powerful; he has a scepticism and distrust, a *refinement* of distrust of everything "good" that is there honoured—he would fain persuade himself that the very happiness there is not genuine. On the other hand, *those* qualities which serve to alleviate the existence of sufferers are brought into prominence and flooded with light; it is here that sympathy, the kind, helping hand, the warm heart, patience, diligence, humility, and friendliness attain to honour; for here these are the most useful qualities, and almost the only means of supporting the burden of existence.

Slave-morality is essentially the morality of utility. Here is the seat of the origin of the famous antithesis "good" and "evil":—power and

dangerousness are assumed to reside in the evil, a certain dreadfulness, subtlety, and strength, which do not admit of being despised. According to slave-morality, therefore, the "evil" man arouses fear; according to master-morality, it is precisely the "good" man who arouses fear and seeks to arouse it, while the bad man is regarded as the despicable being. The contrast attains its maximum when, in accordance with the logical consequences of slave-morality, a shade of depreciation—it may be slight and well-intentioned—at last attaches itself to the "good" man of this morality; because, according to the servile mode of thought, the good man must in any case be the *safe* man: he is good-natured, easily deceived, perhaps a little stupid, *un bonhomme.* Everywhere that slave-morality gains the ascendancy, language shows a tendency to approximate the significations of the words "good" and "stupid."

A. J. AYER
Emotivism

A. J. AYER (1910–1989), English philosopher, was highly influential in the logical positivist movement, which tried to show that many of our ordinary ways of talking, including ethics, are nonsense. This excerpt is from his Language, Truth, and Logic.

I T is our business to give an account of "judgements of value" which is both satisfactory in itself and consistent with our general empiricist principles. We shall set ourselves to show that in so far as statements of value are significant, they are ordinary "scientific" statements; and that in so far as they are

not scientific, they are not in the literal sense significant, but are simply expressions of emotion which can be neither true nor false. . . .

The ordinary system of ethics, as elaborated in the works of ethical philosophers, is very far from being a homogeneous whole. Not only is it apt to contain pieces of metaphysics, and analyses of non-ethical concepts: its actual ethical contents are themselves of very different kinds. We may divide them, indeed, into four main classes. There are, first of all, propositions which express definitions of ethical terms, or judgements about the legitimacy or possibility of certain definitions. Secondly, there are propositions describing the phenomena of moral experience, and their causes. Thirdly, there are exhortations to moral virtue. And, lastly, there are actual ethical judgements. It is unfortunately the case that the distinction between these four classes, plain as it is, is commonly ignored by ethical philosophers: with the result that it is often very difficult to tell from their works what it is that they are seeking to discover or prove.

In fact, it is easy to see that only the first of our four classes, namely that which comprises the propositions relating to the definitions of ethical terms, can be said to constitute ethical philosophy. The propositions which describe the phenomena of moral experience, and their causes, must be assigned to the science of psychology, or sociology. The exhortations to moral virtue are not propositions at all, but ejaculations or commands which are designed to provoke the reader to action of a certain sort. Accordingly, they do not belong to any branch of philosophy or science. As for the expressions of ethical judgements, we have not yet determined how they should be classified. But inasmuch as they are certainly neither definitions nor comments upon definitions, nor quotations, we may say decisively that they do not belong to ethical philosophy. A strictly philosophical treatise on ethics should therefore make no ethical pronouncements. But it should, by giving an analysis of ethical terms, show what is the category to which all such pronouncements belong. And this is what we are now about to do.

A question which is often discussed by ethical philosophers is whether it is possible to find definitions which would reduce all ethical terms to one or two fundamental terms. But this question, though it undeniably belongs to ethical philosophy, is not relevant to our present enquiry. We are not now concerned to discover which

term, within the sphere of ethical terms, is to be taken as fundamental; whether, for example, "good" can be defined in terms of "right" or "right" in terms of "good," or both in terms of "value." What we are interested in is the possibility of reducing the whole sphere of ethical terms to nonethical terms. We are enquiring whether statements of ethical value can be translated into statements of empirical fact.

That they can be so translated is the contention of those ethical philosophers who are commonly called subjectivists, and of those who are known as utilitarians. For the utilitarian defines the rightness of actions, and the goodness of ends, in terms of the pleasure, or happiness, or satisfaction, to which they give rise; the subjectivist, in terms of the feelings of approval which a certain person, or group of people, has towards them. Each of these types of definition makes moral judgements into a subclass of psychological or sociological judgements; and for this reason they are very attractive to us. For, if either was correct, it would follow that ethical assertions were not generically different from the factual assertions which are ordinarily contrasted with them; and the account which we have already given of empirical hypotheses would apply to them also.

Nevertheless we shall not adopt either a subjectivist or a utilitarian analysis of ethical terms. We reject the subjectivist view that to call an action right, or a thing good, is to say that it is generally approved of, because it is not self-contradictory to assert that some actions which are generally approved of are not right, or that some things which are generally approved of are not good. And we reject the alternative subjectivist view that a man who asserts that a certain action is right, or that a certain thing is good, is saying that he himself approves of it, on the ground that a man who confessed that he sometimes approved of what was bad or wrong would not be contradicting himself. And a similar argument is fatal to utilitarianism. We cannot agree that to call an action right is to say that of all the actions possible in the circumstances it would cause, or be likely to cause, the greatest happiness, or the greatest balance of pleasure over pain, or the greatest balance of satisfied over unsatisfied desire, because we find that it is not self-contradictory to say that it is sometimes wrong to perform the action which would actually or probably cause the greatest happiness, or the greatest balance of pleasure over pain, or of satisfied over unsatisfied desire. And since it is not self-contradictory to say that some pleasant things are not good, or that some bad things are desired, it cannot be the case that the sentence "x is good" is equivalent to "x is pleasant," or "x is desired." And to every other variant of utilitarianism with which I am acquainted the same objection can be made. And therefore we should, I think, conclude that the validity of ethical judgements is not determined by the felicific tendencies of actions, any more than by the nature of people's feelings; but that it must be regarded as "absolute" or "intrinsic," and not empirically calculable. . . .

In admitting that normative ethical concepts are irreducible to empirical concepts, we seem to be leaving the way clear for the "absolutist" view of ethics—that is, the view that statements of value are not controlled by observation, ordinary empirical propositions are, but only by a mysterious "intellectual intuition." A feature of this theory, which is seldom recognized by its advocates, is that it makes statements of value unverifiable. For it is notorious that what seems intuitively certain to one person may seem doubtful, or even false, to another. So that unless it is possible to provide some criterion by which one may decide between conflicting intuitions, a mere appeal to intuition is worthless as a test of a proposition's validity. But in the case of moral judgements, no such criterion can be given. Some moralists claim to settle the matter by saying that they "know" that their own moral judgements are correct. But such an assertion is of purely psychological interest, and has not the slightest tendency to prove the validity of any moral judgement. For dissentient moralists may equally well "know" that their ethical views are correct. And, as far as subjective certainty goes, there will be nothing to choose between them.

When such differences of opinion arise in connection with an ordinary empirical proposition, one may attempt to resolve them by referring to, or actually carrying out, some relevant empirical test. But with regard to ethical statements, there is, on the "absolutist" or "intuitionist" theory, no relevant empirical test. We are therefore justified in saying that on this theory ethical statements are held to be unverifiable. . . .

Considering the use which we have made of the principle that a synthetic proposition is significant only if it is empirically verifiable, it is clear that the acceptance of an "absolutist" theory of ethics would undermine the whole of our main argument. And as we have already rejected the "naturalistic" theories which are commonly supposed to provide the only alternative to "absolutism" in ethics, we seem to have reached a difficult position. We shall meet the difficulty by showing that the correct treatment of ethical statements is afforded by a third theory, which is wholly compatible with our radical empiricism.

We begin by admitting that the fundamental ethical concepts are unanalysable, inasmuch as there is no criterion by which one can test the validity of the judgements in which they occur. So far we are in agreement with the absolutists. But, unlike the absolutists, we are able to give an explanation of this fact about ethical concepts. We say that the reason why they are unanalysable is that they are mere pseudo-concepts. The presence of an ethical symbol in a proposition adds nothing to its factual content. Thus if I say to someone, "You acted wrongly in stealing that money," I am not stating anything more than if I had simply said, "You stole that money." In adding that this action is wrong I am not making any further statement about it. I am simply evincing my moral disapproval of it. It is as if I had said, "You stole that money," in a peculiar tone of horror, or written it with the addition of some special exclamation marks. The tone, or the exclamation marks, adds nothing to the literal meaning of the sentence. It merely serves to show that the expression of it is attended by certain feelings in the speaker.

If now I generalise my previous statement and say, "Stealing money is wrong," I produce a sentence which has no factual meaning—that is, expresses no proposition which can be either true or false. It is as if I had written "Stealing money!!"—where the shape and thickness of the exclamation marks show, by a suitable convention, that a special sort of moral disapproval is the feeling which is being expressed. It is clear that there is nothing said here which can be true or false. Another man may disagree with me about the wrongness of stealing, in the sense that he may not have the same feelings about stealing as I have, and he may quarrel with me on account of my moral sentiments. But he cannot, strictly speaking, contradict me. For in saying that a certain type of action is right or wrong, I am not making any factual statement, not even a statement about my own state of mind. I am merely expressing certain moral sentiments. And the man who is ostensibly contradicting me is merely expressing his moral sentiments. So that there is plainly no sense in asking which of us is in the right. For neither of us is asserting a genuine proposition.

What we have just been saying about the symbol "wrong" applies to all normative ethical symbols. Sometimes they occur in sentences which record ordinary empirical facts besides expressing ethical feeling about those facts: sometimes they occur in sentences which simply express ethical feeling about a certain type of action, or situation, without making any statement of fact. But in every case in which one would commonly be said to be making an ethical judgement, the function of the relevant ethical word is purely "emotive." It is used to express feeling about certain objects, but not to make any assertion about them.

SIMONE DE BEAUVOIR
Freedom and Morality

SIMONE DE BEAUVOIR *(1908–1986) was a French novelist and philosopher and a lifelong companion of Jean-Paul Sartre, with whom she shared a radical and profound view about the centrality of freedom in human life. In the following excerpt from her* Ethics of Ambiguity, *she contrasts the essential role of freedom to morality and its opposition to what she (and Sartre) calls mere "facticity" (thing-ness).*

THERE is no way for a man to escape from this world. It is in this world that—avoiding the pitfalls we have just pointed out—he must realize himself morally. Freedom must project itself toward its own reality through a content whose value it establishes. An end is valid only by a return to the freedom which established it and which willed itself through this end. But this will implies that freedom is not to be engulfed in any goal; neither is it to dissipate itself vainly without aiming at a goal. It is not necessary for the subject to seek to be, but it must desire that there *be* being. To will oneself free and to will that there be *being* are one and the same choice, the choice that man makes of himself as a presence in the world. We can neither say that the free man wants freedom in order to desire being, nor that he wants the disclosure of being by freedom. These are two aspects of a single reality. And whichever be the one under consideration, they both imply the bond of each man with all others.

This bond does not immediately reveal itself to everybody. A young man wills himself free. He wills that there be being. This spontaneous liberality which casts him ardently into the world can ally itself to what is commonly called egoism. Often the young man perceives only that aspect of his relationship to others whereby others appear as enemies. In the preface to *The Inner Experience* Georges Bataille emphasizes very forcefully that each individual wants to be All. He sees in every other man and particularly in those whose existence is asserted with most brilliance, a limit, a condemnation of himself. "Each consciousness," said Hegel, "seeks the death of the other." And indeed at every moment others are stealing the whole world away from me. The first movement is to hate them. But this hatred is naive, and the desire immediately struggles against itself. If I were really everything there would be nothing beside me; the world would be empty. There would be

nothing to possess, and I myself would be nothing. If he is reasonable, the young man immediately understands that by taking the world away from me, others also give it to me, since a thing is given to me only by the movement which snatches it from me. To will that there be being is also to will that there be men by and for whom the world is endowed with human significations. One can reveal the world only on a basis revealed by other men. No project can be defined except by its interference with other projects. To make being "be" is to communicate with others by means of being.

This truth is found in another form when we say that freedom cannot will itself without aiming at an open future. The ends which it gives itself must be unable to be transcended by any reflection, but only the freedom of other men can extend them beyond our life. I have tried to show in *Pyrrhus and Cineas* that every man needs the freedom of other men and, in a sense, always wants it, even though he may be a tyrant; the only thing he fails to do is to assume honestly the consequences of such a wish. Only the freedom of others keeps each one of us from hardening in the absurdity of facticity. And if we are to believe the Christian myth of creation. God himself was in agreement on this point with the existentialist doctrine since, in the words of an anti-fascist priest, "He had such respect for man that He created him free."

JONATHAN BENNETT
The Conscience of Huckleberry Finn

JONATHAN BENNETT *is a historian of philosophy and an analytic philosopher who has written widely on modern philosophers and a great many topics. In one of his*

Bennett, Jonathan, "The Conscience of Huckleberry Finn," from *Journal of Philosophy*, Vol. 49, no. 188 (1974), pp. 123–134. Reprinted with the permission of Cambridge University Press.

best-known pieces, he uses Mark Twain's boy-hero Huck Finn to exemplify a traumatic
conflict between what one feels, as a matter of sympathy, and what one "knows" one ought
to do.

ALL that I can mean by a "bad morality" is a morality whose principles I deeply disapprove of. When I call a morality bad, I cannot prove that mine is better; but when I here call any morality bad, I think you will agree with me that it is bad; and that is all I need.

There could be dispute as to whether the springs of someone's actions constitute a *morality*. I think, though, that we must admit that someone who acts in ways which conflict grossly with our morality may nevertheless have a morality of his own—a set of principles of action which he sincerely assents to, so that for him the problem of acting well or rightly or in obedience to conscience is the problem of conforming to *those* principles. The problem of conscientiousness can arise as acutely for a bad morality as for any other: rotten principles may be as difficult to keep as decent ones.

As for "sympathy": I use this term to cover every sort of fellow-feeling, as when one feels pity over someone's loneliness, or horrified compassion over his pain, or when one feels a shrinking reluctance to act in a way which will bring misfortune to someone else. These *feelings* must not be confused with *moral judgments*. My sympathy for someone in distress may lead me to help him, or even to think that I ought to help him; but in itself it is not a judgment about what I ought to do but just a *feeling* for him in his plight. We shall get some light on the difference between feelings and moral judgments when we consider Huckleberry Finn. . . .

Huck Finn has been helping his slave friend Jim to run away from Miss Watson, who is Jim's owner. In their raft-journey down the Mississippi river, they are near to the place at which Jim will become legally free. Now let Huck take over the story:

Jim said it made him all over trembly and feverish to be so close to freedom. Well, I can tell you it made me all over trembly and feverish, too, to hear him, because I begun to get it through my head that he *was* most free—and who was to blame for it? Why, *me*. I couldn't get that out of my conscience, no how nor no way. . . . It hadn't ever come home to me, before, what this thing was that I was doing. But now it did; and it stayed with me, and scorched me more and more. I tried to make out to myself that *I* warn't to blame, because *I* didn't run Jim off from his rightful owner; but it warn't no use, conscience up and say, every time: "But you knowed he was running for his freedom, and you could a paddled ashore and told somebody." That was so—I couldn't get around that, no way. That was where it pinched. Conscience says to me: "What had poor Miss Watson done to you, that you could see her nigger go off right under your eyes and never say one single word? What did that poor old woman do to you, that you could treat her so mean? . . ." I got to feeling so mean and so miserable I most wished I was dead.

Jim speaks of his plan to save up to buy his wife, and then his children, out of slavery; and he adds that if the children cannot be bought he will arrange to steal them. Huck is horrified:

Thinks I, this is what comes of my not thinking. Here was this nigger which I had as good as helped to run away, coming right out flat-footed and saying he would steal his children—children that belonged to a man I didn't even know; a man that hadn't ever done me no harm.

I was sorry to hear Jim say that, it was such a lowering of him. My conscience got to stirring me up hotter than ever, until at last I says to it: "Let up on me—it ain't too late, yet—I'll paddle ashore at first light, and tell." I felt easy, and happy, and light as a feather, right off. All my troubles was gone.

This is bad morality all right. In his earliest years Huck wasn't taught any principles, and the only ones he has encountered since then are those of rural Missouri, in which slave-owning is just one kind of ownership and is not subject to critical pressure. It hasn't occurred to Huck to question those principles. So the action, to us abhorrent, of turning Jim in to the authorities presents itself *clearly* to Huck as the right thing to do.

For us, morality and sympathy would both dictate helping Jim to escape. If we felt any conflict, it would have both these on one side and something else on the other—greed for a reward, or fear of punishment. But Huck's morality conflicts with his sympathy, that is, with his unargued, natural feeling for his friend. The conflict starts when Huck sets off in the canoe towards the shore, pretending that he is going to reconnoitre, but really planning to turn Jim in:

> As I shoved off, [Jim] says: "Pooty soon I'll be a-shout'n for joy, en I'll say, it's all on accounts o' Huck I's a free man . . . Jim won't ever forgit you, Huck: you's de bes' fren' Jim's ever had; en you's de *only* fren' old Jim's got now."
>
> I was paddling off, all in a sweat to tell on him; but when he says this, it seemed to kind of take the tuck all out of me. I went along slow then, and I warn't right down certain whether I was glad I started or whether I warn't. When I was fifty yards off, Jim says:
>
> "Dah you goes, de ole true Huck; de on'y white genlman dat ever kep' his promise to ole Jim." Well, I just felt sick. But I says, I *got* to do it—I can't get *out* of it.

In the upshot, sympathy wins over morality. Huck hasn't the strength of will to do what he sincerely thinks he ought to do. Two men hunting for runaway slaves ask him whether the man on his raft is black or white:

> I didn't answer up prompt. I tried to, but the words wouldn't come. I tried, for a second or two, to brace up and out with it, but I warn't man enough—hadn't the spunk of a rabbit. I see I was weakening; so I just give up trying, and up and says: "He's white."

So Huck enables Jim to escape, thus acting weakly and wickedly—he thinks. In this conflict between sympathy and morality, sympathy wins.

One critic has cited this episode in support of the statement that Huck suffers "excruciating moments of wavering between honesty and

respectability." That is hopelessly wrong, and I agree with the perceptive comment on it by another critic, who says:

> The conflict waged in Huck is much more serious: he scarcely cares for respectability and never hesitates to relinquish it, but he does care for honesty and gratitude—and both honesty and gratitude require that he should give Jim up. It is not, in Huck, honesty at war with respectability but love and compassion for Jim struggling against his conscience. His decision is for Jim and hell: a right decision made in the mental chains that Huck never breaks. His concern for Jim is and remains *irrational*. Huck finds many reasons for giving Jim up and none for stealing him. To the end Huck sees his compassion for Jim as a weak, ignorant, and wicked felony.

Huck Finn, whose sympathies are wide and deep, opts for the only alternative he can see—to give up morality altogether. After he has tricked the slave-hunters, he returns to the raft and undergoes a peculiar crisis:

> I got aboard the raft, feeling bad and low, because I knowed very well I had done wrong, and I see it warn't no use for me to try to learn to do right; a body that don't get *started* right when he's little, ain't got no show—when the pinch comes there ain't nothing to back him up and keep him to his work, and so he gets beat. Then I thought a minute, and says to myself, hold on—s'pose you'd a done right and give Jim up; would you feel better than what you do now? No, says I, I'd feel bad—I'd feel just the same way I do now. Well, then, says I, what's the use you learning to do right, when it's troublesome to do right and ain't no trouble to do wrong, and the wages is just the same? I was stuck. I couldn't answer that. So I reckoned I wouldn't bother no more about it, but after this always do whichever come handiest at the time.

Huck clearly cannot conceive of having any morality except the one he has learned—too late, he thinks—from his society. He is not entirely a prisoner of that morality, because he does after all reject it; but for him that is a decision to relinquish morality as such; he cannot envisage revising his morality, altering its content in face of the various pressures to which it is subject, including pressures from his sympathies. For example, he does not begin to approach the thought that slavery should be rejected on moral grounds, or the thought that what he is doing is not theft because a person cannot be owned and therefore cannot be stolen. The basic trouble is that he cannot or will not engage in abstract intellectual operations of any sort. In chapter 33 he finds himself "feeling to blame, somehow" for something he knows he had no hand in; he assumes that this feeling is a deliverance of conscience; and this confirms him in his belief that conscience shouldn't be listened to:

> It don't make no difference whether you do right or wrong, a person's conscience ain't got no sense, and just goes for him *anyway*. If I had a yaller dog that didn't know no more than a person's conscience does, I would pison him. It takes up more room than all the rest of a person's insides, and yet ain't no good, nohow.

CLAUDIA CARD
A Feminist View of Ethics

CLAUDIA CARD *is professor of philosophy and women's studies at the University of Wisconsin at Madison and the author of several books on feminist philosophy. In this selection, she considers the work of Harvard psychologist Carol Gilligan and her now famous suggestion that women may have a different ethical perspective from men in the context of contemporary ethics.*

A number of feminist scholars are sympathetic to the idea, popularly associated with the work of Carol Gilligan, that an ethic of care is more characteristic of women or is more apt to be implicit in the experience and ideals of women and that an ethic of justice or rights, or abstract action-guiding principle, is more implicit in the experience of men. If some such hypothesis were true, we might expect a bias in ethical theory toward justice or rights, or at least toward abstract action-guiding principles, given the history of sexism. Such a bias appears evident in the contractarianism and utilitarianism of modern Western ethics. Yet these theories have not always been dominant. A more modest hypothesis—less exciting, perhaps less romantic—also found in Carol Gilligan's work but often not distinguished from the "justice and care" hypothesis, is that *the responsibilities of different kinds of relationships* yield different ethical preoccupations, methods, priorities, even concepts. Different kinds of relationships have been differently distributed among women and men in patriarchal society: a larger share of the responsibilities of certain personal and informal relationships to women, a larger share of the responsibilities of formal and impersonal relationships defined by social institutions

Card, Claudia, "One Feminist View of Ethics," from *Identity, Character and Morality* by Owen Flanagan and Amelie Rorty (MIT Press, 1990).

to men. It is plausible that a result has been the creation of a significant difference in ethical orientation. Putting it this way opens better to philosophical inquiry the questions of how good these relationships have been, what their virtues and vices are, their major values, their roles in a good life, in a good society. It allows us, for example, to explore the place of fairness in friendship and to note its absence as a flaw.

The hypothesis in terms of *relationships* puts us into a better position than the justice and care hypothesis to identify moral damage resulting from and perpetuating sex oppression. We need to be sensitive to the possibility, easily disguised by the honorific language of "justice" and "care," that what often pass for virtues for both sexes are vices (see Houston 1987). Histories of oppression require us to read between the lines of what we say. The privileged are liable to arrogance with its blindness to others' perspectives. The oppressed are liable to low self-esteem, ingratiation, and affiliation with abusers ("female masochism"), as well as to a tendency to dissemble, a fear of being conspicuous, and chameleonism—taking on the colors of our environment as protection against assault. Histories of exploitation lead us to identify with service, to find our value in our utility or ability to please. Moral damage among both privileged and oppressed tends to be unselfconscious, mutually reinforcing, and stubborn. Where our identities are at stake, oppression is hard to face. Beneficiaries face guilt issues and are liable to defensiveness. The oppressed face damage to an already precarious self-esteem in admitting impotence. . . .

Sigmund Freud criticized women as deficient in the sense of justice. As Carol Gilligan observes, the behavior underlying this common criticism of women by men is also often cited under different descriptions as evidence of women's "special goodness"—caring, sensitivity, responsiveness to others' needs, and appreciation of the concrete particular. Both the criticism and the praise are part of the tradition of modern Western moral philosophy. "The very thought of seeing women administer justice raises a laugh," said Arthur Schopenhauer. He thought women

"far less capable than men of understanding and sticking to universal principles," yet also that "they surpass men in the virtues of *philanthropy* and *lovingkindness [Menschenliebe],* for the origin of this is . . . intuitive." On women and principles he followed Immanuel Kant, who exclaimed, "I hardly believe the fair sex is capable of principles," and speculated instead, "Providence has put in their breast kind and benevolent sensations, a fine feeling for propriety, and a complaisant soul." The contradiction is acute in Immanuel Kant, whose views on women and on morality seem to imply that good women lack moral character.

I refer loosely to the above views from the academic canon as "the patriarchal view." Women criticize this view from different angles. Some, like Carol Gilligan, defend the moral responses attributed to women as "different but also valuable," arguing that theories by which women appear deficient are faulty. I call this "the rosy view" because it presents a fairly romantic picture of the insights of women and men. Everyone comes out looking good though not perfect; the insights of each sex, basically sound, need to be supplemented by those of the other. Other critics, like Mary Wollstonecraft reject so-called "women's goodness" as a euphemism for vices that make it easier for women to be controlled by men. Mary Wollstonecraft argued that women under sexist institutions become morally deformed, neither loving nor just. Noticing similarities between the vices of women and those of the relatively powerless men in military service, she disagreed with her contemporaries, Jean-Jacques Rousseau and Immanuel Kant, on the gender relatedness of virtues. Her view was that *duties* might vary but *virtues* are the same for everyone. She ridiculed the idea that powerless, abused, uneducated women have a special kind of goodness. I call this view, generously, "the skeptical view," for it suggests skepticism about the likelihood that the perspectives of oppressed women yield special moral insights. The correlative idea, that oppressors' perspectives are no wiser, is not developed by Mary Wollstonecraft, who was writing in

1792 to an audience of men without benefit of a supporting women's community. It is implicit in her approach, however. On this view, the problem with "women's ethics" and "men's ethics" is not that they are incomplete or underdeveloped but that they are warped from the start.

However mutually incompatible they appear, the protests of both Carol Gilligan and Mary Wollstonecraft initially seem right. I have wanted to find more truth in the rosy view. Yet the skeptical view refuses to let go of me. If the two views are to be reconciled, it seems to me utterly crucial not to deny the truths of the skeptical view. . . .

In friendship both fairness and caring are valuable. Although friendship does not usually center on formulating rules and applying them to cases, it typically does involve, as Marilyn Friedman has pointed out, a division of responsibilities in a more or less extensive mutual support system. A good friendship is fair about such divisions. Such fairness may even be a requirement of caring. Fairness in friendship also requires responsiveness to personal deserts or worthiness. If anything, to be a good friend one needs a *better* sense of fairness than to be a good citizen or soldier, an idea that makes good sense of Aristotle's report that people say that "when [we] are friends [we] have no need of justice, while when [we] are just [we] need friendship as well, and the truest form of justice is thought to be a friendly quality." If "justice" here is meant to suggest enforcement, the idea seems sound. Responsiveness where enforcement is not forthcoming is a greater test of one's fairness than where there is possible recourse to sanctions. If the idea is that the values of justice are superficial, however, it seems confused. For what makes sense of friends not needing justice is that they have the relevant values so well internalized. . . .

Women's connectedness is not always a good thing. When our *primary* relationships lack reciprocity of valuing, we risk losing (or failing to develop) self-esteem. Valuing others independently of their utility is at the core of both respect and love, and being so valued is important to self-esteem. In respect we appreciate others as like ourselves in certain fundamental ways; in love we also cherish their particularities. Identifying and valuing ourselves in terms of relationships to others who likewise identify and value themselves in relation to us can leave us with enriched self-esteem. But when our primary attachments are to those who define and value themselves by what they take to be their own achievements while they define and value us in terms of our relationships to them, we are encouraged at best to assimilate, not really to affiliate. We risk becoming extensions, tools. Our caring does not have the same meaning that it has when it is valued because it comes from us. It is not the same source of self-esteem. . . .

The promising idea I find in the hypothesis that "women's ethics" can deepen and correct modern Western ethical theory is that the informal and personal relationships salient in women's lives raise issues of the ethics of attachment that are not reducible to the issues of control that have preoccupied contractualist and utilitarian theorists. Informal, personal relationships are as basic as any relationships in our lives. Acknowledging this does not imply that women have more or better knowledge of the ethics of such relationships. What women more clearly have had is more than our share of the responsibility for maintaining these kinds of relationships and less than our share of the responsibilities of participating in and defining formal institutions.

ROBERT KANE
Through the Moral Maze

ROBERT KANE *teaches philosophy at the University of Texas and has written books on ethics and free will. His primary focus is on questions of ethical pluralism and tolerance, and he summarizes those concerns here.*

A TOWER OF BABEL

THE ancient image of the Tower of Babel has been used by more than a few modern writers to describe the current state of discourse about ethics and values. There is no one "spirit of the times," but many—*too* many in fact—too many competing voices, philosophies, and religions, too many points of view on moral issues, too many interpretations of even our most sacred documents, our Bibles and Constitutions. Only the most unthinking persons can fail to be affected by this pluralism of points of view and not wonder, as a consequence, about the truth of their own beliefs. . . .

Among the consequences of the modern Tower of Babel is a pervasive temptation to embrace relativism, the view that there are no objective or "absolute" values that hold for *all* persons and *all* times. Judgments about the good and the right, it is said, can only be correct for some persons or societies or times, but not for all persons, societies, or times. In support of such a view, there are widespread doubts about the very possibility of making absolute or universal judgments that transcend our always limited points of view. New trends in the social sciences and humanities, some of them with popular names like "postmodernism" or "poststructuralism," make much of the fact that all our views about the world are historically and culturally conditioned. We always see things from a particular point of view (a "conceptual framework," or

"language game," or "cultural tradition"). How can we therefore show that our point of view, or any other, is the right one and competing views wrong, when we must assume the basic presuppositions of some particular point of view to support our claims? How can we climb out of our historically and culturally limited perspectives to find an Archimedean point, an absolute standpoint above the particular and competing points of view?

This problem haunts the modern intellectual landscape. One sees variations of it everywhere in different fields of study, and everywhere it produces doubts among reflective persons about the possibility of justifying belief in objective intellectual, cultural, and moral standards. Many modern thinkers, to be sure, deplore the resulting drift toward relativism or skepticism, arguing that we need to restore belief in objective truth and value. But it is one thing to say this and another to show how it can be done. For the problem of finding an Archimedean point above the pluralism of competing points of view is a complex one, which thinkers have been wrestling with for centuries.

I no longer believe the older ways of solving this problem will work as they did for past generations. . . . If we are not to drift into relativism, therefore, some new ways of thinking about the problem of value are needed. Alasdair MacIntyre is right, I think, to say that the current state of moral discourse is one of grave disrepair, but I am not entirely satisfied with his or any

Kane, Robert, "Through the Moral Maze," from *Through the Moral Maze* (Paragon Books, 1994), pp. 1–6. Reprinted by permission Paragon House.

other contemporary suggestion for repair. Some fundamental possibilities, it seems to me have been overlooked in all traditional and modern searches for absolute value. . . .

The root of present problems about values, is the existence of a pluralism of points of views about the right way to live, with no evident ways of settling disagreements between them. The ancient Tower of Babel is a fitting image for this modern condition. . . .

Mircea Eliade, the distinguished historian of religions, has said that what religions provided for their believers through the ages was a spiritual centering. Primitive peoples often identified a sacred mountain or some other place near their home as the center of the universe. The axis of the world went through that point and reached directly to the heavens. It was the spiritual center of their world and the place through which people found access to the divine.

One of the stories of modern civilization is a gradual undermining of this sense of spiritual centering. When Copernicus said that the earth was not at the center of the universe, European civilization was shocked. It was shocked even more when Giordano Bruno suggested that there were perhaps many other worlds or galaxies. So shocked, indeed, that Bruno—a less cautious man than Copernicus—was burned at the stake for bringing such bad news. This reaction was crude, but not unnatural. For the spatial center of the universe and our nearness to it had always been an image of the spiritual center and our nearness to it. The loss of one seemed a loss of the other.

But the physical center of the universe was only an image of the spiritual center for ancient peoples, and perhaps it was too crude an image. It is also possible to believe that, no matter where we are in the physical universe, we can find the spiritual center if we hold the right beliefs, those that are absolutely true, true for all persons at all times. Realizing this, primitive peoples also thought that *their* beliefs were the true beliefs and their gods *the* true gods, just as they thought that their mountain was the physical center of the universe.

But this approach to the spiritual center has also been challenged by modern civilization—in this case, not by scientific discoveries alone, but also by the existence of a Tower of Babel of conflicting beliefs. In a modern world full of diverse and conflicting religions, sects, cults, denominations, and spiritual movements, we can no longer afford to think about a spiritual center as the ancients did without considerable soul searching. Hans Küng points out that the greatest challenge for Christians in the twentieth century is coming to grips with the diversity of the world's religions and religious points of view whose presence in the global community can no longer be ignored or lightly dismissed. The same challenge exists for all religious believers. It is the threatened loss of a spiritual center—the religious counterpart of the Tower of Babel and the spiritual counterpart of discovering many worlds or galaxies beyond our own. As Huston Smith has put it, using Nietzsche's image, in the modern world we are summoned to become Cosmic Dancers, who may "have our own perspectives, but they can no longer be cast in the hard molds of oblivion to the rest."

LOSS OF MORAL INNOCENCE: PERELANDRA

A second important consequence of the encounter with a pluralism of points of view is that it takes away what might be called our *moral innocence.* How this occurs is nicely illustrated by a scene in C. S. Lewis's fantasy novel *Perelandra.* Lewis describes the journey of a man named Ransom to the planet Venus, called "Perelandra" in the novel, an idyllic world of islands floating on water and covered with exotic foliage (a veritable Eden, unlike the real Venus which is the image of hell). Ransom meets only one humanlike creature there, a green-skinned woman who tells him of her God, Maleldil, and his command that she search for a man of her own kind who also inhabits this world. Ransom and the woman talk until he complains that the floating islands are making his stomach queasy and suggests they move over to the fixed land. The woman is shocked by this suggestion and tells him that Maleldil has commanded that no one should set foot on the fixed land. This is the one thing she is forbidden to do. Ransom's response troubles and confuses her, for he says that in his world, on earth, everyone lives on the fixed land and no one believes it is wrong. Is it possible, she wonders, that there are different meanings of right and wrong and that Maleldil commands one group of people to do one thing and others to live differently? In her confusion she is tempted to move to the fixed land: if others can do it, why can't she?

As the conversation proceeds, Ransom suddenly realizes they are reenacting the story of Eve and the serpent in the Garden of Eden, and *he is playing the serpent,* tempting Eve to do the one thing that God has commanded her not to do: eat of the fruit of the tree of "knowledge of good and evil." In the biblical version, Eve eats of that fruit, Adam does so also, and as a consequence of knowing good and evil they are banished from the Garden. According to the traditional interpretation, this coming to "know good and evil" is coming to know sin through succumbing to temptation. But in *Perelandra* Lewis is suggesting another, modern interpretation of knowing good and evil. The new knowledge that tempts us to sin is the realization that there may be more than one right or wrong way of doing things, and that therefore our way may not be the only "right way." It tempts us because it weakens commitment to our own beliefs. In the resulting confusion we say, like the woman, "if others can do it, why can't we?"

Such a realization that other points of view may be right in their own ways brings an end to moral innocence—the secure feeling that the rights and wrongs learned in childhood are the only correct or true ones, unchallengeable and unambiguous. It hurls persons out of moral innocence into moral confusion, out of the Eden of childhood into the real world of conflict and ambiguity, tempting them to think that since rules are not absolutely unchallengeable or unambiguous, including their own, perhaps none is absolutely binding. One form this challenge takes

is the realization that traditional moral commandments ("Thou shalt not kill, lie, steal . . .") have exceptions in the real world; their absoluteness is questioned. But once exceptions are admitted (for example, in cases of self-defense or war), it becomes problematic where the line on exceptions is to be drawn (capital punishment? abortion? euthanasia?). Disagreements proliferate and the question asked by the woman of Perelandra returns: if others can do it, why can't I?

Failing to grasp these possibilities is to live in moral innocence. To grasp them is to learn something about the complexities of good and evil, but it is learning that comes with a bitter taste. Having tasted the fruit of the tree of knowledge of good and evil in this conspicuously modern manner, we live, so to speak, "after the modern Fall." Beliefs formerly held may survive, but they can no longer be looked upon with the same certainty and innocence. Some people have not crossed this divide, even in the modern world. But those who have crossed it cannot easily go back; any more than they can go back to believing that the earth is flat or situated at the center of the universe. . . .

PLURALISM AND UNCERTAINTY

To lose moral innocence in the modern sense of the *Perelandra* story is to be troubled by two things: *pluralism* and *uncertainty*. Being troubled by pluralism means recognizing the possibility that there are many correct senses of right and wrong (some people are required to live on the fixed land, but others are not) and so there may not be one true or absolute right or wrong. This is the Tower of Babel problem.

Now we are often told that pluralism, or diversity of points of view, does not of itself show that there are no absolute values. The mere existence of competing points of view is compatible with the fact that one of them is right and the others mistaken. This observation is true enough, but it does not go very far toward relieving uneasiness about relativism, if we are also uncertain about how to show which of the competing views is right. In other words, it is not pluralism alone that causes problems about relativism, but pluralism *plus* uncertainty about how to resolve disagreements between conflicting points of view. The two together conspire to erode convictions about the truth of one's own beliefs, just as they did for the woman on Perelandra. In Nietzsche's image, recognizing a thousand different tribes beating to a thousand different drums, we become the first people in history who are not convinced we own the truth.

The uncertainty that conspires with pluralism is actually based on a deeper philosophical problem. If we confront a plurality of conflicting points of view, how can we show that any one of them is the absolute or correct one? To argue that our own view is the right one we must present evidence. But the evidence will inevitably be collected and interpreted from our own point of view. If the debate is about good and evil, the critical evidence will include our views about good and evil, which are not going to be accepted by others who have major disagreements with our point of view in the first place. For this reason, there is a tendency to go around in circles when defending absolutes. The circularity may not always be as evident as "The Bible is absolutely right because it says so" or "I am absolutely right because I believe I am," but it seems that circularity will emerge in some form or another because we are faced with the task of defending the absolute status of our point of view *from* our point of view, which, it seems, is going to beg the question and fail in principle.

This problem of circularity lies behind those popular intellectual trends, . . . which make much of the fact that we must always see things from a particular conceptual framework or cultural tradition, and therefore can never climb out of our framework or tradition to see things from an absolute or neutral perspective above the fray. How can it be shown that our point of view, or any other, is the right one and that all competing views are wrong, when we must assume the basic presuppositions of a particular, and therefore limited, point of view in order to support our claims?

OPENNESS

I want to address those who are troubled in this way by pluralism and uncertainty, but who also have not given up the possibility of believing in absolute values or the search for them. They have lost moral innocence in the sense of the *Perelandra* story, but they are not yet willing to succumb to relativism or skepticism in ethical matters.

Ordinary persons in such a situation often have the following thought. They think to themselves that since it seems impossible to demonstrate that their view is the right one from their point of view (because of the circularity problem), and since everyone else seems to be in the same condition, the only proper attitude for everyone to take is an attitude of "openness" or tolerance, not passing judgment on other points of view from one's own. Judgments about good and evil, right and wrong, they reason, are personal matters and should be made for ourselves only and not imposed on others without their consent. Is it not true that many of the evils of the past—persecutions and wars, slavery and injustice, exploitation and oppression—have come from the opposite attitude of persons believing that they have absolute right on their side? "Evil takes root," Russian poet Joseph Brodsky has said, "when one man begins to think he is superior to another."

This line of reasoning seems natural to many persons in the face of pluralism and uncertainty, especially those who have been brought up in free and democratic societies. But it is often disparaged by theorists and philosophers. Allan Bloom thinks such an attitude is perverse. "Openness," he says, "and the relativism that makes it the only plausible stance in the face of . . . various ways of life . . . is the great insight of our time. The point is not to correct the mistakes and really be right; rather it is not to think you are right at all." Bloom thinks such an attitude of openness—an "openness of indifference," as he calls it—is the scourge of our times, infecting society, education, and young people in perverse ways because it creates an indifference to objective truth and absolute right.

Now if Bloom were correct about the consequences of this line of reasoning which ordinary persons are tempted to follow—from pluralism and uncertainty to openness or tolerance—then the results might be as perverse as he thinks they are. But I want to argue that he is wrong about where such a line of reasoning leads. Ordinary persons who think this way when faced with pluralism and uncertainty are on to something important. Their reasoning does not lead to an "openness of indifference," nor to many of the other consequences that trouble Bloom, but rather to the conclusion that some things are universally right and others universally wrong. Persons who reason in this way may not have thought out what they want to say as clearly as they should, but their instincts are sound and not perverse as Bloom charges.

CHAPTER SEVENTEEN

I LIKE IT, BUT IS IT ART?

No doubt you have some painting or poster on your wall that you look at appreciatively from time to time. You probably also have a favorite CD or cassette that you play while you are relaxing. What is it that you like about them? Why do they give you such special pleasure? Why not just hang an old newspaper on your wall and listen to the sound of two cats fighting while you relax? What is the special place in our lives of those objects that we call "art"? What makes something, a piece of printed paper or a piece of music, art? What makes something a piece of *good* art, as opposed to bad art or not art at all?

The philosophy of art is as rich and varied as the arts themselves, ranging from questions of quality, such as, what is good art and what is bad art? and what makes a piece of music great? to questions of ontology, such as, what is an "original" work of art? and what makes an object a work of art in the first place? The subject of aesthetics—which originally meant the study of sensory experience but later came to mean the study of beauty—is, like ethics, fundamentally a set of questions about values. The ultimate question in the philosophy of art is not only what art is but also what its purpose, function, and importance are in our lives. Great literature, one might suggest, is important because it provides information and carries down the essential stories of a culture. But much of literature, especially poetry, and most of art and music do not necessarily "tell a story" and may not actually convey any information (in the sense of story). Sometimes, of course, the arts are decorative, a pleasant painting to cover an otherwise bare wall, some soothing music to make a hectic day of running errands more relaxing. But such daily uses of art seem to trivialize and demean it. Beethoven's great symphonies, Rembrandt's striking self-portraits, the epics of Homer, Dante, and Tolstoy—these works inspire an almost religious fervor, and we define an entire civilization in terms of them.

And yet, there is always that nagging question about the "subjectivity" of taste. "There is no disputing over tastes," wrote David Hume, quoting some ancient writers. You enjoy watching Three Stooges reruns on television; your friend prefers reading Kafka. Is there a difference? You find yourself moved by a song that has been in the Top 40 for five weeks, which you will tire of in another three weeks, and then

557

never hear again. Your friend prefers Bach's Brandenberg concertos, and although she admits that they are hard to dance to, she nevertheless insists on her taste over yours. Is there any ground for this claim, or is she just being a snob? Is there any arguing over tastes in art? Is there, apart from established social conventions, any meaning to the term "good taste"? Is it enough that we know what we like even if we don't know what's good?

Questions of taste sometimes extend, in a fascinating philosophical way, to the nature of the object itself. What justification could there be, for example, for celebrating the artistic merit of a seven-ton slab of concrete, carefully placed in the middle of an urban mall, at great expense to the taxpayers? What justification can there be to the introduction of a soup can label or, ninety years ago, a urinal into an art museum collection? What makes one piece a work of art and another just a photograph, or just a soup can label? And what distinguishes a copy—even a first-rate copy—from the original? Why isn't the poster you buy in a museum shop for five dollars just as much a work of art as the original? In the case of music, this raises special problems: What counts as the original in any case? The first performance of a piece is often clumsy, badly done, perhaps confused, or even misinterpreted. Is this the original? Or is it the sheet music itself? The idea in the mind of the composer? Why is an original worth so much more, even more than a copy that may be superior because the original has deteriorated? Is this just a historical matter, a question of nostalgia and market value rather than aesthetics?

Until this century, there was more or less general agreement about what counted as art (or music or literature); the main source of disagreement involved questions of quality: Is this piece of art good art or bad art? The question is not just a matter of popular appeal. We all know that Rembrandt's paintings were often rejected by his clients and left to languish in Dutch attics and that Beethoven and Stravinsky were sometimes booed on the first performances of their greatest works. We want to say that these works were great even when they were not appreciated and that we (in our superior wisdom and hindsight) recognize what their contemporaries did not. But today, matters have become even more complicated. Not only do we disagree on which contemporary pieces are good, great, or terrible, but also we no longer agree even on what counts as art. A composer sits silently at a piano for ten minutes; a painting is a black canvas; a book of literature contains no punctuation and no recognizable grammar. Arthur Danto tackles this question head-on by considering some examples of modern art in which there does not seem to be any difference between the work of art and its non-art counterpart.

Traditionally, there have been two answers to the question, "What makes art good art?" The first answer holds that a good or great work of art is so by virtue of inherent *objective* qualities—that is, in the object itself. In his classic *Poetics*, Aristotle defends this approach in his definition of tragedy. The second answer instead insists that what makes a work of art good or great is its effect on the observer or audience. The Russian novelist Leo Tolstoy, in particular, argued that the observer (in his case, the reader) should be "infected by the author's condition of soul." Unlike the first, objective answer, this *subjective* answer does not guarantee any agreement about taste because different audiences, different readers, or different observers may be affected very differently by the same piece. It might even suggest that anyone's reaction to and judgment of a piece are as good as anyone else's reaction and judgment. Thus, it is still said today, "there is no disputing over tastes." In philosophy, however, there is still much disputing over the question of whether there is any disputing over tastes.

David Hume held that the maxim is true, that aesthetic judgment is subjective and that a work of art is beautiful only if it evokes a certain kind of sentiment. Hume disagreed, however, with the conclusion that aesthetic judgments could not be agreed upon.

Beauty, he argued, appeals to the "common sentiments" of mankind, and although opinions might vary, the emotional response would be universal, or at least to every observer with sound judgment. The problem is that many people lack such judgment because they are uncultivated, uneducated, inexperienced, confused, or in poor health. Durable admiration—for example, the lasting admiration for the classics, for classical authors, for the great books and works of art—may be a reliable indicator of great art, but this may be of little help when we are trying to judge the value of works produced in our own time. Hume warns against the "caprices of mode and fashion" and "the mistakes of ignorance and envy." But Mary Devereaux will warn us that this traditional sense of beauty may also have an insidious male bias as evidenced in its emphasis on the female nude.

For many years, the battle has raged in Hollywood between those who believe that adults should be allowed to choose to see (or not see) whatever movies they wish and those who believe that certain subjects and depictions are inappropriate or immoral and should be prohibited. We thus include a selection from the infamous Hays Commission responsible for setting the standards for Hollywood movies until the sixties, a set of standards which continues to cast its shadow over films and television made today. We then offer a piece by the German "Critical Theorists" Theodor Adorno and Max Horkheimer, who discuss what they called the "culture industry," the idea that culture is manufactured for ideological and political purposes. Tom Wolfe gives us a different picture of the function of art in America, and he compares our current attitudes toward art as fundamentally similar to a religion. He abandons aesthetic interpretation and instead emphasizes the social function of art, as a means of rejecting the world but at the same time legitimating wealth. Needless to say, his analysis has brought down the wrath of much of the art world.

In Arthur Danto's essay, *The Art World*, he defends the idea of art as context-dependent. What counts as a work of art in a museum might not be so considered if encountered on the street. Art, in other words, has its own "world." Then, by contrast, Kathleen Higgins considers the world of music, arguing that it is not a world unto itself but rather bound up in interesting ways with everyday life, culture, and morality. Finally, Mary Devereaux presents her controversial view on *The Male Gaze*.

ARISTOTLE

The Nature of Tragedy

ARISTOTLE's (384–322 B.C.) theory of tragedy remained the definitive work on the subject for over two thousand years, and his view that tragedy depends on some fatal flaw in character is still the basis of many modern tragedies. In the following excerpt from the Poetics, *Aristotle describes the basic ingredients of this old and noble art form.*

LET us proceed now to the discussion of Tragedy; before doing so, however, we must gather up the definition resulting from what has been said. A tragedy, then, is the imitation of an action that is serious and also, as having magnitude, complete in itself; in language with pleasurable accessories, each kind brought in separately in the parts of the work; in a dramatic, not in a narrative form; with incidents arousing pity and fear, wherewith to accomplish its catharsis of such emotions.

. . . There are in the natural order of things, therefore, two causes. Thought and Character, of their actions, and consequently of their success or failure in their lives. Now the action (that which was done) is represented in the play by the Fable or Plot. The Fable, in our present sense of the term, is simply this, the combination of the incidents, or things done in the story; whereas Character is what makes us ascribe certain moral qualities to the agents; and Thought is shown in all they say when proving a particular point or, it may be, enunciating a general truth. There are six parts consequently of every tragedy, as a whole (that is) of such or such quality, viz. a Fable or Plot, Characters, Diction, Thought, Spectacle, and Melody. . . .

The most important of the six is the combination of the incidents of the story. Tragedy is essentially an imitation not of persons but of action and life, of happiness and misery. All human happiness or misery takes the form of action; the end for which we live is a certain kind of activity, not a quality. Character gives us qualities, but it is in our actions—what we do— that we are happy or the reverse. In a play accordingly they do not act in order to portray the Characters; they include the Characters for the sake of the action. So that it is the action in it, i.e., its Fable or Plot, that is the end and purpose of the tragedy; and the end is everywhere the chief thing. . . . We maintain, therefore, that the first essential, the life and soul, so to speak, of Tragedy is the Plot; and that the Characters come second—compare the parallel in painting, where the most beautiful colours laid on without order will not give one the same pleasure as a simple black-and-white sketch of a portrait. We maintain that Tragedy is primarily an imitation of action, and that it is mainly for the sake of action that it imitates the personal agents. Third comes the element of Thought, i.e., the power of saying whatever can be said, or what is appropriate to the occasion. This is what, in the speeches in Tragedy, falls under the arts of Politics and Rhetoric; for the older poets make their personages discourse like statesmen, and the modern like rhetoricians. One must not confuse it with Character. Character in a play is that which reveals the moral purpose of the agents, i.e., the sort of thing they seek or avoid, where that is not obvious—hence there is no room for Character in a speech on a purely indifferent subject. Thought, on the other hand, is shown in

Aristotle, "The Nature of Tragedy," from *Oxford Translation of Aristotle,* Volume 11: Rhetoric & Poetics, edited by W. D. Ross, translated by Ingram Bywater, Chps. VI–XVI, sec. 1449b–1454b (Oxford University Press, 1925). Used by permission of Oxford University Press.

all they say when proving or disproving some particular point, or enunciating some universal proposition.

Having thus distinguished the parts, let us now consider the proper construction of the Fable or Plot, as that is at once the first and the most important thing in Tragedy. We have laid it down that a tragedy is an imitation of an action that is complete in itself, as a whole of some magnitude; for a whole may be of no magnitude to speak of. Now a whole is that which has beginning, middle, and end. A beginning is that which is not itself necessarily after anything else, and which has naturally something else after it; an end is that which is naturally after something itself, either as its necessary or usual consequent, and with nothing else after it; and a middle, that which is by nature after one thing and has also another after it. A well-constructed Plot, therefore, cannot either begin or end at any point one likes; beginning and end in it must be of the forms just described. Again: to be beautiful, a living creature, and every whole made up of parts, must not only present a certain order in its arrangement of parts, but also be of a certain definite magnitude. Beauty is a matter of size

and order, and therefore impossible either (1) in a very minute creature, since our perception becomes indistinct as it approaches instantaneity; or (2) in a creature of vast size—one, say, 1,000 miles long—as in that case, instead of the object being seen all at once, the unity and wholeness of it is lost to the beholder. Just in the same way, then, as a beautiful whole made up of parts, or a beautiful living creature, must be of some size, but a size to be taken in by the eye, so a story or Plot must be of some length, but of a length to be taken in by the memory. As for the limit of its length, so far as that is relative to public performances and spectators, it does not fall within the theory of poetry. If they had to perform a hundred tragedies, they would be timed by waterclocks, as they are said to have been at one period. The limit, however, set by the actual nature of the thing is this: the longer the story, consistently with its being comprehensible as a whole, the finer it is by reason of its magnitude. As a rough general formula, "a length which allows of the hero passing by a series of probable or necessary stages from misfortune to happiness, or from happiness to misfortune," may suffice as a limit for the magnitude of the story.

DAVID HUME
Of the Standard of Taste

DAVID HUME *(1711–1776) wrote on art and manners in England as well as on philosophy and history. It was Hume, more than anyone, who promoted the popular view that "there is no disputing of tastes."*

Hume, David, "Of the Standard of Taste," from *Essays: Moral, Political, and Literary,* Volume I, ed. T. H. Green and T. H. Grose, London: Logmans, Green & Co. Ltd., 1882.

THE great variety of Taste, as well as of opinion, which prevails in the world, is too obvious not to have fallen under every one's observation. Men of the most confined knowledge are able to remark a difference of taste in the narrow circle of their acquaintance, even where the persons have been educated under the same government, and have early imbibed the same prejudices. But those, who can enlarge their view to contemplate distant nations and remote ages, are still more surprised at the great inconsistence and contrariety. We are apt to call *barbarous* whatever departs widely from our own taste and apprehension: But soon find the epithet of reproach retorted on us. And the highest arrogance and self-conceit is at last startled, on observing an equal assurance on all sides, and scruples, amidst such a contest of sentiment, to pronounce positively in its own favour.

As this variety of taste is obvious to the most careless inquirer, so will it be found, on examination, to be still greater in reality than in appearance. The sentiments of men often differ with regard to beauty and deformity of all kinds, even while their general discourse is the same. There are certain terms in every language, which impart blame, and others praise; and all men, who use the same tongue, must agree in their application of them. Every voice is united in applauding elegance, propriety, simplicity, spirit in writing; and in blaming fustian, affectation, coldness, and a false brilliancy: But when critics come to particulars, this seeming unanimity vanishes; and it is found, that they had affixed a very different meaning to their expressions. In all matters of opinion and science, the case is opposite: The difference among men is there oftener found to lie in generals than in particulars; and to be less in reality than in appearance. An explanation of the terms commonly ends the controversy; and the disputants are surprised to find, that they had been quarreling, while at bottom they agreed in their judgment. . . .

It is natural for us to seek a *Standard of Taste;* a rule, by which the various sentiments of men may be reconciled; at least, a decision, afforded, confirming one sentiment, and condemning another.

There is a species of philosophy, which cuts off all hopes of success in such an attempt, and represents the impossibility of ever attaining any standard of taste. The difference, it is said, is very wide between judgment and sentiment. All sentiment is right; because sentiment has a reference to nothing beyond itself, and is always real, wherever a man is conscious of it. But all determinations of the understanding are not right; because they have a reference to something beyond themselves, to wit, real matter of fact; and are not always comformable to that standard. Among a thousand different opinions which different men may entertain of the same subject, there is one, and but one, that is just and true; and the only difficulty is to fix and ascertain it. On the contrary, a thousand different sentiments, excited by the same object, are all right: Because no sentiment represents what is really in the object. It only marks a certain conformity or relation between the object and the organs or faculties of the mind; and if that conformity did not really exist, the sentiment could never possibly have being. Beauty is no quality in things themselves: It exists merely in the mind which contemplates them; and each mind perceives a different beauty. One person may even perceive deformity, where another is sensible of beauty; and every individual ought to acquiesce in his own sentiment, without pretending to regulate those of others. To seek the real beauty, or real deformity, is as fruitless an enquiry, as to pretend to ascertain the real sweet or real bitter. According to the disposition of the organs, the same object may be both sweet and bitter; and the proverb has justly determined it to be fruitless to dispute concerning tastes. It is very natural, and even quite necessary, to extend this axiom to mental, as well as bodily taste; and thus common sense, which is so often at variance with philosophy, especially with the skeptical kind, is found, in one instance at least, to agree in pronouncing the same decision.

But though this axiom, by passing into a proverb, seems to have attained the sanction of common sense; there is certainly a species of common sense which opposes it, at least serves to modify and restrain it. Whoever would assert an equality of genius and elegance between Ogilby and Milton, or Bunyan and Addison, would be thought to defend no less an extravagance, than if he had maintained a molehill to be as high as [a mountain], or a pond as extensive as the ocean. Though there may be found persons, who give the preference to the former authors; no one pays attention to such a taste; and we pronounce without scruple the sentiment of these pretended critics to be absurd and ridiculous. The principle of the natural equality of tastes is then totally forgot, and while we admit it on some occasions, where the objects seem near an equality, it appears an extravagant paradox, or rather a palpable absurdity, where objects so disproportioned are compared together.

It is evident that none of the rules of composition are fixed by reasonings *a priori*, or can be esteemed abstract conclusions of the understanding, from comparing those habitudes and relations of ideas, which are eternal and immutable. Their foundation is the same with that of all the practical sciences, experience; nor are they any thing but general observations, concerning what has been universally found to please in all countries and in all ages. Many of the beauties of poetry and even of eloquence are founded on falsehood and fiction, on hyperboles, metaphors, and an abuse or perversion of terms from their natural meaning. To check the sallies of the imagination, and to reduce every expression to geometrical truth and exactness, would be the most contrary to the laws of criticism; because it would produce a work, which, by universal experience, has been found the most insipid and disagreeable. But though poetry can never submit to exact truth, it must be confined by rules of art, discovered to the author either by genius or observation. If some negligent or irregular writers have pleased, they have not pleased by their transgressions of rule or order, but in spite of these transgressions: They have possessed other beauties, which were conformable to just criticism; and the force of these beauties has been able to overpower censure, and give the mind a satisfaction superior to the disgust arising

from the blemishes.... If they are found to please, they cannot be faults; let the pleasure, which they produce, be ever so unexpected and unaccountable.

But though all the general rules of art are founded only on experience and on the observation of the common sentiments of human nature, we must not imagine, that, on every occasion, the feelings of men will be conformable to these rules. Those finer emotions of the mind are of a very tender and delicate nature, and require the concurrence of many favourable circumstances to make them play with facility and exactness, according to their general and established principles. The least exterior hindrance to such small springs, or the least internal disorder, disturbs their motion, and confounds the operation of the whole machine. When we would make an experiment of this nature, and would try the force of any beauty or deformity, we must choose with care a proper time and place, and bring the fancy to a suitable situation and disposition. A perfect serenity of mind, a recollection of thought, a due attention to the object; if any of these circumstances be wanting, our experiment will be fallacious, and we shall be unable to judge of the catholic and universal beauty. The relation, which nature has placed between the form and the sentiment will at least be more obscure; and it will require greater accuracy to trace and discern it. We shall be able to ascertain its influence not so much from the operations of each particular beauty, as from the durable admiration, which attends those works, that have survived all the caprices of mode and fashion, all the mistakes of ignorance and envy....

It appears then, that, amidst all the variety and caprice of taste, there are certain general principles of approbation or blame, whose influence a careful eye may trace in all operations of the mind. Some particular forms or qualities, from the original structure of the internal fabric, are calculated to please, and others to displease; and if they fail of their effect in any particular instance, it is from some apparent defect or imperfection in the organ. A man in a fever would not insist on his palate as able to decide concerning flavours; nor would one, affected with the jaundice, pretend to give a verdict with regard to colours. In each creature, there is a sound and a defective state; and the former alone can be supposed to afford us a true standard of taste and sentiment. If, in the sound state of the organ, there be an entire or a considerable uniformity of sentiment among men, we may thence derive an idea of the perfect beauty; in like manner as the appearance of objects in daylight, to the eye of a man in health, is denominated their true and real colour, even while colour is allowed to be merely a phantasm of the senses.

Many and frequent are the defects in the internal organs, which prevent or weaken the influence of those general principles, on which depends our sentiment of beauty or deformity. Though some objects, by the structure of the mind, be naturally calculated to give pleasure, it is not to be expected, that in every individual the pleasure will be equally felt. Particular incidents and situations occur, which either throw a false light on the objects, or hinder the true from conveying to the imagination the proper sentiment and perception.

One obvious cause, why many feel not the proper sentiment of beauty, is the want of that *delicacy* of imagination, which is requisite to convey a sensibility of those finer emotions. . . .

It is impossible to continue in the practice of contemplating any order of beauty, without being frequently obliged to form *comparisons* between the several species and degrees of excellence, and estimating their proportion to each other. A man, who had no opportunity of comparing the different kinds of beauty, is indeed totally unqualified to pronounce an opinion with regard to any object presented to him. By comparison alone we fix the epithets of praise or blame, and learn how to assign the due degree of each. . . .

But to enable a critic the more fully to execute this undertaking, he must preserve his mind free from all *prejudice,* and allow nothing to enter into his consideration, but the very object which is submitted to his examination. We may observe, that every work of art, in order to produce its due effect on the mind, must be surveyed in a certain point of view, and cannot be fully relished by persons, whose situation, real or imaginary, is not conformable to that which is required by the performance. . . .

It is well known, that in all questions, submitted to the understanding, prejudice is destructive of sound judgment, and perverts all operations of the intellectual faculties: It is no less contrary to good taste; nor has it less influence to corrupt our sentiment of beauty. It belongs to *good sense* to check its influence in both cases; and in this respect, as well as in many others, reason, if not an essential part of taste, is at least requisite to the operations of this latter faculty. In all the nobler productions of genius, there is a mutual relation and correspondence of parts; nor can either the beauties or blemishes be perceived by him, whose thought is not capacious enough to comprehend all those parts, and compare them with each other, in order to perceive the consistence and uniformity of the whole. Every work of art has also a certain end or purpose, for which it is calculated; and is to be deemed more or less perfect, as it is more or less fitted to attain this end. The object of eloquence is to persuade, of history to instruct, of poetry to please by means of the passions and the imagination. These ends we must carry constantly in our view, when we peruse any performance; and we must be able to judge how far the means employed are adapted to their respective purposes. Besides, every kind of composition, even the most poetical is nothing but a chain of propositions and reasonings; not always, indeed, the justest and most exact, but still plausible and specious, however disguised by the coloring of the imagination. The persons introduced in tragedy and epic poetry, must be represented as reasoning, and thinking, and concluding, and acting, suitably to their character and circumstances; and without judgment, as well as taste and invention, a poet can never hope to succeed in so delicate an undertaking. Not to mention, that the same excellence of faculties which contributes to the improvement of reason, the same clearness of conception, the same exactness of distinction, the same vivacity of apprehension, are essential to the operations of true taste, and are its infallible concomitants. It seldom, or never happens, that a man of sense, who has experience in any art, cannot judge of its beauty; and it is no less rare to meet with a man who has a just taste without a sound understanding.

Thus, though the principles of taste be universal, and, nearly, if not entirely the same in all men; yet few are qualified to give judgment on any work of art, or establish their own sentiment as the standard of beauty. . . . Strong sense, united to delicate sentiment, improved by practice, perfected by comparison, and cleared of all prejudice, can alone entitle critics to his valuable character; and the joint verdict of such, wherever they are to be found, is the true standard of taste and beauty.

But where are such critics to be found? By what marks are they to be known? How distinguish them from pretenders? These questions are embarrassing; and seem to throw us back into the same uncertainty, from which, during the course of this essay, we have endeavoured to extricate ourselves.

But if we consider the matter aright, these are questions of fact, not of sentiment. Whether any particular person be endowed with good sense and a delicate imagination, free from prejudice, may often be the subject of dispute, and be liable to great discussion and enquiry: But that such a character is valuable and estimable will be agreed in by all mankind. Where these doubts occur, men can do no more than in other disputable questions, which are submitted to the understanding: They must produce the best arguments, that their invention suggests to them; they must acknowledge a true and decisive standard to exist somewhere, to wit, real existence and matter of fact; and they must have indulgence to such as differ from them in their appeals to this standard. It is sufficient for our present purpose, if we have proved, that the taste of all individuals is not upon an equal footing, and that some men in general, however difficult to be particularly pitched upon, will be acknowledged by universal sentiment to have a preference above others.

LEO TOLSTOY

What Is Art?

LEO TOLSTOY *(1828–1910), the author of such classics as* War and Peace *and* Anna Karenina, *also wrote extensively on art and religion. His theory of art as the sincere expression and communication of the artist's moral and religious feelings has been extremely influential and is still being vigorously argued by artists and writers today.*

EVERY work of art causes the receiver to enter into a certain kind of relationship both with him who produced, or is producing, the art, and with all those who, simultaneously, previously, or subsequently, receive the same artistic impression.

Speech, transmitting the thoughts and experiences of men, serves as a means of union among them, and art acts in similar manner. The peculiarity of this latter means of intercourse, distinguishing it from intercourse by means of words, consists in this, that whereas by words a man transmits his thoughts to another, by means of art he transmits his feelings.

The activity of art is based on the fact that a man, receiving through his sense of hearing or sight another man's expression of feeling, is capable of experiencing the emotion which moved the man who expressed it. To take the simplest example: one man laughs, and another who hears becomes merry; or a man weeps, and another who hears feels sorrow. A man is excited or irritated, and another man seeing him comes to a similar state of mind. By his movements or by the sounds of his voice, a man expresses courage and determination or sadness and calmness, and this state of mind passes on to others. A man suffers, expressing his sufferings by groans and spasms, and this suffering transmits itself to other people; a man expresses his feeling of admiration, devotion, fear, respect, or love to certain objects, persons, or phenomena, and others are infected by the same feelings of admiration, devotion, fear, respect, or love to the same objects, persons, and phenomena.

And it is upon this capacity of man to receive another man's expression of feeling and experience those feelings himself, that the activity of art is based.

If a man infects another or others directly, immediately, by his appearance or by the sounds he gives vent to at the very time he experiences the feeling; if he causes another man to yawn when he himself cannot help yawning, or to laugh or cry when he himself is obliged to laugh or cry, or to suffer when he himself is suffering— that does not amount to art.

Art begins when one person, with the object of joining another or others to himself in one and the same feeling, expresses that feeling by certain external indications. To take the simplest example: a boy, having experienced, let us say, fear on encountering a wolf, relates that encounter; and, in order to evoke in others the feeling he has experienced, describes himself, his condition before the encounter, the surroundings, the wood, his own lightheartedness, and then the wolf's appearance, its movements, the distance between himself and the wolf, etc. All this, if only the boy, when telling the story, again experiences the feelings he had lived through and infects the hearers and compels them to feel what the narrator had experienced, is art. If even the boy had not seen a wolf but had frequently been afraid of one, and if, wishing to evoke in others the fear he had felt, he invented an encounter with a wolf and recounted it so as to make his hearers share the feelings he experienced when he feared the wolf, that also would be art. And just in the same way it is art if a man, having experienced either the fear of suffering or the attraction of enjoyment (whether in reality or in imagination), expresses these feelings on canvas or in marble so that others are infected by them. And it is also art if a man feels or imagines to himself feelings of delight, gladness, sorrow, despair, courage, or despondency and the transition from one to another of these feelings, and expresses these feelings by sounds so that the hearers are infected by them and experience them as they were experienced by the composer.

The feelings with which the artist infects others may be most various—very strong or very weak, very important or very insignificant, very bad or very good: feelings of love for one's own country, self-devotion and submission to fate or to God expressed in a drama, raptures of lovers described in a novel, feelings of voluptuousness expressed in a picture, courage expressed in a triumphal march, merriment evoked by a dance, humor evoked by a funny story, the feeling of quietness transmitted by an evening landscape or by a lullaby, or the feeling of admiration evoked by a beautiful arabesque—it is all art.

If only the spectators or auditors are infected by the feelings which the author has felt, it is art.

To evoke in oneself a feeling one has once experienced, and having evoked it in oneself, then, by means of movements, lines, colors, sounds, or forms expressed in words, so to transmit that feeling that others may experience the same feeling—this is the activity of art.

Art is a human activity consisting in this, that one man consciously, by means of certain external signs, hands on to others feelings he has lived through, and that other people are infected by these feelings and also experience them. . . .

There is one indubitable indication distinguishing real art from its counterfeit, namely, the infectiousness of art. If a man, without exercising effort and without altering his standpoint on reading, hearing, or seeing another man's work, experiences a mental condition which unites him with that man and with other people who also partake of that work of art, then the object evoking that condition is a work of art. And however poetical, realistic, effectual, or interesting a work may be, it is not a work of art if it does not evoke that feeling (quite distinct from all other feelings) of joy and of spiritual union with another (the author) and with others (those who are also infected by it).

It is true that his indication is an *internal* one, and that there are people who have forgotten what the action of real art is, who expect something else from art (in our society the great majority are in this state), and that therefore such people may mistake for this aesthetic feeling the feeling of diversion and a certain excitement which they receive from counterfeits of art. But though it is impossible to undeceive these people, just as it is impossible to convince a man suffering from colorblindness that green is not red, yet, for all that, this indication remains perfectly definite to those whose feeling for art is neither perverted nor atrophied, and it clearly distinguishes the feeling produced by art from all other feelings.

The chief peculiarity of this feeling is that the receiver of a true artistic impression is so united to the artist that he feels as if the work were his own and not someone else's—as if what it expresses were just what he had long been wishing to express. A real work of art destroys, in the consciousness of the receiver, the separation between himself and the artist—not that alone, but also between himself and all whose minds receive this work of art. In this freeing of our personality from its separation and isolation, in this uniting of it with others, lies the chief characteristic and the great attractive force of art.

If a man is infected by the author's condition of soul, if he feels this emotion and this union with others, then the object which has effected this is art; but if there be no such infection, if there be not this union with the author and with others who are moved by the same work—then it is not art. And not only is infection a sure sign of art, but the degree of infectiousness is also the sole measure of excellence in art.

The stronger the infection, the better is the art as art, speaking now apart from its subject matter, i.e., not considering the quality of the feelings it transmits.

And the degree of the infectiousness of art depends on three conditions:

1. On the greater or lesser individuality of the feeling transmitted:

2. On the greater or lesser clearness with which the feeling is transmitted:

3. On the sincerity of the artist, i.e., on the greater or lesser force with which the artist himself feels the emotion he transmits.

The more individual the feeling transmitted the more strongly does it act on the receiver, the more individual the state of soul into which he is transferred, the more pleasure does the receiver obtain, and therefore the more readily and strongly does he join it.

The clearness of expression assists infection because the receiver, who mingles in consciousness with the author, is the better satisfied the more clearly the feeling is transmitted, which, as it seems to him, he has long known and felt, and for which he has only now found expression.

But most of all is the degree of infectiousness of art increased by the degree of sincerity in the artist. As soon as the spectator, hearer, or reader feels that the artist is infected by his own production, and writes, sings, or plays for himself, and not merely to act on others, this mental condition of the artist infects the receiver; and contrariwise, as soon as the spectator, reader, or hearer feels that the author is not writing, singing or playing for his own satisfaction—does not himself feel what he wishes to express—but is doing it for him, the receiver, a resistance immediately springs up, and the most individual and the newest feelings and the cleverest technique not only fail to produce any infection but actually repel.

I have mentioned three conditions of contagiousness in art, but they may be all summed into one, the last, sincerity, i.e., that the artist should be impelled by an inner need to express his feeling. That condition includes the first; for if the artist is sincere he will express the feeling as he experienced it. And as each man is different from everyone else, his feeling will be individual for everyone else; and the more individual it is—the more the artist has drawn it from the depths of his nature—the more sympathetic and sincere will it be. And this same sincerity will impel the artist to find a clear expression of the feeling which he wishes to transmit.

Therefore this third condition—sincerity—is the most important of the three. It is always complied with in peasant art, and this explains why such art always acts so powerfully; but it is a condition almost entirely absent from our upper-class art, which is continually produced by artists actuated by personal aims of covetousness or vanity.

Such are the three conditions which divide art from its counterfeits, and which also decide the quality of every work of art apart from its subject matter.

The absence of any one of these conditions excludes a work from the category of art and relegates it to that of art's counterfeits. If the work does not transmit the artist's peculiarity of feeling and is therefore not individual, if it is unintelligibly expressed, or if it has not proceeded from the author's inner need for expression—it is not a work of art. If all these conditions are present, even in the smallest degree, then the work, even if a weak one, is yet a work of art.

The presence in various degrees of these three conditions—individuality, clearness, and sincerity—decides the merit of a work of art as art, apart from subject matter. All works of art take rank of merit according to the degree in which they fulfil the first, the second, and the third of these conditions. In one the individuality of the feeling transmitted may predominate; in another, clearness of expression; in a third, sincerity; while a fourth may have sincerity and individuality but be deficient in clearness; a fifth, individuality and clearness but less sincerity; and so forth, in all possible degrees and combinations.

Thus is art divided from that which is not art, and thus is the quality of art as art decided, independently of its subject matter, i.e., apart from whether the feelings it transmits are good or bad.

THE HAYS COMMISSION
The Motion Picture Production Code

WILL H. HAYS *was known for his campaigns against "smut" before he became the first president of the Motion Picture Producers and Distributors in 1922. He inspired the Motion Picture Production Code, written in 1930, which censored the sexual and social content of films.*

FOREWORD

MOTION picture producers recognize the high trust and confidence that have been placed in them by the people of the world and that have made motion pictures a universal form of entertainment.

They recognize their responsibility to the public because of this trust and because entertainment and art are important influences in the life of a nation.

Hence, though regarding motion pictures primarily as entertainment without any explicit purposes of teaching or propaganda, they know that the motion picture within its own field of entertainment may be directly responsible for spiritual or moral progress, for higher types of social life, and for much correct thinking.

On their part, they ask from the public and from public leaders a sympathetic understanding of the problems inherent in motion picture production and a spirit of cooperation that will allow the opportunity necessary to bring the motion picture to a still higher level of wholesome entertainment for all concerned.

THE PRODUCTION CODE
General Principles

1. No picture shall be produced which will lower the moral standards of those who see it. Hence the sympathy of the audience shall never be thrown to the side of crime, wrongdoing, evil, or sin.

2. Correct standards of life, subject only to the requirements of drama and entertainment, shall be presented.

3. Law—divine, natural, or human—shall not be ridiculed, nor shall sympathy be created for its violation.

Particular Applications:

Crime

1. Crime shall never be presented in such a way as to throw sympathy with the crime as against law and justice, or to inspire others with a desire for imitation.

2. Methods of crime shall not be explicitly presented or detailed in a manner calculated to glamorize crime or inspire imitation.

3. Action showing the taking of human life is to be held to the minimum. Its frequent presentation tends to lessen regard for the sacredness of life.

4. Suicide, as a solution of problems occurring in the development of screen drama, is to be discouraged unless absolutely necessary for the development of the plot, and shall never be justified, or glorified, or used specifically to defeat the ends of justice.

5. Excessive flaunting of weapons by criminals shall not be permitted.

6. There shall be no scenes of law-enforcing officers dying at the hands of criminals, unless such scenes are absolutely necessary to the plot.

Hays Commission, "The, The Motion Picture Production Code," reprinted from C. Gardener, *Censorship Papers* (Dodd & Mead, New York), 1987, pp. 207–212.

7. Pictures dealing with criminal activities in which minors participate, or to which minors are related, shall not be approved if they tend to incite demoralizing imitation on the part of youth.

8. Murder:

   The technique of murder must not be presented in a way that will inspire imitation.

   • Brutal killings are not to be presented in detail.

   • Revenge in modern times shall not be justified.

   • Mercy killing shall never be made to seem right or permissible.

9. Drug addiction or the illicit traffic in addiction-producing drugs shall not be shown if the portrayal:

   • Tends in any manner to encourage, stimulate, or justify the use of such drugs; or

   • Stresses, visually or by dialog, their temporarily attractive effects; or

   • Suggests that the drug habit may be quickly or easily broken; or

   • Shows details of drug procurement or of the taking of drugs in any manner; or

   • Emphasizes the profits of the drug traffic; or

   • Involves children who are shown knowingly to use or traffic in drugs.

10. Stories on the kidnapping or illegal abduction of children are acceptable under the code only

    • when the subject is handled with restraint and discretion and avoids details, gruesomeness and undue horror; and

    • the child is returned unharmed.

Brutality

Excessive and inhuman acts of cruelty and brutality shall not be presented. This includes all detailed and protracted presentation of physical violence, torture, and abuse.

Sex

The sanctity of the institution of marriage and home shall be upheld. No film shall infer that casual or promiscuous sex relationships are the accepted or common thing.

1. Adultery and illicit sex, sometimes necessary plot material, shall not be explicitly treated, nor shall they be justified or made to seem right and permissible.

2. Scenes of passion:

   • These should not be introduced except where they are definitely essential to the plot.

   • Lustful and open-mouthed kissing, lustful embraces, suggestive posture and gestures are not to be shown.

   • In general, passion should be treated in such manner as not to stimulate the baser emotions.

3. Seduction or rape:

   • These should never be more than suggested, and then only when essential to the plot. They should never be shown explicitly.

   • They are never acceptable subject matter for comedy.

   • They should never be made to seem right and permissible.

4. The subject of abortion shall be discouraged, shall never be more than suggested, and when referred to shall be condemned. It must never be treated lightly or made the subject of comedy. Abortion shall never be shown explicitly or by inference, and story must not indicate that an abortion has been performed. The word "abortion" shall not be used.

5. The methods and techniques of prostitution and white slavery shall never be presented in detail, nor shall the subjects be presented unless shown in contrast as such may not be shown.

6. Sex perversion or any inference of it is forbidden.

7. Sex hygiene and venereal diseases are not acceptable subject matter for theatrical motion pictures.

8. Children's sex organs are never to be exposed. This provision shall not apply to infants.

Vulgarity

Vulgar expressions and double meanings having the same effect are forbidden. This shall include, but not be limited to, such words and expressions as chippie, fairy, goose, nuts, pansy, S.O.B., son-of-a. The treatment of low, disgusting, unpleasant, though not necessarily evil, subjects should be guided always by the dictates of good taste and a proper regard for the sensibilities of the audience.

Obscenity

1. Dances suggesting or representing sexual actions or emphasizing indecent movements are to be regarded as obscene.

2. Obscenity in words, gesture, reference, song, joke, or by suggestion, even when likely to be understood by only part of the audience, is forbidden.

Blasphemy and Profanity

1. Blasphemy is forbidden. Reference to the Deity, God, Lord, Jesus, Christ shall not be irreverent.

2. Profanity is forbidden. The words "hell" and "damn," while sometimes dramatically valid, will, if used without moderation, be considered offensive by many members of the audience. Their use shall be governed by the discretion and prudent advice of the Code Administration.

Costumes

1. Complete nudity, in fact or in silhouette, is never permitted, nor shall there be any licentious notice by characters in the film of suggested nudity.

2. Indecent or undue exposure is forbidden. The foregoing shall not be interpreted to exclude actual scenes photographed in a foreign land of the natives of that land, showing native life, provided:

   • Such scenes are included in a documentary film or travelogue depicting exclusively such land, its customs, and civilization; and

   • Such scenes are not in themselves intrinsically objectionable.

Religion

1. No film or episode shall throw ridicule on any religious faith.

2. Ministers of religion, or persons posing as such, shall not be portrayed as comic characters or as villains so as to cast disrespect on religion.

3. Ceremonies of any definite religion shall be carefully and respectfully handled.

Special Subjects

The following subjects must be treated with discretion and restraint within the careful limits of good tastes:

1. Bedroom scenes.

2. Hangings and electrocutions.

3. Liquor and drinking.

4. Surgical operations and childbirth.

5. Third-degree methods.

National Feelings

1. The use of the flag shall be consistently respectful.

2. The history, institutions, prominent people, and citizenry of all nations shall be represented fairly.

3. No picture shall be produced that tends to incite bigotry or hatred among peoples of differing races, religions, or national origins. The use of such offensive words as Chink, Dago, Frog, Greaser, Hunkie, Kike, Nigger, Spic, Wop, Yid should be avoided.

Titles

The following titles shall not be used:

1. Titles which are salacious, indecent, obscene, profane, or vulgar.

2. Titles which violate any other clause of this code.

Cruelty to Animals

In the production of motion pictures involving animals the producer shall consult with the authorized representative of the American Humane Association and invite him to be present during the staging of such animal action. There shall be no use of any contrivance or apparatus for tripping or otherwise treating animals in any unacceptably harsh manner.

THEODOR ADORNO AND MAX HORKHEIMER

The Culture Industry

Enlightenment as Mass Deception

THEODOR ADORNO *(1903–1969) and* MAX HORKHEIMER *(1895–1973)*
were two of the leading "Critical Theorists" who led the German philosophical revolt
against National Socialism. This famous piece originated in their book, The Dialectic of
Enlightenment.

THE sociological theory that the loss of the support of objectively established religion, the dissolution of the last remnants of precapitalism, together with technological and social differentiation or specialization, have led to cultural chaos is disproved every day for culture now impresses the same stamp on everything. Films, radio and magazines make up a system which is uniform as a whole and in every part. Even the aesthetic activities of political opposites are one in their enthusiastic obedience to the rhythm of the iron system. The decorative industrial management buildings and exhibition centers in authoritarian countries are much the same as any where else. The huge gleaming towers that shoot up everywhere are outward signs of the ingenious planning of international concerns, toward which the unleashed entrepreneurial system (whose monuments are a mass of gloomy houses and business premises in grimy, spiritless cities) was already hastening. Even now the older houses just outside the concrete city centers look like slums, and the new bungalows on the outskirts are at one with the flimsy structures of world fairs in their praise of technical progress and their built-in demand to be discarded after a short while like empty food cans. Yet the city housing projects designed to perpetuate the individual as a supposedly independent unit in a small hygienic dwelling make him all the more subservient to his adversary—the absolute power of capitalism. Because the inhabitants, as producers and as consumers, are drawn into the center in search of work and pleasure, all the living units crystallize into well-organized complexes. The striking unity of microcosm and macrocosm presents men with a model of their culture: the false identity of the general and the particular. Under monopoly all mass culture is identical, and the lines of its artificial framework begin to show through. The people at the top are no longer so interested in concealing monopoly: as its violence becomes more open, so its power grows. Movies and radio need no longer pretend to be art. The truth that they are just business is made into an ideology in order to justify the rubbish they deliberately produce. They call themselves industries; and when their directors' incomes are published, any doubt about the social utility of the finished products is removed.

Interested parties explain the culture industry in technological terms. It is alleged that because millions participate in it, certain reproduction processes are necessary that inevitably require identical needs in innumerable places to be satisfied with identical goods. The technical contrast between the few production centers and the

Adorno, Theodor and Max Horkheimer, "The Culture Industry," from *Dialectic of Enlightenment*, translated by John Cummins (New York: Herder and Herder). Copyright © 1972 Continuum Publishing Co.

large number of widely dispersed consumption points is said to demand organization and planning by management. Furthermore, it is claimed that standards were based in the first place on consumers' needs, and for that reason were accepted with so little resistance. The result is the circle of manipulation and retroactive need in which the unity of the system grows ever stronger. No mention is made of the fact that the basis on which technology acquires power over society is the power of those whose economic hold over society is greatest. A technological rationale is the rationale of domination itself. It is the coercive nature of society alienated from itself. Automobiles, bombs, and movies keep the whole thing together until their leveling element shows its strength in the very wrong which it furthered. It has made the technology of the culture industry no more than the achievement of standardization and mass production, sacrificing whatever involved a distinction between the logic of the work and that of the social system. This is the result not of a law of movement in technology as such but of its function in today's economy. The need which might resist central control has already been suppressed by the control of the individual consciousness. The step from the telephone to the radio has clearly distinguished the roles. The former still allowed the subscriber to play the role of subject, and was liberal. The latter is democratic: it turns all participants into listeners and authoritatively subjects them to broadcast programs which are all exactly the same. No machinery of rejoinder has been devised, and private broadcasters are denied any freedom. They are confined to the apocryphal field of the "amateur," and also have to accept organization from above. But any trace of spontaneity from the public in official broadcasting is controlled and absorbed by talent scouts, studio competitions and official programs of every kind selected by professionals. Talented performers belong to the industry long before it displays them; otherwise they would not be so eager to fit in. The attitude of the public, which ostensibly and actually favors the system of the culture industry, is a part of the system and not an excuse for it. If one branch of art follows the same formula as one with a very different medium and content; if the dramatic intrigue of broadcast soap operas becomes no more than useful material for showing how to master technical problems at both ends of the scale of musical experience—real jazz or a cheap imitation; or if a movement from a Beethoven symphony is crudely "adapted" for a film soundtrack in the same way as a Tolstoy novel is garbled in a film script: then the claim that this is done to satisfy the spontaneous wishes of the public is no more than hot air. We are closer to the facts if we explain these phenomena as inherent in the technical and personnel apparatus which, down to its last cog, itself forms part of the economic mechanism of selection. In addition there is the agreement—or at least the determination—of all executive authorities not to produce or sanction anything that in any way differs from their own rules, their own ideas about consumers, or above all themselves.

In our age the objective social tendency is incarnate in the hidden subjective purposes of company directors, the foremost among whom are in the most powerful sectors of industry—steel, petroleum, electricity, and chemicals. Culture monopolies are weak and dependent in comparison. They cannot afford to neglect their appeasement of the real holders of power. . . . The dependence of the most powerful broadcasting company on the electrical industry, or of the motion picture industry on the banks, is characteristic of the whole sphere, whose individual branches are themselves economically interwoven. All are in such close contact that the extreme concentration of mental forces allows demarcation lines between different firms and technical branches to be ignored. The ruthless unity in the culture industry is evidence of what will happen in politics. Marked differentiations such as those of A and B films, or of stories in magazines in different price ranges, depend not so much on subject matter as on classifying, organizing, and labeling consumers. Something is provided for all so that none may escape; the distinctions are emphasized and extended. The public is catered for with a hierarchical range of mass-produced products of varying quality, thus advancing the rule of complete quantification. Everybody must behave (as if spontaneously) in accordance with his previously determined and indexed level, and choose the category of mass product turned out for his type. Consumers appear as statistics on research organization charts, and are divided by income groups into red, green, and blue areas; the technique is that used for any type of propaganda.

How formalized the procedure is can be seen when the mechanically differentiated products prove to be all alike in the end. That the difference between the Chrysler range and General Motors products is basically illusory strikes every child with a keen interest in varieties. What connoisseurs discuss as good or bad points serve only to perpetuate the semblance of competition and range of choice. The same applies to the Warner Brothers and Metro Goldwyn Mayer productions. But even the differences between the more expensive and cheaper models put out by the same firm steadily diminish: for automobiles, there are such differences as the number of cylinders, cubic capacity, details of patented gadgets; and for films there are the number of stars, the extravagant use of technology, labor, and equipment, and the introduction of the latest psychological formulas. The universal criterion of merit is the amount of "conspicuous production," of blatant cash investment. The varying budgets in the culture industry do not bear the slightest relation to factual values, to the meaning of the products themselves. Even the technical media are relentlessly forced into uniformity. Television aims at a synthesis of radio and film, and is held up only because the interested parties have not yet reached agreement, but its consequences will be quite enormous and promise to intensify the impoverishment of aesthetic matter so drastically, that by tomorrow the thinly veiled identity of all industrial culture products can come triumphantly out into the open, derisively fulfilling the Wagnerian dream of the *Gesamtkunstwerk*—the fusion of all the arts in one work. The alliance of word,

image, and music is all the more perfect than in *Tristan* because the sensuous elements which all approvingly reflect the surface of social reality are in principle embodied in the same technical process, the unity of which becomes its distinctive content. This process integrates all the elements of the production, from the novel (shaped with an eye to the film) to the last sound effect. It is the triumph of invested capital, whose title as absolute master is etched deep into the hearts of the dispossessed in the employment line; it is the meaningful content of every film, whatever plot the production team may have selected.

The man with leisure has to accept what the culture manufacturers offer him. Kant's formalism still expected a contribution from the individual, who was thought to relate the varied experiences of the senses to fundamental concepts; but industry robs the individual of his function. Its prime service to the customer is to do his schematizing for him. Kant said that there was a secret mechanism in the soul which prepared direct intuitions in such a way that they could be fitted into the system of pure reason. But today that secret has been deciphered. While the mechanism is to all appearances planned by those who serve up the data of experience, that is, by the culture industry, it is in fact forced upon the latter by the power of society, which remains irrational, however we may try to rationalize it; and this inescapable force is processed by commercial agencies so that they give an artificial impression of being in command. There is nothing left for the consumer to classify. Producers have done it for him. Art for the masses has destroyed the dream but still conforms to the tenets of that dreaming idealism which critical idealism balked at. Everything derives from consciousness: for Malebranche and Berkeley, from the consciousness of God; in mass art, from the consciousness of the production team. Not only are the hit songs, stars, and soap operas cyclically recurrent and rigidly invariable types, but the specific content of the entertainment itself is derived from them and only appears to change. The details are interchangeable. The short interval sequence which was effective in a hit song, the hero's momentary fall from grace (which he accepts as good sport), the rough treatment which the beloved gets from the male star, the latter's rugged defiance of the spoilt heiress, are, like all the other details, ready-made cliches to be slotted in anywhere; they never do anything more than fulfill the purpose allotted them in the overall plan. Their whole *raison d'être* is to confirm it by being its constituent parts. As soon as the film begins, it is quite clear how it will end, and who will be rewarded, punished, or forgotten. In light music, once the trained ear has heard the first notes of the hit song, it can guess what is coming and feel flattered when it does come. The average length of the short story has to be rigidly adhered to. Even gags, effects, and jokes are calculated like the setting in which they are placed. They are the responsibility of special experts and their narrow range makes it easy for them to be apportioned in the office. The development of the culture industry has led to the predominance of the effect, the obvious touch, and the technical detail over the work itself—which once expressed an idea, but was liquidated together with the idea. When the detail won its freedom, it became rebellious and, in the period from Romanticism to Expressionism, asserted itself as free expression, as a vehicle of protest against the organization. In music the single harmonic effect obliterated the awareness of form as a whole; in painting the individual color was stressed at the expense of pictorial composition; and in the novel psychology became more important than structure. The totality of the culture industry has put an end to this. Though concerned exclusively with effects, it crushes their insubordination and makes them subserve the formula, which replaces the work. The same fate is inflicted on whole and parts alike. The whole inevitably bears no relation to the details—just like the career of a successful man into which everything is made to fit as an illustration or a proof, whereas it is nothing more than the sum of all those idiotic events. The so-called dominant idea is like a file which ensures order but not coherence. The whole and the parts are alike; there is no antithesis and no

connection. Their prearranged harmony is a mockery of what had to be striven after in the great bourgeois works of art. In Germany the graveyard stillness of the dictatorship already hung over the gayest films of the democratic era.

The whole world is made to pass through the filter of the culture industry. The old experience of the movie-goer, who sees the world outside as an extension of the film he has just left (because the latter is intent upon reproducing the world of everyday perceptions), is now the producer's guideline. The more intensely and flawlessly his techniques duplicate empirical objects, the easier it is today for the illusion to prevail that the outside world is the straightforward continuation of that presented on the screen. This purpose has been furthered by mechanical reproduction since the lightning takeover by the sound film.

Real life is becoming indistinguishable from the movies. The sound film, far surpassing the theater of illusion, leaves no room for imagination or reflection on the part of the audience, who is unable to respond within the structure of the film, yet deviate from its precise detail without losing the thread of the story; hence the film forces its victims to equate it directly with reality. The stunting of the mass-media consumer's powers of imagination and spontaneity does not have to be traced back to any psychological mechanisms; he must ascribe the loss of those attributes to the objective nature of the products themselves, especially to the most characteristic of them, the sound film. They are so designed that quickness, powers of observation, and experience are undeniably needed to apprehend them at all; yet sustained thought is out of the question if the spectator is not to miss the relentless rush of facts. Even though the effort required for his response is semi-automatic, no scope is left for the imagination. Those who are so absorbed by the world of the movie—by its images, gestures, and words—that they are unable to supply what really makes it a world, do not have to dwell on particular points of its mechanics during a screening. All the other films and products of the entertainment industry which they have seen have taught them what to expect; they react automatically. The might of industrial society is lodged in men's minds. The entertainments manufacturers know that their products will be consumed with alertness even when the customer is distraught, for each of them is a model of the huge economic machinery which has always sustained the masses, whether at work or at leisure—which is akin to work. From every sound film and every broadcast program the social effect can be inferred which is exclusive to none but is shared by all alike. The culture industry as a whole has molded men as a type unfailingly reproduced in every product.

In the culture industry the notion of genuine style is seen to be the aesthetic equivalent of domination. Style considered as mere aesthetic regularity is a romantic dream of the past. The unity of style not only of the Christian Middle Ages but of the Renaissance expresses in each case the different structure of social power, and not the obscure experience of the oppressed in which the general was enclosed. The great artists were never those who embodied a wholly flawless and perfect style, but those who used style as a way of hardening themselves against the chaotic expression of suffering, as a negative truth. The style of their works gave what was expressed that force without which life flows away unheard. Those very art forms which are known as classical, such as Mozart's music, contain objective trends which represent something different to the style which they incarnate. As late as Schönberg and Picasso, the great artists have retained a mistrust of style, and at crucial points have subordinated it to the logic of the matter. What Dadaists and Expressionists called the untruth of style as such triumphs today in the sung jargon of a crooner, in the carefully contrived elegance of a film star, and even in the admirable expertise of a photograph of a peasant's squalid hut. [Style represents a promise in every work of art. That which is expressed is subsumed through style into the dominant forms of generality, into the language of music, painting, or words, in the hope that it will be reconciled thus with the idea of true generality. This promise held out by the work of art that it will create truth by lending new shape to the conventional social forms is as necessary as it is hypocritical. It unconditionally posits the real forms of life as it is by suggesting that fulfillment lies in their aesthetic derivatives. To this extent the claim of art is always ideology too.] However, only in this confrontation with tradition of which style is the record can art express suffering. That factor in a work of art which enables it to transcend reality certainly cannot be detached from style; but it does not consist of the harmony actually realized, of any doubtful unity of form and content, within and without, of individual and society; it is to be found in those features in which discrepancy appears: in the necessary failure of the passionate striving for identity. Instead of exposing itself to this failure in which the style of the great work of art has always achieved self-negation, the inferior work has always relied on its similarity with others—on a surrogate identity.

In the culture industry this imitation finally becomes absolute. Having ceased to be anything but style, it reveals the latter's secret: obedience to the social hierarchy. Today aesthetic barbarity completes what has threatened the creations of the spirit since they were gathered together as culture and neutralized. To speak of culture was always contrary to culture. Culture as a common denominator already contains in embryo that schematization and process of cataloging and classification which bring culture within the sphere of administration. And it is precisely the industrialized, the consequent, subsumption which entirely accords with this notion of culture. By subordinating in the same way and to the same end all areas of intellectual creation, by occupying men's senses from the time they leave the factory in the evening to the time they clock in again the next morning with matter that bears the impress of the labor process they themselves have to sustain throughout the day, this subsumption mockingly satisfies the concept of a unified culture which the philosophers of personality contrasted with mass culture.

ARTHUR C. DANTO
The Art World

ARTHUR DANTO *is a well-known art critic and philosopher who writes regularly for* The Nation *and taught at Columbia University for most of his career. Among his many books on art are* The Transfiguration of the Commonplace *and* The Philosophical Disenfranchisement of Art. *In "The Art World," Danto considers modern art in particular and asks the question "what distinguishes art from non-art, especially where the objects seem to be the same?" He shows us the example of Andy Warhol's famous Brillo boxes and asks when is a Brillo box not just a Brillo box but a work of art?*

———

HAMLET
Do you see nothing there?

THE QUEEN
Nothing at all; yet all that is I see.

—SHAKESPEARE
Hamlet, Act III, Scene IV

HAMLET and Socrates, though in praise and deprecation respectively, spoke of art as a mirror held up to nature. As with many disagreements in attitude, this one has a factual basis. Socrates saw mirrors as but reflecting what we can already see; so art, insofar as mirrorlike, yields idle accurate duplication of the appearances of things, and is of no cognitive benefit whatsoever. Hamlet, more acutely, recognized a remarkable feature of reflecting surfaces, namely that they show us what we could not otherwise perceive our own face and form—and so art, insofar as it is mirrorlike, reveals us to ourselves, and is, even by Socratic criteria, of some cognitive utility after all. As a philosopher, however, I find Socrates' discussion defective on other, perhaps less profound grounds than these. If a mirror-image of *o* is indeed an imitation of *o*, then, if art is imitation, mirror-images are art. But in fact mirroring objects no more is art than returning weapons to a madman is justice; and reference to mirrorings would be just the sly sort of counterinstance we would expect Socrates to bring forward in rebuttal of the theory he instead uses them to illustrate. If that theory requires us to class *these as* art, it thereby shows its inadequacy: "is an imitation" will not do as a sufficient condition for "is art" Yet, perhaps because artists *were* engaged in imitation, in Socrates' time and after, the insufficiency of the theory was not noticed until the invention of photography. Once rejected as a sufficient condition, mimesis was quickly discarded as even a necessary one; and since the achievement of Kandinsky, mimetic features have been relegated to the periphery of critical concern, so much so that some works survive in spite of possessing those virtues,

"The Art World" by Arthur C. Danto, from *Journal of Philosophy*, LXI, 19 (Oct. 15, 1964), pp. 571–584. Reprinted by permission of the author and The Journal of Philosophy.

excellence in which was once celebrated as the essence of art, narrowly escaping demotion to mere illustrations.

It is, of course, indispensable in Socratic discussion that all participants be masters of the concept up for analysis, since the aim is to match a real defining expression to a term in active use, and the test for adequacy presumably consists in showing that the former analyzes and applies to all and only those things of which the latter is true. The popular disclaimer notwithstanding, then, Socrates' auditors purportedly knew what art was as well as what they liked; and a theory of art, regarded here as a real definition or "Art," is accordingly not to be of great use in helping men to recognize instances of its application. Their antecedent ability to do this is precisely what the adequacy of the theory is to be tested against, the problem being only to make explicit what they already know. It is our use of the term that the theory allegedly means to capture, but we are supposedly able, in the words of a recent writer, "to separate those objects which are works of art from those which are not, because . . . we know how correctly to use the word 'art' and to apply the phrase 'work of art.'" Theories, on this account, are somewhat like mirror-images on Socrates' account, showing forth what we already know, wordy reflections of the actual linguistic practice we are masters in.

But telling artworks from other things is not so simple a matter, even for native speakers, and these days one might not be aware he was on artistic terrain without an artistic theory to tell him so. And part of the reason for this lies in the fact that terrain is constituted artistic in virtue of artistic theories, so that one use of theories, in addition to helping us discriminate art from the rest, consists in making art possible. Glaucon and the others could hardly have known what was art and what not: Otherwise they would never have been taken in by mirror-images.

. . . Two of our pioneers—Robert Rauschenberg and Claes Oldenburg—have made genuine beds.

Rauschenberg's bed hangs on a wall, and is streaked with some desultory housepaint. Old-enburg's bed is a rhomboid, narrower at one end than the other, with what one might speak of as a built-in perspective: ideal for small bedrooms. As beds, these sell at singularly inflated prices, but one *could sleep* in either of them: Rauschenberg has expressed the fear that someone might just climb into his bed and fall asleep. Imagine, now, a certain Testadura—a plain speaker and noted philistine—who is not aware that these are art, and who takes them to be reality simple and pure. He attributes the paint streaks on Rauschenberg's bed to the slovenliness of the owner, and the bias in the Oldenburg bed to the ineptitude of the builder or the whimsy, perhaps, of whoever had it "custom-made." These would be mistakes, but mistakes of rather an odd kind, and not terribly different from that made by the stunned birds who pecked the sham grapes of Zeuxis. They mistook art for reality. And so has Testadura. . . .

How shall we describe Testadura's error? What, after all, prevents Oldenburg's creation from being a misshapen bed? This is equivalent to asking what makes it art, and with this query we enter a domain of conceptual inquiry where native speakers are poor guides: they are lost themselves.

To mistake an artwork for a real object is no great feat when an artwork is the real object one mistakes it for. The problem is how to avoid such errors, or to remove them once they are made. The artwork is a bed, and not a bed-illusion; so there is nothing like the traumatic encounter against a flat surface that brought it home to the lords of Zeuxis that they had been duped. Except for the guard cautioning Testadura not to sleep on the artworks, he might never have discovered that this was an artwork and not a bed; and since, after all, one cannot discover that a bed is not a bed, how is Testadura to realize that he has made an error? . . .

There is an *is* that figures prominently in statements concerning artworks which is not the *is* of either identity or predication; nor is it the *is* of existence, of identification, or some special *is* made up to serve a philosophic end. Nevertheless, it is in common usage, and is readily

mastered by children. It is the sense of *is* in accordance with which a child, shown a circle and
a triangle and asked which is him and which his
sister, will point to the triangle saying "That is
me"; or, in response to my question, the person
next to me points to the man in purple and says
"That one is Lear"; or in the gallery I point, for
my companion's benefit, to a spot in the painting
before us and say "That white dab is Icarus." We
do not mean, in these instances, that whatever is
pointed to stands for, or represents, what is said
to be, for the word "Icarus" stands for or represents Icarus: yet I would not in the same sense of
is point to the word and say "That is Icarus."
The sentence "That *a* is *b*" is perfectly compatible with "That *a is not b*" when the first employs
this sense of is and the second employs some
other, though *a* and *b* are used nonambiguously
throughout. Often, indeed, the truth of the first
requires the truth of the second. The first, in fact,
is incompatible with "That *a is not b*" only when
the *is* is used nonambiguously throughout. For
want of a word I shall designate this the is of
artistic identification; in each case in which it is
used, the *a* stands for some specific physical
property of, or physical part of, an object; and, finally, it is a necessary condition for something to
be an artwork that some part or property of it be
designable by the subject of a sentence that employs this special is. It is an is, incidentally,
which has near-relatives in marginal and mythical pronouncements. (Thus, one is Quetzalcoatl;
those *are* the Pillars of Hercules.) . . .

. . . Testadura, having hovered in the wings
throughout this discussion, protests [on looking
at two indiscernible paintings] that *all he sees is
paint:* a white painted oblong with a black line
painted across it. And how right he really is: that
is all he sees or that anybody can, we aesthetes
included. So, if he asks us to show him what
there is further to see, to demonstrate through
pointing that this is an artwork *(Sea and Sky),* we
cannot comply, for he has overlooked nothing
(and it would be absurd to suppose he had, that
there was something tiny we could point to and
he, peering closely, say "So it is! A work of art
after all!"). We cannot help him until he has

mastered the *is of artistic identification* and so
constitutes it a work of art. If he cannot achieve
this, he will never look upon artworks: he will be
like a child who sees sticks as sticks.

But what about pure abstractions, say something that looks just like A but is entitled No. 7?
The Tenth Street abstractionist blankly insists
that there is nothing here but white paint and
black, and none of our literary identifications
need apply. What then distinguishes him from
Testadura, whose philistine utterances are indiscernible from his? And how can it be an artwork
for him and not for Testadura, when they agree
that there is nothing that does not meet the eye?
The answer, unpopular as it is likely to be to
purists of every variety, lies in the fact that this
artist has returned to the physicality of paint
through an atmosphere compounded of artistic
theories and the history of recent and remote
painting, elements of which he is trying to refine
out of his own work; and as a consequence of
this his work belongs in this atmosphere and is
part of this history. He has achieved abstraction
through rejection of artistic identifications, returning to the real world from which such identifications remove us (he thinks), somewhat in
the mode of Ch'ing Yuan, who wrote:

> Before I had studied Zen for thirty years, I saw
> mountains as mountains and waters as waters.
> When I arrived at a more intimate knowledge, I
> came to the point where I saw that mountains are
> not mountains, and waters are not waters. But now
> that I have got the very substance I am at rest. For it
> is just that I see mountains once again as mountains,
> and waters once again as waters.

His identification of what he has made is logically dependent upon the theories and history
he rejects. The difference between his utterance
and Testadura's "This is black paint and white
paint and nothing more" lies in the fact that he is
still using the *is* of artistic identification, so that
his use of "That black paint is black paint" is not
a tautology. Testadura is not at that stage. To see
something as art requires something the eye
cannot decry—an atmosphere of artistic theory,
a knowledge of the history of art: an artworld.

Mr. Andy Warhol, the Pop artist, displays facsimiles of Brillo cartons, piled high, in neat stacks, as in the stockroom of the supermarket. They happen to be of wood, painted to look like cardboard, and why not? To paraphrase the critic of the *Times*, if one may make the facsimile of a human being out of bronze, why not the facsimile of a Brillo carton out of plywood? The cost of these boxes happens to be 2×10^1 that of their homely counterparts in real life—a differential hardly ascribable to their advantage in durability. In fact the Brillo people might, at some slight increase in cost, make their boxes out of plywood without these becoming artworks, and Warhol might make *his* out of cardboard without their ceasing to be art. So we may forget questions of intrinsic value, and ask why the Brillo people cannot manufacture art and why Warhol cannot but make artworks. Well, his are made by hand, to be sure. Which is like an insane reversal of Picasso's strategy in pasting the label from a bottle of Suze onto a drawing, saying as it were that the academic artist, concerned with exact imitation, must always fall short of the real thing: so why not just *use* the real thing? The Pop artist laboriously reproduces machine-made objects by hand, e.g., painting the labels on coffee cans (one can hear the familiar commendation "Entirely made by hand" falling painfully out of the guide's vocabulary when confronted by these objects). But the difference cannot consist in craft: a man who carved pebbles out of stones and carefully constructed a work called *Gravel Pile* might invoke the labor theory of value to account for the price he demands; but the question is, What makes it art? And why need Warhol *make* these things anyway? Why not just scrawl his signature across one? Or crush one up and display it as *Crushed Brillo Box* ("A protest against mechanization . . .") or simply display a Brillo carton as *Uncrushed Brillo Box* ("A bold affirmation of the plastic authenticity of industrial . . .")? Is this man a kind of Midas, turning whatever he touches into the gold of pure art? And the whole world consisting of latent artworks waiting, like the bread and wine of reality, to be transfigured, through some dark mystery, into the indiscernible flesh and blood of the sacrament? Never mind that the Brillo box may not be good, much less great art. The impressive thing is that it is art at all. But if it is why are not the indiscernible Brillo boxes that are in the stockroom? Or has the whole distinction between art and reality broken down?

Suppose a man collects objects (ready-mades), including a Brillo carton; we praise the exhibit for variety, ingenuity, what you will. Next he exhibits nothing but Brillo cartons, and we criticize it as dull, repetitive, self-plagiarizing—or (more profoundly) claim that he is obsessed by regularity and repetition, as in Marienbad. Or he piles them high, leaving a narrow path; we tread our way through the smooth opaque stacks and find it an unsettling experience, and write it up as the closing in of consumer products, confining us as prisoners: or we say he is a modern pyramid builder. True, we don't say these things about the stockboy. But then a stockroom is not an art gallery, and we cannot readily separate the Brillo cartons from the gallery they are in, any more than we can separate the Rauschenberg bed from the paint upon it. Outside the gallery, they are pasteboard cartons. But then, scoured clean of paint, Rauschenberg's bed is a bed, just what it was before it was transformed into art. But then if we think this matter through, we discover that the artist has failed, really and of necessity, to produce a mere real object. He has produced an artwork, his use of real Brillo cartons being but an expansion of the resources available to artists, a contribution to artists' materials, as oil paint was, or *tuche*.

What in the end makes the difference between a Brillo box and a work of art consisting of a Brillo box is a certain theory of art. It is the theory that takes it up into the world of art, and keeps it from collapsing into the real object which it is (in a sense of is other than that of artistic identification). Of course, without the theory, one is unlikely to see it as art, and in order to see it as part of the artworld, one must have mastered a good deal of artistic theory as well as a considerable amount of the history of recent New York painting. It could not have been art fifty years ago. But then there could not have been, everything being equal, flight insurance in the Middle Ages, or Etruscan typewriter erasers. The world has to be ready for certain things, the artworld no less than the real one. It is the role of artistic theories, these days as always, to make the artworld, and art, possible. It would, I should think, never have occurred to the painters of Lascaux that they were producing *art* on those walls. Not unless there were neolithic aestheticians.

Brillo boxes enter the artworld with that same tonic incongruity the *commedia dell'arte* characters bring into *Ariadne auf Naxos*. Whatever is the artistically relevant predicate in virtue of which they gain their entry, the rest of the artworld becomes that much the richer in having the opposite predicate available and applicable to its members. And, to return to the view of Hamlet with which we began this discussion, Brillo boxes may reveal us to ourselves as well as anything might: as a mirror held up to nature, they might serve to catch the conscience of our kings.

KATHLEEN M. HIGGINS
The Music of Our Lives

KATHLEEN HIGGINS *is professor of philosophy at the University of Texas, author of several books on Nietzsche and aesthetics, and the editor of* Aesthetics in Perspective.

BENEVOLENCE is akin to music," Confucius tells us; Plato claims that "musical training is a more potent instrument than any other, because rhythm and harmony find their way into the inward places of the soul, on which they mightily fasten, imparting grace, and making the soul of him who is rightly educated graceful, or of him who is ill-educated ungraceful." The pervasive influence of music, and its intimate connection with our ethical outlook, has been a matter of cross-cultural comment for millennia. The world's philosophical traditions have often treated music as a central tool for the promotion of harmonious living for both society and the individual.

But this idea seems foreign to most contemporary Americans. When I've mentioned my interest in writing a book on music and ethics, more than one acquaintance has asked, "Do you mean the controversy between Frank Zappa and Tipper Gore?" For most Americans, "rock lyrics gone wrong" is the paradigm case of music having an ethical impact. Only occasionally does one hear of the ethical impact of music apart from lyrics, and then usually as a complaint. Allan Bloom's controversial *Closing of the American Mind* devotes an entire chapter to lambasting the depravity of rock music, which in his view has "one appeal only, a barbaric appeal, to sexual desire." His vitriolic attack on a whole

Higgins, Kathleen, "The Music of Our Lives," from *The Music of Our Lives* by Kathleen Higgins, pp. 1–3, 150–154. Reprinted by permission of the author.

species of music lacks even the qualified tolerance that Nikita Khrushchev voiced when he conceded, "We are not against all jazz music. . . . But there is music which makes one feel like vomiting, and causes colic in one's stomach." Bloom at least "remembers" music serving a positive ethical function, although he despairs of its operation in a society that dances to rock 'n' roll.

Bloom is right in thinking that music can provide "cultivation of the soul" and express humanity's "noblest activities . . . while providing a pleasure extending from the lowest bodily to the highest spiritual" aspects of the human being. But he is wrong to withhold this praise from any but our tradition's classical repertoire. In this, he makes a common and pernicious rhetorical move. Bloom praises the glories of a fictitious past when everyday folks (at least the well-to-do) found spiritual sustenance in classical music (which in Bloom's usage comprises the output of a single continent over twice as many centuries). But this praise demeans our actual musical lives, in which most of us hear music almost continuously and have unprecedented resources for experiencing the wealth of music produced throughout the world and the course of our own history.

Bloom's move is pernicious because it reinforces the poverty that *does* characterize our everyday musical experience, while failing to acknowledge that it is a poverty of riches. Music is so pervasive in our environment that many of us are startled by silence; but we often feel its presence as an intrusion. For most of us, our everyday encounters with music are neither "encounters" nor "experience" in any meaningful sense. No wonder, then, that the thought of "spiritual experience" or "ethical edification" from music seems as foreign to us as Bloom's lament suggests.

The irony is that musical experience is more available than ever before. Developments in recording technology have done more than produce stars and millionaires. Recorded music can give us experiential access to an incredible range of music, a range spanning centuries and the world's cultures. While serious questions remain regarding the appropriate way to approach the music of other cultures, we have the unprecedented opportunity to *experience* it. But for the most part—with exciting exceptions like "Afro-Pop"—we take little advantage of this possibility, either as institutions or as individuals. We hear more music than our ancestors in any other era of history, and yet our sense of music's contribution to life is singularly impoverished.

• • •

As a society we regard our everyday lives as virtually immune to transformative aesthetic experience, as John Dewey complained in *Art as Experience*. Dewey blamed this on Americans' tendency to put "art" on a distant pedestal. If what he says is true with respect to all art—and I think it is—his complaint is particularly apt with respect to music. Philosophy in America, moreover, has contributed to the problem by reinforcing the divorce between "objects worthy of its consideration" and the everyday world. To be sure, philosophical discussion may not have wide-ranging cultural impact on American musical habits, but that in itself is a manifestation of the dissociation between musical aesthetics and everyday life.

Contemporary American philosophy has little place for music, let alone for the music of everyday life. Musical aesthetics is a marginal phenomenon within aesthetics, and the whole field of aesthetics is treated as a "fringe" of philosophical concern. I suspect that, in response to this marginalization, aestheticians frequently adopt more "impressive" stylistic models from other, "technical" areas of philosophy, describing the arts in overly serious and somber dissections, with as many gestures toward precision as possible. Although most willingly admit that aesthetics cannot aspire to "more precision than it admits of," in Aristotle's phrase, recent writers have assumed that it admits of a remarkable degree of precision—distorting, I argue, both the arts and aesthetic sensibility.

In musical aesthetics, such endeavors have a built-in scaffold. Western musical notation is designed to provide precise indications of pitch and rhythm. Thus, musical aestheticians have frequently set to work on the musical score, ignoring or even denying the importance of the performer and, for that matter, the listener. Nelson Goodman, for instance, considers the score the sine qua non of the musical work, so much so that if one departs in the slightest detail from the written score, one has not, on his analysis, performed the work.

The problem with this is that the score just isn't the music. Not that most philosophers are likely to say that it is. Francis Sparshott calls it a "recipe" that provides an "opportunity" for the experiences of musical performance and listening. And few besides Goodman would consider it "the truth, the whole truth" about a musical work. But the score receives undue attention. And as a consequence, the sphere of discussion becomes quite narrow. Improvisation, for example, is treated as aberrant, even though this characterization describes most of the world's music. And nonnotated features of musical experience—the vital character of performance as well as the where, the when, and the circumstances of listening—are rarely discussed.

Conservatism, ethnocentrism, and divorce from experience characterize the now established philosophical approach to music. They result from what is seen as a requirement of philosophical procedure: restriction of one's topic to yield precise results. But such restrictive analysis involves deliberate disregard for the points of connection that one phenomenon may have with another. If the idea of discussing music's connection with ethics sounds bizarre to today's philosophical audience, this is partially due to a methodological obsession with keeping subject matters distinct and isolating music not only from morals and social philosophy but even from its performance and enjoyment.

• • •

The nonstructural components of musical experience suggest reasons for believing that music has an "ethical aspect." Music's affective character, which involves intersubjective empathy and often shared delight, makes listeners socially aware of their intimate connection with others—and does so in a context in which social and individual existence are not at odds. Engaging in satisfying shared experience heightens our receptivity and emotional sensitivity. Music's motivation of listeners to appreciate the range of affective experience (and often its nuances) without the situational pressures that would lead them to decisive action (and to taking emotional sides) also enhances sensitivity to the motivations and emotional perspectives of other human beings. By so developing our potential to understand others, music serves a role of decided ethical significance. Aesthetic recognition of the importance and the extent of the emotional texture of musical experience should, therefore, lead to an appreciation of these "ethical" effects.

• • •

These claims do not entail that every human encounter with music has a positive effect on ethics, or even that every such encounter is desirable in some respect. I am assuming that the typical American's life includes at least some musical experiences that he or she values, and that the reasons for this are relevant to life outside the experience of music.

I am convinced, in addition, that openness to a broad range of musical possibilities is of value to developing ethically valuable capacities, such as openness to other human beings in general. But my basic case does not depend on the breadth or narrowness of particular listeners' musical exposure. The general features of musical experience that I depend on—such as the implicit sociability of musical experience, the multiple aspects of the listener that are simultaneously addressed, the susceptibility of "humanly organized sound" to symbolic interpretation, and its suitability to provoke analogical thought—are common to experiences of music of virtually all types and for everyone.

Admittedly, my discussion is located in a context—specifically, the context of American listening experience. I do not presume to discuss the nature of what every musical listener in the world gets out of music. Instead, I focus on the range of musical experience available within my own society. But—and I think this is important—the range of music available to Americans is incredibly large. Recording technology has made music from around the world available for American consumption. Our *own* musical experience involves the music of other societies (and the "fusion" productions of diverse cultural interactions) as well as that of many popular traditions, in addition to Western classical music.

This diversity is another reason I talk about "musical experience" generally. I am interested in

the diversity of musics available to us, and the diverse contributions that they might make to our lives. Insofar as some musics give more prominence to particular inherent potentials of sound for experience, and insofar as some of these potentials provide the basis for a comparison with certain features of ethical life, consideration of the range of our experience is essential to my effort. Music is a means of exploring the wealth of our ethical world.

MARY DEVEREAUX
The Male Gaze

MARY DEVEREAUX *teaches philosophy, feminism, and aesthetics at the University of California, San Diego.*

A T the heart of recent feminist theorizing about art is the claim that various forms of representation—painting, photography, film—assume a "male gaze." The notion of the gaze has both a literal and a figurative component. Narrowly construed, it refers to actual looking. Broadly, or more metaphorically, it refers to a way of thinking about, and acting in, the world.

In literal terms, the gaze is male when men do the looking. Men look both as spectators and as characters within works. In figurative terms, to say that the gaze is male refers to a way of seeing which takes women as its object. In this broad sense, the gaze is male whenever it directs itself at, and takes pleasure in, women, where women function as erotic objects. Many feminists claim

that most art, most of the time, places women in this position. . . .

Feminist theorists, like many other theorists, take as basic the tenet that no vision, not even artistic vision, is neutral vision. All vision is colored by the "spectacles" through which we see the world. The notion that all seeing is "a way of seeing" contrasts sharply with the traditional realist assumption that observation can be cleanly separated from interpretation, at least under certain ideally specified conditions. In part, feminist theorists can be understood as reiterating a familiar, but still important, objection to the naive notion of the innocent eye. As E. H. Gombrich convincingly argues, observation is never innocent. In his words, "Whenever we receive a visual impression, we react by docketing it, filing

Deveraux, Mary, "The Male Gaze," from *Journal of Aesthetics and Art Criticism*, vol. 48, 1990. Used by permission.

it, grouping it in one way or another, even if the impression is only that of an inkblot or a fingerprint. . . . [T]he postulate of an unbiased eye demands the impossible." Observation is always conditioned by perspective and expectation.

Yet, feminist claims that our representations inscribe a male gaze involve more than a denial of the eye's innocence. They involve asserting the central role that gender plays in formulating those expectations. Feminist theorists insist, moreover, that these expectations are disproportionately affected by male needs, beliefs and desires. Both men and women have learned to see the world through male eyes. So, for example, women throughout their lives expend enormous amounts of time and energy and money making themselves "beautiful." In undertaking this costly process, women judge themselves according to internalized standards of what is pleasing to men. As Sandra Bartky observes, adolescent girls "learn to appraise themselves as they are shortly to be appraised." In this sense, the eyes are female, but the gaze is male.

Feminist theorists object to seeing the world "through male eyes." They equate the male gaze with patriarchy. The notion of patriarchy is key here. Defined as a social system structured upon the supremacy of the father and the legal dependence of wives and children, patriarchy makes women depend upon men not only for status and privilege, but for their very identity. The assumption is that this arrangement oppresses women. It also, as both feminists and non-feminists have argued, oppresses men, although not necessarily in the same way as it oppresses women. . . .

For this reason, much of feminist theorizing about art is critical in tone. From its perspective, the artistic canon is androcentric, and hence, politically repressive. . . . Briefly summarized, the feminist critique of representation rests on the equation: the medium five male five patriarchal five oppressive.

Some will greet this equation as exaggerated, even absurd. The idea that art is political or ideologically charged contradicts the deeply held belief that art speaks to and for all human beings. Socrates' charges against the poets notwithstand-

ing, the Western European tradition characterizes art as liberating, enlightening, uplifting. Art's effects are positive; the experiences it offers intrinsically valuable. In categorizing art with other forms of patriarchal oppression, feminist theorists reject the division of art and politics basic to Anglo-American aesthetics.

The implications of this rejection are important and far-reaching. In dividing the artworld into male and female, feminist theorists irrevocably link the production and consumption of art with issues of power and control. Outside the Anglo-American paradigm, this linkage is not new. The Marxist tradition in aesthetics has long placed the concept of power at the center of the discussion of art. Marxism's emphasis on how class and other social forces and practices enter into the reading of any text lays the groundwork for feminist investigations of how gender enters the exchange with the text. . . .

To this end, I want to investigate how gendered vision works in one specific representational practice, namely film. Film is a natural choice for such a study because it is a medium so fundamentally built around the activity of looking. It is also, not surprisingly, the medium where the male gaze has been most extensively discussed. . . .

Despite the extensive literature which refers to and relies upon it, the concept of the male gaze remains difficult to understand. It is so in part because, as noted above, the male gaze refers both to literal and metaphorical vision. A further difficulty in understanding the male gaze arises from the failure to distinguish three different gazes: that of film-maker, the characters within the film and the spectator. With each of these gazes, literal and figurative seeing interact in a variety of ways.

In the first case, that of the film-maker, someone looks through the viewfinder of a camera, someone (often the same person) looks at the rushes after the day's shooting and someone looks at the film's final cut. This person may be male, but need not be. Women, too, make movies and have done so since the early days of the medium (e.g., Maya Deren, Dorothy Artner, Leni Riefenstahl).

What does it mean then to say that at this level the gaze is male? It means that despite the presence of women directors and screenwriters, the institutions of film-making remain largely populated by men. Not all films have male authors, but whoever makes movies must work nonetheless within a system owned and operated by men. At the level of the film-maker, then, men do not always do the looking, but they generally control who does. The male gaze is not always male, but *it is always male-dominated.*

By male-dominated, feminist theorists mean male-gendered, not simply possessed of male anatomy. A key move distinguishes sex from gender. A child is born sexed; through education and experience, it acquires gender. On this account, education and experience create the particular way of seeing which the term, "the male gaze," describes. Male institutional control thus refers not to the anatomy of film world personnel, which includes both men and women, but to the way film, however authored, contributes to the hegemony of men over women.

From a feminist point of view, this control matters because it "builds in" a preference for a particular type of film, i.e., one which positions women in ways consistent with patriarchal assumptions. Movies promote a way of seeing which takes man as subject, women as object. Simone de Beauvoir's *The Second Sex* puts the point succinctly. "Representation of the world, like the world itself, is the work of men; they describe it from their own point of view, which they confuse with absolute truth."

As de Beauvoir explains, women, unlike men, do not learn to describe the world from their own point of view. As the "other," woman learns to submerge or renounce her subjectivity. She finds her identity in the subjectivity of the men to whom she is attached (father, husband, lover). In the eyes of men, she finds her identity as the object of men's desire. . . .

Within the Hollywood film there is a long tradition of women performing for the camera. Women sing, dance, dress and undress, all before the steady, often adoring, gaze of an implied spectator. Frequently, female performance plays a role in the plot, as when Vivian sings for Marlowe and the audience at Eddie Mars' nightclub. But whether playing fictional characters who sing and dance before an audience or not, Marlene Dietrich, Marilyn Monroe, Ingrid Bergman and other female "stars," perform *for* the camera. As Stanley Cavell has pointed out, in photographing beautiful women, the cinema has found one of the subjects most congenial to it. But "congenial" here means the congeniality of men making films for men.

The male-controlled institutions of film-making thus place women on screen in a particular position. As eroticized objects, women are doubly victimized. As Ann Kaplan argues, the male gaze involves more than simply looking; it carries with it the threat of action and possession. This power to act and possess is not reciprocal. Women can receive and return a gaze, but they cannot act upon it.

To be fully operative as a mechanism of oppression, the male gaze depends upon a second condition. Not only must looking come with some "back-up"—physical, economic, social— but "being looked at" must also activate some level of female narcissism. Women themselves must not be indifferent to the gaze turned upon them; they must have internalized a certain assignment of positions. . . .

It would be useful at this point to make a distinction, one between objectification, aestheticization and degradation. "Objectification," as I am using the term, means no more than to make someone or something the object of my gaze. There is nothing inherently oppressive about objectification understood in this way. Nor is the filmic male gaze any more objectifying than any other gaze. Aestheticization, defined here, means simply treating people or things as objects of aesthetic contemplation. There is nothing inherently oppressive about aestheticization. Both objectification and aestheticization may be degrading, but they need not be. "Degradation" is a complex notion, associated with such concepts as respect, human dignity and worth. To degrade is to demean or debase someone, where this involves not only failing to respect, but also, in some sense, actively diminishing the value or dignity of the person.

PART SIX

JUSTICE AND RESPONSIBILITY

CHAPTER EIGHTEEN

AM I FREE TO CHOOSE WHAT I DO?

There is perhaps no topic in philosophy that inspires more public debate than the question of freedom and responsibility. Take the case of a criminal who was raised in a slum, surrounded by poverty, crime, and drugs. He went to a school in which the most academic activity was writing graffiti (most of it misspelled) on walls. He was abused as a child, beaten up as a teenager, and harassed as a young adult. His act of violence, his defense attorney argues, was nothing but the product of his environment and his upbringing. It is society's fault; he is not to blame. The prosecutor is incensed. Thousands of children grow up in similar circumstances, she argues, and they do not turn to crime. A person is free and responsible for what he or she does, she concludes, and crime must be paid for. In another case, a young would-be assassin is said to be "disturbed." He was taking drugs; he had delusions; he did not know right from wrong. His defense attorney also argues that he is not responsible. He had no choice in what he did. The public is enraged. How could a person not be responsible for an act that was planned? And so the argument goes, on the front pages of our newspapers.

Freedom and responsibility go hand in hand. We hold people responsible because we believe that they are free to act or not act in certain ways. People have choices; they make decisions. They act on the basis of knowledge and in accordance with certain values. They are not robots. It is particularly disturbing, therefore, to realize that some of our basic beliefs about the universe contradict this treasured supposition. Once upon a time, people believed (much more than we do today) in fate—the idea that everything that happens is somehow ordained to happen beforehand. For example, the ancient Greeks accepted the idea that we are often caught in horrible conflicts from which there is no acceptable escape—which is what they called *tragedy*. Saint Augustine worried how it is possible for us to be free if God, in his omniscience, knows in advance everything that we will do. God may have given us "free will," but it doesn't seem to make much sense to speak of freedom of choice if what you are going to do is already known ahead of time (even if *you* don't know it).

Modern science presents us with an even more formidable doubt about freedom. One of our basic beliefs about the world is that every event has a cause. Science may not yet have an explanation for a certain event because it may be very complicated. But we do not doubt that someday, with enough knowledge, we will explain it. And even if we cannot explain some strange event, we do not doubt that there is an explanation—even if we never find it out. This thesis is called determinism, which can be summarized as the principle that every event has a cause. But human actions and decisions are events, and if they, too, are caused or "determined" to be one way rather than another, then a very real question is whether or not it makes any sense to say that we are free to make our own decisions. We may only *seem* to be doing so, but this experience of making a decision, like our action itself, may be nothing but the result of a long sequence of causes and conditions that determines everything we do.

This is the "free will problem." It has tormented philosophers and juries for centuries, and it has practical implications that go far beyond criminal law. If we are in fact "pawns of the universe," then not only does it make no sense to hold us responsible for what we do, but also what we do is just a matter of what or who controls the determining causes. It is with this in mind that Harvard psychologist and behaviorist B. F. Skinner attacks the idea of freedom and suggests that well-meaning behavioral psychologists could and should arrange a less chaotic and more civilized deterministic environment than the one we now live in.

As science closes its explanatory grip on one realm of events after another, it would seem that determinism becomes less and less avoidable as a conclusion. But events in science itself sometimes undermine the determinist picture. In the heyday of hard determinism in about the eighteenth century (represented here by the French Baron d'Holbach), it made sense to think about the universe as composed of innumerable particles in causal relationship to one another, and this made the determinist thesis "hard" indeed. But twentieth-century physics has overthrown this picture of "matter in motion" and replaced it with a complicated model of subatomic "particles" that do not follow the classic laws of causality. Contemporary quantum theory, for instance, rejects the idea of predictable cause-and-effect relations at the fundamental level of reality, and without predictions and cause and effect, the determinist thesis does not have a foothold on our thinking. On the other hand, many scientists who accept the determinist picture insist that there is, nevertheless, room for freedom and responsibility. The great psychologist William James, for example, accepted the determinist premise but insisted that we still make decisions and can be held responsible for what we do—a position called soft determinism. Jean-Paul Sartre insists that, from one's own point of view, it makes no sense to believe that one's actions and decisions are determined.

In the following selections, we have included Aristotle's classic definition of voluntary action as that which is done neither out of "compulsion" nor out of ignorance. Baron d'Holbach states the classic case for determinism. Then Nietzsche returns to the ancient notion of "fate" and argues that the the very idea of "free will" is one of the "Four Great Errors," which have mainly to do with the scientific conceptions of "cause and effect." Instead, Nietzsche defends an existential holism, the idea that no one has any choice about whether or not to be born, or about the circumstances of life. John Hospers uses the Freudian notion of the unconscious to throw into total confusion Aristotle's definition, because compelling forces are acting within us as well as on us from the outside. Jean-Paul Sartre offers an existentialist defense of freedom, which holds that even if determinism is true, there can be no escaping the freedom and responsibility that are always ours, in every action. B. F. Skinner presents his case for behaviorist control, and philosopher Robert Kane replies. Finally, Iris Young discusses the serious problem of oppression, the denial of freedom at the hands of others.

ARISTOTLE
Voluntary and Involuntary Action

ARISTOTLE *(394–322 B.C.) uses Book III of his* Nicomachean Ethics *to understand the difference between voluntary and involuntary action. An excerpt follows.*

WE have found that moral excellence or virtue has to do with feelings and actions. These may be voluntary or involuntary. It is only to the former that we assign praise or blame, though when the involuntary are concerned we may find ourselves ready to condone and on occasion to pity. It is clearly, then, incumbent on the student of moral philosophy to determine the limits of the voluntary and involuntary. Legislators also find such a definition useful when they are seeking to prescribe appropriate rewards and punishments.

Actions are commonly regarded as involuntary when they are performed *(a)* under compulsion, *(b)* as the result of ignorance. An act, it is thought, is done under compulsion when it originates in some external cause of such a nature that the agent or person subject to the compulsion contributes nothing to it. Such a situation is created, for example, when a sea captain is carried out of his course by a contrary wind or by men who have got him in their power. But the case is not always so clear. One might have to consider an action performed for some fine end or through fear of something worse to follow. For example, a tyrant who had a man's parents or children in his power might order him to do something dishonourable on condition that, if the man did it, their lives would be spared; otherwise not. In such cases it might be hard to say whether the actions are voluntary or not. A similar difficulty is created by the jettison of cargo in a storm. When the situation has no complications you never get a man voluntarily throwing away his property. But if it is to save the life of himself and his mates, any sensible person will do it. Such actions partake of both qualities, though they look more like voluntary than involuntary acts. For at the time they are performed they are the result of a deliberate choice between alternatives, and when an action is performed the end or object of that action is held to be the end it had at the moment of its performance. It follows that the terms "voluntary" and "involuntary" should be used with reference to the time when the acts were being performed. Now in the imaginary cases we have stated the acts are voluntary. For the movement of the limbs instrumental to the action originates in the agent himself, and when this is so it is in a man's own power to act or not to act. Such actions therefore are voluntary. But they are so only in the special circumstances; otherwise of course they would be involuntary. For nobody would choose to do anything of the sort purely for its own sake. Occasionally indeed the performance of such actions is held to do a man credit. This happens when he submits to some disgrace or pain as the only way of achieving some great or splendid result. But if his case is just the opposite he is blamed, for it shows a degraded nature to submit to humiliations with only a paltry object in view, or at any rate not a high one. But there are also cases which are thought to merit, I will not say praise, but condonation. An example is provided when a man does something wrong because he is afraid of torture too severe for flesh and blood to endure. Though surely there are some things which a

Aristotle, "Voluntary and Involuntary Action," from *The Nicomachean Ethics,* trans J. E. C. Welldon. Book III, Chapter I. London: Macmillan Publishing Co., 1912, pp. 426–428.

man cannot be compelled to do—which he will rather die than do, however painful the mode of death. Such a deed is matricide; the reasons which "compelled" Alcmaeon in Euripides' play to kill his mother carry their absurdity on the face of them. Yet it is not always easy to make up our minds what is our best course in choosing one of two alternatives—such and such an action instead of such and such another—or in facing one penalty instead of another. Still harder is it to stick to our decision when made. For, generally speaking, the consequences we expect in such imbroglios are painful, and what we are forced to do far from honourable. Then we get praised or blamed according as we succumb to the compulsion or resist it.

What class of actions, then, ought we to distinguish as "compulsory"? It is arguable that the bare description will apply to any case where the cause of the action is found in things external to the agent when he contributes nothing to the result. But it may happen that actions, though, abstractly considered, involuntary, are deliberately chosen at a given time and in given circumstances in preference to a given alternative. In that case, their origin being in the agent, these actions must be pronounced voluntary in the particular circumstances and because they are preferred to their alternatives. In themselves they are involuntary, yet they have more of the voluntary about them, since conduct is a sequence of particular acts, and the particular things done in the circumstances we have supposed are voluntary. But when it comes to saying which of two alternative lines of action should be preferred—then difficulties arise. For the differences in particular cases are many.

If it should be argued that the pleasurable and honourable things exercise constraint upon us from without, and therefore actions performed under their influence are compulsory, it may be replied that this would make every action compulsory. For we all have some pleasurable or honourable motive in everything we do. Secondly, people acting under compulsion and against their will find it painful, whereas those whose actions are inspired by the pleasurable

and the honourable find that these actions are accompanied by pleasure. In the third place it is absurd to accuse external influences instead of ourselves when we fall an easy prey to such inducements and to lay the blame for all dishonourable deeds on the seductions of pleasure, while claiming for ourselves credit for any fine thing we have done. It appears, then, that an action is compulsory only when it is caused by something external to itself which is not influenced by anything contributed by the person under compulsion.

Then there are acts done through ignorance. Any act of this nature is other than voluntary, but it is involuntary only when it causes the doer subsequent pain and regret. For a man who has been led into some action by ignorance and yet has no regrets, while he cannot be said to have been a voluntary agent—he did not know what he was doing—nevertheless cannot be said to have acted involuntarily, since he feels no compunction. We therefore draw a distinction. *(a)* When a man who has done something as a result of ignorance is sorry for it, we take it that he has acted involuntarily. *(b)* When such a man is not sorry, the case is different and we shall have to call him a "non-voluntary" agent. For it is better that he should have a distinctive name in order to mark the distinction. Note, further, that there is evidently a difference between acting *in consequence* of ignorance and acting *in* ignorance. When a man is drunk or in passion his actions are not supposed to be the result of ignorance but of one or other of these conditions. But, as he does not realize what he is doing, he is acting *in* ignorance. To be sure every bad man is ignorant of what he ought to do and refrain from doing, and it is just this ignorance that makes people unjust and otherwise wicked. But when we use the word "involuntary" we do not apply it in a case where the agent does not know what is for his own good. For involuntary acts are not the consequence of ignorance when the ignorance is shown in our choice of ends; what does result from such ignorance is a completely vicious condition. No, what I mean is not general ignorance—which is what gives ground for censure—but particular ignorance, ignorance that is to say of the particular circumstances or the particular persons concerned. In such cases there may be room for pity and pardon, because a man who acts in ignorance of such details is an involuntary agent. . . .

An involuntary act being one performed under compulsion or as the result of ignorance, a voluntary act would seem to be one of which the origin or efficient cause lies in the agent, he knowing the particular circumstances in which he is acting. I believe it to be an error to say that acts occasioned by anger or desire are involuntary. For in the first place if we maintain this we shall have to give up the view that any of the lower animals, or even children, are capable of voluntary action. In the second place, when we act from desire or anger are none of our actions voluntary? Or are our fine actions voluntary, our ignoble actions, involuntary? It is an absurd

distinction, since the agent is one and the same person. It is surely paradoxical to describe as "involuntary" acts inspired by sentiments which we quite properly desire to have. There are some things at which we *ought* to feel angry, and others which we *ought* to desire—health, for instance, and the acquisition of knowledge. Thirdly, people assume that what is involuntary must be painful and what falls in with our own wishes must be pleasant. Fourthly, what difference is there in point of voluntariness between wrong actions which are calculated and wrong actions which are done on impulse? Both are to be avoided; and the further reflection suggests itself, that the irrational emotions are no less typically human than our considered judgement. Whence it follows that actions inspired by anger or desire are equally typical of the human being who performs them. Therefore to classify these actions as "involuntary" is surely a very strange proceeding. . . .

BARON D'HOLBACH
Are We Cogs in the Universe?

BARON D'HOLBACH *(1723–1789) was a French aristocrat during the Enlightenment who believed in a thoroughgoing materialism. He argued that the universe is nothing but "matter in motion" and human behavior nothing but the result of the deterministic behavior of this matter. He argues his version of "hard" determinism in the selection that follows.*

IN whatever manner man is considered, he is connected to universal nature, and submitted to the necessary and immutable laws that she imposes on all beings she contains, according to their peculiar essences or to the respective properties with which, without consulting them, she endows each particular species. Man's life is a line that nature commands him to

D'holbach, Baron, "Are We Cogs in the Universe?" from *A System of Nature,* trans. H. D. Robinson, Boston: J.P. Mendum, 1889, pp. 357–358.

describe upon the surface of the earth, without his ever being able to swerve from it, even for an instant. He is born without his own consent; his organization does in nowise depend upon himself; his ideas come to him involuntarily; his habits are in the power of those who cause him to contract them; he is unceasingly modified by causes, whether visible or concealed, over which he has no control, which necessarily regulate his mode of existence, give the hue to his way of thinking, and determine his manner of acting. He is good or bad, happy or miserable, wise or foolish, reasonable or irrational, without his will being for anything in these various states. Nevertheless, in spite of the shackles by which he is bound, it is pretended he is a free agent, or that independent of the causes by which he is moved, he determines his own will, and regulates his own condition.

However slender the foundation of his opinion, of which everything ought to point out to him the error, it is current at this day and passes for an incontestable truth with a great number of people, otherwise extremely enlightened; it is the basis of religion, which supposing relations between man and the unknown being she has placed above nature, has been incapable of imagining how man could merit reward or deserve punishment from this being, if he was not a free agent. Society has been believed interested in his system; because an idea has gone abroad, that if all the actions of man were to be contemplated as necessary, the right of punishing those who injure their associates would no longer exist. At length human vanity accommodated itself to a hypothesis which, unquestionably, appears to distinguish man from all other physical beings, by assigning to him the special privilege of a total independence of all other causes, but of which a very little reflection would have shown him the impossibility.

The will, as we have elsewhere said, is a modification of the brain, by which it is disposed to action, or prepared to give play to the organs. This will is necessarily determined by the qualities, good or bad, agreeable or painful, of the object or the motive that acts upon his sense, or

of which the idea remains with him, and is resuscitated by his memory. In consequence, he acts necessarily, his action is the result of the impulse he receives either from the motive, from the object, or from the idea which has modified his brain, or disposed his will. When he does not act according to this impulse, it is because there comes some new cause, some new motive, some new idea, which modified his brain in a different manner, gives him a new impulse, determines his will in another way, by which the action of the former impulse is suspended: thus, the sight of an agreeable object, or its idea, determines his will to set him in action to procure it; but if a new object or a new idea more powerfully attracts him, it gives a new direction to his will, annihilates the effect of the former, and prevents the action by which it was to be procured. This is the mode in which reflection, experience, reason, necessarily arrests or suspends the action of man's will: without this he would of necessity have followed the anterior impulse which carried him towards a then desirable object. In all this he always acts according to necessary laws from which he has no means of emancipating himself.

In short, the actions of man are never free; they are always the necessary consequence of his temperament, of the received ideas, and of the notions, either true or false, which he has formed to himself of happiness; of his opinions, strengthened by example, by education, and by daily experience. So many crimes are witnessed on the earth only because every thing conspires to render man vicious and criminal; the religion he has adopted, his government, his education, the examples set before him, irresistibly drive him on to evil: under these circumstances, morality preaches virtue to him in vain. In those societies where vice is esteemed, where crime is crowned, where venality is constantly recompensed, where the most dreadful disorders are punished only in those who are too weak to enjoy the privilege of committing them with impunity, the practice of virtue is considered nothing more than a painful sacrifice of happiness. Such societies chastise, in the lower orders, those excesses which they respect in the higher ranks; and frequently have the injustice to condemn those in the penalty of death, whom public prejudices, maintained by constant example, have rendered criminal.

Man, then, is not a free agent in any one instant of his life; he is necessarily guided in each step by those advantages, whether real or fictitious, that he attaches to the objects by which his passions are roused: these passions themselves are necessary in a being who unceasingly tends towards his own happiness; their energy is necessary, since that depends on his temperament; his temperament is necessary, because it depends on the physical elements which enter into his composition; the modification of this temperament is necessary, as it is the infallible and inevitable consequence of the impulse he receives from the incessant action of moral and physical beings.

FRIEDRICH NIETZSCHE
Twilight of an Error

FRIEDRICH NIETZSCHE *(1844–1900) delighted in throwing into question the most treasured presuppositions of his philosophical predecessors, for instance, the doctrine of "free will." In the following selection from "The Four Great Errors" (in his book,* Twilight of the Idols*), he attacks the very idea of free will as not only a philosophical error but also as an insidious falsification of human nature and responsibility.*

THE FOUR GREAT ERRORS

1

THE ERROR OF MISTAKING CAUSE FOR CONSEQUENCE.—There is no more dangerous error than that of *mistaking the consequence for the cause:* I call it reason's intrinsic form of corruption. Nonetheless, this error is among the most ancient and most recent habits of mankind: it is even sanctified among us, it bears the names "religion" and "morality." *Every* proposition formulated by religion and morality contains it; priests and moral legislators are the authors of this corruption of reason.—I adduce an example. Everyone knows the book of the celebrated Cornaro in which he recommends his meagre diet as a recipe for a long and happy life—a virtuous one, too. . . . The reason: mistaking the consequence for the cause. The worthy Italian saw in his diet the *cause* of his long life: while the prerequisite of long life, an extraordinarily slow metabolism, a small consumption, was the cause of his meagre diet. He was not free to eat much *or* little as he chose, his frugality was *not* an act of "free will": he became ill when he ate more. But if one is not a bony fellow of this sort one does not merely do well, one positively needs to eat *properly*. . . .

2

The most general formula at the basis of every religion and morality is: "Do this and this, refrain from this and this—and you will be happy! Otherwise. . . ." Every morality, every religion *is* this imperative—I call it the great original sin of reason, *immortal unreason*. In my mouth this formula is converted into its reverse—*first* example of my "revaluation of all values": a well-constituted human being, a "happy one," *must* perform certain actions and instinctively shrinks from other actions, he transports the order of which he is the physiological representative into his relations with other human beings and with things. In a formula: his virtue is the *consequence* of his happiness. . . . Long life, a plentiful posterity is *not* the reward of virtue, virtue itself is rather just that slowing down of the metabolism which also has, among other things, a long life, a plentiful posterity, as its outcome.—The Church and morality say: "A race, a people perishes through vice and luxury." My *restored* reason says: when a people is perishing, degenerating physiologically, vice and luxury (that is to say the necessity for stronger and stronger and more and more frequent stimulants, such as every exhausted nature is acquainted with) *follow* therefrom. A young man grows prematurely pale and faded. His friends say: this and that illness is to blame. I say: *that* he became ill, *that* he failed to resist the illness, was already the consequence of an impoverished life, an hereditary exhaustion. . . .

3

THE ERROR OF A FALSE CAUSALITY.—We have always believed we know what a cause is: but whence did we derive our knowledge, more precisely our belief we possessed this knowledge? From the realm of the celebrated "inner facts," none of which has up till now been shown to be factual. We believed ourselves to be causal agents in the act of willing; we at least thought we were there *catching causality in the act*. It was likewise never doubted that all the *antecedentia* of an action, its causes, were to be sought in the consciousness and could be discovered there if

one sought them—as "motives": for otherwise one would not have been *free* to perform it, *responsible* for it. Finally, who would have disputed that a thought is caused? that the ego causes the thought? . . . Today we do not believe a word of it. The "inner world" is full of phantoms and false lights: the will is one of them. The will no longer moves anything, consequently no longer explains anything—it merely accompanies events, it can also be absent. The so-called "motive": another error. Merely a surface phenomenon of consciousness, an accompaniment to an act, which conceals rather than exposes the *antecedentia* of the act: And as for the ego! It has become a fable, a fiction, a play on words: it has totally ceased to think, to feel and to will! . . .

7

THE ERROR OF FREE WILL.—We no longer have any sympathy today with the concept of "free will": we know only too well what it is—the most infamous of all the arts of the theologian for making mankind "accountable" in his sense of the word, that is to say for *making mankind dependent on him*. . . . I give here only the psychology of making men accountable.—Everywhere accountability is sought, it is usually the instinct for *punishing and judging* which seeks it. One has deprived becoming of its innocence if being in this or that state is traced back to will, to intentions, to accountable acts: the doctrine of will has been invented essentially for the purpose of punishment, that is of *finding guilty*. The whole of the old-style psychology, the psychology of will, has as its precondition the desire of its authors, the priests at the head of the ancient communities, to create for themselves a *right* to ordain punishments—or their desire to create for God a right to do so. . . . Men were thought of as "free" so that they could become *guilty*: consequently, every action *had* to be thought of as willed, the origin of every action as lying in the consciousness (—whereby the most *fundamental* falsification *in psychologicis* was made into the very principle of psychology). . . . Today, when we have started to move in the *reverse* direction, when we immoralists especially are trying with all our might to remove the concept of guilt and the concept of punishment from the world and to purge psychology, history, nature, the social institutions and sanctions of them, there is in our eyes no more radical opposition than that of the theologians, who continue to infect the innocence of becoming with "punishment" and "guilt" by means of the concept of the "moral world-order." Christianity is a hangman's metaphysics. . . .

8

What alone can *our* teaching be?—That no one *gives* a human being his qualities: not God, not society, not his parents or ancestors, not *he himself* (—the nonsensical idea here last rejected was propounded, as intelligible freedom, by Kant, and perhaps also by Plato before him). *No one* is accountable for existing at all, or for being constituted as he is, or for living in the circumstances and surroundings in which he lives. The fatality of his nature cannot be disentangled from the fatality of all that which has been and will be. He is *not* the result of a special design, a will, a purpose; he is *not* the subject of an attempt to attain to an "ideal of man" or an "ideal of happiness" or an "ideal of morality"—it is absurd to want to *hand over* his nature to some purpose or other. *We* invented the concept "purpose": in reality purpose is *lacking*. . . . One is necessary, one is a piece of fate, one belongs to the whole, one *is* in the whole—there exists nothing which could judge, measure, compare, condemn our being, for that would be to judge, measure, compare, condemn the whole. . . . *But nothing exists apart from the whole!*

JOHN HOSPERS
Meaning and Free Will

JOHN HOSPERS *was professor of philosophy at the University of Southern California and the author of a number of books on ethics. He ran several times for president of the United States on the Libertarian ticket. In the following he argues for a thoroughgoing determinism, not based on the model of physics but rather on psychoanalysis, which declares that all our behavior is based on unconscious motivation.*

PERHAPS the most obvious conception of freedom is this: an act is free if and only if it is a voluntary act. A response that occurs spontaneously, not as a result of your willing it, such as a reflex action, is not a free act. I do not know that this view is ever held in its pure form, but it is the basis for other ones. As it stands, of course, it is ambiguous: does "voluntary" entail "premeditated"? Are acts we perform semi-automatically through habit to be called

Hospers, John, "Meaning and Free Will," from *Philosophy and Phenomenological Research*, Vol. 10, No. 3, March 1950, pp. 313–321, 324–325, 327. Copyright by Philosophy and Phenomenological Research. Reprinted by permission of the publisher.

free acts? To what extent is a conscious decision to act required for the act to be classified as voluntary? What of sudden outbursts of feeling? They are hardly premeditated or decided upon, yet they may have their origin in the presence or absence of habit-patterns due to self-discipline which may have been consciously decided upon. Clearly the view needs to be refined.

Now, however we may come to define "voluntary," it is perfectly possible to maintain that all voluntary acts are free acts and vice versa; after all, it is a matter of what meaning we are giving to the word "free" and we can give it this meaning if we choose. But it soon becomes apparent that this is not the meaning which most of us *want* to give it: for there *are* classes of actions which we want to refrain from calling "free" even though they are voluntary (not that we have this denial in mind when we use the word "free"—still, it is significant that we do not use the word in some situations in which the act in question is nevertheless voluntary).

When a man tells a state secret under torture, he does choose voluntarily between telling and enduring more torture; and when he submits to a bandit's command at the point of a gun, he voluntarily chooses to submit rather than to be shot. And still such actions would not generally be called free; it is clear that they are performed under compulsion. Voluntary acts performed under compulsion would not be called free; and the cruder view is to this extent amended.

For some persons, this is as far as we need to go. Schlick, for example, says that the free-will issue is the scandal of philosophy and nothing but so much wasted ink and paper, because the whole controversy is nothing but an inexcusable confusion between compulsion and universal causality. The free act is the uncompelled act, says Schlick, and controversies about causality and determinism have nothing to do with the case. When one asks whether an act done of necessity is free, the question is ambiguous: if "of necessity" means "by compulsion," then the answer is no; if, on the other hand, "of necessity" is a way of referring to "causal uniformity" in nature—the sense in which we may misleadingly

speak of the laws of nature as "necessary" simply because there are no exceptions to them—then the answer is clearly yes; every act is an instance of some causal law (uniformity) or other, but this has nothing to do with its being free in the sense of uncompelled.

For Schlick, this is the end of the matter. Any attempt to discuss the matter further simply betrays a failure to perceive the clarifying distinctions that Schlick has made.

> Freedom means the opposite of compulsion; a man is *free* if he does not act under *compulsion,* and he is compelled or unfree when he is hindered from without in the realization of his natural desires. Hence he is unfree when he is locked up, or chained, or when someone forces him at the point of a gun to do what otherwise he would not do. This is quite clear, and everyone will admit that the everyday or legal notion of the lack of freedom is thus correctly interpreted, and that a man will be considered quite free . . . if no such external compulsion is exerted upon him.

This all seems clear enough. And yet if we ask whether it ends the matter, whether it states what we "really mean" by "free," many of us will feel qualms. We remember statements about human beings being pawns of their environment, victims of conditions beyond their control, the result of causal influences stemming from parents, etc., and we think, "Still, are we really free?" We do not want to say that the uniformity of nature itself binds us or renders us unfree: yet is there not something in what generations of wise men have said about man being fettered? Is there not something too facile, too sleight-of-hand, in Schlick's cutting of the Gordian knot?

It will be noticed that we have slipped from talking about acts as being free into talking about human beings as free. Both locutions are employed, I would say about 50-50. Sometimes an attempt is made to legislate definitely between the two: Stebbing, for instance, says that one must never call acts free, but only the doers of the acts.

Let us pause over this for a moment. If it is we and not our acts that are to be called free, the most obvious reflection to make is that we are free to do some things and not free to do other things; we are free to lift our hands but not free to lift the moon. We cannot simply call ourselves free or unfree *in toto;* we must say at best that we are free in respect of certain actions only. G. E. Moore states the criterion as follows: we are free to do an act if we can do it *if* we want to; that which we can do if we want to is what we are free to do. Some things certain people are free to do while others are not: most of us are free to move our legs, but paralytics are not; some of us are free to concentrate on philosophical reading matter for three hours at a stretch while others are not. In general, we could relate the two approaches by saying that a *person* is free *in respect of* a given action if he can do it if he wants to, and in this case his *act* is free.

Moore himself, however, has reservations. . . . He adds that there *is* a sense of "free" which fulfills the criterion he has just set forth; but that there may be *another* sense in which man cannot be said to be free in all the situations in which he could rightly be said to be so in the first sense.

And surely it is not necessary for me to multiply examples of the sort of thing we mean. In practice most of us would not call free many persons who behave voluntarily and even with calculation aforethought, and under no compulsion either of any obvious sort. A metropolitan newspaper headlines an article with the words "Boy Killer Is Doomed Long before He Is Born," and then goes on to describe how a twelve-year-old boy has just been sentenced to thirty years in Sing Sing for the murder of a girl; his family background includes records of drunkenness, divorce, social maladjustment, epilepsy, and paresis. He early displays a tendency to sadistic activity to hide an underlying masochism and "prove that he's a man"; being coddled by his mother only worsens this tendency, until, spurned by a girl in his attempt on her, he kills her—not simply in a fit of anger, but calculatingly, deliberately. Is he free in respect of his criminal act, or for that matter in most of the acts of his life? Surely to ask this question is to answer it in the negative. Perhaps I have taken

an extreme case; but it is only to show the superficiality of the Schlick analysis the more clearly. Though not everyone has criminotic tendencies, everyone has been moulded by influences which in large measure at least determine his present behavior; he is literally the product of these influences, stemming from periods prior to his "years of discretion," giving him a host of character traits that he cannot change now even if he would. So obviously does what a man is depend upon how a man comes to be, that it is small wonder that philosophers and sages have considered man far indeed from being the master of his fate. It is not as if man's will were standing high and serene above the flux of events that have moulded him; it is itself caught up in this flux, itself carried along on the current. An act is free when it is determined by the man's character, say moralists; but when there was nothing the man could do to shape his character, and even the degree of will power available to him in shaping his habits and disciplining himself to overcome the influence of his early environment is a factor over which he has no control, what are we to say of this kind of "freedom"? Is it not rather like the freedom of the machine to stamp labels on cans when it has been devised for just that purpose? Some machines can do so more efficiently than others, but only because they have been better constructed.

It is not my purpose here to establish this thesis in general, but only in one specific respect which has received comparatively little attention, namely, the field referred to by psychiatrists as that of unconscious motivation. In what follows I shall restrict my attention to it because it illustrates as clearly as anything the points I wish to make.

Let me try to summarize very briefly the psychoanalytic doctrine on this point. The conscious life of the human being, including the conscious decisions and volitions, is merely a mouthpiece for the unconscious—not directly for the enactment of unconscious drives, but of the compromise between unconscious drives and unconscious reproaches. There is a Big Three behind the scenes which the automaton called the conscious personality carries out: the id, an "eternal gimme," presents its wish and demands its immediate satisfaction; the superego says no to the wish immediately upon presentation, and the unconscious ego, the mediator between the two, tries to keep peace by means of compromise.

To go into examples of the functioning of these three "bosses" would be endless; psychoanalytic case books supply hundreds of them. The important point for us to see in the present context is that it is the unconscious that determines what the conscious impulse and the conscious action shall be. Hamlet, for example, had a strong Oedipus wish, which was violently counteracted by super-ego reproaches; these early wishes were vividly revived in an unusual adult situation in which his uncle usurped the coveted position from Hamlet's father and won his mother besides. This situation evoked strong strictures on the part of Hamlet's super-ego, and it was this that was responsible for his notorious delay in killing his uncle. A dozen times Hamlet could have killed Claudius easily; but every time Hamlet "decided" not to: a free choice, moralists would say—but no, listen to the super-ego: "What you feel such hatred toward your uncle for, what you are plotting to kill him for, is precisely the crime which you yourself desire to commit: to kill your father and replace him in the affections of your mother. Your fate and your uncle's are bound up together." This paralyzes Hamlet into inaction. Consciously all he knows is that he is unable to act; this conscious inability he rationalizes, giving a different excuse each time.

We have always been conscious of the fact that we are not masters of our fate in every respect—that there are many things which we cannot do, that nature is more powerful than we are, that we cannot disobey laws without danger of reprisals, etc. Lately we have become more conscious, too, though novelists and dramatists have always been fairly conscious of it, that we are not free with respect to the emotions that we feel—whom we love or hate, what types we admire, and the like. More lately still we have been reminded that there are unconscious motivations

for our basic attractions and repulsions, our compulsive actions or inabilities to act. But what is not welcome news is that our very acts of volition, and the entire train of deliberations leading up to them, are but facades for the expression of unconscious wishes, or rather, unconscious compromises and defenses.

A man is faced by a choice: shall he kill another person or not? Moralists would say, here is a free choice—the result of deliberation, an action consciously entered into. And yet, though the agent himself does not know it, and has no awareness of the forces that are at work within him, his choice is already determined for him: his conscious will is only an instrument, a slave, in the hands of a deep unconscious motivation which determines his action. If he has a great deal of what the analyst calls "free-floating guilt," he will not; but if the guilt is such as to demand immediate absorption in the form of self-damaging behavior, this accumulated guilt will have to be discharged in some criminal action. The man himself does not know what the inner clockwork is; he is like the hands on the clock, thinking they move freely over the face of the clock.

A woman has married and divorced several husbands. Now she is faced with a choice for the next marriage: shall she marry Mr. A, or Mr. B, or nobody at all? She may take considerable time to "decide" this question, and her decision may appear as a final triumph of her free will. Let us assume that A is a normal, well-adjusted, kind, and generous man, while B is a leech, an impostor, one who will become entangled constantly in quarrels with her. If she belongs to a certain classifiable psychological type, she will inevitably choose B, and she will do so even if her previous husbands have resembled B, so that one would think that she "had learned from experience." Consciously, she will of course "give the matter due consideration," etc., etc. To the psychoanalyst all this is irrelevant chaff in the wind—only a camouflage for the inner workings about which she knows nothing consciously. If she is of a certain kind of masochistic strain, as exhibited in her previous set of symptoms, she *must* choose B: her super-ego, always out to maximize the torment in the situation, seeing what dazzling possibilities for self-damaging behavior are promised by the choice of B, compels her to make the choice she does, and even to conceal the real basis of the choice behind an elaborate facade of rationalizations.

A man is addicted to gambling. In the service of his addiction he loses all his money, spends what belongs to his wife, even sells his property and neglects his children. For a time perhaps he stops; then, inevitably, he takes it up again, although he himself may think he chose to. The man does not know that he is a victim rather than an agent; or, if he sometimes senses that he is in the throes of something-he-knows-not-what, he will have no inkling of its character and will soon relapse into the illusion that he (his conscious self) is freely deciding the course of his own actions. What he does not know, of course, is that he is still taking out on his mother the original lesion to his infantile narcissism, getting back at her for her fancied refusal of his infantile wishes—and this by rejecting everything identified with her, namely education, discipline, logic, common sense, training. At the roulette wheel, almost along among adult activities, chance—the opposite of all these things—rules supreme; and his addiction represents his continued and emphatic reiteration of his rejection of Mother and all she represents to his unconscious.

This pseudo-aggression of his is of course masochistic in its effects. In the long run he always loses; he can never quit while he is winning. And far from playing in order to win, rather one can say that his losing is a *sine qua non* of his psychic equilibrium (as it was for example with Dostoyevsky): guilt demands punishment, and in the ego's "deal" with the superego the super-ego has granted satisfaction of infantile wishes in return for the self-damaging conditions obtaining. Winning would upset the neurotic equilibrium.

A man has wash-compulsion. He must be constantly washing his hands—he uses up perhaps 400 towels a day. Asked why he does this, he says, "I need to, my hands are dirty"; and if it is pointed out to him that they are not really dirty, he says "They feel dirty anyway, I feel

better when I wash them." So once again he washes them. He "freely decides" every time; he feels that he must wash them, he deliberates for a moment perhaps, but always ends by washing them. What he does not see, of course, is the invisible wires inside him pulling him inevitably to do the thing he does: the infantile id-wish concerns preoccupation with dirt, the super-ego charges him with this, and the terrified ego must respond, "No, I don't like dirt, see how clean I like to be, look how I wash my hands!" . . .

Let us take, finally, a less colorful, more everyday example. A student at a university, possessing wealth, charm, and all that is usually considered essential to popularity, begins to develop the following personality-pattern: although well taught in the graces of social conversation, he always makes a *faux pas* somewhere, and always in the worst possible situation; to his friends he makes cutting remarks which hurt deeply—and always apparently aimed in such a way as to hurt the most: a remark that would not hurt A but would hurt B he invariably makes to B rather than to A, and so on. None of this is conscious. Ordinarily he is considerate of people, but he contrives always (unconsciously) to impose on just those friends who would resent it most, and at just the times when he should know that he should not impose: at 3 o'clock in the morning, without forewarning, he phones a friend in a near-by city demanding to stay at his apartment for the weekend; naturally the friend is offended, but the person himself is not aware that he has provoked the grievance ("common sense" suffers a temporary eclipse when the neurotic pattern sets in, and one's intelligence, far from being of help in such a situation, is used in the interest of the neurosis), and when the friend is cool to him the next time they meet, he wonders why and feels unjustly treated. Aggressive behavior on his part invites resentment and aggression in turn, but all that he consciously sees is other's behavior toward him—and he considers himself the innocent victim of an unjustified "persecution."

Each of these choices is, from the moralist's point of view, free: he chose to phone his friend at 3 A.M.; he chose to make the cutting remark that he did, etc. What he does not know is that an ineradicable masochistic pattern has set in. His unconscious is far more shrewd and clever than is his conscious intellect; it sees with uncanny accuracy just what kind of behavior will damage him most, and unerringly forces him into that behavior. Consciously, the student "doesn't know why he did it"—he gives different "reasons" at different times, but they are all, once again, rationalizations cloaking the unconscious mechanism which propels him willy-nilly into actions that his "common sense" eschews.

The more of this sort of thing you see, the more you can see what the psychoanalyst means when he talks about "the illusion of free-will." And the more of a psychiatrist you become, the more you are overcome with a sense of what an illusion this precious free-will really is. In some kinds of cases most of us can see it already: it takes no psychiatrist to look at the epileptic and sigh with sadness at the thought that soon this person before you will be as one possessed, not the same thoughtful intelligent person you knew. But people are not aware of this in other contexts, for example when they express surprise at how a person whom they have been so good to could treat them so badly. Let us suppose that you help a person financially or morally or in some other way, so that he is in your debt; suppose further that he is one of the many neurotics who unconsciously identify kindness with weakness and aggression with strength, then he will unconsciously take your kindness to him as weakness and use it as the occasion for enacting some aggression against you. He can't help it, he may regret it himself later; still, he will be driven to do it. If we gain a little knowledge of psychiatry, we can look at him with pity, that a person otherwise so worthy should be so unreliable— but we will exercise realism too and be aware that there are some types of people that you cannot be good to: in "free" acts of their conscious volition, they will use your own goodness against you.

Sometimes the persons themselves will become dimly aware that "something behind the scenes" is determining their behavior. The divorcee will sometimes view herself with detachment, as if she were some machine (and indeed the psychoanalyst does call her a "repeating-machine"): "I know I'm caught in a net, that I'll fall in love with this guy and marry him and the whole ridiculous merry-go-round will start all over again."

We talk about free will, and we say, yes, the person is free to do so-and-so if he can do so *if* he wants to—and we forget that his wanting to is itself caught up in the stream of determinism, that unconscious forces drive him into the wanting or not wanting to do the thing in question. The idea of the puppet whose motions are manipulated from behind by invisible wires, or better still, by springs inside, is no mere figure of speech. The analogy is a telling one at almost every point. . . .

Now, what of the notion of responsibility? What happens to it on our analysis?

Let us begin with an example, not a fictitious one. A woman and her two-year-old baby are riding on a train to Montreal in mid-winter. The child is ill. The woman wants badly to get to her destination. She is, unknown to herself, the victim of a neurotic conflict whose nature is irrelevant here except for the fact that it forces her to behave aggressively toward the child, partly to spite her husband whom she despises and who loves the child, but chiefly to ward off super-ego charges of masochistic attachment. Consciously she loves the child, and when she says this she says it sincerely, but she must behave aggressively toward it nevertheless, just as many children love their mothers but are nasty to them most of the time in neurotic pseudo-aggression. The child becomes more ill as the train approaches Montreal; the heating system of the train is not working, and the conductor advises the woman to get off the train at the next town and get the child to a hospital at once. The woman says no, she must get to Montreal. Shortly afterward, the child's condition worsens, and the mother does all she can do keep it alive, without, however, leaving the train, for she declares that it is absolutely necessary that she reach her destination. But before she gets there the child is dead. After that, of course, the mother grieves, blames herself, weeps hysterically, and joins the church to gain surcease from the guilt that constantly overwhelms her when she thinks of how her aggressive behavior has killed her child.

Was she responsible for her deed? In ordinary life, after making a mistake, we say, "Chalk it up to experience" Here we say, "Chalk it up to the neurosis." No, she is not responsible. She could not help it if her neurosis forced her to act this way—she didn't even know what was going on behind the scenes, she merely acted out the part assigned to her. This is far more true than is generally realized: criminal actions in general are not actions for which their agents are responsible; the agents are passive, not active—they are victims of a neurotic conflict. Their very hyperactivity is unconsciously determined.

To say this is, of course, not to say that we should not punish criminals. Clearly, for our own protection, we must remove them from our midst so that they can no longer molest and endanger organized society. And, of course, if we use the word "responsible" in such a way that justly to hold someone responsible for a deed is by definition identical with being justified in punishing him, then we can and do hold people responsible. But this is like the sense of "free" in which free acts are voluntary ones. It does not go deep enough. In a deeper sense we cannot hold the person responsible: we may hold his neurosis responsible, but he is not responsible for his neurosis, particularly since the age at which its onset was inevitable was an age before he could even speak.

The neurosis is responsible—but isn't the neurosis a part of *him?* We have been speaking all the time as if the person and his unconscious were two separate beings; but isn't he one personality, including conscious and unconscious departments together?

I do not wish to deny this. But it hardly helps us here; for what people want when they talk about freedom, and what they hold to when they champion it, is the idea that the *conscious* will is the master of their destiny. "I am the master of my fate, I am the captain of my soul"—and they surely mean their conscious selves, the self that they can recognize and search and introspect. Between an unconscious that willy-nilly determines your actions, and an external force which pushes you, there is little if anything to choose. The unconscious is just *as if* it were an outside force; and indeed, psychiatrists will assert that the inner Hitler can torment you far more than any external Hitler can. Thus the kind of freedom that people want, the only kind they will settle for, is precisely the kind that psychiatry says that they cannot have. . . .

Let us . . . put the situation schematically in the form of a deductive argument.

1. An occurrence over which we had no control is something we cannot be held responsible for.

2. Events E, occurring during our babyhood, were events over which we had no control.

3. Therefore events E were events which we cannot be held responsible for.

4. But if there is something we cannot be held responsible for, neither can we be held responsible for something that inevitably results from it.

5. Events E have as inevitable consequence Neurosis N, which in turn has as inevitable consequence Behavior B.

6. Since N is the inevitable consequence of E and B is the inevitable consequence of N, B is the inevitable consequence of E.

7. Hence, not being responsible for E, we cannot be responsible for B.

JEAN-PAUL SARTRE
Freedom and Responsibility

JEAN-PAUL SARTRE's (1905–1980) "existentialism" features a powerful emphasis on the freedom and responsibility of each individual. The following is taken from his Being and Nothingness.

ALTHOUGH the considerations which are about to follow are of interest primarily to the ethicist, it may nevertheless be worthwhile after these descriptions and arguments to return to the freedom of the for-itself and try to understand what the fact of this freedom represents for human destiny.

The essential consequence of our earlier remarks is that man being condemned to be free carries the weight of the whole world on his shoulders; he is responsible for the world and for himself as a way of being. We are taking the word "responsibility" in its ordinary sense as "consciousness (of) being the incontestable author of an event or of an object." In this sense the responsibility of the for-itself is overwhelming since he is the one by whom it happens that *there is* a world; since he is also the one who makes himself be, then whatever may be the situation in which he finds himself, the for-itself must wholly assume this situation with its peculiar coefficient of adversity, even though it be insupportable. He must assume the situation with the proud consciousness of being the author of it, for the very worst disadvantages or the worst threats which can endanger my person have meaning only in and through my project; and it is on the ground of the engagement which I am that they appear. It is therefore senseless to think of complaining since nothing foreign has decided what we feel, what we live, or what we are.

Furthermore this absolute responsibility is not resignation; it is simply the logical requirement of the consequences of our freedom. What happens to me happens through me, and I can neither affect myself with it nor revolt against it nor resign myself to it. Moreover everything which happens to me is *mine*. By this we must understand first of all that I am always equal to what happens to me *qua* man, for what happens to a man through other men and through himself can be only human. The most terrible situations of war, the worst tortures do not create a nonhuman state of things; there is no nonhuman situation. It is only through fear, flight, and recourse to magical types of conduct that I shall decide on the non-human, but this decision is human, and I shall carry the entire responsibility for it. But in addition the situation is *mine* because it is the image of my free choice of myself, and everything which it presents to me is *mine* in that this represents me and symbolizes me. Is it not I who decide the coefficient of adversity in things and even their unpredictability by deciding myself?

Thus there are no *accidents* in life; a community event which suddenly bursts forth and involves me in it does not come from the outside. If I am mobilized in a war, this war is *my* war; it is in my image and I deserve it. I deserve it first because I could always get out of it by suicide or by desertion; these ultimate possibles are those which must always be present for us when there is a question of envisaging a situation. For lack of getting out of it, I have *chosen* it. This can be due to inertia, to cowardice in the face of public

Sartre, Jean-Paul, "Freedom and Responsibility," from *Being and Nothingness,* New York: Philosophical Library Publishers, 1943, pp. 406–408.

opinion, or because I prefer certain other values to the value of the refusal to join in the war (the good opinion of my relatives, the honor of my family, *etc.*) Any way you look at it, it is a matter of a choice. This choice will be repeated later on again and again without a break until the end of the war. Therefore we must agree with the statement by J. Romains, "In war there are no innocent victims." If therefore I have preferred war to death or to dishonor, everything takes place as if I bore the entire responsibility for this war. Of course others have declared it, and one might be tempted perhaps to consider me as a simple accomplice. But this notion of complicity has only a juridical sense, and it does not hold there. For it depended on me that for me and by me this war should not exist, and I have decided that it does exist. There was no compulsion here, for the compulsion could have got no hold on a freedom. I did not have any excuse; . . . the peculiar character of human-reality is that it is without excuse. Therefore it remains for me only to lay claim to this war.

But in addition the war is *mine* because by the sole fact that arises in a situation which I cause to be and that I can discover it there only by engaging myself for or against it, I can no longer distinguish at present the choice which I make of myself from the choice which I make of the war. To live this war is to choose myself through it and to choose it through my choice of myself. There can be no question of considering it as "four years of vacation" or as a "reprieve," as a "recess," the essential part of my responsibilities being elsewhere in my married, family, or professional life. In this war which I have chosen I choose myself from day to day, and I make it mine by making myself. If it is going to be four empty years, then it is I who bear the responsibility for this.

Finally, . . . each person is an absolute choice of self from the standpoint of a world of knowledges and of techniques which this choice both assumes and illumines; each person is an absolute upsurge at an absolute date and is perfectly unthinkable at another date. It is therefore a waste of time to ask what I should have been if this war

had not broken out, for I have chosen myself as one of the possible meanings of the epoch which imperceptibly led to war. I am not distinct from this same epoch; I could not be transported to another epoch without contradiction. Thus I *am* this war which restricts and limits and makes comprehensible the period which preceded it. In this sense we may define more precisely the responsibility of the for-itself if to the earlier quoted statement, "There are no innocent victims," we add the words, "We have the war we deserve." Thus, totally free, undistinguishable from the period for which I have chosen to be the meaning, as profoundly responsible for the war as if I had myself declared it, unable to live without integrating it in *my* situation, engaging myself in it wholly and stamping it with my seal, I must be without remorse or regrets as I am without excuse; for from the instant of my upsurge into being, I carry the weight of the world by myself alone without anything or any person being able to lighten it.

Yet this responsibility is of a very particular type. Someone will say, "I did not ask to be born." This is a naïve way of throwing greater emphasis on our facticity. I am responsible for everything, in fact, except for my very responsibility, for I am not the foundation of my being. Therefore everything takes place as if I were compelled to be responsible. I am *abandoned* in the world, not in the sense that I might remain abandoned and passive in a hostile universe like a board floating on the water, but rather in the sense that I find myself suddenly alone and without help, engaged in a world for which I bear the whole responsibility without being able, whatever I do, to tear myself away from this responsibility for an instant. For I am responsible for my very desire of fleeing responsibilities. To make myself passive in the world, to refuse to act upon things and upon Others is still to choose myself, and suicide is one mode among others of being-in-the-world. Yet I find an absolute responsibility for the fact that my facticity (here the fact of my birth) is directly inapprehensible and even inconceivable, for this fact of my birth never appears as a brute fact but always across a projective reconstruction of my for-itself. I am ashamed of being born or I am astonished at it or I rejoice over it, or in attempting to get rid of my life I affirm that I live and I assume this life as bad. Thus in a certain sense I *choose* being born. This choice itself is integrally affected with facticity since I am not able not to choose, but this facticity in turn will appear only in so far as I surpass it toward my ends. Thus facticity is everywhere but inapprehensible; I never encounter anything except my responsibility. That is why I cannot ask, "*Why* was I born?" or curse the day of my birth or declare that I did not ask to be born, for these various attitudes toward my birth—*i.e.*, toward the *fact* that I realize a presence in the world—are absolutely nothing else but ways of assuming this birth in full responsibility and making it *mine*. Here again I encounter only myself and my projects so that finally my abandonment—*i.e.*, my facticity—consists simply in the fact that I am condemned to be wholly responsible for myself. I am the being which *is* in such a way that in its being its being is in question. And this "is" of my being *is* as present and inapprehensible.

Under these conditions since every event in the world can be revealed to me only as an *opportunity* (an opportunity made use of, lacked, neglected, *etc.*), or better yet since everything which happens to us can be considered as a *chance* (*i.e.*, can appear to us only as a way of realizing this being which is in question in our being) and since other as transcendences-transcended are themselves only *opportunities* and *chances*, the responsibility of the for-itself extends to the entire world as a peopled-world. It is precisely thus that the for-itself apprehends itself in anguish; that is, as a being which is neither the foundation of its own being nor of the Other's being nor of the in-itselfs which form the world, but a being which is compelled to decide the meaning of being—within it and everywhere outside of it. The one who realizes in anguish his condition as *being* thrown into a responsibility which extends to his very abandonment has no longer either remorse or regret or excuse; he is no longer anything but a freedom which perfectly reveals itself and whose being resides in this very revelation. But as we pointed out . . . , most of the time we flee anguish in bad faith.

B. F. SKINNER
Freedom and the Control of Men

B. F. SKINNER *(1904–1990) was professor of psychology at Harvard and the best-known American "behaviorist." His best-known experiment, "Walden Two," was a rigidly reinforced community governed by behaviorist theory. In the following he argues his polemical thesis against the importance of what we call "freedom" and urges more scientific control over the conditions influencing people's behavior.*

THE second half of the twentieth century may be remembered for its solution of a curious problem. Although Western democracy created the conditions responsible for the rise of modern science, it is now evident that it may never fully profit from that achievement. The so-called "democratic philosophy" of human behavior to which it also gave rise is increasingly in conflict with the application of the methods of science to human affairs. Unless this conflict is somehow resolved, the ultimate goals of democracy may be long deferred.

Just as biographers and critics look for external influences to account for the traits and achievements of the men they study, so science ultimately explains behavior in terms of "causes" or conditions which lie beyond the individual himself. As more and more causal relations are demonstrated, a practical corollary becomes difficult to resist: it should be possible to *produce* behavior according to plan simply by arranging the proper conditions. Now, among the specifications which might reasonably be submitted to a behavioral technology are these: Let men be happy, informed, skillful, well behaved, and productive.

This immediate practical implication of a science of behavior has a familiar ring, for it recalls the doctrine of human perfectibility of eighteenth and nineteenth-century humanism. A science of man shares the optimism of that philosophy and supplies striking support for the working faith that men can build a better world and, through it, better men. The support comes just in time, for there has been little optimism of late among those who speak from the traditional point of view. Democracy has become "realistic," and it is only with some embarrassment that one admits today to perfectionistic or utopian thinking.

The earlier temper is worth considering, however. History records many foolish and unworkable schemes for human betterment, but almost all the great changes in our culture which we now regard as worthwhile can be traced to perfectionistic philosophies. Governmental, religious, educational, economic, and social reforms follow a common pattern. Someone believes that a change in a cultural practice—for example, in the rules of evidence in a court of law, in the characterization of man's relation to God, in the way children are taught to read and write, in permitted rates of interest, or in minimal housing standards—will improve the condition of men: by promoting justice, permitting men to seek salvation more effectively, increasing the literacy of a people, checking an inflationary trend, or improving public health and family relations, respectively. The underlying hypothesis is always the same: that a different physical or cultural environment will make a different and better man.

The scientific study of behavior not only justifies the general pattern of such proposals; it promises new and better hypotheses. The earliest cultural practices must have originated in sheer accidents. Those which strengthened the group survived with the group in a sort of natural selection. As soon as men began to propose and carry out changes in practice for the sake of possible consequences, the evolutionary process must have accelerated. The simple practice of making changes must have had survival value. A further acceleration is now to be expected. As laws of behavior are more precisely stated, the changes in the environment required to bring about a given effect may be more clearly specified. Conditions which have been neglected because their effects were slight or unlooked for may be shown to be relevant. New conditions may actually be created, as in the discovery and synthesis of drugs which affect behavior.

This is no time, then, to abandon notions of progress, improvement, or, indeed, human perfectibility. The simple fact is that man is able, and now as never before, to lift himself by his own bootstraps. In achieving control of the world of which he is a part, he may learn at last to control himself.

Timeworn objections to the planned improvement of cultural practices are already losing much of their force. Marcus Aurelius was probably right in advising his readers to be content with a haphazard amelioration of mankind.

"Never hope to realize Plato's republic," he sighed, ". . . for who can change the opinions of men? And without a change of sentiments what can you make but reluctant slaves and hypocrites?" He was thinking, no doubt, of contemporary patterns of control based upon punishment or the threat of punishment which, as he correctly observed, breed only reluctant slaves of those who submit and hypocrites of those who discover modes of evasion. But we need not share his pessimism, for the opinions of men can be changed. The techniques of indoctrination which were being devised by the early Christian Church at the very time Marcus Aurelius was writing are relevant, as are some of the techniques of psychotherapy and of advertising and public relations. Other methods suggested by recent scientific analyses leave little doubt of the matter.

The study of human behavior also answers the cynical complaint that there is a plain "cussedness" in man which will always thwart efforts to improve him. We are often told that men do not want to be changed, even for the better. Try to help them, and they will outwit you and remain happily wretched. Dostoevsky claimed to see some plan in it. "Out of sheer ingratitude," he complained, or possibly based, "man will play you a dirty trick, just to prove that men are still men and not the keys of a piano. . . . And even if you could prove that a man is only a piano key, he would still do something out of sheer perversity—he would create destruction and chaos—just to gain his point. . . . And if all this could in turn be analyzed and prevented by predicting that it would occur, then man would deliberately go mad to prove his point." This is a conceivable neurotic reaction to inept control. A few men may have shown it, and many have enjoyed Dostoevsky's statement because they tend to show it. But that such perversity is a fundamental reaction of the human organism to controlling conditions is sheer nonsense.

So is the objection that we have no way of knowing what changes to make even though we have the necessary techniques. That is one of the great hoaxes of the century—a sort of booby trap left behind in the retreat before the advancing front of science. Scientists themselves have unsuspectingly agreed that there are two kinds of useful propositions about nature—facts and value judgments—and that science must confine itself to "what is," leaving "what ought to be" to others. But with what special sort of wisdom is the nonscientist endowed? Science is only effective knowing, no matter who engages in it. Verbal behavior proves upon analysis to be composed of many different types of utterances, from poetry and exhortation to logic and factual description, but these are not all equally useful in talking about cultural practices. We may classify useful propositions according to the degrees of confidence with which they may be asserted. Sentences about nature range from highly probable "facts" to sheer guesses. In general, future events are less likely to be correctly described than past. When a scientist talks about a projected experiment, for example, he must often resort to statements having only a moderate likelihood of being correct; he calls them hypotheses.

Designing a new cultural pattern is in many ways like designing an experiment. In drawing up a new constitution, outlining a new educational program, modifying a religious doctrine, or setting up a new fiscal policy, many statements must be quite tentative. We cannot be sure that the practices we specify will have the consequences we predict, or that the consequences will reward our efforts. This is in the nature of such proposals. They are not value judgments—they are guesses. To confuse and delay the improvement of cultural practices by quibbling about the word *improve* is itself not a useful practice. Let us agree, to start with, that health is better than illness, wisdom better than ignorance, love better than hate, and productive energy better than neurotic sloth.

Perhaps the most crucial part of our democratic philosophy to be reconsidered is our attitude toward freedom—or its reciprocal, the control of human behavior. We do not oppose all forms of control because it is . . . "human nature" to do so. The reaction is not characteristic of all men under all conditions of life. It is an attitude which has been carefully engineered, in large part by what we call the "literature" of democracy. With respect to some methods of control (for example, the threat of force), very little engineering is needed, for the techniques or their immediate consequences are objectionable. Society has suppressed these methods by branding them "wrong," "illegal," or "sinful." But to encourage these attitudes toward objectionable forms of control, it has been necessary to disguise the real nature of certain indispensable techniques, the commonest examples of which are education, moral discourse, and persuasion. The actual procedures appear harmless enough. They consist of supplying information, presenting opportunities for action, pointing out logical relationships, appealing to reason or "enlightened understanding," and so on. Through a masterful piece of misrepresentation, the illusion is fostered that these procedures do not involve the control of behavior; at most, they are simply ways of "getting someone to change his mind." But analysis not only reveals the presence of well-defined behavioral processes, it demonstrates a kind of control no less inexorable, though in some ways more acceptable, than the bully's threat of force.

Let us suppose that someone in whom we are interested is acting unwisely—he is careless in the way he deals with his friends, he drives too fast, or he holds his golf club the wrong way. We could probably help him by issuing a series of commands: don't nag, don't drive over sixty, don't hold your club that way. Much less objectionable would be "an appeal to reason." We could show him how people are affected by his treatment of them, how accident rates rise sharply at higher speeds, how a particular grip on the club alters the way the ball is struck and corrects a slice. In doing so we resort to verbal mediating devices which emphasize and support certain "contingencies of reinforcement"—that is, certain relations between behavior and its consequences—which strengthen the behavior we wish to set up. The same consequences would possibly set up the behavior without our help, and they eventually take control no matter which form of help we give. The appeal to reason has certain advantages over the authoritative command. A threat of punishment, no matter how subtle, generates emotional reactions and tendencies to escape or revolt. Perhaps the controllee merely "feels resentment" at being made to act in a given way, but even that is to be avoided. When we "appeal to reason," he "feels freer to do as he pleases." The fact is that we have exerted *less* control than in using a threat; since other conditions may contribute to the result, the effect may be delayed or, possibly in a given instance, lacking. But if we have worked a change in his behavior at all, it is because we have altered relevant environmental conditions, and the processes we have set in motion are just as real and just as inexorable, if not as comprehensive, as in the most authoritative coercion.

"Arranging an opportunity for action" is another example of disguised control. The power of the negative form has already been exposed in the analysis of censorship. Restriction of opportunity is recognized as far from harmless. As Ralph Barton Perry said in an article which appeared in the Spring, 1953, *Pacific Spectator,* "Whoever determines what alternatives shall be made known to man controls what that man shall choose *from*. He is deprived of freedom in proportion as he is denied access to *any* ideas, or is confined to any range of ideas short of the totality of relevant possibilities." But there is a positive side as well. When we present a relevant state of affairs, we increase the likelihood that a given form of behavior will be emitted. To the extent that the probability of action has changed, we have made a definite contribution. The teacher of history controls a student's behavior (or, if the reader prefers, "deprives him of freedom") just as much in *presenting* historical facts as in suppressing them. Other conditions will no doubt affect the student, but the contribution made to his behavior by the presentation of material is fixed and, within its range, irresistible.

The methods of education, moral discourse, and persuasion are acceptable not because they recognize the freedom of the individual or his right to dissent, but because they make only *partial* contributions to the control of his behavior. The freedom they recognize is freedom from a more coercive form of control. The dissent which they tolerate is the possible effect of other determiners of action. Since these sanctioned methods are frequently ineffective, we have been able to convince ourselves that they do not represent control at all. When they show too much strength to permit disguise, we give them other names and suppress them as energetically as we suppress the use of force. Education grown too powerful is rejected as propaganda or "brainwashing," while really effective persuasion is described as "undue influence," "demagoguery," "seduction," and so on.

If we are not to rely solely upon accident for the innovations which give rise to cultural evolution, we must accept the fact that some kind of control of human behavior is inevitable. We cannot use good sense in human affairs unless someone engages in the design and construction of environmental conditions which affect the behavior of men. Environmental changes have always been the condition for the improvement of cultural patterns, and we can hardly use the more effective methods of science without making changes on a grander scale. We are all controlled by the world in which we live, and part of that world has been and will be constructed by men. The question is this: Are we to be controlled by accident, by tyrants, or by ourselves in effective cultural design?

The danger of the misuse of power is possibly greater than ever. It is not allayed by disguising the facts. We cannot make wise decisions if we continue to pretend that human behavior is not controlled, or if we refuse to engage in control when valuable results might be forthcoming. Such measures weaken only ourselves, leaving the strength of science to others. The first step in a defense against tyranny is the fullest possible exposure of controlling techniques. A second step has already been taken successfully in restricting the use of physical force. Slowly, and as yet imperfectly, we have worked out an ethical and governmental design in which the strong man is not allowed to use the power deriving from his strength to control his fellow men. He is restrained by a superior force created for that purpose—the ethical pressure of the group, or more explicit religious and governmental measures. We tend to distrust superior forces, as we currently hesitate to relinquish sovereignty in order to set up an international police force. But it is only through such counter-control that we have achieved what we call peace—a condition in which men are not permitted to control each other through force. In other words, control itself must be controlled.

Science has turned up dangerous processes and materials before. To use the facts and techniques of a science of man to the fullest extent without making some monstrous mistake will be difficult and obviously perilous. It is no time for self-deception, emotional indulgence, or the assumption of attitudes which are no longer useful. Man is facing a difficult test. He must keep his head now, or he must start again—a long way back.

ROBERT KANE
The Significance of Free Will
Old Dispute, New Themes

ROBERT KANE *is professor of philosophy of The University of Texas at Austin and the author of* The Significance of Free Will *and other books and articles on freedom.*

"THERE is a disputation that will continue till mankind are raised from the dead, between the Necessitarians and the partisans of free will." These are the words of twelfth-century Persian poet, Jalalu'ddin Rumi. The problem of free will and necessity (or determinism), of which Rumi speaks, has puzzled the greatest minds for centuries—including famous philosophers, literary figures, theologians, scientists, legal theorists and psychologists—as well as many ordinary people. It has affected and been affected by both religion and science.

In his classic poem, *Paradise Lost,* John Milton describes the angels debating how some of them could have sinned of their own free wills given that God had made them intelligent and happy. Why would they have done it? And why were they responsible for it rather than God, since God had made them the way they were and had complete foreknowledge of what they would do. While puzzling over such questions, even the angels, Milton tells us, were "in Endless Mazes lost" (not a comforting thought for us humans). On the scientific front, issues about free will lead us to ask about the nature of the physical universe and our place in it (are we determined by physical laws and movements of the atoms?), about human psychology and the springs of action (can our actions be predicted by those who know our psychology?), about social conditioning, moral responsibility, crime and punishment, right and wrong, good and evil, and much more.

To dive into these questions, the best way to begin is with the idea of *freedom* itself. Nothing could be more important than freedom to the modern world. All over the globe, the trend (often against resistance) is toward societies that are more free. But why do we want freedom? The simple, and not totally adequate, answer is that to be more free is to have the capacity and opportunity to satisfy more of our desires. In a free society we can walk into a store and buy almost anything we want. We can choose what movies to see, what music to listen to, whom to vote for.

But these are what you might call *surface* freedoms. What is meant by *free will* runs deeper than these everyday freedoms. To see how, suppose we had maximal freedom to make such choices to satisfy our desires and yet the choices we actually made were manipulated by others, by the powers that be. In such a world we would have a great deal of everyday freedom to do whatever we wanted, yet our free *will* would be severely limited. We would be free to *act* or choose as we will, but would not have the ultimate say about what it is that we will. Someone else would be pulling the strings, not by coercing us against our wishes, but by manipulating us into having the wishes they wanted us to have.

You may be thinking that, to some extent, we do live in such a world, where we are free to make numerous choices, but are manipulated into making many choices we do make by advertising, television, public relations, spin doctors, salespersons, marketers, and sometimes indeed by friends, parents, relatives, rivals or enemies. One indication of how important free will is to us is that people generally feel revulsion at such manipulation and feel demeaned by it when they find out they have been subjected to it. You may think you are your own person because you have chosen in accord with your own wishes, but then find out that these wishes were manipulated by others who wanted you to choose in just the way you did. Such situations are demeaning because we realize we were not our own persons; and having free will is about being your own person.

The problem is brought out in a striking way by twentieth-century utopian novels, like Aldous Huxley's *Brave New World* and B. F. Skinner's *Walden Two*. In the fictional societies described in these famous works, people can have and do what they will or choose, but only to the extent that they have been conditioned by behavioral engineers or neuro-chemists to will or choose what they can have and do. In *Brave New World*, the lower-echelon workers are under the influence of powerful drugs so that they do not dream of things they cannot have. They are quite content to play miniature golf all weekend. They can do what they want, though their wants are meager and controlled by drugs.

The citizens of *Walden Two* have a richer existence than the workers of *Brave New World*. Yet their desires and purposes are also covertly controlled, in this case by behavioral engineers. Walden Two-ers live collectively in a kind of rural commune; and because they share duties of farming and raising children, they have plenty of leisure. They pursue arts, sciences, crafts, engage in musical performances and enjoy what appears to be a pleasant existence. The fictional founder of Walden Two, a fellow named Frazier, forthrightly says that their pleasant existence is brought about by the fact that, in his community, persons can do whatever they want or

choose because they have been behaviorally conditioned since childhood to want and choose only what they can have and do. In other words, they have maximal *surface freedom* of action and choice (they can choose or do anything they want), but they lack a *deeper freedom* of the will because their desires and purposes are created by their behavioral conditioners or controllers. Their wills are not of "their own" making. Indeed, what happens in Walden Two is that their surface freedom to act and choose *as* they will is maximized by minimizing the deeper freedom to have the ultimate say in what they will.

Thus Frazier can say that Walden Two "is the freest place on earth" (p. 297), since he has surface freedoms in mind. For there is no *coercion* in Walden Two and no *punishment* because no one has to be forced to do anything against his or her will. The citizens can have anything they want because they have been conditioned not to want anything they cannot have. As for the deeper freedom, or free will, it does not exist in Walden Two, as Frazier himself admits (p. 257). But this is no loss, according to Frazier. Echoing *Walden Two's* author, B. F. Skinner (a foremost defender of behaviorism in psychology), Frazier thinks the deeper freedom of the will is an illusion in the first place. We do not have it anyway, inside or outside Walden Two. In our ordinary lives, he argues, we are just as much the products of upbringing and social conditioning as the citizens of Walden Two, though we may delude ourselves into thinking otherwise. In our case, the conditioners are parents, teachers, coaches, schoolmates, peers, makers of TV programs, films, videos and other creators of the cultures and societies in which we live. The difference is that, unlike Walden Two, such everyday conditioning is often haphazard, incompetent and harmful.

Why then, Skinner asks, reject the maximal surface freedom and happiness of Walden Two for a deeper freedom of the will that is something we do not and cannot have anyway? Along with many other scientists, he thinks the idea that we could be *ultimate* determiners of our own ends or purposes (which is what the deeper freedom of the will would require) is an impossible ideal that cannot fit into the modern scientific picture of the world. To have such freedom, we would have to have been the original creators of our own wills—of ourselves. But if we trace the psychological springs of action back further and further to childhood, we find that we were less free back then, not more, and more subject to conditioning. We thus delude ourselves into thinking that we have sacrificed some real (deeper) freedom for the happiness of Walden Two. Rather we have gained a maximum amount of the only kind of freedom we really can have (surface freedom), while giving up an illusion (free will).

Seductive as these arguments may be, there are many people who continue to believe that something important is missing in Walden Two and that the deeper freedom is not a mere illusion. Such persons want to be the ultimate designers of their own lives as Frazier was for the lives of Walden Two. They want to be the creators, as he was, not the pawns—at least for their own lives. What they long for is what was traditionally meant by "free will."

Here is yet another way of looking at it. Free will in this deeper sense is also intimately related to notions of moral responsibility, blameworthiness and praiseworthiness. Suppose a young man is on trial for an assault and robbery in which his victim was beaten to death. Let us say we attend his trial on a daily basis. At first, our thoughts of the young man are filled with anger and resentment. But as we listen daily to how he came to have the mean character and perverse motives he did have—a sordid story of parental neglect, child abuse, sexual abuse, bad role models—some of our resentment against the young man is shifted over to the parents and others who abused and influenced him. We begin to feel angry with them as well as him. Yet we aren't quite ready to shift all of the blame away from the young man himself. We wonder whether some residual responsibility may not belong to him. Our questions become: to what extent is *he* responsible for becoming the sort of person he now is? Was it *all* a question of bad parenting, societal neglect, social conditioning, and the like, or did he have any role to play in it?

These are crucial questions about free will and they are questions about what may be called *ultimate responsibility*. We know that parenting and society, genetic make-up and upbringing, have an influence on what we become and what we are. But were these influences entirely *determining* or did they "leave anything over" for us to be responsible for? That's what we wanted to know about the young man. The question of whether he is merely a victim of his bad circumstances or has some residual responsibility for being what he is depends on whether these other factors were or were not *entirely* determining.

Turning this around, if there were factors or circumstances that entirely determined what he did, then to be ultimately responsible, he would have had to be responsible to some degree for some of those factors by virtue of earlier acts through which he formed his present character. As Aristotle put it centuries ago: if a man is responsible for the wicked acts that flow from his character, then he must at one time in the past have been responsible for forming the character from which these acts flow. But, of course, if *all* of our choices and actions were entirely determined by prior circumstances, we would have had to be responsible to some degree for some of these circumstances by still earlier acts, and so on indefinitely backwards in time—an impossibility for finite creatures like ourselves. At some point, if we are to be ultimately responsible for being what we are, there must be acts in our life histories in which parenting and society, genetic make-up and other factors did not completely determine how we acted, but left something over for us to be responsible for then and there. This is why many people have thought that the deeper freedom of the will is not compatible with being completely determined by the past. Surface freedoms (to do or choose what we will) may be compatible with determinism, but free will does not seem to be (as Skinner himself realized).

Yet such thoughts only lead to a further problem that has haunted free will debates for centuries: if this deeper freedom is not compatible with determinism, it does not seem to be compatible with *indeterminism* either. An event which is undetermined might occur or might not occur, given the entire past. (A determined event *must* occur, given the entire past.) Thus, whether or not an undetermined event actually occurs, given its past, is a matter of chance. But chance events occur spontaneously and are not under the control of anything, hence not under the control of agents. How then could they be free actions? If, for example, a choice occurred by virtue of a quantum jump or other undetermined event in one's brain, it would seem a fluke or accident rather than a responsible choice. Undetermined events in the brain or body it seems would inhibit or interfere with our freedom, occurring spontaneously and not under our control. They would turn out to be a nuisance—or perhaps a curse, like epilepsy—rather than an enhancement of our freedom.

Or look at the problem in another way that goes a little deeper. If my choice is really undetermined, that means I could have made a different choice *given exactly the same past* right up to the moment when I did choose. That is what indeterminism and the denial of determinism mean: exactly the same past, different outcomes. Imagine, for example, that I had been deliberating about where to spend my vacation, in Hawaii or Colorado, and after much thought and deliberation had decided I preferred Hawaii and chose it. If the choice was undetermined, then exactly the same deliberation, the same thought processes, the same beliefs, desires and other motives—not a sliver of difference—that led up to my favoring and choosing Hawaii over Colorado, might by chance have issued in my choosing Colorado instead. That is very strange. If such a thing happened it would seem a fluke or accident, like that quantum jump in the brain just mentioned, not a rational choice. Since I had come to favor Hawaii and was about to choose it, when by chance I chose Colorado, I would wonder what went wrong and perhaps consult a neurologist. For reasons such as these, people have argued that undetermined free choices would be "arbitrary," "capricious," "random," "irrational," "uncontrolled," and "inexplicable," not really free

and responsible choices at all. If free will is not compatible with determinism, it does not seem to be compatible with indeterminism either.

These charges are powerful ones and defenders of free will have made some extraordinary claims attempting to respond to them. Free will requires indeterminism alright, they have said, but it cannot *merely* be indeterminism or chance. Some "extra factors" must be involved in free will that go beyond ordinary scientific or causal understanding. Immanuel Kant said we can't explain free will in scientific and psychological terms. To account for it we have to appeal to the agency of what he called a "noumenal self" outside space and time that could not be studied in scientific terms. Others have appealed to what Nobel physiologist John Eccles calls a "transempirical power center," which would intervene in the brain, filling the causal gaps left by indeterminism or chance. Still others have appealed to a special kind of agent or immanent causation that cannot be explained in terms of the ordinary scientific modes of causation in terms of events or occurrences.

These unusual stratagems, which are common among defenders of free will, have unfortunately reinforced the view, now widespread among philosophers and scientists, that traditional notions of free will requiring indeterminism are mysterious and have no place in the modern scientific picture of the world. Such stratagems, to their critics, are reminiscent of the old debates about vital forces in biology of the nineteenth century, where obscure forces were postulated to explain what otherwise could not be explained about living things. They remind us of the Arkansas farmer when he first saw an automobile. He listened intently to the explanation of how the internal combustion engine worked and nodded in agreement, but insisted on looking under the hood anyway because, as he said, "there must be a horse in there somewhere." (In Arkansas, this is a story about a Texas farmer.)

Can we do more to explain indeterminist free will and reconcile it with modern science without appealing to such stratagems? I think we can if we are willing to do some new thinking about the problem. The first thing to note is that indeterminism does not have to be a factor in all acts done "of our own free wills." Not all of them have to be undetermined. Frequently in everyday life we act from our existing motives without having to think or deliberate about what to do. At such times, we may very well be determined by our existing characters and motives. Yet we may also be acting "of our own free wills" to the extent that we formed our present characters and motives (our wills) by earlier choices or actions that were not themselves determined. Let us call these earlier choices or actions "self-forming" choices or actions.

Now I believe that such undetermined self-forming choices or actions occur at those difficult times of life when we are torn between competing visions of what we should do or become; and they are more frequent than we think. Perhaps we are torn between doing the moral thing or acting from ambition, or between powerful present desires and long-term goals, or we are faced with difficult tasks for which we have aversions. In all such cases, we are faced with competing motivations and have to make an effort to overcome temptation to do something else we also strongly want. There is tension and uncertainty in our minds about what to do at such times that, I suggest, is reflected in appropriate regions of our brains by movement away from thermodynamic equilibrium—in short, a kind of stirring up of chaos in the brain that makes it sensitive to micro-indeterminacies at the neuronal level. The uncertainty and inner tension we feel at such soul-searching moments of self-formation would thus be reflected in the indeterminacy of our neural processes themselves. What is experienced personally as uncertainty would correspond physically to the opening of a window of opportunity that temporarily screens off complete determination by influences of the past. (By contrast, when we act from predominant motives or settled dispositions, the uncertainty or indeterminacy is muted. If it did play a role in such cases, it *would* be a mere nuisance or fluke.)

When we do decide under such conditions of uncertainty, the outcome is not determined because of the preceding indeterminacy—and yet it can be willed (and hence rational and voluntary) either way owing to the fact that in such self-formation, the agents prior wills are divided by conflicting motives. Consider a businesswoman who faces a conflict of this kind. She is on the way to a business meeting important to her career when she observes an assault taking place in an alley. An inner struggle ensues between her moral conscience, to stop and call for help, and her career ambitions which tell her she cannot miss this meeting. She has to make an effort of will to overcome the temptation to go on to her meeting. If she overcomes this temptation, it will be the result of her effort, but if she fails, it will be because she did not *allow* her effort to succeed. And this is due to the fact that, while she wanted to overcome temptation, she also wanted to fail, for quite different and incommensurable reasons. When we, like the businesswoman, decide in such circumstances, and the indeterminate efforts we are making become determinate choices, we *make* one set of competing reasons or motives prevail over the others at that moment *by deciding*. . . .

One might object that a residual arbitrariness remains in such undetermined self-forming choices since there cannot in principle be sufficient or overriding *prior* reasons for making one choice and one set of reasons prevail over the other. (This of course does not mean the agent lacks good prior reasons for choosing, but only that they are not overriding, until made so by choosing.) I would grant this, but argue that such arbitrariness relative to prior reasons tells us something important about free will. It tells us that "every undetermined self-forming free choice is the initiation of a 'value experiment' whose justification lies in the future and is not fully explained by the past. In making such a choice we say, in effect, 'Let's try this. It is not required by my past, but is consistent with my past and is one branching pathway my life can now meaningfully take. I am willing to take responsibility for it one way or the other.'"

It is worth noting in this connection that the term "arbitrary" comes from the Latin *arbitium* which means "judgment"—as in *liberum arbitrium voluntatis*, "free judgment of the will" (the medieval designation for free will). Imagine a writer in the middle of a novel. The novel's heroine faces a crisis and the writer has not yet developed her character in sufficient detail to say exactly how she will act. The author makes a judgment about this that is not determined by the heroine's already formed past which does not give unique direction.

In this sense, the judgment *(arbitrium)* of how she will react is "arbitrary" but not entirely so. It had input from the heroine's fictional past and in turn gave input to her projected future. In a similar way, agents who exercise free will are both authors of and characters in their own stories all at once. By virtue of "self-forming" judgments of the will *(arbitria voluntatis)*, they are "arbiters" of their own lives, "making themselves" out of past that, if they are truly free, does not limit their future pathways to one.

IRIS YOUNG

Oppression

IRIS YOUNG *teaches feminism, philosophy, and politics at the University of Pittsburgh. She is author of* Justice and the Politics of Difference *and* Intersecting Voices: Dilemmas of Gender, Political Philosophy, and Policy.

Someone who does not see a pane of glass does not know that he does not see it.

Someone who, being placed differently, does see it, does not know the other does not see it.

When our will finds expression outside ourselves in actions performed by others, we do not waste our time and our power of attention in examining whether they have consented to this. This is true for all of us. Our attention, given entirely to the success of the undertaking, is not claimed by them as long as they are docile. . . .

Rape is a terrible caricature of love from which consent is absent. After rape, oppression is the second horror of human existence. It is a terrible caricature of obedience.

—SIMONE WEIL

I have proposed an enabling conception of justice. Justice should refer not only to distribution, but also to the institutional conditions necessary for the development and exercise of individual capacities and collective communication and cooperation. Under this conception of justice, injustice refers primarily to two forms of disabling constraints, oppression and domination. While these constraints include distributive patterns, they also involve matters which cannot easily be assimilated to the logic of distribution: decision-making procedures, division of labor, and culture.

Many people in the United States would not choose the term "oppression" to name injustice in our society. For contemporary emancipatory social movements, on the other hand—socialists, radical feminists, American Indian activists, Black activists, gay and lesbian activists—oppression is a central category of political discourse. Entering the political discourse in which oppression is a central category involves adopting a general mode of analyzing and evaluating social structures and practices which is incommensurate with the language of liberal individualism that dominates political discourse in the United States.

A major political project for those of us who identify with at least one of these movements must thus be to persuade people that the discourse of oppression makes sense of much of our social experience. We are ill prepared for this task, however, because we have no clear account of the meaning of oppression. While we find the term used often in the diverse philosophical and theoretical literature spawned by radical social movements in the United States, we find little direct discussion of the meaning of the concept as used by these movements.

I offer some explication of the concept of oppression as I understand its use by new social movements in the United States since the 1960s. My starting point is reflection on the conditions of the groups said by these movements to be oppressed: among others women, Blacks, Chicanos, Puerto Ricans and other Spanish-speaking Americans, American Indians, Jews, lesbians, gay men, Arabs, Asians, old people, working-class people, and the physically and mentally disabled. I aim to systematize the meaning of the concept of oppression as used by these diverse political movements, and to provide normative argument to clarify the wrongs the term names.

Obviously the above-named groups are not oppressed to the same extent or in the same ways. In the most general sense, all oppressed people suffer some inhibition of their ability to develop and exercise their capacities and express their needs, thoughts, and feelings. In that abstract sense all oppressed people face a common condition. Beyond that, in any more specific sense, it is not possible to define a single set of criteria that describe the condition of oppression of the above groups. Consequently, attempts by theorists and activists to discover a common description or the essential causes of the oppression of all these groups have frequently led to fruitless disputes about whose oppression is more fundamental or more grave. The contexts in which members of these groups use the term oppression to describe the injustices of their situation suggest that oppression names in fact a family of concepts and conditions, which I divide into five categories: exploitation, marginalization, powerlessness, cultural imperialism, and violence. . . .

One reason that many people would not use the term oppression to describe injustice in our society is that they do not understand the term in the same way as do new social movements. In its traditional usage, oppression means the exercise of tyranny by a ruling group. Thus many Americans would agree with radicals in applying the term oppression to the situation of Black South Africans under apartheid. Oppression also traditionally carries a strong connotation of conquest and colonial domination. The Hebrews were oppressed in Egypt, and many uses of the term oppression in the West invoke this paradigm.

Dominant political discourse may use the term oppression to describe societies other than our own, usually Communist or purportedly Communist societies. Within this anti-Communist rhetoric both tyrannical and colonialist implications of the term appear. For the anti-Communist, Communism denotes precisely the exercise of brutal tyranny over a whole people by a few rulers, and the will to conquer the world, bringing hitherto independent peoples under that tyranny. In dominant political discourse it is not legitimate to use the term oppression to describe our society, because oppression is the evil perpetrated by the Others.

New left social movements of the 1960s and 1970s, however, shifted the meaning of the concept of oppression. In its new usage, oppression designates the disadvantage and injustice some people suffer not because a tyrannical power coerces them, but because of the everyday practices of a well-intentioned liberal society. In this new left usage, the tyranny of a ruling group over another, as in South Africa, must certainly be called oppressive. But oppression also refers to systemic constraints on groups that are not necessarily the result of the intentions of a tyrant. Oppression in this sense is structural, rather than the result of a few people's choices or policies. Its causes are embedded in unquestioned norms, habits, and symbols, in the assumptions underlying institutional rules and the collective consequences of following those rules. It names, as Marilyn Frye puts it, "an enclosing structure of forces and barriers which tends to the immobilization and reduction of a group or category of people." In this extended structural sense oppression refers to the vast and deep injustices some groups suffer as a consequence of often unconscious assumptions and reactions of well-meaning people in ordinary interactions, media and cultural stereotypes, and structural features of bureaucratic hierarchies and market mechanisms—in short, the normal processes of everyday life. We cannot eliminate this structural oppression by getting rid of the rulers or making some new laws, because oppressions are systematically reproduced in major economic, political, and cultural institutions.

The systemic character of oppression implies that an oppressed group need not have a correlate oppressing group. While structural oppression involves relations among groups, these relations do not always fit the paradigm of conscious and intentional oppression of one group by another. Foucault suggests that to understand the meaning and operation of power in modern society we must look beyond the model of power as "sovereignty," a dyadic relation of ruler and subject, and instead analyze the exercise of power as the effect of often liberal and "humane" practices of education, bureaucratic administration, production and distribution of consumer goods, medicine, and so on. The conscious actions of many individuals daily contribute to maintaining and reproducing oppression, but those people are usually simply doing their jobs or living their lives, and do not understand themselves as agents of oppression.

I do not mean to suggest that within a system of oppression individual persons do not intentionally harm others in oppressed groups. The raped woman, the beaten Black youth, the locked-out worker, the gay man harassed on the street, are victims of intentional actions by identifiable agents. I also do not mean to deny that specific groups are beneficiaries of the oppression of other groups, and thus have an interest in their continued oppression. Indeed, for every oppressed group there is a group that is *privileged* in relation to that group.

The concept of oppression has been current among radicals since the 1960s partly in reaction to Marxist attempts to reduce the injustices of racism and sexism, for example, to the effects of class domination or bourgeois ideology. Racism, sexism, ageism, homophobia, some social movements asserted, are distinct forms of oppression with their own dynamics apart from the dynamics of class, even though they may interact with class oppression. From often heated discussions among socialists, feminists, and antiracism activists in the last ten years a consensus is emerging that many different groups must be said to be oppressed in our society, and that no single form of oppression can be assigned causal or moral primacy. The same discussion has also led to the recognition that group differences cut across individual lives in a multiplicity of ways that can entail privilege and oppression for the same person in different respects. Only a plural explication of the concept of oppression can adequately capture these insights.

CHAPTER NINETEEN

WHAT DO I JUSTLY DESERVE?

We demand and expect justice in society, and we object when it is not in evidence. One person pays more in taxes than another person with the same income, and we want to know why. One child receives an excellent education, whereas another who is just as bright and talented does not, and we want to know why. One man is convicted of a criminal offense and is sentenced to lifetime imprisonment, whereas another is convicted of the same offense and is put on probation for two years, and we want to know why. One way to understand the theory of justice—admittedly a very modern way of doing so—is to think of a theory of justice as a general explanation about why people are treated differently. For example, some people *should* be taxed more because they have a different kind of income or fewer children to support. Some criminals should be punished more than others because they have committed prior offenses and are more likely to do so again. One person is called to serve in the army while another is allowed to pursue a career because his career is in "the national interest." A theory of justice is a kind of decision procedure through which legislators, judges, administrators, and, ultimately, all of us can figure out what is fair and what is not, who should get what and how much.

We often hear that "life isn't fair"—sometimes from someone who is trying to defend a recent injustice. This bit of cynicism isn't at all new; Plato considered it and rejected it more than twenty-five hundred years ago in *The Republic*. In the first of the following selections, Socrates considers the thesis that the only real justice is strength and that the strong can do whatever they can get away with. In other words, "might makes right." But Socrates shows that this cannot be what justice is. The strong can be wrong. A different way of understanding "life isn't fair" is the basis of Thomas Hobbes' famous account of justice in *The Leviathan*. In the state of nature, he argues, there is no such thing as justice, but in human society, justice comes about as a matter of convention. Thus, the question of whether life is fair or not is quite irrelevant, according to Hobbes; the important thing is that we are just and that we arrange our society so that justice is realized in it.

One of the presumptions of justice—although the word takes on many meanings and interpretations—is equality. Thus, John Stuart Mill defends his "utilitarian" theory of justice on the premise that everyone "counts for one and no more than one." John Rawls presents a brief version of his influential recent theory of justice as fairness in which equality is also a central consideration, and Robert Nozick supplies a short rejoiner and a brief introduction to his own theory of "entitlements."

The final selections are more practical in their focus—David Brooks on tax inequality, Peter Singer on wealth and poverty, Iris Young on "The Myth of Merit," Amartya Sen on world poverty in terms of basic human rights, Malcolm X on the difference between human rights and civil rights, and Cheshire Calhoun, who argues for a reorientation of discussions of justice along feminist lines.

PLATO
Does Might Make Right?

PLATO's *(427–347 B.C.)* Republic *takes justice as its central concern. In the following selection, Socrates holds that justice is a kind of harmony, in an individual as well as in the ideal state. He therefore argues against Thrasymachus, who insists that justice is whatever is in the interests of the stronger.*

LISTEN, then, [Thrasymachus] said; I proclaim that justice is nothing else than the interest of the stronger. And now why do you not praise me. But of course you won't.

Let me first understand you, [Socrates] replied. Justice, as you say, is the interest of the stronger. What, Thrasymachus, is the meaning of this? You cannot mean to say that because Polydamas is stronger than we are, and finds the eating of beef conductive to his bodily strength, that to eat beef is therefore equally for our good who are weaker than he is, and right and just for us?

That's abominable of you, Socrates; you take the words in the sense which is most damaging to the argument.

Not at all, my good sir, I said; I am trying to understand them; and I wish that you would be a little clearer.

Well, he said, have you never heard that forms of government differ; there are tyrannies and there are democracies, and there are aristocracies?

Yes, I know.

And the government is the ruling power in each state?

Certainly.

And the different forms of government make laws democratical, aristocratical, tyrannical, with a view to their several interests; and these laws, which are made by them for their own interests, are the justice which they deliver to their subjects, and him who transgresses them they punish as a breaker of the law, and unjust. And that is what I mean when I say that in all states there is the same principle of justice, which is the interest of the government; and as the government must be supposed to have power, the only reasonable conclusion is, that everywhere there is one principle of justice, which is the interest of the stronger.

Now I understand you, I said; and whether you are right or not I will try to discover. But let me remark, that in defining justice you have yourself used the word "interest" which you forbade me to use. It is true, however, that in your definition the words "of the stronger" are added.

A small addition, you must allow, he said.

Great or small, never mind about that: we must first enquire whether what you are saying is the truth. Now we are both agreed that justice is interest of some sort, but you go on to say "of the stronger"; about this addition I am not so sure, and must therefore consider further.

Proceed.

I will; and first tell me, Do you admit that it is just for subjects to obey their rulers?

I do.

But are the rulers of states absolutely infallible, or are they sometimes liable to err?

To be sure, he replied, they are liable to err.

Then in making their laws, they may sometimes make them rightly, and sometimes not?

True.

Plato, "Does Might Make Right?" from *Republic*, Book 1, pp. 46–52, translated Benjamin Jowett, New York: Heritage Press, 1944.

When they make them rightly, they make them agreeably to their interest; when they are mistaken, contrary to their interest; you admit that?

Yes.

And the laws which they make must be obeyed by their subjects,—and that is what you call justice?

Doubtless.

Then justice, according to your argument, is not only obedience to the interest of the stronger but the reverse?

What is that you are saying? He asked.

I am only repeating what you are saying, I believe. But let us consider: Have we not admitted that the rulers may be mistaken about their own interest in what they command, and also that to obey them is justice? Has not that been admitted?

Yes.

Then you must also have acknowledged justice not to be for the interest of the stronger, when the rulers unintentionally command things to be done which are to their own injury. For if, as you say, justice is the obedience which the subject renders to their commands, in that case, O wisest of men, is there any escape from the conclusion that the weaker are commanded to do, not what is for the interest, but what is for the injury of the stronger?

Nothing can be clearer, Socrates, said Polemarchus.

Yes, said Cleitophon, interposing, if you are allowed to be his witness.

But there is no need of any witness, said Polemarchus, for Thrasymachus himself acknowledges that rulers may sometimes command what is not for their own interest, and that for subjects to obey them is justice.

Yes, Polemarchus,—Thrasymachus said that for subjects to do what was commanded by their rulers is just.

Yes, Cleitophon, but he also said that justice is the interest of the stronger, and, while admitting both these propositions, he further acknowledged that the stronger may command the weaker who are his subjects to do what is not for his own interest; whence follows that justice is

the injury quite as much as the interest of the stronger. But, said Cleitophon, he meant by the interest of the stronger what the stronger thought to be his interest,—this was what the weaker had to do; and this was affirmed by him to be justice.

Those were not his words, rejoined Polemarchus.

Never mind, I replied, if he now says that they are, let us accept his statement. Tell me, Thrasymachus, I said, did you mean by justice what the stronger thought to be his interest, whether really so or not?

Certainly not, he said. Do you suppose that I call him who is mistaken the stronger at the time when he is mistaken?

Yes, I said, my impression was that you did so, when you admitted that the ruler was not infallible but might be sometimes mistaken.

You argue like an informer, Socrates. Do you mean, for example, that he who is mistaken about the sick is a physician in that he is mistaken? Or that he who errs in arithmetic or grammar is an arithmetician or grammarian at the time when he is making the mistake, in respect of the mistake? True, we say that the physician or arithmetician or grammarian has made a mistake, but this is only a way of speaking; for the fact is that neither the grammarian nor any other person of skill ever makes a mistake in so far as he is what his name implies; they none of them err unless their skill fails them, and then they cease to be skilled artists. No artist or sage or ruler errs at the time when he is what his name implies; though he is commonly said to err, and I adopted the common mode of speaking. But to be perfectly accurate, since you are such a lover of accuracy, we should say that the ruler, in so far as he is a ruler, is unerring, and, being unerring, always commands that which is for his own interest; and the subject is required to execute his commands; and therefore, as I said at first and now repeat, justice is the interest of the stronger.

Indeed, Thrasymachus, and do I really appear to you to argue like an informer?

Certainly, he replied.

And do you suppose that I ask these questions with any design of injuring you in the argument?

Nay, he replied, "suppose" is not the word—I know it, but you will be found out, and by sheer force of argument you will never prevail.

I shall not make the attempt, my dear man; but to avoid any misunderstanding occurring between us in future, let me ask, in what sense do you speak of a ruler or stronger whose interest, as you were saying, he being the superior, it is just that the inferior should execute—is he a ruler in the popular or in the strict sense of the term?

In the strictest of all senses, he said. And now cheat and play the informer if you can: I ask no quarter at your hands. But you never will be able, never.

And do you imagine, I said, that I am such a madman as to try and cheat Thrasymachus? I might as well shave a lion.

Why, he said, you made the attempt a minute ago, and you failed.

Enough, I said, of these civilities. It will be better that I should ask you a question: Is the physician, taken in that strict sense of which you are speaking, a healer of the sick or a maker of money? And remember that I am now speaking of the true physician.

A healer of the sick, he replied.

And the pilot—that is to say, the true pilot—is he a captain of sailors or a mere sailor?

A captain of sailors.

The circumstance that he sails in the ship is not to be taken into account; neither is he to be called a sailor; the name pilot by which he is distinguished has nothing to do with sailing, but is significant of his skill and of his authority over the sailors.

Very true, he said.

Now, I said, every art has an interest?

Certainly.

For which the art has to consider and provide?

Yes, that is the aim of art.

And the interest of any art is the perfection of it—this and nothing else?

What do you mean?

I mean what I may illustrate negatively by the example of the body. Suppose you were to ask me whether the body is self-sufficing or has wants, I should reply: Certainly the body has wants; for the body may be ill and require to be cured, and has therefore interests to which the art of medicine ministers; and this is the origin and intention of medicine, as you will acknowledge. Am I not right?

Quite right, he replied.

But is the art of medicine or any other art faulty or deficient in any quality in the same way that the eye may be deficient in sight or the ear fail of hearing, and therefore requires another art to provide for the interests of seeing and hearing—has art in itself, I say, any similar liability to fault or defect, and does every art require another supplementary art to provide for its interests, and that another and another end? Or have the arts to look only after their own interests? Or have they no need either of themselves or of another?—having no faults or defects, they have no need to correct them, either by the exercise of their own art or of any other; they have only to consider the interest of their subject-matter. For every art remains pure and faultless while remaining true—that is to say, while perfect and unimpaired. Take the words in your precise sense, and tell me whether I am not right.

Yes, clearly.

Then medicine does not consider the interest of medicine, but the interest of the body?

True, he said.

Nor does the art of horsemanship consider the interests of the art of horsemanship, but the interests of the horse; neither do any other arts care for themselves, for they have no needs; they care only for that which is the subject of their art?

True, he said.

But surely, Thrasymachus, the arts are the superiors and rulers of their own subjects?

To this he assented with a good deal of reluctance.

Then, I said, no science or art considers or enjoins the interests of the stronger or superior, but only the interest of the subject and weaker?

He made an attempt to contest this proposition also, but finally acquiesced.

Then, I continued, no physician, in so far as he is a physician, considers his own good in what he prescribes, but the good of his patient; for the true physician is also a ruler having the human body as a subject, and is not a mere money-maker; that has been admitted?

Yes.

And the pilot likewise, in the strict sense of the term, is a ruler of sailors and not a mere sailor?

That has been admitted.

And such a pilot and ruler will provide and prescribe for the interest of the sailor who is under him, and not for his own or the ruler's interest?

He gave a reluctant "Yes."

Then, I said, Thrasymachus, there is no one in any rule who, in so far as he is a ruler, considers or enjoins what is for his own interest, but always what is for the interest of his subject or suitable to his art; to that he looks, and that alone he considers in everything which he says and does.

When we had got to this point in the argument, every one saw that [Thrasymachus'] definition of justice had been completely upset.

THOMAS HOBBES
Justice and the Social Contract

THOMAS HOBBES *(1588–1679) was a political reformer and the author of a bold book,* The Leviathan, *in which, among other things, he argues against the divine right of kings. He begins the book by considering what life might be like in "the state of nature"— before the formation of societies (see pp. 466–467). In nature, he says, there is no such thing as justice. In nature, there is only a war—"of all against all." Justice arises as part of the "social contract" that creates society. The following is from* The Leviathan.

TO this war of every man, against every man, this also is consequent; that nothing can be unjust. The notions of right and wrong, justice and injustice have there no place. Where there is no common power, there is no law: where no law, no injustice. Force, and fraud, are in war the two cardinal virtues. Justice, and injustice are none of the faculties neither of the body, nor mind. If they were, they might be in a man that were alone in the world, as well as his senses, and passions. They are qualities, that relate to men in society, not in solitude. It is consequent also to the same condition, that there be no propriety, no dominion, no *mine* and *thine* distinct; but only that to be every man's, that he can get: and for so long, as he can keep it. And thus much for the ill condition, which man by mere nature is actually placed in; though with a possibility to come out of it, consisting partly in the passions, partly in his reason.

Hobbes, Thomas, "Justice and the Social Contract," from *Leviathan,* Oxford: Oxford University Press, 1909, Part I, Chs. 14 and 15; Part II, Ch. 18.

The passions that incline men to peace, and fear of death; desire of such things as are necessary to commodious living; and a hope by their industry to obtain them. And reason suggesteth convenient articles of peace, upon which men may be drawn to agreement. These articles, are they, which otherwise are called the Laws of Nature. . . .

The RIGHT OF NATURE, which writers commonly call *jus naturale,* is the liberty each man hath, to use his own power, as he will himself, for the preservation of his own nature; that is to say, of his own life; and consequently, of doing any thing, which in his own judgment, and reason, he shall conceive to be the aptest means thereunto.

By LIBERTY is understood, according, to the proper signification of the word, the absence of external impediments: which impediments, may oft take away part of a man's power to do what he would; but cannot hinder him from using the power left him, according as his judgment, and reason shall dictate to him.

A LAW OF NATURE, *lex naturalis,* is a precept or general rule, found out by reason, by which a man is forbidden to do that, which is destructive of his life, or taketh away the means of preserving the same; and to omit that, by which he thinketh it may be best preserved. For though they that speak of this subject, use to confound *jus,* and *lex, right* and *law:* yet they ought to be distinguished; because RIGHT, consisteth in liberty to do, or to forbear: whereas LAW, determineth, and bindeth, to one of them: so that law, and right, differ as much, as obligation, and liberty; which in one and the same matter are inconsistent.

And because the condition of man, as hath been declared in the precedent chapter, is a condition of war of every one against every one; in which case every one is governed by his own reason; and there is nothing he can make use of, that may not be a help unto him, in preserving his life against his enemies; it followeth, that in such a condition, every man has a right to every thing; even to one another's body. And therefore, as long as this natural right of every man to everything endureth, there can be no security to any man, how strong or wise soever he be, of living out the time, which nature ordinarily

alloweth men to live. And consequently it is a precept, or general rule of reason, *that every man, ought to endeavour peace, as far as he has hope of obtaining it; and when he cannot obtain it, that he may seek, and use, all helps, and advantages of war.* The first branch of which rule, containeth the first, and fundamental law of nature; which is, *to seek peace, and follow it.* The second, the sum of the right of nature; which is, *by all means we can, to defend ourselves.*

From this fundamental law of nature, by which men are commanded to endeavour peace, is derived this second law; that a man be willing, when others are so too, as far-forth, as for peace, and defense of himself he shall think it necessary, to lay down this right to all things; and be contented with so much liberty against other men, as he would allow other men against himself. For as long as every man holdeth this right, of doing any thing he liketh; so long are all men in the condition of war. But if other men will not lay down their right, as well as he; then there is no reason for any one, to divest himself of his; for that were to expose himself to prey, which no man is bound to, rather than to dispose himself to peace. This is that law of the Gospel: *whatsoever you require that others should do to you, that do ye to them.* And that law of all men, *do not do to others what you do not want them to do to you.*

Whensoever a man transferreth his right, or renounceth it; it is either in consideration of some right reciprocally transferred to himself: or for some other good he hopeth for thereby. For it is a voluntary act: and of the voluntary acts of every man, the object is some *good to himself.* And therefore there be some rights, which no man can be understood by any words, or other signs, to have abandoned, or transferred. As first a man cannot lay down the right of resisting them, that assault him by force, to take away his life; because he cannot be understood to aim thereby, at any good to himself. The same may be said of wounds, and chains, and imprisonment; both because there is no benefit consequent to such patience; as there is to the patience of suffering another to be wounded, or imprisoned: as also because a man cannot tell, when he seeth men proceed against him by violence, whether they intend his death or not. And lastly the motive, and end for which this renouncing, and transferring of right is introduced, is nothing else but the security of a man's person, in his life, and in the means of so preserving life, as not to be weary of it. And therefore if a man by words, or their signs, seem to despoil himself on the end, for which those signs were intended; he is not to be understood as if he meant it, or that it was his will; but that he was ignorant of how such words and actions were to be interpreted. . . .

A covenant not to defend myself from force, by force, is always void. For, as I have showed before, no man can transfer, or lay down his right to save himself from death, wounds, and imprisonment, the avoiding whereof is the only end of laying down any right; and therefore the promise of not resisting force, in no covenant transferreth any right; nor is obliging. For though a man may covenant thus, *unless I do so, or so, kill me;* he cannot covenant thus, *unless I do so, or so, I will not resist you, when you come to kill me.* For man by nature chooseth the lesser evil, which is danger of death in resisting; rather than the greater, which is certain and present death is not resisting. And this is granted to be true by all men, in that they lead criminals to execution, and prison, with armed men, notwithstanding that such criminals have consented to the law, by which they are condemned.

From that law of nature, by which we are obliged to transfer to another, such rights, as being retained, hinder the peace of mankind, there followeth a third; which is this, *that men perform their covenants made:* without which, covenants are in vain, and but empty words; and the right of all men to all things remaining, we are still in the condition of war.

And in this law of nature, consisteth the fountain and original of JUSTICE. For where no covenant hath preceded, there hath no right been transferred, and every man has right to every thing; and consequently, no action can be unjust. But when a covenant is made, then to break it is *unjust:* and the definition of INJUSTICE, is no other than *the not performance of covenant.* And whatsoever is not unjust, is *just.*

But because covenants of mutual trust, where there is a fear of not performance on either part, as hath been said in the former chapter, are invalid; though the original of justice be the making of covenants; yet injustice actually there can be none, till the cause of such fear be taken away; which while men are in the natural condition of war, cannot be done. Therefore before the names of just, and unjust can have place, there must be some coercive power, to compel men equally to the performance of their covenants, by the terror of some punishment, greater than the benefit they expect by the breach of their covenant; and to make good that propriety, which by mutual contract men acquire, in recompense of the universal right they abandon: and such power there is none before the erection of a commonwealth. And this is also to be gathered out of the ordinary definition of justice in the Schools: for they say, that *justice is the constant will of giving to every man his own.* And therefore where there is no *own,* that is no propriety, there is no injustice; and where there is no coercive power erected, that is, where there is no commonwealth, there is no propriety; all men having right to all things: therefore where there is no commonwealth, there nothing is unjust. So that the nature of justice, consisteth in keeping of valid covenants: but the validity of covenants begins not but with the constitution of a civil power, sufficient to compel men to keep them: and then it is also that propriety begins.

A commonwealth is said to be *instituted,* when a *multitude* of men do agree, and *covenant, every one, with every one,* that to whatsoever *man,* or *assembly of men,* shall be given by the major part, the *right to present* the person of them all, that is to say, to be their *representative;* every one, as well he that *voted for it,* as he that *voted against it,* shall *authorize* all the actions and judgments, of that man, or assembly of men, in the same manner, as if they were his own, to the end, to live peaceably amongst themselves, and be protected against other men.

From this institution of a commonwealth are derived all the *rights,* and *faculties* of him, or them, on whom the sovereign power is conferred by the consent of the people assembled.

First, because they covenant, it is to be understood, they are not obliged by former covenant to any thing repugnant hereunto. And consequently they that have already instituted a commonwealth, being thereby bound by covenant, to own the actions, and judgments of one, cannot lawfully make a new covenant, amongst themselves, to be obedient to any other, in any thing whatsoever, without his permission. And therefore, they that are subjects to a monarch, cannot without his leave cast off monarchy, and return to the confusion of a disunited multitude; nor transfer their person from him that beareth it, to another man, or other assembly of men: for they are bound, every man to every man, to own, and be reputed author of all, that he that already is their sovereign, shall do, and judge fit to be done: so that any one man dissenting, all the rest should break their covenant made to that man, which is injustice: and they have also every man given the sovereignty to him that beareth their person; and therefore if they depose him, they take from him that which is his own, and so again it is injustice. Besides, if he that attempteth to depose his sovereign, be killed, or punished by him for such attempt, he is author of his own punishment, as being by the institution, author of all his sovereign shall do: and because it is injustice for a man to do any thing, for which he may be punished by his own authority, he is also upon that title, unjust. And whereas some men have pretended for their disobedience to their sovereign, a new covenant, made, not with men, but with God; this also is unjust: for there is no covenant with God, but by mediation of somebody that representeth God's person; which none doth but God's lieutenant, who hath the sovereignty under God. But this pretence of covenant with God, is so evident a lie, even in the pretenders' own consciences, that it is not only an act of an unjust, but also of a vile, and unmanly disposition.

Secondly, because the right of bearing the person of them all, is given to him they make sovereign, by covenant only of one to another, and not of him to any of them; there can happen no breach of covenant on the part of the sovereign; and consequently none of his subjects, by any pretence of forfeiture, can be freed from his subjection. That he which is made sovereign maketh no covenant with his subjects beforehand, is manifest; because either he must make it with the whole multitude, as one party to the covenant; or he must make a several covenant with every man. With the whole, as one party, it is impossible; because as yet they are not one person: and if he make so many several covenants as there be men, those covenants after he hath the sovereignty are void; because what act soever can be pretended by any one of them for breach thereof, is the act both of himself, and of all the rest, because done in the person, and by the right of every one of them in particular. Besides, if any one, or more of them, pretend a breach of the covenant made by the sovereign at his institution; and others, or one other of his subjects, or himself alone, pretend there was no such breach, there is in this case, no judge to decide the controversy; it returns therefore to the sword again; and every man recovereth the right of protecting himself by his own strength, contrary to the design they had in the institution. It is therefore in vain to grant sovereignty by way of precedent covenant. The opinion that any monarch receiveth his power by covenant, this is to say, on condition, proceedeth from want of understanding this easy truth, that covenants being but words and breath, have no force to oblige, contain, constrain or protect any man, but what it has from the public sword; that is, from the untied hands of that man, or assembly of men that hath the sovereignty, and whose actions are avouched by them all, and performed by the strength of them all, in him united. But when an assembly of men is made sovereign; then no man imagineth any such covenant to have passed in the institution; for no man is so dull as to say, for example, the people of Rome made a covenant with the Romans, to hold the sovereignty on such or such conditions; which not performed, the Romans might lawfully depose the Roman people. That men see not the reason to be alike in a monarchy, and in a popular government, proceedeth from the ambition of some, that are kinder to the government of an assembly, whereof they may hope to participate, than of monarchy, which they despair to enjoy.

Thirdly, because the major part hath by consenting voices declared a sovereign; he that dissented must now consent with the rest; that is, be contented to avow all the actions he shall do, or else justly be destroyed by the rest. For if he voluntarily entered into the congregation of them that were assembled, he sufficiently declared thereby his will, and therefore tacitly covenanted, to stand to what the major part should ordain: and therefore if he refuse to stand thereto, or make protestation against any of their decrees, he does contrary to his covenant, and therefore unjustly. And whether he be of the congregation, or not; and whether his consent be asked, or not, he must either submit to their decrees, or be left in the condition of war he was in before; wherein he might without injustice be destroyed by any man whatsoever.

Fourthly, because every subject is by this institution author of all the actions, and judgment of the sovereign instituted; it follows that whatsoever he doth, it can be no injury to any of his subjects; nor ought he to be any of them accused of injustice. For he that doth anything by authority from another, doth therein no injury to him by whose authority he acteth: but by this institution of a commonwealth, every particular man is author of all the sovereign doth: and consequently he that complaineth of injury from his sovereign, complaineth of that whereof he himself is author; and therefore ought not to accuse any man but himself; no nor himself of injury; because to do injury to one's self, is impossible. It is true that they that have sovereign power may commit iniquity; but not injustice, or injury in the proper signification.

Fifthly, and consequently to that which was said last, no man that hath sovereign power can justly be put to death, or otherwise in any manner by his subjects punished. For seeing every subject is author of the actions of his sovereign; he punisheth another for the actions committed by himself.

JOHN STUART MILL
A Utilitarian Theory of Justice

JOHN STUART MILL *(1806–1873) insists that justice is part and parcel of his ethical view, called "utilitarianism," which calls for "the greatest good for the greatest number." The problem for his view is that it is not clear how justice can be a matter only of utility rather than of rights and obligations. First, Mill analyzes the various ingredients in justice. Then he defends the idea that justice is indeed a function of utility. The following is from Mill's* Utilitarianism.

Mill, John Stuart, "A Utilitarian Theory of Justice," from *Utilitarinism,* Longmans & Green, 1907.

IN the case of this, as of our other moral sentiments, there is no necessary connexion between the question of its origin and that of its binding force. That a feeling is bestowed on us by nature does not necessarily legitimate all its promptings. The feeling of justice might be a peculiar instinct, and might yet require, like our other instincts, to be controlled and enlightened by a higher reason. If we have intellectual instincts leading us to judge in a particular way, as well as animal instincts that prompt us to act in a particular way, there is no necessity that the former should be more infallible in their sphere than the latter in theirs; it may as well happen that wrong judgments are occasionally suggested by those, as wrong actions by these.

In the first place, it is mostly considered unjust to deprive anyone of his personal liberty, his property, or any other thing which belongs to him by law. Here, therefore, is one instance of the application of the terms "just" and "unjust" in a perfectly definite sense, namely, that it is just to respect, unjust to violate, the *legal rights* of anyone. But this judgment admits of several exceptions, arising from the other forms in which the notions of justice and injustice present themselves. For example, the person who suffers the deprivation may (as the phrase is) have forfeited the rights which he is so deprived of—a case to which we shall return presently. But also—

Secondly, the legal rights of which he is deprived may be rights which ought not to have belonged to him; in other words, the law which confers on him these rights may be a bad law. When it is so or when (which is the same thing for our purpose) it is supposed to be so, opinions will differ as to the justice of infringing it. Some maintain that no law, however bad, ought to be disobeyed by an individual citizen; that his opposition to it, if shown at all, should only be shown in endeavoring to get it altered by competent authority. This opinion (which condemns many of the most illustrious benefactors of mankind, and would often protect pernicious institutions against the only weapons which, in the state of things existing at the time, have any chance of succeeding against them) is defended by those who hold it on grounds of expediency, principally on that of the importance to the common interest of mankind, of maintaining inviolate the sentiment of submission to law. Other persons, again, hold the directly contrary opinion that any law, judged to be bad, may blamelessly be disobeyed, even though it be not judged to be unjust but only inexpedient, while others would confine the license of disobedience to the case of unjust laws; but, again, some say that all laws which are inexpedient are unjust, since every law imposes some restriction on the natural liberty of mankind, which restriction is an injustice unless legitimated by tending to their good. Among these diversities of opinion it seems to be universally admitted that there may be unjust laws, and that law, consequently, is not the ultimate criterion of justice, but may give to one person a benefit, or impose on another an evil, which justice condemns. When, however, a law is thought to be unjust, it seems always to be regarded as being so in the same way in which a breach of law is unjust, namely, by infringing somebody's right, which, as it cannot in this case be a legal right, receives a different appellation and is called a moral right. We may say, therefore, that a second case of injustice consists in taking or withholding from any person that to which he has a *moral right.*

Thirdly, it is universally considered just that each person should obtain that (whether good or evil) which he *deserves*, and unjust that he should obtain a good or be made to undergo an evil which he does not deserve. This is, perhaps, the clearest and most emphatic form in which the idea of justice is conceived by the general mind. As it involves the notion of desert, the question arises what constitutes desert? Speaking in a general way, a person is understood to deserve good if he does right, evil if he does wrong: and in a more particular sense, to deserve good from those to whom he does or has done good, and evil from those to whom he does or has done evil. The percept of returning good for evil has never been regarded as a case of the fulfillment of justice, but as one in which the claims of justice are waived, in obedience to other considerations.

Fourthly, it is confessedly unjust to *break faith* with anyone: to violate an engagement, either express or implied, or disappoint expectations raised by our own conduct, at least if we have raised those expectations knowingly and voluntarily. Like the other obligations of justice already spoken of, this one is not regarded as absolute, but as capable of being overruled by a stronger obligation of justice on the other side, or by such conduct on the part of the person concerned as is deemed to absolve us from our obligation to him and to constitute a *forfeiture* of the benefit which he has been led to expect.

Fifthly, it is, by universal admission, inconsistent with justice to be *partial*—to show favor or preference to one person over another in matters to which favor and preference do not properly apply. Impartiality, however, does not seem to be regarded as a duty in itself, but rather as instrumental to some other duty; for it is admitted that favor and preference are not always censurable, and, indeed, the cases in which they are condemned are rather the exception than the rule. A person would be more likely to be blamed than applauded for giving his family or friends no superiority in good offices over strangers when he could do so without violating any other duty; and no one thinks it unjust to seek one person in preference to another as a friend, connection, or companion. Impartiality where rights are concerned is of course obligatory, but this is involved in the more general obligation of giving to everyone his right. A tribunal, for example, must be impartial because it is bound to award, without regard to any other consideration, a disputed object to the one of two parties who has the right to it. There are other cases in which impartiality means being solely influenced by desert, as with those who, in the capacity of judges, preceptors, or parents, administer reward and punishment as such. There are cases, again, in which it means being solely influenced by consideration for the public interest, as in making a selection among candidates for a government employment. Impartiality, in short, as an obligation of justice, may be said to mean being exclusively influenced by the considerations which it is supposed ought to influence the particular case in hand, and resisting solicitation of any motives which prompt to conduct different from what those considerations would dictate.

Nearly allied to the idea of impartiality is that of *equality,* which often enters as a component part both into the conception of justice and into the practice of it, and, in the eyes of many persons, constitutes its essence. But in this, still more than in any other case, the notion of justice varies in different persons, and always conforms in its variations to their notion of utility. Each person maintains that equality is the dictate of justice, except where he thinks that expediency requires inequality. The justice of giving equal protection to the rights of all is maintained by those who support the most outrageous inequality in the rights themselves. Even in slave countries it is theoretically admitted that the rights of the slave, such as they are, ought to be as sacred as those of the master, and that a tribunal which fails to enforce them with equal strictness is wanting in justice; while, at the same time, institutions which leave to the slave scarcely any rights to enforce are not deemed unjust because they are not deemed inexpedient. Those who think that utility requires distinctions of rank do not consider it unjust that riches and social privileges should be unequally dispensed; but those who think this inequality inexpedient think it unjust also. Whoever thinks that government is necessary sees no injustice in as much inequality as is constituted by giving to the magistrate powers not granted to other people. Even among those who hold leveling doctrines, there are differences of opinion about expediency. Some communists consider it unjust that the produce of the labor of the community should be shared on any other principle than that of exact equality; others think it just that those should receive most whose wants are greatest; while others hold that those who work harder, or who produce more, or whose services are more valuable to the community, may justly claim a larger quota in the division of the produce. And the sense of natural justice may be plausibly appealed to in behalf of every one of these opinions.

Justice implies something which it is not only right to do, and wrong not to do, but which some individual person can claim from us as his moral right. No one has a moral right to our generosity or beneficence because we are not morally bound to practice those virtues toward any given individual. And it will be found with respect to this as to every correct definition that the instances which seem to conflict with it are those which most confirm it. For if a moralist attempts, as some have done, to make out that mankind generally, though not any given individual, have a right to all the good we can do them, he at once, by that thesis, includes generosity and beneficence within the category of justice. He is obliged to say that our utmost exertions are *due* to our fellow creatures, thus assimilating them to a debt; or that nothing less can be a sufficient *return* for what society does for us, thus classing the case as one of gratitude; both of which are acknowledged cases of justice, and not of the virtue of beneficence; and whoever does not place the distinction between justice and morality in general, where we have now placed it, will be found to make no distinction between them at all, but to merge all morality in justice.

To recapitulate: the idea of justice supposes two things—a rule of conduct and a sentiment which sanctions the rule. The first must be supposed common to all mankind and intended for their good. The other (the sentiment) is a desire that punishment may be suffered by those who infringe the rule. There is involved, in addition, the conception of some definite person who suffers by the infringement, whose rights (to use the expression appropriated to the case) are violated by it. And the sentiment of justice appears to me to be the animal desire to repel or retaliate a hurt or damage to oneself or to those with whom one sympathizes, widened so as to include all persons, by the human capacity of enlarged sympathy and the human conception of intelligent self-interest. From the latter elements the feeling derives its morality; from the former, its peculiar impressiveness and energy of self-assertion. . . .

If the preceding analysis, or something resembling it, be not the correct account of the notion of justice—if justice be totally independent of utility, and be a standard *per se*, which the mind can recognize by simple introspection of itself—it is hard to understand why that internal oracle is so ambiguous, and why so many things appear either just or unjust, according to the light in which they are regarded.

We are continually informed that utility is an uncertain standard, which every different person interprets differently, and that there is no safely but in the immutable, ineffaceable, and unmistakable dictates of justice, which carry their evidence in themselves and are independent of the fluctuations of opinion. One would suppose from this that on questions of justice there could be no controversy; that, if we take that for our rule, its application to any given case could leave us in as little doubt as a mathematical demonstration. So far is this from being the fact that there is as much difference of opinion, and as much discussion, about what is just as about what is useful to society. Not only have different nations and individuals different notions of justice, but in the mind of one and the same individual, justice is not some one rule, principle, or maxim, but many which do not always coincide in their dictates, and, in choosing between which, he is guided either by some extraneous standard or by his own personal predilections. . . .

. . . [For instance] in co-operative industrial association, is it just or not that talent or skill should give a title to superior remuneration? On the negative side of the question it is argued that whoever does the best he can deserves equally well, and ought not in justice to be put in a position of inferiority for no fault of his own; that superior abilities have already advantages more than enough, in the admiration they excite, the personal influence they command, and the internal sources of satisfaction attending them, without adding to these a superior share of the world's goods; and that society is bound in justice rather to make compensation to the less favored for this unmerited inequality of advantages than to aggravate it. On the contrary side it is contended that society receives more from the more efficient laborer; that, his services being more useful, society owes him a larger return for them; that a greater share of the joint result is actually his work, and not to allow his claim to it is a kind of robbery; that, if he is only to receive as much as others, he can only be justly required to produce as much, and to give a smaller amount of time and exertion, proportioned to his superior efficiency. Who shall decide between these appeals to conflicting principles of justice? Justice has in this case two sides to it, which it is impossible to bring into harmony, and the two disputants have chosen opposite sides; the one looks to what it is just that the individual should receive, the other to what it is just that the community should give. Each, from his own point of view, is unanswerable; and any choice between them, on grounds of justice, must be perfectly arbitrary. Social utility alone can decide the preference.

The considerations which have now been adduced resolve, I conceive, the only real difficulty in the utilitarian theory of morals. It has always been evident that all cases of justice are also cases of expediency; the difference is in the peculiar sentiment which attaches to the former, as contradistinguished from the latter. If this characteristic sentiment has been sufficiently accounted for; if there is no necessity to assume for it any peculiarity of origin; if it is simply the natural feeling of resentment, moralized by being made co-extensive with the demands of social good; and if this feeling not only does but ought to exist in all the classes of cases to which the idea of justice corresponds—that idea no longer presents itself as a stumbling block to the utilitarial ethics. Justice remains the appropriate name for certain social utilities which are vastly more important, and therefore more absolute and imperative, than any others are as a class (though not more so than others may be in particular cases); and which, therefore, ought to be, as well as naturally are, guarded by a sentiment, not only different in degree, but also in kind; distinguished from the milder feeling which attaches to the mere idea of promoting human pleasure or convenience at once by the more definite nature of its commands and by the sterner character of its sanctions.

JOHN RAWLS
Justice as Fairness

JOHN RAWLS *(1921–2002) was a professor of philosophy at Harvard University and the author of* A Theory of Justice. *In the following essay, he discusses some of the main ideas of his theory "justice as fairness."*

1 It might seem at first sight that the concepts of justice and fairness are the same, and that there is no reason to distinguish them, or to say that one is more fundamental than the other. I think that this impression is mistaken. In this paper I wish to show that the fundamental idea in the concept of justice is fairness; and I wish to offer an analysis of the concept of justice from this point of view. To bring out the force of this claim, and the analysis based upon it, I shall then argue that it is this aspect of justice for which utilitarianism, in its classical form, is unable to account, but which is expressed, even if misleadingly, by the idea of the social contract.

To start with I shall develop a particular conception of justice by stating and commenting upon two principles which specify it, and by considering the circumstances and conditions under which they may be thought to arise. The principles defining this conception itself, are, of course, familiar. It may be possible, however, by using the notion of fairness as a framework, to assemble and to look at them in a new way. Before stating this conception, however, the following preliminary matters should be kept in mind.

Throughout I consider justice only as a virtue of social institutions, or what I shall call practices. The principles of justice are regarded as formulating restrictions as to how practices may define positions and offices, and assign thereto powers and liabilities, rights and duties. Justice as a virtue of particular actions or of persons I do not take up at all. It is important to distinguish these various subjects of justice, since the meaning of the concept varies according to whether it is applied to practices, particular actions, or persons. These meanings are, indeed, connected, but they are not identical. I shall confine my discussion to the sense of justice as applied to practices, since this sense is the basic one. Once it is understood, the other senses should go quite easily.

Justice is to be understood in its customary sense as representing but *one* of the many virtues of social institutions, for these may be antiquated, inefficient, degrading, or any number of other things, without being unjust. Justice is not to be confused with an all-inclusive vision of a good society; it is only one part of any such conception. It is important, for example, to distinguish that sense of equality which is an aspect of the concept of justice from that sense of equality which belongs to a more comprehensive social ideal. There may well be inequalities which one concedes are just, or at least not unjust, but which, nevertheless, one wishes on other grounds, to do away with. I shall focus attention, then, on the usual sense of justice in which it is essentially the elimination of arbitrary distinctions and the establishment, within the structure of a practice, of a proper balance between competing claims.

Finally, there is no need to consider the principles discussed below as *the* principles of justice. For the moment it is sufficient that they are typical of a family of principles normally associated with the concept of justice. The way in which the principles of this family resemble one another, as shown by the background against which they may be thought to arise, will be made clear by the whole of the subsequent argument.

2 The conception of justice which I want to develop may be stated in the form of two principles as follows: first, each person participating in a practice, or affected by it, has an equal right to the most extensive liberty compatible with a like liberty for all; and second, inequalities are arbitrary unless it is reasonable to expect that they will work out for everyone's advantage, and provided the positions and offices to which they attach, or from which they may be gained, are open to all. These principles express justice as a complex of three ideas: liberty, equality, and reward for services contributing to the common good.

• • •

The first principle holds, of course, only if other things are equal; that is, while there must always be a justification for departing from the initial position of equal liberty (which is defined by the pattern of rights and duties, powers and liabilities, established by a practice), and the burden of proof is placed on him who would depart from it, nevertheless, there can be, and often there is, a justification for doing so. Now, that similar particular cases, as defined by a practice, should be treated similarly as they arise, is part of the very concept of a practice; it is involved in the notion of an activity in accordance with rules. The first principle expresses an analogous conception, but as applied to the structure of practices themselves. It holds, for example, that there is a presumption against the distinctions and classifications made by legal systems and other practices to the extent that they infringe on the original and equal liberty of the persons participating in them. The second principle defines how this presumption may be rebutted.

It might be argued at this point that justice requires only an equal liberty. If, however, a greater liberty were possible for all without loss or conflict, then it would be irrational to settle on a lesser liberty. There is no reason for circumscribing rights unless their exercise would be incompatible, or would render the practice defining them less effective. Therefore no serious distortion of the concept of justice is likely to follow from including within it the concept of the greatest equal liberty.

The second principle defines what sorts of inequalities are permissible; it specifies how the presumption laid down by the first principle may be put aside. Now by inequalities it is best to understand not *any* differences between offices and positions, but differences in the benefits and burdens attached to them either directly or indirectly, such as prestige and wealth, or liability to taxation and compulsory services. Players in a game do not protest against there being different positions, such as batter, pitcher, catcher, and the like, nor to there being various privileges and powers as specified by the rules; nor do the citizens of a country object to there being the different offices of government such as president, senator, governor, judge, and so on, each with their special rights and duties. It is not differences of this kind that are normally thought of as inequalities, but differences in the resulting distribution established by a practice, or made possible by it, of the things men strive to attain or avoid. Thus they may complain about the pattern of honors and rewards set up by a practice (e.g., the privileges and salaries of government officials) or they may object to the distribution of power and wealth which results from the various ways in which men avail themselves of the opportunities allowed by it (e.g., the concentration of wealth which may develop in a free price system allowing large entrepreneurial or speculative gains).

It should be noted that the second principle holds that an inequality is allowed only if there is reason to believe that the practice with the inequality, or resulting in it, will work for the advantage of *every* party engaging in it. Here it is important to stress that *every* party must gain from the inequality. Since the principle applies to practices, it implies that the representative man in every office or position defined by a practice, when he views it as a going concern, must find it reasonable to prefer his condition and prospects with the inequality to what they would be under the practice without it. The principle excludes, therefore, the justification of inequalities on the grounds that the disadvantages of those in one position are outweighed by the greater advantages of those in another position. This rather simple restriction is the main modification I wish to make in the utilitarian principle as usually understood.

·   ·   ·

3 Given these principles one might try to derive them from a priori principles of reason, or claim that they were known by intuition. These are familiar enough steps and, at least in the case of the first principle, might be made with some success. Usually, however, such arguments, made at this point, are unconvincing. They are not likely to lead to an understanding of the basis of the principles of justice, not at least as principles of justice. I wish, therefore, to look at the principles in a different way.

Imagine a society of persons amongst whom a certain system of practices is *already* well established. Now suppose that by and large they are mutually self-interested; their allegiance to their established practices is normally founded on the prospect of self-advantage. One need not assume that, in all senses of the term "person," the persons in this society are mutually self-interested. If the characterization as mutually self-interested applies when the line of division is the family, it may still be true that members of families are bound by ties of sentiment and affection and willingly acknowledge duties in contradiction to self-interest. Mutual self-interestedness in the relations between families, nations, churches, and the like, is commonly associated with intense loyalty and devotion on the part of individual members. Therefore, one can form a more realistic conception of this society if one thinks of it as consisting of mutually self-interested families, or some other association. Further, it is not necessary to suppose that these persons are mutually self-interested under all circumstances, but only in the usual situations in which they participate in their common practice.

Now suppose also that these persons are rational: they know their own interests more or less accurately; they are capable of tracing out the likely consequences of adopting one practice rather than another; they are capable of adhering to a course of action once they have decided upon it; they can resist present temptations and the enticements of immediate gain; and the bare knowledge or perception of the difference between their condition and that of others is not, within certain limits and in itself, a source of great dissatisfaction. Only the last point adds anything to the usual definition of rationality. This definition should allow, I think for the idea that a rational man would not be greatly downcast from knowing, or seeing, that others are in a better position than himself, unless he thought their being so was the result of injustice, or the consequence of letting chance work itself out for no useful common purpose, and so on. So if these persons strike us as unpleasantly egoistic, they are at least free in some degree from the fault of envy.

Finally, assume that these persons have roughly similar needs and interests, or needs and interests in various ways complementary, so that fruitful cooperation amongst them is possible; and suppose that they are sufficiently equal in power and ability to guarantee that in normal circumstances none is able to dominate the others. This condition (as well as the others) may seem excessively vague; but in view of the conception of justice to which the argument leads, there seems no reason for making it more exact here.

Since these persons are conceived as engaging in their common practices, which are already established, there is no question of our supposing them to come together to deliberate as to how they will set these practices up for the first time. Yet we can imagine that from time to time they discuss with one another whether any of them has a legitimate complaint against their established institutions. Such discussions are perfectly natural in any normal society. Now suppose that they have settled on doing this in the following way. They first try to arrive at the principles by which complaints, and so practices themselves, are to be judged. Their procedure for this is to let each person propose the principles upon which he wishes his complaints to be tried with the understanding that, if acknowledged, the complaints of others will be similarly tried, and that no complaints will be heard at all until everyone is roughly of one mind as to how complaints are to be judged. They each understand further that the principles proposed and acknowledged on this occasion are binding on future occasions. Thus each will be wary of proposing a principle which would give him a peculiar advantage, in his present circumstances, supposing it to be accepted. Each person knows that he will be bound by it in future circumstances the peculiarities of which cannot be known, and which might well be such that the principle is then to his disadvantage. The idea is that everyone should be required to make *in advance* a firm commitment, which others also may reasonably be expected to make, and that no one be given the opportunity to tailor the canons of a legitimate complaint to fit his own special condition, and then to discard them when they no longer suit his purpose. Hence each person will propose principles of a general kind which will, to a large degree, gain their sense from the various applications to be made of them, the particular circumstances of which being as yet unknown. These principles will express the conditions in accordance with which each is the least unwilling to have his interests limited in the design of practices, given the competing interests of the others, on the supposition that the interests of others will be limited likewise. The restrictions which would so arise might be thought of as those a person would keep in mind if he were designing a practice in which his enemy were to assign him his place.

The two main parts of this conjectural account have a definite significance. The character and respective situations of the parties reflect the typical circumstances in which questions of justice arise. The procedure whereby principles are proposed and acknowledged represents constraints, analogous to those of having a morality, whereby rational and mutually self-interested persons are brought to act reasonably. Thus the first part reflects the fact that questions of justice arise when conflicting claims are made upon the design of a practice and where it is taken for granted that each person will insist, as far as possible, on what he considers his rights. It is typical of cases of justice to involve persons who are pressing on one another their claims, between which a fair balance or equilibrium must be found. On the other hand, as expressed by the second part, having a morality must at least imply the acknowledgment of principles as impartially applying to one's own conduct as well as to another's, and moreover principles which may constitute a constraint, or limitation, upon the pursuit of one's own interests. There are, of course, other aspects of having a morality: the acknowledgment of moral principles must show itself in accepting a reference to them as reasons for limiting one's claims, in acknowledging the burden of providing a special explanation, or excuse, when one acts contrary to them, or else in showing shame and remorse and a desire to make amends, and so on. It is sufficient to remark here that having a morality is analogous to having made a firm commitment in advance; for one must acknowledge the principles of morality even when to one's disadvantage. A man whose moral judgements always coincided with his interests could be suspected of having no morality at all.

Thus the two parts of the foregoing account are intended to mirror the kinds of circumstances in which questions of justice arise and the constraints which having a morality would impose upon persons so situated. In this way one can see how the acceptance of the principles of justice might come about, for given all these conditions as described, it would be natural if the two principles of justice were to be acknowledged. Since there is no way for anyone to win special advantage for himself, each might consider it reasonable to acknowledge equality as an initial principle. There is, however, no reason why they should regard this position as final; for if there are inequalities which satisfy the second principle, the immediate gain which equality would allow can be considered as intelligently invested in view of its future return. If, as is quite likely, these inequalities work as incentives to draw out better efforts, the members of this society may look upon them as concessions to human nature: they, like us, may think that people ideally should want to serve one another. But as they are mutually self-interested, their acceptance of these inequalities is merely the acceptance of the relations in which they actually stand, and a recognition of the motives which lead them to engage in their common practices. *They* have no title to complain of one another. And so provided that the conditions of the principle are met, there is no reason why they should not allow such inequalities. Indeed, it would be short-sighted of them to do so, and could result, in most cases, only from their being dejected by the bare knowledge, or perception, that others are better situated. Each person will, however, insist on an advantage to himself, and so on a common advantage, for none is willing to sacrifice anything for the others.

ROBERT NOZICK
The Principle of Fairness

ROBERT NOZICK (1938–2002) was a professor of philosophy at Harvard University, and in the following selection he expresses his reservations about the theory of justice formulated and made famous by his colleague, John Rawls.

A principle suggested by Herbert Hart, which (following John Rawls) we shall call the *principle of fairness,* would be of service here if it were adequate. This principle holds that when a number of persons engage in a just, mutually advantageous, cooperative venture according to rules and thus restrain their liberty in ways necessary to yield advantages for all, those who have submitted to these restrictions have a right to similar acquiescence on the part of those who have benefited from their submission. Acceptance of benefits (even when this is not a giving of express or tacit undertaking to cooperate) is enough, according to this principle, to bind one. If one adds to the principle of fairness the claim that the others to whom the obligations are owed or their agents may *enforce* the obligations arising under this principle (including the obligation to limit one's actions), then groups of people in a state of nature who agree to a procedure to pick those to engage in certain acts will have legitimate rights to prohibit "free riders." Such a right may be crucial to the viability of such agreements. We should scrutinize such a powerful right very carefully, especially as it seems to make *unanimous* consent to coercive government in a state of nature *unnecessary!* . . .

The principle of fairness, as we stated it following Hart and Rawls, is objectionable and unacceptable. Suppose some of the people in your neighborhood (there are 364 other adults) have found a public address system and decide to institute a system of public entertainment. They post a list of names, one for each day, yours among them. On his assigned day (one can easily switch days) a person is to run the public address system, play records over it, give news bulletins, tell amusing stories he has heard, and so on. After 138 days on which each person has done his part, your day arrives. Are you obligated to take your turn? You *have* benefited from it, occasionally opening your window to listen, enjoying some music or chuckling at someone's funny story. The other people *have* put themselves out. But must you answer the call when it is your turn to do so? As it stands, surely not. Though you benefit from the arrangement, you may know all along that 364 days of entertainment supplied by others will not be worth your giving up *one* day. You would rather not have any of it and not give up a day than have it all and spend one of your days at it. Given these preferences, how can it be that you are required to participate when your scheduled time comes? It would be nice to have philosophy readings on the radio to which one could tune in at any time, perhaps late at night when tired. But it may not be nice enough for you to want to give up one whole day of your own as a reader on the program. Whatever you want, can others create an obligation for you to do so by going ahead and starting the program themselves? In this case you can choose to forgo the benefit by not turning on the radio; in other cases the benefits may be unavoidable. If each day a different person on your street sweeps the entire street, must you do so when your time comes? Even if you don't care that much about a clean street? Must you imagine dirt as you traverse the street, so as not to benefit as a free rider? Must you refrain from turning on the radio to hear the philosophy readings? Must you mow your front lawn as often as your neighbors mow theirs?

At the very least one wants to build into the principle of fairness the condition that the benefits to a person from the actions of the others are greater than the costs to him of doing his share. How are we to imagine this? Is the condition satisfied if you do enjoy the daily broadcasts over the PA system in your neighborhood but would prefer a day off hiking, rather than hearing these broadcasts all year? For you to be obligated to give up your day to broadcast mustn't it be true, at least, that there is nothing you could do with a day (with that day, with the increment in any other day, by shifting some activities to that day) which you would prefer to hearing broadcasts for the year? If the only way to get the broadcasts was to spend the day participating in the arrangement, in order for the condition that the benefits outweigh the costs to be satisfied, you would have to be willing to spend it on the broadcasts rather than to gain *any* other available thing.

If the principle of fairness were modified so as to contain this very strong condition, it still would be objectionable. The benefits might only barely be worth the costs to you of doing your share, yet others might benefit from *this* institution much more than you do; they all treasure listening to the public broadcasts. As the person least benefited by the practice, are you obligated to do an equal amount for it? Or perhaps you would prefer that all cooperated in *another* venture, limiting their conduct and making sacrifices for *it*. It is true, *given* that they are not following your plan (and thus limiting what other options are available to you), that the benefits of their venture *are* worth to you the costs of your cooperation. However, you do not wish to cooperate, as part of your plan to focus their attention on your alternative proposal which

they have ignored or not given, in your view at least, its proper due. (You want them, for example, to read the Talmud on the radio instead of the philosophy they are reading.) By lending the institution (their institution) the support of your cooperating in it, you will only make it harder to change or alter.

On the face of it, enforcing the principle of fairness is objectionable. You may not decide to give me something, for example a book, and then grab money from me to pay for it, even if I have nothing better to spend the money on. You have, if anything, even less reason to demand payment if your activity that gives me the book also benefits you; suppose that your best way of getting exercise is by throwing books into people's houses, or that some other activity of yours thrusts books into people's houses as an unavoidable side effect. Nor are things changed if your inability to collect money or payments for the books which unavoidably spill over into others' houses makes it inadvisable or too expensive for you to carry on the activity with this side effect. One cannot, whatever one's purposes, just act so as to give people benefits and then demand (or seize) payment. Nor can a group of persons do this. If you may not charge and collect for benefits you bestow without prior agreement, you certainly may not do so for benefits whose bestowal costs you nothing, and most certainly people need not repay you for costless-to-provide benefits which yet *others* provided them. So the fact that we partially are "social products" in that we benefit from current patterns and forms created by the multitudinous actions of a long string of long-forgotten people, forms which include institutions, ways of doing things, and language . . . does not create in us a general floating debt which the current society can collect and use as it will.

Perhaps a modified principle of fairness can be stated which would be free from these and similar difficulties. What seems certain is that any such principle, if possible, would be so complex and involved that one could not combine it with a special principle legitimating *enforcement* within a state of nature of the obligations that have arisen under it. Hence, even if the principle could be formulated so that it was no longer open to objection, it would not serve to obviate the need for other persons' *consenting* to cooperate and limit their own activities.

THE ENTITLEMENT THEORY

The subject of justice in holdings consists of three major topics. The first is the *original acquisition of holdings,* the appropriation of unheld things. This includes the issues of how unheld things may come to be held, the process, or processes, by which unheld things may come to be held, the things that may come to be held by these processes, the extent of what comes to be held by a particular process, and so on. We shall refer to the complicated truth about this topic, which we shall not formulate here, as the principle of justice in acquisition. The second topic concerns the *transfer of holdings* from one person to another. By what processes may a person transfer holdings to another? How may a person acquire a holding from another who holds it? Under this topic come general descriptions of voluntary exchange, and gift and (on the other hand) fraud, as well as reference to particular conventional details fixed upon in a given society. The complicated truth about this subject (with placeholders for conventional details) we shall call the principle of justice in transfer. (And we shall suppose it also includes principles governing how a person may divest himself of a holding, passing it into an unheld state.)

If the world were wholly just, the following inductive definition would exhaustively cover the subject of justice in holdings.

1. A person who acquires a holding in accordance with the principle of justice in acquisition is entitled to that holding.

2. A person who acquires a holding in accordance with the principle of justice in transfer, from someone else entitled to the holding, is entitled to the holding.

3. No one is entitled to a holding except by (repeated) application of 1 and 2.

The complete principle of distributive justice would say simply that a distribution is just if everyone is entitled to the holdings they possess under the distribution.

A distribution is just if it arises from another just distribution by legitimate means. The legitimate means of moving from one distribution to another are specified by the principle of justice in transfer. The legitimate first "moves" are specified by the principle of justice in acquisition. Whatever arises from a just situation by just steps is itself just. The means of change specified by the principle of justice in transfer preserve justice. As correct rules of inference are truth-preserving, and any conclusion deduced via repeated application of such rules from only true premises is itself true, so the means of transition from one situation to another specified by the principle of justice in transfer are justice-preserving, and any situation actually arising from repeated transitions in accordance with the principle from a just situation is itself just. The parallel between just-preserving transformations and truth-preserving transformations illuminates where it fails as well as where it holds. That a conclusion could have been deduced by truth-preserving means from premises that are true suffices to show its truth. That from a just situation a situation *could* have arisen via justice-preserving means does *not* suffice to show its justice. The fact that a thief's victims voluntarily *could* have presented him with gifts does not entitle the thief to his ill-gotten gains. Justice in holdings is historical; it depends upon what actually has happened. We shall return to this point later.

Not all actual situations are generated in accordance with the two principles of justice in holdings: the principle of justice in acquisition and the principle of justice in transfer. Some people steal from others, or defraud them, or enslave them, seizing their product and preventing them from living as they choose, or forcibly exclude others from competing in exchanges. None of these are permissible modes of transition from one situation to another. And some persons acquire holdings by means not sanctioned by the principle of justice in acquisition. The existence of past injustice (previous violations of the first two principles of justice in holdings) raises the third major topic under justice in holdings: the rectification of injustice in holdings. If past injustice has shaped present holdings in various ways, some identifiable and some not, what now, if anything, ought to be done to rectify these injustices? What obligations do the performers of injustice have toward those whose position is worse than it would have been had the injustice not been done? Or, than it would have been had compensation been paid promptly? How, if at all, do things change if the beneficiaries and those made worse off are not the direct parties in the act of injustice, but, for example their descendants? Is an injustice done to someone whose holding was itself based upon an unrectified injustice? How far back must one go in wiping clean the historical slate of injustices? What may victims of injustice permissibly do in order to rectify the injustices being done to them, including the many injustices done by persons acting through their government? I do not know of a thorough or theoretically sophisticated treatment of such issues. Idealizing greatly, let us suppose theoretical investigation will produce a principle of rectification. This principle uses historical information about previous situations and injustices done in them (as defined by the first two principles of justice and rights against interference), and information about the actual course of events that flowed from these injustices, until the present, and it yields a description (or descriptions) of holdings in the society. The principle of rectification presumably will make use of its best estimate of subjunctive information about what would have occurred (or a probability distribution over what might have occurred, using the expected value) if the injustice had not taken place. If the actual description of holdings turns out not to be one of the descriptions yielded by the principle, then one of the descriptions yielded must be realized.

The general outlines of the theory of justice in holdings are that the holdings of a person are just if he is entitled to them by the principles of justice in acquisition and transfer, or by the principle of rectification of injustice (as specified by the first two principles). If each person's holdings are just, then the total set (distribution) of holdings is just.

HISTORICAL PRINCIPLES AND END-RESULT PRINCIPLES

The general outlines of the entitlement theory illuminate the nature and defects of other conceptions of distributive justice. The entitlement theory of justice in distributions is *historical;* whether a distribution is just depends upon how it came about. In contrast, *current time-slice* principles of justice hold that the justice of a distribution is determined by how things are distributed (who has what) as judged by some *structural* principle(s) of just distribution. A utilitarian who judges between any two distributions by seeing which has the greater sum of utility and, if the sums tie, applies some fixed equality criterion to choose the more equal distribution, would hold a current time-slice principle of justice. As would someone who had a fixed schedule of trade-offs between the sum of happiness and equality. According to a current time-slice principle, all that needs to be looked at, in judging the justice of a distribution, is who ends up with what; in comparing any two distributions one need look only at the matrix presenting the distributions. No further information need be fed into a principle of justice. It is a consequence of such principles of justice that any two structurally identical distributions are equally just. (Two distributions are structurally identical if they present the same profile, but perhaps have different persons occupying the particular slots. My having ten and your having five, and my having five and your having ten are structurally identical distributions.) Welfare economics is the theory of current time-slice principles of justice. The subject is conceived as operating on matrices representing only current information about distribution. This, as well as some of the usual conditions (for example, the choice of distribution is invariant under relabeling of columns), guarantees that welfare economics will be a current time-slice theory, with all of its inadequacies.

Most persons do not accept current time-slice principles as constituting the whole story about distributive shares. They think it relevant in assessing the justice of a situation to consider not only the distribution it embodies, but also how that distribution came about. If some persons are in prison for murder or war crimes, we do not say that to assess the justice of the distribution in the society we must look only at what this person has, and that person has, and that person has . . . at the current time. We think it relevant to ask whether someone did something so that he deserved to be punished, *deserved* to have a lower share. Most will agree to the relevance of further information with regard to punishments and penalties. Consider also desired things. One traditional socialist view is that workers are entitled to the product and full fruits of their labor; they have earned it; a distribution is unjust if it does not give the workers what they are entitled to. Such entitlements are based upon some past history. No socialist holding this view would find it comforting to be told that because the actual distribution A happens to coincide structurally with the one he desires D, A therefore is no less just than D, it differs only in that the "parasitic" owners of capital receive under A what the workers are entitled to under D, and the workers receive under A what the owners are entitled to under D, namely very little. This socialist rightly, in my view, holds onto the notions of earning, producing, entitlement, desert, and so forth, and he rejects current time-slice principles that look only to the structure of the resulting set of holdings. (The set of holdings resulting from what? Isn't it implausible that how holdings are produced and come to exist has no effect at all on who should hold what?) His mistake lies in his view of what entitlements arise out of what sorts of productive processes.

We construe the position we discuss too narrowly by speaking of *current* time-slice principles. Nothing is changed if structural principles operate upon a time sequence of current time-slice profiles and, for example, give someone more now to counterbalance the less he has had earlier. A utilitarian or an egalitarian or any mixture of the two over time will inherit the difficulties of his more myopic comrades. He is not helped by the fact that *some* of the information others consider relevant in assessing a distribution is reflected, unrecoverably, in past matrices. Henceforth, we shall refer to such unhistorical principles of distributive justice, including the current time-slice principles, as *end-result principles* or *end-state principles*.

In contrast to end-result principles of justice, *historical principles* of justice hold that past circumstances or actions of people can create differential entitlements or differential deserts to things. An injustice can be worked by moving from one distribution to another structurally identical one, for the second, in profile the same, may violate people's entitlements or deserts; it may not fit the actual history.

DAVID BROOKS

The Triumph of Hope Over Self-Interest

DAVID BROOKS *is a columnist for* The New York Times, *a regular commentator on* PBS, *and the author of* Bobos in Paradise: The New Upper Class and How They Got There. *He explains why people accept what would seem to be unfair and disadvantageous tax arrangements.*

WHY don't people vote their own self-interest? Every few years the Republicans propose a tax cut, and every few years the Democrats pull out their income distribution charts to show that much of the benefits of the Republican plan go to the richest 1 percent of Americans or thereabouts. And yet every few years a Republican plan wends its way through the legislative process and, with some trims and amendments, passes.

The Democrats couldn't even persuade people to oppose the repeal of the estate tax, which is explicitly for the mega-upper class. Al Gore, who ran a populist campaign, couldn't even win the votes of white males who didn't go to college, whose incomes have stagnated over the past decades, and who were the explicit targets of his campaign. Why don't more Americans want to distribute more wealth down to people like themselves?

Well, as the academics would say, it's overdetermined. There are several reasons.

People vote their aspirations.

The most telling polling result from the 2000 election was from a *Time* magazine survey that asked people if they are in the top 1 percent of earners. Nineteen percent of Americans say they are in the richest 1 percent and a further 20 percent expect to be someday. So right away you have 39 percent of Americans who thought that when Mr. Gore savaged a plan that favored the top 1 percent, he was taking a direct shot at them.

It's not hard to see why they think this way. Americans live in a culture of abundance. They have always had a sense that great opportunities lie just over the horizon, in the next valley, with the next job or the next big thing. None of us is really poor; we're just pre-rich.

Americans read magazines for people more affluent than they are (*W, Cigar Aficionado, The New Yorker, Robb Report, Town and Country*) because they think that someday they could be that guy with the tastefully appointed horse farm. Democratic politicians proposing to take from the rich are just bashing the dreams of our imminent selves.

Income resentment is not a strong emotion in much of America.

If you earn $125,000 a year and live in Manhattan, certainly, you are surrounded by things you cannot afford. You have to walk by those buildings on Central Park West with the 2,500-square-foot apartments that are empty three-quarters of the year because their evil owners are mostly living at their other houses in L.A.

But if you are a middle-class person in most of America, you are not brought into incessant contact with things you can't afford. There aren't Lexus dealerships on every corner. There are no snooty restaurants with water sommeliers to help you sort though the bottled eau selections. You can afford most of the things at Wal-Mart or Kohl's and the occasional meal at the Macaroni Grill. Moreover, it would be socially unacceptable for you to pull up to church in a Jaguar or to

Brooks, David, "Triumph of Hope Over Self-Interest," from *The New York Times* (January 12, 2003).

hire a caterer for your dinner party anyway. So you are not plagued by a nagging feeling of doing without.

Many Americans admire the rich.

They don't see society as a conflict zone between the rich and poor. It's taboo to say in a democratic culture, but do you think a nation that watches Katie Couric in the morning, Tom Hanks in the evening and Michael Jordan on weekends harbors deep animosity toward the affluent?

On the contrary. I'm writing this from Nashville, where one of the richest families, the Frists, is hugely admired for its entrepreneurial skill and community service. People don't want to tax the Frists—they want to elect them to the Senate. And they did.

Nor are Americans suffering from false consciousness. You go to a town where the factories have closed and people who once earned $14 an hour now work for $8 an hour. They've taken their hits. But odds are you will find their faith in hard work and self-reliance undiminished, and their suspicion of Washington unchanged.

Americans resent social inequality more than income inequality.

As the sociologist Jennifer Lopez has observed: "Don't be fooled by the rocks that I got, I'm just, I'm just Jenny from the block." As long as rich people "stay real," in Ms. Lopez's formulation, they are admired. Meanwhile, middle-class journalists and academics who seem to look down on megachurches, suburbia, and hunters are resented. If Americans see the tax debate as being waged between the economic elite, led by President Bush, and the cultural elite, led by Barbra Streisand, they are going to side with Mr. Bush, who could come to any suburban barbershop and fit right in.

Most Americans do not have Marxian categories in their heads.

This is the most important reason Americans resist wealth redistribution, the reason that subsumes all others. Americans do not see society as a layer cake, with the rich on top, the middle class beneath them and the working class and underclass at the bottom. They see society as a high school cafeteria, with their community at one table and other communities at other tables. They are pretty sure that their community is the nicest, and filled with the best people, and they have a vague pity for all those poor souls who live in New York City or California and have a lot of money but no true neighbors and no free time.

All of this adds up to a terrain incredibly inhospitable to class-based politics. Every few years a group of millionaire Democratic presidential aspirants pretends to be the people's warriors against the overclass. They look inauthentic, combative rather than unifying. Worst of all, their basic message is not optimistic.

They haven't learned what Franklin and Teddy Roosevelt and even Bill Clinton knew: that you can run against rich people, but only those who have betrayed the ideal of fair competition. You have to be more hopeful and growth-oriented than your opponent, and you cannot imply that we are a nation tragically and permanently divided by income. In the gospel of America, there are no permanent conflicts.

PETER SINGER
Rich and Poor

PETER SINGER, *for many years a professor in Australia, is now part of the Center for Values at Princeton University. He is the author of* Animal Liberation *and many books on ethics. In a powerful and radical way, he advocates sharing our resources with those worse off.*

SOME FACTS ABOUT POVERTY

CONSIDER these facts: by the most cautious estimates, 400 million people lack the calories, protein, vitamins and minerals needed to sustain their bodies and minds in a healthy state. Millions are constantly hungry; others suffer from deficiency diseases and from infections they would be able to resist on a better diet. Children are the worst affected. According to one study, 14 million children under five die every year from the combined effects of malnutrition and infection. In some districts half the children born can be expected to die before their fifth birthday.

Nor is lack of food the only hardship of the poor. To give a broader picture, Robert McNamara, when president of the World Bank, suggested the term "absolute poverty." The poverty we are familiar with in industrialised nations is relative poverty—meaning that some citizens are poor, relative to the wealth enjoyed by their neighbours. People living in relative poverty in Australia might be quite comfortably off by comparison with pensioners in Britain, and British pensioners are not poor in comparison with the poverty that exists in Mali or Ethiopia. Absolute poverty, on the other hand, is poverty by any standard. In McNamara's words:

Poverty at the absolute level . . . is life at the very margin of existence. The absolute poor are severely deprived human beings struggling to survive in a set of squalid and degraded circumstances almost beyond the power of our sophisticated imaginations and privileged circumstances to conceive.

Compared to those fortunate enough to live in developed countries, individuals in the poorest nations have:

- An infant mortality rate eight times higher
- A life expectancy one-third lower
- An adult literacy rate 60 per cent less
- A nutritional level, for one out of every two in the population, below acceptable standards;
- And for millions of infants, less protein than is sufficient to permit optimum development of the brain.

McNamara has summed up absolute poverty as "a condition of life so characterised by malnutrition, illiteracy, disease, squalid surroundings, high infant mortality and low life expectancy as to be beneath any reasonable definition of human decency." . . .

Death and disease apart, absolute poverty remains a miserable condition of life, with inadequate food, shelter, clothing, sanitation, health services and education. The Worldwatch Institute estimates that as many as 1.2 billion people—or 23 per cent of the world's population—live in absolute poverty. For the purposes of this estimate, absolute poverty is defined as "the lack of sufficient income in cash or kind to meet the most basic biological needs for food, clothing, and shelter." Absolute poverty is probably the principal cause of human misery today. . . .

The problem is not that the world cannot produce enough to feed and shelter its people.

Singer, Peter, "Rich and Poor," from *Practical Ethics*, 2/e (Cambridge University Press, 1993). Reprinted with the permission of Cambridge University Press.

People in the poor countries consume, on average, 180 kilos of grain a year, while North Americans average around 900 kilos. The difference is caused by the fact that in the rich countries we feed most of our grain to animals, converting it into meat, milk, and eggs. Because this is a highly inefficient process, people in rich countries are responsible for the consumption of far more food than those in poor countries who eat few animal products. If we stopped feeding animals on grains and soybeans, the amount of food saved would—if distributed to those who need it—be more than enough to end hunger throughout the world.

These facts about animal food do not mean that we can easily solve the world food problem by cutting down on animal products, but they show that the problem is essentially one of distribution rather than production. The world does produce enough food. Moreover, the poorer nations themselves could produce far more if they made more use of improved agricultural techniques.

So why are people hungry? Poor people cannot afford to buy grain grown by farmers in the richer nations. Poor farmers cannot afford to buy improved seeds, or fertilisers, or the machinery needed for drilling wells and pumping water. Only by transferring some of the wealth of the rich nations to the poor can the situation be changed.

That this wealth exists is clear. Against the picture of absolute poverty that McNamara has painted, one might pose a picture of "absolute affluence." Those who are absolutely affluent are not necessarily affluent by comparison with their neighbours, but they are affluent by any reasonable definition of human needs. This means that they have more income than they need to provide themselves adequately with all the basic necessities of life. After buying (either directly or through their taxes) food, shelter, clothing, basic health services, and education, the absolutely affluent are still able to spend money on luxuries. The absolutely affluent choose their food for the pleasures of the palate, not to stop hunger; they buy new clothes to look good, not to keep warm; they move house to be in a better

neighborhood or have a playroom for the children, not to keep out the rain; and after all this there is still money to spend on stereo systems, video-cameras, and overseas holidays.

At this stage I am making no ethical judgments about absolute affluence, merely pointing out that it exists. Its defining characteristic is a significant amount of income above the level necessary to provide for the basic human needs of oneself and one's dependents. By this standard, the majority of citizens of Western Europe, North America, Japan, Australia, New Zealand, and the oil-rich Middle Eastern states are all absolutely affluent. To quote McNamara once more:

> The average citizen of a developed country enjoys wealth beyond the wildest dreams of the one billion people in countries with per capita incomes under $200.

These, therefore, are the countries—and individuals—who have wealth that they could, without threatening their own basic welfare, transfer to the absolutely poor.

At present, very little is being transferred. Only Sweden, the Netherlands, Norway, and some of the oil-exporting Arab states have reached the modest target, set by the United Nations, of 0.7 per cent of gross national product (GNP). Britain gives 0.31 per cent of its GNP in official development assistance and a small additional amount in unofficial aid from voluntary organisations. The total comes to about £2 per month per person, and compares with 5.5 per cent of GNP spent on alcohol, and 3 per cent on tobacco. Other, even wealthier nations, give little more: Germany gives 0.41 per cent and Japan 0.32 per cent. The United States gives a mere 0.15 per cent of its GNP. . . .

THE OBLIGATION TO ASSIST

The Argument for an Obligation to Assist

The path from the library at my university to the humanities lecture theatre passes a shallow ornamental pond. Suppose that on my way to give a lecture I notice that a small child has fallen in and is in danger of drowning. Would anyone deny that I ought to wade in and pull the child out? This will mean getting my clothes muddy and either cancelling my lecture or delaying it until I can find something dry to change into; but compared with the avoidable death of a child this is insignificant.

A plausible principle that would support the judgment that I ought to pull the child out is this: if it is in our power to prevent something very bad from happening, without thereby sacrificing anything of comparable moral significance, we ought to do it. This principle seems uncontroversial. It will obviously win the assent of consequentialists; but non-consequentialists should accept it too, because the injunction to prevent what is bad applies only when nothing comparably significant is at stake. Thus the principle cannot lead to the kinds of actions of which non-consequentialists strongly disapprove—serious violations of individual rights, injustice, broken promises, and so on. If non-consequentialists regard any of these as comparable in moral significance to the bad thing that is to be prevented, they will automatically regard the principle as not applying in those cases in which the bad thing can only be prevented by violating rights, doing injustice, breaking promises, or whatever else is at stake. Most non-consequentialists hold that we ought to prevent what is bad and promote what is good. Their dispute with

consequentialists lies in their insistence that this is not the sole ultimate ethical principle: that it is an ethical principle is not denied by any plausible ethical theory.

Nevertheless the uncontroversial appearance of the principle that we ought to prevent what is bad when we can do so without sacrificing anything of comparable moral significance is deceptive. If it were taken seriously and acted upon, our lives and our world would be fundamentally changed. For the principle applies, not just to rare situations in which one can save a child from a pond, but to the everyday situation in which we can assist those living in absolute poverty. In saying this I assume that absolute poverty, with its hunger and malnutrition, lack of shelter, illiteracy, disease, high infant mortality, and low life expectancy, is a bad thing. And I assume that it is within the power of the affluent to reduce absolute poverty, without sacrificing anything of comparable moral significance. If these two assumptions and the principle we have been discussing are correct, we have an obligation to help those in absolute poverty that is no less strong than our obligation to rescue a drowning child from a pond. Not to help would be wrong, whether or not it is intrinsically equivalent to killing. Helping is not, as conventionally thought, a charitable act that it is praiseworthy to do, but not wrong to omit; it is something that everyone ought to do.

IRIS YOUNG
The Myth of Merit

IRIS YOUNG *teaches feminism, philosophy, and politics at the University of Pittsburgh. She is author of* Justice and the Politics of Difference.

A widely held principle of justice in our society is that positions and rewards should be distributed according to individual merit. The merit principle holds that positions should be awarded to the most qualified individuals, that is, to those who have the greatest aptitude and skill for performing the tasks those positions require. This principle is central to legitimating a hierarchical division of labor in a liberal democratic society which assumes the equal moral and political worth of all persons. Assuming as given a structural division between scarce highly rewarded positions and more plentiful less rewarded positions, the merit principle asserts that this division of labor is just when no group receives privileged positions by birth or right, or by virtue of arbitrary characteristics such as race, ethnicity, or sex. The unjust hierarchy of caste is to be replaced by a "natural" hierarchy of intellect and skill.

• • •

Use of a principle of merit to allocate scarce and desirable positions in a job hierarchy, and in the educational institutions that train people for those jobs, is just only if several conditions are met. First, qualifications must be defined in terms of technical skills and competence, independently of and neutral with respect to values and culture. By technical competence I mean competence at producing specified results. If merit criteria do not distinguish between technical skills and normative or cultural attributes, there is no way to separate being a "good" worker of a certain sort from being the sort of person—with the right background, way of life, and so on. Second, to justify differential job privilege the purely technical skills and competencies must be "job related," in that they operate as predictors for excellent performance in the position. Third, for merit criteria to be applied justly, performance and competence must be judged individually. In order to say that one individual is more qualified than another, finally, the performances and predicted performances of individuals must be compared and ranked according to

measures which are independent of and neutral with respect to values and culture.

Proponents of a merit principle rarely doubt that these conditions can be met. Fishkin, for example, finds it obvious that the technical competence of individuals can be measured and predicted apart from values, purposes, and cultural norms. "It is hard to believe," he says, "in a modern industrial society, with a complex differentiation of tasks that qualifications that are performance related could not be defined so as to predict better performances." It may be hard to believe, but in fact such normatively and culturally neutral measures of individual performance do not exist for most jobs. The idea of merit criteria that are objective and unbiased with respect to personal attributes is a version of the ideal of impartiality, and is just as impossible.

First, most jobs are too complex and multifaceted to allow for a precise identification of their tasks and thus measurement of levels of performance of those tasks. Precise, value-neutral, task-specific measures of job performance are possible only for jobs with a limited number of definable functions, each of which is a fairly straightforward identifiable task, requiring little verbal skill, imagination, or judgment. Data entry work or quality control sorting may satisfy these requirements, but a great many jobs do not. A travel agent, for example, must keep records, communicate effectively on the telephone and through ever-changing computer networks of information, and study and keep at hand options in tour packages for many places. Service sector work, a vastly expanding portion of jobs, in general can rarely be evaluated in terms of the criteria of productivity and efficiency applied to industrial production, because it makes much less sense to count services rendered than items that come off the assembly line.

Second, in complex industrial and office organizations, it is often not possible to identify the contribution that each individual makes, precisely because the workers cooperate in producing an outcome or product. The performance of a team, department, or firm may be measurable, but this is of little use in justifying the position or level of reward of any particular team members.

Third, a great many jobs require wide discretion in what the worker does and how best to do it. In many jobs the worker's role is more negative than positive; he or she oversees a process and intervenes to prevent something from going wrong. In automated processes, from individual machines to entire factories, for example, workers routinely contribute little to the actual making of things, but they must be vigilant in tending the machines to make sure the process goes as it should. The negative role increases worker discretion about whether, when and how often to intervene. Perhaps there is one easily identifiable and measurable way to perform many positive actions. But there are many ways of preventing a process from going wrong, and it is not usually possible to measure a worker's productivity level in terms of the costs that would have been incurred if she or he had not intervened, or the costs that would have been saved if she or he had intervened differently.

Finally, the division of labor in most large organizations means that those evaluating a worker's performance often are not familiar with the actual work process. Modern organizational hierarchies are what Claus Offe calls task discontinuous hierarchies. In a task continuous hierarchy, like that exemplified by medieval guild production, superiors do the same kind of work as their subordinates, but with a greater degree of skill and competence. In the task discontinuous hierarchies of contemporary organizations, job ladders are highly segregated. Superiors do not do the same kind of work as subordinates, and may never have done that sort of work. Thus the superior is often not competent to evaluate the technical work performance itself, and must rely on evaluating workers' attitudes, their compliance with the rules, their self-presentation, their cooperativeness—that is, their social comportment.

While these four impediments to a normatively and culturally neutral definition and assessment of job performance occur in many types of work, they are most apparent in professional and managerial work. These types of work usually involve a wide diversity of skills and tasks. Most or all of these tasks rely on the use of judgment, discretion, imagination, and verbal acuity, and none of these qualities is precisely measurable according to some objective, value-neutral scale. The achievement of professional and managerial objectives usually involves a complex series of social relationships and dependencies, to the extent that it is often unreasonable to hold professionals responsible for not meeting objectives. Professional and managerial jobs, finally, often are evaluated not only by superiors in a task discontinuous hierarchy, but by clients who are even less aware of the nature of the jobs and the skills required, and who are thus not in a position to apply criteria of technical performance that are normatively and culturally neutral.

In very tentative conclusion, it seems that the principle of equality (in the version that rests on needs rather than that which requires "perfect equality") and the principles of contribution and effort (where nonarbitrarily applicable, and only *after* everyone's basic needs have been satisfied) have the most weight as determinants of economic justice, whereas all forms of the principle of merit are implausible in that role. The reason for the priority of basic needs is that, where there is economic abundance, the claim to life itself and to minimally decent conditions are, like other human rights, claims that all men make with perfect equality. As economic production increases, these claims are given ever greater consideration in the form of rising standards for distinguishing basic needs from other wanted goods. But no matter where that line is drawn, when we go beyond it into the realm of economic surplus or "luxuries," non-egalitarian considerations (especially contribution and effort) come increasingly into play.

AMARTYA SEN
Property and Hunger

AMARTYA SEN *is professor of economics at Harvard University and is author of many books, including* Ethics and Economics. *In 1998 he won the Nobel Prize for his work on economics and social justice. In this essay, he insists that questions of justice be appealed not just to abstract theory but also to the concrete facts of human life—especially the facts revealed by economies and by pervasive human misery.*

I N an interesting letter to Anna George, the daughter of Henry George, Bernard Shaw wrote: "Your father found me a literary dilettante and militant rationalist in religion, and a barren rascal at that. By turning my mind to economics he made a man of me." [I] am not able to determine what making a man of Bernard Shaw would exactly consist of, but it is clear that the kind of moral and social problems with which Shaw was deeply concerned could not be sensibly pursued without examining their economic aspects. For example, the claims of property rights, which some would defend and some (including Shaw) would dispute, are not just matters of basic moral belief that could not possibly be influenced one way or the other by any empirical arguments. They call for sensitive moral analysis responsive to empirical realities, including economic ones.

Moral claims based on intrinsically valuable rights are often used in political and social arguments. Rights related to ownership have been invoked for ages. But there are also other types of rights which have been seen as "inherent and inalienable," and the American Declaration of Independence refers to "certain unalienable rights," among which are "life, liberty and the pursuit of happiness." The Indian constitution talks even of "the right to an adequate means of livelihood." The "right not to be hungry" has often been invoked in recent discussions on the obligation to help the famished.

RIGHTS: INSTRUMENTS, CONSTRAINTS, OR GOALS?

Rights can be taken to be morally important in three different ways. First, they can be considered to be valuable *instruments* to achieve other goals. This is the "instrumental view," and is well illustrated by the utilitarian approach to rights. Rights are, in that view, of no intrinsic importance. Violation of rights is not in itself a bad thing, nor fulfillment intrinsically good. But the acceptance of rights promotes, in this view, things that are ultimately important, to wit, utility. Jeremy Bentham rejected "natural rights" as "simple nonsense," and "natural and imprescriptible rights" as "rhetorical nonsense, nonsense upon stilts." But he attached great importance to rights as instruments valuable to the promotion of a good society, and devoted much energy to the attempt to reform appropriately the actual system of rights.

The second view may be called the "constraint view," and it takes the form of seeing rights as *constraints* on what others can or cannot do. In this view rights *are* intrinsically important. However, they don't figure in moral accounting as goals to be generally promoted, but only as constraints that others must obey. As Robert Nozick has put it in a powerful exposition of this "constraint view": "Individuals have rights, and there are things no person or group may do to them (without violating their rights)."

Rights "set the constraints within which a social choice is to be made, by excluding certain alternatives, fixing others, and so on."

The third approach is to see fulfillments or rights as goals to be pursued. This "goal view" differs from the instrumental view in regarding rights to be intrinsically important, and it differs from the constraint view in seeing the fulfillment of rights as goals to be generally promoted, rather than taking them as demanding only (and exactly) that we refrain from violating the rights of others. In the "constraint view" there is no duty to help anyone with his or her rights (merely not to hinder), and also in the "instrumental view" there is no duty, in fact, to help unless the right fulfillment will also promote some other goal such as utility. The "goal view" integrates the valuation of rights—their fulfillment and violation—in overall moral accounting, and yields a wider sphere of influence of rights in morality.

I have argued elsewhere that the goal view has advantages that the other two approaches do not share, in particular, the ability to accommodate integrated moral accounting including inter alia the intrinsic importance of a class of fundamental rights. I shall not repeat that argument here. But there is an interesting question of dual roles of rights in the sense that some rights may be *both* intrinsically important and instrumentally valuable. For example, the right to be free from hunger could—not implausibly—be regarded as being valuable in itself as well as serving as a good instrument to promote other goals such as security, longevity or utility. If so, both the goal view and the instrumental view would have to be simultaneously deployed to get a comprehensive assessment of such a right. This problem of comprehensiveness is a particularly important issue in the context of Henry George's discussion of rights, since he gave many rights significant dual roles.

The instrumental aspect is an inescapable feature of every right, since irrespective of whether a certain right is intrinsically valuable or not, its acceptance will certainly have other consequences as well, and these, too, have to be assessed along with the intrinsic value of rights (if any). A right that is regarded as quite valuable in itself may nevertheless be judged to be morally rejectable if it leads to disastrous consequences. This is a case of the rights playing a *negative* instrumental role. It is, of course, also possible that the instrumental argument will *bolster* the intrinsic claims of a right to be taken seriously. I shall presently argue that such is the case in George's analysis with the right of labor to its produce.

There are two general conclusions to draw, at this stage, from this very preliminary discussion. First, we must distinguish between (1) the intrinsic value of a right, and (2) the overall value of a right taking note inter alia of its intrinsic importance (if any). The acceptance of the intrinsic importance of any right is no guarantee that its overall moral valuation must be favorable. Second, no moral assessment of a right can be independent of its likely consequences. The need for empirical assessment of the effects of accepting any right cannot be escaped. Empirical arguments are quite central to moral philosophy.

PROPERTY AND DEPRIVATION

The right to hold, use and bequeath property that one has legitimately acquired is often taken to be inherently valuable. In fact, however, many of its defenses seem to be actually of the instrumental type, e.g., arguing that property rights make people more free to choose one kind of a life rather than another. Even the traditional attempt at founding "natural property rights" on the principles of "natural liberty" (with or without John Locke's proviso) has some instrumental features. But even if we do accept that property rights may have some intrinsic value, this does not in any way amount to an overall justification of property rights, since property rights may have consequences which themselves will require assessment. Indeed, the causation of hunger as well as its prevention may materially depend on how property rights are structured. If a set of property rights leads, say, to starvation, as it well might, then the moral approval of these rights would certainly be compromised severely. In general, the need for consequential analysis of property rights is inescapable whether or not such rights are seen as having any intrinsic value.

Consider Henry George's formula of giving "the product to the producer." This is, of course, an ambiguous rule, since the division of the credits for production to different causal influences (e.g., according to "marginal productivities" in neoclassical theory, or according to human efforts in classical labor theory) is inevitably somewhat arbitrary, and full of problems involving internal tensions. But no matter how the ambiguities are resolved, it is clear that this rule would give no part of the socially produced output to one who is unemployed since he or she is producing nothing. Also, a person whose productive contribution happens to be tiny, according to *whichever* procedure of such accounting we use, can expect to get very little based on this so-called "natural law." Thus, hunger and starvation are compatible with this system of rights. George thought that this would not occur, since the economic reforms he proposed (including the abolition of land rights) would eliminate unemployment, and provision for the disabled would be made through the sympathetic support of others. These are empirical matters. If these empirical generalizations do not hold, then the outlined system of rights would yield a serious conflict. The property rights to one's product (however defined) might be of some intrinsic moral importance, but we clearly must also take note of the moral disvalue of human misery (such as suffering due to hunger and nutrition-related diseases). The latter could very plausibly be seen as having more moral force than the former. A positive intrinsic value of the right to one's product can go with an overall negative value, taking everything into account.

This type of problem arises most powerfully in assessing the ethical force of some of the standard theories of rights. For example, neither a straightforward moral theory asserting inalienable property rights, nor an elaborate theory of an entitlement system of the kind outlined by Robert Nozick, can escape having to face the possibility that when applied to an actual society, the rights in question may yield hunger, starvation, and even large-scale famine. I have tried to argue elsewhere—not in the context of disputing these moral theories but in trying to understand the causation of famines in the modern world—that famines are, in fact, best explained in terms of failures of entitlement systems. The entitlements here refer, of course, to legal rights and to practical possibilities, rather than to moral status, but the laws and actual operation of private ownership economies have many features in common with the moral system of entitlements analyzed by Nozick and others.

The entitlement approach to famines need not, of course, be confined to private ownership economies, and entitlement failures of other systems can also be fruitfully studied to examine famines and hunger. In the specific context of private ownership economies, the entitlements are substantially analyzable in terms, respectively, of what may be called "endowments" and "exchange entitlements." A person's endowment refers to what he or she initially owns (including the person's own labor power), and the exchange entitlement mapping tells us what the person can obtain through exchanging what he or she owns, either by production (exchange with nature), or by trade (exchange with others), or a mixture of the two. A person has to starve if neither the endowments, nor what can be obtained through exchange, yields an adequate amount of food.

If starvation and hunger are seen in terms of failures of entitlements, then it becomes immediately clear that the total availability of food in a country is only one of several variables that are relevant. Many famines occur without any decline in the availability of food. For example, in the Great Bengal famine of 1943, the total food availability in Bengal was not particularly bad (considerably higher than two years earlier when there was no famine), and yet three million people died, in a famine mainly affecting the rural areas, through rather violent shifts in the relative purchasing powers of different groups, hitting the rural laborers the hardest. The Ethiopian famine of 1973 took place in a year of average per capita food availability, but the cultivators and other occupation groups in the province of Wollo had lost their means of subsistence (through loss of crops and a decline of economic activity, related to a local drought) and had no means of commanding food from elsewhere in the country. Indeed, some food moved *out* of Wollo to more prosperous people in other parts of Ethiopia, repeating a pattern of contrary movement of food that was widely observed during the Irish famine of the 1840s (with food moving out of famine-stricken Ireland to prosperous England which had greater power in the battle of entitlements). The Bangladesh famine of 1974 took place in a year of *peak* food availability, but several occupation groups had lost their entitlement to food through loss of employment and other economic changes (including inflationary pressures causing prices to outrun wages). Other examples of famines without significant (or any) decline in food availability can be found, and there is nothing particularly surprising about this fact once it is recognized that the availability of food is only one influence among many on the entitlement of each occupation group. Even when a famine is associated with a decline of food availability, the entitlement changes have to be studied to understand the particular nature of the famine, e.g., why one occupation group is hit but not another. The causation of starvation can be sensibly sought in failures of entitlements of the respective groups.

The causal analysis of famines in terms of entitlements also points to possible public policies of prevention. The main economic strategy would have to take the form of increasing the entitlements of the deprived groups, and in general, of guaranteeing minimum entitlements for everyone, paying particular attention to the vulnerable groups. This can, in the long run, be done in many different ways, involving both economic growth (including growth of food output) and distributional adjustments. Some of these policies may, however, require that the property rights and the corresponding entitlements of

the more prosperous groups be violated. The problem, in fact, is particularly acute in the short run, since it may not be possible to engineer rapid economic growth instantly. Then the burden of raising entitlements of the groups in distress would largely have to fall on reducing the entitlements of others more favorably placed. Transfers of income or commodities through various public policies may well be effective in quashing a famine (as the experience of famine relief in different countries has shown), but it may require substantial government intervention in the entitlements of the more prosperous groups.

There is, however, no great moral dilemma in this if property rights are treated as purely *instrumental*. If the goals of relief of hunger and poverty are sufficiently powerful, then it would be just right to violate whatever property rights come in the way, since—in this view—property rights have no intrinsic status. On the other hand, if property rights are taken to be morally inviolable irrespective of their consequences, then it will follow that these policies cannot be morally acceptable even though they might save thousands, or even millions, from dying. The inflexible moral "constraint" of respecting people's legitimately acquired entitlements would rule out such policies.

In fact this type of problem presents a reductio ad absurdum of the moral validity of constraint-based entitlement systems. However, while the conclusion to be derived from that approach might well be "absurd," the situation postulated is not an imaginary one at all. It is based on studies of actual famines and the role of entitlement failures in the causation of mass starvation. If there is an embarrassment here, it belongs solidly to the consequence-independent way to seeing rights.

I should add that this dilemma does not arise from regarding property rights to be of intrinsic value, which can be criticized on other grounds, but not this one. Even if property rights *are* of intrinsic value, their violation may be justified on grounds of the favorable consequences of that violation. A right, as was mentioned earlier, may be intrinsically valuable and still be justly violated taking everything into account. The "absurdum" does not belong to attaching intrinsic value to property rights, but to regarding these rights as simply acceptable, regardless of their consequences. A moral system that values both property rights and other goals—such as avoiding famines and starvation, or fulfilling people's right not to be hungry—can, on the one hand, give property rights intrinsic importance, and on the other, recommend the violation of property rights when that leads to better overall consequences (*including* the disvalue of rights violation).

The issue here is not the valuing of property rights, but their alleged inviolability. There is no dilemma here either for the purely instrumental view of property rights or for treating the fulfillment of property rights as one goal among many, but specifically for consequence-independent assertions of property rights and for the corresponding constraint-based approaches to moral entitlement of ownership.

That property and hunger are closely related cannot possibly come as a great surprise. Hunger is primarily associated with not owning enough food and thus property rights over food are immediately and directly involved. Fights over that property right can be a major part of the reality of a poor country, and any system of moral assessment has to take note of that phenomenon. The tendency to see hunger in purely technocratic terms of food output and availability may help to hide the crucial role of entitlements in the genesis of hunger, but a fuller economic analysis cannot overlook that crucial role. Since property rights over food are derived from property rights over other goods and resources (through production and trade), the entire system of rights of acquisition and transfer is implicated in the emergence and survival of hunger and starvation.

THE RIGHT NOT TO BE HUNGRY

Property rights have been championed for a long time. In contrast, the assertion of "the right not to be hungry" is a comparatively recent phenomenon. While this right is much invoked in political debates, there is a good deal of skepticism about treating this as truly a right in any substantial way. It is often asserted that this concept of "right not to be hungry" stands essentially for nothing at all ("simple nonsense," as Bentham called "natural rights" in general). That piece of sophisticated cynicism reveals not so much a penetrating insight into the practical affairs of the world, but a refusal to investigate what people mean when they assert the existence of rights that for the bulk of humanity, are not in fact guaranteed by the existing institutional arrangements.

The right not to be hungry is not asserted as a recognition of an institutional right that already exists, as the right to property typically is. The assertion is primarily a moral claim as to what should be valued, and what institutional structure we should aim for, and try to guarantee if feasible. It can also be seen in terms of Ronald Dworkin's category of "background rights"—rights that provide a justification for political decisions by society in abstract. This interpretation serves as the basis for a reason to change the existing institutional structure and state policy.

It is broadly in this form that the right to "an adequate means of livelihood" is referred to in the Constitution of India: "The state shall, in particular, direct its policy towards securing . . . that the citizens, men and women equally, have the right to an adequate means of livelihood." This does not, of course, offer to each citizen a guaranteed right to an adequate livelihood, but the state is asked to take steps such that this right could become realizable for all.

In fact, this right has often been invoked in political debates in India. The electoral politics of India does indeed give particular scope for such use of what are seen as background rights. It is of course, not altogether clear whether the reference to this right in the Indian constitution has in fact materially influenced the political debates. The constitutional statement is often cited, but very likely this issue would have figured in any case in these debates, given the nature of the moral and political concern. But whatever the constitutional contribution, it is interesting to ask whether the implicit acceptance of the value of the right to freedom from hunger makes any difference to actual policy.

It can be argued that the general acceptance of the right of freedom from acute hunger as a major goal has played quite a substantial role in preventing famines in India. The last real famine in India was in 1943, and while food availability per head in India has risen only rather slowly (even now the food availability per head is no higher than in many sub-Saharan countries stricken by recurrent famines), the country has not experienced any famine since independence in 1947. The main cause of that success is a policy of public intervention. Whenever a famine has threatened (e.g., in Bihar in 1967–68, in Maharashtra in 1971–73, in West Bengal in 1978–79), a public policy of intervention and relief has offered minimum entitlements to the potential famine victims, and thus have the threatening famines been averted. It can be argued that the quickness of the response of the respective governments (both state and central) reflects a political necessity, given the Indian electoral system and the importance attached by the public to the prevention of starvation. Political pressures from opposition groups and the news media have kept the respective governments on their toes, and the right to be free from acute hunger and starvation has been achieved largely because it has been seen as a valuable right. Thus the recognition of the intrinsic moral importance of this right, which has been widely invoked in public discussions, has served as a powerful political instrument as well.

On the other hand, this process has been far from effective in tackling pervasive and persistent undernourishment in India. There has been no famine in post-independence India, but perhaps a third of India's rural population is perennially undernourished. So long as hunger remains non-acute and starvation deaths are avoided (even though morbidity and mortality rates are enhanced by undernourishment), the need for a policy response is neither much discussed by the news media, nor forcefully demanded even by opposition parties. The elimination of famines coexists with the survival of widespread "regular hunger." The right to "adequate means" of *nourishment* does not at all seem to arouse political concern in a way that the right to "adequate means" to *avoid starvation* does.

The contrast can be due to one of several different reasons. It could, of course, simply be that the ability to avoid undernourishment is not socially accepted as very important. This could be so, though what is socially accepted and what is not is also partly a matter of how clearly the questions are posed. It is, in fact, quite possible that the freedom in question would be regarded as a morally important right if the question were posed in a transparent way, but this does not happen because of the nature of Indian electoral politics and that of news coverage. The issue is certainly not "dramatic" in the way in which starvation deaths and threatening famines are. Continued low-key misery may be too familiar a phenomenon to make it worthwhile for political leaders to get some mileage out of it in practical politics. The news media may also find little profit in emphasizing a non-spectacular phenomenon—the quiet survival of disciplined, non-acute hunger.

If this is indeed the case, then the implications for action of the goal of eliminating hunger, or guaranteeing to all the means for achieving this, may be quite complex. The political case for making the quiet hunger less quiet and more troublesome for governments in power is certainly relevant. Aggressive political journalism might prove to have an instrumental moral value if it were able to go beyond reporting the horrors of visible starvation and to portray the pervasive, non-acute hunger in a more dramatic and telling way. This is obviously not the place to discuss the instrumentalities of practical politics, but the endorsement of the moral right to be free from hunger—both acute and non-acute—would in fact raise pointed questions about the means which might be used to pursue such a goal.

MORAL ASSESSMENT AND SOCIAL RELATIONS

Henry George's advice to Bernard Shaw to study economics may well be supplemented by advising the economist to study politics and sociology, and the "moral scientist," to use an old-fashioned term, to study them all. When fulfillments of such rights as freedom from hunger are accepted as goals (among other possible goals), the moral assessment of actions and institutions will depend crucially on economic, social, and political analyses of how best to pursue these goals.

If there is one thing that emerges sharply from the discussion I have tried to present in this paper, it is the importance of factual analysis for moral assessment, including moral scrutiny of the acceptability and pursuit of specific rights. This is so even when the right in question is acknowledged to have intrinsic moral value, since valuing a right is not the same thing as accepting it. To affirm acceptability independently of consequences can be peculiarly untenable, as was discussed in analyzing entitlements and hunger. In assessing the claims of property rights, or the right not to be hungry, the examination cannot be confined to issues of basic valuation only, and much of the challenge of assessment lies in the empirical analysis of causes and effects. In the world in which we live—full of hunger as well as wealth—these empirical investigations can be both complex and quite extraordinarily important. The big moral questions are frequently also deeply economic, social, or political.

MALCOLM X
Human Rights, Civil Rights

MALCOLM X *(1925–1965), originally named Malcolm Little, was a controversial civil rights leader, a powerful organizer, and a spectacular spokesperson for human rights in America. Initially he advocated separatism and black nationalism, but as a result of his conversion to Islam and a pilgrimage he made to Mecca, he revised his political views. Shortly before he was assassinated he adopted a platform of brotherhood and equality. Here he distinguishes between human rights and civil rights.*

[INTERVIEWER]

One question that I've wondered about—in several of your lectures you've stressed the idea that the struggle of your people is for human rights rather than civil rights. Can you explain a bit what you mean by that?

Malcolm X, "Human Rights, Civil Rights," from his speech at Militant Labor Reform on "Prospects for Freedom in 1965." Pathfinder Press and Betty Shabazz.

MALCOLM X:

Civil rights actually keeps the struggle within the domestic confines of America. It keeps it under the jurisdiction of the American government, which means that as long as our struggle for what we're seeking is labeled civil rights, we can only go to Washington, D.C., and then we rely upon either the Supreme Court, the President or the Congress or the senators. These senators—many of them are racists. Many of the congressmen are racists. Many of the judges are racists and oftentimes the president himself is a very shrewdly camouflaged racist. And so we really can't get meaningful redress for our grievances when we are depending upon these grievances being redressed just within the jurisdiction of the United States government.

On the other hand, human rights go beyond the jurisdiction of this government. Human rights are international. Human rights are something that a man has by dint of his having been born. The labeling of our struggle in this country under the title civil rights of the past 12 years has actually made it impossible for us to get outside help. Many foreign nations, many of our brothers and sisters on the African continent who have gotten their independence, have restrained themselves, have refrained from becoming vocally or actively involved in our struggle for fear that they would be violating U.S. protocol, that they would be accused of getting involved in America's domestic affairs.

On the other hand, when we label it human rights, it internationalizes the problem and puts it at a level that makes it possible for any nation or any people anywhere on this earth to speak out in behalf of our human rights struggle.

So we feel that by calling it civil rights for the past 12 years, we've actually been barking up the wrong tree, that ours is a problem of *human* rights.

Plus, if we have our human rights, our civil rights are automatic. If we're respected as a human being, we'll be respected as a citizen; and in this country the black man not only is not respected as a citizen, he is not even respected as a human being.

And the proof is that you find in many instances people can come to this country from other countries—they can come to this country from behind the Iron Curtain—and despite the fact that they come here from these other places, they don't have to have civil-rights legislation passed in order for their rights to be safeguarded.

No new legislation is necessary for foreigners who come here to have their rights safeguarded. The Constitution is sufficient, but when it comes to the black men who were born here—whenever we are asking for our rights, they tell us that new legislation is necessary.

Well, we don't believe that. The Organization of Afro-American Unity feels that as long as our people in this country confine their struggle within the limitations and under the jurisdiction of the United States government, we remain within the confines of the vicious system that has done nothing but exploit and oppress us ever since we've been here. So we feel that our only real hope is to make known that our problem is not a Negro problem or an American problem but rather, it has become a human problem, a world problem, and it has to be attacked at the world level, at a level at which all segments of humanity can intervene in our behalf.

CHESHIRE CALHOUN
Justice, Care, and Gender Bias

CHESHIRE CALHOUN *teaches philosophy and is head of the women's studies program at Colby College in Maine.*

CAROL Gilligan poses two separable, though in her work not separate, challenges to moral theory. The first is a challenge to the adequacy of current moral theory that is dominated by the ethics of justice. The ethics of justice, on her view, excludes some dimensions of moral experience, such as contextual decision making, special obligations, the moral motives of compassion and sympathy, and the relevance of considering one's own integrity in making moral decisions. The second is a challenge to moral theory's presumed gender neutrality. The ethics of justice is not gender neutral, she argues, because it advocates ideals of agency, moral motivation, and correct moral reasoning which women are less likely than men to achieve; and because the moral dimensions excluded from the ethics of justice are just the ones figuring more prominently in women's than men's moral experience. The adequacy and gender bias charges are, for Gilligan, linked. She claims that the ethics of justice and the ethics of care are two different moral orientations. Whereas individuals may use both orientations, the shift from one to the other requires a Gestalt shift, since "the

terms of one perspective do not contain the terms of the other." The exclusion of the care perspective from the ethics of justice simultaneously undermines the adequacy of the ethics of justice (it cannot give a complete account of moral life) and renders it gender-biased.

Some critics have responded by arguing that there is no logical incompatibility between the two moral orientations. Because the ethics of justice does not in principle exclude the ethics of care (even if theorists within the justice tradition have had little to say about care issues), it is neither inadequate nor gender-biased. Correctly applying moral rules and principles, for instance, requires, rather than excludes, knowledge of contextual details. Both orientations are crucial to correct moral reasoning and an adequate understanding of moral life. Thus, the ethics of justice and the ethics of care are not in fact rivaling, alternative moral theories. The so-called ethics of care merely makes focal issues that are already implicitly contained in the ethics of justice.

Suppose the two are logically compatible. Would the charge of gender bias evaporate? Yes, so long as gender neutrality only requires that

Calhoun, Cheshire, "Justice, Care and Gender Bias," from *The Journal of Philosophy*, Vol. LXXXV, 9 (September 1988), pp. 451–463. Used by permission of The Journal of Philosophy.

the ethics of justice could, consistently, make room for the central moral concerns of the ethics of care. But perhaps gender neutrality requires more than this. Since the spectre of gender bias in theoretical knowledge is itself a moral issue, we would be well advised to consider the question of gender bias more carefully before concluding that our moral theory speaks in an androgynous voice. Although we can and should test the ethics of justice by asking whether it could consistently include the central moral issues in the ethics of care, we might also ask what ideologies of the moral life are likely to result from the repeated inclusion or exclusion of particular topics in moral theorizing.

Theorizing that crystallizes into a tradition has nonlogical as well as logical implications. In order to explain why a tradition has the contours it does, one may need to suppose general acceptance of particular beliefs that are not logically entailed by any particular theory and might be denied by individual theorists were those beliefs articulated. When behavioral researchers, for example, focus almost exclusively on aggression and its role in human life, neglecting other behavioral motives, their doing so has the nonlogical implication that aggression is, indeed, the most important behavioral motive. This is because only a belief like this would explain the rationality of this pattern of research. Such nonlogical implications become ideologies when politically loaded (as the importance of aggression is when coupled with observations about women's lower level of aggression).

When understood as directed at moral theory's nonlogical implications, the gender-bias charge takes a different form. Even if the ethics of justice could consistently accommodate the ethics of care, the critical point is that theorists in the justice tradition have not said much, except in passing, about the ethics of care, and are unlikely to say much in the future without a radical shift in theoretical priorities; and concentrating almost exclusively on rights of noninterference, impartiality, rationality, autonomy, and principles creates an ideology of the moral domain which has undesirable political implications

for women. This formulation shifts the justice-care debate from one about logical compatibility to a debate about which theoretical priorities would improve the lot of women.

I see no way around this politicization of philosophical critique. If we hope to shape culture, and not merely to add bricks to a philosophical tower, we will need to be mindful of the cultural/political use to which our thoughts may be put after leaving our word processors. This mindfulness should include asking whether our theoretical work enacts or discredits a moral commitment to improving the lot of women.

Providing us with some way of envisioning our shared humanity, and thus our equal membership in the moral community, is certainly an important thing for moral theory to do. But too much talk about our similarities as moral selves, and too little talk about our differences has its moral dangers. For one, unless we are also quite knowledgeable about the substantial differences between persons, particularly central differences due to gender, race, and class, we may be tempted to slide into supposing that our common humanity includes more substantive similarities than it does in fact. For instance, moral theorists have assumed that moral selves have a prominent interest in property and thus in property rights. But property rights may have loomed large on the moral horizons of past moral theorists partly, or largely, because they were themselves propertied and their activities took place primarily in the public, economic sphere. Historically, women could not share the same interest in property and concern about protecting it, since they were neither legally entitled to hold it nor primary participants in the public, economic world. And arguably, women do not now place the same priority. (I have in mind the fact that equal opportunity has had surprisingly little impact on either sex segregation in the workforce or on women's, but not men's, accommodating their work and work schedules to childrearing needs. One explanation is that income matters less to women than other sorts of considerations. The measure of a woman, unlike the measure of a man, is not the size of her paycheck.) Seyla Benhabib summarizes this point by suggesting that a single-minded emphasis on common humanity encourages a "substitutionalist universalism" where universal humanity "is defined surreptitiously by identifying the experiences of a specific group of subjects as the paradigmatic case of all humans."

In addition to encouraging us to overlook how our basic interests may differ depending on our social location, the emphasis on common humanity, because it is insensitive to connections between interests, social location, and power, deters questions about the possible malformation of our interests as a result of their development within an inegalitarian social structure. Both dangers plague the role-reversal test, some version of which has been a staple of moral theorizing. Although the point of that test is to eliminate egoistic bias in moral judgments, without a sensitivity to how our (uncommon) humanity is shaped by our social structure, role-reversal tests may simply preserve, rather than eliminate, inequities. This is because role-reversal tests either take individuals' desires as givens, thus ignoring the possibility that socially subordinate individuals have been socialized to want the very things that keep them socially subordinate (e.g., Susan Brownmiller argues that women have been socialized to want masochistic sexual relationships); or, if they take into account what individuals ought to want, role-reversal tests typically ignore the way that social power structures may have produced an alignment between the concept of a normal, reasonable desire and the desires of the dominant group (so, for example, much of the affirmative action literature takes it for granted that women ought to want traditionally defined male jobs with no consideration of the possibility that women might prefer retailoring those jobs so that they are less competitive, less hierarchical, and more compatible with family responsibilities).

In short, without adequate knowledge of how very different human interests, temperaments, lifestyles, and commitments may be, as well as a knowledge of how those interests may be malformed as a result of power inequities, the very egoism and group bias that the focus on common humanity was designed to eliminate may slip in as a result of that focus.

CHAPTER TWENTY

How Should I Make (and Spend) Money?

How do you intend to make a living? This might seem like a rather vulgar question for a philosophy course, but contrary to its reputation, philosophy is deeply involved in even the most practical aspects of our lives. In particular, the very question about "making a living"—as opposed to being granted the necessities of life by the government, for example—already points to an entire philosophy of life: the idea that you should *earn* your keep, that you have a *choice* in how you will do this, and that it is alright that you might or might not make more money and live more luxuriously than other people. The nineteenth-century name for the economic system that encourages this philosophical view of life and work is capitalism, and it is just as much a system of ethics as it is of economics. Although people all too often say that "business is unethical," the truth is that business is defined by its ethics. There are right and wrong ways for you to make money and there are better and worse ways to spend your many. Business ethics is the name of a new discipline (though it goes back to ancient times) that maps out the guidelines of ethics in business.

The broad principles of ethics—such as "treat people as ends and never merely as means" and "do not cause unnecessary harm"—apply in virtually every aspect of our lives, and perhaps, too, in every nation and culture. But most of ethics requires a more specific understanding of the particular practices in which human beings participate. The ethics of good sportsmanship will be very different (even when similar in vocabulary) from the ethics of war. Perhaps the most important single context for understanding ethics in contemporary American society is the world of business. It would not be an overstatement to say that a great many of our primary American values are either derived from or are part of business ethics. These include the traditional virtues of thrift, planning, and honoring one's contracts, as well as the skills of negotiating, trying to produce the highest quality product for the best price, and looking for the best bargain. Business—the production and sale of goods and services and the purchase of them—provides the context in which most of us live. Activities that once were the province of religion or the state (for example, the arts) are now very much part of the business world. And yet, it is often joked that "business ethics is a contradiction in terms" and that "there is no ethics in business." Such humor betrays an important problem in our thinking. On the one hand, business provides the value system upon which much of our society depends for its ethics and its understanding of what is right and wrong, fair and unfair. On the other hand, business itself is too often thought to be opposed to ethics, if it is not unethical, and value-free, except for the all-important "bottom line," the value of making a dollar (or a million of them).

Business ethics is a relatively new concern, in one sense. As a subject of serious concern, an attempt to understand how business actually works and what its implicit rules of fairness are, business ethics is only a few decades old. It is the product of both the power and success of American business and the increased awareness, if not frequency, of business scandals and abuses—automobiles that might have been fixed in the factory that explode upon collision, securities firms that fiddle with clients' funds or trade illegally on "insider" information, American companies abroad caught bribing foreign officials for contracts. But although the focus of business ethics is often upon such scandals and wrongdoing, the presumption is that most people and most companies in business are indeed ethical and conscientious. They really do try to serve not only their customers and stockholders but also their employees and the surrounding community. So business ethics like ethics in general is the attempt to spell out the rules for proper conduct that are already followed by most of the businesspeople in America.

In another, less flattering sense, business ethics has been around since ancient times, but almost always in the form of an all-out attack on business and its values. The materialism on which a consumer society is based has often been thought to be unethical to the core. And the so-called profit motive, on which most of business is based, was condemned for centuries and even called a sin—"avarice." This entirely negative attitude toward business did not change in Europe until the seventeenth century, just about the time that America—the foremost business society—was being settled.

The philosophical problems of business fall roughly into two categories. First there are the very broad questions about business as such—what the nineteenth-century philosophers named capitalism. These include whether "free enterprise" is indeed the best way to make a society prosper and its citizens happy and whether it is a fair way to distribute the wealth, goods, and advantages of a society to all its citizens. The father of modern economics and most famous prophet of capitalism, Adam Smith, wrote in his *Wealth of Nations* that the free enterprise system is indeed the best way to make a society prosper and provide all its citizens with comforts and even luxuries unimaginable in any other society. (His book was published in England in 1776, the same year the Declaration of Independence in America was signed.)

But as capitalism (and the industrial revolution that provided its technology) developed in England and elsewhere, it became evident that not all people were prospering equally. Those who worked as much as sixteen hours a day in the mines and factories—including many young children—remained desperately poor, while their bosses often became fabulously wealthy. The unfairness of this situation was particularly evident to a young German named Karl Marx, who had come to live in London in the mid-nineteenth century. He and his friend Friedrich Engels (who was himself a wealthy businessman) wrote what is still the most devastating attack on this new world. In fact, many of the reforms urged by Marx and Engels have been carried out in most businesses today. But the question remains to what extent business—the private production and sale of the material goods and services—is the best and fairest way of running the economy of a society. Many authors advocate more government control of who makes what and who gets what, or at least regulation of businesses so that certain minimal standards of quality, safety, and fairness are maintained. Many other authors and businesspeople insist that such control and regulation are best accomplished by business themselves and by the consumer, who in his or her freedom to buy or not a certain product in fact controls the business world more effectively than can any government.

The second category of problems in business ethics is more particular and applies to the activities of particular businesses. The business world has changed a great deal since Adam Smith and Marx wrote their treatises on capitalism. They were looking at a world of small shopkeepers and (what we would consider) modest industries. The business world of today is dominated instead by enormous corporations, some of which have hundreds of thousands of employees and offices in almost every country in the world. Accordingly, many of the problems of business ethics today have to do with the size, the power, and, consequently, the social responsibilities of corporations. It has been argued that corporations have only a single purpose—to make a profit, on the assumption that a corporation that is making a profit must also be providing quality goods and services to its consumers. It has also been argued that business is much more like a game of poker than it is a socially responsible institution, with the conclusion that businesspeople should not be expected to follow the same ethical principles as everyone else. On the other hand, it has been argued that businesses, like very powerful citizens, have special obligations that go beyond their responsibilities to their stockholders and customers. These arguments are kept in the public eye by such familiar headlines as "XYZ corporation indicted for taking kickbacks on defense contracts" or "Manufacturer knew that XXX causes cancer." One could claim even that a proper appreciation of business ethics is the condition for businesses' continued respect and success in the world.

The importance of ethics in business became obvious in 2002, when one of the largest corporations in the United States, Enron of Houston, Texas, collapsed and declared bankruptcy, leaving its loyal employees without jobs and without pensions, devastating retirement funds and the portfolios of stockholders around the country. It soon became evident that the whole company was built on a foundation of dubious and possibly illegal "creative accounting." William Greider has written about many financial topics, but in his "Crime in the Suites" he lays down a heavy indictment of not only a company but a system that encourages corrupt practices and betrayed obligations.

The chapter begins with some sage words on business by Confucius, writing some two millennia ago, and ends with advice from Joseph Campbell, summarizing the wisdom of the world's collective mythologies. In between are selections which include Adam Smith's classic statement about capitalism and an excerpt from Marx and Engels. Also included is Milton Friedman's controversial denial of the social responsibilities of business. By considering the career of entrepreneur-turned-criminal Ivan Boesky, Peter Singer raises the question of what it is ultimately worth to "make a lot of money." As a bit of internal evidence in the conflict concerning the social responsibility of corporations, we include a memo from the Ford Motor Company concerning one of the more notorious cases of the past several decades. An essay by Joanne Ciulla raises deep questions concerning the meaning of work. William Greider indicts both Enron and the system that spawned it in his "Crime in the Suites."

Turning to the consumption side of the topic, we ask, "What responsibilities do we have as consumers?" Jim Hightower raises the question of buying clothes made in sweatshops in which poor people work for cheap wages in awful conditions: such goods are typically less expensive, but is it right to buy them? Then we consider the controversial question of downloading music—of getting music for free but cutting out any payment to the artists and producers who made it. Is it right to do this? We include a statement for the World Trade Organization on "intellectual property," and a statement from an admitted downloader defending his behavior. Finally, Robert Solomon argues for a vision of business that incorporates integrity and the virtues, and we include a last word from mythologist Joseph Campbell.

CONFUCIUS
On Business

CONFUCIUS *(551–479 B.C.) was a famous Chinese sage and teacher. He sought to effect social change by holding a political office but was unable to secure such a position. Instead, he acquired a small group of dedicated students, and his philosophy is now world renowned. (China is one of the world's oldest business societies.)*

2 Tzu-chang asked Master K'ung, saying, What must a man do, that he may thereby be fitted to govern the land? The Master said, He must pay attention to the Five Lovely Things and put away from him the Four Ugly Things. Tzu-chang said, What are they that you call the Five Lovely Things? The Master said, A gentleman "can be bounteous without extravagance, can get work out of people without arousing resentment, has longings but is never covetous, is proud but never insolent, inspires awe but is never ferocious."

Tzu-chang said, What is meant by being bounteous without extravagance? The Master said, If he gives to the people only such advantages as are really advantageous to them, is he not being bounteous without extravagance? If he imposes upon them only such tasks as they are capable of performing, is he not getting work out of them without arousing resentment? If what he longs for and what he gets is Goodness, who can say that he is covetous? A gentleman, irrespective of whether he is dealing with many persons or with few, with the small or with the great, never presumes to slight them. Is not this indeed being "proud without insolence"? A gentleman sees to it that his clothes and hat are put on straight, and imparts such dignity to his gaze

that he imposes on others. No sooner do they see him from afar than they are in awe. Is not this indeed inspiring awe without ferocity?

Tzu-chang said, What are they, that you call the Four Ugly Things? The Master said, Putting men to death, without having taught them (the Right); that is called savagery. Expecting the completion of tasks, without giving due warning; that is called oppression. To be dilatory about giving orders, but to expect absolute punctuality, that is called being a tormentor. And similarly, though meaning to let a man have something, to be grudging about bringing it out from within, that is called behaving like a petty functionary.

14 The Master said, He does not mind not being in office; all he minds about is whether he has qualities that entitle him to office. He does not mind failing to get recognition; he is too busy doing the things that entitle him to recognition.

7 The Master said, Gentlemen never compete. You will say that in archery they do so. But even then they bow and make way for one another when they are going up to the archery-ground, when they are coming down and at the subsequent drinking bout. Thus even when competing, they still remain gentlemen.

ADAM SMITH
Benefits of the Profit Motive

ADAM SMITH's *(1723–1790)* Wealth of Nations *is often called the Bible of capitalism. It also marks the beginning of modern economic theory. The following selection from that work is a discussion of the value of the division of labor and the advantages of the capitalist system.*

THE greatest improvement in the productive power of labor, and the greater part of the skill, dexterity, and judgment with which it is anywhere directed, or applied, seem to have been the effects of the division of labor. . . .

To take an example, therefore, from a very trifling manufacture; but one in which the division of labor has been very often taken notice of, the trade of the pin-maker; a workman not educated to this business (which the division of labor has rendered a distinct trade), nor acquainted with the use of the machinery employed in it (to the invention of which the same division of labor has probably given occasion), could scarce, perhaps, with his utmost industry, make one pin a day, and certainly could not make twenty. But in the way in which this business is now carried on, not only the whole work is a peculiar trade, but it is divided into a number of branches, of which the greater part are likewise peculiar trades. One man draws out the wire, another straights it, a third cuts it, a fourth points it, a fifth grinds it at the top for receiving the head; to make the head requires two or three distinct operations; to put it on is a peculiar business, to whiten the pins is another; it is even a trade by itself to put them into the paper; and the important business of making a pin is, in this manner, divided into about eighteen distinct operations, which, in some manufactories, are all performed by distinct hands, though in others the same man will sometimes perform two or three of them. I have seen a small manufactory of this kind where ten men only were employed, and where some of them consequently performed two or three distinct operations. But though they were very poor, and therefore but indifferently accommodated with the necessary machinery, they could, when they exerted themselves, make among them about twelve pounds of pins in a day. There are in a pound upwards of four thousand pins of a middling size. Those ten persons, therefore, could make among them upwards of forty-eight thousand pins in a day. Each person, therefore, making a tenth part of forty-eight thousand pins, might be considered as making four thousand eight hundred pins in a day. But if they had all wrought separately and independently, and without any of them having been educated to this peculiar business, they certainly could not each of them have made twenty, perhaps not one pin in a day; that is, certainly, not the two hundred and fortieth, perhaps not the four thousand eight hundredth part, of what they are at present capable of performing in consequence of a proper division and combination of their different operations.

In every other art and manufacture, the effects of the division of labor are similar to what they are in this very trifling one; though in many of them, the labor can neither be so much subdivided, nor reduced to so great a simplicity of operation. The division of labor, however, so far as it can be introduced, occasions, in every art, a proportionable increase of the productive powers of labor. . . .

Smith, Adam, "Benefits of the Profit Motive," from *An Inquiry Into the Nature and Courses of the Wealth of Nations,* Book I, Chs. 1–2 and Book 4, Ch. 2. ed. James Rogers, Oxford: Clarendon Press, 1880.

This great increase of the quantity of work, which, in consequence of the division of labor, the same number of people are capable of performing, is owing to three different circumstances: first, to the increase of dexterity in every particular workman; secondly, to the saving of the time which is commonly lost in passing from one species of work to another; and lastly, to the invention of a great number of machines which facilitate and abridge labor, and enable one man to do the work of many.

First, the improvement of the dexterity of the workman necessarily increases the quantity of the work he can perform; and the division of labor, by reducing every man's business to some one simple operation and by making this operation the sole employment of his life, necessarily increases very much the dexterity of the workman. A common smith, who, though accustomed to handle the hammer, has never been used to make nails, if upon some particular occasion he is obliged to attempt it, will scarce, I am assured, be able to make about two or three hundred nails in a day, and those too very bad ones. A smith who has been accustomed to make nails, but whose sole or principal business has not been that of a nailer, can seldom with his utmost diligence make more than eight hundred or a thousand nails in a day. I have seen several boys under twenty years of age who had never exercised any other trade but that of making nails, and who, when they exerted themselves, could make, each of them, upwards of two thousand three hundred nails in a day. The making of a nail, however, is by no means one of the simplest operations. The same person blows the bellows, stirs or mends the fire as there is occasion, heats the iron, and forges every part of the nail: In forging the head too he is obliged to change his tools. The different operations into which the making of a pin or of a metal button is subdivided, are all of them much more simple; and the dexterity of the person, of whose life it has been the sole business to perform them, is usually much greater. The rapidity with which some of the operations of those manufactures are performed exceeds what the human hand could, by those who had never seen them, be supposed capable of acquiring.

Secondly, the advantage which is gained by saving the time commonly lost in passing from one sort of work to another is much greater than we should at first view be apt to imagine it. It is impossible to pass very quickly from one kind of work to another, that is carried on in a different place, and with quite different tools. A country weaver who cultivates a small farm must lose a good deal of time in passing from his loom to the field, and from the field to his loom. When the two trades can be carried on in the same workhouse, the loss of time is no doubt much less. It is even in this case, however, very considerable. . . .

Thirdly, and lastly, every body must be sensible how much labor is facilitated and abridged by the application of proper machinery. . . .

. . . A great part of the machines made use of in those manufactures in which labor is most subdivided were originally the inventions of common workmen, who, being each of them employed in some very simple operation, naturally turned their thoughts toward finding out easier and readier methods of performing it. Whoever has been much accustomed to visit such manufacturers must frequently have been shown very pretty machines which were the inventions of such workmen in order to facilitate and quicken their own particular part of the work. In the first fire-engines, a boy was constantly employed to open and shut alternately the communication between the boiler and the cylinder, according as the piston either ascended or descended. One of those boys, who loved to play with his companions, observed that, by tying a string from the handle of the valve which opened this communication to another part of the machine, the valve would open and shut without his assistance, and leave him at liberty to divert himself with his play-fellows. One of the greatest improvements that has been made upon this machine, since it was first invented, was in this manner the discovery of a boy who wanted to save his own labor. . . .

It is the great multiplication of the productions of all the different arts, in consequence of the division of labor, which occasions, in a well-governed society, that universal opulence which extends itself to the lowest ranks of people. Every workman has a great quantity of his own work to dispose of beyond what he himself has occasion for; and every other workman being exactly in the same situation, he is enabled to exchange a great quantity of his own goods for a great quantity, or, what comes to the same thing, for the price of a great quantity of theirs. He supplies them abundantly with what they have occasion for, and they accommodate him as amply with what he has occasion for, and a general plenty diffuses itself through all the different ranks of the society. . . .

This division of labor, from which so many advantages are derived, is not originally the effect of any human wisdom which foresees and intends that general opulence to which it gives occasion. It is the necessary, though very slow and gradual, consequence of a certain propensity in human nature which has in view no such extensive utility: the propensity to truck, barter, and exchange one thing for another.

. . . In almost every other race of animals each individual, when it is grown up to maturity, is entirely independent, and in its natural state has occasion for the assistance of no other living creature. But man has almost constant occasion for the help of his brethren, and it is in vain for him to expect it from their benevolence only. He will be more likely to prevail if he can interest their self-love in his favor, and show them that it is for their own advantage to do for him what he requires of them. Whoever offers to another a bargain of any kind, proposes to do this. Give me that which I want, and you shall have this which you want, is the meaning of every such offer; and it is in the manner that we obtain from one another the far greater part of those good offices which we stand in need of. It is not from the benevolence of the butcher, the brewer, or the baker, that we expect our dinner, but from their regard to their own interest. We address ourselves, not to their humanity but to their self-love, and never talk to them of our own necessities but of their advantages. Nobody but a beggar chooses to depend chiefly upon the benevolence of his fellow-citizens. Even a beggar does not depend on it entirely. The charity of well-disposed people, indeed, supplies him with the whole fund of his subsistence. But though this principle ultimately provides him with all the necessaries of life which he has occasion for, it neither does nor can provide him with them as he has occasion for them. The greater part of his occasional wants are supplied in the same manner as those of other people, by treaty, by barter, and by purchase. With the money which one man gives him he purchases food. The old clothes which another bestows upon him he exchanges for other old clothes which suit him better, or for lodging, or for food, or for money, with which he can buy either food, clothes, or lodging, as he has occasion.

As it is by treaty, by barter, and by purchase that we obtain from one another the greater part of those mutual good offices which we stand in need of, so it is this same trucking disposition which originally gives occasion to the division of labor. In a tribe of hunters or shepherds a particular person makes bows and arrows, for example, with more readiness and dexterity than any other. He frequently exchanges them for cattle or for venison with his companions; and he finds at last that he can in this manner get more cattle and venison than if he himself went to the field to catch them. From a regard to his own interest, therefore, the making of bows and arrows grows to be his chief business, and he becomes a sort of armorer. Another excels in making the frames and covers of their little huts or movable houses. He is accustomed to be of use in this way to his neighbors, who reward him in the same manner with cattle and with venison till at last he finds it his interest to dedicate himself entirely to this employment, and to become a sort of house carpenter. In the same manner a third becomes a smith or a brazier, a fourth a tanner or dresser of hides or skins, the principal part of the clothing of savages. And thus the certainty of being able to exchange all that surplus part of the produce of his own labor, which is over and above his own consumption, for such parts of the produce of other men's labor as he may have occasion for, encourages every man to apply himself to a particular occupation, and to cultivate and bring to perfection whatever talent or genius he may possess for that particular species of business.

The difference of natural talents in different men is, in reality, much less than we are aware of; and the very different genius which appears to distinguish men of different professions, when grown up to maturity, is not upon many occasions so much the cause as the effect of the division of labor. The difference between the most dissimilar characters, between a philosopher and a common street porter, for example, seems to arise not so much from nature as from habit, custom, and education. When they came into the world, and for the first six or eight years of their existence, they were, perhaps, very much alike, and neither their parents nor play-fellows could perceive any remarkable difference. About that age, or soon after, they come to be employed in very different occupations. The difference of talents comes then to be taken notice of, and widens by degrees, till at last the vanity of the philosopher is willing to acknowledge scarce any resemblance. But without the disposition to truck, barter, and exchange, every man must have procured to himself every necessary and conveniency of life which he wanted. All must have had the same duties to perform, and the same work to do, and there could have been no such difference of employment as could alone give occasion to any great difference of talents. . . .

Every individual is continually exerting himself to find out the most advantageous employment for whatever capital he can command. It is his own advantage, indeed, and not that of the society, which he has in view. But the study of his own advantage, naturally, or rather necessarily, leads him to prefer that employment which is most advantageous to the society. . . .

As every individual, therefore, endeavors as much as he can both to employ his capital in the support of domestic industry, and so to direct that industry that its produce may be of the greatest value, every individual necessarily labors to render the annual revenue of the society as great as he can. He generally, indeed, neither intends to promote the public interest, nor knows how much he is promoting it. By preferring the support of domestic to that of foreign industry, he intends only his own security: and by directing that industry in such a manner as its produce may be of the greatest value, he intends only his own gain, and he is in this, as in many other cases, led by an invisible hand to promote an end which was no part of his intention. Nor is it always the worse for the society that it was no part of it. By pursuing his own interest he frequently promotes that of the society more effectually than when he really intends to promote it. I have never known much good done, by those who affected to trade for the public good. It is an affectation, indeed, not very common among merchants, and very few words need be employed in dissuading them from it. . . .

If we examine, I say, all those things . . . we shall be sensible that without the assistance and cooperation of many thousands, the very meanest person in a civilized country could not be provided, even according to what we very falsely imagine, the easy and simple manner in which he is commonly accommodated. Compared indeed with the more extravagant luxury of the great, his accommodation must no doubt appear extremely simple and easy; and yet it may be true, perhaps, that the accommodation of a European prince does not always so much exceed that of an industrious and frugal peasant, as the accommodation of the latter exceeds that of many an African king, the absolute master of the lives and liberties of the thousand naked savages.

KARL MARX AND FRIEDRICH ENGELS

The Immorality of Capitalism

KARL MARX *(1818–1883) and* FRIEDRICH ENGELS *(1820–1895) were the founders of modern communism. Their* Communist Manifesto, *reproduced in part here, was their 1848 battle cry, formulated in the name of the newly organized working class— the "proletariat."*

THE history of all hitherto existing society is the history of class struggles.

Freeman and slave, patrician and plebeian, lord and serf, guildmaster and journeyman, in a word, oppressor and oppressed, stood in constant opposition to one another, carried on an uninterrupted, now hidden, now open fight, a fight that each time ended, either in a revolutionary reconstitution of society at large, or in the common ruin of the struggling classes.

In the earlier epochs of history, we find almost everywhere a complicated arrangement of society into various orders, a manifold gradation of social rank. In ancient Rome we have patricians, knights, plebeians, slaves; in the Middle Ages, feudal lords, vassals, guildmasters, journeymen, apprentices, serfs; and in almost all of these particular classes, again, other subordinate gradations.

The modern bourgeois society that has sprouted from the ruins of feudal society has not done away with class antagonisms. It has only established new classes, new conditions of oppression, new forms of struggle in place of the old ones.

Our epoch, the epoch of the bourgeoisie, shows, however, this distinctive feature: it has simplified the class antagonisms. Society as a whole is more and more splitting up into two great hostile camps, into two great classes directly facing each other: *bourgeoisie* and *proletariat.* . . .

Modern industry has established the world market, for which the discovery of America paved the way. This market has given an immense development to commerce, to navigation, to communication by land. This development has, it its turn, reacted on the extension of industry; and in proportion as industry, commerce, navigation, railways extended, in the same proportion the bourgeoisie developed, increased its capital, and pushed into the background every class handed down from the Middle Ages.

We see, therefore, how the modern bourgeoisie is itself the product of a long course of development, of a series of revolutions in the modes of production and of exchange. . . .

The need of a constantly expanding market for its products chases the bourgeoisie over the whole surface of the globe. It must nestle everywhere, settle everywhere, establish connections everywhere.

The bourgeoisie has through its exploitation of the world market given a cosmopolitan character to production and consumption in every country. To the great chagrin of reactionaries, it has drawn from under the feet of industry the national ground on which it stood. All old-established national industries have been destroyed or are daily being destroyed. They are dislodged by new industries, whose introduction becomes a life and death question for all civilized nations, by industries that no longer work up indigenous raw material, but raw material drawn from the remotest zones; industries whose products are consumed, not only at home, but in every quarter of the globe. In place of the old wants, satisfied by the productions of the country, we find new wants requiring for their satisfaction the products of distant lands and climates. In place of the old local and national seclusion and self-sufficiency, we have intercourse in every direction, universal interdependence of nations. And as in material, so also in intellectual production. The intellectual creations of individual nations become common property. National one-sidedness and narrowmindedness become more and more impossible, and from the numerous national and local literatures, there emerges a world literature.

The bourgeoisie, by the rapid improvement of all instruments of production, by the immensely facilitated means of communications, draws all, even the most backward, nations into civilization. The cheap prices of its commodities are the heavy artillery with which it batters down all Chinese walls, with which it forces the underdeveloped nations' intensely obstinate hatred of foreigners to capitulate. It compels all nations, on pain of extinction, to adopt the bourgeois mode of production; it compels them to introduce what it calls civilization into their midst, *i.e.,* to become bourgeois themselves. In one word, it creates a world in its own image. . . .

MILTON FRIEDMAN

The Social Responsibility of Business Is to Increase Its Profits

MILTON FRIEDMAN *is a well-known economist, author, columnist, and defender of the free market system. The following is a notorious essay he wrote for the* New York Times *in 1970.*

W HEN I hear businessmen speak eloquently about the "social responsibilities of business in a free-enterprise system," I am reminded of the wonderful line about the Frenchman who discovered at the age of seventy that he had been speaking prose all his life. The businessmen believe that they are defending free enterprise when they declaim that business is not concerned "merely" with profit but also with promoting desirable "social" ends; that business has a "social conscience" and takes seriously its responsibilities for providing employment, eliminating discrimination, avoiding pollution and whatever else may be the catchwords of the contemporary crop of reformers. In fact they are—or would be if they or anyone else took them seriously—preaching pure and unadulterated socialism. Businessmen who talk this way are unwitting puppets of the intellectual forces that have been undermining the basis of a free society these past decades.

The discussions of the "social responsibilities of business" are notable for their analytical looseness and lack of rigor. What does it mean to say that "business" has responsibilities? Only people can have responsibilities. A corporation is an artificial person and in this sense may have artificial responsibilities, but "business" as a whole cannot be said to have responsibilities, even in this vague sense. The first step toward clarity to examining the doctrine of the social responsibility of business is to ask precisely what it implies for whom.

Presumably, the individuals who are to be responsible are businessmen, which means individual proprietors or corporate executives. Most of the discussing of social responsibility is directed at corporations, so in what follows I shall mostly neglect the individual proprietors and speak of corporate executives.

In a free-enterprise, private-property system, a corporate executive is an employee of the owners of the business. He has direct responsibility to his employers. That responsibility is to conduct the business in accordance with their desires, which generally will be to make as much money as possible while conforming to the basic rules of the society, both those embodied in law and those embodied in ethical custom. Of course, in some cases his employers may have a different objective. A group of persons might establish a corporation for an eleemosynary purpose—for example, a hospital or a school. The manager of such a corporation will not have money profit as his objectives but the rendering of certain services.

In either case, the key point is that, in his capacity as a corporate executive, the manager is the agent of the individuals who own the corporation or establish the eleemosynary institution, and his primary responsibility is to them.

Needless to say, this does not mean that it is easy to judge how well he is performing his task. But at least the criterion of performance is straightforward, and the persons among whom a voluntary contractual arrangement exists are clearly defined.

Of course, the corporate executive is also a person in his own right. As a person, he may have many other responsibilities that he recognizes or assumes voluntarily—to his family, his conscience, his feelings of charity, his church, his clubs, his city, his country. He may feel impelled by these responsibilities to devote part of his income to causes he regards as worthy, to refuse to work for particular corporations, even to leave his job, for example, to join his country's armed forces. If we wish, we may refer to some of these responsibilities as "social responsibilities." But in these respects he is acting as a principal, not an agent; he is spending his own money or time or energy, not the money of his employers or the time or energy he has contracted to devote to their purposes. If these are "social responsibilities," they are the social responsibilities of individuals, not of business.

What does it mean to say that the corporate executive has a "social responsibility" in his capacity as businessman? If this statement is not pure rhetoric, it must mean that he is to act in some way that is not in the interest of his employers. For example, that he is to refrain from increasing the price of the product in order to contribute to the social objective of preventing inflation, even though a price increase would be in the best interests of the corporation. Or that he is to make expenditures on reducing pollution beyond the amount that is in the best interests of the corporation or that is required by law in order to contribute to the social objective of improving the environment. Or that, at the expense of corporate profits, he is to hire "hard core" unemployed instead of better qualified available workmen to contribute to the social objective of reducing poverty.

In each of these cases, the corporate executive would be spending someone else's money for a general social interest. Insofar as his actions in accord with his "social responsibility" reduce returns to stockholders, he is spending their money. Insofar as his actions raise the price to customers, he is spending the customers' money.

Insofar as his actions lower the wages of some employees, he is spending their money.

The stockholders or the customers or the employees could separately spend their own money on the particular action if they wished to do so. The executive is exercising a distinct "social responsibility," rather than serving as an agent of the stockholders or the customers or the employees, only if he spends the money in a different way than they would have spent it.

But if he does this, he is in effect imposing taxes, on the one hand, and deciding how the tax proceeds shall be spent, on the other.

This process raises political questions on two levels: principle and consequences. On the level of political principle, the imposition of taxes and the expenditure of tax proceeds are governmental functions. We have established elaborate constitutional, parliamentary and judicial provisions to control these functions, to assure that taxes are imposed so far as possible in accordance with the preferences and desires of the public—after all, "taxation without representation" was one of the battle cries of the American Revolution. We have a system of checks and balances to separate the legislative function of imposing taxes and enacting expenditures from the executive function of collecting taxes and administering expenditure programs and from the judicial function of mediating disputes and interpreting the law.

Here the businessman—self-selected or appointed directly or indirectly by stockholders—is to be simultaneously legislator, executive and jurist. He is to decide whom to tax by how much and for what purpose, and he is to spend the proceeds—all this guided only by general exhortations from on high to restrain inflation, improve the environment, fight poverty and so on and on.

The whole justification for permitting the corporate executive to be selected by the stockholder is that the executive is an agent serving the interests of his principal. This justification disappears when the corporate executive imposes taxes and spends the proceeds for "social" purposes. He becomes in effect a public employee, a civil servant, even though he remains in name an employee of a private enterprise. On grounds of political principle, it is intolerable that such civil servants—insofar as their actions in the name of social responsibility are real and not just window-dressing—should be selected as they are now. If they are to be civil servants, then they must be elected through a political process. If they are to impose taxes and make expenditures to foster "social" objectives, then political machinery must be set up to make the assessment of taxes and to determine through a political process the objectives to be served.

This is the basic reason why the doctrine of "social responsibility" involves the acceptance of the socialist view that political mechanisms, not market mechanisms, are the appropriate way to determine the allocation of scarce resources to alternative uses.

On the grounds of consequences, can the corporate executive in fact discharge his alleged "social responsibilities"? On the one hand, suppose he could get away with spending the stockholders' or customers' or employees' money. How is he to know how to spend it? He is told that he must contribute to fighting inflation. How is he to know what action of his will contribute to that end? He is presumably an expert in running his company—in producing a product or selling it or financing it. But nothing about his selection makes him an expert on inflation. Will his holding down the price of his product reduce inflationary pressure? Or, by leaving more spending power in the hands of his customers, simply divert it elsewhere? Or, by forcing him to produce less because of the lower price, will it simply contribute to shortages? Even if he could answer these questions, how much cost is he justified in imposing on his stockholders, customers and employees for this social purpose? What is his appropriate share and what is the appropriate share of others? . . .

. . . [T]he doctrine of "social responsibility" taken seriously would extend the scope of the political mechanism to every human activity. It does not differ in philosophy from the most explicitly collectivist doctrine. It differs only by professing to believe that collectivist ends can be attained without collectivist means. That is why, in my book "Capitalism and Freedom," I have called it a "fundamentally subversive doctrine" in a free society, and have said that in such a society, "there is one and only one social responsibility of business—to use its resources and engage in activities designed to increase its profits so long as it stays within the rules of the game, which is to say, engages in open and free competition without deception or fraud."

The Ford Pinto Memo

In the early 1970s, there were a number of fatal accidents involving Ford Pintos, in which the gas tank burst into flames following a relatively minor rear-end collision. Subsequent investigation established that the Ford Motor Company knew about the defect in advance and turned up a study that Ford had prepared for the federal government, breaking down "costs and benefits" of allowing the accidents to happen as opposed to fixing the defect. The summary of that study is reproduced here.

BENEFITS [OF FIXING THE CARS]

Savings:	180 burn deaths, 180 serious burn injuries, 2,100 burned vehicles
Unit Cost:	$200,000 per death, $67,000 per injury, $700 per vehicle.
Total Benefit:	180 × (200,000) + 180 × ($67,000) + 2,100 × ($700) = $49.5 million

COSTS

Sales:	11 million cars, 1.5 million light trucks
Unit Cost:	$11 per car, $11 per truck
Total Cost:	11,000,000 × ($11) + 1,500,000 × ($11) = $137 million

CALCULATION OF "COST OF DEATH" AT $200,000:

Component	1971 Costs
Future Productivity Losses	
Direct	$132,000
Indirect	41,300
Medical Costs	
Hospital	700
Other	425
Property Damage	1,500
Insurance Administration	4,700
Legal and Court	3,000
Employer Losses	1,000
Victim's Pain and Suffering	10,000
Funeral	900
Asset (Lost Consumption)	5,000
Miscellaneous	200
Total per fatality	$200,725

Ford Motor Company's "The Ford Pinto Memo" was released by J. C. Echold, in the Division of Auto Safety, Ford Motor Co., and was first published by Mark Dowie, *Mother Jones*, Sept.–Oct. 1977, p. 28. This was taken from Robert C. Solomon, *It's Good Business* (New York: Harper and Row, 1985).

PETER SINGER
Ivan Boesky's Choice

PETER SINGER, *for many years a professor in Australia, is now part of the Center for Values at Princeton University. He is the author of* Animal Liberation *and many books on ethics.*

IN 1985 Ivan Boesky was known as "the king of the arbitragers," a specialized form of investment in the shares of companies that were the target of takeover offers. He made profits of $40 million in 1981 when Du Pont bought Conoco; $80 million in 1984 when Chevron bought Gulf Oil; and in the same year, $100 million when Texaco acquired Getty Oil. There were some substantial losses too, but not enough to stop Boesky making *Forbes* magazine's list of America's wealthiest 400 people. His personal fortune was estimated at between $150 and $200 million.

Boesky had achieved both a formidable reputation, and a substantial degree of respectability. His reputation came, in part, from the amount of money that he controlled. "Ivan," said one colleague, "could get any Chief Executive Officer in the country off the toilet to talk to him at seven o'clock in the morning." But his reputation was also built on the belief that he had brought a new "scientific" approach to investment, based on an elaborate communications system that he claimed was like NASA's. He was featured not only in business magazines, but also in the *New York Times* Living section. He wore the best suits, on which a Winston Churchill-style gold watch chain was prominently displayed. He owned a twelve-bedroom Georgian mansion set on 190 acres in Westchester County, outside New York City. He was a notable member of the Republican Party, and some thought he cherished political ambitions. He held positions at the American Ballet Theater and the Metropolitan Museum of Art.

Unlike other arbitragers before him, Boesky sought to publicize the nature of his work, and aimed to be recognized as an expert in a specialized area that aided the proper functioning of the market. In 1985 he published a book about arbitrage entitled *Merger Mania*. The book claims that arbitrage contributes to "a fair, liquid, and efficient market" and states that "undue profits are not made: there are no esoteric tricks that enable arbitragers to outwit the system . . . profit opportunities exist only because risk arbitrage serves an important market function." *Merger Mania* begins with a touching dedication:

Dedication

My father, my mentor, William H. Boesky (1900–1964), of beloved memory, whose courage brought him to these shores from his native Ykaterinoslav, Russia, in the year 1912. My life has been profoundly influenced by my father's spirit and strong commitment to the well-being of humanity, and by his emphasis on learning as the most important means to justice, mercy, and righteousness. His life remains an example of returning to the community the benefits he had received through the exercise of God-given talents.

With this inspiration I write this book for all who wish to learn of my specialty, that they may be inspired to believe that confidence in one's self and determination can allow one to become whatever one may dream. May those who read my book gain some understanding for the opportunity which exists uniquely in this great land.

In the same year that his autobiography was published, at the height of his success, Boesky entered into an arrangement for obtaining inside information from Dennis Levine. Levine, who was himself earning around $3 million annually in salary and bonuses, worked at Drexel Burnham Lambert, the phenomenally successful Wall Street firm that dominated the "junk bond" market. Since junk bonds were the favoured way of raising funds for takeovers, Drexel was involved in almost every major takeover battle, and Levine was privy to information that, in the hands of someone with plenty of capital, could be used to make hundreds of millions of dollars, virtually without risk.

The ethics of this situation are not in dispute. When Boesky was buying shares on the basis of the information Levine gave him, he knew that the shares would rise in price. The shareholders who sold to him did not know that, and hence sold the shares at less than they could have obtained for them later, if they had not sold. If Drexel's client was someone who wished to take a company over, then that client would have to pay more for the company if the news of the intended takeover leaked out, since Boesky's purchases would push up the price of the shares. The added cost might mean that the bid to take over the target company would fail; or it might mean that, though the bid succeeded, after the takeover more of the company's assets would be sold off, to pay for the increased borrowings needed to buy the company at the higher price. Since Drexel, and hence Levine, had obtained the information of the intended takeover in confidence from their clients, for them to disclose it to others who could profit from it, to the disadvantage of their clients, was clearly contrary to all accepted professional ethical standards. Boesky has never suggested that he dissents from these standards, or believed that his circumstances justified an exception to them. Boesky also knew that trading in inside information was illegal. Nevertheless, in 1985 he went so far as to formalize the arrangement he had with Levine, agreeing to pay him 5 percent of the profits he made from purchasing shares about which Levine had given him information.

Why did Boesky do it? Why would anyone who has $150 million, a respected position in society, and—as is evident from the dedication to his book—values at least the appearance of an ethical life that benefits the community as a whole, risk his reputation, his wealth, and his freedom by doing something that is obviously neither legal or ethical? Granted, Boesky stood to make very large sums of money from his arrangement with Levine. The Securities and Exchange Commission was later to describe several transactions in which Boesky had used information obtained from Levine; his profits on these deals were estimated at $50 million. Given the previous track record of the Securities and Exchange Commission, Boesky could well have thought that his illegal insider trading was likely to go undetected and unprosecuted. So it was reasonable enough for Boesky to believe that the use of inside information would bring him a lot of money with little chance of exposure. Does that mean that it was a wise thing for him to do? In these circumstances, where does wisdom lie? In choosing to enrich himself further, in a manner that he could not justify ethically, Boesky was making a choice between fundamentally different ways of living. I shall call this type of choice an "ultimate choice." When ethics and self-interest seem to be in conflict, we face an ultimate choice. How are we to choose?

Most of the choices we make in our everyday lives are restricted choices, in that they are made from within a given framework or set of values. Given that I want to keep reasonably fit, I sensibly choose to go for a walk rather than slouch on the sofa with a can of beer, watching the football on television. Since you want to do something to help preserve rainforests, you join a coalition to raise public awareness of the continuing destruction of the forests. Another person wants a well-paid and interesting career, so she studies law. In each of these choices, the fundamental values are already assumed, and the choice is a matter of the best means of achieving what is valued. In ultimate choices, however, the fundamental values themselves come to the fore. We are no longer choosing within a framework that assumes that we want only to maximize our own interests, nor within a framework that takes it for granted that we are going to do whatever we consider to be best, ethically speaking. Instead, we are choosing between different possible ways of living: the way of living in which self-interest is paramount, or that in which ethics is paramount, or perhaps some trade-off between the two. (I take ethics and self-interest as the two rival viewpoints because they are, in my view, the two strongest contenders. Other possibilities include, for example, living by the rules of etiquette, or living in accordance with one's own aesthetic standards, treating one's life as a work of art; but these possibilities are not the subject of this book.)

Ultimate choices take courage. In making restricted choices, our fundamental values form a foundation on which we can stand when we choose. To make an ultimate choice we must put in question the foundations of our lives. In the fifties, French philosophers like Jean-Paul Sartre saw this kind of choice as an expression of our ultimate freedom. We are free to choose what we are to be, because we have no essential nature, that is, no given purpose outside ourselves. Unlike, say, an apple tree that has come into existence as a result of someone else's plan, we simply exist, and the rest is up to us. (Hence the name given to this group of thinkers: existentialists.) Sometimes this leads to a sense that we are standing before a moral void. We feel vertigo, and want to get out of that situation as quickly as possible. So we avoid the ultimate choice by carrying on as we were doing before. That seems the simplest and safest thing to do. But we do not really avoid making the ultimate choice in that way. We make it by default, and it may not be safe at all. Perhaps Ivan Boesky continued to do what would make him richer because to do anything else would have involved questioning the foundations of most of his life. He acted as if his essential nature was to make money. But of course it was not: he could have chosen living ethically ahead of money-making.

Even if we are ready to face an ultimate choice, however, it is not easy to know how to make it. In more restricted choice situations we

know how to get expert advice. There are financial consultants and educational counsellors and health care advisers, all ready to tell you about what is the best for your own interest. Many people will be eager to offer you their opinions about what would be the right thing to do, too. But who is the expert here? Suppose that you have the opportunity to sell your car, which you know is about to need major repairs, to a stranger who is too innocent to have the car checked properly. He is pleased with the car's appearance, and a deal is about to be struck, when he casually asks if the car has any problems. If you say, just as casually, "No, nothing that I know of," the stranger will buy the car, paying you at least $1,000 more than you would get from anyone who knew the truth. He will never be able to prove that you were lying. You are convinced that it would be wrong to lie to him, but another $1,000 would make your life more comfortable for the next few months. In this situation you don't see any need to ask anyone for advice about what is in your best interest; nor do you need to ask what it would be right to do. So can you still ask *what to do?*

Of course you can. Some would say that if you know that it would be wrong to lie about your car, that is the end of the matter; but this is wishful thinking. If we are honest with ourselves, we will admit that, at least sometimes, where self-interest and ethics clash, we choose self-interest, and this is not just a case of being weak-willed or irrational. We are genuinely unsure what it is rational to do, because when the clash is so fundamental, reason seems to have no way of resolving it.

We all face ultimate choices, and with equal intensity, whether our opportunities are to gain, by unethical means, $50 or $50 million. The state of the world in the late twentieth century means that even if we are never tempted at all by unethical ways of making money, we have to decide to what extent we shall live for ourselves, and to what extent for others. There are people who are hungry, malnourished, lacking shelter, or basic health care: and there are voluntary organizations that raise money to help these people. True, the problem is so big that one individual cannot make much impact on it; and no doubt some of the money will be swallowed up in administration, or will get stolen, or for some other reason will not reach the people who need it most. Despite these inevitable problems, the discrepancy between the wealth of the developed world and the poverty of the poorest people in developing countries is so great that if only a small fraction of what you give reaches the people who need it, that fraction will make a far greater difference to the people it reaches than the full amount you give could make to your own life. That you as an individual cannot make an impact on the entire problem seems scarcely relevant, since you can make an impact on the lives of particular families. So will you get involved with one of these organizations? Will you yourself give, not just spare change when a tin is rattled under your nose, but substantial amounts that will reduce your ability to live a luxurious lifestyle?

Some consumer products damage the ozone layer, contribute to the greenhouse effect, destroy rainforests, or pollute our rivers and lakes. Others are tested by being put, in concentrated form, into the eyes of conscious rabbits, held immobilized in rows of restraining devices like medieval stocks. There are alternatives to products that are environmentally damaging, or tested in such cruel ways. To find the alternatives can, however, be time-consuming, and a nuisance. Will you take the trouble to find them?

We face ethical choices constantly in our personal relationships. We have opportunities to use people and discard them, or to remain loyal to them. We can stand up for what we believe, or make ourselves popular by going along with what the group does. Though the morality of personal relationships is difficult to generalize about because every situation is different, here too we often know what the right thing to do is, but are uncertain about what to do.

There are, no doubt, some people who go through life without considering the ethics of what they are doing. Some of these people are just indifferent to others; some are downright vicious. Yet genuine indifference to ethics of any sort is rare. Mark "Chopper" Read, one of Australia's nastiest criminals, recently published (from prison) an horrific autobiography, replete with nauseating details of beatings and forms of torture he inflicted on his enemies before killing them. Through all his relish for violence, however, the author shows evident anxiety to assure his readers that his victims were all in some way members of the criminal class who deserved what they got. He wants his readers to be clear that he has nothing but contempt for an Australian mass murderer—now one of Read's fellow-prisoners—who opened up on passersby with an automatic rifle. The psychological need for ethical justification, no matter how weak that justification may be, is remarkably pervasive.

We should each ask ourselves: what place does ethics have in my daily life? In thinking about this question, ask yourself: what do I think of as a good life, in the fullest sense of that term? This is an ultimate question. To ask it is to ask: what kind of a life do I truly admire, and what kind of life do I hope to be able to look back on, when I am older and reflect on how I have lived? Will it be enough to say: "It was fun"? Will I even be able to say truthfully that it *was* fun? Whatever your position or status, you can ask what—within the limits of what is possible for you—you want to achieve with your life.

WILLIAM GREIDER

Crime in the Suites

WILLIAM GREIDER *The collapse of Enron devastated its employees and stockholders and much of the community in Houston. It seems that the company was built on a foundation of dubious and possibly illegal "creative accounting." In what follows, William Greider condemns not only the company but the system that supported it.*

THE collapse of Enron has swiftly morphed into a go-to-jail financial scandal, laden with the heavy breathing of political fixers, but Enron makes visible a more profound scandal—the failure of market orthodoxy itself. Enron, accompanied by a supporting cast from banking, accounting and Washington politics, is a virtual piñata of corrupt practices and betrayed obligations to investors, taxpayers and voters. But these matters ought not to surprise anyone, because they have been familiar, recurring outrages during the recent reign of high-flying Wall Street. This time, the distinctive scale may make it harder to brush them aside. "There are many more Enrons out there," a well-placed Washington lawyer confided. He knows because he has represented a couple of them.

The rot in America's financial system is structural and systemic. It consists of lying, cheating and stealing on a grand scale, but most offenses seem depersonalized because the transactions are so complex and remote from ordinary human criminality. The various cops-and-robbers investigations now under way will provide the story line for coming months, but the heart of the matter lies deeper than individual venality. In this era of deregulation and laissez-faire ideology, the essential premise has been that market forces discipline and punish the errant players more effectively than government does. To produce greater efficiency and innovation, government was told to back off, and it largely has.

"Transparency" became the exalted buzzword. The market discipline would be exercised by investors acting on honest information supplied by the banks and brokerages holding their money, "independent" corporate directors and outside auditors, and regular disclosure reports required by the Securities and Exchange Commission and other regulatory agencies. The Enron story makes a sick joke of all these safeguards.

But the rot consists of more than greed and ignorance. The evolving new forms of finance and banking, joined with the permissive culture in Washington, produced an exotic structural nightmare in which some firms are regulated and supervised while others are not. They converge, however, with *kereitzu*-style backscratching in the business of lending and investing other people's money. The results are profoundly conflicted loyalties in banks and financial firms—who have fiduciary obligations to the citizens who give them money to invest. Banks and brokerages often cannot tell the truth to retail customers, depositors or investors without potentially injuring the corporate clients that provide huge commissions and profits from investment deals. Sometimes bankers cannot even tell the truth to themselves because they have put their own capital (or government-insured deposits) at risk in the deals. These and other deformities will not be cleaned up overnight (if at all, given the bipartisan political subservience to Wall Street interests). But

Greider, William, "Crime in the Suites," reprinted with permission from the February 4, 2002, issue of *The Nation*. For subscription information, call 1-800-333-8536. Portions of each week's *Nation* magazine can be accessed at http://www.thenation.com

Enron ought to be seen as the casebook for fundamental reform.

The people bilked in Enron's sudden implosion were not only the 12,000 employees whose 401(k) savings disappeared while Enron insiders were smartly cashing out more than $1 billion of their own shares. The other losers are working people across America. Enron was effectively owned by them. On June 30, before the CEO abruptly resigned and the stock price began its terminal decline, 64 percent of Enron's 744 million shares were owned by institutional investors, mainly pension funds but also mutual funds in which families have individual accounts. At midyear, the company was valued at $36.5 billion, having fallen from $70 billion in less than six months. The share price is now close to zero. Either way you figure it, ordinary Americans—the beneficial owners of pension funds—lost $25–$50 billion because they were told lies by the people and firms they trusted to protect their interests. . . .

The disorder writ large by the Enron story is this regular plundering of ordinary Americans, who are saving on their own or who have accepted deferred wages in the form of future retirement benefits. Major pension funds can and do sue for damages when they are defrauded, but this is obviously an impotent form of discipline. Labor Department officials have known the

vulnerable spots in pension-fund protection for many years and regularly sent corrective amendments to Congress—ignored under both parties. In the financial world, the larceny is effectively decriminalized—culprits typically settle in cash with fines or settlements, without admitting guilt but promising not to do it again. If jail time deters garden-variety crime, maybe it would be useful therapy for corporate and financial behavior.

The most important reform that could flow from these disasters is legislation that gives employees, union and nonunion, a voice and role in supervising their own pension funds as well as the growing 401(k) plans. In Enron's case, the employees who were not wiped out were sheet-metal workers at subsidiaries acquired by Enron whose union locals insisted on keeping their own separately managed pension funds. Labor-managed pension funds, with holdings of about $400 billion, are dwarfed by corporate-controlled funds, in which the future beneficiaries are frequently manipulated to enhance the company's bottom line. Yet pension funds supervised jointly by unions and management give better average benefits and broader coverage (despite a few scandals of their own). If pension boards included people whose own money is at stake, it could be a powerful enforcer of responsible behavior. . . .

JIM HIGHTOWER
SweatX Is Chic

JIM HIGHTOWER *is a regular contributor to the* Texas Observer *and many other magazines. He has also been Texas Railroad Commissioner and has a popular talk show. He wrote this piece for* The Nation.

Hightower, Jim, "SweatX Is Chic," reprinted with permission from the June 24, 2002, issue of *The Nation*. For subscription information, call 1-800-333-8536. Portions of each week's *Nation* magazine can be accessed at http://www.thenation.com

A couple of years ago, Susan DeMarco and I were doing our radio talk show, *Chat & Chew*, on the topic of sweatshop goods. A lady from Jackson, Mississippi, called to say that whenever she goes into a store to shop for clothing, she always tries to find a manager and asks, "Can you tell me where your made-in-the-USA section is?" Good question. Go into any clothing department and everything in there—from overcoats to undies, hats to shoes—bears labels that shout: made in China, Bangladesh, El Salvador, the Philippines . . . everywhere but the US of A. This is not only in the Wal-Marts and Targets but also in the upscale Talbotses and Abercrombie & Fitches.

It's not that Americans are unable to make quality stuff, but the ugly fact is that corporations have abandoned US workers and communities in hot pursuit of ever-fatter profits, rushing off to the lowest-wage hellholes they can find to cut and sew their garments. Instead of paying even a minimum wage of $5.15 an hour here, they can get wage slaves at 13 cents an hour in China—then ship the goods back here without lowering the price they charge us. The corporations gleefully pocket the difference in labor costs—and claim that this is the "magic" of the new global market at work. It is certainly magic for them.

For us it is globaloney—just the same old greed. But what's a consumer to do? Even if a garment is made in the United States, some companies also run sweatshops here, with workers, usually recent immigrants, crammed into basement "contract shops," making less than minimum wage. How can we combat the scourge of sweatshops everywhere? Government could take action, but even under Bill Clinton, it was Nike, Gap, Ralph Lauren, and other bigwigs that dominated the discussion, so Washington did nothing but dabble and dawdle. Of course, under King George the W, even discussion has stopped.

The good news is that people themselves—especially children and young people—see sweatshops as a moral abomination, putting them (yet again) well ahead of officialdom. Major groups like United Students Against Sweatshops, the National Labor Committee, Global Exchange, and the garment union UNITE have been aggressively exposing, agitating, and organizing against sweatshop labor. As this political organizing expands, an important assault on sweatshops has come from the one place the multibillion-dollar industry least expects: The marketplace itself.

SweatX is a new brand of garment in every sense of the word. The Hot Fudge Social Venture Fund, set up by Ben Cohen, the puckish entrepreneur and social activist of Ben & Jerry's ice cream fame, has invested $1 million to date in a brand-new garment business in Los Angeles. The business, called *teamX*, is based on a thoroughly radical principle: "Garment workers don't have to be exploited in order to operate a financially successful apparel factory." Imagine.

Inspired and informed by Spain's Mondragon Industrial Cooperatives (a fifty-year-old network of successful employee-owned businesses), *teamX* is organized as a worker-owned co-op that (1) is a union shop organized by UNITE; (2) pays a living wage starting at $8.50 an hour; (3) provides good healthcare, a pension and a share of profits through co-op ownership; (4) practices the "solidarity ratio," in which no executive is paid more than eight times what the lowest-paid worker gets; and (5) intends to make a profit, grow, and spread its progressive seed.

This is no touchie-feelie, froufrou social exercise but a bottom-line business initiative to show that doing well can also mean doing good. Pierre Ferrari's twenty-five years in the corporate world ranges from being VP of Coca-Cola to being director of Ben & Jerry's . . . to now being CEO of *teamX*. These entrepreneurial folks believed that there had to be a better way than sweatshops. Ferrari immersed himself in the economics of garment production. His most shocking (and enlightening) discovery was that a sweatshop worker in the United States gets about 25 cents to make a T-shirt that retails for as much as 18 bucks. Let's say that a worker grosses about $9,000 a year. Poverty. What if you doubled the wage—to 50 cents per shirt? The increase would not affect the buyer, but that worker would suddenly be getting $18,000 a year. Not exactly a fortune, but a livable wage. "Come on," says Ferrari, "they're exploiting people for a lousy 25 cents?"

BUILDING THE BRAND

This March, twenty *teamX* employee-owners, many of whom previously had been sweatshop workers, began production in Los Angeles on their company's first line of stylish shirts, shorts, caps, and other casual wear, working with state-of-the-art equipment in a brand-new factory. "I've been working in clothing for twenty years, and I never had a paid holiday before this," one of the employees told the *Los Angeles Times*. A small, experienced team of managers has been assembled, drawing especially on some older managers who are not merely chasing bucks but looking to add a moral dimension to their work lives.

To build the brand identity, *teamX* is initially targeting the activist community—campuses, unions, churches, local governments, nonprofits, etc. (The T-shirts for my Rolling Thunder Downhome Democracy Tour proudly bear the SweatX label.) This "market of conscience" alone has a huge and virtually untapped potential—as Ferrari discovered, for example, unions buy a lot of T-shirts for rallies, organizing drives, and such. After Oprah recently featured *teamX* on her show, the phones began ringing off the hook with orders, and Ferrari now expects this upstart startup to break even by July—an investment miracle by anyone's standards.

By tapping this growing market of conscience, SweatX not only can be successful but will put the lie to the garment industry's cynical assertion that low wages are an inevitable component of globalization. We can help by talking to our local organizations, clothing store managers, school board members, and others, introducing them to the SweatX possibility, showing with our dollars that commerce and conscience can cohabitate.

On Intellectual Property

The question of intellectual property has energized artists, manufacturers, producers, and consumers. The World Trade Organization has taken a strong stand on this, but enforcement and cooperation has been difficult. The WTO's Agreement on Trade-Related Aspects of Intellectual Property Rights (TRIPS), negotiated in the 1986–94 Uruguay Round, introduced intellectual property rules into the multilateral trading system for the first time.

ORIGINS: INTO THE RULE-BASED TRADE SYSTEM

IDEAS and knowledge are an increasingly important part of trade. Most of the value of new medicines and other high technology products lies in the amount of invention, innovation, research, design, and testing involved. Films, music recordings, books, computer software, and on-line services are bought and sold because of the information and creativity they contain, not usually because of the plastic, metal, or paper used to make them. Many products that used to be traded as low-technology goods or commodities now contain a higher proportion of invention and design in their value—for example, brand-named clothing or new varieties of plants.

Creators can be given the right to prevent others from using their inventions, designs or other creations—and to use that right to negotiate payment in return for others using them. These are "intellectual property rights." They take a number of forms. For example, books, paintings, and films come under copyright; inventions can be patented; brand-names and product logos can be registered as trademarks; and so on. Governments and parliaments have given creators these rights as an incentive to produce ideas that will benefit society as a whole.

The extent of protection and enforcement of these rights varied widely around the world; and as intellectual property became more important in trade, these differences became a source of tension in international economic relations. New internationally-agreed trade rules for intellectual property rights were seen as a way to introduce more order and predictability, and for disputes to be settled more systematically.

The Uruguay Round achieved that. The WTO's TRIPS Agreement is an attempt to narrow the gaps in the way these rights are protected around the world, and to bring them under common international rules. It establishes minimum levels of protection that each government has to give to the intellectual property of fellow WTO members. In doing so, it strikes a balance between the long term benefits and possible short term costs to society. Society benefits in the long term when intellectual property protection encourages creation and invention, especially when the period of protection expires and the creations and inventions enter the public domain. Governments are allowed to reduce any short term costs through various exceptions, for example, to tackle public health problems. And, when there are trade disputes over intellectual property rights, the WTO's dispute settlement system is now available.

The agreement covers five broad issues:

how basic principles of the trading system and other international intellectual property agreements should be applied

how to give adequate protection to intellectual property rights

how countries should enforce those rights adequately in their own territories

how to settle disputes on intellectual property between members of the WTO

special transitional arrangements during the period when the new system is being introduced

BASIC PRINCIPLES: NATIONAL TREATMENT, MFN, AND BALANCED PROTECTION

As in GATT and GATS, the starting point of the intellectual property agreement is basic principles. And as in the two other agreements, non-discrimination features prominently: national treatment (treating one's own nationals and (foreigners equally), and most-favoured-nation treatment (equal treatment for nationals of all trading partners in the WTO). National treatment is also a key principle in other intellectual property agreements outside the WTO.

The TRIPS Agreement has an additional important principle: intellectual property protection should contribute to technical innovation and the transfer of technology. Both producers and users should benefit, and economic and social welfare should be enhanced, the agreement says.

COPYRIGHT

The TRIPS agreement ensures that computer programs will be protected as literary works under the Berne Convention and outlines how databases should be protected.

It also expands international copyright rules to cover rental rights. Authors of computer programs and producers of sound recordings must have the right to prohibit the commercial rental of their works to the public. A similar exclusive right applies to films where commercial rental has led to widespread copying, affecting copyright-owners' potential earnings from their films.

The agreement says performers must also have the right to prevent unauthorized recording, reproduction, and broadcast of live performances (bootlegging) for no less than 50 years. Producers of sound recordings must have the right to prevent the unauthorized reproduction of recordings for a period of 50 years.

TRADEMARKS

The agreement defines what types of signs must be eligible for protection as trademarks, and what the minimum rights conferred on their owners must be. It says that service marks must be protected in the same way as trademarks used for goods. Marks that have become well-known in a particular country enjoy additional protection.

GEOGRAPHICAL INDICATIONS

A place name is sometimes used to identify a product. This "geographical indication" does not only say where the product was made. More importantly, it identifies the product's special characteristics, which are the result of the product's origins.

Well-known examples include "Champagne," "Scotch," "Tequila," and "Roquefort" cheese. Wine and spirits makers are particularly concerned about the use of place-names to identify products, and the TRIPS Agreement contains special provisions for these products. But the issue is also important for other types of goods.

Using the place name when the product was made elsewhere or when it does not have the usual characteristics can mislead consumers, and it can lead to unfair competition. The TRIPS Agreement says countries have to prevent this misuse of place names.

COREY BERGSTEIN
Downloading in Canada

This exemplary piece on evasion is by Corey Bergstein (from the Web).

I download music from the Internet. I do this without the permission of the owners of the copyrights in either the composition or the recording. There, I've said it! In fact, I'm not the least bit afraid to admit that I do it all the time. That's because there is nothing illegal about what I am doing.

Copying music for the purpose of private use is legal in Canada. What!? you exclaim. Well, it all came to a head in the mid 1990's when the Canadian music industry lobby stepped up its complaints that people were getting rich off the illegal copying of music. What people you ask? Bootleggers? Street Vendors? Underground Black Marketeers? No. The people the music industry were after were the likes of Maxell, Fuji, TDK, Sony and all the other blank media producers who were selling millions of dollars worth of cassette tapes onto which all this music was being copied, with the even greater threat of CD-Rs just over the horizon.

So the Canadian government stepped in and granted the music industry's wish for a levy on Blank Audio Media. Through the levy, we all pay a little bit more for our blank cassette tapes and CD-Rs and the extra funds are distributed to artist members of the various Canadian music industry collectives, such as the Canadian Musical Reproduction Rights Agency (CMRRA) and the Society of Composers, Authors, and Music Publishers of Canada (SOCAN).

However, Parliament could not impose a levy (a kind of tax) based on a premise of illegal activity. So, in 1998, simultaneously with the imposition with the levy, the Canadian Copyright Act was amended to provide for the express exclusion of copying for private use from being an infringement of copyright. That exclusion is now found in section 80 of the Copyright Act and reads, in part:

"80(1) Subject to subsection (2), the act of reproducing all or any substantial part of . . . (c) a sound recording in which a musical work . . . is embodied, onto an audio recording medium for the private use of the person who makes the copy, does not constitute an infringement of the copyright in the . . . sound recording."

Let's look at these sections. The first part of 80(1) is concerned with reproducing a sound recording onto an "audio recording medium." Since the levy only applies to audio recording media, the exception only applies to copies recorded onto an "audio recording medium." Section 79 of the Copyright Act defines "audio recording medium" as follows:

"79 'audio recording medium' means a recording medium, regardless of its material form, onto which a sound recording may be reproduced and that is of a kind ordinarily used by individual consumers for that purpose. . . ."

The Canadian Copyright Board, who is responsible for authorizing the amount of the levy, has stated that the term "ordinarily" is used to describe what is "regular, normal, average, recurring, or consistent." It goes on to state that "the

levy is applicable to recording media which a non-marginal number of consumers use for private copying in a way that is not marginal."

Well, this obviously covers such media as cassette tapes and blank CDs, but is a computer's hard drive an "audio recording medium"? Well, no levy is currently imposed against computer hard drives. However, when I download a song from the Internet to my computer, I am physically altering my hard drive with a representation of the sound recording. I may not be able to see this alteration with the naked eye, but that does not change the fact that a physical change occurs. This is, in a very real way, no different from running a needle over a slab of wax or imposing a magnetic impression on a strip of tape. A detailed discussion of the physics behind this process is beyond the scope of this article; suffice to say that the sound recording is reproduced on my hard drive.

Additionally, I would submit that members of the public "ordinarily" use their hard drives to copy music. How many of you reading this have a sound recording on your hard drive right now? It would not be a stretch to say that most of you do. Clearly, this is far from marginal use. Furthermore, the words "regardless of its material form" found in the definition easily broaden the scope of media covered by this definition to include one's hard drive.

Simply because no levy is currently imposed on hard drives doesn't remove such media from inclusion in the construction of section 80. Of course, the ordinary use of a medium to copy sound recordings must necessarily precede the inclusion of that medium in the levy. Also, the fact that certain media are not exclusively used to copy sound recordings is already taken into account in the fixing of the amount of the levy. The Copyright Board has recognized the evolving market for recording media and has stated that, as of 2001, the data available on the downloading of music from the Internet was too uncertain to be considered in fixing the amount of the levy, "although it could become of central concern in future tariff application." It reasonably follows that a hard drive is an "audio recording medium."

So, now that I know that I am reproducing a sound recording onto an audio recording medium, the question remains whether I am doing so for my "private use." Basically, "private" use is the opposite of "public" use. The test involves a review of what I am doing with the sound recording I have copied. A private use is one that is made for my own personal musical benefit and includes such uses as sitting at home listening to it play on my stereo or on my computer or burning it to a compact disc and playing it in my car for my own personal enjoyment. In contrast, public uses would include playing it in my restaurant or nightclub or burning multiple copies and selling them on the street, all for the musical benefit of others.

Those of you who know me know that the use to which I put my downloaded sound recordings is home or car listening for my own personal enjoyment. There could not be a clearer private use than that to which I put the music I copy to my hard drive from Internet sources.

But aren't the Internet sources just illegal copies anyway? Isn't that the fruit of the poisonous tree? Well, no. Not when Parliament intentionally refused to impose the requirement that the source or target be lawfully owned—a fact confirmed by the Copyright Board.

As a result, when I download music from the Internet, I am making a copy of a sound recording on an audio recording medium for my own private use. As such, section 80(1) of the Copyright Act deems my copying not to constitute an infringement of copyright.

JOANNE CIULLA
Honest Work

JOANNE CIULLA *teaches business ethics and management at the Jepson School of Leadership at the University of Richmond. She is the author of* This Working Life *and* The Ethics of Leadership.

———

Suppose that every tool we had could perform its function, either at our bidding, or itself perceiving the need, and suppose that shuttles in a loom could fly to and fro and a plucker on a lyre all self-moved, then manufacturers would have no need of workers nor master of slaves.

—ARISTOTLE
Politics

IT'S been more than 2,300 years since Aristotle mused about a life without work. Today, the tools and machines that Aristotle dreamed of are becoming the furniture of everyday life in industrialized countries, as the demands of a competitive market catapult us toward a world in which machines replace or simplify most jobs. Aristotle might have rejoiced at this, but Americans don't. Instead of greeting this era with joy, we cling ever more tightly to our work.

Ours is a work-oriented society—one where "all play and no work makes Jack a big jerk." We live in a paradoxical culture that both celebrates work and continually strives to eliminate it. While we treasure economic efficiency, we seek interesting jobs that will offer fulfillment and meaning to our lives.

A SOURCE OF IDENTITY

Perhaps the demand for meaningful work grows because we see the supply shrinking.

For many people, work promises more than most jobs can deliver. The corporation is not capable of providing meaningful work for all of its employees.

As things now stand, we have gone beyond the work ethic, which endowed work with moral value, and expect our jobs to be the source of our identity, the basis of our individual worth and the mainspring of happiness. Furthermore, we want our work to substitute for the fulfillment that used to be derived from friends, family and community.

Over the past 60 years, management has capitalized on this "loaded" meaning of work. The social engineer has replaced the time-study man—corporations have become "cultures" that seek to transform employees into a happy family.

The problem of alienation has been licked by "entertaining" that encroaches on employees' leisure time in the guise of business dinners, corporate beer busts and networking parties. Managers, charged with the task of making work meaningful, create new ways of persuading employees to invest more of themselves in their work than their jobs may require. So, banal work is sometimes dressed up to look meaningful.

EMOTIONAL DEMANDS

Under the old school of scientific management, the alienated worker did what he or she was told, got paid and went home. The work might have been boring and the wages unfair, but at least everyone knew where they stood.

Today, the transaction is not as honest. While we still trade our labor, we are also required to give away a slice of our private lives.

Workers of the past were often overworked; today, many of us are overmanaged. The exhaustion that pains the faces of office workers at the end of the day may not be physical but emotional, because management may be demanding more of the self than the timely and efficient performance of the task at hand actually requires.

"WHAT DO YOU DO?"

Work determines our status and shapes our social interactions. One of the first things Americans ask when they met someone new is, "What do you do?" This used to be considered a rude question in Europe, but in recent years it's being asked more and more. To be retired or unemployed in a work-oriented society is to be relegated to the status of a nonentity.

Young people fanatically pursue careers as if a good job were the sole key to happiness—whether that happiness is derived from the status of the job itself or from the wages that they believe will eventually buy it. They are willing to take drug tests, wear the right clothes and belong to the right clubs, all in the name of obtaining a position that will eventually give them freedom to choose. Many argue that they'll work 70-hour weeks, make their fortunes and retire at forty—few ever do. This attitude has taken a social toll in terms of loneliness, divorce, child abuse and sometimes even white-collar crime.

ONE-WAY COMMITMENTS

A consequence of this loaded meaning of work is that people willingly put their happiness in the hands of the market and their employers. Unlike social institutions such as church and community, corporations frequently do not possess a clear moral vision of what is good for people. It is ironic that in an era of hostile takeovers, corporations seem to offer less security but want more commitment and trust from their employees. Yet traits such as trust and loyalty are based on a reciprocal relationship.

In this environment, managers are challenged to find ways of motivating people who want jobs that satisfy a variety of abstract desires and needs, such as self-development and self-fulfillment.

While there doesn't seem to be much consensus on what "self-development" means or what people self-develop for, many feel that this is what they *should* want. So managers, consultants and psychologists guess at employees' needs and develop programs and policies that carry the implicit promise of fulfilling them. This results in a vicious circle—employees desire more, management promises more and the expectation of finding meaning in work rises. Both sides grope in the dark for ways to build a workplace "El Dorado."

The authenticity of a corporation's moral commitment is questionable if the drive for meaningful work is merely another motivating tool or a mask for authority. Young people who enter the work force are wise to attempts to manipulate them under the guise of caring and skeptical of programs prescribed by the latest management fad that are supposed to create excitement. Managers cannot continually jump-start employees into action. And unlike the organized workers of old, today's young worker doesn't rebel or exert power by picketing with his or her colleagues, but instead stages his or her own silent strike of passive resistance.

WORTHWHILE WORK

In Search of Excellence and the pop management books that followed it charged managers with the task of "making meaning." Peters and Waterman wrote, "We desperately need mean-

ing in our lives and will sacrifice a great deal for it to the institution that provides it for us." We first have to ask: What is it that a corporation has a right to ask people to sacrifice? Their families? Their personal lives? Their leisure? Their beliefs?

Over the past 20 years, the workplace has become more appealing to people's tastes and lifestyles. But we're discovering that some of the values that have emerged from business life are not very attractive or satisfying. Corporate scandals and employee crimes have forced us to rethink the values that have been bred in the workplace and the marketplace. What we have seen in the 1980s is the moral crisis of work, which I would also characterize as a crisis of meaning.

What *is* meaningful work? Is it something that an institution can define or is it something that people discover? The British designer and social critic William Morris had some interesting insights into the nature of what he calls "worthwhile work."

Morris states that work can be either a "lightening to life" or "burden to life."

The difference lies in the fact that in the first type of work there is hope while in the second there is none. According to Morris, it is hope that makes work worth doing. He says, "Worthy work carries with it the hope of pleasure in rest, the hope of pleasure in our using what it makes, and the hope of pleasure in our daily creative skill."

MEANING IS INDIVIDUAL

The concept of hope is a useful one for understanding the nature of meaningful work.

Academics who write about work often make the mistake of assuming that everyone wants work like theirs. Interview a variety of workers, and you soon discover that this simply isn't true. There is a wide variance in the kinds of work that people like to do and the ways in which they find meaning.

Morris' characterization of worthy work has both a subjective and objective element to it. It is subjective in the sense that hope is a potential that the individual worker may or may not actualize. It is objective in the sense that leisure, usefulness and the exercise of skill require that these elements be present in the nature of the work itself. Morris further asserts, "If work cannot be made less repulsive by either shortening it, making it intermittent or having a special usefulness to the man who freely performs it, then the product of such work is not worth the price."

And, while institutions can provide general frameworks for meaning, it is up to individuals to interpret these meanings for themselves. For example, our liberal society guarantees life and liberty, but it only offers us the *pursuit* of happiness. If a corporation defined and dictated "meaningful work," the freedom of employees to find it and shape it into the context of their lives would be diminished.

Employers do, however, have a moral responsibility to do all they can to redesign jobs and to carefully think through the impact of technology on employees.

Where jobs can't be made more interesting, companies need to think of ways to accommodate employees so that their jobs do not stand in the way of their leading satisfying lives outside of work.

TOWARD A MORE JUST WORKPLACE

Employers have an ethical obligation to recognize that employees have a right to meaningful lives. Businesses might begin by eliminating policies and practices that interfere with that right. Because not all jobs are exciting or engaging, perhaps efforts should be made to make work fit better into people's lives instead of forcing people's lives to fit into work.

The main reasons people give for why they are unhappy at work are that they feel powerless, they do not trust the organization and they feel they are not being treated fairly.

Throughout history, work has involved a relationship of unequal power. Real innovation in management will come when issues like the balance of power are acknowledged and management seeks to create a more just workplace.

In the 8th century B.C., the Greek poet Hesiod pointed out that justice is what makes work worthwhile. He wrote, "Neither famine nor disaster ever haunt men who do true justice; but lightheartedly they tend the fields which are all their care."

PATRICIA H. WERHANE
A Bill of Rights for Employees and Employers

PATRICIA H. WERHANE *teaches business ethics at the University of Virginia. Much of her work focuses on Wittgenstein, aesthetics, and professional ethics. Her books include* Art and Nonart, Ethical Issues in Business, *and* Persons, Rights, and Corporations.

EMPLOYEE RIGHTS

1. Every person has an equal right to a job and a right to equal consideration at the job. Employees may not be discriminated against on the basis of religion, sex, ethnic origin, race, color, or economic background.

2. Every person has the right to equal pay for work, where "equal work" is defined by the job description and title.

3. Every employee has rights to his or her job. After a probation period of three to ten years every employee has the right to his or her job. An employee can be dismissed only under the following conditions:

   • He or she is not performing satisfactorily the job for which he or she was hired.

   • He or she is involved in criminal activity either within or outside the corporation.

   • He or she is drunk or takes drugs on the job.

   • He or she actively disrupts corporate business activity without a valid reason.

   • He or she becomes physically or mentally incapacitated or reaches mandatory retirement age.

   • The employer has publicly verifiable economic reasons for dismissing the employee, e.g., transfer of the company, loss of sales, bankruptcy, etc.

   • Under no circumstances can an employee be dismissed or laid off without the institution of fair due process procedure.

4. Every employee has the right to due process in the workplace. He or she has the right to a peer review, to a hearing, and if necessary, to outside arbitration before being demoted or fired.

5. Every employee has the right to free expression in the workplace. This includes the right to object to corporate acts that he or she finds illegal or immoral without retaliation or penalty. The objection may take the form of free speech, whistle-blowing, or conscientious objection. However, any criticism must be documented or proven.

6. The Privacy Act, which protects the privacy and confidentiality of public employees, should be extended to all employees.

7. The polygraph should be outlawed.

8. Employees have the right to engage in outside activities of their choice.

9. Every employee has the right to a safe workplace, including the right to safety information and participation in improving work hazards. Every employee has the right to legal protection that guards against preventable job risks.

10. Every employee has the right to as much information as possible about the corporation, about his or her job, work hazards, possibilities for future employment, and any other information necessary for job enrichment and development.

11. Every employee as the right to participate in the decision-making processes entailed in his or her job, department, or in the corporation as a whole, where appropriate.

12. Every public and private employee has the right to strike when the foregoing demands are not met in the workplace.

EMPLOYER RIGHTS

1A. Any employee found discriminating against another employee or operating in a discriminatory manner against her employer is subject to employer reprimand, demotion, or firing.

2A. Any employee not deserving equal pay because of inefficiency should be shifted to another job.

3A. No employee who functions inefficiently, who drinks or takes drugs on the job, commits felonies or acts in ways that prevent carrying out work duties has a right to a job.

4A. Any employee found guilty under a due process procedure should be reprimanded. (e.g., demoted or dismissed), and, if appropriate, brought before the law.

5A. No employer must retain employees who slander the corporation or other corporate constituents.

6A. The privacy of employers is as important as the privacy of employees. By written agreement employees may be required not to disclose confidential corporate information or trade secrets unless not doing so is clearly against the public interest.

7A. Employers may engage in surveillance of employees at work (but only at work) with their foreknowledge and consent.

8A. No employee may engage in activities that literally harm the employer, nor may an employee have a second job whose business competes with the business of the first employer.

9A. Employees shall be expected to carry out job assignments for which they are hired unless these conflict with common moral standards or unless the employee was not fully informed about these assignments or their dangers before accepting employment. Employees themselves should become fully informed about work dangers.

10A. Employers have rights to personal information about employees or prospective employees adequate to make sound hiring and promotion judgments so long as the employer preserves the confidentiality of such information.

11A. Employers as well as employees have rights. Therefore the right to participation is a correlative obligation on the part of both parties to respect mutual rights. Employers, then, have the right to demand efficiency and productivity from their employees in return for the employee right to participation in the workplace.

12A. Employees who strike for no reason are subject to dismissal.

Any employee or employer who feels he or she has been unduly penalized under a bill of rights may appeal to an outside arbitrator.

ROBERT C. SOLOMON
Making Money and the Importance of the Virtues

ROBERT C. SOLOMON *teaches philosophy at the University of Texas and has written books on existentialism and on business ethics. He consults with a number of corporations, and this piece elaborates on the importance of business ethics and virtuous living even in the rough-and-tumble world of business.*

TWENTY years ago, I was invited by a friend in the business school to speak to a group of business executives in a special program at the University of Texas. I was a budding young philosophy professor and, quite frankly, I had little business sense or sympathies. But I did it, I enjoyed it, and I've been working with groups of business people and corporations ever since. As a philosopher, I am still talking about the meaning of life and morals in business. I no longer fear, as I once did, that hard-headed business people would have no interest in ethics. Quite the contrary, I find the level of interest so keen that I fear that I might not be able to satisfy it. They rightly wonder (and sometimes ask), "I am already a moral person, so what do you have to teach me?"

That seems to me to be exactly the right question. I do not have to teach anyone "the difference between right and wrong." (Indeed, if I did, I would not know how to go about doing so.) But what bothers virtually every one of my clients, from the CEO of one of New York's largest banks to the welder at our local IBM plant, is how to firm up the connection between the "bottom line" demands of business and ethics. And that is something well worth talking about.

HOW WE TALK ABOUT BUSINESS

Every discipline or profession has its own self-glorifying vocabulary. It is how they justify themselves. It is how they sell themselves. It is how they think of themselves and what they do.

Politicians bask in the concept of "public service" even while they pursue personal power and exploit the fears and prejudices of their constituents. But who would question the virtue of devoting oneself to public service?

Lawyers defend "justice" and our "rights" on a handsome contingency basis as they lead us through a thicket of regulations and liabilities created by—other lawyers. But who would question the virtue of devoting oneself to justice and rights?

Physicians (even those with bulging portfolios) "heal" and "save lives," an undeniably noble cause. Who would question the value of human life and well-being?

University professors immodestly celebrate what they do in the noble language of "truth and knowledge" even when they spend most of their time and energy battling each other for status in exquisitely petty but vicious campus politics. But who would question their dedication to the truth, to enlightening young minds and to preserving the values of Civilization?

In the case of business, however, the language of self-description is hardly noble or self-glorifying. One of my businessman friends told me, "in business you always know how well you are doing. You just have to put your hand in your pocket." (I did not pursue the ambiguity of the suggestion.) The simple phrase, "the bottom line," and the vulgar verb, "making money," summarize a one-dimensional image of business that is notoriously unflattering and, in the public perception, extremely destructive.

We can readily understand why we should applaud people who devote themselves to public service, or defend our rights, or cure illness and save lives, or search for truth and knowledge. It is not so easy to understand why we should cheer for those who (as they themselves seem to claim) are out only for material gain for themselves. There is more than enough cynicism in the world about the callous attitudes in business. Business people themselves should be loathe to confirm such cynicism. One can put as much faith as one wishes in Adam Smith's "invisible hand" and the theory that individual self-interest yields collective prosperity, but it does not follow that we should describe what we do in business merely as "making money."

DOWN FROM
THE MOUNTAIN TOP

It is often said, by way of a joke, that business ethics is a "contradiction in terms," an oxymoron.

To some extent, this only reflects normal skepticism. We have all been cheated by some bad apple auto mechanic or taken in by some mail order scam at some point in our lives. We all know businesses that cut corners, and most of us have been in positions ourselves where our sense of doing right has been pressured or compromised. But I think that the skepticism about business ethics goes deeper than that, into our very way of thinking about both business and ethics.

So I begin my seminars with a story about ethics:

> Moses went to the top of the mountain, and there God *handed down* to him a set of Commandments, sanctioned by Himself, most of which begin, "Thou shalt not. . . ." Moses turned around, went down the mountain and handed the Law down to his people, who were not, if you recall, particularly receptive.

This is how we often think about ethics. As "*handed down,*" imposed from above, primarily in the form of prohibitions and constraints. It is an understandable way of thinking about ethics, given how most of us learn about morals in the first place.

> Mother yells, "Stop it! Don't tease your baby brother."
> The older child responds, "Why not?!"
> Mother replies (as she should), "Because I said so!"

Here is ethics "from the top," "*handed down*" or imposed by a recognized authority (with the power to punish). And so it is natural for us to think of ethics in terms of prohibitions and constraints. But when we think of ethics this way, whether our response is obedience or rebellion ("Why not?!") our ethics is not, in an all-important sense, "our own."

Then I tell another story, this one about business:

> The great economist Adam Smith taught us all the power of the Law of Supply and Demand, that free enterprise produces prosperity, but that free enterprise must be, above all, *free.* The proper attitude of all non-business concerns toward business should be "*laissze-faire,*" "leave it alone."

Insofar as ethics is thought of as a set of constraints, imposed by the law or other moral authorities, there will be a practical contradiction with business as "free enterprise," by its very nature free from external constraints. But to so think of ethics as constraint and business as free from constraint leads to an impoverishment of both, and it quite naturally gives rise to the following kind of not so unfamiliar story:

> Moe the shyster meets Larry the liquidator and together they strike up a deal to take over hardworking entrepreneur Curly's business. They fire Curly and all of his employees and sell off the business in pieces. They agree that the ethics is dubious, but "it's legal," and, after all, "*business is business.*"

Business is not "free" in the sense of being an amoral, unethical activity. And ethics is not merely a matter of obeying the law or some other set of external constraints. And so what I proceed to explore for the next several hours or days, and in this book, is how ethics in business is not only possible but necessary, how markets can be both "free" and moral, and why "business ethics" is not, after all, a contradiction but rather the precondition of any long-term, flourishing business enterprise.

The best answer to the charge of contradiction, I believe, lies in the concept of virtue. A virtue, unlike an externally imposed constraint, is very much our own. Our virtues (and vices) make us the person we are. But virtues, in turn, presuppose values. A value simply espoused, even if it is sincerely believed, is worth very little if it is not translated into action. Virtues are values turned into action. Virtues and values come together in visions of business, and of the role of business in life more generally. Our vision dictates our values and informs our virtues, so virtue is not just action. It is intelligent, visionary action, expressing one's sense of what the world must be like. And virtues, I then go on to show, provide the foundation of both ethical living and success in business.

BACK TO THE MOUNTAIN: LIVING OUR VALUES

Here is another story. It is called "The Parable of the Sadhu."

> A successful Wall Street banker travels to the Himalayas for a much-needed vacation, to engage

in a long-term dream he has had, to trek across one of the world's most challenging mountain passes. He is a religious man. He is an ambitious man.

About halfway up to the pass, he and his group are approached by a group of New Zealanders, who hand over the half-frozen but still living body of a Sadhu, a holy man, who has come down over the pass in the wrong direction and gotten lost in the freezing cold and the snow and ice of the mountain.

If he and his group take the Sadhu down to safety, the wind and snow will close the mountain pass and they will have to give up their attempt. If they do not, he will surely die. One of the group, an anthropologist, decides that the Sadhu must be saved. The banker insists on going over the pass. The anthropologist takes the Sadhu halfway down, then hands him to a group of Japanese, who give him some food but refuse to carry him any further. The anthropologist then hurries to meet his friend over the pass.

When they join together, the anthropologist angrily asks the banker, "how does it feel to have contributed to the death of another human being?" The banker, surprised, defensively insists, "we all did our bit. There was nothing else we could do. If we had taken him down, the whole trip would have been for nothing!"

Two years later, he wrote a confession of what he did (or did not do) for the most prestigious business journal, for everyone in his world to read.

I ask, What do you make of this story, with regard to business life?

The conversation is almost always brisk and keen. Virtually everyone sees the obvious analogy between "climbing the corporate ladder" (or otherwise pursuing your own personal objectives) and climbing a mountain. They also see an undeniable ethical lapse, an unforgivable neglect of the plight of another human being, in this case, in a life-or-death situation. Several participants talk about the breakdown in teamwork, both between and within the groups, their collective failure to coordinate a rescue effort. No one, but no one, was willing to take on the final responsibility (not even the anthropologist, who found himself caught between his good intention to save the Sadhu and the need to get across the pass and join his friend).

But the discussion turns truly active when the nature of the banker's action (or lack of appropriate action) comes into question. He was not ignorant of the difference between right and wrong, or of the value of human life—perhaps the most important value of all. It was not as if he did not recognize his obligations. But, rather, he was blinded by his own objective, and no doubt by the perseverance that had made him such a success on Wall Street too. His very virtues became vices, obstacles to his doing what he surely knew he ought to do.

Moreover, he *rationalized*. He found all sorts of reasons why *not* saving the Sadhu was the right (or at least the permissible) thing to do. He insists, for example, that they had made a considerable investment in the trip, in terms of time, effort and expense.

Indeed they had, as we all make investments in our careers, our projects, our lives. But, sometimes, those investments have to be abandoned or compromised for a greater good, a more important value.

The banker insists that they had their "own safety to think about."

Indeed they did, but, apart from the normal dangers of mountain climbing, they would not have put themselves in any further danger by taking the Sadhu down the mountain.

The banker complains that their "altitude sickness was getting worse." But the one piece of advice given in every pamphlet, article or book on mountain climbing regarding altitude sickness is this: *go down.* Quite the contrary of making the rescue effort more difficult, altitude sickness would seem to provide a motive for the climbers to rescue the Sadhu, thus giving themselves an honorable excuse for giving up the climb and making themselves feel better.

There is also the nasty question of racism that emerges: the anthropologist, now angry, asks, "would the banker have behaved in the same way if the victim were a Western woman instead of an exotic stranger?" That in turn raises the tricky question of "relativism," whether one has the obligation to behave according to one's own values when dealing with people whose values may be very different. (One group of bright young MBAs turned the question on its head, demanding "what right do we have to interfere with the Sadhu's activity, whatever it may have been? Moreover, why should we take responsibility for someone else's *ir*responsibility?" Hard and important questions indeed.)

But what the story and the discussion illustrate to almost everyone's satisfaction is that believing in values alone is not enough. Values have to be translated into action, and that means that acting according to our values cannot merely be an abstract obligation but must get "built into" our ways of dealing with the world. That is what a virtue is, and that is what good business, and business ethics, and this book, are all about.

WHY VIRTUE IS NECESSARY

At a recent conference on the environment, a particularly belligerent critic hammered away at "International Capital" for degrading the ecology of the planet. The statistics of such degradation are frightening, of course. The ethical and political solutions suggested seemed to me impractical. What fascinated me, however, was that one obvious solution to the problem was never even mentioned, namely, the idea that the multi- and trans-national corporations he so abused and accused might themselves feel some sense of obligation to look after the environment. Or, rather, the board and executives and employees and customers of those companies might feel some such obligation. Instead, the corporate world was treated as an impersonal monolith. There were no heroes, just one villain, "International Capital."

The speaker lamented the fact that there were no social or political forces available to combat this monolith, and, in a sense, what he said was certainly true. But what was wrong was the idea of a monolith in the first place. Quite apart from the question of effective international legal sanctions and monitoring organizations, there is first and foremost the question of corporate virtue—the virtues, that is, of all of the people who make up, patronize and invest in the many different corporations that make up so much of the business world. In the absence of such virtues, I would feel compelled to join the pessimists in worrying desperately about our collective future. But I see such virtues all around me in the business world, and at all levels. Without such virtues, we would surely enter a new "dark ages." But with them, we might indeed see some semblance of "a new world order" in which humanity and not only profits become the measure. The choice is up to us, not to the mindless workings of "International Capital."

This tendency to depersonalize, to see corporations as all of a piece, defined by legalities and buried under a handful of economic abstractions, is the target of this book. There is no such thing as "International Capital." There is no such entity as "Corporate America." There is only Motorola, and AT&T, Chase Manhattan and Citibank, IBM, Compaq and Apple, Merck and Upjohn, Johnson & Johnson, Exxon, Nike, and Freeport-McMoran, or, more accurately, the people who make up these companies. There are, to be sure, a few exemplary good guys and some despicable bad guys, but there are thousands of companies and many millions of executives, managers and employees who are neither saints nor monsters but just people trying to live a decent, happy life and doing their jobs accordingly. Corporations are not faceless forces or monoliths. We have to remind and convince ourselves that they are nothing but people and relationships, flesh and blood, working together in cooperation and mutual self-interest, trying, most of them, to do the right thing.

Problematic too is that abstraction called "the market" ("the institutionalization of irresponsibility," in the delicious phrase of the great "Buddhist" economist, E. F. Schumacher). "The market" may be the product of our collective psychology but it is not, obviously, within our personal control. Even the most powerful among us feels constrained and powerless in the face of "market forces." But what tends to get left out of the picture is our own free will and responsibility. As employees and managers, as consumers and as stockholders, we are always making choices, and as we choose, we create ourselves. We build reputations as we display our virtues and our vices too. The foundation of free enterprise is not the iron laws of economics but the personal question, "who are you, and what do you (really) want?" Whether addressed to one individual or a multi-national corporation with a hundred thousand employees and managers, we want to know: "What are your virtues, and why should we trust and support you?" It is my purpose here to define and defend those virtues, right in the bowels of business.

The problems of business today are first and foremost profoundly ethical and philosophical problems. They are questions about the very nature of the business enterprise and the nature of the corporation. For example, the very conception of the corporation as a "legal fiction" defined in terms of obligations to its stockholders implies that corporations are not moral or morally responsible agencies and suggests (at best) a morally ambiguous sense of responsibility for the executives and employees of the corporation. It is not surprising, then, that some major, once respectable companies find themselves riddled and ruined by scandals in which the rubber check of corporate responsibility bounces up and down the hierarchy and seems to get cashed out nowhere.

So, too, business activity itself is misconceived in an amoral way, subsumed (or hidden) under the all-purpose imagery of "competitiveness." But "competition" is but one of a large number of relationships that people and companies have with one another, and an overemphasis on competition can be disastrous for the sense of community and for the underlying cooperation that is necessary for any successful business activity. The need to be more "competitive" is more often than not better cast as the need to be more cooperative, to earn the loyalty, trust and understanding of one's customers, employees and investors. Ethics, to put the matter bluntly, is good business.

How we do business—and what business does to us—has everything to do with how we think about business, talk about business,

conceive of business, practice business. If we think, talk, conceive and practice business as a ruthless, cut-throat, "dog-eat-dog" activity, then that, of course, is what it will become. And, so too, it is what we will become, no matter how often (in our "off" hours and personal lives) we insist otherwise. If, on the other hand, business is conceived—as it has often been conceived—as an enterprise based on trust and mutual benefits, an enterprise for civilized, virtuous people, then that, in turn, will be equally self-fulfilling. It will also be much more amiable, secure, enjoyable and, last but not least, profitable.

It is undeniable that a person becomes what he or she does. We are molded by our peers, by the rigors and language of our jobs, by the culture of the organization or the industry. This is not to deny personal choices and responsibility, but it is to say the obvious: if you spend (more than) half of your adult waking life working, including the most creative hours of most of your days, what you do, the people you work with and the values of the organization you work for are going to be an inescapable influence on who and what you are. (And consider how much of the other half of your life is taken up by travel to and from work, trips to the supermarket or the dry cleaner, emergency visits to the vet, cleaning up the basement, disciplining the kids, mindlessly watching television, personal grooming, not to mention the work you take home with you, etc.) It is a distinctively contemporary version of what used to be called "existentialism"—*you are what you do*.

In place of the brutally competitive and disruptive imagery and "bottom line" thinking that is so pervasive in business these days, I want to underscore the importance of integrity. It may be true, as pundits from Alvin Toffler to Tom Peters have suggested, that most of us will have a half dozen or more careers in our working lifetimes. But it does not follow from this that the transition from career to career needs to be as utterly traumatic and disruptive, as threatening to mental health and the well-being of families and whole communities as it now threatens to be. The way to a future without "future shock" is the main theme of ethics, remembering who we are, what we really need, and what we stand for. What endures, what keeps us whole, is our integrity.

AN "ARISTOTELEAN" APPROACH TO BUSINESS

The good life, according to Aristotle, is the happy life, the flourishing life, "doing well." The point is not that we should stop thinking about money or trying to make a living. It is a question of perspective, and a question of what that living amounts to. Is it, in fact, just a means to make money? Or is it, as it should be, a worthwhile activity that provides the meaningful substance of our adult lives, the source of our sense of self-worth and where we meet our closest friends? Is the company we work for a white-collar version of Hell, or is it a community where we are glad to see our colleagues and get on with the work of the day? It was Aristotle who insisted on the virtues or "excellences" as the basic constituents of individual and collective happiness. The underlying assumption was that a person is who he or she is by virtue of his or her place and role in the community, and the virtues of the community, in turn, nurture and encourage each of its members be "a good person." It takes little leap of philosophical imagination to recognize this same relationship between the individual employee, manager or executive and the modern corporation. On the "Aristotelean" approach to business, a good corporation is one that is not only profitable but provides a morally rewarding environment in which good people can develop not only their skills but their virtues.

JOSEPH CAMPBELL
Follow Your Bliss

JOSEPH CAMPBELL *(1904–1987) is best known for his extensive work on world mythology and his PBS television series with Bill Moyers on that subject. The following excerpt expresses one of his best-known expressions, "follow your bliss."*

THE man who never followed his bliss . . . may have a success in life, but then just think of it—what kind of life was it? What good was it—you've never done the thing you wanted to do in all your life. I always tell my students, go where your body and soul want to go. When you have the feeling, then stay with it, and don't let anyone throw you off. . . .

That is following your bliss. . . .

When I taught at Sarah Lawrence, I would have an individual conference with every one of my students at least once a fortnight, for a half hour or so. Now, if you're talking on about the things that students ought to be reading, and suddenly you hit on something that the student really responds to, you can see the eyes open and the complexion change. The life possibility has opened there. All you can say to yourself is, "I hope this child hangs on to that." They may or may not, but when they do, they have found life right there in the room with them. . . .

It is miraculous. I even have a superstition that has grown on me as the result of invisible hands coming all the time—namely, that if you do follow your bliss you put yourself on a kind of track that has been there all the while, waiting for you, and the life that you ought to be living is the one you are living. When you can see that, you begin to meet people who are in the field of your bliss, and they open the doors to you. I say, follow your bliss and don't be afraid, and doors will open where you didn't know they were going to be.